Norway
p313

Iceland
p248

Faroe
Islands
p120

Finland
p150

Sweden
p419

St Petersburg
p237

Tallinn
p228

Denmark
p38

THIS EDITION WRITTEN AND RESEARCHED BY
Andy Symington
Carolyn Bain, Cristian Bonetto, Mark Elliott, Anthony Ham
Becky Ohlsen, Fran Parnell, Simon Richmond

welcome to Scandinavia

Outdoors

The great outdoors is rarely greater than in Europe's big north. Epic expanses of wilderness – forests, lakes, volcanoes – and intoxicatingly pure air mean that engaging with nature is a pleasure. A network of well-cared-for, protected areas stretches across the region, offering some of Europe's best hiking as well as anything from kayaking to glacier walking to bear watching. Spectacular coasts, whether rugged fjords, cliffs teeming with seabirds, or archipelagos so speckled with islands it looks like the artist who designed this canvas flicked a paintbrush at it, invite exploration from the sea. It's rare to find such inspiring landscapes that are so easily accessed.

City Style

Stolid Nordic stereotypes dissolve completely in the region's vibrant capitals. Crest-of-the-wave design can be seen across them all, backed up by outstanding modern architecture, excellent museums, imaginative solutions for 21st-century urban living, some of Europe's most acclaimed restaurants and a nightlife that fizzes along wildly despite the hefty beer prices. Live music is a given: you're bound to come across some inspiring local act whether your taste is Viking metal or chamber music. Style here manages to be conservative and innovative at the same time, or perhaps it's just that the new and the old blend with less effort here than in other places. A side trip to glo-

Effortlessly chic cities balance remote forests, enchanting style gurus and wilderness hikers alike. Endless day, perpetual night. Rocking festivals, majestic aurora borealis. Scandinavia's menu is anything but bland.

(left) Norwegian fjord, near Molde
(below) Aurora borealis (Northern Lights), Lofoten Islands (p387), Norway

rious St Petersburg or seductive Tallinn will add an eastern Baltic kick to your Scandinavian city experiences.

Seasons

They have proper seasons up here. Long, cold winters with feet of snow carpeting the ground and the sun making only cameo appearances – if at all. Despite the scary sub-zero temperatures, there's a wealth of things to do: skiing, sledding behind huskies or reindeer, taking snowmobile safaris to the Arctic Sea, dangling a fishing line through a hole in the ice, spending romantic nights in snow hotels, visiting Santa Claus and gazing at the soul-piercing Northern Lights. Spring sees nature's tentative awakening before the explosive summer with its long, long days, filled with festivals, beer terraces and wonderful boating, hiking and cycling. The autumn, in Scandinavia's forested lands, can be the most beautiful of all, as the birches and other deciduous trees display a glorious array of colours, offering marvellous woodland walking before the first snows.

Green Choices

You'll rarely come across the word *ecotourism* in Scandinavia, but those values have long been an important part of life here. Generally, green, sustainable solutions are a way of life here, rather than a gimmick to attract visitors.

❭ Scandinavia

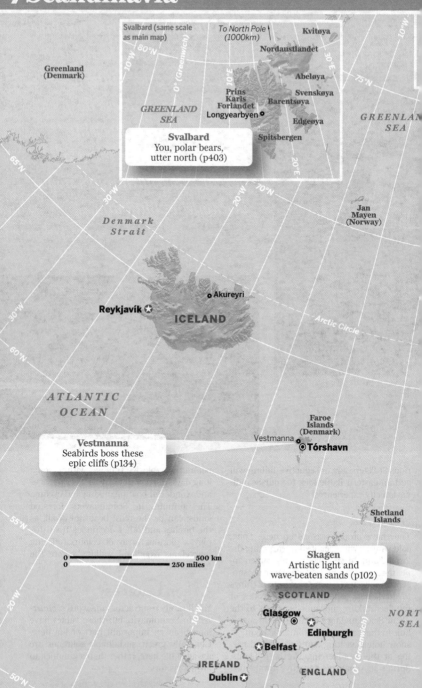

Svalbard (same scale as main map)

Greenland (Denmark)

Kvitøya

Nordaustlandet

Abeløya

GREENLAND SEA

Prins Karls Forlandet

Svenskøya

Barentsøya

Longyearbyen

Edgeøya

Spitsbergen

GREENLAND SEA

To North Pole (1000km)

Svalbard
You, polar bears, utter north (p403)

Denmark Strait

Jan Mayen (Norway)

Akureyri

Reykjavík

ICELAND

Arctic Circle

ATLANTIC OCEAN

Faroe Islands (Denmark)

Vestmanna
Seabirds boss these epic cliffs (p134)

Vestmanna

Tórshavn

Shetland Islands

Skagen
Artistic light and wave-beaten sands (p102)

0   500 km
0   250 miles

SCOTLAND

Glasgow

Edinburgh

NORTH SEA

Belfast

IRELAND

Dublin

ENGLAND

Svalbard
(Greenwich)
(Norway)

See Svalbard inset

Novaya
Zemlya
(Russia)

*BARENTS
SEA*

Lofoten Islands
Epic rock, timeless fishing
communities (p387)

Hermitage, St Petersburg
One of the world's
great galleries (p238)

Nordkapp ○

○ Vardø

● Murmansk

Tromsø ○

Inarijärvi

*ORWEGIAN
SEA*

Narvik ○

Lofoten
Islands

○ Kiruna

Bodø ○

○ Rovaniemi

Fjords
nvestigate these awesome
eological serrations (p340)

Oulu
○

SWEDEN

FINLAND

RUSSIA

*Lake
Onega*

NORWAY

Umeå ○

● Kuopio

Oulujärvi

Trondheim ○

○ Östersund

○ Vaasa

Jyväskylä

Saimaa

Lappeenranta

*Lake
Ladoga*

● **Ålesund**

Galdhøpiggen
(2469m) ▲

*Gulf of
Bothnia*

Tampere ○

● **Vyborg**

Lillehammer ○

Turku ○

Helsinki ●

● **St Petersburg**

Åland

Gulf of Finland

● **Bergen**

Oslo ✪

○ Uppsala

● **Tallinn**

*Lake
Peipsi*

Västerås ○

✪ **Stockholm**

ESTONIA

RUSSIA

Örebro ○

● **Stavanger**

Vänern

○ Norrköping

○ Linköping

Kristiansand
○

Vättern

Skagen ○

○ Jönköping

Gotland

*BALTIC
SEA*

Rīga ✪

LATVIA

Skagerrak

Göteborg

● **Aalborg**

Öland

LITHUANIA

Tallinn
Evocative medieval
city centre (p228)

Århus ○

Helsingør ○

○ Helsingborg

ENMARK

Copenhagen ●

Esbjerg ○

Odense ○

Funen

○ **Malmö**

Bornholm

Vilnius ✪

Kaliningrad ◎ **RUSSIA**

✪ **Minsk**

55°N

BELARUS

19 TOP EXPERIENCES

National Park Hiking

1 Scandinavia's unspoilt wilderness areas are the finest in Europe. If you like dark pine woods populated by foxes and bears, head for northeastern Finland's Karhunkierros trail (p206). Norway's Jotunheimen National Park (p338) encompasses hundreds of lofty mountain peaks and crystal-blue lakes. Lying inside the Arctic Circle, Abisko National Park in Sweden begins the epic 440km Kungsleden hiking trail (p500). Walkers will never forget the bleak volcanic slopes, steaming pools and mossy valleys of Iceland's Landmannalaugar to Þórsmörk trek (p298). Abisko National Park (p499, above)

GRAEME CORNWALLIS / LONELY PLANET IMAGES ©

Fjords, Norway

2 The drama of Norway's fjords (p340) is difficult to overstate. Seen from above, the fjords cut deep gashes into the Norwegian interior, adding texture and depth to the map of northwestern Scandinavia. Up close, sheer rock walls plunge from high, green meadows into water-filled canyons shadowed by pretty fjord-side villages. Sognefjorden, over 200km long, and Hardangerfjord are Norway's most extensive fjord networks, but the quiet, precipitous beauty of Nærøyfjorden (part of Sognefjorden), Lysefjord and – the king of Norwegian fjords – Geirangerfjord are prime candidates for Scandinavia's most beautiful corner.

Aurora Borealis, Lapland & Iceland

3 Whether caused by the collision of charged particles in the upper atmosphere, or sparked, as Sámi tradition tells, by a giant snow fox swishing its tail as it runs across the Arctic tundra, the haunting, humbling splendour of the aurora borealis, or Northern Lights, is an experience never to be forgotten. Though it is theoretically visible year-round, it's much easier to see and more spectacular in the darker winter months. The further north, such as the Lapland region (p207) in Finland, the better your chances of gazing on nature's light show.

DAVID TIPLING / LONELY PLANET IMAGES ©

The Hermitage, St Petersburg

JONATHAN CHESTER / LONELY PLANET IMAGES ©

4 Housed in the Winter Palace, the Hermitage (p238), centrepiece of St Petersburg, embodies the opulence and extravagance of the tsarist regime. Climb the impossibly grand staircases to discover dazzling staterooms decorated with enormous chandeliers. You'll also find gallery after gallery stuffed with an eye-boggling collection of glorious artworks and rare artefacts, ranging from Egyptian mummies and Scythian gold to treasures of the Italian Renaissance, not to mention some of the most famous images created by 19th- and 20th-century Impressionist and post-Impressionist painters.

Lofoten Islands, Norway

5 Few visitors forget their first sighting of the Lofoten Islands (p387), laid out in summer greens and yellows or drowned in the snows of winter, their razor-sharp peaks poking dark against a cobalt-clear sky. In the pure, exhilarating air, there's a constant tang of salt and, in the villages, more than a whiff of cod, that giant of the seas whose annual migration brings wealth. A hiker's dream and nowadays linked by bridges, the islands are simple to hop along, whether by bus, car or bicycle.

CRAIG PERSHOUSE / LONELY PLANET IMAGES ©

Svalbard, Norway

6 The subpolar archipelago of Svalbard (p403) is a true place of the heart. Deliciously remote and yet surprisingly accessible, Svalbard is Europe's most evocative slice of the polar north and one of the continent's last great wilderness areas. Shapely peaks, massive ice fields (60% of Svalbard is covered by glaciers) and heartbreakingly beautiful fjords provide the backdrop for a rich array of Arctic wildlife (including around one-fifth of the world's polar bears, which outnumber people up here) and for summer and winter activities that get you out amid the ringing silence of the snows.

JONATHAN SMITH / LONELY PLANET IMAGES ©

Old Town, Tallinn

7 The jewel in Tallinn's crown is its Unesco-protected Old Town (p229), a 14th- and 15th-century two-tiered jumble of turrets, spires and winding streets. Most travellers' experiences of Tallinn begin and end with the cobblestoned, chocolate-box landscape of intertwining alleys and picturesque courtyards. Enjoy it on high (climb one of the observation towers) or down below (refuel in one of the vaulted cellars turned into cosy bars and cafes), or simply stroll and soak up the medieval magic.

CHRISTIAN ASLUND / LONELY PLANET IMAGES ©

Island Cycling

8 A lazy bike ride around the perimeters of Gotland (p465), the holiday-friendly Baltic Sea island, is one of the most rewarding ways to spend your time in Sweden: the mostly flat, paved Gotlandsleden cycle path (p490) circles the island, passing fields of poppies, shady woodlands, historic churches and ancient rune stones at regular intervals. Also a short ferry ride from Stockholm, the autonomous Åland islands (p172) have a network of bridges and ferries that makes them a pleasure to pedal around. Or try the 105km-long ride around Bornholm (p68), one of Denmark's National Routes, from the hilly north to the flat, scenic south. Cycling in Bornholm, Denmark (above)

NIKOLAI LINARES / CORBIS

New Nordic Food

9 When Noma (p52) topped S.Pellegrino's 2010 'World's 50 Best Restaurants' list, Copenhagen's culinary prowess was confirmed. Once known for smørrebrød (open sandwiches) and *frikadeller* (meatballs), Denmark's capital has reinvented itself as a hotbed of gastronomic innovation, where restaurants like Orangeriet (p50) and Kødbyens Fiskebar (p51) are revamping Nordic cuisine. Other countries have followed Denmark's lead, and exciting new restaurants now stock all the region's capitals, with more popping up like chanterelle mushrooms. Chefs at Noma, Copenhagen (above)

W KORALL / PHOTOLIBRARY

Ice Hotel, Sweden

11 Somewhere between a chandelier and an igloo, the famed Ice Hotel (p499) at Jukkasjärvi is a justifiably popular destination – it may be a gimmick, but it's also really cool (and not just literally). Sleep among bearskin rugs in a hotel sculpted anew from ice each winter; hang out in the attached Icebar, sipping chilled vodka out of ice glasses. Beyond its own appeal, the hotel makes a good base for admiring the aurora borealis and learning about Sámi culture in this part of Lapland.

PETER UNGER / LONELY PLANET IMAGES ©

Skagen, Denmark

10 Sweeping skies, moving sands and duelling seas: the appeal of Skagen (p102) is both ephemeral and constant. The lure of the light has drawn many – packing paintbrushes – from far beyond its coastline, and its blending colour of sky, sea and sand can inspire awe in the most hardened of souls. This is both Jutland's northern tip and Denmark's 'end of the line', where gentle fields give way to ghostly dunes, a buried church and the shape-shifting headland of Grenen, where the Baltic meets its murky North Sea rival.

Thermal Springs & Saunas

12 Geothermal pools are Iceland's pride. The most famous is the Blue Lagoon (p268) spa, whose waters are packed with skin-softening minerals. Visitors can also relax in warm milky-blue waters at Mývatn Nature Baths, or even inside a volcanic crater at nearby Viti (p284). The sauna (p193) is as deeply entrenched in Finnish tradition: participants steam in the nude, whisk themselves with birch twigs and cool off with a cold shower or icy plunge. Experience the soothing springs and saunas yourself, and emerge from your visit a calmer, wiser person. Blue Lagoon (left)

Vestmanna Cliffs, Faroe Islands

13 Boats and birds are the great attractions of the Faroe Islands and the two combine in thrilling fashion when sailing from Vestmanna (p134) to the region's teeming bird cliffs. You can't be sure of fine weather but even in cloud and drizzle the ride is utterly memorable as you approach these seabird empires, with clouds of razorbills, guillemots and fulmars wheeling overhead as your boatman steers past rocky spikes and soaring cliffs.

Bog Bodies, Denmark

14 If you've ever read Seamus Heaney's 'bog people' poems, you'll know all about the eerily preserved, millennia-old bodies exhumed from Denmark's peat bogs. Skin still intact and frown lines clear, these ancient locals seem caught in perpetual slumber. The Grauballe Man (p86) near Århus is a compelling Bronze Age whodunit: was he a noble sacrifice or the victim of foul play? More serene is the Tollund Man (p93), his face so breathtakingly preserved that people mistook him for a modern-day crime victim upon discovery in 1950. Tollund Man (left)

Sledding

15 Once there's healthy snow cover in the north, a classic experience is to hitch up a team of reindeer or husky dogs (p412) to a sled and swish away under the pale winter sun. Short jaunts are good for getting the hang of steering, stopping and letting the animals know who's boss; once your confidence is high, take off on an overnight trip, sleeping in a hut in the wilderness and thawing those deserving bones with a steaming sauna.

Bar Life

16 In Reykjavík (p250), Helsinki (p153) and Stockholm (p422) summer is short and winter is long and bitter. Driving away the darkness is a necessity – so it's no wonder that a near-legendary nightlife has evolved in these cities. After all, what could be better than gathering your friends into a snug, sleek bar to talk, drink, joke, sing, laugh, flirt and dance the night away? Natural Nordic reserve melts away with the application of *brennivín* (Iceland), *salmiakkikossu* (Finland), *snaps* or aquavit (Sweden), or plain old beer – join the party and make new friends fast. Reykjavík *runtur* (left)

Design Shopping

17 If design is defined as making the practical beautiful, then Scandinavia rules the roost. Elegant, innovative yet functional takes on everyday items mean that you won't have to look far before you get an 'I need that!' moment. There's great design and handicrafts to be found right across the region, but Copenhagen (p54) and Helsinki (p163), closely followed by Stockholm (p439), are where modern flagships can be found alongside the best of the edgier new ideas. Stilleben, Copenhagen (right)

18 Wooden buildings are a feature of Scandinavia, once comprising whole towns. However, 'great fires' – whether through somebody smoking in bed or burning the toast – were understandably common and comparatively few of these historic districts remain. They are worth seeking out for their quaint, unusual beauty; among others, Rauma (p183), Bergen (p340) and Göteborg (p465) preserve excellent 'timbertowns', perfect neighbourhoods for strolling around. Bryggen area in Bergen, Norway (left)

JONATHAN SMITH / LONELY PLANET IMAGES ©

A Cottage Somewhere

19 Vast numbers of Scandinavians head for summer cottages (p221). The typical one is simple, by a lake or on an island, with few modern comforts but probably a rowing boat or canoe, a barbecue, a bit of old fishing line and maybe a sauna. The holidays are spent enjoying nature and getting away from city life. Across the region there are numerous rental cottages that can become venues for you to experience a slice of authentic Nordic peace. Jostedalsbreen, Norway (above)

need to know

Buses
» Comprehensive network throughout the region. The only choice in further-flung corners like Lapland.

Trains
» Efficient services in the continental nations, none in Iceland or the Faroe Islands.

When to Go

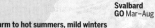

Warm to hot summers, mild winters
Warm to hot summers, cold winters
Mild year round
Mild summers, cold to very cold winters
Polar climate

Svalbard
GO Mar–Aug

Iceland
GO Jun–Aug

Lapland
GO Feb–Mar, Aug–Sep

Faroe Islands
GO Jun–Aug

Fjords
GO Mar–Sep

St Petersburg/ Tallinn
GO Jun–Jul

Copenhagen
GO May–Oct, Dec

High Season
(Jun–Aug)

» Expect warm, long days through most of the region.

» Hotel prices are down in many countries.

» Christmas and February to March are very busy in winter-sports destinations.

Shoulder Season (Apr–May, Sep–Oct)

» Expect chilly nights and even snow.

» It's not the cheapest time to travel as summer hostels and camping grounds have closed.

» Many attractions close or shorten opening hours.

Low Season
(Nov–Mar)

» Outside the cities, it's very quiet except in winter-sports centres.

» Prepare for serious cold.

» Most outdoor attractions are shut and other tourist services closed or severely restricted.

Set Your Budget

Budget Less than €140

» Dorm beds: €15–40

» Supermarkets and market halls for self-caterers

» Cheap lunch specials: €8–15

» National parks: free

Midrange €140–250

» Double room: €80–150

» Car hire: €50–80 per day

» Lunch and light dinner in restaurants

» Major museum admission: €7–15

Top End Over €250

» Double room: €140–220

» Three-course meal for two with wine: €150–200

» Cocktail in the glitziest designer bar: €15–25

Driving

» Drive on the right. Car hire is easy but not cheap. Few motorways so travel times can be long. Compulsory winter tyres mean hassle-free snow driving.

Ferries

» Top way to travel the region: great-value network around the Baltic; spectacular Norwegian coastal ferry, and a service to the Faroe Islands and Iceland.

Bicycles

» Very bike-friendly cities and lots of options for longer cycling routes. Most ferries, buses and trains carry bikes for little or no charge.

Planes

» Decent network of budget flights connecting major centres. Full-fare flights with the major carriers are comparatively expensive.

Websites

» **Lonely Planet** (www.lonelyplanet.com/europe) Destination information, accommodation bookings, traveller forum and more.

» **Go Scandinavia** (www.goscandinavia.com) Combined tourist board website for the five major Nordic countries.

» **IceNews** (www.icenews.is) Presents the latest English news snippets from the Nordic nations.

» **Direct Ferries** (www.directferries.co.uk) Useful booking site for Baltic and Atlantic ferries.

Money

» Debit and credit cards used throughout; ATMs widespread, accept all cards

» Finland and Tallinn use the euro; St Petersburg uses the rouble

» Iceland (króna), Norway (krone), Sweden (krona) and Denmark/Faroe Islands (krone) each have their own currency

» The euro is commonly accepted in major centres; all major currencies are easily exchanged throughout the region

Visas

» With the exception of Russia (St Petersburg, p246) and the Faroe Islands (p147), all countries in this guide are part of the Schengen area.

» A valid passport or EU identity card is required to enter the Schengen area. Citizens of the EU, USA, Canada, Australia and New Zealand don't need a tourist visa for stays of less than three months; others may need a Schengen visa. See each country's directory section for further information.

Arriving in Scandinavia

» **Copenhagen Kastrup Airport**
Trains: every 10 minutes into the centre
Taxis: Around Dkr250 for the 15-minute ride

» **Stockholm Arlanda Airport**
Trains: express trains run all day from Stockholm; airport buses are cheaper but slower
Taxis: Think Skr450 for the 45-minute drive

» **Helsinki Vantaa Airport**
Buses: regular standard and express buses into the centre
Taxis: dedicated airport taxis cost €27 and take half an hour

What to Take

» For winter visits: decent thermal underwear, waterproof boots and top layer, woolly hat, gloves and a neck warmer

» A credit or debit card: plastic's an easy option throughout, and saves working out which country that 50-krone banknote is from

» An HI membership card, towel and sleep sheet if you plan to use hostels

» A tent and sleeping bag if you're going hiking – huts fill up fast

» Powerful insect repellent in summer, especially in Finland and Iceland

» An eye mask for sleeping under the never-setting summer sun

» Swimsuit: there are lots of hot springs, spa hotels and lakes to jump in

» Mobile phone: buying a local SIM card is the easiest way to get connected

if you like...

Coastal Scenery

Scoured by glaciers, speckled with islands and buffeted by wind and rain, the Nordic coastlines are spectacular and capable of inspiring profound awe. The Atlantic coasts are the most jagged, while the more sedate Baltic archipelagos offer a gentler beauty.

Grenen Stand in two seas at Denmark's northern tip (p102)

Island thieves Mythology claims that the dramatic rocky sea stacks Risin and Kellingin were a villainous couple who attempted to drag the Faroes away to Iceland but became petrified when caught in the act (p137)

The High Coast See northern Sweden's dramatic Höga Kusten (p491)

Lofoten Marvel at nature's sheer improbability in these northern Norwegian islands (p387)

Svalbard Be spellbound where vast glaciers meet the Arctic Ocean at this remote outpost (p403)

Jökulsárlón Watch glaciers float to sea from this glittering lagoon (p289)

Ingólfshöfði An isolated Iceland headland and nature reserve, accessible only by tractor-towed hay cart (p290)

Hiking

Wide open spaces, majestic landscapes and bracing, clean air make the Nordic lands excellent for hiking. Multiday treks are easily accomplished thanks to the great network of national parks, camping grounds and overnight huts. Norway and Iceland offer the most scenic trails, while Finland and Sweden are particularly good for walking through the colours of the spectacular autumn forest.

Northern Sweden Trek along the Kungsleden (King's Trail) in Swedish Lapland (p500)

Norwegian peaks Traverse the roof of Norway in the Jotunheimen National Park (p338)

Rjukan Hike in search of wild reindeer atop Norway's Hardangervidda plateau (p334)

Hornstrandir Accessible only by boat in high summer, this isolated Icelandic peninsula is the ultimate escape (p275)

Landmannalaugar To Þórsmörk Trek Iceland's most famous hike, over rainbow-coloured mountains and through deserts of pumice (p298)

Finnish Lapland Hit Lapland's UKK National Park for some top trekking in one of Europe's last great wildernesses (p213)

Cycling

Bikes are a way of life in Scandinavia, and the cities are full of cycle lanes, grab-a-bike stands and marked cycling routes. There are also great options for multiday cycling holidays, particularly in the Baltic islands. It's easy to take bikes on public transport throughout the region.

Bornholm Pedal your way across this perfect Danish island (p68)

Tallinn Get out of the Old Town and take a bike tour to the far-flung corners of the capital (p233)

Cycling the Faroes The islands are compact yet stunning and traffic is graciously light (p148)

Gotland Make the easy loop around this Swedish island (p465)

Rjukan Ride across Norway's Hardangervidda, Europe's highest mountain plateau (p334)

Mývatn The best way to explore Lake Mývatn's charms is on a day-long bicycle circuit (p283)

Åland This archipelago between Finland and Sweden is ideal for two-wheeled touring, with numerous flat islands to explore (p172)

CHRISTIAN ASLUND / LONELY PLANET IMAGES ©

» Cross-country skiing in Tromsø (p395), Norway

Vikings

Whether you're interested in the structured society, extensive trade networks, dexterous handicrafts and well-honed navigational skills of this advanced civilisation or you glorify in tales of plunder, pillage, horned helmets, dragonships and the twilight of the gods, there's something for you in western Scandinavia.

Roskilde Set sail on a faithful Viking replica in Denmark (p63)

Ribe Vikingecenter Schmooze with modern-day Danish Vikings (p107)

Gotland Visit this Swedish island's numerous rune stones and ship settings (p486)

Oslo Board a Viking longboat at Oslo's marvellous Viking-skipshuset (p319)

Reykjavík 871+/-2 Fascinating hi-tech exhibition, based around an original Viking longhouse (p251)

Saga Museum A kind of Viking Madame Tussauds, this Reykjavík museum is heaps of fun (p251)

Northern seas Follow the mighty wake of the Viking colonists by taking the boat from Denmark to the Faroes and Iceland (p30)

The Active Winter

Once the snow has firmly carpeted the land, northern Scandinavia is a wonderful place to get active. March and April is the best time to enjoy winter sports, with much more daylight and less-extreme temperatures than you get earlier in the winter.

Sled safaris Head out pulled by huskies or reindeer, or aboard a snowmobile to explore the frozen wildernesses. There are excellent places to do this right across northern Norway, Sweden and Finland, whether it's a short hour-long swoosh or a multiday adventure (p412).

Skiing and snowboarding There are excellent resorts in Norway and flatter, family-friendly slopes in northern Sweden and Finland. These places usually offer a host of other wintry activities like snowshoe treks and ice fishing (p221).

Breaking the ice Crunch a passage through the frozen Gulf of Bothnia aboard an icebreaker and go for a dip – with a hi-tech drysuit – at Kemi in Finland (p211)

Winter Wonders

Winter's magic isn't confined to the active. There are other enticing attractions aplenty up north, and the southern cities are feel-good places in December, with spectacular street lighting and festive drinks.

Snow hotels It's tough to beat the romance of snow hotels, ethereally beautiful creations sculpted from snow and ice. The most famous is at Jukkasjärvi (near Kiruna) in Sweden (p499) but others we like are at Alta (p398) and Kirkenes (p401) in Norway, and Kemi (p211) in Finland.

Santa Claus Visit the world's most famous beardie in his eerie Finnish grotto (p207)

Stockholm Christmas Shop at Gamla Stan's delightful Christmas Market (p422)

Tivoli Put the magic back into Christmas with wonderful lights and warming mulled wine (p41)

Aurora borealis (Northern Lights) Get as far north as you can. Find a place without much light. Then you'll need patience and a slice of luck. One of the best viewing spots is Abisko in Sweden (p499).

» Architect Steven Holl designed Kiasma, a museum in Helsinki, Finland (p156)

Food & Drink

Once pooh-poohed by the gourmets, Scandinavia is now at the forefront of modern gourmet and molecular cuisine. Michelin stars twinkle across the region's capitals: Copenhagen's the place to head for the most sophisticated restaurant scene, but heartier traditional cookery still warms the cockles in local restaurants throughout the region.

Noma Push the culinary envelope in Copenhagen, at the world's hottest restaurant (p52)

Vodka Sample different types of vodka and eat fine Russian cuisine at Russian Vodkaroom No 1 (p245)

Puffins They're charming to watch but can also end up in the Faroese cooking pot (p145)

Smörgåsbord Try the Verandan at the Grand Hôtel, Stockholm, open all year (p436)

Brennivín Known as 'Black Death', this Icelandic schnapps is swiggable in all good bars (p264)

Rudolf and friends Reindeer is a staple in Lapland; elk and bear make regular appearances on menus in other parts of Finland (p219)

Canoeing & Kayaking

It's hard to beat this region for kayaking and canoeing. Numerous suppliers, handily placed camping grounds and plenty of wildlife to silently approach make it a pleasure, whether you're planning a multiday sea-kayaking or afternoon lake-canoeing adventure.

Danish Lake District Glide silent lakes in bucolic Jutland (p93)

Stockholm Rent a canoe for the day from Djurgårdsbrons Sjöcafe (p432)

Sweden Set out on a longer canoe trip (p506)

Norway Kayak through some of Norway's prettiest corners from Svalbard to the fjords (p411)

Ísafjörður This Icelandic destination is perfect for beginners (p273)

Seyðisfjörður Guided kayaking tours with the affable Hlynur in Iceland (p287)

Åland Paddle around the low, rocky islands of this quietly picturesque Finnish archipelago (p172)

Seal Lakes Explore these watery Finnish national parks by boat and try to spot a rare inland seal (p191)

Modern Art & Architecture

Nordic lands tend to be at the forefront of these things, with designers and artists given a freer rein than elsewhere. The region has a huge amount to offer for anyone interested in contemporary art and architecture.

Louisiana Art meets vistas at this Copenhagen modern-art must (p57)

ARoS Walk among giants at this Danish cultural showpiece (p86)

Island art The Faroes' imaginative national gallery is a feast of modernist expression (p123)

Stockholm Visit one of Scandinavia's best modern-art museums, Moderna Museet (p427)

Malmö Marvel at the Turning Torso (p457)

Oslo Enjoy Scandinavia's newest architectural icon: the Oslo Opera House (p315)

Helsinki Iconic Kiasma still turns heads with its exuberant exterior and excellent exhibitions (p156)

Alvar Aalto Make an architectural pilgrimage to Jyväskylä, the city where one of the giants made his name (p191)

If you like... choppers, then the Faroes is the place for you, offering both cheap, scenic helicopter flights and motorcycle hires (p148)

If you like... Sámi culture Visit reindeer at Kiruna (p498) or Inari (p214), and experience cultural activities in Lemmenjoki National Park (p215).

Historic Buildings & Churches

It's not all out-with-the-old and bring-in-the-new in Scandinavia. Creaky, ancient wooden churches dot the countryside, and the older towns and cities in the region are replete with treasures. A series of muscular castles fortified the kingdoms around the ever-turbulent Baltic.

Kronborg Slot Channel Shakespeare at Hamlet's old haunt in Helsingør (p59)

St Petersburg Be dazzled by the candy-coloured swirls and brilliant mosaic decoration on the Church of the Saviour on Spilled Blood (p238)

Tallinn Weaving your way around the medieval Old Town's narrow, cobbled streets is like strolling back to the 14th century (p229)

Gotland Historic churches dot this Swedish island (p486)

Norwegian stave churches Admire World Heritage–listed Urnes Stave Church on the banks of a fjord (p368)

Olavinlinna Finland's most spectacular castle, delicately perched on a rocky islet, lords it over the centre of one of its prettiest towns (p187)

Wildlife Watching

The clamour of seabirds fills the air across the Atlantic while whales roll in the ocean. Elk are widespread, Finnish forests harbour serious carnivores and the mighty polar bear still lords it – for now – over Svalbard. Low population densities make it excellent for observing wildlife in summer.

Fanø Witness mass migration of the feathered kind in Denmark (p109)

Bird boating To and through the spectacular Faroese bird cliffs (p134)

Reindeer These roam at will across the north of Sweden, Norway and Finland; learn about reindeer in Jukkasjärvi, in Sweden (p498)

Central Norway Track down the prehistoric musk ox (p339)

Svalbard Watch out for Europe's last polar bears in Svalbard (p403)

Whale watching Head to Norway's Lofoten Islands (p387) or Húsavík in Iceland (p307)

Látrabjarg These dramatic cliffs are the world's biggest bird breeding grounds (p275)

Bear watching Head out to the Finnish forests on a bear-watching excursion (p201)

Design

Why is Scandinavian design so admired? Because substance comes first and style second. The mainland cities are full of innovative and beautiful creations, but an underlying efficiency and practicality keeps contact with the region's rural past. In the north Sámi artists weave modern interpretations and ancient traditions.

Copenhagen Hit the Dansk Design Center (p45) then revamp your home at Hay House, a Danish design mecca (p55)

Helsinki A design epicentre with everything from flagship stores to cutting-edge studios (p163)

Faroese woolcrafts Organic wool turned into designer knitwear (p129)

Stockholm DesignTorget puts chic gadgetry within reach (p440)

Bergen Browse designer jewellery around the ancient warehouses of Bryggen (p349)

Hafnarhús This central modern-art gallery sells cutting-edge Icelandic design (p254)

Lapland Hit workshops at Inari (p214) for the best Sámi handicrafts and browse jewellery that evokes the Arctic north in Kautokeino (p403)

month by month

Top Events

1 **Midsummer,** June

2 **Sled Safaris and Skiing,** March

3 **Roskilde Festival,** June

4 **Aurora Watching,** November

5 **Christmas,** December

January

It's cold. Very cold and very dark. But this is the beginning of the active winter; there's enough snow for ice hotels, and sledding, snowmobiling and skiing are reliable.

 **Kiruna Snöfestivalen, Sweden**

This Lapland snow festival (www.kirunalapland. se), based around a snow-sculpting competition that draws artists from all over, is on the last weekend in January. There's also a husky dog competition and a handi-crafts fair.

Skábmagovat, Finland

In the third week of January, this film festival with an indigenous theme is held in the Finnish Sámi village of Inari. Associated cultural events also happen here throughout the winter.

February

There's enough light now for it to be prime skiing season in northern Scandinavia. Local holidays mean it gets very busy (and pricey) on the slopes around the middle of the month.

 Þorrablót, Iceland

Held all across the country, nominally in honour of the god Thor, this midwinter festival's centrepiece is a feast for the fearless that includes delicacies such as putrid shark.

March

As the hours of light dramatically increase and temperatures begin to rise again, this is an excellent time to take advantage of the hefty snow cover and indulge in some winter activities.

Reindeer Racing, Finland

Held over the last weekend of March or first of April, the King's Cup (www.pa liskunnat.fi) is the grand finale of Finnish Lapland's reindeer-racing season and a great spectacle.

 Vasaloppet, Sweden

Held on the first Sunday in March, this ski race (www. vasaloppet.se) salutes Gus-tav Vasa's history-making flight on skis in 1521; it has grown into a week-long ski fest and celebration with different races – short, gru-elling or just for fun.

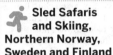 **Sled Safaris and Skiing, Northern Norway, Sweden and Finland**

Whizzing across the snow pulled by a team of hus-kies or reindeer is a pretty spectacular way to see the northern wildernesses. Add snowmobiling or skiing to the mix and it's a top time to be at high latitude.

April

Easter is celebrated in a traditional fashion across the region. Spring is underway in Denmark and the southern parts, but there's still solid snow cover in the northern reaches.

 Sámi Easter Festival, Norway

Thousands of Sámi par-ticipate in reindeer racing, theatre and cultural events (www.samieasterfestival. com) in the Finnmark towns of Karasjok and Kautokeino. The highlight is the Sámi Grand Prix, a singing and *yoiking* contest attended by artists from across Lapland.

Valborgsmässoafton, Sweden

This public holiday (Walpurgis Night) on 30 April is a pagan hold-over that's partly to welcome the arrival of spring. Celebrated across the country, it involves lighting huge bonfires, singing songs and forming parades.

Jazzkaar, Tallinn

Late April sees jazz greats from all around the world converge on Estonia's picturesque capital for a series of performances (www.jazzkaar.ee).

May

A transitional month in the north, with snow beginning to disappear and signs of life emerging after the long winter. In the south, spring's in full flow. This is a quiet but rewarding time to visit.

Copenhagen Marathon, Denmark

Scandinavia's largest marathon (www.copenhagenmarathon.dk) is on a Sunday in mid-May and draws around 5000 participants and tens of thousands of spectators. A series of shorter, lead-up races in the preceding months are a fun way to see the city.

Reykjavík Arts Festival, Iceland

Running for two weeks from late May to June, this wide-ranging festival (www.artfest.is) sees Iceland's capital taken over by local and international theatre performances, films, lectures and music.

Bergen International Festival, Norway

One of the biggest events on Norway's cultural calendar, this two-week festival (www.fib.no), beginning in late May, showcases dance, music and folklore presentations. It's at once international and a return to the city's roots.

June

Midsummer weekend in late June is celebrated with great gusto, but it's typically a family event; unless you've got local friends it's not the best moment to visit. Lapland's muddy, but the rest of the region is warm and welcoming.

Old Town Days, Tallinn

This week-long Estonian festival (www.vanalinnapaevad.ee) in early June features dancing, concerts, costumed performers and plenty of medieval merrymaking in the heart of Tallinn's stunning historic centre.

Stockholm Jazz Festival, Sweden

Held on the island of Skeppsholmen, this internationally known jazz fest (www.stockholmjazz.com) brings artists from all over, including big names like Van Morrison and Mary J Blige.

Skagen Festival, Denmark

Held over four days in late June, this festival (www.skagenfestival.dk, in Danish) at Denmark's picturesque northern tip features folk and world music performed by Danish and international artists.

Moldejazz, Norway

Norway has a fine portfolio of jazz festivals, but Molde's version (www.moldejazz.no) in mid-July is the most prestigious. With 100,000 spectators, world-class performers and a reputation for consistently high-quality music, it's easily one of Norway's most popular festivals.

Independence Day, Iceland

Held on 17 June, this is the largest nationwide festival in the country. It commemorates the founding of the Republic of Iceland in 1944 with big parades and general celebration.

Roskilde Festival, Denmark

Northern Europe's largest music festival (www.roskilde-festival.dk) rocks Roskilde for four consecutive days each summer. It takes place from late June to early July, but advance ticket sales are on offer in December and the festival usually sells out. p62

Midsummer, Denmark, Norway, Sweden, Finland

The year's biggest event in continental Nordic Europe sees fun family feasts, joyous celebrations of the summer, heady bonfires and copious drinking, often at peaceful lakeside summer cottages. It takes place on the weekend that falls between 19 June and 26 June.

White Nights, St Petersburg

The Russian city is vibrant from May through to July with gala opera, ballet and music performances, as well as the boisterous Scarlet Sails night, with concerts and fireworks attended by a million people, including many students celebrating the end of the academic year.

Extreme Sports Festival, Norway

Adventure junkies from across the world converge on Voss in late June for a week of skydiving, paragliding, parasailing and base jumping (www.ekstrems portveko.com); local and international music acts keep the energy flowing.

July

Peak season sees long, long days and sunshine. This is when the region really comes to life, with many festivals, boat trips, activities, cheaper hotels and a celebratory feel. Insects in Lapland and Iceland are a nuisance.

Frederikssund Vikingespil, Denmark

Held in Frederikssund over a two-week period from late June to early July, this Viking festival (www.vikingespil. dk) includes a costumed open-air drama followed by a banquet with Viking food and entertainment.

Copenhagen Jazz Festival, Denmark

This is the biggest entertainment event of the year in the capital, with 10 days of music at the beginning of July. The festival (www. jazz.dk) features a range of Danish and international jazz, blues and fusion music, with over 500 indoor and outdoor concerts.

Ólavsøka, Faroe Islands

The largest and most exciting traditional festival in the Faroes celebrates the 10th-century Norwegian king Olav the Holy, who spread Christian faith on the isles. The big days are 28 and 29 July.

Savonlinna Opera Festival, Finland

A month of excellent performances (www.operafestival. fi) in the romantic location of one of Europe's most picturesquely situated castles makes this Finland's biggest summer drawcard for casual and devoted lovers of opera. p188

Ruisrock, Finland

Finland's oldest and possibly best rock festival (www. ruisrock.fi) takes place in early July on an island just

outside the southwestern city of Turku. Top Finnish and international acts take part.

Wife-Carrying World Championships, Finland

Finland's, nay, the world's premier wife-carrying event (www.eukonkanto.fi) is held in the village of Sonkajärvi in early July. Winning couples (marriage not required) win the woman's weight in beer as well as significant kudos. p196

August

Most Scandinavians are back at work, so it's quieter than July but there's still decent weather across most of the region. It's a great time for hiking in Lapland, biking the islands or cruising the archipelagos.

Medieval Week, Sweden

Find yourself an actual knight in shining armour at this immensely popular annual Swedish fest (www. medeltidsveckan.se) in Visby, Gotland's medieval jewel. It takes place over a week in early August.

Århus Festival, Denmark

The 10-day Århus Festival (www.aarhusfestuge.dk) starts in late August and features scores of music performances, theatre, ballet, modern dance, opera, films and sports events at indoor and outdoor venues across Denmark's second-largest city.

Air Guitar World Championships, FInland

Tune your imaginary instrument and get involved in this crazy rockstravaganza (www.airguitarworldchampionships.com) held in Oulu in late August. This surfeit of cheesy guitar classics and seemingly endless beer is all in the name of world peace.

Reykjavík Jazz Festival, Iceland

A fun, yearly cultural event is the Reykjavík Jazz Festival (www.reykjavikjazz.is) with jazz concerts around the city. It tends to move around the calendar, so be sure to check the month.

Copenhagen Cooking, Denmark

Scandinavia's largest food festival (www.copenhagencooking.dk) focuses on the gourmet. It's a busy event that will let you catch up on the latest trends in fashionable new Nordic cuisine.

September

The winter is fast approaching: pack something warm for those chilly nights. Autumn colours are spectacular in northern forests, making it another great month for hiking. Many attractions and activities close down or go onto winter time.

Reykjavík International Film Festival, Iceland

This annual event (www.riff.is) is right at the end of September sees blockbusters make way for international art films in cinemas across the city, as well as talks from film directors from home and abroad.

Ruska Hiking, Finland and Sweden

Ruska is the Finnish word for the autumn colours, and there's a mini high season in Finnish and Swedish Lapland as hikers take to the trails to enjoy nature's brief artistic flourish.

October

Snow is already beginning to carpet the region's north. It's generally a quiet time to be in Scandinavia, as locals face the realities of yet another long winter approaching.

Iceland Airwaves, Iceland

This five-day event (www.icelandairwaves.is) in Reykjavík is one of the world's most cutting-edge music festivals: don't expect to sleep. It focuses on new musical trends rather than mainstream acts.

November

Once the clocks change in late October, there's no denying the winter. November's bad for winter sports as there's little light and not enough snow. It can be a good month to see the aurora borealis (Northern Lights), though.

Aurora Watching, Iceland, Norway, Sweden, Finland

Whether you are blessed with seeing the aurora borealis is largely a matter of luck, but the further north you are, the better the chances. Dark, cloudless nights, patience and a viewing spot away from city lights are other key factors.

Stockholm International Film Festival, Sweden

Screenings of new international and independent films, director talks and discussion panels draw cinephiles to this important annual festival (www.stockholmfilmfestival.se); tickets go quickly, so book early.

December

The Christmas period is celebrated enthusiastically across the region, with cinnamon smells, warming mulled drinks, romantic lights and festive traditions putting the meaning back into the event.

Christmas, Region-wide

Whether visiting Santa and his reindeer in Finnish Lapland, admiring the magic of Copenhagen's Tivoli at night or sampling home-baked delicacies, Christmas – especially if you know a friendly local family to spend it with – is a heart-warming time to be here.

Itineraries
Scandinavia in a Nutshell
One or Two Weeks

For those short on time, this is a quick hop around the classic sights of southern Scandinavia. With just a week, it's essentially one city in each of Denmark, Sweden and Norway; extra time allows more detailed exploration and side trips.

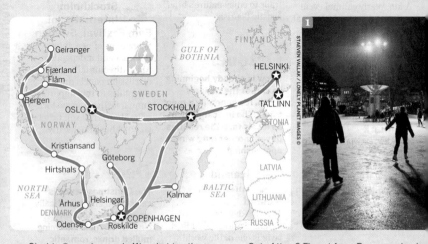

» Start in Copenhagen (p41), admiring the waterfront and museums, and enjoying the lights of Tivoli at night.

» Take a day trip to the cathedral and Viking Ship Museum at Roskilde (p62) or 'Hamlet's' castle at Helsingør (p59).

» Next, take the train to Stockholm (p422) and get into the design scene, as well as admire the stately, watery centre of town.

» An overnight train takes you to Oslo (p315), where you can check out much of Munch's work.

» From Oslo, a long but very scenic day includes the rail trip to Flåm (p365) and a combination boat/bus journey along the Sognefjord to Bergen (p340), Norway's prettiest city.

» Out of time? Fly out from Bergen or back to Copenhagen.

» Otherwise, head to Kristiansand (p331), where there's a ferry to Hirtshals (p104).

» Nose on down to Århus (p86) – don't miss the ARoS art museum. From here, it's an easy train ride to Copenhagen.

» Extra days? A side trip from Stockholm on a Baltic ferry could take you to Helsinki (p153) or picturesque Tallinn (p228).

» Other stops could include Göteborg (p465) or Kalmar (p483); more fjord-y Norwegian experiences at Fjærland (p369) and Geiranger (p371); or extra Danish time at Odense (p75)

Clockwise from top left
1. Ice skating in Oslo 2. Stockholm's Gamla Stan 3. Tivoli, Copenhagen

Finland and the Baltic

Two to Three Weeks

Starting in Stockholm, this itinerary follows the old trading routes around the Baltic and covers plenty of Finland, including the capital, Helsinki, and beautiful Lakeland, also taking in the sumptuous Baltic cities of Tallinn and St Petersburg.

» Kick things off in **Stockholm** (p422), for centuries a Baltic trading powerhouse.

» From here, take advantage of the cheap, luxurious overnight ferries to Finland. Disembark in **Helsinki** (p153) – get a good view of the spectacular arrival – and investigate the cathedrals, modern architecture and design scene. Catch a classical or rock concert too.

» From Helsinki, it's an easy boat trip across the Baltic to medieval **Tallinn** (p228), a historic treasure trove that's worth a couple of days' exploration. If time's short, take a day trip.

» Returning to Helsinki, take the train or ferry to **St Petersburg** (p237). Normally you need a visa, but it can be waived for short stays when arriving by boat. After this enchanting, imperial city – the Hermitage museum and the ballet are top draws – return to Helsinki.

» In summer, take the train to the shimmering lakes of **Savonlinna** (p187), with its awesome medieval castle and opera festival, or **Kuopio** (p192), to steam up in its large smoke sauna.

» Then head to the dynamic cultural city of **Tampere** (p177), visiting its quirky museums and taking a lake cruise.

» Hit intriguing **Turku** (p166), then return by ferry to Stockholm via the **Åland islands** (p172). Stop off for as long as you wish and tour by bike.

Clockwise from top left
1. Savonlinna's castle, Olavinlinna 2. Mariinsky Theatre (p246), St Petersburg 3. Tallinn 4. Helsinki's Kiasma (p156), designed by Steven Holl

Beyond the Arctic Circle

Three Weeks

This thorough visit to the north takes in Santa, Sámi culture, spectacular coastal scenery viewed from the sea and opportunities for excellent activities. It'll be a completely different experience in summer or in winter.

» Take the overnight train from Helsinki (p153) to Rovaniemi (p207). Visit the fabulous Arktikum, chat with Santa and prepare for the wilderness.

» Cross the Arctic Circle to Saariselkä (p213) for great activities, whether summer hiking in the UKK National Park or husky-sledding trips in winter.

» From here it's a short hop to the Sámi village of Inari (p213), where Siida is a wonderful exhibition on Lapland's nature and indigenous cultures.

» From Inari summer buses run right to Nordkapp (p399), where you can stand at the top of Europe and gaze out towards the utter north.

» Catch the *Hurtigruten* coastal steamer to the stunning Lofoten Islands (p387), possibly stopping in lively Tromsø (p393).

» The boat heads right down to Bergen, but jump off in Narvik (p384) and take the train to Kiruna (p498), a remote mining town, and in winter, home to the famous Ice Hotel.

» Take side trips to stunning Abisko National Park (p499) and the Sámi village of Jokkmokk (p496).

» From here, head back to Helsinki via Tornio (p212) or fly, train or bus all the way south to Stockholm (p422).

Clockwise from top left
1. Sámi people handicrafts 2. Arktikum, Rovaniemi
3. Coastline from the *Hurtigruten* 4. The chapel at the Ice Hotel (p499), near Kiruna

Northern Islands

Four Weeks

Of course you can fly to the northern islands, but it's much more fun to do it like the Vikings did and go by boat. Start in Denmark and head into the North Atlantic to fabulous Iceland, with a stop in the Faroes en route.

» Fly into **Copenhagen** (p41), taking some time to absorb its addictive atmosphere.

» Then hit north Jutland and the beautiful dunes at **Skagen** (p102).

» Jump aboard the weekly (biweekly in summer) ferry *Norröna*, leaving from nearby **Hirtshals** (p104).

» Take advantage of your free stop in the remote **Faroe Islands** (p120), but keep an eye on the boat timetables: you may have to spend a week here.

» Giggle at the comical puffins on the awesome cliffs of **Mykines** (p134) and take a boat trip to visit the immense seabird colonies at **Vestmanna** (p134).

» The ferry (mid-April to October) continues to Iceland, arriving at **Seyðisfjörður** (p287).

» From here journey to Reykjavík along the south coast past **Skaftafell** (p290).

» In **Reykjavík** (p250), visit the Saga Museum and take trips to the Viking village of Hafnarfjörður and the Blue Lagoon.

» If you've got time to explore, head to the desolate interior for the amazing geo-scapes of **Landmannalaugar** (p298). Take the spectacular three-day hike to Þórsmörk, one of Europe's most spectacular walks.

» Travel around the Ring Rd, including an R&R stop at peaceful fjord-side **Akureyri** (p276).

» Head back to Denmark on the ferry if you're still game, otherwise fly back from Reykjavík.

Clockwise from top left
1. Mykines 2. On the Landmannalaugar to Þórsmörk trek
3. Skaftafell 4. Fjallabak Nature Reserve (p298), Iceland

countries at a glance

The seductive call of the north is one of wild landscapes, crisp air and cutting-edge city style coloured by the epic changes of the Scandinavian seasons.

Scenically, it's hard to beat. Norway's noble, breathtaking coastline, serrated with fjords, competes with Iceland's harsh, volcanic majesty. Soothing Swedish and Finnish lake- and forest-scapes offer a gentler beauty.

Though the towns and cities all have a definite allure – Copenhagen and St Petersburg are the ones worth the most time – the big attraction is the outdoors. There are so many ways to get active on land, water and snow. Hiking, kayaking and wildlife watching are among Europe's best, while the bike-friendly culture makes it great for cyclists too, particularly Denmark, southern Sweden and various Baltic islands.

Denmark

Cycling ✓✓✓
History ✓✓
Gastronomy ✓✓

Two-wheeled Pleasure
With a highest point as lofty as your average big-city office building, it's no surprise to find that Denmark is a paradise for cycling. With thousands of kilometres of dedicated cycle routes and islands designed for two-wheeled exploration, it's the best way to get around.

Past Echoes
Denmark's historical sites are excellent. Hauntingly preserved bog bodies take us back to prehistoric times, while Roskilde's Viking boats and majestic cathedral are important remnants of other periods. Hamlet may have been a fictional character, but his home, Elsinore Castle, is a major attraction.

New Nordic Cuisine
Nordic food has taken a big upward swing, and Denmark is at the forefront of modern trends in Scandinavian cuisine. Copenhagen has a great eating scene, with Noma one of the world's most highly regarded restaurants.

p38

PLAN YOUR TRIP COUNTRIES AT A GLANCE

Faroe Islands

Birdlife ✓✓✓
Helicopter Rides ✓✓
Village Hopping ✓

Seabird Cities

Far out in the north Atlantic, the Faroes make the perfect base for vast squadrons of seabirds, whether you're dodging dive-bombing skuas on Skúvoy, admiring the teeming bird cliffs around Vestmanna or charmed by the delightful puffin colonies on Mykines.

Views from Upstairs

Helicopters are normally an expensive pastime, but the Faroes' subsidised inter-island flights make taking to the skies an affordable option. Buzz across the emerald green pastures and craggy coastlines on dramatic chopper flights that are some of the best value activities you'll find anywhere.

Village Life

The traditional villages of the Faroes are a delight to explore, especially around the northern parts of the island of Eysturoy. Rent a car and conduct a leisurely investigation of these quaintly colourful, spectacularly situated fishing settlements.

p120

Finland

Hiking ✓✓
Winter Activities ✓✓
Design ✓✓✓

Wild Nature

Finland's vast forested wildernesses are some of Europe's least-populated areas. Large national parks with excellent networks of trails, huts and camping grounds make this prime hiking country. Kayaking and canoeing are also great options.

Active Winters

Northern Finland's numerous ski resorts aren't very elevated but are great for beginners and families. Skiing's just the start, though: snowy wildernesses crossed in sleds pulled by reindeer or huskies, snowmobile safaris, icebreaker cruises, nights in snow hotels and a personal audience with Santa Claus are other wintry delights.

Design & Architecture

Finnish design is world famous; browsing Helsinki's shops, from flagship emporia to edgy bohemian studios, is one of the city's great pleasures. Some of the world's finest modern architecture can also be found scattered around Finland's towns.

p150

Tallinn

Medieval Streets ✓✓✓
Culture ✓
Bars & Cafes ✓✓

Historic Jewel

A short trip across the water from Helsinki, Estonia's capital, Tallinn, is the jewel of the nation. The medieval Old Town is its highlight, and weaving your way along its narrow, cobbled streets is like strolling back to the 14th century.

Traditional Culture

Despite (or perhaps because of) centuries of occupation, Estonians have tenaciously held onto their national identity and are deeply, emotionally connected to their history, folklore and national song traditions.

Bar Life

Tallinn has numerous cosy cafes decorated in plush style, ideal spots to while away a few hours if the weather's not being kind. Nightlife, with alcohol not such a wallet drain as in other Nordic countries, is pretty vibrant.

p228

St Petersburg

Art ✓✓✓
Palaces ✓✓
Performances ✓✓✓

Glorious Gallery
A jaunt to this marvellous city at the end of the Baltic is easily accomplished from Finland. The Hermitage is one of the world's great art galleries, and it doesn't disappoint, with an immense collection of European art of the highest quality. Budget a lot of time to see it.

Plush Palaces
The tsars weren't averse to a bit of glamorous living, and their palaces are appropriately opulent creations, with hall after hall of gilt inlay, chandeliers and ornament, all overlooking vast, meticulously planned gardens.

Tutu Draw
The Kirov company has a deserved reputation as one of the world's best, and its home, the Mariinsky Theatre, is a gorgeous historic performance space in the old style. Be sure to go, especially for ballet, which is just wonderful.

p237

Iceland

Scenery ✓✓✓
Activities ✓✓
Wildlife ✓✓

Volcanic Landscapes
Iceland, forged in fire, has a scenic splendour matched by few other nations. It's a bleak, epic grandeur that seems designed to remind visitors of their utter insignificance in the greater scheme of things. Getting among the steaming pools, spouting geysers and majestic glaciers is Iceland's number-one experience.

Outdoors
There are so many ways to get active. Truly spectacular hikes give awesome perspectives of Iceland's natural wonder; kayaks let you see it all from the seaward side. And what better way to soothe those aching muscles than luxuriating in a thermal spring?

Whales & Birds
The land may seem inhospitable, but the seas and skies teem with life. Iceland is one of the world's premier spots for whale watching, and the quantity of seabirds has to be seen to be believed.

p248

Norway

Fjords ✓✓✓
Activities ✓✓
Wildlife ✓✓

Coastal Majesty
The famous serrations of the coast are justly renowned; from base to tip, Norway's jagged geography is deeply momentous, inspiring profound awe.

Outdoor Appeal
The rough and rugged contours make this a prime outdoors destination. Mountains and plateaux attract hikers and cyclists, while the coastline invites getting out on the water in anything from a kayak to a cruise ship. Winter switches over to husky-sledding and snowmobile safaris, as well as the region's best skiing.

Unusual Creatures
For a modern European country, Norway has an impressive range of beasts, from whales sporting offshore to roaming elk and reindeer. There's even a reintroduced population of the weird-looking musk ox, as well as plentiful seabird life. Right up north, Svalbard is bossed by polar bears and walruses.

p313

Sweden

Winter Activities ✓✓
Museums ✓✓
Boating ✓✓

Snowy Seduction

Northern Sweden has several top-drawer winter attractions, one of which is the aurora borealis (Northern Lights). Dark places like Abisko, in the country's top-left corner, make great observatories; other attractions up here include dog-sledding, skiing and Kiruna's famous Ice Hotel.

Proud Heritage

Sweden, which once controlled much of northern Europe, has a rich history and proud artistic heritage, which is displayed at great galleries and museums in the country. But it's not all about the rich and famous. Excellent open-air displays dotted across the country document the humbler traditions of everyday life.

Water World

The abundance of water once the snow melts means it's a country that's beautifully set up for boating, whether you're canoeing inland waterways or exploring the coastline in a yacht or kayak.

p419

Look out for these icons:

 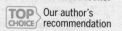 Our author's recommendation

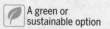 A green or sustainable option

 No payment required

See the Index for a full list of destinations covered in this book.

On the Road

Denmark

Includes »

Best Places to Eat

» Noma (p52)

» Kødbyens Fiskebar (p51)

» Schønnemann (p50)

» Restaurant Kadeau (p71)

» Nordisk Spisehus (p90)

Best Places to Stay

» Hotel Nimb (p48)

» CPH Living (p49)

» Dragsholm Slot (p61)

» Pension Vestergade 44 (p85)

» Stammershalle Badehotel (p73)

Why Go?

Denmark is the bridge between Scandinavia and northern Europe. To the rest of Scandinavia, the Danes are fun-loving, frivolous party animals, with relatively liberal, progressive attitudes. Their culture, food, architecture and appetite for conspicuous consumption owe as much, if not more, to their German neighbours to the south than to their former colonies – Sweden, Norway and Iceland to the north.

Packed with intriguing museums, shops, bars, nightlife and award-winning restaurants, Denmark's capital, Copenhagen, is one of the hippest, most accessible cities in northern Europe. And while Danish cities such as Odense and Århus harbour their own cultural gems, Denmark's other chief appeal lies in its picture-perfect countryside, sweeping coastline and historic sights such as neolithic burial chambers, the bodies of well-preserved Iron Age people exhumed from their slumber in peat bogs, and atmospheric Viking ruins and treasures.

When to Go
Copenhagen

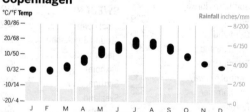

Jun & Jul Long days, buzzing beachside towns, Copenhagen Jazz, and A-list rock fest Roskilde.

Sep & Oct Fewer crowds, golden landscapes and cosy nights by crackling open fires.

Dec Twinkling Christmas lights, ice-skating rinks, and gallons of warming *gløgg* (mulled wine).

Connections

Denmark's modern, efficient transport network is well connected to the region and the rest of the world. Located in Copenhagen, its main airport, Kastrup, offers excellent and numerous long- and short-haul connections, while Billund and Århus in Jutland (regional airports) offer numerous European short-haul options. Good road and rail connections link Sweden and Germany to Denmark. Plentiful ferries link Denmark with all major Baltic destinations and with Atlantic Coast destinations in Norway, the Faroe Islands, Iceland and the UK.

ITINERARIES

One Week

You could comfortably spend five days in Copenhagen exploring the museums, hunting down Danish design and taste-testing its lauded restaurants and bars. A trip north along the coast to the magnificent modern-art museum, Louisiana, and then further north still to Helsingborg Slot, before returning south via Frederiksborg Slot, would be a great way to spend the other two days. If the weather is on your side, head for the north coast of Zealand for historic fishing villages and gorgeous sandy beaches.

Two Weeks

After time in Copenhagen, a quick catamaran ride will take you to the Baltic island of Bornholm, reputedly the sunniest slice of Denmark, and famed for cycling, beaches and its cheap, tasty smoke-houses. Alternatively, head west, stopping off on the island of Funen to see Hans Christian Andersen's birthplace in Odense. Continue further west to the Jutland peninsula for the bustling city of Århus and further north to magnificent Skagen, where the Baltic and North Seas clash.

Essential Food & Drink

» **Smørrebrød** Rye bread topped with anything from beef tartar to egg and shrimp, the open sandwich is Denmark's most famous culinary export.

» **Sild** Smoked, cured, pickled or fried, herring is a local staple and best washed down with generous serves of akvavit (schnapps).

» **Kanelsnegle** A calorific delight, 'cinnamon snails' are sweet, buttery scrolls, sometimes laced with chocolate.

» **Akvavit** Denmark's best-loved spirit is caraway-spiced akvavit from Aalborg, drunk straight down as a shot, followed by a chaser of øl (beer).

» **Lashings of beer** Carlsberg may dominate, but Denmark's expanding battalion of microbreweries includes Ølfabriken, Brøckhouse and Grauballe.

AT A GLANCE

» **Capital** Copenhagen
» **Area** 43,094 sq km
» **Population** 5.5 million
» **Country code** ☑45
» **Language** Danish
» **Currency** krone

Exchange Rates

Australia	A$1	Dkr5.48
Canada	C$1	Dkr5.28
Europe	€1	Dkr7.46
Japan	¥100	Dkr6.16
New Zealand	NZ$1	Dkr4.03
UK	UK£1	Dkr8.38
USA	US$1	Dkr5.03

Set Your Budget

» **Budget hotel room** Dkr500
» **Two-course evening meal** Dkr300
» **Museum entrance** free–Dkr75
» **Beer** Dkr45
» **Copenhagen transport pass (72 hours)** Dkr180

Resources

» **Visit Denmark** (www.visitdenmark.com) Comprehensive tourist information

» **Kopenhagen** (www.kopenhagen.dk) Contemporary art exhibitions in Copenhagen

» **AOK** (www.aok.dk) Events, restaurants, bars and nightlife in Copenhagen

» **Danish State Railways** (www.dsb.dk) Timetables, ticket prices and a useful journey planner

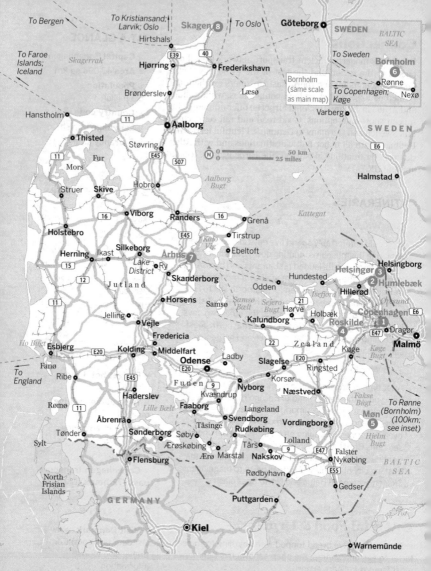

Denmark Highlights

1 Shop, nosh and chill in Scandinavia's capital of cool, **Copenhagen** (p39)

2 Be inspired by the art and the views at the sublime **Louisiana Museum of Modern Art** (p57) in HumlebæK

3 Snoop around **Kronborg Slot** (p59), Hamlet's epic home in Helsingør

4 Get your groove on at Denmark's top annual music event **Roskilde Festival** (p62)

5 Tackle the Colgate-white cliffs of **Møns Klint** (p66) on picture-perfect Møn

6 Lose yourself in nature and smoked fish on the Baltic island of **Bornholm** (p68)

7 See Århus through Technicolor glass at top-notch art museum **ARoS** (p86)

8 Watch angry seas collide above luminous, northern **Skagen** (p102)

COPENHAGEN

POP 1.8 MILLION

Stockholm might be more grandiose and Oslo more spectacularly located, but there is no more dynamic, cosmopolitan and downright cool a city in Scandinavia than Copenhagen.

While this thousand-year-old harbour town has managed to retain much of its historic good looks – think copper spires, cobbled squares and pastel-coloured gabled abodes – the focus here is on the innovative and cutting edge. Denmark's over-achieving capital is home to a thriving design scene, a futuristic metro system, and clean, green developments. Its streets are awash with effortlessly hip shops, cafes and bars; world-class museums and art collections; brave new architecture; and no fewer than 12 Michelin-starred restaurants. This is also a royal city, home to the multitalented Queen Margrethe II and her family.

And as if this wasn't impressive enough, a bounty of beautiful beaches, wooded parks and elegant lakes await just minutes away.

History

For more millennia than anyone can be sure of, Copenhagen was a fishermen's settlement on the shores of what we now call the Øresund Strait, the narrow belt of water between Denmark and Sweden.

Wendish pirates, who marauded the coast in the 12th century, prompted the locals, led by Bishop Absalon, to build a fort on a small island in the harbour – where the modern-day Danish parliament stands on Slotsholmen; you can still see the foundations of the original fort in the cellar museum.

The city of København ('købe' means 'to buy', 'havn' is 'harbour') gradually grew to the north of Slotsholmen, where the restaurants of Gammel Strand now stand, founded on the wealth that came from the herring caught by the local fishermen. But it wasn't until the 15th century that Copenhagen took over as the capital of Denmark from Roskilde.

Denmark's great Renaissance king, Christian IV (1588–1648), transformed Copenhagen into an impressive capital. From there he controlled much of Scandinavia – with numerous ambitious buildings including Rosenborg Slot and the Rundetårn. Eventually Christian IV brought the country to its knees with overspending and reckless foreign forays.

By the early 19th century the once mighty Danish empire was greatly diminished. Twice in the early 19th century the British navy bombarded the city but its people bounced back with a cultural Golden Age, led by the likes of Hans Christian Andersen and Søren Kierkegaard.

⊙ Sights

Two of the great things about Copenhagen are its accessibility and size. You can walk across the city centre in an hour, and travel further with great ease thanks to the cycle paths, metro, trains and buses, all of which means you can pack many of the sights into two days.

Tivoli
AMUSEMENT PARK

(www.tivoli.dk; adult/child Dkr95/50, multiride ticket Dkr205/170; ⊙11am-11pm Sun-Thu, to 12.30am Fri, to midnight Sat, high season) Copenhagen's historic amusement park has been Denmark's number-one tourist attraction pretty much since the day it opened more than 160 years ago. It's not Disneyland, but Tivoli has an innocent, old-fashioned charm, particularly after dark when its wonderful illuminations work their magic. There are flower beds, food pavilions, amusement rides, carnival games and various stage shows.

FREE Nationalmuseet
MUSEUM

(National Museum; www.natmus.dk; Ny Vestergade 10; ⊙10am-5pm Tue-Sun) For a whistle-stop tour through the history of Denmark, nothing can beat the Nationalmuseet: here you will find the world's most extensive collection of Danish artefacts from the Palaeolithic period to the 19th century. Naturally, the stars of the show are the Vikings, those much maligned but actually very sophisticated Scandinavian marauders. Highlights include Bronze Age burial remains in oak coffins and various examples of *lur* (musical horns) that were used for ceremony and communication, ancient rune stones, a golden sun chariot and Viking weaponry. But the displays don't stop with the Vikings; there are excellent collections covering the Middle Ages and Renaissance period too, plus delightful Egyptian and classical antiquities, as well as frequently changing special exhibitions. There's even an excellent, hands-on Children's Museum.

Rosenborg Slot
CASTLE

(www.rosenborgslot.dk; adult/child Dkr75/free; ⊙castle & treasury 10am-5pm daily Jun-Aug, closed

DENMARK COPENHAGEN

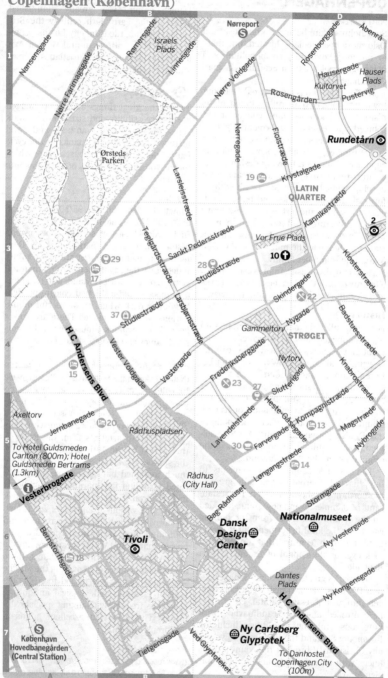

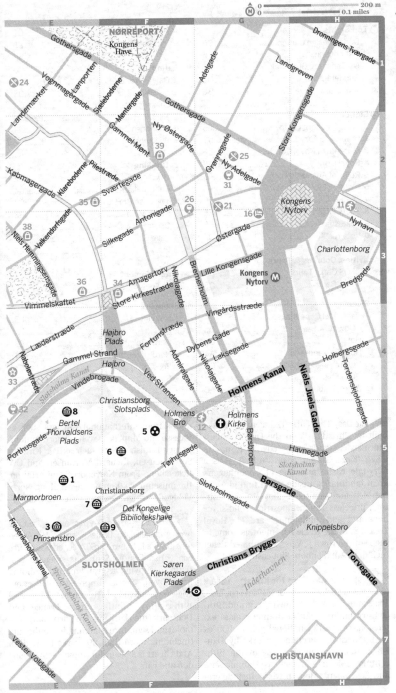

N

0   200 m
0   0.1 miles

NØRREPORT

Kongens Have

Dronningens Tværgade

Gothersgade
Vognmagergade
Landemærket
Lønporten
Skæleboderne
Møntergade
Adelgade
Landgreven
Store Kongensgade

24

Gammel Mønt

Gothersgade

Ny Østergade

39

Købmagergade
Klareboderne
Pilestræde
Sværtegade

35

Grønnegade
Ny Adelgade
25
31

Kongens
Nytorv

11

Nyhavn

38

Valkendorfsgade
Niels Hemmingsensgade

Antonigade
Silkegade

26

21

16

Østergade

Charlottenborg

Bredgade

36

34

Amagertorv
Nikolajgade
Store Kirkestræde

Vimmelskaftet

Lille Kongensgade
Bremerholm

Kongens
Nytorv M

Vingårdsstræde

Læderstræde

Højbro
Plads

Fortunstræde

Dybens Gade

Nikolajgade
Laksegade

Holmens Kanal

Niels Juels Gade

Holbergsgade

Tordenskjoldsgade

Nabolosstræde

33

Gammel Strand
Slotsholms Kanal

Højbro
Vindebrogade

Ved Stranden

Admiralgade

32

8

Christiansborg
Slotsplads

Bertel
Thorvaldsens
Plads

5

6

Holmens
Bro

12

Holmens
Kirke

Børsbroen

Havnegade

Slotsholms
Kanal

Børsgade

Porthusgade

1

Christiansborg

7

Tøjhusgade

Slotsholmsgade

Marmorbroen

3

9

Det Kongelige
Bibilioteks have

Frederiksholms Kanal

Prinsensbro

Knippelsbro

SLOTSHOLMEN

Søren
Kierkegaards
Plads

Christians Brygge

Torvegade

4

Inderhavnen

Vester Voldgade

Frederiksholms Kanal

CHRISTIANSHAVN

Copenhagen (København)

early-late Dec) This early 17th-century castle, built by Christian IV in the Dutch Renaissance style, stands at the edge of **Kongens Have** (King's Gardens; admission free). It is a fairy-tale castle and one of Copenhagen's great landmarks. Inside you'll find glorious marbled and painted ceilings, gilded mirrors, priceless Dutch tapestries, solid-silver lions, and gold- and enamelware. The Royal Treasury, in the castle basement, is home to the Danish crown jewels. A combined ticket including Amalienborg Slot costs Dkr100.

FREE **Statens Museum for Kunst** MUSEUM (www.smk.dk; Sølvgade 48-50; ⊙10am-5pm Tue & Thu-Sun, to 8pm Wed) Occupying a grand 19th-century building and a dramatic glass extension, Denmark's national gallery houses an impressive collection of works by Danish artists, particularly those of the 19th-century Golden Age such as Hammershøj and Eckersberg. Modern works include cre-

ations from international A-listers such as Picasso and Munch, as well as more contemporary Danish artists such as Per Kirkeby, Søren Jensen, Richard Mortensen and CW Eckersberg. From Nørreport S-train station, the museum is 800m northeast along Nørre Voldgade (which becomes Øster Voldgade).

TOP CHOICE **Ny Carlsberg Glyptotek** MUSEUM (www.glyptoteket.dk; Dantes Plads 7, HC Andersens Blvd; adult/child Dkr60/free, admission free Sun; ⊙11am-5pm Tue-Sun) This splendid museum, occupying a grand period building near Tivoli, has an impressive collection. Highlights include Etruscan art, 18th- and 19th-century paintings from France and Denmark (the Gauguins are particularly notable) and sculpture spanning five millennia (including more than 30 works by Rodin). At its heart is a beautiful tropical winter garden and cafe.

COPENHAGEN IN...

Two Days

Orientate yourself with a **canal tour** before taking in **Nyhavn**, shopping for Danish design at **Hay House** and **Illums Bolighus**, and devouring pastries at **Lagkagehuset**. Dive into Danish history at the **Nationalmuseet**, enjoy a lazy lunch at **Bastionen og Løven**, then explore free-spirited **Christiania**. Book dinner at trendy **Kødbyens Fiskebar** and cap off the evening at artist-designed **Karrierebar**. The following day, visit **Statens Museum for Kunst**, sample smørrebrød at **Schønnemann** and take in the panorama atop **Rundetårn**. After a wardrobe revamp at **Pop Cph** and **Storm**, savour New Nordic nosh at **Noma** (assuming you booked months ahead!). If it's summer, indulge your inner child at twinkling **Tivoli**. If it's not, warm up with perfect cocktails at **1105**.

Four Days

Spend day three gazing at art and Sweden at the stunning **Louisiana Museum of Modern Art** or head further north to Hamlet's 'home' in Helsingør, **Kronborg Slot**. Head back into town for dinner at **Fischer**, followed by beer and culture at **Gefährlich** or jazz at swinging **La Fontaine**. Spend day four exploring **Ny Carlsberg Glyptotek**, lunching at romantic **Orangeriet** and eyeing the crown jewels at **Rosenborg Slot**. After dark, catch an aria at architectural diva **Copenhagen Opera House**.

Dansk Design Center   GALLERY
(www.ddc.dk; HC Andersens Blvd 27; adult/child Dkr50/free; ☉10am-5pm Mon, Tue, Thu & Fri, to 9pm Wed, 11am-4pm Sat & Sun) Denmark's temple to design has an excellent permanent exhibition of local design through the decades in the basement and a regularly changing temporary exhibition on the ground floor. Clued up on local design, stock up at the gift shop for a bit of domestic name-dropping.

Slotsholmen   DISTRICT
An island separated from the city centre by a moat-like canal on three sides and the harbour on the other side, Slotsholmen is the site of **Christiansborg Palace**, home to Denmark's parliament. There are many sites on the island, including a **teatermuseet** (theatre museum), a museum housing the **royal coaches**, and a magnificent **Tøjhusmuseet** (Royal Arsenal; armoury museum), but the grandest is the **Slots-og Ejendomsstyrelsen** (Royal Reception Chambers; www.ses.dk; admission Dkr75; ☉guided tours in English 1pm & 2.30pm Sat & Sun Jul-Sep), the ornate Renaissance hall where the queen entertains heads of state.

The **Ruins of Absalon's Fortress** (adult/child Dkr40/20; ☉10am-4pm, closed Mon Oct-Apr) are the excavated foundations of Bishop Absalon's original castle of 1167 and of its successor, Copenhagen Slot. They can be visited in the basement of the present palace.

Thorvaldsens Museum (www.thorvaldsens museum.dk; Bertel Thorvaldsens Plads; adult/child Dkr20/free, admission free Wed; ☉10am-5pm Tue-Sun) features imposing statues by the famed Danish sculptor Bertel Thorvaldsen, who was heavily influenced by Greek and Roman mythology. Enter from the direction of Vindebrogade.

The **Royal Library** (www.kb.dk; Søren Kierkegaards Plads; ☉9am-9pm Mon-Fri, to 5pm Sat mid-Aug–Jun) dates from the 17th century, but the focal point these days is its ultramodern walkway-connected extension dubbed the 'Black Diamond' for its shiny black granite facade. The sleek, seven-storey building houses 21 million books and other literary items such as Hans Christian Andersen's original manuscripts. The building itself is open for visits and has a cafe and restaurant.

Rundetårn   OBSERVATION TOWER
(www.rundetaarn.dk; Købmagergade 52; adult/child Dkr25/5; ☉10am-8pm daily end May–end Sep) The Round Tower provides a fine vantage point for viewing the old city. Christian IV built it in 1642 as an astronomical observatory for the famous silver-nosed astronomer Tycho Brahe. Halfway up the 209m-high spiral walkway is a hall with changing exhibits. The tower houses the oldest functioning observatory in Europe and offers evening **astronomy programs** (☉7-10pm Tue & Wed mid-Oct–mid-Mar); and by day you may also be

lucky enough to see a dramatic, live projection of the sun.

Latin Quarter
NEIGHBOURHOOD

Also known as Pisserenden (which needs no translation), the historic university quarter is a grid of narrow streets and, often, half-timbered town houses to the north of Strøget filled with independent shops and cafes.

Opposite the university stands **Vor Frue Kirke** (⊙8am-5pm, closed to viewing during services & concerts), Copenhagen's neoclassical cathedral. The building dates from 1829, but stands on the site of earlier churches. Inside are imposing neoclassical statues of Christ and the 12 apostles, the most acclaimed works of the Golden Age sculptor Bertel Thorvaldsen. A couple of blocks east of the cathedral is the pretty square of **Gråbrødre Torv**, which has several medium-priced restaurants with outdoor seating. On the northern side of the Latin Quarter is **Kultorvet**, a lively square known for its impromptu street entertainment, beer gardens, flower stalls and produce stands.

Christianshavn
NEIGHBOURHOOD

A kind of alternative commune, known as the Freetown of Christiania ever since its 1960s heyday, Copenhagen's picturesque canal quarter once did a roaring open trade in soft drugs. A clampdown and police raids have put a stop to that and it's less of a circus these days, although the alternative, hippie ideal lives on. Built on reclaimed land in the 17th century by Christian IV, it's a great place to wander beside the canals and visit the quarter's pleasant cafes.

To get there, walk over the bridge from the northeastern side of Slotsholmen or you can take the Metro from Kongens Nytorv or Nørreport direct to Christianshavnstorv.

Vor Frelsers Kirke
CHURCH

(www.vorfrelserskirke.dk; Sankt Annæ Gade 29; admission free, tower adult/child Dkr25/10; ⊙11am-3.30pm, closed during services, tower 11am-4pm Apr-Oct) Close to Freetown of Christiania is the 17th-century Vor Frelsers Kirke, which has an impressive baroque altar and an elaborately carved pipe organ, propped up by two unhappy-looking decorative elephants. For a panoramic view of the city and across to Sweden, climb the 400 steps of the church's 95m-high spiral tower. The last 160 steps run spectacularly along the outside rim, narrowing to the point where they disappear at the top.

Carlsberg Brewery
BREWERY

(www.visitcarlsberg.dk; Gamle Carlsberg Vej 11; adult incl 1 beer Dkr65, 12-17yr/under 12yr Dkr50/free; ⊙10am-5pm Tue-Sun, to 7.30pm Thu May-Aug) At the Carlsberg Brewery Visitor Centre you can find out about the history of Danish beer and the modern-day brewing process for the self-proclaimed 'probably best' beer in the world. The experience is capped off with a sampling of the present-day product. The brewery is a little outside the centre of the city to the west: take bus 6A westbound or the S-Tog (S-Train, whose 10 lines pass through Central Station) to Enghave station.

Waterfront
NEIGHBOURHOOD

Just east of Kongens Nytorv, the bustling waterfront and surrounding area are home to a number of iconic city landmarks. The home of the royal family since 1794, **Amalienborg Palace** (www.ses.dk; adult/child Dkr60/free; ⊙10am-4pm May-Oct & mid-late Dec) comprises four austere mansions surrounding the central square and guarded by sentries, who are relieved at noon by a ceremonial changing of the guard. You can view the interior of the northwestern mansion, with its royal memorabilia and study rooms of three kings. A combined ticket including Rosenborg Slot costs Dkr100.

Inland along Frederiksgade is the splendid **Frederikskirken** (www.marmorkirken.dk; admission free, dome adult/child Dkr25/10; ⊙10am-5pm Mon, Tue, Thu & Sat, 10am-6.30pm Wed, noon-5pm Fri & Sun, dome 1pm & 3pm mid-Jun–Aug). It's known universally as Marmorkirken (Marble Church) and the view from its great dome is spectacular.

Back on Amalienborg Plads, and 500m north along Amaliegade, is Churchillparken, where you'll find **Frihedsmuseet** (admission free; ⊙10am-5pm Tue-Sun May-Sep), with moving relics from the history of the Danish Resistance against Nazi occupation.

About 150m north of the Frihedsmuseet you pass the spectacular **Gefion Fountain**, which features the goddess Gefion ploughing the island of Zealand with her four sons yoked as oxen. Another 400m north along the waterfront is the statue of the unjustly famed **Little Mermaid** (Den Lille Havfrue), a rather forlorn statue that is actually one of the least interesting of all Copenhagen's many sights.

The **Copenhagen Opera House** (☑33 69 69 69; www.kglteater.dk; ⊙guided tours in English Dkr100 Jul–mid-Aug, see website for schedule), on the island of Holmen facing Amalienborg across the harbour, is well worth a visit. Tickets often sell out months in advance, though any unsold tickets for a performance are offered at a bargain 50% off from 6pm at the box office. There are two restaurants and you can take a guided tour of Henning Larsen's controversial glass-fronted masterpiece with its vast roof, attacked by critics as ungainly and out of proportion in its waterfront setting.

The latest architectural addition to the city's waterfront is the striking, Dkr900-million, three-stage Skuespilhuset (Royal Danish Playhouse; ☑33 69 69 69; www.kglteater. dk; Sankt Anne Plads 36; guided tours in English are only for groups Dkr2500), the country's new national theatre overlooking the harbour directly across from the new Opera House. Most productions are in Danish. Tickets must be bought in advance from www. kglteater.dk, www.billetnet.dk, or at the box office.

Gardens
GARDEN

The stretch of gardens along Øster Voldgade offers a refuge from the city traffic. **Kongens Have**, the large public park behind Rosenborg Slot, is a popular sunbathing spot.

The Botanisk Have (Botanical Gardens; main entrance Gothersgade 140; ☺8.30am-6pm daily May-Sep) on the western side of Rosenborg Slot has fragrant trails. Its Palmehus (☺10am-3pm daily May-Sep, closed Mon Oct-Apr) is a large, walk-through glasshouse growing a variety of tropical plants. The gardens also house the Botanic Museum (Gothersgade 130; admission free; ☺varies).

Activities

Weather permitting, there are reasonably good opportunities to swim and sunbathe on stretches of beach around 5km from the city centre at the spectacularly redeveloped Amager Strand; take the Metro to Amager Strand and then walk east for about 300m. Alternatively, come summer there is a lively 'beach' scene on the city-centre harbour front itself in and around the Islands Brygge open-air harbour pool, right in the heart of the city (open only from June to August). Alternatively, there's the heated circular indoor pool at the DGI-Byen Centre (www.dgi-byen. dk; Tietgensgade 65, Vesterbro) near the station.

☞ Tours

Rickshaw & Bike Tours

Copenhagen Rickshaw
CITY

(☑35 43 01 22; www.rickshaw.dk, in Danish; 30min tour Dkr160) These two-seater, open carriages

Opening hours can vary significantly between high and low seasons. Hours provided in this book are for the high season. There is no strict rule defining 'high season' and it can vary from sight to sight. Most commonly, high season refers to the period from late June to mid-August (sometimes even early June to late August, though in some places the season covers May to September, inclusive). Where there are no seasonal hours specified, the hours apply year-round.

powered by fit, young pedal-pushers operate daily and can be found at most main squares. They can also be used as taxis – the price starts at Dkr40 and you pay Dkr4 per minute thereafter. Each rickshaw seats two adults and one child.

The company also runs city bike tours (adult/under 14yr Dkr280/140; ☺10.30am daily), departing from Vodroffsvej 55 (near Forum metro station) and lasting 2½ to 3 hours. Reservations are not required.

Canal Tours

The best way to see Copenhagen is from the water. There are several ways to take a boat tour around the city's canals and harbour, with multilingual guides giving a commentary in English.

DFDS Canal Tours
CITY

(www.canaltours.com; adult/child Dkr60/40; ☺9.15am & up to every 15min until 5.30pm mid-May–Jun, to 7.30pm mid-Jun–early Sep) Tours leave from the head of Nyhavn or the Marriott Hotel, and take 50 minutes, passing by the *Little Mermaid,* Christianshavn and Christiansborg Palace.

Netto-Boats
CITY

(www.netto-baadene.dk; adult/child Dkr30/15; ☺10am-5pm 2-5 times per hour, late March–mid-Oct, to 7pm Jul & Aug) Departing from Holmens Kirke and from Nyhavn.

Festivals & Events

Copenhagen Jazz Festival
MUSIC

(www.jazz.dk) The city's largest music event invigorates the whole city with 10 days of music in early July. The festival presents a wide range of Danish and international jazz, blues and fusion music in more than

HOP-ON, HOP-OFF BOATS

In addition to offering boat tours, canal boats make an excellent, traffic-free alternative for getting to some of Copenhagen's waterfront sites. **DFDS Canal Tours** charges Dkr60 for a one-day 'waterbus' pass (Dkr40 for children) or Dkr40 per trip (Dkr30 for children) from mid-May to mid-September. The boats, which leave Nyhavn every 40 to 60 minutes between 10am and 5.30pm mid-May to early September, make a dozen stops, including at the *Little Mermaid*, Nationalmuseet and Vor Frelsers Kirke (with no commentary), allowing you to get on and off as you like. Bear in mind that not all tour boats have roofs and the weather is ever-changing in Copenhagen harbour, so be sure to pack for all conditions.

500 indoor and outdoor venues, with music wafting out of practically every public square, park, pub and cafe from Strøget to Tivoli.

Copenhagen Cooking   FOOD
(www.copenhagencooking.dk) Scandinavia's largest food festival, with dozens of events taking place during one week at the end of August.

🛏 Sleeping

Copenhagen's range of hotels has expanded massively in the last few years, from the likes of Nimb and Skt Petri at the top end, to the cheap (for this part of the world at least) and chic Wakeup Copenhagen and ever-fabulous Danhostel on HC Andersens Blvd. Camping options remain limited, however, not least by the weather.

The city's traditional hotel quarter is centred behind Central Station, on and around Istedgade. Here you will find numerous bland business hotels and medium-range chains. This also happens to be the city's redlight district, with some fruity shop window displays and the occasional group of rowdy winos and glazed addicts.

The tourist office can book rooms in private homes (Dkr350/500 for singles/doubles); there is a Dkr100 booking fee if you do it via the tourist office when you arrive, otherwise it is free online.

You can also visit the website www.bedandbreakfast.dk for B&B accommodation throughout Denmark.

TOP CHOICE Hotel Nimb   HOTEL €€€
(☑88 70 00 00; www.nimb.dk; Bernstorffsgade 5; r Dkr2500-8500; @) Copenhagen's first proper boutique hotel opened in Tivoli in early 2008 to international acclaim. With a beautiful interior, two excellent restaurants, a fabulous cocktail bar, and every conceivable luxury – overnight it became the place to stay in the Danish capital.

Hotel Fox   HOTEL €€
(☑33 95 77 55; www.hotelfox.dk; Jarmers Plads 3; r Dkr690-1790) Though some of the rooms could use a fresh lick of paint, the Fox remains exciting for its outrageous, one-off rooms, each designed by a group of international artists and designers. The hotel restaurant transforms into a DJ bar by night. Located five minutes from the town hall square (Rådhuspladsen) and Strøget, it's on the fringe of the Latin Quarter.

🖋 Hotel Guldsmeden Bertrams, Carlton & Axel   HOTEL €€€
(☑33 25 04 05/22 15 00/31 32 66, 33 31 32 66; www.hotelguldsmeden.dk; Vesterbrogade 107 & 66, Helgolandsgade 7; s/d Dkr935/1053; @) Sandra and Marc Weinert's excellent Guldsmeden group now has three attractive and welcoming hotels in Copenhagen. The Axel boasts a spa and is vaguely Balinese style, while both Bertrams and Carlton are decked out in the chain's characteristic French-colonial style. The Axel is four-star, Bertrams and the Carlton are three-star. The Axel is the most central, while Bertrams and Carlton are close to the hipster nightlife and shops of Vesterbro.

Wakeup Copenhagen   HOTEL €€
(☑44 80 00 10; www.wakeupcopenhagen.com; Carsten Niebuhrs Gade 11; s Dkr400-900, d Skr500-1000; @) Cheap meets chic at this new 510-room budget hotel, located 1km south of Central Station. While the foyer is a slick combo of concrete, glass and Arne Jacobsen chairs, rooms are compact, fresh and stylish, complete with pod-like showers. Clean linen is under the bed (cost-cutting in action) and three floors feature wooden flooring for the allergy-inclined. Book online for the cheapest rates.

CPH Living
HOTEL €€€

(☎61 60 85 46; www.cphliving.com; Langebrogade 1c; r Dkr1000-1300) Following HC Andersens Blvd southeast from Tivoli you'll come to Langebro bridge. Just to the east of the bridge sits this freight-boat-turned-floating-hotel: each of its 12 stylish rooms features harbour and city views. Perks include flat-screen TVs, modern bathrooms with rainforest shower, and a communal sun deck for summertime lounging. Breakfast is a simple continental affair, while the central location makes it an easy to walk to the city centre, Christianshavn and the harbour beach at Islands Brygge.

Square
HOTEL €€€

(☎33 38 12 00; www.thesquarecopenhagen.com; Rådhuspladsen 14; s Dkr990-1825, d Dkr1090-2085) This relative newcomer on Copenhagen's town hall square could not be better located nor better equipped, with attractive, modern, minimalist rooms and breakfast included. There are cheaper hotels in town, but few offer as much style for the money, particularly if you are lucky to bag one of the frequent special offers.

Hotel Alexandra
HOTEL €€€

(☎33 74 44 44; www.hotel-alexandra.dk; HC Andersens Blvd 8; s Dkr925-1425, d Dkr995-1745; P @) The lovely, cosy Alexandra is packed with classic Danish furniture to really get you in the mood for a stay in this great design capital. As well as an excellent restaurant, Bistroen, it boasts a Green Key environmental award, judged on more than 50 environmental criteria.

Hotel d'Angleterre
HOTEL €€€

(☎33 12 00 95; www.dangleterre.dk; Kongens Nytorv 34; s Dkr1430-2830, d Dkr1930-3330; @) This lavish and, let's be honest, ever so slightly camp five-star hotel has long reigned un-challenged as the city's top overnight spot for celebrities, Eurotrash and minor royalty. It doesn't skimp on the extras, including a top-notch health club in the basement, but other newer arrivals on the Copenhagen hotel scene probably hold greater appeal for younger guests.

Hotel Nyhavn 71
HOTEL €€€

(☎33 43 62 00; www.71nyhavnhotel.com; Nyhavn 71; s Dkr1290-1785, d Dkr1490-2085) Superbly located at the harbour end of Nyhavn, this beautiful converted grain house boasts four-star luxury, albeit with sometimes rather small rooms. It's close to the excellent night-life of the Nyhavn canal.

Hotel 27
HOTEL €€€

(☎70 27 56 27; www.hotel27.dk; Løngangstræde 27; s/d Dkr1086/1395; P) This very centrally located hotel, just 220m from Tivoli and Rådhuspladsen, is the epitome of a contemporary Danish design hotel with many extras including satellite TV and three bars (yes, there's even an ice bar). If you're a light sleeper, request a room away from the bars.

Hotel Skt Petri
HOTEL €€€

(☎33 45 91 00; www.hotelsktpetri.com; Krystalgade 22; s Dkr995-2695, d Dkr1195-2895; @) Despite looking a little tired in parts, Skt Petri remains one of Copenhagen's coolest luxury hotels. The rooms are cosseting, and some have balconies or enchanting city views or both: request a room on level 4 or higher for the best outlook. Guests have access to the gym next door, while the bright, high foyer seems tailor-made for sipping cocktails in.

Copenhagen Island
HOTEL €€€

(☎33 38 96 00; www.copenhagenisland.com; Kalvebod Brygge 35; s Dkr860-1755, d Dkr960-2060; P @) The ubersleek Kim Utzon design and stunning views across the western harbour more than make up for Copenhagen Island's slightly out-of-the-way location (1.2km from Tivoli and Central Station from the city centre proper or one stop on the S-Tog from nearby Dybbelsbro station to Central Station). The rack rates might look high but the Island often has very special bargain rates (Dkr860 to Dkr960) online.

Danhostel Copenhagen City
HOSTEL €

(☎33 11 85 85; www.danhostel.dk/copenhagencity; HC Andersens Blvd 50; dm Dkr130-195; @) The best of Copenhagen's hostels occupies a modern high-rise overlooking the harbour a short walk from Central Station. With a

LAST-MINUTE CHEAP SLEEPS

If you arrive in Copenhagen without a hotel booking, luck may yet be on your side. The Copenhagen Visitor Centre (p55) offers over-the-counter, last-minute deals on hotel rooms at very low prices. A double room at a four-star hotel can cost as little as Dkr700, with three-star options at around Dkr500 per night. Breakfast is often included, as well as the perk of a central location.

reception that resembles a boutique hotel, a great cafe and a 25% discount on the facilities at the DGI-Byen swimming pool and sports centre included in the price, it is a good idea to book ahead.

Danhostel Copenhagen Downtown HOSTEL €
(☎70 23 21 10; www.copenhagendowntown.com; Vandkunsten 5; dm/d from Dkr130/499) This characterful, buzzing hostel could not be more centrally located, right beside the main pedestrian shopping street, Strøget, and prides itself on its cultural dynamism, with several artists in residence. The refurbished attic features new rooms, each accommodating six people and each with private bathroom. Equally novel is the new batch of IP phones, allowing guests to make cheap international calls.

Cab Inn City HOTEL €€
(☎33 46 16 16; www.cabinn.com; Mitchellsgade 14; s/d/tr Dkr545/675/805; @) Cab Inns are modern, rather clinical but boast good facilities (including kettle and TV) and reliable levels of comfort (although the ship's-cabin – cab-in, geddit? – style means small rooms and rather narrow bunk-style beds). This is the best located of all Copenhagen's Cab Inns, considering it's a short walk south of Tivoli. There's free foyer internet access. You do usually have to book well in advance here as it is pretty much unrivalled for price and location.

City Public Hostel HOSTEL €
(☎36 98 11 66; www.citypublichostel.dk; Absalonsgade 8; dm Dkr125-170; ⊙early May–end Aug) A central, friendly, well-run hostel with dorms sleeping six to 66; they are both mixed and separate gender. Breakfast costs Dkr40 and there is an outdoor barbecue area.

Camping Charlottenlund Fort CAMPING GROUND €
(☎39 62 36 88; www.campingcopenhagen.dk; Strandvejen 144, Charlottenlund; campsites per adult/tent Dkr95/40; ⊙mid-Apr–Sep) Located 6km north of the city centre beside a delightful sandy beach overlooking the Øresund sea. Take bus 14 for a half-hour trip.

✖ Eating
Copenhagen's dining scene is the country's most dynamic, with options spanning Michelin-starred, modern-Scandinavian hot spots to hip restaurant–bar combos to historic eateries dishing up smørrebrød (open sandwiches), herring and akvavit.

You'll find many of the city's coolest restaurants in the Vesterbrø neighbourhood, while bohemian Nørrebro has its fair share of cheaper, student-friendly cafes. If you're a kroner-conscious gourmand, look out for special, pared-back lunch menus, available at several of the city's most-sought-after New Nordic restaurants.

AROUND STRØGET
Orangeriet MODERN SCANDINAVIAN €€€
(☎33 11 13 07; www.restaurant-orangeriet.dk; Kronprinsessegade 13; fixed menus Dkr335; ⊙lunch & dinner Tue-Sat, lunch Sun) Enviably set in a soothing conservatory in Kongens Have, Orangeriet is one of the best new restaurants in Copenhagen. At the helm is award-winning chef Jasper Kure, whose contemporary Nordic creations focus on simplicity and premium seasonal produce. Book ahead.

Schønnemann DANISH €€
(☎33 12 07 85; Hauser Plads 16; meals Dkr59-148; ⊙11.30am-5pm Mon-Sat) Schønnemann has been filling bellies with smørrebrød (open sandwiches) and schnapps since 1877. It was originally a hit with peasant farmers; its current fan base includes René Redzepi, head chef at world-famous Noma. Not much else has changed, from the sawdust-sprinkled floors to the stoic Danish soul food. It's a local institution, so call ahead.

Café Victor FRENCH, DANISH €€
(Ny Østergade 8; meals Dkr65-225; ⊙8am-1am Mon-Wed, 8am-2am Thu-Sat, 11am-midnight Sun) An old-school (actually, it was the first in Denmark) Parisian-style brasserie replete with zinc bar, cafe and restaurant, Victor is a chichi melange of Chanel-clad glamour pusses, French Champagne and divine Franco-Danish dishes. See and be seen.

Lagkagehuset BAKERY €
(www.lagkagehuset.dk; Frederiksberggade 21; sandwiches & salads Dkr45; ⊙7.30am-8pm) One of the best bakeries in town lies right on bustling Strøget in the heart of the city and is highly recommended for sandwiches and salads. It has another convenient location at Torvegade 45 (open 6am to 7pm Monday to Friday, and to 6pm Saturday and Sunday) in Christianshavn.

Wokshop Cantina THAI, VIETNAMESE €€
(www.wokshop.dk; Ny Adelgade 6; curries Dkr119-140; ⊙lunch & dinner Mon-Fri, dinner Sat) This basement canteen in a street just off

WANT MORE?

For in-depth information, reviews and recommendations at your fingertips, head to the Apple App Store to purchase Lonely Planet's *Copenhagen City Guide* iPhone app.

Alternatively, head to Lonely Planet (www.lonelyplanet.com/denmark/copenhagen) for planning advice, author recommendations, traveller reviews and insider tips.

Kongens Nytorv (beside the grand Hotel d'Angleterre) serves excellent and cheap Thai and Vietnamese staples.

La Glace CAFE €
(www.laglace.dk; Skoubougade 3; slices Dkr47; ⊙8.30am-5.30pm Mon-Thu, to 6pm Fri, 9am-5pm Sat, 11am-5pm Sun, closed Sun Apr-Sep) The best and oldest cake shop in Copenhagen serves sensational gateaus and does a wicked hot chocolate.

NØRREBRO
An easy walk northwest of the city centre, across Peblinge Sø (lake), the neighbourhood of Nørrebro is a great place to eat, with countless cool cafes and bars. Head for Elmegade for contemporary takeaways (sushi, bagels, sandwiches, coffee, beer), Blågardsgade for healthy snacks, or Sankt Hans Torv for stylish cafes and ice-cream parlours (and the nightclub Rust is around the corner). Further north, elegant Østerbro is home to several worthy restaurants, including an authentic Italian gem.

Nørrebro Bryghus BREWERY €€
(www.noerrebrobryghus.dk; Ryesgade 3; lunch dishes under Dkr149, 3 courses Dkr325; ⊙Mon-Sat) This celebrated contemporary beer cathedral brews its own lager, stout, ale and weiss beers in-house and serves excellent, refined brasserie food (venison with lingonberry purée, or smoked scallops with lobster cream, for instance), to a cool, young clientele.

Fischer ITALIAN €€
(www.hosfischer.dk, in Danish; Victor Borges Plads 12; dinner mains Dkr135-195; ⊙lunch & dinner Mon-Sat, 10.30am-3pm Sun) Set in a converted working-men's bar, neighbourly Fischer serves Italian soul food such as freshly made linguini with *aglio e olio* (pasta with garlic, olive oil and chilli). That it's all seriously good isn't surprising considering

owner and head chef David Fischer worked the kitchen at Rome's Michelin-starred La Pergola.

AROUND TIVOLI & VESTERBRO

Kødbyens Fiskebar MODERN SCANDINAVIAN €€€
(✆32 15 56 56; www.fiskebaren.dk; Flæsketorvet 100; mains Dkr195-225; ⊙dinner Tue-Sat) Occupying a former factory in trendy Kødbyen (Copenhagen's meat-packing district), this Michelin-listed hot spot is *the* place for seafood. Seasonal produce shines through in dishes like Limfjorden blue mussels with steamed apple cider and herbs, while desserts may include divine English liquorice with sea buckthorn and white-chocolate ice cream.

Cofoco FRENCH, DANISH €€€
(✆33 13 60 60; www.cofoco.dk; Abel Cathrines Gade 7; 4 courses Dkr250; ⊙dinner Mon-Sat) One of several top-quality, fixed-menu places owned by the same team, Cofoco offers a glamorous setting and refined Franco-Danish food (foie gras, pear and pork terrine, for instance, or duck leg with Jerusalem artichoke and mushrooms), on a budget. **Les Trois Cochons** (✆33 31 70 55; Værndemsvej 10) is another great-value restaurant from the same people, which we also heartily recommend.

Paté Paté EUROPEAN €€
(✆39 69 55 57; www.patepate.dk; Slagterboderne 1; mains Dkr145-195; ⊙8am-midnight Sun-Wed, 8-1am Thu, 8-3am Fri & Sat, kitchen closes 11pm) Another Kødbyen must, this pâté factory-turned-restaurant-and-wine bar gives Euro classics a modern twist (think poussin with liver crostini, pickled cherries and summer truffle). It's hip yet convivial; bonus extras include clued-up staff, a well-versed wine list and welcoming alfresco summertime tables.

Nimb DANISH €€
(✆88 70 00 00; www.nimb.dk; Bernstorffsgade 5; lunch mains Dkr160-195, dinner mains Dkr185-235) Copenhagen's most exclusive hotel also houses a luxury restaurant (with the unlikely name of Hermann) and this slick, more affordable Scandinavian brasserie with a terrace overlooking Tivoli. Lunch focuses on simple, classically influenced Danish fare, while dinner cranks up the options and contemporary twists (think hay-baked celeriac with roasted purée and consommé, sweet onions, hazelnut and poached egg).

AROUND NYHAVN

TOP CHOICE **Damindra** JAPANESE €€
(www.damindra.dk; Holbergsgade 26; lunches Dkr150-368, dinner mains Dkr115-155, 7-course sushi menus Dkr368; ⊙Tue-Sat) Unforgettable Japanese dishes define this little-known gem, whose owner designed almost everything in sight, including the cutlery and chairs. From the buttery sashimi to an unforgettable prawn tempura, it's all obscenely fresh, flavoursome and beautifully presented.

Le Sommelier FRENCH, DANISH €€€
(☎33 11 45 15; www.lesommelier.dk; Bredgade 63; mains Dkr195-225; ⊙lunch & dinner Mon-Fri, dinner Sat & Sun) White-linen tables, wooden floorboards and vintage French and Italian posters set the scene at Le Sommelier, where French traditions merge with seasonal Nordic produce (think Norwegian lobster with lobster bisque and crab salad). Flavours are clean and comforting, and the wine list has an impressive French selection.

Cap Horn DANISH, EUROPEAN €€
(Nyhavn 21; mains Dkr179-210) Amid many a middling canal-side restaurant, Cap Horn stands out, serving excellent, fresh Danish seafood including grilled langoustine and aioli.

CHRISTIANSHAVN & CHRISTIANIA

Noma MODERN SCANDINAVIAN €€€
(☎32 96 32 97; www.noma.dk; Strandgade 93; fixed menus Dkr900; ⊙Tue-Sat) Topping the S.Pellegrino 'World's 50 Best Restaurants' list in 2010, this Michelin-starred must sources its ingredients exclusively – and often foraged – from the Nordic countries. Chef René Redzepi is an innovative genius, not afraid to overturn conventions. Drooling? Book three months ahead.

TOP CHOICE **Bastionen og Løven** DANISH €€
(www.bastionen-loven.dk; Christianshavn Voldgade 50; mains Dkr185-195) Housed beside a historic windmill on the city ramparts just south of Christiania, charming Bastionen og Løven serves gorgeous, seasonal Danish dishes without the stodge. Its weekend brunch is one of the city's best and the front garden is perfect for alfresco noshing on a sunny day.

Cafe Wilder EUROPEAN €€
(Wildersgade 56; mains Dkr85-185) This archetypal Christianshavn cafe serves simple, beautiful dishes such as goat's cheese au gratin on bruschetta, or roasted cockerel breast with butter-sautéd asparagus, pak choi and baby carrots to loyal locals.

Morgenstedet VEGETARIAN €
(www.morgenstedet.dk; Langgaden; mains Dkr70; ⊙Tue-Sun) This long-established vegetarian and vegan place has a pretty garden in the heart of Christiania. Its dish of the day is usually a curry.

Drinking

Drinking is one of the Danes' chief pastimes and Copenhagen is packed with a huge range of places from cosy, old-school cellar bars or 'bodegas', to the cavernous fleshpots close to Rådhuspladsen, and the many more, quirky, grungy, boozy, artsy, and stylish places elsewhere. The line between cafe, bar and restaurant is often blurred, with many places changing role as the day progresses. Nørrebro and Vesterbro (especially along Istedgade, west of the red-light district, and Kødbyen, closer to the station) are well worth exploring.

Bibendum BAR
(www.vincafeen.dk; Nansensgade 45; ⊙Mon-Sat) This cosy little cellar is home to the best wine bar in Copenhagen, run by an exceptionally knowledgeable, and blessedly snobbery-free crowd of wine enthusiasts serving a broad range of, often New World, wines by the glass.

Karrierebar BAR
(www.karrierebar.com; Flæsketorvet 57-67; ⊙Thu-Sat) Forget the food, which is middling. This cool bar in the heart of the city's old meat-packing quarter remains one of the destination venues in the city for the late-20s, early-30s media and art crowd right now. With lighting by Olafur Eliasson no less.

1105 BAR
(www.1105.dk; Kristen Bernikows Gade 4; ⊙Wed-Sat) Domain of legendary barman Gromit Eduardsen, this luxe cocktail bar peddles perfect libations such as the No. 4 (Tanqueray gin, cardamom seeds, pepper, lime and honey). Whisky connoisseurs will be equally enthralled.

Union Bar BAR
(www.theunionbar.dk; Store Strandstræde 19; ⊙Wed-Sat) Inspired by the speakeasy bars of old New York (even the cocktails are named after 1920s slang), the Union hides behind an unmarked black door. Ring the buzzer and head down the stairs to a suitably dim, decadent scene of handsome bartenders, in-the-know revellers and smooth tunes.

RUNE RK: DJ & MUSIC PRODUCER

To experience Copenhagen's electronic music scene...

...don't miss **Culture Box**, especially if the locals are playing. **Simons** is the new hang-out for in-the-know clubbers. Scan the flyers at www.hifly.dk for upcoming club events.

Top electronic music festivals in Copenhagen...

...include Raw (www.rawcph.com) and the ever-crazy Copenhagen Distortion (www.cphdistortion.dk), both held in June. The latter is a collection of street parties around the city playing some pop and lots of underground electronica. Strøm (www.stromcph.dk) in August is more civilised and family friendly.

Danish electronica...

...has exploded with talent like Lulu Rouge, Noir and Lasbas. Andres Trentemøller has strongly influenced the local sound, which is equally melancholic, atmospheric and danceable.

I wrote my hit 'Calabria'...

...after playing a gig in the Italian region. My records were stolen, there were mobsters, and the organisers wouldn't pay up. Contrary to popular belief, it is not a tribute to the place.

Ruby   BAR
(www.rby.dk; Nybrogade 10; ☺Mon-Sat) If you are looking for one of the coolest cocktail bars in Copenhagen, this discreet (from the outside at least) place beside the canal is it. There are self-proclaimed cocktail nerds behind the bar, and the city's most dazzling youth in front of it.

Coffee Collective   CAFE
(www.coffeecollective.dk; Jægersborggade 10; ☺7.30am-8pm Mon-Fri, 9am-6pm Sat, 10am-6pm Sun) Coffee snobs gravitate to this bolt-hole espresso bar and on-site roaster. On up-and-coming Jægersborggade in Nørrebro, its passionate team of young baristi peddle complex, flavoursome brews that outshine the competition.

Palæ Bar   PUB
(Ny Adelgade 5; ☺11am-1am Mon-Wed, 11am-3am Thu-Sat, 4pm-1am Sun) Cosy Palæ is one of Copenhagen's best old-school drinking dens, with a loyal crowd spanning journalists and writers to beer-swilling politicians.

☆ Entertainment

Weekday nights, which can be a little quiet, are when the cafes and cocktail bars come into their own, but Copenhagen really revs into gear from Thursday to Saturday, when it turns into a genuine 24-hour party city. Club admission is usually around Dkr70, but you can often get in for free before a certain time in the evening. Major international rock acts often play the national stadium, Parken in Østerbro, at Forum in Frederiksberg or Valbyhallen in Valby, but you can just as easily catch the likes of Rufus Wainwright or the Kaiser Chiefs playing at Vega. Visit www.hifly.dk or www.aok.dk (in Danish) for listings.

Denmark's stunning, new national DR Koncerthus (concert hall; ☏35 20 30 40; www.dr.dk/koncerthuset; Emil Holms Kanal 20, Amager; admission varies), designed by French architect Jean Nouvel, promises more than 200 concerts a year, predominantly by Danmarks Radio's own symphony orchestra, but also a wide range of classical and contemporary performers. Be warned: concerts sell out well in advance, but returns and unsold tickets are available at the box office and online two hours before the show commences on any given day.

Live Music & Nightclubs

Copenhagen Opera House   OPERA
(☏33 69 69 69; www.kglteater.dk) The city's most bombastic building, overlooking the waterfront, houses world-class opera as well as the odd curve-ball act such as Elvis Costello and Nick Cave. Tickets must be bought in advance from either www.billetnet.dk or at the box office. Unsold tickets to a specific performance are available at half-price from 6pm at the box office.

Gefährlich   BAR, CULTURAL CENTRE
(www.gefahrlich.dk; Fælledvej 7, Nørrebro; admission usually free; ⊙11am-midnight Tue, 11-2am Wed, 11-3am Thu, 11-3.30am Fri, 10-3.30am Sat) This deeply groovy bar-club-restaurant-lounge-cafe-hairdresser-art space (really) has made a major splash on the Nørrebro nightlife scene. It gets packed on weekends, and the incriminating evidence is usually posted on MySpace by midweek.

Simons   CLUB
(www.simonscopenhagen.com; Store Strandstræde 14; ⊙Fri & Sat) Occupying a former art gallery, hip Simons' biggest (and smallest) claims to fame are top-shelf DJ talent and dwarfs behind the bar. Expect selective electronica and an even more selective door policy (Fridays are more accessible than Saturdays). If you have a Danish SIM card, register for updates online.

Rust   LIVE MUSIC, CLUB
(www.rust.dk; Guldbergsgade 8; admission varies) Rust remains the edgiest of Copenhagen's major clubs. Spaces range from nightclub to live-music hall and lounge, with an equally diverse musical policy. From 11pm, entrance is available only to over 18s (Wednesday and Thursday) and over 20s (Friday and Saturday).

Vega   LIVE MUSIC, CLUB
(www.vega.dk; Enghavevej 40) Vega is the daddy of all Copenhagen's live-music and club venues, with two stages (Store, or 'Big' Vega, and Lille, or, you guessed it, 'Little' Vega), plus two bars, all housed in a fabulous 1950s former trade union HQ by Vilhelm Lauritizen. Admission is usually free to the Vega Natklub (11pm to 5am Friday and Saturday) if you arrive before 1am, or usually Dkr60 thereafter. Some special club nights do charge admission. Book tickets through www.vega.dk.

TOP CHOICE **La Fontaine**   LIVE MUSIC
(www.lafontaine.dk, in Danish; Kompagnistræde 11, Strædet, ⊙7pm-5am, live music 11pm-3am Fri & Sat & 9pm-1am Sun) Cosy La Fontaine is a stalwart of the city's thriving jazz scene. Expect live gigs Friday to Sunday and legendary late-night jam sessions.

Culture Box   CLUB
(www.culture-box.com; Kronprinsessegade 54a; ⊙bar 8pm-late Fri & Sat, club midnight-6am Fri & Sat but variable) A genuinely world-class showcase for – mainly – electronica (techno,

house, drum'n'bass etc) with a relaxed, non-commercial, non-up-itself atmosphere.

Cinemas

There are numerous cinemas showing first-release movies, and most of them lie within 200m of Rådhuspladsen. It is customary in Denmark to show foreign-language films in the original language with subtitles.

Gay & Lesbian Venues

Denmark was the first country to permit same-sex marriage and has had a gay scene for more than 30 years – initially centred on Centralhjørnet – so it's not surprising that it remains welcoming to gays and lesbians, with numerous bars, cafes and clubs. For more information and listings visit www.copenhagen-gay-life.dk.

Oscar Bar & Cafe   CAFE, BAR
(www.oscarbarcafe.dk; Rådhuspladsen 77; ⊙noon-midnight Sun-Wed, noon-2am Thu-Sat, kitchen noon-10pm) A corner cafe–bar near Rådhuspladsen, and especially popular with the city's eye-candy men, this is a good place to get up to speed with what's happening on the Copenhagen gay scene.

Jailhouse CPH   BAR
(www.jailhousecph.dk; Studiestræde 12; ⊙bar Mon-Sun, dinner Thu-Sat) This popular themed bar and restaurant promises plenty of penal action, with uniformed 'guards' and willing guests.

Never Mind   BAR
(www.nevermindbar.dk; Nørre Voldgade 2; ⊙10pm-6am) Tiny, smoky and often packed to the rafters, Never Mind is a seriously fun spot for shameless pop and late-night flirtation.

Central Hjørnet   BAR
(www.centralhjornet.dk; Kattetsundet 18; ⊙noon-2am) The oldest gay bar in the village remains at the heart of the gay scene.

🛍 Shopping

Copenhagen is a superb, if expensive, shopping city. The city heaves with small, independent boutiques selling – in particular – unique ceramics, glasswares, homewares and fashion, often made by the person manning the till.

Take note that nearly everything closes on Sunday, although some grocers and supermarkets remain open in residential areas, such as Istedgade and Nørrebrogade.

Strøget (City Centre) Local and global fashion chains, Danish design stores, department stores; downmarket at its western end, upmarket at its eastern end.

Kronprinsensgade, Store Regnegade, Pilestræde, Købmagergade (City Centre) High-end independent fashion labels, local jewellery and homewares.

Istedgade (Vesterbro) Street fashion, vintage threads, shoes and food.

Elmegade, Blågårdsgade & Ravnsborggade (Nørrebro) Antiques, hipster fashion labels, homewares.

Bredgade (Nyhavn) Upmarket art and antiques.

Hoff
JEWELLERY

(Kronprinsensgade 12) Ingrid Hoff selects only the best Danish contemporary art jewellery for her showroom. Though her designers mix gold and silver with acrylic and nylon, this is not just of-the-moment fashion jewellery, but one-off and limited-run pieces to last a lifetime.

Pop Cph
CLOTHING

(www.popcph.dk; Gråbrødretorv 4) Mikkel Kristensen and Kasper Henriksen began hosting parties for Copenhagen's creative community in 2005. The parties continue to inspire the duo's fashion creations, which span graphic-print T-shirts to dinner-party glamour fused with subversive detailing.

Illums Bolighus
DESIGN

(www.illumsbolighus.dk; Amagertorv 8-10, Strøget) Raid this department store for sleek interior design, clothing, jewellery and furniture from big-name local and international designers.

Hay House
DESIGN

(www.hay.dk; Østergade 61, Strøget) Rolf Hay's fabulous interior design store sells well-chosen Danish furniture as well as irresistible design gifts such as ceramic cups, funky textiles and art books.

Storm
CLOTHING, ACCESSORIES

(www.stormfashion.dk; Store Regnegade 1) Copenhagen's cool crew head here for in-the-know labels such as Sixpack France, Yuketen and Anne Demeulemeester. Extras include design books, fashion magazines, CDs and fragrances.

Nordisk Korthandel
BOOKS, MAPS

(www.scanmaps.dk; Studiestræde 26-30) Offers a superb but pricey collection of travel guides and maps.

❶ Information

Internet Access

Hovedbiblioteket (15 Krystalgade; ☉10am-7pm Mon-Fri, 10am-2pm Sat, to 4pm Sat Oct-Mar) A public library offering free internet access on nine computers.

Sidewalk Express (www.sidewalkexpress.com; Central Station, Bernstorffsgade; per 90min Dkr29; ☉11am-5.30pm Mon-Thu, to 6pm Fri, 10am-3pm Sat) Self-service computer terminals with internet access.

Medical Services

Frederiksberg Hospital (☑38 16 35 22; Nordre Fasanvej 57) West of the city centre; has a 24-hour emergency ward.

Steno Apotek (Vesterbrogade 6c; ☉24hr) Pharmacy opposite Central Station.

Money

Banks, all of which charge transaction fees, are found throughout the city centre. Banks in the airport arrival and transit halls are open 6am to 10pm daily.

The **Forex exchange booth** (Central Station; ☉8am-9pm) has the lowest fees but you will find other exchange shops all along Strøget.

Post

Central Station Post Office (☉8am-9pm Mon-Fri, 10am-4pm Sat & Sun)

Post office (Købmagergade 33) Offers poste-restante services.

Tourist Information

Copenhagen Visitor Centre (☑70 22 24 42; www.visitcopenhagen.com; Vesterbrogade 4a; ☉9am-6pm Mon-Sat, 10am-2pm Sun May & Jun, 9am-8pm Mon-Sat, 10am-6pm Sun Jul & Aug, 9am-6pm Mon-Sat early-end Sep) This tourist office distributes a free city map, and brochures covering Copenhagen and all of Denmark's regions.

DENMARK COPENHAGEN

Travel Agencies

Kilroy Travels (www.kilroytravels.com; Skindergade 28)

Getting There & Away

Air

Copenhagen's international airport is in Kastrup, 10km southeast of the city centre. Flights connect frequently with most major Danish and Scandinavian destinations.

Boat

The ferry to Oslo, operated by **DFDS Seaways** (www.dfdsseaways.co.uk; Dampfærgevej 30), departs from the Nordhavn area north of the city (past Kastellet).

Bus

International buses leave from Central Station; advance reservations on most routes can be made at **Eurolines** (www.eurolines.dk; Halmtorvet 5).

Car & Motorcycle

The main highways into Copenhagen are the E20, which goes west to Funen and east to Malmö, Sweden; and the E47, which connects to Helsingør. If you're coming into Copenhagen from the north on the E47, exit onto Lyngbyvej (Rte 19) and continue south to get into the heart of the city.

As well as airport booths, the following rental agencies have city branches:

Avis (70 24 77 07; www.avis.com; Kampmannsgade 1)

Budget (33 55 05 00; www.budget.com; Vester Farimagsgade 7)

Europcar (89 33 11 33; www.europcar.com; Gammel Kongevej 13)

Hertz (33 17 90 20; www.hertzdk.dk; Ved Vesterport 3)

Train

Long-distance trains arrive and depart from Central Station (Hovedbanegården). *Billetautomats* (coin-operated ticket machines) are the quickest way to purchase a ticket, but only if you've mastered the zone-system prices.

They are best for S-Tog tickets. **DSB Billetsalg** (5.45am-11.30pm; international ticket sales 9.30am-6pm) is best for reservations and for purchasing international train tickets. Alternatively, you can make reservations at www.dsb.dk, which has an English-language option.

Central Station (per 24hr small/large locker Dkr40/50, max 72hr; 5.30-1am Mon-Sat, 6-1am Sun) also offers left luggage services – lockers are in the lower level near the Reventlowsgade exit.

Getting Around

To/From the Airport

TRAIN (www.dsb.dk) Links the airport with Central Station (Dkr36, 12 minutes, every 10 minutes).

METRO (www.m.dk) Links the airport with the eastern side of the city, stopping at Christianshavn Torv, Kongens Nytorv and Nørreport stations (www.m.dk; Dkr48, 13 minutes, every five minutes).

TAXI (35 35 35 35) Costs about Dkr250 from the city centre, with a journey time of around 15 minutes.

Bicycle

City Bikes offers free-use bikes from April to November at 110 City Bike racks throughout central Copenhagen. Deposit a Dkr20 coin in the stand to release the bike. You can return the bicycle to any rack to get your money back. Except during weekday rush hours, you can carry bikes on S-trains for free.

Københavns Cykler (www.rentabike; Reventlowsgade 11) At Central Station beneath platform 12; rents out bikes from Dkr75 a day.

Bus & Train

Copenhagen has a large, modern and efficient public transport system. Buses, Metro and trains use a common fare system based on zones. The basic fare of Dkr24 for up to two zones covers most city runs and allows transfers between buses and trains on a single ticket within one hour. If you're day-tripping it to Louisiana Museum for Modern Art, Helsingør and other North Zealand coastal sites, purchase a 24-hour pass

 COPENHAGEN CARD

The **Copenhagen Card** (www.visitcopenhagen.com; 24hr card adult/child Dkr239/125, 72hr card Dkr469/235, adult card covers 2 children under 10yr) secures unlimited travel on buses and trains around Copenhagen and North Zealand, and on the city's waterbuses. It also gives free or discounted admission to around 60 of the region's museums and attractions. Cards are sold at the Copenhagen tourist office, Central Station, major Danske Statsbaner (DSB) stations and at many hotels, camping grounds and hostels. Be aware, though, that several of the city's attractions are either free or at least free one day of the week.

(adult/child Dkr130/65), which allows unlimited travel in all zones. Two children under 12 travel free when accompanied by an adult.

METRO (www.m.dk) Consists of two lines (M1 and M2) and runs a minimum of every three minutes. Connects Nørreport and Kongens Nytorv (near Nyhavn) to Christianshavn and the airport. Purchase tickets from *billetautomats* at the station. Trains run around the clock, with reduced frequency at night.

S-TOG (S-train; www.dsb.dk) Operates seven metropolitan lines, each passing through Central Station (København H). Handy destinations include Helsingør and Køge. Purchase tickets at the station and punch them in the yellow time clock on the platform.

BUS (www.moviatrafik.dk, in Danish) Copenhagen's vast bus system has its main terminus at Rådhuspladsen. Night buses (12.30am to 5am) run on a few major routes. Purchase tickets on board from the driver.

Car & Motorcycle

Weekday morning and evening rush hour aside, traffic is usually manageable, though parking can be hard to find. It's far better to explore sights within the city centre on foot or by using public transport.

For kerbside parking, buy a ticket from a street-side *parkomat* and place it inside the windscreen. Parking costs from Dkr3 to Dkr29 depending on the time of day or night and how close you are to the city centre.

Taxi

Taxis with signs saying '*fri*' (meaning 'free') can be flagged down or you can phone ☑35 35 35 35. The basic fare is Dkr24 (Dkr37 if you book over the phone), plus Dkr12.50 per kilometre between 7am and 4pm, Dkr13.50 between 4pm and 7am Monday to Friday and all day Saturday and Sunday, and Dkr16.80 from 11pm to 7am Friday to Saturday and on public holidays. Fares include a service charge, so tipping is not expected. Taxis accept credit cards.

Klampenborg

Klampenborg is a favourite spot for family outings from Copenhagen. It is only 20 minutes from Central Station on the S-train's line C (Dkr46). Bellevue Beach, 400m east of Klampenborg station, is a sandy strand that gets packed with sunbathers in summer. A large grassy area behind the beach absorbs some of the overflow.

About 700m west from the station is Bakken (www.bakken.dk; Dyrehavevej 62; ⊗noon-midnight Mon-Sat, noon-10pm Sun Jul-Aug), the world's oldest amusement park. A blue-collar version of Copenhagen's Tivoli, it's a pleasantly old-fashioned carnival of bumper cars, slot machines and beer halls.

Bakken is on the southern edge of Dyrehaven, an extensive expanse of beech woods and meadows crossed with peaceful walking and cycling trails. Dyrehaven was established in 1669 as a royal hunting ground and is the capital's most popular picnic area – it's excellent for cycling and running too. At its centre, 2km north of Bakken, is the old manor house Eremitagen, a good vantage point for spotting herds of deer.

Louisiana Museum of Modern Art

Denmark's foremost modern-art museum (www.louisiana.dk; Gl Strandvej 13; adult/child Dkr95/free; ⊗11am-11pm Tue-Fri, 11am-6pm Sat & Sun) is housed in several low-level galleries atmospherically located beside the Øresund sea. It is surrounded by beautiful grounds full of sculptures by the likes of Henry Moore and Alexander Calder. The museum's permanent collection features works by Giacometti, Picasso, Warhol, Rauschenberg and many more, and there are outstanding changing exhibitions. It's a terrific spot even if you're not passionate about modern art. There's also a diverting **Children's Wing** and a lakeside garden, cafe and restaurant with fantastic views across the water to Sweden.

The museum is situated about 900m north on Strandvej from Humlebæk station, which is 36 minutes on the S-train's line C from Copenhagen. If you're day-tripping it from Copenhagen, it's cheaper to buy a 24-hour transport pass (Dkr130) from ticket vending machines.

ZEALAND

Though, naturally, Copenhagen is the centre of gravity for most visitors to Denmark's eastern island, there is plenty to make it worth your while to explore beyond the city limits. Zealand is an island with a rich history, beautiful coastline and plenty of gentle rolling countryside; and of course there's Helsingør Slot, better known as Hamlet's castle, Elsinore, and Frederiksborg Slot, a magnificent Renaissance castle. Older still are the remarkable Viking ships of Roskilde, excavated from Roskilde fjord in the 1950s and housed in a purpose-built museum.

North Zealand

One of the most popular day trips from Copenhagen is a loop tour taking in Frederiksborg Slot in Hillerød and Kronborg Slot in Helsingør. With an early start you might even have time to reach one of the northshore beaches before making your way back to the city, although it is more rewarding to allow an extra day for wandering between shoreline towns along this idyllic coastline.

If you're driving between Helsingør and Copenhagen, ignore the motorway and take the coastal road, Strandvej (Rte 152), which is far more scenic, although it can get crowded on summer weekends.

FREDERIKSBORG SLOT

Hillerød, 30km northwest of Copenhagen, is the site of Frederiksborg Slot (www.frederiks borgmuseet.dk; adult/child Dkr60/15; ⊘10am-5pm Apr-Oct), an impressive Dutch Renaissance castle that's spread across three islands. The oldest part of the castle dates from Frederik II's time, though most of the present structure was built by his son Christian IV in the early 17th century. After parts of the castle were ravaged by fire in 1859, Carlsberg beer baron JC Jacobsen spearheaded a drive to restore the castle and make it a national museum.

The sprawling castle has a magnificent interior, with gilded ceilings, full wall-sized tapestries, royal paintings and antiques. The richly embellished Riddershalen (Knights' Hall) and the coronation chapel, where Danish monarchs were crowned between 1671 and 1840, are well worth the admission fee.

The S-train (E line) runs every 10 minutes between Copenhagen and Hillerød (one-way Dkr103.50), a 40-minute ride. From Hillerød station follow the signs to Torvet, then continue along Slotsgade to the castle, a 1.5km walk in all. Alternatively, take bus 701 or 702, which can drop you at the gate.

North Zealand

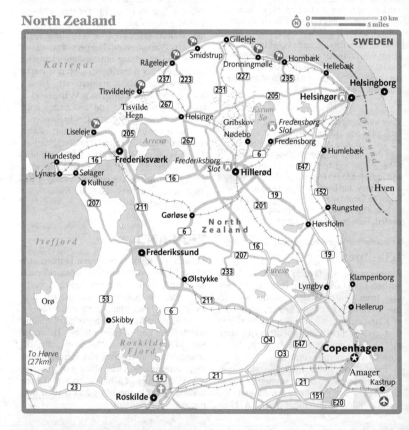

HELSINGØR (ELSINORE)
POP 46,200

Generally, visitors come to the charming harbour town of Helsingør, at the northeastern tip of Zealand, for one of two reasons. If they are Swedish, they come to stock up on cheap(er) booze (this is the closest point to Sweden, and ferries shuttle back and forth across the Øresund every half-hour). More likely is that they have come to soak up the atmosphere of Denmark's most famous and awe-inspiring castle, Elsinore, home of Shakespeare's indecisive antihero, Hamlet. The tourist office (☏49 21 13 33; www.visit nordsjaelland.com; Havnepladsen 3; ☺10am-5pm Mon-Fri, to 2pm Sat late Jun–early Aug) is opposite the train station.

◉ Sights

Kronborg Slot   CASTLE
(www.kronborg.dk; adult/6-14yr/under 6yr Dkr75/25/free; ☺10.30am-5pm daily May-Sep, 11am-4pm Tue-Sun Apr & Oct) Helsingør's top sight is Kronborg Slot, made famous as the Elsinore Castle of Shakespeare's Hamlet (it has been, and remains, the venue for summer performances of the play in recent years during the annual Hamlet festival – often with major English or US stars in the lead role). Kronborg's primary function was not as a royal residence, but rather as a grandiose tollhouse, wresting taxes (the infamous and lucrative 'Sound Dues') for more than 400 years from ships passing through the narrow Øresund. Stand by the cannons facing Sweden and you immediately see what a key strategic military and naval choke point this was. The castle is on the northern side of the harbour within easy walking distance of the station.

Medieval Quarter
& Around   HISTORIC AREA, MUSEUM
From the tourist office head up Brostræde and along Sankt Anna Gade. This will take you through the medieval quarter and past the old cathedral, Sankt Olai Kirke (St Anna Gade 12, ☺10am-4pm Mon-Sat May-Aug); the small City History Museum (admission free; ☺noon-4pm Tue-Fri, 10am-2pm Sat, noon-4pm Sun); and Sct Mariæ Kirke and Karmeliterklostret (adult/child Dkr20/5; church ☺10am-3pm Tue-Sun mid-May–mid-Sep, guided tours 2pm Fri & Sat mid-Jun–mid-Sep), one of Scandinavia's best-preserved medieval monasteries. From here Sudergade leads to the tree-lined, cobbled central square of Axeltorv, where you will find several cafes and takeaways. Further out of town are Danmarks Tekniske Museum (www.tekniskmuseum.dk, in Danish; Fabriksvej 25; adult/child Dkr65/free; ☺10am-5pm Tue-Sun), with historic aeroplanes and motor cars among other exhibits, and Øresundsakvariet (www.oresundsakvariet.ku.dk, in Danish; Strandpromenaden 5; adult/child Dkr55/35; ☺10am-5pm daily Jun-Aug), an aquarium with local sea life.

Fredensborg Slot   CASTLE
(www.ses.dk; adult/child Dkr50/20; ☺garden tours 1pm & 4.30pm) A 20-minute train ride southwest of Helsingør takes you to a very different kind of royal castle from Kronborg Slot. Fredensborg Slot evolved during the early 18th century as a royal hunting lodge. Its present-day role is as the royal family's summer residence and number-one party palace: this is where the wedding reception of Crown Prince Frederik and Tasmanian Mary Donaldson took place. It is a peaceful spot for a stroll or a picnic, with lush rolling lawns, forest and formal gardens beside Esrum Sø (Lake Esrum). The private gardens, herb garden and orangerie most closely surrounding the house are open only during July.

🛏 Sleeping

The tourist office website (www.visitnord sjaelland.com) offers a list of private accommodation options, with links to each property. Prices start at Dkr450 for both singles and doubles.

Danhostel Helsingør   HOSTEL €
(☏49 28 49 49; www.helsingorhostel.dk; Nordre Strandvej 24; dm Dkr175, r Dkr475-850; Ⓟ@) Housed in the imposing red-brick Villa Moltke, 2km northwest of the centre, this hostel is right by the water with its own beach. Rooms are simple but clean. From Helsingør train station, catch bus 340 or take the lokalbanen (local train) from Helsingør to Marienlyst station.

Hotel Sleep2Night   MOTEL €€
(☏49 27 01 00; www.sleep2night.com; Industrivej 19; s/d Dkr760/875; Ⓟ@) This wooden chalet-style accommodation is Denmark's beautifully designed take on the US motel, with simple but well-equipped rooms and free internet connections throughout. It's good value (check the website for discounted-rate offers) but it's a 20-minute journey from the centre of town, to the south of Helsingør. From the train station, take bus 801, 802 or 805.

Hotel Marienlyst HOTEL €€€
(📞49 21 40 00; www.marienlyst.dk; Nordre Strand-vej 2; s/d Dkr1070/1170) This is the closest things get to glamour and luxury in these parts, as this modern conference hotel has a casino, swimming pool and views across the sea to Sweden.

Helsingør Camping CAMPING GROUND €
(📞49 28 49 50; www.helsingorcamping.dk; Stran-dalleen 2; campsites per adult/child Dkr60/30, cabins from Dkr350) A well-spaced beachside camping ground that is east of the hostel and close to one of the area's best beaches.

✗ Eating & Drinking

Madam Sprunck CAFE, EUROPEAN €€
(www.madamsprunck.dk; Stengade 48; salads Dkr92-96, restaurant mains Dkr198-225) This Hels-ingør institution, housed in a building dating back to 1781, is situated around a charming courtyard with outdoors seating in summer. As well as serving great evening meals in its restaurant, it does a lavish brunch (Dkr135) and a two-course lunch menu for Dkr160.

Hispania SPANISH €€
(www.cyberastur.es/hispania/; Stengade 7; mains Dkr175-185, tapas Dkr65-98) For some reason a finding a real, authentic Spanish tapas bar in Helsingør took us a bit by surprise, but the kitchen staff are Spanish, and this is the real deal, with a charmingly eclectic interior and a good range of Spanish wines. Try the excellent chorizo croquettes.

Gæstgivergården DANISH €€
(Kampergade 11; smørrebrød Dkr59-69, mains Dkr89-149) This traditional Danish pub of-fers a good-value lunch menu.

Café Vivaldi CAFE €€
(Stengade 9; lunches Dkr79-105, mains Dkr129-209) Part of a small chain, this pleasant French–Italian cafe at the end of the high street serves salads, sandwiches and omelettes.

❶ Getting There & Away

BOAT **Scandlines** (📞33 15 15 15; www.scan dlines.com) sails around 75 times daily from Helsingør to Helsingborg, in Sweden (return ticket adult/car with nine passengers from Dkr48/355).

TRAIN Trains between Copenhagen and Helsingør run several times hourly (one-way Dkr108, 45 minutes). If you're day-tripping it from Copenhagen, buy a 24-hour pass (Dkr130). Trains between Helsingør and Hillerød (Dkr69, 30 minutes) run at least once hourly.

Zealand's North Coast

The entire stretch of coast from Helsingør west to Liseleje is in effect Zealand's holi-day zone, with literally thousands of tradi-tional Danish summer houses packing the woodlands and beachfronts. The festive atmosphere that takes over the charm-ing, half-timbered fishing villages, such as Gilleleje and Hornbæk, and the long, sandy, impeccably clean beaches, make it worth visiting.

Hornbæk, the next main town west of Helsingør, has the best and most easily accessible beach on the north coast. The beach is a vast expanse of white sand and grassy dunes that run the entire length of the town, and it has a Blue Flag eco-friend-ly label. From the train station, it's just a five-minute walk directly down Havnevej to the harbour, where you'll find a great seafood kiosk and the yacht marina. Simply climb the dunes to the left and you're on the beach. The library doubles as the **tour-ist office** (www.hornbaek.dk; Vestre Stejlebakke 2a; ⏱1-5pm Mon & Thu, 10am-3pm Tue, Wed & Fri, to 2pm Sat).

Zealand's northernmost town, Gilleleje, has the island's largest fishing port. Visitors usually head straight for the harbour and adjacent sandy beach. The harbour has sev-eral wonderful seafood kiosks, selling fresh-ly caught crayfish platters, fish and chips and even sushi. The **tourist office** (www. visitnordsjaelland.com; Hovedgade 6f; ⏱10am-5pm Mon-Fri, to 3pm Sat late-Jun–mid-Aug) is in the centre. There are excellent beaches ei-ther side of the town and others along the coast to the west, especially at Rågeleje, Dronningmølle and at Smidstrup Strand, where conditions are often good for wind-surfing. All have Blue Flags.

Tisvildeleje is a pleasant seaside village known for its bohemian and artistic com-munities, with a long, straggling main street that leads to an even longer beach. It really transforms in July when the holidaymakers arrive. Out of season it's somewhat desolate. The **tourist office** (www.visitnordsjaelland.com; Banevej 8; ⏱12.30-4.30pm Mon-Fri, 10am-noon Sat late-Jun–mid-Aug, closed rest of yr) is at the train station. Behind the beach is Tisvilde Hegn, a windswept forest of twisted trees and heather-covered hills laced with good walking paths.

DRAGSHOLM SLOT

Fancy a night in a culinary castle? Then pack your bag and your appetite and check in at **Dragsholm Slot** (59 65 33 00; www.dragsholm-slot.dk; Dragsholm Allé, Hørve; s/d from Dkr1795/1995; P). Located at the edge of Zealand's fertile Lammefjorden (Denmark's most famous 'vegetable garden'), its medieval walls are home to **Slotskøkkenet** (Castle Kitchen; 3/5/7 courses Dkr550/650/800; dinner Tue-Sat summer, dinner Fri & Sat winter), a New Nordic hot spot headed by ex-Noma chef Claus Henriksen. From the area's prized carrots to herbs from the castle's own garden, 'locally sourced' is the catch-cry here. The end result is deceptively simple, sublime creations such as candied herbs with skyr and celeriac. Upstairs, the more casual **Spisehuset** (lunch dishes Dkr80-165, 3-course dinners Dkr295) offers cheaper, pared-back Nordic dishes using the same top-notch ingredients (think herb-marinated herring or hay-smoked salmon). Bookings are a must for Slotskøkkenet and recommended for Spisehuset.

Nosh aside, whitewashed Dragsholm is famed for its 800-year history, which includes the imprisonment of Roskilde's last Catholic bishop and the secret burial of a love-struck girl in the castle walls (eerily visible behind a plexiglass panel). While some rooms – spread across the castle and the nearby porter's lodge – feature contemporary styling, most ooze a distinguished baronial air, with anything from canopy beds to fleur-de-lis wallpaper and (in some cases) jacuzzis. Add to this a string of Late Romantic salons and ballrooms and rambling fairy-tale gardens, and you'll soon be feeling like a well-fed noble.

Check the website for dinner and accommodation packages (often cheaper than the official room rates), and request a room with field or garden views. Dragsholm Slot is located 91km west of Copenhagen via motorway 21.

Sleeping

Dronningmølle Strandcamping
CAMPING GROUND €

(49 71 92 90; www.dronningmolle.dk; Strandkrogen 2b, Dronningmølle; campsites per adult/child Dkr85/55, tent Dkr155) This excellent, four-star camping ground is on the coast road between Hornbæk and Gilleleje. You have to cross the main road to get to the beach, but it is a beauty and has a Blue Flag. Tent sites come with all amenities – electricity, water and in some cases, even cable TV.

Hotel Villa Strand
HOTEL €€

(49 70 00 88; www.villastrand.dk; Kystvej 2; s/d from Dkr895/995) Villa Strand is a pleasant, quiet place to the west of Hornbæk centre and very close to the beach. There are cheaper doubles in garden bungalows, and plusher rooms with balconies in the main building.

Gilleleje Badehotel
HOTEL €€€

(48 30 13 47; www.gillelejebadehotel.dk; Hulsøvej 15, Gilleleje; d Dkr1190-1390; P) On Gilleleje beach, the grandest of the north coast's bathing hotels has been renovated in Gustavian style. Request a room with a sea view.

Helenekilde Badehotel
HOTEL €€€

(48 70 70 01; www.helenekilde.com; Strandvejen 25, Tisvildeleje; s Dkr995-2395; d Dkr1095-2495; P) A beautiful, renovated bathing hotel that is built on the cliffs overlooking the beaches at Tisvildeleje; it's about a 10-minute walk from the main street.

Ewaldsgården Guest House
GUESTHOUSE €€

(49 70 00 82; www.ewaldsgaarden.dk; Johannes Ewalds Vej 5, Hornbæk; s/d Dkr550/850; end Jun–mid-Aug; P) Though not close to the beach, this cosy and elegant guesthouse is excellent value and has pretty, light-filled rooms.

Hotel Bretagne
HOTEL €€€

(49 70 16 66; www.hotelbretagne.dk; Sauntevej 18, Hornbæk; s/d Dkr995/1195) This is an imposing, whitewashed former clinic with lovely, modern, comfy rooms and good facilities, including wi-fi.

Eating

For eating out along Zealand's northern coast you can't beat the seafood restaurants – usually little more than a few kiosks, really – that you find in the harbours.

Fiskehuset Hornbæk
SEAFOOD €

(Havenevej 32, Hornbæk; fish & chips Dkr50; vary) Hornbæk's seafood kiosk is the Fiskehuset. Here you can dine like a lord, albeit outdoors with paper serviettes, on smoked cod's roe, cured herring, smoked mackerel, fresh prawns, *fiskfrikadeller* (Danish fish cakes), mussel soup and all manner of wonderful, fresh, local seafood – for under Dkr60.

Adamsen's Fish
SEAFOOD €€
(Gilleleje Harbour; ⊙Jun-Aug) Adamsen's is the reason why Gilleleje harbour is such a great place to hang out in the summer. Its seafood takeaways – fish cakes Dkr55, sushi Dkr125, shellfish platter Dkr135 – draw the crowds, who while away sunny afternoons on the picnic benches here. You can buy fresh fish here year-round, too.

Restaurant Søstrene Olsen
FRENCH, DANISH €€€
(☑49 70 05 50; www.sostreneolsen.dk; Øresundsvej 10, Hornbæk; mains Dkr168-298; ⊙Mar-Oct) Hornbæk is hardly a gourmet mecca, but you will find well-executed, refined, ambitious Franco-Danish food at husband-and-wife team Thorleif and Minne Aagaard's charming thatched cottage right on the beach.

Restaurant Hansens Café
DANISH, EUROPEAN €€
(☑49 70 04 79; www.hansenscafe.dk; Havnevej 19, Hornbæk; mains Dkr168-225; ⊙dinner Mon-Sat, lunch & dinner Sun) This half-timbered, thatched cottage restaurant with garden seating serves traditional Danish food and French/Mediterranean-inspired dishes such as roast beef with horseradish and pickles, or fresh fish served with radish tzatziki and new Danish potatoes.

⊙ Getting There & Away
Train connections to/from Helsingør include the following:

Hornbæk Dkr34.50, 25 minutes, every 30 minutes on weekdays, hourly on weekends

Gilleleje Dkr69, 43 minutes, every 30 minutes on weekdays, hourly on weekends

Tisvildeleje via Hillerød Dkr80.50, one hour, hourly

On Sundays, Tisvildeleje is reached by taking bus 390R from Helsingør to Helsinge (one hour, hourly). From here, trains continue to Tisvildeleje.

Although buses service the area, trains are usually the quicker, more convenient option. Hillerød trains run to Gilleleje and to Tisvildeleje (Dkr57.50, 30 minutes, every 30 minutes Monday to Saturday, hourly on Sunday), though with no rail link between the two.

Roskilde
POP 46,700

Most foreigners who have heard of Roskilde know it either as the home of one of northern Europe's best outdoor music festivals, or the sight of several remarkable Viking ship finds, now housed in an excellent, purpose-built museum. To the Danes, however, it is a city of great royal and religious significance, as it was the capital city long before Copenhagen and is still the burial place of 39 monarchs stretching back several hundred years. Located on the southern tip of Roskilde Fjord, the city was a thriving trading port throughout the Middle Ages. It was also the site of Zealand's first Christian church, built by Viking king Harald Bluetooth in AD 980.

The **Roskilde Festival** (www.roskilde-festival.dk; 2011 festival pass Dkr1725) takes place over a long weekend in early July, in fields just outside the city centre. It attracts the biggest international rock and pop names (Prince, Prodigy, Patti Smith and Gorillaz all performed in 2010), along with 75,000 music fans. It is renowned for its relaxed, friendly atmosphere. Most visitors camp on-site, as the accommodation in Roskilde itself tends to get booked up well in advance.

⊙ Sights

Roskilde Domkirke
CHURCH
(www.roskildedomkirke.dk; Domkirkepladsen; adult/child/under 7yr Dkr25/15/free; ⊙9am-5pm Mon-Sat, 12.30-5pm Sun Apr-Sep) Though most of Roskilde's medieval buildings have vanished in fires over the centuries, the imposing twin-spired cathedral still dominates the city centre. Started by Bishop Absalon in 1170, Roskilde Domkirke has been rebuilt and added to so many times that this mighty brick edifice represents a millennium of Danish church architectural styles. It's protected under Unesco's World Heritage list.

The cathedral has tall spiky **spires**, eye-catching in their disproportionate slenderness compared with the solidity of the rest of the building. The cathedral interior is splendid; its **crypts** contain the sarcophagi of 39 Danish kings and queens. Some are lavishly embellished and guarded by marble statues of knights and women in mourning. Others are simple and unadorned. There's something quite affecting about being able to stand so close to the remains of so many of Scandinavia's powerful historical figures. For light relief, take a look at the 15th-century

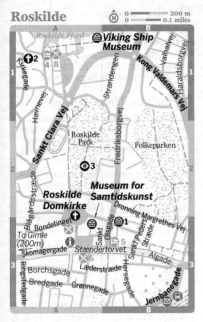

DENMARK ROSKILDE

in a replica Viking ship. As well as this, MS *Sagafjord* is a veteran cruiser that offers sailing **tours** (adult/child Dkr98/39) of the fjord from April to October (daily from June to August).

clock above the entrance, where a tiny St George on horseback marks the hour by slaying a yelping dragon (a pair of bellows and three out-of-tune organ pipes create its yelp).

Viking Ship Museum   MUSEUM
(www.vikingskibsmuseet.dk; Vindeboder 12; adult/child May-Sep Dkr100/free, Oct-Apr Dkr70/free; ◎10am-5pm) From the northern side of the cathedral, walk across a field where wildflowers blanket the unexcavated remains of Roskilde's original medieval town, and continue through a green belt all the way to the well-presented Viking Ship Museum. Here you'll find five reconstructed Viking ships (c 1000), excavated from Roskilde Fjord in 1962 and brought to shore in thousands of fragments. The five ships – all different – had been filled with stones and scuttled to block the entrance to the fjord to protect the town (at that time, the capital of Denmark) from attack by Norwegian Vikings. The museum also incorporates fascinating **waterfront workshops** where replicas of Viking ships are built using Viking-era techniques. The smells and sounds here are just as they would have been 1000 years ago.

From May to the end of September, you can take a **trip** (excl museum admission Dkr75; ◎daily Jun–end Aug, check with the museum for other times) on the waters of Roskilde Fjord

Other Sights   HISTORIC AREA, MUSEUM
West of the Viking Ship Museum is the **Sankt Jørgensbjerg quarter**, where the cobbled Kirkegade walkway leads through a neighbourhood of old straw-roofed houses into the courtyard of the 11th-century **Sankt Jørgensbjerg Kirke**.

Back in the town, a terrific surprise awaits art fans at the **Museum for Samtidskunst** (www.samtidskunst.dk; Stændertorvet 3d; adult/child Dkr40/free, admission free Wed; ◎11am-5pm Tue-Fri, noon-4pm Sat & Sun). Housed in the elegant 18th-century Roskilde Palace, this is a surprisingly cutting-edge contemporary art space, fond of perplexing installations by Danish and international artists.

Roskilde Museum (www.roskildemuseum.dk; Sankt Olsgade 18; adult/child Dkr25/free; ◎11am-4pm) has displays on Roskilde's rich history.

If the Viking Ship Museum has given you a taste for the history of the region, 7km southwest of Roskilde is the fascinating **Sagnlandet Lejre** (www.sagnlandet.dk; Slangealleen 2, Lejre; adult/child Dkr125/85; ◎10am-5pm daily end Jun–mid-Aug), a historic, 43-hectare open-air park – they call it a centre for 'experimental archaeology' – with recreated buildings from the Iron Age, Stone Age, Viking era and the 19th century, and variety of activities and special events. You get there by train from Roskilde (Dkr23, six minutes).

🍴 Sleeping & Eating

The tourist office books rooms in private homes for Dkr450 for doubles only, plus a Dkr45 booking fee.

Danhostel Roskilde   HOSTEL €

(☑46 35 21 84; www.danhostel.dk/roskilde; Vindeboder 7; dm Dkr180-200, r Dkr400-600; P) This harbourside hostel is especially smart and modern, even by Danish hostel standards. Though made up of small three-, four-, five-, six- or eight-bed dorms, most are offered as private rooms. It's adjacent to the Viking Ship Museum.

Restaurant Snekken   EUROPEAN €€€

(www.snekken.dk; Vinderboder 16; ◷11.30am-11pm; mains Dkr228-285) This modern, glassy restaurant is in a great spot overlooking the fjord and a few metres from the Viking Ship Museum and Roskilde Danhostel. The food perhaps is not worth a trip on its own, but the menu offers some ambitious mains (think grilled guinea hen with smoked mashed potatoes, peas, leeks and a thyme glaze), as well as lighter lunch fare.

Café Vivaldi   CAFE, RESTAURANT €€

(Stændertorvet 8; mains Dkr129-209; ◷10am-10pm Sun-Thu, to 11.30pm Fri & Sat) Right on the main square with views to the cathedral is this contemporary chain serving wraps, sandwiches, burgers and pasta dishes (Dkr79 to Dkr99), as well as evening main courses.

Gimle   CAFE €

(www.gimle.dk, in Danish; Helligkorsvej 2; meals Dkr35-85; ◷noon-midnight Tue & Wed, to 2am Thu & Fri, 10-2am Sat, 10am-5pm Sun, kitchen closes 8pm) Gimle covers all bases, from laidback cafe and cultural hub, to live-music venue and weekend nightclub. Pull up a retro chair and munch on simple, tasty grub such as bagels, salads, nachos and burgers (including a vegetarian version). Wi-fi is free.

Hotel Prindsen   HOTEL €€€

(☑46 30 91 00; Algade 13; www.prindsen.dk; s Dkr895-1435, d Dkr995-1590) The town's grandest accommodation, with plenty of chintz and all the trimmings.

Rådhuskælderen   DANISH, EUROPEAN €€€

(www.raadhuskaeldern.dk; Fondens Bro 1; mains Dkr168-300; ◷11am-11pm Mon-Sat) Right next to the cathedral, this atmospheric, red-brick cellar serves simple modern European and Danish dishes.

ℹ️ Information

Nordea Bank (Algade 4)

Post office (Jernbanegade 3)

Tourist office (www.visitroskilde.com; Stændertorvet 1; ◷10am-5pm Mon-Fri, 10am-1pm Sat Apr-Jun, to 2pm Sat Jul & Aug)

ℹ️ Getting There & Around

Trains from Copenhagen to Roskilde are frequent (Dkr92, 25 minutes). From Copenhagen by car, Rte 21 leads to Roskilde; upon approaching the city, exit onto Rte 156, which leads into the centre.

Parking discs are required in Roskilde. There are free car parks at Gustav Weds Plads and near the Viking Ship Museum.

Jupiter Cykler (www.jupitercykler.dk; Gullandsstræde 3; per day Dkr75-90), just off Skomagergade, rents out bikes.

Køge

POP 34,900

Køge is a pretty town that, if not worth a special visit, offers a pleasant diversion if you're passing through on your way by ferry to Bornholm. The one-time medieval trading centre, 42km south of Copenhagen, retains an engaging core of historic buildings that line the narrow streets leading off the broad and busy main square, Torvet.

A short stroll through the central part of Køge takes you to Denmark's oldest half-timbered building (c 1527) at Kirkestræde 20, a marvellous survivor with a fine raked roof. Køge's historical museum (Nørregade 4; adult/child Dkr30/free; ◷11am-5pm Tue-Sun Jun-Aug) is in a splendid building that dates from 1619. Another gem is Brogade 23, decorated with cherubs carved by the famed 17th-century artist Abel Schrøder. Elsewhere best efforts have been made to improve a not very attractive industrial harbour with open-air cafes and restaurants. Finally, Køge also has Denmark's only museum dedicated to the artistic process, KØS (www.koes.dk; Vestergade 1; adult/child Dkr50/free; ◷10am-5pm Tue-Sun), which includes the sketches for the statue of the *Little Mermaid* and for Queen Margrethe II's birthday tapestries.

🍴 Sleeping & Eating

The tourist office can book double rooms in private homes from Dkr400.

Hotel Hvide Hus   HOTEL €€€

(☑56 65 36 90; www.helnan.info; Strandvejen 111; s Dkr695-1295, d Dkr925-1495; P) Well located if a little characterless, this 127-room modern hotel is on the beach, and has a cafe and restaurant.

🛏 Danhostel Køge HOSTEL €

(📞56 67 66 50; www.danhostel.dk/koege; Vamdrupvej 1; dm Dkr200, r from Dkr380; ⊘Feb–mid-Dec; 🅿) The hostel (with wi-fi) is 2km northwest of the centre.

StigAnn EUROPEAN €€€

(www.stigann.dk; Sankt Gertruds Stræd 2; lunches Dkr65-100, dinners Dkr195-265, 3-course menus Dkr325; ⊘4-11pm Mon-Thu, noon-midnight Fri & Sat) One of Køge's best restaurants by some margin, StigAnn offers refined and ambitious retro-classic dishes such as Tournedos Rossini and Chateaubriand.

ℹ Information

Tourist office (📞56 67 60 01; www.visitkoege. com; Vestergade 1; ⊘9am-5pm Mon-Fri, 9am-2pm Sat Jun-Aug) Just off the square.

ℹ Getting There & Away

You can park in Torvet, but for one hour only during the day; there are longer-term car parks near the train station. Time discs are required.

Boat

Bornholmer Færgen (📞56 95 18 66; www. bornholmerfaergen.dk; adult/12-15yr/under 11yr Dkr266/133/free, car incl 5 passengers Dkr1532-1550) operates an overnight service from Køge to Bornholm, departing daily at 12.30am and arriving at 6am. It is quicker and almost as cheap to take a train via Copenhagen to Ystad in Sweden, and then a catamaran to Rønne from there (total journey time would be around 3½ hours), although it can make sense to sleep while you sail if your itinerary is tight.

Train & Bus

Køge's train and bus stations are at Jernbanegade 12 on the east side of town. The train station is the last stop on the E line on Copenhagen's S-Tog network. Trains to Copenhagen run at least three times an hour (Dkr103.50, 40 minutes). The bus to Copenhagen (Dkr103.50, one hour) leaves from outside the train station.

Trelleborg

In the countryside of southern Zealand Trelleborg (www.vikingeborg.dk; Trelleborg Allé 4, Hejninge; adult/child Dkr60/free; ⊘10am-4pm Tue-Sun Apr, May, Sep & Oct, to 5pm Tue-Sun Jun-Aug) is the best preserved of Denmark's four Viking ring fortresses.

There isn't an awful lot to see here, it must be said – there is a reconstructed Viking hall, a small visitor centre and the earthen-walled fortress itself, dating from AD 980. This is made up of various grassy earthworks, hillocks and trenches divided into four symmetrical quadrants. In Viking times, each quadrant contained four long elliptical buildings of wood that surrounded a courtyard. Each of the 16 buildings, which served as barracks, was exactly 100 Roman feet (29.5m) long. Concrete blocks mark the outlines of the house foundations. Plaques point out burial mounds and other features.

Trelleborg is 7km west of Slagelse. To get there, take the train to Slagelse (Dkr69, 33 minutes from Roskilde) and then either catch the hourly bus 312 to Trelleborg (Dkr26, 12 minutes) or take a taxi from Slagelse (Dkr170 weekdays, Dkr190 weekends).

South Islands

The three islands of Møn, Falster and Lolland mark the southernmost part of Denmark. Of these, Møn and Falster are the most beautiful. Though just a 1½-hour drive from Copenhagen, these rural oases with their gently rolling, unspoiled landscape can seem centuries removed. Though bridges connect all three islands to each other and Zealand, they often appear disconnected from the modern world, which of course is part of their appeal. Cycling holidays are popular here, as is fishing, sailing, birdwatching and hiking, and there are several good golf courses. There is also a thriving arts scene on Møn, although the island is most celebrated for its striking chalk sea cliffs.

VORDINGBORG

POP 11,500

Though it isn't actually on the south islands, you will most likely have to pass through the southern Zealand harbour town of Vordingborg, the largest in the region, to reach them. It is worth spending an hour or so in this busy, culturally interesting town, once home to one of the most important defensive fortresses in Denmark, built by Valdemar the Great as a Baltic power base. The remnants of that 14th-century fortress, the 26m Gåsetårnet (Goose Tower), is the town's most prominent landmark today and marks the start of the high street. Beside the Goose Tower is **Danmarks Borgcenter** (Slotsruinen 1; adult/

child Dkr45/free, incl admission to the Goose Tower; ⊙10am-5pm May-Sep, 10am-4pm Tue-Sun Oct-Apr) with historically themed exhibitions and, during the summer, a wide range of re-enactment and archaeological activities. It is also home to the **Vordingborg tourist office** (☑55 34 11 11; ⊙10am-5pm daily Jul-Sep).

MØN
POP 9900

Ask any Dane, and they will tell you that the white cliffs of eastern Møn (Møns Klint) are one of the great natural 'wonders' of Denmark. That isn't saying much, of course – but the cliffs are rather majestic, and the beaches that ring the island are as good as any in Denmark. Inland you'll find woodland, narrow lanes, medieval churches and prehistoric remains.

One downside is that the island's bus service is sketchy, and to get the best out of Møn, having your own transport helps.

Stege, the main settlement on Møn, is an everyday place, but it is enlivened by its role as the island's gateway town and main commercial centre.

◎ Sights & Activities

Møns Klint   NATURE, MUSEUM
The chalk cliffs of Møns Klint, at the eastern tip of the island, were created during the last Ice Age when the calcareous deposits from aeons of compressed seashells were lifted from the ocean floor. The gleaming white cliffs rise sharply for 128m above an azure sea, presenting one of the most striking landscapes in Denmark. The chalk subsoil of the land above the cliffs supports a terrific variety of wildflowers including vivid orchids. There is a strict embargo on picking wildflowers.

The woods of Klinteskoven, behind the cliffs, have a network of paths and tracks. From near the cafeteria you can descend the cliffs by a series of wooden stairways. It's quite a long descent and a strenuous return up the 500-odd stairs. From the base of the steps, turn south along the narrow beach, which leads in about 1km to another stairway at Gråryg Fald. These take you steeply to the top of the cliff, from where a path leads back to the car park (Dkr25). Warning notices and barriers should be heeded. The reasons for this and the history of the cliffs themselves are now explained at the swish museum **Geocenter Møns Klint** (www.moensklint.dk; Stengårdsvej 8, Borre; adult/child Dkr115/70; ⊙10am-6pm end Jun–Aug), which also houses a collection of fossils found on the beaches here. The museum is located on the clifftop at Borre and has a lovely cafe-restaurant with views over the sea.

During summer, **boat tours** (☑21 40 41 81; www.sejlkutteren-discovery.dk, in Danish) of the coast around the cliffs run with MS *Discovery* from Klintholm harbour every two hours from 10am to 4pm.

Passage Graves   HISTORIC SITE
Møn has a wealth of prehistoric remains, although many are vestigial burial mounds. The best-preserved sites are the late–Stone Age passage graves of **Kong Asgers Høj** and **Klekkende Høj**. Both are on the west side of the island within a 2km radius of the village of Røddinge, from where they are signposted. Kong Asgers Høj is close to the narrow road and parking space is limited. The site is extremely well preserved and comprises a grassy mound pierced by a low passageway that leads to a splendid stone-lined chamber. Take a torch and mind your head. **Klekkende Høj** is on a hilltop amid fields. From a car park, follow a signposted track to reach the site. The grave has a double chamber and again you need a torch and some agility to creep inside.

FREE **Stege Kirke**   CHURCH
(Provstestræde; ⊙9am-5pm Tue-Sat, 9am-noon Sun Apr-Sep) Stege Kirke has unique medieval frescos and a pulpit carved with entertaining visual interpretations of biblical scenes.

Cycling   CYCLING
Although testing at times, cycling on Møn is rewarding given the island's uncharacteristic hilliness. The tourist office has a route map and an excellent printout guide in English to themed bike tours on the island.

⫟ Sleeping & Eating

You can find a list of Møn's many guesthouses and B&Bs at www.visitvordingborg.dk. In Stege, there are bakeries and supermarkets and a handful of cafes.

TOP CHOICE **Bakkegaard Gæstgiveri** GUESTHOUSE €
(☑55 81 93 01; www.bakkegaarden64.dk; Busenevej 64, Busene; r with/without view Dkr405/355, subsequent nights Dkr350/300; P@) Artists and the artistically inclined will adore this guesthouse. Within walking distance of Møns Klint and set on peaceful grounds with sea views, its 12 cosy rooms are decorated by 13 local artists. The cultural theme continues with a small gallery and occasional art classes, while

A FEAST OF FRESCOS

Given Møn's artistic sensibility, it seems apt that the island should claim some of the best-preserved primitive frescos in Denmark. You'll find them in many of Møn's churches, most of which are of medieval origin. The frescos depict biblical scenes, often interpreted through light-hearted rustic imagery. Fearful of what they saw as too much Roman exuberance, post-Reformation Lutherans whitewashed them, ironically preserving the artworks. The style of Møn fresco painting owes much to the Emelundemestteren (the Elmelunde Master), an accomplished stylist whose name is unknown. Some of his finest work can be seen at Elmelunde Kirke (Kirkebakken 41; admission free; ⊘8am-5pm May-Sep) on the road to Møns Klint.

the in-house cafe (lunch Dkr65 to Dkr120, dinner mains Dkr130) serves mostly organic, local produce.

Elmehøj   GUESTHOUSE €
(🖉55 81 35 35; www.elmehoj.dk; Kirkebakken 38, Elmelunde; s/d/tr/q Dkr315/420/600/800; P) This large family-run guesthouse is in the centre of the island right beside Elmelunde Church. This ivy-covered manor house is imposing and located in pleasant grounds with views over Steve Cove. Though slightly dated, the simple rooms are homely, and all have shared bathrooms. The beach is a short drive away, and there is a horse-riding school nearby.

Camping Møns Klint   CAMPING GROUND €
(🖉55 81 20 25; www.campingmoensklint.dk; Klinte-vej 544, Børre Møn; campsites per adult/child/tent Dkr82/57/25; ⊘Apr-Oct) The best located of Møn's camping grounds is about 3km from the cliffs. The camping ground is in a pleasant woodland setting with swimming pool and tennis court as well as horse riding.

David's   FRENCH, DANISH €€
(www.davids.nu, in Danish; Storegade 11a, Stege; lunches Dkr 80-135, 2-course menus Dkr245; ⊘10am-5pm Mon-Thu, to 10pm Fri & Sat, kitchen closes 8pm) Ambitious modern Franco-Danish food using locally sourced ingredients is on offer here, for very reasonable prices. Local fish is one of David's specialities, as well as the Nordic-twist 'tapas' plate (Dkr135).

Danhostel Møns Klint   HOSTEL €
(🖉55 81 20 30; www.danhostel.dk/moen; Langeb-jergvej 1, Borre; dm/d/tr/q Dkr165/330/420/460; ⊘May-mid-Sep; P) This two-star hostel 5km from the beach and cliffs occupies an enchanting lakeside spot opposite the camping ground.

Bryguset Møn   MICROBREWERY €€
(Storegade 18, Stege; burgers & lunch plates Dkr59-89, dinners Dkr59-159; ⊘11am-9pm daily end May-Sep, closed Jan) This casual micro-brewery is a sound bet for simple, honest grub. It has outdoor seating in summer.

ⓘ Information

Møn tourist office (🖉55 86 04 00; www.visit vordingborg.dk; Storegade 2; ⊘9.30am-5pm Mon-Fri, 9am-6pm Sat mid-Jun-Aug) is at the entrance to Stege. As well as offering informa-tion on the island, the website allows you to book accommodation online out of hours.

ⓘ Getting There & Around

From Copenhagen take the train to Vordingborg (Dkr121, 1¼ hours; at least once hourly); from there it's a 40-minute ride to Stege on bus 660R (Dkr45; hourly Monday to Saturday, every two hours on Sunday). From Stege, bus 667 travels towards Møns Klint (Dkr15, 20 minutes, hourly on weekdays, every two hours on weekends), stopping within about 6km of Møns Klint itself. From late June to mid-August, bus 667 stops at the hostel and camping ground en route.

FALSTER
POP 43,400

Falster is the middle of the three islands to the south of Zealand and, as with Møn and Lolland, the people who live here – most of whom live in the only town of any sig-nificance, Nykøbing – are largely concerned with farming and tourism. The east coast of Falster is lined with white sandy beaches that attract huge numbers of German and Danish holidaymakers, many of whom own tree-shrouded cabins along the wooded coastline.

The most glorious stretch of beach is at Marielyst, which is 12km from Nykøbing. The beach draws crowds in summer, but it's so long that you can always achieve some sense of escape. The southern tip of the island, Gedser Odde, is the southernmost point of Denmark.

🛏 Sleeping

Danhostel Nykøbing Falster   HOSTEL €
(🖉54 85 66 99; www.danhostel.dk/nykoebingfal-ster; Østre Allé 110; dm Dkr250, s Dkr340-610, d

Dkr 465-610; ⊘mid-Jan–mid-Dec; P) This is the nearest hostel to Marielyst, being just 1km east of Nykøbing, Falster's train station. It is a large, institutional-style place about 10km from the beach.

Marielyst Camping   CAMPING GROUND €

(☎54 13 53 07; www.marielyst-camping.dk; Marielyst Strandvej 36; campsites per adult/child Dkr80/40) This central camping ground has a long season and is popular with families. It's 400m from the beach.

Hotel Nørrevang   HOTEL €€€

(☎54 13 62 62; www.norrevang.dk; Marielyst Strandvej 32; s/d Dkr870/1095) This thatched, half-timbered house 500m from the beach in Marielyst has 26 rooms, a pool, tennis court and restaurant.

ℹ Information

The **tourist office** (www.visitlolland-falster.com; Marielyst Strandpark 3; ⊘9am-4pm Mon-Fri, to 5pm Sat, to 2pm Sun Jul & Aug) is in a modern complex on the western entrance to the resort as you come in from the E55. Go left at the big roundabout. There is also a tourist office in **Nykøbing** (Østergågade 7; ⊘10am-5pm Mon-Fri, to 1pm Sat).

ℹ Getting There & Around

BOAT From Gedser **Scandlines ferries** (www.scandlines.com) reach Rostock, Germany (per person/car including five passengers from Dkr45/650; 1¾ hours, at least eight daily). Tickets booked online in advance can be significantly cheaper than the prices listed here.

TRAIN Trains leave Copenhagen several times each hour for Nykøbing (Dkr151, two hours) on the western side of the island, from where it's a Dkr30 bus ride to Marielyst on the east (25 minutes) or Gedser (50 minutes) further south.

BORNHOLM

POP 42,200

Bornholm is a little Baltic pearl: a Danish island, yet it lies some 200km east of the mainland, north of Poland. It boasts more hours of sunshine than any other part of the country, as well as gorgeous sandy beaches, idyllic fishing villages, numerous historic sights, endless cycle paths and a burgeoning reputation for culinary curiosities and ceramic artists and glassmakers.

Unique among Bornholm's attractions are its four 12th-century round churches, splendid buildings whose whitewashed walls, 2m thick, are framed by solid buttresses and crowned with black, conical roofs. Each was designed as both a place of worship and a fortress against enemy attacks, with a gun-slot-pierced upper storey. All four churches are still used for Sunday services, but are otherwise open to visitors. The island's tourist website, with information on accommodation, activities, and transport, is at www.bornholm.info.

History

Bornholm's history reflects its position at the heart of the Baltic and, in its time, Sweden, Germany and Soviet Russia have occupied it. A Danish possession since the Middle Ages, the island fell into Swedish hands in the 17th century, but was won back for Denmark by a fierce local rebellion.

The island suffered cruelly in the chaos at the end of WWII. It was occupied by the Nazis, but when Germany surrendered in May 1945 the commander on Bornholm resisted and Rønne and Nexø suffered heavy damage from Soviet air raids. On 9 May the island was handed over to the Soviets, who remained in situ until the following year, when Bornholm was returned to Denmark.

ℹ Getting There & Away

Air

Cimber Air (www.cimber.dk) has several flights a day between Copenhagen and Bornholm (one-way around Dkr500, 35 minutes). Book ahead for cheaper prices.

Boat

Bornholmer Færgen (☎56 95 18 66; www.bornholmerfaergen.dk; adult Dkr266, car Dkr1532-1550) operates an overnight ferry service from Køge, just south of Copenhagen, to Bornholm. The ferry departs daily at 12.30am and arrives at 6am. Køge is around 30 minutes south of Copenhagen by train, which is an additional cost and time if you are travelling from Copenhagen.

Train

From Copenhagen, **DSB** (www.dsb.dk) offers a combined train/catamaran ticket (one-way Dkr294, three hours) that includes train travel to Ystad (Sweden) and high-speed catamaran from Ystad to Rønne on Bornholm. This is the most cost- and time-effective option from Copenhagen. It's also possible to drive to Ystad and cross with a car from there.

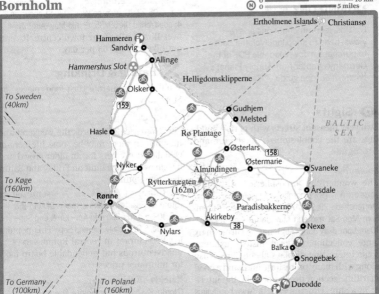

Ertholmene Islands — Christiansø

BALTIC SEA

To Sweden (40km)
To Køge (160km)
To Germany (100km)
To Poland (160km)

Hammeren
Sandvig
Hammershus Slot
Allinge
Helligdomsklipperne
Olsker
159
Gudhjem
Melsted
Hasle
Rø Plantage
Østerlars
158
Nyker
Almindingen
Østermarie
Svaneke
Rytterknægten (162m)
Rønne
Årsdale
Paradisbakkerne
Åkirkeby
38
Nexø
Nylars
Balka
Snogebæk
Dueodde

DENMARK RØNNE

ⓘ Getting Around

To/From the Airport

Bornholms Lufthavn is 5km southeast of Rønne, on the road to Dueodde. Buses 7 and 8 stop on the main road in front of the airport.

Bicycle

Bornholm is criss-crossed by more than 200km of bike trails. Download cycle routes free at www.bornholm.info, or purchase a more detailed cycling booklet with maps (Dkr119) from the island's tourist offices.

In Rønne, **Bornholms Cykeludlejning** (www. bornholms-cykeludlejning.dk, in Danish; Nordre Kystvej 5; per day/week Dkr70/360), next to the tourist office, has bikes for hire. Rental bikes are commonly available at hostels and camping grounds for about Dkr60 a day.

Bus

Bornholms Amts Trafikselskab (BAT; www. bat.dk, in Danish; pass per day adult/child Dkr150/75, per week Dkr500/250) operates bus services on the island. Fares cost Dkr12 per zone; the maximum fare is for five zones. Ask the bus driver about a 'RaBATkort' (10 rides), which can be used by more than one person and saves about 20%. From mid-April to mid-October, bus 7 leaves from the Rønne ferry terminal twice daily (10.10am and 2.20pm), travelling anticlockwise around the island, stopping at Dueodde beach and major coastal villages before terminating at Hammershus. Bus 8 follows the same route but in a clockwise direction, also departing from the Rønne ferry terminal at 10.10am and 2.20pm. There are more evening buses in the peak season from late June to the end of August. Other buses make direct runs from Rønne to Nexø, Svaneke, Gudhjem and Sandvig.

Car & Scooter

Europcar (☎56 95 43 00; www.europcar.com; Nordre Kystvej 1, Rønne) rents out motor scooters (per day Dkr299) or cars (per day Dkr590). The office is in the petrol station just along the road from the ferry terminal. **Avis** (☎70 24 77 19; www.avis.dk; Dampskibskajen 3-5, Rønne), further into town, and at Rønne airport, offers similar rates.

Rønne

POP 14,000

Though Rønne is not the most charming of the island's harbour towns, virtually everyone who visits Bornholm will end up spending time here. The town boasts engaging museums and an old quarter of cobbled streets flanked by pretty single-storey dwellings, as well as having a reasonable-sized shopping area. It is the island's largest settlement and is a popular shopping destination for Swedes on day trips.

MOVING ON?

For tips, recommendations and re-views, head to shop.lonelyplanet.com to purchase a downloadable PDF of the Germany chapter from Lonely Planet's *Western Europe* guide.

Sights

Two very pleasant streets with period build-ings are the cobblestoned Laksegade and Storegade.

Museums   MUSEUMS

The wonderfully atmospheric Bornholms Museum (www.bornholmsmuseum.dk; Sankt Mortensgade 29; adult/child Dkr50/free; ☉10am-5pm Mon-Sat mid-end May, Jun & Sep–mid-Oct, 10am-5pm daily Jul & Aug) has a surprisingly large collection of local history exhibits, some interesting displays about Christiansø along with many prehistoric finds and a good maritime section decked out like the interi-or of a ship. Hjorths Fabrik (www.bornholms museer.dk, in Danish; Krystalgade 5; adult/child Dkr50/free; ☉10am-5pm daily Jul & Aug, closed Sun Sep-Jun) is a ceramics museum complete with working features. Admission to either one of these museums includes admission to the other.

Nylars Rundkirke   CHURCH

This handsome round church, built in 1150 and decorated with 13th-century frescos, is surrounded by Viking rune stones. It's only a 15-minute ride from Rønne on bus 6.

Sleeping

The tourist office books rooms in private homes for singles (Dkr225) and doubles (Dkr400).

BB-Hotel   HOTEL €

(☎70 22 55 30; www.bbhotels.dk; Store Torv 17, Rønne; d/tr/q Dkr500/650/800; P) Accommo-dation doesn't get much more spartan than this self-service place above some shops on the main square, but the rooms are clean and all have en suite bathroom, plus breakfast is included in the price. Above all, it's cheap.

Danhostel Rønne   HOSTEL €

(☎56 95 13 40; www.danhostel-roenne.dk; Arsenalvej 12; dm/s/d/tr Dkr150/300/420/480; P) Immaculately kept and close to town, rooms here sleep up to eight. There is a shared kitchen, laundry, minigolf and bike rental on site.

Galløkken Camping   CAMPING €

(☎56 95 23 20; www.gallokken.dk; Strandvejen 4; adult/child Dkr69/35; ☉mid-May–Aug) Just over 1km south of the town centre. It rents out bikes for Dkr65 per day.

Eating & Drinking

You'll find numerous fast-food places on Store Torv.

O'Malley's   PUB

(Store Torvegade 2) Towards the weekend and in summer, there may be some life here at O'Malley's; it caters for an older crowd and has an over-21 age limit on Friday and Satur-day from 9pm.

Restaurant Fyrtøjet   RESTAURANT €€

(Store Torvegade 22, Rønne; mains Dkr145-168; ☉5.30-9pm Tue-Sun mid-Apr–Jun & end Sep–mid-Dec, 5-9pm daily Jul–end Sep) This popular local restaurant in central Rønne serves unadventurous but dependable bistro food for midrange prices.

Kvickly supermarket   SUPERMARKET €

(Nordre Kystvej 28) Opposite the tourist office; its good bakery opens at 9am (7am weekends), and its handy bistro offers sandwiches (Dkr50 to Dkr70) and hearty hot meals (Dkr60 to Dkr105).

Information

There's free internet access at the **public library** (Pingels Allé; ☉10am-7pm Mon & Tue, to 6pm Wed-Fri, to 2pm Sat); you must book a slot first.

Tourist office (Bornholms Velkomstcenter; ☎56 95 95 00; www.bornholm.info; Nordre Kystvej 3; ☉9am-2pm Sat early-end Jun, 9am-5.30pm end Jun–mid-Aug, 9am-4pm Mon-Sat mid-end Aug) A few minutes' walk from the harbour; has masses of information on all of Bornholm.

Dueodde

Dueodde has a vast stretch of white-sand beach backed by woodlands and dunes. The only 'sight' is the slender lighthouse (adult/child Dkr10/5; ☉11am-2pm Tue-Thu, 11.30am-3pm Sun May–end Jun & mid-Aug–Sep, 11.30am-4pm daily end Jun–mid-Aug), which you can climb for views of sea and strand that stretch to the horizon. There's no village, just a bus stop with a single hotel, a restaurant, a clus-ter of kiosks selling ice cream and hot dogs, and necessary public toilets to cope with the rush from tour coaches in summer. It can be a crowded trek for a couple of hundred metres along boardwalks to reach the superb beach. Once there, head left or right for wide-open spaces.

🛏 Sleeping & Eating

Bornholms Familie Camping   CAMPING GROUND €
(☑56 48 81 50; www.bornholms-familiecamping.dk; Krogegårdsvejen 2; adult/child/tent Dkr72/42/62, apartments per week Dkr4000-5000, 4-person tent per day Dkr500; ℗) One of the loveliest camping grounds in Denmark, this place is set amid beech and pine trees right beside the wonderful soft, white-sand beach at Dueodde. Facilities include laundry, shared kitchen, minigolf, table tennis, and sauna.

Restaurant Kadeau   MODERN SCANDINAVIAN €€€
(☑56 97 82 50; www.kadeau.dk; in Danish; Baunevej 18; lunch mains Dkr120-240, 2-/3-/4-course dinners Dkr395/425/465; ⊙daily Jul & Aug, Wed-Sun May, Jun & Sep) A short drive west of Dueodde, beachside Kadeau overlooks lapping waves, sand dunes and little else. Expect contemporary Nordic cuisine of a uniquely high and ambitious standard (think salt- and sugar-cured salmon with smoked cheese, seasonal vegetables, or pork belly with pickled and raw beets, malt crumble and sorrel). Book ahead.

Dueodde Vandrerhjem (Youth Hostel) & Camping   HOSTEL, CAMPING GROUND €
(☑56 48 81 19; www.dueodde.dk; Skorkkegårdsvejen 17; s/d/tr/q Dkr225/375/450/530, campsites adult/child Dkr65/35, tent Dkr25-33; ⊙May-Sep; ▣) Another lovely, low-cost spot to stay on Dueodde beach is this cabin-style, single-storey hostel and camping ground. It has an indoor pool, sauna and solarium, among other facilities.

Dueodde Camping   CAMPING GROUND €
(☑56 48 81 49; Duegårdsvej 2; campsites adult/child Dkr71/42; ▣) This picturesque camping ground right beside the beach boasts an open-air pool, tennis court, sauna, solarium and plenty of children's activities.

Bornholm's East Coast

Bornholm's east coast tends to be fairly built-up and is punctuated by several settlements, all with some interest as stopping-off places.

Snogebæk is a small shore-side fishing village that hangs on to its authenticity because of its small fleet of working boats and its scattering of fishing huts and cabins.

Just north of Snogebæk is the fine beach of **Balka Strand**.

Nexø is Bornholm's second-largest town. It took a hammering from Soviet bombers in WWII and today much of what you see from the harbour outwards is a fairly functional reconstruction. **Nexø Museum** (Havnen 2; adult/child Dkr30/10; ⊙10am-4pm Mon-Fri, 10am-2pm Sat Jul & Aug) is at the harbour and is packed with maritime flotsam and jetsam including an old-fashioned diving suit, cannons, WWII mines and the inner workings of a lighthouse. **Nexø-Dueodde Turistinformation** (Sdr Hammer 2g; ⊙10am-5pm Mon-Fri, 9am-2pm Sat May-Aug) is down by the harbour.

Three kilometres northwest of Nexø lies **Paradisbakkerne**, a natural wonderland of forest, high-heath bogs, and rift valleys. To get here from Nexø, take Paradisvej (which becomes Klintebyvejen) inland and turn right at Lisegårdsvejen, which leads to a car park and kiosk selling a map (Dkr10) of the area's walking tracks.

The harbour town of **Svaneke** has award-winning historic buildings, especially those near the village church, a few minutes' walk south of the centre. The **tourist office** (Peter F. Heerings Gade 7; ⊙10am-4pm Mon-Fri Jun-Aug) is open only in summer.

🛏 Sleeping

Hostel Møbelfabrikken   HOSTEL €€
(☑70 22 08 98; www.mobelfabrikken.dk; Gammel Rønnevej 17a, Nexø; s Dkr375-485, d Dkr495-595, q Dkr625-750) One of the more unusual places to stay on Bornholm is this major glass and ceramic workshop and hostel on the outskirts of Nexø. It hosts various events, courses and exhibitions throughout the year, and you can even rent the workshop. Rooms are extremely basic, but clean and tidy.

Hotel Balka Strand   HOTEL €€
(☑56 49 49 49; www.hotelbalkastrand.dk; Boulevarden 9; s/d from Dkr750/895; ℗@) A good base in the Snogebæk–Nexø area, this friendly, smart hotel is about 150m from Balka Strand beach.

Danhostel Svaneke   HOSTEL €
(☑56 49 62 42; www.danhostel-svaneke.dk; Reberbanevej 9; dm/s/d Dkr160/440/490; ⊙Apr-Oct) This quiet complex of bungalow-style chalet dorms and rooms is 1km south of the centre of Svaneke and close to the water.

🍴 Eating & Drinking

Rogeriet i Svaneke   SMOKE-HOUSE €
(Fiskergade 12; counter items Dkr30-85) Perhaps the best smoke-house on the island. Down

RASMUS KOFOED: SOMMELIER

Bornholm native Rasmus Kofoed is the founder of Dueodde's Restaurant Kadeau.

Must-eats

Don't miss smoked herring and a beer at a *rogeri* (smoke-house). Smoke-houses are part of Bornholm's history, and one of the island's simple pleasures. Bornholm is famous for its dairy products and **Svaneke Is** makes some of the best ice cream. If you're adventurous, try the blue-cheese ice cream with marinated or smoked salmon.

Must-dos

Walk around **Svaneke**. The locals have been very active in protecting its built heritage and I think it's the most beautiful town on Bornholm. Then there's **Paradisbakkerne**, with its changing landscapes and sublime views. It's called 'Paradise Hills' with good reason.

Did You Know?

We can grow figs on Bornholm. The island is one of the mildest areas of Denmark. It takes a while to warm up in June but then it stays warm for longer, which allows some exotic things to grow. Bornholm is also home to Denmark's biggest chef competition, **Sol Over Gudhjem** (Sun Over Gudhjem; www.solovergudhjemkonkurrence.dk, in Danish). It takes place in June and sees some of the country's best chefs battle it out using local produce. It's a growing hit with visitors and is broadcast on TV.

by the harbour, it serves smoked trout, cod's roe, herring and fish *frikadeller,* traditionally washed down with a cool beer while sitting at the outdoor picnic tables.

Bryghuset   MICROBREWERY €€
(Torv 5; lunches Dkr59-99, dinner mains Dkr139-209, set 2-/3-course dinners Dkr199/259) This friendly microbrewery brews a number of excellent beers, ideal for washing down all of that smoked fish. If you haven't already eaten, it also serves decent pub grub, for less than Dkr120.

Svaneke Is   ICE CREAM €
(www.svaneke-is.dk; Postgade 3) Ditch the diet at Svaneke Is, which uses seasonal and local ingredients to make heavenly ice creams, sorbets and sherbets.

Gudhjem

POP 750

Is this the perfect Danish seaside holiday village? We think it might well be. Gudhjem is just big enough to offer enough for a week's holiday without being too swamped by tourists. There are plenty of places to eat and stay, and excellent beaches within a kilometre or so. Its charming half-timbered houses and sloping streets rolling down to

the pleasant harbour front make it one of the island's most attractive towns.

Gudhjem has narrow streets and parking is difficult. There's a public car park northwest of the harbour. This is also where you catch the boat to Christiansø.

⊙ Sights

A bike path leads inland 4km south from Gudhjem to the thick-walled, buttressed **Østerlars Rundkirke**, the most impressive of the island's round churches – buses 1 and 4 go by the church.

Oluf Høst Museet   MUSEUM
(www.ohmus.dk; Løkkegade 35; adult/child Dkr75/35; ⊙11am-5pm Tue-Sun early May–early Jun, 11am-5pm Mon-Sun early Jun–end Sep) The former home and studio of 20th-century Danish painter Oluf Høst is now a beautiful museum dedicated to his life and work. Though inspired by Cézanne, Høst's work is distinctly Scandinavian in his depiction of Bornholm's light and moods. The beautiful backyard hosts a tiny cafe and children's art space, as well as Høst's former summer atelier.

Bornholms Kunstmuseum   MUSEUM
(www.bornholms-kunstmuseum.dk; Helligdommen, Rø; adult/child Dkr70/free; ⊙10am-5pm Tue-Sun Apr, May, Sep & Oct, 10am-5pm Jun-Aug) Six kilometres north of Gudhjem along the coast

road is Bornholm's leading art museum. Housed in a striking modern building overlooking the famously vertiginous Heligdoms cliffs and coastal path, it boasts some of the finest 19th- and early 20th-century art to have been made on the island by Danish artists such as Richard Mortensen and Michael Ancher. There is also an excellent cafe. Buses 1 and 4 reach the museum.

🛏 Sleeping & Eating

Stammershalle Badehotel   HOTEL €€€
(📞56 48 42 10; www.stammershalle-badehotel.dk; Sdr Strandvej 128, Rø; s Dkr790, d Dkr1090-1490; 🅿) This has to be one of the island's most charismatic places to stay. This imposing 19th-century bathing hotel overlooking a rocky part of the coast a few kilometres north of Gudhjem has bags of charm and elegance with light, bright decor, a superior restaurant and gorgeous views across the sea to Christiansø.

Gudhjem Rogeri   SMOKE-HOUSE €
(buffet Dkr98) Dating from 1910, this waterfront smoke-house is the oldest on the island. It has an all-you-can-eat buffet and some challenging seating, including on the upper floor, which is reached by rope ladder. There's live folk, country and rock music most nights in summer.

🍴 Gudhjem Mølle   CAFE €
(www.gudhjemmoelle.dk, in Danish; Møllebakken 4c; sandwiches Dkr75, salads Dkr65-100; ⏰10am-6pm Jun–mid-Aug, varies rest of yr) Built in 1893, Denmark's biggest windmill now houses a gourmet cafe and provedore. Nibble on freshly made salads, sandwiches, tapas and cakes, many of them made using local produce. Take-home treats include Bornholm cheeses, sausages, aquavit and beer.

Jantzens Hotel   HOTEL €€€
(📞56 48 50 17; www.jantzenshotel.dk; Brøddegade 33; s Dkr700-900, d Dkr975-1200) The central Jantzens Hotel is a fine old building with stylish, modern rooms.

Danhostel Gudhjem   HOSTEL €
(📞56 48 50 35; www.danhostel-gudhjem.dk; dm/s/d Dkr195/340/440) About 50m from the harbourside bus stop, this hostel is in an attractive spot by the harbour with small, cosy, bright-white six-bed dorms.

Therns Hotel   HOTEL €€
(📞56 48 50 99; www.therns-hotel.dk; Brøddegade 31; s Dkr750, d Dkr850-1050) The management

from Danhostel Gudhjem also handles this pleasant place to stay.

❶ Information

Tourist office (📞56 48 52 10; Åbogade 7; ⏰8.30am-noon & 12.30-3.15pm Mon-Tue & Thu-Fri) A block inland from the harbour, alongside the library.

Sandvig & Allinge

Sandvig and Allinge have grown together over the years and are generally referred to as Sandvig-Allinge. They are tucked away to the east of Bornholm's rocky northwestern tip and boast an excellent sandy beach to add to their beguiling appeal. Sandvig is a small fishing village, while Allinge has as good a range of restaurants, grand hotels and nightlife as you will find outside Rønne. Bornholm's best-known sight, Hammershus Slot, is 3km south on the road to Rønne. The impressive, substantial ruins of this 13th-century castle are the largest of their kind in Scandinavia. They are perched dramatically over the sea, flanked by cliffs and a deep valley. One of the best ways of reaching the castle is by following footpaths from Sandvig through the heather-covered hills of Hammeren – a wonderful hour-long hike. The trail begins by the camping ground. If there is a must-see sight on Bornholm, this castle is it.

🛏 Sleeping

Byskrivergarden   HOTEL €€
(📞56 48 08 86; www.byskrivergaarden.dk; Løsebækegade 3, Allinge; s/d Dkr670/900; ⏰mid-May–mid-Sep; 🅿) An enchanting, white-walled, black-beamed converted farmhouse right on the water in Allinge. The rooms are smartly, if sparsely, decorated in contemporary style; try to get the sea-facing ones. There's a pleasant garden and swimmable, kelp-filled rock pools around the corner if you fancy braving the water.

Gæstgiveren   GUESTHOUSE, APARTMENT €€
(📞56 44 62 30; Theatrestræde 2, Allinge; d/tr Dkr800/900, 3-bedroom apt per week Dkr8000 Jul, apt price negotiable rest of yr; ⏰Jun–mid-Aug, apt rental yr-round) A lively place to stay in the heart of Allinge is this... Well, we're not sure how best to describe it really – it's part holiday guesthouse, part live-music venue, part outdoor grill restaurant and bar. If you stay here you can expect to become part of the

seasonal, Copenhagen-by-sea community of creative, bohemian types who spend the summer in Allinge... and not to get much sleep.

Hotel du Nord
APARTMENT €€€

(☎20 95 12 53; www.hotel-du-nord.dk; Storegade 4, Allinge; apt 3 nights Dkr3500-7000, apt weekly end Jun–mid-Aug Dkr6000-11000; @) In the centre of Allinge, this chic little hotel actually consists of three beautifully appointed apartments (two with eight beds and one with six beds). From late June to mid-August, rental is on a weekly basis only. At all other times, there is a minimum three-night stay. Annoyingly, bed sheets and towels are not provided.

✖ Eating

Nordbornholms Rogeri
SMOKE-HOUSE €

(Kæmpestranden 2, Allinge; meals Dkr54-85) If you ask us, you can't have too many good smokehouses, and this is another great one, right on the harbour in Allinge. The Dkr169 all-you-can-eat fish buffet is truly sumptuous.

Lassens Restaurant
FRENCH, DANISH €€€

(☎56 48 03 44; Strandvejen 68; 3-/4-course dinners Dkr350/395; ⊙dinner Tue-Sun) More classically French influenced than Dueodde's Kadeau, Hotel Romantik's in-house restaurant is another sound bet for gastronomes. The monthly changing menu offers interesting combinations, such as smoked eel with crispy malt, cream of chives, cucumber and radish. Request a window seat with sea views.

Café Sommer
CAFE, RESTAURANT €€

(Havnegade 19; mains Dkr110-175) A popular place to refuel, Café Sommer's lunch grub includes salads, burgers and sandwiches, as well as great smørrebrød (three for Dkr120 including fried local salted herring with beets, onions and mustard). Dinner is a slightly more ambitious affair, and there's a cosy little harbour-facing terrace to boot.

Christiansø

POP 100

Charmingly preserved, tiny Christiansø (it's about 500m long) is a 17th-century fortress-island an hour's sail northeast of Bornholm. It's well worth making time for a day trip, as more than 70,000 visitors do each year (only 3000 spend the night). It has been a seasonal fishing hamlet since the Middle Ages. Christiansø fell briefly into Swedish hands in 1658, after which Christian V decided to turn the island into an invincible naval fortress. Bastions and barracks were built; church, school and prison followed.

By the 1850s the island was no longer needed as a forward base against Sweden and the navy withdrew. Soldiers who wanted to stay on as fishermen were allowed to live as free tenants in the old cottages. Their offspring, and a few latter-day fisherfolk and artists, currently comprise Christiansø's 100 residents. The entire island is an unspoiled reserve – there are no cats or dogs, no cars and no modern buildings – allowing the rich birdlife, including puffins, to prosper.

There's a small local history museum in Frederickson's tower and a great 360-degree view from Christiansø lighthouse. Otherwise the main activity is walking the footpaths along the fortified walls and batteries that skirt the island. There are skerries with nesting seabirds and a secluded swimming cove on Christiansø's eastern side.

In summer, camping is allowed in a small field at the Duchess Battery (tent per night Dkr75 to Dkr100). Christiansø Gæstgiveriet (☎56 46 20 15; s/d incl breakfast Dkr950/1050), the island's only inn, has six rooms with shared bathroom, and a restaurant. Booking ahead for a room is advised. There's a small food store and a kiosk.

Christiansøfarten (☎56 48 51 76) sails daily to Christiansø from Gudhjem and Allinge between mid-May and mid-September. The mail boat from Gudhjem sails Monday to Friday year-round. Boats from Gudhjem charge Dkr220 per adult and Dkr110 per child for a return journey. Boats from Allinge charge Dkr250 per adult and Dkr125 per child. Dogs or other pets are forbidden on Christiansø.

FUNEN

POP 454,300

As a stepping stone from Zealand to the Jutland peninsula, the rural island of Funen is often overlooked by visitors, who perhaps make a whistle-stop visit to Hans Christian Andersen's birthplace and museum in the island's capital, Odense. But there is more to Funen (Fyn in Danish): the towns of Svendborg and Faaborg have a gentle charm, particularly in summer, and there are excellent, clean beaches all around the island. And then there are Funen's 123 manor houses and castles. Dating from as far back as the

14th century, most open their grounds to the public.

Funen is connected to Zealand by the Storebælts Forbindlesen (Great Belt's Bridge) and to Jutland by the Lillebælts Bro (Little Belt's Bridge). In all, the impressive span, which runs between the industrial towns of Korsør and Nyborg, covers 18km – even longer than the Øresunds Fixed Link. If you're taking a train, the cost of crossing is included in your fare; however, if you're driving, there's a costly bridge toll each way (under-6m/over-6m vehicle Dkr220/335; Dkr115 for a motorbike). For more information, go to www.storebaelt.dk.

If you are visiting Funen by bike – as many Danish holidaymakers do – a useful guide is the *Cykelguide Fyn* (Dkr119), available from most tourist offices, which shows cycle routes throughout Funen and its neighbouring islands. Virtually all towns on Funen have places that rent bicycles by the day or week from around Dkr75 per day.

Odense

POP 166,300

There's plenty more to Odense than the legacy of its – and Denmark's – most famous son, the writer and traveller Hans Christian Andersen. Nevertheless, HCA's (as he's known in these parts) birthplace and adjoining museum are the number-one draw, even if there is no concrete evidence to show he ever lived in the house in question (the man himself denied it, in fact). Elsewhere in the country's third-largest city there are some excellent restaurants; one of the best shopping zones outside Copenhagen; a thriving cultural and exhibition space, Brandts Klædefabrik; and the largest stage in Scandinavia in Odense Koncerthus. For more information on the city, go to www.visitodense.com.

⊙ Sights

HC Andersens Hus   MUSEUM
(www.museum.odense.dk; Bangs Boder 29; adult/child Dkr60/free; ⊙9am-5pm end Jun–Aug) Amid the picturesque houses of the old, working-class part of Odense, now often referred to as the 'HCA Quarter', this museum was expanded to mark Andersen's 200th anniversary in 2005. It contains a thorough and lively telling of the amazing life Andersen lived, put into an interesting historical context and leavened by some good audiovisual material. Andersen was supposedly born in the corner room of the building, although the author himself denied this in later life and there is no concrete evidence to support this view.

Fyrtøjet – Et Kulturhus for Børn   CULTURAL CENTRE
(Tinderbox – A Cultural Centre for Children; www.fyrtoejet.com; Hans Jensens Stræde 21; admission Dkr85; ⊙10am-5pm end Jun–mid-Aug) Next door to the museum is the charming Fyrtøjet – Et Kulturhus for Børn, where youngsters can explore the magical world of Hans Christian Andersen through storytelling and music (in English as well as Danish during summer), and by dressing up and pretending to be some of Andersen's most famous characters. There is a good cafe here (meals Dkr75 to Dkr99, two-course menu Dkr265).

HC Andersens Barndomshjem   MUSEUM
(Munkemøllestræde 3-5; adult/child Dkr25/free; ⊙11am-3pm Tue-Sun Jan–end Jun & Sep-Dec, 10am-4pm daily end Jun–Aug) This museum has a couple of rooms of exhibits in the small house where Hans Christian lived from the age of two to 14, when he left to seek his fortune in Copenhagen. This is the house he describes in his autobiographies and which features in a couple of his fairy stories.

Brandts   CULTURAL CENTRE
(www.brandts.dk; Brandts Passage; combined ticket adult/child Dkr80/free; ⊙10am-5pm Tue, Wed & Fri-Sun, noon-9pm Thu) The former textile mill has been converted into an impressive cultural centre with a photography museum (Dkr40), a modern art gallery (Dkr50) and a media museum (Dkr40). The superb exhibition spaces often present excellent temporary exhibitions from artists from all over the world. There's also an excellent art book and gift shop on the ground floor.

Den Fynske Landsby   MUSEUM
(www.museum.odense.dk; Sejerskovvej 20; adult/child Dkr80/free, admission free Jan-Mar; ⊙11am-3pm Jan-Mar, 10am-5pm Tue-Sun Apr–end Jun & mid-Aug–mid-Oct, 10am-6pm daily end Jun–mid-Aug, 10am-7pm mid-Jun–mid-Aug) This is a delightful open-air museum, furnished with period buildings authentically laid out like a small country village, complete with barnyard animals, a duck pond, apple trees and flower gardens. Note that while the grounds are open on Sundays from January to March, the visitor centre and houses are closed.

The museum is in a green zone 4km south of the city centre. Both buses 111 (towards Skt Klemens) and 110 (towards Assens/

DENMARK FUNEN

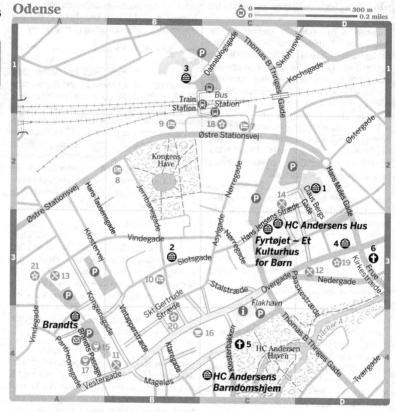

Odense

Haarby) stop very close to the museum. From May to early September you can take a boat (www.aafart.dk; adult/child under 12 years Dkr60/45) from Munke Mose down the river to Erik Bøghs Sti, from where it's a 15-minute woodland walk along the river to Den Fynske Landsby.

Sankt Knuds Kirke   CHURCH
(Flakhaven; admission free; ☺10am-4pm Mon-Sat, noon-5pm Sun, to 5pm Sat Apr-Oct) Odense's 13th-century Gothic cathedral reflects Odense's medieval wealth and stature. The stark white interior has a handsome rococo pulpit, a dazzling 16th-century altarpiece and a gilded wooden triptych crowded with more than 300 carved figures and said to be one of the finest pieces of religious art in northern Europe.

Fyns Kunstmuseum   MUSEUM
(www.museum.odense.dk; Jernbanegade 13; adult/child Dkr40/free; ☺10am-4pm Tue-Sun) In a stately, neoclassical building, this museum has a serene atmosphere and contains a quality collection of Danish art from the 18th century to the present. There are small collections of fine sculptures and contemporary art; changing exhibitions are also staged.

Jernbanemuseet   MUSEUM
(www.jernbanemuseet.dk; Dannebrogsgade 24; adult/child Dkr80/40 end-Jun–mid-Aug, Dkr60/30 rest of yr; ☺10am-4pm) Railway buffs should not miss the collection of 19th-century locomotives at the rail museum just behind the train station. There are also mini railways for children of all ages to ride on.

FREE Carl Nielsen Museet   MUSEUM
(Claus Bergs Gade 11; ☺11am-3pm Wed-Sun Jun-Aug, 3-7pm Thu & Fri, 11am-3pm Sat & Sun Sep-May) This museum in Odense's concert hall details the career of the city's native son Carl Nielsen, Denmark's best-known composer.

Møntergården   MUSEUM
(Overgade 48-50; adult/child Dkr40/free; ☺10am-4pm Tue-Sun) Odense's modest city museum has various displays on the city's history from the Viking Age and a couple of 16th- and 17th-century half-timbered houses.

🛏 Sleeping

First Hotel Grand   HOTEL €€€
(☎66 11 71 71; www.firsthotels.dk; Jernbanegade 18; s/d incl breakfast from Dkr795/995) Close to the station, this refurbished member of the

First Hotels chain is the height of modernity compared with most of Odense's accommodation. It has slick, modern Danish decor and a spacious, glamorous brasserie bar, the Brasserie Grand (open lunch and dinner Monday to Saturday, closed July).

🗹 Clarion Collection
Hotel Plaza   HOTEL €€€
(☎66 11 77 45; www.millinghotels.dk; Østre Stationsvej 24; s Dkr795-1445, d Dkr895-1645; @) Overlooking the green spaces of Kongens Have in the centre of town, this comfortable hotel is one of Odense's best. Its spacious rooms are decorated in a rather chintzy, provincial Old English style but are fairly luxurious. There's a gym and free snacks between 3pm and 6pm. You get the best rates online.

Pia's B&B   APARTMENT €€
(☎66 13 02 38; www.pias-bb.dk; Absalonsgade 14; d/tr/q Dkr565/675/800, breakfast extra Dkr50 per person; P@) If you are in town for a while, you could consider this cosy apartment in a pretty little cottage close to the main shopping street. It has a fully equipped kitchen, washing machine, computer and private entrance, and is excellent value.

Alberte Bed & Breakfast   GUESTHOUSE €
(☎66 12 30 12; www.albertte.dk; Sophie Breums Vej 10; s/d/tr/q Dkr440/475/575/680; @) A few minutes' walk north east of the train station is this cosy, clean, tidy suburban house B&B with cooking facilities and TVs in rooms. Breakfast costs Dkr 35 to Dkr50.

Cab Inn   HOTEL €€
(☎63 14 57 00; www.cabinn.com; Østre Stationsvej 7; s Dkr485, d Dkr675-805; @) The reliably cheap and modern bargain hotel chain has arrived in Odense with a 200-plus-room establishment right beside the station.

Danhostel Odense City   HOSTEL €
(☎63 11 04 25; www.cityhostel.dk; Østre Stationsvej 31; dm/s/d/tr incl breakfast from Dkr200/400/500/500; @) An excellent, modern 139-bed place, with four- and six-bed dorms, a kitchen and laundry facilities, located alongside the train and bus stations. All rooms have a bathroom.

DCU Camping   CAMPING GROUND €
(☎66 11 47 02; www.camping-odense.dk; Odensevej 102; adult/child/tent Dkr74/45/45) Just under 4km south from the city centre, this camping ground is top-notch, with an

A PERFECT STROLL

The east side of Odense's city centre has some of the city's oldest buildings. You can follow a rewarding walking route from the centre by crossing the busy Torvegade and strolling down Nedergade, a cobblestoned street lined with leaning, half-timbered houses and antique shops, and then returning via Overgade. En route you'll pass the 13th-century **Vor Frue Kirke** (◷10am-3pm Mon-Fri, 10am-noon Sat). From Overgade turn right into Overstræde, left into Bangs Boder, and then immediately right into what is a continuation of Bangs Boder. Awaiting is a charming cobbled-stoned street lined with pastel-coloured cottages. At the end of Bangs Boder, turn left into Hans Jensens Stræde, which leads back to busy Thomas B Thriges Gade and the centre of town beyond (note the Hans Christian Andersen–themed pedestrian lights!).

open-air pool, various sports facilities and 13 chalets for rent.

✕ Eating

Numerous, mainly fast-food, places line Kongensgade.

Odense Banegård Center, which incorporates the train and bus stations, has low-priced options including bakery **Bager From** (◷5.45am-6.30pm Mon-Fri, 7am-5.30pm Sat & Sun), a supermarket and a pub.

TOP CHOICE Kvægtorvet MODERN SCANDINAVIAN €€€
(☏65 91 50 01; www.kvaegtorvet.com; Rugårdsvej 25; 6-/12-course tasting menus Dkr375/595; ◷lunch Fri, dinner Mon-Sat) Klavs Styrbæk is one of Funen's leading chefs and his superb restaurant is renowned for its accomplished, ambitious modern Danish food made using locally sourced meat and seafood, such as pheasant with chestnuts and grilled scallops with coconut and lime. The restaurant is 1km west of the train station.

Munkebo Kro FRENCH, DANISH €€€
(☏65 97 40 30; www.thomaspasfall.dk; Fjordvej 56, Munkebo; 2-course lunches Dkr298, 4-/5-/6-course tasting menus Dkr595/695/795) Fiercely expensive his food may be, but chef Thomas Pasfill's dishes are renowned throughout Denmark for their refinement and creativity (monkfish and king crab ballontine bisque is one classic dish). His restaurant is housed in a delightful thatched coaching inn dating from 1826 and overlooking a small fjord 15km north of Odense. There are 22 rooms on site, with prices from Dkr1195/1395 per single/double.

Under Lindetræt FRENCH, DANISH €€€
(☏66 12 92 86; www.underlindetraet.dk; Ramsherred 2; 2 courses Dkr370; ◷dinner Tue-Sat) Right opposite HC Andersens Hus is one of the city's leading restaurants, housed in a lovely 18th-century cottage. Chef Brian Madsen's refined, classic dishes pay significant homage to Alsace and Tuscany.

Den Gamle Kro FRENCH, DANISH €€
(Overgade 23; open sandwiches Dkr69-139, 3 courses Dkr348) One of Odense's most atmospheric restaurants is spread throughout several rooms of a half-timbered, 17th-century house serving traditional Franco-Danish food with a twist (think green pea soup with cava, smoked salmon and whipped cream).

Gertruds CAFE, BAR
(www.gertruds.dk; Jernbanegade 8; sandwiches Dkr79-92, salads Dkr118-128, dinner mains Dkr189-238) On a fountain-studded square, this modern cafe–bistro peddles everything from morning croissants and eggs to gourmet sandwiches, grilled meats and seasonal dishes such as asparagus risotto. DJs hit the decks on Friday and Saturday nights, with monthly live jazz and stand-up comedy gigs to boot.

Cuckoo's Nest CAFE
(www.cuckoos.dk; Vestergade 73; salads Dkr87-92, mains Dkr159-169) A great stalwart of Odense's nightlife scene is this cavernous bar and restaurant on the corner of the main shopping street and Brandts Passage. A lengthy and wide-ranging menu includes everything from nachos and burgers to *confit de canard*.

Il Gusto ICE CREAM €
(☏66 19 26 04; Vindegade 84-86; gelato 2 flavours Dkr25; ◷11.30am-10pm Mon-Sat, 12.30-10pm Sun summer, times vary rest of yr, closed Nov-Feb) Run by Sicilian expat Stefano Di Gaetano, this tiny gelateria is a mecca for gelato connoisseurs. Flavours are seasonal and everything is made from scratch, the proper Italian way. For a double dose of dolce vita, knock back a mighty espresso.

Drinking

Room CAFE, CLUB
(Brandts Passage 6-8; ⊙10am-10pm Sun-Wed, 10am-midnight Thu, 1am to 3am Sat, to 6pm Sun) One of Odense's trendiest venues is this light, bright modern cafe–nightclub in the Brandt's Passage area. Kick back at an alfresco table or head in on Thursday to Saturday nights for DJ-spun house.

Joe & the Juice JUICE BAR
(Vestergade 20; juices Dkr38, sandwiches Dkr45; ⊙10am-6pm Mon-Thu, to 8pm Fri, to 5pm Sun) Attached to the Magasin department store, this hip chain squeezes fresh juices with names like 'Stress Down' and 'Total Rehab'. You'll also find decent coffee and freshly made sandwiches.

Envy-Lounge CAFE, BAR
(Brandts Passage 31; ⊙11am-11pm Tue-Thu, to 1am Fri & Sat) Smooth libations and Scandi-chic interiors define this trendy cafe-cum-cocktail lounge.

☆ Entertainment

Nightlife is centred on Brandts Passage, a pedestrian corridor lined with boutiques, restaurants, bars and cafes, many with outdoor seating in summer, leading to Brandts Klædefabrik.

On Thursdays, from July to mid-August, Kongens Have is the setting for free and highly popular weekly music concerts. Tunes span anything from '60s pop to contemporary rock, mostly performed by Danish acts. Concerts normally start at 7pm, though it's best to check www.odense.dk for updates.

Franck A CLUB
(www.francka.dk; Jernbanegade 4; ⊙10am-1am Sun-Wed, to 3am Thu-Sat) Everyone knows Franck A's, one of the main nightlife venues in the city, with a large, sleek, raw-brick cafe–bar-restaurant serving burgers, brunches and Franco-Danish bistro grub throughout the day, and DJs playing Thursday to Saturday. It attracts a younger crowd at weekends.

Club Retro CLUB
(www.retro.dk, in Danish; Overgade 45; admission varies; ⊙vary, usually midnight-6am Sat) One of a chain of two clubs in Denmark, the Odense branch hosts local and international DJs, usually on Saturday only. Age restrictions apply most nights (ie over 21s).

Cafe Biografen CINEMA
(Brandts Klædefabrik; tickets Dkr70-90) Shows first-run movies on three screens. Bio-

city (Odense Banegård Center) is another multiplex cinema, on the 2nd floor of the train station.

Brandts LIVE MUSIC
(☑65 20 70 01; Brandts Passage) Has an outdoor amphitheatre that's a venue for free summer weekend concerts.

Jazzhus Dexter LIVE MUSIC
(www.dexter.dk; Vindegade 65) Jazzhus Dexter has good live-music (mostly of the jazz variety) groups virtually every night of the week starting around 8pm or 9pm.

ℹ Information

Internet Access
Odense Central Library (Odense Banegård Center; ⊙10am-7pm Mon-Thu, to 4pm Fri, to 2pm Sat, also open to 2pm Sun Oct-Mar) Offers free use of the internet.

Money
Nordea (Vestergade 64)

Post
Post office (Brandts Passage; ⊙10am-6pm Mon-Fri, to 1pm Sat)

Tourist Information
Tourist office (☑66 12 75 20; www.visitodense.com; Vestergade 2; ⊙9.30am-6pm Mon-Fri, 10am-3pm Sat, 11am-2pm Sun Jul & Aug) Located on Rådhus, a 900m walk from the train station, the tourist office rents out bikes (per day/week Dkr100/500).

ℹ Getting There & Away

At the train station, left-luggage lockers cost Dkr20 to Dkr40 for 24 hours. Also at the eastern end of Vestergade, close to HC Andersens Hus, is another left-luggage place, which charges Dkr15 to Dkr30 for 24 hours.

Odense is on the main railway line between Copenhagen (Dkr244, 1½ hours, at least twice hourly), Århus (Dkr212, 1¾ hours, twice hourly), Aalborg (Dkr327, three hours, once or twice hourly) and Esbjerg (Dkr193, 1¾ hours, one to three times hourly). Buses leave from the rear of the train station.

Odense is just north of the E20; access from the highway is clearly marked. Rte 43 connects Odense with Faaborg; Rte 9 connects Odense with Svendborg.

ℹ Getting Around

Odense is best seen on foot or on a bicycle. Bikes can be rented at the tourist office.

You'll find substantial car parks around Brandts Klædefabrik and the Carl Nielsen Museet. Parking costs around Dkr12 per hour.

Car-rental companies in town include the following:

Avis (☑70 24 77 87; www.avis.com; Rugaardsvej 3)

Europcar (☑66 14 15 44; www.europcar.com; Vestre Stationsvej 13)

Vikingemuseet Ladby (Ladby Viking Museum)

This historical site (www.vikingemuseetladby. dk; Vikingevej 123, Ladby; adult/child Dkr50/free; ⏰10am-5pm Jun-Aug) comprises the remains of a 22m-long Viking ship that once formed the tomb of a 10th-century Viking chieftain. All the wooden planks from the Ladby ship decayed long ago, leaving the imprint of the hull moulded into the earth, along with iron nails, an anchor and the partial remains of the dogs and horses that were buried with their master. There's a separate visitor centre at the arrival car park with a 1:10-scale model of the ship and background information about the site.

To get here by car, in Ladby, 4km southwest of Kerteminde via Odensevej, turn north onto Vikingevej, a one-lane road through fields that ends after 1.2km at the Ladbyskibet car park. You enter through the little museum, from where it's a few minutes' walk along a field path to the mound.

From Banegården Plads C in Odense, catch bus 151 or 152 to Kerteminde (Dkr40, 40 minutes, hourly), then change to bus 482 for the village of Ladby (30 minutes, hourly). Once in Ladby, you'll have to walk the Vikingevej section to the museum about 25 minutes away. The last bus back to Kerteminde leaves Ladby at 4.50pm.

Egeskov Slot

This magnificent castle (www.egeskov.dk; combined ticket for all sights except castle adult/child Dkr150/80, plus castle interior Dkr195/105; ⏰10am-5pm May, Jun, early-end Aug & Sep–early Oct, to 7pm Jul–early Aug), complete with moat and drawbridge, is an outstanding example of the lavish efforts that sprang up during Denmark's Golden Age, the Renaissance. There are enough sights and activities here to keep anyone happily occupied for a day. The castle exteriors are the best features. The interior is heavily Victorian in its furnishings and hunting trophies of now rare beasts. The grounds include century-old privet hedges, free-roaming peacocks, topiary, aerial woodland walkways, English gardens and a bamboo grass labyrinth.

The castle grounds usually stay open an hour longer than the castle. Admission to the grounds includes entry to a large antique-car museum, which also features some vintage aircraft swooping from the rafters.

Egeskov Slot is 2km west of Kvændrup on Rte 8. From Odense take the Svendborg-bound train to Kvændrup station (Dkr57, 24 minutes, hourly) and continue on foot or by taxi.

Faaborg & Around

POP 7200

Faaborg is a pretty, historic fishing town on the south coast of Funen. Though its small shopping quarter has rather fallen into decline in recent years, its harbour is flourishing once again and the art museum justly renowned. In the 17th century it was home to one of Denmark's largest commercial fleets and it retains many vestiges of that earlier era in its picturesque, cobblestone streets and leaning, half-timbered houses. This is where you take the ferries to the quiet, time-warp southern islands, most notably Ærø.

◉ Sights & Activities

Torvet   MONUMENT, MUSEUM

Faaborg's main square, Torvet, is a pleasant spot to linger. It features the Svendborg sculptor Kai Nielsen's striking bronze fountain group *Ymerbrønd;* a naked giant suckling at the udders of a cow (depicting a Norse fertility myth), it caused quite a stir after it was unveiled. A handsome, 18th-century merchant's house is now the town museum, **Den Gamle Gaard** (Holkegade 1; adult/child Dkr30/free; ⏰10am-4pm early Jun–mid-Aug), complete with period furnishings.

Faaborg Museum for Fynsk Malerkunst   MUSEUM

(www.faaborgmuseum.dk; Grønnegade 75, Faaborg; adult/child Dkr60/free; ⏰10am-4pm daily Apr-Oct) The small Faaborg Museum for Fynsk Malerkunst is a former winery, which contains a fine collection of Funen art, including works by artists such as Peter Hansen, Jens Birkholm and Anna Syberg. Kai Nielsen's original granite sculpture of the *Ymerbrønd* is also here. The town landmark is the near-by belltower of **St Nikolai**.

Islands
ISLANDS

There are numerous daily ferries to the nearby islands of Avernakø and Lyø (Dkr110 return, bicycle Dkr30, car Dkr180) and a passenger service that travels to Bjørnø (Dkr54 return).

🛏 Sleeping & Eating

The tourist office can book rooms in private homes for Dkr250 for single travellers and Dkr400 for doubles, plus a Dkr25 booking fee. There are a couple of unremarkable cafes and fast-food places in the town square and more upmarket restaurants along the harbour front.

Hotel Færgegaarden HOTEL €€
(☑62 61 11 15; www.hotelfg.dk; Christian IX Vej 31, Faaborg; s/d Dkr795/950) Faaborg's oldest hotel was refurbished recently and is located close to the harbour and town centre. Its restaurant is oriented to the tourists who flock here in summer, featuring dishes such as veal schnitzel and gazpacho with locally sourced ham (mains Dkr135 to Dkr185).

Falsled Kro MODERN SCANDINAVIAN €€€
(☑62 68 11 11; www.falsledkro.dk; Assensvej 513, Millinge; r Dkr1975-3175, ste Dkr3375; ⊙lunch & dinner Tue-Sun May-Aug, lunch Wed-Sat, dinner Tue-Sun Sep-Apr) This enchanting thatched coaching inn dates back to the 15th century and is home to celebrated Danish chef Per Hallundbaek. The food (lunch/dinner mains Dkr245/450) blends the best local ingredients with French techniques and modern Scandi twists. The individually decorated, modern country-house–style rooms are as beautiful. It is 7km northwest along the coast road to Assens from Faaborg.

TOP CHOICE Steensgaard

Manor FRENCH, DANISH €€€
(☑62 61 94 90; www.herregaardspension.dk; Steensgaard 4, Millinge; 4-/5-/7-courses Dkr555/625/760) Remarkably, there are not one but two atmospheric manor-inns close to Faaborg. Steensgaard (singles/doubles from Dkr1195/1475) is grander still architecturally, with a moat, beautiful gardens and an interior packed with antiques. The food is slightly more classic, but still exceptional quality (think foie gras de canard with smoked duck breast and pickled blackberries). It is just off the road to Assens.

Det Hvide Pakhus FRENCH, DANISH €€
(Christian IXs Vej 2; www.dethvidepakhus.dk; Faaborg Harbour; lunches Dkr82-155, dinner mains Dkr192-240; ⊙lunch & dinner daily high season, closed Mon, Tue & Sun low season, closed Dec & Jan) This light, airy converted warehouse serving fresh seafood and classic Franco-Danish dishes has been central to the rejuvenation of Faaborg's harbour. It's as popular with locals as it is with tourists.

Danhostel Faaborg HOSTEL €
(☑62 61 12 03; www.danhostel.dk/faaborg; Grønnegade 71-72, Faaborg; dm/s/d Dkr175/300/350; ⊙May-Sep; 🅿) This 69-bed, three-star hostel occupies two handsome historic buildings, close to the Faaborg Museum and the town's indoor swimming baths.

Hotel Faaborg HOTEL €€
(☑62 61 02 45; www.hotelfaaborg.dk; Torvet, Faaborg; s/d Dkr750/950; 🅿@) This very central hotel in Faaborg has good, welcoming rooms.

Faaborg Røgeri SMOKE-HOUSE €
(Vestkaj, Faaborg; fish dishes Dkr26-68) Situated to the west of the harbour, this takeaway serves cheap, tasty, home-smoked fish, and ice cream to boot.

ℹ Information

Tourist office (☑62 61 07 07; www.visitfaaborg-midtfyn.dk; Banegårdspladsen 2a; ⊙9am-5pm Mon-Sat Jun-Aug) Adjacent to the bus station and car park on the harbour front. You can hire bikes here for Dkr60 a day.

ℹ Getting There & Away

Bus

Fynbus (www.fynbus.dk) routes 111 and 141 from Odense (Dkr69, 1¼ hours) run at least hourly to 11pm. Bus 931 from Svendborg (Dkr50, 50 minutes, at least hourly) also runs frequently throughout the day.

Car

From the north, simply follow Rte 43, which is called Odensevej as it enters town.

Svendborg

POP 27,100

This pretty, relaxed 750-year-old harbour town is a major sailing and kayaking centre, with a small but well-stocked shopping quarter and several good dining options. The marine heritage counterbalances the fairly soulless modern docks that dominate the waterfront. It really picks up in summer when tourists flock to nearby Langeland.

◉ Sights & Activities

Sejlskibsbroen
WATERFRONT

At the southern end of Havnepladsen's cobbled quayside, opposite where the Ærø ferry docks, is Sejlskibsbroen, a jetty lined with splendidly preserved sailing ships and smaller vessels and with an adjoining marina catering for the great number of yachts that sail local waters. Ask at the tourist centre about the various trips that can be arranged on the old sailing ships.

Tåsinge
CASTLE

Just over the bridge from Svendborg is the island of Tåsinge, with its pretty harbourside village of Troense and the nearby 17th-century castle **Valdemars Slot** (www.valdemarsslot.dk; Slotsalléen 100; adult/child Dkr85/40; ☺10am-5pm daily Jun-Aug & mid-Oct). The castle was built in the early 17th century by Denmark's great Renaissance king, Christian IV, for his son, but later awarded to the naval hero Admiral Niels Juel; it remains in his family to this day. Its lavish interior is crammed with paintings and eccentric objects. In the grounds are the **Danish Yachting Museum**, **Denmark's Toy Museum** and the **Big Game Trophy Museum**, packed with vintage playthings. The grounds of the castle and the nearby white-sand beach have free access. You can get to Valdemars Slot by bus but a better way is by MS *Helge*, an old-style ferry that carries passengers from Svendborg to Troense and Valdemars Slot every few hours (adult/child Dkr120/60) from mid-May to mid-September. The castle also has a good Danish **restaurant** (open sandwiches Dkr55-94, meals Dkr88-168; ☺11.30am-4pm daily May–end Sep), which sells picnic baskets for Dkr160 to Dkr200.

Outdoor Activities
CYCLING, KAYAKING

You can rent bicycles at **Svendborg Cykeludlejning** (www.svendborgcykeludlejning.dk; Jessens Mole 9b). For kayak rental and tours, head to **Nicus Nature** (www.nicusnature.com, in Danish; Vindebyoerevej 31b).

🛏 Sleeping & Eating

The nearest camping grounds are located on Tåsinge.

🍴 Hotel Svendborg
HOTEL €€€

(☑62 21 17 00; www.hotel-svendborg.dk; Centrumpladsen 1; s/d Dkr995/1195; ℗@) A functional business-style hotel with an excellent location in the heart of the shopping district. It has a neighbouring sister hotel, the Hotel Garni, which has slightly cheaper rooms and fewer frills.

Anders Granhøj
FRENCH, DANISH €€€

(☑62 61 10 01; www.andersgranhoej.dk; Torvet 10; 2-course lunches Dkr195, 3-course dinners Dkr395; ☺Tue-Sat) This is perhaps the last place you'd expect to find a chef of the quality and experience of Anders Granhøj, a former *chef de partie* of the esteemed Hotel Meurice in Paris, but we're grateful he's here cooking his sophisticated, modern food from the best local and luxury ingredients. Expect delicious, juicy Funen mussels, local game and langoustine to feature on an enticing menu.

🍴 Restaurant Number 5
DANISH €€

(☑72 18 55 55; Havneplads 3a; mains Dkr175-205, 3-course dinners Dkr395; ☺lunch & dinner Jun-Aug, dinner Tue-Sat Sep-May) This top-end restaurant is housed in a converted 19th-century warehouse right on the harbour front by the historic ships. It serves ambitious Scandinavian food using fresh, seasonal produce (think cold cured salmon with radicchio, radish, herbs, beer-bread crisps and cold potato salad).

Hotel Ærø
HOTEL €€

(☑62 21 07 60; www.hotel-aeroe.dk, in Danish; Brogade 1; s/d Dkr825/995; ℗) Right by the water, the Ærø has large, modern chalet-style rooms. There's a good restaurant serving traditional fare, including light lunches, smørrebrød and more-substantial mains (Dkr48 to Dkr238).

Danhostel Svendborg
HOSTEL €

(☑62 21 66 99; www.danhostel-svendborg.dk; Vestergade 45; dm/s/d Dkr250/490/520; ℗@) This five-star–rated hostel occupies a renovated 19th-century iron foundry in the town centre. Dorm beds are available only from July to mid-September.

ℹ Information

Tourist office (☑62 23 57 00; www.visitsydfyn.dk; Centrumpladsen 4; ☺9.30am-6pm Mon-Fri, to 2pm Sat end Jun–mid-Aug) Has lots of information on south Funen as a whole.

ℹ Getting There & Around

The train and bus stations are two blocks northwest of the dock.

Trains run from Odense to Svendborg (Dkr69, 45 minutes, hourly). **Car ferries** (☑62 52 40 00;

www.aeroe-ferry.com) run to Ærøskøbing (return per adult/child/car Dkr179/101/396; 75 minutes) five to six times daily; the last one departs at 10.30pm.

Langeland
POP 13,300

The long, narrow grain-producing island of Langeland, connected by bridge to Funen via Tåsinge, is a natural haven and popular holiday destination for Danes. It has some excellent sandy beaches, enjoyable cycling and rewarding birdwatching. A large part of the island around Dovns Klint has been protected as a wildlife reserve. It is also well known in Denmark for its annual Langeland Festival (www.langelandsfestival.dk, in Danish, ☉late Jul–early Aug), a popular family-oriented music festival often referred to as 'Denmark's largest garden party'.

◉ Sights & Activities

Tranekær Slot   CASTLE GARDEN, MUSEUM
Langeland's top sight is the red stucco Tranekær Slot, a handsome medieval castle that has been in the hands of the one family since 1672. The castle is not open to the public, but its grounds are home to the Tickon (Tranekær International Centre for Art & Nature; admission to grounds adult/child Dkr25/free), a collection of intriguing art installations created by international artists and sited around the wooded grounds and lake. Tranekær Slot Museum and the Souvenir Museum are in the castle's old water mill and old theatre respectively.

Situated about 1km north of the castle is the Castle Mill (Lejbølleveje; adult/child Dkr25/free; ☉11am-5pm daily Jul & Aug, 11am-4pm Mon-Thu & 11-5pm Sun May, Jun & Sep), a 19th-century windmill, with its remarkable wooden mechanics still intact.

Rudkøbing   TOWN CENTRE, NATURE
Langeland's main town of Rudkøbing has a fairly desolate harbour area, but the town centre is attractive and there are some fine old buildings around Rudekøbing Kirke, to the north of Brogade, the street leading inland from the harbour to the main square of Torvet. For beaches, head for Ristinge about 15km south of Rudkøbing; for birdwatching you'll find a sighting tower at Tryggelev Nor, 5km south of Ristinge, and a sanctuary at Gulstav Bog, the island's southern tip.

Cycling is a good way to explore Langeland. The tourist office has an excellent English-language cycling map (Dkr30) that describes six bike routes on the island. Bikes can be hired at Lapletten (☑62 51 10 98; Engdraget 1, Rudkøbing; per day Dkr60).

🛏 Sleeping

The tourist office and its website (www.turist.langeland.dk) maintain a list of rooms for rent in private homes, with doubles costing about Dkr400 to Dkr600.

Skrøbelev Gods   HOTEL €€€
(☑62 51 45 31; www.ritz-resorts.com; Skrøbelev Hedevej 4; r from Dkr1695) This secluded converted manor farm 3km from Rudkøbing in the centre of the island is based in buildings dating from the 17th century. The decor is wonderfully camp and over the top, and there is a very impressive wine cellar.

🍃 Damgården   GUESTHOUSE €€
(☑62 59 16 45; www.damgaarden.dk; Emmerbøllevej 5, Emmerbølle, Tranekær; s/d Dkr400/600; P) Denmark's first organic B&B offers bright, spacious rooms in a pretty farmhouse with a large garden and serves great homemade breakfasts. The owners can organise tours and outings.

Danhostel Rudkøbing   HOSTEL €
(☑62 51 18 30; www.danhostel.dk/rudkobing; Engdraget 11; campsites/dm/d Dkr60/150/450; ☉Apr–end Oct) A basic hostel, less than ideally located a way back from the centre or the water. There's also space for tents.

❶ Information

Pick up information about the island from Langeland's **tourist office** (www.langeland.dk; Torvet 5, Rudkøbing; ☉9am-5pm Mon-Fri, to 3pm Sat Jul-Aug).

❶ Getting There & Away

Boat

Car ferries (☑62 52 40 00; www.aeroe-ferry.com) sail from Rudkøbing to Marstal in Ærø (return per adult/child/car Dkr179/101/396, one hour) four to six times daily. The ticket is valid for any one of Ærø's four ferry routes. A ferry service also sails from Spodsbjerg to Tårs in Lolland.

Bus

Buses make the 25-minute run from Svendborg to Rudkøbing (Dkr41) at least hourly weekdays,

HAVE YOUR SAY

Found a fantastic restaurant that you're longing to share with the world? Disagree with our recommendations? Or just want to talk about your most recent trip?

Whatever your reason, head to lonelyplanet.com, where you can post a review, ask or answer a question on the Thorntree forum, comment on a blog, or share your photos and tips on Groups. Or you can simply spend time chatting with like-minded travellers. So go on, have your say.

with reduced service on weekends; most connect onwards to Tranekær.

Ærø

POP 6800

Just 30km long and 8km wide, Ærø (pronounced 'with difficulty') holds a special place in the hearts of Danes. Mention it and they will sigh wistfully and perhaps recall a long-ago childhood visit to the quaint old town of Ærøskøbing, or cycling holidays amid the beautiful, gentle countryside peppered with crooked, half-timbered houses with traditional hand-blown glass windows and decorative doorways beautified by hollyhocks. Most young residents leave as soon as they can, however, as, though Ærø is one of the most enchanting of all the islands of the south Funen archipelago, there isn't a great deal going on here out of season. There are some good, small beaches, one of the best being Risemark Strand on the southern tip of the island; it's a great place to tour by bicycle, not least as this is in keeping with the spirit of an island that is run almost entirely on sustainable energy sources such as wind and solar power.

Ærø has three main towns: Ærøskøbing, Marstal and Søby. The island's tourist website is www.aeroeisland.com.

ÆRØSKØBING

POP 975

The words 'higgledy' and 'piggledy' could have been invented to describe the idyllic town of Ærøskøbing. A prosperous merchants' town in the late 17th century, Ærøskøbing's narrow, winding cobblestone streets are lined with 17th- and 18th-century houses. The tourist office sells an illustrated leaflet (Dkr10) describing the finest buildings in the town, many of them very well preserved.

Apart from Ærøskøbing's overall charm, the main tourist attraction is Flaske Peters Samling (Smedegade 22; admission incl Ærø Museum adult/child Dkr30/free; ☺10am-5pm end Jun–mid-Aug), a museum in the former poorhouse with displays of local folk art. There are also examples of the work of ship's cook Peter Jacobsen, 'Bottle Peter', who crafted 1700 ships-in-a-bottle during his long life. Ærø Museum (www.arremus.dk; Brogade 3-5; admission incl Flaske Peters Samling adult/child Dkr30/free; ☺10am-4pm mid-Jun–early Sep) charts the local cultural history.

Ærøskøbing tourist office (Ærøskøbing Havn 4; ☺9am-6pm Mon-Fri, 10am-6pm Sat & Sun mid-Jul–early Aug) is by the waterfront.

SØBY

This quiet little port has a shipyard, which happens to be the island's biggest employer, a sizeable fishing fleet and a busy yacht marina. Five kilometres beyond Søby, at Ærø's northern tip, there's a pebble beach with clear water and a stone lighthouse with a view.

MARSTAL

On the southeastern end of the island, Marstal is Ærø's most modern-looking town and has a web of busy shopping streets at its centre. Marstal has an emphatically maritime history; even its street names echo the names of ships and famous sailors. Its Søfartsmuseum (Prinsensgade 1; adult/child Dkr50/free; ☺9am-6pm Jul & Aug, to 5pm Jun) has an absorbing collection of nautical artefacts including 250 ships' models and full-size boats. There is a reasonably good beach on the southern side of town.

Marstal tourist office (Havnegade 5; ☺10am-4pm Mon-Fri, to 1pm Sat & Sun Jun-Aug) is a few minutes' walk south of the harbour.

ANCIENT ÆRØ

Ærø once had more than 100 prehistoric sites and, although many have been lost, the island still has some atmospheric Neolithic remains, especially in its southeast district, to the west of Marstal. At the small village of Store Rise is the site of Tingstedet, the remains of a passage grave in a field behind an attractive 12th-century church.

At Lindsbjerg is the superb hilltop site of a long barrow and two passage graves, one of which has a nicely poised capstone. Just over 1km south of here, following signs and right on the coast, is the fascinating medieval relic of **Sankt Albert's Kirke**. It's within a Viking defensive wall from about the 8th century.

Another striking site is at **Kragnæs**, about 4km west of Marstal. Head through the village of Græsvænge and follow the signs for 'Jættestue' along narrow lanes to reach a small car park, from where it's about 600m along field tracks to the restored grave site.

Sleeping

The island's tourist offices have a list of countryside B&Bs around the island for around Dkr330/500 per single/double. There are camping grounds at **Søby** (☑62 58 14 70; www. soeby-camping.dk), **Ærøskøbing** (☑62 52 18 54; www.aeroecamp.dk) and **Marstal** (☑63 52 63 69; www.marstalcamping.dk).

TOP CHOICE Pension

Vestergade 44 GUESTHOUSE €€

(☑62 52 22 98; www.vestergade44.com; Vestergade 44, Ærøskøbing; r Dkr790-990; P) Next door to Hotel Ærohus is this delightful 18th-century house with beautifully appointed, cosy interiors. Host Susanna Greve is impeccably gracious and we won't be surprised if you consider staying an extra night or two. Single rooms cost Dkr600 per night outside the summer period.

Hotel Ærøhus HOTEL €€€

(☑62 52 10 03; www.aeroehus.dk; Vestergade 38, Ærøskøbing; s/d Dkr990/1250; P) This hotel occupies a large period building near the harbour. Rooms are comfortable and modern; there's a smart garden annexe and two tennis courts. The in-house restaurant (three courses Dkr375) specialises in local seafood. Rent a bike for Dkr75 per day.

Vindeballe Kro GUESTHOUSE €€

(☑62 52 16 13; Vindeballevej 1, Ærøskøbing; s/d Dkr500/700) A cheap accommodation option 5km from Ærøskøbing, this characterful inn has 10 rooms run by Maria and Steen Larsen.

Danhostel Marstal HOSTEL €

(☑62 53 39 50; www.marstalvandrerhjem. dk; Færgestræde 29; dm Dkr175, s/d from Dkr325/375; ⊘May–mid-Sep; P) South of Marstal harbour, this modest, bright and neatly kept hostel is right by the sea.

Villa Blomberg HOSTEL €

(☑62 52 10 44; www.villablomberg.dk; Smedevejen 158, Ærøskøbing; dm/d Dkr130/230; P) This hostel is 1km from town on the road to Marstal. You can rent bikes (per day/week Dkr55/275) and kayaks (per hour Dkr100).

Eating & Drinking

All three towns have bakeries, restaurants and food stores.

Den Grønne Gren CAFE €€

(www.dengronnegren.dk; Vester Bregninge 17, Bregninge Æ; lunches Dkr69-132, dinners Dkr115-210; ⊘daily Jul & Aug, closed Mon & Tue May, Jun & Sep) Janni Bidstrup's charming, guesthouse (singles/doubles Dkr495/740) and cafe – actually 9km west of Ærøskøbing – serves mainly organic food and killer espresso. Pizzas (served on Fridays and Sunday evenings) are a speciality.

Ærøskøbing Røgeri SMOKE-HOUSE €

(Havnen 15, Ærøskøbing; ⊘11am-8pm Jun-Aug, to 6pm Apr–end Jun & mid-Aug–end Sep) This traditional fish smoke-house in Ærøskøbing harbour serves excellent-value plates for Dkr26 to Dkr70 – you eat outside on picnic benches.

Café Aroma CAFE €€

(Havnepladsen, Ærøskøbing; lunches Dkr75-98, dinners Dkr148-185; ⊘mid-Jun–Aug) This eclectic cafe serves simple, quality grub, including salads, smørrebrød (open sandwiches) and burgers made with homemade bread and dressing. Even the ice cream is proudly homemade.

Getting There & Away

Car ferries (☑62 52 40 00; www.aeroe-ferry .dk; return per adult/child/bike/car Dkr179/101/38/396) run year-round. If you have a car it's a good idea to make reservations, particularly at weekends and in midsummer.

Ferry routes to/from Ærø are as follows:

ROUTE	FREQUENCY (PER DAY)	DURATION (MINS)
Faaborg-Søby	5-6 (Mon-Fri), 2-3 (Sat & Sun)	60
Fynshav-Søby	4 (Mon-Fri), 2-5 (Sat), 3-4 (Sun)	70
Svendborg-Ærøskøbing	6 (Mon-Fri), 5 (Sat), 5-6 (Sun)	75
Rudkøbing-Marstal	5-6 (Mon-Fri), 4 (Sat), 5 (Sun)	60

❶ Getting Around

Bicycle

Pilebækkens Cykel og Servicestation (☑62 52 11 10; Pilebækken 11; per day Dkr55-75), opposite the car park on the outskirts of Ærøskøbing, rents out bikes.

Søby Cykeludlejning (☑62 58 14 60; Havnevejen 2; per day Dkr60) rents out bikes in Søby. Both the tourist office in Ærøskøbing and Marstal sell a Dkr20 cycling map of the island.

Bus

Bus 790 runs from Søby to Marstal via Ærøskøbing (17 times daily weekdays, eight times daily on weekends).

JUTLAND

Denmark doesn't have a North–South divide; culturally, spiritually and to a great extent politically, it is divided into Jutland... and all the rest. Jutlanders are different. Sturdy, down to earth, unpretentious, hardworking. You will find an old-fashioned hospitality here and an engaging frankness; the landscape is the most epic in all of Denmark (that's not saying much, but there are at least some hills, as well as vast and spectacular sandy beaches); and there are several engaging and characterful cities and towns.

Århus

POP 242,900

Always the bridesmaid, never the bride, Århus (the second-largest city in Denmark) has tended to labour in the shadows of Copenhagen in terms of its cultural draw for visitors, and it is probably also true that few young Danes grow up with dreams of moving here rather than the capital. But – and it's a big 'but' – this is a terrific city in which to spend a day or two.

It is the cultural and commercial heart of Jutland and has one of Denmark's best music and entertainment scenes (there is a very large student population on account of the city's university). There's also a well-preserved historic quarter, and plenty to see and do, ranging from fantastic museums – not least ARoS, one of the best art museums in Denmark – and period churches in the centre, to picturesque woodland trails and beaches along the city's outskirts.

◉ Sights & Activities

TOP CHOICE AROS   MUSEUM
(www.aros.dk; adult/child Dkr95/free; ⊙10am-5pm Thu-Sun & Tue, to 10pm Wed) One of the top three art galleries in Denmark, AROS is home to a comprehensive collection of 19th- and 20th-century Danish art and a wide range of arresting and vivid contemporary art. There are pieces here from Warhol and Lichtenstein and, in colourfully lit pickling jars, a work by Danish artist Bjørn Nørgaard consisting of parts of a horse he sacrified in protest at the Vietnam War (long before British artist Damien Hirst started chopping up animals in the name of art). Hard to miss is Ron Mueck's startlingly lifelike giant *Boy* and Olafur Eliasson's whimsical *Your Rainbow Panorama,* a 360-degree rooftop walkway offering technicolour views of the city. There's also an in-house cafe and restaurant for peckish culture vultures.

Den Gamle By   MUSEUM
(Old Town; www.dengamleby.dk; Viborgvej 2; adult/child Dkr125/free; ⊙9am-6pm end Jun–early Sep) The Danes' seemingly limitless enthusiasm for dressing up and recreating history reaches its zenith at Den Gamle By. It's an engaging open-air museum of 75 half-timbered houses brought here from around Denmark and reconstructed as a provincial town, complete with a functioning bakery, silversmith and bookbinder. Recreated neighbourhoods from 1927 and 1974 are the latest additions. The museum is on Viborgvej, 1.1km from the central train station. Buses 3, 14, 25 and 55 will take you there.

The **Botanisk Have** (Botanical Gardens), with its thousands of plants and recreated Jutland environments, occupies the high ground above Den Gamle By and can be reached through an exit from the old town or directly from Vesterbrogade.

Moesgård   NATURE, MUSEUM
Visit Moesgård, 5km south of the city centre, for its glorious beech woods and the trails threading through them towards sandy beaches. Visit for the well-presented history exhibits from the Stone Age to the Viking Age at **Moesgård Museum of Prehistory** (adult/child Dkr60/free; ⊙10am-5pm Apr-Sep). But above all else, visit Moesgård for the museum's most dramatic exhibit: the 2000-year-old **Grauballe Man**, or Grauballe-manden, whose astonishingly well preserved

body was found in 1952 at the village of Grauballe, 35km west of Århus.

The superb display on the Grauballe Man is part history lesson, part forensics lesson. Was he a sacrifice to Iron Age fertility gods, an executed prisoner perhaps, or simply a victim of murder? Either way, the broken leg and the gaping neck wound suggest that his death, sometime in the last century BC, was a horribly violent one. His body and skin, tanned and preserved by the unique chemical and biological qualities of the peat bogs, are remarkably intact, right down to hair and fingernails.

Away from all this death and violence, there's an enjoyable **trail** dubbed the 'prehistoric trackway' or Oldtidsstien leading from behind the museum across fields of wildflowers, past grazing sheep and through beech woods down to **Moesgård Strand**, Århus' best sandy beach. The trail, marked by red-dotted stones, passes reconstructed historic sights including a dolmen, burial cists and an Iron Age house. The museum has a brochure with details. You can walk one way and catch a bus back to the city centre, or follow the trail both ways as a 5km round trip. It's all well worth a half-day or full-day visit, with a picnic perhaps if the weather behaves itself.

Bus 6 from Århus train station terminates at the museum year-round and runs twice an hour.

Århus Domkirke
CHURCH

(Bispetorv; admission free; ☉9.30am-4pm Mon & Wed-Sat, 10.30am-4pm Tue) This impressive cathedral is Denmark's longest, with a lofty nave that spans nearly 100m. The original Romanesque chapel at the eastern end dates from the 12th century, while most of the rest of the church is 15th-century Gothic.

Like other Danish churches, the cathedral was once richly decorated with **frescos** that served to convey biblical parables to unschooled peasants. After the Reformation, church authorities who felt the frescos smacked too much of Roman Catholicism had them all whitewashed, but many have now been uncovered and restored. They range from fairy-tale paintings of St George slaying a dragon, to scenes of hellfire. The cathedral's splendid, five-panel, gilt **altarpiece** is a highlight. It was made in Lübeck by the renowned woodcarver Bernt Notke in the 15th century.

Vor Frue Kirke
CHURCH

(Frue Kirkeplads; admission free; ☉10am-4pm Mon-Fri, to 2pm Sat) This church, off Vestergade, has a carved wooden **altarpiece** dating from the 1530s. But far more interesting is what's in its basement: the **crypt** of the city's original cathedral, dating from about 1060. Enter via the stairway beneath the altar. To enter a third chapel, this one with 16th-century frescos, go through the courtyard and take the left door.

FREE Vikinge-Museet
MUSEUM

(Sankt Clements Torv 6; ☉10am-4pm Mon-Wed & Fri, to 5.30pm Thu) There's more than the expected vaults in the basement of Nordea bank, where there's a small exhibition of artefacts from the Viking Age town that were excavated at this site in 1964 during the bank's construction. The display includes a skeleton, a reconstructed house, 1000-year-old carpentry tools and pottery, and photos of the excavation.

Swimming
SWIMMING

There are sandy beaches on the outskirts of Århus. The most popular one to the north is **Bellevue**, about 4km from the city centre (bus 6 or 16), while the favourite to the south is Moesgård Strand.

✺ Festivals & Events

Århus Festival
ARTS

(www.aarhusfestuge.dk) This 10-day festival in late August and/or early September turns the city into a stage for nonstop revelry, with world-class jazz, rock, classical music, theatre and dance. Events take place all over the city and there is a fringe element also.

Sculpture by the Sea
ARTS

(www.sculpturebythesea.dk) This biennial, month-long festival transforms the city's beachfront into an outdoor gallery, with around 60 sculptures from both Danish and foreign artists displayed beside (and in) the water.

🛏 Sleeping

The tourist office books rooms in private homes for around Dkr400/500 per single/double, plus a Dkr50 booking fee.

Hotel Guldsmeden
HOTEL €€€

(☎86 13 45 50; www.hotelguldsmeden.com; Guldsmedgade 40; s/d from Dkr9995/1050, with shared bathroom from Dkr695/895) On the northern side of the city centre, this is our midrange

Århus

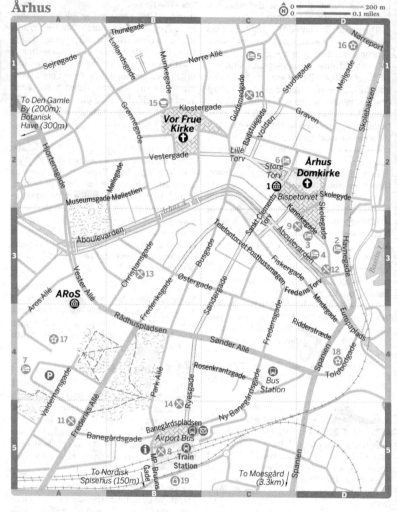

choice in town for friendly staff, delightfully bright French-colonial–style rooms with polished wood floors, large four-poster beds with soft white linen, a small garden terrace and a generally relaxed, stylish ambience. Further perks include organic toiletries and good (mainly organic) breakfasts.

Hotel Ferdinand
HOTEL €€€

(☎87 32 14 44; www.hotelferdinand.dk, in Danish; Åboulevarden 28; studio s/d from Dkr950/1150, ste s/d from Dkr1100/1300) Right on the buzzing canal-side, this boutique hotel is divided into simple, fully equipped studio apartments (washing machine and dryer included!) and svelte, stylish suites. The brilliant downstairs brasserie is one of the best-value nosh spots in town. Ask about special packages, which may include breakfast (usually Dkr95) and dinner.

Cab Inn Århus
HOTEL €€

(☎86 75 70 00; www.cabinn.com; Kannikegade 14; s Dkr485-545, d Dkr615-675; @) In an ideal central location opposite the Domkirke, the style here is standard Cab Inn, with small, rather bare but usually clean rooms. If you're a light sleeper, request a room not facing Åboulevarden, especially on Thursday to

Saturday nights. Parking costs Dkr60. Free internet and wi-fi access.

Danhostel Århus　　HOSTEL €€
(☎86 21 21 20; www.aarhus-danhostel.dk; Marienlundsvej 10; dm Dkr165, r Dkr570-810; ⊘Jan–midDec; P) It may be 4km north of the city centre but it's well worth considering for the lovely parkland setting in a renovated 1850s dance hall. It's at the edge of the Risskov Woods and a few minutes from the beach. Buses 6 and 9 pass nearby.

Århus City Sleep-In　　HOTEL €
(☎86 19 20 55; www.citysleep-in.dk; Havnegade 20; dm Dkr170, d with/without bathroom Dkr490/430; ⊘24hr; @) Run by a youth organisation, the Århus City Sleep-In is in a central former mariners' hotel. It's casual, the rooms are a bit run-down, but it's a cheerful place and by far the best budget option in the centre. Sheet hire costs Dkr50 and padlocks are Dkr25 if you don't have your own.

Hotel Royal　　HOTEL €€€
(☎86 12 00 11; www.hotelroyal.dk; Store Torv 4; s Dkr1450, d from Dkr1850; @) Built in 1838, this is Århus' answer to Copenhagen's Hotel d'Angleterre – opulent, ornate, luxurious and wonderfully atmospheric, with all modern luxuries. Check the website for special offers.

🎖 **Radisson BLU Scandinavia**　HOTEL €€€
(☎86 12 86 65; www.radissonblu.dk; Margrethepladsen; r Dkr845-1495; @) Right beside

ARoS and Århus Koncerthus, this massive, modern hotel includes a restaurant–bar, gym access (per day Dkr75), and free wi-fi for guests.

Århus Camping　　CAMPING GROUND €
(☎86 23 11 33; www.aarhusnord.dk; Randersvej 400, Lisbjerg; adult/child/tent Dkr81/44/25; ⊘yr-round) This large, quite decent, three-star camping ground is about 8.5km north of Århus.

✗ Eating & Drinking

The Åboulevarden canal area is the place to head for the most high-profile restaurants and cafes – during the summer high season, the canal-side throngs with restaurant tables and there is a buzzing party atmosphere at weekends.

Nearby Skolegade is packed with popular, studenty pubs and clubs. Less touristy than Åboulevarden, the narrow streets of the 'Latin Quarter' north of the cathedral are also thick with cafes serving Danish and ethnic foods.

The train station has a convenience store, two fast-food outlets and a small **supermarket** (⊘to midnight). Adjoining the station is **Bruuns Galleri**, a major shopping centre with a larger supermarket, bakery and several fast-food options.

Two blocks west of the station is **Føtex supermarket** (Frederiks Allé), with a cheap bakery and deli.

TOP CHOICE **Nordisk Spisehus** MODERN SCANDINAVIAN €€€

(☎86 17 70 99; www.nordiskspisehus.dk; MP Bruunsgade 31; mains Dkr180-255, 3 courses Dkr350, weekend brunches Dkr149) A kind of budget Noma (see p52), this clean, simple, modern-Scandinavian restaurant, a short walk west of the station, serves regional delicacies such as local free-range veal, Nordic cheeses and fjord shrimp. We recommend the home-smoked salmon, which is given an extra last-minute hay-smoking beneath a glass cloche at your table. It is served with a dazzlingly fresh salad with salt-cured apples, radish and cucumber (Dkr98). Service is friendly and knowledgeable.

Malling & Schmidt MODERN SCANDINAVIAN €€€

(☎86 17 70 88; www.mallingschmidt.dk; Jægergårdsgade 81; 4-/6-/8 courses Dkr595/795/995; ☺dinner Wed-Sat) Run by the Nordisk Spisehus team, Århus' culinary A-lister is home to respected chef Thorsten Schmidt and his inspired takes on Nordic ingredients (think free-range Danish beef with dark berries and wild herbs, or goat's cheese and smoked herring ice cream). Book ahead. To get here from the train station, head south about 200m down MP Bruunsgade, turning right into Jægergårdsgade.

Brasserie Ferdinand FRENCH, DANISH €€€

(☎87 32 14 44; www.hotelferdinand.dk; Åboulevarden 28; lunches Dkr85-225, dinner mains Dkr165-265, Saturday brunches Dkr165; ☺Mon-Sat) Seasonal, local, organic produce informs the Franco-Danish dishes at this chic, canal-side brasserie. The three-course dinner (Dkr345) is particularly good value, while pan-fried foie gras (Dkr165) and classic beef tartar (Dkr135) are dependable menu staples. The clued-up waitstaff offer sound advice on wine pairings, and the Saturday brunch (from 10am to noon) is arguably the city's best.

Sigfred's Kaffebar CAFE €

(Ryesgade 28; sandwiches Dkr44-54; ☺8.30am-6.30pm Mon-Thu, to 8pm Fri, midnight Mon-Thu, 9.30am-6pm Sat) Sigfred's has quite possibly the best coffee in Jutland, brewed by expert baristi and sipped by ever-faithful regulars. Accompaniments include flaky pastries (the *pain au raisin* is addictive) and Italian-inspired panini. There's a supercosy second **branch** (☺10am-5.30pm Mon-Thu, to 7pm Fri, 10am-4pm Sat) inside the Vangsgaards bookstore at Ryesgade 3.

Manu Italienskis ICE CREAM €

(Frederiksgade 88; gelato 2 scoops Dkr25; ☺noon-10pm daily Mar-Oct, noon-6pm Wed-Sat Nov & Dec, closed Jan & Feb) Head here for sublime gelato, made by Florentine expat Emanuele ('Manu') Iezzi. Flavours include Lakrids (liquorice), watermelon and Manu's favourite, mango (made with Indian mangos).

Bryggeriet Sct Clemens MICROBREWERY €€

(www.bryggeriet.dk; Kannikegade 10 & 12; mains Dkr100-270; ☺Mon-Sat) This cosy microbrewery is a short walk from Åboulevarden and serves a range of home-brewed beers, as well as a decent range of cheapish fast food. This is part of the Hereford Beefstouw chain, so the menu is predictably steak-centric (although, less predictably, this includes Wagyu beef).

Globen Flakket CAFE, RESTAURANT €€

(www.globen-flakket.dk; Åboulevarden 18; sandwiches Dkr58-98, mains Dkr132-178; ☺8.45am-midnight Mon-Thu, to 3am Fri, 9am-3am Sat, to 11pm Sun) This slinky riverside cafe-cum-restaurant covers all the bases. Tuck into tapas, burgers, brunch and bistro mains such as pasta and hearty risotto. The Friday and Saturday dinner buffet (Dkr148, 6pm to 9pm) and weekend brunch buffet (Dkr98, 10am to 2pm) are both good value.

Café Gemmestedet CAFE, BAR

(Gammel Munkegade 1; ☺10am-midnight Mon-Wed, to 1am Thu, to 2am Fri & Sat, 10am-7pm Sun) A cosy jumble of chandeliers, candles, board games and piano, this bohemian cafe-bar is famed for its original, kookily named cocktails ('When something happened that made everything different and exciting', anyone?). There's an interesting choice of beers, organic juices, and tasty daytime grub (including a popular 'tapas platter').

Emmery's CAFE €

(Guldsmedgade 24-26; brunches Dkr100-130; ☺7.30am-5.30pm Mon-Thu, to 6.30pm Fri, to 3.30pm Sat, to 3pm Sun) A stylish and friendly cafe–delicatessen–wine shop hybrid that serves its own delicious bread and sandwiches (Dkr55 to Dkr70), some with vegetarian fillings.

ARoS CAFE/RESTAURANT €€

(sandwiches Dkr45, mains Dkr135-198; ☺10.30am-3pm Tue, Thu-Sun, to 9pm Wed) A good bet for a snack, the art museum's downstairs cafe serves tasty sandwiches, tapas and lovely sweet treats; go upstairs for good, simple brasserie food.

⭐ Entertainment

Århus has a vibrant music scene. For the lowdown on what's happening around town, click onto www.visitaarhus.com.

Train   LIVE MUSIC, CLUB
(www.train.dk; Toldbodgade 6; ⊙vary) One of the biggest venues in Denmark stages concerts by international rock, pop and country stars. Expect late-night clubbing events most Fridays and Saturdays.

Musikcaféen   LIVE MUSIC
(www.musikcafeen.dk, in Danish; Mejlgade 53; ⊙Mon-Sat) This and the adjacent Gyngen are alternative and often vibrant venues, with rock, jazz and world music. They are a showcase for hopefuls and up-and-coming acts.

Musikhuset Århus   LIVE MUSIC
(www.musikhusetaarhus.dk; Thomas Jensens Allée 2) The city concert hall presents dance, opera and concerts by Danish and international performers.

ℹ Information

Emergency
Århus Universitetshospital (☎89 49 27 16; Nørrebrogade 44) Has a 24-hour emergency room.

Post
Post office (Banegårdspladsen) Beside the train station.

Tourist Information
The **tourist office** (☎87 31 50 10; www.visit aarhus.com; Banegårdspladsen; ⊙10am-5pm Mon-Thu, to 4pm Fri) is well stocked with brochures on Århus, Jutland and the rest of Denmark. Here you can buy the Århus Card, a 24-hour or 48-hour pass that includes public-transport usage and admission to various attractions (24 hours adult/child Dkr119/59, 48 hours Dkr149/69). Information kiosks were set to replace the current office in September 2011. Check www.vistaarhus.com for details.

ℹ Getting There & Away

Air
SAS (www.flysas.com) and **Cimber Air** (www.cimber.dk) have frequent daily connections to Copenhagen (one-way ticket around Dkr300). Budget airline **Ryanair** (www.ryanair.com) operates one daily flight between Århus and London-Stansted. The airport is in Tirstrup, 44km northeast of Århus.

Boat
Mols-Linien (☎70 10 14 18; www.mols-linien.dk) runs car ferries from Århus to Odden in northwest Zealand (adult/child Dkr325/162, car and five passengers Dkr725, 65 minutes).

Bus
The bus station (Fredensgade) has a DSB cafe and a small supermarket. **Abildskou buses** (www.abildskou.dk) run a few times daily between Århus and Copenhagen's Valby station and the airport, stopping in Odense on the way (adult/child Dkr290/145, three hours). For information on travel to other destinations in Jutland visit www.dsb.dk. Bus-station lockers cost Dkr10 for 24 hours.

Car & Motorcycle
The main highways to Århus are the E45 from the north and south and Rte 15 from the west. The E45 curves around the western edge of the city as a ring road. There are a number of turn-offs from the ring road into the city, including Åohavevej from the south and Randersvej from the north.

Cars can be rented from **Europcar** (☎89 33 11 11; www.europcar.com; Sønder Allé 35).

Train
Århus is well connected by train. Destinations include the following:

Copenhagen via Odense adult/child Dkr339/170, three hours, twice hourly

Aalborg adult/child Dkr171/86, 1½ hours, twice hourly

Esbjerg Dkr235/118, 2½ hours; once or twice hourly

There's a ticket-queuing system at the station: red for internal; green for international. For local journeys, unless you have mastered use of the quicker ticket machines, be prepared for quite long waits at busy times. Friday trains are always very busy and it's advisable to reserve a seat for long journeys. Train-station lockers cost Dkr20 to Dkr40 for 24 hours.

ℹ Getting Around

To/From the Airport
The airport bus to Århus train station costs Dkr95/70 per adult/child and takes approximately 45 minutes. Check times to the airport at the stands outside the train station; some services start only in August. The taxi fare to the airport is about Dkr750.

Bicycle
Bikes4Rent (www.bikes4rent.dk; Skander-borgvej 107, Viby J; ⊙8am-7pm; per day Dkr75) rents out good-quality bikes.

City Bikes (www.aarhusbycykel.dk) offers free-use bikes from some 56 City Bike racks around the city from April to October. If you're lucky enough to find a bike rack with an actual bike in it, simply deposit a Dkr20 coin in the stand to release the bike. You can return the bicycle to any rack to get your money back.

Bus

Most in-town buses stop in front of the train station or around the corner on Park Allé. City bus tickets (Dkr20) are bought from a machine at the back of the bus and allow unlimited rides within the time period stamped on the ticket, which is two hours.

The Århus Card includes both bus travel and entry into many Århus museums. You can buy tickets and passes at the tourist office.

Car & Motorcycle

A car is convenient for getting to sights such as Moesgård on the city outskirts, though the city centre is best explored on foot. There's paid parking along many streets and in municipal car parks, including one on the southern side of Musikhuset Århus. Fees range from Dkr12 to Dkr15 for one hour. Overnight (7pm to 9am) is free, as is Saturday from 4pm and all day Sunday.

Taxi

Taxis congregate outside the Århus mainline station and at Store Torv. Expect to pay between Dkr70 and Dkr200 for destinations within the greater city.

Randers Regnskov

One of the most popular attractions in Jutland is Randers' state-of-the-art indoor rainforest and tropical zoo (www.regnskoven.dk; Tørvebryggen 11, Randers; adult/3-11yr/under 3yr Dkr165/95/free; ⊙10am-6pm daily end Jun–mid-Aug, to 5pm daily mid–end Aug). It is a spectacular space in which you can get close to, and in some cases handle, a wide range of tropical animals. It is housed in three individual, connected glass domes that artificially recreate the natural tropical environments of South America, Africa and Asia – there's also an aquarium, and a petting zoo outside.

Expect to see 250 different animal species including various monkeys, frogs, sloths, butterflies, birds and crocodiles (the latter, thankfully, do not roam free).

The zoo is in Randers, 40km north of Århus on the E45 motorway to Aalborg. By train Aalborg is 45 to 56 minutes away (adult/child Dkr98/49); Århus is 36 minutes (Dkr59/43).

Jelling

The tiny, apparently nondescript village of Jelling is a kind of spiritual touchstone for the Danes, and virtually all of them will visit it at some point during their lives. This is the location of one of Denmark's most important historic sites, the Jelling Kirke. Inside the small whitewashed church are frescos dating from the 12th century, and outside the door are two impressive and historically significant rune stones.

The smaller stone was erected in the early 900s by King Gorm the Old, Denmark's first king, in honour of his wife, Queen Thyra. The larger one, raised by Harald Bluetooth and dubbed 'Denmark's baptismal certificate', is adorned with the oldest representation of Christ found in Scandinavia and reads: 'Harald king bade this be ordained for Gorm his father and Thyra his mother, the Harald who won for himself all Denmark and Norway and made the Danes Christians.'

Two huge burial mounds flank the church; the one on the northern side is said to be that of King Gorm and the other of Queen Thyra, although excavators in the 19th century found no human remains and few artefacts. This could suggest much earlier grave robbing.

During the 1970s archaeologists excavated below Jelling Kirke and found the remains of three wooden churches. The oldest of these was thought to have been erected by Harald Bluetooth. A burial chamber within this site was also uncovered and revealed human bones and gold jewellery that shared characteristics with artefacts previously discovered within the large northern burial mound. One suggestion is that the bones found beneath the church ruins are those of King Gorm and they were moved there from the old pagan burial mound by Harald Bluetooth out of respect for his recently acquired Christian faith. Queen Thyra remains ephemeral. The Jelling mounds, church and rune stones are a designated Unesco World Heritage site.

Kongernes Jelling (Gormsgade 23; admission free; ⊙10am-5pm Tue-Sun Jun-Aug, noon-4pm Tue-Sun Sep-May, closed end Dec), the information and exhibition centre just across the road from the church, offers a good insight into the history of the Jelling monuments and of early Denmark.

Jelling makes a good two-hour side trip off the Odense–Århus run. Change trains at

Vejle for the ride to Jelling (Dkr28, 15 minutes). The church is 100m straight up Stationsvej from the Jelling train station.

The Lake District

This is a perhaps misleading name for what is more like a gently hilly region with a few medium-sized lakes and Denmark's highest point, Yding Skovhøj, but, though it is unlikely to induce nosebleeds, this is a delightful area for rambling. There is also ample opportunity for canoeing, biking and longer-distance hiking here. This is also where you'll find Denmark's longest river, the Gudenå, and Mossø, Jutland's largest lake. This area is south and southwest of Silkeborg, slap bang in the centre of Jutland, half an hour's drive west of Århus.

SILKEBORG
POP 42,400

Silkeborg overcomes its rather bland modern character with a friendly openness. It is the Lake District's biggest town and is an ideal base for exploring the surrounding forests and waterways. The town has some good restaurants and lively bars and cafes. A compelling reason to visit is to see the Tollund Man, the body of a preserved Iron Age 'bog man' who looks as if he's merely asleep.

◉ Sights

Silkeborg Museum   MUSEUM
(www.silkeborgmuseum.dk; Hovedgårdsvej 7; adult/child Dkr50/free; ◷10am-5pm daily May–end Oct) The main (actually virtually the only) attraction at the Silkeborg Museum is the Tollund Man. He is believed to have been executed in 300 BC and his leathery body, complete with the rope still around the neck, was discovered in a bog in 1950. The well-preserved face of the Tollund Man is hypnotic in its detail, right down to the stubble on his chin. The museum is about 150m east of the main town square.

Kunst Centret Silkeborg Bad   ART GALLERY
(www.silkeborgbad.dk; Gjessøvej 40; adult/child Dkr60/free; ◷10am-5pm Tue-Sun May-Sep, noon-4pm Tue-Fri, 11am-5pm Sat & Sun Oct-Apr) Kunst Centret Silkeborg Bad, a former spa dating from 1883, is now a beautiful, modern art space – Art Centre Silkeborg Baths – with permanent works and changing exhibitions of art, sculpture, ceramics, glassware, design and architecture, surrounded by parkland

featuring contemporary sculpture. It's about 2km southwest of the town.

Museum Jorn   MUSEUM
(www.museumjorn.dk; Gudenåvej 7-9; adult/child Dkr70/free; ◷10am-5pm Tue-Sun Apr-Oct) Fresh from a major renovation, Museum Jorn (formerly Silkeborg Kuntsmuseum) contains some striking work, such as the large ceramic walls by Jean Dubuffet and Pierre Alechinsky that greet visitors at the entrance. It displays many of the works of native son Asger Jorn and other modern artists, including Max Ernst, Le Corbusier and Danish artists from the influential COBRA group. It's 1km south of the town centre.

Aqua   AQUARIUM
(www.ferskvandscentret.dk/aqua; Vejsøvej 55; adult/child Dkr115/60; ◷10am-6pm end Jun–early Aug, closed early-end Dec) Situated 2km south of central Silkeborg, Aqua is an entertaining aquarium and exhibition centre exploring the ecosystems of the lakes and surrounding area with lots of fishy creatures, otters and fishing birds among the imaginative displays.

⚘ Activities

Outdoor activities are at the heart of the Lake District's appeal. The track of the old railway from Silkeborg to Horsens is now an excellent **walking** and **cycling** trail of about 50km or so. It passes through the beech forest of **Nordskoven**, itself criss-crossed with hiking and bike trails. To reach Nordskoven head south down Åhavevej from the tourist office, then go left over the old railway bridge down by the hostel.

Canoeing is a marvellous way to explore the Lake District and you can plan trips for several days staying at lakeside camping grounds along the way. The canoe-hire places can help plan an itinerary. Rent canoes for Dkr100/380 per hour/day at **Slusekiosken** (☑86 80 30 03; www.silkeborgkanocenter.dk; Østergade 36) at the harbour.

The world's oldest operating **paddle steamer** (☑86 82 07 66; www.hjejlen.com; times & prices vary) offers tours on the lake during summer, departing opposite Slusekiosken.

⊨ Sleeping

Budget and midrange options in town are limited, making B&B accommodation an especially good option. The tourist office publishes a B&B booklet, with singles/doubles costing around Dkr250/500.

Radisson BLU Hotel   HOTEL **€€€**
(☑88 82 22 22; www.radissonblu.com; Papirfabrikken 12; s Dkr995-1345, d Dkr995-1845; P@) A comfortable, business-class hotel in a converted mill by the riverbank, the Radisson is simply the best place to stay in town. The huge rooms in a simple, appealing modern Scandinavian style, have large beds and all modern conveniences. There's a bar and restaurant, plus discounted use of a nearby fitness centre.

Danhostel Silkeborg   HOSTEL **€**
(☑86 82 36 42; www.danhostel-silkeborg.dk; Åhavevej 55; dm/r Dkr250/650; ☺Mar–end Nov; P@) The riverbank location (650m southeast of the town's main square), modern facilities and lack of decent alternative options make this hostel very popular, so book ahead. It's east of the train station. Dorms are available only from July to mid-September, while private rooms are available all year.

Gammel Skovridergaard   HOTEL **€€€**
(☑87 22 55 00; www.glskov.dk; Marienlundsvej 36; s/d Dkr1150/1450) This magnificent former manor farm is now a hotel and conference centre with oodles of charm and an idyllic location close to the lakes and forests of Silkeborg, yet only a 1.9km walk south from the main town square.

✗ Eating

Nygade, lined with grill bars and pizza places, is the street to head to for quick, inexpensive fast food.

There are a number of cheap food outlets on Søndergade, the pedestrianised main street. The **Føtex supermarket** (Torvet) has a bakery and an inexpensive cafe.

The riverside Papirfabrik (Paper Factory) cultural centre is home to the excellent **Række 1 Cafe** (www.papirfabrikken.nu; Papirfabriksame; ☺11am-midnight Jun-Aug, to 5pm Sep-May) and **Michael D Lounge & Brasserie** (Papirfabriksame; 3 courses Dkr350), which serves French brasserie classics and a more refined tasting menu.

Restaurant Gastronomisk   EUROPEAN **€€€**
(www.gastronomiske.dk; Søndergade 20; lunches Dkr85-135, dinner mains Dkr230-255, 4/5 courses Dkr348/423; ☺Tue-Sat) This cosy brasserie–restaurant, located 200m south of the main square, serves good salads, steaks, sandwiches and soups for lunch and more ambitious, modern European dishes in the evenings.

Den Gyldne Ovn   CAFE, BAKERY **€**
(Tværgade 4-6; sandwiches/wraps Dkr32-48, salads Dkr35-37; ☺7.30am-5pm Mon-Fri, 9am-2.30pm Sat) Located 150m southwest of the main square, this refreshingly healthy, trendy chain peddles tasty wraps, baguettes and salads. Naughtier options include mini pizzas, muffins, cookies and buttery pastries. Eat in or take away.

❶ Information

Library (Hostrupsgade 41) Has free internet terminals.

Jsyke Bank (Vestergade 16) Branch with an ATM.

Tourist office (www.silkeborg.com; Åhavevej 2a; ☺9.30am-5.30pm Mon-Fri, 10am-2pm Sat Jul–late Aug) Near the harbour; has lots of leaflets including detailed route descriptions of walks and cycle routes.

❶ Getting There & Away

Hourly or half-hourly trains connect Silkeborg with Skanderborg (Dkr47, 30 minutes) and Århus (Dkr65, 49 minutes) via Ry. There are regular daily buses to Århus (Dkr65, 48 minutes).

SKANDERBORG & RY

Two smaller, quieter Lake District towns east of Silkeborg are Ry and Skanderborg. Ry, the closer of the two to Silkeborg, is a particularly peaceful place from which to base your exploration of the Lake District. Skanderborg is a rather humdrum town, but with a lovely setting on Skanderborg Lake. It is best known in Denmark for the Skanderborg Festival.

◉ Sights & Activities

Himmelbjerget   NATURE AREA
The Lake District's most visited spot is the whimsically named Himmelbjerget (Sky Mountain), which, at just 147m, is one of Denmark's highest hills. It was formed by water erosion during the final Ice Age as a 'false hill' or *kol,* the sides of which are quite steep. There are a number of interesting memorials surrounding the hilltop's crowning glory, the 25m-tower (admission Dkr10), reached via a marked 6km footpath north east of Ry, or by bus or boat.

Outdoor Activities   CANOEING, CYCLING
If you want to explore the lakes in the district, **Ry Kanofart** (www.kanoferie.dk, in Danish; Kyhnsvej 20, Ry) rents out canoes for Dkr360 per day. For walking and cycling routes, ask at Ry's tourist centre for walking and cycling leaflets (Dkr40). **Cykeludlejning** (www.

THE HEART OF ART

If you're a fan of modern art, chances are you've heard of Italian conceptual artist Piero Manzoni (1933–63). What you may not know is that the biggest public collection of his work is not in Milan, but on the eastern fringe of Herning, a regional textile centre 40km west of Silkeborg. You'll find Manzoni's work, and that of visionaries like Mario Merz and Man Ray, at **HEART** (www.heartmus.dk; Birk Centerpark 8, Herning; admission Dkr75; ⏱10am–5pm Tue, Wed & Fri-Sun, to 10pm Thu), Herning's striking contemporary-art museum. Designed by US architect Steven Holl, its shirt-like crumpled walls and sleeve-inspired roof honour the collection's founder, Danish shirt manufacturer and passionate art collector Aage Damgaard (1917–91). In the summers of 1960 and 1961, Damgaard invited Manzoni to indulge his creative spirit in Herning. The result was a string of masterpieces and the forging of Herning's Manzoni legacy. But HEART doesn't stop at 20th-century conceptual art, with several world-class exhibitions of contemporary art staged annually.

Across the street, the **Carl-Henning Pedersen and Else Alfelt Museum** (www.chpeamuseum.dk; Birk Centerpark 1; adult/child Dkr40/free; ⏱10am–5pm Tue-Sun May-Oct) showcases the riotously colourful paintings, watercolours, mosaics, ceramics and sculptures of artists Carl-Henning (1913–2007) and Else Alfelt (1910–74). Next door to HEART stands Danish architect Jørn Utzon's 1970-designed **Prototype House** (closed to the public), while further south on Birk Centerpark street you'll stumble across artist Ingvar Cronhammar's ominous **Elia**. Attracting lightning, shooting random flames of gas, and looking straight off a *Dr Who* set, it's northern Europe's largest sculpture.

HEART and its neighbours aside, there's little else to keep you in Herning, so consider it a day trip from Silkeborg, easily reached by train (one-way Dkr57, 40 minutes). Alight at Birk Centerpark station (not at Herning station), from where the sights are a quick walk up the street.

rycykler.dk, in Danish; Parallelvej 9b, Ry) rents out bikes for Dkr75 a day.

✦ Festivals & Events

Skanderborg Festival　　　　　MUSIC
(www.smukfest.dk) The Skanderborg Festival bills itself as Denmark's most beautiful, and is second only to Roskilde in terms of scale. It takes place during the second weekend in August in Dyrehaven, a parkland a couple of kilometres east of the town, and attracts up to 45,000 people with an entertaining mix of – mostly Danish – rock and pop artists.

⌂ Sleeping & Eating

The butcher's shop opposite Ry train station has fried fish and a few other takeaway selections. The bakery next door serves decent coffee.

Knudhule　　　　CABIN, BUNGALOW €€
(☎86 89 14 07; www.knudhule.dk, in Danish; Randersvej 88, Ry; 5-person cabin per week from Dkr1995) Knudhule is an appealing budget holiday camp on a picturesque lake. There are cabins without bathrooms, and bungalows (sleeping up to four) with bathrooms. There's also a small restaurant, minigolf,

boat hire and swimming/diving platforms on the lake. To get there from the train station, cross the tracks, turn left and go 2.5km.

Ry Park Hotel　　　　　HOTEL €€€
(☎86 89 19 11; www.ryparkhotel.dk, in Danish; Kyhnsvej 2, Ry; s/d from Dkr690/1050; P@) Ry's largest hotel was about to undergo a major renovation when we visited, which is good news as the otherwise clean, comfortable rooms could use a little freshening up. Located right on the lake (you can rent canoes), facilities include an indoor pool and midrange European restaurant, **La Saison** (mains Dkr188 to Dkr220).

Pizzeria Italia　　　　ITALIAN €€
(Skanderborgvej 3, Ry; fish & meat mains Dkr109-147) There are several restaurants and fast-food places on Skanderborgvej, including Pizzeria Italia, which offers tasty pastas (Dkr69 to Dkr79) and a three-course menu (Dkr159).

❶ Information

Ry's **tourist office** (☎86 69 66 00; www.visit skanderborg.com; Klostervej 3, Ry; ⏱7am–5pm Mon-Fri, 10am-2pm Sat mid-Jul–mid-Aug) is in the train station.

ℹ Getting There & Away

Twice-hourly trains connect Ry and Skanderborg with Silkeborg and Århus. See www.dsb.dk for details.

VIBORG
POP 35,200

Quieter and sleepier than Silkeborg, Viborg has a pretty, compact town centre and an important historic and religious heritage, and makes another good base for exploring the nearby lakes and surrounding woodland. In 1060 Viborg became one of Denmark's eight bishoprics and grew into a major religious centre. Prior to the Reformation the town had 25 churches and abbeys, though ecclesiastical remnants from that period are few.

◉ Sights & Activities

The tourist office has excellent printouts, including English-language versions, which describe walks around the town with historical and cultural themes. Sankt Mogens Gade, between the cathedral and the tourist office, has some handsome old houses, including Hauchs Gård at No 7 and the Willesens House at No 9, both dating back to around 1520.

During summer you can take a trip on the Viborg lakes on the *Margrethe I* (adult/child Dkr50/30). The boat departs from the jetty at Golf Salonen.

Viborg Domkirke   CHURCH
(Sankt Mogens Gade 4; admission Dkr10; ⊙11am-4pm Mon-Sat, noon-4pm Sun) This multitowered marvel is one of Denmark's largest granite churches and dominates the town. The first church on the site dated from the Viking period. The interior is awash with frescos painted over five years (1908–13) by artist Joakim Skovgaard and featuring scenes from the Old Testament and the life of Christ.

Skovgaard Museet   MUSEUM
(www.skovgaardmuseet.dk; Domkirkestræde 2-4; adult/child Dkr40/free; ⊙10am-5pm Tue-Sun Jun-Aug) Skovgaard Museet lies to the south of Viborg Domkirke. It also features work by Joakim Skovgaard, but here the scenes are more down to earth and include portraits, landscapes and nudes. The museum also features regularly changing exhibitions.

Kunsthallen Brænderigården   ART GALLERY
(www.braenderigaarden.dk, in Danish; Riddergade 8; adult/child Dkr40/free; ⊙1-5pm Tue-Sun) An interesting modern art space showcasing changing exhibitions of architecture, photography, art and sculpture.

Viborg Stiftsmuseum   MUSEUM
(www.viborgstiftsmuseum.dk, in Danish; Hjultorvet 4; adult/child Dkr40/free; ⊙11am-5pm Tue-Sun mid-Jun–Aug, 1-4pm Tue-Fri, 11am-5pm Sat & Sun Sep–mid-Jun) Viborg Stiftsmuseum is a local history museum that tells the story of Viborg's rich religious past.

🛏 Sleeping & Eating

The tourist office website (www.viborg.dk) has a list of private accommodation options with singles/doubles starting at Dkr200/350.

The Sankt Mathias Gade Centre has cafes, a supermarket, bakery, fruit shop and a butcher.

Palads Hotel   HOTEL €€€
(☎86 62 37 00; www.hotelpalads.dk; Sankt Mathias Gade; s Dkr895, d Dkr995-1195; P @) Straddling four sites, this chintzy yet charming hotel is part of the Best Western chain and has bright, pleasant rooms (some with kitchenettes). It's just a short walk north of the train station.

Danhostel Viborg   HOSTEL €
(☎86 67 17 81; www.danhostel.dk/viborg; Vinkelvej 36; dm Dkr150, s/d from Dkr305/380; ⊙mid-Jan–early Dec; P) This lovely, modern hostel is adjacent to DCU-Viborg Camping and also handy for lakeside activities (and very quiet); it's a 2km walk from town.

DCU-Viborg Camping   CAMPING GROUND €
(☎86 67 13 11; www.camping-viborg.dk; Vinkelvej 36b; campsites per adult/child/tent Dkr75/46/45; ⊙end Mar–end Oct) Viborg is a well-ordered, three-star camping ground at a pleasant, leafy location on the east side of Lake Søndersø.

Café Morville   CAFE
(Hjultorvet; sandwiches & salads Dkr80-115, tapas brunches Dkr75-105, pastas Dkr110-130) A bustling place on the main square with sleek, modern decor, some good bistro-style dishes, and smooth espresso.

Kafé Arthur   CAFE, RESTAURANT €€
(Vestergade 4; mains Dkr169-248) Bare-brick, stripped floors and candlelight make for a cosy setting.

ℹ Information

The **post office** and several banks with **ATMs** line Sankt Mathias Gade, just south of the main square.

Tourist office (☎87 87 88 88; www.visitviborg.dk; Nytorv 9; ⊙9am-5pm Mon-Fri, to 2pm Sat Jun-Aug) Located in the centre of town; rents out bikes (per day Dkr100).

ⓘ Getting There & Around

Viborg is 66km northwest of Århus on Rte 26 and 41km west of Randers on Rte 16. Trains from Århus (Dk121, 70 minutes) run once or twice hourly on weekdays, and hourly at weekends. There is ample and convenient free parking behind the Sankt Mathias Gade Centre on the south side of town, but you must use a time disc.

Aalborg

POP 123,400

Though at the time of going to press they were in the process of tearing half of Aalborg down, we get the feeling things are on the up for what is, at heart, an attractive town. There is a major redevelopment under way on Aalborg's waterfront, and at its centre is architecture and design museum the Utzon Center, named after the celebrated, late architect of Australia's Sydney Opera House. As well as this, Aalborg has a vibrant nightlife thanks to a large student population, and several other worthwhile sites, not least the remarkable Lindholm Høje, Denmark's largest Viking burial ground. True, there is a fair bit of industrial and commercial development surrounding the town, but the centre contains enough ancient half-timbered buildings to give you an idea of the affluence its Renaissance merchants enjoyed.

⊙ Sights

Old Town   HISTORIC AREA, MUSEUM

The whitewashed **Buldolfi Domkirke** marks the centre of the old town, and has colourful frescos in the foyer. About 75m west of the cathedral is the **Aalborg Historiske Museum** (Algade 48; adult/child Dkr30/free; ⊙10am-5pm Tue-Sun), with artefacts from prehistory to the present and furnishings and interiors that hint at the wealth Aalborg's merchants enjoyed during the Renaissance.

The alley between the museum and church leads to the rambling **Monastery of the Holy Ghost** (CW Obels Plads; adult/child Dkr50; ⊙guided tours in English 2pm Tue Jul–mid-Aug), which dates from 1431 and features frescos from the early 16th century. Northeast of the cathedral on Østerågade are three noteworthy historic buildings: the **old town hall** (c 1762), the five-storey **Jens Bangs Stenhus** (built c 1624 by wealthy merchant Jens Bangs) and **Jørgen Olufsens House** (c 1616).

In addition, the half-timbered neighbourhoods around **Vor Frue Kirke** are worth a stroll, particularly the cobbled Hjelmerstald.

Aalborghus Slot, near the waterfront, is more administrative office than castle, but there's a small **dungeon** (⊙8am-3pm Mon-Fri May-Oct) you can enter for free.

Utzon Center   CULTURAL CENTRE

(www.utzoncenter.dk; Slotspladsen 4; adult/child Dkr40/free; ⊙10am-5pm Tue-Sun, also open Mon Jul & Aug) An impressive 700-sq-metre design and architecture space, the Utzon Centre, with its distinctive silver roofscape, is right on the harbour front close to Aalborghus Slot. It bills itself as 'a dynamic and experimental centre of culture and knowledge' and is close to where the celebrated Danish architect, Jørn Utzon (1918–2008), who died shortly after the centre was finished, went to school. It hosts a changing program of exhibitions on architecture, design, industrial design and art. One of the permanent exhibitions is *Sisu*, a spidsgatter-class yacht designed by Aage Utzon, Utzon's father. A combined ticket including Kunsten costs adult/child Dkr60/free.

Kunsten   MUSEUM

(www.kunsten.dk; Kong Christian Allé 50; adult/child incl Utzon Center Dkr60/free; ⊙10am-5pm Tue-Sun, to 9pm Tue Feb-Apr & Sep-Nov) This regional art museum, in a stark, modular building designed by Finnish architect Alvar Aalto, has a fine collection of Danish modern and contemporary art, including work by Asger Jorn and JF Willumsen. Temporary exhibitions cover both home-grown and foreign talent.

To get to the museum, take the tunnel beneath the train station; it leads to Kildeparken, a green space with statues and water fountains. Go directly through the park, cross Vesterbro and then continue through a wooded area to the museum, a 10-minute walk in all. Alternatively, take bus 15 from the centre of town.

FREE Lindholm Høje   HISTORIC SITE

(⊙dawn-dusk) The Limfjorden (chalk fjord) was a kind of Viking motorway providing easy and speedy access to the Atlantic for longboat raiding parties. It's perhaps not surprising then that by far the most important piece of Aalborg's historical heritage is a predominantly Viking one. The hugely atmospheric Lindholm Høje is a Viking burial ground where nearly 700 graves from the Iron Age and Viking Age are strewn around a hilltop pasture ringed by a wall of tall beech trees. Many of the Viking graves are marked by stones placed in the outline of a Viking ship, with two larger end stones as stem and

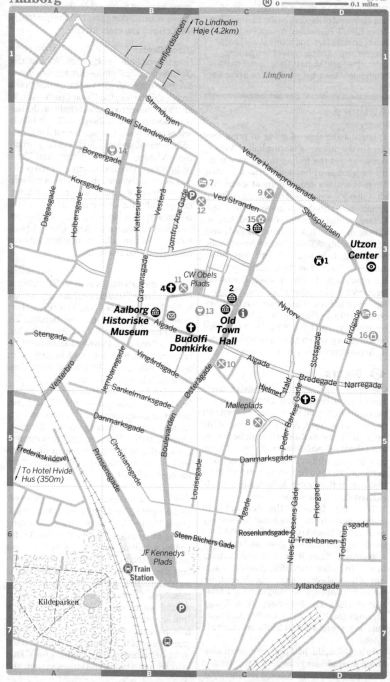

0   200 m
0   0.1 miles

To Lindholm
Høje (4.2km)

Limfjordsbroen

Limfjord

Strandvejen

Gammel Strandvejen

Vestre Havnepromenade

Borgergade 14

Korsgade

Dalgasgade

Holbergsgade

Kattesundet

Vesterå

Jomfru Ane Gade

Ved Stranden 7

9

Slotspladsen

15
3

Utzon
Center

1

Gravensgade

CW Obels
Plads

4 11

2

13

Aalborg
Historiske
Museum

Algade

Old
Town
Hall

Budolfi
Domkirke

Nytorv

Fjordgade 6

16

Stengade

Vesterbro

Vingårdsgade

Jernbanegade

Sankelmarksgade

Østerågade

10

Algade

Hjelmer

Stald

Slotsgade

Bredegade

Nørregade

5

Danmarksgade

Christiansgade

Prinsensgade

Boulevarden

Mølleplads

Peder Barkes Gade

8

Danmarksgade

Frederikskildevej

To Hotel Hvide
Hus (350m)

Louisegade

Agade

Steen Blichers Gade

Rosenlundsgade

Niels Ebbesens Gade

Trækbanen

Priorgade

Toldstrup

sgade

JF Kennedys
Plads

Kildeparken

Train
Station

Jyllandsgade

stern. The museum ([📞]99 31 74 40; adult/child Dkr60/free; [🕐]10am-5pm daily Apr-Oct), adjacent to the field, depicts the site's history, while huge murals behind the exhibits speculate on what the people of Lindholm looked like and how they lived. Lindholm Høje is 15 minutes from Aalborg centre on bus 2.

FREE Kunsthall Nord ART GALLERY
(www.kunstvaerket.dk, in Danish; Nordkraft, Kjellerups Torv 5; [🕐]vary, usually noon-5pm Tue, Thu & Fri, to 8pm Wed, to 3pm Sat & Sun) Located inside a power station-turned-cultural centre, this gallery curates interesting, temporary exhibitions of Danish and international artists. Check the website (in Danish) for upcoming shows.

🛏 Sleeping

Accommodation options are pretty good in town, inexpensive compared with other Danish destinations and not generally in massive demand.

Cab Inn Aalborg HOTEL **€€**
([📞]96 20 30 00; www.cabinn.com; Fjordgade 20; s Dkr615-675; [@]) The cheap and reliable Cab Inn chain recently added Aalborg to its portfolio with this modern, centrally located hotel. All 239 rooms have TV and private bathroom, and the waterfront is a short walk away.

Hotel Hvide Hus HOTEL **€€€**
([📞]98 13 84 00; www.helnan.info, in Danish; Vesterbro 2; s Dkr795-975, d 995-1195) A quick walk from the city centre, this large, modern hotel may not be especially characterful, but its rooms are attractive and modern, the views are superb, and the rates are good for a hotel of this class in Denmark.

🏅Radisson BLU Limfjord HOTEL **€€€**
([📞]98 16 43 33; www.radissonblu.com; Ved Stranden 14-16; s/d Dkr1315/1515) This is the top-end place in town, occupying a grandstand position overlooking the fjord and close to all the main attractions, restaurants and shops. While the rooms could use an update, they remain smart and comfortable. Facilities include free wi-fi, solarium, gym and an Italian restaurant.

Danhostel Aalborg HOSTEL **€**
([📞]98 11 60 44; www.danhostelaalborg.dk; Skydebanevej 50; dm/s/d Dkr288/460/530; [P][@]) Handy for boating activities on the fjord but hardly central, the hostel is at the marina 4km west of the centre. It also runs an adjacent camping ground with cabins. Otherwise the facilities are rather basic.

Aalborg Camping CAMPING GROUND **€**
([📞]98 11 60 44; www.aalborgcamping.dk; Skydebanevej 50; adult/child/tent Dkr50/25/45) This pleasant two-star camping ground is popular with naturists.

🍴 Eating

Eating out in Aalborg is very much a never-mind-the-quality, feel-the-width kind of scenario, and there are precious few genuinely good or original options. A clutch of new places dotted around the town centre caters well enough to all low and midrange budgets and tastes. If it's just ballast you want with your alcohol, then Jomfru Ane Gade, a lively, pedestrian street jammed solid with fast-food-style restaurants and bars, is the place to go.

Mortens Kro
FRENCH, DANISH €€€

(☎98 12 48 60; www.mortenskro.dk; Møllea 4-6; 4/5/6 courses Dkr548/648/748; ☺dinner Mon-Sat) Hands down both the best and priciest place to eat in town, Mortens Kro serves lavish, inventive Franco-Danish fare such as lobster and pumpkin soup with roasted langoustine tails, or veal tenderloin marinated in truffle, cognac and olive oil. Bookings advised, especially in summer.

Mundgott Brasserie
EUROPEAN €€

(www.mundgott.dk, in Danish; Toldbod Plads 2; lunches Dkr68-128, dinner mains Dkr110-245; ☺Mon-Sat) One of the more upmarket places to eat in the centre of town, this spacious, well-run brasserie has a solid kitchen that turns out mostly classic brasserie dishes such as coq au vin, made with chickens from Bornholm. Lunch options are generally lighter.

Penny Lane
CAFE €

(Boulevarden 1; cakes from Dkr35; ☺10am-6pm Mon-Fri, 9.30am-2pm Sat) This is one of the most charming cafes in Jutland, featuring a well-stocked delicatessen, wines, quirky decor (the owner has a collection of more than 5000 English pastry-cutters – 'People are strange,' he shrugs, by way of explanation) and terrific cakes and pastries.

SushiSushi
JAPANESE €€

(www.sushisushi.dk; Ved Stranden 11b; menus Dkr115-220; ☺lunch & dinner Mon-Sat, dinner Sun) Sit and enjoy, or pay and take away terrific, fresh sushi from this small place around the corner from Jomfru Ane Gade.

Pingvin
TAPAS €€

(www.cafepingvin.dk, in Danish; Adelgade 12; tapas platters Dkr178-248, lunch sandwiches & salads Dkr88-98; ☺Mon-Sat) This chic, contemporary wine and tapas bar serves tasty dishes that are perfect for a light meal.

Drinking & Entertainment

If it's a flirt, a drink or loud repetitive beats in the form of banging techno, Euro-rock or house music you're after, trawl Jomfru Ane Gade, Aalborg's take-no-prisoners party street. The venues themselves are pretty homogenous, so it's best to explore until you hear your kind of music.

Wharf
PUB

(Wharf, Borgergade 16; ☺2pm-midnight Mon-Wed, to 1am Thu, noon-2am Fri & Sat, 3-8pm Sun) This

surprising slice of the UK in deepest Jutland is dedicated to cask ale and serves up to 44 different British, Belgian, Irish and German beers the length of its capacious bar. There's also a good selection of rare single-malt whiskies.

Studenterhuset
BAR, LIVE MUSIC

(Student Union; Gammeltorv 10; ☺closed Sun & mid-Jul–mid-Aug) This is a convivial budget drinking and entertainment option. Lined with bookshelves, it's surprisingly upmarket and, well, studious for a students' union. There's inexpensive beer, regular live bands and DJ nights.

Irish House
PUB

(www.theirishhouse.dk; Østerågade 25; ☺1pm-1am Mon-Wed, 1pm-2am Thu, noon-4am Fri & Sat, 2pm-midnight Sun) A lively Irish pub with a convivial atmosphere and live music, mostly on Thursday to Saturday nights.

ⓘ Information

Behind Vor Frue Kirke, **Danish Emigration Archives** (www.emiarch.dk; Arkivstræde 1; ☺10am-4pm Mon-Wed, to 5pm Thu, to 3pm Fri) helps foreigners of Danish descent trace their roots.

Hovedbiblioteket (City library; Rendsburggade 2; ☺10am-7pm Mon-Thu, to 6pm Fri, to 2pm Sat) Free internet access.

Jyske Bank (Nytorv 1)

Post office (Algade 42)

Tourist office (www.visitaalborg.com; Østerågade 8; ☺11am-8pm Mon-Fri, 10am-2pm Sat) Friendly and helpful, with masses of information, including a diary of events, What's on in Aalborg.

ⓘ Getting There & Away

Bus & Train

Trains run to Århus (Dkr171, 1½ hours, at least hourly) and Frederikshavn (Dkr99, one hour, hourly). **Abildskou buses** (www.abildskou.dk) run to Copenhagen (bus 888, Dkr330, 5½ hours, twice daily Sunday to Friday, once daily Saturday).

Car & Motorcycle

The E45 bypasses the city centre, tunnelling under the Limfjord, whereas the connecting Rte 180 leads into the centre. To get to Lindholm Høje or points north from Aalborg centre, take Rte 180 (Vesterbro), which bridges the Limfjord.

Avis (☎70 24 77 40; www.avis.com) is at the train station. **Europcar** (☎98 13 23 55; www.europcar.com; Jyllandsgade 6) is a short distance to the east.

ⓘ Getting Around

City buses leave from the intersection of Østerågade and Nytorv. The bus fare is Dkr18 to any place in greater Aalborg.

Despite a few one-way streets and the often-confusing outer roads that may have you driving in circles, central Aalborg is a fairly easy place to get around by car. There's metered parking in the city centre (Dkr13 to Dkr16 per hour) and time-limited, free parking along many side streets, but you need to use a parking disc. The new **Friis Shopping Centre** (Nytorv) allows three hours of free undercover parking, though you will still need to validate your ticket at the automated pay machine before exiting.

Frederikshavn

POP 23,300

A transport hub rather than a compelling destination, the bustling port town of Frederikshavn nevertheless has a certain appeal, a couple of interesting sights and a pleasant enough pedestrianised centre.

◉ Sights

Bangsbo   MUSEUM, NATURE

It's well worth exploring this area, about 3km from the centre on the southern edge of town. The main drawcard is **Bangsbo Museum** (www.bangsbo.com; Margrethesvej 6; adult/child Dkr50/free; ⊙10am-4pm Mon-Fri, 11am-4pm Sat & Sun), an old country estate with an interesting mix of exhibits. The manor house displays antique furnishings and collectables, while the old farm buildings hold ship figureheads, military paraphernalia and exhibits on Danish resistance to the German occupation. The most intriguing exhibit is the Ellingå ship, reconstructed remains of a 12th-century Viking-style merchant ship that was dug up from a nearby stream bed. Bus 3 from central Frederikshavn stops near the entrance to the estate, from where it's an enjoyable 500m walk through the woods to the museum. The adjoining **Bangsbo Botanisk Have** (Botanical Gardens) has a deer park and is a pleasant place to stroll or enjoy a picnic.

Bangsbo Fort (Understedvej 21; adult/child Dkr50/free; ⊙10am-4pm Mon-Fri, 11am-4pm Sat & Sun Jun-Sep, closed Oct-May), about 800m over the wooded ridge from the gardens, is an atmospheric WWII bunker complex housing some big guns and commanding wonderful views across to Frederikshavn and out to sea.

(Kragholmen 1; adult/child Dkr15/free; ⊙10am-4pm Tue-Fri, 11am-4pm Sun Jun-Aug) The white-washed Krudttårnet is a striking old gun tower and powder magazine that once formed part of the 17th-century citadel that protected the port. Various pieces of artillery are on display at the top.

🛌 Sleeping

Unsurprisingly, given the captive custom of those awaiting onward connections, good-value sleeping options are limited, prices higher and standards lower here compared with other towns in the region. The tourist office books rooms in private homes from Dkr175/350 for singles/doubles, plus a Dkr50 booking fee.

Hotel Herman Bang   HOTEL €€€

(✆98 42 21 66; www.hermanbang.dk, in Danish; Tordenskjoldsgade 3; s/d Dkr595/795, s/d with bathroom from Dkr795/995; @) The mid-priced rooms here are bright and comfortable, the most expensive are huge, new and luxurious. Avoid the cheapest, which are bland, need new carpets and generally offer poor value. There's an upmarket spa next door for beauty and relaxation treatments.

Danhostel Frederikshavn   HOSTEL €

(✆98 42 14 75; www.danhostel.dk/frederikshavn; Buhlsvej 6; dm/s/d Dkr100/350/400; ⊙Feb-Nov; P) A pleasant place with chalet-style, six-bed dorms located 2km north of the ferry terminal.

🍴 Eating

Numerous, mainly fast-food, places line central Danmarkgade.

Møllehuset   CAFE, RESTAURANT €€

(Skovalléen 45; lunches Dkr85-185, dinner mains Dkr185-205; ⊙11am-9pm Tue-Sat, to 5pm Mon & Sun) An appealing cafe and restaurant in a leafy setting across the roundabout from the botanic gardens, serving simple fresh lunches – such as homemade fish crépinettes, and good cheese platters – along with more polished dinners.

Frank's   RESTAURANT €€€

(✆98 42 22 88; www.franks.dk, in Danish; Silovej 8; lunches Dkr79-159, dinner mains Dkr200; ⊙Tue-Sat) Towering nine storeys above the port's gritty industrial heart in a former grain silo, Frank's offers a thrilling bird's-eye view of the dockside loading, unloading and maritime comings and goings. The fine-dining menu doesn't always live up to the views but is strong on fish. Book ahead to bag a window seat.

Super Best SUPERMARKET €
(Læsøgade 16; ⊙8am-7pm Mon-Fri, 7.30am-6pm Sat & Sun) Next to the tourist office, this supermarket is a good place to pick up provisions, especially if you're going on to expensive Norway.

❶ Information

An overhead walkway leads from the ferry terminal to the **tourist office** (☑98 42 32 66; www.visitfrederikshavn.dk; Skandiatorv 1; ⊙9am-4pm Mon-Sat, 10am-1pm Sun late Jun-early Aug).

❶ Getting There & Away

The train station and adjacent bus terminal are a 10-minute walk north of the tourist office.

Boat

From Frederikshavn **Stena Line** (☑96 20 02 00; www.stenaline.dk, in Danish) runs ferries four to eight times daily (adult/child four to 14 years from Dkr100/70, car with five passengers from Dkr460, two to 3½ hours) to Göteborg, Sweden.

Train

Frederikshavn is the northern terminus of the DSB train line. Trains run about hourly south to Aalborg (Dkr99) and then onto Copenhagen (Dkr393). **Nordjyske Jernbaner** (www.njba. dk, in Danish) runs trains to Skagen (Dkr54) hourly on weekdays and roughly every two hours on weekends. Trains to Hirtshals (Dkr63) run roughly every hour.

Skagen

POP 8600

Skagen is a magical place, both bracing and beautiful. If you are driving from the south, to get there you pass through kilometre after kilometre of, well, pretty much nothing really, until first pine forests and then an extraordinary landscape of grassy sand dunes herald this popular vacation region. The town of Skagen (pronounced 'skane') is a busy working harbour and is Denmark's northernmost settlement, just a couple of kilometres from the dramatic sandy spit where the country finally peters out at Grenen, a slender point of wave-washed sand, where seals bask and seagulls soar.

Artists discovered Skagen's luminous light and its colourful, wind-blasted, heath-and-dune landscape in the mid-19th century

and fixed eagerly on the romantic imagery of the area's fishing life that had earned the people of Skagen a hard living for centuries. Painters such as Michael and Anna Ancher and Oscar Björck followed the contemporary fashion of painting *en plein air* (out of doors), often regardless of the weather. Their work established a vivid figurative style of painting that became known internationally as the 'Skagen School'.

Today, Skagen is a very popular tourist resort, which is completely packed during high summer. But the sense of a more picturesque Skagen survives and the town's older neighbourhood, Gammel Skagen, 5km west, is filled with distinctive, single-storey, yellow-walled (they're traditionally painted every Whitsuntide with lime and ochre), red-roofed houses.

The peninsula is lined with fine beaches, including a sandy stretch on the eastern end of Østre Strandvej, a 15-minute walk from the town centre.

The Skagen music festival (www.skagen festival.dk, in Danish) packs the town out with official performers, buskers and appreciative visitors during the last weekend of June.

◉ Sights

Grenen NATURE AREA
Appropriately for such a neatly kept country, Denmark doesn't end untidily at its northernmost point, but on a neat finger of sand just a few metres wide. You can actually paddle at its tip where the waters of the Kattegat and Skagerrak clash and you can put one foot in each sea; but not too far. Bathing is strictly forbidden here because of the ferocious tidal currents and often turbulent seas that collide to create mane-tossing white horses.

The tip is the culmination of a long, curving sweep of sand at Grenen, about 3km northeast of Skagen along Rte 40. Where the road ends there's a car park, cafe-restaurant, souvenir shop plus, in high summer, what seems like the entire population of Denmark. Crowds head along the last stretch of beach for the 30-minute walk to the tip. From Easter to October, a special tractor-drawn bus, the *Sandormen,* leaves from the car park every half-hour, waits for 15 minutes at the beach end, then returns (adult/child return Dkr20/10). From late June to early August, buses run from Skagen station to Grenen hourly (Dkr15) five times daily until 5pm. Taxis, available at the train station, charge about Dkr75 to Grenen.

Skagens Museum   MUSEUM
(www.skagensmuseum.dk; Brøndumsvej 4; adult/child Dkr80/free; ☺10am-5pm Thu-Tue, to 9pm Wed May-Aug, closed Jan) This fine museum showcases the paintings of Michael and Anna Ancher, PS Krøyer, and of other artists who flocked to Skagen between 1830 and 1930, many of them kitchen-sink portraits of the lives and deaths of the fishing community.

Tilsandede Kirke   NATURE AREA
(adult/child Dkr10/5; ☺11am-5pm Jun-Sep) This whitewashed medieval church tower still rises above the sand dunes that buried the church and surrounding farms in the late 18th century. The tower, in a nature reserve, is 5km south of Skagen and well signposted from Rte 40. By bike, take Gammel Landevej from Skagen.

Råbjerg Mile   NATURE AREA
These undulating 40m-high hills comprise Denmark's largest expanse of shifting dunes and are great fun to explore. Råbjerg Mile is 16km south of Skagen, off Rte 40 on the road to Kandestederne. From May to September, bus 99 runs six times a day from Skagen station (Dkr18, 25 minutes).

Michael & Anna Ancher's Hus   MUSEUM
(www.anchershus.dk; Markvej 2-4; adult/child Dkr70/free; ☺10am-5pm daily May-Sep) This poignant domestic museum occupies the house that the Anchers bought in 1884 and in which their daughter Helga lived until 1960.

🛏 Sleeping
Hotel accommodation can be scarce at summer weekends, especially during the Skagen Festival at the end of June and in weeks 28 and 29 (mid-July), when Denmark's VIP party crowd hits town to party. The tourist office books singles/doubles in private homes for around Dkr300/425, plus a Dkr75 booking fee for the first night and Dkr25 for subsequent nights.

Marienlund Badepension   GUESTHOUSE €€
(☎98 44 13 20; www.marienlund.dk; Fabriciusvej 8; s/d Dkr595/995) A modern, comfortable, immaculately kept place that is situated on the quieter western side of town near the open-air museum.

Grenen Camping   CAMPING GROUND €
(☎98 44 25 46; www.grenencamping.dk; Fyrvej 16; adult/child Dkr85/50) A fine seaside location, semiprivate campsites and pleasant four-bunk huts, 1.5km northeast of Skagen centre. The only downside is the rather tightly bunched sites.

Danhostel Skagen   HOSTEL €
(☎98 44 22 00; www.danhostel.dk/skagen; Rolighedsvej 2; dm Dkr150, s/d Dkr500/600; ☺mid-Feb–Nov; P) Well kept, very popular and 1km from the centre; book ahead in summer. Rates drop sharply in low season.

Skagen Sømandshjem   HOTEL €€
(☎98 44 25 88; Østre Strandvej 2; s/d Dkr615/975, without bathroom Dkr515/795) A harbourside hotel that has simple, comfy rooms.

🍴 Eating & Drinking
Around half a dozen seafood shacks line the harbour selling good seafood to eat inside, outside or takeaway. Freshly caught prawns are the favourite fare, costing around Dkr95 for a generous helping. Here you'll also find a bakery.

You'll find a couple of pizzerias, Mexican restaurants, a burger joint and an ice-cream shop clustered near each other on Havnevej. The supermarket **Super Brugsen** (Sankt Laurentii Vej 28) has a bakery.

Ruths Hotel   FRENCH, DANISH €€€
(☎98 44 11 24; www.ruths-hotel.dk; Hans Ruths Vej 1; brasserie mains Dkr130-265; gourmet 3/4/5 courses Dkr650/750/950; ☺brasserie yr-round, gourmet restaurant Apr–mid-Oct) This is one of Denmark's grand bathing hotels, beautifully modernised and close to the beach. It also has two excellent restaurants, overseen by French chef Michel Michaud, formerly of Falsled Kro. The brasserie is lighter and cheaper, with dishes such as home-smoked salmon, snails, rib eye and oysters, while **Ruths Gourmet** is more formal, with titanic dishes like pigeon cassoulet.

Brøndum's Hotel   FRENCH, DANISH €€
(☎98 44 15 55; www.broendums-hotel.dk, in Danish; Anchersvej 3; lunches Dkr125-195, dinner mains Dkr180-300) French cuisine is the main influence on the otherwise classic Danish dishes, with lots of fresh seafood such as lobster and turbot, as well as tenderloin and chateaubriand. Meals are served in the old-world ambience of the cosy dining room and, in the warmer months, a picture-perfect garden. Rooms (single/double Dkr850/1350) were fully renovated in 2008.

Restaurant Pakhuset   DANISH, EUROPEAN **€€**

(Rødspættevej 6; light lunches Dkr80-125, mains Dkr195-220) There's a mix of great fresh fish mains and cheaper light lunches (such as fish cakes with remoulade, cranberry compote and salad for Dkr90). It has long hours and a superb ambience both outdoors (right among the bustle of the harbour) and indoors (a lovely wooden-beamed interior sprinkled with jovial ship mastheads). Its downstairs cafe offers cheaper dishes.

Jakobs   CAFE, RESTAURANT **€€**

(Havnevej 4; dinner mains Dkr185-220) Jakobs is a popular restaurant on Skagen's busy main street. It does good homemade brunches (Dkr58 to Dkr115), salads and pasta (Dkr75 to Dkr125). By night it's a popular bar staging live music at weekends (usually cover bands).

Buddy Holly's   BAR, CLUB

(Havnevej 16) There's nothing cutting edge or elegant about Buddy Holly's, but the predictable sonic menu of dance and disco classics from the '70s, '80s and '90s gets a 30- and 40-something crowd up and dancing.

ℹ Information

Sankt Laurentii Vej, Skagen's main street, runs almost the entire length of this long thin town, and is never more than five minutes from the waterfront.

Tourist office (☎98 44 13 77; www.skagen -tourist.dk; Vestre Strandvej 10; ⊘9am-4pm Mon-Sat, 10am-2pm Sun late Jun-late Aug) is by the harbour.

ℹ Getting There & Away

Nordjyske Jernbaner (www.njba.dk, in Danish) runs trains to Frederikshavn (Dkr54, 35 minutes, once or twice hourly on weekdays, every two hours on weekends). Bus 99 runs between Hirtshals and Skagen (Dkr45, one hour 20 minutes, two to four daily) from late June to early August only. The same bus continues on to Hjørring and Løkken.

ℹ Getting Around

Cycling is an excellent way of exploring Skagen and the surrounding area. Close to the tourist office, **Cykelhandler** (Vestre Strandvej 4; per day Dkr70) rents out bicycles through the liquor shop next door.

Skagen is very busy with traffic in high season. There is little free parking but you will find convenient car parks (Dkr12 per hour, free between 6pm and 9am) by the harbour; one between the tourist office and the waterfront, the other just to the left of the tourist office.

Hirtshals

POP 6300

A busy, modern little town thanks to a large commercial fishing harbour and ferry terminal, Hirtshals has an easy, friendly character, an excellent aquarium and some fine stretches of beach, although its looks aren't likely to take your breath away. The main street, pedestrianised Nørregade, is lined with a mix of cafes and shops, and with supermarkets that cater to Norwegian shoppers piling off the ferries to load up with relatively cheap Danish meats and groceries. The seaward end of Nørregade opens out into a wide, airy space, Den Grønne Plads (Green Square), which overlooks the fishing harbour and its tiers of blue-hulled boats.

⊙ Sights

In the surrounding area there are coastal cliffs and a lighthouse on the town's western side. If you want beaches, there's a lovely unspoiled stretch at Tornby Strand, 5km south.

Nordsøen Oceanarium   AQUARIUM

(www.nordsoenoceanarium.dk; Willemoesvej 2; adult/child Dkr145/70; ⊘9am-6pm daily Jul & Aug, to 5pm daily Apr-Jun, Sep & Oct, closed Jan) Hirtshals' big draw is this impressive aquarium that recreates a slice of the North Sea in a massive four-storey tank, containing elegantly balletic schools of thousands of fish. Divers feed the fish at 1pm and the seals at 11am and 3pm.

🛏 Sleeping & Eating

Staff at the tourist office can book rooms in private homes from around Dkr150/250 per single/double, plus a Dkr50 booking fee.

There are cafes at the northern end of Hjørringgade, and there are also a couple of pizza and kebab places on Nørregade.

Danhostel Hirtshals   HOSTEL **€**

(☎98 94 12 48; www.danhostelnord.dk/hirtshals; Kystvejen 53; dm/s/d Dkr150/400/520; ⊘Mar-Oct; ℗) Occupying a bland building and offering basic facilities about 1km from the centre, the saving grace of this hostel is its location a bucket and spade's throw from the beach.

Hotel Hirtshals   HOTEL **€€**

(☎98 94 20 77; www.hotelhirtshals.dk; Havnegade 2; s/d Dkr795/895) On the main square above the fishing harbour, the Hirtshals has bright, comfortable rooms with high, steepled ceilings and good sea views at the front.

Hirtshals Kro
DANISH €€

(Havnegade; lunches Dkr55-189, dinner mains Dkr148-228) A delightful restaurant in a very old *kro* that has retained its character. Not surprisingly, the menu offers several tasty seafood dishes, including a mixed fish plate for Dkr208.

❶ Information

Tourist office (☏98 94 22 20; www.visithirt shals.com; Nørregade 40; ⊙9am-4pm Mon-Sat Jun-Aug).

❶ Getting There & Away

Boat

Color Line (☏99 56 19 77; www.colorline.com) runs year-round ferries to the following towns in Norway:

Larvik 3¾ hours, once or twice daily

Kristiansand three to four hours, once or twice daily

Fares on both routes range from Dkr200/100 per adult/child midweek in the low season to Dkr500/250 on summer weekends for passengers, Dkr310 to Dkr660 for cars.

Fjord Line (☏97 96 30 00; www.fjordline.dk) runs year-round ferries to the following ports in Norway:

Bergen adult/car with five passengers from Dkr261/1232, 19¼ hours, three times weekly

Stavanger adult/car with five passengers from Dkr130/765, 11½ hours, four times weekly

From mid-April to mid-September, Fjord Line also runs a high-speed catamaran to Kristiansand in Norway (adult/car with five passengers Dkr139/532, 2¼ hours, twice daily). **Smyril Line** (in Denmark ☏96 55 03 60, in Faroe Islands 345 900; www.smyril-line.com) connects Hirtshals to Tórshavn (Faroe Islands) and Seyðisfjörður (Iceland) via the ferry *Norröna*. Seyðisfjörður from €114, 13 hours, once weekly (Apr-Oct only). Tórshavn from €97, seven hours, once weekly.

Bus

From late June to early August a **bus** (☏72 30 80 49) from Hirtshals station to Hjørring (Dkr27) stops en route at Tornby Strand four times a day.

Train

Hirtshals' main train station is 500m south of the ferry harbour. There is a second stop near the Color Line terminal. The privately run line connects Hirtshals with Hjørring (Dkr24, 20 min-

utes). Trains run at least hourly. From Hjørring you can take a DSB train to Aalborg (Dkr81, 45 minutes, once or twice hourly) or Frederikshavn (Dkr54, 30 minutes, once or twice hourly).

Esbjerg

POP 71,500

As with many industrial ports, most visitors to Esbjerg rush through as quickly as possible. That said, there are attractive parts to this interesting town, as well as one or two excellent attractions. Esbjerg is the centre of Denmark's extensive North Sea oil activities and in recent years the export of wind turbines has replaced the fishing industry as a major source of income. Although Esbjerg has its fair share of early 20th-century buildings, if period charm is what you're after then head straight to nearby Ribe.

⊙ Sights & Activities

Esbjerg Kunstmuseum
MUSEUM

(Havnegade 20; adult/child Dkr50/free; ⊙10am-4pm) The single most worthwhile place to visit in town is the Esbjerg Kunstmuseum, an impressive gallery with an important collection of Danish modern art, including work by Asger Jorn.

Esbjerg Museum
MUSEUM

(Torvegade 45; adult/child Dkr30/free, admission free Wed; ⊙10am-4pm daily Jun–mid-Sep) Also in the town centre, the small Esbjerg Museum contains a few historical artefacts from the area and an amber display, offering a short diversion if it's raining.

🛏 Sleeping

There's a good range of reasonably priced accommodation in town. The tourist office books rooms in private homes at around Dkr210/330 for singles/doubles.

Ådalens Camping
CAMPING GROUND €

(☏75 15 88 22; www.adal.dk; Gudenåvej 20; campsites adult/child Dkr75/47; 🐾) The nearest camping to Esbjerg (5km north of the city via bus 1 or 7), this place has great facilities including a pool, solarium and jacuzzi.

Cab Inn Esbjerg
HOTEL €€€

(☏75 18 16 00; www.cabinn.com; Skolegade14; s Dkr750-895, d Dkr1010-1130; 🅿@) Clean, functional but good-value, cabin-style rooms (with small dimensions and rather narrow bunk beds) right in the centre. The superior rooms are larger and less clinical. Free internet access.

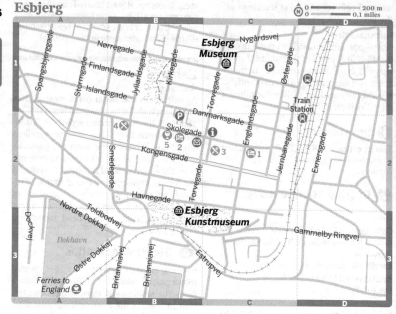

Esbjerg

Esbjerg Museum

Esbjerg Kunstmuseum

Ferries to England

Danhostel Esbjerg
HOSTEL €

(☎75 12 42 58; www.danhostel.dk/esbjerg; Gammel Vardevej 80; dm Dkr180, s/d Dkr500/600, without bathroom Dkr350/480; ⊙Feb–mid-Dec; ℗) Occupying a handsome former high school 3km northwest of the city centre, this hostel is close to sports facilities including a pool. Take bus 4.

Hotel Ansgar
HOTEL €€€

(☎75 12 82 44; www.hotelansgar.dk; Skolegade 36; s Dkr750-850, d Dkr1050-1150; ℗@) Ansgar offers large, comfortable rooms decorated in simple classic Scandinavian style.

✖ Eating & Drinking

Most restaurants and grocery stores are east of Torvet on Kongensgade.

Sand's Restaurant
DANISH €€

(www.sands.dk, in Danish; Skolegade 60; lunches Dkr49-169, mains Dkr109-229) You'll find superb, authentic Danish staples such as smørrebrød, Danish hash, meatballs, smoked eel and *pariserbof* (a fried beef patty on bread with a raw egg yolk, pickles and fresh horseradish) in this cosy, old-fashioned dining room.

Dronning Louise
CAFE, RESTAURANT €€

(www.dr-louise.dk, in Danish; Torvet 19; lunches Dkr49-100, mains Dkr130-245) This jack-of-all-trades place turns out decent salads, bagels and burgers for under Dkr110, as well as slightly more ambitious brasserie fare and pastries from the cafe counter. There's a disco upstairs on Friday and Saturday nights, with tunes spanning Top 40 pop to commercial dance.

Paddy Go Easy
PUB

(Skolegade 42) A friendly Irish pub actually run by Irish proprietors, just off the main square.

ℹ Information

Central Library (Nørregade 19; ⊙10am-7pm Mon-Thu, to 5pm Fri, to 2pm Sat) Free internet access.

Danske Bank (Torvet 18)

Post office (Torvet 20)

Tourist office (☎75 12 55 99; www.visitesbjerg.com; Skolegade 33; ⊙10am-5pm Mon-Fri, to 2.30pm Sat Jul & Aug).

ℹ Getting There & Away

DFDS Seaways (www.dfdsseaways.co.uk) sails from Esbjerg to Harwich (UK) at least twice a week.

Esbjerg

◎ **Top Sights**

Esbjerg Kunstmuseum B3
Esbjerg Museum.................................C1

◎ **Sleeping**

1 Cab Inn Esbjerg......................................C2
2 Hotel Ansgar..B2

◎ **Eating**

3 Dronning Louise.....................................C2
4 Sand's Restaurant..............................B2

◎ **Drinking**

5 Paddy Go Easy B2

If you're driving into Esbjerg from the east, the E20 leads into the city centre. If you're coming from the south, Rte 24 merges with the E20 on the city outskirts. From the north, Rte 12 makes a beeline into the city, ending at the harbour.

Trains to Copenhagen (Dkr339, 2¼ hours, hourly) run until 9.41pm.

❶ Getting Around

Most city-bound buses (Dkr18) call at the train station. Parking is free in Esbjerg. There's also a convenient car park on Danmarksgade, but it has a two-hour limit; some unlimited parking is available in the car park on Nørregade, east of the library.

Legoland

Children under 12 years of age will love Legoland (www.legoland.dk; adult/3-13 yr Dkr279/249; ⊙Apr-Oct, see website for times), a theme park dedicated to the little plastic blocks from which many of the miniature cities, interactive play areas, safari animals, pirates, princesses, astronauts, Vikings and other displays and attractions here are built. There are some excellent younger children's amusement rides, but for wilder rides suited to older children and adults, Legoland compares unfavourably to Copenhagen's Tivoli. The rides close one or two hours before the park does.

Legoland is 63km northeast of Esbjerg. Bus 913X (www.xbus.dk, in Danish) connects Esbjerg to Legoland (adult/child Dkr84/56, 65 minutes, five daily on weekdays, two daily on Saturday, three daily on Sunday) and Århus beyond.

Ribe

POP 8200

The charming crooked, cobblestone streets of Ribe date from AD 869, making it one of Scandinavia's oldest and Denmark's most attractive towns. It is a delightful chocolate-box confection of half-timbered, 16th-century houses, clear-flowing streams and water meadows. Almost everything, including the hostel and train station, is within a 10-minute walk of Torvet, the town square, which is dominated by the huge Romanesque cathedral.

◉ Sights & Activities

For a pleasant stroll that takes in some of Ribe's handsome half-timbered buildings and winding cobbled lanes, head along any of the streets radiating out from Torvet, in particular Puggårdsgade or Grønnegade, from where narrow alleys lead down and across Fiskegarde to Skibbroen and the picturesque old harbour.

Ribe Domkirke   CHURCH
(Torvet; steeple adult/child Dkr10/5; ⊙10am-5pm Mon-Fri, 10am-5.30pm Sat, noon-5.30pm Sun) Dominating the heart of the town, Ribe Domkirke boasts a variety of hugger-mugger styles from Romanesque to Gothic. The cathedral's monumental presence is literally sunk into the heart of Ribe. The highlight is the climb up the steeple for breathtaking views.

Ribes Vikinger   MUSEUM
(www.ribesvikinger.dk; Odins Plads 1; adult/child Dkr60/free; ⊙10am-6pm Jul & Aug, to 4pm Apr-Jun, Sep & Oct) Ribes Vikinger is a substantial museum opposite the train station; it has archaeological displays of Ribe's Viking past, including a reconstructed marketplace and Viking ship, with lots of hands-on features.

Ribe Vikingecenter   MUSEUM
(www.ribevikingecenter.dk; Lustrupvej 4; adult/child Dkr90/45; ⊙11am-5pm daily mid-Jun–Aug, 10am-3.30pm Mon-Fri May–mid-Jun & Sep–end Oct) Located 3km south of the centre, this recreated Viking village is complete with working artisans and interpreters decked out in period costumes. There are hands-on activities, such as woodwork and archery, to take part in during May and August, and there are plenty of ponies to pet. Bus 717 (Dkr20) will take you there from Ribe.

Old Town Hall   MUSEUM
(adult/child Dkr15/free; ☺1-5pm daily Jun-Aug,
1-5pm Mon-Fri mid–end May & early–mid-Sep)
The town also has a couple of interesting
local-history museums, including one at
the Old Town Hall, the former debtors' prison, displaying a small arsenal of viciously
spiked medieval weaponry and the formidable axe of the town executioner.

Night Watchman   TOUR
There isn't any new-fangled CCTV fad in
Ribe; instead, a costumed night watchman
takes care of security, making the rounds
from Torvet at 10pm from May to mid-
September (also at 8pm June to August).
You can follow him for free as he sings his
way through the old streets.

Ribe Kunstmuseum   MUSEUM
(www.ribe-kunstmuseum.dk; Sankt Nicolajgade 10;
adult/child Dkr70/free; ☺10am-5pm Thu-Tue, to
8pm Wed Jul & Aug) Ribe Kunstmuseum has a
fine collection of 19th-century Golden Age
and Silver Age Danish art, including Ludvig
Abelin Schou's dramatic *Death of Chione*.

🛏 Sleeping

The tourist office maintains a list of singles/
doubles in private homes from around
Dkr300/400.

Weis Stue   HOTEL €
(☎75 42 07 00; www.weisstue.dk; Torvet; s/d
Dkr395/495) This is the poorer, quirkier but
no less charming alternative to the Dagmar
opposite. A small, ancient wooden-beamed
house, it has rather small, crooked rooms
right above its restaurant, but they have
bags of character. The restaurant offers
hearty plates of herring, salmon or meatballs (Dkr139 to Dkr245) in delightfully
cosy wooden dining rooms.

📝 Danhostel Ribe   HOSTEL €
(☎75 42 06 20; www.danhostel-ribe.dk; Sankt
Pedersgade 16; dm Dkr170, s Dkr340-580, d
Dkr380-580; ☺mid-Feb–mid-Dec; P) The modern, 170-bed hostel has friendly staff and
a good, uncrowded location. The rooms at
the top are especially appealing and worth
the extra cost. In July, a bed in a larger
dorm (with shared bathroom) will set you
back Dkr120.

Ribe Byferie   RESORT €€€
(☎79 88 79 88; www.ribe-byferie.dk; Damvej 34;
apt for 2-4 people Dkr945-1995; P) This unusual
development consists of several terraces of
new-built, self-catering cottages, to the south
west of the town centre. It is, in effect, a holiday centre within the town and perfect for
families of up to seven. There is a children's
club, canoes and bicycles to rent, various
other sports facilities and, of course, all the
various attractions within Ribe itself.

Hotel Dagmar   HOTEL €€€
(☎75 42 00 33; www.hoteldagmar.dk, in Danish;
Torvet; s/d from Dkr1045/1245) The central
Hotel Dagmar claims to be the oldest
hotel in Denmark; it has plush (if mostly
rather small) rooms and a great period
atmosphere.

🍴 Eating & Drinking

Sælhunden   DANISH €€
(Skibbroen 13; mains Dkr115-225; ☺11am-9.30pm
mid-May–Aug) This cosy, old restaurant is
right on the quayside. Look out for a West
Jutland speciality called *bakskuld* (Dkr85),
consisting of dried, salted and smoked dab
(flatfish) served with rye bread. A tasty lunch
of herring or smoked ham costs Dkr99; it's
also a good spot for a coffee and (if you're
lucky) crêpes.

Vægterkælderen   EUROPEAN €€
(Torvet; mains Dkr160-175) The basement
restaurant in the Hotel Dagmar shares a
kitchen with the hotel's classy upstairs restaurant but it has cheaper dishes, including good steaks and fresh fish.

Café Valdemar   CAFE, BAR
(Sct Nicolajgade 6; ☺1-7pm Tue, to 11pm Wed,
to 2am Thu, to 5am Fri, 3pm-5am Sat) This
buzzing cafe and bar offers frequent live
music, youthful flirting and, most attractive of all, a waterside terrace in the heart
of the old town.

ℹ Information

Danske Bank (Saltgade 10-14)
Post office (Sct Nicolaj Gade)
Tourist office (☎75 42 15 00; www.visitribe.
dk; Torvet 3; ☺9am-6pm Mon-Fri, 10am-5pm
Sat, to 2pm Sun Jul & Aug)

ℹ Getting There & Away

There are trains from Esbjerg to Ribe (Dkr60, 40
minutes, once or twice hourly) and from Århus
to Ribe (Dkr244, two hours 40 minutes, hourly).

Fanø

POP 3200

If Esbjerg has one silver lining, it is that one of the treasures of the Danish Wadden Sea – famed for its seals, birdlife and recently declared national park status – is just a short ferry ride away. The island of Fanø, a popular holiday island for Danes and Germans, pulls in the punters with its picture-postcard villages; stunning, broad, endless sandy beaches; and lively summer-season atmosphere. Its two fishing villages, at either end of the island, Nordby (to the north is the main town, where the majority of the islanders live) and Sønderho (on the southern tip), are exceptionally pretty, assiduously preserved jumbles of historic thatched cottages in which time seems to have stood still for the past century or three. Sønderho in particular is one of Denmark's most charming villages. It dates from the 16th century and has more than a hint of Middle Earth to its low-level, half-timbered thatched houses.

Fanø, 16km long and only 5km at its widest point, was once home to the largest fleet outside Copenhagen, and over a period of 150 years was the site for the construction of more than 1000 vessels. In 1741 the Danish king, Christian VI, was forced to sell the island to raise money for the public coffers.

◎ Sights & Activities

Beaches
BEACH

Families and water-sports fans come to Fanø above all else for the magnificent beaches – the best of which are around Rindby Strand, Sønderho and Fanø Bad (Denmark's first international seaside resort). All three villages have shops and restaurants. Further north is the vast and breathtaking sand spit, Søren Jessens Sand. The interior of the island features Fanø Klitplantage, a protected nature reserve that is richly rewarding for ornithologists. Amber hunters also flock to the island to hunt along Fanø's beaches.

Museums
MUSEUM

Fanø Skibsfarts og Dragtsamling (www.fanoskibs-dragt.dk; Hovedgaden 28, Nordby; adult/child Dkr25/5; ⊙11am-4pm Mon-Sat May-Sep) is a small museum that covers the nautical history of this ancient fishing island.

Fanø Museum (www.fanomuseerne.dk, in Danish; Skolevej 2, Nordby; adult/child Dkr25/5; ⊙11am-2pm Mon-Sat Jun & early–mid-Sep, 11am-4pm Mon-Fri Jul & Aug) is housed in a 300-year-old building and is a companion museum to the Skibsfarts og Dragtsamling. It covers the rest of the island's history and boasts a particularly good collection of period furniture.

Fanø Kunstmuseum (www.fanoekunst museum.dk; Nordland 5, Sønderho; adult/child Dkr30/15; ⊙2-5pm Tue-Sat, 11am-5pm Sun Jun-Aug) features paintings from the 19th and early 20th century by Fanø artists and other Danish artists who have been inspired by the timeless lifestyle and wonderful light of the island.

Fanø Golf Links
GOLF

(www.fanoe-golf-links.dk; Golfvejen 5, Fanø Bad; 18 holes Dkr340) Fanø Golf Links is Denmark's only links course and offers an – often literally – breathtaking 18 holes beside the sea. You can rent equipment, but booking is advised during the summer.

🛏 Sleeping & Eating

There are seven campsites on Fanø, virtually all within a short walk of the coast. For more information see www.visitfanoe.dk. There are supermarkets in shops in all the main villages on the island.

For rental of holiday homes or apartments, from historic thatched cottages, to modern summer houses, contact **Fanø Hus** (☎75 16 26 00; www.fanohus.dk, in Danish & German; Hovedgaden 12, Nordby).

There is a small supermarket, **Merko** (Kirkevejen 32), in Rindby, with an in-house baker and butcher.

TOP CHOICE **Sønderho Kro**
GUESTHOUSE €€€

(☎75 16 40 09; www.sonderhokro.dk; Kropladsen 11, Sønderho; d Dkr1100-1800; ℗) The loveliest place to stay on the island (and renowned around the country) is this thatched inn dating from 1722; its 14 individually decorated rooms are filled with charming local antiques. The inn also has a notable gourmet restaurant (lunch Dkr118 to Dkr 168, dinner three/seven courses Dkr460/750), which serves local lamb, seafood and other seasonal Danish offerings in a refined, French style.

Fanø Rogeri
SMOKE-HOUSE €€

(www.fanoeroegeri.dk; Postvejen 16, Rindby; dinner mains Dkr175-200; ⊙lunch & dinner Tue-Sat, lunch Sun Jun-mid-Aug) Salmon, shellfish, eel and herring are among the delicacies smoked on the premises and served in the garden during the summer. The fantastic lunch buffet (Dkr149; Tuesday, Saturday and Sunday) and dinner buffet (Dkr189; Tuesday and Sunday) are particularly good value. There is a delicatessen here too, selling meats, wine, cheese, charcuterie and fish to go.

Hotel Fanø Badeland RESORT **€€€**
(☑75 16 60 00; www.fanoebadeland.dk; Strand-vejen 52, Fanø Bad; apt Dkr1024-1635; **P**) This holiday centre has modern self-catering apartments beside the beach, with an indoor swimming pool and tennis court, massage service and restaurant. Rates drop significantly after the first night.

ℹ Information

Tourist office (☑70 26 42 00; www.visitfanoe. dk; Færgevej 1, Nordby; ⏰10am-5pm Mon-Fri, 10am-2pm Sat Apr-Jun, Sep & Oct, 9am-5pm Mon-Fri, 10am-4pm Sat & Sun Jul & Aug) Close to the harbour in Nordby.

ℹ Getting There & Around

You can rent bicycles in Nordby from **Fanø Cykler** (www.fanoecykler.dk; Hovedgaden 96, Nordby & Kirkevejen 67, Rindby; per day Dkr50) and from **Unika Cykler** (www.unikacykler.dk, in Danish; Mellemgaden 12, Fanø; per day Dkr75).

Fanø Færgen (☑70 23 15 15; www.fanoefaer-gen.dk; car May-Oct/Nov-Apr incl passengers Dkr380/275, adult/child yr-round Dkr 35/20) ferries depart from Esbjerg for Nordby at least once an hour (more during summer) from 5am to midnight (to around 2.15am on Friday and Saturday nights). The trip takes 12 minutes.

Once on the island, there is a limited local bus service connecting Nordby with Fanø Bad, Rindby Strand and Sønderho.

UNDERSTAND DENMARK

History

Humble Hunters to Mighty Vikings

First settled around 4000 BC, most prob-ably by prehistoric hunter-gatherers from the south, Denmark has been at the centre of Scandinavian civilisation ever since, and there are plenty of reminders of that past in the shape of the ancient burial chambers that pepper the countryside and the traces of fortifications at, for example, Trelleborg.

The Danes themselves are thought to have migrated south from Sweden in around AD 500 but it was their descendants of who were initially a peaceful, farming people who

are better known today. What we think of as modern Denmark was an important trad-ing centre within the Viking empire and the physical evidence of this part of the coun-try's history is to be found throughout the country today. In the late 9th century, war-riors led by the Viking chieftain, Hardegon, conquered the Jutland peninsula. The Dan-ish monarchy, Europe's oldest, dates back to Hardegon's son, Gorm the Old, who reigned in the early 10th century. Gorm's son, Harald Bluetooth, completed the conquest of Den-mark and spearheaded the conversion of the Danes to Christianity; his story and his legacy is well showcased in the tiny hamlet of Jelling. Successive Danish kings sent their subjects to row their longboats to England and conquer most of the Baltic region. They were accomplished fighters, sword-smiths, shipbuilders and sailors, qualities well illus-trated at the excellent Viking Ship Museum in Roskilde.

Reformation, Renaissance & a 30-year War

In 1397 Margrethe I of Denmark estab-lished a union between Denmark, Norway and Sweden to counter the influence of the powerful Hanseatic League that had come to dominate the region's trade. Sweden with-drew from the union in 1523 and over the next few hundred years Denmark and Swe-den fought numerous border skirmishes and a few fully fledged wars, largely over control of the Baltic Sea. Norway remained under Danish rule until 1814.

In the 16th century the Reformation swept through the country, accompanied by church burnings and civil warfare. The fighting ended in 1536, the Catholic Church was ousted and the Danish Lutheran Church headed by the monarchy was established.

Denmark's Golden Age was under Chris-tian IV (1588–1648), with Renaissance cities, castles and fortresses flourishing through-out his kingdom. A superb example is Eges-kov Slot on Funen. In 1625 Christian IV, hoping to neutralise Swedish expansion, entered an extremely ill-advised and pro-tracted struggle known as the Thirty Years War. The Swedes triumphed and won large chunks of Danish territory. Centuries worth of Danish kings and queens are laid to rest in sarcophagi on dramatic display at Roskil-de's cathedral.

The Modern Nation

Literature, the arts, philosophy and populist ideas flourished in the 1830s, and Europe's Year of Revolution in 1848 helped inspire a democratic movement in Denmark. Overnight, and in typically orderly Danish fashion, the country adopted male suffrage and a constitution on 5 June 1849, forcing King Frederik VII to relinquish most of his power and become Denmark's first constitutional monarch. Denmark lost the Schleswig and Holstein regions to Germany in 1864.

Denmark remained neutral throughout WWI and also declared its neutrality at the outbreak of WWII. Nevertheless, on 9 April 1940 the Germans invaded, albeit allowing the Danes a degree of autonomy. For three years the Danes managed to walk a thin line, running their own internal affairs under Nazi supervision, until in August 1943 the Germans took outright control. The Danish Resistance movement mushroomed and 7000 Jewish Danes were smuggled into neutral Sweden.

Although Soviet forces heavily bombarded the island of Bornholm, the rest of Denmark emerged from WWII relatively unscathed. Postwar Social Democrat governments introduced a comprehensive social welfare state in the postwar period, and still today Denmark provides its citizens with extensive cradle-to-grave social security.

Denmark joined NATO in 1949, and the European Community, now the EU, in 1973. The Danes offer tepid support for an expanding EU. In 1993 they narrowly voted to accept the Maastricht Treaty, which established the terms of a European economic and political union, only after being granted exemptions from common-defence and single-currency provisions. They also voted not to adopt the euro in 2000.

Contemporary Fairy Tales & Controversies

In 2004 the country's most eligible bachelor, Crown Prince Frederik, married Australian Mary Donaldson in a hugely popular and exhaustively covered storybook wedding. They now have four children.

It has not all been fairy tales, though. In late 2005 and early 2006 Denmark made world headlines when a right-wing Jutland newspaper published inflammatory cartoons depicting the Prophet Mohammed. The ensuing outcry saw the Danish flag burned in city streets throughout the Middle East.

Accustomed to being a blameless paragon of international virtue, Denmark has also experienced harsh criticism from some unusual quarters. Critics say its increasingly tough immigration laws are proof of creeping xenophobia and racism, earning it a rebuke from the European Council and the UN High Commissioner for Refugees.

The laws were introduced by long-serving prime minister Anders Fogh Rasmussen, who ended his seven-year reign in office in 2009 to become Secretary General of NATO. Succeeding him is current prime minister Lars Løkke Rasmussen (no relation), whose leadership of the 2009 UN Climate Conference in Copenhagen was undermined by the leaking of the Danish Text: prepared by the Danish government, the document clearly advantaged developed nations over poorer members of the conference.

The Danes

Denmark's 5.5 million people are a generally relaxed bunch. It takes a lot to shock a Dane, and even if they are, they probably won't show it. This was the first country in the world to legalise same-sex marriages, and it became (in)famous during the 1960s for its relaxed attitudes to pornography.

They are an outwardly serious people, yet with an ironic sense of humour. They have a strong sense of family and an admirable environmental sensitivity. Above all, they are the most egalitarian of people – they officially have the smallest gap between rich and poor in the world – proud of their social equality in which none have too much or too little.

The vast majority of Danes are members of the National Church of Denmark, an Evangelical Lutheran denomination (a proportion of each Dane's income tax goes directly to the church), but less than 5% of the population are regular churchgoers.

Arts

Famous Danish Authors

By far the most famous Danish author is Hans Christian Andersen. Other prominent Danish writers include religious philosopher Søren Kierkegaard, whose writings were a forerunner of existentialism, and Karen Blixen, who under the name Isak Dinesen penned *Out of Africa* and *Babette's Feast*, both made into acclaimed movies in the

1980s. One of Denmark's foremost contemporary authors is Ib Michael, a magic realist who has seen many of his novels and poems translated into English.

Architecture & Design

For a small country Denmark has had a massive global impact in the fields of architecture and design. Arne Jacobsen, Verner Panton, the late Jørn Utzon and Hans J Wegner are now considered among the foremost designers of the 20th century, and the tradition of great furniture and interior design remains strong in the country's design schools, museums and independent artisanal workshops. In recent years, a new league of eco-conscious architectural firms has emerged on the world stage. Among them is Effekt, designers of Tallinn's striking new Estonian Academy of Arts building, and BIG (Bjarke Ingels Group), whose head-turning projects include the cascading VM Bjerget housing complex in Copenhagen's Ørestad district. Indeed, Copenhagen is Denmark's architectural and design powerhouse, with museums such as the Danish Design Center and architectural show-stealers like the Opera House and Royal Library extension maintaining the country's enviable international reputation.

The Danish Screen

As with its design prowess, Denmark's success and influence in the realm of cinema has far exceeded what you might expect from a country of this size. Denmark has scored regular Oscar success with films such as *Babette's Feast,* Gabriel Axel's adaptation of a Karen Blixen novel; Bille August's *Pelle the Conqueror;* and Anders Thomas Jensen's short film *Valgaften.* In 2010, Mads Brügger's subversively comic documentary about North Korea, *The Red Chapel,* won the World Cinema Documentary Jury Prize at the Sundance Film Festival.

The last decade or so has seen director Lars von Trier stir up repeated controversy – and win numerous international film prizes – with his challenging films such as *Breaking the Waves, Dancer in the Dark* and *Dogville,* starring Nicole Kidman. Von Trier was a leading member of the Dogme95 film movement with its famous list of cinematic dos and don'ts. The movement scored notable international hits such as Thomas Vinterberg's *Festen* (The Party) and Lone Scherfig's *Italian for Beginners.* Another influential artistic figure is film director and experimental documentary maker Jørgen Leth.

Art: From the Skagen School to Contemporary Cool

Before the 19th century, Danish art consisted mainly of formal portraiture, exemplified by the works of Jens Juel (1745–1802). A Golden Age ushered in the 19th century with such fine painters as Wilhelm Eckersberg (1783–1853) and major sculptors like Bertel Thorvaldsen (1770–1844), although he chose to spend most of his life in Rome.

Later in the century the Skagen School evolved from the movement towards alfresco painting of scenes from working life, especially of fishing communities on the northern coasts of Jutland and Zealand. Much of it is exhibited at the Skagens Museum. Leading exponents of the Skagen School were PS Krøyer and Michael and Anna Ancher. In the mid-20th century, a vigorous modernist school of Danish painting emerged, of which Asger Jorn (1914–73) was a leading exponent. Many of his works are on display at the art museum in Silkeborg.

A number of contemporary Danish artists enjoy international acclaim, including conceptual artists Jeppe Hein, duo Elmgreen & Dragset, and Danish–Icelandic Olafur Eliasson. The latter's famously large-scale projects have included four temporary 'waterfalls' along New York's East River, as well as a whimsical multicoloured walkway atop the acclaimed ARoS gallery in Århus.

Like Århus, many Danish towns and cities contain a vibrant selection of home-grown and international contemporary art; even the smallest towns can surprise. Two of the best small art museums and galleries outside the capital are Faaborg's art museum and Herning's contemporary-art museum, HEART. Topping it all off is the magnificent Louisiana Museum of Modern Art, on the coast north of Copenhagen.

Green Travel

If you want to travel sustainably Denmark is the place to do it. Creating a modest carbon footprint and minimising your environmental impact are made very easy indeed. For starters there's the excellent public transport network and the fact that it's easy to cycle almost everywhere.

Arriving in Denmark by plane at Copenhagen airport, you will see the country's ma-

THE WATERWAY REVIVAL

Following its ambitious plan to restore wetlands and re-establish marshes and streams throughout the country, Denmark inaugurated its third national park, **Nationalpark Vadehadet** (Wadden Sea National Park), in 2010. Stretching along Jutland's west coast from Ho Bugt to the German border, and incorporating the popular island Fanø, its marshlands provide food and rest for millions of migratory birds.

jor contribution to improving the global environment: a row of wind turbines, technology the country has made its own. Danes also lead the way in their consumption of organic produce, recycling and environmentally friendly transport: more Danes commute by bicycle than any other European nationality.

Wildlife

Still commonly seen in Denmark are wild hare, deer and many species of birds, including magpies, coots, swans and ducks. Returning the wetlands should help endangered species such as the freshwater otter make a comeback. The Danes are particularly proud of their eagles – they have two pairs of golden eagles who live in Lille Vildmose, close to Aalborg on Jutland, and are national celebrities. Twitchers may also spot kingfishers *(isfugl)*, black storks (sort stork) and European honey buzzards *(hvepsevåge)*.

Danish Cuisine

Denmark has rebranded itself from 'dining dowager' to 'cutting-edge gastronome' in less than two decades. At the heart of the revolution is Copenhagen, home to 13 Michelin-starred restaurants and 2010 S.Pellegrino World's Best Restaurant winner, Noma. Along with restaurants like Kødbyens Fiskebar and Orangeriet, Noma has helped redefine Nordic cuisine by showcasing native produce and herbs, prepared using traditional techniques and contemporary experimentation, and focused on clean, natural flavours.

Staples & Specialities

Proud of it though they are, even the Danes would concede that their traditional cuisine is rather heavy and unhealthy. They eat a great deal of meat, mostly pork and usually accompanied by something starchy and a gravy-like sauce. However, one Danish speciality has conquered the world: smørrebrød, or the Danish open sandwich.

Other commonly encountered dishes include *frikadeller* (meatballs), *flæskesteg* (roast pork with crackling... actually it's mostly crackling), *hvid labskovs* (beef-and-potato stew) and *hakkebøf* (beefburger with fried onions). The Danes are great smokers too; you'll find smoke-houses preserving herring, eel, cod livers, shrimp and other seafood all around the coast of the country. The most renowned are on Bornholm.

Where to Eat & Drink

Beyond Copenhagen, Denmark's food scene is less inspiring. Though culinary destinations like Zealand's Dragsholm Slot, Bornholm's Restaurant Kadeau, and Århus' Malling & Schmidt and Nordisk Spisehus fly the flag for quality and innovation, most restaurant food outside the capital is limited to pizza, burgers and kebabs, and perhaps the odd second-rate Italian, Chinese or Thai place.

That said, outside Copenhagen you can still find great Danish home cooking in the country's traditional *kroer* or 'inns'.

Drinking

The Danes are enthusiastic drinkers, and not just of their world-famous domestic beers. The most popular spirit in Denmark is caraway-spiced Aalborg aquavit; it's drunk straight down as a shot, followed by a chaser of beer. Øl (beer), *vin* (wine) and spirits are reasonably cheap and easily bought here compared with other Scandinavian countries.

SURVIVAL GUIDE

Directory A–Z

Accommodation

In this chapter accommodation prices are based on a double room with private, indoor bathroom and breakfast unless stated otherwise. The following price indicators apply:

€€€ more than Dkr1000

€€ Dkr350 to Dkr1000

€ less than Dkr350

CAMPING & CABINS

Denmark's 478 camping grounds typically charge from Dkr70 to Dkr85 per person to pitch a tent. A camping pass (available at any camping ground) is required (Dkr100) and covers a family group with children aged under 18 years for the season. If you do not have a seasonal pass you pay an extra Dkr35 a night for a transit pass. The Danish Camping Association (☑39 27 88 44; www. campingraadet.dk; Campingrådet, Mosedalvej 15, Valby) inspects and grades Danish camping grounds using a star system and carries a full list on its website.

HOSTELS

The national Hostelling International office is Danhostel (☑33 31 36 12; www.danhostel.dk; Vesterbrogade 39, 1620 Copenhagen V).

Most of Denmark's 95 *vandrerhjem* (hostels) in its Danhostel association have private rooms in addition to dorms, making hostels an affordable and popular alternative to hotels (so book ahead from June to August).

Dorm beds cost from about Dkr150, while private rooms range from about Dkr300 to Dkr500 for singles, and Dkr400 to Dkr500 for doubles. Blankets and pillows are provided, but not sheets; bring your own or hire them for Dkr50 to Dkr75. Sleeping bags are not allowed.

A Hostelling International Card costs Dkr160. Without one you pay Dkr35 extra a night. You can buy them at all Danhostels. Outside Copenhagen, check-in is generally between 4pm and 8pm or 9pm (but a few places close as early as 6pm).

HOTELS

Budget hotels start at around Dkr500/650 for singles/doubles. *Kros,* a name that implies country inn but is more often the Danish version of a motel, are generally cheaper, and often occupy homely period houses. Both hotels and *kros* usually include an all-you-can-eat breakfast. You can find out more about some of Denmark's inns and make online bookings at www.krohotel.dk.

Rates listed in this chapter include all taxes and are for rooms with toilet and shower, unless otherwise specified. Many large chain or business-oriented hotels offer discounts at weekends year-round and from May to September when business travel is light.

OTHER ACCOMMODATION

Many tourist offices book rooms in private homes for a small fee, or provide a free list of the rooms on their website so travellers can book online or phone on their own. Rates vary, averaging about Dkr400/600 for singles/ doubles. Standards of accommodation vary widely. Dansk Bed & Breakfast (☑39 61 04 05; www.bbdk.dk) handles more than 300 homes throughout Denmark, offering private rooms at similar rates.

Activities

CYCLING

Cycling is a popular holiday activity and there are thousands of kilometres of established cycling routes. Those around Bornholm, Funen and Møn, as well as the 440km Old Military Rd (Hærvejen) through central Jutland, are among the most popular.

Dansk Cyklist Forbund (DCF; ☑33 32 31 21; www.dcf.dk; Rømersgade 5, 1362 Copenhagen K) publishes a 1:500,000-scale cycling map of the entire country (Dkr25), as well as more detailed regional cycling maps.

DCF also publishes *Overnatning i det fri* (Dkr129), which lists hundreds of farmers who provide cyclists with a place to pitch a tent for Dkr20 a night. Cycling maps can be purchased online from DCF.

WALKING

Though Denmark lacks substantial forests, many small tracts of woodland are crisscrossed by pleasant walking trails.

Skov og Naturstyrelsen (Forest & Nature Bureau, ☑72 54 20 00; www.skovognatur.dk) produces brochures with sketch maps that show trails in nearly 100 such areas; PDFs of these brochures are available free on its website.

WATER SPORTS

Canoeing possibilities on Denmark's inland lakes, such as canoe touring between lakeside camping grounds in Jutland's Lake District, are superb. You can hire canoes and equipment at many camping grounds or in main centres such as Silkeborg. The lakes are generally undemanding as far as water conditions go, although some experience is an advantage.

Denmark's remarkable coastline offers terrific windsurfing and kitesurfing possibilities. Good areas are along the northern coast of Zealand at places such as Smidstrup Strand, and in northwest Jutland. The Limfjord area of northwest Jutland is particularly suited to windsurfing and canoeing.

Business Hours

In this chapter, opening hours have been provided only when they differ from the following standard hours:

Banks 9.30am-4pm Mon-Fri, to 5 or 6pm Thu

Bars 4pm-2, 3, 4 or 5am

Post offices 9 or 10am-5 or 6pm Mon-Fri, to noon or 2pm Sat

Restaurants 11am-2.30pm & 5-10pm

Stores 9.30am-5.30pm Mon-Thu, to 7pm Fri, to 2pm Sat

Supermarkets 9am-7 or 8pm Mon-Fri, 8 or 9am-5pm Sat

Children

Denmark is a particularly child-friendly country. Children under 18 years are admitted free to many attractions, and educational play areas are common at many museums. Festivals often cater to families, and the country's collection of amusement parks and outdoor activities will keep young ones happily occupied. For more information on family travel in Denmark, see www.visitdenmark.com.

Food

Generally speaking, eating out in Denmark is not cheap. You can expect to pay Dkr350 for a decent three-course meal in the capital, rising easily to Dkr1000 and above in the best places.

Throughout this chapter, the following price indicators have been used (prices refer to the cost of a main course):

€€€ more than Dkr190

€€ Dkr100 to Dkr190

€ less than Dkr100

Gay & Lesbian Travellers

Denmark is a popular destination for gay and lesbian travellers. Copenhagen in particular has an active, open gay community with numerous bars and nightlife options.

Landsforeningen for Bøsser og Lesbiske (LBL; ☐33 13 19 48; www.lbl.dk; Nygade 7, Copenhagen) is the national organisation for gay men and lesbians. Branch offices in main towns are mentioned in relevant sections in this chapter. Copenhagen Gay Life (www.copenhagen-gay-life.dk) is a good English-language website with links to LBL and other gay organisations, as well as listings of gay

venues and events. QX (www.qx.se) is a free monthly magazine available in Copenhagen, Stockholm, Göteborg and Malmö.

Internet Access

Wi-fi hot spots,, many of them free, are mushrooming across Denmark. Most public libraries offer free access to internet-enabled computers. Most hotels, guesthouses and hostels offer wi-fi access, often free. Internet cafes are increasingly rare.

Money

ATMs Major bank ATMs accept Visa, MasterCard and the Cirrus and Plus bank cards.

Credit & debit cards All major credit and debit cards are accepted throughout Denmark. A surcharge of up to 3.75% is imposed on foreign credit card transactions in some restaurants, shops and hotels.

Travellers cheques All common travellers cheques are accepted in Denmark. Buy your travellers cheques in higher denominations; bank fees for changing money are a hefty Dkr25 to Dkr30 per cheque, with a Dkr40 minimum. Travellers cheques command a better exchange rate than cash by about 1%.

Changing money If you're exchanging cash, there's a Dkr25 fee for a transaction. Post offices exchange foreign currency at comparable rates to those at banks.

Euros Denmark remains outside the euro zone, though acceptance of euros is commonplace. Most hotels and restaurants will take euros, as do many bars, cafes and shops, although you may find reluctance to do so in more remote areas or from very small businesses. Government institutions do not accept euros.

Tipping Restaurant bills and taxi fares include service charges in the quoted prices. Further tipping is not expected. If you're particularly pleased with service at a restaurant, consider leaving a small – 10% to 15% – tip for your waiter/waitress.

Public Holidays

Summer holidays for schoolchildren begin around 20 June and end around 10 August. Many Danes go on holiday during the first three weeks of July. The following public holidays are observed in Denmark:

New Year's Day 1 January

Maundy Thursday Thursday before Easter

Good Friday to Easter Monday March/April

Common Prayer Day fourth Friday after Easter

Ascension Day fifth Thursday after Easter

Whit Sunday fifth Sunday after Easter

Whit Monday fifth Monday after Easter

Constitution Day 5 June

Christmas Eve 24 December from noon

Christmas Day 25 December

Telephone

To call Denmark from abroad dial your country's international access code, then ☎45 (Denmark's country code), then the local number. There are no regional area codes within Denmark.

To call internationally from Denmark dial ☎00, then the country code for the country you're calling, followed by the area code (without the initial zero if there is one) and the local number.

Local calls at coin phones costs Dkr5. Phonecards (Dkr50 to Dkr100) are available from post offices and newspaper kiosks. Domestic calls are cheapest between 7.30pm and 8am daily and all day Sunday.

Time

Denmark is normally one hour ahead of GMT/UTC. Clocks are moved forward one hour for daylight-saving time from the last Sunday in March to the last Sunday in October. Denmark uses the 24-hour clock.

Tourist Information

Visit Denmark (www.visitdenmark.com), Denmark's official tourism website, lists tourist offices throughout the country, including their opening hours.

Travellers with Disabilities

Overall, Denmark is a user-friendly destination for travellers with disabilities. The **Danish Tourist Board** (www.visitdenmark.com) has to date accredited, in association with local disability organisations, more than 1300 locations as 'accessible to all' throughout Denmark. See the website for further information.

Visas

Denmark is one of 25 member countries of the Schengen Agreement, under which 22 EU countries (all but Bulgaria, Cyprus, Ireland, Romania and the UK) plus Iceland, Norway and Switzerland have abolished checks at common borders. Citizens of the USA, Canada, Australia and New Zealand need a valid passport to visit Denmark, but do not need a visa for stays of less than three months. Citizens of EU countries and other Scandinavian countries with a valid passport or national identity card do not require visas.

Women Travellers

Kvindehuset (☎33 14 28 04; Gothersgade 37, Copenhagen) is a help centre and meeting place for women. Dial ☎112 for rape crisis or other emergencies.

Getting There & Away

Air

If you're coming from European destinations consider flying into an airport other than Copenhagen, such as Århus or Billund; airfares are competitive, and the airports are well connected by bus with neighbouring towns and afford fast access to Northern and Central Jutland.

Main Danish airports:

Copenhagen (www.cph.dk) Nonstop flights include most major European destinations, New York, Washington DC, Chicago, Toronto, Bangkok, Beijing, Shanghai, Singapore, Tokyo, Tel Aviv, Cairo and Damascus

Århus (www.aar.dk) Nonstop flights include London (Stansted), Stockholm, Gothenburg, Oslo, Girona (Barcelona) and Málaga.

Billund (www.bll.dk) Nonstop flights include London (Stansted), Manchester, Edinburgh, Stockholm, Oslo, Helsinki, Frankfurt, Düsseldorf, Amsterdam, Brussels, Paris, Milan (Bergamo), Rome, Pisa, Girona (Barcelona) and Málaga.

Land

GERMANY

The E45 is the main motorway running between Germany and Denmark's Jutland peninsula.

Bus

Eurolines (www.eurolines.com) operates buses from Copenhagen to 18 destinations in Germany.

Berlin Dkr282, seven hours, one to two daily

Frankfurt Dkr734, 13 hours, one daily

Hamburg Dkr297, six hours, one to two daily

Services to Germany also depart from Århus and Aalborg. Note that fares booked online in advance can be substantially cheaper than the prices listed here.

Train

There is one daily direct service between Copenhagen and Berlin, with several more nondirect services. Direct trains cost around Dkr1010, with a journey time of 6¾ hours. A direct overnight service to Frankfurt departs daily. The price is around Dkr1180, with a journey time of 12½ hours. Faster ICE trains, requiring one change, depart three times daily to Frankfurt. The price is around Dkr1260, with a journey time of 8¼ hours. Fares booked in advance can be substantially cheaper than the prices listed here, see www.db.de for more information.

NORWAY

Bus

Eurolines (www.eurolines.com) offers three to four weekly services between Oslo and Copenhagen (Dkr385, nine hours) via Göteborg.

Train

One daily train connects Copenhagen with Oslo via Göteborg, Sweden (2nd-class around Dkr830, eight hours). Fares fluctuate and booking in advance can be cheaper than the price listed here. See www.sj.se for more information.

SWEDEN

Bus

Eurolines (www.eurolines.com) runs three weekly buses to Göteborg (Dkr275, 4½ hours) and Stockholm (Dkr385, 9¾ hours).

Train

Trains run many times a day between Denmark and Sweden via the Øresund bridge linking Copenhagen with Malmö (Dkr90, 40 minutes). From Copenhagen, other Swedish connections include the following:

Göteborg Dkr395, 3½ hours, 20 daily

Stockholm Dkr975, five hours, 16 daily

If you're travelling by train, the bridge crossing is included in the fare, but for those travelling by car, there's a Dkr295 toll per ve-

hicle. For train timetables, ticket offers and bookings, see www.sj.se.

Sea

GERMANY

Scandlines (☎33 15 15 15; www.scandlines.com) connects Rødby to Puttgarden, Germany (from Dkr499 including car and five passengers, 45 minutes, every 30 minutes). It also runs services between Gedser and Rostock, Germany (from Dkr699, 1¾ hours, nine times daily).

BorholmerFærgen (☎56 95 18 66; www.bornholmerfaergen.dk) connects Rønne to Sassnitz, Germany (Dkr797 to Dkr1585 including car and five passengers, 3½ hours, three to eight times daily) from April to October.

ICELAND & THE FAROE ISLANDS

Smyril Line (in Denmark ☎96 55 03 60, in Faroe Islands 345 900; www.smyril-line.com) connects Hirtshals to Tórshavn (Faroe Islands) and Seyðisfjörður (Iceland); see the boxed text, p526, for further details about this service.

Seyðisfjörður from €114, 13 hours, once weekly (Apr-Oct only)

Tórshavn from €97, seven hours, once weekly

NORWAY

DFDS (☎33 42 30 10; www.dfdsseaways.com) operates an overnight ferry between Copenhagen and Oslo (from Dkr895, 16½ hours, daily).

Stena Line (☎96 20 02 00; www.stenaline.co.uk) connects Frederikshavn and Oslo (from Dkr330 including car and five passengers, 8½ hours, six to seven times weekly).

Colorline (☎99 56 19 77; www.colorline.com) sails from Hirtshals to the following ports in Norway:

Kristiansand Dkr539 including car and five passengers, three to four hours, one to two daily

Larvik Dkr539 including car and five passengers, 3¾ hours, one to two daily

Fjord Line (☎97 96 30 00; www.fjordline.dk) runs from Hirtshals to the following ports in Norway:

Bergen adult/car with five passengers from Dkr261/1232, 19¼ hours, three times weekly

Stavanger adult/car with five passengers from Dkr130/765, 11½ hours, four times weekly

From mid-April to mid-September, Fjord Line also runs a high-speed catamaran to Kristiansand, Norway (adult/car with five passengers Dkr139/532, 2¼ hours, twice daily).

Always check websites for special offers, which can be significantly cheaper than the prices listed here.

POLAND
Polferries (☑ 33 13 52 23; www.polferries.pl) operates ferries to Świnoujście from both Copenhagen (from Dkr470, 10 hours, three times weekly) and Rønne (from Dkr300, three to four hours, Saturday only). Check the website for promotions and last-minute offers.

SWEDEN
Scandlines (☑ 33 15 15 15; www.scandlines.com) sails around 75 times daily between Helsingør and Helsingborg (return ticket adult/car including 9 passengers from Dkr48/355). Book online for the cheapest fares.

Stena Line (☑ 96 20 02 00; www.stenaline.co.uk) connects Frederikshavn to Göteborg (from Dkr460 including car and five passengers, 3½ hours, four to eight times daily).

BorholmerFærgen (☑ 56 95 18 66; www.bornholmerfaergen.dk) runs ferries between Rønne and Ystad (Dkr1051 including car and five passengers, 1¼ to 2½ hours, three to eight times daily).

UK
DFDS Seaways (☑ in the UK 08705 333 000; in Denmark 33 42 30 00; www.dfdsseaways.co.uk) sails from Esbjerg to Harwich (cabin from £142, 19 hours, three to four times weekly).

Getting Around

Air

Most internal flights cost around Dkr500 for a standard ticket and can be cheaper if booked in advance.

Cimber Air (☑ 70 10 12 18; www.cimber.dk) Services include Copenhagen to Århus (35 minutes, six daily on weekdays, at least two on weekends), Aalborg (50 minutes, at least five daily), Rønne (Bornholm, 35 minutes, at least four daily), Billund (Legoland, 45 minutes, six daily on weekdays, at least three daily on weekends), and Karup (Central Jutland, 50 minutes, 11 daily on weekdays, at least four daily on weekends).

SAS (☑ 70 10 20 00; www.flysas.com) Links Copenhagen with Aalborg (at least five times daily) and Århus (at least four times daily).

Bicycle

Cycling is a practical way to get around Denmark. There are extensive bike paths linking towns throughout the country and bike lanes through most city centres.

You can rent bikes in most towns for around Dkr75 per day, plus a deposit of about Dkr250. Bikes can be taken on ferries and most trains for a modest cost. From May to August, you must make a reservation to carry a bicycle on InterCity and InterCity-Lyn, either at the station or by calling ☑ 70 13 14 15. Bikes can be carried for free on Copenhagen's S-trains outside rush hours.

Boat

Ferries links virtually all of Denmark's populated islands. Where there's not a bridge, there's usually a ferry, most of which take cars. Specific information is given under individual destination sections. Scandlines (☑ 33 15 15; www.scandlines.com) operates many domestic ferry services. Timetables are widely available in tourist offices and train stations.

Bus

All large cities and towns have a local and regional bus system; many connect with trains. There are also a few long-distance bus routes, including from Copenhagen to Aalborg or Århus.

Travelling by bus on long-distance routes costs about 20% less than travel by train, although it's slower.

The main bus companies operating in Denmark include the following:

Abildskou (☑ 70 21 08 88; www.abildskou.dk) Runs from Copenhagen to Århus, Silkeborg and Aalborg.

Bornholmerbussen (☑ 56 95 21 21; www.bat.dk, in Danish) Operates the bus services on Bornholm.

Gråhund Bus (☑ 44 68 44 00; www.graahundbus.dk, in Danish) Operates between Copenhagen and Bornholm, Copenhagen and Malmö and Copenhagen and Berlin.

Thinggaard Expressbusser (☑ 98 11 66 00; www.ekspresbus.dk, in Danish) Operates between Frederikshavn and Esbjerg via Aalborg.

Car & Motorcycle

Denmark is perfect for touring by car. Roads are in good condition and well signposted. Traffic is manageable, even in major cities such as Copenhagen (rush hours excepted). Denmark's extensive network of ferries carries motor vehicles for reasonable rates. It's always a good idea for drivers to call ahead and make reservations.

AUTOMOBILE ASSOCIATIONS

Denmark's main motoring organisation is **Forenede Danske Motorejere** (FDM; ☑32 66 01 00/70 13 30 40; www.fdm.dk, in Danish; Firskovvej 32, 2800 Lyngby).

CAR HIRE

The following applies when renting a car:
» You must be 21.
» You must have a valid home driving licence.
» You must have a major credit card.
» You may need to supply a passport.
» Independent local companies are often much cheaper than the international chains, but the big companies offer one-way rentals.
» You'll generally get the best deal by booking through an international rental agency before you arrive in Denmark.
» Check car-rental websites for special online deals.
» Drivers aged 21 to 25 may need to pay an additional 'young driver fee' (Dkr100 per day)
» Europcar offers unlimited kilometres and generally has the cheapest deals (from Dkr470 per day), but it's always wise to call around and compare.

Car-hire companies in Denmark:

Avis (www.avis.com)

Europcar (www.europcar.com)

Hertz (www.hertzdk.dk)

INSURANCE

Check with your insurance company that your policy is valid for driving in Denmark before you depart.

ROAD RULES

» In Denmark you drive on the right, and use of seatbelts is mandatory.
» Unless otherwise posted, the speed limits for cars and motorcycles are as follows:
  • *50km/h in built-up areas*
  • *80km/h on main highways*
  • *110km/h or 130km/h on motorways.*
» The legal blood-alcohol limit is 0.05%.
» The use of dipped headlights is compulsory at all times.

Train

With the exception of a few short private lines, **Danish State Railways** (DSB; www.dsb.dk) runs all Danish train services. Overall, train travel in Denmark is not expensive, in large part because distances are short.

Reservations Sleek intercity (IC) trains generally require reservations (Dkr 30). The older, slower interregional (IR) trains make more stops and don't require reservations. Both cost the same, apart from the InterCity-Lyn, a pricier express train.

Discounts & Passes People aged 65 and older are entitled to a 25% discount on Friday and Sunday and a 50% discount on other days. Children under the age of 12 years usually travel for free if accompanied by an adult, and one adult can bring two children for free. This offer is not available in 1st class. Rail passes don't cover reservation fees or surcharges.

Faroe Islands

Why Go?

The Faroes (Føroyar) form an 18-piece jigsaw puzzle of majestic grass-coated rocks jutting out of the frothing North Atlantic swells. Midway between Iceland and Scotland, this is a largely undiscovered slice of Scandinavia where multi-coloured cottages and grass-roofed wooden churches add focus to grandly stark, treeless moorlands. Terms like 'remote' and 'windswept' often feel inadequate as you ramble along cairn-marked footpaths criss-crossing craggy layer-cake mountains and skirting some of Europe's tallest sea cliffs. Yet even the tiniest, once-remote hamlets are now linked by an extraordinary series of road tunnels. And layered over the islands' fascinating Old Norse culture is a savvy modern society whose tight-knit rural communities are remarkably alive with art and music. Even if the weather proves uncooperative, this self-assured little demi-nation is likely to surprise and delight even the most cynical traveller.

Best Places to Eat

» Áarstova (p127)
» Matstovan Elisabeth (p140)
» Kgl Handil Pub (p142)

Best Places to Stay

» Gjáargarður (p136)
» Gistingarhúisið Undir Heygnum (p141)
» Krákureiðrið (p135)

When to Go
Tórshavn

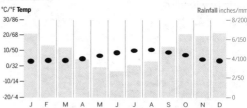

Jun Days are dreamily long; most hotels and museums are open but tourist numbers are low.

Jul & Aug The main tourist season, with traditional boat races and festivals, notably Ólavsøka.

Sep-May Rain abounds, and much infrastructure is shut, but meditative tourists are welcome.

Connections

In summer there's a twice-weekly flight to London Stansted. Otherwise the only connections are to/from Denmark and Iceland either by air or using the comfortable Norröna car ferry (once or twice weekly).

ITINERARIES

Two Nights/Three Days

Take a boat ride along the Vestmanna bird cliffs. Drive to Gjógv with side trips to Saksun and Eiði outbound, returning via Funningur, Elduvík and Kirkjubøur. Spend the last night in Tórshavn strolling the historic Tinganes district and exploring the lively pubs.

Ten Days

Fly in on a Wednesday afternoon, walk or cycle from the airport to Sørvágur, then the next morning take the boat to Mykines. After a day with the puffins, hop on the Friday helicopter to Kirkja, walk to Hattarvík and return by ferry the same afternoon to Klaksvík. After an excursion to Kallur, walk up to Klakkur in the evening. Head for Suðuroy via Tórshavn, then on Wednesday at lunchtime take the helicopter from Froðba to Skúvoy. Having seen the skuas, jump on the last ferry-bus combo trip back to Tórshavn. Spend the last days as per the short itinerary above. Be sure to prebook the transport.

Essential Food & Drink

» **Turrur fiskur** Dried, pounded fish.

» **Skerpikjøt** Jamon-style wind-dried mutton.

» **Grind og spik** Whale meat and blubber, traditionally popular though availability is now sporadic.

» **Seyðahøvd** Sheep's head.

» **Seabirds** Puffins and guillemots (and their eggs) occasionally find their way onto local plates.

» **Tap water** Fine to drink.

» **Alcoholic drinks** Klaksvík-based **Föroya Bjor** (www.bjor.fo) creates several decent brews, including rich, dark Black Sheep (5.8%). Not stocked in supermarkets or grocery shops.

AT A GLANCE

» **Capital** Tórshavn

» **Area** 1399 sq km

» **Population** 48,700

» **Country code** 298

» **Languages** Faroese, Danish

» **Currency** Faroese króna and Danish krone (Dkr)

Exchange Rates

Australia	A$1	Dkr5.48
Canada	C$1	Dkr5.28
Europe	€1	Dkr7.46
Japan	¥100	Dkr6.16
New Zealand	NZ$1	Dkr4.03
UK	UK£1	Dkr8.38
USA	US$1	Dkr5.03

Set Your Budget

» **Budget hotel room** Dkr650–800

» **Two-course evening meal** Dkr220–350

» **Museum entrance** Dkr20–50

» **Beer** Dkr35–50

» **Tórshavn transport ticket** free

Resources

» **Official website** (www.faroeislands.com)

» **Village by village** (www.faroeislands.dk)

» **Tourist board** (www.visitfaroeislands.com)

» **Philatelic service** (www.faroestamps.fo)

» **Hoppa listings** (http://hoppa.com/eu/nor/fo)

» **Comprehensive transport info** (www.ssl.fo)

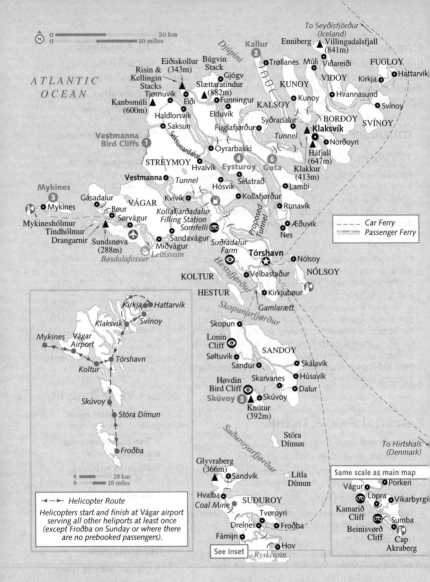

Faroe Islands Highlights

1. Brave the waves on a magical boat trip beneath the towering **Vestmanna Bird Cliffs** (p134)

2. Hike to **Kallur lighthouse** (p139) for a breathtaking panorama of cliffs and headlands

3. Stroll across spectacular clifftops to the lively puffin colonies of peaceful **Mykines** (p134)

4. Drive around **northern Eysturoy** (p136) visiting many of the Faroes' cutest villages, grandest fjords and highest peaks

5. Beat off dive-bombing skuas on **Skúvoy** (p132)

6. Discover Faroese rock music at July's beachside festival, **G!** (p136), in Gøta

7. See the Faroes at their most dramatic on great value **helicopter trips** (p148)

TÓRSHAVN

POP 19,700

The capital and by far the Faroes' biggest city, Tórshavn (Thor's Harbour) counterpoints its modern buildings with pockets of turf-roofed timber cottages set around busy, boat-filled harbours. It's a very pleasant, laidback town that merits a day's exploration. And its transport links, good restaurants and hotels make Tórshavn an excellent base from which to explore the rest of the country.

History

Tórshavn's central location attracted the Faroes' first *ting* (parliament) here in AD 1000 but poor soils kept the town relatively small for centuries. That changed after 1856, once the Danish trading monopoly was replaced by free trade, and Tórshavn rapidly evolved into the islands' main trading hub. It has been growing ever since.

◉ Sights & Activities

CENTRAL AREA

Old Tórshavn   NEIGHBOURHOOD
(Map p126) The little Tinganes Peninsula is Tórshavn's historical heart, a captivating jumble of turf-roofed cottages and bigger red-painted stone-and-timber buildings, many of which are occupied by the islands' government offices. Most date from after a devastating 1673 fire. Guides can explain the history of each structure but random strolling is enough for most visitors. The distinctive little 'cathedral', **Havnarkirkja** (Bringsnagøta; ⊘2.30-4.30pm Tue-Fri, 10am-2pm Sat), has a gilt-trimmed clock tower and an interior that's relatively ornate by austere Faroese standards. A row of colourful old wharf buildings (Undir Bryggjubakka) lines the inner harbour that bobs photogenically with yachts and sloops.

FREE **Skansin Fort**   RUINS
(Map p126) Turf-softened bastions are all that remain of the 1629 fort, first built to defend the Royal Trade Monopoly at Tinganes from pirates. Today it's topped by a **lighthouse** and four baby-sized 18th-century cannons. Lower down, two bigger naval guns recall the WWII era when the fortress served as a British HQ.

Løgting   PARLIAMENT
(Map p126; Tinghúsvegur) A barnlike wooden house fused improbably to what looks like a 1990s public library together form a complex housing one of the world's smallest yet oldest parliaments. In an age of global security paranoia it's refreshing to be able to walk up to a seat of government and press your nose up against the window even when the chamber's in session.

Norðlýsið   SEA EXCURSIONS
(Map p126; ☑218520; www.nordlysid.com; excursions adult Dkr200-250, child Dkr100-125) Moored in the Western Harbour, this antique wooden sailing boat looks great in port and even better at sea. Regular **fishing trips** and three-hour **sightseeing cruises** usually run on Tuesdays and Thursdays, but check the website. Most famous are occasional excursions to Hestur (some Tuesdays in summer) for a concert played in a reverberant sea cave where slapping wave sounds are an integral part of the effect.

GREATER TÓRSHAVN

Føroya Fornminnissavn   MUSEUM
(Map p124; www.fornminni.fo; adult/child Dkr30/ free; ⊘10am-5pm Mon-Fri, 2-5pm Sat & Sun mid-May–mid-Sep) The excellent Føroya Fornminnissavn is split between two sites in Hoyvík, 3km north of the centre.

The main site (Brekkutún 6) displays Faroese artefacts from Viking rune stones to early-20th-century open-decked boats. Don't miss the Faroes' greatest artistic treasure: 15th-century church fittings from Kirkjubøur, including the widely photographed carving of the Virgin Mary meeting Elisabeth (mother of John the Baptist).

The museum's peaceful second site, Hoyvíksgarður (Kúrdalsvegur 18), fills a superbly preserved 1920s farmstead with period fittings including a bell telephone and a functioning grandfather clock. There's a full set of turf-roofed outhouses and the bucolic setting feels a world away from the city. Yet it's just 300m off major Hvítanesvegur where buses 2 and 3 drop you off.

Listasavn Føroya   ART GALLERY
(Map p124; www.art.fo; Gundadalsvegur 9; adult/student/child Dkr50/20/free; ⊘11am-5pm Mon-Fri, 2-5pm Sat & Sun May-Aug, 2-5pm Tue-Sun Sep-Apr) This wonderfully light-suffused gallery houses an imaginative collection of Faroese modern and contemporary art, including moving, death-haunted canvases by the great Sámal Joensen-Mikines, large-scale abstract canvases by Ingálvur av Reyni, and quirkier pieces such as Beinta av Reyni's portrait of Eminem as an angel. Around the

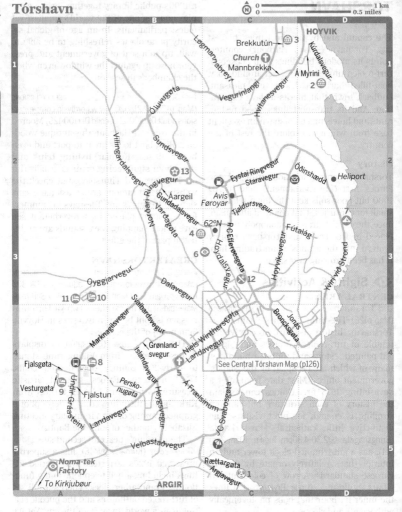

museum, **Viðarlundin** is a wild park where trees and sculptures mingle.

Vesturkirkjan
CHURCH

(Map p124; Landavegur; ⊘3-5pm Mon-Fri mid-Jun–Aug) This 1970s church dominates views of the town with its pyramidal apse. While hardly beautiful the structure is iconic, and inside a corona of afternoon light powerfully illuminates the bare, modern interior.

Náttúrugripasavn
MUSEUM

(Map p126; www.ngs.fo; VU Hammershaimbsgøta 13; adult/child Dkr20/free; ⊘10am-4pm Mon-Fri, 3-5pm Sat & Sun Jun-Aug, Sun only Sep-May) This child-friendly nature museum features an informative geological section, a big selection of taxidermy, and a gigantic whale's skull.

Aquarium
AQUARIUM

(Map p124; Rættargøta; adult/child Dkr40/20; ⊘2-5pm mid-Jun–Aug, Sat & Sun only Sep–mid-Jun) This small but fascinating introduction to the marine life of the Faroes includes anemones, curious 'mine' urchins and over 30 types of live fish; exact numbers depend on how many have been eaten by their tank-share friends.

Tórshavn

◎ Sights

Hiking to Kirkjubøur HIKING
A classic, very well-trodden mountain trail to Kirkjubøur taking around two hours starts at the Noma-Tek factory (Map p124), on Tórshavn's city bus 3 route. **Berg Hestar** (☑316896, 216896; www.berghestar.com; ☺by appointment) will take groups the same way riding Icelandic horses.

🛏 Sleeping

The limited accommodation options can get booked up early. For B&Bs or apartment rentals see p146.

CENTRAL AREA

Hotel Tórshavn HOTEL €€€
(Map p126; ☑350000; www.hoteltorshavn.fo; Tórsgøta 4; s/d/ste Dkr1100/1400/3000; ☺closed Christmas; @) The closest Tórshavn comes to a boutique hotel, with sleek decor and wonderful views across to the church and harbour from desirable corner suites and most 'superior' rooms. Bathrooms are cramped in cheaper rooms and singles come with narrow beds. For half the price there are six bargain-value 'small' singles that aren't actually much smaller and are OK if you don't mind overlooking pipes and vents. Rates include breakfast.

Bládýpi HOSTEL €
(Map p126; ☑500600; www.hostel.fo; Dr Jakobsensgøta 14-16; dm without/with sheets Dkr200/250, s/tw/tr Dkr600/800/1000, without bathroom Dkr450/650/850; ☺reception 8am-6pm Mon-Fri, 4-8pm Sat & Sun) Tórshavn's best budget option, this central, well-run hostel-cum-hotel is spotlessly clean and prices include a good buffet breakfast. Spacious dorms share sitting areas and an equipped kitchen. Private rooms with shared bathrooms are bright if small, but if you want a private bathroom the co-owned Skansin is a marginally better option. Prices drop slightly out of season.

Guesthouse Skansin BUDGET HOTEL €€
(Map p126; ☑500606; www.hostel.fo; Jekaragøta 8; s/d Dkr600/800, without bathroom Dkr450/650) Bright, well-kept rooms with fridge, TV and quality beds come in various shapes and sizes. The best are en-suite room 20, 'family size' room 22 and corner room 23 with its harbour views. Breakfast is included and there's free street parking nearby. No alcohol allowed.

Hotel Streym HOTEL €€
(Map p126; ☑355500, 533900; www.hotelstreym.com; Yviri við Strond 19; s/d Dkr795/995; ☺reception 6.30am-10.30pm) What this well-run hotel lacks in location it makes up for in Scandi style, lime-green details and humorous notes painted onto corridor walls. Rooms are simple and stripped down, with desks and plenty of space except in the small singles. Wi-fi is limited to newer rooms.

Hotel Hafnia BUSINESS HOTEL €€€
(Map p126; ☑313233; www.hafnia.fo; Áarvegur 4-10; s/d/ste incl breakfast Dkr1450/1650/3000; P@) Rooms have framed modern-art prints and that dark-wood neoclassical furniture beloved of business hotels worldwide. Bathrooms are small and slightly dated and wi-fi is patchy, but it's very central and good deals (around Dkr900 for a double including buffet breakfast) are often available through online discounters.

GREATER TÓRSHAVN

Hotel Føroyar HOTEL €€€
(Map p124; ☑317500; www.hotelforoyar.com; Oyggjarvegur; s/d Dkr1500/1800, ste Dkr2200-7000; P@) The city's top hotel is turf roofed in a nod to tradition, but dark and soothing inside without being overly trendy. All the rooms are spacious, have bathtubs and enjoy great views over town, a 3km drive

Central Tórshavn

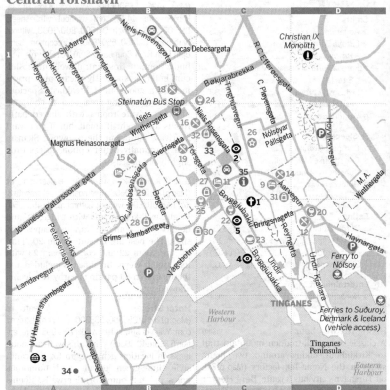

below. The Clinton Room (Dkr2200), where Bill bedded down in 2007, isn't especially memorable unless you take the optional attached conference room. Wedding suites (Dkr3000) are a better option for space and luxury.

Kerjalon Hostel
HOSTEL €

(Map p124; ☑318910; www.hosteltorshaven.fo; Oyggjarvegur 49; dm/d Dkr175/410, sheets Dkr65; ℙ@) Sleeping up to 98 people, the Kerjalon has timber-clad bunk-bed rooms that share bathrooms, a laundry (Dkr30) and a large kitchen. Tiny lockers (Dkr5) are available for valuables. The hilltop location is around 25 minutes' walk from the centre using shortcuts. Check-in (from 4pm) at the Hotel Føroyar across the same car park. No wi-fi.

Guesthouses Undir Fjalli & Marknagil
GUESTHOUSES €€

(Map p124; ☑605010; www.undirfjalli.com; Vesturgøta 15-17 & Marknagilsvegur 75; s/d incl breakfast Dkr495/655; ☺Jul–mid-Aug) Somewhat worn, en-suite student accommodation is rented to tourists during the summer vacation with online bargain rates starting from Dkr295. Both sites are accessed via bus 1 to Handilsskúlin. Smaller Undir Fjalli has a communal kitchen. Breakfast (included) is served at Marknagil ('Skúlaheim').

Camping Ground
CAMPING GROUND €

(Map p124; ☑265801; Yvir við Strond; per adult/child Dkr70/35; ☺Jun-Aug) Two handkerchiefs of grass between a busy road and a wind-battered rocky beach share decent showers and washing machines (Dkr25 per load). Book through the tourist office.

✗ Eating

Central Tórshavn has, by far, the Faroes' best and most varied dining options. Restaurants tend to be relatively expensive but lunch buffets are great money-savers and several pubs and cafes serve much cheaper bar meals.

Etika
JAPANESE, VEGETARIAN €€

(Map p126; ✆319319; www.etika.fo; Áarvegur 3; mains Dkr135-175; ⏱11am-midnight Mon-Sat, 5pm-midnight Sun, kitchen till 10pm) Black walls and copper-coloured seats give this little cafe–wine bar an arty feel. Japanese-influenced specialities include 'Nordic Sushi' (nigiri from Dkr22 per piece) and vegie options including a Dkr135 tofu steak meal.

Marco Polo
PUB €€

(Map p126; Sverrisgøta 12; mains Dkr155-215; ⏱11.30am-10pm Mon-Fri, 5-10pm Sat & Sun) A notionally nautical theme puts the atmosphere slightly beyond that of a typical pub, though the beery smell rather lingers. Menu options include ribs, seafood and fish of the day, but the real attraction is the Dkr85 lunch buffet, available weekdays only till 2pm.

Restaurant Hafnia
INTERNATIONAL, SEAFOOD €€€

(Map p126; ✆313233; Hotel Hafnia, Áarvegur 4-10; mains Dkr225; ⏱11.30am-2pm & 6-9.30pm) The main drawcard of this upmarket hotel restaurant is the mouth-watering seafood buffet (Dkr325) served Tuesday and Thursday evenings in summer. Reservations essential.

Glasstovan
NORDIC €€€

(Map p124; ✆317500; www.hotelforoyar.com; Oyggjarvegur 45; lunch mains Dkr130-165, 2-/3-/4-course dinner Dkr340/420/490; ⏱7-10am, noon-2pm & 6-10pm) Tórshavn's top chef has brought new culinary flair to the Hotel Føroyar's sleek restaurant featuring a copper bar, black walls, white tablecloths and sweeping city views.

Borðkrókur
SALADS €

(Map p124; Nordic House; mains Dkr35-50; ⏱10am-5pm Mon-Sat) The bargain here is the modest, buffet salad bar (Dkr50) with 18 options including pickled garlic and dried tomatoes.

Carello
PIZZA €€

(Map p126; ✆320360; Havnargøta; mains Dkr80-125; ⏱11.30am-10pm Sun-Thu, 11.30am-11pm Fri, 1-11pm Sat) White woodwork, red upholstery and sepia photos create a well-pitched blend of ancient and modern. For sunny summer days there's an open terrace, albeit overlooking the bus station across a noisy road.

Rio Bravo
STEAKHOUSE €€

(Map p126; www.riobravo.fo; Tórsgøta 11; mains Dkr155-185, pasta Dkr125; ⏱11.30am-10pm Mon-Fri, 5-10pm Sat & Sun) The Dkr95 buffet

Restaurants

TOP CHOICE **Áarstova**
NORDIC €€€

(Map p126; ✆333000; www.aarstova.fo; Gongin 1; mains/starters Dkr245/125; ⏱6pm-midnight, kitchen till 9.30pm) Obliging, well-trained staff serve divine, locally sourced food in a 300-year-old former inn whose stripped wooden interior gives it a fresh feel while maintaining the building's historic character. Flavours are delectable but the regularly changing menu offers only three main-course choices, with fish dishes prominent. Book ahead.

Hvonn Brasserie
INTERNATIONAL €€

(Map p126; ✆350035; Tórsgøta 4; mains Dkr75-240; ⏱noon-10pm) The casually contemporary restaurant of the Hotel Tórshavn has a very wide-ranging international menu encompassing curry, fajitas, mezes, pastas, Thai soup and pizza. Vegetarians can find some solace at the buffet salad bar (Dkr78/35 as main course/accompaniment).

at this Wild West–themed steakhouse is available for both lunch (daily) and dinner (not Saturday).

Quick Eats
Fast-food outlets can be found at the **SMS Shopping Mall** (Map p124), near the bus station, and around Tórsgøta/Niels Finsensgøta, a nightlife district that comes merrily to life on summer weekend nights.

Pizza Kjallarin   PIZZA €
(Map p126; ☎353353; Niels Finsensgøta; pizzas Dkr60-90; ☺11am-midnight Mon-Thu, 11am-5am Fri, 5pm-5am Sat, 5pm-midnight Sun) Swiftly made thin-crust pizzas to go.

Self-Catering
Miklagarður   SUPERMARKET €
(Map p124; SMS Shopping Mall) Large, well stocked with mix-your-own salads (Dkr10.50 per 100g).

Fk Supermarket   SUPERMARKET €
(Map p126; Dr Jakobsensgøta; ☺7am-7pm Mon-Fri, 7am-5pm Sat) Central and relatively inexpensive.

Mylnun   GROCERY STORE €
(Map p126; Frúuróð; ☺7am-11pm daily) Relatively late opening hours.

Drinking

Where there's beer and live music, watch how the characteristic Faroese reserve crumbles. While most pubs close by midnight on weekdays, Friday and Saturday nights see a dozen central drinking spots still open around 4am, several providing live music.

As well as the listings below, Marco Polo and Rio Bravo restaurants have popular pubs, and Etika doubles as a wine bar.

Hvonn Café   LOUNGE
(Map p126; Tórsgøta 4; beers from Dkr35; ☺noon-midnight) This cosmopolitan lounge is a popular meeting place for Tórshavn's 30-something crowd enjoying cocktails, bar food and a choice of 10 draft beers (Faroese, Belgian and Danish). It's particularly busy on Tuesdays/Thursdays when there's free live jazz/blues.

Kaffihúsið
COFFEE HOUSE

(Map p126; www.kaffihusid.fo; Undir Bryggjubakka; ◷10am-9pm Mon-Sat, noon-9pm Sun) Great coffee (Dkr20 to Dkr47) served behind a rust-sculpted arty facade where fashionable decor contrasts with rough stone walls. On sunny days tables spill onto an open terrace facing the yachts of the western harbour.

Sirkus
PUB

(Map p126; www.facebook.com/sirkus.fo; Gríms Kambans Gøta 2; beers Dkr35; ◷noon-midnight Sun-Thu, noon-4am Fri & Sat) Tórshavn's alternative crowd congregates on two floors of idiosyncrasies with graffiti-cool toilets, cartoon walled stairs and DJ sets from Thursday to Saturday. Sandwiches and burgers are served.

Café Natúr
PUB

(Map p126; Áarvegur 7; beers from Dkr30) This partly timbered, turf-roofed pub offers a short list of good-value bar snacks (tortillas, pitas, salad) until 8pm. Live music at weekends. Smokers can stay warm while puffing away on the almost glassed-in terrace.

Irish Pub
IRISH PUB

(Map p126; Gríms Kambansgøta 13; beer/Guinness Dkr35/60; ◷11am-midnight Sun-Thu, 11am-3am Fri & Sat) Dark wood dividers, lantern-style lamps, and a view over the Western Harbour make for a convivial if predictable drinking den. Bar meals (till 9pm) are good value and at weekends there are late-night snacks till 3am.

Mica
CAFE, BAR

(Map p126; Niels Finsensgøta 12; beers Dkr30; ◷11am-midnight Mon-Thu, 11am-4am Fri & Sat, 5-11pm Sun) This intimate wooden bungalow has a whitewashed contemporary look and hides a beer garden at the back for summer weekends. Serves nachos, pitas, soup and smoothies before 10pm.

Kafe Vágsbotn
BEER TERRACE

(Map p126; Undir Bryggjubakka 3; juice/beer Dkr38/50; ◷11am-10pm Sun-Thu, noon-3am Fri & Sat May-Aug) Wrap up in a blanket (provided) to sip freshly squeezed juices or draft beers at this outdoor spot whose harbourside perch is somewhat marred by passing traffic. Summer only.

Kafe Kaspar
BAR, CAFE

(Map p126; www.hafnia.fo; Undir Bryggjubakka) Hip, low-key, '70s-retro lounge serving coffee and cake by day, and cocktails later.

☆ Entertainment

The events-listing pamphlet *Havnartíðindi* (in Faroese) is available free from the tourist office.

Norðurlandahúsið
CULTURAL CENTRE

(Nordic House; Map p124; ☑351351; www.nlh.fo; Norðari Ringvegur 10; ◷10am-5pm Mon-Sat, 2-5pm Sun) Turf-roofed yet modern, this architecturally interesting cultural centre hosts concerts, plays, exhibitions and conferences.

Havnar Bio
CINEMA, CLUBS

(Map p126; ☑311956; www.bio.fo; Tinghúsvegur 8; tickets Dkr80) Two-screen cinema showing original films with Danish subtitles. In the same grungy building is a pizzeria, Chinese restaurant and two nightclubs: **Rex** (3rd fl; ◷midnight-4am Fri & Sat) and bigger, darker **Deep** (◷11pm-4am Fri & Sat). Both typically charge Dkr100 cover but free Fridays are possible.

⌂ Shopping

HN Jacobsens
BOOKS

(Map p126; www.hnj.fo; Mylnugøta) Sells maps and books plus souvenir cuddly puffin toys. It is attached to the tourist office.

Andreas í Vágsbotni
SOUVENIRS

(Gríms Kambansgøta) Souvenirs, knitwear, T-shirts and costumed dolls.

Galerie Focus
ART

(www.galeriefocus.com; Gríms Kambansgøta 20; ◷4-6pm Tue-Sat) Intimate gallery.

Glarsmiðjan Gallery
ART

(www.glarsmidjan.fo; Dr Jakobsensgøta 7; ◷10am-5.30pm Mon-Fri) Modern Faroese paintings.

Sirri
DESIGNER CLOTHING

(www.sirri.fo; Áarvegur 10) Produces elegant garments from organic, dye-free wool. Also sells sheepskins from Stóra Dímun.

TUTL
MUSIC

(www.tutl.com; Niels Finsensgøta 9) Cooperative of local musicians whose shop lets you to listen to a vast range of Faroese artists (CDs Dkr120 to Dkr169). There's a free 4pm mini-concert each summer weekday.

M&M
SECONDHAND CDS

(Vágsbotnur 14) Small selection from Dkr50.

ⓘ Information

Internet Access

Býarbókasavnið (Town Library; Niels Finsensgøta 7; ◷10am-6pm Mon-Fri, 10am-2pm Sat) Sign up for free half-hour slots.

TÓRSHAVN ENTERTAINMENT

Føroya Landsbókasavn (National Library; www.flb.fo; JC Svabosgøta 16; ◷10am-6pm Mon-Thu, 10am-5pm Fri Sep-Jun, 10am-3pm Mon-Fri Jul & Aug) Free internet access.
Tourist office (Mylnugøta; per hr Dkr40) Two computers.

Medical Services

Landssjúkrahúsið (Map p124; ☎1870; www. lsh.fo; JC Svabosgøta) Modern hospital with casualty ward. Between 4pm and 8am you can get an emergency doctor's consultation. Emergency dental service from 1pm to 2pm on weekends.

Money

Outside banking hours, the Hotel Hafnia can exchange cash at poor rates. Banks (with ATMs) include **Eik Banki** (Tinghúsvegur 49) and **Føroya Banki** (Niels Finsensgøta 15).

Post

Main post office (Óðinshædd 2) The post office is well out of the centre but there's also an automated postal machine within the much more central Snarskivan (city hall) building, accessible 9am to 4pm weekdays.

Tourist Information

Tourist office (Kunningarstovan; ☎315788; www.visittorshavn.fo; Mylnugøta; ◷8am-5.30pm Mon-Fri, 9am-2pm Sat Jun-Aug, 9am-5.30pm Mon-Fri, 10am-2pm Sat Sep-May) Assists with accommodation and tour bookings, provides great free brochures and maps. Bookshop attached.

❶ Getting There & Away

Ferries to Suðuroy, Iceland and Denmark plus all long-distance buses depart from a combined bus-ferry station (the **Farstøðin Transport Terminal**) which has luggage lockers (small/big Dkr15/30), an ATM and a taxi stand. The ferry to Nólsoy uses a separate jetty nearby.

❶ Getting Around

To/From the Airport

CAR HIRE Companies' airport booths are only staffed given advance bookings. Hefty airport supplements apply, plus there's the Vagar tunnel toll to pay.

MINIBUS **Airport Shuttle** (☎332473; www. shuttlebuss.com) picks up from selected hotels around 6.30am, 9am, 1pm and 3pm (Dkr150 or €25). Book ahead.

PUBLIC BUS From the Farstøðin Transport terminal, regular bus 300 takes 55 minutes (Dkr90).

TAXI Costs around Dkr600. **Bil** (☎323232; www.airporttaxi.fo; per person Dkr175) offers an airport taxi-share service. Book one day ahead.

City Bus

COSTS Red city buses are free.
FREQUENCY Half-hourly weekdays, hourly weekends and evenings.
USEFUL ROUTES From the central Steinatún stop, bus 2 loops anticlockwise around town passing close to Hotel Streym, main post office, Føroya Fornminnissavn and Norðurlandahúsið, returning past the SMS Shopping Mall before heading south to Argir via the hospital. Bus 3 does virtually the same loop clockwise then heads west on Landavegur.

Taxi

Companies include **Auto** (☎311234) and **Bil** (☎323232; www.taxi.fo). Taxis are metered, with fares starting around Dkr65 for under 2km (or Dkr90 between midnight and 6am). Longer rides work out between Dkr12 and Dkr16 per km by day; it's 16% more after 5pm and 35% more after midnight.

AROUND TÓRSHAVN

Nólsoy

POP 250

This hunchbacked grassy island makes a quick, easy rural escape from the capital. Views of Tórshavn from the ferry (Dkr45 return, 20 minutes, five to seven times daily) are part of the appeal. You'll arrive in architecturally neutral Nólsoy village where the harbour sports an 1863 church, whale-bone gateway and tourist office (☎327060; www.visitnolsoy.fo; ◷10am-5pm), which has an inviting little cafe and can get you into the sweet little Brunn House. Some visitors make the three-hour hike to the lighthouses on the island's southern end, but you need only walk 20 minutes to get a wide series of headland panoramas, passing some archaic stone fish-drying barns and a very lumpy set of Viking ruins en route.

Ornithologists come to Nólsoy to visit the 'worlds' biggest' colony of storm petrels, best observed at dusk. Jens-Kjeld Jensen runs guided bird tours (☎327064; www.jenskjeld.info; ◷mid-Jun–late Aug) costing Dkr450 including accommodation. Book way ahead.

The four-room B&B-cafe Kaffistovan (☎327175; s/d Dkr250/500) has three neat but compact rooms in the eaves plus a bigger one with balcony and views, albeit as stylistically dated as the shared bathroom.

Kirkjubøur

POP 80

Sprinkled along the base of a craggy sea-facing bluff, Kirkjubøur (*cheer*-chi-ba) consists of around 20 tar-blackened chalet homes, some with turf roofs and stone bases. For centuries this was the Faroes' religious and cultural centre. Behind the simple, whitewashed St Olav's church (AD 1111) lies the shell of the never-completed 13th-century Magnus Cathedral (admission free; ☺24hr). Work stopped when local villagers, fed up with paying the taxes to fund it, revolted and killed the bishop. Today its hefty basalt wall-tops are wrapped with protective black metal cladding that converts the ruins into an incongruous statement of contemporary art. Facing it is the beautiful turf-roofed farmhouse Roykstovan (Smoke Chamber; ☎328089; www.patursson.com; adult/child Dkr30/free; ☺10am-5.30pm Mon-Sat, 2-5.30pm Sun May-Aug or by appointment) built upon the 900-year-old foundation platform of the long-disappeared bishop's palace. The exterior is detailed with 19th-century pseudo-Viking carvings picked out in vivid red and turquoise. Although a private home (in the Patursson family for 17 generations, no less), two rooms are usually open for public viewing. Their driftwood timbers are scented with history and draped with fascinating artefacts, each telling its own story. By advance arrangement you can even organise a feast at the great banqueting bench fashioned from the life-saving plank of an 1895 shipwreck.

If driving consider making a cliff-clinging side trip towards Syðradalur farm for some memorable views towards Koltur.

From Tórshavn, the 8.10am, 10.30am, 4.30pm and 6.30pm departures of bus 101 to Gamlarætt port (Dkr20, 30 minutes) will continue 2km further to Kirkjubøur by advance request. Call ☎343030.

SANDOY & SKÚVOY

Though close to the capital and very attractive in parts, these islands lack must-see attractions and are often overlooked by visitors.

❶ Getting There & Away

Unless you come by helicopter, all visits to Sandoy and Skúvoy start with the ro-ro vehicle ferry linking Skopun (northern Sandoy) to Gamlarætt

WORTH A TRIP

THE FAROES' CUTEST VILLAGES

» Elduvík (p136)
» Mykines (p134)
» Skarvanes (p132)
» Funningur (p136)

(Streymoy) seven times daily (last northbound service 10.30pm most days).

Passenger boats (☎505207) to Skúvoy leave Sandur four or five times per day (Dkr45 return, 35 minutes) but you must make a reservation in advance. Bus 600 from Skopun to Sandur (Dkr20, 20 minutes, six times a day) connects to both ferries and links to Skálavík on the eastern shore. Bus 601 connects both Húsavík and Dalur to Sandur (Dkr20) four times daily.

There's no ferry from Skúvoy to Suðuroy.

Sandur

POP 1390

Sandoy's main settlement, Sandur is mostly flat and somewhat diffuse but has banks, an ATM and shops, if no restaurants. Its very helpful tourist office (☎361836; www.visitsandoy.fo; Mørkin Mikla 3; ☺9am-noon & 1-4pm Mon-Fri Apr-Aug, 1-4pm Sep-Mar) can organise hiking, birdwatching and seaborne tours of the bird cliffs of both Sandoy and Skúvoy.

The black timber cube opposite Heimasandsvegur 28 is a new, two-level art gallery (Listasavnið Á Sandi; adult/child Dkr40/free; ☺2-4pm Tue-Sun mid-May–Sep, Sun only Oct–mid-May) featuring 20th-century Faroese work, including distinctive semi-abstract canvases by Ingálvur av Reyni. Norðara Koyta (Heimasandsvegur 81; adult/child Dkr30/free; ☺2-4pm Jun-Sep, Sun only Oct–May) is a sweet little 1812 house-museum with turf roof and seven tiny rooms featuring 19th-century furnishings. Neither is worth a major detour.

Often misnamed a 'hostel', Ísansgarður (☎508008; louisahenze@gmail.com; 117 Heimasandsvegur; s/d without bathroom Dkr300/420) is a pleasant guesthouse set back off the main road 500m north of the tourist office in Sandur. There are nine simple, clean rooms, one with private bathroom (Dkr480). Book well ahead as the owner stays in Tórshavn when no guests are expected.

The Faroese term *siða*, sometimes translated in tourist brochures as rappelling, is the traditional lowering of people on ropes down cliff faces, originally to collect birds' eggs. For groups of eight or more, Sandoy's tourist office can organise a fully harnessed *siða* experience dropping you 200m, halfway down the Lonin sea cliffs, to a ledge where you get time to explore before being hoisted back up. Equipment, including helmet and walkie-talkie, is included as is the guided 90-minute access hike from Søltuvik.

Around Sandur

Single-track lanes undulate across moorlands and edge around Sandoy's coastal slopes. The finest runs southeast off the Sandur–Húsavík road to the very photogenically huddled 10-house hamlet of Skarvanes. Another adorable lane winds 5km west of Sandur to Søltuvik, a lonely single house above a beach with a pair of antique crossed anchors.

In Húsavík a grassy area punctuated with medieval stone outhouses faces a sandy beach that's pounded by furious waves. Around a precarious headland road, Dalur is set back from a stony beach in a gloriously green bowl-valley. For the very satisfying Dalur–Skarvanes moorland hike (around 90 minutes, best westbound), start up Gerðavegur, which soon becomes an unpaved farm track. Leave the track 1.1km beyond Dalur's last house then follow the cairns. Keep right once you've descended to the west-coast clifftop path then find your way down through sheep gates. Annoyingly there's no public transport back from Skarvanes to the Húsavík–Sandur road (6km).

Pleasantly set but architecturally dull, Skopun features the world's biggest postbox on a suburban hilltop.

A few weekends per year boat-builder Jóan Petur Clementsen (✆361019, 286119; tojo@olivant.fo) takes adventurous groups by sea to the Faroes' most isolated island, Stóra Dímun (population five). You'll climb through puffin fields (somewhat nerve-rackingly at times using ropes) to the island's single farmstead for coffee and cake. Cost per person is around DKr500.

Sandur tourist office can arrange B&Bs (s/d incl breakfast Dkr350/450) and basic campsites (Dkr60) in Sandur, Húsavík and Dalur. Hanna Sórensen's B&B (✆266417; Sjógøta 13) at Húsavík has great beach views from the 'pink room' and if you're lucky you might even get to taste a morsel of Hanna's home-hung *skerpikjøt* (air-dried mutton).

Skúvoy (Skúgvoy)

POP 50

Named after its large population of great skuas, Skúvoy slopes steadily but not steeply up from its single-port village to the very attractive Høvdin bird cliffs. These are alive with clouds of fulmars and oystercatchers and reached by a mostly tame stroll (no vehicles) taking around 45 minutes each way. Follow red-painted wooden stakes after the only road peters out and bring a stick to protect your head in case you're dive-bombed by swooping skuas.

In the village, Harry Jensen has a comfortable three-room B&B (✆361459, 210028; harryj@olivant.fo; s/d Dkr350/500) just across the stream from the church and helipad. He's knowledgeable about local birdlife, provides hearty meals (lunch/dinner Dkr100/150) and has almost completed an attached cafe that's due to open in 2011.

THE WESTERN ISLANDS

Vágar

POP 3060

If you fly into the Faroes you'll arrive on Vágar (*vow*-whar). While most travellers dash straight off to Tórshavn, Vágar itself has a dramatic cliff-edged western coast that's most entertainingly viewed from the mini-ferry to loveable Mykines. Six to nine times daily, bus 300 links Tórshavn and Sørvágur (Dkr100, one hour) via the airport (Dkr90, 55 minutes) and Miðvágur. One or two daily buses will continue from Sørvágur to Bøur if you reserve on ✆215610 at least two hours ahead.

MIÐVÁGUR & SANDAVÁGUR

Miðvágur is home to Vágar's banks, supermarkets and **tourist office** (☑213455; www.visitvagar.fo; ☺9am-4pm Mon-Fri). Within the tourist office, the three-room **War Museum** (Krigssavnið; adult Dkr50) commemorates the Faroe Islands' role in WWII and the roughly 5000 British troops stationed on Vágar (1940–1944) who, among other things, built the airport.

On a hillside just above town, **Kálvalið** (☑332425, 275325; adult/child Dkr30/free; ☺call to arrange) is a two-room, turf-roofed stone hovel that was used from 1632 as a home for widows of local priests. One such resident woman outlived three holy husbands. Retaining original mud floors, ceiling timbers from shipwrecks and wooden beds, it's probably the Faroes' oldest surviving house, and the small but fascinating collection of traditional tools and household implements is engagingly explained by the caretaker who opens the place at short notice on request.

Sandavágur, with its fanciful 1917 **church**, is 2.5km further east. Between the two, **Á Giljanesi** (☑333465; www.giljanes.fo; dm/s/d Dkr200/350/450) is a simple, almost totally unstaffed hostel with a decent kitchen and smallish, fair-value rooms. Bring a sleeping bag or pay Dkr50 for sheets. Even-numbered rooms have bay views toward Koltur's craggy rear end. Camping costs Dkr75 per adult.

AROUND MIÐVÁGUR

A leisurely but rewarding 1½-hour hike follows the eastern bank of **Leitisvatn**, the country's largest lake. Start on Heiðagøta, the side road beside the small police station (*politi*). Turn right, go through the gate and follow a path through often boggy land which forms rich breeding grounds for oystercatchers, whimbrels and snipe. The path ends above **Bøsdalafossur**, a 30m waterfall formed where the lake water tumbles directly into the foaming sea surf below. For particularly inspiring views of the soaring cliff-edged coastline, climb the raised rocks slightly to the east. On your return look out for a spindly rocky spire evocatively nicknamed the **Trøllkonufingur** (Witch's Finger) on the other side of Miðvágur.

Another way to enjoy the scenery of Leitisvatn is on a three-hour **lake cruise** (☑333123; www.lakeside.fo; adult/child Dkr275/175; ☺10am Mon-Sat Apr-Sep) or the same company's **evening cruise** (adult/child Dkr440/275; ☺6pm Jun-Aug), which includes dinner.

SØRVÁGUR

POP 1030

Just 1.5km west of the airport, **Sørvágur** curves somewhat blandly around the eastern end of an otherwise handsome fjord. The main attraction is a twice-daily summer boat service to Mykines leaving from a harbour at the town's southwestern limit. That's near the petrol station and snack bar, some 150m west of **Sørvágs Bygdarsavn** (☑253757; www.bygdarsavnid.com; Rossatrøðin 13; admission Dkr30; ☺by appointment), a one-room museum of traditional Faroese tools. Exhibits, including horse-hair cliff-egg raiders' ropes and *kveistur* bird-wing dusters, are similar to those displayed at the more interesting Kálvalið in Miðvágur.

Ró Guesthouse (☑332036, 532036; www.ro.fo; 13 Í Geilini; s/d Dkr400/700) has bright if small new rooms with flat-screen TVs, virginal white linen and bathrooms in all but two tiny singles. The totally unmarked building is set one block back from the harbour road. There's not even a doorbell so phone ahead to arrange arrival details. Guests can use the washing machine, dryer and a shared, if almost windowless, kitchen and lounge.

AROUND SØRVÁGUR

Picturesque **Bøur** (population 70) is a bayside huddle of old Faroese homes, several

VÁGAR AIRPORT (VÁGA FLOGHAVEN)

The Faroes' only **airport** (www.floghavn.fo) has a tourist information desk, a cafeteria and free wi-fi for Atlantic Airways passengers. There's an ATM but no bank. If you're desperate you can exchange cash at poor rates in the recently refurbished **62°N Airport Hotel** (Hotel Vágar; ☑309090; www.62n.fo; s/d Dkr925/1210), three minutes' walk west of the terminal. Unremarkable rooms there feel overpriced but the hotel's **restaurant** (mains Dkr145-225; ☺11am-9pm) has pleasant views and a good-value weekday lunch buffet (Dkr99) plus Vágar's only bar (beer Dkr35). The hotel rents low-tech **bicycles** (per half-day Dkr75) plus **canoes** (half-/full day Dkr300/500) on the nearby lake.

with turf roofs. An intimidatingly tall amphitheatre of *hamrar* (stepped cliffs) stands behind. The 4km trip from Sørvágur is amply justified by bewitching views of Tindhólmur, a serrated islet of vertical rock that rises from the frothing waves like a Tolkienesque fantasy castle. Surreally sliced, Tindhólmur seems to have had its western half mistakenly erased in postproduction. It's one of the Faroes' landscape icons.

Another 4km west of Bøur, Gásadalur (*gwa-sa-dal-wur;* population 22) occupies an even grander amphitheatre. The village homes are less photogenic than those of Bøur, but Tindhólmur makes a fine backdrop. Road access (no bus) is via an illuminated 1.5km tunnel. Alternatively, a perilous hike via the former postman's trail (2½ hours) starts 700m south of the tunnel's eastern entrance (guide essential).

Mykines

POP 20

The Faroes' westernmost island, dramatic Mykines (*mitch*-i-ness), is one of the Faroes' best birdwatching spots. The island's eponymous and only village is an absolute charmer made up of traditional turf-roofed houses overlooking a precipitous harbour where landing can be a true adventure in inclement weather.

All transport on Mykines is on foot. The star attraction is hiking to the 1909 Mykinesholmur Lighthouse (allow three hours return) through densely packed puffin burrows and across a 35m footbridge over a sea gorge brimming with birdlife. Glimpse the Faroes' only significant gannet colonies on stacks near the lighthouse.

🛏 Sleeping

Kristianshús   LODGE €
(📞312985, 212985; www.mikines.fo; campsites per adult Dkr50, r per person without/with linen Dkr150/250; ☺May-Aug) In Mykines village, this unpretentious lodge can hold up to 30 people in three simply furnished houses. One hosts a communal lounge and kitchen, another a dining room serving hearty setmenu suppers (Dkr140), plus a minishop selling beer (Dkr30), hot dogs (Dkr25) and chocolate bars. Bathrooms are shared.

Yellow House   HOTEL €
(📞532614; www.gulahusid.com; per person without/with linen Dkr150/250; ☺Jun-Aug) Directly opposite Kristianshús, standards at Yellow House are slightly better if you score one of the bright homestay-style rooms upstairs. However, the basement bunk rooms are claustrophobically cramped. A kitchen and washing machine are available but bring your food with you from Vágar. When it's unstaffed get the key from the sheep-scented 'post office', an entirely unmarked red house 100m away.

ℹ Getting There & Away

Transport should be booked ahead, but it's still highly weather-dependent so allow leeway in case you get stranded among the puffins.

Boat

The partly uncovered mini-ferry **Brynhild** (📞343030; Dkr60) leaves Sørvágur at 10.20am and 4.20pm from May to August, taking around 40 minutes, then returning immediately.

Helicopter

Three days weekly, fog allowing, the helicopter arrives in Mykines from Vágar (Dkr145, 10 minutes). It returns immediately then continues after a short break to Tórshavn then to Froðba (Wednesday), Klaksvík and Flugloy (Friday) or Skúvoy (Sunday). On Fridays you can arrive from Froðba, Skúvoy or Tórshavn.

Northern Streymoy

KVÍVÍK

POP 370

Worth a very brief stop if you're driving to Vestmanna, Kvívík village is noted for the ruins of a Viking farmstead but the minimalist site consists of just two foot-high horseshoes of excavated stones topped with protective turf. From the 1903 church they're 100m away across the stream that divides the village in two.

VESTMANNA

POP 1260

Vestmanna is layered around a large, steep-sided fjord end that drips with several waterfalls.

◉ Sights & Activities

Although the scenery is marred by hydroelectric feeder pipes, warehouses and harbour workings, the town remains unmissable as the starting point for inspirational two-hour boat tours (adult/child Dkr250/125; ☺May-Sep) to the Vestmanna Bird Cliffs. Tour boats bob beneath towering cliff faces, pass spiky rock pinnacles and sometimes squeeze beneath tight stone arches. You'll spy the breeding areas of guillemots and razorbills as screeching fulmars and kittiwakes soar above like thousands of white dots. Bring warm, waterproof clothing.

Two operators, Lamhauge (☎424155; www.sightseeing.fo) and Skúvadal (☎471600; www.puffin.fo), work together offering various-sized boats to fit passenger numbers (minimum five). There are zero to five departures daily from May to September, according to demand and weather conditions. A 2pm sailing is the most reliable but typically also the most crowded.

Tickets are sold through the tourist centre (☎471500, 771500; www.visit-vestmanna.com; ☺9am-5pm May-Sep) whose little Saga Museum (adult/child Dkr90/75) tells 11 gory tales of Faroese history/folklore using a half-hour audio guide and professionally lifelike wax figures. Museum tickets aren't quite as preposterously overpriced if combined with a bird-cliff tour (combo adult/child Dkr300/150).

ATV Mountain Tours (☎289090; www.atv.fo; ☺by arrangement year-round) offer a variety of quad-bike trips into the sheep-grazed mountains behind town. The shortest two-hour trips (Dkr650 per person, minimum two) depart up to four times daily and can be combined with Magni Blástein's Fishing Trips (☎581582; www.fishingwithblastein.com; adult/child Dkr400/150), tentatively time-tabled for 9.30am and 2.30pm. Advanced bookings are essential.

All the above organisations are at the 'tourist harbour' (former car-ferry dock) but central Vestmanna's post office, banks and commercial port are 900m further west.

🛏 Sleeping & Eating

Krákureiðrið (☎424747, 764747; jf.egilsnes@kallnet.fo; Niðarivegur 34; s/tw Dkr400/500) is a superneat six-room guesthouse with good shared showers and a great kitchen with partial views across the tourist harbour. Breakfast and make-your-own coffee are free. Phone the friendly owners to announce your arrival as there's neither reception nor bell. The tourist centre can call for you and is itself home to Vestmanna's only restaurant, Fjørðurkrógvin (☎471505; mains Dkr188-220; ☺9am-5pm May-late Sep), where beers cost Dkr35 and coffee-and-cake sets you back Dkr55. The Magn Filling Station (tourist harbour; ☺7am-11pm Mon-Sat, 9am-11pm Sun) sells hot dogs and limited groceries for those interested in self-catering.

🛈 Getting There & Away

Public buses from Tórshavn (Dkr50, one hour) run eight times each weekday, thrice daily at weekends. Almost all require changing from bus 300 (airport service) to bus 100 at the Kollafjarðadalur (kotla-furdla) petrol station. When travelling by car, choose the starkly barren old mountain road (Rte 10) and consider brief detours to pretty Norðradalur hamlet and to Kvívík. Tora tours (☎315505; www.tora.fo; adult/child Dkr685/340 return; ☺8.30am Wed, 4pm Sat) do most of this, collecting you from Tórshavn hotels and connecting with Vestmanna boat trips (included).

NORTHERN STREYMOY

Northern Streymoy's hotel-less villages make enchanting detours by car. However, most visitors find they're not quite stunning enough to justify the awkward access by rare buses from Oyrarbakki.

SAKSUN
POP 30

Over 10km of lonely moorland valley leads from Hvalvík to tiny Saksun. Fork right at the village's scrappy southwestern end and continue 1km to find the solitary turf-roofed church. It's dramatically perched high above a tidal lake, impressively ringed by crags and waterfalls, forming one of the Faroes' most photographed sights. From road's end look back at the proud 19th-century farmstead, which has an almost medieval appearance. It's strictly private property, but in summer the oldest section opens as Dúvugarður Folk Museum (☎210700; admission Dkr30; ☺2-5pm Fri-Wed mid-Jun–mid-Aug) showing three distinct sections furnished in period style. One was used by the farmer, another by servants and a third housed the village priest.

TJØRNUVÍK
POP 70

A gently satisfying 14km drive northwest from Oyrarbakki passes a 'forest' of cairns (just beyond Langasandur), an impressive roadside waterfall (1.4km further) and Haldlorsvik's octagonal church. A cliff-ledge road leads on into Tjørnuvík. Clasped tightly in a rocky claw of backing mountains, the village is a mostly modern huddle hiding just a few turf-roofed cottages. Great views look across a wave-pounded, grey-sand beach towards the distinctive sea stacks Risin and Kellingin (p135). Serious hikers could trek south across a partially treacherous mountain trail to Saksun (three to four hours).

Northern Eysturoy

With jaw-dropping scenery everywhere you turn, travelling between the villages of northern Eysturoy makes for one of the most magical experiences in the country.

❶ Getting There & Away

You'll need a car to really enjoy this area. The only regular buses run Tórshavn–Gøta–Klaksvík plus Oyrarbakki–Eiði (Dkr20, 25 minutes, seven times every weekday and four times on Saturday). By advance request, **bus 201** (☑343030) connects Gjógv to Oyrarbakki three times each weekday (Dkr40, 40 minutes) via Funningur but there's no summer service to Elduvík.

EIÐI
POP 640

The large village of Eiði (*ay-ee*) rises steeply from a lake-dappled green isthmus, affording memorable views across the sound to Streymoy. The main attraction here is hiking up **Eiðiskollur** to a lively fulmar bird cliff that plummets over 350m, offering heart-stopping views down upon the classic twin sea stacks, **Risin and Kellingin**. For those OK with steep gradients, the walk takes around 45 minutes out, 30 minutes back. The route is cairn-marked once you've climbed a small fence from the village's uppermost road end (beyond Mali-fløta 13).

Behind a sturdy 1881 **church**, Eiði's old core consists of tightly folded alleys hiding **Eiðis Bygdasavn** (☑423597; adult/child Dkr30/free; ☺4-6pm Mon & Sun Jun & Jul or by arrangement), a little turf-roofed folk museum. The interiors have been reworked in 19th-century style and there are numerous photos to illustrate changing lifestyles over several generations.

Erling Petersen offers **B&B rooms** (☑423194, 213194; Esturi í Túni 8) in the lane that starts across the tiny park from the museum, but catching him in can be a challenge.

GJÓGV
POP 40

Tiny Gjógv (*jek*-v) is clustered around the short, picturesque sea gorge for which it's named. In one of several traditional cottages, **Debesar Shop-Café** (☑423523; www.gjogvadventure.fo; Niðari í Stovu; coffee Dkr15; ☺10am-5.30pm May-Sep) sells souvenirs, ice creams and Gjógv liquorice rock. Proceeds from its Dkr30 local hiking maps support local environmental projects, though a map

isn't necessary for Gjógv's most popular short **hike** up the western cliff-side where fulmars soar and a few puffins nest.

Gjógv's unique guesthouse, **Gjáargarður** (☑423171; www.gjaargardur.fo; Viking-style s/d Dkr350/600, s/d Dkr750/890, superior d Dkr990; ☺closed 15 Dec-15 Jan; ℗@), is a three-storey turf-roofed chalet where so-called 'Viking style' beds are built into the upper-floor eaves like in medieval Faroese farmhouses. These are great fun for one person but claustrophobically over-cosy for two. A couple of timber-clad rooms share the same communal bathrooms and have great private balconies. If you want en suite bathroom facilities and a lockable door there are unrefined 'standard' rooms downstairs plus considerably bigger and more stylish 'superior' options in the annexe next door, featuring tiled floors and tasteful ceramics. Much of the guesthouse is wheelchair accessible and breakfast is included. Set dinners (Dkr170) are copious and well prepared; fish on Monday, Wednesday and Friday, a mixed buffet on Sunday. Lunches by arrangement.

ELDUVÍK
POP 30

Facing Kalsoy's jagged northern tip, Elduvík is a dreamily cute snaggle of tar-blackened traditional cottages divided into two photogenic clumps by the meandering mouth of the Stóra stream. The cafe and B&B have closed but there are a couple of hook-ups for caravans at the otherwise unequipped little **campsite** (☑306900).

FUNNINGUR
POP 80

Set beneath some of the Faroes' tallest peaks, the old village of Funningur is home to a particularly photogenic 1847 **church** with turf roof, tar-coated shutters and an idyllic little stream running beside it. For bird's-eye views down onto Funningur and fabulous panoramas in all directions, zigzag up the dizzying roads to Eiði and Gjógv.

GØTA
POP 1060

Caught in a fjord end between two jagged mountain arms, Gøta is in fact a sprawling trio of villages. Syðrugøta's sandy little beach is the improbable venue for the Faroes' foremost rock festival, **G!** (www.gfestival.com; ☺late Jul). There's a celebrated modern church in Gøtugjógv. But the main attraction is Norðragøta's **Blásastova** (☑222717; www.blasastova.fo; adult/child

Risin (the Giant) and Kellingin (the Hag) were a mythical couple sent by the giants of Iceland to steal the Faroes under cover of darkness. However, in lassoing the islands near Eiði the cliffs fractured and by the time they had started to drag the Faroes away, the sun had risen and turned them into rock stacks. These petrified figures are visible from Tjørnuvík and from the scenic Eiði–Gjógv road (use the free binocular stand). Or gaze down on them from Eiðiskollur above Eiði.

Dkr40/10; ⊗2-4pm Fri-Tue mid-May–mid-Sep), a historical museum that incorporates half a dozen turf-roofed buildings, including the village church. Stones in the basement of one such house are supposedly remnants of the home of saga-era anti-hero Tronður i Gøtu, whose statue looks towards it from a bizarre horizontal posture.

Southern Eysturoy

Prosperous **Runavík** (www.visiteysturoy.fo) is the centre of a semi-urban sprawl that lines much of the Skálafjord. The area isn't worth a detour but if you're driving this way there are moorland and headland views from the wind farm above forgettable Æðuvik, while **Nes** has ancient and modern churches plus a one-gun WWII sea-defence emplacement. Villages **Lambi** and **Selatrað** have the area's most picturesque rural settings. In contrastingly urban Runavík, **Cafe-Bar Pêche** (☑447040; mains Dkr80-180) is a relatively suave snack restaurant with Dkr70 lunch buffets (weekdays), chicken wings or fish and chips.

KLAKSVÍK & THE NORTHERN ISLES

Klaksvík

POP 4670

The colourful fjord-side port of Klaksvík forms an urban horseshoe hemmed by stepped pyramidal peaks. It's a logical base for exploring the northern isles and while short on specific sights, photogenic viewpoints abound in and around town.

◉ Sights & Activities

Klakkur   HIKE, VIEWPOINT
A steady grassy climb brings you to the top of this 413m cliff with truly splendid views

encompassing the fjordland drama of surrounding islands. The city below looks especially magnificent as the lights come on at dusk. The trail is obvious if occasionally steep, taking 45 minutes from a tiny car park where unpaved Astarbreyt dead ends 2km northwest of the heliport.

Norðoya Fornminnissavn   FOLK MUSEUM
(☑456287; Klaksvíksvegur 86; adult/child Dkr20/free; ⊗1-4pm mid-May–mid-Sep) The top attraction of Klaksvík's little museum is a nostalgic, fully preserved old pharmacy shop room that operated until 1961.

Leikalund   HISTORIC BUILDING
(☑457151; Klaksvíksvegur 84; ⊗1-6pm Mon-Fri, 10am-2pm Sat) Dating from the Danish trading monopoly days, this restored wooden-beamed store now sells souvenirs, books and Faroese CDs and serves coffee (Dkr10). The back room hosts changing art exhibitions and intimate live concerts (first weekend of most months).

Christianskirkjan   CHURCH
(Kirkjubrekka; ⊗11am-noon & 2-4pm Mon-Sat Jun-Aug) An intriguing, if far from handsome, attempt to meld Viking-era design with modern architecture, the 1963 Christianskirkjan is most interesting for its transplanted 1901 altar mural and the full-size rowing boat dangling high above the nave.

Summar Festivalur   FESTIVAL
(www.summarfestivalur.fo) This major music festival takes place in early August.

☞ Tours

Fishing and/or sightseeing trips (circumnavigating Fugloy or rounding Enniberg) depend on group size, currents, weather and availability. Make contact well in advance or ask the tourist office, preferably a day or two ahead.

Alpha Pilot   BOAT TRIPS
(☑289508; www.northadventures.fo; adult/child Dkr300/150; ⊗12.10pm & 4.15pm daily Jul & Aug)

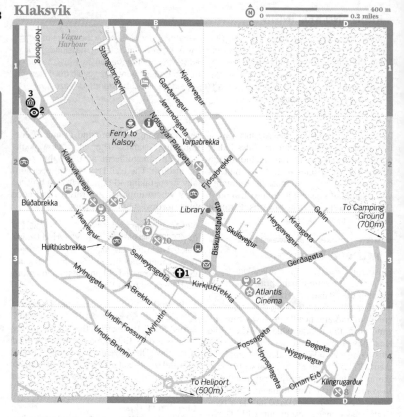

^(N) 0 _____ 400 m
      0 _____ 0.2 miles

Sightseeing excursions start from Hvannasund, 20-minutes' drive north.

Dragin BOAT TRIPS

(☎756661; www.dragin.fo; adult/child Dkr250/100; ⊙6pm Jun-Aug) This 1940s wooden boat offers bracing four-hour sightseeing cruises (minimum 10, maximum 30 people) including coffee and soup. Book through the tourist office by 2pm.

Komet BOAT TRIPS

(☎291507; www.komet.fo; adult/child Dkr400/200; ⊙4pm) Four-hour sea-angling trips.

🛏 Sleeping

Hotel Klaksvík HOTEL €€

(☎455333; www.hotelklaksvik.fo; Víkavegur 38; s/d incl breakfast Dkr795/995; ⊙reception 7am-9pm) Candle lanterns welcome you into a modest foyer, the stairways are scuffed but the rooms are sizeable and spotlessly clean.

Some command great bay views. Rates include feeble wi-fi and good buffet breakfasts. Other meals are available but the whole establishment is alcohol-free. Four storeys, no lift.

Norðoya Vallaraheim UNSTAFFED HOSTEL €
(Stangavegur 16; s/d/tr Dkr350/450/550; ⊗Jun-Aug) This four-room hostel with shared kitchen and bathroom must be booked ahead via the tourist office, whose staff can also arrange rooms at three central B&Bs and some self-catering apartments given enough notice.

Camping Ground UNMANNED CAMPSITE €
(Uti-I-Grov; tent & up to 4 people Dkr150) Book and pay at the tourist office to use this small, flat hillside lawn with simple toilet block and heated kitchen cabin. It's 1km east of the church, hidden behind an isolated kindergarten. The car park has four caravan hook-ups (Dkr150).

✖ Eating & Drinking

Hereford STEAKHOUSE €€€
(☑456434; Klaksvíksvegur 45; mains Dkr215-265; ⊗6-10pm Tue-Sun) Busts and candles lead up to a pine-walled room of dining booths where excellent pepper steak, tournedos or lamb are the mainstays. It's head and shoulders above the (decidedly limited) competition.

Hjá Jórun BAKERY, CAFE €
(☑455314; Klingrugarður 6; ⊗7am-10pm) Although entered inauspiciously from a light-industrial estate, this large modern bakery has seating at picture windows that survey the eastern fjord. Luscious bread, cakes and open sandwiches are available all day; pizzas (from Dkr75), kebabs (Dkr98) or steak meals (Dkr140) after 5pm.

Pizza 67 PIZZA €
(☑456767; Klaksvíksvegur 22; pizzas from Dkr47; ⊗5-11pm Sun-Thu, 5pm-5am Fri & Sat) The well-cooked pizzas are tasty, albeit slightly stingy on the toppings. Takeaway or eat in one tiny stool room admiring faded Elvis pictures.

Roykstovan PUB €
(Klaksvíksvegur 41; beer from Dkr20; ⊗11am-midnight Sun-Thu, noon-4am Fri & Sat) This graffiti-muralled house contains a rough-edged pub that's ideal for meeting (and hopefully not fighting with) razzed-up seamen.

Maverik PUB €
(Gerðagøta; ⊗6pm-late Thu-Sun) Has a small outdoor triangle of concrete beer garden opposite the Atlantis cinema.

Kiosk Var GROCERY STORE
(Klaksvíksvegur 56; ⊗9am-11pm) Hot dogs, late-night groceries.

Fk Supermarket SUPERMARKET
(Nólsoyar Pálsgøta 8; ⊗8am-10pm Mon-Sat, 10am-10pm Sun) Central supermarket.

Føroya Bjór BREWERY
(Klaksvíksvegur; ⊗10am-5pm Mon-Thu, 10am-5.30pm Fri) Beneath the Faroes' main brewery, a store sells its beers but only in six-packs.

ℹ Information

Eik (Bøgøta), **Føroya Banki** (Klaksvíksvegur 7) and **Norðoya Sparikassi** (Ósavegur 1) are banks with ATMs.

Library (Tingstøðin; ⊗1-6pm Mon-Fri, 10am-3pm Sat) Two computers with free internet access.

Tourist office (Norðoya Kunningarstova; ☑456939; www.visitnordoy.fo; Nólsoyar Pálsgøta 32; ⊗10am-noon & 1-4pm Mon-Fri Sep-May) Accommodation and tour bookings.

ℹ Getting There & Away

BUS Route 400 to Tórshavn (Dkr90, 1¾ hours) runs five to 11 times daily.

CAR Colourfully illuminated, the 6.3km Norðoya tunnel to Leirvík costs Dkr130 per car, payable westbound only at Effo petrol stations.

HELICOPTER Three or four times weekly to Fugloy, Fridays to Froðba via Skúvoy, and summer Monday mornings to Mykines.

TAXIS ☑580404, 755555

Kalsoy

This long, thin succession of abrupt peaks and swales is nicknamed the 'flute' for its many tunnel holes. The scenery glimpsed all too briefly between those tunnels is majestic. **Mikladalur** has a photogenic setting and a rusting former goods lift recalling the preroad days. But the highlight is standing beside **Kallur lighthouse** at the island's northernmost tip for spectacular views encompassing six different headlands. Reaching the lighthouse takes around 45 minutes on foot from **Trøllanes**. From the red gate at the end of the village climb a short, steep slope then contour around to the right of Borgarin peak aiming for a midway course

Hunting long-finned pilot whales *(grind)* is a controversial but age-old Faroese tradition called *grindadráp* (see www.whaling.fo). Boats herd pods of these whales into a shallow bay where local people stand waiting on the beach. They insert steel gaffs into the whales' blowholes then cut the jugular and carotid blood vessels with long knives. Loss of blood pressure causes a rapid death. The method is considered the quickest and the least painful way to kill whales. The whale meat is divided up among villagers according to a strict hierarchical code.

See p302 for a discussion of the pros and cons of whaling throughout Scandinavia.

(bring a stick to defend yourself from possible skua attacks). Cross the snipe-rich depression beyond to reach the Kallur headland. Confusingly, the lighthouse isn't visible until relatively shortly before you reach it.

Kalsoy is reached from Klaksvík by a small car ferry that crosses to functional Syðradalur harbour up to eight times daily (pedestrian/car Dkr45/160 return, 20 minutes). Connecting with some boats, minibus 506 runs to Trøllanes (Dkr30, 40 minutes) but check timetables carefully and book ahead on ☑505220.

Kunoy

POP 90

Dominating Klaksvík harbour with its sculpted rear end, Kunoy island is connected to Borðoy by a sinuous rock causeway. The road then burrows 3km straight through the mountain to access Kunoy village where a handful of old stone-walled buildings (amid newer homes) are backed by a towering mountain amphitheatre.

Viðoy & Viðareiði

POP 350

The amorphous village of Viðareiði (vee-ar-*oy*-ye) nestles in a green swale between perfectly pyramidal Malinsfjall (750m) and the jagged amphitheatre of Villingadalsfjall (841m). The scene is prettiest at the village's western end where a dainty, 1892 church sits above the disused former boat slipway. Climbing part-way up Villingadalsfjall reveals some magnificent views across the headlands of Borðoy, Kunoy and Kalsoy. Climbing further you'll encounter steep scree, but when fog and low clouds allow, experienced trekkers can scramble over the summit, along a knife-edge ridge and on to Enniberg, one of Europe's highest sea cliffs.

Hotel Norð (☑451244; www.hotelnord.fo; Eggjarvegur 1; s/d Dkr700/900; ☺mid-Jun–Sep or by arrangement for groups) has 15 scrupulously clean rooms. Those facing south offer sweeping views. However, despite a 2007 makeover, the place shows many minor signs of wear, and the skeleton staff can be hard to track down. Wi-fi is limited to the sizeable restaurant where breakfast is included. Dinner is by reservation only.

A few doors away the eight-table house-restaurant **Matstovan Elisabeth** (☑451275; Eggjarvegur 13; mains Dkr180-240; ☺noon-9pm mid-May–mid-Aug) serves up flavoursome fish of the day, steak meals and open sandwiches (from Dkr26). More interesting are seasonal local specialities like roast puffin or braised *lomvigi* (guillemot, a seabird) but for those you may need to book a day beforehand.

From Klaksvík bus 500 runs to Viðareiði (Dkr30, 30 minutes, three daily) via Hvannasund (Dkr20, 20 minutes) whence boats leave to Fugloy.

Fugloy

POP 40

Clinging valiantly to Fugloy's steep southern tip, the slopes above Kirkja (*cheer*-cha) survey an array of islands. Somewhat gloomier Hattarvík is nestled deep in a sweeping valley that rises steeply to east-coast bird cliffs. Hattarvík's red-roofed 1899 stone church stares wistfully out across the endless Atlantic surf. Neither village has a protected harbour and for some travellers the real thrill of visiting Fugloy is the dicey, wave-buffeted landing as they disembark from the passenger-only ferry. Schedules vary notoriously according to weather, wind direction and whether a detour to Svínoy is added. However, typically departures are at least twice daily from Hvannasund, taking around 45 minutes then returning immediately. On Wednesdays and summer Sundays you could take the 8.45am boat from Hvannasund to Hattarvík, then walk to Kirkja (around 1½ hours) with plenty of time to get the helicopter out to Klaksvík or Tórshavn. But don't forget to book. If the copter's cancelled you'll still be able to escape on the 3.45pm boat. There's no formal accommodation.

SUÐUROY

The most southerly of the Faroes, Suðuroy is indented with fjords and has its share of dramatic clifftop scenery, especially along the western coast. There are several good choices for part-day hikes and the island's population is considered the nation's friendliest and most outgoing.

Tvøroyri

POP 1110

Suðuroy's pleasant chief town, Tvøroyri (tver-*oi*-ree) sprawls gently along the northern slopes of Trongisvágsfjord. It's the logical base for visiting Suðuroy with the Faroes' most atmospheric pub, a good-value waterfront guesthouse and some fine DIY hiking. Dominated by a distinctive 1908 church, the town's central core is around the town hall.

◉ Sights & Activities

Museum   HISTORIC BUILDING
(Doktoragøta 5; admission Dkr20; ⊙2.30-5.30pm Sun or by appointment) This grass-roofed building was built in 1852 and retains a selection of period mementos, but the greatest attractions are the lively explanations of curator **Einar Larsen** (✆228241), who can usually open the museum up given an hour or two's notice.

Outside of the museum, leading down to the commercial port, is a rough **cobble-slope** originally used for fish drying. The nearby 1836 **Thomsen monopoly-house** contains the brilliant Kgl Handil pub.

Gallari Oyggin   GALLERY, GARDEN
(✆227938; Sjógøtoa 186; admission Dkr20; ⊙3-6pm Tue-Sun or by arrangement) Somewhat brutal metallic sculptures are displayed in the layered garden of a local house that features imaginative paintings and a small

cafe (coffee/beer Dkr25/30). The greenhouse grows what's probably the Faroes' only banana plant.

Froðbiarnakkur   WALK
This easy hike (45 minutes up, 35 minutes back) climbs gently to the communications mast on 325m Nakkur for clifftop views encompassing virtually all of the eastern islands. Follow the rocky tractor road that starts 1.8km east of Tvøroyri church, just beyond the house at Froðbiavegur 252. Some short cuts are possible.

Hvannhagi   HIKE
An appealing 1½-hour circular hike to Hvannavatan Lake starts from the point where Ovari Vegur peters out (there's a tiny car park). The fairly clear trail crosses a gentle 206m pass then descends a narrow gully into an emerald-green swale bracketed by sea cliffs. Looping back you'll need to ascend a short, very steep stretch on loose rocks, but it's not unduly difficult given reasonable fitness.

Fámijnsgøtan   HIKE
This satisfying two-hour trek leads right across the island to Fámijn (p143), offering a wide range of moorland views and landscapes (remember to book your return bus, last service around 4.30pm). Start walking from a clearly marked stile 1.3km off Rte 20 up Havammavegur. Follow cairns through two clefts between peaks, keeping right after each, but then once descending steeply, keeping to the left of the lake on the lower plateau. This route is much harder to follow in reverse.

🛏 Sleeping

The tourist office organises rooms at two central unstaffed guesthouses – the **Old Police Station Guesthouse** (Sornhúsvegur 10) and **Virgin Cape Guesthouse** (Miðbrekka 12) – and at B&Bs and rental homes across the island.

TOP CHOICE Gistingarhúsið Undir Heygnum   GUESTHOUSE €
(✆372046, 223925; www.guest-house.dk; Undir Heygnum; s/d from Dkr300/500) The 'guesthouse under the hill' is a model of Scandinavian style and cleanliness with new pine floors and dazzling white linens. Many rooms have great fjord views, some are slightly small and all share bathrooms, but there's a splendidly equipped kitchen and

FAROE ISLANDS SUÐUROY

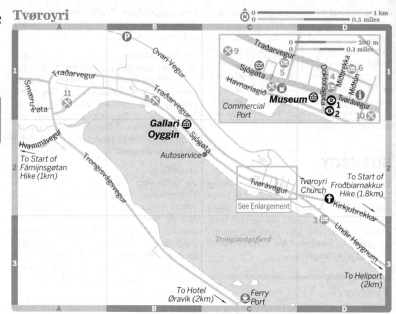

lounge with satellite TV, CD player and more views. Wi-fi costs Dkr25 per day.

Hotel Tvøroyri   HOTEL €€
(✆371171; fax 372171; Miðbrekka 5; s/d Dkr675/775, without bathroom Dkr500/650) The dead-whale photo makes a disconcerting welcome and some of the cheaper little single rooms lack style, but the en suite rooms have been tastefully refreshed (sizes vary), there's a top-floor TV room and the flat roof has outdoor seating if you can find your way up.

✗ Eating

Hotel Øravík   FISH, PIZZA €€
(✆371302; www.oravik.com; Øravík; pizza Dkr60-80, 1-/2-/3-course meals Dkr180/220/260; ◷5-10pm) Decor and guest rooms are lacklustre, but some tables in the restaurant have lovely views of a trickling stream. Choose from pizza, steak or fish of the day. You'll need wheels as it's nearly 6km south of town.

Hotel Tvøroyri   PIZZA €
(Miðbrekka 5; ◷6-10pm Fri-Sun) At weekends, Hotel Tvøroyri's restaurant serves pizzas (from Dkr65). Otherwise with advance notice it offers very good set lunches (Dkr100 at noon) and dinners (Dkr125 to Dkr200 at 6pm).

Gaard's Bakarí   BAKERY   €
(✆371175; Sjógøta 264; ◷6am-6pm Mon-Fri, 7am-noon Sat, 6-9am Sun) Fresh bread and pastries.

Magn Petrol Station   FAST FOOD, SELF-CATERING
(◷7.30am-11pm Mon-Sat, 9-11am & 1-11pm Sun) Sells hot dogs and groceries.

Bónus Supermarket   FAST FOOD, SELF-CATERING
(◷9am-6pm Mon-Fri, 9am-1pm Sat) Sells hot dogs and groceries.

🍷 Drinking

TOP CHOICE / Kgl Handil Pub   HISTORIC PUB
(Krambúðin Hja Thomsen; ✆371007; beer from Dkr25; ◷8am-11pm Mon-Thu, 8am-4am Fri & Sat, 3-9pm Sun) Complete with sepia photos, shop drawers, a 19th-century office room and the original 1882 cash register, this beautifully restored wooden shophouse is a must-see even if you're not thirsty. Simple snacks are available.

❶ Information

Money
Eik Banki (Sjógøta 15) Has an ATM.
Føroya Banki (Sjógøta 4) Has an ATM.

Tvøroyri

Tourist Information

Suðuroy Kunningarstovan (☎372490; www.
visitsuduroy.fo; Tøråvegur 37; ☺9am-noon &
1-4pm Mon-Thu, to 3pm Fri) Near the town hall;
organises accommodation and guided hikes.

❶ Getting There & Away

Car

To explore Suðuroy consider bringing a vehicle
from Tórshavn or rent one:

Autoservice (☎222328, 268851; Remus-
Borh2004@hotmail.com; Sjógøta 79; ☺8am-
5.30pm Mon-Fri, 9am-1pm Sat) A repair shop
with three somewhat aging cars (Dkr500/400
first/subsequent day).

Magn Petrol Station (☎371466; sit@post.oli-
vant.fo; Ósavegur, Trongisvágur) The mechanic,
Jákup Midjord, rents one 10-year-old Toyota
(Dkr400 per day).

Ferry

The impressively sleek, comfortable *Smyril*
car ferry (two hours, twice daily) sails between
Tórshavn and Drelnes, directly across the
fjord from central Tvøroyri but 4.5km by road.
Linking bus services connect to Tvøroyri and
other Suðuroy villages. Return ticket costs
Dkr90/40/60/40/225 per adult/child/student/
pensioner/car. As you pay on board, northbound
only, the ride is effectively free if you sail south-
bound then return by helicopter.

Helicopter

Runs to/from Tórshavn (Dkr215, 30 minutes)
or beyond via Skúvoy and Stóra Dímun. Flights
are twice-weekly (thrice-weekly June to August)
from **Froðba Heliport** (Á Høvdanum 57), 2km
east of central Tvøroyri.

Northern Suðuroy

After an unlit tunnel, Rte 29 passes Suðuroy's
minuscule last coal mine then descends to
unexpectedly sandy bays at Hvalba and
Sandvík. Both villages frame views of the
craggy, uninhabited island of Lítla Dímun.
However, the greatest attraction of a trip
north is to continue west from Sandvík up
a lane called Heiðavegur. This later becomes
Oyggarvegurin, a gated, increasingly rocky
unpaved farm track that's driveable by car if
you're careful. After 3km you reach a sharp
bend from where there are great views down
towards the spiky rock-stack island of Ás-
mundarstakkur, tightly ringed with vast,
dark cliffs. And immediately to your southwest are the plunging bird cliffs of Glyvrab-
erg. Hike carefully on the grassy tops here
as they are sliced almost invisibly by peril-
ously vertical chasms. For a true adrenalin
rush seek out a hidden, wobbly plank bridge
that crosses one such sphincter-tighteningly
deep chasm.

Tvøroyri to Hvalba buses (up to five daily)
only continue to Sandvík (Dkr30, 30 minutes)
given advance reservations; call ☎212324.

FÁMJIN

Fámjin's colourful, if architecturally ordinary,
houses are dotted about an emerald-green
bowl-valley carpeted with flowers, dripping
with waterfalls and backed by an impressively grand, layered amphitheatre. The
original Mikkelsen Merkið flag is displayed
in Fámjin's sober 1876 church, whose key is
kept by Margrit Nielsen (☎371921), who lives
in the blue-and-white house behind. The tiny
Krambúðin á Brúgvaroyri (☎225201, 372044;
coffee/burger Dkr10/25; ☺during fine weather May-
Aug) is a quaint if over-restored harbour-front
shop-cafe dating from 1880.

If reserved on ☎212324, a minibus will
whisk you along the grandly photogenic
9km switchback road to/from Øravík and
on to Tvøroyri (sometimes changing at
Øravík). If walking one way, the hike is best
made westbound from Tvøroyri (see p141).
Another trail continues south with some
steep sections to Ryskivatn lake whence a
drivable track links on to Vágur.

Southern Suðuroy

Both **Hov** and **Porkeri** have turf-roofed **churches**. Fjord-side **Vágur**, Suðuroy's lacklustre second town, has a one-room **museum** (Vágsvegur 101; admission Dkr30; ⊘1-3pm Mon-Fri) devoted to the work of local artist Ruth Smith, but you'll probably need to ask the friendly **tourist office** (✆374342; vagur@ visitsuduroy.fo; Vágsvegur 30; ⊘9am-4pm Mon-Fri) to have it opened for you. Vágur's **wool workshop** (Suðuroyar Ullvirki; ✆374006) is due to resume operations in 2011. **Hotel Bakkin** (✆373961; www.hotelbakkin.com; Vágsvegur 69; s/d Dkr600/700, without bathroom Dkr500/600) has clean, functional rooms and an evening-only restaurant serving mostly pizza (from Dkr45). **Messan** (✆374222; Vágsvegur 109; burgers Dkr22-45, steaks Dkr209-265; ⊘noon-2pm & 6-10pm Mon-Sat, 6-10pm Sun) is a charming little restaurant just off the bayside road where it curves at the fjord end.

The Vágur area's main attraction is the awesome view of plunging vertical headlands seen from the top of **Kamarið Cliff**. That's 2km up Eggjarvegur, the first asphalt road beyond the Magn petrol station, heading diagonally right off Rte 20.

Even more stupendous is the dizzying **Beinisvørð Cliff** plunging 469m into the sea, a 20m stroll from a bend in the old mountain route to Sumba (just before the conspicuous communications mast).

With a lighthouse and some puffin burrows, **Cap Akraberg** is the Faroes' southernmost point and a photogenic spot despite the two vast TV masts.

Bus 700 runs to Vágur (Dkr40, 35 minutes) six times each school day from Tvøroyri with two more daily from Drelnes port. By advance request (✆239551) some services continue to Sumba (Dkr50, 55 minutes). However, all buses bypass the main view-points by several kilometres, so for visiting southern Suðuroy you'll really need wheels.

UNDERSTAND THE FAROE ISLANDS

History

Archaeological evidence now supports the long-held view that Celtic monks were living in eremitic seclusion on the Faroes by AD 630. Their isolation was ended in the 9th century when the first Norse farmers arrived escaping tyranny in Scandinavia, setting up a parliament (*ting*) on the Tinganes peninsula, now central Tórshavn. Around AD 1000, Skúvoy-born Sigmundur Brestisson attempted to forcefully convert the islands to Christianity in the name of the Norwegian king. His failure and dramatic swimming escape to Sandvík make him a tragic hero of the classic Faroese sagas. However, Brestisson's opponent, Tróndur í Gøtu, is currently undergoing something of a re-evaluation from heathen bad guy to pro-independence freedom fighter, as you'll discover when visiting his former farm at Gøta. Tróndur's resistance was in vain and after his death in 1035, the Faroes were Christianised by Brestisson's son-in-law, becoming a self-governing part of the Kingdom of Norway. The first bishop's seat was established in Kirkjubøur.

Even after Norway fell to Denmark in 1380, the Faroese parliament retained a certain judicial and administrative role, though this was reduced in 1660 and the *ting* was abolished altogether in 1816 (restored in 1852). Between 1535 and 1856, all trade was governed by the Danish monopoly for which the great stores of Tinganes were developed.

FLAG DAY

The Merkið, the Faroe Islands' 'national' flag, is a red Scandinavian cross, edged with blue on a white ground. Invented by Fámijn students in 1919, it had limited local usage in the 1930s but came into its own in 1940: WWII was at its height and Denmark had fallen to Nazi Germany. The Faroes, however, remained pro-Allies and continued to supply Britain with fish despite considerable wartime dangers. As flying the 'enemy' Danish flag was no longer acceptable to British warships, Hans Mikkelsen, captain of the Faroese ship *Eysturoy*, suggested using the Merkið. Winston Churchill approved the use of the flag on 25 April 1940. It was the first international recognition of the flag and the date is still celebrated as Faroese Flag Day.

In 1849, the Danish parliament incorporated the islands as a 'county' of Denmark. This provoked strong independence movements, which were reignited by the British occupation of the islands during WWII, when the islands proved that they could effectively run themselves. In 1948 the Danish compromise was to upgrade the Faroes' status to the 'self-governing community within the Kingdom of Denmark', which it remains today. When Denmark joined the EEC (now EU), the Faroes refused to follow. This smart move protected their fishery-based economy from ruthless EU competition. Following a sharp recession, bank defaults and a population drain in the 1990s, the economy rebounded impressively in the early 21st century. The Faroe Islands weathered the 2008 global economic downturn relatively well despite worries over fishing quotas and setbacks in the search for offshore oil. As of 2010 the oil hunt continues, while vast infrastructure projects aim to extend the airport runway and to drill an incredible new road tunnel between Tórshavn and Runavík.

The Faroese

The majority of Faroese are of Nordic Viking origin. Many display a self-contained reserve that can feel disconcerting at first. But spend some time here and you'll discover a rich vein of hospitality. Nearly half of the Faroese population now live in greater Tórshavn…at least on weekdays. But on summer weekends many return 'home' and suddenly village populations grow up to fivefold. Christianity is fundamental to Faroese culture; 84% of the population belong to the Evangelical-Lutheran Church, with around 10% Plymouth Brethren and a small minority of Roman Catholics. The Faroese language, *Føroyskt*, is related to Old Norse. Useful phrases include *góðan dag* (hello), *takk* (thanks), *farvæl* (goodbye) and *orsaka meg* (excuse me).

The Arts

William Heinesen and Heðin Brú are the internationally best-known Faroese writers. However, before written Faroese developed (after 1846), the language had been kept alive through a strong tradition of oral epic poetry (*kvæði*) recited as accompaniment to the classic stomping ring-form 'chain dances', which are still a mainstay of summer Ólavsøkan festivities. Today the range of Faroese musical talent is nothing short of astonishing, with a vibrant recording industry (www.tutl.com) and several summer festivals, including classical showcase Summartónar Festival (www.composers.fo) and the Gøta beach rock-fest G! (www.gfestival.com).

Best known of the Faroes' modern painters is Sámal Joensen Mikines (1906–79), whose most accessible canvases are impressionistic landscapes. Several towns (Klaksvík, Gøta, Tórshavn) feature oddly upended sculptures by Hans Pauli Olsen (www.hanspauliolsen.dk).

Landscape

Adrift between Iceland and Scotland, these 18 treeless, grassy islands are the remnants of a flat-capped volcanic continent that covered the Atlantic region 100 million years ago. Ice ages have since sculpted characteristic fjords while the sea has etched out numerous sheer cliffs and chasms. The highest peak is Slættaratindur (882m) on Eysturoy.

Wildlife

More than 100 species of birds find summer nesting homes on the Faroe Islands. The coastal cliffs teem with fulmars (*havhestur*), guillemots (*lomvigi*), razorbills (*álka*), various gulls and lovable puffins (*lundi*). Gannets (*súla*) are easiest to spot on Mykines. Ubiquitous oystercatchers (*tjaldur*, the Faroes' national bird) nest on clifftop moors amid the alien warbles of long-billed snipe (*mýrisnípa*) and the dive-bombing antics of predatory great skua (*skúgvur*) and Arctic skua (*kjógvi*), best seen on Skúvoy. Nólsoy has a big colony of storm petrels (*drunnhvíti*).

Ubiquitous sheep, the most common land mammal, have helped shape the islands' distinctively bare, green appearance. Pilot whales are the best-known inhabitants of Faroese waters (see boxed text, p140) along with various other species of whale, plentiful saltwater fish, farmed trout and salmon, plus a few seals, traditionally considered to be the reincarnations of ancestral spirits.

Faroese Cuisine

Traditional Faroese cuisine is a decidedly hearty affair, built around fish, lamb and potatoes. Wind-drying is a classic method of preservation. Only the capital, Tórshavn, has much of a selection of dining options. Elsewhere some settlements have pizzerias while grill booths and some petrol stations sell hot dogs and burgers, occasionally adding British-style fish and chips. Vegetarian options are uncommon.

Alcoholic drinks were only fully legalised in 1992. They're served at pubs and some restaurants but otherwise only sold (daytime only, not Sundays) through brewery depots and at *rúsdrekkasøla* (state liquor stores). The only exception is weak (2.8%) 'light' beer, which can be purchased in grocery shops.

SURVIVAL GUIDE

Directory A–Z

Accommodation

While larger hotels and some guesthouses operate year-round, much accommodation opens only in summer. Booking ahead is strongly advised, since most guesthouses, some hostels and even certain hotels are only staffed when visitors are expected. You'll often need to prearrange arrival times, so carrying a mobile phone is wise.

Price ranges for two people in a double room including breakfast:

€€€ more than Dkr1000

€€ Dkr500 to Dkr1000

€ less than Dkr500

B&Bs In unpretentious family homes (singles/doubles from Dkr350/450). Along with **house/apartment rentals** (two-bed flats from Dkr600, plus a one-off cleaning fee), these can be arranged through tourist offices Greengate (www.greengate.fo/eng/overnatning) or 62°N (www.62n.fo). You'll generally need to give notice of a day or two to arrange things.

Camping (Dkr60 per person) Only permitted at recognised camping grounds. Generally pretty basic, these are often operated by tourist offices or attached to hostels. The inevitably wet and windy weather can make camping challenging. It's technically illegal to park campervans or caravans overnight at a roadside lay-by or viewpoint.

Guesthouses (*gistingarhús*) Typically offer a communal kitchen and have mostly shared bathroom facilities.

Hostels (*vallaraheim*) These charge Dkr150 to Dkr250 for dormitory beds. This assumes you have a sleeping bag. If you don't, expect an additional Dkr65 to Dkr100 bed-linen charge.

Hotels (from Dkr700/900 per single/double) Typically neat and clean, if utilitarian, with private bathrooms whose showers usually flow straight onto the floor.

Activities

Birdwatching and hiking These are the greatest attractions in the region. Bookshops sell accurate 1:20,000 scale topographic maps (Dkr80 per sheet). Tourist office brochures describe key hiking routes.

Boat cruises The best way to observe bird cliffs and needle-shaped rocky islets known as 'stacks'.

Fishing River and lake fishing require licences (Dkr300/500 per day/season). Check details, open seasons and top fishing spots with tourist offices. If bringing your own fishing tackle it must be thoroughly cleaned, disinfected and dried before leaving home. Find fish name translations at www.frs.fo/fish.asp?LangId=3.

Business Hours

Banks From 9.30am to 4pm Monday to Friday.

Petrol stations and their kiosks From 7.30am to 11pm. Some close on Sunday mornings.

Pubs Until 11pm Sunday to Thursday, until 4am Friday to Saturday.

Shops From 9.30am to 5.30pm Monday to Friday and 9am to 1pm Saturday. Some supermarkets open later and on Sundays.

Children

The Faroes aren't equipped with adventure parks or high-profile attractions for children, but kids may find the whole country an adventure with its wide-open spaces and close proximity to birdlife. Parents will find a land that's free of most urban dangers, but do keep toddlers away from those cliffs.

Food

Price ranges for main courses:

€€€ more than Dkr220

€€ Dkr80 to Dkr220

€ less than Dkr80

Gay & Lesbian Travellers

Forget trying to find a local gay scene – there simply isn't one. The law respects gay rights but does not forbid discrimination against homosexuals. Conservative attitudes mean that gay travellers should exercise discretion.

Internet Access

There are no internet cafes, but major libraries have free access on their computers. Unless noted, hotels have free wi-fi.

Maps

Tourist offices distribute an excellent free 1:200,000 scale *Faroe Islands Map* that includes basic street plans of larger settlements. Bookshops sell 1:20,000 maps (Dkr80), perfect for hikers, and *Føroyar Topografiskt Atlas* (Dkr125), a comprehensive atlas-booklet of six 1:100,000 scale maps.

Money

Currency Faroese króna and Danish krone (Dkr) are worth exactly the same and are used interchangeably. Coins only come in Danish designs but notes have Faroese variants. The latter are technically valid in mainland Denmark but play safe and swap any remaining cash to Danish designs before departure.

Access Bigger branches of Føroya Banki and Eik Banki change travellers cheques and major foreign currencies, and have multicard ATMs.

Tax-free shopping Allows foreigners spending over Dkr300 in around 220 shops marked 'Tax-free' to claim back the 25% VAT: fill in a Tax Refund Cheque in the shop and get it stamped by the sales clerk.

Public Holidays

Holidays really are holidays in the Faroes: most transport stops running and everything closes down.

New Year's Day 1 January

Easter Maundy Thursday to Easter Monday, March/April

Flag Day 25 April

Labour Day 1 May

Prayer Day April/May

Ascension Day May/June

Whit Sunday, Whit Monday May/June

Constitution Day 5 June

Ólavsøka Faroese National Days, 28 and 29 July

Christmas 24 to 26 December

New Year's Eve 31 December

Telephone

Prepaid SIM cards for unlocked GSM handsets cost Dkr100, including Dkr100 call credit on both the FøroyaTele (www.ft.fo) and Vodafone (www.vodafone.fo) networks. The latter is marginally cheaper for local calls (Dkr2.95/1.75 per minute during peak/off-peak times). SMS text messages worldwide cost Dkr0.70 on either network. International roaming agreements are limited.

Time

Same as London (ie GMT/UTC in winter), five hours ahead of New York, 11 hours behind Sydney.

Tourist Information

Friendly English-speaking tourist offices (*kunningarstovan*) in each main town can help arrange accommodation and tours. Great free maps and brochures.

Visas

EU, US, Canadian, Australian and New Zealand citizens need only a valid passport for visits up to three months. Citizens of Nordic countries need only a valid identity card. Those requiring a visa for the Faroes (including South Africans) must have one that specifically identifies the Faroes: ie not just a standard Danish or Schengen visa. Apply to the Danish embassy in your country of residence.

Getting There & Away

Air

The Faroe Islands' fog-prone and only airport is on Vágar (☑354400; www.floghavn.fo), see the boxed text, p133.

Atlantic Airways (☑341060; www.atlantic.fo) National airline serves Copenhagen and

ⓘ PLANNING YOUR TRIP

Before arriving use www.ssl.fo to plan your travel itinerary, remembering that services may run at different times on each day of the week. Book helicopter rides and accommodation well in advance, building in leeway in case of cancellations. On arrival get the tourist office's country map and comprehensive 112-page *Faroe Islands Tourist Guide*. Both are free.

Billund in Denmark daily, plus Reykjavík (Iceland) twice weekly. In summer, also flies to Aalborg (Denmark, four times a week) and London Stansted (UK, twice weekly).

Air Iceland (☑341000; www.airiceland.is) Has flights to Reykjavík.

Sea

In summer, a Denmark–Iceland ticket allows a stop-off in the Faroes at no extra cost providing you prearrange it and continue on the subsequent sailing.

To Denmark Smyril Line (☑345900; www.smyrilline.com; Jonas Broncksgøta 37, Tórshavn; ☺8am-5pm Mon-Fri) operates the gigantic *Norröna* car-ferry (see boxed text, p526) once or twice weekly between Tórshavn and the Danish port of Hirtshals, taking between 30 and 38 hours. Foot passengers pay €54/78 each way in the low/high season, and a car with two adults costs €261/392. Add €14 booking fee. Quoted prices include a bed in a six-bunk, windowless dorm. For better cabins add a supplement of anywhere from €23/55 per berth to €425/849 for the 'suite'.

To Iceland Once a week (April to October only), the ferry also does a return trip from Tórshavn to Seyðisfjörður in Iceland (passengers low/high season Dkr185/277, car with driver Dkr400/791).

Getting Around

The website of the national transport company **Strandfaraskip Landsins** (☑343030; www.ssl.fo) lists all ferry, bus and helicopter timetables. Note that 'x' on a timetable means 'weekdays'. The SL Visitor Travelcard (Dkr500/700 for four/seven days) gives un-

limited travel on all buses and most ferries (not to Mykines), but is unlikely to save you much money. Certain services offer small discounts to students or for 10-trip tickets. Read timetable footnotes very carefully: services might run only on certain dates and some require you to phone in a booking in advance.

Air

At only Dkr85 to Dkr360 per journey, scenic rides in an eight-seater helicopter *(tyrlan)* are the Faroes' greatest travel bargain. Book early by contacting **Atlantic Airways** (☑341060; station@atlantic.fo; ☺8am-4pm Mon-Fri) then pay on departure (cash only). Beware that bad weather can cause cancellations, and stops are skipped when nobody has prebooked.

On each operation day (three weekly, or four in summer) helicopters depart from Vágar airport, hopping in quick succession to all other heliports (except on Sunday when Froðba is missed out). The order varies; timetables are on www.atlantic.fo.

Bicycle

Surfaced roads, minimal traffic, light summer nights and stunning scenery all make riding a bicycle *(súkklur)* a tempting proposition. However steep hills, wind, rain and fog argue against it. Road tunnels are cyclists' greatest hazard. Many are freakily dark, others potentially life-threatening due to carbon monoxide build-up. Best avoided.

Good lighting and wind-/waterproof clothing is essential. If things get rough you can pop your bike on certain buses for Dkr30.

Boat

On ferries, cars cost Dkr160 (including driver); extra passengers pay the standard Dkr45 pedestrian fare. Exceptions are the big Tórshavn–Suðuroy ferry (p143) and the pedestrian-only ferry to Mykines (p134). Timetables are on www.ssl.fo.

Bus

Bus and ferry timetables are sensibly coordinated, and combined bus-ferry tickets (purchased aboard) are cheaper than the two separate fares. If you're the only prebooked passenger on minor bus routes you might find that your 'bus' is actually a taxi (albeit charging standard bus fares).

Car & Motorcycle

Driving allows you to see vastly more of the Faroes' remote villages and valleys in a short time. Roads are quiet, well maintained and accurately signposted.

HIRE

Costs From around Dkr400 per day including partial insurance; Dkr300 for longer hires.

Conditions Minimum driver age is 20, with one year's driving experience.

Airport pick-up Generally adds Dkr200 each way plus the Dkr130 tunnel toll.

Rental Companies

62°N (☑340050; www.62n.fo; Gundadalsvegur, Tórshavn; ☺8am-5pm Mon-Fri) Agents for Hertz, Sixt and Europcar.

Avis Føroyar (☑313535, after hr 217535; www.avis.fo; Staravegur 1-3; ☺8am-5pm Mon-Fri) Only 100km per day free mileage.

BVK (☑283310; www.bvk.fo; Millum Svalir 2, Leirvík; ☺8am-5pm Mon-Fri) Delivers to your hotel for Dkr100.

Harley Davidson (☑210405; www.hd.fo; Jónas Bronncksgøta 33, Tórshavn; ☺4.30-6pm Tue-Fri, noon-2pm Sat) Yes! Easyriders can tour the isles by Harley from Dkr875 per day including gear and insurance.

Rentacar (☑232121; http://rentacar.fo; í Homrum 19, Kollafjøður; ☺8am-5pm Mon-Fri) Its office is out in Kollafjøður; Tórshavn pick-ups cost Dkr100 extra.

ROAD RULES

Alcohol Driving after even a single alcoholic drink is forbidden.

Driving Right-hand side.

Headlights Always on when driving.

Hazards Beware of sheep leaping onto the road; if you hit one, you must call the police (☑351448) and have your insurance pay the damages.

Licences EU, US, Canadian, Australian and New Zealand licences are valid. Otherwise, bring an international driving permit.

Parking Free but time-limited in central areas of Tórshavn, Klaksvík and Runavík during business hours (9am to 6pm Monday to Saturday). 'P' signs state the number of minutes or hours *(tíma)* permitted. Display your arrival time using a parking disc, available free from banks.

Seatbelts Compulsory front and rear.

Speed limits Set at 80km/h (open highways), 60km/h (with caravan), 50km/h (built-up areas). You can lose your licence on the spot for driving over 110km/h.

Tunnels One-lane tunnels and roads have passing bays (marked 'M' in tunnels) every few hundred metres: priority is always given to one direction – you have to pull in and let cars coming the other way pass you when the bays are on your right. The two-lane Vágar–Streymoy and Eysturoy–Borðoy undersea tunnels each cost Dkr130 return for small vehicles. Pay at Effo petrol stations or, if driving a rental car, you can just give the money to the agency.

Finland

Includes »

Best Places to Eat

» Musta Lammas (p195)
» Demo (p159)
» Figaro (p192)
» Tuulensuu (p180)

Best Places to Stay

» Hotel Yöpuu (p191)
» Lossiranta Lodge (p189)
» Dream Hostel (p180)
» Hotel GLO (p158)
» Hotelli Helka (p157)
» Lumihotelli (p211)

Why Go?

There's something pure in the Finnish air and spirit that's incredibly vital and exciting. It's an invitation to get out and active year-round. A post-sauna dip in an ice hole under the majestic aurora borealis, after whooshing across the snow behind a team of huskies, isn't a typical winter's day just anywhere. And hiking or canoeing under the midnight sun through pine forests populated by wolves and bears isn't your typical tanning-oil summer either.

Although socially and economically in the vanguard of nations, large parts of Finland remain gloriously remote; trendsetting modern Helsinki is counterbalanced by vast pine- and birch-forested wildernesses in the north and east.

Nordic peace in a lakeside cottage, summer sunshine on convivial beer terraces, avant-garde Helsinki design, dark melodic music and cafes warm with baking cinnamon aromas are other facets of Suomi seduction. As are the independent, loyal, warm and welcoming Finns, who tend to do their own thing and are much the better for it.

When to Go

Helsinki

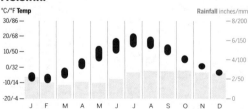

Mar There's still plenty of snow, but enough daylight to enjoy winter sports.

Jul Everlasting daylight, countless festivals and discounted accommodation.

Sep The stunning colours of the autumn *ruska* season make this prime hiking time up north.

Connections

Road connections with Norway and Sweden are way up in the north, but ferries are big on the Baltic; an overnight boat can take you to Stockholm or even as far as Germany. Helsinki's harbour also offers quick and easy boat connections to Tallinn in Estonia, launch pad for the Baltic states and Eastern Europe. Finland's also a springboard for Russia, with boat, bus and train services available, some visa-free.

ITINERARIES

One Week

Helsinki demands at least a couple of days and is a good base for a day trip to Tallinn (Estonia) or Porvoo. In summer, head to the eastern Lakeland and explore Lappeenranta, Savonlinna and Kuopio (catch a lake ferry between the latter towns). In winter, take an overnight train or budget flight to Lapland (Rovaniemi) for a few days, visiting Santa, exploring Sámi culture and mushing with the huskies. A Helsinki–Savonlinna–Kuopio–Rovaniemi–Helsinki route is a good option.

Two Weeks

Spend a few days in Helsinki and Porvoo, visit the harbour town of Turku and lively Tampere. Next stops are Savonlinna and Kuopio in the beautiful eastern Lakeland. Head up to Rovaniemi, and perhaps as far north as Inari. You could also fit in a summer festival, some hiking in Lapland or North Karelia, or a quick cycling trip to Åland.

Essential Food & Drink

» **Coffee** To fit in, eight or nine cups a day is about right, best accompanied with a cinnamon-flavoured pastry.

» **Offbeat meats** Unusual meats appear on menus: reindeer is a staple up north, elk is commonly eaten, and bear is also seasonally available.

» **Fresh food** The kauppahalli (market hall) is where to go for a stunning array of produce. In summer, stalls at the kauppatori (market square) sell delicious fresh vegetables and fruit.

» **Alcoholic drinks** Beer is a staple. Finns also love dissolving things in vodka; try a shot of *salmiakkikossu* (salty-liquorice flavoured) or *fisu* (Fisherman's Friend–flavoured).

» **Fish** Salmon is ubiquitous; tasty lake fish include arctic char, pike-perch and scrumptious fried *muikku* (vendace).

AT A GLANCE

» **Capital** Helsinki

» **Area** 338,145 sq km

» **Population** 5.4 million

» **Country code** ☑358

» **Languages** Finnish, Swedish, Sámi languages

» **Currency** euro

Exchange Rates

Australia	A$1	€0.73
Canada	C$1	€0.71
Japan	¥100	€0.83
New Zealand	NZ$1	€0.54
UK	UK£1	€1.12
USA	US$1	€0.67

Set Your Budget

» **Budget hotel room** €60

» **Two-course evening meal** €40

» **Museum entrance** €6

» **Beer** €5.50

» **City transport ticket** €3

Resources

» **Finnish Tourist Board** (www.visitfinland.com)

» **Helsingin Sanomat** (www.hs.fi/english) News

» **Matkahuolto** (www.matkahuolto.fi) Bus travel

» **Metsähallitus** (www.outdoors.fi) Great hiking resource

» **This is Finland** (www.finland.fi) Informative and entertaining

» **VR** (www.vr.fi) Train travel

Finland Highlights

1 Immerse yourself in harbourside **Helsinki** (p153), creative melting pot for the latest in Finnish design and nightlife

2 Marvel at the shimmering lakescapes of handsome **Savonlinna** (p187), and see top-quality opera in its medieval castle

3 Cruise Lakeland waterways, gorge on tiny fish, and sweat it in the huge smoke sauna at **Kuopio** (p192)

4 Cross the Arctic Circle, hit the awesome Arktikum museum, and visit Santa in his official grotto at **Rovaniemi** (p207)

5 Trek the Bear's Ring Trail in the **Oulanka National Park** (p206)

6 Learn about Sámi culture and reindeer at **Inari** (p213)

7 Cycle the picturesque islands of the **Åland archipelago** (p172)

8 Check out the quirky **museums** (p177) of Tampere

9 Take an unusual pub crawl around the offbeat watering holes of **Turku** (p166)

10 Crunch out a shipping lane aboard an icebreaker and spend a night in the ethereal **Snow Castle** (p211) at Kemi

One Day

Finns are the world's biggest coffee drinkers, so first-up it's a caffeine shot with a cinnamon *pulla* (bun) at one of the centre's classic cafes. Then, head down to the kauppatori, and investigate the fresh produce in the adjacent kauppahalli market building. Grab a picnic and take the harbour boat to the island fortress of Suomenlinna. Once back, hit Senate Square and nearby Uspenski Cathedral. Then get the metro to the legendary Kotiharjun Sauna for a predinner sweat. Eat traditional Finnish at Sea Horse or Kosmos, then take in a concert at Tavastia or a couple of beers at a bar in the Punavuori district.

Two Days

With an extra day, you can start to investigate the art and design scene. Head to the Ateneum for a perspective on the Golden Age of Finnish painting, and then see cutting-edge contemporary works at the still-iconic Kiasma. If you're tired of being on your feet, catch tram 3 for a circular sightseeing trip around town, before browsing some of the design shops around the centre of town. In the evening, head up to the Ateljee bar for great views.

HELSINKI

🎵09 / POP 583,400

It's fitting that harbourside Helsinki, capital of a country with such a watery geography, melds so graciously into the Baltic Sea. Half the city seems to be liquid, and the tortured writhings of the complex coastline includes any number of bays, inlets and a smattering of islands.

Though Helsinki can seem like a younger sibling to other Scandinavian capitals, it's the one that went to art school, scorns pop music, is working in a cutting-edge design studio and hangs out with friends who like black and plenty of piercings. The city's design shops are legendary and its music and pub scene kicking.

On the other hand, much of what is lovable in Helsinki is older. Its understated yet glorious art nouveau buildings, the spacious elegance of its centenarian cafes, the careful preservation of Finnish heritage in its dozens of museums, and restaurants that have changed neither menu nor furnishings since the 1930s are all part of the city's quirky charm.

Like all of Finland, though, Helsinki has a dual nature. In winter, although it still hums along with skaters, cafe chat and cultural life, you can sometimes wonder where all the people are. In spring and summer they are back again, though, packing green spaces and outdoor tables to get a piece of blessed sun, whirring around on thousands of bicycles, and revving the city's nightlife into overdrive.

History

Helsinki (Swedish: Helsingfors) was founded in 1550 by the Swedish king Gustav Vasa, who hoped to compete with the Hanseatic trading port of Tallinn across the water. In the 18th century the Swedes built a mammoth fortress on the nearby island of Suomenlinna, but it wasn't enough to keep the Russians out. Once the Russians were in control of Finland, they needed a capital closer to home than the Swedish-influenced west coast. Helsinki was it, and took Turku's mantle in 1812. Helsinki grew rapidly, with German architect CL Engel responsible for many noble central buildings. In the bitter postwar years, the 1952 Olympic Games symbolised the city's gradual revival.

ℹ️ **SCANDINAVIA? NOT US!**

Despite its proximity, Finland isn't actually geographically part of Scandinavia, and Finns will be quick to remind you of the fact. Technically, Scandinavia refers to the Scandinavian Peninsula (Norway plus Sweden) along with Denmark. Linguistically, Scandinavia includes Iceland, the Faroe Islands and Swedish-speaking Finns, while the term Nordic countries is a more general term for all these lands.

FINLAND HELSINKI

Helsinki

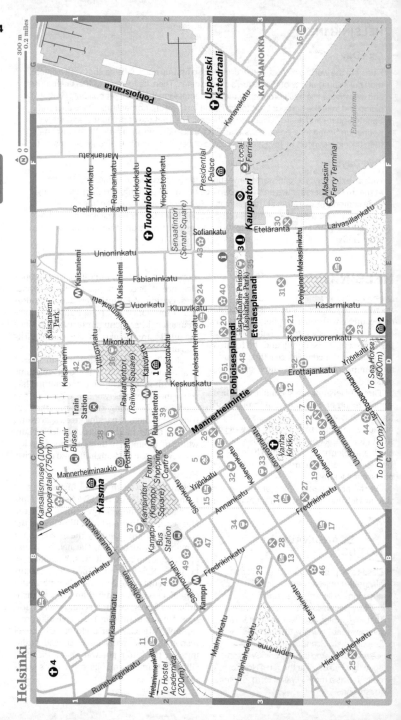

300 m
0.2 miles

⊙ Sights

Kauppatori   MARKET SQUARE
Finnish cities are traditionally centred around their market square; Helsinki's sits right by the passenger harbour in the old part of town. It's a forum for selling fish fresh off the boats, as well as other fresh garden produce and seasonal berries. Check out the fountain and mermaid **Havis Amanda statue**, a symbol of Helsinki.

FREE **Tuomiokirkko & Uspenskin**
Katedraali   CATHEDRALS
Presiding over Senate Square just north of the kauppatori, chalk-white neoclassical

Tuomiokirkko (Lutheran Cathedral; Unioninkatu 29; ⊙9am-6pm Sep-May, 9am-midnight Jun-Aug) was designed by CL Engel but not completed until 1852, 12 years after his death. Its interior is fairly unadorned, unlike that of the red-brick **Uspenskin Katedraali** (Uspenski Cathedral; Kanavakatu 1; ⊙9.30am-4pm Mon-Sat, noon-3pm Sun) on nearby Katajanokka island. The two cathedrals face each other high above the city like two queens on a theological chessboard. Built as a Russian Orthodox church in 1868, it features classic onion-topped domes and now serves the Finnish Orthodox congregation. The high, square interior has a lavish iconostasis.

HELSINKI CARD

If you plan to see a lot of sights, the Helsinki Card gives you free travel, entry to more than 50 attractions in and around Helsinki, and discounts on day tours to Porvoo and Tallinn. It costs €34/45/55 per 24/48/72 hours for adults, €13/16/19 for children. It's cheaper to buy it online (www.helsinki-card.fi); otherwise get it at the tourist office, hotels, R-kioskis and transport terminals.

Suomenlinna   ISLAND
The 'fortress of Finland' is just 15 minutes by boat from the kauppatori and makes an ideal day or half-day trip from town, especially if it's sunny and you pack a picnic or book a table for alfresco eating on this Unesco World Heritage–listed island.

Built in 1748 as Sveaborg to protect against the Russians, the impressive island fortress once held more people than Helsinki but was finally conquered after a prolonged assault in 1808.

At the bridge connecting the two main islands, Iso Mustasaari and Susisaari, is the **Inventory Chamber Visitor Centre** (www.suomenlinna.fi; walking tours €7, free with Helsinki Card; ☉10am-6pm May-Sep, 10.30am-4.30pm Oct-Apr, walking tours depart 11am & 2pm Jun-Aug), which has tourist information, maps and guided walking tours daily in summer and weekends only in winter. Here too is **Suomenlinna Museum** (admission €5), featuring a scale model of Suomenlinna as it looked in 1808 and a 30-minute audiovisual display.

Ramble around the various fortifications to your heart's content. There's a blue-signposted walking path that takes in many of the main attractions, which include several naval- and military-themed museums.

There's an HI hostel on Suomenlinna, as well as a supermarket for self-caterers, several good cafes and a couple of classy restaurants. Locals like to picnic among the fortress ruins with a few drinks. At around 5.15pm it's worth finding a spot to watch the enormous Baltic ferries pass through the narrow gap.

HKL ferries run from the passenger quay at the kauppatori (return €3.80, 15 minutes, three times hourly from 6.20am to 2.20am).

Kiasma   GALLERY
(www.kiasma.fi; Mannerheiminaukio 2; adult/child €8/free; ☉10am-5pm Tue, 10am-8.30pm Wed-Fri, 10am-6pm Sat & Sun) Now just one of a series of elegant contemporary buildings in this part of town, curvaceous and quirky metallic Kiasma, designed by Steven Holl and finished in 1998, is still a symbol of the city's modernisation. It exhibits an eclectic collection of Finnish and international modern art and keeps people on their toes with its striking contemporary exhibitions.

Kiasma's outstanding success is that it's been embraced by the people of Helsinki. Its sleek, glass-sided cafe and terrace are hugely popular, locals sunbathe on the grassy fringes, and skateboarders perform aerobatics under the stern gaze of Mannerheim's statue outside.

Ateneum   GALLERY
(www.ateneum.fi; Kaivokatu 2; adult/child €8/free; ☉10am-6pm Tue & Fri, 10am-8pm Wed & Thu, 11am-5pm Sat & Sun) Visit Finland's national gallery for a course in the 'who's who' of Finnish art. It houses Finnish paintings and sculptures from the 18th century to the 1950s including works by Albert Edelfelt, the prolific Akseli Gallen-Kallela, the Von Wright brothers and Pekka Halonen. Pride of place goes to Gallen-Kallela's triptych from the Kalevala depicting Väinämöinen's pursuit of the maiden Aino. There's also a small but interesting collection of 19th- and early 20th-century foreign art. Downstairs is a cafe, a good bookshop and a reading room with internet terminals.

Kansallismuseo   MUSEUM
(www.kansallismuseo.fi; Mannerheimintie 34; adult/child €7/free; ☉11am-8pm Tue, 11am-6pm Wed-Sun) The impressive National Museum, built in National Romantic style in 1916, looks a bit like a Gothic church with its heavy stonework and tall square tower. This is Finland's premier historical museum and is divided into rooms covering different periods of Finnish history, including prehistory and archaeological finds, church relics, ethnography and changing cultural exhibitions. It's a very thorough, old-style museum – you might have trouble selling this one to the kids – but it provides a comprehensive overview.

Temppeliaukio Kirkko   CHURCH
(Lutherinkatu 3; ☉10am-8pm Mon-Fri, to 6.45pm Wed, 10am-6pm Sat, noon-1.45pm & 3.30-6pm Sun) The Temppeliaukio church, designed

by Timo and Tuomo Suomalainen in 1969, remains one of Helsinki's foremost attractions. Hewn into solid stone, it feels close to a Finnish ideal of spirituality in nature – you could be in a rocky glade were it not for the stunning 24m-diameter roof covered in 22km of copper stripping. There are regular concerts, with great acoustics.

Seurasaaren Ulkomuseo MUSEUM
(Seurasaari Open-Air Museum; www.seurasaari.fi; adult/child €6/free; ☉11am-5pm) The peaceful, forested island of Seurasaari, northwest of the centre, is home to this sprawling open-air folk museum with more than 80 wooden buildings from the 18th and 19th centuries. In summer, guides dressed in traditional costume demonstrate folk dancing and crafts.

Seurasaari is the best place in Helsinki to see the **Midsummer bonfires**, a popular local tradition on Midsummer's Eve.

For Seurasaari, take bus 24 from central Helsinki, or tram 4 and walk.

Design Museum MUSEUM
(www.designmuseum.fi; Korkeavuorenkatu 23; adult/child €8/free; ☉11am-8pm Tue, 11am-6pm Wed-Sun Sep-May, 11am-6pm daily Jun-Aug) This museum has a permanent collection that looks at the roots of Finnish design in the nation's traditions and nature. Changing exhibitions focus on contemporary design, such as the recent Fennofolk movement.

🏃 Activities

Yrjönkadun Uimahalli POOL
(Yrjönkatu 21; swimming €5, swimming plus saunas €12; ☉men 6.30am-9pm Tue, Thu & Sat, women noon-9pm Sun & Mon, 6.30am-9pm Wed & Fri) For a sauna and swim, head to this sleek art deco Helsinki institution – a fusion of soaring Nordic elegance and Roman baths. There are separate hours for men and women. Nudity is compulsory in the saunas; bathing suits are optional in the pool.

Kotiharjun Sauna SAUNA
(www.kotiharjunsauna.fi; Harjutorinkatu 1; adult/child €10/5; ☉2-8pm Tue-Fri, 1-7pm Sat, sauna time until 10pm) A traditional public wood-fired sauna dating back to 1928. These largely disappeared with the advent of shared saunas in apartment buildings, but it's a classic experience, where you can also get a scrub-down and massage. There are separate saunas for men and women. It's a short stroll from Sörnäinen metro station.

👉 Tours

There are several cruise companies departing hourly on harbour jaunts from the kauppatori in summer. These cost between €15 and €20, or around €35 with lunch or dinner on board.

Leaving from near the tourist office, **Helsinki Expert** (☎2288 1600; www.helsinkiexpert.fi; adult/child €26/15; ☉on the hr 10am-2pm summer, 11am winter) runs multilingual 90-minute sightseeing tours in its bright orange bus. The same company offers walking tours.

An excellent budget alternative is to catch the 3T/3B tram and pick up the free *Sightseeing on 3T/3B* brochure as your guide around the city centre and out to Kallio.

✨ Festivals & Events

There's something going on in Helsinki year-round. Some of the biggies:

Vappu STUDENT GRADUATION
Held on May Day. The student graduation festival is celebrated by gathering around the Havis Amanda statue, which receives a white 'student cap'.

Helsinki Day CITY FESTIVAL
Free events celebrating the city's anniversary on June 12.

Helsinki Festival ARTS FESTIVAL
(Helsingin Juhlaviikot; www.helsinginjuhlaviikot.fi; tickets €10-50) From late August to early September, this arts festival features chamber music, jazz, theatre, opera and more.

Baltic Herring Market FOOD
(www.portofhelsinki.fi) In the first week of October, fisherfolk and chefs gather at the kauppatori to cook the time-honoured fish.

🛏 Sleeping

Bookings are advisable from mid-May to mid-August (and essential for Helsinki Day). Helsinki has plenty of big, central business hotels, including the Sokos, Radisson, Scandic and Cumulus chains.

Helsinki Expert (www.hotelbooking.fi) has a useful online booking service; you can also book accommodation at their sales points at the train station and the tourist office.

[TOP CHOICE] **Hotelli Helka** HOTEL €€€
(☎613 580; www.helka.fi; Pohjoinen Rautatiekatu 23A; s/d €151/189; [P] [@]) One of the centre's best midrange hotels – you can nearly always bag it cheaper than the listed price –

the Helka has competent, friendly staff and excellent facilities, including free parking if you can bag one of the limited spots. Best are the rooms, which smell of pine with their Artek furniture, ice-block bedside lights and prints of an autumn forest that hang over the beds and are backlit to give rooms a moody glow. They hire bikes to guests in summer at €15 per day.

TOP CHOICE Hotelli Finn   HOTEL €€

(☑684 4360; www.hotellifinn.fi; Kalevankatu 3B; s/d with toilet €65/75, with toilet & shower €75/90) Offering top value for Helsinki high in a central city building, this small, friendly hotel was under gradual refurbishment when we last passed by. The corridors were darkly done out in sexy chocolate and red, but the rooms were all bright white and blond parquet. This, and the rates, may change but it'll remain a great choice.

Hotel Fabian   HOTEL €€€

(☑040-521 0356; www.hotelfabian.fi; Fabianinkatu 7; r around €150; @) Central, but in a quiet part without the bustle of the other designer hotels, this place hasn't been open long but is getting everything right. Elegant standard rooms with whimsical lighting and chessboard tiles are extremely comfortable; they vary substantially in size. Higher grade rooms add extra features and a kitchenette. There's no restaurant, but breakfast is cooked in front of you by the chef. Staff seem very happy to be there.

Hostel Academica   HOSTEL €

(☑1311 4334; www.hostelacademica.fi; Hietaniemenkatu 14; dm €24, s/d €56/69; ☉Jun-Aug; P@☀) Finnish students live well, so in summer take advantage of this residence, a superclean spot packed with features (pool and sauna) and cheery staff. The modern rooms are great, and all come with bar fridges and their own bathrooms. Dorms have only four bunks so even the cheapest rooms feel uncrowded. They're also environmentally sound, offsetting all their carbon emissions among other positive steps. HI discount.

Hotel GLO   HOTEL €€€

(☑010-344 4400; www.palacekamp.fi; Kluuvikatu 4; r around €200; @) There are no starched suits at reception at this laidback designer offshoot of the Hotel Kämp, and the relaxed atmosphere continues through the comfortably modish public areas to the rooms. Beds:

exceptionally inviting. Facilities: top notch and mostly free. Highlight: the stuffed tiger toy atop the covers. Location: on a pedestrian street in the heart of town. Online prices are the best; if there's not much difference between the standard and the standard XL, go for the latter as you get quite a bit more space. Service is friendly and excellent and they'll stick an extra bed in free for under-15s.

Klaus K   HOTEL €€€

(☑020 770 4700; www.klauskhotel.com; Bulevardi 2; s/d from €120/175; @) Part of the new generation of design hotels, this snazzy spot has Kalevala quotes woven into the gold walls of the lobby with the thread running a framed verse in every room. It's distinctly Finnish, with luxurious toiletries, space-conscious architecture and sauna-style bathroom ceilings. But there are worldly comforts like high-speed wi-fi and DVDs in all rooms, plus two good restaurants and frostily cool bar.

Hellsten Helsinki Parliament

APARTMENTS €€

(☑251 1050; www.hellstenhotels.fi; Museokatu 18; studio apt €80-180; ☉reception 8am-8pm Mon-Fri; @) A step-up in style and comfort from many hotels, the apartments here have sleek modern furnishings, kitchenette, internet connections and cable TV. Prices vary seasonally and there are discounts for longer stays. In a great location. They'll give you a key code if you arrive after hours.

Scandic Grand Marina   HOTEL €€€

(☑16661; www.scandic-hotels.com; Katajanokanlaituri 7; s/d €164/184; P@) In a converted brick harbour warehouse near the Viking Line terminal on Katajanokka, the Grand Marina is an outstanding hotel with one of Helsinki's best outlooks. Facilities are top notch, with spacious, refurbished rooms, a business centre, a gym, restaurant and bar. Discounts at weekends and in summer.

Rastila Camping   CAMPING GROUND €

(☑0310 78517; www.rastilacamping.fi; Karavaanikatu 4; tent sites €10 plus per person €5, 2-4 person cabins €45-70, cottages €124-167; hostel dm/s/d €19/30/55; P@MRastila) Only 20 minutes on the metro from the heart of town, in a pretty waterside location, this camping ground makes sense. As well as tent and van sites, there are wooden cabins and more upmarket log cottages, as well as a summer hostel (open July and August). There are all sorts of facilities including rowing boat and canoe hire. Great for families.

WANT MORE?

Head to Lonely Planet (www.lonely planet.com/finland/helsinki) for planning advice, author recommendations, traveller reviews and insider tips.

Hostel Erottajanpuisto   HOSTEL €
(☑642 169; www.erottajanpuisto.com; Uudenmaankatu 9; dm/s/d €26/49/65; @) Helsinki's smallest and most laidback hostel occupies the top floor of a building in a lively street of bars and restaurants close to the heart of the city. Forget curfews, lockouts, school kids and bringing your own sleeping sheet – this is more like a guesthouse with (crowded) dormitories. Private rooms offer more peace. Great lounge and friendly folk.

Eurohostel   HOSTEL €
(☑622 0470; www.eurohostel.fi; Linnankatu 9; s €43-48, d €51-58; @) On Katajanokka island less than 500m from the Viking Line terminal, this HI-affiliate is busy but a bit soulless and offers both backpacker and 'hotel' rooms. Both share common bathrooms. The small cafe–bar serves a breakfast buffet (€7.70) and other meals, and there's a morning sauna included. HI discount. Tram 4 stops right alongside.

Omenahotelli   HOTEL €€
(☑0600 18018; www.omena.com; r €80-95) Eerikinkatu (Eerikinkatu 24); Lönnrotinkatu (Lönnrotinkatu 13); Yrjönkatu (Yrjönkatu 30) This staffless hotel chain is good value and has three handy Helsinki locations. As well as a double bed, rooms have a fold-out sofa that can sleep two more, plus there's a microwave and minifridge. Book online or via a terminal in the lobby.

Hostel Stadion   HOSTEL €
(☑477 8480; www.stadionhostel.fi; Pohjoinen Stadiontie 3; dm/s/d €20/38/47; P@) An easy tram ride from town, this well-equipped hostel is actually part of the Olympic Stadium. There are no views, though, and it feels old-style with big dorms and not much light-heartedness. It's the cheapest bed in town, so sometimes there's the odd curious character about. HI discount.

Traveller's Home   APARTMENTS €€
(☑044 2119 526; www.travellershome.fi; Lönnrotinkatu 16D; d/q €85/105) These guys kit you out with a fully furnished apartment somewhere in the city centre so you'll feel like you're living in Helsinki. Some are better than others; you may have to walk a while from the office, which is open only from 2pm to 6pm.

✕ Eating

Helsinki has by far Finland's best range of Finnish and international cafes and restaurants. In summer, several island restaurants serve lavish plates of seafood.

Restaurants

TOP CHOICE Kosmos   FINNISH €€
(☑647 255; www.kosmos.fi; Kalevankatu 3; mains €17-26; ⊗11.30-1am Mon-Fri, 4pm-1am Sat, closed Jul) Designed by Alvar Aalto, this classical place could qualify as an institution on that fact alone, but the great formal service and reliably excellent food make it a real Helsinki redoubt. A Finnish antipasto plate (including smoked reindeer and Baltic herring) is the ideal start before moving on to meaty mains such as Russian chicken breast served with roe and sauerkraut or lamb kidneys with pilaf.

TOP CHOICE Demo   MODERN FINNISH €€€
(☑2289 0840; www.restaurantdemo.fi; Uudenmaankatu 9; mains €26-40; ⊗dinner Tue-Sat) Book to get a table at this chic spot, where young chefs wow a designer-y crowd with modern Finnish cuisine. The quality is excellent, the combinations innovative, the presentation top notch and the slick contemporary decor appropriate. A place to be seen, but not a place for quiet contemplation.

Juuri   MODERN FINNISH €€
(☑635 732; www.juuri.fi; Korkeavuorenkatu 27; mains €24; ⊗lunch Mon-Sat, dinner daily) Creative takes on classic Finnish ingredients draw the crowds to this stylish modern restaurant, but the best way to eat is to sample the 'sapas', which are tapas with a Suomi twist (€4.30 a plate). You might graze marinated fish, smoked beef or homemade sausages.

Sea Horse   FINNISH €€
(☑010-837 5700; www.seahorse.fi; Kapteeninkatu 11; mains €14-24; ⊗10.30am-midnight) Sea Horse dates back to the '30s and is as traditional a Finnish restaurant as you'll find anywhere. Locals gather in the gloriously unchanged interior to meet and drink over hefty dishes of Baltic herring, Finnish meatballs and cabbage rolls.

Chez Dominique   FRENCH €€€
(☎612 7393; www.chezdominique.fi; Rikhardinkatu 4; mains €55, set menus €98-136; ☺lunch & dinner Tue-Fri, dinner Sat, closed Jul) Helsinki's most renowned restaurant is still one of its best. The focus these days is increasingly on its degustation menus, which present quality Finnish fare alongside French gourmet morsels and avant-garde combinations. The à la carte options have a more traditionally Gallic feel. There's an excellent wine list, with various matched suites available to accompany the set menus.

Boathouse   SEAFOOD €€€
(☎6227 1070; www.palacekamp.fi; Liuskasaari; mains €26-31; ☺dinner Mon-Sat, May-Sep) The most breezy and welcoming of the upmarket island restaurants, this circular two-deck affair is on Liuskasaari, with ferries from the jetty at Merisatamanranta. The restaurant does great seafood platters and tuna steaks. Instead of a guestbook, visitors pin notes to the lobby's chandelier.

Zucchini   VEGETARIAN €
(Fabianinkatu 4; lunch €7-10; ☺lunch Mon-Fri) One of the city's few vegetarian eateries, this covers a lot of bases with friendliness and freshly baked quiches and piping-hot soups. The sunny terrace out the back is stunning in summer.

Café Bar 9   CAFE €
(www.bar9.net; Uudenmaankatu 9; mains €8-10) It's tough to find low-priced food at dinnertime in Helsinki that's not shaved off a spinning stick, so this place stands out. It would anyway, with its retro red formica tables and unpretentious artsy air. Plates vary, with some solid Finnish fare backed up by big sandwiches, Thai-inspired stir-fries and pasta. Portions are generous so don't overdo it: you can always come back.

Konstan Mölja   FINNISH €
(☎694 7504; www.konstanmolja.fi; Hietalahdenkatu 14; lunch/dinner buffet €8/18; ☺lunch & dinner Tue-Fri, dinner Sat) The maritime interior of this old sailors' eatery hosts an impressive husband-and-wife team who turn out a great-value Finnish buffet for lunch and dinner. Though these days it sees plenty of tourists, it provides solid traditional fare with salmon, soup, reindeer and friendly explanations of what goes with what. They close for a month in summer, so ring ahead to check it's open.

Bar Tapasta   TAPAS €
(www.marcante.fi; Uudenmaankatu 13; tapas €4-7; ☺4.30pm-late Mon-Sat) This is an intimate and welcoming bar with quirky Mediterranean decor, an elegant young crowd and friendly staff. The tapas are cheap and generous; there is also a selection of wines by the glass and popular sangria.

Ravintola Martta   FINNISH €
(www.ravintolamartta.fi; Lapinlahdenkatu 3; lunches €7-9; ☺lunch Mon-Sat, dinner Tue-Sat) One of the best-value lunch stops around, Martta is run by a historic women's organisation. The light, bright dining room is matched by the tasty, wholesome food.

Orchid Thai Restaurant   THAI €
(www.thaimaalainenravintola.com; Eerikinkatu 20; mains €10-16) This cheap and cheerful little spot does tasty Thai with scrumptious stir-fried duck alongside classics such as green curry and cashew-nut chicken.

Koto   JAPANESE €
(www.ravintola-koto.fi; Lönnrotinkatu 22; mains €10-16, lunch €9-15; ☺lunch & dinner Mon-Sat) It's blonde-wood zen at this Japanese joint that does sashimi, yakitori and brilliant sushi.

Kuu   FINNISH €€
(☎2709 0973; www.ravintolakuu.info; Töölönkatu 27; mains €14-26; ☺lunch & dinner) Excellent choice for traditional Finnish fare. On a corner behind the Crowne Plaza hotel on Mannerheimintie.

Cafes

TOP CHOICE Tamminiementien Kahvila   CAFE €
(www.villaangelica.fi; Tamminiementie 8; ☺11am-7pm Apr-Oct) This memorable cafe is in lovely parkland; follow signs for the Urho Kekkonen Museum. It's like a cross between a Chekhov play and a flower-loving granny's country cottage and is utterly curious and charming. Catch tram 4 or bus 24. Opens until 10pm in high summer.

Karl Fazer   CAFE €
(www.fazer.fi; Kluuvikatu 3; lunches €8-12; ☺7.30am-10pm Mon-Fri, 9am-10pm Sat) Another historic cafe worth delving into, this is a huge space with plenty of character, classic decor and a small terrace. Founded in 1891 by the Finnish confectionery-making family (you'll see Fazer sweets and chocolate everywhere), it does amazing ice-cream sundaes and also sells cakes and tea to take away.

Café Strindberg
CAFE €

(www.palacekamp.fi; Pohjoisesplanadi 33; ⊙9am-10pm Mon-Sat, 10am-10pm Sun) This upmarket cafe is a classic place to see and be seen on the Esplanade, with a terrace whose waiter-served seats are much in demand. There's a sumptuous lounge and classy bistro upstairs too. Due to reopen in 2011 with new decor.

Café Ekberg
CAFE €

(www.cafeekberg.fi; Bulevardi 9; buffet breakfast weekday/weekend €9/18; ⊙7.30am-7pm Mon-Fri, 8.30am-5pm Sat, 10am-5pm Sun) There's been a cafe of this name in Helsinki since 1861, and today it continues to be a family-run place renowned for its pastries such as the Napoleon cake. Their buffet breakfasts and lunches are also popular, and there's fresh bread to take away.

Tin Tin Tango
CAFE €

(www.tintintango.info; Töölöntorinkatu 7; light meals €7-10; ⊙7am-midnight Mon-Fri, 9am-2am Sat, 10am-midnight Sun) This buzzy neighbourhood cafe decorated with prints from the quiffed Belgian's adventures has a bit of everything. There's a laundry and a sauna (handy if you need to wash your only pair of jeans), as well as cosy tables to sip a drink or get to grips with delicious rolls absolutely stuffed full. The welcoming, low-key bohemian vibe is the real draw, though. It's on a square a block west of Mannerheimintie some 750m north of Kiasma.

Quick Eats & Self-Catering
In summer there are food stalls, fresh produce and expensive berries at the kauppatori.

Vanha Kauppahalli
SELF-CATERING

(Old Market Hall; Eteläranta 1; ⊙8am-6pm Mon-Fri, 8am-4pm Sat, 10am-4pm Sun summer only) The real picnic treats are here, where you can get filled rolls, cheese, breads, fish and an array of Finnish snacks and delicacies (plus there's a small Alko).

Hakaniemi Kauppahalli
SELF-CATERING

(⊙8am-6pm Mon-Fri, 8am-4pm Sat) The fabulous traditional market hall by Hakaniemi metro station is less visited by tourists. Here you'll find some great salmon-on-rye sandwiches.

Soppakeittiö
QUICK EATS

(soups €7-9; ⊙11am-5pm Mon-Fri) A great place to warm the cockles in winter. There's a branch at each kauppahalli.

♥ Drinking

Helsinki has some of Scandinavia's most diverse nightlife. In winter locals gather in cosy bars while, in summer, early-opening beer terraces sprout all over town.

The centre is full of bars and clubs, with the Punavuori area around Iso-Roobertinkatu one of the most worthwhile for trendy alternative choices. For the cheapest beer in Helsinki (under €3 a pint during the seemingly perpetual happy hours), hit working-class Kallio (near Sörnäinen metro station), north of the centre.

Teerenpeli
PUB

(www.teerenpeli.com; Olavinkatu 2) Get away from the Finnish lager mainstream with this excellent pub right by the bus station. It serves very tasty ales, stouts and berry ciders from a microbrewery in Lahti in a long, split-level place with romantically low lighting and intimate tables. A top spot.

Corona Bar & Kafe Moskova
BAR

(www.andorra.fi; Eerikinkatu 11-15; ⊙bar 11am-2am daily, cafe 6pm-2am Mon-Sat) Those offbeat film-making Kaurismäki brothers are up to their old tricks with this pair of conjoined drinking dens. Corona plays the relative straight man with pool tables and cheap beer, while Moskova is back in the USSR with a bubbling samovar and Soviet vinyl. At closing they clear the place out by playing Brezhnev speeches. But wait, there's more: Dubrovnik, in the same complex, does regular live jazz, and Roska ('rubbish'), downstairs, is completely decorated in recycled materials.

Bar Loose
BAR

(www.barloose.com; Annankatu 21; ⊙4pm-2am Mon & Tue, 4pm-4am Wed-Sat, 6pm-4am Sun) The opulent blood-red interior and comfortably cosy seating seem too stylish for a rock bar, but this is what this is, with portraits of guitar heroes lining one wall and an eclectic mix of people filling the upstairs, served by two bars. Downstairs is a club area, with live music more nights than not.

Ateljee Bar
BAR

(Sokos Hotel Torni, Yrjönkatu 26; ⊙2pm-2am Mon-Thu, noon-2am Fri & Sat, 2pm-1am Sun) It's worth heading up to this tiny perch on the roof of the Sokos Hotel Torni for the city panorama. Downstairs, the courtyard Tornin Piha is a cute little terrace with good wines by the glass. The rooftop bars of the Palace and the

Sokos Vaakuna hotels are also notable for their great views.

Kappeli
BAR, RESTAURANT

(www.kappeli.fi; Eteläesplanadi 1; ⊙10am-midnight) In the middle of the park near the kauppatori, this has one of the most popular summer terraces, facing a stage where various bands and musicians regularly play in summer. Inside, there's a vaulted cellar bar, which is fantastic later in the evening or when the sun's not shining. There are also restaurant and cafe sections.

Zetor
PUB, RESTAURANT

(www.ravintolazetor.fi; Mannerheimintie 3-5; ⊙11.30am-4am Tue-Sat, noon-midnight Sun & Mon) A fun Finnish restaurant and pub with deeply ironic tractor decor. It's owned by film-maker Aki Kaurismäki and designed by the Leningrad Cowboys. It's worth going in just for a drink and a ride on a tractor, but the food is decent value too (mains €12 to €22), and served until very late.

Vltava
PUB, BISTRO

(www.vltava.fi; Elielinaukio 2; ⊙11am-3am) Right by the train station, this Czech pub has an excellent terrace, tasty beers, hearty food to soak it up (bar meals €12 to €24), and classier upstairs bistro seating.

Pub Tram Spårakoff
PUB TRAM

(www.koff.net; tickets €8; ⊙departs hourly 2-3pm & 5-8pm Tue-Sat late May-late Aug) Not sure whether to go sightseeing or booze the day away? Do both in this bright-red pub tram, the tipsy alternative to traditional tours around town. Departs from Mikonkatu, east of the train station.

Roskapankki
PUB

(Helsinginkatu 20; ⊙9am-2am) There's a string of earthy local pubs along Helsinginkatu, such as this grungy local favourite – whose name means 'trash bank'.

☆ Entertainment

Nightclubs

Helsinki has a dynamic club scene; some nights have age limits.

Tiger
CLUB

(www.thetiger.fi; Urho Kekkosen katu 1A; admission €10; ⊙10pm-4am Fri-Sun) Ascend into clubbing heaven at this super-slick club with stellar lighting and high-altitude cocktails. Music runs from chart hits to R&B; drinks are expensive but the view from the terrace is stunning. Entrance via Kamppi Square.

Kuudes Linja
CLUB

(www.kuudeslinja.com; Hämeentie 13; tickets €8-12; ⊙9pm-3am Sun & Tue-Thu, 10pm-4am Fri & Sat) Between Hakaniemi and Sörnäinen metro stops, this is the place to find Helsinki's more experimental beats from top visiting DJs playing techno, industrial, post-rock and electro. There are also live gigs.

Teatteri
CLUB, BAR

(www.royalravintolat.com; Pohjoisesplanadi 2; ⊙Mon-Sat) In a stylish former Swedish theatre, this club has three floors of fun, from the sophisticated Long bar, with its modernist paintings and web-spun light fixtures, to the summer-swelling terraces. It's got an older, more relaxed crowd and can be packed on weekends.

Cinemas

Cinemas in Helsinki show original versions with Finnish and Swedish subtitles.

Kino Engel
CINEMA

(☏020-155 5801; www.cinemamondo.fi; Sofiankatu 4; adults €8) This independent theatre shows art-house and Finnish indie film.

FinnKino
CINEMA

(☏0600 007 007; www.finnkino.fi; adult €7-11.50) Tennispalatsi (Salomonkatu 15); Maxim (Kluuvikatu 1) Operates several Helsinki cinemas with big-name films.

Gay & Lesbian Venues

Helsinki has a low-key but solid gay scene. Check out www.gayfinland.fi for more listings. There's also a list of gay-friendly places at www.visithelsinki.fi, following the 'For You' and 'Gay Visitors' links.

Lost & Found
BAR

(www.lostandfound.fi; Annankatu 6; ⊙10pm-4am) This sophisticated gay and hetero bar is still a hugely popular late-night hang-out with people of all persuasions. Head downstairs to the grotto-like dance floor and wait for your favourite chart hits to spin.

DTM
CAFE, CLUB

(www.dtm.fi; Iso Roobertinkatu 28; club €2-10; ⊙9am-4am Mon-Sat, noon-4am Sun; @) Scandinavia's biggest gay club (Don't Tell Mum) is a multilevel complex with an early-opening cafe–bar. There are a couple of dance floors with regular club nights as well as drag shows or women-only sessions.

Room Albert
BAR

(www.roombar.fi; Kalevankatu 36; ⊙2pm-2am) A slick bar for gay men, with laidback tunes.

Theatre & Concerts

For upcoming performances, see *Helsinki This Week,* inquire at the tourist office, or check the website of ticket outlet Lippu-piste (☑0600 900 900; www.lippu.fi).

Musiikkitalo
CONCERT HALL

(Helsinki Music Centre; www.musiikkitalo.fi; Mannerheimintie 13) By the time you read this, this ongoing building project should be open next to Kiasma. The striking building will have a main auditorium and several smaller ones: a fitting venue for the city's wonderful classical concerts.

Oopperatalo
THEATRE

(Opera House; ☑4030 2211; www.opera.fi; Helsinginkatu 58; tickets from €14) Opera and ballet performances.

Kansallisteatteri
THEATRE

(☑1733 1331; www.kansallisteatteri.fi; Läntinen teatterikuja 1) Hosts Finnish National Theatre performances, near the train station.

Live Music

Various bars and clubs around Helsinki host live bands. Big-name rock concerts and international acts often perform at Hartwall Areena.

Tavastia & Semifinal
BAR, VENUE

(www.tavastiaklubi.fi; Urho Kekkosenkatu 4; tickets from €15; ☉9pm-late) One of Helsinki's legendary rock venues, this attracts both up-and-coming local acts and bigger international groups. There's a band every night of the week. Also check out what's on at Semifinal, the smaller venue next door (tickets €6 to €8).

Storyville
JAZZ

(www.storyville.fi; Museokatu 8; ☉6pm-late Tue-Sat) Helsinki's number-one jazz club attracts a refined older crowd swinging to boogie-woogie, trad jazz, Dixieland and New Orleans most nights. There's a cool outside terrace in summer. It's on a corner just south of the Kansallismuseo.

Juttutupa
BAR, RESTAURANT

(www.juttutupa.com; Säästöpankinranta 6) This imposing stone building near Hakaniemi metro is one of Helsinki's top live-music bars, focusing on contemporary jazz and rock fusion. The best day is Wednesday, when there's nearly always a high-quality jazz act.

Virgin Oil Co
BAR, CLUB

(www.virginoil.fi; Mannerheimintie 5) While it does pizzas and has a cosy front bar area and weekend nightclub, the big attraction of this central spot is the top-drawer Finnish bands it attracts on a regular basis.

Sport

Hartwall Areena
SPORTS

(☑tickets 0600 900 900; www.hartwall-areena.com; Areenakuja 1) If you're around between September and April, take the opportunity to see an ice hockey game. Big matches are played at this huge arena in Pasila, north of the centre (tram 7A or 7B). The stadium is home to Helsinki superleague side Jokerit. Tickets cost €15 to €35.

Shopping

Known for design and art, Helsinki is an epicentre of Nordic cool from fashion to the latest furniture and homewares. The central but touristy Esplanadi has the chic boutiques of Finnish classics like Marimekko, Stockmann, Aarikka and Artek. The hippest area is definitely Punavuori, which has several good boutiques and art galleries to explore.

Design Forum Finland
DESIGN

(☑6220 810; www.designforum.fi; Erottajankatu 7 ☉10am-7pm Mon-Fri, 10am-6pm Sat, noon-6pm Sun) For design, you can get some good pointers at this place, which operates a shop that hosts many designers' work. You're often better off price-wise to hunt down your own bargains, though.

Design District Helsinki
DESIGN

(www.designdistrict.fi) A loose confederation of innovative design shops spread through the central area, particularly between Esplanadi and Punavuori. Grab their brochure map from the tourist office.

Akateeminen Kirjakauppa
BOOKSHOP

(www.akateeminenkirjakauppa.fi; Pohjoisesplanadi 39; ☉9am-9pm Mon-Fri, 9am-6pm Sat, noon-6pm Sun) Finland's biggest bookshop has a huge travel section, maps, Finnish literature and an impressive English section.

ℹ Information

Emergency

Ambulance, fire and police (☑112)
24-hour medical advice (☑10023)

Internet Access

Internet access at various public libraries is free. Large parts of the city centre have free wi-fi, as do many bars and cafes – some also have terminals for customers' use.

MOVING ON?

For tips, recommendations and reviews, head to shop.lonelyplanet.com to purchase a downloadable PDF of the Western European Russia chapter from Lonely Planet's *Russia* guide.

Kirjasto 10 (Elielinkatu 2; ⊙10am-10pm Mon-Thu, 10am-6pm Fri, noon-6pm Sat & Sun) On the 1st floor of the main post office. Several half-hour terminals and others are bookable.

mbar (www.mbar.fi; Mannerheimintie 22; per hr €5; ⊙9am-midnight, later at weekends) In the Lasipalatsi building. Heaps of terminals and proper drinks.

Sidewalk Express (www.sidewalkexpress.com; per hr €2). There are several of these no-staff stand-up access points around town. Buy your ticket from the machine; it's valid for all of them. Handy locations include the central train station (far left as you look at the trains) and Kamppi bus station (outside the ticket office).

Medical Services

Haartman Hospital (☑3106 3231; Haartmaninkatu 4; ⊙24hr) For emergency medical assistance.

Yliopiston Apteekki Mannerheimintie (Mannerheimintie 96; ⊙24hr); city centre (Mannerheimintie 5; ⊙7am-midnight) Pharmacies; the branch in the city centre is more convenient.

Money

There are currency-exchange counters at the airport and ferry terminals. ATMs ('Otto') are plentiful in the city.

Forex (www.forex.fi; ⊙8am-9pm Mon-Fri, 9am-7pm Sat & Sun) At Pohjoisesplanadi 27 and at the train station; the best place to change cash or travellers cheques.

Post & Telephone

Main post office (www.posti.fi; Mannerheiminaukio 1; ⊙7am-9pm Mon-Fri, 10am-6pm Sat & Sun) Between the bus and train stations. There are almost no phone booths in Finland, but there's a call centre here.

Tourist Information

Helsinki City Tourist Office (☑3101 3300; www.visithelsinki.fi; Pohjoisesplanadi 19; ⊙9am-8pm Mon-Fri, 9am-6pm Sat & Sun) Busy multilingual office with booking desk. In summer, they send out uniformed 'Helsinki Helpers' – grab one on the street and ask away. A cut-down version of the city tourism website can be delivered to your mobile at www.helsinki.mobi.

 **Getting There & Away**

AIR There are direct flights to Helsinki from many major European cities and several intercontinental ones. The airport is at Vantaa, 19km north of Helsinki.

Boat

International ferries travel the Baltic from Helsinki. See p224.

TERMINALS There are five main terminals, three close to the centre: Katajanokka terminal is served by bus 13 and trams 2, 2V and 4, and Olympia and Makasiini terminals by trams 3B and 3T. Länsiterminaali (West Terminal) is served by bus 15, while further-afield Hansaterminaali (Vuosaari) can be reached on bus 90A.

FERRY TICKETS May be purchased at the terminal, from a ferry company's office (and often its website) or (in some cases) from the city tourist office. Book in advance during the high season (late June to mid-August).

Bus

Regional and long-distance buses dock at underground **Kamppi Bus Station** (www.matkahuolto.fi), below the Kamppi Centre off Salomonkatu or Frederikinkatu. There are services to all major towns in Finland.

Left Luggage

Small/large lockers cost €2/4 per 24 hours at the bus and train station. There are similar lockers and left-luggage counters at the ferry terminals.

Train

Helsinki's **train station** (rautatieasema; www.vr.fi; ⊙tickets 6.30am-9.30pm) is central. It's linked to the metro (Rautatientori stop), and is a short walk from the bus station.

The train is the fastest and cheapest way to get from Helsinki to major centres: express trains run daily to Turku, Tampere, Kuopio and Lappeenranta among others, and there's a choice of day and overnight trains to Oulu, Rovaniemi and Joensuu. There are also daily trains to Russia (p224).

 Getting Around

To/From the Airport

BUS Bus 615 (€3.40, 45 minutes) shuttles between Vantaa airport and Rautatientori by the train station. Bus stops are marked with a blue sign featuring a plane. Faster Finnair buses (€5.90, 30 minutes, every 20 minutes) also depart from the train station, stopping once en route.

TAXI Door-to-door **airport taxis** (☑0600 555 555; www.airporttaxi.fi) need to be booked the previous day before 6pm if you're leaving Helsinki (one to two people costs €27).

Bicycle

Helsinki is ideal for cycling, as it's flat and has well-marked bicycle paths.

MAP Pick up a copy of the *Helsinki Cycling Map* from the tourist office.

HIRE There are free City Bikes at stands around the centre. Deposit a €2 coin into the stand that locks them, then reclaim it when you return the bike to any stand. For something more sophisticated, **Greenbike** (☑050 404 0400; www.greenbike.fi; Bulevardi 32; 3-speed bike per day/24hr/week €20/25/75; ☺10am-6pm May-Aug) rents out quality bikes including 24-speed hybrids.

Local Transport

The city's public transport system, **HKL** (www.hkl.fi) operates buses, metro and local trains, trams and the Suomenlinna ferry. A one-hour ticket for any HKL transport costs €2.50 when purchased on-board, or €2 when purchased in advance. The ticket allows unlimited transfers but must be validated in the stamping machine on-board when you first use it. Day or multiday tickets (€6.80/10.20/13.60 for 24/48/72 hours) are the best option if you're in town for a short period of time. The Helsinki Card gives you free travel anywhere within Helsinki (see p156).

HKL offices (☺7.30am-7pm Mon-Thu, 7.30am-5pm Fri, 10am-3pm Sat) at the Kamppi Bus Station and the Rautatientori and Hakaniemi metro stations sell tickets and passes, as do many of the city's R-kioskis and the tourist office. The *Helsinki Route Map*, available at HKL offices and the city tourist office, is an easily understood public-transport map.

Porvoo

☑019 / POP 47,900

A great day trip from Helsinki, charming medieval Porvoo is Finland's second-oldest town (founded in 1346). There are three distinct sections to the city: the Old Town, the new town and the 19th-century Empire quarter, built Russian-style under the rule of Tsar Nicholas I of Russia.

◉ Sights

Vanha Porvoo (Old Town) HISTORIC AREA
The Old Town, with its tightly clustered wooden houses, cobbled streets and riverfront setting, is one of the most picturesque in Finland. During the day, its craft shops are bustling with visitors; if you can stay the night, you'll have it more or less to yourself. The old painted buildings are spectacular in the setting sun. Crossing the old bridge to the west bank of the Porvoonjoki (Porvoo River)

provides a fantastic view of the photogenic, rust-red **shore houses** lining the river bank.

Tuomiokirkko CATHEDRAL
(cathedral; ☺10am-6pm Mon-Fri, 10am-2pm Sat, 2-5pm Sun) The historic stone-and-timber cathedral sits atop a hill looking over the quaint Old Town. Vandalised by fire in 2006, it has been completely restored, so you can admire the ornate pulpit and tiered galleries. The magnificent exterior, with freestanding belltower, remains the highlight.

Porvoo Museo MUSEUM
(www.porvoonmuseo.fi; Vanha Raatihuoneentori; adult/child €6/3; ☺10am-4pm Mon-Sat, 11am-4pm Sun) Porvoo is located in two adjacent buildings on the beautiful cobbled Old Town Hall Square.

⏢ Sleeping

Hotelli Onni HOTEL €€€
(☑044 534 8110; www.hotelonni.fi; Kirkkotori 3; s/d €150/180) Right opposite the cathedral, this gold-coloured wooden building couldn't be better placed. There's a real range here, from the four-poster bed and slick design of the Funk room to the rustic single Peasant room. Breakfast is downstairs in the terraced cafe that serves as a popular coffee shop.

Gasthaus Werneri GUESTHOUSE €
(☑0400 494 876; www.werneri.net; Adlercreutzinkatu 29; s/d/tr €45/60/90) This cosy family-run guesthouse, in an apartment block a 10-minute walk from the Old Town (the street is about seven blocks east of the bridge along the main road Mannerheiminkatu), is decent value for Finland with just five rooms (with shared bathrooms) and a self-contained apartment.

Porvoon Retkeilymaja HOSTEL €
(☑523 0012; www.porvoohostel.fi; Linnankoskenkatu 1-3; dm/s/d €18/33/44; ☺check-in 4-7pm; ▣) A 10-minute walk southeast of the Old Town, this historic wooden house holds a well-kept hostel in a grassy garden. It's a bit old school, but it's the cheapest bed in town. There's a great indoor pool and sauna complex over the road. HI discount.

✕ Eating & Drinking

Porvoo's most atmospheric cafes, restaurants and bars are in the Old Town and along the riverfront. Porvoo is famous for its sweets; the Runeberg pastry is ubiquitous.

Timbaali   FINNISH €€
(☑523 1020; www.timbaali.com; Jokikatu 43; mains
€20-26; ☺11am-11pm Mon-Sat, 11am-6pm Sun) In
the heart of the Old Town, this rustic restaurant specialises in slow food: locally farmed
snails (€15 for half a dozen) prepared in a
variety of innovative ways. There's also a
broad menu of gourmet Finnish cuisine,
served in quaint dining rooms or the inner
courtyard.

TOP CHOICE Porvoon Paahtimo   CAFE, PUB
(www.porvoonpaahtimo.fi; Mannerheiminkatu 2;
☺10am-11pm) Right at the main bridge, this
atmospheric red-brick former storehouse is
a cosy, romantic spot for drinks of any kind:
they roast their own coffee and have tap
beer and several wines by the glass. There's
a terrace and boat deck, which come with
blankets on cooler evenings. It opens till
3am at weekends.

Brunberg   CONFECTIONER
(www.brunberg.fi; Välikatu 4) Does legendary
chocolate and liquorice.

❶ Information
Tourist office (☑520 2316; www.porvoo.fi; Ri-
hkamakatu 4; ☺9am-6pm Mon-Fri, 10am-4pm
Sat & Sun; @) Southern edge of Old Town.

❶ Getting There & Away
BOAT The historic steamship **JL Runeberg**
(☑524 3331; www.msjlruneberg.fi) sails daily,
except Thursday, from Helsinki (one-way/
return €24/35) in summer (exact dates vary).
The trip takes 3½ hours each way, so you may
prefer to return by bus or, on Saturday only, on
the **vintage diesel train** (combined ferry and
train ticket €31).
BUS The bus station is on the kauppatori;
buses run every half-hour between Porvoo
and Helsinki's bus station (€11, one hour), but
the best way to reach Porvoo in summer is by
boat.

SOUTH COAST

The south coast of Finland meanders east
and west of Helsinki, revealing harbour
towns, marinas, islands and farmland. This
is something of a summer playground for
Finnish families, with a handful of fading
resort towns and the pretty bays, beaches
and convoluted islands and waterways of the
southern archipelago. Medieval churches,
old manors and castles show the strong influence of early Swedish settlers, and Swedish is still a majority language in some of the
coastal towns.

Turku
☑02 / POP 176,100
Turku is Finland's oldest town, but today
it's a modern maritime city, brimming
with museums and boasting a robust harbourside castle and magnificent cathedral.
Its heart and soul is the lovely Aurajoki, a
broad ribbon spilling into the Baltic Sea
harbour and lined with riverboat bars and
restaurants.

Once the capital under the Swedes, Turku
(Swedish: Åbo) was founded in 1229, and
grew into an important trading centre despite being ravaged by fire many times. In
2011 it shone again as one of the EU's Capitals of Culture.

❖ Sights & Activities
Soak up Turku's summertime vibe by walking or cycling along the riverbank between
the cathedral and the castle, crossing via
bridges or the pedestrian ferry (föri) – pick
up a walking-tour brochure from the tourist office.

Turun Linna   CASTLE
(Turku Castle; www.museumcentreturku.fi; admission €7, guided tours €2; ☺10am-6pm Tue-Sun) A
visit to lofty Turku Castle, near the harbour,
should be your first stop. Founded in 1280
at the mouth of the Aurajoki, the castle has
been rebuilt a number of times since. Notable occupants have included Count Per
Brahe, founder of many towns in Finland,
and Sweden's King Eric XIV, who was im-
prisoned in the castle's Round Tower in the
late 16th century, having been declared in-
sane. Guided tours of the stronghold area
are available in English with advance notice, or daily at midday in June, but do not
include the Renaissance rooms on the upper floor, or the extensive museums in the
bailey section of the castle, so allow time to
explore those yourself.

Aboa Vetus & Ars Nova   MUSEUM, GALLERY
(☑250 0552; www.aboavetusarsnova.fi; Itäinen
Rantakatu 4-6; admission €8; ☺11am-7pm, English-
language tour 11.30am daily Jul & Aug) Aboa Vetus and Ars Nova are two museums under
one roof. Aboa Vetus is an absolutely fascinating museum of live archaeology. You
descend into the comprehensively excavated remains of medieval Turku; these are

Turku

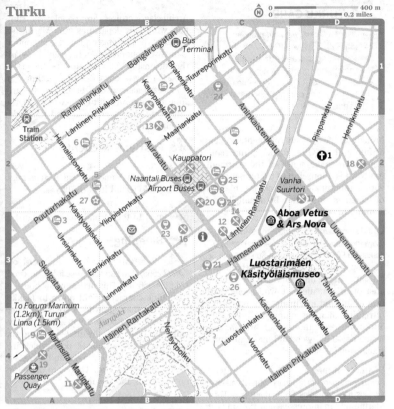

Turku

ℹ️ TURKU CARD

The **Turku Card** (www.turkutouring.fi; 24/48hr €21/28) gives free admission to most museums and attractions in the region, free public transport and various other discounts. Available from the tourist office or any participating attraction.

brought to life by lively commentary, plenty of info and activities for kids, and replica items that make sense of the fragments. Ars Nova is a museum of contemporary art with temporary exhibitions, the highlight of which is the Turku Biennaali, held in summer in odd years.

Luostarimäen Käsityöläismuseo   MUSEUM
(www.museumcentreturku.fi; Vartiovuorenkatu 2; admission €6; ⊘10am-6pm Tue-Sun Feb–mid-Sep) The open-air Luostarinmäki Handicrafts Museum, in the only surviving 18th-century area of this medieval town, is one of the best of its kind in Finland and much more intriguing than the name suggests – it's a Turku must-see. In summer, artisans work inside its 40 old wooden houses, and musicians stroll its paths.

Forum Marinum   MUSEUM
(www.forum-marinum.fi; Linnankatu 72; admission €7, plus museum ships €5; ⊘11am-7pm) Forum Marinum is an impressive maritime museum near Turku Castle. As well as a nautically crammed exhibition space devoted to Turku's shipping background, it incorporates a fleet of **museum ships** including the mine layer *Keihässalmi*, the three-masted barque *Sigyn* and the impressive 1902 sailing ship *Suomen Joutsen* (Swan of Finland). The ships can be visited independently of the museum.

FREE Turun Tuomiokirkko   CATHEDRAL
(www.turunseurakunnat.fi; ⊘9am-7pm) Commanding Turku Cathedral, dating from the 13th century, is the national shrine and 'mother church' of the Lutheran Church of Finland. In the south gallery of the cathedral is a small museum (adult/child €2/1) containing church relics and artworks. The cathedral opens until 8pm in summer. Opposite the cathedral, the **Vanha Suurtori** was once the main town square. It's surrounded by elegant buildings, the old town hall and trading mansions.

Cruises   BOAT TRIPS
Archipelago cruises are popular in summer, with daily departures from Martinsilta bridge at the passenger quay. The best option is the two-hour cruise out to Naantali aboard the steamship **SS Ukkopekka** (www.ukkopekka.fi; one-way/return €22/27, ⊘9.30am, 2pm & 7pm early Jun–mid-Aug). From May to early June and mid-August to mid-September, the same boat does a cruise around the Turku Archipelago (€28).

⭐ Festivals & Events

Ruisrock   MUSIC
(www.ruisrock.fi) A major music festival held on Ruissalo island in early July.

Turku Music Festival   MUSIC
(www.tmj.fi) In the second week in August.

🛏️ Sleeping

TOP CHOICE Park Hotel   HOTEL €€€
(☑273 2555; www.parkhotelturku.fi; Rauhankatu 1; s/d €124/156; P) This art nouveau house is a genuine character right down to Jaakko, the parrot that squawks a welcome when you check in. Rooms themselves are lavishly decorated in individual styles and the other facilities, such as a pool table, fireplace-warmed drawing room and breakfast, make for a great stay. There are discounts on weekends and in summer.

Bed & Breakfast Tuure   B&B €
(☑233 0230; www.tuure.fi; Tuureporinkatu 17C; s/d/tr €38/52/75; @) Very handy for the bus station, and close to the market square, this tidy and friendly guesthouse makes an excellent place to stay. The rooms are bright and thoughtfully decorated, you get your own keys, and there's a microwave, a fridge and free internet use for guests.

Centro Hotel   HOTEL €€
(☑211 8100; www.centrohotel.com; Yliopistonkatu 12; s/d €98/108; P@) Central but far enough from the raucous kauppatori to still be quiet, this place has a good balance. Attentive service always feels friendly, and blonde-wood rooms are a good compromise between size and price, with superiors that have a more designer feel. The breakfast buffet has fresh pastries and a varied spread that's worth getting out of bed for. There are discounts on weekends and in summer.

Turku Hostel

HOSTEL €

(☑262 7680; www.turku.fi/hostelturku; Linnankatu 39; dm/s/tw €18/38/45; P@) Well located on the river close to the town centre, this is a neat place with good lockers, spacious dorms, keycard security and a minifridge in each private room. There's also bike hire and internet. There's a 2am curfew if you're dorming it. HI discount.

Bridgettine Convent Guesthouse

GUESTHOUSE €

(☑250 1910; www.kolumbus.fi/birgitta.turku; Ursininkatu 15A; s/d €45/65; P) This clean, simple B&B guesthouse, run by the nuns of a Catholic convent, is a haven of peace, without being too officious – silence is expected around the corridors and reception areas after 10pm.

Sokos Hamburger Börs & City Börs

HOTEL €€

(☑337 381; www.sokoshotels.fi; Kauppiaskatu 6; City Börs s/d €88/102, Hamburger Börs €118/128; @☒) Towering over the market square, this is the town's biggest hotel. The City Börs option is across the road and has simpler, cheaper rooms. The main hotel comes with the lot: free sauna, flat-screen TVs and tastefully decorated rooms with solid doors that could take a battering ram. The included breakfast is extensive and includes a Japanese option.

Ruissalo Camping

CAMPING GROUND €

(☑262 5100; www.turku.fi; campsites €14, plus per person €4, 2-/4-person r €35/70; ☺Jun-Aug) On Ruissalo island, 10km west of the city centre, this camping ground has lots of room for tents and a few cabins, along with saunas, a cafeteria and nice beaches. It's the bunkhouse for Ruisrock so expect it to be booked out around festival time (early July). Bus 8 runs from the kauppatori to the camping ground.

Omenahotelli

HOTEL €

(☑0600 18018; www.omena.com; Humalistonkatu 7; r €50-65) This larger hotel, part of a chain that takes internet bookings, is in a refurbished Alvar Aalto–designed building. It represents the usual excellent value of the 'apple hotels' with spaces that can sleep up to four. You can also book via the lobby terminal.

✘ Eating

There are plenty of cheap eateries on and around Turku's bustling central kauppatori.

(☑251 5880; www.bossa.fi; Kauppiaskatu 12; mains €19-25, ☺4pm-10pm Mon-Fri, 2-11pm Sat, 3-9pm Sun) Buzzy and inviting, this L-shaped Brazilian restaurant is decorated with arty photos of the carnival capital. There's excellent, authentic eating to be done here: *feijoada* (hearty bean and meat stew), *moqueca* (Bahian prawn casserole with a distinctive palm-oil flavour), or *acarajé* (bean and cashew fritters). Portions are generous and service is excellent. Live music on Tuesdays.

Bistrot Le Porc

FRENCH €€

(☑230 0030; www.porc.fi; Martinkatu 3; mains €14-18; 11am-10pm Mon-Fri, 2-10pm Sat, 2-8pm Sun) This newcomer on the Turku scene has quickly won a loyal fan base (read: book ahead at weekends) with its classic French bistro fare served at more-than-fair prices. The delicious changing menu, no-nonsense contemporary decor and caring service soon won us over, too.

Enkeliravintola

FINNISH €€

(☑231 8088; www.enkeliravintola.fi; Kauppiaskatu 16; mains €19-25; ☺dinner Tue-Sun, lunch daily) You can't help feeling the celestial presence in the 'angel restaurant', an atmospheric old restaurant serving thoughtfully prepared Finnish cuisine with the winged wonders omnipresent. Dishes like roast goose banish any winter chills.

Trattoria Romana

ITALIAN €€

(Hämeenkatu 9; pizza & pasta €10-15) With that reliably comfortable trattoria decoration, this intimate spot adds to the tried-and-tested favourites with some more interesting combinations, including a changing list of daily specials. Get the waiter to translate them for you, as they're very worthwhile, and better value than the à la carte meat dishes. Delicious salads are available here too.

CaféArt

CAFE €

(www.cafeart.fi; Läntinen Rantakatu 5; ☺11am-7pm Mon-Sat) In a noble old waterfront building on one of Turku's most pleasant stretches, this hospitable cafe has tables out along the river. There's good espresso and superelaborate lattes and hot chocolates. Opens on Sunday in summer.

Vaakahuoneen Paviljonki

FINNISH, ASIAN €

(www.vaakahuone.fi; Linnankatu 38; mains €11-24, fish buffet €10; ☺food served 11am-10pm May-Aug) This riverfront jazz restaurant is the place to go for great-value food and entertainment in summer. As well as an à la carte menu there's a daily 'archipelago fish buffet' (June to August), plus a changing Asian buffet, all served to foot-tapping live trad-jazz bands.

Blanko   BISTRO, BAR €€

(www.blanko.net; Aurakatu 1; mains €13-20) This chic place by the main bridge is a top spot for its creative menu of wok dishes, salads and pasta. There's an outdoor terrace great for watching Turku life; it opens late at weekends, when there are DJs once the washing up is done.

Viikinkiravintola Harald   SCANDINAVIAN €€

(☑044 766 8204; www.ravintolaharald.fi; Aurakatu 3; menus €29-54, mains €16-28) Dust off your horned helmet for this Viking restaurant where subtlety is run through with a berserker's broadsword.

Baan Thai   THAI €

(Kauppiaskatu 15; mains €9-13) Authentic spicy Thai food with great-value lunch specials.

Teini   FINNISH €€

(☑010 764 5391; www.tokravintolat.fi; Uudenmaankatu 1; mains €16-25; ☺lunch & dinner Mon-Sat) Local institution for traditional Finnish cuisine.

☑Kauppahalli   SELF-CATERING

(Eerikinkatu 16; ☺7am-5.30pm Mon-Fri, 7am-3pm Sat) Packed with produce, a sushi bar and a cool cafe in a converted train carriage.

🍷 Drinking & Entertainment

Turku also has some of Finland's most eccentric bars that make for an offbeat pub crawl.

Boat Bars   BARS

Summer drinking begins on the decks of any of the boats lining the south bank of the river. Although most serve food, they are primarily floating beer terraces with music and shipboard socialising. If the beer prices make you wince, join locals gathering on the grassy riverbank drinking takeaway alcohol.

Panimoravintola Koulu   PUB, RESTAURANT

(www.panimoravintolakoulu.fi; Eerikinkatu 18; ☺11am-2am) They've done their homework at this brewery pub, set in a former school, with nine of their own beers and ciders. As well as inkwells and school desks, there's a rowing boat on the roof. The restaurant upstairs (closed Sunday) is good too, and there's a garden with minigolf.

Teerenpeli   PUB

(www.teerenpeli.com; Eerikinkatu 8; ☺noon-2am) On the corner of the kauppatori and offering an elegance that's not always visible at nights on that square, this is an excellent venue for a drink, with several really tasty beers and ciders from a microbrewery in Lahti. There's good service and a fine range of malts – they even distil one of their own.

Puutorin Vessa   PUB

(www.puutorinvessa.fi; Puutori; ☺noon-midnight) In the middle of a small square near the bus terminal, this novel bar was a public toilet in a former life. Toilet humour and memorabilia adorn the walls and you can even have your drink in a tin potty.

Uusi Apteeki   PUB

(www.uusiapteeki.fi; Kaskenkatu 1; ☺10am-2am) This characterful bar was once a pharmacy; the antique shelving and desks have been retained, but they are filled with hundreds of old beer bottles. It's a locals' spot, great for a quiet drink; there's an array of good international beers on tap.

Edison   PUB

(www.tokravintolat.fi; Kauppiaskatu 4; ☺3pm-late) While there's nothing particularly quirky about this corner pub, it's a comfortable, spacious spot, and can be livelier than the other options we list here. On boisterous weekend evenings it's a great place to meet the locals.

Klubi   BAR, NIGHTCLUB

(www.klubi.net; Humalistonkatu 8A; ☺10pm-4am Sun-Tue, 8pm-4am Wed-Sat) This massive complex has several speeds from the casual drinking of Kolo ('cave') to the DJ-fuelled nightclub of Ilta, plus regular big Finnish bands at Live. It's part-owned by a local record label, which means it snares its fair share of prominent bands.

ℹ Information

Forex (www.forex.fi; Eerikinkatu 13; ☺9am-7pm Mon-Fri, 10am-3pm Sat) The best place to change cash and travellers cheques.

Hansa CyberCafé (Hansa Arcade; per hr €3.60) Coin-op internet. Also at Turku Hostel.

Library (☑262 3611; Linnankatu 2; ☺11am-8pm Mon-Thu, 11am-6pm Fri, 11am-4pm Sat) Free internet terminals (15-minute maximum).

Main Post Office (Humalistonkatu 1)

Tourist Office (☑262 7444; www.turkutouring. fi; Aurakatu 4; ☺8.30am-6pm Mon-Fri, 9am-4pm Sat & Sun, 10am-3pm winter weekends;

@) Busy, very helpful and with information on the entire region.

ⓘ Getting There & Away

AIR **Finnair** (www.finnair.com) fly regularly between Helsinki and Turku airport, 8km north of the city. **Blue1** (✆06000 25831; www.blue1.com) has cheap flights to Copenhagen and Stockholm. Wizzair and AirBaltic service various eastern European cities.

BOAT The harbour, southwest of the centre, has terminals for **Tallink/Silja Line** (✆0600 15700; www.tallinksilja.fi) and **Viking Line** (✆0600 41577; www.vikingline.fi). Both companies sail to Stockholm (11 hours) and Mariehamn (six hours). Prices vary widely according to season and class, with deck class one-way tickets to Stockholm ranging from €20 to €50.

BUS From the main **bus terminal** (Aninkaistenkatu 20) there are hourly express buses to Helsinki (€28.50, 2¼ hours) and frequent services to Tampere (€23.20, three hours) and other points in southern Finland.

TRAIN The train station is a short walk northwest of the centre; trains also stop at the ferry harbour and at Kupittaa train station east of the centre. Bus 32 shuttles between the centre and the main train station. Express trains run frequently to and from Helsinki (from €26.50, two hours), Tampere (from €23.90, 1¾ hours) and beyond.

ⓘ Getting Around

BICYCLE Various places hire bikes; the best quality ones can be found at **Hertz** (www.hertz.fi; Lonttistentie 9; per day €15-20, per week €75-100), whose bikes you can also rent at the tourist office. Ask there about the 250km route around the Turku archipelago, covered in more detail in Lonely Planet's *Finland* guide.

BUS Bus 1 runs between the kauppatori and the airport (€2.50, 25 minutes). This same bus also goes from the kauppatori to the harbour. City and regional buses are frequent and you pay €2.50 for a two-hour ticket or €5.50 for a 24-hour ticket.

Naantali

✆02 / POP 14,100

The lovely seaside town of Naantali is just 18km from Turku and is set around a picturesque horseshoe-shaped harbour. It's a delightfully peaceful, historic sort of spot…or it would be, were it not for the presence of its extraordinarily popular main attraction. The village itself was developed after the founding of a convent in the 1440s.

◉ Sights

Today the harbour, lined with cafes and restaurants, the delightful cobbled Old Town and the huge Convent Church are enough incentive for a day trip here from Turku. Outside the tourist summer season, Naantali is practically deserted.

Muumimaailma   AMUSEMENT PARK
(Moomin World; www.muumimaailma.fi; 1-/2-day pass €21/30; ◉10am-6pm early Jun–mid-Aug, noon-6pm late Aug) A sort of Disneyland based on Tove Jansson's Moomintroll books, situated near the centre on Kailo Island. It's one of the country's most popular attractions in summer for young families and comes strongly recommended by readers.

🛏 Sleeping & Eating

Although an easy day trip from Turku, Naantali has some lovely guesthouses.

Villa Antonius   GUESTHOUSE €€
(✆435 1938; www.cafeantonius.fi; Mannerheiminkatu 9; d €120-150, ste €180) In the heart of the old town, Antonius is a romantic boutique B&B with a variety of rooms across three buildings decked out with historical memorabilia and furnishings. They're all pictured on the website, so have a think about which one you want when reserving. Downstairs is a charming old-world cafe with light meals, mouth-watering sweets and the house speciality: homemade gingerbread.

Villa Saksa   GUESTHOUSE €€€
(✆040-761 8384; www.villasaksa.doldrums.fi; Rantakatu 6; apt €155) With views across to the president's summer palace, this dignified old wooden villa is one of the real finds in Naantali. The apartment is richly decorated in antique pieces and has a small kitchen. Prices drop sharply outside the summer high season – think €90 from late August to the end of May.

Naantali Spa Hotel   HOTEL €€€
(✆44550; www.naantalispa.fi; Matkailijantie 2; s/d €132/152; P@☒) The last word in pampering, this spa hotel is ranked one of the best in Finland. Luxurious rooms, exotic restaurants, awesome spa and health facilities – there's even a stationary cruise ship docked outside where you can stay in luxury shipboard cabins. It's like something out of Vegas. If this is too much for the budget, nonguests can use the spa and pool facilities (€14 to €17 for three hours).

Merisali   BUFFET RESTAURANT €
(www.merisali.fi; Nunnakatu 1; buffet lunch/dinner
€10/12; ⊘breakfast, lunch & dinner May-Sep) Just
below the Convent Church, this iconic restaurant in an old waterfront spa pavilion has
a shaded terrace and a mind-blowing smorgasbord for lunch and dinner, including lavish seafood and salads – pack an appetite!
It's slightly more expensive on Sundays.

❶ Information

Naantalin Matkailu (☏435 9800; www.
naantalinmatkailu.fi; Kaivotori 2; ⊘9am-6pm
Mon-Fri, 10am-4pm Sat & Sun; @) Tourist
information near the harbour; also hires bikes.

❶ Getting There & Away

Buses to Naantali (routes 11 and 110) run every
15 to 30 minutes from the kauppatori in Turku
(€5, 30 minutes). In summer the steamship
Ukkopekka cruises between Turku and Naantali
several times daily (see p168).

Hanko
☏019 / POP 9590

With its sweep of beach and bustling marina, Hanko (Swedish: Hangö) is easily the
pick of Finland's south-coast resorts. In the
late 19th and early 20th centuries it was a
popular and glamorous summer retreat for
Russian nobles and artists. These cashed-
up holidaymakers built lofty wooden villas
on the sandy shore east of the harbour, and
with several of them now converted into
charming guesthouses, they continue to attract tourists with a taste for the romantic.

🛏 Sleeping & Eating

Across from East Harbour is a string of restaurant–bars in converted wooden storehouses, most specialising in seafood, but
also pizza and pasta.

Villa Tellina   GUESTHOUSE €€
(☏Jun-Aug 248 6356, Sep-May 523 0856; www.tel-
lina.com; Appelgrenintie 2; s/d €70/90, with bathroom from €60/90; P) Right by the beach, this
rambling place has basic rooms that can be
a little tight. The same owners operate Villa
Eva (Kaivokatu 2) and Villa Thalatta (Appelgrenintie 1), so it's a good first stop during
busy periods.

Villa Maija   GUESTHOUSE €€
(☏248 2900; www.villamaija.fi; Appelgrenintie 7;
d €85-160; P) Maija is another outstanding
19th-century timber house, with loads of

imperial character. The newer rooms have
bathrooms and those with sea views have
superb glassed-in verandahs or balconies.
Some rooms are in other buildings around
the same yard. Breakfasts feel like a step
back to the grandest days of the Russian
Empire in a lovely setting with plenty of
choices.

❶ Information

Tourist office (☏220 3411; www.hanko.fi;
Raatihuoneentori 5; ⊘9am-4pm Mon-Fri, plus
10am-4pm Sat & Sun Jun & Jul) Can help with
the myriad summer activities in town.

❶ Getting There & Away

There's at least one daily bus to/from Helsinki
(€23.50, 2¼ hours). The train from Helsinki
(€23.20, two hours) requires a change to a local train or bus
at Karjaa.

ÅLAND
☏018 / POP 27,700

Little known beyond the Baltic, this sweeping archipelago spattered between Finland
and Sweden is a curious geopolitical entity
that belongs to Finland but has its own parliament, speaks Swedish, flies its own flag
proudly from every pole and issues its own
national stamps.

There are well over 6000 islands, although many of these are merely little
mounds of granite rising centimetres above
the sea. Indeed, the islands are all remarkably flat: Ålanders are even less thrilled by
global warming than most.

This flatness, however, makes the islands
ideal for exploration by bike. The main central island (Åland) is connected with those
around it by bridge and cable ferry while,
northeast and southeast of here, the archipelago islands are even more rural and
remote: on places like Kökar you could be
forgiven for believing you have stepped right
back in time. Throughout Åland, traditions
such as the Midsummer celebration bear a
marked local character.

❶ Information

INTERNET RESOURCES The website www.
visitaland.com is very helpful, and www.aland
sresor.fi lets you book much of the island's
accommodation online.

FINLAND ÅLAND

Åland

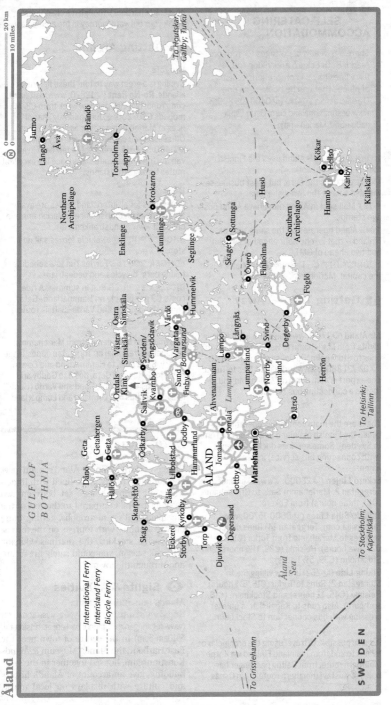

Legend:
— International Ferry
– – Interisland Ferry
···· Bicycle Ferry

GULF OF BOTHNIA

Northern Archipelago

Southern Archipelago

ÅLAND

Åland Sea

SWEDEN

To Houtskär; Galtby; Turku

To Helsinki; Tallinn

To Stockholm; Kapellskär

To Grisslehamn

Place names:
Jurmo, Långö, Åva, Brändö, Torsholma, Lappo, Krokarno, Kumlinge, Enklinge, Seglinge, Skaget, Sottunga, Överö, Finholma, Föglö, Husö, Kökar, Hellsö, Karlby, Hamnö, Källskär, Östra Simskäla, Västra Simskäla, Sveden/Tengsödavik, Vargata, Vårdö, Hummelvik, Lumpo, Långnäs, Svinö, Degerby, Ordals Klint, Kvarnbo, Sund, Finby, Bomarsund, Ahvenanmaan, Lumparland, Norrby, Lemland, Herrön, Getabergen, Geta, Dånö, Hällö, Ödkarby, Godby, Hammarland, Jomala, Gottby, Mariehamn, Salvik, Jällbolstad, Säls, Kyrkoby, Skarpnåtö, Skag, Eckerö, Storby, Torp, Djurvik, Degersand, Järsö, Lumparn, Ahvenanmaan

SELF-CATERING ACCOMMODATION

There's a wealth of cottages for rent on Åland. Both Eckerö and Viking (p224) ferry lines have a comprehensive list of places that can be booked, as does **Destination Åland** (☑0400 108 800; www.destinationaland.com; Östra Esplanadgatan 7, Mariehamn).

MOBILE PHONES Åland uses the Finnish mobile-phone network.

MONEY It uses the euro, but most businesses will also accept the Swedish krona.

POST Mail sent in Åland must have Åland postage stamps.

TIME Åland operates on the same time as Finland – that is, one hour ahead of Sweden, and two ahead of GMT.

TOURIST OFFICE The main tourist office is in the capital, Mariehamn.

Getting There & Away

Air

Air Åland (☑17110; www.airaland.ax) has daily flights from Mariehamn to Helsinki and weekday ones to Stockholm. Business airline **Turku Air** (☑02-721 8800; www.turkuair.fi) flies to Turku. The airport is 4km north of Mariehamn and there's a connecting bus service.

Boat

These are the main companies operating between the Finnish mainland and Åland (and on to Sweden). Some services dock at Långnäs (with connecting bus service) instead of Mariehamn:

Eckerö Linjen (☑28000; www.eckerolinjen.ax; Torggatan 2, Mariehamn) Sails to Grisslehamn (€10, three hours) from Eckerö.

Tallink/Silja Lines (☑0600-15700; www.tallinksilja.com; Torggatan 14) Runs direct services to Mariehamn from Turku (€16 to €27, five hours), Helsinki (€29, 11½ hours) and Stockholm (€39, 5½ hours).

Viking Line (☑26211; www.vikingline.fi; Storagatan 2) Runs to Turku (€16, 5½ hours), Helsinki (€45, 11 hours) and Stockholm (€16, six hours). Also runs to Kapellskär, a quicker crossing with bus connection to Stockholm.

It's also possible to travel using the archipelago ferries to and from mainland Finland via Korpo (southern route, from Galtby passenger harbour) or Kustavi (northern route, from Osnäs

passenger harbour), though it's cheaper to break your outward journey in the archipelago.

Getting Around

Bicycle

Cycling is a great way to tour these flat, rural islands. **Ro-No Rent** (☑12820; www.visitaland.com/rono; bicycles per day/week from €8/40, mopeds €80/200; ⊙Jun–mid-Aug) has offices at Mariehamn harbour as well as Eckerö. Off-season you can arrange a hire by calling ☑0400-529 315, preferably a few days in advance. Green-and-white signs trace the excellent routes through the islands.

Boat

Timetables for all interisland ferries are available at the main tourist office in Mariehamn and online at www.alandstrafiken.ax.

SHORT TRIPS Free vehicle ferries sail nonstop.

LONGER ROUTES Ferries run to a schedule taking cars, bicycles and pedestrians.

BICYCLE FERRIES Run in summer. A ride costs €9 per bicycle on Hammarland–Geta, Lumparland–Sund and Vårdö–Saltvik routes.

Bus

Five main bus lines depart from Mariehamn's regional bus terminal on Torggatan opposite the library. Bus 1 goes to Hammarland and Eckerö, bus 2 to Godby and Geta, bus 3 to Godby and Saltvik, bus 4 to Godby, Sund and Vårdö (Hummelvik) and bus 5 to Lemland and Lumparland (Långnäs).

Mariehamn

☑018 / POP 11,200

Village-y Mariehamn is Åland's main port and capital, a pretty place lined with linden trees and timber houses set between two large harbours. Compared to the rest of the archipelago, it's a metropolis, getting quite busy in summer with tourists off the ferries, and yachts stocking the marinas. Outside the peak season, you could safely fire a cannon through the town.

Sights & Activities

Ålands Museum & Ålands Konstmuseum   MUSEUM, GALLERY
(www.regeringen.ax; Stadhusparken; admission €4; ⊙10am-5pm) In the centre of town near the East Harbour, the Ålands Museum & Ålands Konstmuseum, housed together in the same building, give an account of Åland's history and culture with displays on local music,

seafaring, wildlife and festivals. There's little info in English. The art museum features a permanent collection of works by Åland artists – check out the works on cardboard by Joel Pettersson, the 'Åland Van Gogh' – as well as changing exhibitions. It's free from October to April.

Sjöfartsmuseum   MUSEUM

(Maritime Museum; www.sjofartsmuseum.ax; Hamngatan 2) The stalwarts of Åland are mariners and the best place to get a feel for their exploits is down at the West Harbour. The Sjöfartsmuseum was undergoing a major renovation when we last visited, and was closed until 2012.

Pommern   MUSEUM

(www.pommern.aland.fi; admission €5; ☺9am-5pm May-Aug, 10am-4pm Sep) You can still visit, anchored outside the Sjöfartsmuseum, the museum ship *Pommern,* a beautifully preserved four-masted barque built in Glasgow in 1903. The audio guide (€3.50) can help bring the old ship to life. It opens until 7pm in July.

Sjökvarteret   BOATYARD

(Maritime Quarter; www.sjokvarteret.com) Over at the East Harbour is a marina, boat-building yard and museum (adult/child €4/free; ☺9am-5pm Mon-Fri, 10am-6pm Sat) with exhibitions on shipbuilding, craft workshops and a cafe.

Boating   WATER SPORTS

There are various options for getting out on the water yourself. Ro-No Rent (p225) hires kayaks – kayaking around the archipelago is a great way to see Åland – and small boats; for more luxurious seafaring, the Linden (www.saaristoseikkailu.fi) offers Friday and Saturday lunch and dinner cruises (from €55) in a lovely old schooner.

🛏 Sleeping

Rates for Mariehamn's hotels and guest-houses peak in July and August.

Pensionat Solhem   GUESTHOUSE €

(☎16322; www.visitaland.com/solhem; Lökskärsvägen; s/d €50/69; ☺May-Oct; P) Although it might be 3km south of the centre, it's only 2km from the ferries to this delightful seaside spot that can feel like your very own villa. Rooms are basic with shared bathrooms, but cheerful staff keep the place running like clockwork. Guests also have use of the

rowing boats and sauna. Local buses (routes B and D) stop nearby.

Park Alandia Hotel   HOTEL €€

(☎14130; www.vikingline.fi/parkalandiahotel; Norra Esplanadgatan 3; s/d €94/112; P🏊) The Park is a modern, comfortable hotel on Mariehamn's main boulevard. A range of smart rooms with TV – some with kitchenette and bath-tub – are complemented by a small swimming pool and sauna. Rooms are a bargain on a Sunday, and Viking Lines offers ferry-plus-hotel deals. There's a good restaurant, a cafe and a lively terrace bar at the front.

Gröna Udden Camping   CAMPING GROUND €€

(☎21121; www.gronaudden.com; campsite €7, plus per adult €7, 2-/4-person cabins €80/105, r €80; ☺May–mid-Sep) A kilometre south of the centre, this camping ground is a family favourite, with a safe swimming beach, minigolf course, bike hire and sauna. If the tent plots are a little small, then opt for the spruce red cabins, which are fully equipped.

Gästhem Kronan   GUESTHOUSE €€

(☎12617; www.visitaland.com/kronan; Neptunigatan 52; s/d €49/71; P) Mariehamn has no hostels, but Kronan is a good-value guesthouse with basic but spotless, renovated rooms with shared bathroom. It's in a quiet street a short walk from the ferry terminal. It's a lot cheaper outside high season, though breakfast isn't included. Call ahead out of season as they're not always there. Expensive wi-fi.

🍴 Eating & Drinking

Mariehamn's many cafes serve the local speciality, *Ålandspannkaka* (Åland pancakes), a fluffy square pudding made with semolina and served with stewed prunes.

Indigo   SCANDINAVIAN €€

(☎16550; www.indigo.ax; Nygatan 1; mains €22-27; ☺lunch & dinner Mon-Fri, dinner Sat, bar until 3am weekends) Attractive and upmarket, this restaurant is in a historic brick-and-timber building but the menu is contemporary Scandinavian. Upstairs, in a beautiful loft space, they serve a good-value bistro menu in the evenings (dishes €12 to €18). It's also a stylish spot for a weekend drink.

Umbra   ITALIAN €€

(☎51550; www.umbra.ax; Norra Esplanadgatan 2; mains €13-18, lunch €9.90; ☺11am-midnight May-Aug, lunch Mon-Fri Sep-Apr) This smartly rustic

Italian spot is a welcome new Mariehamn arrival. Scrumptious homemade pasta sits alongside stylish antipasti and generously proportioned mains; lunch is a choice of two great specials that are filling and tasty.

Café Bönan   CAFE €
(www.cafebonan.ax; Sjökvarteret; lunch buffet €8; ⊙10.30am-1.30pm Mon-Fri) This vegetarian place does healthy salad buffets all sourced from ethical producers so it's total guilt-free lunching. Opens weekends in summer.

Dino's Bar & Grill   BAR, BISTRO €€
(www.dinosbar.com; Strandgatan 12; mains €12-20; ⊙lunch & dinner Mon-Sat, dinner Sun) Popular as a meeting spot, this bar does thick burgers and creative pasta and steaks, best eaten on its great outdoor deck. It's a good place to hang around for a few beers, especially when the house band is playing.

ⓘ Information

Tourist office (⊉24000; www.visitaland.com; Storagatan 8; ⊙9am-5pm Mon-Fri, 9am-4pm Sat & Sun; @) Plenty of island info. Books tours. Open 9am to 6pm daily in the height of summer; there's also a booth at the ferry terminal.

Around the Islands

SUND

Crossing the bridge into the municipality of Sund brings you to Åland's most striking attraction: the medieval 14th-century Kastelholms Slott (admission €5; ⊙10am-5pm May–mid-Sep, to 6pm Jul, English tours 2pm late Jun-early Aug), a striking and beautifully situated castle. Next to the castle, Jan Karlsgårdens Friluftsmuseum (admission free; ⊙10am-5pm May–mid-Sep) is a typical open-air museum consisting of about 20 wooden buildings, including three windmills, transported here from around the archipelago.

Further east, the ruins of the Russian fortress at Bomarsund are accessible all year. The impressive fortifications date from the 1830s and were destroyed during the Crimean War (1853–56). Near Bomarsund, Puttes Camping (⊉44040; www.visitaland.com/puttes-camping; campsites per person €2.50, plus per tent or vehicle €2, cabins from €30; ⊙May-Aug; P) is a large, well-equipped site with a beach sauna, a cafe and cabins.

ECKERÖ

Finland's westernmost municipality, Eckerö is all blonde hair and tanned bodies in summer, packed with holidaying Swedish families making the short ferry-hop across. Storby (Big Village), at the ferry terminal, is the main centre, with a tourist office (⊉38095; www.eckero.ax), petrol station and bank. The best beach is at Degersand in the south, but away from the coast, Eckerö is typical rural Åland, with winding country lanes and tiny villages.

Storby was once the western extremity of the Russian Empire, and the Bear wanted a show of power for Europe, so CL Engel was commissioned to design a massive, er, post office. The Post och Tullhuset is enormous and now houses a cafe, post office, exhibition gallery and the small mailboat museum (admission €2; ⊙10am-3pm Tue-Sun early Jun–mid-Aug), which tells the story of the gruelling archipelago mail route that cost many lives over 2½ centuries. Bus 1 runs to Mariehamn.

EASTERN ARCHIPELAGO ROUTES

If you have a bit of time on your hands it's possible to island-hop eastwards through the northeast and southeast archipelago routes. Accommodation options are limited so carry a tent or make advance bookings.

To the north you can travel through Vårdö then take the ferry to Kumlinge. Another 1½ hours by ferry via Lappo brings you to Torsholma on the scattered island group of Brändö. It's then possible to hop via Jurmo all the way to Turku. By public transport, take bus 4 from Mariehamn to Hummelvik harbour on Vårdö island. From Turku, take a bus to Kustavi, and on to Vartsala island to reach the harbour of Osnäs (Vuosnainen).

To the south, it's an easier trip to the port of Långnäs, from where you can hop via Föglö and Sottunga to the far-flung but picturesque island of Kökar, with hiking trails, a 14th-century abbey and an 18th-century church. By local transport from Mariehamn, take bus 5 to Långnäs harbour. From Kökar there are ferries to Galtby harbour on Korppoo island (two hours), then it's 75km by bus to Turku.

If taking a car on these ferries, it's substantially cheaper if you spend a night en route between Finland and mainland Åland.

SOUTHWESTERN FINLAND

Tampere

☑03 / POP 211,600

For many visitors, Tampere is Finland's number-one city, and it's easy to see why. It combines Nordic sophistication with urban vitality and a most scenic location between two vast lakes. Through its centre churn the Tammerkoski rapids, whose grassy banks contrast with the red brick of the imposing but picturesque chimneys of the fabric mills that once gave the city the moniker 'Manchester of Finland'.

A popular weekend destination thanks to its budget flight connection, Tampere doesn't disappoint: its students ensure plenty of evening action, and its regenerated industrial buildings house quirky museums, enticing shops, pubs, cinemas and cafes.

◎ Sights

Tuomiokirkko   CATHEDRAL
(Tuomiokirkonkatu 3; ⊙10am-5pm Jun-Aug, 11am-3pm Sep-Apr) Tampere's intriguing cathedral is one of the most notable examples of National Romantic architecture in Finland. The famous artist Hugo Simberg was responsible for the frescos and stained glass; once you've seen them you'll appreciate that they were controversial at the time. A procession of ghostly childlike apostles holds the 'garland of life', the garden of death shows graves and plants tended by skeletal figures, while another image shows a wounded angel being carried off on a stretcher by two children. There's a solemn, almost mournful feel about it; the altarpiece, by Magnus Enckell, is a dreamlike Resurrection in similar style. The symbolist stonework and disturbing colours of the stained glass add to the haunting ambience.

Finlayson Centre   LEISURE COMPLEX
(Satakunnankatu 18) Tampere's era as an industrial city began with the arrival of Scot James Finlayson, who established a small workshop by the Tammerkoski here in 1820. He later erected a huge cotton mill, now sensitively converted into a mall of cafes and shops; you'll also find a cinema here, as well as a great brewery–pub and the offbeat Vakoilumuseo.

Vakoilumuseo   MUSEUM
(Spy Museum; www.vakoilumuseo.fi; Finlayson Centre, Satakunnankatu 18; adult/child €7/5.50; ⊙10am-6pm Mon-Sat, 11am-5pm Sun). This plays to the budding secret agent in all of us: as well as histories of famous Finnish and foreign spies, it has numerous Bond-style gadgets and some interactive displays. For a little extra, the kids can take a suitability test for KGB cadet school.

Lenin-Museo   MUSEUM
(www.lenin.fi; Hämeenpuisto 28; adult/child €5/3; ⊙9am-6pm Mon-Fri, 11am-4pm Sat & Sun) Admirers of bearded revolutionaries won't want to miss the small Lenin Museum, housed in the Workers' Hall where Lenin and Stalin first met at a conference in 1905. His life is documented by way of photos and documents; it's a little dry, but it's fascinating to see, for example, Vladimir's old school report (a straight-A student). There's a crazy gift shop where you can buy Lenin pens, badges, T-shirts and other souvenirs of the Soviet era.

Muumilaakso   MUSEUM
(Moomin Valley Museum; www.tampere.fi; Hämeenpuisto 20; adult/child €7/2; ⊙9am-5pm Tue-Fri, 10am-6pm Sat & Sun) Explore the creation of Tove Jansson's enduringly popular Moomins in this museum in the basement of the public library building. It contains original drawings and elaborate models depicting stories from Moomin Valley (English explanations available), computer displays, toys and other memorabilia. Naturally, there's a gift shop.

Amurin Työläismuseokortteli   MUSEUM
(www.tampere.fi/amuri; Satakunnankatu 49; adult/child €6/1; ⊙10am-6pm Tue-Sun mid-May–mid-Sep) An entire block of 19th-century wooden houses, including 32 apartments, a bakery, a shoemaker, two general shops and a cafe is preserved in the Amuri Museum of Workers' Housing. It's one of the most realistic house-museums in Finland – many homes look as if the tenant had left just moments ago to go shopping.

Särkänniemi   AMUSEMENT PARK
(www.sarkanniemi.fi; adult/child day pass up to €33/28; ⊙rides noon-7pm mid-May–Aug) On the northern edge of town, this promontory amusement park is a large complex with several attractions, including a good art gallery and an aquarium. There's a bewildering system of entry tickets and opening times depending on what your interest is; it's cheaper to book online. A day pass is valid

FINLAND SOUTHWESTERN FINLAND

Tampere

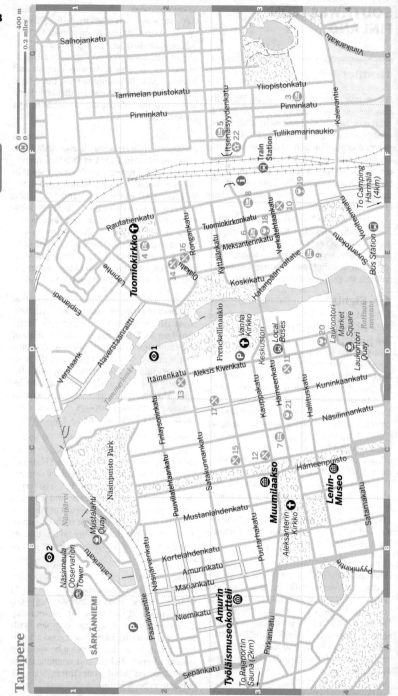

for all sights and unlimited rides, while €8 will get you up the observation tower, and into the gallery and farm zoo. Take bus 4 from the train station.

🏃 Activities

Pyynikki   WALKING TRAILS
Rising between Tampere's two lakes, Pyynikki is a forested ridge of walking and cycling trails with fine views on both sides. There's a stone observation tower (Näkötorni; ⊙9am-8pm; adult/child €2/0.50) on the ridge with a cafe serving Tampere's best doughnuts (€1.50 each). The tower is a 20-minute walk from the centre of town, west along Satamakatu, bearing left at a small park, then right up the hill.

Rajaportin Sauna   SAUNA
(www.rajaportinsauna.fi; Pispalan Valtatie 9; adult/child €6/1; ⊙6-10pm Mon & Wed, 3-9pm Fri, 2-10pm Sat) This is Finland's oldest operating traditional public sauna. It's a great chance to experience the softer steam from a traditionally heated sauna rather than the harsher electric ones. It's a couple of kilometres west of the centre; buses 1, 13 and 22 among others head out there. There's a cafe on-site, and massages can be arranged. Take a towel or rent one there.

🚶 Tours

Trips on Tampere's two magnificent lakes are extremely popular in summer and there are plenty of options. Trips on Näsijärvi leave from Mustalahti quay, while Laukontori quay serves Pyhäjärvi. All cruises can be booked at the tourist office.

SS Tarjanne   BOAT TRIPS
(☎010 422 5600; www.runoilijantie.fi) From Mustalahti quay, the glorious steamship SS *Tarjanne* does evening cruises with optional dinner, but is best boarded for the **Poet's Way**, one of the finest lake cruises in Finland. A one-way ticket costs €39 to Ruovesi (4¾ hours) and €50 to Virrat (8¼ hours). For €35 per person, you can sleep in this old boat before or after your trip. Day use of a cabin is also €30. Bicycles can be taken on board for a small fee. You can book a day trip to Virrat or Ruovesi, with one of the legs made by bus (return to Virrat/Ruovesi costs €67/55).

Suomen Hopealinja   BOAT TRIPS
(Finnish Silverline; ☎212 3889; www.hopealinja.fi) Runs cruises to Visavuori (one-way/return €34/51, five hours, 9.30am, Wednesday to Saturday June to mid-August), continuing to Hämeenlinna (one-way/return €44/66, 8½ hours).

🎉 Festivals & Events

There are events in Tampere almost year-round.

Tampere Film Festival   FILM FESTIVAL
(www.tamperefilmfestival.fi) Usually held in early March, this is a respected international festival of short films.

Tammerfest ROCK-MUSIC FESTIVAL
(www.tammerfest.fi) The city's premier rock-music festival, held over four days in mid-July with concerts at various stages around town.

Tampere Jazz Happening JAZZ FESTIVAL
(www.tamperemusicfestivals.fi) October or early November brings this award-winning event featuring Finnish and international jazz musicians.

Tampere Illuminations LIGHTS FESTIVAL
(www.valoviikot.fi) From mid-October to early January, 40,000 coloured lights brighten the city streets.

🛏 Sleeping

TOP CHOICE Dream Hostel HOSTEL €
(☎045-236 0517; www.dreamhostel.fi; Åkerlundinkatu 2; dm €22.50-27.50, tw/q €65/110; @) Sparky and spacious, this new arrival is just about Finland's best hostel. Helpful staff, super-comfortable wide-berth dorms in various sizes (both unisex and female are available), a heap of facilities, original decor and the right attitude about everything make it a real winner. It's a short walk from the train station in a quiet area.

Scandic Tampere City HOTEL €€€
(☎244 6111; www.scandichotels.com; Rautatienkatu 16; s/d €172/192; @) Right opposite the train station, this hotel has modern Nordic lines and a fistful of facilities including a sauna, a gym, various restaurants and a cocktail bar. The rooms are spacious and spotless with a clean wooden feel. You can borrow bikes or walking poles from reception.

Hotelli Victoria HOTEL €€
(☎242 5111; www.hotellivictoria.fi; Itsenäisyydenkatu 1; s/d around €109/142; P@⊠) Just on the other side of the train station from the centre, this friendly hotel offers sound summer value with its spruce rooms, free internet and a commendable breakfast spread including waffles, sausage omelette and berry pudding options. Bike hire; discounts on weekends and in summer.

Hostel Sofia HOSTEL €€
(☎254 4020; www.hostelsofia.fi; Tuomiokirkonkatu 12A; dm/s/d €28/59/75; P@) This comfortable hostel is right opposite the cathedral and fills up fast. A recent refit has left it looking very spruce, offering rooms with comfortable beds (no bunks), large windows and stepladder shelves, as well as good showers

and a kitchenette on every floor. Two floors allow small groups to virtually have their own apartment, and breakfast and laundry are available. If you're going to arrive late, they'll text you a door code. HI discount and bike rental.

Omenahotelli HOTELS €
(☎0600 18018; www.omena.com; r to €65; @) With two locations at the western (Hämeenkatu 28) and eastern (Hämeenkatu 7) ends of the main drag – the latter very handy for the station – this receptionless hotel offers the usual comfortable rooms with twin beds, a microwave, a kettle and a fold-out couch. Internet is expensive but the rooms are great value for a family of four or two couples. Book online or via the terminal at the entrance.

Camping Härmälä CAMPING GROUND €
(☎020 719 9777; www.suomicamping.fi; Leirintätu 8; campsites €14, plus per person €5, cabins €48-76; ☉mid-May–mid-Sep; P) Four kilometres south of the centre (take bus 1), this is a spacious camping ground on the Pyhäjärvi lakeshore. There's a cafe, saunas and rowing boats, as well as an adjacent summer hotel with self-contained rooms (singles/doubles €45/59, open June to August).

Sokos Hotel Ilves HOTEL €€
(☎020-123 4631; www.sokoshotels.fi; Hatanpään valtatie 1; s/d €140/150; P@⊠) This huge tower hotel has over 300 rooms, bright with turquoise paint and light wood, and offering excellent views over the heart of town or the Tammerkoski below.

🍴 Eating

Tampere's speciality, *mustamakkara,* is a mild sausage made with cow's blood, black-pudding style. It's normally eaten with lingonberry jam and is tastier than it sounds. You can get it at the kauppahalli, or a summer kiosk at Laukontori market.

TOP CHOICE Tuulensuu GASTROPUB €€
(www.gastropub.net/tuulensuu; Hämeenpuisto 23; mains €13-20; ☉food 4pm-midnight Mon-Fri, noon-midnight Sat, 5pm-midnight Sun) The best of a range of gastropubs that have recently sprouted, this corner spot has a fine range of beers and wines, as well as a lengthy port and cigar menu. The food is lovingly prepared and features staples such as liver and schnitzel, as well as more elaborate plates like duck *confit* and an excellent cassoulet (vegie version available too). Even the bar

snacks are gourmet: fresh-roasted almonds. It's closed Sundays in summer.

Neljä Vuodenaikaa
BISTRO €

(4 Saisons; www.4vuodenaikaa.fi; Kauppahalli; dishes €8-18; ⊗breakfast Tue-Fri, lunch Mon-Sat) Tucked into a corner of the kauppahalli, this recommended spot brings a Gallic flair to the Finnish lunch hour with delicious plates such as bouillabaisse and French country salad augmented by excellent daily specials and wines by the glass.

Panimoravintola Plevna
BEER HALL €€

(www.plevna.fi; Itäinenkatu 8; mains €10-19; ⊗food served 11am-10pm) Inside the old Finlayson textile mill, this big barn of a place offers a wide range of delicious beer, cider and perry brewed on the premises, including an excellent strong stout. Meals are large and designed for soaking it all up: massive sausage platters and enormous slabs of pork in classic beer-hall style as well as more Finnish fish and steak dishes. 'Vegetables' here means potatoes and onions, preferably fried, but it's all tasty, and service is fast.

Bodega Salud
SPANISH €€

(🕾233 4400; www.salud.fi; Tuomiokirkonkatu 19; mains €21-30) Enduringly popular for its cosy atmosphere and good salad, fruit and cheese bar, this place blends Spanish and Finnish choices with more offbeat snails, gnu steak and Rocky Mountain oysters. You get a certificate if you eat the oysters – shellfish are scarce in Colorado, but rams have been heard bleating in countertenor tones.

🖊 Kauppahalli
MARKET HALL €

(Hämeenkatu 19; ⊗8am-6pm Mon-Fri, 8am-3pm Sat) This intriguing indoor market is one of Finland's best, with picturesque wooden stalls serving a dazzling array of wonderful meat, fruit, baked goodies and fish.

Runo
CAFE €

(www.kahvilaruno.fi; Ojakatu 3; sandwiches €3-5; ⊗9am-8pm Mon-Sat, 10am-8pm Sun) With an arty crowd and bohemian feel, Runo (meaning 'poem') is an elegant, almost baroque cafe with books, paintings, decent coffee and huge windows that allow you to keep tabs on the weather.

Oluthuone Esplanadi
GASTROPUB €€

(www.esplanadi.fi; Kauppakatu 16; bar food €8-9, mains €10-18; ⊗food dinner daily, lunch Fri & Sat) Offering all the Plevna beers but in a more intimate central location. There are burgers and sausages on the bar menu,

but better is the pike-perch (zander) from the local lake.

Vohvelikahvila
CAFE €

(www.vohvelikahvila.com; Ojakatu 2; waffles €4-6.50; ⊗10am-8pm Mon-Sat, 11am-7pm Sun) This cosy and quaint little place does a range of sweet delights, but specialises above all in fresh waffles, which come laden with cream and chocolate.

Wanha Vanilja
CAFE €

(Kuninkaankatu 15; light meals €4-7; ⊗11am-6pm Tue-Fri, noon-5pm Sat) True to its name, this homelike cafe, a treasure-trove of time-worn furniture, is bursting with the aroma of vanilla, which they add to the coffee.

🍷 Drinking & Entertainment

Panimoravintola Plevna and Tuulensuu are also fine places for a beer or two.

Café Europa
PUB, CAFE

(Aleksanterinkatu 29; ⊗noon-late) Furnished with 1930s-style horsehair couches and chairs, this is a romantic old-world European type of place complete with Belgian and German beers, board games, ornate mirrors and chandeliers, and an excellent summer terrace.

Teerenpeli
PUB

(www.teerenpeli.com; Hämeenkatu 25; ⊗noon-late) On the main street, this is another good place with excellent microbrewery beer and cider. There's a relaxing, candle-lit interior, heated terrace and heaps of choice at the taps. There's a huge downstairs space too, with comfy seating.

O'Connell's
PUB

(www.oconnells.fi; Rautatienkatu 24; ⊗4pm-1am) Popular with both Finns and expats, this rambling Irish pub is handy for the train station and has plenty of time-worn, comfortable seating and an air of bonhomie. Its best feature is the range of interesting beers on tap and carefully selected bottled imports.

Suvi
BOAT BAR

(www.laivaravintolasuvi.fi; Laukontori; ⊗10am-late Jun-Sep) Moored alongside the Laukontori quay, this is a typical Finnish boat bar offering no-nonsense deck-top drinking. Prepare a boarding party and lap up the afternoon sun.

Tullikamari Klubi
BAR, VENUE

(www.klubi.net; Tullikamarinaukio 2; ⊗Mon-Sat, to 4am Wed-Sat) This cavernous place, near the train station, is Tampere's main indoor live-music venue; there are usually several bands playing every week, and big Finnish names regularly swing by for concerts.

ⓘ Information

Forex (www.forex.fi; Hämeenkatu 4; ⊙9am-9pm Mon-Fri, 9am-6pm Sat, noon-6pm Sun) Moneychangers in the Stockmann Building. There's another branch that's by the main square and open shorter hours.

GoTampere Oy (tourist office; ✆5656 6800; www.gotampere.fi; Rautatienkatu 25; ⊙9.30am-5pm Sat & Sun; @) In the train station. Has a booking desk.

Internet Café Madi (Tuomiokirkonkatu 36; per hr €3; ⊙10am-10pm Mon-Fri, 11am-10pm Sat & Sun) Free tea and coffee.

ⓘ Getting There & Away

Air

AirBaltic (www.airbaltic.com) Connects Tampere with Rovaniemi as well as Riga.

Blue 1 (✆06000 25831; www.blue1.com) Flies direct to Stockholm.

Finnair (www.finnair.com) Flies to Helsinki – though it's more convenient on the train – and serves other major Finnish cities.

Ryanair (✆0200 39000; www.ryanair.com) Has daily services to several European destinations including London Stansted, Edinburgh, 'Frankfurt' Hahn, Oslo and Milan. Note that there's no ATM at the Ryanair terminal, but you can buy bus tickets with a card if you're euro-less.

Wingo (✆0600 95020; www.wingo.fi) Flies to Turku and Oulu.

Bus

The **bus station** (Hatanpään valtatie 7) is in the south of town. Regular express buses run from Helsinki (€24.60, 2½ hours) and Turku (€23.20, two to three hours), and most other major towns in Finland are served from here.

Train

The **train station** (www.vr.fi; Rautatienkatu 25) is in the centre at the eastern end of Hämeenkatu. Express trains run hourly to/from Helsinki (€26.30, two hours). There are direct trains to Turku (€24, 1¾ hours), Oulu (€57 to €67, 4½ to seven hours) and other cities.

ⓘ Getting Around

Tampere's bus service is extensive and a one-hour ticket costs €2. A 24-hour Tourist Ticket costs €6. Buses (€2) run between the airport and the centre. A separate company serves Ryanair flights (€6).

Hämeenlinna

♪03 / POP 66.500

Dominated by its namesake, majestic Häme Castle, built in the 13th century, Hämeenlinna (Swedish: Tavastehus) is the oldest inland town in Finland. The town is quiet but picturesque, and its wealth of museums will keep you busy for a day or two. It makes a good stop between Helsinki and Tampere, and you could head on to the latter by lake boat.

The **tourist office** (✆621 3373; www.hameenlinna.fi; Raatihuoneenkatu 11; ⊙9am-4.15pm Mon-Fri, 11am-3pm Sat) has plenty of information and free internet. It opens until 5pm on Mondays.

Hämeenlinna means **Häme Castle** (www.nba.fi; adult/child €5/3; ⊙10am-6pm) so it's no surprise that this bulky twin-towered red-brick fortress is the town's pride and most significant attraction. It never saw serious military action and, after the Russian takeover, was converted into a jail. The interior is a little disappointing, with a modern exhibition annex tacked on to the original building, whose bare rooms don't really evoke its past. The guided tour is recommended.

By the castle are three worthwhile museums, which can be visited with the castle on a combined ticket (adult/child €12/6). The most interesting is the **Prison Museum**, set in a prison block that only closed in 1997.

Finland's most famous composer, Jean Sibelius, was born in Hämeenlinna in 1865 and his childhood home is now an unassuming **museum** (Hallituskatu 11; adult/child €4/1; ⊙10am-4pm Tue-Sun) whose four rooms contain photographs, letters, his upright piano and some family furniture.

Finland loves its house-museums and **Palanderin Talo** (Linnankatu 16; adult/child €4/1; ⊙noon-3pm Tue-Sun Jun-Aug, weekends only Sep-May) is among the best, as it offers a wonderful insight into well-off 19th-century Finnish life, thanks to excellent English-speaking guided tours.

There are no hostels in town, but there are hostel-style rooms as well as camping and cabins at **Aulangon Lomakylä** (✆675 9772; www.aulangonlomakyla.fi; Aulangonheikkiläntie 168; campsites €20, d €45, cabins/cottages €50/80; Ⓟ) on the edge of a nature park, 6km north of the centre. It's a lovely spot.

Hotelli Emilia (✆612 2106; www.hotelliemilia.fi; Raatihuoneenkatu 23; s/d €96/115), on the pedestrian street, is a privately owned hotel and a good deal with its summer discounts.

Hämeenlinna is located on the Helsinki–Tampere motorway and rail line, so trains and express buses to both cities are frequent and fast. In summer you can cruise on a lake ferry to or from Tampere (see p179).

Rauma
🎵 02 / POP 39,800

👁 Sights

Old Town   HISTORIC AREA
Some 600 wooden houses from the 18th and 19th centuries make up Vanha Rauma (Old Rauma), a Unesco site and the main attraction of this seaside town. With its narrow cobbled streets, cafes, house museums (combined ticket €7) and 15th-century stone Church of the Holy Cross, the Old Town makes modern-day Rauma worthy of a stop along the west coast.

🛏 Sleeping & Eating

Hotelli Vanha Rauma   HOTEL €€
(☑8376 2200; www.hotelvanharauma.fi; Vanhankirkonkatu 26; s/d €123/148; ℗) Newly refurbished, this sleek hotel is set in a one-time fish market on the edge of the Old Town. Despite Rauma's creaky wooden feel, rooms here are modern and chic, with flat-screen TV, comfy chairs and views into the park or courtyard. There are only 20, so book ahead. Good weekend and summer deals can be found on their website.

Rauman Kesähotelli   HOSTEL €
(☑050-511 8855; www.kesahotellirauma.fi; Satamakatu 20; s/d/f €46/62/75; ⊙Jun-Aug; ℗) About 1km west of the Old Town, this summer hostel is student accommodation most of the year. It's clean and the facilities are excellent, with a private kitchen and bathrooms shared between two rooms.

Poroholma   CAMPING GROUND €
(☑8388 2500; www.poroholma.fi; Poroholmantie; campsites €10, plus per person €5, cottages €80-100; ⊙May-Aug; ℗) On pretty Otanlahti Bay about 2km northwest of the town centre, this pleasant camping ground has fabulous facilities and a range of cottages. A tourist 'train' chugs out there from the centre in peak season.

Wanhan Rauman Kellari   FINNISH €€
(☑866 6700; www.wanhanraumankellari.fi; Anundilankatu 8; mains €11-22) On the edge of Vanha Rauma, this stone-and-timber cellar restaurant is a great place to splurge on Finnish specialities, seafood and steak. The rooftop beer terrace is terrific in summer. Excellent value.

Café Sali   CAFE, BISTRO €
(www.cafesali.fi; Kuninkaankatu 22; lunch €9; ⊙lunch & dinner Tue-Fri, dinner Sat) On the kauppatori, this enormous restored historic building is part cafe, part restaurant and part lounge bar. It does great coffee and is the town favourite for lunchtime salads and daily hot specials.

ℹ Information

Tourist office (☑834 3512; www.visitrauma.fi; Nortamonkatu 5; ⊙Mon-Fri Sep-Apr) Publishes the helpful pamphlet *A Walking Tour in the Old Town* (free). In summer it relocates to the Old Town Hall at Kauppakatu 13 and opens daily.

ℹ Getting There & Away

Rauma is connected by regular buses to Pori (45 minutes) and Turku (€20, 1½ hours).

Vaasa
🎵 06 / POP 59,200

The Gulf of Bothnia gets wasp-waisted around here, and Sweden's a bare 45 nautical miles away, so it's no surprise that a cultural duality exists in Vaasa (Swedish: Vasa). A quarter of the population speaks Swedish and the city has a feel all of its own. You'll hear conversations between friends and colleagues in restaurants and bars flitting between Finnish and Swedish, often in the same sentence.

👁 Sights

Pohjanmaan Museo   MUSEUM
(www.museo.vaasa.fi; Museokatu 3; admission €5; ⊙10am-5pm Tue-Fri, 10am-8pm Wed, noon-5pm Sat & Sun) This two-in-one museum is Vaasa's must-see. The art collection upstairs is extraordinary. There's an excellent range of works from the Golden Age of Finnish painting; more surprisingly, there's also a high-quality selection of European masters, purchased for virtually nothing in the chaos of Russia after the revolution. Downstairs,

WORTH A TRIP

KVARKEN ARCHIPELAGO

This part of the Gulf of Bothnia is a World Heritage area known as the **Kvarken** (www.kvarken.fi); the land is still rising as the crust 'rebounds' after the last ice age weighed it down. New islets appear, expand and join other islands, forming a fascinating changing landscape across the shallow sea. You can drive or bike out to Replot to examine the phenomenon, but the area cries out for exploration by canoe; the tourist office has details of people who can set this up. Terra Nova, in the Pohjanmaan Museo, is the best place to go for more info about the area.

Terra Nova is devoted to the ecosystem of the local environment.

Vaskiluoto Island   AMUSEMENT PARKS
On Vaskiluoto island, linked by a bridge to the town centre, is the amusement park, **Wasalandia** (www.wasalandia.fi; day pass €18; ⊙from 11am mid-Jun–mid-Aug, closing varies 4-7pm) and a water park, **Tropiclandia** (www.tropiclandia.fi; admission €21; ⊙8am-9pm Mon-Fri, 10am-9pm Sat & Sun, closed most of Sep), both popular with Finnish families and great for young kids.

Kuntsi   GALLERY
(www.kuntsi.fi; Rantakatu; admission €6; ⊙11am-5pm Tue-Sun, to 8pm Wed) Vaasa styles itself as an art town, and there are several galleries. Retro-contemporary Kuntsi is by the water.

🛏 Sleeping

TOP CHOICE Kenraali Wasa Hostel   GUESTHOUSE €
(☎0400-668 521; www.kenraaliwasahostel.com; Korsholmanpuistikko 6-8; s/d/tr €50/60/65; P @) Decorated true to its origins as a former military hospital, this place is more guesthouse than hostel, with cosy rooms, an intimate, peaceful feel, bike hire and a good kitchen.

Hotel Astor   HOTEL €€
(☎326 9111; www.astorvaasa.fi; Asemakatu 4; s/d €124/143; P @) This stylish, intimate hotel opposite the train station is in a lovely old building with a classy, noble interior. The nicest rooms are in the old wing of the building, with polished floors and dark-wood furnishings. Weekend and summer discounts.

Omenahotelli   HOTEL €
(☎0600 18018; www.omena.com; Hovioikeudenpuistikko 23; r €45-60) This is one of the smaller hotels in this chain that takes internet bookings (you can also book using the terminal in the foyer). Rooms are newish,

with a twin bed and fold-out couch that can accommodate a couple for the same price.

Hostel Vaasa   HOSTEL €
(☎324 1555; www.hostelvaasa.fi; Niemeläntie 1; dm/s/d €25/48/58; P @) A 20-minute bus-less walk across the water from the centre (turn right after crossing the bridge), this is part of the Hotel Fenno. Vaasa's cheapest option, but dorm rates are available only in summer. HI discount.

🍴 Eating & Drinking

Strampen   FINNISH €€
(☎041-451 4512; www.strampen.com; Rantakatu 5; mains €14-23, lunch buffet €9-11; ⊙lunch & dinner Mon-Sat) A waterfront favourite that manages to do top-end meals inside and affordable burgers and pasta for drinkers on its harbourside terrace.

Fondis   FINNISH, BAR €€
(☎280 0400; www.fondis.fi; Hovioikeudenpuistikko 15; mains €12-20) There's a bit of everything here on the main pedestrian thoroughfare; Fondis has hearty Finnish meals with good service, there's a stylish lounge bar with sunny terrace and an upstairs nightclub, and around the corner in El Gringo you'll find just about the cheapest beer in town.

Sky   BAR
(www.sky.fi; Kauppatori) For a drink with a bird's-eye view over the city, head here to the rooftop of the Sokos Hotel Vaakuna.

ℹ Information

Tourist office (☎325 1145; www.visitvaasa.fi; Raastuvankatu 30; ⊙9am-6pm Mon-Fri, 10am-6pm Sat & Sun Jun-Aug, 9am-4pm Mon-Fri Sep-May; @) Books accommodation and rents bikes.

ℹ Getting There & Away

BUS & TRAIN From the combined bus and train station, there are frequent buses up and down the coast, and trains connecting via Seinäjoki to Tampere (€34.50, 2½ hours) and Helsinki (€54, four to five hours).

FERRY From May to September there are daily ferries (adults/cars €60/65, four hours) between Vaasa and the Swedish town of Umeå (Finnish: Uumaja) with **RG Lines** (☑020-771 6810; www.rgline.com). The ferry terminal is on the western side of Vaskiluoto (take bus 10).

Jakobstad

☑06 / POP 19,700

The quaint town of Jakobstad (Finnish: Pietarsaari), about 100km north of Vaasa, has a Swedish-speaking majority and is one of the most distinctive and enchanting spots on this part of the Finnish west coast known as *parallelsverige* (parallel Sweden).

◉ Sights

Skata   HISTORIC AREA
Skata is filled with around 300 wonderfully preserved 18th-century wooden houses. It is just north of the centre and is Jakobstad's highlight.

🛏 Sleeping & Eating

There are cheap places to eat and drink along the partly pedestrian Kanalesplanaden, one block north of the market square.

Jugend Home   HOTEL, HOSTEL €€
(☑781 4300; www.visitjugend.fi; Skolgatan 11; hostel s/d/f €39/49/60; hotel s/d €69/89; ℗@) A good all-round option on the edge of Skata, this large building has cosy hostel rooms nestled around a good central kitchen and lounge area. Hotel-style rooms are smart and modern, and come with breakfast. Other facilities include a sauna, bar and pool table.

Westerlunds Inn   GUESTHOUSE €
(☑723 0440; www.multi.fi/westerlund; Norrmalmsgatan 8; s/d/tr €29/45/55; ℗) Old-fashioned charm in the heart of the historic Skata part of town makes this lovely family-run guesthouse a romantic choice. There are kitchen facilities, a sauna and spotless shared bathrooms. Breakfast is €5 extra. Look for the signs saying Resandehem/Matkustajakoti. No wi-fi.

Hostel Lilja   HOSTEL, CAFE €
(☑050-516 7301; www.aftereight.fi/hostel; Storgatan 6; s/d/tr €40/50/60, ste €80, ◔9am-4pm Mon-Fri; ℗@) This stylish, modern hostel in the town centre is attached to the funky After Eight music cafe. Spotless rooms have

that Scandinavian style; there's a TV room, wood-fired sauna and cheap bike rental.

ℹ Information

After Eight (Storgatan; ◔10am-3pm Mon-Fri) A music cafe and local youth meeting centre. There's free internet access. You can hire bikes cheaply here too.

Tourist office (☑723 1796; www.jakobstad.fi; Runebergsgatan 12; ◔8am-6pm Mon-Fri, 9am-3pm Sat Jun-Aug, 8am-4pm Mon-Fri Sep-May) Next to the town square.

ℹ Getting There & Away

BUS There are regular buses to Jakobstad from Vaasa (€19.90, 1½ to 2½ hours) and other towns along the west coast.

TRAIN Bennäs (Finnish: Pännäinen), 11km away, is the closest train station to Jakobstad. A shuttle bus (€4, 10 minutes) meets arriving trains.

LAKELAND, KARELIA & THE EAST

Most of southern Finland could be dubbed 'lakeland', but this spectacular area takes it to extremes. It often seems there's more water than land here, and what water it is: sublime, sparkling and clean, reflecting sky and forests cleanly as a mirror. It's a land that leaves an indelible impression on every visitor.

The greater Lakeland area encompasses Karelia, once the symbol of Finnish distinctiveness and the totem of the independence movement. Most of Karelia today lies over the other side of the Russian border; much of the gruelling attrition of the Winter and Continuation Wars against the Soviet Union was in this area, and large swathes of territory were lost.

Lappeenranta

☑05 / POP 71,900

On the southern shores of vast Lake Saimaa, the South Karelian capital of Lappeenranta is an animated Lakeland town with a visible history, a giant sandcastle and a canal that goes all the way to Russia.

Lappeenranta was a frontier garrison town until the construction of the Saimaa Canal in 1856 made it an important trading centre. These days the canal is a major attraction for tourists, with boats cruising as far as Vyborg, Finland's second-largest city until it was lost to Russia. Finland's largest lake spreads out from Lappeenranta's harbour, and the town itself is vibrant, with plenty of historical links in its old fortress; it's a good place to sample Karelian food and culture.

◉ Sights & Activities

Linnoitus
FORTRESS, MUSEUMS

(www.lappeenranta.fi/linnoitus; adult/child combined ticket €8/free. fortress free; ◷10am-6pm Mon-Fri, 11am-5pm Sat & Sun) On a small hill overlooking the harbour, Linnoitus is a fortress started by the Swedes and finished by the Russians in the 18th century. Some of the fortress buildings house galleries and craft workshops; others have been turned into museums. These include the **South Karelia Museum**, with a variety of folk costumes, local history and a scale model of Vyborg as it looked before it fell to the Russians in 1939, and the **South Karelia Art Museum**, with a permanent collection of paintings by Finnish and Karelian artists.

FREE Hiekkalinna
SANDCASTLE

(◷10am-9pm mid-Jun–Aug) Another daunting fortress sits just below, on the lake side. Hiekkalinna is a giant sandcastle that uses around 3 million kg of sand for its ramparts and themed sculptures. It's great for kids, and has a small village of nearby rides (many free).

Beach Sauna
SAUNA

(admission €4.50; ◷women 4-8pm Wed & Fri, men 4-8pm Tue & Thu) At Myllysaari, east of the harbour area.

☞ Tours

Cruises on Lake Saimaa and the Saimaa Canal are popular, and there are daily departures from late May to mid-September from the passenger quay at the harbour. The cruise along the Saimaa Canal to Vyborg (Russia) is one of Lappeenranta's biggest drawcards. At the time of research you didn't need a visa, even if you stayed overnight in Vyborg, but check this ahead of time.

Saimaan Matkaverkko
CRUISES

(☏0541 0100; fax 541 0140; www.saimaatravel.fi; Valtakatu 49) Runs various trips. They need a copy of your passport at least three days before departure to arrange the 'visa-free' trip to Russia. Booking these cruises well in advance is advisable in any case, as they are very popular. It's on the roundabout at the eastern end of the main street through town.

🛏 Sleeping

Contact the Lappeenranta tourist office for details of some of the many appealing farmhouse stays available in the area.

Huhtiniemi
CAMPING GROUND, HOSTEL €

(☏451 5555; www.huhtiniemi.com; Kuusimäenkatu 18; campsites €12 plus per person €4.50, 2-/4-person cottages €35/45, apt €75; ◷mid-May–Sep; P) This large complex 2km west of the centre has a bed for just about everyone. There's the expansive camping ground by the lake (mosquito repellent is a must in summer) as well as tidy cottages with bunks and fridges, and self-contained apartments. Buses 1, 3 and 5 run past; most incoming intercity buses will also stop here.

Guesthouse Kantolankulma
GUESTHOUSE €€

(☏050-328 7595; www.gasthauslappeenranta.com; Kimpisenkatu 19; s/d €56/82; P) Close to the harbour and town centre, this is a spiffing guesthouse with apartment-style rooms ranging from a studio to four-room apartment, but all have full kitchen with utensils, cable TV and bathroom. Call ahead as it is quite often unstaffed. It's just off the roundabout at the eastern end of Valtakatu.

ABCiti Motel
GUESTHOUSE €

(☏415 0800; www.abcitimotel.ru; Kannelkatu 1; s/d €49/59; P@) The cheapest bed outside the summer season, this laissez-faire Russian-run spot a block south of the tourist office has decent rooms with fridge and shared bathroom. You get breakfast and a private evening sauna session too.

Huhtiniemi Hostel
HOSTEL

(☏451 5555; www.huhtiniemi.com; dm €10; ◷Jun-Aug) HI hostel at the camping ground. Has two simple six-bed dorms.

Finnhostel Lappeenranta
HOTEL

(☏451 5555; www.huhtiniemi.com; s/d €60/75) Offers good hotel-style rooms with bathrooms and breakfast, and pool and sauna access in a nearby sport centre. At the Huhtiniemi camping ground.

✗ Eating & Drinking

Stalls at the harbour, kauppatori and kauppahalli sell local Karelian specialities such as *vety* (bread roll or pie with smoked ham, sliced boiled egg, mince and spices), rice pie, or waffles with jam and whipped cream.

In town, Kauppakatu and Valtakatu each have a lively strip of bars and clubs.

Kahvila Majurska
CAFE €

(www.majurska.com; Kristiinankatu 1; pastries €2-5; ⊕10am-7pm) In a beautifully furnished 18th-century wooden building at the fortress complex, Majurska oozes charm and does a good range of homemade cakes and quiches.

Tassos
GREEK €€

(☑010-762 1452; www.tassos.fi; Valtakatu 33; mains €18-28) This temple-like building in the heart of town offers Greek-inspired cooking. Hellenic classics such as dolmades, tzatziki and souvlaki appear alongside pasta bursting with vegies, and the house special: duck breast in sherry and gooseberry sauce. Portions aren't huge, but include a salad bar with tasty homemade bread. The lunch buffet (€14) offers better value.

Wanha Makasiini
BISTRO €

(www.ravintolawanhamakasiini.fi; Satamatie 4; mains €9-20; ⊕lunch Sat & Sun, dinner daily) Pizza, pasta, salads and more in a cosy ambience in an old storehouse by the water below the fortress. Opens daily in summer.

SS Suvi-Saimaa & Prinsessa Armaada
BOAT BAR

In summer, the best place for a drink is down at the harbour where these two boats welcome you to their busy beer terraces.

❶ Information

Tourist kiosks (⊕9am-8pm) Open from June to mid-August by the harbour, at the fortress and at the sandcastle.

Tourist office (☑667 788; www.gosaimaa.fi; Kauppakatu 40D; ⊕9am-5pm Mon-Fri; @) On the ground floor of the Maakuntagalleria shopping complex, on Kauppakatu, midway between the train station and the fortress.

❶ Getting There & Away

AIR From Lappeenranta's airport, Ryanair serves Brussels Charleroi and Düsseldorf Weeze, while AirBaltic flies to Kuopio, Kuusamo, Tallinn and Riga. Take bus 4 to the airport.

BUS & TRAIN The bus and train stations are together about 500m south of the centre along Ratakatu, though most buses stop in the centre too. Trains are speedier and cheaper than buses to Helsinki (€34.50, 2½ hours) and

Joensuu (€34.50, 2¼ hours). For Savonlinna, change trains at Parikkala. For Kuopio change at Mikkeli.

Savonlinna
☑015 / POP 27,800

Often considered Finland's prettiest town, Savonlinna shimmers on a sunny day as the water ripples around its centre. Set on two islands between Haapavesi and Pihlajavesi lakes, it's a classic Lakeland settlement with a major attraction: perched on a rocky islet, one of Europe's most visually dramatic castles lords it over the picturesque centre and hosts July's world-famous opera festival in a spectacular setting.

◎ Sights & Activities

Olavinlinna
CASTLE

(www.olavinlinna.fi; adult/child €5/3.50; ⊕10am-6pm Jun–mid-Aug, last tour leaves 1hr before close) Standing immense and haughty on a rock in the lake, 15th-century Olavinlinna is one of the most spectacular castles in northern Europe and, as well as being an imposing fortification, is also the spectacular venue for the month-long Savonlinna Opera Festival. The castle's been heavily restored after fire damage, but is still seriously impressive, not least in the way it's built directly on the rock in the middle of the lake. To visit the interior, including original towers, bastions and chambers, you must join a guided tour (around 45 minutes). Tours are multilingual and depart on the hour. Guides are good at bringing the castle to life.

Savonlinnan Maakuntamuseo
MUSEUM

(www.savonlinna.fi/museo; Riihisaari; adult/child €5/1; ⊕10am-5pm daily, closed Mon Sep-May) Across from the castle, the provincial museum tells of local history and the importance of water transport. Here also is Nestori, a national parks visitor and information centre for the Saimaa region. Moored alongside are four historic ships, all with exhibitions open from May to September during museum hours (same ticket).

Cruises
BOAT TRIPS

(€10-15) Dozens of 1½-hour scenic cruises leave from the harbour near the kauppatori daily in summer. **SS Heinävesi** (www.savonlinnanlaivat.com) runs daily at 11am to Retretti art gallery in Punkaharju (one-way/return €24/32, kids €9/14, two hours, mid-June to mid-August), giving you 2½ hours there.

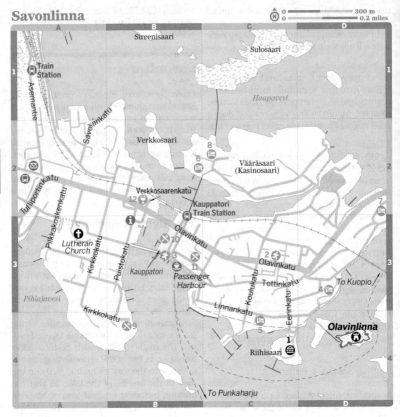

Polkupyörähuolto Koponen   BIKE HIRE
(☎533 977; Olavinkatu 19; per day €10; ◷9am-
5pm Mon-Fri May-Sep) Hires out bikes. The
Savonlinna area is great for bicycle touring, and bikes can be carried on board
lake-boats for a small fee.

Boating   BOATING
To rent canoes and rowing boats, visit
Vuohimäki camping ground (p189).

⭐ Festivals

TOP
CHOICE **Savonlinna Opera
Festival**   OPERA FESTIVAL
(☎476 750; www.operafestival.fi; Olavinkatu 27)
Finland's most famous festival, with an enviably dramatic setting: the covered courtyard
of Olavinlinna Castle. It offers four weeks of
high-class opera performances from early
July to early August. The atmosphere in town
during the festival is reason enough to come;
it's buzzing, with restaurants serving post-

show midnight feasts, and animated discussions and impromptu arias on all sides.

The festival's excellent website details the
program. There are tickets in various price
bands. The top grades (€117 to €159) are fine,
but the penultimate grade (€80 to €101) puts
you in untiered seats, so it helps to be tall.
The few cheap seats (€40) have a severely
restricted view. Buy tickets up to a year in
advance from **Lippupalvelu** (☎0600 10800;
www.lippupalvelu.fi) or from Savonlinna Travel.

Ballet Festival   BALLET FESTIVAL
(www.savonlinnaballet.net) When the opera's
done, this important festival runs for four
days in early August.

🛏 Sleeping

Prices rise sharply during the opera festival,
when hotel beds are scarce. Fortunately, students are out of town and their residences
are converted to summer hotels and hostels.

Book accommodation well in advance if you plan to visit during July.

TOP CHOICE Lossiranta Lodge   HOTEL €€
(☎044-511 2323; www.lossiranta.net; Aino Acktén Puistotie; r €110-160; [P]) This beautifully designed boutique villa boasts a stunning lakeside location and the closest possible view of Olavinlinna. The five unique rooms are impossibly cute, lovingly designed and surprisingly functional. It's recommended but it's best to book ahead during summer. Run by the same people, Tavis (Kalkkiuuninkatu) is further along the lakeshore.

Perhehotelli Hospitz   HOTEL €€
(☎515 661; www.hospitz.com; Linnankatu 20; s/d €85/95; [P][@]) This cosy place near the castle is a Savonlinna classic, built in the 1930s and redolent of that period's elegance, with striped wallpaper, ornate public areas and an orchard garden down to the water. The rooms are also stylish, although beds are narrow and bathrooms small.

Spa Hotel Casino   HOTEL €€
(☎73950; www.spahotelcasino.fi; Kasinosaari; s/d €95/110, large d €110/135; [P][@][≋]) Charmingly situated on an island across a footbridge from the kauppatori, this is a good option. Nearly all rooms have a balcony; those that don't, have their own sauna. In 'small' rooms, the beds are arranged toe-to-toe. The rooms aren't luxurious for this price, but guests have unlimited access to the excellent spa facilities, and the location is fantastic.

Vuorilinna   HOTEL, HOSTEL €
(☎73950; www.fontana.fi; Kylpylaitoksentie; dm/s/d €30/65/85; ☺Jun-Aug; [P]) Set in several buildings mostly used by students, this

friendly complex shares the spa hotel's appealing location across a footbridge from the centre. Rooms are clean and comfortable; the cheaper ones share bathroom and kitchen between two. Dorm rates get you the same deal, and there's an HI discount.

Vuohimäki   CAMPING GROUND €
(☎537 353; www.fontana.fi; campsites €13.50, plus per person €4, 4-person r €58-76, 4-/6-person cabins €76/84; ☺early Jun-late Aug; [P]) Located 7km southwest of town, this has good facilities but fills quickly in July. Prices for rooms and cabins are cheaper in June and August. It hires canoes, bikes and rowing boats.

SS Heinävesi   BOAT €
(☎533 120; www.savonlinnanlaivat.fi; cabins upper/lower deck per person €33/28) During summer this steamer offers cramped but cute two-bunk cabins after the last cruise every afternoon or evening. It's moored right in the centre of things.

Lake Star & Lake Seal   BOAT €
(☎0400 200 117; www.lakestar.info; d €40) Also offer cabins.

🍴 Eating & Drinking

The lively lakeside kauppatori is the place for casual snacking. A *lörtsy* (turnover) is typical and comes savoury with meat (*lihalörtsy*) or sweet with apple (*omenalörtsy*) or cloudberry (*lakkalörtsy*). Savonlinna is also famous for fried *muikku* (vendace, tiny lake fish); try these at Kalastajan Koju on the kauppatori, or the Muikkubaari on the top floor of the Seurahuone hotel. The opera festival peps up Savonlinna's nightlife, with restaurants open late and pubs thronged with post-performance merriment. Near the castle, on lovely Linnankatu, several handsome cafe–bars compete for the pre- and post-opera crowd with mini bottles of fizz and traditional, if priced-up, Finnish plates.

Majakka
FINNISH €€

(☑206 2825; www.ravintolamajakka.fi; Satamakatu 11; mains €12-20) This restaurant has a deck-like terrace fitting the nautical theme (the name means 'lighthouse'). Local meat and fish specialities are tasty, generously sized and fairly priced and the select-your-own appetiser plate is a nice touch. It's child-friendly too.

Huvila
FINNISH €€

(☑555 0555; www.panimoravintolahuvila.fi; Puistokatu 4; mains €23-24; ☻noon-midnight Jun-Aug) This noble wooden building was formerly a fever hospital but writes happier stories these days as an excellent microbrewery and smart restaurant. The food focuses on fresh local ingredients, and one of the delicious beers will match your plate perfectly, whether it be fresh, hoppy Joutsen, traditional sweet *sahti,* or the deliciously rich dessert stout. The terrace is a wonderful place on a sunny afternoon; there are also two cosy, compact attic rooms (doubles €120 during opera festival, €75 at other times).

Olutravintola Sillansuu
PUB

(Verkkosaarenkatu 1; ☻2pm-late) Savonlinna's best pub by some distance is compact and cosy, offering an excellent variety of international bottled beers, a decent whisky selection and friendly service. There's a downstairs area with a pool table; during the festival, amateur arias are sometimes sung as the beer kegs empty.

Liekkilohi
FISH €€

(www.liekkilohi.fi; fish buffet per kg €39; ☻Jun–mid-Aug) This bright-red pontoon, anchored just off the kauppatori, specialises in 'flamed' salmon, a delicious plate that forms part of an excellent pay-by-weight fish buffet.

Information

Savonlinna Travel (☑517 510; www.savonlinna.travel; Puistokatu 1; ☻9am-5pm Mon-Fri Aug-Jun, 9am-7pm daily Jul) Tourist information including accommodation reservation, farmstays, festival tickets and tours. Free internet.

ℹ Getting There & Away

Air

Finnair/Finncomm fly daily between Helsinki and Savonlinna in summer, and more seldom in winter. The airport is 15km from the centre and a **taxi shuttle** (☑040 536 9545) meets arriving flights in July and August (€12, 20 minutes).

Boat

KUOPIO From mid-June to mid-August, **MS Puijo** (www.mspuijo.fi) travels to Kuopio on Monday, Wednesday and Friday at 9am (€79 one-way, 10½ hours), returning on Tuesday, Thursday and Saturday. You can book a return from Savonlinna with overnight cabin accommodation for €159.

LAPPEENRANTA MS Kristina Brahe (www.kristinacruises.com) heads to/from Lappeenranta (€85, 8½ hours) once a week during summer; the fare includes lunch and return bus transfer to Savonlinna.

Bus

HELSINKI (€48.40, 4½ to 5½ hours, several per day)
JOENSUU (€23.80, three hours)
KUOPIO (€29.70, three hours)
MIKKELI (€21.70, 1½ hours, hourly)

Train

Trains departing from Helsinki (€55.60, five hours) and Joensuu (€29.10, 2¼ hours), both require a change in Parikkala. For Kuopio, Jyväskylä and Tampere, rail buses will shuttle you for the two-hour trip to Pieksämäki to connect with trains. The main train station is a walk from the centre of Savonlinna; board and alight at the Kauppatori station instead.

Around Savonlinna

PUNKAHARJU

Situated between Savonlinna and Parikkala, Punkaharju is a renowned sand ridge covered with pines; the surrounding forest and lakes are also beautiful and it is a great area for some cycling or walking. Worth the trip in itself is wonderful **Retretti** (www.retretti.fi; adult/child €16/5, with Lusto €23/9; ☻10am-6pm Jun-Aug), one of the world's most unusual galleries. An innovative annual exhibition of contemporary art is displayed inside an enormous subterranean cavern complex, artificial but authentic in atmosphere.

Not far away, **Lusto** (www.lusto.fi; adult/child €10/5, with Retretti €23/9; ☻10am-7pm) is dedicated to forests and forestry and is a good visit, with plenty of English information.

Trains between Savonlinna and Parikkala stop at Retretti, Lusto and Punkaharju train stations (€3.90 to €4.90, 35 minutes, five to six daily). You can also get here on less regular buses from Savonlinna or by boat (p187).

KERIMÄKI

The world's largest wooden **church** (www.kerimaki.fi; ⏱10am-6pm Jun–mid-Aug, to 7pm Jul, 10am-4pm mid-end Aug) can be found here, about 23km east of Savonlinna. It was built in 1847 to seat a (very optimistic) congregation of 5000 people. Regular buses run here from Savonlinna.

Jyväskylä

🕿014 / POP 129,700

Vivacious and young at heart, central Lakeland's main town has a wonderful waterside location and an optimistic feel that makes it a real drawcard. Thanks to Alvar Aalto, the city also has a global reputation for its architecture, and petrolheads know it as the legendary venue for the Finnish leg of the World Rally Championships.

◉ Sights & Activities

Alvar Aalto-Museo MUSEUM
(www.alvaraalto.fi; Alvar Aallon katu 7; adult/child €6/free; ⏱11am-6pm Tue-Sun) Alvar Aalto, a giant of 20th-century architecture, was schooled here, opened his first offices here and spent his summers in nearby Muuratsalo. The city has dozens of Aalto buildings, but stop first at one of his last creations: the Alvar Aalto Museum, near the university to the west of the centre. It's very engaging, and you get a real feel for the man and his philosophy; buy a copy of the *Architectural Map Guide* (€2), which plots well over a

hundred buildings in and around Jyväskylä, designed by Aalto and other notable figures. They rent simple bikes (€10/15 for one/two days) to help you explore them. Outside town, at Säynätsalo Town Hall, you can sleep in a room that the man himself slept in, and at Muuratsalo you can visit his experimental summer cottage.

Jyväskylä has several other worthwhile museums, all free on Friday, and closed on Monday.

Cruises BOAT TRIPS
(www.jyvaskyla.fi) In summer, there are numerous cruise options, from short lake trips to longer journeys on the Keitele canal or to Lahti.

Laajavuori Winter Sports Centre SKIING
(www.laajavuori.com; Laajavuorentie) Has five modest slopes open in winter, plus a kids' run and 62km of cross-country trails.

⏍ Sleeping

TOP
CHOICE **Hotel Yöpuu** BOUTIQUE HOTEL €€
(🕿333 900; www.hotelliyopuu.fi; Yliopistonkatu 23; s/d/ste €105/146/175; [P][@]) Among Finland's most enchanting boutique hotels, this exquisite spot has lavishly decorated rooms, all individually designed in markedly different styles (the Africa room is really something to behold). There's an excellent restaurant too, and discounts on weekends.

Kesähotelli Harju/Amis HOTEL €
(🕿443 0100; www.hotelliamis.com; Sepänkatu 3; s/d/tr €49/60/72; ⏱Jun-early Aug; [P][@]) Five minutes uphill from the centre, this excellent summer hotel has modern, light and spacious student rooms with kitchenette (no utensils, but there's an equipped kitchen downstairs) and good bathrooms. It's a real

---

WORTH A TRIP

THE SEAL LAKES

Linnansaari and Kolovesi, two primarily watery national parks in the Savonlinna area, offer fabulous lake-scapes dotted with islands; all best explored by hiring a canoe or rowing boat. Several outfitters offer these services, and free camping spots dot the lakes' shores.

This is the habitat of the Saimaa ringed seal, an endangered freshwater species whose population levels have stabilised and are on the increase, although there remain only a precarious 300-odd of the noble greyish beasts.

The parks both have information points, but a good place to start is Nestori centre in the Savonlinna museum. **Saimaaholiday** (www.saimaaholiday.net) and **Kolovesi Retkeily** (🕿040 558 9163; www.sealtrail.com) are experienced operators for Linnansaari and Kolovesi respectively.

bargain, especially given that breakfast and an evening sauna are included.

Retkeilyhotelli Laajari HOSTEL €
(☑266 7053; www.laajavuori.com; Laajavuorentie 15; dm/s/d €29/45/64; **P**) Part of Laajavuori sports complex 4km from town, this hostel is easily accessed on bus 25 and has institutional rooms and a burger cafe. HI members get a discount. Breakfast and sauna included.

✗ Eating & Drinking

TOP CHOICE Figaro FINNISH €€
(☑212 255; www.figaro-restaurant.com; Asemakatu 4; mains €21-27) With a warm drawing-room feel and cordial service, this backs up the atmosphere with really excellent food served in generous portions. A delicate pike carpaccio might be followed with aromatic and succulent salmon with coriander and ginger, sizeable steaks on a mountain of fried onion, or reindeer doused in creamy chanterelle sauce.

Ye Old Brick's Inn PUB €€
(www.oldbricksinn.fi; Kauppakatu 41; mains €13-20; ⊙11am-2am) In the liveliest part of the pedestrian zone, this warm and welcoming pub has several excellent beers on tap, a cosy interior and an outdoor terrace as well as an upmarket bar menu (mains €13 to €22). Kitchen shuts 9pm on Mondays and 11pm other days.

Katriinan Kasvisravintola VEGETARIAN €
(www.maijasilvennoinen.fi; Kauppakatu 11; lunch €6-9; ⊙lunch Mon-Fri) A couple of blocks west of the pedestrian zone, this vegetarian lunch restaurant is an excellent bet. Six euros gets you soup and salad bar, €7 buys a hot dish instead of the soup, and €9 gets you the lot. It changes daily – you might get pasta, ratatouille or curry – but it's always tasty.

Sohwi PUB
(www.sohwi.fi; Vaasankatu 21; ⊙noon-late Mon-Sat, 2pm-midnight Sun) A short walk from the centre is an excellent bar with a spacious wooden terrace, a good menu of snacks and soak-it-all-up bar meals, and plenty of lively student and academic discussion lubricated by a range of good bottled and draught beers. There's an internet terminal too. A great place.

❶ Information

Tourist office (☑266 0113; www.jyvaskylaregion.fi; Asemakatu 6; ⊙9am-5pm Mon-Fri, also 9am-2pm Sat Jun-Aug; @) Good info and ticket

sales, including day passes for the local buses (€7.50), good value if you're going to catch three or more.

❶ Getting There & Away

Air
Finnair operate several flights from Helsinki to Jyväskylä each weekday and fewer on weekends. Jyväskylä airport is 21km north of the centre; buses run to/from the bus station for €5 each way.

Bus
The bus terminal shares the Matkakeskus building with the train station and has many daily express buses connecting Jyväskylä to southern Finnish towns, including hourly departures to Helsinki (€45.50, 4½ hours), some requiring a change.

Train
The train station is between the town and the harbour, in the Matkakeskus building. There are regular trains from Helsinki (€47.70, three to 3½ hours), some requiring a change at Tampere.

Kuopio

☑017 / POP 92,700

Most things a reasonable person could desire from a summery lakeside town are in Kuopio, with pleasure cruises on the azure water, spruce forests to stroll in, wooden waterside pubs, and local fish specialities to taste. And what better than a traditional smoke sauna to give necessary impetus to jump into the admittedly chilly waters?

◉ Sights & Activities

Jätkänkämppä Savusauna SMOKE SAUNA
(☑030-60830; www.rauhalahti.fi; adult/child €12/6; ⊙4-10pm Tue, also Thu from Jun-Aug) Time your visit for a Tuesday (or Thursday in summer) so you can sweat in Jätkänkämppä smoke sauna, a memorable and sociable experience that draws locals and visitors. This giant *savusauna* (smoke sauna) seats 60; it's mixed, and guests are given

> ❶ **DISCOUNT MUSEUM CARD**
>
> If you're going to visit a few Kuopio museums, grab the Museum Card, which gives discounted entry to six of them. It costs €12 and can be bought at any museum or the tourist office.

Nothing is more traditionally or culturally Finnish than the sauna. For centuries it has been a place to bathe, meditate, warm up during cold winters and even give birth, and most Finns still use the sauna at least once a week. An invitation to bathe in a family's sauna is an honour.

There are three principal types of sauna around these days. The most common is the electric sauna stove, which produces a fairly dry harsh heat compared with the much-loved chimney sauna, which is driven by a log fire and is the staple of life at Finnish summer cottages. Even rarer is the true *savusauna* (smoke sauna), which is without a chimney.

Bathing is done in the nude (there are some exceptions in public saunas, which are almost always sex-segregated anyway) and Finns are quite strict about the nonsexual – even sacred – nature of the sauna.

According to sauna etiquette you should wash or shower first. Once inside the sauna (with a temperature of 80°C to 100°C), water is thrown onto the stove using a *kauhu* (ladle), producing *löyly* (steam). A *vihta* (whisk of birch twigs and leaves) is sometimes used to lightly strike the skin, improving circulation. Once you're hot enough, go outside and cool off with a cold shower or preferably by jumping into a lake or pool – enthusiastic Finns do so even in winter by cutting a hole in the ice. Repeat the process. The sauna beer afterwards is also traditional.

towels to wear. Bring a swimsuit for a dip in the lake – devoted locals and brave tourists do so even when it's covered with ice. The **restaurant** in the adjacent loggers' cabin serves traditional dinner (adult/child buffet €19/9) when the sauna's on, with accordion entertainment and a lumberjack show. Bus 7 goes every half-hour from the kauppatori to the Rauhalahti hotel complex, from where it's a 600m walk to the sauna, or you could take the lake boat from the passenger harbour in summer.

Puijo
HILL, OBSERVATION TOWER

In a country as flat as Finland, Puijo Hill is highly regarded. Take the lift to the top of the 75m-high **Puijon Torni** (Puijo Tower; www.puijo. com; adult/child €6/3; ⊙9am-10pm) for vast perspectives of (yes, you guessed correctly) lakes and forests. The spruce-forested hill is a popular spot for mountain biking, walking and, in winter, cross-country skiing, and there's a giant all-season ski jump here where you can often see jumpers in training. There's no public transport but you can walk to the top from the town centre in 30 to 40 minutes.

Kuopion Museo
MUSEUM

(www.kuopionmuseo.fi; Kauppakatu 23; adult/child €5/3; ⊙10am-5pm Tue, Thu & Fri, 10am-7pm Wed, 11am-5pm Sat & Sun) In a castle-like art nouveau mansion, this museum has a wide scope. The top two floors are devoted to cultural history, but the real highlight is the natural history display, with a wide variety of beautifully presented Finnish wildlife, including a mammoth and an ostrich wearing snow boots. There's little information in English.

Kuopion Korttelimuseo
MUSEUM

(www.korttelimuseo.kuopio.fi; Kirkkokatu 22; adult/child €4/free; ⊙10am-5pm Tue-Sun) A block of old townhouses and a real delight. Several homes – all with period furniture and decor – are very detailed and thorough, and the level of information (in English) is excellent.

Suomen Ortodoksinen Kirkkomuseo
MUSEUM

(Orthodox Church Museum; www.ortodoksinen kirkkomuseo.fi; Karjalankatu 1; adult/child €5/1; ⊙10am-4pm Tue & Thu-Sun, 10am-6pm Wed) A fascinating, well-presented collection brought here from monasteries, churches and *tsasounas* (chapels) in occupied Karelia. It was being renovated at last visit, but should be open by the time this book goes to press.

Pikku-Pietarin Torikuja
MARKET

(⊙10am-5pm Mon-Fri, 10am-3pm Sat Jun-Aug) Pikku-Pietarin Torikuja is an atmospheric narrow lane of renovated red wooden houses converted into quirky shops stocking jewellery, clothing, handicrafts and other items. Halfway along is an excellent **cafe** (open from 8am).

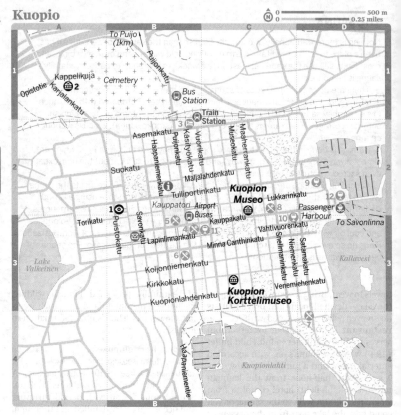

N ⬆ 0 _____ 500 m
0 _____ 0.25 miles

Lake Cruises

BOAT TRIPS

In summer there are regular lake and canal cruises from the harbour. Ninety-minute jaunts cost €11 (half-price for children) and depart hourly from 11am to 6pm. There are cruises to Rauhalahti tourist centre (€13 return) Monday to Saturday from early June to mid-August; a good way to get to the smoke sauna. Special theme cruises include dinner and dancing, wine tasting or a trip to a local berry farm. There are also canal cruises and a monastery cruise to Valamo and Lintula, with return bus transport (€69). For short cruises, pay on the boat; for longer ones, book at the tourist office or near the harbour at Minna Canthinkatu 4. One of the companies offering most options is Roll (www.roll.fi).

✦ Festivals & Events

Kuopion Tanssii ja Soi   DANCE FESTIVAL
(www.kuopiodancefestival.fi) In mid-June. There are open-air classical and modern dance performances, comedy and theatre gigs, and the town is generally buzzing at this time.

🛏 Sleeping

Spa Hotel Rauhalahti   SPA HOTEL €€
(☏030-60830; www.rauhalahti.com; Katiskaniementie 8; s/d €104/136; P@☆) Situated at the Rauhalahti centre, 5km south of town, this place has spa facilities, and there's a restaurant, cafe and popular dance club. Entrance to the spa is €12 for nonguests. Take bus 7 from town.

Hostelli Rauhalahti (s/d €76/90) is in the Spa Hotel complex but cheaper, with simple Nordic rooms and full use of the hotel's facilities. Also in the Spa Hotel complex is **Apartment Hotel** (2-/4-person apt from €112/170), with excellent modern pads that have all the trimmings, including, for not much extra dough, a sauna.

Kuopio

Matkustajakoti Rautatie   GUESTHOUSE €
(☏580 0569; www.kuopionasemagrilli.com; Ase-makatu 1; s/d with bathroom €55/79, without bathroom €45/60; P) This friendly place, run out of the grilli at the train station, actually offers en-suite rooms in the station itself, which are very comfortable, exceedingly spacious and surprisingly peaceful. Across the road, at Vuorikatu 35, they have some cheaper but also acceptable rooms, this time with shared bathroom.

Matkailukeskus Rauhalahti
CAMPING GROUND €
(☏473 000; www.rauhalahti.com; Kiviniementie; campsites €13, plus per person €4, cabins €30-57, cottages €110; ☉late May-Aug; P) Next to the Rauhalahti spa complex, this place has a great location, plenty of facilities and is well set up for families. Bus 7 or 16 will get you here.

Hostelli Hermanni   HOSTEL €
(☏040-910 9083; www.hostellihermanni.fi; Her-manninaukio 3E; dm/s/d €25/40/50; P@) Tucked away in a quiet area 1.5km south of the kauppatori (follow Haapaniemenkatu and bear left when you can: the hostel's in the Metsähallitus building), this is a well-run little hostel with comfy wooden bunks and beds, high ceilings and decent shared

bathrooms and kitchen. Check-in is between 2pm and 9pm; if you are going to arrive lat-er, call ahead. Bus 1 from the centre makes occasional appearances nearby.

✖ Eating

TOP CHOICE Musta Lammas   FINNISH €€€
(☏581 0458; www.mustalammas.net; Satamakatu 4; mains €25-29, degustation menu €54; ☉dinner Mon-Sat) One of Finland's best restaurants, the Black Sheep has a golden fleece. Set in an enchantingly romantic brick-vaulted space, it offers delicious gourmet mains with Finnish ingredients and French flair.

🍽 Kauppahalli   MARKET
(☉8am-5pm Mon-Fri, 8am-3pm Sat) At the southern end of the kauppatori is a classic Finnish indoor market hall. Here stalls sell local speciality *kalakukko,* a large rye loaf stuffed with whitefish and then baked. It's delicious hot or cold. A whole one – a sub-stantial thing – costs around €20, but the bakery by the western door sells mini-ones for €2 if you just want a taste.

Kummisetä   FINNISH €€
(www.kummiseta.com; Minna Canthinkatu 44; mains €14-21. ☉dinner daily, lunch Sat) The sober brown colours of the 'Godfather' restaurant give it a traditional and romantic feel that's replicated on the menu, with country pâté, pike-perch, chanterelle sauces and berries all making welcome appearances alongside chunky steaks. Food and service are both ex-cellent. There's also a popular back terrace and an attractive bar.

Vapaasatama Sampo   FINNISH €
(www.wanhamestari.fi; Kauppakatu 13; muikku dish-es €9-14) Have it stewed, fried, smoked or in a soup, but it's all about *muikku* (vendace) here. This is one of Finland's most famous spots to try the small lake fish that drives Savo stomachs. The 70-year-old restaurant is cosy and most typical.

Kaneli   CAFE €
(www.kahvilakaneli.net; Kauppakatu 22; ☉noon-6pm Mon-Fri, 11am-4pm Sat, noon-4pm Sun) This cracking cafe just off the kauppatori evokes a bygone age with much of its decor, but offers modern comfort in its shiny espresso ma-chine, as well as many other flavoured cof-fees to accompany your toothsome and sticky *pulla* (bun). Opens longer hours in summer.

SHE AIN'T HEAVY, SHE'S MY WIFE

If the thought of grabbing your wife by the legs, hurling her over your shoulder and running for your life sounds appealing, make sure you're in Sonkajärvi, 100km north of Kuopio near the town of Iisalmi, in early July, for the **Wife-Carrying World Championships** (www.eukonkanto.fi). What began as a heathenish medieval habit of pillaging neighbouring villages in search of nubile women has become one of Finland's oddest – and most publicised – events.

The championship is a race over a 253.5m obstacle course, where competitors must carry their 'wives' through water traps and over hurdles to achieve the fastest time. Dropping your cargo means a 15-second penalty. The winners get the wife's weight in beer and, of course, the prestigious title of Wife-Carrying World Champions. To enter, you need only €50 and a consenting female.

There's also a sprint and a team competition; the championship is accompanied by a weekend of drinking, dancing and typical Finnish frivolity, with a big-name band on the Thursday night.

Buses and trains connect Kuopio with Iisalmi, from where buses run to Sonkajärvi, 18km northeast.

Puijon Torni FINNISH €€
(☎255 5255; www.puijo.com; mains €19-27 ⊙9am-10pm) Revolving restaurants usually plunge on the culinary altimeter, but the food atop Puijo tower is pretty good, although the decor won't feature in *Finnish Design Yearbook* any time soon. Choices focus on Suomi specialities, including reindeer, Arctic char and pikeperch, and there are a few set menus (€35 to €46). Last orders are when the tower shuts.

 Drinking

Kuopio's nightlife area is around Kauppakatu, east of the kauppatori. There are many options in this block, some with summer terraces.

Henry's Pub PUB
(www.henryspub.net; Käsityökatu 17; ⊙9pm-4am) An atmospheric underworld with bands playing several times a week.

Wanha Satama PUB
(www.wanhasatama.net; mains €14-18; ⊙11am-11pm Sun-Tue, 11am-4am Wed-Sat summer) Down by the harbour in a massive wooden warehouses. Has a summer terrace.

Albatrossi PUB
(www.ravintolaalbatrossi.fi; ⊙11am-midnight May-Sep) Also by the harbour. Definitely the place to be on a sunny day, if you're not on the water itself.

Helmi BAR
(www.satamanhelmi.fi; Kauppakatu 2; ⊙11am-midnight or later) A downmarket bar with an excellent terrace. It has no frills but does four things, and does them well: pizzas, panini, salads and seriously cheap beer.

ⓘ Information

Kuopio Tourist Service (☎182 585; www.kuopioinfo.fi; Haapaniemenkatu 17; ⊙9.30am-4.30pm Mon-Fri, also 9.30am-3pm Sat Jul) By the kauppatori. Information on regional attractions and accommodation.

ⓘ Getting There & Away

Air

Kuopio airport is 14km north of town. **Buses** (☎020 141 5710) leave from the kauppatori by the Anttila department store 55 minutes before most departures (€5 one-way, 30 minutes).
AirBaltic (www.airbaltic.com) Flies to Riga (Latvia) via Lappeenranta.
Blue1 (☎06000 25831; www.blue1.com) Daily flights to Helsinki.
Finnair (☎580 7400; www.finnair.com) Daily flights to Helsinki.

Boat

From mid-June to mid-August, **MS Puijo** (www.mspuijo.fi) travels to Savonlinna (€79 one-way, 10½ hours) on Tuesday, Thursday and Saturday at 9am, returning on Monday, Wednesday and Friday. It passes through scenic waterways, canals and locks. A return with overnight cabin accommodation costs €159.

Bus

The bus terminal is just north of the train station. Regular express services to/from Kuopio
HELSINKI (€60.20, 6½ hours)
JYVÄSKYLÄ (€23.20, 2¼ hours)
KAJAANI (€31.50, 2¾ hours)
SAVONLINNA (€29.70, three hours)

Train

The train station is 400m north of the centre on Asemakatu.

HELSINKI (€58.10, 4½ hours)
KAJAANI (€23.90, 1¾ hours)
OULU (€45.30, four hours)

Joensuu

📞 013 / POP 72,700

The provincial capital of North Karelia, Joensuu is mainly a jumping-off point for hikes into surrounding wilderness areas. During school term it's a lively university town with students cruising around on bikes, and there are enough bars and restaurants to keep you occupied in the evening. The gentle Pielisjoki rapids divide the town into two parts: most of the town centre is west of the river, but the bus and train stations are to the east.

👁 Sights & Activities

Carelicum   MUSEUM
(www.pohjoiskarjalanmuseo.fi; Koskikatu 5; admission €4.50; ⏰10am-5pm Mon-Fri, 10am-3pm Sat & Sun) One of the finest museums to be found in the eastern Lakeland area. The exhibits

chart the history, traditions and culture of Karelia, part of which is now in Russia.

Ilosaarirock   ROCK-MUSIC FESTIVAL
(www.ilosaarirock.fi) Held over a weekend in mid-July, this is a highly charged rock festival.

🛏 Sleeping

TOP CHOICE Finnhostel Joensuu   HOSTEL €
(📞267 5076; www.islo.fi; Kalevankatu 8; s without bathroom €46, s/tw with bathroom €56/70) This super spot offers great value in sizeable new rooms with mini-kitchen and small balconies, across the road from reception, located in a sports institute. Cheaper singles share bathroom and kitchen with one other room. Prices include breakfast and access to facilities that include a sauna and gym. HI discount.

Hotel GreenStar   HOTEL €
(📞010-423 9390; www.greenstar.fi; Torikatu 16; r €55; 🅿) This bright newish hotel has all the usual facilities without environmental guilt: it's designed for low energy consumption. Rooms sleep up to three for the same price with a pullout armchair for a third bed.

> ### WORTH A TRIP
>
> ## VALAMO MONASTERY
>
> Finland's only Orthodox monastery, **Valamo** (📞017-570 111; www.valamo.fi; Valamontie 42, Uusi-Valamo) is one of Lakeland's most popular attractions. One of the great, ancient Russian monasteries, old Valamo was eventually re-established here, after the Revolution and the Winter War. Monks and novices, almost a thousand strong at old Valamo a century ago, now number just five, but the complex in general is thriving.
>
> The first church was made by connecting two sheds; the rustic architecture contrasts curiously with the fine gilded icons. The new church, completed in 1977, has an onion dome and is redolent with incense.
>
> Visitors are free to roam and enter the churches; services take place at 6am and 6pm Monday to Saturday, and 9am and 6pm Sunday, with an extra one daily at 1pm from June to August. A **guided tour** (€4; 1hr) is highly recommended for insights into the monastery and Orthodox beliefs
>
> Valamo makes an excellent place to stay, more peaceful once evening descends. Two **guesthouses** (s/d €32/54; 🅿) in picturesque wooden buildings provide comfortable, no-frills sleeping with shared bathroom; the **hotel** (s/d/apt €75/110/140; 🅿) offers a higher standard of accommodation. The complex's eatery, **Trapesa** (⏰7am-9pm), has high-quality buffet spreads (€12 to €15), Russian-style high tea (€8) and evening meals with not a hint of monastic frugality; try the monastery's range of berry wines.
>
> Valamo is clearly signposted 4km north of the main Varkaus–Joensuu road. A couple of daily buses run to Valamo from Joensuu and from Helsinki via Mikkeli and Varkaus. From Heinävesi change at Karvio.
>
> The most pleasant way to get to Valamo (and nearby Lintula Convent, which also has simple accommodation) in summer is on a **Monastery Cruise** (📞015 250 250; www.mspuijo.fi; adult/child €69/35) from Kuopio.

There's automatic check-in in the foyer as well as internet booking.

Kesähotelli Elli
HOTEL €

(☑010 421 5600; www.summerhotelelli.fi; Länsikatu 18; s/d/f €50/62/70, apt €100; ☺Jun-Aug; ℗) This student apartment building becomes a summer hotel in a spot that's pleasantly far from the centre of town. The facilities, including sauna, laundry and shared kitchens and bathrooms between two rooms, will make you think about enrolling in a Finnish university.

Linnunlahti Camping
CAMPING GROUND €

(☑126 272; www.linnunlahticamping.fi; Linnunlahdentie 1; campsites €12, plus per person €4, 4-6-person cabins €35-42; ☺mid-Jun–early Aug; ℗) Just south of the centre and right next to the Ilosaari festival stage, this site has a pleasant lakeside location and good-value cottages.

Eating & Drinking

The kauppatori is packed with grillis and stalls selling cheap snacks: try the *karjalanpiirakka*, a savoury rice pastry of local origin but eagerly munched all over Finland.

Astoria
HUNGARIAN €€

(☑229 766; www.astoria.fi; mains €18-27; ☺dinner daily, lunch Sat & Sun) This rustic but stylish riverfront restaurant specialises in Hungarian cuisine with a paprika kick, as well as a wide range of roast meats, mostly for two or more diners. There's a great summer terrace and bar.

Wanha Jokela
PUB

(www.ravintolawanhajokela.fi; Torikatu 26, 10am-late) The oldest and best pub in town, this bohemian hang-out is always interesting. It's full of characters and cheap beer and also has inexpensive rooms (single/double €35/50) with shared bathroom upstairs in case you have one too many.

Houkutus
CAFE €

(www.houkutus.fi; Torikatu 24; lunch €5.50; ☺7.30am-7pm Mon-Fri, 8.30am-5pm Sat) Lively central café with great cakes, wraps, salads and filling soup lunches.

Tuulaaki
CAFE

(Rantakatu; ☺11am-3am May-Aug) In summer there's plenty of drinking, socialising and live music at this harbour cafe, where the passenger ferries dock.

❶ Information

Karelia Expert (☑0400 239 549; www.visitkarelia.fi; Koskikatu 5; ☺9am-5pm Mon-Fri, also 10am-3pm Sat mid-May–mid-Sep, 10am-3pm Sun Jul; @) In the Carelicum; functions as the tourist information office.

❶ Getting There & Away

AIR Finnair flies daily to/from Helsinki. Joensuu's airport is 11km from town; the bus service costs €5 one-way and departs weekdays only from the bus station.

BOAT In summer MS *Vinkeri II* operates at least weekly from Joensuu to Koli (one-way/return €40/60, 6½ hours), from where you can connect with another ferry to Lieksa, across Lake Pielinen. Book with **Satumaa Risteilyt** (☑050-566 0815; www.satumaaristeilyt.fi).

BUS The bus is across the river on Itäranta. Local buses go to Savonlinna (€23.80, three hours), Kuopio (€27.10, 2½ hours) as well as Helsinki and closer Karelian destinations.

TRAIN The train station is next to the bus station across the river. Direct trains run frequently to/from Helsinki (€61.20, 4½ hours) and Lieksa (€13.40, 1¼ hours). For northern and western destinations change at Pieksämäki; for Savonlinna change at Parikkala.

Ilomantsi

☑013 / POP 5970

Pushing up against the border that separates Finland from Russia, Ilomantsi is Finland's most Karelian, Orthodox and eastern municipality, and the centre of a charming region where a wealth of wilderness hiking opens up before you.

The excellent tourist centre, **Karelia Expert** (☑0400 20 072; www.visitkarelia.fi; Kalevalantie 13; ☺8am-4pm Mon-Fri) can help with just about everything, from cottage reservations to information on trekking routes and hire of camping equipment, snowshoes and cross-country ski gear.

Parppeinvaara (www.parppeinvaara.fi; adult/child €5/free; ☺10am-4pm Jun-Aug, to 6pm Jul) is the oldest and most interesting of Finland's Karelian theme villages, where you can hear the *kantele* (Karelian stringed instrument) played and try traditional food at the excellent **Parppeinpirtti** (www.parppeinpirtti.fi; lunch €18; ☺lunch Mon-Fri mid-May–Sep, also Sat & Sun Jun–mid-Aug).

Ilomantsi celebrates **Petru Praasniekka** on 28 and 29 June and **Ilja Praasniekka** on 19 and 20 July every year.

Contact Karelia Expert about cottages in the surrounding region. **B&B Kaksi Karhua** (☑040-561 0930; www.kaksikarhua.fi; Mantsintie 26; s/d €35/60) is set among greenery and a few pecking chickens, lending it a relaxed country-house vibe, although it's very handily located for the town centre and ski trails in winter. Rooms are freshly painted and smallish, but there's a cheerful welcome and hearty breakfast. En-suite rooms are slightly pricier than rooms with a shared bathroom.

Originally built in 1751, **Anssilan Monola** (☑040-543 1526; www.ilomantsi.com/anssila; Anssilantie; s/d €30/60, 4-person cottages €120; **P**), a former dairy farm, is on a hill 4km south of the village and about 500m off the main road. It's family-friendly with rides on horses and sleds for kids; rooms are available in a range of converted farmhouse buildings.

Treks Around Karelia

Karelia's best trekking routes form the **Karjalan Kierros** (Karelian Circuit), a loop of really lovely marked trails with a total length of over 1000km between Ilomantsi and Lake Pielinen. For more information on these and other routes contact Karelia Expert (☑0400 20 072; www.kareliaexpert.fi) in Ilomantsi or Lieksa, or Metsähallitus (www.outdoors.fi).

KARHUNPOLKU

The **Bear's Trail** (not to be confused with the Bear's Ring near Kuusamo) is a 133km marked hiking trail of medium difficulty leading north from Patvinsuo National Park near Lieksa, through a string of stunning national parks and peaceful nature reserves along the Russian border. The trail ends at Teljo, about 50km south of Kuhmo. You will need to arrange transport from either end.

SUSITAIVAL

The 90km **Wolf's Trail** is a marked trail running south from the marshlands of Patvinsuo National Park to the forests of Petkeljärvi National Park, 21km east of Ilomantsi. This links with the Bear's Trail. It's a three-day trek of medium difficulty (the marshland can be wet underfoot). It passes through some important Winter War battlegrounds near the Russian border.

Lake Pielinen Region

In a land full of lakes, Pielinen, Finland's sixth-largest lake, is pretty special. In summer it's the shimmering jewel of North Karelia and is surrounded by some of the most beautiful wilderness areas and action-packed countryside in southeast Finland.

KOLI NATIONAL PARK

Finns consider the views from the heights of Koli, overlooking Lake Pielinen, as the best in the country – the same views inspired several Finnish artists from the National Romantic era. In summer, the national park offers scenic hiking routes, and there's a ferry service between Koli and Lieksa (1½ hours) or Joensuu (see p198). In winter, Koli attracts skiers, with two slalom centres and more than 60km of cross-country trails, including 24km of illuminated track.

The hill has road access with a short funicular (free) from the lower car park to the hotel. From here it's a brief walk to Ukko-Koli, the highest point and 200m further is Akka-Koli, another peak. At the car park, Luontokeskus Ukko (www.outdoors.fi; adult/child €5/2; ⊙10am-5pm) is a modern visitor centre with exhibitions on history, nature and the park's geology, and information on hiking.

In Koli village, 3km below the Luontokeskus, the tourist office (☑045 138 7429; www.koli.fi; Ylä-Kolintie 2; ⊙Mon-Sat, plus Sun Jul & Aug) books activities and has a comprehensive range of information and maps. The village also has a post office, supermarket and coin-op internet, but the last stop for banks and fuel is Kollinporti.

The family-run Kolin Retkeilymaja (☑050-343 7881; www.vanhankoulunmajatalo.fi; Niinilahdentie 47; dm/s/d €28/35/50; **P**), on a gravel road 6km from the bus stop, is a basic hostel set in the countryside and offering good-sized twins with a kitchen and smoke sauna, plus a traditional Sámi *kota* (wigwam-like tent). HI discount.

Apart from the boat, year-round *kimppakyyti* shuttle taxis (☑0100 9986) run from Joensuu to Koli (€20, one hour), picking up at hotels. It's best to book the service the day before; if your phone Finnish isn't great, get the tourist office or your hotel to call for you.

LIEKSA & RUUNAA
☑013 / POP 12,800

The small lakeside town of Lieksa is primarily a base and service town if you're planning any outdoor activities in the region. In winter, husky tours and snowmobile safaris along the Russian border are popular; in summer, hiking, fishing and white-water rafting are all the rage.

◉ Sights & Activities

Pielisen Museo MUSEUM
(www.lieksa.fi/museo; Pappilantie 2; adult/child €4.50/1.50; ⊙10am-6pm mid-May–mid-Sep) One of Finland's largest open-air museums is a slightly jumbled complex of almost 100 Karelian buildings (many relocated from Russia) and historical exhibits – along with an indoor museum of local war and folk history. The indoor hall is also open (€3, 10am to 3pm Tuesday to Friday) in winter.

Ruunaa Recreation Area ACTIVITY PARK
(www.outdoors.fi) Karelia Expert in Lieksa handles information and bookings for all manner of activities around Lieksa and at this park, 30km east. This is a superb, carefully managed wilderness area perfect for fishing, white-water rafting, wildlife spotting and easy hiking. The drawback is that public transport barely exists, but you should be able to hitch (or go with an organised tour) in summer.

⊨ Sleeping

There are numerous options in the countryside around Lieksa. In town, there's a campsite, a hostel and a pair of hotels.

TOP
CHOICE **Kestikievari
Herranniemi** FARMSTAY, HOSTEL €€
(📞0400 482 949; www.herranniemi.com; Vuonislahdentie 185; dm €15, cabins €30-70, cottage €130; B&B s/d €54/74; 🅿) It's worth going out of the way and catching a train to Vuonislahti, 28km south of Lieksa, for this brilliant lakeside retreat. The welcoming farm property has a restaurant, a dormitory outbuilding, a range of comfortable rooms and cottages, two lakeside saunas, rowing boats and even massage and herbal therapy. HI discount.

Ruunaan Retkeilykeskus CAMPING GROUND €
(📞040-579 5684; www.ruunaa.fi; campsites €12, plus per person €3, cabins/cottages €35/100; 🅿) At Ruunaa, in addition to accommodation and services at Naarajoki, the Hiking Centre has a large cafe (May to October), campsites, a kitchen, a sauna and cabins ranging from simple to luxurious. A boardwalk goes a short distance from here to the Neitikoski rapids, a popular fishing and kayaking spot.

Hotelli Puustelli HOTEL €€
(📞511 5500; www.puustelliravintolat.fi; Hovileirinkatu 3; s/d €90/105; 🅿@) By the riverside in Lieksa, with good-sized rooms with affordable rates that include breakfast and sauna. Popular restaurant; discounts on weekends and in summer.

Timitranlinna HOSTEL €
(📞044 333 4044; www.timitra.fi; Timitrantie 3; dm €25-35; 🅿) On the way to the camping ground in Lieksa, this offers good budget accommodation in single beds.

❶ Information

Karelia Expert (📞0400 175 323; www.visit karelia.fi; Pielisentie 19; ⊙9am-5pm Mon-Fri, 9am-2pm Sat) On the main street, this is the place to stop at for information on accommodation and activities.

❶ Getting There & Away

Buses head from Joensuu and Nurmes to Lieksa, as do trains. A **car ferry** (📞0400 889 845; www.pielis-laivat.fi; adult/child/car/bicycle €15/8/11/2) runs once to twice daily between Lieksa and Koli from early June to August.

NURMES
📞013 / POP 8560
On the northern shores of Lake Pielinen, Nurmes is another base for activities such as snowmobiling, ice fishing, dog-sledding and cross-country skiing tours in winter, and canoeing, hiking and farmhouse tours in summer. It's a pleasant town in its own right though, with an 'old town' area (Puu-Nurmes) of historical wooden buildings along Kirkkokatu. A highlight is **Bomban Talo**, part of a re-created Karelian village 3km east of the centre featuring a summer market, craft shops and cafes.

Karelia Expert (📞050 336 0707; www.visit karelia.fi; Kauppatori 3; ⊙9am-5pm Mon-Fri, 9am-2pm Sat) has local information and bookings. It's opposite the bus and train stations.

The best places to stay in Nurmes are side by side on the lake shore about 3.5km east of the town centre. **Hyvärilä** (📞020-741 6780; www.hyvarila.com; Lomatie 12; campsites €14.50, cabins €46-59, hostel dm/s €11.50/21, hotel s/d €75/93; 🅿) is a sprawling lakefront holiday resort with a manicured camping ground, two youth hostels, an upmarket hotel, a restaurant and even a golf course. **Holiday Club Bomba** (📞687 200; www.holidayclubhotels.fi; Tuulentie 10; d €111, apt from

€128; P@⊠), near the Karelian village, is a stylish set-up of rooms and cottages, where you can pamper yourself with the spa and sauna facilities.

Buses run regularly to Joensuu, Kajaani and Lieksa. For Kuhmo there are direct buses Monday to Friday during the school year; otherwise change at Sotkamo. Trains go to Joensuu via Lieksa.

NORTH-CENTRAL FINLAND

Kajaani

✏08 / POP 38,300

Essentially a one-street town, Kajaani makes a handy stopover between Lakeland and the north but has little to keep you beyond the pretty riverside. The city was long an important station on the Kainuu tar transportation route; other claims to fame are that Elias Lönnrot, creator of the *Kalevala*, worked here for a period, using it as a base for his travels, and long-reigning president Urho Kekkonen lived here as a student.

Picturesquely set on a river island, the Kajaani Castle ruins show all the signs of thorough damage by war, time and more recent mischief. It's a fine spot to bask on the grass on a sunny day. Nearby there's a tar-boat channel with a lock built in 1846 to enable the boats laden with tar barrels to pass the Ämmäkoski rapids.

The most interesting sight is at Paltaniemi, 9km northwest of Kajaani. Its enchantingly weathered wooden church (✏687 5334; Paltaniementie 851; ◷10am-6pm mid-May–mid-Aug) was built in 1726, and has some of Finland's most interesting church paintings, rustic 18th-century works full of life and colour that enliven the roof and walls. Take bus 4 from Kajaani (weekdays only).

Once you're this far north, eating choice narrows rapidly. The few options that do exist are along the partly pedestrianised Kauppakatu. If you are staying overnight, Kartanohotelli Karolineburg (✏613 1291; www.karolineburg.com; Karoliinantie 4; s/d from €70/80, d with sauna €110, ste €120-250; P), set in a wooden manor house and outbuildings across the river from town, makes a refreshing change from sterile business hotels. Run by a friendly family, it offers a wide range of chambers, from suites with their own sauna and terrace, to simpler modern rooms. Elegant furnishings, bosky grounds and classy restaurant fare make it a romantic choice. Prices drop a little in summer.

Kajaani Info (✏6155 2555; www.visitkajaani. fi; Kauppakatu 21; ◷9am-5pm Mon-Fri, 9am-2pm Sat) is the helpful tourist office, just off the tiny town square.

Finnair flies to/from Helsinki, and trains run to Helsinki (€69.90, 6½ hours, four daily) via Kuopio, and northwest to Oulu. Buses serve Kuhmo (€18.40, 1¾ hours) and other towns in the region during the week, with fewer departures at weekends.

Kuhmo

✏08 / POP 9600

Kuhmo, once a major tar producer, is a good launch pad for the wilderness; it makes a natural base for hiking the UKK (Urho K Kekkonen) route, Finland's longest marked trek. The vast taiga forest runs from here right across Siberia and harbours 'respect' animals like wolves, bears and lynx. Kuhmo is also the unofficial capital of Vienan Karjala, the Karelian heartland that is now in Russia. This was the region that artists explored in the Karelian movement, such a crucial part of the development of Finnish national identity.

◉ Sights & Activities

Hiking is the big drawcard in Kuhmo, but there are plenty of other ways to get active; the tourist office can help organise things like white-water rafting, while Petola visitor centre has more walking info and can arrange fishing permits.

WILDLIFE WATCHING

The deep forests in eastern and northeastern Finland offer excellent wildlife-spotting opportunities. While you're unlikely to spot bears, wolves, lynx or wolverines on a casual hike, there are plenty of reliable operators throughout the region that specialise in trips to watch these creatures in their domain. The excellent birdlife, both migratory and local, offers further opportunities. Ask at tourist offices for local services.

Kalevalakylä (Kalevala Village)
AMUSEMENT PARK

(☎0440 755 500; www.kalevalaspirit.fi) Four kilometres from the centre of town is this theme park about traditional Karelian life, with a number of Karelian wooden buildings including a sauna, craft shops and Pohjolantalo, a large hall that functions as cafe, restaurant and gallery. There's also the **Kalevala Spirit Experience** (adult/child €30/15; ☺late-Jun–Jul), a two-hour tour in Finnish or English that tests your inherent Finnishness with costumed guides, sauna, tar-making, fishing, woodcarving and so on. You need to book it ahead.

Petola Luontokeskus
NATURE CENTRE

(www.luontoon.fi; Lentiirantie 342; ☺9am-5pm) An excellent nature centre focusing on carnivore species. On the main road near the Kalevala turnoff.

Juminkeko
CULTURAL CENTRE

(www.juminkeko.fi; Kontionkatu 25; adult/child €4/free; ☺noon-6pm Sun-Thu, daily in Jul) If you are interested in the *Kalevala* or Karelian culture, pay a visit to the excellent centre, which offers everything from audiovisual presentations, to Finland's largest collection of *Kalevala* books and multimedia translations.

Wild Brown Bear
WILDLIFE-WATCHING TRIPS

(☎040-546 9008; www.wildbrownbear.fi) Organises wildlife safaris and bear-viewing from hides for around €150.

Taiga Spirit
WILDLIFE-WATCHING TRIPS

(☎040-746 8243; www.taigaspirit.com) Organises wildlife safaris and bear-viewing from hides for around €150.

Kuhmon Kamarimusiikki
MUSIC FESTIVAL

(Kuhmo Chamber Music Festival; ☎652 0936; www.kuhmofestival.fi) Runs for two weeks in late July and has a full program of about 80 top-quality concerts performed by a variety of Finnish and international musicians. Tickets are a steal at around €15 for most events.

🛏 Sleeping

Hotelli Kalevala
HOTEL €€

(☎655 4100; www.hotellikalevala.fi; Väinämöinen 9; s/d €85/122; 🅿@☒) Four kilometres away, by the Kalevala village, this striking building of wood and concrete is a great place to stay. The pretty rooms in yellow colours mostly have tantalising lake views, with the sound of the lapping water. The restaurant's great

too, but it's the facilities that win you over here: they organise anything from snowmobile safaris to spa treatments.

Matkakoti Parkki
GUESTHOUSE €

(☎655 0271, matkakoti.parkki@elisanet.fi; Vientie 3; s/d/tr €30/50/70; 🅿) Run in a most kindly manner, this quiet and handsome little family guesthouse offers excellent value near the centre of town. Rooms share bathrooms, are spotless, and need to be booked ahead during the festival. There's a kitchen you can use, and breakfast is included.

Kalevala Camping
CAMPING GROUND €

(☎0440 755 500; www.kalevalaspirit.fi; Väinämöinen 13; campsites €10, 2-person cabins €35, cottages €90-110; ☺Jun–mid-Aug) This has basic facilities but a most attractive lakeside location, 4km from town and among tall pines. The heated cottages are open May to September.

ℹ Information

The main tourist information points are at **Kalevala Spirit** (☎0440 755 500; www.kalevalaspirit.fi; Väinämöinen; ☺8am-10pm) at the entrance to the Kalevala Village and at Petola Luontokeskus. The nature centre, bookshop and Hotelli Kainuu in the centre of town also give out info.

ℹ Getting There & Away

Numerous daily buses head to/from Kajaani (€18.40, 1¾ hours), and to Nurmes, usually requiring a change at Sotkamo. For other destinations, you'll have to go via Kajaani.

Oulu

☎08 / POP 139,200

Prosperous Oulu is spread across several islands, elegantly connected by pedestrian bridges, and water never seems far away. In summer, the angled sun bathes the kauppatori in light and all seems well with the world. Locals, who appreciate daylight when they get it, crowd the terraces, and stalls groan under the weight of Arctic berries.

Founded in 1605, Oulu grew prosperous in the 18th-century from tar, which was floated down the river from the Kainuu region and shipped to Sweden for shipbuilding. Although pulp factories are a major industry, it's the IT boom that's leading the way in Oulu now and plenty of professional expats live and work here.

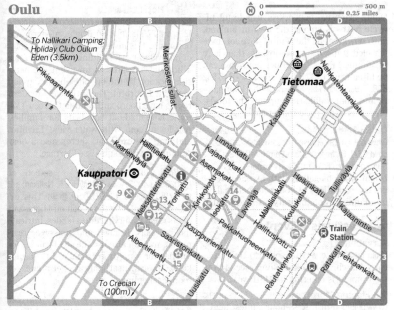

Oulu

◉ Sights & Activities

Kauppatori MARKET SQUARE

By the waterside, this is one of the liveliest and most colourful in Finland with its red wooden storehouses (now housing restaurants, bars and craft shops), market stalls, bursting summer terraces and the rotund *Toripolliisi* statue, a humorous representation of the local police.

Tietomaa MUSEUM

(www.tietomaa.fi; Nahkatehtaankatu 6; adult/child €15/11; ⊙10am-5pm or 6pm) Scandinavia's largest science museum can occupy kids for the best part of a day with a giant Imax screen, hands-on interactive exhibits on planets and the human body, and an observation tower. It opens until 8pm on some Wednesdays; see the website for exact schedules.

Cycling
BIKE TRAILS

Oulu's extensive network of wonderful **bi-cycle paths** is among the best in Finland, and nowhere is the Finns' love of two-wheeled transport more obvious than here in summer. Bikes (€2/15 per hour/day) can be hired from Kiikeli hire shed (☎0440 552 808; ☺9am-6pm May-Sep) near the kauppatori, and from Nallikari Camping. The tourist office has a free cycle-route map.

Oulun Taidemuseo
GALLERY

(www.ouka.fi/taidemuseo; Kasarmintie 7; adult/child €3/1, Fri free; ☺10am-5pm Tue-Thu, Sat & Sun, noon-7pm Fri) Oulu's art museum is a bright spacious gallery with excellent temporary exhibitions of both international and Finnish contemporary art, and a cafe.

✹✹ Festivals & Events

Tervahiihto
SKIING

(Oulu Tar Ski Race; www.tervahiihto.fi) Held in early March. This 70km skiing race (40km for women) is entering its 113th year.

Ice-Fishing Marathon
ICE FISHING

(www.oulutourism.fi) A 48-hour contest held on the open sea in late March (when the ice is still thick) that draws more than 400 participants.

Roviantti
FOOD FESTIVAL

(www.roviantti.info) Pack the breath-mints for this culinary festival held over a weekend in mid-July, one day of which is devoted wholly to garlic. Eats on offer include everything from garlic-flavoured beer to ice cream – all enhanced by festivities and live entertainment.

Oulu Music Video Festival
MUSIC FESTIVAL

(www.omvf.net) In late August. Includes the **Air Guitar World Championships** (www.airguitarworldchampionships.com). Contestants from all over the world take the stage to show what they can do with their imaginary instruments.

🛏 Sleeping

There's precious little budget accommodation in Oulu, but many places have good discounts in summer. As this book went to press, a new hotel, **Forenom Hotel Oulu** (☎020-198 3420; www.forenom.fi; Rautatienkatu 9; s/d €75/85; Ⓟⓐ) was opening opposite the train station. Reception is open only on weekdays 9am to 5pm, but they can give you a door code if you'll arrive at another time.

TOP CHOICE ⟩ Hotel Lasaretti
HOTEL €€

(☎020-757 4700; www.lasaretti.com; Kasarmintie 13; s/d €127/148; Ⓟⓐ☆) Bright, modern and optimistic, this inviting hotel sits in a group of renovated brick buildings that were once a hospital. It's close to town but the parkside location by the bubbling-bright stream makes it feel rural. The artistically modern rooms have floorboards and flat-screen TVs; some have fold-out sofa-beds for families. Ask for a room with water view. Facilities and staff are excellent; there's also a busy restaurant with a sun-kissed terrace.

Holiday Club Oulun Eden
SPA HOTEL €€

(☎020-123 4905; www.holidayclub.fi; Nallikari; s/d €130/150, superior €150/170; Ⓟⓐ☆) This excellent spa hotel by the beach on Hietasaari offers great watery facilities (slides, intricate indoor pools, saunas) and massage treatments. You can also use the spa facilities for the day for a pretty reasonable €15 (€9 for kids). You can nearly always get a cheaper room deal online.

Hotel Scandic Oulu
HOTEL €€€

(☎543 1000; www.scandic-hotels.com; Saaristonkatu 4; s/d €148/165; ⓐ) This sleek, recently opened hotel occupies half a city block right in the middle. From the space-opera lights in its spacious foyer to the high-ceilinged rooms with clean Nordic decor and flat-screen, it's a temple to efficiency, hygiene and modern design (art, individuality: look elsewhere).

Nallikari Camping
CAMPING GROUND €

(☎044-703 1353; www.nallikari.fi; Hietasaari; campsites €13-16, plus per adult/child €4/1, cabins €36-42, cottages €98-139; Ⓟⓐ) Resembling a small town, this excellent camping ground offers all sorts of options in a location close to the beach on Hietasaari, a 40-minute walk to town via pedestrian bridges. Bus 17 gets you there from the kauppatori, as does the tourist train.

🍴 Eating

Local specialities can be found in and around the lively kauppatori.

📗 Kauppahalli
SELF-CATERING

(☺8am-6pm Mon-Fri, 8am-3pm Sat) On the square, the kauppahalli has freshly filleted salmon glistening in the market stalls and plenty of spots to snack on anything from cloudberries to sushi.

Café Bisketti
CAFE €

(www.cafebisketti.fi; Kirkkokatu 8; lunches €5-8; ⊘8am-9.30pm Mon-Thu, 8am-11.30pm Fri & Sat, 11am-9.30pm Sun) This top double-sided spot transforms itself throughout the day. Think twice before getting that pastry with your morning coffee; they're enormous and might not leave room for lunch, with cheap deals on soup, salad, coffee and a pastry, and hot dishes for not much extra. In the evenings, the terrace is a decent spot for people-watching with a beer.

Puistola
BISTRO, RESTAURANT €€

(☑020-792 8210; www.ravintolapuistola.fi; Pakkahuoneenkatu 15; bistro mains €15-23, restaurant mains €20-32) This ambitious new arrival offers a deli–cafe and two restaurant areas. The entry-level bistro is a comfortable space, and turns out tasty, imaginative dishes from its open kitchen with plenty of flair, and also does good-value lunches. Downstairs is a more formal restaurant (open dinner only, Tuesday to Saturday), with somewhat higher prices. Service throughout is excellent. Be sure to check out the toilets – highly original.

Crecian
GREEK €€

(www.crecian.fi; Kirkkokatu 55; mains €20-27) It's worth the short stroll from the centre to this popular neighbourhood restaurant, predictably decked out in blue and white, though the owner's actually Cypriot. The dishes are tasty and generously proportioned, and service is welcoming.

Sokeri-Jussin Kievari
FINNISH €€

(☑376 628; www.sokerijussi.net; Pikisaarentie 2; mains €19-30; ⊘11am-10pm) An Oulu classic, this timbered local on Pikisaari was once a sugar warehouse and has outdoor tables that have good views of the centre. Although the renovated interior has lost a bit of the original character, it's still an attractive spot to eat, with no-frills traditional dishes, including reindeer in summer, and more up-market fare in winter.

Indian Cuisine
INDIAN €

(www.indiancuisine.fi; Kajaaninkatu 38; mains €13-15) Opposite the station, this is the best Indian food in town, and probably for quite a few hundred kilometres. Excellent service.

Café Saara
CAFE €

(www.cafesaara.fi; Asemakatu 7; cakes €3-6; ⊘8am-7pm Mon-Fri, 10am-6pm Sat, 11am-6pm Sun) Delicious gooey cakes, good coffee and glasses of wine in this elegant central cafe.

🍸 Drinking & Entertainment

There's plenty going on in Oulu at night. The kauppatori is the spot to start in summer: the terraces lick up every last drop of the evening sun. Keltainen Aitta and Makasiini are the main ones, set in traditional wooden warehouses.

TOP CHOICE Never Grow Old
BAR

(www.ngo.fi; Hallituskatu 17; ⊘6pm-2am) This enduringly popular bar hits its stride after 10pm, with plenty of dancing, DJs and revelry in the tightly packed interior. The goofy decor includes some seriously comfortable and extremely uncomfortable places to sit, and a log-palisade bar that seems designed to get you to wear your drink. It opens earlier in summer.

Kaarlenholvi Jumpru Pub
PUB

(www.jumpru.fi; Kauppurienkatu 6; ⊘11am-2am Mon & Tue, 11am-4am Wed-Sat, noon-2am Sun) This Oulu institution is a great place for meeting locals and its enclosed outdoor area always seems to be humming with cheerfully sauced-up folk. There's a warren of cosy rooms inside, as well as a nightclub opening from 10pm Wednesday to Saturday.

Graali
PUB

(www.graali.fi; Saaristonkatu 5; ⊘2pm-2am) When it's cold and snowy outside, there's nowhere cosier than this pub, decorated with suits of armour and sporting trophies. Sink into a leather armchair by the open fire and feel the warmth return to your bones.

St Michaels
PUB

(www.stmichael.fi; Hallituskatu 17; ⊘2pm-2am) On the same block as Never Grow Old is convivial St Michaels, an Irish bar with decent Guinness and a good whisky selection.

Sarkka
PUB

(www.tervahovi.fi; Hallituskatu 17; ⊘9am-3am) An old-time Finnish bar that charges a €2 entrance fee at night but is worth it for the downbeat traditional atmosphere and heroic opening hours.

45 Special
NIGHTCLUB

(www.45special.com; Saaristonkatu 12; ⊘8pm-4am) This grungy three-level club pulls a youngish crowd for its downstairs rock and chartier top floor. There's a €7 cover at weekends and regular live gigs.

Information

Wireless internet is available throughout the city centre on the PanOulu network.

Tourist office (📞044-703 1330; www.visit oulu.fi; Torikatu 10; ⏰9am-5pm Mon-Thu, 9am-4pm Fri) Publishes the useful guide *Look at Oulu*.

❶ Getting There & Away

Air

Bus 19 runs between the centre and the airport (€3.60, 25 minutes, every 20 minutes).

AIRBALTIC Flights to Turku, Riga and Stockholm and probably more places by the time you read this.

BLUE1 Several daily direct flights from Helsinki.

FINNAIR Several daily direct flights from Helsinki.

Bus

The bus station, near the train station, has services connecting Oulu with all the main centres.

HELSINKI (€89.10, 10 hours)
KAJAANI (€28.50, 2½ hours)
ROVANIEMI (€39.80, 3½ hours)
TORNIO (€22.80, 2½ hours)

Train

The station is just east of the centre. Six to 10 trains a day (€71.50, seven to nine hours) run from Helsinki to Oulu; the Pendolino service takes only six hours (€77.20). There are also trains via Kajaani, and trains north to Rovaniemi.

Kuusamo

📞08 / POP 16,500

Kuusamo is a remote frontier town 200km northeast of Oulu and close to the Russian border. Wonderful canoeing, hiking and wildlife-watching is available in the surrounding area; nearby Ruka also draws the winter crowds.

There are many possibilities for cross-country skiing, hiking and fishing as well as fast, rugged rapids on the **Kitkajoki** and **Oulankajoki**. **Karhuntassu** (📞0306 502 540; www.kuusamo.fi; Torangintaival 2; ⏰9am-8pm Mon-Fri, 10am-6pm Sat & Sun) at the highway junction has comprehensive tourist information, free internet, a national parks info point and a cottage-rental booking desk. There are many tour operators based in Kuusamo and Ruka, offering a full range of winter and summer activities. The Ruka

website, www.ruka.fi, is a good place to look for active ideas.

Numerous holiday cottages dot the area. Contact the tourist office, **FinFun** (📞0203 70021; www.finfun.fi), which has a portfolio of hundreds, or **ProLoma** (📞020-792 9700; www.proloma.fi).

Kuusamon Kansanopisto (📞050-444 1157; http://edu.kuusamo.fi/kansanopisto; Kitkantie 35; s/d €30/50, with shared shower €25/42; 🅿) is around the corner from the bus. This folk high school offers great budget accommodation in comfortable spacious rooms with en suites; the bad news is that you have to arrive during office hours (8am to 3.45pm Monday to Friday).

A cordial welcome is guaranteed at sweet main-street **Hotelli Kuusanka** (📞852 2240; www.kuusanka.fi; Ouluntie 2; s/d €60/80; 🅿), whose blue-shaded rooms are so clean you can smell it.

Finnair flies to Helsinki. Buses run daily from Kajaani, Oulu and Rovaniemi.

Oulanka National Park

This is one of the most visited national parks in Finland, thanks mainly to the 80km **Karhunkierros** (Bear's Ring Trail), a spectacular three- or four-day trek through rugged cliffs, deep gorges and swinging suspension bridges, starting from either the Hautajärvi Visitor Centre or the Ristikallio parking area and ending at the resort village of Ruka, which is located 25km north of Kuusamo.

There are shelters and free overnight huts on the trail. The *Rukatunturi-Oulanka Map* (1:40,000) has trail and hut information. The best online resource is the excellent Metsähallitus website, www.outdoors.fi.

Juuma is another gateway to the region, with accommodation and accessibility to some of the main sights, such as the charming, idyllic **Myllykoski** and **Jyrävä** waterfalls.

If you don't have the time or resources for the longer walk, you can do the 12km **Pieni Karhunkierros** (Little Bear's Ring) from Juuma in around four hours. The trail starts at **Lomakylä Retki-Etappi** (📞863 218; www.retkietappi.fi; Juumantie 134; campsites €10; cabins from €30; ⏰Jun-Sep; 🅿), where there are campsites and cabins.

It's important to pick your time in Lapland carefully. In the far north there's no sun for 50 days of the year, and no night for 70-odd days. In June it's very muddy, and in July insects can be hard to deal with. If you're here to walk, August is great, and in September the *ruska* (autumn) colours can be seen. There's thick snow cover from mid-October to May; the best time for skiing and husky/reindeer/snowmobile safaris is March and April, when you get a decent amount of daylight and less extreme temperatures.

LAPLAND

Lapland, extending hundreds of kilometres above the Arctic Circle, is Finland's true wilderness and casts a powerful spell. While you won't see polar bears or rocky fjords, there is something intangible here that makes it magical. The midnight sun, the Sámi peoples, the aurora borealis (Northern Lights) and the wandering reindeer are all components of this magic, as is good old ho-ho-ho himself, who 'officially' resides in this part of the world.

Lapland has awesome wild spaces and is *the* place in Finland to get active. Opportunities to get out and experience this vastness are endless. In winter you can mush with husky-dogs, ski in downhill resorts, cheer for reindeer races on frozen lakes, drill a hole and go ice fishing, or snowmobile through forests. In summer, hike through pristine national parks in endless daylight and raft down white-water rivers. The only limitation here is your budget.

Rovaniemi

📞 016 / POP 59,900

Expanding rapidly on the back of a tourism boom, the 'official' terrestrial residence of Santa Claus is the capital of Finnish Lapland and a more-or-less obligatory northern stop. Its wonderful Arktikum museum is the perfect introduction to the mysteries of these latitudes, and Rovaniemi is a good place to organise activities.

Thoroughly destroyed by the retreating Wehrmacht in 1944, the town was rebuilt to a plan by Alvar Aalto, with the major streets in the shape of a reindeer's head and antlers (don't worry, it took us years to work it out). Its unattractive buildings are compensated for by its marvellous location on the fast-flowing (when it's not frozen over...) Kemijoki.

Though the museum is by far the most impressive sight, the tour buses roll north of town, where everyone's favourite beardie-weirdie has an impressive grotto among an array of tourist shops that straddle the Arctic Circle marker. It's free to visit, if not to photograph, the personable chap.

◉ Sights & Activities

TOP CHOICE **Arktikum**   MUSEUM

(www.arktikum.fi; Pohjoisranta 4; adult/child/family €12/5/25; ⊙9am-7pm mid-Jun–mid-Aug, 10am-6pm Tue-Sun rest of yr) With its beautifully designed glass tunnel stretching out to the Ounasjoki, Arktikum is one of Finland's best museums and well worth the admission fee if you are interested in the north. There are two main exhibitions; one side deals with Lapland, with some information on Sámi culture. The highlight, though, is the other side, with a wide-ranging display on the Arctic itself, with superb static and interactive displays focusing on Arctic flora and fauna, as well as on the peoples of Arctic Europe, Asia and North America.

Napapiiri & Santa Claus Village   TOURIST COMPLEX

The southernmost line at which the sun doesn't set at least one day a year, the Arctic Circle, is called Napapiiri in Finland. It crosses the road here, 8km north of Rovaniemi – and built right on top of it is the 'official' Santa Claus Village (www.santaclausvillage.info; admission free; ⊙9am-6pm Jun-Aug), a touristy complex of shops. Here too is the Santa Claus Post Office (www.santaclaus.posti.fi; FIN-96930 Arctic Circle), which receives nearly three-quarters of a million letters each year from children all over the world. Your postcard sent from here will bear an official Santa stamp, and you can arrange to have it delivered at Christmas time.

But the big attraction is, of course **Santa** himself, who sees visitors year-round in a rather impressive grotto (www.santaclauslive.com; admission free; ⊙9am-6pm Jun-Aug), where a huge clock mechanism (it slows the earth's rotation so that Santa can visit the world's children on Christmas night) eerily surrounds those queuing for an audience.

Rovaniemi

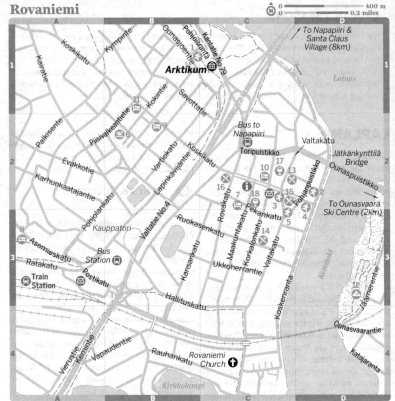

FINLAND LAPLAND

The portly saint is quite a linguist, and an old hand at chatting with kids and adults alike. A private chinwag with the man is absolutely free, but you can't photograph the moment...and official photos of your visit start at an outrageous €25.

Bus 8 heads to Napapiiri from the train station, passing through the centre (adult/child €6.60/3.80 return).

Ounasvaara Ski Centre   SKIING
(www.ounasvaara.fi) Across the Ounasjoki and 3km above town, the centre has six downhill ski slopes and three ski jumps, plus a summer tobogganing run and the Ounasvaara Sky Hotel. It's a good spot for hiking in summer.

Europcar   BIKE HIRE
(Pohjanpuistikko 2) Rent bicycles for €20 a day.

Vesihiisi   SWIMMING, SAUNA
(Nuortenkatu 11; admission €5.50) Has an outdoor and indoor pool as well as sau-

nas, with separate times and sections for men and women. It's cheaper in summer.

Festivals & Events

Napapiirinhiihto   SKIING
(www.napapiirinhiihto.fi) In March, Rovaniemi hosts skiing and ski-jumping competitions as well as a reindeer race in the centre of town.

Jutajaiset   CULTURAL FESTIVAL
(www.jutajaiset.fi) A celebration of Lapland folklore by various youth ensembles, in late June.

Christmas   RELIGIOUS FESTIVAL
A huge festival here, and there are plenty of festive activities throughout December.

☞ Tours

Rovaniemi is Lapland's most popular base for winter and summer activities, offering the convenience of frequent departures and professional trips with multilingual guides.

In summer, tours offered by many operators include guided walks, mountain biking (€55 to €60), river cruises (€25), visits to a reindeer farm (€50 to €60) or huskies (€80), rafting, canoeing and wilderness camping. Winter activities are snowmobiling (€97 to €155 for a two- to six-hour trip), snowshoe-walking (€49), reindeer-sledding (€104 to €111), husky-sledding (€68 to €240), cross-country skiing (€50 to €60), or a combination. These can include ice fishing, a sauna, a shot at seeing the aurora borealis or an overnight trip to a wilderness cottage (€350 to €450). Recommended operators include the following:

Lapland Safaris   SUMMER, WINTER
(☑331 1200; www.laplandsafaris.fi; Koskikatu 1) Reliable and well-established outfit for most of the above activities.

Eräsetti Wild North   SUMMER, WINTER
(☑020-564 6980; www.erasettiwildnorth.fi; Pilke, Ounasjoentie 6). Experienced operator with another office at Santa's village.

Husky Point   DOG-SLEDDING
(☑0400 790 096; www.huskypoint.fi; Koskikatu 9) From short rides to multiday treks.

Safartica   SUMMER, WINTER
(☑311 485; www.safartica.com; Valtakatu 18) One of the best for snowmobiling and river activities.

🛏 Sleeping

Most places offer good discounts in summer.

TOP CHOICE **City Hotel**   HOTEL €€
(☑330 0111; www.cityhotel.fi; Pekankatu 9; s/d €107/124; P@) There's something pleasing about this warm and welcoming place a block off the main drag and cheerfully tucked between the convivial ambience of its own restaurant and bar. It retains an intimate feel, with excellent service and plenty of extras included free of charge. All the rooms are commodious and compact: it's worth the small upgrade to the recently refurbished 'comfort' rooms with their new beds and plush maroon and brown fabrics.

Hotel Santa Claus   HOTEL €€€
(☑321 321; www.hotelsantaclaus.fi; Korkalonkatu 29; s/d €149/179; @) Thankfully this excellent hotel is devoid of sleigh bells and 'ho-ho-ho' kitsch. It's right in the heart of town and very upbeat and busy, with helpful staff and a great bar and restaurant. The rooms have all the trimmings and are spacious, with a sofa and good-sized beds; a small supplement gets you a superior room, which is slightly bigger.

Hostel Rudolf   HOSTEL €
(☑321 321; www.rudolf.fi; Koskikatu 41; dm/s/d €46/60/85; P) Run by Hotel Santa Claus, where you inconveniently have to go to check in, this staffless hostel is Rovaniemi's only one and can fill up fast. Dorms are comfortable, and the private rooms good for the price, with spotless bathrooms, solid desks

and bedside lamps; there's also a kitchen available but no wi-fi. HI discount.

Guesthouse Borealis
GUESTHOUSE €

(☎342 0130; www.guesthouseborealis.com; Asemieskatu 1; s/d/tr €45/56/81; P@) The cordial hospitality and proximity to the train station make this family-run spot a winner. The rooms have no frills but are bright and clean; some have a balcony. The airy dining room is the venue for breakfast, which features Finnish porridge; there's also a sauna for a small extra charge.

Hotelli Aakenus
HOTEL €€

(☎342 2051; www.hotelliaakenus.net; Koskikatu 47; s/d €70/90; P@) Offering excellent summer value from mid-May right through until the end of August, this friendly, efficient little hotel is a short distance west of the centre of town and only a short stroll from the Arktikum. The bright rooms vary in furnishings and size, but they are all spacious and comfortable.

Ounaskoski Camping
CAMPING GROUND €

(☎345 304; Jäämerentie 1; campsites €15, plus per adult/child €5/3; ⊙late May–mid-Sep) Just across the elegant bridge from the town centre, this camping ground is perfectly situated on the riverbank.

🍴 Eating

Kauppayhtiö
CAFE €

(Valtakatu 24; light meals €4-7; ⊙10.30am-8pm Mon-Thu, 10.30am-2am Fri & Sat; @) Rovaniemi's best cafe, this is an oddball collection of retro curios with a coffee-bean and gasoline theme and colourful plastic tables. An espresso machine, bottomless coffee, outdoor seating, salads, sundaes and a bohemian Lapland crowd keep the place ticking.

Gaissa
FINNISH €€€

(☎321 321; www.hotelsantaclaus.fi; Korkalonkatu 29; mains €19-31; ⊙dinner Mon-Sat, plus Sun Dec & Jan) Part of the upstairs restaurant of the Hotel Santa Claus, elegant Gaissa offers petite, reindeer-heavy upmarket cuisine including slow-roasted lamb that falls off the bone.

ZoomUp
BRASSERIE €€

(☎321 321; www.hotelsantaclaus.fi; Korkalonkatu 29; ZoomUp mains €14-20; ⊙lunch & dinner) Upstairs alongside Gaissa at the Hotel Santa Claus, ZoomUp serves excellent salads, pasta, grilled meats, and succulent tuna and

salmon steaks in a more casual atmosphere aimed at pulling a local crowd.

Nili
FINNISH €€€

(☎0400 369 669; www.nili.fi; Valtakatu 20; mains €19-28; ⊙dinner Mon-Sat) There's much more English than Finnish heard at this popular central restaurant, with an attractive interior and a Lapland theme. There are a few glitches – the staff, who wear 'Lapp' smocks, are obviously instructed to sell as much as they can – but the meals are very tasty, with wild-mushroom sauces garnishing fish, reindeer, and even bear dishes.

Mariza
FINNISH €

(www.ruokahuonemariza.fi; Ruokasenkatu 2; lunch €8.20; ⊙lunch Mon-Fri) A couple of blocks from the centre in untouristed territory, this simple lunch place is a real find, and offers a buffet of home-cooked Finnish food, including daily changing hot dishes, soup and salad. Authentic and excellent.

Xiang Long
CHINESE €

(Koskikatu 21; mains €11-17) This main-street Chinese restaurant has friendly service, tasty steamed prawn dim-sum, a salad bar and several reindeer dishes, including one served on a sizzling platter. The lunch buffet (€8.80 Monday to Friday) is great value.

🍸 Drinking & Entertainment

Excluding ski resorts, Rovaniemi is the only place north of Oulu with a half-decent nightlife.

ZoomIt
CAFE, BAR

(www.hotelsantaclaus.fi; Koskikatu; ⊙11am-11pm) Large light, modern ZoomIt is a popular, buzzy central bar and cafe, a good place for a drink or coffee while you scope out Rovaniemi. Right in the heart of town, its terrace is the spot to be on a sunny afternoon and its spacious interior gives room to stretch out with a book if it's raining.

Roy Club
BAR, NIGHTCLUB

(www.royclub.fi; Maakuntakatu 24; ⊙9pm-4am) This friendly bar has a sedate, comfortable top half with cosy seating, a very cheap happy hour until 1am nightly, and well-attended Tuesday karaoke. There's also a downstairs nightclub that gets cheerily boisterous with students and goes late.

Irish Times
PUB

(Valtakatu 33; ⊙2pm-3am) A convivial Irish bar with a distinctly Finnish flavour, this is a fine choice for an animated night of pubbing. It has an excellent heated terrace at the back, and regular live music and karaoke, while the downstairs bar has pool tables. There's a cover charge at weekends, when it's at its best.

ⓘ Information

There are lockers (€2 per 24 hours) at both train and bus stations, and a storage counter at the train station.

Metsähallitus (☑020-564 7820; pilke@metsa. fi; Pilke, Ounasjoentie 6; ◷8am-4pm Mon-Fri) Information centre for the national parks, with information on hiking and fishing in Lapland and an exhibition on sustainable forestry. The office sells maps and fishing permits, and books cottages.

Tourist Information (☑346 270; www.visitro-vaniemi.fi; Maakuntakatu 29; ◷9am-5pm Mon-Fri) On the square in the middle of town. Free internet. They open until 6pm from mid-June to mid-August, when they also open weekends from 9am to 1pm. They use the same opening hours over the Christmas high season.

ⓘ Getting There & Away

Air

There are numerous winter charter flights from all around Europe. Buses meet each arriving flight (€7, 15 minutes). Airport buses leave the bus station an hour before departures, doing hotel pick-ups.

AIRBALTIC Flies to Riga and Tampere.

BLUE1 Flies to Helsinki.

FINNAIR Flies daily from Helsinki and Oulu.

Bus

Rovaniemi is Lapland's main transport hub. Daily connections serve just about everywhere in Lapland: see destination sections for details. Some buses head on north into Norway.

HELSINKI (€118, 12½ hours) Night buses.

KEMI (€23.20, 1½ hours) Frequent express buses.

OULU (€39.80, 3½ hours) Frequent express buses.

Train

HELSINKI (€79 to €83, 10 to 12 hours) Quicker, cheaper and more commodious than the bus. There are three daily direct services (via Oulu), including overnight services (high-season total prices go from €93 in a berth up to €169 in a smart modern cabin with en suite) with car transport possibilities.

ⓘ Getting Around

Major car-rental agencies have offices in the centre and at the airport. **Europcar** (☑0403

062 870; www.europcar.fi; Pohjanpuistikko 2) is at the Rantasipi Pohjanhovi hotel.

Kemi
☑016 / POP 22,600

Kemi is an industrial town and important deepwater harbour. Although not hugely appealing (in summer only the gem museum and wide waterfront have any sort of siren song), Kemi is home to two of Finland's blockbuster winter attractions: the Arctic icebreaker *Sampo,* and the Lumilinna (Snow Castle), complete with ice hotel.

⊙ Sights

Sampo   SHIP
Plough through the Gulf of Bothnia pack ice aboard the *Sampo,* a genuine Arctic icebreaker ship. The four-hour cruise includes lunch and ice-swimming in special drysuits – a remarkable experience. The *Sampo* sails two or more times weekly from late December to mid-April, and costs €240 per adult. If you choose to approach and leave the good ship on snowmobiles (with a reindeer visit included), the price is €387. The best time to go is when the ice is thickest, usually in March. Contact **Sampo Tours** (☑256 548; www.sampotours.com; Kauppakatu 16), inside the tourist information office, for departure dates and to book.

Snow Castle   CASTLE
(☑259 502, www.snowcastle.net; adult/child €8/4; ◷10am-7pm end of Jan–mid-Apr) Few things conjure the fairy-tale romance of a snow castle, and few can compete with Kemi's, a favoured destination for weddings, honeymoons, or just general marvelling at the weird light and sumptuously realised decoration of the multistoreyed interior. The design changes every year but always includes an ethereally beautiful chapel (hope the vows last longer than those ice wedding rings), a **snow hotel** and a restaurant (3-course menus €35-47).

🛏 Sleeping

TOP CHOICE **Lumihotelli**   SNOW HOTEL €€€
(☑258878; www.snowcastle.net; s/d/ste €175/280/320; ℗) Between late January and early April you can spend the night in the snow hotel. The interior temperature is -5°C, but a woolly sheepskin and sturdy sleeping bag keep you warm(ish) atop the ice bed. In the morning you can thaw out in the sauna of a nearby hotel.

Hotelli Palomestari
HOTEL €€

(☎257117; www.hotellipalomestari.com; Valtakatu 12; s/d €75/85; P@) This likeable family place is one block south and one west of the train and bus stations and offers friendly service and decent rooms with trademark Finnish furniture including a desk and sofa. There's also a convivial bar.

❶ Information

Kemin Matkailu (☎258878; www.visitkemi.fi; Kauppakatu 16; ⊙9am-5pm Mon-Fri) Kemi's tourist office. The gemstone gallery also has tourist information.

❶ Getting There & Away

AIR Kemi/Tornio airport is 6km north, and Finncomm have regular Helsinki flights. A trip in a shared airport taxi costs €12.

BUSES Run to Tornio (€6.10, 45 minutes) more than hourly (fewer at weekends), Rovaniemi (€23.20, 1½ hours) and Oulu (€19.90, 1¾ hours) among other places.

TRAINS From Helsinki, Oulu and Rovaniemi.

Tornio

☑016 / POP 22,500

Right on the impressive Tornionjoki, the longest free-flowing river in northern Europe, Tornio is joined to its Swedish counterpart Haparanda (Finnish: Haaparanta) by short bridges. Cross-border shopping has boomed here in recent years, with new malls popping up like mushrooms. Don't forget that Finland is an hour ahead of Sweden.

◉ Sights

Churches
CHURCHES

Interesting sights near the town centre include the beautiful wooden **Tornio Church** (1686) on Seminaarinkatu, and the tiny **Orthodox Church** (⊙10am-6pm Tue-Sat Jun-early Aug) on Lukiokatu, built by order of Tsar Alexander I.

Aineen Taidemuseo
GALLERY

(www.tornio.fi/aine; Torikatu 2; adult/child €4/free; ⊙11am-6pm Tue-Thu, 11am-3pm Fri-Sun) Has a big collection of Finnish art from the 19th and 20th centuries.

🏃 Activities

River-rafting is popular in summer on the Kukkolankoski, using inflatable rubber rafts or traditional wooden boats. There are also kayaking trips and winter excursions such as snowmobile, reindeer and husky safaris. The tourist office can make bookings for all trips and handles **fishing** permits; there are several excellent spots along the Tornionjoki.

Green Zone golf course
GOLF

(☎431711; www.golf.fi/mlgk; Näräntie) The famous course straddles Finland and Sweden, allowing you to fire shots into a different country and time zone, or play under the midnight sun. You'll need a Green Card or handicap certificate. There's also a driving range and pitch-and-putt course here.

🛏 Sleeping & Eating

There's a good hostel and upmarket hotel across the bridge in Haparanda (p496).

E-City Matkakoti
GUESTHOUSE €

(☎044-509 0358; www.ecitybedandbreakfast.com; Saarenpäänkatu 39; s/d €40/60; P) Tornio's best budget option, this is a friendly guesthouse north of the brewery, and run by a welcoming young family. Cosy rooms feature comfortable beds and colourful fabrics; the shared bathrooms are clean and have good showers, and breakfast includes traditional Finnish porridge.

Kaupunginhotelli
HOTEL €€

(☎43311; www.tornionkaupunginhotelli.fi; Itäranta 4; s/d €116/131; P@⛱) Tornio's only real hotel has decent facilities, including a small pool, restaurant, bar, karaoke and nightclub. The rooms are attractive, with colourful bedspreads and plenty of natural light (in summer at least), though closer examination might have you calling for a pot of varnish and a tin of paint to touch things up.

Umpitunneli
TEX-MEX, PUB €

(www.umpitunneli.fi; Hallituskatu 15; mains €12-17; ⊙food served Mon-Fri 3pm-9.30pm, Sat 1-9.30pm, Sun 1-8pm) The 'Dead-End Tunnel' may be a road to nowhere, but it's a most enjoyable one, with a huge terrace, plenty of pissed-up patrons adding entertainment value at weekends, and large plates of food, from creamy pasta to steaks and Tex-Mex. There are often live bands.

Camping Tornio
CAMPING GROUND €

(☎445 945; www.campingtornio.com; Matkaili-jantie; campsites €12, plus per adult/child €4/2, cabins €36-59; ⊙May-Sep; P) Three kilometres from town, off the road to Kemi. Boat and bike hire, tennis and a beach.

ℹ Information

Green Line Centre (📞050 590 0562; www. haparandatornio.com; ⊘8am-8pm Mon-Fri, 10am-6pm Sat & Sun; @) Acts as the tourist office for both towns.

ℹ Getting There & Away

There are a few daily buses from Rovaniemi (€15.50, two hours), although there are more connections (bus and train) via Kemi (€6.10, 45 minutes, more than hourly, less at weekends, free with rail pass). Many Tornio-bound buses continue to Haparanda, although the distance is so short you can walk.

From Haparanda, there are buses to Luleå, from where buses and trains run to other Swedish destinations.

Rovaniemi to Inari

North from Rovaniemi, Hwy 4 (E75) heads up to the vast, flat expanse of northern Lapland and Sápmi, home of the Sámi people and their domesticated reindeer herds wandering the forests and fells. Subtle landscape changes become more severe as you head north, and the feeling of entering one of Europe's last great wildernesses is palpable. The resort town of Saariselkä is the base for hiking or ski-trekking do-it-yourself itineraries in the wonderful UKK National Park, while the Sámi capital of Inari is the place to learn about their traditions and a base for visiting the Lemmenjoki National Park.

SODANKYLÄ
📍016 / POP 8790

Likeable Sodankylä is the main service centre for one of Europe's least-populated areas, which has a population density of just 0.75 people per sq km. It makes a decent staging post on the way between Rovaniemi and the north.

The **tourist office** (📞040-746 9776; www. sodankyla.fi; Jäämerentie 3; ⊘9am-5pm Mon-Fri, 10am-3pm Sat) is at the intersection of the Kemijärvi and Rovaniemi roads. Next to it, the **old church** (⊘9am-6pm Jun-Aug, by request rest of yr) is the region's oldest and dates back to 1689.

Sodankylä books out in mid-June for the **Midnight Sun Film Festival** (www.msfilmfestival.fi), which has a comprehensive range of intriguing screenings in three venues.

Across the river from the town, **Camping Sodankylä Nilimella** (📞612 181; www.naturexventures.fi; campsites €6, plus per adult/child €4/2, 2-/4-person cabins €36/52, apt €65/95; ⊘Jun-

Sep; P) has simple but spacious cabins, as well as cottage apartments with private kitchen and sauna. You can hire bikes for €15 per day.

Majatalo Kolme Veljestä (📞0400-539 075; www.majatalokolmeveljesta.fi; Ivalontie 1; s/d/tr €46/64/75; P@), 500m north of the centre, has small but spotless rooms that share a decent bathroom. Price includes kitchen use, breakfast, a sauna and free tea and coffee. Central **Hotelli Karhu** (📞0201 620 610; www. hotel-bearinn.com; Lapintie 7; s/d €72/86; P) is a great deal, offering buzzy staff, offbeat lobby decor and really inviting chambers, with big fluffy beds, greywood floors and great modern bathrooms.

There are plenty of cafes, supermarkets, takeaways and a couple of bars lined up along the main street, Jäämerentie.

There are regular buses from Rovaniemi, Ivalo and Kemijärvi. The bus terminal is on the main road.

SAARISELKÄ
📍016

Between Sodankylä and Inari, this collection of enormous hotels and holiday cottages makes a great stop for the active. It's on the edge of one of Europe's great wilderness areas, much of which is covered by the UKK National Park. You could hike for weeks here; there's a good network of huts and a few marked trails. In winter, this is a ski resort and a very popular base for snowmobiling and husky trips. In the Siula centre there's tourist information and a **national parks office** (📞020-564 7200; www.outdoors.fi; ⊘9am-5pm Mon-Fri, 9am-3pm Sat & Sun) that sells maps and reserves wilderness cabins. Hit the website www.saariselka.fi for cottage accommodation; the cheapest place to stay is **Saariselän Panimo** (📞675 6500; www. saariselanpanimo.fi; s/d €44/58; P), a cosy brewpub whose spacious, clean rooms are a real bargain. Buses run regularly to Ivalo (€6.80, 30 minutes) and further north, and south to Rovaniemi.

Inari
📍016 / POP 550

You might miss the tiny village of Inari (Sámi: Anár), if you're not paying attention. Don't, for this is the place to begin to learn something of Sámi culture, and has the wonderful Siida museum, as well as excellent handicrafts shops. It's also a great base for heading off to further-flung locations like Lemmenjoki National Park.

Inari is the seat of the Finnish Sámi parliament, and building is underway on a Sámi cultural centre that will hold it, as well as a library and music archive. The village sits on Lapland's largest lake, Inarijärvi, a spectacular body of water with more than 3000 islands in its 1153-sq-km area.

◎ Sights & Activities

An excellent year-round activities program is operated by Inari Event (☏040-777 4339; www.visitinari.fi), based at the Inarin Kultahovi hotel.

TOP CHOICE Siida   MUSEUM
(www.siida.fi; adult/child €8/4; ⊙9am-8pm Jun-Sep, 10am-5pm Tue-Sun Oct-May) One of Finland's finest museums, Siida should not be missed. It's a comprehensive overview of the Sámi and their Arctic environment that's actually two museums skilfully interwoven. Outside is the original museum, a complex of **open-air buildings** that reflect post-nomadic Sámi life. There's also a fine craft shop and a cafe with a decent lunch deal.

Siida's website is worth a mention itself: via the 'web exhibitions' page you can access a series of excellent pages on the Inari and Skolt Sámi cultures.

Inarin Porofarmi   REINDEER FARM
(☏673 912; www.reindeerfarm.fi; Kittiläntie 1445) Inarin Porofarmi is a reindeer farm that runs sled-trips in winter and visits in summer with plenty of information on reindeer herding and Sámi culture. The two-hour visit costs €20, or €50 including transport from Inari.

Walking Track   WALKING
There's a marked 7.5km walking track (starting from the Siida parking area) to the 18th-century Pielpajärvi wilderness church. If you have a vehicle, there's another parking area 3km closer. In winter or spring you'll need snowshoes and a keen attitude to tackle this walk.

✎ Handicrafts   CRAFT WORKSHOPS
Inari is the main centre for Sámi handicrafts and there are several studios and boutique shops in the village. Sámi Duodji Ry (Inarintie 51; ⊙10am-6pm daily Jul & Aug, 10am-5pm Mon-Fri, 10am-3pm Sat Sep-Jun), on the main road, is the main shop of the Finnish association of Sámi craftspeople.

Lake & Snow   BOAT TRIPS
(☏671 108; www.saariselka.fi/lakesnow; Inarintie 26) Daily cruises sail on Inarijärvi from mid-June (as soon as the ice melts) to mid-August (€16, two hours).

✮ Festivals & Events

Skábmagovat   FILM FESTIVAL
(www.skabmagovat.fi) A recommended film festival in the third week of January, with an indigenous theme.

King's Cup   REINDEER RACING
(www.paliskunnat.fi) Held over the last weekend of March or first of April, the King's Cup is the grand finale of Lapland's reindeer-racing season and a great spectacle as the de-antlered beasts race around the frozen lake, jockeys sliding like waterskiers behind them.

⊨ Sleeping & Eating

Inarin Kultahovi   HOTEL €€
(☏511 7100; www.hotelkultahovi.fi; Saarikoskentie 2; s/d €69/90, new wing €109/125; P) Just off the main road towards Lemmenjoki, this cosy family-run place overlooks the rapids and has spruce rooms: the ones in the newer 'River House' have riverside balconies and saunas. There's a restaurant (mains €14 to €25, open 11am to 11pm) that serves well-presented, tasty Lappish specialities.

Villa Lanca   GUESTHOUSE €€
(☏040-748 0984; www.villalanca.com; s/d €52/75, with kitchen €63/89; P) On the main road in the heart of town, this is Inari's most characterful lodging, with boutique rooms decorated with Asian fabrics, feather charms and real artistic flair. The cute attic rooms are spacious and cheaper but lack a bit of headroom. Breakfast included.

Lomakylä Inari   CAMPING GROUND €
(☏671 108; www.saariselka.fi/lomakylainari; 2-/4-person cabins €43/48, with bathroom €65/75, cottages €80-170, campsites for 1/2/4 people €10/15/18; ⊙Jun-Sep; P@) The closest cabin accommodation to town, this is 500m south of the centre and a good option. Some cottages are available in winter.

❶ Information

Tourist office (☏040-168 9668; www.inari.fi) In the Siida museum and open the same hours. There's also a nature information point here.

ℹ️ Getting There & Away

FROM IVALO (€7.50, 30 minutes) Ivalo has a popular winter airport.

FROM ROVANIEMI (€54.50, 5¼ hours) Two daily buses hit Inari and continue to Norway, one to Karasjok and on to Nordkapp in summer, another to Tana Bru.

TO KIRKENES In summer.

Lemmenjoki National Park

Lemmenjoki is Finland's largest national park, covering a remote wilderness area between Inari and Norway. It's prime hiking territory, with desolate wilderness rivers, rough landscapes and the mystique of gold, with solitary prospectors sloshing away with their pans in the middle of nowhere. Boat trips on the river allow more leisurely exploration of the park.

Lemmenjoki Nature Centre (www.out doors.fi; ☺9am-6pm early Jun-Sep) is near the park entrance just before the village of Njurgulahti, about 50km southwest of Inari.

As well as hiking and gold panning, there's a boat cruise along the Lemmenjoki valley in summer, from Njurgulahti village to the Kultahamina wilderness hut at Gold Harbour. A 20km marked trail also follows the course of the river, so you can take the boat one way, then hike back. There are several places offering camping and/or cabin accommodation, food and boat trips. Inside the park, a dozen wilderness huts provide free accommodation.

There is one taxi-bus running Monday to Saturday between Inari and Njurgulahti from early June to early August. Otherwise, check school-bus times with the tourist office.

Northwestern Lapland

There's plenty going on above the Arctic Circle in northwestern Lapland, with several ski resorts (Levi, Ylläs, Olos), and a wonderful range of activities in Muonio, including memorable husky-sled treks. The long, lonely journey up Finland's left 'arm' culminates in Kilpisjärvi, tucked in between Sweden and Norway. These are Finland's 'highlands' and, though not especially high altitude, they offer excellent walking and some outstanding views.

MUONIO
🗷016

The village of Muonio is the last significant stop on Rd 21 before Kilpisjärvi and Norway.

It sits on the scenic Muonionjoki that forms the border between Finland and Sweden, and is a fine base for summer and winter activities. There are plenty of places to stay around here and there's low-key skiing in winter.

Three kilometres south, the excellent Harriniva centre (🗷530 0300; www.harriniva. fi) has a vast program of summer and winter activities, ranging from short jaunts to multiday adventures. In summer these include guided hikes, canoe and boat trips, horse trekking, quad safaris and fishing on the salmon-packed Muonionjoki. You can also rent bikes, boats and rods here, and there are various accommodation options. In winter, there are wonderful **dog-sledding safaris** from 1½ hours (€70) to two days (€530), or trips of a week or longer, perhaps adding reindeer-sledding and snowmobiling to the mix. In summer you can visit the **Arktinen Rekikoirakeskus** (Arctic sled-dog centre) with over 400 lovable dogs, all with names and personalities. A great guided tour of their town (for that is what it is) is €7/4 per adult/child.

LEVI
🗷016

Levi is one of Finland's two most popular ski resorts, but it's also a very popular destination for *ruska* season hiking and a cheap base in summer. The tourist office (🗷639 3300; www.levi.fi; Myllyojantie 2; ☺9am-4.30pm Mon-Fri, 11am-4pm Sat & Sun) should be your first stop for accommodation bookings as well as activities like snowmobile safaris and dog-sled treks.

The ski resort (www.levi.fi) has 47 downhill slopes, many of which are lit. Opportunities for cross-country skiing are also good, with trails totalling 230km.

Accommodation prices go through the roof in December, and between February and May. Virtually the whole town consists of holiday apartments and cottages, typically sleeping four to six, with sauna, fully equipped kitchen and many other mod cons. In summer, they are a real bargain, costing €45 to €60 per night; in winter €1100 a week is average. Four to five daily buses run between Rovaniemi and Levi (€31.50, 2½ hours).

HETTA/ENONTEKIÖ & PALLAS-YLLÄSTUNTURI NATIONAL PARK
🗷016 / POP 1970

One of the easiest long-distance walks in Lapland is the excellent 55km trekking route between the northern village of Hetta (also known as Enontekiö) and **Hotelli Pallas** (☎323 355; www.laplandhotels.com; s/d €150/180; **P**). The marked trail passes through Pallas-Yllästunturi National Park, Finland's third-largest, and can easily be completed in four days. There are free wilderness huts, but these can be packed with people in summer so it is wise to carry your own tent. See www.outdoors.fi for details of the route and huts.

The village of Hetta has a large Sámi population and, though a bit spread-out, makes a good stop for a night or two. Here, **Skierri** (☎0205 647 950; www.outdoors.fi; ⊙9am-5pm) is the combined local tourist office and a visitor centre for the national park. At the southern end of the trek, the **Pallastun-turi Luontokeskus** (☎0205 647 930; www.outdoors.fi; ⊙10am-5pm) at Pallastunturi provides information and can also make hut reservations.

Hetan Majatalo (☎554 0400; www.hetan-majatalo.fi; hotel s/d €65/90, guesthouse €40/64; **P@**) is in the centre of town, but set back in its own garden away from the road. This welcoming pad offers two types of accommodation in facing buildings: clean and simple guesthouse rooms sharing bathrooms, and very handsome and spacious wood-clad hotel rooms. It's an excellent deal that includes breakfast and sauna.

Buses from Hetta head out to the main road to Rovaniemi (€51.60, five hours) and Kilpisjärvi (€28.20, 3¼ hours) via a swapover at Palojoensuu. There's a summer service from Rovaniemi to Tromsø in Norway via Hetta, Kautokeino and Alta.

KILPISJÄRVI
☎016

The remote village of Kilpisjärvi, the northernmost settlement in the 'arm' of Finland, is on the doorstep of both Norway and Sweden. At 480m above sea level, this small border post, wedged between the lake of Kilpisjärvi and the magnificent surrounding fells, is also the highest village in Finland.

The Kilpisjärvi area offers fantastic long and short hikes. The ascent to slate-capped **Saana Fell** (1029m) takes two to three hours return. Also popular is the route through **Malla Nature Park** to the Kolmen Valtakunnan Raja, a concrete block in a lake that marks the **treble border** of Finland, Sweden and Norway. Alternatively, a summer **boat service** (☎0400 669 392) drops you a light 3km away (one-way/return €15/20, 30 minutes).

Lining the main road are several camping grounds with cabins. Many places are open only during the trekking season, which is from June to September.

Two daily buses connect Rovaniemi and Kilpisjärvi (€66, six to eight hours) via Kittilä, Levi and Muonio, with a connection to Hetta. In summer, one heads on to Tromsø in Norway.

UNDERSTAND FINLAND

History

Finland's story is that of a wrestling mat between two heavyweights, Sweden and Russia, and the nation's eventful emergence from their grip to become one of the world's most progressive and prosperous nations.

Prehistory

Though evidence of pre–ice age habitation exists, it wasn't until around 9000 years ago that settlement was re-established after the big chill. Things are hazy, but the likeliest scenario seems to be that the Finns' ancestors moved in to the south and drove the nomadic ancestors of the Sámi north towards Lapland.

Sweden and Russia

The 12th and 13th centuries saw the Swedes begin to move in, Christianising the Finns in the south, and establishing settlements and fortifications. The Russians were never far away, though. There were constant skirmishes with the power of Novgorod, and in the early 18th century Peter the Great attacked and occupied much of Finland. By 1809 Sweden was in no state to resist, and Finland became a duchy of the Russian Empire. The capital was moved to Helsinki, but the communist revolution of October 1917 brought the downfall of the Russian tsar and enabled Finland to declare independence.

The Winter and Continuation Wars

Stalin's aggressive territorial demands in 1939 led to the Winter War between Finland and the Soviet Union, conducted in horribly low temperatures. Little Finland resisted heroically, but was defeated and forced to cede a 10th of its territory. When pressured for more, Finland accepted assistance from Germany. This 'Continuation War' against the Russians cost Finland almost 100,000 lives. Eventually Mannerheim negotiated an armistice with the Russians, ceding more land, and then waged a bitter war in Lapland to oust the Germans. Against the odds, Finland remained independent, but at a heavy price.

Recent Times

Finland managed to take a neutral stance during the Cold War, and once the USSR collapsed, it joined the EU in 1995, and adopted the euro in 2002.

In the new millennium, Finland has boomed on the back of a strong technology sector, the traditionally important forestry industry, design and manufacturing and, increasingly, tourism. It's a major success story of the new Europe with a strong economy, robust social values and super-low crime and corruption.

The Finns

Finland is one of Europe's most sparsely populated countries, with 17 people per sq km, falling to fewer than one in parts of Lapland. Both Finnish and Swedish are official languages, with some 5.5% of Finns having Swedish as their mother tongue, especially on the west coast and the Åland archipelago. Just over 2% of all Finnish residents are immigrants, one of the lowest percentages of any European country.

Finland's minorities include some 6000 Roma in the south and, in the north, the Sámi, from several distinct groups. About 84% of Finns describe themselves as Lutherans, 1.1% are Orthodox and most of the remainder unaffiliated. Only 4% of Finns are weekly churchgoers, one of the world's lowest worship rates.

A capacity for silence and reflection are the traits that best sum up the Finnish character, though this seems odd when weighed against their global gold medal in coffee consumption, their production line of successful heavy bands, and their propensity for a tipple. The image of a log cabin with a sauna by a lake tells much about Finnish culture: independence, endurance (*sisu* or 'guts') and a deep love of nature.

Architecture

Finland's modern architecture – sleek, functionalist and industrial – has been admired throughout the world ever since Alvar Aalto started making a name for himself during the 1930s. His works can be seen all over Finland today, from the angular Finlandia Talo in Helsinki to the public buildings and street plan of Rovaniemi. Jyväskylä is another obligatory stop for Aalto fans.

Earlier architecture in Finland can be seen in churches made from stone or wood – Kerimäki's oversized church is worth seeing, as are the cathedrals at Turku and Tampere. Low-rise Helsinki boasts a patchwork of architectural styles, including the neoclassical buildings of Senate Square, the rich ornamentation of art nouveau (Jugendstil), the modern functionalism of Aalto's buildings and the postmodern Kiasma museum.

Finnish Design

Finland, like Scandinavia as a whole, is also famous for its design. Aalto again laid a foundation with innovative interior design, furniture and the famous Savoy vase. Finns have created and refined their own design style through craft tradition and using natural materials such as wood, glass and ceramics. Glassware and porcelain such as Iittala and Arabia are world famous, while Marimekko's upbeat, colourful fabrics are a Finnish icon. A new wave of young designers is keeping things from stagnating. Stereotypes are cheerfully broken without losing sight of the roots: an innate practicality and the Finns' almost mystical closeness to nature.

Finnish Cinema

Although around 20 films are produced in Finland annually, few make it onto screens beyond the Nordic countries. The best-known Finnish filmmaker is Aki Kaurismäki, who won the Grand Prix at Cannes in 2002 for his wonderful film *Man Without a Past,* an ultimately life-affirming story about a man who loses his memory. His brother, Mika, has made a reputation for insightful documentaries like *Sonic Mirror* (2008), partially looking at Finland's jazz scene

Recent home-grown hits include *Musta jää* (Black Ice; 2007), a characteristically complex Finnish film of infidelity, and *The*

Home of Dark Butterflies (2008), a stark look at a Finnish boys' home. For something completely different, check out *Dudesons Movie* (2006), featuring the painful madness of a group of Finnish TV nuts in the style of *Jackass,* or *Miesten Vuoro* (Steam of Life; 2010), a fabulous doco-film featuring Finnish men sweating and talking about life in the confessional of the sauna.

Hollywood's most famous Finn is Renny Harlin, director of action movies such as *Die Hard II, Cliffhanger* and *Deep Blue Sea*. At time of research he was back home working on the bio-pic *Mannerheim,* based on the life of Finland's wartime leader.

Finland hosts some quality film festivals, notably the Midnight Sun Film Festival in Sodankylä and the Tampere International Short Film Festival.

Literature

The *Kalevala,* a collection of folk stories, songs and poems compiled in the 1830s by Elias Lönnrot, is Finland's national epic and a very entertaining read. Aleksis Kivi's novel *Seven Brothers* is regarded as the founding novel of modern Finnish literature. Its back-to-nature escapism touches something inherent in the forest-loving Finnish character. The theme is echoed in *The Year of the Hare,* written by Arto Paasilinna in the 1970s. Other 20th-century novelists include Mika Waltari who gained fame with *The Egyptian,* and FE Sillanpää, who received the Nobel Prize for literature in 1939. The national bestseller during the postwar period was *The Unknown Soldier* by Väinö Linna. The late Tove Jansson is internationally famous for her Moominland children's stories, and Leena Lander is a contemporary Finnish novelist whose *Tummien perhosten koti* (The Home of the Dark Butterflies) was made into a popular film.

A Musical Nation

Music is huge in Finland, and in summer numerous festivals all over the country revel in everything from mournful Finnish tango to stirring symphony orchestras to crunchingly potent metal.

Revered composer Jean Sibelius (1865–1957) was at the forefront of the nationalist movement. His stirring tone-poem *Finlandia* has been raised to the status of a national hymn. Classical music is thriving in Finland, which is an assembly line of orchestral and operatic talent: see a performance if you can.

The Karelian region has its own folk-music traditions, typified by the stringed *kantele,* while the Sámi passed down their traditions and beliefs not through the written word but through the songlike chant called the *yoik*.

Finnish bands have made a big impact on the heavier, darker side of the music scale in recent years. The Rasmus, Nightwish, Apocalyptica, Lordi, HIM and the 69 Eyes are huge worldwide. But there is lighter music, such as the Von Hertzen Brothers, indie band Disco Ensemble, emo-punks Poets of the Fall and melodic Husky Rescue. Then there are unstoppable legends like Hanoi Rocks, Flaming Sideburns and the unicorn-quiffed Leningrad Cowboys.

Dance

Finns' passion for dance is typified by the tango, which, although borrowed from Latin America, has been refined into a uniquely Finnish style. Older Finns are tango-mad and every town has a dance hall or dance restaurant. A similar form of Finnish dancing is the waltz-like *humppa*.

Finnish Art

Finland's Golden Age was the 19th-century National Romantic era, when artists such as Akseli Gallen-Kallela, Albert Edelfelt, Pekka Halonen and the Von Wright brothers were inspired by the country's forests and pastoral landscape. Gallen-Kallela is probably Finland's most famous artist. He is known for his *Kalevala*-inspired works – don't miss his frescos on display in the Kansallismuseo (National Museum) in Helsinki.

The best of Finnish art can be seen at Ateneum (National Gallery) in Helsinki, but there's an art gallery *(taidemuseo)* in just about every Finnish city.

A Country of Forests and Lakes

People often describe Finland offhand as a country of 'forests and lakes', and the truth is that they are spot on. Some 10% of Suomi is taken up by bodies of water, and nearly 70% is forested with birch, spruce and pine. It's a fairly flat expanse of territory: though the fells of Lapland add a little height to the picture, they are small change compared to the muscular mountainscapes of Norway.

Measuring 338,000 sq km and weighing in as Europe's seventh-largest nation, Finland hits remarkable latitudes: even its southernmost point is comparable with Anchorage in Alaska, or the lower reaches of Greenland. Its watery vital statistics are also impressive, with 187,888 large lakes and numerous further wetlands and smaller bodies of water. Geographers estimate that its total coastline, including riverbanks and lakeshores, measures 315,000km, not far off the distance to the moon.

Finland has one of the world's highest tree coverages; much of this forest is managed, and timber-harvesting and the associated pulp-milling is an important industry.

Wildlife

Brown bears, lynx, wolverines and wolves are native to Finland, although sightings are rare. You're more likely to see an elk, though hopefully not crashing through your windscreen; drive cautiously. In Lapland, the Sámi keep commercial herds of some 230,000 reindeer. Finland is a bird-watcher's paradise, with species like the capercaillie and golden eagle augmented by hundreds of migratory arrivals in spring and summer.

National Parks

Finland's excellent network of national parks and other protected areas is maintained by Metsähallitus (www.outdoors.fi), the Finnish Forest & Park Service. In total, over 30,000 sq km, some 9% of the total area, is in some way protected land. The largest and most pristine national parks are in northern Finland, particularly Lapland, where vast swathes of wilderness invite trekking, cross-country skiing, fishing and canoeing.

Sustainable Finland

As a general model for environmentally sustainable nationhood, Finland does very well. Though it has a high per-capita carbon-emission rate, this is largely due to its abnormal heating requirements and is offset in many ways. As in much of northern Europe, cycling and recycling were big here decades ago, littering and waste-dumping don't exist, and sensible solutions for keeping the houses warm and minimising heat loss were a question of survival, not virtue. Finns in general have a deep respect for and understanding of nature and have always trodden lightly on it, seeing the forest as friend, not foe.

But they're not a nation of tree-huggers. Most of the forests are periodically logged, and privately owned plots are long-term investments for many Finns. Hunting is big here, and animals are kept at an 'optimum' population level by the keen shooting contingent.

And, despite the rushing rivers and clean air, Finland manages to produce only some 16% of its energy needs from hydro- and wind-generated sources. Nevertheless, it plans to meet EU targets for 38% of energy to be produced from renewables by 2020, with wood-based energy a large part of the proposal.

Finland is a strong supporter of nuclear energy, with several operational reactors.

Finnish Cuisine

Typically Finnish food is similar to the fare you get elsewhere in Scandinavia – lots of fish, such as Baltic herring, salmon and whitefish, along with heavy food such as potatoes, meatballs, sausages, soups, stews and dark rye bread. Finns tend to make lunch the main meal of the day. Breakfast can be anything from coffee and a *pulla* to a buffet of cold cuts, porridge, eggs, berries and pickled fish.

Staples & Specialities

Simple hamburgers, hot dogs and kebabs are a cheap, common snack, served from grillis. Fish is a mainstay of the Finnish diet. Fresh salmon, herring and Arctic char are common, and the tiny lake fish *muikku* is another treat. Elk and bear make occasional appearances, while in Lapland, reindeer is a staple on every menu.

Regional specialities from Karelia include *vety*, a sandwich made with ham, eggs and pickles, and the *karjalanpiirakka*, a savoury rice pasty folded in a thin, open crust. In Tampere, try *mustamakkara*, a thick sausage made from cow's blood. In Savo, especially Kuopio, a highlight is *kalakukko*, fish baked in a rye loaf. Åland is known for its fluffy semolina pancakes. Seasonal berries are a delight in Finland – look out for cloudberries and lingonberries from Lapland, and market stalls selling blueberries, strawberries and raspberries.

Finns drink plenty of beer, and among the big local brews are Lapin Kulta and Karhu. Cider is also popular, as is *lonkero,* a ready-made mix of gin and fruity soft drink, usually grapefruit. Other uniquely Finnish drinks include *salmiakkikossu,* which combines dissolved liquorice sweets with the iconic Koskenkorva vodka (an acquired taste); *fisu,* which does the same but with Fisherman's Friend pastilles; *sahti,* a sweet, high-alcohol beer; and cloudberry or cranberry liqueurs.

Where to Eat & Drink

Big towns all have a kauppahalli (market hall), the place to head for all sorts of Finnish specialities, breads, cheeses, fresh fish and cheap sandwiches and snacks. The summer kauppatori (market square) also has food stalls and market produce.

Meals in a *ravintola* (restaurant) can be expensive, particularly dinner, but Finns tend to eat their main meal in the middle of the day, so most restaurants and some cafes put on a generous *lounas* (lunch) buffet for between €7 and €10. These include all-you-can-eat salad, bread, coffee and dessert, plus big helpings of hearty fare – sausage and potatoes or fish and pasta are common.

Finns are big lovers of chain restaurants (Golden Rax Pizza Buffet, Rosso, Amarillo, Koti Pizza, Hesburger, Fransmanni and many more), which can be found in most towns. Quality isn't wonderful, but they can be cheap refuelling options and tend to open long hours.

Finns are the world's biggest coffee drinkers, so cafes are everywhere, ranging from 100-year-old imperial classics to trendy networking joints and simple country caffeine stops.

Beer, wine and spirits are sold by the state network, beautifully named Alko. There are stores in every town. The legal age for drinking is 18 for beer and wine, and 20 for spirits. Beer and cider with less than 5% alcohol can be bought easily at supermarkets, service stations and convenience stores.

Vegetarians & Vegans

Most medium-sized towns in Finland will have a *kasvisravintola* (vegetarian restaurant), usually open weekday lunchtimes only. It's easy to self-cater at markets, or eat only the salad and vegetables at lunch buffets (which is usually cheaper). Many restaurants also have a salad buffet. The website www.vegaaniliitto.fi has a useful listing of vegetarian and vegan restaurants; follow 'ruoka' and 'kasvisravintoloita' (the Finnish list is more up-to-date than the English one).

SURVIVAL GUIDE

Directory A–Z

Accommodation

Sleeping listings in this chapter are divided into three price categories, based on the cost of a standard double room at its most expensive. In the budget category expect shared bathrooms; midrange will have private bathroom, good facilities and breakfast buffet included, while top end has business-class or five-star facilities.

€€€ more than €150

€€ €70 to €150

€ less than €70

CAMPING

Most camping grounds are open only from June to August (ie summer) and popular spots are crowded during July and the Midsummer weekend. Campsites usually cost around €12 plus €4 per person. Almost all camping grounds have cabins or cottages for rent, which are usually excellent value from €35 for a basic double cabin to €120 for a cottage with kitchen, bathroom and sauna.

The Camping Card Scandinavia offers useful discounts. You can buy it at most campsites for €7. The Finnish Camping Association (www.camping.fi) carries an extensive listing of campsites across the country.

Finland's *jokamiehenoikeus* (everyman's right) allows access to most land and means you can pitch a tent almost anywhere on public land or at designated free campsites in national parks.

HOSTELS & SUMMER HOTELS

For solo travellers, hostels generally offer the cheapest bed, and can be good value for twin rooms. Finnish hostels are invariably clean, comfortable and very well equipped, though most are in somewhat institutional buildings.

Some Finnish hostels are run by the Finnish Youth Hostel Association (SRM), and many more are affiliated. It's worth being a member of HI (www.hihostels.com), as members save €2.50 per night at affiliated places. You'll save money with a sleeping sheet or your own linen, as hostels tend to charge €4 to €8 for this.

From June to August, many student residences are made over as summer hostels and hotels. These are often great value, as you usually get your own room, with kitchen (bring your own utensils, though) and bathroom either to yourself or shared between two.

HOTELS

Most hotels in Finland cater to business travellers and the majority belong to one of a few major chains, including Sokos (www.sokoshotels.fi), Scandic (www.scandichotels.com) and Cumulus (www.cumulus.fi). Finlandia (www.finlandiahotels.fi) is an association of independent hotels, while Omenahotelli (www.omena.com) offers great-value staffless hotels booked online.

Hotels in Finland are designed with business travellers in mind and tend to charge them robustly. But at weekends and during the summer holidays, they bring their prices crashing down to try and lure people who aren't on company expense accounts. Prices in three- and four-star hotels tend to drop by 40% or so at these times; so take advantage. Prices listed in this guide are weekday prices unless otherwise specified.

All Finnish hotels have a large, plentiful and delicious buffet breakfast included in the rate and most include a sauna session.

FARMSTAYS

A growing, and often ecologically sound, accommodation sector in Finland is that of farmstays. Many rural farms, particularly in the south, offer B&B accommodation, a unique opportunity to meet local people and experience their way of life. Plenty of activities are also usually on offer. ECEAT (www.eceat.fi) lists a number of organic, sustainable farms in Finland that offer accommodation. Local tourist offices keep lists of farmstay options in the surrounding area; the website www.visitfinland.com links to a few (click on accommodation), and Lomarengas (☑095-766 3350; www.lomarengas.fi) also has many listed on its website. In general, prices are good – from around €30 per person per night, country breakfast included. Evening meals are also usually available. Your hosts may not speak much English; if you have difficulties the local tourist office will be happy to help arrange the booking.

SELF-CATERING ACCOMMODATION

One of Finland's joys is its plethora of cottages for rent, ranging from simple camping cabins to fully equipped bungalows with electric sauna and gleaming modern kitchen. These can be remarkably good value and are perfect for families. There are tens of thousands of cabins and cottages for rent in Finland, many in typical, romantic foresty lakeside locations. By far the biggest national agent for cottage rentals is Lomarengas (☑0306 502 502; www.lomarengas.fi; Eteläesplanadi 22, Helsinki). Another good choice is Villi Pohjola (☑020-344 122; www.wildnorth.net). This arm of the Finnish Forest & Park Service has cottages and cabins for rent all over Finland, but especially in Lapland and the north. Local tourist offices and town websites also have lists.

Activities

Boating, Canoeing, Kayaking Every waterside town has a place (most frequently the camping ground) where you can rent a canoe, kayak or rowing boat by the hour or day. Rental cottages often have rowing boats that you can use free of charge to investigate the local lake and its islands. Canoe and kayak rentals range in price from €15 to €30 per day, and €80 to €200 per week. The website www.canoeinfinland.com has details of several Lakeland routes.

Fishing Several permits are required of foreigners (between the ages of 18 and 64) but they are very easy to arrange. Buy them online via the website www.mmm.fi or talk to the local campsite, tourist office or fishing shop. Ice fishing is popular and requires no licence.

Hiking Hiking is best from June to September, although in July mosquitoes and other biting insects can be a big problem in Lapland. Wilderness huts line the northern trails (both free shared ones and private bookable ones). According to the law, a principle of common access to nature applies, so you are generally allowed to hike in any forested or wilderness area. The website www.outdoors.fi provides comprehensive information on trekking routes and huts in national parks.

Skiing The ski season in Finland runs from late November to early May and slightly longer in the north, where it's possible to ski from October to May. You can rent all skiing or snowboarding equipment at major ski resorts for about €30/110 per day/week. A one-day lift pass costs around €30/160 per day/week. Cross-country skiing is popular: it's best during January and February in southern Finland, and from December to April in the north.

Saunas Many hotels, hostels and camping grounds have saunas that are free with a night's stay. See p193 for more sauna information.

Snowmobiles (Skidoos) You'll need a valid drivers licence to use one.

Business Hours

Following are usual business hours in Finland. Opening hours aren't given in the book unless they differ significantly from the list below.

Alko (state alcohol store) 9am-8pm Mon-Fri, to 6pm Sat

Banks 9am-4.15pm Mon-Fri

Nightclubs As late as 4am

Post offices 9am-6pm Mon-Fri

Pubs 11am-1am (often later on Fri & Sat)

Restaurants 11am-10pm, lunch 11am-3pm

Shops 9am-6pm Mon-Fri, to 3pm Sat

Children

Finland is a very easy country to travel in with children. All hotels will put extra beds in rooms, restaurants have family-friendly features and there are substantial transport discounts.

Food

Restaurants in this chapter have been categorised as follows:

€€€ more than €25

€€ €15 to €25

€ less than €15

Gay & Lesbian Travellers

Finland's cities are open, tolerant places and Helsinki, though no Copenhagen or Stockholm, has a small but welcoming gay scene (see p162).

Internet Access

Public libraries Always have at least one free internet terminal.

Tourist offices Most have an internet terminal that you can use for free (usually 15 minutes).

Wireless internet access Very widespread; several cities have extensive networks, and nearly all hotels, as well as many restaurants, cafes and bars, offer free access to customers and guests.

Money

Currency Finland adopted the euro (€) in 2002. Euro notes come in five, 10, 20, 50, 100 and 500 denominations and coins in five, 10, 20, 50 cents and €1 and €2.

ATMs Using ATMs with a credit or debit card is by far the easiest way of getting cash in Finland. ATMs have a name, Otto, and can be found even in small villages.

Credit cards Widely accepted; Finns are dedicated users of the plastic even to buy a beer or cup of coffee.

Moneychangers Travellers cheques and cash can be exchanged at banks; in the big cities, independent exchange facilities such as **Forex** (www.forex.fi) usually offer better rates.

Tipping Service is considered to be included in bills, so there's no need to tip at all unless you want to reward exceptional service.

Public Holidays

Finland grinds to a halt twice a year: around Christmas and New Year, and during the Midsummer weekend. National public holidays:

New Year's Day 1 January

Epiphany 6 January

Good Friday March/April

Easter Sunday & Monday March/April

May Day 1 May

Ascension Day May

Whit Sunday late May or early June

Midsummer's Eve & Day weekend in June closest to 24 June

All Saints' Day first Saturday in November

Independence Day 6 December

Christmas 24 & 25 December

Boxing Day 26 December

Telephone

Public telephones Basically no longer exist on the street in Finland, so if you don't have a mobile you're reduced to making expensive calls from your hotel room or talking over the internet.

Mobile phones The cheapest and most practical solution is to purchase a Finnish SIM card and pop it in your own phone. Make sure your phone isn't blocked from doing this by your home network first. If coming from outside Europe, check that it will work in Europe's GSM 900/1800 network. You can buy a prepaid SIM-card at any R-kioski. There are always several deals on offer, and you might be able to pick up a card for as little as €10, including some call credit. Top the credit up at the same outlets, online, or at ATMs.

Phonecards At the R-kioski you can also buy cut-rate phone cards that substantially lower the cost of making international calls.

Phone codes The country code for Finland is ☑358. To dial abroad it's ☑00. The number for the international operator is ☑020208.

Time

Finland is on Eastern European Time (EET), an hour ahead of Sweden and Norway and two hours ahead of UTC/GMT (three hours from late March to late October).

Toilets

Public toilets are widespread in Finland but expensive – often €1 a time.

Tourist Information

The main website of the Finnish Tourist Board is www.visitfinland.com. Local tourist offices and websites are mentioned throughout the chapter.

Visas

Finland is one of 25 member countries of the Schengen Agreement, under which 22 EU countries (all but Bulgaria, Cyprus, Ireland, Romania and the UK) plus Iceland, Norway and Switzerland have abolished checks at common borders. Citizens of the USA, Canada, Australia and New Zealand need a valid passport to visit Finland, but do not need a visa for stays of less than three months. Citizens of EU countries and other Scandi-

navian countries with a valid passport or national identity card do not require visas. For more information contact the nearest Finnish embassy or consulate, or check the website www.formin.finland.fi.

Getting There & Away

Air

Airlines Finland is easily reached by air, with a growing number of direct flights to Helsinki from European, American and Asian destinations. Finnair (☑0600 140140; www.finnair.fi) and cheaper Finncomm (www.fc.fi) fly to 20 Finnish cities, usually at least once per day. Blue1 (☑06000 25831; www.blue1.com) has budget flights to a handful of Finnish destinations; check www.whichbudget.com for a complete list. Scandinavian Airlines and AirBaltic also serve Finland from various European countries.

Airports Most flights to Finland land at Helsinki-Vantaa airport (☑0200 14636; www.helsinki-vantaa.fi), situated 19km north of the capital. Winter charters hit Rovaniemi (www.finavia.fi), Lapland's main airport.

Land

Border crossings There are several border crossings from northern Sweden and Norway to northern Finland, with no passport or customs formalities. There are nine main border crossings between Finland and Russia, including several in the southeast and two in Lapland. They are more serious frontiers; you must already have a Russian visa.

Vehicles Can easily be brought into Finland on the Baltic ferries provided you have registration papers and valid insurance (Green Card). See p226 for information about driving in Finland.

SWEDEN

The only bus route between Finland and Sweden is between the linked towns of Tornio, Finland, and Haparanda, Sweden, from where you can get onward transport into their respective countries. The other possible crossing point are the towns of Kaaresuvanto (Finland) and Karesuando (Sweden), separated by a bridge and both served sporadically by buses.

NORWAY

There are five daily routes linking Finnish Lapland with northern Norway, some running only in summer. These are operated by Eskelisen Lapin Linjat (www.eskelisen-lapin-linjat.com), whose website has detailed maps and timetables, as does the Finnish bus website for Matkahuolto (www.matkahuolto.fi).

All routes originate or pass through Rovaniemi; the three northeastern routes continue via Inari to either Kirkenes, Tanabru/Vadsø or Karasjok. The Karasjok bus continues in summer to Nordkapp (North Cape). On the western route, one Rovaniemi-Kilpisjärvi bus runs on daily to Tromsø in summer, and a Rovaniemi–Hetta bus continues to Kautokeino and Alta.

RUSSIA
Bus

There are daily express buses to Vyborg and St Petersburg from Helsinki and Lappeenranta (one originates in Turku). These services appear on the website of Matkahuolto (www.matkahuolto.fi). Helsinki–Vyborg one-way is €34 (five hours) and to St Petersburg it's €39 (8½ to nine hours). Book at the bus station in Helsinki. There are also semi-official buses and minibuses that can be cheaper options. Costs and travel times vary substantially. Think €15 to €20 in a bus, or around €25 in a minibus, which is faster, and also quicker at the border.

Goldline (www.goldline.fi) runs three weekly buses from Rovaniemi via Ivalo to Murmansk, and there are also cross-border services from Kuhmo.

Train

The only international train links with Finland are to/from Moscow and St Petersburg. All trains go via the Finnish towns of Lahti and Kouvola, and the Russian city of Vyborg. Tickets are sold at the international ticket counter at Helsinki station. You must have a valid Russian visa; passport checks are carried out onboard.

Fares There are two high-speed *Allegro* train services daily from Helsinki to the Finland Station in St Petersburg (2nd/1st class €84/134, 3½ hours). The *Tolstoi* sleeper runs from Helsinki via St Petersburg (Ladozhki station) to Moscow (2nd/1st class €103/155, 13 hours). The fare includes a sleeper berth. There are a number of more upmarket sleepers costing up to €393. Return fares are double, and there are significant discounts for families and small groups. See www.vr.fi for details.

Sea

Services are year-round between major cities: book ahead in summer, at weekends and if travelling with a vehicle. The boats are amazingly cheap if you travel deck class (without a cabin). Many ferry lines offer 50% discounts for holders of Eurail, Scanrail and InterRail passes. Some offer discounts for seniors, and for ISIC and youth-card holders; inquire when purchasing your ticket. There are usually discounts for families and small groups travelling together.

Ferry companies have detailed timetables and fares on their websites. Fares vary according to season. Operators with their Finnish contact numbers:

Eckerö Line (☎06000 4300) Tallinn (www.eckeroline.fi); Åland (www.eckerolinjen.fi)

Finnlines (☎010-343 4500; www.finnlines.com)

Linda Line (☎06000 668 970; www.lindaliini.ee)

RG Line (☎0207-716 810; www.rgline.com)

St Peter Line (☎010-346 7820; www.stpeterline.com)

Tallink/Silja Line (☎0600 15700; www.tallinksilja.com)

Viking Line (☎0600 41577; www.vikingline.fi)

SWEDEN

The daily Stockholm–Helsinki, Stockholm–Turku and Kapellskär–Mariehamn (Åland) routes are dominated by Tallink/Silja and Viking Lines. Viking Line is the cheaper, with a passenger ticket between Stockholm and Helsinki costing from €36 to €50 (up to €62 on Friday). You can doss down in chairs or the floor; the cheapest berths start at €45 in peak season.

Helsinki Tallink/Silja doesn't offer deck tickets on the Helsinki run: the cheapest cabins start at €122 for the crossing.

Turku Tickets cost €20 in summer on the day ferries (11 to 12 hours). Note that Åbo is Swedish for Turku.

Eckerö Eckerö Linjen sails from Grisslehamn, north of Stockholm, to Eckerö in Åland. It's by far the quickest, at just two hours, and, with prices around €6 to €10 return and €10 for a car, it's an amazing bargain. There's a connecting bus from Stockholm and Uppsala.

Vaasa RG Lines sails to Umeå, Sweden (€60 per person plus €65 per car, 4½ hours) almost daily year-round.

Naantali Finnlines runs a simple cargo ferry, which connects Naantali, near Turku, with Kapellskär three times daily.

ESTONIA

Several ferry companies ply the Gulf of Finland between Helsinki and Tallinn in Estonia. Car ferries cross in 3½ hours, catamarans and hydrofoils in about 1½ hours, although in winter there are fewer departures and traffic is slower due to the ice.

Ferries The cheapest option: Tallink, Viking Line and Silja Line have several daily departures (€22 to €38 one-way). Vehicle space costs from €19 to €30. Eckerö Line has fewer departures but is the cheapest. Tallink has vehicle space on its fast ferry (€28 to €38 one-way for standard-size cars).

Catamarans and hydrofoils Cost between €30 and €40 one-way, but online deals, advance purchase specials, and offers can knock this as low as €20. Linda Line and Tallink offer these routes. On the websites you can easily see which departures are offering cheaper rates.

GERMANY & POLAND

To Travemünde Finnlines runs from Helsinki (from €196 one-way from June to August plus €100 per vehicle, 28 hours), with connecting bus service to Hamburg.

To Gdynia Finnlines also runs to Poland (from 21 hours).

To Rostock Tallink/Silja also runs a fast ferry from Helsinki (27 hours), with seats costing from €73 to €98 and berths starting at €127. Vehicle places are available from €115/196 one-way/return.

RUSSIA

St Petersburg St Peter Line connects with Helsinki three times weekly, an overnight trip of 14 hours that costs €38 to €61 per passenger and €35 per vehicle. Cabins start at €120. A significant added benefit of arriving in Russia this way is a visa-free stay of up to three days in St Petersburg. You'll need to be travelling as a group of two or more and have confirmation of a hotel reservation.

Finland is well served by public transport. A great source to find the best way between two points is the online route planner at www.matka.fi, which gives you bus and train options and even walking distances between stations and town centres.

Air

Finnair runs a fairly comprehensive domestic service, mainly out of Helsinki. Standard prices are expensive, but check the website for offers. Budget carriers offer the cheapest fares for advance internet bookings.

Major airlines flying domestically:

AirBaltic (☑0600 18181; www.airbaltic.com) Offers several low-budget domestic routes.

Blue1 (☑06000 25831; www.blue1.com) Budget flights from Helsinki to Kuopio, Oulu, Rovaniemi and Vaasa.

Finnair (☑81881; www.finnair.com) Extensive domestic network.

FinnComm (☑094-243 2000; www.fc.fi) Finnair affiliate offering budget fares; book via its website or Finnair offices.

Bicycle

Bikes can be carried on most trains, buses and ferries.

Bike paths Finland is flat and as bicycle-friendly as any country you'll find, with many kilometres of bike paths. The Åland islands are particularly good cycling country.

Bike hire Daily/weekly hire from €15/70 is possible in most cities. Camping grounds, hotels and hostels often have cheap bikes available for local exploration.

Boat

Lake and river passenger services were once important means of summer transport in Finland. These services are now largely kept on as cruises, and make a great, leisurely way to journey between towns.

Popular routes Tampere–Hämeenlinna, Savonlinna–Kuopio, Lahti–Jyväskylä and Joensuu–Koli–Lieksa.

Main coastal routes Turku–Naantali, Helsinki–Porvoo and the archipelago ferries to the Åland islands.

Bus

Ticket offices Long-distance bus ticketing is handled by Matkahuolto ([image]0200 4000; www.matkahuolto.fi), whose excellent website has all timetables. Each town has a *linja-autoasema* (bus terminal), with local timetables displayed (*lähtevät* is departures, *saapuvat* arrivals). Ticket offices work normal business hours, but you can always buy the ticket from the driver.

Fares Buses may be *pikavuoro* (express) or *vakiovuoro* (regular). Fares are based on distance travelled. The one-way fare for a 100km trip is €16.90/19.90 for normal/express.

Discounts For student discounts you need to be studying full-time in Finland and buy a student coach discount card (€8) from any bus station. If booking three or more adult tickets together, a 25% discount applies: great for groups.

Car & Motorcycle

Petrol Expensive in Finland. Many petrol stations are unstaffed, so have bank notes handy for the machine: they don't accept foreign cards. Change is not given.

HIRE

Costs Car rental is expensive, but between a group of three or four it can work out at a reasonable cost. From the major rental companies a small car costs from €60/280 per day/week with 300km free per day. As ever, the cheapest deals are online. While the daily rate is high, the weekly rate offers some respite. Best of all, though, are the weekend rates. These can cost little more than the rate for a single day, and you can pick up the car early afternoon on Friday and return it late Sunday or early Monday.

Rental companies:

Avis ([image]09-859 8356; www.avis.fi)

Budget ([image]0207 466 600; www.budget.fi)

Europcar ([image]0200 12154; www.europcar.fi)

Hertz ([image]0200 11 22 33; www.hertz.fi)

Sixt ([image]0200 111 222; www.sixt.fi) One of the cheapest.

ROAD CONDITIONS & HAZARDS

Road network Finland's road network is excellent, although there are only a few motorways. When approaching a town or city, look for signs saying *keskusta* (town centre). There are no road tolls but lots of speed cameras.

Wildlife Beware of elk and reindeer, which don't respect vehicles and can dash onto the road unexpectedly. This sounds comical, but elks especially constitute a deadly danger. Notify the police if there is an accident involving these animals. Reindeer are very common in Lapland: slow right down if you see one, as there will be more nearby.

Snow and ice Possible from September to April, and as late as June in Lapland, make driving a serious undertaking. Snow chains are illegal: instead, people use either snow tyres, which have metal studs, or special all-weather tyres. The website http://alk.tiehallinto.fi has road webcams around Finland, good for checking conditions on your prospective route.

ROAD RULES

Alcohol The blood alcohol limit is 0.05%.

Driving Finns drive on the right.

Headlights Use at all times.

Right of way An important feature of Finland is that there are fewer give-way signs than in many countries. Traffic entering an intersection from the right has right of way. While this doesn't apply to highways or main roads, you'll find that in towns cars will nip out from the right without looking: you must give way, so be careful at every intersection.

Seatbelts Compulsory for all.

Speed limit Set at 50km/h in built-up areas, from 80km/h to 100km/h on highways, and 120km/h on motorways.

Train

Finnish trains are run by the state-owned Valtion Rautatiet (VR; [image]0600 41900; www.vr.fi) and are an excellent service: they are fast, efficient and cheaper than the bus.

VR's website has comprehensive timetable information and some ticket sales. Major stations have a VR office: this is where to buy your ticket, as the automated machines accept only Finnish bank cards. You can also board and pay the conductor, but if the ticket office was open, you'll be charged a small penalty fee (€3 to €6).

CLASSES

The main classes of trains are the high-speed Pendolino (the fastest and most expensive class), fast Intercity (IC), Express and Regional trains. The first three have both 1st- and 2nd-class sections, while regional trains ('H' on the timetable), are the cheapest and slowest services, and have only 2nd-class carriages.

On longer routes there are two types of sleeping carriage currently in operation. The traditional blue ones offer berths in one-/two-/three-bed cabins; the newer sleeping cars offer single and double compartments in a double-decker carriage. There are cabins equipped for wheelchair use, and ones with bathroom. Berths cost from €19 to €82 in high season. Sleeper trains transport cars, handy if you've brought your own vehicle.

COSTS

Second class A one-way ticket for a 100km express train journey costs approximately €15.50.

First class Cost 50% more than a 2nd-class ticket.

Return fare About 10% less than two one-way tickets.

Discounts Children under 17 pay half-price, and children aged under six travel free (but without a seat). A child travels free with every adult on long-distance trips, and there are also discounts for seniors, local students and any group of three or more adults travelling together.

TRAIN PASSES

International rail passes accepted in Finland include the Eurail Scandinavia Pass, Eurail Global Pass and InterRail Global Pass.

Finland Eurail Pass Gives you €131/172/234 for three/five/10 days' 2nd-class travel in a one-month period within Finland.

InterRail Finland Pass Offers travel only in Finland for three/four/six/eight days in a one-month period, costing €112/139/189/229 in 2nd class.

Finnrail Pass Available to travellers residing outside Finland and offers a similar deal to the Finland Eurail pass at a similar price. See the VR website for details.

Tallinn

Best Places to Eat

» nAnO (p234)

» Ö (p234)

» Olde Hansa (p234)

Best Places to Stay

» Tallinn Backpackers (p233)

» Old House Hostel & Guesthouse (p233)

» Nordic Hotel Forum (p234)

Why Go?

These are heady days for Estonia. In only one generation this diminutive country has shaken off the dead weight of the Soviet era and turned its focus to the West, and to promises of a richer, shinier future. It's clearly taking its cues from its Nordic neighbours, especially Finland – a country with which it shares strong linguistic and cultural ties. A Tallinn visit from Helsinki is just too easy to over-look – ferries ply the 85km separating the two capitals so frequently that Finns almost think of Tallinn as a distant suburb.

And what a 'suburb'! Tallinn fuses Eastern European and Nordic moods, medieval and modern architecture, cobblestoned and cosmopolitan charms. It's an intoxicating mix of Gothic church spires, glass-and-chrome sky-scrapers, wine cellars inside 15th-century basements, beer terraces on sun-filled Raekoja plats and bike paths to beaches and forests – with a few Soviet throwbacks in the mix, for added spice.

When to Go

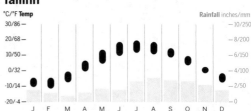

Tallinn

Apr & May See the country shake off winter's gloom.

Jun-Aug White nights, beach parties and loads of summer festivals.

Dec Christmas markets, mulled wine and long cosy nights.

⊙ Sights

The medieval Old Town, just south of Tallinn Bay, comprises Toompea (the upper town) and the lower town, still surrounded by much of its 2.5km defensive wall. Its centre is Raekoja plats (Town Hall Square). Immediately east of Old Town is the modern city centre.

Raekoja plats   TOWN SQUARE
Raekoja plats has been the heart of Tallinn life since the 11th century; bathed in sunlight or sprinkled with snow, it's always a photogenic spot. It's dominated by northern Europe's only surviving Gothic town hall (www.tallinn.ee/raekoda; Raekoja plats; adult/student €4/2; ☺10am-4pm Mon-Sat Jul & Aug), built between 1371 and 1404. Climb the tower (adult/student €3/1; ☺11am-6pm May–mid-Sep) for fine Old Town views.

The nearby Town Council Pharmacy (Raeapteek; Raekoja plats 11) is another ancient Tallinn institution; there's been a pharmacy or apothecary here since 1422. An arch beside it leads into narrow Saiakang (White Bread Passage), at the far end of which is the striking 14th-century Gothic Holy Spirit Church (adult/concession €1/0.50; ☺9am-5pm Mon-Sat May-Sep, 10am-3pm Mon-Fri Oct-Apr).

Lower Old Town   HISTORIC NEIGHBOURHOOD
From the Holy Spirit Church, stroll along Pikk (Long Street), which runs north to the Great Coast Gate – the medieval exit to Tallinn's port. Pikk is lined with the 15th-

GOODBYE KROON, HELLO EURO

On 1 January 2011, Estonia bid a fond farewell to its national currency, the kroon (EEK; introduced in 1992 to replace the Soviet rouble). The official currency of Estonia is now the euro.

Prices in this chapter were researched when the kroon was still in place, and have been converted at the official exchange rate (€1 = EEK15.65). Visitors to Estonia should expect some changes to listed prices as the euro settles in.

century houses of merchants and gentry (check out the fabulous facade of the gallery at No 18).

At the northern end of Pikk stands a chief Tallinn landmark, the gargantuan St Olaf's Church (entry at Lai 50). Viewseekers unafraid of a bit of sweat should head up to the observation tower (adult/student €2/1; ☺10am-6pm Apr-Oct). Just south of the church is the former KGB headquarters (Pikk 59), whose basement windows were sealed to conceal the sounds of cruel interrogations.

A medieval merchant's home houses the City Museum (www.linnamuuseum.ee; Vene 17; adult/student €3.20/1.90; ☺10.30am-5 or 6pm Wed-Mon), which traces Tallinn's development from its beginnings through to 1940 with some quirky displays and curious artefacts.

The street of Vene is home to some photogenic passageways and courtyards – check out Katariina käik (Vene 12), housing artisans' studios, and Master's Courtyard (Vene 6), a cobblestoned charmer, some of it dating from the 13th century. It's full of craft stores and a sweet cafe-chocolaterie.

The majestic St Nicholas' Church (Niguliste Kirik), now known as the Niguliste Museum (www.ekm.ee; Niguliste 3; adult/student €3.20/1.90; ☺10am-5pm Wed-Sun), stages concerts and serves as a museum of medieval church art.

Toompea   HISTORIC NEIGHBOURHOOD
A regal approach to Toompea is through the red-roofed 1380 gate tower at the western end of Pikk in the lower town, and then uphill along Pikk jalg (Long Leg). Alternatively, a winding stairway connects Lühike jalg (Short Leg), off Rataskaevu, to Toompea.

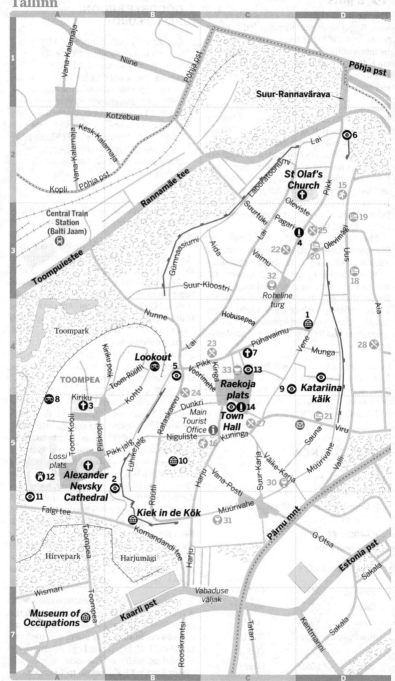

TALLINN

A · B · C · D

1

Niine

Põhja pst

Põhja pst

Suur-Rannavärava

Kotzebue

Vana-Kalamaja
Vana-Kalamaja
Kesk-Kalamaja
Kopli
Põhja pst

Rannamäe tee

Toompuiestee

Central Train
Station
(Balti Jaam)

Lai
◎◎ 6

St Olaf's
Church
✚ Oleviste
Pikk
✚ 15

Laboratooriumi
Suurtüki
Pagari
① 4
✕ 25
🏢 19

Aida
Lai
Vaimu
22 ◎
20 ◎
Uus

Gümnaasiumi

Suur-Kloostri

32 ◎
Roheline
turg

🏢 18

Nunne

Toompark

Lai
Hobusepea
Pühavaimu
1 🏛

Vene
Munga

28 ✕

Kiriku põik

Lookout
◎◎
5 ◎

Toom-Rüütli

23 ✕
Pikk
Voorimehe
Kinga

✚ 7

33 ▢ ◎ 13

Raekoja
plats
9 ◎ Katariina
käik

TOOMPEA

Kohtu

Pikk jalg

Rataskaevu

Dunkri
24 ◎
Main
Tourist
Office
Niguliste
① 16

◎① 14
Town
Hall
✉ 27

21 🏢

Kiriku
◎◎ 8
✚ 3

Kuninga
Sauna
Viru

Piiskopi
Toom-Kooli

10 🏛

Harju
Vana-Posti
Suur-Karja
Väike-Karja
Müürivahe
Valli

Lossi
plats
🏰 12

✚
Alexander
Nevsky
Cathedral
2 ◎

Lühike jalg
Rüütli

30 ◎

Falgi tee
◎ 11

Kiek in de Kõk
🏰

Müürivahe
31 ◎

Pärnu mnt

Komandandi tee

G Otsa

Hirvepark

Harjumägi

Estonia pst
Sakala

Wismari

Toompea

Museum of
Occupations 🏛

Kaarli pst

Vabaduse
väljak

Roosikrantsi

Tatari

Kentmanni

Sakala

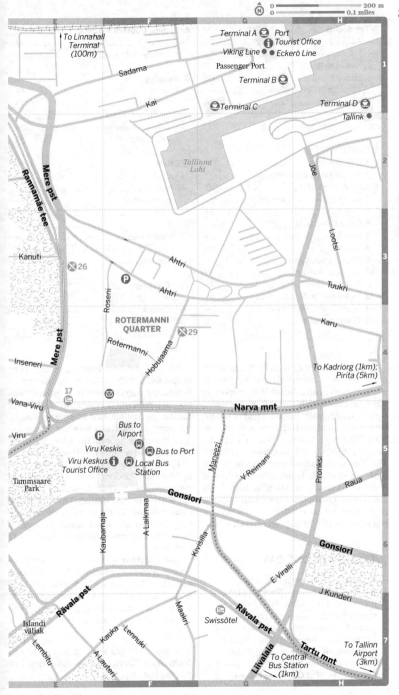

TALLINN

To Linnahall
Terminal
(100m)

Terminal A — Port
Tourist Office
Viking Line ● ● Eckerö Line
Passenger Port
Terminal B

Sadama

Kai

Terminal C

Terminal D
Tallink ●

Tallinna
Laht

Joe

Mere pst

Rannamäe tee

Kanuti

Lootsi

26

Ahtri

Roseni

Ahtri

Tuukri

Karu

ROTERMANNI
QUARTER

29

Rotermanni

Hobujaama

To Kadriorg (1km);
Pirita (5km)

Inseneri

Mere pst

Vana-Viru

17

Narva mnt

Viru

Bus to
Airport

Viru Keskis
Viru Keskus
Tourist Office

Bus to Port

Local Bus
Station

Tammsaare
Park

Magdeezi

V Reimani

Pronksi

Raua

Gonsiori

Kaubamaja

A Laikmaa

Kiivsilla

Gonsiori

Rävala pst

Islandi
väljak

Lembitu

Kauka

A Lauteri

Lennuki

Maakri

E Viralli

J Kunderi

Rävala pst

Swissôtel

Liivalaia

Tartu mnt

To Central
Bus Station
(1km)

To Tallinn
Airport
(3km)

Tallinn

The 19th-century Russian Orthodox Alexander Nevsky Cathedral (Lossi plats) greets you at the top in all its onion-domed glory. It was built strategically across from Toompea Castle, traditionally Estonia's seat of power. Only a section of the Old Town wall and the Pikk Hermann bastion, from which the state flag flies, are left from medieval times. The Riigikogu (parliament) meets in the pink, baroque-style building in front, which is an 18th-century addition. A path leads down from Lossi plats through an opening in the wall to the Danish King's Courtyard, where, in summer, artists set up their easels.

TALLINN IN ONE DAY

First, get your bearings by climbing the Town Hall tower on **Raekoja plats**, then explore the cobbled Old Town streets below – museums, churches, courtyards, cafes, whatever takes your fancy. In the afternoon, catch a tram to leafy, lovely **Kadriorg** and check out its quality museums. Finish with a locally flavoured feast at **Ö** or **Olde Hansa**.

Kiek in de Kök (Komandandi tee; adult/ student €4.50/2.60; ◎10.30am-5pm Tue-Sun), a formidable cannon tower built around 1475, houses a museum documenting the birth of Tallinn, its bastions and its military events. Its name means 'Peep into the Kitchen' – from the upper floors of the tower, medieval voyeurs could see into Old Town kitchens.

The Lutheran Dome Church (Toom-Kooli 6; ◎9am-5pm Tue-Sun), sombre and austere, was founded in 1233, though this edifice dates from the 14th century. From the Dome Church, follow Kohtu to the city's favourite lookout over the lower town. Be sure to have your cameras at the ready, as the vista is superb.

The absorbing Museum of Occupations (www.okupatsioon.ee; Toompea 8; adult/student €1.90/1; ◎11am-6pm Tue-Sun), just downhill from Toompea, focuses on Estonia's 20th-century occupations (Nazi and Soviet) – and the joy of a happy ending.

Kadriorg   PARK, MUSEUMS

To reach Kadriorg Park, 2km east of Old Town along Narva maantee, take tram 1 or 3 to the last stop.

This lovely, wooded park and its palace were designed for Peter the Great (1672–1725, r 1682–1725) for his wife Catherine I. The park's original centrepiece is **Kadriorg Palace** (1718–36), now home to the **Kadriorg Art Museum** (www.ekm.ee; Weizenbergi 37; adult/student €4.15/2.25; ⊙10am-5pm Tue-Sun May-Sep, 10am-5pm Wed-Sun Oct-Apr). The 17th- and 18th-century foreign art is mainly unabashedly romantic, and the palace unashamedly splendid.

The grand 21st-century showpiece of Kadriorg is **KUMU** (www.ekm.ee; Weizenbergi 34; adult/student €5.75/3.20; ⊙11am-6pm Tue-Sun May-Sep, 11am-6pm Wed-Sun Oct-Apr), also known as the Art Museum of Estonia. It's a spectacular modern structure of limestone, glass and copper, and it contains the largest repository of Estonian art in the country, plus constantly changing contemporary exhibits.

☞ Tours

From June to August, **360° Adventures** (☎5555 8785; www.360.ee) offers twice-weekly guided kayaking trips giving you four hours out on Tallinn Bay (€30) and a new perspective on Tallinn's sights.

City Bike (☎511 1819; www.citybike.ee; Uus 33) rents bikes for city- or country-wide exploring, and has a range of Tallinn tours, as well as tours (cycling or bus) to Lahemaa National Park, the perfect rural retreat from the capital.

The guys behind the excellent **Traveller Info Tent** (☎5554 2111; www.traveller.ee; Niguliste) run entertaining, good-value walking city tours or cycling city tours. They also run a pub crawl). Their finest offering to tightwads is a free, two-hour walking tour of Tallinn. From June to August, tours run daily from the tent itself; the rest of the year these tours need to be booked in advance via email or phone (minimum three participants).

★✩ Festivals & Events

Expect an extra-full calendar of events in 2011 as Tallinn celebrates its status as a European City of Culture; check www.tallinn2011.ee. For a complete list of Tallinn festivals, visit the 'Experience' pages of www.tourism.tallinn.ee.

Jazzkaar   MUSIC
(www.jazzkaar.ee) Jazz greats from around the world converge on Tallinn in late April.

Old Town Days   ARTS, CULTURE
(www.vanalinnapaevad.ee) Week-long festival in early June featuring dancing, concerts and plenty of medieval merrymaking.

Õllesummer   MUSIC
(Beer Summer; www.ollesummer.ee) Rock-music extravaganza over four days in early July.

Black Nights Film Festival   FILM
(www.poff.ee) Films and animations bring life to cold nights from mid-November to mid-December.

🛏 Sleeping

Each place to stay is accompanied by one of the following symbols (prices relate to the cost of a double room):

€€€ more than €130

€€ €40 to €130

€ less than €40

Tallinn Backpackers   HOSTEL €
(☎644 0298; www.tallinnbackpackers.com; Olevimägi 11; dm with shared bathroom €9-13; @) In an ideal Old Town location, this 26-bed place has a global feel and a roll-call of traveller-happy features: happy hours, cheap dinners, free wi-fi and internet, lockers, free sauna, bike rental and day trips to nearby attractions. Staff organise pub crawls and city tours that anyone can join, and a shuttle bus to Rīga. Private rooms are available at the offshoot **Viru Backpackers** (☎644 6050; 3rd fl, Viru 5; s/d/tw/q with shared bathroom €25/36/36/48), which has less atmosphere but does boast a good central location; its only downside is the shortage of shared bathrooms.

Old House Hostel & Guesthouse   GUESTHOUSES €
(☎641 1464; www.oldhouse.ee; Uus 22 & Uus 26; dm/s/tw/tr/q with shared bathroom from €19/29/42/63/83; P@) Although one is called a hostel, these twin establishments feel much more like cosy guesthouses (antiques, plants, lamps and bedspreads, with minimal bunks), and they're a long way

TALLINN FOR FREE

» Absorb the medieval magic wandering **Old Town** – on your own or on Traveller Info Tent's **free tour**.

» Get a breath of fresh air at **Kadriorg Park**.

» Hit the beach at **Pirita** (northeast of the centre; bus 1A, 8, 34A and 38) or retro-Soviet **Stroomi** (4km due west of the centre; bus 40).

» Browse the artisans' studios of **Katariina käik** and **Master's Courtyard**.

from earning the 'party hostel' tag. Dorms and private rooms are available at both (all bathrooms are shared); guest kitchen, free wi-fi and parking are quality extras. Management also rents fantastic Old Town apartments at reasonable prices (see the website).

Nordic Hotel Forum　　　　HOTEL **€€**
(☑622 2900; www.nordichotels.eu; Viru väljak 3; r €86-150; P@≋) The Forum shows surprising style and personality for a large, business-style hotel – witness the artwork on the hotel's facade and the trees on the roof. It stands out among its competitors for the facilities, laid on thick (including a lovely 'relaxation centre' with saunas and indoor pool); welcoming staff; and prime location.

🍴 Eating

See the options listed under Drinking for more good eating choices. Restaurants in this chapter have been categorised by the price of an average main course, as follows:

€€€ more than €20

€€ €10 to €20

€ less than €10

There's a small, 24-hour grocery store, **Kolmjalg** (Pikk 11), in Old Town. For first-rate picnic fodder, stock up at **Bonaparte Deli** (Pikk 47). Otherwise, try **Rimi** (Aia 7) supermarket, on the outskirts of Old Town.

TOP CHOICE nAnO　　　　CAFE **€**
(☑5552 2522; Sulevimägi 5; meals around €5; ⊙noon-3pm Mon-Fri) There's no real sign to indicate you've found this place, nor are there firm hours, or a written menu. Instead, this

is a whimsical world concocted by Beatrice, an Estonian model, and Priit, her DJ husband, who welcome guests into part of their colourful home. Beatrice and Priit feed diners fresh, home-style meals along the lines of herb-filled borscht, Russian-style pastries and pasta with in-season chanterelles or salmon. It's a treat for all the senses. Call ahead to check hours – at research time there was talk of opening for dinner too.

Ö　　　　MODERN ESTONIAN **€€€**
(☑661 6150; www.restoran-o.ee; Mere pst 6e; mains €17-24) With angelic chandelier sculptures and charcoal-and-white overtones, the dining room at award-winning Ö is an understated work of art – as are the meals coming out of the kitchen, showcasing winning ways with seasonal local produce. Bookings are advised.

Olde Hansa　　　　MEDIEVAL **€€**
(www.oldehansa.ee; Vana turg 1; mains €10-23) Candlelit Olde Hansa is the place to indulge in a gluttonous feast. And if the medieval music, communal wooden tables, and aromas of red wine and roast meats sound a bit much, take heart – the chefs have done their research in producing historically authentic fare. It may sound a bit touristy, but even the locals rate this place.

Vapiano　　　　ITALIAN **€**
(Hobujaama 10; pizzas & pastas €4-8) Choose your pasta or salad from the appropriate counter and watch as it's prepared in front of you. If it's pizza you're after, you'll receive a pager to notify you when it's ready. This is 'fast' food done healthy, fresh and cheap, in a bright, buzzing spot.

Kompressor　　　　PANCAKES **€**
(Rataskaevu 3; pancakes €2.60-3.70) Under an industrial ceiling you can plug any holes in your stomach with cheap pancakes of the sweet or savoury persuasion. By night, this is a decent detour for a budget drink. It's low on aesthetics but high on value.

🍷 Drinking

Hell Hunt　　　　PUB
(Pikk 39) See if you can score a few of the comfy armchairs out the back of this trouper of the pub circuit. It boasts an amiable air and reasonable prices for local-brewed beer and cider, plus decent pub grub. Don't let

the menacing-sounding name put you off – it means 'Gentle Wolf'.

Kehrwieder   CAFE
(Saiakang 1) Sure there's seating on Raekoja plats, but inside the city's cosiest cafe is where ambience is found in spades – you can stretch out on a couch, read by lamplight and bump your head on the arched ceilings. Open until midnight.

Drink Bar & Grill   PUB
(Väike-Karja 8) You know a bar means business when it calls itself Drink. This place takes its beer seriously, and offers plenty of beer-friendly accompaniments: traditional pub grub, happy hour from 5pm to 7pm, big-screen sports, quiz nights.

Gloria Wine Cellar   WINE BAR
(Müürivahe 2) This mazelike cellar has a number of nooks and crannies where you can secrete yourself with a date and/or a good bottle of shiraz. The dark wood, antique furnishings and flickering candles add to the allure.

ℹ Information

Internet Access
The city is bathed in wi-fi, much of it free.

Metro Internet (basement, Viru Keskus, Viru väljak 4; per hr €1.60) By the bus terminal under Viru Keskus shopping centre.

Money
Tavid (Aia 5; ⊙24hr) Reliably good rates. Night-time rates aren't as good as those during business hours.

Post
Central post office (Narva mnt 1)

Tourist Information
Tallinn In Your Pocket (www.inyourpocket.com) The king of the region's listings. Its booklets are on sale at bookshops, or can be downloaded free from its website.

Tallinn tourist information centre (www.tourism.tallinn.ee; cnr Kullassepa & Niguliste; ⊙9am-5pm Mon-Fri, 10am-3pm Sat Oct-Apr, 9am-6pm or later Mon-Fri, 10am-5pm Sat & Sun May-Sep) A block south of Raekoja plats. There are also information desks at the port (Terminal A), and inside Viru Keskus shopping centre. None of these centres book accommodation.

Traveller Info Tent (www.traveller-info.com; Niguliste; ⊙9am-9 or 10pm Jun-Aug) Fabulous source of information, set up by young locals in a tent opposite the official tourist info centre. It produces an invaluable map of Tallinn with

recommended places, dispenses lots of local tips, keeps a 'what's on' board, and operates entertaining, well-priced walking and cycling tours.

ℹ Getting There & Away

Air
The national carrier, **Estonian Air** (☎640 1163; www.estonian-air.ee), links Tallinn with some 15 cities in Europe and Russia. Other airlines serving **Tallinn airport** (www.tallinn-airport.ee) include **Finnair** (☎626 6309; www.finnair.com), with frequent flights to Helsinki.

Boat
Tallinn's main sea-passenger terminal is at the end of Sadama, a short, 1km walk northeast of Old Town; most ferries to/from Helsinki dock here.

FINLAND Oodles of ferries ply the 85km separating Helsinki and Tallinn (ships take two to 3½ hours, hydrofoils approximately 1½ hours). In high winds or bad weather, hydrofoils are often cancelled; they operate only when the sea is free from ice, while larger ferries sail year-round.

All companies provide concessions. Prices are cheaper on weekdays, and outside summer. There's lots of competition, so shop around.

Eckerö Line (☎664 6000; www.eckeroline.ee; Terminal A) Sails once daily back and forth year-round (adult one way €19 to €23, three to 3½ hours).

Linda Line (☎699 9333; www.lindaliini.ee; Linnahall Terminal) Small, passenger-only hydrofoils up to seven times daily from late March to late December (€19 to €45, 1½ hours).

Tallink (☎640 9808; www.tallinksilja.com; Terminal D) At least five services daily in each direction, year-round. The huge *Baltic Princess* takes 3½ hours; newer high-speed ferries take two hours. Adult prices range from €26 to €44.

Viking Line (☎666 3966; www.vikingline.ee; Terminal A) Operates a giant car ferry, with two departures daily (adult €22 to €39, 2½ hours).

SWEDEN **Tallink** (☎640 9808; www.tallinksilja.com) sails every night between Tallinn's Terminal D and Stockholm, via the Åland islands (cabin berth from €144, 16 hours). Book ahead.

MOVING ON?

For tips, recommendations and reviews, head to shop.lonelyplanet.com to purchase a downloadable PDF of the Estonia chapter from Lonely Planet's *Eastern Europe* guide.

ⓘ Getting Around

Tallinn has an excellent network of buses, trolleybuses and trams running from 6am to midnight; all three modes of transport use the same ticket system. Buy *piletid* (tickets) from street kiosks (€1, or a book of 10 single tickets for €6.40) or from the driver (€1.60). Validate your ticket using the machine or hole-puncher inside the vehicle – watch a local to see how it's done.

The major bus terminal for local buses is at the basement level of Viru Keskus shopping centre or the surrounding streets (just east of Old Town). Public transport timetables are at www.tallinn.ee.

City Bike (☑ 511 1819; www.citybike.ee; Uus 33; rental per hr/day/week €2.30/13/51.10) can help you get around by bike, within Tallinn and around Estonia.

Taxis are plentiful, but it's best to order one by phone: try **Krooni Takso** (☑ 1212, 638 1212) or **Reval Takso** (☑ 621 2111).

St Petersburg

Includes »

Best Places to Eat

Best Places to Stay

Why Go?

'St Petersburg is Russia, but it is not Russian.' The opinion of Nicholas II, the empire's last tsar, on his one-time capital still resonates. The city, affectionately know as Piter to locals and an easy excursion from Finland, is a fascinating hybrid where one moment you can be sniffing incense inside a mosaic-covered Orthodox church or wandering the gilded halls of a palace, the next knocking back vodka shots in a groovy bar or posing at a contemporary-art event.

Europe's fourth-largest city is also a visual delight. The Neva River and surrounding canals reflect unbroken facades of handsome 18th- and 19th-century buildings that house a spellbinding collection of cultural storehouses, culminating in the incomparable Hermitage. This environment, warts and all, was the inspiration for many of Russia's greatest artists, including the writers Pushkin, Gogol and Dostoevsky, and musical maestros such as Rachmaninoff, Tchaikovsky and Shostakovich. Plus the city is one of the most tourist-friendly places in Russia.

When to Go

St Petersburg

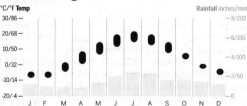

May Enjoy warmer weather and a couple of big festival parades.

Jun & Jul Party all night during St Petersburg's White Nights.

Dec-Jan Winter arts festivals and the snow make St Petersburg look magical.

NEED TO KNOW

At a Glance

» **Population** 4.6 million
» **Country code** ☑7; area code ☑812
» **Language** Russian
» **Currency** rouble

Exchange Rates

Australia	A$1	R30.00
Canada	C$1	R28.91
Europe	€1	R40.81
Japan	¥100	R33.74
New Zealand	NZ$1	R22.04
UK	UK£1	R45.84
USA	US$1	R27.52

⊙ Sights

Hermitage & Dvortsovaya Ploshchad
MUSEUM

(Map p244; ☑571 3465; www.hermitagemuseum.org; Dvortsovaya pl 2; adult R400, student & under 17yr free; ⊙10.30am-6pm Tue-Sat, to 5pm Sun) Headquartered in the magnificent Winter Palace, and stacked with treasures, ranging from Egyptian mummies and Scythian gold to early 20th-century European art by Matisse and Picasso, the Hermitage is a must-do. Avoid queuing for tickets by booking online through the museum's website.

The main entrance is from **Dvortsovaya ploshchad** (Palace Sq), one of the city's most impressive and historic spaces. Stand back to admire the palace and the central 47.5m **Alexander Column**, named after Alexander I and commemorating the 1812 victory over Napoleon.

Church of the Saviour on Spilled Blood
CHURCH

(Spas na Krovi; Map p244; www.cathedral.ru; Kony ushennaya pl; adult/student R320/170; ⊙11am-7pm Thu-Tue Oct-Apr, 10am-8pm Thu-Tue May-Sep) This multidomed dazzler of a church, partly modelled on St Basil's in Moscow, was built between 1883 and 1907 on the spot where Alexander II was assassinated in 1881 (hence its gruesome name). The interior's 7000 sq metres of mosaics fully justify the entrance fee.

Russian Museum
MUSEUM

(Russy Muzey; Map p244; ☑595 4248; www.rusmuseum.ru; Inzhenernaya ul 4; adult/student R350/150; ⊙10am-5pm Mon, to 6pm Wed-Sun) The Mikhailovsky Palace now houses one of Russia's finest collections of local art; visit to view masterpieces by the likes of Karl Bryulov, Vasily Kandinsky and Ilya Repin, Russia's best-loved artist. The gardens behind are also worth a stroll.

St Isaac's Cathedral
CHURCH, MUSEUM

(Isaakievsky Sobor; Map p244; www.cathedral.ru; Isaakievskaya pl; adult/student R320/170; ⊙11am-7pm Thu-Tue) The golden dome of this cathedral dominates the city skyline. Its lavish interior is a **museum**, but if you're pushed for time the best thing to do is buy the separate ticket to climb the 262 steps up to the **colonnade** (R100; ⊙11am-6pm Thu-Tue) around the dome's drum for panoramic views.

Behind the cathedral is **ploshchad Dekabristov** (Decembrists' Sq), named after the Decembrists' Uprising of 14 December 1825, and Falconet's famous statue of Peter the Great, the **Bronze Horseman**.

Nevsky Prospekt
ARCHITECTURE

Walking at least part of Nevsky pr (Map p244), Russia's most famous street, is a St Petersburg ritual. Starting at Dvortsovaya pl, notice the gilded spire of the **Admiralty** to your right as you head southeast down Nevsky towards the Moyka River. Across the Moyka, Rastrelli's baroque **Stroganov Palace** houses a branch of the Russian Museum.

A block beyond the Moyka, the great arms of the **Kazan Cathedral** (Kazansky Sobor; ☑571 4826; Kazanskaya pl 2; admission free; ⊙10am-7pm, services 10am & 6pm) reach out towards the avenue. Opposite is the **Singer Building**, a Style Moderne (Russia's take on art nouveau) beauty restored to all its splendour when it was the headquarters of the sewing machine company; inside is a bookshop and a good cafe with a great view of the street.

WANT MORE?

For in-depth information, reviews and recommendations at your fingertips, head to the Apple App Store to purchase Lonely Planet's *St Petersburg City Guide* iPhone app.

CONTEMPORARY ART GALLERIES

Once an artists' squat, the legendary Pushkinskaya 10 (Map p240; ☎764 5371; www.p-10.ru; Ligovsky pr 53; ☺3-7pm Wed-Sun) is now a fully legit nonprofit organisation, packed with small galleries. The building is also home to the music clubs Fish Fabrique Nouvelle (http://vkontakte.ru/club250531; Ligovsky pr 53; cover R100-150; ☺3pm-late) and Experimental Sound Gallery (GEZ-21; www.tac.spb.ru; 3rd fl, Ligovsky pr 53; cover R100-150; ☺concerts from 9pm). The entrance to the complex is through the archway at Ligovsky pr 53.

Loft Project Floors (Loft Proekt Etazhi; Map p240; www.loftprojectetagi.ru; Ligovsky pr 74; some galleries free; ☺2-10pm Tue-Sat) is located in the former Smolensky Bread Bakery. It consists of four large and industrial-looking gallery spaces, the main one being Globe Gallery (www.globegallery.ru; admission free), next to the chic Loft Wine Bar (www.loft winebar.ru). Also in the building is arty **Hostel Ligovsky 74**, an excellent inexpensive cafe, Green Room (☺9am-10pm), and several shops.

Further along you'll pass the covered arcades of historic department store Bolsoy Gostiny Dvor, another Rastrelli creation dating from 1757–85.

An enormous statue of Catherine the Great stands at the centre of ploshchad Ostrovskogo, commonly referred to as the Catherine Gardens; at the southern end of the gardens is Aleksandrinksy Theatre, where Chekhov's *The Seagull* premiered in 1896.

Nevsky pr crosses the Fontanka Canal on the Anichkov most, with its dramatic statues of rearing horses at its four corners.

Yusupov Palace   MUSEUM
(Map p240; ☎314 9883; www.yusupov-palace. ru; nab reki Moyki 94; adult/student R500/380; ☺11am-5pm) Best known as the place where Rasputin met his untimely end, this dazzler of a palace sports a series of richly decorated rooms culminating in a gilded jewel box of a theatre, where performances are still held. Admission includes an audio tour in English or several other languages. At 1.45pm, tag along for the Russian-language tour *Murder of Rasputin* (adult/student R300/180), the only way to see the room where the deed was done.

Peter & Paul Fortress   HISTORIC BUILDING
(Petropavlovskaya krepost; Map p240; ☎238 4550; www.spbmuseum.ru; ☺grounds 6am-10pm, exhibitions 11am-6pm Thu-Mon, to 5pm Tue) Founded in 1703 as the original military fortress for the new city, the Peter and Paul Fortress was mainly used as a political prison up to 1917.

It's also home to the Sts Peter & Paul Cathedral (adult/student R200/90), with its landmark needle-thin spire and magnificent baroque interior. All Russia's tsars since Peter the Great have been buried here.

Individual tickets are needed for each of the fortress' attractions, so the best deal is the combined entry ticket (adult/student R350/170; valid 2 days). This ticket allows access to most of the exhibitions that are on the island.

Menshikov Palace   MUSEUM
(Menshikovsky Dvorets; Map p240; ☎323 1112; www.hermitagemuseum.org; Universitetskaya nab 15; adult/student R200/100; ☺10.30am-6pm Tue-Sat, to 5pm Sun) The best of many museums gathered on Vasilevsky Island is this riverside palace, built in 1707 for Peter the Great's confidant Alexander Menshikov. Now a branch of the Hermitage, the impressively

ST PETERSBURG IN TWO DAYS

Touring the **Hermitage** can easily gobble up a day, but leave some time to be dazzled by the mosaic interior of the **Church of the Saviour on Spilled Blood** and to climb up the colonnade of **St Isaac's Cathedral** for a bird's-eye view of the city.

On day two head across the Neva River to explore the **Peter & Paul Fortress**. Continue around to the **Strelka** to see the museums here, or at least take in the view. Art lovers will also want to drop by the splendid **Russian Museum**, then catch a performance at the **Mariinsky Theatre**.

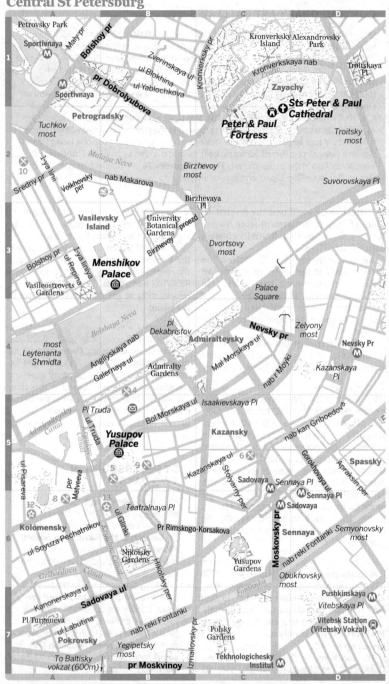

ST PETERSBURG

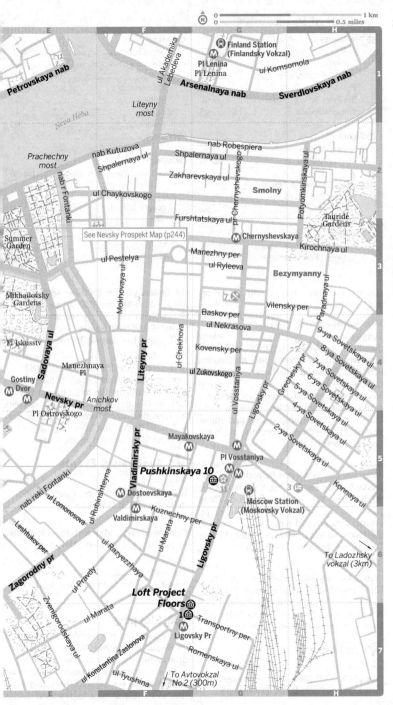

ST PETERSBURG

0 — 1 km
0 — 0.5 miles

Petrovskaya nab

Neva Heba

Finland Station
(Finlandsky Vokzal)
Pl Lenina
Pl Lenina
ul Komsomola

ul Akademika Lebedeva

Arsenalnaya nab

Sverdlovskaya nab

Liteyny most

Prachechny most

nab Kutuzova
Shpalernaya ul
Shpalernaya ul

nab Robespiera

nab r Fontanki

ul Chaykovskogo

Zakharevskaya ul

pr Chernyshevskogo

Smolny

Potyomkinskaya ul

Furshtatskaya ul

Tauride Gardens

Summer Garden

Chernyshevskaya

Kirochnaya ul

Mikhailovsky Gardens

ul Pestelya

Manezhny per
ul Ryleeva

Bezymyanny

Paradnaya ul

Pl Iskusstv

Mokhovaya ul

7

Vilensky per

Baskov per
ul Nekrasova

9-ya Sovetskaya ul
8-ya Sovetskaya ul

Sadovaya ul

Manezhnaya Pl

Liteyny pr

ul Chekhova

Kovensky per

ul Zukovskogo

Grechesky pr

7-ya Sovetskaya ul
6-ya Sovetskaya ul
5-ya Sovetskaya ul
4-ya Sovetskaya ul

Gostiny Dvor

Nevsky pr

Anichkov most

Pl Ostrovskogo

ul Vosstaniya

Ligovsky pr

2-ya Sovetskaya ul

Mayakovskaya

Pl Vosstaniya

Vladimirsky pr

Pushkinskaya 10

Konnaya ul

nab reki Fontanki
ul Lomonosova

ul Rubinshteyna

Dostoevskaya

Kuznechny per

11

Moscow Station
(Moskovsky Vokzal)

3

Leshtukov per

Valdimirskaya

ul Marata

Ligovsky pr

Zagorodny pr

ul Razyezzhaya

To Ladozhsky
vokzal (3km)

ul Pravdy

Zvengorodskaya ul

Loft Project
Floors

1

ul Marata

ul Konstantina Zaslonova

ul Tyushina

Transportny per

Ligovsky Pr

Romenskaya ul

To Avtovokzal
No 2 (300m)

See Nevsky Prospekt Map (p244)

restored interiors are filled with period art and furniture.

Museum of Anthropology & Ethnography   MUSEUM
(Kunstkamera; Map p244; ☑328 1412; www.kunstkamera.ru; Tamozhenny per; adult/student R250/150; ⊙11am-6pm Tue-Sun) Crowds still flock to see Peter the Great's ghoulish collection of monstrosities, notably preserved freaks, two-headed mutant foetuses and odd body parts. The anthropological and ethnographic displays from around the world are pretty interesting, too.

Strelka   MONUMENTS
Sweeping city views can be had from Vasilevsky Island's eastern 'nose', known as the Strelka. The two Rostral Columns (Map p244) on the point, studded with ships' prows, were oil-fired navigation beacons in the 1800s; on some holidays, such as Victory Day, gas torches are still lit on them.

FREE **Summer Garden**   GARDEN
(Map p240; Letny Sad; ⊙10am-10pm May-Sep, 10am-8pm Oct–mid-Apr) Laid out in the early 18th century and recently renovated, this is a delightful place to relax beneath leafy trees and beside classical statues.

⚡ Activities

Holiday Club Spa & Wellness   SPA
(Map p240; ☑335 2200; www.sokosrestaurants.ru; Sokos Hotel Palace Bridge, Birzhevoy per

2-4, Vasilevsky Ostrov; R600 7am-4pm Mon-Fri, R1200 4-10pm Mon-Fri, R1300 all day Sat & Sun; ⊙7am-10pm) This luxury spa and swim complex has eight saunas, including one built like a Russian log house.

Anglo Tourismo   BOAT, WALKING
(Map p244; ☑921-989 4722; www.anglotourismo.com; nab reki Fontanki; adult/student from R500/400) During the main tourist season (May to October) there are plenty of boats for hire. Boat tours leave from beside the Anichkov Bridge and offer English commentary. Also offers walking tours.

🎊 Festivals & Events

9 May   CULTURE
Big military parades and a public holiday mark the end of WWII.

City Day   CULTURE
Celebrated on 27 May with mass festivities including a parade along Nevsky pr.

White Nights Festival   CULTURE
The umbrella name for various arts events that run from late May to the end of July.

🛏 Sleeping

Room prices are at a premium between May and September. Outside this period, rates can drop up by up to 30% on those quoted here.

In this chapter, each place to stay is accompanied by one of the following symbols (the price relates to a high-season double room with private bathroom and, unless stated otherwise, includes breakfast):

€€€ more than R10,000

€€ R3000 to R10,000

€ less than R3000

TOP CHOICE Anichkov
Pension   PENSION, APARTMENT **€€€**
(Map p244; ☎314 7059; www.anichkov.com; Nevsky pr 64, apt 4; s/d incl breakfast from R5860/7200, apt s/d R8280/9980; @) The six rooms and gorgeous apartment here are decorated in soft shades of beige and cream with walnut veneer furniture and antique-themed wallpaper. The lounge offers balcony views of the bridge from which the pension takes its name.

Hostel Ligovsky 74   HOSTEL **€€**
(Map p240; ☎329 1274; www.hostel74.ru; Ligovsky pr 74; dm/tw/designer room R600/1500/2500; @) This hostel is part of Loft Project Floors (see boxed text, p239). The dorm beds are OK, but it's the three fab design rooms, all with en suite, that are the standouts. Everyone gets a souvenir photo and rates include a basic breakfast.

Stony Island Hotel   HOTEL **€€**
(Map p244; ☎740 1588; www.stonyisland.ru; ul Lomonosova 1; d or tw incl breakfast from R4500; @) Exposed-brick walls and chic contemporary furnishings give this supercentral hotel the design edge.

Cuba Hostel   HOTEL **€**
(Map p244; ☎921 7115, 315 1558; www.cubahostel. ru; Kazanskaya ul 5; dm/tw R490/1250; @) Cool

---

ℹ HOMESTAYS & FLAT RENTALS

243

Try the following for non-hotel and hostel accommodation:

» **HOFA** (☎8-911-766 5464; www.hofa.ru)

» **City Realty** (☎570 6342; www. cityrealtyrussia.com; Muchnoy per 2)

» **Ost-West Kontaktservice** (Map p240; ☎327 3416; www.ostwest.com; Nevsky pr 100)

Cuba presses all the right buttons in terms of atmosphere, friendliness, price and location. Each of the dorms is painted a different colour, and arty design is used throughout.

Location Hostel   HOTEL **€**
(Map p244; ☎490 6429; www.location-hostel. ru; Admiralteisky pr 8; dm/tw incl breakfast from R600/1400; @) So chic it even has Philippe Starck chairs in its well-equipped kitchen! The grand stairwell acts as a photo exhibition space.

 Eating

St Petersburg offers a broad range of quality restaurants and cafes serving many different cuisines.

Restaurants in this chapter have been categorised by the price of an average main course, as follows:

€€€ more than R1500

€€ R600 to R1500

€ less than R600

WORTH A TRIP

PETER'S COUNTRY RETREAT

Among the several palace estates that the tsars built around St Petersburg, the one not to miss is **Petrodvorets** (☎427 0073; http://peterhofmuseum.com; ul Razvodnaya 2), 29km west of the city and also known as Peterhof.

This courtly retreat's highlight is its **Grand Cascade & Water Avenue**, a symphony of over 140 fountains and canals located in the **Lower Park** (Nizhny Park; adult/student R350/180; ⊙9am-8pm Mon-Fri, to 9pm Sat & Sun). The fountains only work from mid-May to early October (from 11am to 5pm Monday to Friday and 11am to 6pm Saturday and Sunday), but the gilded ensemble looks marvellous at any time of the year.

Buses and *marshrutky* (minibuses) to Petrodvorets (R50, 30 minutes) run frequently from outside metro stations Avtovo, Leninsky pr and pr Veteranov. There's also the K404 bus from outside the Baltisky vokzal (R50, 40 minutes). All stop near the main entrance to the Upper Garden.

From May to September, the *Meteor* **hydrofoil** (www.boattrip.ru; one way/return R500/800; ⊙9.30am-7pm) goes every 20 to 30 minutes from the jetty in front of St Petersburg's Hermitage (30 minutes).

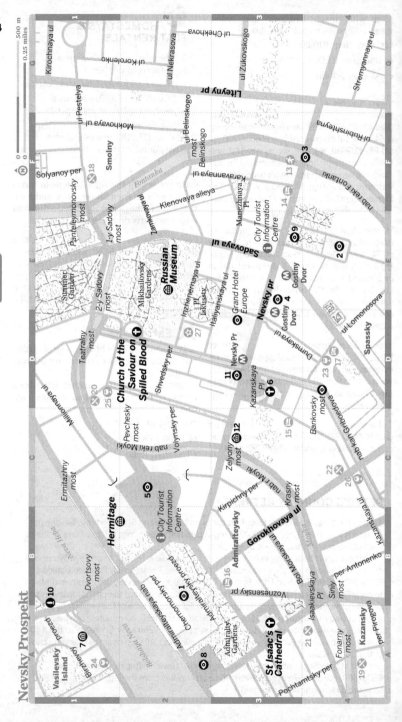

Teplo

RUSSIAN/EUROPEAN €€

(Map p244; ☎570 1974; Bolshaya Morskaya ul 45; mains R260-500) You'll instantly warm to Teplo's cosy living-room atmosphere, liberally scattered with cuddly soft toys. The food – roast chicken, salmon in Savoy cabbage, sweet and savoury pies and pastries baked daily – is equally comforting.

TOP CHOICE Sadko

RUSSIAN €€

(Map p240; ☎903 2373; www.sadko-rst.ru; ul Glinki 2; mains R260-650) Ideal as a pre- or post-Mariinsky Theatre dining option, Sadko serves fine renditions of all the Russian favourites. It also has a lovely traditional floral-design decor and singing waiters!

Russian Vodkaroom No 1

RUSSIAN €€€

(Map p240; ☎570 6420; www.vodkaroom.ru; Konnogvardeysky bul 4; mains R500-1300) Before dining in this elegant restaurant it's worth taking the English guided tour of the attached small **Vodka Museum** and doing a tasting of three vodkas (R450). If that whets your appetite, there are some 140 vodkas on the menu to sample.

Botanika

VEGETARIAN €€

(Map p244; ☎272 7011; www.cafebotanika.ru; ul Pestelya 7; mains R200-300) Piter's best range of vegetarian food – from Russian salads to Indian and Japanese dishes – is offered at this stylish restaurant with pretty decorative touches by students from the art academy across the road.

Stolle

RUSSIAN €

(www.stolle.ru; pies R60-100; ☺8am-10pm); Konyushennaya per (Map p244; Konyushennaya per 1/6); ul Vosstaniya (Map p240; ul Vosstaniya 32); ul Dekabristov 19 (Map p240; ul Dekabristov 19); ul Dekabristov 33 (Map p240; ul Dekabristov 33); Vasilyevsky Island (Map p240; 1-ya linii 50) We can't get enough of Stolle's traditional Russian savoury and sweet pies. It's easy to make a meal of it with soups and other dishes that can be ordered at the counter.

St-Leninsbar

RUSSIAN €

(Map p240; www.leninsbar.restoran.ru; Grivtsova per 7; ☺noon-midnight) This tiny, cheeky homage to Lenin is a great place to sample well-executed classics of Russian cuisine at socialist prices. Its place mats also provide a lesson on how to drink vodka.

ST PETERSBURG

VISAS

Visas are required by all – apply well in advance of your trip! Try either **Express to Russia** (www.expresstorussia.com) or **Zierer Visa Services** (✆1-866 788 1100; www.zvs.com) for assistance.

Zoom Café　　　　RUSSIAN/EUROPEAN **€**
(Map p244; www.cafezoom.ru; Gorokhovaya ul 22; mains R200-400) Popular, relaxed hang-out with regularly changing art exhibitions. Serves unfussy, tasty European and Russian food.

Café Idiot　　　　RUSSIAN, VEGETARIAN **€€**
(Map p244; nab reki Moyki 82; meals R400; ⊙11am-1am) This long-running cafe charms with its prerevolutionary atmosphere. It's ideal for a nightcap or late supper.

Drinking & Entertainment

The strip of dive bars, including Dacha, Fidel and Belgrad, along ul Dumskaya gets packed with youthful revellers who spill onto the streets from midnight to dawn.

Atelierbar　　　　BAR, CAFE
(Map p244; www.atelierbar.ru; ul Lomonosova 1; ⊙9am-6am) Attitude free, shabby chic and youthful – just what you'd expect from the groovesters behind Cuba Hostel. During the day it's a cafe on the ground floor; late at night is when the bar/club on the two upper floors cranks up.

Stirka　　　　CAFE-BAR
(Map p244; Kazanskaya ul 26; ⊙11am-1am Sun-Thu, to 4am Fri & Sat) Hipsters' hang-out where you can play chess or listen to the DJ, while also doing your laundry – what a good idea! A 5kg wash costs R150; the dryer R100; and a mug of excellent Vasileostrovskoe beer R120.

Mariinsky Theatre　　　　THEATRE
(Map p240; ✆326 4141; www.mariinsky.ru; Teatralnaya pl 1) Top of our list for highbrow entertainment, the Mariinsky is home to the world-famous Kirov Ballet and Opera company. Book tickets in advance on the website for here and for the acoustically splendid concert hall (ul Pisareva 20).

Also mounting excellent opera and ballet productions in an equally historic building is the **Mikhailovsky Opera & Ballet Theatre** (Map p244; ✆585 4305; www.mikhailovsky.ru; pl Iskusstv 1).

Other Side　　　　BAR, LIVE MUSIC
(Map p244; www.theotherside.ru; Bolshaya Konyushennaya ul 1; ⊙noon to last customer, concerts 8pm Sun-Thu, 10pm or 11pm Fri & Sat) There's live music Friday and Saturday at this gastrobar, which serves decent food (mains R200 to R500). Most people turn up to enjoy its several beers on tap.

Grad Petrov　　　　MICROBREWERY, RESTAURANT
(Map p244; ✆326 0137; http://die-kneipe.ru; Universitetskaya nab 5; ⊙noon to last customer) The refreshing ales and German-style sausages are reason enough to stop by this fine microbrewery with a view across the Neva from its outdoor tables.

❶ Information

Internet Access

Café Max (www.cafemax.ru; Nevsky pr 90/92; per hr R40; ⊙24hr) Wi-fi available here. Also has a branch in the Hermitage.

Tvoyo (Nevsky pr 66; per hr R60; ⊙24hr) Enter from Liteyny pr.

Media

The following English-language publications are available free at many hotels, hostels, restaurants and bars across the city:

St Petersburg in Your Pocket (www.inyourpocket.com/city/st_petersburg.html) Monthly listings booklet with useful up-to-date information and short features.

St Petersburg Times (www.sptimes.ru) Published Tuesday and Friday, this plucky little newspaper has been fearlessly telling it like it really is for over 15 years.

Tourist Information

City tourist information centre (www.visit-petersburg.ru) main office (Map p244; ✆982 8253; Sadovaya ul 14/52; ⊙10am-7pm Mon-Fri, noon-6pm Sat); Hermitage booth (Map p244; Dvortsovaya pl 12; ⊙10am-7pm daily) There are also branches at the Pulkovo-1 and Pulkovo-2 air terminals (open 10am to 7pm Monday to Friday).

❶ Getting There & Away

Air

Pulkovo-1 and **Pulkovo-2** are, respectively, the domestic and international terminals of St Petersburg's **Pulkovo airport** (www.pulkovoairport.ru/eng).

Boat

Linking Helsinki and St Petersburg three times a week is the Finnish ferry **St Peter Line** (✆322 6699; www.stpeterline.com); coming from Helsinki, passengers are allowed to stay in St Petersburg visa-free for up to 72 hours.

Bus

St Petersburg's main bus station, **Avtovokzal No 2** (www.avokzal.ru; nab Obvodnogo kanala 36) – there isn't a No 1 – has both international and European Russia services.

There are regular buses from St Petersburg to Helsinki, Finland (from €40, eight hours, four to six daily). A couple of operators are **Ardis Finnord** (☑314 8951; Italiyanskaya ul 37), which runs two buses daily, and **Sovavto** (☑702 2550; www.sovavto.ru; Vitebsky pr 3), with daily departures to Helsinki and Turku (11 hours). The latter's buses are timed to arrivals and departures of the Silja Line and Viking Line ferries from Turku to Stockholm.

Euroline (www.luxexpress.eu) buses (from R950, 7½ hours, seven daily) from **Baltisky vokzal** (Baltic Station) provide connections to Tallinn.

Train

The new high-speed **Allegro** (www.vr.fi/allegro) service (€84, 3½ hours, four daily) connects St Petersburg and Helsinki. Departures are from **Finlandsky vokzal** (Finland Station; pl Lenina 6). There's also the overnight *Tolstoy* service connecting Helsinki with Moscow via St Petersburg's **Ladozhsky vokzal** (Ladoga Station, Zhanevsky pr 73).

Buy Russian rail tickets in Helsinki at the special ticket counter in the central station. In St Petersburg tickets can be purchased at the train stations, the **central train ticket office** (☑762 3344; nab kanala Griboedova 24; ☉8am-8pm Mon-Sat, 8am-4pm Sun) and many travel agencies around town.

❶ Getting Around

To/From the Airport

From Moskovskaya metro station, bus 39 runs to Pulkovo-1, the domestic terminal, and bus 13

MOVING ON?

For tips, recommendations and reviews, head to shop.lonelyplanet.com to purchase a downloadable PDF of the Russia chapter from Lonely Planet's *Eastern Europe* guide.

runs to Pulkovo-2, the international terminal. There are also plenty of *marshrutky* (minibuses). The trip takes about 15 minutes and costs just R16 to R22. Alternatively, buses and *marshrutky* K3 go all the way from the airport to Sennaya pl in the city centre or K39 to pl Vosstaniya (R35).

By taxi it's around R600 to get to the city (R400 from the city to the airport). Most drivers will request more from foreigners, so be prepared to haggle or take the bus.

Public Transport

The **metro** (single ride/10 trips in a week R22/185; ☉5.30am-midnight) is usually the quickest way around the city. *Zhetony* (tokens) and credit-loaded cards can be bought from booths in the stations.

Marshrutky are faster than the regular buses and trolleybuses. Costs vary with the route, but the average fare is R20 and fares are displayed prominently inside each van.

Taxi

Hold your arm out to stop unofficial taxis. Don't get in if there's more than one person in there already and agree a price before setting off – R100 should be fine for 1km trips, R200 to R300 for slightly longer. To book a taxi call either **Ladybird** (☑900 0504; www.ladybird-taxi.ru), which has women drivers and child car seats, or **Peterburgskoe taksi 068** (☑068, 324 7777; www.taxi068.spb.ru).

Iceland

Why Go?

Iceland is literally a country in the making, a vast volcanic laboratory where mighty forces shape the earth: geysers gush, mudpots gloop, sulphurous clouds puff from fissures and glaciers grind great pathways through the mountains. Experience the full weirdness of Icelandic nature by bathing in turquoise pools, kayaking under the midnight sun or crunching across a dazzling-white ice cap.

Iceland's creatures are larger than life too: minke, humpback and even blue whales are common visitors to the deeper fjords. Record-breaking numbers of birds nest in the sea cliffs: cutest are the fearless puffins who flutter and bill here in their millions.

The landscape is infectious: hidden energy and a desire to shape the world are Icelandic traits. Clean, green Reykjavík must contain the world's highest concentration of dreamers, authors, poets and musicians. The recession hit Iceland particularly hard, but natives are facing it with stoicism; and for visitors, at least, a weaker króna means a cheaper holiday.

Best Places to Eat

» Fish Company (p262)
» Við Tjörnina (p262)
» Vox (p262)
» Við Fjöruborðið (p270)

Best Places to Stay

» Castle House & Embassy Apartments (p259)
» Three Sisters (p259)
» Hótel Borg (p259)
» Hótel Aldan (p288)

When to Go

Reykjavík

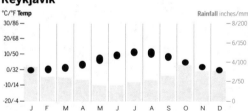

May & Jun Prime birdwatching season happily coincides with the two driest months of the year.

Aug Reykjavík runs at full throttle, culminating in the Culture Night arts festival and firework display.

Nov-Apr The best months for viewing the aurora borealis (Northern Lights).

Connections

Little Iceland, way out on the edge of nothing, is nevertheless connected by regular flights from Keflavík airport to Denmark (Copenhagen), Finland (Helsinki), Norway (Bergen, Oslo and Stavanger) and Sweden (Göteborg and Stockholm) – see p309 for details.

For those who like more romance, the ferry from Denmark (p310) along the jaw-dropping fjord to Seyðisfjörður is the most stylish way to arrive.

ITINERARIES

Three Days

Arrive in Reykjavík on Friday to catch the decadent *runtur* (pub crawl). Sober up in Laugadalur geothermal pool, admire the views from Hallgrímskirkja, then absorb some Viking history at the National Museum. On Sunday, visit Gullfoss, Geysir and Þingvellir on a Golden Circle tour. Stop to soak in the Blue Lagoon on the way home.

One Week

Head for the countryside: chill out on serene Snæfellsnes in the west; view the volcanic Vestmannaeyjar with their immense puffin colonies; or drive east to Skaftafell for wonderful hiking and glacier walking.

Essential Food & Drink

» **Traditional Icelandic dishes** These reflect a nightmarish historical need to eat every last scrap: brave souls might try *svið* (singed sheep's head), *súrsaðir hrútspungar* (pickled ram's testicles) and *hárkarl* (putrefied shark meat), bought from the butcher, fishmonger or old-school workers' canteens. More palatable offerings include *harðfiskur* (dried strips of haddock with butter), *plokkfiskur* (a hearty fish-and-potato gratin) and delicious yoghurt-like *skyr*.

» **Succulent specialities** Icelandic lamb is some of the tastiest on the planet – sheep roam free in the mountains all summer, grazing on sweet grass and wild thyme. Iceland also takes great pride in its fishing industry, and superfresh fish dishes grace most menus. Pink-footed goose and reindeer meat from the eastern highlands are high-end treats.

» **Whale meat controversy** Although whales are a protected species, many Icelandic restaurants serve whale meat: the International Fund for Animal Welfare (IFAW) points out that only 1.1% of Icelanders regularly eat whale, and that tourists consume an appreciable proportion of the catch.

» **Favourite drinks** The traditional alcoholic brew *brennivín* is schnapps made from potatoes and caraway seeds. It's fondly known as *svarti dauði* (black death). Coffee is a national institution.

AT A GLANCE

» **Capital** Reykjavík
» **Area** 103,000 sq km
» **Population** 318,200
» **Country code** ☎354
» **Language** Icelandic
» **Currency** króna (Ikr)

Exchange Rates

Australia	A$1	Ikr121.04
Canada	C$1	Ikr116.63
Europe	€1	Ikr164.67
Japan	¥100	Ikr136.15
New Zealand	NZ$1	Ikr88.92
UK	UK£1	Ikr184.97
USA	US$1	Ikr111.06

Set Your Budget

» **Budget hotel room** Ikr17,000
» **Two-course evening meal** Ikr4000
» **Museum entrance** free–Ikr1000
» **Beer (500mL)** Ikr800
» **Reykjavík bus ticket** Ikr280

Resources

» **Icelandic Tourist Board** (www.visiticeland.com) With links to regional websites

» **Reykjavík Tourist Office** (www.visitreykjavik.is)

REYKJAVÍK

POP 117,500

Iceland's pint-size capital is cute and complex and runs entirely on coffee. It's packed with cosy cafes, top-quality restaurants, fine museums, swirling music and state-of-the-art geothermal pools – all the trappings of a large 21st-century European city but shrunk down to a minute, manageable size. All

these delectable diversions are layered over a foundation of rich Viking history. The froth on top is Reykjavík's eccentric and excessive *runtur,* a wild pub crawl that starts on Friday night around small, superstylish clubs and bars, and ends in Sunday brunch and a city-wide hangover.

The world's most northerly capital offers a bewitching combination of small-town

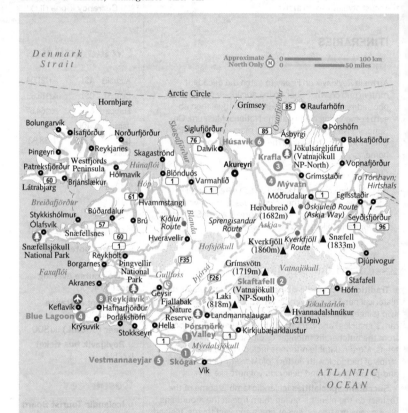

Iceland Highlights

① Hike from **Þórsmörk to Skógar** (p292) and see the new lava formed in the 2010 Eyjafjallajökull eruptions

② Walk up a glinting glacier at **Skaftafell** (p290)

③ Tour the smouldering volcanic wastelands of **Krafla** (p284)

④ Swim through steam clouds at Iceland's world-famous **Blue Lagoon** (p268) spa or **Mývatn Nature Baths** (p284)

⑤ Visit the **Vestmannaeyjar** (p293) to experience life in a close-knit island community...and see puffins

⑥ See ocean giants roll from the waves on a **whale-watching** (p307) trip in Húsavík

⑦ Rocket down rapids in a **raft** (p306)

⑧ Cavort with happy drunks on the Reykjavík **runtur** (p264)

innocence and mischievous energy. As if that wasn't enough, nature herself adds a powerful extra dimension: snow-topped mountains and volcanoes line the horizon; the ocean rolls right up to the very edge of town; and the air is as cold and clean as frozen diamonds.

The international airport is an hour's drive away at Keflavík but getting to the capital is easy. See p267 for details.

⊙ Sights

TOP
CHOICE Hallgrímskirkja   CHURCH
(Map p256; ☎510 1000; www.hallgrimskirkja. is; Skólavörðuholt; ⊙9am-5pm mid-Aug–mid-Jun, 9am-7pm mid-Jun–mid-Aug) This immense concrete church is Reykjavík's most attention-seeking building, visible from 20km away. Its sweeping frontage represents columns of volcanic basalt and took a staggering 34 years to build. Recently it was discovered that the original builders skimped on materials; extensive repair work was needed to replace the defective concrete. The church is now free from scaffolding and back in business: admire the elongated, ultrastark interior; then, for an unmissable view of the city, take an elevator trip up the 75m tower (adult/7-14yr Ikr500/100).

Outside, a statue of Leifur Eiríksson, the first European to visit America, gazes proudly forth. It was a present from the USA on the 1000th anniversary of the Alþing, Iceland's parliament.

From July to mid-August, the church's mighty 15m-high organ pipes up for a popular program of **concerts** (tickets lunchtime/evening Ikr1000/1500), held at lunchtime on Wednesday, Thursday and Saturday, and on Sunday evening.

National Museum   MUSEUM
(Map p256; www.natmus.is; Suðurgata 41; adult/under 18yr/concession Ikr1000/free/500, admission free Wed; ⊙10am-5pm daily May–mid-Sep, 11am-5pm Tue-Sun mid-Sep–Apr) Iceland's 147-year-old national museum gives an award-winning, state-of-the-art overview of Iceland's history and culture. The strongest section is the 1st floor, which shows off swords and silver hoards from the Settlement Era, and one of the nation's most treasured artefacts – a stunning carved 13th-century church door. Upstairs, the journey through Iceland's turbulent past continues with exhibitions on Danish rule,

Arrive on Friday night to experience the city's pub crawl, the **runtur**. Sober up on Saturday with a quick dip in the **Laugadalur geothermal pool**. Don't miss the panoramic view from **Hallgrímskirkja** and wider mountain views from **Perlan**. Book a **whale-watching trip** for Sunday morning, then spend a leisurely afternoon at the **National Museum**.

the growth of the fishing industry and the country's dramatic 20th-century leap from penury to plenty. Walk or catch bus S1, S3-6, 12 or 14.

Reykjavík 871+/-2   MUSEUM
(Settlement Exhibition; Map p256; www.reykjavik871.is; Aðalstræti 16; adult/12-18yr Ikr600/300; ⊙10am-5pm) The city's newest museum is a superb combination of archaeology, technology and imagination. Although the exhibition is compact (it's based around a single Viking longhouse), it's completely absorbing. Best are the tiny wraiths – go and see!

Perlan   LEISURE COMPLEX
(Map p252; www.perlan.is; Öskjuhlíð) The huge water tanks on Öskjuhlíð hill are also a tourist complex known as Perlan (the Pearl), a popular Sunday afternoon outing for families. In the building's atrium, an artificial geyser blasts off every few minutes. Upstairs, a 360-degree viewing deck shares tremendous mountain and city vistas with a cafe and revolving restaurant. Take bus 18 from Lækjartorg.

Saga Museum   MUSEUM
(Map p252; www.sagamuseum.is; adult/child/concession Ikr1500/800/1000; ⊙10am-6pm Apr-Sep, noon-5pm Oct-Mar) Silicon models, thudding axes and blood-curdling screams bring Iceland's history to life at this excellent museum located in the Perlan complex. Don't blame the *brennivín* if you see the characters walking round town – they were modelled on Reykjavík inhabitants.

Þjóðmenningarhúsið   MUSEUM
(Culture House; Map p256; www.thjodmenning. is; Hverfisgata 15; adult/under 16yr Ikr400/free, admission free Wed; ⊙11am-5pm) Fans of the Icelandic sagas should head for the excellent Culture House, which offers intelligent

ICELAND REYKJAVÍK

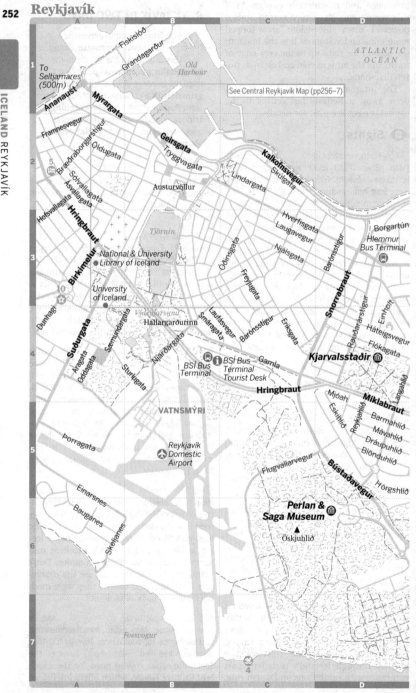

See Central Reykjavík Map (pp256–7)

ATLANTIC OCEAN

To Seltjarnares (500m)

Fiskislóð

Grandagarður

Old Harbour

Ánanaust

Mýrargata

Framnesvegur

Geirsgata

Bræðraborgarstígur

Öldugata

Tryggvagata

Kalkofnsvegur

Skúlagata

Lindargata

Sólvallagata

Ásvallagata

Austurvöllur

Hofsvallagata

Hringbraut

Birkimelur

Tjörnin

National & University
Library of Iceland

University of Iceland

Viðbarsund

Suðurgata

Dunhagi

Arágata

Oddagata

Samundargata

Hallargarðurinn

Njörðargata

Sturlugata

Hverfisgata

Laugavegur

Óðinsgata

Freyjugata

Njálsgata

Laufásvegur

Smáragata

Baronsstígur

Eiríksgata

Snorrabraut

Barónsstígur

Borgartún

Hlemmur
Bus Terminal

Rauðarárstígur

Einholt

Háteigsvegur

Flókagata

BSÍ Bus Terminal

BSÍ Bus Terminal Tourist Desk

Gamla

Kjarvalsstaðir 🏛

Hringbraut

Mjóah

Reykjahlíð

Eskihlíð

Miklabraut

Barmahlíð

Mávahlíð

Dráupuhlíð

Blönduhlíð

Langahlíð

VATNSMÝRI

Þorragata

Reykjavík Domestic Airport ✈

Flugvallarvegur

Bústaðavegur

Hörgshlíð

Einarsnes

Bauganes

Skeljanes

Perlan & Saga Museum 🏛

Öskjuhlíð ▲

Fossvogur

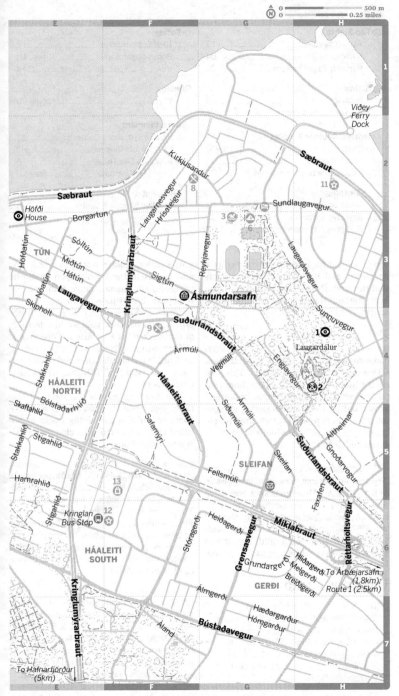

N 0 ——— 500 m
0 ——— 0.25 miles

Viðey Ferry Dock

Sæbraut

11

Sundlaugavegur

Sæbraut

Höfði House

Borgartún

Kirkjusandur

8

Laugarnesvegur

Hrísateigur

Reykjavegur

3

6

Laugarásvegur

Sóltún

TÚN

Miðtún

Hátún

Sigtún

Suðurlandsbraut

Sunnuvegur

Höfðatún

Nóatún

Skipholt

Laugavegur

Kringlumýrarbraut

Ásmundarsafn

9

Armúli

Laugardalur

1

Vegmúli

Engjavegur

2

Stakkahlíð

HÁALEITI NORTH

Bólstaðarhlíð

Skaftahlíð

Stigahlíð

Stakkahlíð

Háaleitisbraut

Safamýri

Armúli

Síðumúli

Althheimar

Hamrahlíð

Fellsmúli

SLEIFAN

Skeifan

Suðurlandsbraut

Gnoðarvogur

Faxafen

Réttarholtsvegur

Stigahlíð

13

Kringlan Bus Stop

12

HÁALEITI SOUTH

Heiðagerði

Miklabraut

Stóragerði

Grensásvegur

Grundargerði

Hlíðargerði

To Meigerði

Breiðagerði

To Árbæjarsafn (1.8km); Route 1 (2.5km)

GERÐI

Álmgerði

Hæðargarður

Hólmgarður

Kringlumýrarbraut

Áland

Bústaðavegur

To Hafnarfjörður (5km)

displays about the history of these medieval narratives and the memorable characters that rise from their pages. Darkened rooms here contain the original vellum manuscripts.

FREE **National Gallery of Iceland** ART GALLERY
(Listasafn Íslands; Map p256; www.listasafn.is; Fríkirkjuvegur 7; ⏰11am-5pm Tue-Sun) This spacious white building on the lake shore contains works by Iceland's most renowned artists and provides an interesting glimpse into the nation's psyche: surreal mud-purple landscapes mingle with visions of ogresses, giants and dead men.

FREE **Listasafn Reykjavíkur** MUSEUM
(Reykjavík Art Museum; www.listasafnreykjavikur.is) Reykjavík Art Museum is split over three sites. At the rather wonderful **Ásmundarsafn** (Ásmundur Sveinsson Sculpture Museum; Map p252; Sigtún; ⏰10am-4pm May-Sep, 1-4pm Sat & Sun Oct-Apr), you'll find the artist's massive concrete sculptures in the garden,

DISCOUNT CARD

The **Reykjavík Welcome Card** (24/48/72hr lkr1500/2000/2500) gives free entry to various galleries, museums, swimming pools and the ferry to Viðey island, and includes a bus pass. Available at several outlets including the tourist offices.

plus smaller, spikier works in wood, clay and metals in the igloo-shaped studio he designed. His themes range from folklore to physics. Bus 14 passes close by.

Jóhannes Kjarval (1885–1972) was a fisherman until his crew paid for him to study at the Academy of Fine Arts in Copenhagen. His unearthly Icelandic landscapes can be seen inside the angular glass-and-wood **Kjarvalsstaðir** (Map p252; Flókagata; ⏰10am-5pm). Catch bus 13.

The third gallery is **Hafnarhús** (Map p256; Tryggvagata 17; ⏰10am-5pm), a severe concrete building containing works by political cartoonist Erró, plus changing modern-art exhibitions.

Einar Jónsson Museum MUSEUM
(Map p256; www.skulptur.is; Njarðargata; adult/under 16yr lkr500/free; ⏰2-5pm Tue-Sun Jun–mid-Sep, to 5pm Sat & Sun mid-Sep–Nov & Feb-May) The weird symbolist creations of sculptor Einar Jónsson are objects you'll either love or hate: find out which at his cube-shaped former home. For a free taster, the garden around the back contains 26 small bronze casts of Einar's work.

Árbæjarsafn MUSEUM
(off Map p252; www.arbaejarsafn.is; Kistuhylur 4; adult/under 18yr lkr600/free; ⏰10am-5pm Jun-Aug, by tour only 1pm Mon, Wed & Fri Sep-May) Quaint old buildings have been uprooted from various places in Iceland, then replanted at this open-air museum, a kind of zoo for houses, 4km from the city centre.

Kids love running around the creaky timber homes. Take bus 19.

Botanic Garden
PARK

(Grasagarður; Map p252; www.grasagardur.is; Skúlatún 2; admission free; greenhouse ☉10am-10pm May-Aug, to 3pm Sep-Apr) Filled with sub-Arctic plant species and colourful seasonal flowers, this is a popular place for picnics. The summer cafe thrums with customers. Buses 14, 15, 17, 19 and S2 pass within 400m.

Old Reykjavík
NEIGHBOURHOOD

Old Reykjavík grew up around Tjörnin (The Pond; Map p256), a large lake that echoes with the honks and hoots of thousands of geese, swans, ducks and gulls. The pleasant park at the southern end is laced with walking and cycling paths.

Rising on stilts from the northern shore of Tjörnin is Reykjavík's postmodern City Hall, Raðhús (Map p256; Tjarnargata 11; ☉8am-7pm Mon-Fri, noon-6pm Sat & Sun). It contains a tourist information desk, a cafe and a huge, impressive 3-D map of Iceland: a mass of mountains, fjords and volcanoes.

The neat grey basalt building on the southern side of Austurvöllur, the main square, houses Alþingi (Map p256; www.althingi.is; Túngata), the Icelandic parliament. Dómkirkja (Map p256; Lækjargata 14a; ☉10am-5pm Mon-Fri) is Iceland's small but perfectly proportioned cathedral.

Volcano Show
CINEMA

(Map p256; ☎845 9548; vknudsen2000@yahoo.com; Red Rock Cinema, Hellusund 6a; 1hr show adult/11-16yr/6-10yr Ikr1200/1000/500, 2hr show Ikr1500/1200/600; ☉11am, 3pm & 8pm in English Jul & Aug, 6.30pm in German Jul & Aug, 1pm Sat in French Jul & Aug, in English 8pm daily Sep-Jun) Eccentric eruption-chaser Villi Knudsen is the photographer, owner and presenter of this awesome film show. His explosive footage captures 50 years' worth of Icelandic volcanoes.

🏃 Activities

Elding Whale Watching
BOAT TRIPS

(Map p256; ☎555 3565; www.elding.is; adult/7-15yr Ikr8000/3500) Iceland is terrific for spotting whales, dolphins and porpoises, with a 97% chance of seeing one (although nature is unpredictable, and sometimes you *might* see nothing but gulls and waves...). Elding runs three-hour trips from the harbour, generally at 9am and 1pm, with additional tours in high season. Tours run year-round, but late spring to early autumn is the best period for sightings.

During bird breeding season (mid-May to mid-August), whale-watching boats also spin round Lundey to look at the **puffins**. For visitors short of time, a dedicated one-hour **puffin tour** (adult/7-15yr Ikr5000/2500) runs at 9.30am and 3pm.

Laugardalslaug
SWIMMING POOL

(Map p252; Sundlaugavegur 30; adult/child Ikr360/120, swimsuit/towel hire Ikr350/350; ☉6.30am-10.30pm Mon-Fri year-round, 8am-10.30pm Sat & Sun Apr-Oct, to 8pm Oct-Mar) The biggest and best of Reykjavík's many geothermal swimming pools is found next door to the camping ground. There's an Olympic-size indoor pool, an outdoor pool, seven jacuzzi-like 'hot pots', a steam bath and a curling 86m water slide for kids big and small. Right next door to Laugardalslaug is a five-star health resort, Laugar (☎553 0000; www.laugarspa.is; admission Ikr4620), with themed saunas, steam rooms and beauty treatments. Catch bus 14 from Lækjartorg or Hlemmur.

🏖 Nauthólsvík Geothermal Beach
BEACH

(Ylströndin; Map p252; admission free; ☉11am-7pm mid-May–mid-Aug) Bringing a touch of the Riviera to Reykjavík, the eco-certified Blue Flag beach is a dinky crescent of golden sand warmed by 18°C to 20°C geothermal water. There are large crowds in sunny weather. Take bus 16 or 19.

SCRUB UP

Reykjavík's many outdoor swimming pools, heated by volcanic water, are the social hubs of the city: children play, teenagers flirt, business deals are made and everyone catches up with the latest gossip.

Geothermal pools are the nation's pride and joy. And as chemical cleaners like chlorine aren't used, it's vital that visitors wash thoroughly without a swimsuit before getting in. To do otherwise is to cause great offence. For further information, see www.spacity.is.

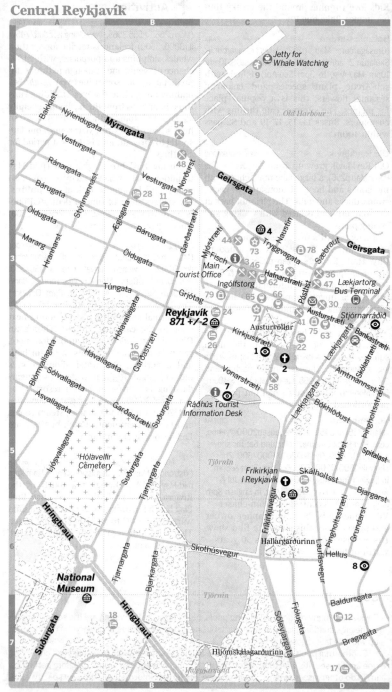

Jetty for
Whale Watching
9

Old Harbour

Mýrargata

Bakkast.

Nýlendugata

Vesturgata

Geirsgata

Ránargata

Styrimannst.

Vesturgata

54

Norðurst.

48

Geirsgata

Bárugata

Ægisgata

Bárugata

Garðastræti

28   11   25

Sæbraut

Geirsgata

Öldugata

Mararg

Öldugata

Hrannarst.

Túngata

Mýöstræti

Garðastræti

44

4
73

Trygvagata

78

Naustin

36

47

Lækjartorg
Bus Terminal

Fisch
Main
Tourist Office

3 46

Hafnarstræti

Ingólfstorg

53

62

Pósthst.

Holavallagata

Grjótag

79

65   66

30

Stjórnarráðið

Reykjavík
871 +/-2

24

Austurstræti

41   75   63

Bankastræti

Skólavörðustr.

Hávallagata

16

Garðastræti

71

Austurvöllur

Amtmannsst.

Blómvallagata

Ásvallagata

26

Kirkjustræti

1   2

22

Bókhlöðust

Þingholtsstræti

Sólvallagata

Garðastræti   Suðurgata

Vonarstræti

58

Lækjargata

Ljósvallagata

7

Ráðhús Tourist
Information Desk

Miðst.

Spítalast

Hólavellir
Cemetery

Tjarnargata

Tjörnin

Fríkirkjan
í Reykjavík

6   13

Skálholtsst.

Þingholtsstræti

Bjargarst.

Hringbraut

Skothúsvegur

Frikirkjuvegur

Hallargarðurinn

Hellus

Laufásvegur

Grundarst.

National
Museum

Tjarnargata

Bjarkargata

Tjörnin

8

Baldursgata

Suðurgata

18

Hringbraut

Söleyjargata

Fjólugata

12

Bragagata

Hljómskálagarðurinn

17

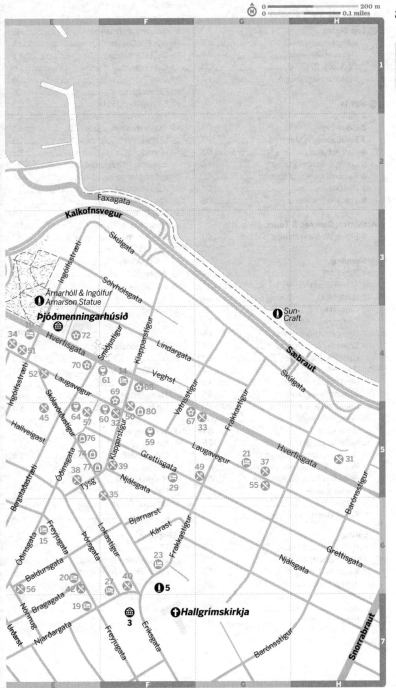

0 — 200 m
0 — 0.1 miles

Faxagata

Kalkofnsvegur

Skúlagata

Ingólfsstræti

Sölvhólsgata

Árnarhóll & Ingólfur
Arnarson Statue

Þjóðmenningarhúsið

Sun-
Craft

Sæbraut

34
51

Hverfisgata

72

Smiðjustígur

Klapparstígur

Lindargata

Skúlagata

70
52

Laugavegur

61

14

Veghst

68

Vatnsstígur

Frakkastígur

Hverfisgata

Skólavörðustígur

69

67

33

31

45

64

60

32

50

80

57

76

59

Laugavegur

21

37

74

77

39

Grettisgata

49

55

38

Óðinsgata

Klapparstígur

Njálsgata

29

Tysg

35

Ingólfsstræti

Hallveigast

Bergstaðastræti

Bjarnarst

Karast

Frakkastígur

Njálsgata

Grettisgata

Baronsstígur

Freyjugata

15

Lokastígur

Þórsgata

23

Óðinsgata

Baldursgata

20

42

27

40

56

Nönnug

Bragagata

19

Njarðargata

3

5

Hallgrímskirkja

Erriksgata

Freyjugata

Urðarst

Baronsstígur

Snorrabraut

ICELAND REYKJAVÍK

◎ Top Sights
Hallgrímskirkja F7
National Museum......................................A7
Reykjavík 871 +/-2 ....C4
Þjóðmenningarhúsið E4

◎ Sights
1 Alþingi..C4
2 Dómkirkja...C4
3 Einar Jónsson Museum.........................F7
4 Hafnarhús...C3
5 Leifur Eiríksson Statue.........................F6
6 National Gallery of Iceland C5
7 Ráðhús..C4
8 Volcano Show...D6

Activities, Courses & Tours
9 Elding Whale Watching..........................C1

🛏 Sleeping
10 101 Hotel E4
11 Álfhóll Guesthouse B2
12 Baldursbrá Guesthouse D7
13 Castle House D5
14 CenterHotel Klöpp..................................F4
15 Draupnir Apartments.............................E6
16 Embassy Apartments.............................B4
17 Galtafell Guesthouse.............................D7
18 Garður Inn..B7
19 Guesthouse Andrea................................E7
20 Guesthouse Aurora.................................E6
Guesthouse Butterfly....................(see 11)
21 Guesthouse Von......................................G5
22 Hótel Borg..D4
23 Hótel Leifur Eiríksson............................F6
24 Hótel Reykjavík Centrum.......................C4
25 Reykjavík Downtown Hostel..................B2
26 Salvation Army Guesthouse..................C4
27 Sunna Guesthouse.................................F6
28 Three Sisters..B2
29 Tower Guesthouse F5

🍴 Eating
30 10-11 Supermarket.................................D3
31 10-11 Supermarket.................................H5
32 Á Næstu Grösum F5
33 Austur Indía Félagið...............................G5
34 b5 ....E4
35 Babalú F5
36 Bæjarins Beztu.......................................D3

37 Bónus Supermarket...............................G5
38 C Is For Cookie.......................................E5
39 Café Garðurinn F5
40 Café Loki...F6
41 Café Paris...D4
42 Eldsmiðjan..E6
43 Emmessís og Pylsur..............................C3
44 Fish Company...C3
45 Grænn Kostur E5
46 Hlölla Bátar..C3
47 Hornið...D3
48 Icelandic Fish & Chips............................B2
49 Indian Mango G5
50 Kaffi Hljómalind F5
51 Kaffi Sólon E4
52 Kofi Tómasar Frænda.............................E4
53 Nonnabiti...C3
54 Sægreifinn..B2
55 Svarta Kaffið G5
56 Þrír Frakkar E6
57 Vegamót E5
58 Við Tjörnina C4

🍷 Drinking
59 Boston..F5
60 Café Oliver..F5
61 Celtic Cross..F4
62 Dubliner..C3
63 Hressingarskálinn..................................D4
64 Kaffibarinn...E5
65 Thorvaldsen C3
66 Vín Búð..C3

🎭 Entertainment
67 Bíó Paradís...F5
68 Café Rosenberg......................................F4
69 Hemmi & Valdi..F4
70 Hverfisbarinn E4
71 NASA...C4
72 National Theatre.....................................E4
73 Sódóma...C3

🛍 Shopping
74 12 Tónar..E5
75 Eymundsson Bookshop..........................D4
76 Eymundsson Bookshop E5
77 Handknitting Association of Iceland.....E5
78 Kolaportið Flea Market...........................D3
79 Kraum C3
80 Smekkleysa...F5

 Festivals & Events

For forthcoming live music festivals, see www.musik.is.

In May, the capital comes awake with the two-week Reykjavík Arts Festival (www.artfest.is), when the city is taken over by local and international theatre performances, films, lectures and music.

August is a big time for celebrations, with the Gay Pride (www.gaypride.is) parade around the second weekend of the month. The Reykjavík Marathon (www.marathon.is) is an atmospheric event held on a Saturday in mid-August – the same day as Culture Night, a lively time of art, music and dance with a grand fireworks finale. The annual Reykjavík Jazz Festival (www.reykjavikjazz.is) has been moved around the calendar a lot, but debuted as an August festival in 2010.

In September, the annual Reykjavík International Film Festival (www.riff.is) sees blockbusters make way for international art films in cinemas across the city.

Iceland Airwaves (www.icelandairwaves.com) is a last blast of music and noise before winter sets in. This five-day event, held in the third week of October, is one of the world's most cutting-edge music festivals: don't expect to sleep.

🛏 Sleeping

Reykjavík is packed in summer: book accommodation well in advance. Breakfast is usually included in room prices (but not for sleeping-bag accommodation). Remember that drunken revellers rule the streets if considering weekend accommodation on Laugavegur, Austurvöllur, Ingólfstorg or neighbouring streets.

TOP CHOICE **Castle House & Embassy Apartments**   APARTMENTS €€
(Map p256; ☎511 2166; http://hotelsiceland.net; Skálholtsstígur 2a & Garðastræti 40; 1-6-person apt Ikr11,000-38,000) Turn to these excellent self-contained apartments at two different sites for satisfyingly central and commendably

quiet accommodation. Much more personal than a hotel, these apartments still come with room service: fresh towels appear daily, and washing up magically cleans itself. Breakfast is not included. The tariff changes depending on demand – cheapest rates are through the website.

Three Sisters   APARTMENTS €€
(Þrjár Systur; Map p256; ☎565 2181; www.threesisters.is; Ránargata 16; 1-/2-person/f apt Ikr12,600/16,600/22,300; ☺mid-May–Aug; @) A twinkly eyed former fisherman runs the Three Sisters, a lovely townhouse in old Reykjavík, now divided into eight studio apartments. Comfy counterpane beds are flanked by old-fashioned easy chairs and new flat-screen TVs. Each room comes with a cute, fully equipped kitchen. A short stroll seawards is a second building with sleeping-bag accommodation in six-bed dorms (around Ikr3000) and a further eight apartments.

Hótel Borg   HISTORIC HOTEL €€€
(Map p256; ☎551 1440; www.hotelborg.is; Pósthússtræti 11; s/d/ste Ikr37,800/47,700/72,300) The city's most historic hotel, Borg is a 1930s art deco palace located in prime position on Austurvöllur square. A major overhaul in 2006 replaced antiquated charm with supersmart, if somewhat masculine-feeling, beige, black and cream decor. Parquet floors, leather headboards and flat-screen Bang & Olufsen TVs are standard throughout. Bathrooms have splendid giant showerheads, and quadruple-glazed windows muffle weekend street noise. Buffet breakfast Ikr3300. Babysitting service.

Sunna Guesthouse   GUESTHOUSE €€
(Map p256; ☎511 5570; www.sunna.is; Þórsgata 26; s/d/apt from Ikr12,000/15,000/19,000; P@) Rooms are simple and sunny with honey-coloured parquet floors. Nine have private bathrooms and those at the front offer good views of Hallgrímskirkja. Families are welcomed: there are four large family apartments, in addition to the eight neat

---

FREE ATTRACTIONS

Reykjavík can be costly, but there are some free sights to enjoy:

» Listasafn Reykjavíkur There's at least a day's worth of viewing at Reykjavík Art Museum, with its three galleries scattered across the city.

» Perlan Gorge on gorgeous views from the top of the city's hot-water tanks.

» Einar Jónsson Museum garden Free sculpture garden behind the museum.

Those travelling with children will find ample facilities (baby-changing tables in toilets, high chairs in restaurants etc) and a gently welcoming attitude. However, the only attraction in Reykjavík aimed specifically at (youngish) children is **Reykjavík Zoo & Family Park** (Map p252; ☎575 7800; www.mu.is; Laugardalur; adult/5-12yr Ikr600/500, 1-/10-/20-ride tickets Ikr200/1800/3400; ☉10am-6pm mid-May–mid-Aug, to 5pm mid-Aug–mid-May). Don't expect lions and tigers: think seals, foxes, farm animals and a small aquarium. The Family Park contains child-size bulldozers, a giant trampoline and mini fairground rides. Buses 14, 15, 17, 19 and S2 pass within 400m.

Tots love to feed the birds on Tjörnin, the city's central lake, and the open-air Árbæjarsafn has plenty of appeal for kids of all ages. The dramatic Saga Museum will delight some but may be too frightening for younger children.

studio apartments (accommodating one to four people). The breakfast room can get cramped during high season.

Reykjavík City Hostel
HOSTEL €

(Map p252; ☎553 8110; www.hostel.is; Sundlaugavegur 34; sleeping bag in 2-/4-/6-bed dm Ikr5300/3500/2500, bed linen Ikr900; P@) The award-winning youth hostel beside the camping ground has many commendable points: it's environmentally friendly, and has helpful staff and excellent facilities (24-hour reception, several kitchens, laundry, large-screen TV room, free wi-fi, bike rental etc). School parties can be noisy – bring ear plugs. Breakfast Ikr1100. The hostel is about 2.5km east of the city centre (bus 14).

Reykjavík Downtown Hostel
HOSTEL €€

(Map p256; ☎553 8120; www.hostel.is; Vesturgata 17; sleeping bag in 4-/10-bed dm Ikr6200/4400, d Ikr16,400, d without bath Ikr13,000, bed linen Ikr950; @) The new 'Downtown' youth-hostel branch, opened in March 2009, still has that fresh-paint smell. It has the same fine staff as its City Hostel cousin and facilities that are *almost* as good, but the focus is on couples and families rather than young backpackers. This, and its amazing Old Town location, mean correspondingly higher prices.

Áskot B&B
B&B €€

(Map p252; ☎662 0183; www.askot.is; Ásvallagata 52; s/d/tr with shared bathrooms Ikr10,500/14,200/18,400; @) This pleasing little family-run place, with more personality than many a Reykjavík guesthouse, is tucked away in a residential district west of the centre. Rooms are decently sized, with an ample number of shared bathrooms and kitchens between them. There are discounts for stays over three days. Breakfast available in summer.

Tower Guesthouse
APARTMENTS €€

(Map p256; ☎899 9998; www.tower.is; Grettisgata 22C; d Ikr 16,900, 1- & 2-bed apt Ikr16,900-29,900) These central apartments are good value for money, with spotless rooms, private bathrooms and airy shared kitchens, located on a quiet street running parallel to Laugavegur. Facilities are great and include a dishwasher and washing machine.

Draupnir Apartments
GUESTHOUSE €€

(Map p256; ☎552 4494; www.ghdraupnir.com; Óðinsgata 15; d Ikr17,000, s/d without bath Ikr10,000/14,000) This reader-recommended place offers single and double rooms, rather than apartments! Slightly misleading name aside, this is a sweet find. It's on a quiet residential street, just a few minutes' walk from the heart of town: its bedrooms are airy, and there's a sitting room and garden that guests can use.

Hótel Reykjavík Centrum
HOTEL €€€

(Map p256; ☎514 6000; www.hotelcentrum.is; Aðalstræti 16; s/d Ikr34,000/40,000) This central hotel has striking architecture – mezzanines and a glass roof unite two buildings, giving the whole place a spry, light feel. Its 89 neatly proportioned rooms come in two styles – 'traditional', with patterned wallpaper and white-painted furniture, and 'deluxe', with leather seats and a more contemporary feel. Both have excellent facilities. Rack rates are high, but look out for good internet deals.

CenterHotel Klöpp
HOTEL €€

(Map p256; ☎595 8520; www.centerhotels.is; Klapparstígur 26; s/d from Ikr14,800/16,000; ☉closed 18-27 Dec; P@) This mellow place has modestly sized rooms with minimal furnishings, but warm woody tones still lend them a cosy feel. All contain a TV, fridge, radio, kettle and an internet connection point. It's worth paying more for a superior 5th-floor room – they're larger and with sea and mountain views. Wi-fi available in lobby only.

Baldursbrá Guesthouse   GUESTHOUSE €€
(Map p256; ☑552 6646; baldursbra@centrum.is; Laufásvegur 41; s/d Ikr10,000/16,000) Situated in the genteel 'Embassy District', Baldursbrá is a little oasis within easy walking distance of the city centre. Blessings include a friendly welcome, spick, span and spacious rooms, and a garden with a hot pot. Bathrooms are shared, but all rooms have a washbasin.

Álfhóll Guesthouse   GUESTHOUSE €€
(Map p256; ☑898 1838; www.islandia.is/alf; Ránargata 8; s/d Ikr10,800/18,500/18,500, d without bathroom Ikr14,500, 2–4-person apt Ikr22,000-27,000; ⊘mid-May–Aug) Run by a family of elf enthusiasts, Álfhóll has rooms that team modern white walls and parquet flooring with old furniture that's full of character, giving the place a bit of soul. Most rooms have washbasins, and the bathroom-to-guest ratio is not *too* bad for an Old Town house. The three apartments represent best value, with private bathrooms and little kitchens.

Guesthouse Butterfly   GUESTHOUSE €€
(Map p256; ☑894 1864; www.kvasir.is/butterfly; Ránargata 8a; s/d/apt Ikr13,700/15,300/23,000; ⊘Jun-Aug) On a quiet residential street within fluttering distance of the centre, Guesthouse Butterfly has neat, simply furnished rooms with a good ratio of shared bathrooms. There's a guest kitchen, and the friendly Icelandic-Norwegian owners make you feel right at home. Three self-contained apartments have kitchens and balconies.

101 Hotel   BOUTIQUE HOTEL €€€
(Map p256; ☑580 0101; www.101hotel.is; Hverfisgata 10; s/d/ste from Ikr54,900/62,900/89,900; @) Reykjavík's newest boutique hotel is devilishly divine. Its 38 sensuous rooms – with yielding king- or queen-sized beds, glass-walled showers and rich wooden floors – may mean you boycott the bars and opt for a night in instead. A spa with masseurs, a small gym and a glitterati bar add to the opulence.

Hótel Leifur Eiríksson   HOTEL €€
(Map p256; ☑562 0800; www.hotelleifur.is; Skólavörðustígur 45; s/d/tr Ikr17,500/21,200/25,000) This hotel glories in one of the best locations in Reykjavík: it's slap on the end of arty Skólavörðustígur, and more than half of the (small) 47 rooms have inspiring views of Hallgrímskirkja. There's no restaurant, but free tea and coffee are available 24 hours in the lobby.

Salvation Army Guesthouse   HOSTEL €
(Map p256; ☑561 3203; www.herinn.is; Kirkjustræti 2; sleeping bag in dm Ikr3100, s/d/tr/q Ikr7400/10,400/14,400/18,200) This is the nearest thing Reykjavík has to a Japanese capsule hotel! The tiny rooms are highly functional and frill-free, but it has a wonderfully central location and beats the Downtown hostel effortlessly on price. There's a bustling, backpacker-y atmosphere, guest kitchen and lounging area. Breakfast costs Ikr800.

Garður Inn   SUMMER HOTEL €€
(Map p256; ☑562 4000 yr-round, 511 5900 Jun-Aug; www.innsoficeland.is; Hringbraut; sleeping bag in dm/tw Ikr4500/6000, s/d Ikr12,500/14,000;⊘Jun-Aug; P@) The university campus, about 1km from the centre, has utilitarian rooms available once students have left for the summer, all with shared bathrooms. The cheapest sleeping-bag accommodation is in 16-person dorms; the most expensive is in twin rooms.

Guesthouse Andrea   GUESTHOUSE €€
(Map p256; ☑899 1773; www.aurorahouse.is; Njarðargata 43; sleeping bag in dm Ikr4000, s/d Ikr11,5000/14,500; ⊘mid-May–Sep; @) Friendly Siggi runs this hidden place, tucked down a side street in a quiet residential area. Its five private rooms have spruce-wood floors and are ideal for self-caterers: each has a sink, cooker, fridge and tiny two-seater table. Siggi also owns two nearby guesthouses, **Aurora** (Freyjugata 24) and **Von** (Laugavegur 55), with similar facilities and identical prices.

Reykjavík Campsite   CAMPING GROUND €
(Map p252; ☑568 6944; www.reykjavikcampsite.is; Sundlaugavegur 32; campsites per person Ikr1100, 2-bed cabins Ikr7500; ⊘mid-May–mid-Sep; P@) There's only one camping ground in Reykjavík and it gets very busy in summer. It holds 650 people, though, so you'd be unlucky not to find a pitch. Laundry and internet facilities. Bus 14.

Galtafell Guesthouse   GUESTHOUSE €€
(Map p256; ☑551 4344, 699 2525; www. galtafell.com; Laufásvegur 46; s/d/apt from Ikr11,700/15,200/19,000; P) This guesthouse has a great location in a quiet, well-to-do suburb within easy walking distance of town. Although the accommodation is nowhere near

as grand as the castellated exterior implies, the four spruce apartments each contain a fully equipped kitchen, cosy seating area and separate bedroom; and the three basement doubles are serviceable.

✖ Eating

Reykjavík's eateries vary from hot-dog stands to world-class restaurants. Two things are consistent: high quality and high prices. The best dishes are generally those made from Iceland's outstanding fresh fish, seafood and juicy, mountain-reared lamb. For a general overview and types of eateries, including the vague distinction between cafes and bars; see p304. For opening hours, see p307.

Reykjavík's dining places are found along Laugavegur, Hverfisgata and Austurstræti. Tips are always included in the bill.

Restaurants

TOP CHOICE **Fish Company** FINE DINING €€€
(Fiskfélagið; Map p256; ☑552 5300; www.fisk felagid.is; Vesturgata 2a; mains Ikr4000-6000; ⏰lunch & dinner) A recent shining star in the Reykjavík dining scene, this atmospheric restaurant serves up a truly ambitious 'round-the-world' menu (despite the name, the focus isn't wholly on fish). A sample meal might begin with slow-cooked Spanish serrano, travel to China for a main of succulent, slow-cooked ginger salmon and finish with Tahitian banana and coconut cake! And the chef's-choice three-course 'Menu around Iceland' option (Ikr7900) is a fabulous way to sample seasonal Icelandic ingredients. Complemented by a snug interior with hotchpotch seating, candles and copper lamps.

TOP CHOICE **Við Tjörnina** SEAFOOD €€€
(Map p256; ☑551 8666; www.vidtjornina.is; Templarasund 3; mains Ikr3800-5000; ⏰dinner) Tucked away on a side street near Tjörnin, this famed seafood establishment serves up beautifully presented Icelandic feasts such as guillemot with port, tender lamb fillet and garlic langoustine. The restaurant itself is cosy and wonderfully distinctive; it feels like a quirky, upper-class, 1930s drawing room.

Vox FINE DINING €€€
(Map p252; ☑444 5050; www.vox.is; Suðurlandsbraut 2; mains Ikr4500-6000; ⏰dinner Tue-Sat) The Hilton's five-star restaurant serves up superb seasonal dishes (think pink-footed goose with caramelised apples), and there's

usually one vegie option. The waiters sometimes bring out extra little treats – like their amazing 'invisible gazpacho' – for you to try.

Þrír Frakkar SEAFOOD €€
(Map p256; ☑552 3939; www.3frakkar.com; Baldursgata 14; mains Ikr3000-4000; ⏰lunch & dinner) Owner-chef Úlfar Eysteinsson has built up an excellent reputation at this snug little restaurant, which has been given the thumbs-up by Jamie Oliver. Specialities include salted cod, anglerfish and *plokkfiskur* (fish stew) with black bread. (Whale meat served.)

Austur Indía Félagið INDIAN €€
(Map p256; ☑552 1630; www.austurindia.is; Hverfisgata 56; mains Ikr3200-4200; ⏰dinner) The northernmost Indian restaurant in the world, Austur Indía Félagið is an upmarket experience, with minimalist interior and a select choice of excellent (mostly tandoori) dishes. The atmosphere is relaxed and the service warm. Apparently this place is a favourite of Harrison Ford's, and who dares argue with Indy?

Indian Mango INDIAN €€
(Map p256; ☑551 7722; cnr Frakkastígur & Grettisgata; mains Ikr2400-4000; ⏰dinner Mon-Sat) A flavoursome experience, Mango specialises in Goan-Icelandic fusion food, if you can imagine that. Its specialities are *svartfugl* (guillemot) marinaded in Indian spices and the sweetest, smoothest mango kulfi made with Goan mangos. Great for vegies.

Á Næstu Grösum VEGETARIAN €
(First Vegetarian; Map p256; ☑552 8410; www.anaes tugrosum.is; Laugavegur 20b; daily specials Ikr1490; ⏰noon-10pm Mon-Sat, 5-10pm Sun) This first-rate, canteen-style vegie restaurant in a cheerful orange room overlooking Laugavegur offers several daily specials. Dishes feature seasonal organic veg and inventive dressings, and portions are huge. There's extra spice on Indian nights (Friday and Saturday). Organic wine and beer are available.

Hornið ITALIAN €€
(Map p256; ☑551 3340; Hafnarstræti 15; 9in pizza around Ikr2200, mains Ikr2600-4000; ⏰11am-11pm) There's an easy-going atmosphere at this bright art deco cafe-restaurant, with its warm terracotta tiles, weeping-fig plants and decently spaced tables. Pizzas are freshly made before your eyes, the prettily presented pasta meals will set you up for the day and you can sample traditional Icelandic fish dishes.

Grænn Kostur
VEGETARIAN €

(Map p256; ✆552 2028; www.graennkostur. is; Skólavörðustígur 8b; daily special Ikr1490; ⌚11.30am-9pm Mon-Sat, 1-9pm Sun) This place serves organic, vegetarian set meals similar to Á Næstu Grösum. It's smaller and harder to find, but persevere! The easiest way to get there is through the car park (parking lot) on Bergstaðastræti.

Sægreifinn
SEAFOOD €€

(Map p256; ✆553 1500; Geirsgata 9; mains Ikr1500-2500; ⌚11.30am-10pm summer, shorter hr winter) Eccentric Sægreifinn serves up fresh seafood in what looks almost like a 1950s English chip shop...except for the barrel seats and stuffed seal. Lobster soup and seafood kebabs are specialities. (Whale meat served.)

Icelandic Fish & Chips
SEAFOOD €€

(Map p256; ✆511 1118; www.fishandchips.is; Tryggvagata 8; mains around Ikr2000; ⌚noon-9pm) A reader-recommended restaurant serving hearty portions of...well, have a guess! It's good-value fare (for Iceland, at least), and the owners have put their own singular slant on it with a range of 'Skyronnaises' – *skyr*-based sauces (eg rosemary and green apple) that add an unusual zing to this most traditional of dishes.

Cafes

Café Paris
BISTRO €€

(Map p256; ✆551 1020; Austurstræti 14; snacks Ikr800-2000; ⌚9am-1am) An old favourite, in spite of sometimes hit-and-miss service. Paris is one of the city's prime people-watching spots, particularly in summer when outdoor seating spills out onto Austurvöllur square. The leather-upholstered interior is atmospheric at night, filled with tunes and tinkling wine glasses. Good selection of light meals (sandwiches, crêpes, burgers, salads and tacos).

Babalú
CAFE €

(Map p256; Skólavörðustígur 22a; ⌚11am-11pm) More inviting than your own living room, this tiny cafe sells tea, coffee, hot chocolate, sweet and savoury crêpes, and delicious New York–style cheesecake. It's a fine place to linger – in winter, snuggle down in a cosy corner; when the sun shines, head for the rooftop terrace to spy on the street below. Occasional live music.

b5
BISTRO €€

(Map p256; ✆552 9600; www.b5.is; Bankastræti 5; light meals Ikr1700-2200; ⌚11am-midnight Sun-Wed, to 1am Thu, to 2am Fri & Sat) Despite its barely there name and supersleek interior, this bistro-bar is actually a very mellow place with comfy seating, light Scandinavian-style meals, games consoles for the kids to borrow and funky tunes on Friday and Saturday nights.

C Is For Cookie
CAFE €

(Map p256; Týsgata 8; snacks Ikr500-1000; ⌚9am-8pm Mon-Sat) Downtown Reykjavík's newest cafe, named in honour of Sesame Street's Cookie Monster, is probably not one that you would stumble across accidentally. It's worth seeking out, though, for its cheerful atmosphere, great homemade cakes and the pretty pictures floating on top of your latte. Come for breakfast or for a light lunch of salad, soup or grilled sandwiches.

Kaffi Sólon
BISTRO €€

(Map p256; ✆562 3232; www.solon.is; Bankastræti 7a; snacks & light meals Ikr1700-2500; ⌚11am-midnight Mon-Wed, to 1am Thu-Sat, noon-midnight Sun) With its huge picture windows, leather seats and glamorous staff, Sólon looks expensive, but this cultivated international bistro is good value and has lots of choice. It becomes a swish bar/club for a beautiful, martini-drinking set by night, with in-demand DJs and (rare in Reykjavík) a dance floor.

Svarta Kaffið
CAFE €

(Map p256; Laugavegur 54; snacks & light meals Ikr1000-1500; ⌚11am-1am Sun-Thu, to 3am Fri & Sat) Order thick, homemade soup (one meat and one veg option daily) at this dark, cave-like cafe – it's served piping hot in pumpkin-like bread bowls. Svarta Kaffið is also a whimsical nightspot, with African masks and dim lighting adding a certain frisson.

Kaffi Hljómalind
ORGANIC €

(Map p256; www.kaffihljomalind.org; Laugavegur 23; snacks Ikr800-1300; ⌚9am-11pm Mon-Fri, 11am-11pm Sat & Sun) This commendable community-run fair-trade cafe is run on a not-for-profit basis. It looks like a 1950s home with 1970s flourishes (prayer flags, patterned chairs, hand-painted cups and saucers), and is a meeting place for Reykjavík's radicals.

Café Garðurinn
VEGETARIAN €

(Map p256; Klapparstígur 37; soup Ikr900, mains Ikr1450; ⌚11am-5pm Mon-Fri, noon-5pm Sat, closed Aug) This tiny but tasteful vegie cafe is based around seven tables and the hum of civilised conversation. Choice is limited, but the food's delicious – we can heartily recommend the Catalonian tofu balls! Half portions available.

Kofi Tómasar Frænda
CAFE €

(Koffin; Map p256; Laugavegur 2; snacks around Ikr800; ⊙10am-1am Mon-Thu, to 5.30am Fri & Sat, 11am-1am Sun) Subterranean Koffin has a student-y feel. Relax with magazines and a snack (nachos, lasagne, sandwiches, cakes or chocolate-coated marzipan) and watch disconnected feet scurry along Laugavegur. At night, it turns into a candlelit bar with DJs spinning tunes.

Vegamót
BISTRO €€

(Map p256; ☑511 3040; www.vegamot.is; Vegamótstígur 4; light meals around Ikr2000; ⊙11am-1am Mon-Thu, to 5am Fri & Sat, noon-1am Sun) A long-running cafe-bar-club, but still a voguish place to eat, drink, see and be seen. There's a startling amount of choice on the 'global' menu, including Mexican salad, sesame-fried monkfish, seafood quesadilla and blackened chicken. The attached takeaway charges 10% less.

Café Loki
ICELANDIC €

(Map p256; www.textil.is; Lokastígur 28; snacks around Ikr950, Icelandic platter Ikr1890; ⊙10am-6pm Mon-Sat, noon-6pm Sun) Ignore the glaring exterior signage: this 1st-floor cafe close to Hallgrímskirkja is quite tasteful inside. It serves up very traditional dishes, from herring on homemade rye bread to Icelandic platters of sheep's-head jelly and shark meat. Popular with curious tourists and (a mark of approval) with locals too.

Quick Eats

Bæjarins Beztu
STREET FOOD €

(Map p256) Icelanders swear it's impossible to get a bad hot dog from this van near the harbour, patronised by Bill Clinton! Use the vital sentence *Eina með öllu* ('One with everything') for mustard, ketchup, remoulade and onions.

Eldsmiðjan
PIZZA €

(Map p256; ☑562 3838; Bragagata 38a; 10in pizza around Ikr1500; ⊙11am-11pm) Wood-fired pizzas, reputedly the best in town. Dare you try the snail topping?

Hlölla Bátar
BUDGET €

(Map p256; Ingólfstorg; subs around Ikr1200; ⊙10am-2am Sun-Thu, to 7am Fri & Sat) Postclub favourite.

Emmessís og Pylsur
BUDGET €

(Map p256; Ingólfstorg)

Nonnabiti
BURGERS €

(Map p256; Hafnarstræti 11; snacks Ikr500-900; ⊙to 2am Sun-Thu, to 5.30am Fri & Sat)

Self-Catering

Bónus
SUPERMARKET

Laugavegur 59 (Map p256; ⊙noon-6.30pm Mon-Thu, 10am-7.30pm Fri, to 6pm Sat); Kringlan (Map p252; ⊙noon-6.30pm Mon-Thu, 10am-7.30pm Fri, to 6pm Sat, 1-6pm Sun) Cheapest supermarket.

10-11
SUPERMARKET

(⊙24hr) Austurstræti (Map p256); Barónsstígur (Map p256); Laugalækur (Map p252) More up-market, with branches all over town.

Drinking

Reykjavík is renowned for its Friday- and Saturday-night *runtur,* when industrious Icelanders abandon work and party with passion (midweek drinking is not part of Icelandic culture). Beer is expensive. Most people visit a government-owned Vín Búð (the only shops licensed to sell alcohol), tipple at home, then hit the town from midnight to 6am. There's a central Vín Búð (Map p256; Austurstræti 10; ⊙11am-6pm Mon-Thu & Sat, to 7pm Fri) and another in Kringlan shopping centre (Map p252) with the same hours.

Some venues have cover charges (about Ikr1000), and 'in' clubs have long queues (lines) at weekends. Things change fast; check *Grapevine* or *Reykjavík This Month* for the latest listings. You should dress up in Reykjavík, although there are pub-style places where you won't feel scruffy in jeans. The minimum drinking age is 20.

Often the only difference between a cafe and a bar is the time of day, see p304.

Boston
BAR

(Map p256; Laugavegur 28b) Boston is cool, arty – and easy to miss: it's accessed through a doorway on Laugavegur that leads you upstairs to its laidback candlelit lounge, decorated in black wallpaper grown over with silver leaves and frequented by a non-conformist crowd. Live music/DJs.

Kaffibarinn
BAR

(Map p256; Bergstaðastræti 1) Damon Albarn from Blur has a stake in this ubertrendy bar, which had a starring role in the cult film *101 Reykjavík*. It's popular with celebs: at weekends you'll need a famous face or a battering ram to get in.

Hressingarskálinn SPORTS BAR
(Map p256; Austurstræti 20) Known colloquially as Hressó, this large, open-plan, rough-and-ready cafe-bar serves a cheap, diverse menu till 10pm daily (everything from porridge to *plokkfiskur,* mains around Ikr1900). At weekends, it concentrates on beer, bar and dancing; a garden out back provides fresh air. There's usually a DJ or live music on Thursday nights.

Café Oliver BAR
(Map p256; www.cafeoliver.is; Laugavegur 20a) Oliver is one of the most in-vogue places for partying late in super style. DJs pump out the tunes on Thursday, Friday and Saturday, with long queues snaking back from the doors.

Thorvaldsen BAR
(Map p256; Austurstræti 8-10) A smart modernist bistro by day (mains Ikr2000 to Ikr3000), this becomes one of the hottest weekend clubs – dress well or you won't get in – and, after midnight, be prepared to queue…and queue. There's a tiny dance floor with weekend DJs. On Thursday the bartenders focus all their creative talents on producing the perfect mojito.

Celtic Cross BAR
(Map p256; Hverfisgata 26) Cosy place, done up like a funeral parlour, with live bands on weekends.

Dubliner PUB
(Map p256; Hafnarstræti 4) Popular with tourists.

☆ Entertainment

Nightclubs
Hverfisbarinn CLUB
(Map p256; www.hverfisbarinn.is; Hverfisgata 20) This trendy bar and club attracts a young, dressy crowd and has long queues at weekends. It's done out in a cool modern-Scandinavian style, which adds to the spacious feel. It has live music on Thursday from 9.30pm, and DJs on Friday and Saturday.

NASA CLUB
(Map p256; www.nasa.is; Austurvöllur) The biggest nightclub in Reykjavík, NASA is a stripped-pine affair filled with Prada-clad crowds. It plays chart music and club anthems, and is also one of the city's biggest live-music venues.

Cinemas
Films are shown in their original language with Icelandic subtitles. Cinemas charge Ikr1100per adult and Ikr550 per child under eight years. The newspaper *Morgunblaðið* lists cinema programs, or click on the 'Bíó' tab at www.kvikmyndir.is.

Reykjavík has seven multiplexes: the closest to the city centre are Sambíóin (Map p252) in Kringlan shopping centre and Laugarásbíó (Map p252; Laugarás) near the youth hostel. A little further out, in the suburb of Kópavogur, five-screen Smárabíó (Smáralind) is Iceland's plushest cinema. Central Bíó Paradís (Map p256; Hverfisgata 54) shows art-house films. Buy tickets at the box offices or online at http://midi.is/cinema.

Theatre
National Theatre THEATRE
(Map p256; ☏585 1200, tickets 551 1200; www.leikhusid.is; Hverfisgata 19; ☺box office noon-6pm & before evening performances, theatre closed Jul & Aug) Puts on around 10 plays, musicals and operas per year, from modern Icelandic works to Shakespeare.

Reykjavík City Theatre THEATRE
(Map p252; ☏568 8000; www.borgarleikhus.is; Listabraut 3, Kringlan; ☺box office 10am-6pm Mon & Tue, to 8pm Wed-Fri, noon-8pm Sat & Sun, theatre closed Jul & Aug) The country's second-largest theatre also stages classic and contemporary plays. The Icelandic Dance Company (www.id.is) is in residence here.

Live Music
Many bars, pubs and clubs have live band performances – try NASA, Hressingarskálinn and Celtic Cross; also try Café Rosenberg (Map p256; ☏551 2442; Klapparstígur 25-27) and (for small, impromptu gigs) Hemmi & Valdi (Map p256; ☏551 6464; Laugavegur 21).

For gig listings, see the excellent English-language newspaper *Grapevine,* available free from cafes, hostels and tourist offices. Also look for flyers or ask the staff in the record shops 12 Tónar or Smekkleysa. Tickets for larger live-music gigs are available at http://midi.is/concerts.

Sódóma BAR
(Map p256; Tryggvagata 22) Opened in 2009, Sódóma is a central bar/club that favours music's rockier end. Its size and brand-new sound system make it one of the city's main live-music venues, with gigs running from Wednesday to Saturday. (Also famous for its urinals, lined with mugshots of Iceland's former bankers!)

Iceland Symphony Orchestra   LIVE MUSIC
(Map p252; ☑545 2500; www.sinfonia.is; Háskólabíó, Hagatorg) The orchestra is due to relocate to the flashy new Harpa: Reykjavík Concert Hall & Conference Centre (http://en.harpa.is) in 2011. There are around 60 classical performances per season, normally on Thursday at 7.30pm.

Iceland Airwaves   MUSIC FESTIVAL
(www.icelandairwaves.com) This five-day festival rocks the city in October.

Shopping

Laugavegur is the main shopping street; Austurstræti and Hafnarstræti contain tourist stores selling puffin-decorated trinkets. Skólavörðustígur sells arty-crafty one-offs.

Handknitting Association of Iceland   HANDICRAFTS
(Map p256; www.handknit.is; Skólavörðustígur 19) Traditional handmade hats, socks and sweaters are on sale here...or buy yarn and knitting patterns, and do it yourself.

Kolaportið Flea Market   MARKET
(Map p256; Geirsgata; ☺11am-5pm Sat & Sun) Rummage through a pleasing tangle of secondhand goods; or try *hákarl* (rotten shark meat) from the fish market if you're brave enough.

Kraum   DESIGN
(Map p256; www.kraum.is; Aðalstræti 10) Beautiful contemporary creations – think fish-skin clothing, silver jewellery, driftwood furniture and ceramic seabirds – fills two storeys of Reykjavík's oldest house.

12 Tónar   MUSIC
(Map p256; www.12tonar.is; Skólavörðustígur 15) For cutting-edge Icelandic tunes, try this hip record shop, with three floors of music and its own recording label. Smaller and edgier is Smekkleysa (Map p256; www.smekkleysa.is; Laugavegur 59), the Sugarcubes' original label.

Eymundsson   BOOKS
(Map p256; Skólavörðustígur 11 & Austurstræti 18; ☺9am-10pm Mon-Fri, 10am-10pm Sat & Sun) Superb choice of English-language books, newspapers, magazines and maps.

Kringlan   SHOPPING CENTRE
(Map p252; www.kringlan.is; Kringlan 4-12) This big shopping mall just outside the city centre also contains a cinema and a Vín Búð.

ℹ Information

Emergency
☑112 for police, ambulance and fire services.

Internet Access
Libraries have the cheapest internet access (Ikr250 per hour).
Aðalbókasafn (Reykjavík City Library; Map p256; www.borgarbokasafn.is; Tryggvagata 15; ☺10am-7pm Mon-Thu, 11am-7pm Fri, 1-5pm Sat & Sun)
G-Zero (Frakkastígur 8; per 15/35/60min Ikr200/350/500; ☺11am-1am Mon-Fri, noon-1am Sat & Sun) A dedicated internet cafe full of game-playing teenagers.

Medical Services
Landspítali University Hospital (☑543 2000; Fossvogur) 24-hour casualty department.
Dentist on duty (☑575 0505)
Health Centre (☑585 2600; Vesturgata 7) Doctor appointments for visitors from Europe cost Ikr2600, for non-Europeans Ikr8000.
Læknavaktin (☑1770) Non-emergency telephone advice between 5pm and 11.30pm.
Lyfja Apótek (☑552 4045; Laugavegur 16; ☺9am-6pm Mon-Fri, 11am-4pm Sat) Central pharmacy.
Lyfja Apótek (☑533 2300; Lágmúli 5; ☺7am-1am) Late-night pharmacy, near the Hilton Reykjavík Nordica Hotel. Take bus S2, 15, 17 or 19.

Money
Commission is high on foreign currency exchange at hotels. There are central branches of all three major Icelandic banks, with ATMs taking MasterCard, Visa, Cirrus, Maestro and Electron cards.
Arion banki (www.arionbanki.is; Austurstræti 5)
Íslandsbanki (www.islandsbanki.is; Lækjargata 12)
Landsbanki Íslands (www.landsbanki.is; Austurstræti 11)

Post
Main post office (Map p256; Pósthússtræti 5; ☺9am-6pm Mon-Fri)

Telephone
Public phones are elusive in mobile-crazy Reykjavík: try the main tourist office, the street opposite Laugavegur 38 and the Kringlan shopping centre.

Tourist Information
Reykjavík has a helpful main tourist office with a booking service. There are satellite tourist desks at the bus terminal and city hall. There are several private offices in the city. Pick up the free booklets *Reykjavík This Month* and *What's On in Reykjavík* for events in the capital. The irreverent English-language newspaper *Grapevine* is widely distributed and has the low-down on what's new in town.

BSÍ bus terminal tourist desk (Map p252; Vatnsmýrarvegur 10)

Main tourist office (Upplýsingamiðstöð Ferðamanna; Map p256; ✆590 1550; www. visitreykjavik.is; Aðalstræti 2; ⏰8.30am-7pm Jun–mid-Sep, 9am-6pm Mon-Fri, to 4pm Sat, to 2pm Sun mid-Sep–May)

Raðhús tourist information desk (Map p256; Tjarnargata 11; ⏰8.30am-4.30pm Mon-Fri, noon-4pm Sat & Sun, closed Sun mid-Sep–mid-May) Inside city hall.

ℹ Getting There & Away

Air

The city airport, Innanlandsflug, serves all domestic destinations, the Faroe Islands and Greenland. Internal flight operator **Flugfélag Íslands** (Air Iceland; ✆570 3030; www.airiceland.is) has a desk here, but internet bookings are cheaper.

International flights operate through **Keflavík airport** (www.keflavikairport.com), 48km west of Reykjavík.

Bus

There are scheduled summer services to other parts of the country from Reykjavík's **BSÍ bus terminal** (Map p252; ✆562 1011; www.bsi.is; Vatnsmýrarvegur 10); winter services are reduced or nonexistent.

To get from Reykjavík to Egilsstaðir (Ikr17,700 or Ikr19,100) involves an overnight stay in Akureyri or Höfn. Daily in summer (Sunday to Friday in winter), it's possible to get to Húsavík (Ikr13,200) in one day, changing in Akureyri. You'll need to break your journey in Akureyri on the way to Mývatn (Ikr13,500).

For Stykkishólmur (Ikr4900, 2½ hours, seven buses per week, daily in July & August), change in Vatnaleið.

ℹ Getting Around

To/From the Airport

It's a 1km walk into town from the city airport terminal (domestic flights), or there's a taxi rank.

The **Flybus** (✆580 5400; www.re.is) to/from Keflavík airport meets all international flights. Buy tickets online before you leave home, or from the machines or ticket booth just inside the airport doors (credit cards accepted). The bus leaves the BSÍ bus terminal two hours before international departures. The hostels and many guesthouses and hotels can arrange transfers to the bus station.

Taxis to/from Keflavík airport cost around Ikr13,500 one way, depending on time of day.

Bicycle

Borgarhjól SF (www.borgarhjol.net; Hverfisgata 50; 4hr/half-day/24hr Ikr2600/3600/4200; ⏰8am-6pm Mon-Fri, 10am-2pm Sat) Bicycle hire (also available from Reykjavík City Hostel and the camping ground).

Bus

Reykjavík's superb **city bus system** (www.straeto.is/english) uses two central terminals: Hlemmur (Map p252) and Lækjartorg (Map p256). Buses only stop at designated bus stops, marked with the letter 'S'.

Fare Adult/6-18yrs Ikr280/100 (exact fare only)

Day buses Run 7am to 11pm or midnight (from 10am Sunday)

BUSES FROM REYKJAVÍK

DESTINATION	DURATION	FREQUENCY	PRICE (IKR, ONE WAY)
Akureyri	6hr	1-2 daily yr-round	10,400
Blue Lagoon	45min	At least 9 daily yr-round	1600
Geysir/Gullfoss	3hr	1-2 daily mid-May–mid-Sep	7200 (return)
Höfn	9hr	1 daily mid-May–mid-Sep, 3 per wk mid-Sep–mid-May	12,200
Landeyjahöfn Harbour (for ferry to Vestmannaeyjar)	2hr	1-2 daily yr-round	3100
Reykholt	2hr	Fri & Sun yr-round	3100
Skaftafell	6½hr	Daily mid-May–mid-Sep, bus (3 per week) stops at Freysnes rest of yr	8900
Þórsmörk	3½hr	1-2 daily mid-Jun–early Sep	5800

FLYBUSES

FLYBUS TICKETS	DESTINATION	PRICE (IKR)	DURATION
Flybus (one way)	BSÍ bus terminal	Adult/12-15yrs 1950/950	50min
Flybus Plus (one way)	Hotel drop-off	Adult/12-15yrs 2500/1250	1–1½hr

Night buses Run until 2am Friday and Saturday

Transfer tickets (*Skiptimiði*) Available from driver if you need two buses to reach your destination.

Reykjavík Welcome Card Includes a bus pass.

Taxi

Taxi prices are high; flag fall starts at around Ikr500. There are usually taxis outside the bus stations, domestic airport, youth hostel, and pubs and bars on weekend nights. Alternatively, call **Borgarbíll** (☑552 2440), **BSR** (☑561 0000) or **Hreyfill-Bæjarleiðir** (☑588 5522). Tipping is not expected.

AROUND REYKJAVÍK

Blue Lagoon

As the Eiffel Tower is to Paris, as Disney World is to Florida, so the **Blue Lagoon** (Bláa Lónið; www.bluelagoon.is; adult/14-15yr Ikr4500/1150, towel/swimsuit/robe hire Ikr800/800/1450, spa treatments from Ikr2250; ⊙9am-9pm Jun-Aug, 10am-8pm Sep-May) is to Iceland...with all the positive and negative connotations that implies. Those who say it's too expensive, too clinical, too crowded are kind of right, but ignore them anyway. The Blue Lagoon is a must see, and you'll be missing something special if you don't go.

Set in a vast black lava field, the milky-blue spa is fed by water (a perfect 38°C, and at Blue Flag standards) from the futuristic Svartsengi geothermal plant, which provides an off-the-planet scene-setter for your swim. Add in steaming silver vents and people coated in silica mud, and you're in another world.

Be careful on the slippery bridges and bring plenty of conditioner for your hair. There's a snack bar, top gourmet restaurant and souvenir shop on site, plus roaming masseurs.

The lagoon is 50km southwest of Reykjavík. Between 10am and 6pm daily year-round, there are nine **Reykjavík Excursions** (☑580 5400; www.re.is) buses from the BSÍ bus terminal (or from your hotel on request). The Ikr6300 cost includes lagoon admission and return fare to Reykjavík (or onward journey to Keflavík airport).

The Golden Circle

Gulp down three of Iceland's most famous natural wonders – Gullfoss, Geysir and Þingvellir – in one day-long circular tour.

⊙ Sights

Gullfoss (Golden Falls) is a spectacular rainbow-tinged double cascade, falling 32m before thundering down a narrow ravine.

All spouting hot springs are named after **Geysir**, 10km away. Tourists clogged the **Great Geysir** in the 1950s with rocks and rubbish, thrown in an attempt to set it off. Since earthquakes in 2000, it has begun erupting again a few times daily. Nearby, the world's most reliable geyser, **Strokkur** (Butter Churn), spouts every six minutes into an impressive 15m to 30m plume.

Þingvellir National Park is Iceland's most important historical site: the Vikings established the world's first democratic parliament, the Alþing, here in AD 930. It also has a superb natural setting, on the edge of an immense rift caused by the separating North American and Eurasian tectonic plates. Þingvellir was (finally!) made a Unesco World Heritage site in 2004. Above the park, on top of the rift, is an interesting **multimedia centre** (admission free; ⊙9am-4pm Apr-Oct) exploring the area's nature and history.

Interesting features, concentrated in a small area of the park, include **Lögberg** (marked by a flagpole), the podium for the Alþing; the remains of **búðir** (booths) where Vikings attending Alþing camped; a **church** and **farm**, now the president's summer house; **Drekkingarhylur**, where adulterous women were drowned; **Þingvallavatn**, Iceland's largest lake; and several fissures, including **Peningagjá** (wishing spring), **Flosagjá** (named after a slave who jumped his way to freedom) and **Nikulásargjá** (after a drunken sheriff discovered dead in the water).

🛏 Sleeping & Eating

There is a discreet cafe (⊙approximately 9am-5pm winter, to 8pm summer) at each of the three sites.

Hótel Geysir   HOTEL €€
(☑480 6800; www.geysircenter.is; Haukadalur; s/d Ikr17,000/21,000; ⊙Apr-Sep; P⧉) Accommodation is in spick, span and tasteful alpine-style cabins. The hotel can also arrange summer horse riding, including day trips to Gullfoss (Ikr13,500). The hotel also has a **camping ground** (per person Ikr1000); generously, campers can use the hotel's hot tub and pool for free.

Hótel Gullfoss   HOTEL €€
(☑486 8979; www.hotelgullfoss.is; Brattholt; s/d/tr Ikr15,000/18,500/25,000; ⊙mid-May–Sep, bookings necessary Oct–mid-May) A few kilometres before the waterfall, tucked into a crevice in the hills, is this simple bungalow hotel with modest en suite rooms, two hot pots and a good restaurant.

Þingvellir camping grounds   CAMPING GROUND €
(☑482 2660; campsites per adult Ikr1000) The Park Service Centre oversees five camping grounds at Þingvellir. The best are those around Leirar (near the centre).

❶ Information

Just by the turnoff to Þingvellir, the Park Service Centre contains a cafe and **seasonal tourist desk** (☑482 2660; www.thingvellir.is; ⊙8.30am-8pm Jun-Aug, 9am-4pm May & Sep, to 4pm Sat & Sun Oct-Apr).

❶ Getting There & Away

Golden Circle day tours from Reykjavík cost around Ikr10,000 (without lunch). Tour operators include **Reykjavík Excursions** (☑580 5400; www.re.is) and **Iceland Excursions**

(☑540 1313; www.grayline.is); you're usually picked up from your accommodation.

From mid-May to mid-September, scheduled buses run at 8.30am from the BSÍ bus station to Geysir (Ikr3700) and Gullfoss (Ikr4000). From mid-June to mid-September, a second service leaving at 8am also swings by Þingvellir.

Hafnarfjörður

POP 25,900

The 'Town in the Lava' rests on a 7000-year-old flow and hides a parallel elfin universe, according to locals. It's worth a quick summer jaunt. The dynamic **tourist office** (☑585 5500; www.visithafnarfjordur.is; Strandgata 6; ⊙8am-4pm Mon-Fri) is inside the town hall.

⊙ Sights & Activities

FREE **Hafnarfjörður Museum**   MUSEUM
(☑585 5780) Hafnarfjörður Museum is spread across several historic buildings in different locations across the town. **Pakkhúsið** (Vesturgata 8; ⊙11am-5pm daily Jun-Aug, to 5pm Sat & Sun Sep-May) is the main section, with interesting displays on the town's history. **Sívertsen Hús** (Vesturgata 6; ⊙11am-5pm Jun-Aug) is an upper-class 19th-century house. At the other end of the social scale is **Siggubær** (Sigga's House; Kirkjuvegur 10; ⊙11am-5pm Sat & Sun Jun-Aug), a restored fisherman's hut.

FREE **Hafnarborg**   ART GALLERY
(☑585 5790; www.hafnarborg.is; Strandgata 34; ⊙noon-5pm Wed-Mon, to 9pm Thu) Well worth a look, this upbeat modern-art gallery has two floors of regularly changing exhibitions and occasional musical concerts.

🎎 Festivals & Events

In mid-June, the peace is shattered as Vikings invade the town for the four-day **Viking Festival**, with staged fights and traditional craft demonstrations.

WORTH A TRIP

GLJÚFRASTEINN LAXNESS MUSEUM

On the way to Þingvellir via Rte 36, literature fans should drop in on the **Gljúfrasteinn Laxness Museum** (☑586 8066; www.gljufrasteinn.is; Mosfellsbær; adult/under 16yrs Ikr800/free; ⊙9am-5pm Jun-Aug, 10am-5pm Tue-Sun Sep-May), former home of Nobel Prize–winning author Halldór Laxness (1902–98). Highlights include the study where Laxness wrote his defining works and the author's beloved Jaguar parked outside (making three-point turns in the car park a nerve-wracking experience!).

From June to August, Sunday music recitals (Ikr1000; 4pm) provide an additional reason to drop by. You'll need your own transport to get here.

WORTH A TRIP

STOKKSEYRI

If you like screaming, it might be worth detouring to tiny Stokkseyri, 60km east of Reykjavík. Creep round 24 dark, dry ice-filled rooms at the Ghost Centre (Draugasetrið; ☎483 1202; www.draugasetrid.is; Hafnargata 9; adult/12-16yr Ikr1500/990; ⊙1-6pm summer) while a 40-minute CD-guide (in English, French or German) tells blood-curdling Icelandic ghost stories. Be warned, it's not for the faint-hearted. Suitable for over-12s.

There's fine dining to be had next door at Við Fjöruborðið (☎483 1550; Eyrarbraut 3a; mains Ikr3000-5000; ⊙5-9pm Mon-Thu, to 10pm Fri, noon-9pm Sat & Sun, closed Mon & Tue winter), a seashore restaurant renowned for its lobster dishes.

❶ Getting There & Away

Hafnarfjörður is a short, easy bus trip from Reykjavík: take bus S1 (Ikr280, 30 minutes, every 15 to 30 minutes) from Hlemmur or Lækjartorg bus stations. The **Flybus** (☎580 5400) to/from Keflavík airport also stops for reserved passengers

Krýsuvík

For a taste of Iceland's weird countryside, Krýsuvík, an abandoned village and volatile geothermal area, makes a fascinating day trip. The area lies about 20km south of Hafnarfjörður; you'll need your own transport or to join a tour. At Seltún, boardwalks meander round eggy-smelling, rainbow-coloured steaming vents, mudpots and solfataras (volcanic steam vents), where the ground temperature reaches about 200°C.

Just down the road is Kleifarvatn, a creepy 1km-deep lake surrounded by volcanic cinders. It's said to be inhabited by a wormlike monster the size of a whale.

The nearby coast is a bleak stretch of seabird cliffs and black beaches. Dozens of hiking tracks criss-cross through this barren area.

THE WEST

Upper Borgarfjörður

A must for saga fans, the lakes and lava flows of this region feature in *Egil's Saga,* and its author, Snorri Sturluson, lived here. Upper Borgarfjörður is 90km north of Reykjavík.

REYKHOLT
POP 40

You'd never guess it, but tiny Reykholt (www.reykholt.is), 22km east of the Ring Rd, was once a political and religious power centre. During the bloodthirsty Sturlung Age

(1230–62), it was the home of Snorri Sturluson, Iceland's greatest saga writer, historian and social climber. Close to the cellar where he was eventually murdered you can see his circular medieval hot tub, Snorri's Pool (Snorralaug). The museum Heimskringla (www.snorrastofa.is; Reykholt; admission Ikr700; ⊙10am-6pm May-Sep, to 5pm Mon-Fri Oct-Apr) explores Snorri's fascinating life.

Sleeping and eating options are limited, but Fosshótel Reykholt (☎435 1260; www.fosshotel.is; Reykholt; s/d Ikr22,000/24,000; [P][@]) has large rooms, hot tubs and a restaurant.

Buses run from Reykjavík to Reykholt (via Deildartunguhver) on Friday and Sunday at 5pm (Ikr3100, two hours). You'll need private transport for Hraunfossar and Barnafoss.

AROUND REYKHOLT

Deildartunguhver, 4km west of Reykholt, is Europe's most powerful, prolific and pongy hot spring, spouting out at 180L per second. About 18km northeast of Reykholt is Hraunfossar, a 1km-long stretch of 'magic waterfalls' mysteriously emerging from beneath a lava flow. Just upstream is Barnafoss, where the Hvítá river thunders through a narrow gorge. According to legend, two children drowned here when a natural bridge collapsed.

Snæfellsnes

[Cue *Twilight Zone* music...] The peninsula is a magnet for UFOs and New Age believers swearing that Snæfellsjökull (1446m) emits a healing aura. It's certainly atmospheric – shadowy mountains, twisting lava flows, tiny fishing villages and scattered farmhouses all sit under the shadow of the glacier. The whole of the peninsula's tip is a national park.

Jules Verne used Snæfell as the gateway to the underworld in *Journey to the Centre of the Earth,* and fragments of the 2008 movie of the same name were filmed here.

STYKKISHÓLMUR

POP 1090

Quaint coastal Stykkishólmur is the largest village in Snæfellsnes, overlooked by a striking church. It makes a serene base for boat trips, horse riding, kayaking or birdwatching. It's also a picturesque shortcut to the Westfjords – car ferries run via Flatey, an island with 19th-century buildings.

The summer-only tourist office (☑433 8120; www.westiceland.is; Borgarbraut; ⊙7am-10pm Mon-Fri, 10am-7pm Sat & Sun Jun-Aug) is inside the swimming pool and sports centre; at other times, consult the knowledgeable staff at the harbourside Sæferðir shop.

◉ Sights & Activities

Súgandisey VIEWPOINT

There are admirable views of Breiðafjörður from Súgandisey, a basalt islet that shelters the picturesque harbour. The shallow waters and myriad islands make the bay a birdwatcher's delight – keep your eyes peeled for Iceland's 'bird king', the white-tailed sea eagle.

Norwegian House MUSEUM

(norskhus@simnet.is; Hafnargata 5; adult/6-16yr lkr500/300; ⊙11am-5pm Jun-Aug) The town's oldest building, it's one of the places William Morris stayed on his 1871 tour of Iceland. Today it contains a sweet little museum and art gallery.

Volcano Museum ART GALLERY

(www.eldfjallasafn.is; Aðalgata 8; adult/under 16yr lkr500/free; ⊙11am-5pm May-Sep) This strange 'museum' is actually the private art collection of vulcanologist Professor Haraldur Sigurðsson, with original works depicting volcanoes not just from Iceland but around the world. Upstairs a large TV shows several fascinating eruption-focused documentaries – maybe one for a rainy day?

ⳤ Tours

Sæferðir BOAT TRIPS

(Seatours; ☑433 2254; www.seatours.is; Smiðjustígur 3; adult lkr6000; ⊙9am-8pm Jun-Aug, 8am-4pm Mon-Fri Sep-May) Sæferðir operates a very popular nature-watching (and eating!) boat trip around the bay. Between June and August, it can help arrange other activities on the peninsula, including horse treks, snowmobiling, kayaking and visits to the nearby farm Bjarnarhöfn to see shark meat being cured.

🛏 Sleeping & Eating

Sjónarhóll Hostel HOSTEL €

(☑861 2517, 438 1417; Höfðagata 1; sleeping bag in dm lkr2500, d lkr6900; ⊙May-Oct; ℗) The dorm rooms in this charming (if rickety) hostel have fantastic views of the harbour. You can also catch fish on its Breiðafjörður boat tours, then barbecue them on the patio.

Hótel Breiðafjörður HOTEL €

(☑433 2200; www.hotelbreidafjordur.is; Aðalgata 8; s/d lkr10,000/16,000; ℗@) The more central of Stykkishólmur's two hotels is this small, friendly, family-run, guesthouse-style place. It offers bright, spacious rooms with modern furniture, neutral decor and new fittings. Breakfast and a free game of golf are included in the price!

Narfeyrarstofa CAFE €€

(Aðalgata 3; mains lkr2500-3500; ⊙11am-11pm Sun-Thu, to 1am Fri & Sat summer, shorter hr winter) This cosy old cafe/bar/restaurant is the best place in town for coffee and cake or a relaxed meal: the varied menu offers hamburgers, soup, fresh mussels, local lamb dishes, catch of the day and one vegie option. In summer demand far outstrips supply and competition for tables is brutal.

DON'T MISS

SETTLEMENT CENTRE, BORGARNES

You could easily zip straight through the elongated settlement of **Borgarnes** without realising you were missing something special. The **Settlement Centre** (Landnámssetur Íslands; www.landnam.is; Brákarbraut 13-15; adult/6-14yrs for one exhibition lkr1800/1400, for both lkr2400/1800; ⊙11am-9pm Jun-Sep, to 5pm Oct-May) comprises two excellent multimedia exhibitions: one covers the settlement of Iceland, and the other recounts the most dramatic parts of *Egil's Saga*, bringing the violent Viking to life with unusual sculptures, lighting and sound effects.

The centre's restaurant, **Búðarklettur** (☑437 1600; mains lkr2000-3500; ⊙10am-9pm), housed in the town's oldest building, is a stylish choice for morning coffee or a more substantial meal, with plenty of traditional Icelandic eats and a good vegie selection.

TROLL TROUBLE

The breathtaking sight of Breiðafjörður's 2700(ish) islands inspired a legend. Three misanthropic trolls decided to separate the Westfjords from the rest of Iceland. All night, they hacked away huge lumps of earth and hurled the pieces into the nearby fjord. The task was so engrossing that they didn't notice the growing light. As the sun touched them, the two male trolls turned instantly to stone. The trollette almost made it home, when she suddenly remembered that she'd left her cow grazing on Grímsey. Stopping to look at it, both she and Daisy came to a rocky end.

Fimm Fiskar   SEAFOOD **€€**
(Frúarstígur 1; mains Ikr2500-3500; ☉11.30am-9.30pm) The other restaurant in town is a less atmospheric spot but makes up for a plain layout with some tasty fish dishes: langoustines dripping with garlic butter, pan-fried plaice, morsels of catfish...and anything else fresh from the fishing boats on the day.

Camping ground   CAMPING GROUND **€**
(☎438 1075; mostri@stykk.is; campsites per person Ikr800) A huge but rather exposed spot on the way into town. Facilities include a laundry.

Bakery   BAKERY **€**
(Nesvegur 1; ☉8.30am-6pm Mon-Fri, 8am-4pm Sat) This sit-down bakery is opposite the camping ground.

❶ Getting There & Away

From June to August, at least one bus plies daily between Reykjavík and Stykkishólmur (Ikr4900, 2½ hours), with a change to a connecting bus in Vatnaleið. No Wednesday or Saturday service in winter.

The ferry **Baldur** (☎433 2254; www.seatours.is; Smiðjustígur 3, Stykkishólmur) operates between Stykkishólmur and Brjánslækur (one way per car/passenger Ikr3950/3950, three hours). Advance booking strongly advised.

DEPART	EARLY JUN–LATE AUG	LATE AUG–EARLY JUN
Stykkishólmur	9am & 3.45pm	3pm Sun-Fri
Brjánslækur	12.15pm & 7pm	6pm Sun-Fri

SNÆFELLSJÖKULL NATIONAL PARK & AROUND

The volcano Snæfell, at the tip of the peninsula, is the heart of Snæfellsjökull National Park. Its glacial summit can be reached when conditions are right: the easiest approach is from the southern end of Rte F570, linking up with one of the **snowmobile tours** run by Snjófell (☎435 6783; www.snjofell.is; Arnarstapi; solo/2-person skidoo ride Ikr15,500/21,000).

Rte F570's northern approach from Ólafsvík is 4WD-only. Park rangers at the visitor centre in Hellnar can provide on-the-spot information, including weather forecasts.

ÓLAFSVÍK
POP 1010

As a base, Stykkishólmur has the best facilities, but Ólafsvík is much closer to the park. It has a sheltered **camping ground** (☎433 9930; campsites per adult/tent Ikr500/500; ☉Jun-Aug) 1km east of the village. Central **Hringhótel Ólafsvík** (☎436 1650; www.hotelolafsvik.is; Ólafsbraut 40; s/d Ikr19,000/22,600; ☉Mar-Oct; ❷) is rather spartan. If you don't mind sharing a bathroom, prices fall by almost 50%.

Eating options in Ólafsvík are limited. The hotel has a rather overpriced restaurant; otherwise there's a fast-food joint and a bakery.

HELLNAR

The spirit of the glacier, Bárður, once lived at tiny Hellnar, 6km outside the main park boundary on the south coast. He couldn't have chosen a more idyllic spot. The park's **visitor centre** (☎436 6888; ☉10am-6pm mid-May–early Sep) and a small cafe overlook a bay in a deep, narrow cleft between hills, echoing with the shrieks of seabirds. Up the hill stands Iceland's only eco-hotel, **Hótel Hellnar** (☎435 6820; www.hellnar.is; s/d with sea view Ikr21,400/24,500, with mountain view Ikr19,100/22,200; ☉mid-May–mid-Sep; ℗). Its twin-bedded rooms are clean, bright and monastically simple, the restaurant uses local organic produce and the guest lounge has marvellous sea views. It's quite common to see whales from the window.

THE WESTFJORDS

The remote Westfjords once had a fearsome reputation for witchcraft, and its abandoned villages, crying seabirds and wild Arctic foxes still cast a haunting spell. A dirt road winds down the edge of a lonely peninsula to Látrabjarg, justly famous for its towering cliffs thick with birdlife. Hornstrandir, accessible only in high summer by boat, is a walker's dream – you could lose yourself for days in its craggy mountains. And the sheer tranquillity of end-of-the-earth-town Ísafjörður might make you question ever returning to the hustle of a city.

Buses to, from and around the Westfjords are patchy and usually only possible in high season. Stjörnubílar (☑456 5518; www.stjornu bilar.is) runs local buses in this region.

Ísafjörður

POP 2680

You feel as though you've reached the end of the earth when you get to Ísafjörður, the Westfjord's largest settlement. Surrounded by vertiginous mountains and deep fjord waters, the town is remote and peaceful, apart from the croaking of ravens.

⊙ Sights

Westfjords Heritage Museum MUSEUM
(www.nedsti.is; Neðstíkaupstaður; adult/under 16yr Ikr550/free; ⊙9am-6pm mid-May–mid-Sep) The knowledgeable staff at the Westfjords Heritage Museum, based in two atmospheric 18th-century wooden warehouses, bring the excellent nautical, whaling and accordion exhibits to life.

⌲ Tours

Ísafjörður itself is a comely but quiet town; but it does make an excellent base for a range of unusual tours available in the surrounding fjords and valleys. Ask the tourist office for detailed **walking** maps.

Westfjords Tours BOAT TRIPS
(Vesturferðir; ☑456 5111; www.vesturferdir.is; Aðalstræti 7; ⊙10am-6pm Mon-Fri) Westfjords Tours specialises in Hornstrandir visits, including a four-hour trip to the abandoned village **Hesteyri** (Ikr7300; ⊙2pm Wed, Fri & Sun, mid-Jun–late Aug). The company also does boat rides to Vigur island, birdwatching tours, fox-watching tours and various cultural excursions. It can also arrange 2½-hour **kayaking** (Ikr7500) sessions in the bay and it hires out **bicycles** (per day Ikr3500).

Borea Adventures ADVENTURE ACTIVITIES
(☑899 3817, 869 7557; www.boreaadventures. com; Hlíðarvegur 38) A new operator offering sea kayaking; fox-watching tours; adventurous multiday yachting trips; journeys to Greenland, Svalbard and Jan Mayen; and winter skiing camps.

ᩃᩬᩊ Festivals & Events

Ísafjörður's usual tranquillity is crumpled up and hurled away in the week after Easter, when the town gears up for two hugely important celebrations: Aldrei Fór Ég Suður and Skíðavikan.

[FREE] **Aldrei Fór Ég Suður** MUSIC
(I Never Went South; www.aldrei.is) Two-day music festival, dreamed up by Ísafjörður-born singer-songwriter Mugison (although the future of the festival was in some doubt at the time of writing).

Skíðavikan SKIING
(Skiing Week; www.skidavikan.is) Annual skiing festival.

Mýrarbolti SOCCER
(www.myrarbolti.com) On the August bank holiday comes the Mýrarbolti tournament, an indescribably filthy day of swamp soccer. Visitors can abandon their sanity too, and register to join a team.

ᩃ Sleeping

[TOP CHOICE] **Gamla Gistihúsið** GUESTHOUSE €€
(☑456 4146; www.gistihus.is; Mánagata 5; sleeping bag in dm from Ikr3300, s/d Ikr9500/13,100; @) This former hospital and old-people's home is a tonic, with sunlight dappling through the windows and homely touches everywhere. The nine neat rooms (with plentiful shared bathrooms) all come with TV, plus there's a guest kitchen and free internet access. Breakfast is Ikr1200 for those in sleeping-bag accommodation.

Hótel Ísafjörður HOTEL €€€
(☑456 4111; www.hotelisafjordur.is; Silfurtorg 2; s/d from Ikr19,500/24,000) On the main square, the town's only hotel is right at the hub of things. Rooms are clean and businesslike – it's worth paying extra for the larger deluxe versions, which come with fine views and bathtubs. Its **Við Pollinn restaurant** (lunch set menu Ikr 2300, mains from Ikr 3000; ⊙breakfast, lunch & dinner) does great grub, and has huge picture windows looking out onto the water.

Hotel Edda SUMMER HOTEL €
(☑444 4960; www.hoteledda.is; sleeping bag in dm from Ikr2100, s/d from Ikr8000/10,000; ⊙mid-Jun–mid-Aug) This is a no-frills summer option, run by Hótel Ísafjörður in the secondary school. Sleeping-bag accommodation is in classrooms, or you can upgrade to a private room.

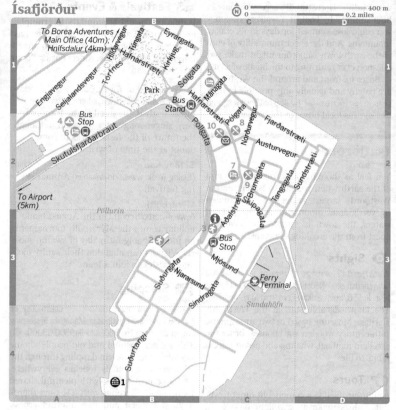

Ísafjörður

Camping ground   CAMPING GROUND €
(☎444 4960; campsites per adult plus tent
Ikr1000; ☉mid-Jun–mid-Aug) Centrally located
behind the secondary school.

✗ Eating

Ísafjörður's eating places seem to be under
a curse – no sooner does a new cafe or restaurant open than it shuts down again. As
we were going to press, news reached us
that the town's two cafe-bars, thriving this
summer, had both closed down. Try the Ed-
inborg cultural centre (where the tourist office is based) to see if a new establishment
has installed itself; otherwise you're left with
few options, including the hotel restaurant
or pizzas and hot dogs from the sweetshop
Hamraborg.

Thai Koon   THAI €
(Hafnarstræti 9; ☉11.30am-9pm Mon-Sat, 5-9pm
Sun) Tiny but popular takeaway in the
shopping centre.

Bakarinn BAKERY €
(Hafnarstræti; ⊘7.30am-6pm Mon-Fri, 9am-
5.30pm Sun) Great for cheap lunches.

Gamla Bakaríð BAKERY €
(Aðalstræti; ⊘7am-6pm Mon-Fri, to 4pm Sat)
Great for cheap lunches of soup, sand-
wiches, pastries and chocolate frogs.

❶ Information

Library (www.isafjordur.is/bokasafn; Eyrartúni;
per hr Ikr200; ⊘1-7pm Mon-Fri, to 4pm Sat)
Internet access is available in the fine library,
once the town's hospital.
Post office (Hafnarstræti 9)
Tourist office (☑450 8060; www.vestfirdir.is;
Aðalstræti 7; ⊘8.30am-6pm Mon-Fri, 11am-
4pm Sat & Sun Jun-Aug, shorter hr in winter)

❶ Getting There & Away

Air

There are twice-daily flights between Reykjavík
and Ísafjörður (Ikr14,900) with **Flugfélag Íslands** (☑570 3030; www.airiceland.is).

Bus

There are two ways of travelling from Reykjavík
to Ísafjörður by bus. One service, via Staðarskáli
and Hólmavík, runs on Tuesday, Friday and Sunday. The second service, via the Stykkishólmur–
Brjánslækur ferry (p272), runs on Monday,
Wednesday and Saturday.

If you're travelling via Staðarskáli and Hólmavík,
you'll need to catch the 8.30am bus from Reykjavík, eventually arriving in Ísafjörður (with luck
and a following wind) at 6pm. The price for this
journey is Ikr13,100, but it makes better sense
to buy a West Iceland & Westfjords bus passport
(see p310 for details).

If you're travelling via the Stykkishólmur–
Brjánslækur ferry, there is a daily bus in summer
that leaves Reykjavík at 8am and arrives in Stykkishólmur at 10.35am.

On the other side of the water, buses meet
both ferry services to Brjánslækur on Monday,
Wednesday and Saturday. The first bus runs to
Ísafjörður (Ikr4000) via Látrabjarg, allowing 1¾
hours at the cliffs; the second bus drives direct
to Ísafjörður. In reverse, buses leave Ísafjörður at
9am Monday, Wednesday and Saturday.

If you want to travel between Ísafjörður and
Akureyri, you'll also need to change in Hólmavík
and Staðarskáli.

Hornstrandir Peninsula

The wildest corner of the Westfjords has
a poignant history: its elderly inhabitants,
left behind with no electricity, roads or telephones, made a collective decision to abandon the peninsula in the 1950s. It's now a
spectacular nature reserve, which solitary
hikers share only with seabirds and Arctic
foxes.

The peninsula is accessible by boat from
Ísafjörður, with one-way fares around
Ikr5500; advance booking strongly recommended – contact the Ísafjörður tourist office for details. There's basic sleeping-bag
accommodation at Hesteyri (☑456 1123, 853
5034, 845 5075; info@hesteyri.net; sleeping bag
Ikr4000; ⊘10 Jun–20 Aug) in four rooms with
kitchen access.

Látrabjarg

The world's biggest bird breeding grounds
are the towering, 14km-long Látrabjarg cliffs.
Fulmars, kittiwakes and fearless puffins fight
for nesting space at the westernmost point of
the Westfjords. It's a truly impressive sight,
but wrap up well; the wind is bitter.

For accommodation, try the beautifully located working farm Breiðavík (☑456 1575; bre
idavik@patro.is; campsites per adult Ikr1500, sleeping
bag in dm Ikr4500, s/d from Ikr9000/12,000; ⊘mid-
May–mid-Sep), on a golden beach 12km from
the cliffs. Nondorm rooms are in a new mini-
hotel extension; it's functional from the outside, but pleasant inside. You can also pitch
tents in a neighbouring field.

THE NORTH

Siglufjörður
POP 1220

Iceland's northernmost town enjoys a dramatic setting at the very tip of the Tröllas-
kagi Peninsula. In the past, herring fishing
brought frenzied activity and untold riches;
today the town's appeal is its peaceful isolation and thrumming community spirit. The
roller-coasting coastal road currently stops
at Siglufjörður, although two new tunnels
(work in progress) will make the town more
accessible.

◉ Sights

Herring Era Museum of Iceland MUSEUM
(Síldarminjasafn Íslands; ☑467 1604; www.
sild.is; Snorragata 15; adult/16-20yr/under 16yr
Ikr1200/600/free; ⊘10am-6pm mid-Jun–mid-Aug,
1-5pm early Jun & mid-Aug–mid-Sep) Lovingly

created over 16 years, this award-winning museum does a stunning job of re-creating Siglufjörður's boom days. Follow the herrings' journey through three harbourside buildings: the full-size night-time harbour; the salting station Roaldsbrakki, looking as though the herring workers have just left; and the fishmeal- and oil-processing plant, with its huge machinery. The museum also functions as the tourist information centre, and as a theatre and music venue in high summer.

Icelandic Folk Music Centre MUSEUM
(Þjóðlagasetur Sr Bjarna Þorsteinssonar; www. siglo.is/setur; Norðurgata 1; admission incl in Herring Museum ticket; ◷10am-6pm mid-Jun–mid-Aug, 1-5pm early Jun & mid-Aug–mid-Sep) Traditional music enthusiasts may be interested in this little museum, which displays 19th-century instruments and offers recordings of Icelandic songs and chants.

✦ Festivals

Herring Adventure Festival CULTURE
Siglufjörður's biggest shindig, this lively festival takes place on the August bank holiday and recreates the gold-rush atmosphere of the town's glory days.

Þjóðlagahátíðin á Siglufirði MUSIC
Folk-music fans will enjoy this festival, a delightfully relaxed five-day affair held in early July.

🛏 Sleeping & Eating

The little camping ground (per person Ikr700; ◷Jun-Aug) is situated right by the town square, and has a toilet block and laundry.

Siglufjörður HI Hostel HOSTEL €
(📞467 1506; siglufjordur@hostel.is; Aðalgata 10; sleeping bag/d Ikr2500/6900) Chipped cherubs and faded gilt make up the endearingly dated decor of this 1930s hotel, whose stately proportions hint at wealthier times. There are 19 charmingly ramshackle rooms with mountain views, a couple of TV lounges, a mighty dining room and a guest kitchen.

Hannes Boy Cafe SEAFOOD, BAR €€
(📞461 7730; Gránugata 23; mains Ikr1700-4000; ◷11.30am-11pm Sun-Thu, to 1am Fri & Sat) An exciting 2010 addition to Siglufjörður, Hannes Boy Cafe is a superstylish place

down by the small-boat harbour, a two-storey, light-filled, airy space where customers sit in seats made from old herring barrels, watched by black-and-white photos of the town's former inhabitants. The menu, naturally, is fish-focused, with lobster soup and catch of the day fresh from the boats outside. At weekends, it becomes a buzzing bar and sometime music venue.

❶ Getting There & Away
You can get from Reykjavík to Siglufjörður year-round by bus, changing at Varmahlíð and Sauðárkrókur. The 8.30am service (Ikr11,000) on Monday, Wednesday, Friday and Sunday will get you to Siglufjörður at either 3.25pm or 7.45pm; on other days the journey may involve an overnight stop in Sauðárkrókur.

Akureyri
POP 17,300
Fertile, sheltered Akureyri, situated alongside Iceland's greatest fjord, has the warmest weather in a cold country. The best restaurants, cafes and cinemas outside the capital nestle beneath a range of snow-capped peaks. It's a place of small pleasures and gentle strolling: admire the flowery gardens, maple trees, sculptures and bobbing boats.

◉ Sights & Activities

Akureyrarkirkja CHURCH
(Eyrarlandsvegur) Akureyrarkirkja was designed by Gudjón Samúelsson, the architect of Reykjavík's Hallgrímskirkja. Although the basalt theme connects them, Akureyrarkirkja looks more like a stylised 1920s US skyscraper than its big-town brother. The church admits visitors in summer; check the board outside for opening times, as they change frequently.

Akureyri Museum MUSEUM
(Minjasafnið Akureyri; www.akmus.is; Aðalstræti 58; adult/under 16yr Ikr600/free; ◷10am-5pm Jun–mid-Sep, 2-4pm Sat mid-Sep–May) Akureyri Museum houses local historical items, including an interesting Settlement Era section. The tranquil garden out front set the fashion for Iceland's 19th-century tree-planting craze.

Nonnahús MUSEUM
(www.nonni.is; Aðalstræti 54; adult/under 16yr Ikr600/free, joint ticket with Akureyri Museum Ikr850; ◷10am-5pm Jun–mid-Sep) Children's writer Reverend Jón Sveinsson (1857–1944) spent his childhood in Akureyri and his old-

fashioned tales of derring-do have a rich Icelandic flavour. You can visit Nonnahús, the author's higgledy-piggledy childhood home, and pick up an English translation of his book *At Skipalón*.

Lystigarður Akureyrar   GARDEN
(www.lystigardur.akureyri.is; Eyrarlandsvegur; admission free; ⊙8am-10pm Mon-Fri, 9am-10pm Sat & Sun Jun-Sep) The most northerly botanical garden in the world makes a delightful picnic spot on sunny days. Opened in 1912, it includes most native Icelandic species and a further 6600 tough plants from high altitudes and latitudes.

Sundlaug Akureyrar   SWIMMING POOL
(Þingvallastræti 21; adult/under 16yr Ikr450/free, sauna Ikr650; ⊙7am-9pm Mon-Fri, 8am-6.30pm Sat & Sun) Akureyri has one of the country's best pools, with hot pots, saunas and flumes.

🛏 Sleeping

Central Akureyri commonly has more visitors than accommodation spaces – bookings are strongly recommended. The tourist office can recommend some very nice farmhouse accommodation (private transport necessary) if everywhere in town is full. **Icelandair** (☑444 4000; www.icelandairhotels.com; Þingvallastræti 23) was due to open a brand-new hotel here over 2011/2012 – see its website for further news.

Akur-Inn   GUESTHOUSE €
(☑461 2500; www.akurinn.is; Brekkugata 27a; sleeping bág per person Ikr4500, s/d with shared bathroom Ikr7200/10,000, d Ikr13,500; @) The seven rooms in this lovely old heritage home have a calm atmosphere and lots of 1930s period charm. Crisp white linens and pale neutral colours add to the simple style. There's a guest kitchen, with coffee always on tap.

TOP CHOICE Hrafninn   GUESTHOUSE €€
(☑661 9050; www.hrafninn.is; Brekkugata 4; s/d Ikr9700/14,200; P) Hrafninn ('The Raven') feels like an elegant manor house without being pretentious or stuffy. The location is ideal, all rooms have en suite bathrooms, prices include a do-it-yourself breakfast and the owner is kind.

Hótel Kea   HOTEL €€€
(☑460 2000; www.keahotels.is; Hafnarstræti 87-9; s/d Ikr22,000/28,400) Akureyri's top hotel has been going since 1944. Rooms here are business-class with slightly old-fashioned

trimmings; the five nicest have balconies overlooking the fjord. Kea is the only hotel in town with facilities for wheelchair users. **Hótel Harpa** (s/d Ikr19,000/24,600) shares Kea's restaurant and reception. In many ways its small rooms are superior: they're recently renovated, with parquet flooring and modern furniture.

Gula Villan   GUESTHOUSE €
(☑896 8464; www.gulavillan.is; Brekkugata 8; sleeping bag/s/d Ikr5000/6500/9800) At this family-friendly place, you'll find spotless, snow-white rooms with leafy patterns stencilled on the walls. The owners have another buttercup-yellow building (Þingvallastræti 14) opposite the swimming pool. Both houses have kitchens, or parties of more than four can order breakfast (Ikr1400 per person).

Stórholt HI Hostel   HOSTEL €
(☑462 3657; www.hostel.is; Stórholt 1; sleeping bag in dm Ikr 3000, s/d Ikr5500/8100; ⊙mid-Jan–mid-Dec; P@) This spotless hostel has a comfy sitting room and two large kitchens, with a summery decking area outside. There are two attractive summer houses, one holding three people (Ikr11,000) and one holding eight (Ikr31,000).

Gistiheimili Akureyri   GUESTHOUSE €€
(☑462 5600; www.hotelakureyri.is; Hafnarstræti 104; s/d Ikr10,700/12,500, s/d with shared bathroom Ikr8300/10,700) This largish place lacks the intimacy of a guesthouse; it's more of a budget hotel with kitchen facilities. The 19 rooms are small but clean, all with TV and washbasins; some have private bathrooms. The sunny, balconied breakfast area (summer only) overlooking bustling Hafnarstræti is the star feature.

Edda Hotel   SUMMER HOTEL €€
(☑444 4000; www.hoteledda.is; Eyrarlandsvegur 28; s/d Ikr14,600/18,300, s/d with shared bathroom Ikr12,900/16,000; ⊙mid-Jun–late Aug; P) Around 200 summer rooms are up for grabs in the grammar school: just over half are superior rooms with TVs and private bathrooms. There's a cafe and large restaurant on site.

Hamrar campsite   CAMPING GROUND €
(☑461 2264; hamrar@hamrar.is; campsites per adult Ikr1000; ⊙mid-May–mid-Sep) This huge camping ground, 1.5km south in a leafy setting by the scout camp at Kjarnaskógur, has newer facilities than Central camping ground and mountain views. Both Hamrar and Central camping areas have kitchen and laundry.

Central camping ground CAMPING GROUND €
(☎462 3379; hamrar@hamrar.is; Þórunnarstræti; campsites per adult Ikr1000; ⊙early Jun-Aug) Central, family-oriented camping ground, close to the swimming pool, supermarket and town.

✗ Eating

TOP
CHOICE **Strikið** GRILL, WORLD €€
(☎462 7100; www.strikid.is; Skipagata 14; mains Ikr2000-4000; ⊙from 11.30am) Huge windows with panoramic fjord views lend a magical glitz to this 5th-floor grill and restaurant.

The menu covers all options: go for pizzas and burgers if you must, or order superb-tasting mains of Icelandic seafood/world cuisine (superfresh trout, honey-roasted pork, salmon with rocket and basil, lobster tails, Thai noodles), washed down with local microbrew Kaldi.

Bautinn FAMILY €€
(☎462 1818; Hafnarstræti 92; mains Ikr1600-3400) Open all day, this restaurant is a favourite for its friendly staff, decent prices and all-you-can-eat salad bar. There's a large glazed conservatory and a more shadowy interior

if you don't enjoy that goldfish-bowl feeling. Dishes include everything from pizzas and salad to puffin and whale.

Rub 23   SEAFOOD €€€
(☎462 2223; www.rub.is; Kaupvangsstræti 6; mains Ikr3700-5000; ☺dinner) This supersleek restaurant revolves around a novel idea: you choose your fish (or meat) main, then pick one of the 11 'rubs', or marinades, that the chef then uses to cook your dish. There's also a separate sushi menu – Icelandic maki prepared with savoury Japanese ingredients. Or treat yourself to the highly recommended chef's selection.

Greifinn   GRILL €€
(☎460 1600; www.greifinn.is; Glerárgata 20; mains Ikr1700-3000; ☺11.30am-10pm) Family-friendly and *always* full to bursting. The good-value menu favours comfort food above all: sizzling Tex-Mex, lamb curry, pasta, burgers, much-praised pizza and big meaty steaks. A bat-phone button on the table summons the waiter.

Café Paris   CAFE €€
(Bláa Kannan; Hafnarstræti 96; ☺8.30am-11.30pm summer, shorter hr winter) This tearoom, with its old wooden interior and swirly-coloured tables, is a peachy place to idle away a morning. In summer outdoor tables mushroom on the main street, and people flock in for the good-value lunch specials (coffee, soup, salad and main), often vegie.

Brauðbúðin   BAKERY €
(Hafnarstræti 108; ☺8am-5.30pm Mon-Fri, 10am-5pm Sat) Sells fresh bread, salad and cakes, with tables to eat them at.

Brynja   ICE CREAM €
(Aðalstræti 3; ☺9am-11.30pm) Slightly out of the centre, this legendary sweetshop is known across Iceland for having the best ice cream in the country.

🍷 Drinking & Entertainment

Compared to Reykjavík, Akureyri's nightlife is quite tame.

Græni Hatturinn   PUB
(Hafnarstræti 96) Similar to a British pub, with frequent live music.

Kaffi Akureyri   CLUB
(Strandgata 7) A dressy venue good for live music and dancing.

Café Amour   CAFE, WINE BAR
(Raðhústorg 9) A cafe, cocktail lounge and wine bar with an upstairs dance floor.

Sjallinn   CLUB
(Geislagata 14) Very large and popular nightclub with chart tunes, DJs and bands.

❶ Information

Hospital (☎463 0100; Eyrarlandsvegur) Just south of the botanical gardens.

Library (☎460 1250; Brekkugata 17; ☺10am-7pm Mon-Fri Jun-Aug, plus noon-5pm Sat Sep-May) Large English-language book section, internet access (per hour Ikr200) and cafe.

Nonni Travel (☎461 1841; www.nonnitravel.is; Brekkugata 5; ☺9am-5pm Mon-Fri mid-May–Sep, 10am-3pm Mon-Fri Oct–mid-May) Tour agency, specialising in trips to Greenland.

Post office (Strandgata 3; ☺9am-6pm Mon-Fri)

Tourist office (☎450 1050; www.visit akureyri.is; Hof Culture House, Strandgata 12; ☺7.30am-7pm mid-Jun–Aug, 8am-4pm Mon-Fri Oct-Apr, also open weekends in shoulder season) Can organise tours.

❶ Getting There & Away

See the Grímsey section for information about travel to Grímsey, including buses to Dalvík (for the ferry).

Air

Flugfélag Íslands (☎570 3030; www.airice land.is) has year-round flights between Akureyri and Reykjavík (Ikr15,000), with at least seven flights daily in summer.

Internationally, **Iceland Express** (www.iceland express.com) has one Saturday flight per week between June and August from Copenhagen (around Ikr 18,000, two hours).

Bus

Buses, mainly operated by **SBA-Norðurleið** (☎550 0700; www.sba.is; Hafnarstræti 82), run from the central bus station.

The **Sterna** (Bílar og fólk; ☎551 1166; www.sterna.is) bus company operates the main route between Reykjavík and Akureyri, with buses departing at least once daily (Ikr10,400, six hours) year-round. SBA-Norðurleið buses travelling over the Kjölur route run from 18 June to 9 September, leaving at 8am daily from both Reykjavík and Akureyri (Ikr12,000, 10½ hours).

A bus to Mývatn (Ikr3100, 1½ hours) runs daily from June to mid-September (four per week rest of year), continuing to Egilsstaðir (a further Ikr4300, two hours), where you can catch another bus (sometimes a good connection, sometimes not) to Seyðisfjörður. Buses to Húsavík (Ikr3100, 1¼ hours) depart one to four times daily, depending on the time of year.

Around Akureyri

South of town is Iceland's most visited 'forest', Kjarnaskógur, popular for family outings. A good day walk from Akureyri follows the Glerárdalur valley as far as Lambi mountain hut. From Akureyri you can hike up and down Mt Sulur (1213m) in about eight hours; if possible, get a lift to the signposted turn-off (it's a dull walk out of town), from where the summit is a 5km climb.

About 50km east of town is the curving waterfall Goðafoss, where Þorgeir Ljósvetningagoði, when asked to decide whether Iceland should adopt Christianity, symboli-cally threw his statues of the old Norse gods. Buses from Akureyri to Mývatn pass the waterfall.

Grímsey

POP 90

The main attraction of Grímsey, a wind-blown island 40km from the north coast, is that it's the only part of Iceland that lies (partly) inside the Arctic Circle. A large sign-post marks the theoretical line; once you've crossed into polar realms, buy a commemorative certificate from the harbourside cafe. Abundant birdlife (puffins, razorbills, guillemots, gulls and Arctic terns) outnumbers the close-knit community by around one million to 89. The boat ride adds to the mystique of reaching this isolated place.

The **Sæfari** (☎458 8970; www.landflutnin gar.is/saefari) sails from Dalvík (44km north of Akureyri) to Grímsey island at 9am on Monday, Wednesday and Friday (return Ikr6480, three hours), returning from Grímsey at 4pm. In summer, connecting buses (Ikr1200) leave Akureyri at 7.45am on Monday, Wednesday and Friday; inconveniently, the last bus back from Dalvík now leaves at 7pm.

From mid-June to mid-August there's one daily scheduled flight at 1pm from Akureyri to Grímsey (return Ikr24,000, 25 minutes). Nonni Travel (p279) can help arrange trips by boat or air.

Húsavík

POP 2230

Most people visit the 'whale-watching capital of Europe' to do just that; in season, you're almost guaranteed to see these awe-inspiring ocean giants feeding in Skjálfandi Bay.

◉ Sights & Activities

TOP
CHOICE/ **Whale Watching**   WHALE WATCHING

From April to October (although the main season is June to August), North Sailing (Norður Sigling; ☎464 7272; www.northsailing.is; Gamli Baukur, Hafnarstétt 11; adult/7-15yr €49/18) and Gentle Giants (Hvalferðir; ☎464 1500; www.gentlegiants.is; Garðarsbraut 6; adult/7-15yr €47/20) offer three-hour whale-watching trips on sturdy oaken boats. There's a 97% chance of sightings – mostly minkes and harbour porpoises, although humpback and blue whales also appear. Buy tickets from the ticket booths opposite the church.

Húsavík

Whale Centre
MUSEUM

(www.whalemuseum.is; Hafnarstétt; adult/6-14yr Ikr1000/450; ⏱9am-7pm Jun-Aug, 10am-5pm May & Sep) The fascinating Whale Centre deserves a couple of hours' attention, preferably *before* you go whale watching. It tells you everything about Icelandic whales and whaling, and the hanging gallery of skeletons allows you to truly appreciate their size.

Safnahúsið
MUSEUM

(Húsavík Museum; www.husmus.is; Stórigarður 17; adult/under 16yrs Ikr600/free; ⏱10am-6pm Jun-Aug, to 4pm Mon-Fri Sep-May) Once you've recovered your land legs, the local museum has impressive maritime and natural history collections, and admission includes a cup of coffee.

Icelandic Phallological Museum
MUSEUM

(www.phallus.is; Héðinsbraut 3a; admission Ikr600; ⏱noon-6pm mid-May–early Sep) This unique

Húsavík

museum contains 204 penises – pickled, dried and stuffed – from local mammals ranging in size from a hamster to a blue whale. The only willy missing is that of *Homo sapiens,* although Páll Arason, who bequeathed his member to the museum 14 years ago, died in January 2011...

🛏 Sleeping

Sigtún GUESTHOUSE €€
(☑464 1674, 846 9364; www.guesthousesigtun.is; Túngata 13; s/d/tr from Ikr10,000/15,500/19,000; @) We can heartily recommend this well-run guesthouse, which offers sparkling rooms and common bathrooms, as well as free internet and laundry. Perched on a hillside at Laugarholt 7e, a second building has the same facilities and sea views. Check-in at the Túngata address between 4pm and 8pm.

Guesthouse Baldursbrekka GUESTHOUSE €
(☑464 1005; onod@simnet.is; Baldursbrekka 20; sleeping bag/s/d Ikr2500/3500/7000) The cheapest option in town, this family home in a quiet cul-de-sac has five dinky rooms, cooking facilities and a garage to hang wet clothes. If it's full, the pleasant lady at No 17 opposite has four rooms and a guest kitchen; prices are similar. Parking is only allowed on one side of the street. Payment by cash only.

Kaldbaks-Kot SELF-CATERING COTTAGES €€
(☑464 1504; www.cottages.is; 2- to 4-person cabins €135-195) For cosy accommodation, try these self-contained little wooden cabins, 2km south of Húsavík and off Rte 85. They contain everything you need (fully equipped kitchen, living room, verandah, TV, barbecue), have mountain-and-sea views, and there are three hot tubs for starlit bathing. Additional costs include linen hire and a final cleaning charge. Larger groups can be catered for.

Vísir Guesthouse GUESTHOUSE €
(☑856 5750; dora@visirhf.is; Garðarsbraut 14; s/d/tr Ikr9000/12,000/17,000; ⊘May-Aug; @) An odd little place based in a fish factory. The 10 bright, simple rooms (half with beautiful sea views, all with shared bathrooms) are set around a rather clatter-y corridor – noisy guests could spell sleepless nights. There's a good kitchen, free washer and dryer, and internet access.

Camping ground CAMPING GROUND €
(☑845 0705; campsites per person Ikr1000; ⊘Jun–mid-Sep) Located at the northern edge of town, with two new utility buildings containing a good kitchen, toilets and washing machine.

🍴 Eating

TOP CHOICE Gamli Baukur PUB €€
(☑464 2442; www.gamlibaukur.is; Hafnarstétt; mains Ikr1400-3700; ⊘11.30am-9pm Sun-Wed, to 1am Thu, 11am-3am Fri & Sat summer) Built from driftwood and with a nautical theme, this cosy harbourside restaurant-bar is the liveliest place in town and serves as the main venue for music and watching football. Fresh scallops, cod, shrimp and herring are on the menu (hamburgers for the fish-disinclined).

Skuld Café CAFE €
(snacks Ikr300-1000; ⊘8am-8pm Jun-Sep) With a smart outdoor deck that overlooks the waterfront, Skuld is a cosy summer cafe and the place for light meals, baked goods or a glass of wine. In winter, get your cake-and-sandwich fix from its supplier, **Heimabakarí Konditori** (Garðarsbraut 15; ⊘8am-5pm Mon-Sat).

Restaurant Salka SEAFOOD €€
(☑464 2551; Garðarsbraut 6; mains Ikr1700-3200; ⊘11.30am-10pm Sun-Thu, to 11pm Fri & Sat) This historic building, which was once Iceland's first cooperative, now houses a good restaurant. The Restaurant Salka has a nice bar and an extensive local menu (with lobster, shrimp, puffin, lamb), plus pizzas and burgers.

ℹ Information

The helpful **tourist information office** (☑464 4300; info@visithusavik.is; Hafnarstétt 1) recently moved into the Whale Centre and has internet access. There's also internet access in the **library** (☑464 6165; Stórigarður 17; per hr Ikr300; ⊘10am-6pm Mon-Thu, to 5pm Fri).

ℹ Getting There & Away

SBA-Norðurleið (☑550 0700; www.sba. is) runs a bus service between Akureyri and Húsavík (Ikr3100, 1¼ hours), at least once daily in winter and up to four times daily in summer. From mid-June to August, there are two services daily to Reykjahlíð at Mývatn (Ikr2500, 40 minutes), and one service Monday to Saturday to Ásbyrgi and the waterfall Dettifoss (Ikr3300, 2¾ hours).

It takes a little while to settle your eye into whale spotting. A cloud of seabirds focused on one point of the sea is a good indicator that whales are present: as a whale chases fish to the surface, the birds descend to steal a share. Another sign is the whale's 'blow' as it snorts out a spray of water vapour – which looks for all the world like a puff of smoke on the water.

Identifying whales at sea can be tough. White-beaked dolphins and shy harbour porpoises (the smallest cetacean) both live around Húsavík, but it's usually dolphins that you'll see, bouncing exuberantly towards the boats.

Of the larger whale species, minkes are most common: small and slim, you'll generally see their pointed snouts poke slightly out of the water, before they become a dark, sleek, shallow curve rolling through the waves.

Humpbacks are wonderful creatures to watch (and don't be surprised if a knobbly head rises next to the boat to watch *you*). They hurl themselves high into the air when they breach; and there's ample time to admire their huge tail flukes as they dive, each with a pattern as individual as a human fingerprint.

Over the last few years, blue whales – the largest animal on earth – have visited the bay in June. You'll recognise them by their huge blow; and of course their jumbo-jet size gives them away.

Húsavík's reputation as Iceland's 'whale-watching capital' is deserved. On a good day in Skjálfandi, shining backs roll from the waves, and blasts of air spout from blowholes in all directions. Some of the whales come so close that you can smell their breath, a rancid stench of month-old fish. Once whiffed, it's never forgotten – but you'll always remember that pungent aroma with a broad smile.

Mývatn

Mývatn is the calm, shallow lake at the heart of a volatile volcanic area. Nature's violent masterpieces are everywhere – crazy-coloured mudpots, huge craters and still-smouldering eruption debris. Once you've had your fill of geology gone wild, mellow out with cycle rides, birdwatching (geese, golden plovers, swans and ducks, including Barrow's goldeneye) and a bathe in the north's version of the Blue Lagoon.

Reykjahlíð (population 173), at the northern end of the lake, is more an assortment of accommodation than a true town, but it makes the best base (Skútustaðir, at the southern end, also has summer facilities). The tourist office (☑464 4390; www.visitmyvatn.is; Hraunvegur 8; ☺9am-midnight Jul & Aug, to 7pm Jun, 10am-4pm May & Sep, to noon Oct-Apr) is in Reykjahlíð, on the main road next to the supermarket, and contains an interesting exhibition on the area's unusual birdlife, geology and volcanic systems.

The down side to Mývatn (Midge Lake) are the dense midge clouds that appear during summer intent on flying up your nose – you may want to bring a head net. Also, if hiking, keep a look out for deep fissures, especially if you are travelling with children.

◉ Sights & Activities

Around the Lake   SCENIC CIRCUIT

One of the best ways to experience the 37-sq-km lake is by either bicycle or horse; there are several places in Reykjahlíð rent them. We recommend a ride round the shores, taking in the forested lava headland of Höfði; pinnacle formations at Kálfaströnd; pseudo-craters at Skútustaðir, where ponds, bogs and marshlands create havens for nesting birds; the climb up Vindbelgjarfjall (529m); and a high-density waterfowl nesting area on the northwestern shore (off-road entry is restricted between 15 May and 20 July), where you'll also find Fuglasafn Sigurgeirs (Sigurgeir's Bird Collection; www.fuglasafn.is; Ytri-Neslönd; adult/7-11yrs Ikr800/400; ☺11am-7pm mid-May–Aug, shorter hr rest of yr), a taxidermic collection of all of Iceland's breeding birds bar one.

Hiking   SCENIC CIRCUIT

One of the most interesting walks around the lake begins at Stóragjá, a hot spring near the village. After a few minutes, the path comes to a dead end at a pipeline. Go left and walk a few hundred metres until the track turns south. It crosses a lava field to Grjótagjá, a 50°C hot spring in a spooky

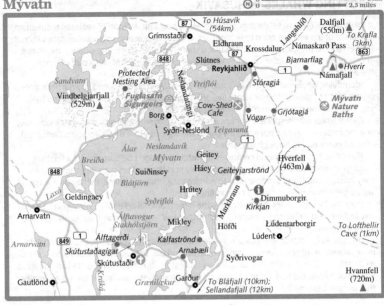

fissure, then continues to the tephra crater **Hverfell** (sadly scarred by graffiti) and **Dimmuborgir**, a 2000-year-old maze of twisted lava whose highlight is the 'Church' (Kirkjan), a natural arched cave that looks manmade.

The new **Dimmuborgir Service Centre** (☎464 1144, 894 1470; www.visitdimmuborgir.is; ⏰9am-10pm Jun-Aug, reduced hr rest of yr), containing a shop and cafe, runs guided walks in this area. Back on the main road, make sure you stop for homemade ice cream at the unusual 'Cow-Shed Cafe'.

TOP CHOICE Mývatn Nature Baths   SPA

(Jarðböðin við Mývatn; www.jardbodin.is; Jarðbaðshólar; adult/12-15yr Ikr2500/1000, towel/swimsuit rental Ikr500/500; ⏰9am-11.30pm Jun-Aug, noon-9.30pm Sep-May) Ease aching muscles at the Mývatn Nature Baths, the north's answer to the Blue Lagoon. Five kilometres east of Reykjahlíð, it's much smaller than the Blue Lagoon but is nicely landscaped, with a hot pot and saunas.

Námafjall & Hverir   VOLCANIC AREA

Vaporous vents cover the pinky-orange Námafjall ridge. At its foot, fumaroles and solfataras in the Hverir geothermal field scream steam and belch mud. The area rests on the mid-Atlantic rift (hence all the activity), and can be seen from quite a distance. It's just off the Ring Rd 6km east of Reykjahlíð.

Krafla   VOLCANIC AREA

The colourful, sulphurous mud hole **Leirhnjúkur** is Krafla's prime attraction. From there you can meander round the **Krafla Caldera**, where several different lava flows overlie each other; some from the 1984 eruptions are still smoking.

Nearby **Stóra-Víti** is a 320m-wide explosion crater and lake (now inactive...allegedly). The 30-megawatt **Kröflustöð power station** sources steam from 17 boreholes around the volcano; step into the **visitor centre** (Gestastofa; ⏰1-5pm Mon-Fri, to 6pm Sat & Sun Jun-Aug) for an explanatory film. One of the power station's preliminary searches produced the whopping crater **Sjálfskapar Víti** (Homemade Hell; near the Krafla car park) when a team drilled into a steam chamber, which exploded. Bits of the rig were found 3km away.

Between 18 June and 31 August, a bus runs from Reykjahlíð (outside the tourist office) to Krafla (Ikr1400) at 8am and 11.30am.

Tours

Hótel Reykjahlíð
VOLCANIC AREA

(☑464 4142; www.reykjahlid.is; Reykjahlíð; ☺mid-Jun–late Sep) Weather permitting, Hótel Reykjahlíð runs daily tours to Dettifoss via Krafla (Ikr19,000, seven hours); to Lofthellir, a lava cave with magnificent natural ice sculptures (Ikr14,500, five hours); and to the cratered wasteland of the Askja caldera (Ikr20,000, 12 hours). Advance bookings are strongly advised.

SBA-Norðurleið
VOLCANIC AREA

(☑550 0700; www.sba.is; ☺mid-Jun–Aug) SBA-Norðurleið operates scheduled buses (less expensive than the Hótel Reykjahlíð tours) to visit Krafla and Dettifoss/Ásbyrgi, which depart from Akureyri, Húsavík and Reykjahlíð. SBA also runs three-day sightseeing tours to Askja, Kverkfjöll and the glacier Vatnajökull – see p297 for details.

Mývatn Tours
VOLCANIC AREA

(☑464 1920; www.askjatours.is; per person Ikr18,000; ☺Jun-Aug) Runs a trip to the Askja caldera and Herðubreiðarlindir nature reserve from the tourist office at Reykjahlíð at 8am daily from 25 June to 31 August.

Sleeping

Sparsely populated Mývatn is overwhelmed by visitors in the summer, and accommodation is often overpriced and leaves a *lot* to be desired (several 'guesthouses' are actually Portakabins). The following options are all in Reykjahlíð, but Skútustaðir, at the southern end of the lake, also has visitor accommodation. Camping at Mývatn is prohibited outside designated areas.

Hótel Reykjahlíð
HOTEL €€€

(☑464 4142; www.reykjahlid.is; s/d/tr Ikr24,700/30,600/37,100; P@) Owners María and Petur refurbished this lakeside hotel in 2006; since then it has been Mývatn's most characterful accommodation choice. Its nine light rooms are a delicate yellow, with thick, billowing curtains and comfy beds; all but one have bathtubs. The hotel has a bar and à la carte restaurant (open summer only) with the best views in town.

Hótel Reynihlíð
HOTEL €€€

(☑464 4170; www.myvatnhotel.is; s/d Ikr27,200/33,600;☺Feb-Oct; P@) The en suite rooms of this smartish business hotel are modern and decorated in bland-but-restful shades. British visitors will appreciate the tea-making facilities. Almost half of the rooms have lake views. It has an upmarket restaurant serving Icelandic specialities, and bicycles for hire.

Ferðaþjónustan Bjarg
CAMPING GROUND €

(☑464 4240; ferdabjarg@simnet.is; Mývatn; campsites per tent Ikr1100, sleeping bag from Ikr3000, d Ikr13,000; ☺May-Sep; @) This is primarily a large, well-equipped camping ground, perfectly situated on the lakeshore. There's a shower block with underfloor heating, a laundry service, summer boat (Ikr2000 per hour) and bike (Ikr2000 for 12 hours) hire, and a nifty kitchen tent. There are also three bright, freshly carpeted rooms in the main building. If you're lucky, you might get to see the owner's smoke-house.

Hlíð Camping Ground
CAMPING GROUND €

(☑464 4103; hlid@isholf.is; Hraunbrún; campsites per person Ikr1200, sleeping bag in dm Ikr4000; @) This large stepped camping ground, 300m inland from the church, has laundry facilities, internet access, free showers and some decent mountain bikes for hire (Ikr1800 per day). Sleeping-bag accommodation is available in four-bed rooms in a Portakabin-style building; just pray your neighbours aren't noisy.

Eating

Eating options in Reykjahlíð are limited to the two hotel restaurants and Gamli Bærinn. Look out for dark, sticky *hverabrauð* (rye bread), baked using geothermal heat. It's sometimes available at the gift shop next to Gamli Bærinn.

Gamli Bærinn
CAFE, BAR €€

(☑464 4270; mains Ikr1700-2800; ☺10am-10pm May-Sep). This atmospheric 'country tavern' is a place of two halves. By day, it's a mellow cafe serving coffee, cakes, quiche and baguettes, while at night it becomes an effervescent bar-restaurant offering simple dishes – Arctic char and chips, *plokkfiskur* and lasagne – and live entertainment.

Cow-Shed Cafe
CAFE €

(Vogafjós; ☑464 4303; www.vogafjos.net; mains around Ikr3000; ☺7.30am-11pm May-Oct) Two kilometres east of Reykjahlíð, the cute 'Cow-Shed Cafe', where you can watch cows being milked and pet the calves, is well worth the walk or cycle. Stop for rich, homemade ice cream during the day and fine-quality trout and lamb mains in the candlelit restaurant at night.

❶ Getting There & Around

The main long-distance bus stop is outside the tourist office in Reykjahlíð. Buses between Mývatn and Akureyri also stop at Skútustaðir. From June to August, there's a daily bus (three per week rest of year) between Akureyri and Mývatn (Ikr3400, 1¾ hours), continuing to Egilsstaðir (a further Ikr4800, two hours).

See p282 for information on buses to/from Húsavík.

See p297 for information on buses to/from Reykjavík via Sprengisandur.

In addition to the accommodation places listed above, you can also hire brand-new 24-gear mountain bikes from **Hike & Bike** (☑899 4845; www.hikeandbike.is; Múlavegur 1, Reykjahlíð; per day Ikr4000). Phone first to arrange pick-up.

Jökulsárgljúfur (Vatnajökull National Park – North)

Sticky-birch forests, orchids and bizarre rock formations fill the rift of Jökulsárgljúfur, sometimes called 'Iceland's Grand Canyon'. One of its major highlights is Ásbyrgi, a hoof-shaped chasm formed by a flood of biblical proportions from a glacier 200km away. The swirls, spirals and strange acoustics at Hljóðaklettar (Echo Rocks) are similarly unearthly, and near the park's southern boundary is Dettifoss, Europe's most forcefully flowing waterfall, where around 200 cu metres of water per second thunder over the edge. Part of the Vatnajökull National Park network, the Jökulsárgljúfur visitor centre (☑470 7100; www.vatnajokulsthjodgardur.is; ◷9am-9pm mid-Jun–mid-Aug, to 7pm early Jun & late Aug, 10am-4pm May & Sep) is located at the entrance to the Ásbyrgi canyon.

Camping is restricted to the official camping grounds: the large Ásbyrgi (campsites per adult Ikr950; ◷mid-May–Sep) camping ground, near the visitor centre, with electricity, hot water and showers; and the small, basic camping ground at Vesturdalur (campsites per adult Ikr950; ◷Jun–mid-Sep), in the heart of the canyon. There is a snack bar and small supermarket inside the Ásbyrgi petrol station (Rte 85).

From 18 June to 31 August, there's a daily bus from Akureyri (Ikr7300, 4¼ hours) and Húsavík (Ikr4700 return, three hours) to major sites in the park. There's also a daily Mývatn–Dettifoss (Ikr3100, one hour) bus

Jökulsárgljúfur (Vatnajökull National Park – North)

via Krafla (Ikr1400, 20 minutes), leaving at 11.30am from the tourist office in Reykjahlíð and returning from Dettifoss at 1.30pm.

THE EAST

Iceland's wild reindeer roam the mountains of the empty east, and Iceland's version of the Loch Ness monster calls the area home. The harsh, inhospitable highlands are a complete contrast to the sparkling fjords, which are surrounded by tumbling waterfalls and dotted with tight-knit communities, such as picturesque Seyðisfjörður. The east is also the site of Iceland's controversial aluminium smelter (see p303).

Egilsstaðir

POP 2280

Egilsstaðir is a rather grey service town and the main regional transport hub. Its saving grace is lovely Lagarfljót (Lögurinn), Iceland's third-largest lake. Since saga times, tales have been told of a monster, the Lagarfljótsörmurinn, who lives in its depths. All amenities are clustered near the central crossroads, including the regional tourist office (☑471 2320; www.east.is; Miðvangur 123; ⊗9am-5pm; @), which moved into a swanky new building right on the crossroads in 2010.

🛏 Sleeping & Eating

Gistiheimilið Egilsstaðir   GUESTHOUSE €€€
(☑471 1114; www.egilsstadir.com; s/d Ikr19,900/ 25,900; P@) The town was named after this splendid heritage guesthouse and farm, 300m west of the crossroads, on the banks of Lagarfljót. Its sensitively renovated en-suite rooms retain a real sense of history, and breakfast/dinner in the lakeside dining room is a delicious experience. The recent price hike is a little eye watering, but you are paying for the most characterful accommodation in town.

Café Nielsen   CAFE €€
(☑471 2626; Tjarnarbraut 1; lunch Ikr1500, dinner mains Ikr2000-4000; ⊗11.30am-11.30pm Mon-Thu, to 2am Fri, 1pm-2am Sat, to 11.30pm Sun) We've never had a duff meal at bustling Café Nielsen, based in Egilsstaðir's oldest house and straddling the divide between bar and restaurant. There's a wide choice, from vegie burgers to reindeer – a speciality of this region.

Hotel Edda   SUMMER HOTEL €€
(☑444 4000; s/d Ikr14,600/18,300; ⊗Jun–mid-Aug) Based at the school opposite the swimming pool, off Tjarnarbraut, Hotel Edda's rooms have private bathrooms, and there's a restaurant with panoramic views.

Camping ground   CAMPING GROUND €
(☑470 0750; tjaldstaedid@egilsstadir.is; Kaupvangur 10; campsites per adult Ikr1000, sleeping bag in dm from Ikr3000; @) Campsites are lined in utilitarian rows, but the facilities are good (including a kitchen, laundry and internet) and there are some dorm beds available.

❶ Getting There & Away

Air

There are up to four **Flugfélag Íslands** (☑570 3030; www.airiceland.is) flights daily between Reykjavík and Egilsstaðir (Ikr17,000).

Bus

Buses stop by Egilsstaðir tourist office. For Akureyri–Mývatn–Egilsstaðir buses, see p280; for Egilsstaðir–Höfn, see p289.

Between mid-June and August, **Ferðaþjónusta Austurlands** (☑472 1515, 852 9250) operates two buses per day Monday, Tuesday and Friday, and three buses per day on Wednesday and Thursday to Seyðisfjörður (Ikr800, 40 minutes). The timetable changes in winter – contact the company for full details.

Taxi

Ferry and bus connections can be less than perfect outside peak season: if you get stuck, a **taxi** (☑892 9247) between Egilsstaðir and Seyðisfjörður costs around Ikr9500.

Seyðisfjörður

POP 700

Things get lively when the Smyril Line's ferry *Norröna* sails majestically up the 17km-long fjord and docks at pretty little Seyðisfjörður. The picturesque houses in the town, snow-capped mountains and cascading waterfalls make the perfect welcome for visitors to Iceland.

❷ Sights & Activities

Blue Church   CHURCH
(www.blaakirkjan.is; Ránargata; tickets Ikr1500-2000; ⊗8.30pm Jul–mid-Aug) Like many of the town's 19th-century timber buildings, this pretty little church was brought in kit form from Norway when the herring boom was at its height. On Wednesday evenings in summer, it's the setting for a popular series of musical performances.

Kayaking & Mountain Biking   KAYAKING, MOUNTAIN BIKING
We highly recommend a guided kayaking trip (☑865 3741; www.iceland-tour.com; 2hr Ikr5000; ⊗Jun-Aug) out on the fjord, led by the good-humoured and informative Hlynur. More experienced paddlers can go on longer trips to Austdalur or Skálanes, or arrange other tailor-made tours. Hlynur also does mountain-bike tours (2hr Ikr2000); or hire a bike and go off on your own (half/full day Ikr1800/3500).

SKÁLANES

You might think Seyðisfjörður is the end of the line, but further retreat is possible. The remote farm **Skálanes** (☎690 6966; www.skalanes.com; sleeping bag Ikr6700; ☺mid-May–mid-Sep), 19km east of Seyðisfjörður along the fjord edge, is a beautiful nature and heritage field centre, surrounded by sea cliffs full of abundant birdlife. Accommodation is simple and cosy; there is a guest kitchen, but meals may be provided on request.

Getting there is an adventure in itself. By foot, you could walk the 19km; you can get there on a hired mountain bike or canoe; the 4WD track is accessible for jeeps; or it may be possible for the centre to pick you up (Ikr8000) from Seyðisfjörður – contact the centre to ask.

Tækniminjasafn Austurlands   MUSEUM
(☎472 1596; Hafnargata 44; adult/under 18yr Ikr600/free; ☺11am-5pm Jun–mid-Sep, 1-4pm Mon-Fri mid-Sep–May) For an insight into the town's fishing and telecommunications history, there's this worthwhile museum.

Hiking   HIKING
The Seyðisfjörður to Vestdalur hike is a fine taste of the countryside around Mt Bjólfur to the Seyðisfjörður–Egilsstaðir road. You could also walk the fjord to Skálanes.

🛏 Sleeping

Hótel Aldan   HOTEL €€€
(☎472 1277; www.hotelaldan.com; Norðurgata 2) This place is split across three old wooden buildings. Reception and the bar-restaurant (where breakfast is served) are at Norðurgata 2. The **Old Bank** (Oddagata 6; s/d/tr Ikr17,900/22,900/27,900; P@) is a truly gorgeous boutique guesthouse with all mod cons. Its luxury rooms are bright, spacious and furnished with antiques, and beds snuggle under hand-embroidered bedspreads. Triple rooms have wicked alcoves. **Snæfell** (Austurvegur 3; s/d/tr Ikr13,900/18,900/22,900; P), the creaky, characterful old post office building, has cheaper rooms. White paintwork, draped muslin curtains and colourful Indian bedspreads give them a fresh and cheerful air.

Hafaldan HI Hostel   HOSTEL €
(☎472 1410; hafaldan@simnet.is; Ránargata 9; sleeping bag in dm Ikr2500, sleeping bag in d Ikr6900, d Ikr7900; @) This peaceful hostel is split over two sites. The main building, a short walk out of town, has harbour views, a sunny lounge, kitchen, laundry and internet access. The annexe used to be the old hospital, but you'd never guess – Indian hangings and funky old furniture cosy it up.

Camping ground   CAMPING GROUND €
(☎472 1521; ferdamenning@sfk.is; Ránargata; campsites per adult Ikr1000; ☺May-Sep) A pleasant, sheltered grassy camping ground with big hedges and picnic benches. Showers and laundry extra.

🍴 Eating

Hótel Aldan   FINE DINING €€€
(☎472 1277; Norðurgata 2; mains Ikr3000-4200; ☺7am-9pm mid-May–mid-Sep) Coffee and light meals are served all day. In the evening, damask tablecloths, crystal wine glasses and flickering candles prettify the tables, and the menu features traditional Icelandic ingredients (eg lamb, lobster, reindeer, fish) with contemporary salads and sauces. The bar buzzes when the boat comes in. (Whale meat served.)

Skaftfell Café   BISTRO €€
(Austurvegur 42; mains Ikr1500-3000; ☺noon-11pm summer; @) This welcoming bistro-bar and internet cafe is a popular place with local artists and musicians. Snacks include bagels, quiche and cakes; the freshly caught seafood is great; and pizzas are a new addition to the menu.

Samkaup-Strax   SUPERMARKET
(Vesturvegur 1; ☺9am-6pm Mon-Fri, 11am-4pm Sat, closed Sun)

ℹ Information

Tourist office (☎472 1551; www.visitsey disfjordur.com; ☺9am-noon & 1-5pm Mon-Fri summer, Tue & Wed only rest of yr) Inside the ferry terminal.

ℹ Getting There & Away

For bus information, see p287. Details of the ferry service from mainland Europe are on p310.

THE SOUTH

Containing glittering glaciers, toppling waterfalls, the iceberg-filled Jökulsárlón lagoon and Iceland's favourite walking area, Skaftafell, it's no wonder that the south is the country's most-visited region. Various places along the coast offer skiing, ice climbing, snowmobiling, dog-sledding and hiking opportunities; or head offshore to the charming Vestmannaeyjar (Westman Islands) to see puffins and experience life on an active volcano.

ℹ Getting There & Away

Sterna (Bílar og fólk; ☑551 1166; www.sterna.is) and **Reykjavík Excursions** (☑580 5400; www.re.is) operate bus routes in the south.

Reykjavík–Kirkjubæjarklaustur–Skaftafell–Jökulsárlón–Höfn (Ikr12,200, 9hr; ☺mid-May–mid-Sep) Departs at 8.30am daily from Reykjavík and at 10am from Höfn. Eastbound from Reykjavík the bus passes Kirkjubæjarklaustur at 1.45pm (Ikr7200), Skaftafell at 2.50pm (Ikr8900) and Jökulsárlón at 4.30pm (Ikr10,300), stopping for a boat tour. Westbound from Höfn it passes Jökulsárlón at 12.10pm (Ikr2300), Skaftafell at 1.10pm (Ikr3900) and Kirkjubæjarklaustur at 2.10pm (Ikr5700).

Skaftafell–Jökulsárlón (Ikr2000; ☺8.30am & 1pm mid-Jun–Aug) Stops for two hours at the lagoon before returning.

Höfn–Stafafell–Egilsstaðir (Ikr6900; ☺mid-May–mid-Sep) This 3¼-hour trip departs from Höfn at 8.30am and from Egilsstaðir at 1.30pm daily. The bus passes Stafafell (east to Egilsstaðir at around 9am, west to Höfn at around 4.30pm).

Reykjavík–Kirkjubæjarklaustur–Skaftafell, via Landmannalaugar (Ikr12,800; ☺mid-Jun–Aug) This 11-hour trip departs from Reykjavík and Skaftafell at 8am daily and stops at Landmannalaugar for three hours. The bus passes through Kirkjubæjarklaustur at 6.30pm eastbound and 9am westbound.

Vatnajökull

Mighty Vatnajökull is Earth's largest ice cap outside the poles. It's 8100 sq km (three times the size of Luxembourg), reaches a thickness of 1km in places and, if you could find a scale big enough, you'd find it weighs 3000 billion tonnes! Scores of glaciers flow down from the centre as rivers of crevassed ice.

In June 2008, **Vatnajökull National Park** (www.vatnajokulsthjodgardur.is) was founded, chiefly to draw attention to the alarming speed at which the ice cap is melting. Its boundaries encompass the ice cap and the former Skaftafell and Jökulsárgljúfur National Parks, forming a 12,000-sq-km megapark that covers 12% of the entire country. A shiny new visitor centre, Snaefellsstofa, opened in 2010 in eastern Iceland, and three other centres will be built in Höfn, Mývatn and Kirkjubæjarklaustur over the next few years.

From June to August, **Vatnajökull Travel** (☑894 1616; www.vatnajokull.is) operates a trip from Höfn to Jöklasel (near the edge of the ice), leaving at 8.30am. You arrive around 10am, allowing time for a bone-shaking one-hour skidoo ride. It returns via Jökulsárlón, where it's possible to take a boat ride on the lagoon, arriving back in Höfn at 5.15pm. Bus, skidoo and boat ticket combined cost €255.

If you have your own transport, you can park at the junction of Rte 1 and F985, and then get a **Glacier Jeep** (☑478 1000; www.glacierjeeps.is; trip incl skidoo ride Ikr16,500; ☺9.30am & 2pm May–mid-Sep) ride up the mountain.

Around Vatnajökull

JÖKULSÁRLÓN

A ghostly procession of luminous-blue icebergs drifts through the 17-sq-km **Jökulsárlón lagoon**, before floating out to sea. This surreal scene (right next to the Ring Rd between Höfn and Skaftafell) is a natural film set: in fact, you might have seen it in *Batman Begins* (2005) and the James Bond film *Die Another Day* (2002). The ice breaks off from Breiðamerkurjökull glacier, an offshoot of Vatnajökull.

Boat trips (☑478 2222; info@jokulsarlon.is; per person Ikr 3000; ☺9am-7pm Jun-Aug, to 5pm late May & early Sep) among the 'bergs are available.

See p289 for information about buses.

HÖFN
POP 1610

Tiny Höfn makes a handy base for trips to the glacier. The tourist office is inside the **Jöklasýning Glacier Exhibition** (☑470 8050; www.rikivatnajokuls.is/is-land; Hafnarbraut 30; adult/under 16yr Ikr1000/free; ☺10am-6pm May-Sep), which has two floors of interesting displays on Vatnajökull and the southeastern corner of Iceland as well as some altogether-too-strange glacial mice. **Vatnajökull Travel** (☑894 1616; www.vatnajokull.is) runs tours to the glacier. Buses leave from outside the N1 petrol station.

WARNING

Dangerous crevasses criss-cross the ice cap – hiking is not recommended without proper equipment and a knowledgeable guide.

🛏 Sleeping

Hótel Höfn HOTEL €€
(📞478 1240; www.hotelhofn.is; Víkurbraut; s/d from Ikr19,250/26,500; 🅿 @) For business-class accommodation, try this friendly hotel where many of the rooms look either out to sea or over the glacier. The extension, opened in 2008, contains larger (and better!) rooms. It also does formal meals, buffets and fast food, including some interesting pizza choices, in its two **dining rooms** (mains Ikr2000-5000; ⏱9am-9pm).

Nýibær HI Hostel HOSTEL €
(📞478 1736; nyibaer@simnet.is; Hafnarbraut 8; sleeping bag in dm Ikr2500, d Ikr6900; 🅿) At the harbour end of town, this is a medium-sized place with laundry facilities. In high season, a second building round the corner welcomes in extra guests.

Camping ground CAMPING GROUND €
(📞478 1606; www.campsite.is; Hafnarbraut 52; campsites per adult Ikr900; ⏱late May–mid-Sep; @) There are 11 log cabins sleeping up to six people, a washer/dryer and cooking facilities, but you'll need your own pans.

🍴 Eating

Kaffi Hornið CAFE €€
(📞478 2600; Hafnarbraut; mains Ikr2400-4200; ⏱11.30am-10pm, closed Sun winter) Kaffi Hornið is an informal log-cabin cafe-bar decorated with local artwork, and the food comes in stomach-stretching portions. There are a couple of vegie options and a Höfn speciality, garlic-toasted lobster, as well as tasty burgers, pasta, fish mains and salads.

Humarhöfnin SEAFOOD €€
(📞478 1200; www.humarhofnin.is; Hafnarbraut 4; mains Ikr3000-5000; ⏱noon-10pm mid-May–Sep) Opened during the 2007 Lobster Festival, rustic-style Humarhöfnin specialises in cooking up pincer-waving little critters.

Skaftafell (Vatnajökull National Park – South)

Skaftafell, now part of the massive Vatnajökull National Park, encompasses a breathtaking collection of peaks and glaciers and is the country's favourite wilderness area. Per year 160,000 visitors come to marvel at thundering waterfalls, twisting birch woods and the brilliant blue-white Vatnajökull ice cap.

The renovated **visitor centre** (📞470 8300; www.vatnajokulsthjodgardur.is; ⏱8am-9pm mid-Jun–mid-Aug, shorter hr rest of yr; @) contains exhibitions and film screenings about the area, and is staffed by people who really know their stuff. It contains a (busy) cafe.

See p289 for information about buses to and from the area.

🏃 Activities

Appearing on postcards and calendars across the land, Skaftafell's most recognisable feature is **Svartifoss**, a gloomy waterfall that thunders over black basalt columns. Due to erosion in this area, rangers are encouraging visitors to explore elsewhere, for example, the easy one-hour return route to **Skaftafellsjökull**. The trail (wheelchair-accessible) begins at the visitor centre and leads to the glacier face, where you can witness the bumps, groans and brilliant blue hues of the ice. The **Icelandic Mountain Guides** (www.mountainguides.is) office (📞587 9999) summer base at Skaftafell (📞894 2959) lead invigorating glacier walks from March to October (two hours Ikr6300; minimum age 10 years).

In fine weather, the circular walk around **Skaftafellsheiði** is a treat. There are some

---

A CART RIDE TO CAPE INGÓLFSHÖFÐI

The dramatic headland Ingólfshöfði is an isolated nature reserve just east of Skaftafell. The only way to access this almost-island, 6km away over treacherous glacial sands, is by **tractor-towed hay cart** (📞894 0894; www.oraefaferdir.is; adult/8-16yrs Ikr4000/1000; ⏱noon Mon-Sat early May–mid-Aug) – the departure point is signposted off the Ring Rd. Once there, local guides take you on a fascinating one-hour bird and nature walk along the 76m-high cliffs and grassy heath, teeming with puffins, guillemots, razorbills, gulls and great skuas.

enjoyable day walks from the camping ground to Kristínartindar (1126m), Kjós or the glacial lagoon in Morsárdalur; plan on about seven hours for each return trip.

☞ Tours

The Laki eruptions of 1783 caused utter devastation to the area. Over 30 billion tonnes of lava spewed from the Laki fissure, the largest recorded flow from a single eruption. The still-volatile Lakagígar area, with its spectacular 25km-long crater, is now part of Vatnajökull National Park. In July and August, daily 11-hour Reykjavík Excursions (☑580 5400; www.re.is) trips from Skaftafell (Ikr12,000, at 8am) and Kirkjubæjarklaustur (Ikr9000, at 9am) visit the craters.

🛏 Sleeping

Book all accommodation ahead in summer, as Skaftafell is immensely popular.

Bölt   FARMHOUSE €
(☑4781626; bolti123@gmail.com; Skaftafellsheiði; sleeping bag in 6-person hut Ikr3600, sleeping bag in d Ikr9000; ☺Mar-Oct) This farm, behind the western edge of the camping ground, is superbly located with dizzying views over the sandur (sand deltas). Accommodation is of the simplest kind – sleeping bags either in six-person bunk-bedded wooden huts, or in tiny double rooms – but who needs a five-star hotel with that scenery to gaze at?

Fosshótel Skaftafell   HOTEL €€€
(☑478 1945; www.fosshotel.is; Freysnes; s/d from Ikr25,000/29,000; ☺Mar-Oct) At Freysnes, 5km east of the park, Skaftafell's 63 rooms (all with bathroom and TV) are functional rather than luxurious; rooms with glacier views cost a little more. The staff are helpful, and the convivial restaurant is the best place to eat in the area.

Camping ground   CAMPING GROUND €
(campsites per adult/13-16 yrs Ikr950/500; ☺Jun–mid-Sep) Camping is permitted only at this large, gravelly location (with laundry facilities), right by the visitor centre.

Kirkjubæjarklaustur

POP 120

Kirkjubæjarklaustur (which translates as 'church-farm-cloister') is a tiny settlement lost in the staggeringly vast and empty san-

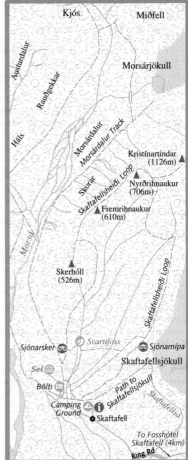

dur. Several sights hark back to its religious beginnings.

A national park visitor centre is planned for the village; in the meantime, the tourist information point (☑487 4620; info@klaustur.is; Kirkjubæjarklaustur Community Centre, opposite church; ☺9am-1pm & 3-9pm Mon-Fri, 10am-8pm Sat, to 6pm Sun Jun-Aug) provides good information. It also contains a small exhibition on the village's history and a recent archaeological dig.

See p289 for information about buses to and from the area.

THE FIRE PRIEST

In 1783, the largest flow of lava in recorded history began spewing from the Laki fissure. Fountains of molten rock shot almost 1.5km into the air, and a fiery flood of lava poured steadily southwards into the lowlands.

On July 20, as a tongue of lava crept towards Kirkjubæjarklaustur, the villagers stumbled to church through thick fog and lightning flashes to hear the Sunday sermon. The Reverend Jón Steingrímsson, who was not expecting his church to survive, prayed fervently to God for mercy as earthquakes shook the building and thunderclaps caused the bells to ring.

After the sermon, the congregation left the building to discover that the all-consuming lava flow had stopped in its tracks. Jón Steingrímsson and his Eldmessa ('Fire Sermon') were given the credit for this miracle, and the humble priest became an Icelandic hero.

◉ Sights

Kirkjugólf's regular basalt columns, cemented with moss, were once mistaken for an old church floor rather than a work of nature, and it's easy to see why. The 'floor' lies in a field about 400m northwest of the petrol station.

Systrastapi (Sisters' Pillar) marks the spot where two nuns were reputedly executed and buried after sleeping with the devil and other no-nos. Systrafoss is the prominent waterfall located near the hotel. The lake Systravatn, a short saunter up the cliffs, was once a place where nuns went to bathe.

See p291 for information about tours to the Lakagígar craters.

🛏 Sleeping & Eating

Hótel Klaustur   HOTEL €€€
(☑487 4900; www.icehotels.is; Klausturvegur 6; s/d from Ikr22,600/26,100) The 57-room Klaustur is run by Icelandair, but is not the same standard as other hotels in the chain. Although rooms are clean and businesslike, it's quite a basic place. The restaurant, however, has an excellent à la carte menu with typical Icelandic mains and some unusual starters – snails, anyone?

Systrakaffi   BISTRO €€
(Klausturvegur 12; light meals Ikr1000-2000, mains Ikr2000-3500; ⊗noon-midnight, to 2am Fri & Sat Jun-Aug, 6-10pm Fri & Sat May & Sep) This ambient little cafe sells a variety of food including chilli burgers, bacon burgers, pizzas and reasonably priced fish and meat dishes, including a bouillabaisse-like seafood soup.

Kirkjubæ II   CAMPING GROUND €
(☑487 4612; kirkjubaer@simnet.is; campsites per adult Ikr900; ⊗Jun-Sep) Pitch tents on the greensward under a pretty waterfall at this pleasant camping spot above town. Hot showers, kitchen and laundry facilities.

Þórsmörk

The Woods of Thor is a stunning glacial valley, full of weird rock formations, twisting gorges, a singing cave, mountain flowers and icy streams. Its proximity to Reykjavík (130km) makes it a popular spot in summer, when tents pile up and the camping grounds become party-ville. Luckily you don't have to go far to escape the crowds.

Wild camping is prohibited, but the three Þórsmörk huts have campsites (per adult Ikr1000) around them. The huts themselves have showers and cooking facilities; reservations are strongly advised, particularly for weekends.

Básar (operated by Útivist; ☑562 1000, 893 2910; www.utivist.is; N 63°40.559, W 19°29.014; sleeping bag in dm Ikr2800)

Húsadalur (operated by HI Iceland; ☑552 8300, 894 1506; www.hostel.is; N 63°41.350, W 19°33.100; sleeping bag in dm Ikr3100)

Þórsmörk/Skagfjörðsskáli (operated by Ferðafélag Íslands; ☑568 2533; www.fi.is; N 63°40.960, W 19°30.890; sleeping bag in dm Ikr4200)

Þórsmörk is the end of the Landmannalaugar–Þórsmörk trek (see p298), although walkers can extend the journey with the 23km Þórsmörk–Skógar hike (Map p299). It crosses Fimmvörðuháls Pass, where a new lava field was formed in the 2010 Eyjafjallajökull eruptions. Go prepared – the terrain is tough, the pass is high and bad weather can descend very quickly even in midsummer. Huts along the Þórsmörk–Skógar stretch are operated by Útivist (☑562 1000; www.utivist.is; Laugavegur 178, Reykjavík; sleeping-bag in hut Ikr2800).

From mid-June to mid-September Reykjavík Excursions (☑580 5400; www.re.is) runs a bus between Reykjavík and Húsadalur (over the hill from Þórsmörk) at 8am daily (Ikr5800, 3½ hours); from mid-June to August, a second service runs daily at 4pm.

Even though Þórsmörk seems tantalisingly close (only 30km from the Ring Rd), you *cannot* drive there without a 4WD: the gravel road surface eventually turns into boulders.

Vestmannaeyjar

POP 4140

Black and brooding, the Vestmannaeyjar islands form 15 eye-catching silhouettes off the southern shore. They were formed by submarine volcanoes around 11,000 years ago, except for sulky-looking Surtsey, the archipelago's newest addition, which rose from the waves in 1963. Ten years later, unforgettable pictures of Heimaey were broadcast across the globe when a huge eruption buried a third of the town under 30 million tonnes of lava. Surtsey was made a Unesco World Heritage site in 2008, but its unique scientific status means that it is not possible to land there.

Heimaey is the only inhabited island. Its little town and sheltered harbour lie between dramatic *klettur* (escarpments) and two ominous volcanoes – blood-red Eldfell and conical Helgafell. Heimaey's cliffs are a breeding ground for 10 million puffin pairs.

◎ Sights & Activities

Skansinn   HISTORICAL AREA
The oldest structure on the island is a ruinous 15th-century fort built by English marauders; nearby is a picturesque replica Norse stave church and an old water tower crushed by the 1973 lava.

Folk Museum   MUSEUM
(Byggðasafn; Raðhússtræti; adult/6-13yr Ikr500/250; ☺11am-5pm Mon-Fri Jun-Aug, 1-5pm Mon-Fri, 11am-2pm Sat Sep-May) There are fascinating photos of Heimaey's 1973 evacuation in the folk museum. Other exhibits deal with fishing, the 17th-century pirate raids…and a case of Nazi memorabilia, left on the museum's doorstep by an anonymous donor!

House Graveyard   LAVA FIELD
Four hundred buildings lie buried under the 1973 lava; on the edge of the flow is an eerie House Graveyard where beloved homes rest in peace. 'Pompeii of the North' (www.pompeinordursins.is) is a faintly puzzling modern 'archaeological' excavation, where 10 crumpled concrete houses are being unearthed along the former street Suðurvegur.

Aquarium & Natural History Museum   MUSEUM
(Fiska- og Náttúrugripasafn; ☑481 1997; Heiðarvegur 12; admission Ikr500; ☺11am-5pm mid-May–mid-Sep, 1-4pm Sat mid-Sep–mid-May) The Aquarium & Natural History Museum has tanks of hideous-looking Icelandic fish as well as a live video link to a puffin colony. A new name – 'Sæheimar' – is pending, and heralds the beginning of a big overhaul, due to take place in 2012.

FREE Surtseyjarstofa   EXHIBITION
(Heiðarvegur 1; ☺11am-5pm mid-May–mid-Sep, 1-4pm Sat mid-Sep–mid-May) Surtsey nature reserve is out of bounds to visitors, but this new,

SKÓGAR

As you're barrelling along the south coast, be sure to stop at the excellent Skógar Museum (www.skogasafn.is; adult/12-15yr Ikr1200/600; ☺museum 9am-6pm Jun-Aug, 10am-5pm May & Sep), built by Þórður Tómasson (who will be 90 in 2011!). There are various restored buildings (church, turf-roofed farmhouse, school building, cowsheds etc) in the grounds, and a hangar-like building at the back houses an interesting transport museum, plus a cafe and souvenir shop. Nearby is the 62m waterfall Skógafoss, shrouded in mist and rainbows.

clever multimedia exhibition explores the island's fiery birth, its subsequent settlement by plants and birds, and its continuing quiet erosion, and considers its future: will anything be left of the Fire God's island by 2050?

Volcanic Film Show   CINEMA
(☑481 1045; Heiðarvegur; adult/under 12yr Ikr800/400; ☺2pm, 3.30pm & 9pm mid-Jun–Aug, 3.30pm late May & early Sep) The explosive hour-long Volcanic Film Show plays at the local cinema, and includes footage of whales and puffin rappelling.

Hiking   HIKING
Opportunities for hiking abound, including walks to Stórhöfði and up the volcanoes Helgafell and Eldfell. It's a treacherous 30-minute climb to the top of **Stóraklif**, 'assisted' by ropes and chains, but worth it for the breathtaking views.

☞ Tours

Viking Tours   BOAT TRIPS
(☑488 4884; www.vikingtours.is; adult/9-14yr Ikr5000/3400; ☺May-Aug) Viking Tours, in the small boats harbour, off Ægisgata, runs daily boat (10.30am and 3.30pm) and bus (1pm) tours of the island, plus whale-watching and fishing trips on request. If nobody's about, ask in nearby Café Kró.

✷ Festivals & Events

Þjóðhátíð Vestmannaeyjar   CULTURE
In 1874, foul weather prevented the islanders from joining the party on the mainland to celebrate the establishment of Iceland's constitution. The earth-shaking Þjóðhátíð Vestmannaeyjar, held on the August bank holiday, has been making up for that day ever since; and these days, half the mainland joins *them* for the wild and drunken celebrations.

Iceland is famous for its puffins (*Fratercula arctica*). It's hard not to get dewy-eyed over these sociable little 'clowns of the ocean', but really they're as tough as old boots, living out on the stormy winter seas and surviving on salt water.

It's easy to spot puffins: they're the clumsiest things in the air. Wings beat frantically 300 to 400 times per minute to keep them aloft, and the birds often crash-land. Underwater, it's a different story – their flight beneath the waves is so graceful that they were once thought to be a bird-fish hybrid.

Every spring, the puffins return to land to breed. They're discerning birds: 60% of the world's population breed in Iceland. From late May to August, the best places to see them include offshore Reykjavík (p255), Látrabjarg (p275) and Heimaey, which has the world's biggest puffin colony. Pufflings start leaving their nests in August. On Heimaey, the young birds are often confused by the town's lights, so every year the town's children stay up late to collect them and point them seawards.

Sadly, a sudden decline in sand eel numbers (the birds' main food source) has led to a corresponding drop in puffin numbers. It remains to be seen whether the populations will recover or continue to fade away. Puffins and their eggs are a traditional part of the Icelandic diet: if you can bring yourself to devour them, you'll often find them on restaurant menus.

🛏 Sleeping

There are lots of guesthouses to choose from, but they fill up fast after the ferry arrives.

Sunnuhöll HI Hostel
HOSTEL €

(☑481 2900; www.hotelvestmannaeyjar.is; Vestmannabraut 28b; sleeping bag in dm from Ikr2500, s/d Ikr4400/6900) We have a soft spot for tiny, homely Sunnuhöll hostel, with its seven plain, neat rooms. The cheapest accommodation is in a (mixed) attic dorm. There is a guest kitchen and sitting room, and you can do laundry in Hótel Mamma across the road. Reception is at Hótel Þórshamar.

Gistiheimilið Hreiðrið
GUESTHOUSE €

(☑481 1045; http://tourist.eyjar.is; Faxastígur 33; sleeping bag/s/d/tr/q Ikr3200/5800/8500/10,800/14,100) Run by the helpful volcano-show people, Ruth and Sigurgeir, this winning guesthouse, spread across two buildings, has a family feel. Features include wall-to-wall puffins, and a well-stocked kitchen and cosy TV lounge in each house. Guests are welcome to use the garden and barbecue.

Hótel Þórshamar
HOTEL €€

(☑481 2900; www.hotelvestmannaeyjar.is; Bárustígur 2; s/d/ste Ikr12,300/17,900/22,500; @) Iceland's first cinema is now a hotel, with pale, pleasant rooms and facilities including sauna, hot tubs and snooker room. Of the older rooms, No 209 is the best, tucked in the corner with its own balcony; otherwise go for the three new suites, all with big beds, modern decor and dark wood floors.

The same family runs several cheaper guesthouses – ask at reception for details.

Herjólfsdalur Camp Ground
CAMPING GROUND €

(☑692 6952; campingisland@gmail.com; campsites per adult Ikr900; ⊙mid-May–Aug) Cupped in the bowl of an extinct volcano, this dandelion-dotted camping ground has hot showers, a laundry room and cooking facilities. It's generally sheltered, but if the wind comes from the wrong angle, it can get rough!

🍴 Eating

Fjólan
SEAFOOD €€

(Vestmannabraut 28; mains from Ikr2200; ⊙7am-11pm) Next door to Hótel Þórshamar, this high-ceiling, gold-column place is the only proper restaurant on the island; it serves probably the best fish in Heimaey. Those ceilings make it rather echoey and draughty, but staff are friendly and accommodating. The buffet breakfast is open to all.

Café Maria
BISTRO €€

(Skólavegur 1; mains Ikr2000-3700; ⊙11.30-1.30am Mon-Fri, to 1am Sat & Sun) A stuffed bird holds the specials board at this pleasantly down-home cafe-restaurant, which is quiet during the day but busy at night. Pizzas, burgers, savoury crêpes, and fresh fish and meat mains are served, including puffin.

Vinaminni Cafe & Bakery
CAFE €

(bakarinn@eyjar.is; Bárustígur) Most of Heimaey's eating options are long-standing affairs with a small-town feel, but this sleek new cafe with gleaming tables and leather banquettes, would not look out of place in Reykjavík. Serves a limited menu of soup, panini etc, and is attached to an excellent bakery.

Pizza 67   PIZZA **€**
(Heiðarvegur 5; pizza Ikr1100-1700; ⊙dinner; @)
Feathered friends are firmly off the menu: chomp crunchy garlic bread instead in a pub-like atmosphere.

Kronan   SUPERMARKET
(Strandvegur 48; ⊙11am-7pm Mon-Fri, to 6pm Sat, to 4pm Sun)

Vöruval   SUPERMARKET
(Vesturvegur 18; ⊙7.30am-7pm Mon-Fri, 10am-7pm Sat, 11am-7pm Sun)

❶ Information

The **tourist office** is a flighty beast, prone to much wandering. At the time of writing, it had settled into a corner of **Penninn bookshop** (☑482 3683; Bárustígur 2; ⊙9am-6pm Mon-Wed, to 9pm Thu & Fri, 10am-6pm Sat, 1-5pm Sun); internet access was also available there. There are **Sparisjóðurinn** and **Íslandsbanki banks** with ATMs near the **post office**. The **library** has internet access (Ikr200 per hour).

❶ Getting There & Away

Air

Flugfélagið Ernir (Eagle Air; ☑562 4200; www.eagleair.is) flies twice daily to and from Reykjavík (Ikr10,500, 20 minutes).

Boat

The **Herjólfur** (☑481 2800; www.herjolfur.is) shuttles between the mainland and the Vestmannaeyjar four times per day. The ferry used to leave from Þorlákshöfn, but since July 2010 it departs from the brand-new Landeyjahöfn harbour 30km southeast of Hvolsvöllur. From the mainland, it leaves at 9am, noon, 4.30pm and 8.30pm; it returns from the island at 7.30am, 10.30am, 3pm and 6pm. The crossing takes 40 minutes. The one-way fare per adult/12 to 15 years is Ikr1000/500, and Ikr1500 per car. Reservations are essential for vehicles, at least 30 minutes prior to departure.

Bus

Sterna (☑553 3737; www.sterna.is) runs some connecting buses from Reykjavík to the new harbour (Ikr3200), setting off around 2½ hours before the ferry departs. However, not all the ferry journeys have a bus connection, and there is nothing whatsoever to do or see at or near Landeyjahöfn, so do check bus schedules carefully.

THE INTERIOR

The desolate interior is so vast, barren and remote that the Apollo astronauts held training exercises here before the 1969 lunar landings. The highlands are truly one of Europe's greatest remaining wilderness areas. There are practically no services, accommodation, mobile-phone signals and bridges, and no guarantees if things go wrong: careful preparations are essential. Routes are only accessible in July and August.

Routes of Central Iceland

Historically, the interior routes were used as summer short cuts between north and south, places of terror to be traversed as quickly as possible. Some *útilegumenn* (outlaws) fled into these harsh highlands: those who survived gained legendary status, like the superhuman Grettir; or Fjalla-Eyvindur, an Icelandic Robin Hood/Butch Cassidy figure.

Routes in this section are summer-only, and (apart from the Kjölur route) are strictly for high-clearance 4WD vehicles. It's recommended that vehicles travel in pairs.

Many mountain huts are run by **Ferðafélag Íslands** (☑568 2533; www.fi.is; Mörkin 6, Reykjavík); accommodation is on a first-come, first-served basis, so book in advance. Facilities tend to be spartan, and if there are kitchens, they generally lack utensils.

KJÖLUR ROUTE

The Kjölur route (35) was once believed to be infested with bloodthirsty outlaws. Nowadays, it's a favourite with visitors: it's greener and more hospitable than the Sprengisandur route; it forms a neat short-cut between Reykjavík and Akureyri; and it's accessible to all vehicles, as there are no rivers to ford (although hire-car companies will still only insure 4WDs for this road). The route's name (Keel) refers to the perceived shape of its topography.

Kjölur's main attraction is **Hveravellir**, a geothermal area of fumaroles and multicoloured hot pools at the northern end of the pass. A camping ground and two mountain huts with kitchens are run by **Hveravallafélag** (☑894 1293; www.hveravellir.is; campsites per adult Ikr1000, sleeping bag in dm/tw Ikr3500/5000, d Ikr14,000).

From 18 June to 9 September, **SBA-Norðurleið** (☎550 0770; www.sba.is) buses travel daily over the Kjölur route between Reykjavík and Akureyri (Ikr12,000, 10½ hours), departing at 8am from both places. See also p310 for details on Reykjavík Excursions' Highland Circle Passport.

SPRENGISANDUR ROUTE

The Sprengisandur route (F26) is long and desolate, but it does offer some wonderful views of Vatnajökull, Tungnafellsjökull and Hofsjökull, as well as Askja and Herðubreið. The bus (see below) passes the photogenic waterfall **Aldeyjarfoss**, which topples over clustered basalt columns.

A good place to break your journey is **Nýidalur**, where there's a **camping ground** (campsites per adult Ikr1000), two Ferðafélag Íslands **huts** (☎860 3334 Jul & Aug; N 64°44.130, W 18°04.350; sleeping bag Ikr4200; ☺Jul & Aug) and numerous hiking possibilities. A recommended, challenging day hike takes you to the **Vonarskarð Pass** (1000m), a colourful saddle between Vatnajökull, Tungnafellsjökull and the green Ógöngur hills.

From July to August, **Reykjavík Excursions** (☎580 5400; www.re.is) buses operate between Landmannalaugar and Mývatn via Sprengisandur. They leave Landmannalaugar at 8.30am on Tuesday, Thursday and Sunday (Ikr11,600, 10 hours); they leave from outside the Mývatn tourist office at 8.30am on Monday, Wednesday and Friday.

Daily buses (Ikr7100, four hours) run between Reykjavík (depart 8am) and Landmannalaugar (depart 3pm) mid-June to mid-September. See also p310 for details on Reykjavík Excursions' Highland Circle Passport.

ÖSKJULEIÐ ROUTE (ASKJA WAY)

Herðubreið and Askja on the Öskjuleið route (F88) are the most visited wonders of the Icelandic desert.

HERÐUBREIÐ

Iceland's most distinctive mountain, Herðubreið (1682m), has been described as a birthday cake, a cooking pot and a lampshade, but the tourist industry calls it (more respectfully) the 'Queen of the Desert'. The track around it makes a nice day hike from **Herðubreiðarlindir Nature Reserve**, a grassy oasis created by springs flowing from beneath the lava. There's a **camping ground** (campsites per adult Ikr1000) and **Þorsteinsskáli Hut** (N 65°11.560, W 16°13.390; sleeping bag Ikr3800; ☺Jun-Aug), with basic kitchen, both run by **Ferðafélag Akureyrar** (Akureyri Touring Club; ☎462 2720; ffa@ffa.is).

ASKJA

Askja is an immense 50-sq-km caldera, created by a colossal explosion of tephra in 1875. Part of the volcano's collapsed magma chamber contains sapphire-blue **Öskjuvatn**, Iceland's deepest lake at 217m. At its northeastern corner is **Víti**, a hot lake in a tephra crater where the water (around 25°C) is ideal for swimming.

The two **Dreki Huts** (N 65°02.520, W 16°35.720; sleeping bag Ikr4200) at **Drekagil** (Dragon Ravine), 8km away, accommodate 60 people and are run by **Ferðafélag Akureyrar** (Akureyri Touring Club; ☎462 2720; ffa@ffa.is).

For tours to the Askja caldera, see p285.

KVERKFJÖLL ROUTE

The 108km-long Kverkfjöll route (F905, F910 and F902) connects Möðrudalur with the Sigurðarskáli hut. This is 3km from the impressive lower **Kverkfjöll ice caves**, where a hot river flows beneath the glacier, melting shimmering patterns on the ice walls. There are other (less impressive) ice caves higher up the glacier and a **hot waterfall** (30°C) at Hveragil, about a five-hour return walk (5.5km) from Sigurðarskáli. Check the route and conditions with the hut warden first – it can be dangerous to enter the caves if the ice is melting.

The 85-bed **Sigurðarskáli hut** (N 64°44.850, W 16°37.890; sleeping bag Ikr3800) and camping ground can be booked through **Ferðafélag Fljótsdalshéraðs** (☎863 5813; ferdafelag@egilsstadir.is).

The simplest way to visit Kverkfjöll is with **SBA-Norðurleið** (www.sba.is; 3-day tour Ikr29,000) Akureyri (☎550 0700); Reykjavík (☎550 0770), with tours departing from Akureyri (8.15am) and the tourist information office at Mývatn (10am) on Monday from early July to mid-August. Tours are just transport and a guide: you must organise your own accommodation and food. Warm clothing, a thick sleeping bag and strong boots are essential.

ICELAND THE INTERIOR

Fjallabak Nature Reserve

The Fjallabak route (F208) is a spectacular alternative to the coast road between Hella and Kirkjubæjarklaustur. It passes through the scenic nature reserve to **Landmannalaugar**, an area of rainbow-coloured rhyolite peaks, rambling lava flows, blue lakes and hot springs, which can hold you captive for days. Much of the route is along (and in!) rivers and therefore unsuitable for 2WD vehicles.

The star attractions around Landmannalaugar are **Laugahraun**, a convoluted lava field; the soothing **hot springs** 200m west of the Landmannalaugar hut; multi-coloured vents at **Brennisteinsalda**; the incredible red crater lake **Ljótipollur**; and the blue lake **Frostastaðavatn**, just over the rhyolite ridge north of Landmannalaugar. **Bláhnúkur**, immediately south of Laugahraun, offers a scree scramble and fine views from the 943m peak.

Ferðafélag Íslands' **hut** (☑ 860 3335 Jul-Sep; N 63°59.600, W 19°03.660; sleeping bag Ikr4200) at Landmannalaugar accommodates 75 people on a first-come, first-served basis and books up quickly with tour groups and club members. Others will probably have to use the **camping ground** (campsites per adult Ikr1000), which has toilet and shower facilities.

See p289 for details of Reykjavík Excursions' Reykjavík–Skaftafell bus route, via Landmannalaugar.

Landmannalaugar To Þórsmörk Trek

The 53km trek from Landmannalaugar to Þórsmörk deserves the same fame as great world walks such as the Inca Trail. The best map is Landmælingar Íslands' *Þórsmörk/Landmannalaugar* (1:100,000), which you can purchase online through **Ferðakort** (www.ferdakort.is).

The track is usually passable from mid-July to early September. You shouldn't have any problems if you're in reasonable condition, but don't take the walk lightly: it requires substantial river crossings, all-weather gear, sturdy boots and sufficient food and water.

Most people walk from north to south (because of the net altitude loss), taking three to four days. Some continue on to Skógar, making it a six-day trip: see p292 for details of the Þórsmörk–Skógar stretch.

Public huts along the track have wardens, although dates when they're there vary from year to year. They can provide information on trail conditions. Huts may be booked out by tour groups; check with **Ferðafélag Íslands** (☑ 568 2533; www.fi.is; Mörkin 6, Reykjavík) before you set out.

From Landmannalaugar hut, cross the **Laugahraun** lava field and ascend **Brennisteinsalda** (840m). Cross some rhyolite hills, then descend to the steaming vents at **Stórihver** and continue across the moors (covered with obsidian chunks and extensive snowfields) and a mountain pass to the **Hrafntinnusker hut**. From Hrafntinnusker, the track bounces over parallel rhyolite ridges before ascending steeply to a ridge studded with hot springs and fumaroles. Cross more ridges of descending altitude then drop steeply from the **Jökultungur** ridge into the **Álftavatn** valley, where a 4WD track leads to two **huts**.

There are several stream crossings south of Álftavatn; after 5km, you'll pass the privately owned **Hvanngil** hut and camping ground. Cross the footbridge over the Kaldaklofskvísl, follow the route posted 'Emstrur/Fljótshlíð' and ford the knee-deep Bláfjallakvísl. The track enters a lonely and surreal 5km stretch of black sand and pumice desert, skirting the pyramid-shaped peak, **Stórasúla**.

The next barrier is the river **Innri-Emstruá**, which is bridged but may have a knee-deep side channel. After the bridge, continue up to the crest and watch on your left for the 'FÍ Skáli' signpost, which directs you through a desolate desert to the **Botnar** (Emstrur) huts.

Cross a small heath then drop steeply to cross the roiling **Fremri-Emstruá** on a small footbridge. From there, the trail is relatively flat to the Ljósá footbridge.

Over the next hill is the more difficult unbridged river **Þrongá**. The onward route on the opposite bank isn't obvious; look for a V-shaped ravine just west of the marked crossing point. There, the track enters the **Þórsmörk** woodland. When you reach a junction, the right fork leads to Reykjavík Excursions' **Húsadalur hut** and the left fork to the Ferðafélag Íslands' **Þórsmörk hut**. Camping is restricted only to sites near the huts. For more information on Þórsmörk, see p292.

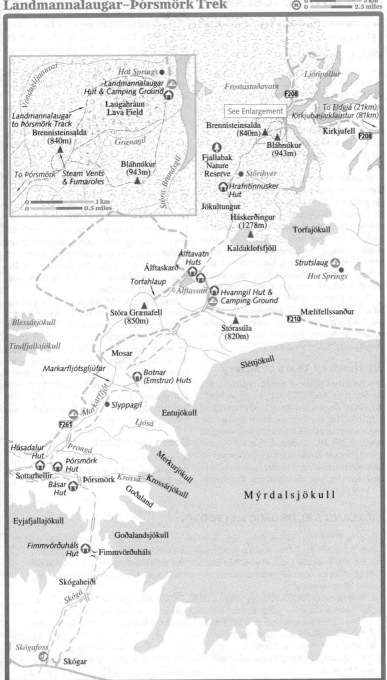

0   5 km
0   2.5 miles

ICELAND LANDMANNALAUGAR TO ÞÓRSMÖRK TREK

Hot Springs ●

Landmannalaugar
Hut & Camping Ground

Laugahraun
Lava Field

Landmannalaugar
to Þórsmörk Track

Brennisteinsalda
(840m) ▲

Grænagil

To Þórsmörk   Steam Vents
& Fumaroles

Bláhnúkur
(943m) ▲

0   1 km
0   0.5 miles

Ljótipollur

Frostastaðavatn

See Enlargement

F208

To Eldgjá (21km);
Kirkjubæjarklaustur (81km)

Kirkjufell

F208

Brennisteinsalda
(840m) ▲ ▲ Bláhnúkur
(943m)

Fjallabak
Nature
Reserve ● Stórihver

Hrafntinnusker
Hut

Jökultungur

Háskerðingur
(1278m)

Torfajökull

Kaldaklofsfjöll

Álftavatn
Huts

Strutslaug

Hot Springs

Álftaskarð

Torfahlaup

Álftavatn   Hvanngil Hut &
Camping Ground

Mælifellssandur

F210

Stóra Grænafell
(850m)

Stórasúla
(820m)

Blessárjökull

Sléttjökull

Tindfjallajökull

Mosar

Markarfljótsgljúfur

Markarfljót

Botnar
(Emstrur) Huts

Slyppagil

Entujökull

Ljósá

F261

Húsadalur
Hut

Þrongá

Þórsmörk
Hut

Merkurjökull

Sottarhellir

Básar
Hut

Þórsmörk   Krossá   Krossá

Krossárjökull

Goðaland

Eyjafjallajökull

Myrdalsjökull

Goðalandsjökull

Fimmvörðuháls
Hut

Fimmvörðuháls

Skógaheiði

Skógá

Skógafoss

Skógar

UNDERSTAND ICELAND

History

Viking Beginnings

Irish monks were probably the first people to come to Iceland in around AD 700. Their solitude was rudely shattered by the Settlement Era (871–930), when a wave of Nordic people descended, driven from the Scandinavian mainland by political clashes. Many raided Ireland and the Scottish islands on the way, bringing Celtic slaves to the new country.

Ingólfur Arnarson, a Norwegian fugitive, became the first official Icelander (AD 871). He settled at Reykjavík (Smoky Bay), which he named after steam he saw rising from geothermal vents. According to 12th-century sources, Ingólfur built his farm on Aðalstræti. Recent archaeological excavations have unearthed a Viking longhouse on that very spot; the dwelling is now the focus of the city's newest museum, Reykjavík 871+/-2.

The settlers rejected monarchy and established the world's first democratic parliament at Þingvellir (Parliament Plains; p268), outside Reykjavík. The country converted to Christianity in the year 1000.

Six-Hundred Years of Misery

Two hundred years of peace ended during the Sturlung Age (1230–62), when Iceland's chieftains descended into bloody territorial fighting. The era is epitomised by the life and violent death of historian and political schemer, Snorri Sturluson (p270). Iceland ceded control of the country to Norway in 1262, then was placed under Danish rule in 1397. For the next six centuries, the forgotten country endured a Dark Age of famine, disease and disastrous volcanic eruptions.

In the early 17th century, the Danish king imposed a trade monopoly that was utterly exploited by foreign merchants. In an attempt to bypass the crippling embargo, weaving, tanning and wool-dyeing factories were built, which led to the foundation of the city of Reykjavík.

Iceland's next calamity was volcanic. In 1783 the vast crater row Lakagígar (Laki) erupted for 10 months, devastating southeastern Iceland and creating a lingering poisonous haze. Nearly 75% of Iceland's livestock and 20% of the human population perished in the resulting famine; an evacuation of the country was discussed.

Birth of a New Nation

In spite (or perhaps because) of such neglectful foreign rule and miserable living conditions, a sense of Icelandic nationalism slowly began to grow. The Republic of Iceland was established on 17 June 1944, symbolically at Þingvellir.

Perversely, while the rest of Europe endured the horrors of WWII, Iceland went from strength to strength. British and then US troops were stationed at Keflavík (right up until September 2006), bringing with them undreamt-of wealth. Subsistence farming gave way to prosperity and a frenzy of new building, funded mainly by American dollars. The Ring Rd, Iceland's main highway that circles the whole country, was finally completed in 1974.

Boom...and Bust

A corresponding boom in the fishing industry saw Iceland extend its fishing limit in the 1970s to 200 miles (322km). This pre-

ICELAND'S ECONOMIC MELTDOWN

In early 2008, Iceland was riding high. However, much of the country's wealth was built over a black hole of debt, and the global recession knocked Iceland flat. By October 2008, the Icelandic stock market had crashed; the króna lost almost half its value overnight; all three national banks went into receivership; and the country teetered on the brink of bankruptcy.

In November 2008 Iceland received a US$2.1 billion International Monetary Fund (IMF) loan and a US$3 billion bailout from Scandinavian neighbours. The government applied for EU membership in 2009, hoping to swap the fluctuating króna for the euro. But in 2010 debate was still rumbling on about Iceland's liability for UK and Dutch losses, incurred when Icesave (a subsidiary of Iceland's national bank Landsbanki) collapsed. The economy is steadying up, but uncertainty and debt look set to haunt the country for years to come.

cipitated the worst of the 'cod wars', when the UK initially refused to recognise the new zone and continued fishing inside what were now deemed to be Icelandic waters. During the seven-month conflict, Icelandic ships cut the nets of British trawlers, shots were fired and ships on both sides were rammed.

Iceland's booming economy suffered when the world financial crisis dealt the country a sledgehammer blow in September 2008, thanks to massive foreign debt and a severely overvalued currency. The government fell following four months of furious protests in the capital. In May 2009 a new left-wing government was elected, headed by Jóhanna Sigurðardóttir, Iceland's first female prime minister. Later that year, the government voted by a narrow margin to apply for EU membership, with a referendum expected in early 2012 should Iceland be invited to join.

In volcano news, the ash cloud from the April 2010 eruption under Eyjafjallajökull glacier shut down European air traffic for six days, causing travel chaos across much of the continent. The airline industry, which is estimated to have lost over US$200 million per day, breathed a sigh of relief when the eruption stopped on May 23 – as did media broadcasters and commentators, who struggled woefully to pronounce the glacier's name correctly.

The Icelanders

Icelanders are reserved but friendly. They value independence and have a live-and-let-live attitude. However, they are fiercely proud of their sea-faring culture and many hold strong prowhaling views. Icelanders recently discovered that much of their genetic makeup is Celtic, suggesting that far more of the Viking settlers had children by their Celtic slaves than originally thought.

Icelanders' names are constructed from a combination of their first name and their father's (or mother's) first name. Girls add the suffix *dóttir* (daughter) to the patronymic and boys add *son*. Therefore, Jón, the son of Einar, would be Jón Einarsson. Guðrun, the daughter of Halldór, would be Guðrun Halldórsdóttir. Icelanders always call each other by their first names.

The country has one of the world's highest life expectancies: 79.7 years for men and 83.3 years for women. Of a population of 318,000, almost half live in Reykjavík.

Iceland officially converted to Christianity around 1000, although followers of the old pagan gods were allowed to worship in private. The Danes imposed Lutheranism in the 1550 Reformation: 84% of Icelanders are Lutheran today.

Arts

Literature

Bloody, black and powerful, the late 12th- and 13th-century sagas are without doubt Iceland's greatest cultural achievement. Written in terse Old Norse, these epics continue to entertain Icelanders and provide them with a rich sense of heritage. One of the best known, *Egil's Saga,* revolves around the complex, devious Egill Skallagrímsson. A renowned poet and skilled lawyer, he's also the grandson of a werewolf and a murderous drunk. You can admire original saga manuscripts in Reykjavík's Þjóðmenningarhúsið.

The best-known modern Icelandic writer is Nobel Prize–winner Halldór Laxness, who lived just outside Reykjavík (p269). His darkly comic work gives a superb insight into Icelandic life. *Independent People,* concerning the fatally proud farmer Bjartur and the birth of the Icelandic nation, is his most famous book and an unmissable read.

Modern Icelandic writers include Einar Kárason, who wrote the outstanding *Devil's Island* (about Reykjavík life in the 1950s); Hallgrímur Helgason, creator of *101 Reykjavík* (about a modern-day city slacker); and Arnaldur Indriðason, whose Reykjavík-based crime fiction, including the award-winning *Silence of the Grave,* regularly tops Iceland's bestseller lists.

Music

Björk is Iceland's most famous musical export. Closely following Björk is Sigur Rós, whose singer Jónsi has also gone on to achieve solo fame. Emiliana Torrini is also popular. The swirling maelstrom of Icelandic popular music constantly throws up new singers and bands. FM Belfast, múm, Hafdís Huld, Ghostigital, Reykjavík!, Dikta, Ólöf Arnalds and Agent Fresco are just some of the many names to look out for. For interesting documentaries about the Icelandic music scene, try *Screaming*

WEIGHING UP THE WHALE DEBATE

After 150 years of hunting, many whale species are now facing extinction. To give populations a chance to recover, the International Whaling Commission (IWC) called for a suspension of commercial whaling in 1986. Most countries complied; however, Iceland continued 'scientific' whaling, a loophole that allows whales to be hunted for DNA samples and then permits the meat to be sold to restaurants.

Following international pressure, there was a lull between 1989 and 2003, after which Icelandic whalers resumed 'scientific' whaling, catching 200 minkes between 2003 and 2007. In 2006, Iceland also began commercial whaling again, with the governmental Icelandic Marine Institute tentatively suggesting that an annual catch of 100 minke and 150 fin whales is sustainable. In response, 26 countries issued a formal protest to the Icelandic government, and conservationists called for a boycott of Iceland and Icelandic goods. The protests appear to have had little impact on the whaling industry: 148 fin whales and 60 minke whales were killed in the 2010 hunting season, according to figures from the Icelandic Ministry of Fisheries and Agriculture.

Whaling is an emotional topic, and has become deeply entwined with national pride. Supporters of the hunt (around 70% of Icelanders polled in 2003, with figures remaining about that level in subsequent polls) believe minke whales are depleting fish stocks and need culling; whereas antiwhalers fear for the animals and for the flourishing whale-watching industry, which brings in about US$18 million annually.

Whaling in Iceland is regulated by the International Whaling Commission. For more information, see the websites of the International Whaling Commission (www.iwcoffice.org), World Wide Fund for Nature (www.wwf.org), Icelandic Ministry of Fisheries and Agriculture (www.fisheries.is) and Greenpeace (www.greenpeace.org).

Masterpiece (2005), *Music from the Moon* (2009) or *Backyard* (2011).

Bands perform live at venues such as NASA, in Reykjavík. The major music event of the year is the international-yet-intimate Iceland Airwaves festival, also in Reykjavík. The Icelandic Music Maffia blog (http://icelandicmusicmaffia.blogspot.com) will keep you up to date with Icelandic gigs and album releases.

Visual Arts

Various artists have wrestled with Iceland's enigmatic soul, including the prolific Ásgrímur Jónsson (1876–1958). His work, depicting Icelandic landscapes and folk tales, can be seen at the National Gallery of Iceland in Reykjavík. Pop-art icon Erró (b 1932) is honoured with a permanent collection in Listasafn Reykjavíkur.

Sculptors are well represented: the mystical work of Einar Jónsson (1874–1954) dwells on death and resurrection, and can be viewed at the Einar Jónsson Museum in Reykjavík. Ásmundur Sveinsson's (1893–1982) sculptures, on display at Ásmundarsafn in Reykjavík, celebrate Iceland and its stories.

Cinema & TV

Baltasar Kormákur has won international audiences for several films. *101 Reykjavík* (2000), based on Hallgrímur Helgason's book of the same name, is the painful, funny tale of a Reykjavík drop-out's fling with his mother's lesbian lover. The thriller *Jar City* (2006), adapted from Arnaldur Indriðason's award-winning novel *Tainted Blood,* follows world-weary Detective Inspector Erlendur as he investigates a brutal murder and some dodgy doings at Iceland's Genetic Research Centre.

For forthcoming films, see the informative www.icelandicfilmcentre.is.

Environment
The Land

Iceland, a juvenile among the world's land masses, is shaped by desert plateaus (52%), lava fields (11%), sandur (sand deltas; 4%) and ice caps (12%). Over half of Iceland lies above 400m and its highest point, Hvannadalshnúkur, rises 2119m above sea level. Only 21% of Iceland is considered habitable.

Iceland's active volcanic zone runs through the middle of the country, from southwest to northeast. Active-zone geological features include lava flows, tubes, geysers, hot springs and volcanoes, and rocks such as basalt, pumice and rhyolite. Geysir, Krýsuvík and Krafla are very accessible active areas.

There are very few trees. Most of the native flora consists of grasses, mosses, lichens and wildflowers. *Plöntukort Íslands* (Botanical Map; Ikr1690), available from Reykjavík's bookshops, is a good guide.

Wildlife

The wild-eyed Arctic fox is the only indigenous land mammal; introduced species include reindeer and mice. Polar bears occasionally turn up on the north coast, but their life expectancy in Iceland is short.

The lack of land mammals is compensated for by vast numbers of birds and marine fauna. Kittiwakes, fulmars and gannets form large coastal colonies (best seen at Látrabjarg); there are Arctic terns, golden plovers, ducks, swans, divers and geese at Mývatn; and Vestmannaeyjar has the largest population of puffins. The website www.fuglar.is lists what rarities are about. *Fuglakort Íslands* (Birdwatcher's Map; Ikr1690), sold in Reykjavík's bookshops, is a good reference.

Four different seal species and 12 species of cetacean have been spotted: boat trips run from various coastal towns, including Reykjavík, although the best sightings are at Húsavík.

National Parks & Nature Reserves

Iceland's national parks *(þjóðgarður)* are Snæfellsjökull (Snæfellsnes); Þingvellir (The Golden Circle), a Unesco World Heritage site; and the newly created Vatnajökull National Park (Vatnajökull), which combines the former Jökulsárgljúfur and Skaftafell parks. There are countless nature reserves *(friðland)*, the most significant being Mývatn. Parks and reserves are open to visitors at all times. Wild camping is restricted. For further information, contact the government's environment agency, **Umhverfisstofnun** (☑591 2000; www.ust.is).

Environmental Issues

Historically, sheep farming and timber extraction caused immense environmental damage. The Iceland Forest Service estimates that a mere 1% of Iceland's original woodland remains. Large-scale aerial seeding and intensive tree-planting programs are combating erosion.

Concerns over declining fish stocks have led the government to invest in other areas, particularly heavy industry (in early 2008, aluminium smelting products accounted for 40% of Iceland's total exports, overtaking fish for the first time). The most controversial project in Icelandic history was the dam built in the Kárahnjúkar peaks in eastern Iceland to power an American aluminium smelting plant. Completed in 2008, it altered the courses of two glacial rivers and flooded a vast area of untouched wilderness.

Iceland is endeavouring to free itself of fossil fuels by 2050, relying instead on geothermal power, hydrogen cells and solar energy.

Icelandic Cuisine

Cafes and restaurants in Reykjavík cater to most tastes, but fresh fish, seafood and Icelandic lamb get top billing on most upmarket menus.

The government levies high taxes on alcohol to discourage excessive drinking. Check out Friday-night Reykjavík to see the success of this policy!

Staples & Specialities

Born from centuries of near-starvation, Iceland's traditional dishes reflect a 'waste not, want not' austerity. Specialities include *svið* (singed sheep's head complete with eyeballs), *súrsaðir hrútspungar* (pickled rams' testicles) and *hákarl* (putrefied shark meat, buried and rotted for three months to make it digestible). These gruesome dishes are generally only eaten nowadays during the February celebration of Þorri. You can try cubes of shark meat at Kolaportið Flea Market in Reykjavík, but be warned that the smell alone makes many foreigners ill! Some restaurants serve whale meat *(hval)* (see boxed text, p302).

Icelanders consume *lundi* (puffin), which looks and tastes like calf liver. Most of the birds are netted on the Vestmannaeyjar. *Harðfiskur* is an everyday snack: these brittle pieces of wind-dried haddock are usually eaten with butter. Delicious yoghurt-like *skyr*, made from curdled milk, is a unique treat; sugar, fruit and cream are often added to turn it into a rich dessert. Around Mývatn look out for a regional pudding: *hverabrauð* (hot-spring bread) is a sweet, dark, sticky loaf, baked in the ground using geothermal heat. *Kleinur* (twisted doughnuts, traditionally deep-fried in lard) are popular snacks to dip in coffee.

Coffee is a national institution, and most cafes offer free refills. The traditional Icelandic alcoholic brew is *brennivín* (burnt wine), a sort of schnapps made from potatoes and caraway seeds with the foreboding nickname *svarti dauði* (black death). Note that if you buy *syrmjolk* from the supermarket, it's sour milk.

Where to Eat & Drink

Reykjavík has no shortage of cosy cafes (commonly open from 11am until 1am, later at weekends) that turn into bars at night. They're great for lingering coffees, light lunches (from about Ikr1500) and late-night beers. Restaurants are more upmarket, often serving gourmet food, with mains from about Ikr2700 to Ikr5000 per person. Some are open for lunch (between 11am and 2pm), and most open nightly (between 6pm and 10pm). In other towns, choice is much reduced and opening times shorter.

Every village has at least one *kaupfélagið* (cooperative supermarket), with Bónus and Netto being the cheapest. Petrol stations and grills sell relatively inexpensive fast-food snacks (a hot dog and chips cost around Ikr800).

Beer, wine and spirits are available to people aged over 20 years from licensed hotels, bars, restaurants and Vín Búð (state monopoly) stores.

Vegetarians & Vegans

Outside Reykjavík, which has three vegan/vegie restaurants, choices are limited. Most places offer one vegie dish, but as this usually involves cheese, vegans may have to self-cater.

SURVIVAL GUIDE

Directory A–Z

Accommodation

Iceland has a full spectrum of accommodation options, from spartan mountain huts through hostels, working farms, guesthouses and school-based summer rooms to luxury hotels. Walls, even in upmarket accommodation, tend to be thin – bring earplugs if you're sensitive to noise.

Sleeping-bag accommodation is a peculiarly Icelandic concept, and a boon for those on a budget. Many hostels and guesthouses let you have a bed without bedding for a discount on their standard prices, if you use your own sleeping bag.

We have given high-season prices throughout. Out of season, prices at some B&Bs, guesthouses and hotels drop by as much as 50%. Many places close in winter; check first.

In this chapter accommodation prices are based on a double room, usually with private bathroom and breakfast. The following price indicators apply:

€€€ more than Ikr22,000

€€ Ikr12,000 to Ikr22,000

€ less than Ikr12,000

CAMPING

Make sure your tent is up to Icelandic weather: storm-force winds and deluges aren't uncommon throughout the year, even in summer. Wild camping is possible in some areas (although not on fenced land without permission, or in national parks and nature reserves), but is often discouraged. With approximately 130 *tjaldsvæði* (organised camping grounds) in towns and at rural farmhouses, there's usually a campsite close at hand. Camping costs around Ikr1000 per person and grounds usually open from June to August.

Campfires are not allowed, so bring a stove. Butane cartridges and petroleum fuels are available in petrol stations and hardware shops.

A free directory, *Útilega: Tjaldsvæði Íslands* (available from tourist offices), lists many of Iceland's camping grounds.

EDDA HOTELS & SUMMER HOTELS

Once, when Icelandic kids from remote regions were sent away to be educated at boarding schools, the school buildings doubled as basic summer hotels when the children returned home in the holidays. Nowadays, most of the summer Edda hotels are used in winter as conference centres, although a couple still serve as student lodgings in term time.

There are 13 Edda Hotels (☑444 4000; www.hoteledda.is); most have restaurants and many have geothermal pools. Accommodation tends to be simple: rooms are plain but functional, usually with twin beds, a washbasin and shared bathrooms, although a few hotels offer rooms with private bathrooms. Some Edda hotels have dormitory sleeping-bag spaces, costing around Ikr3000 per person. Singles/doubles start at Ikr8000/10,000 for a room with washbasin.

Other town and village schools operate their own private summer hotels.

EMERGENCY HUTS

ICE-SAR (Icelandic Association for Search & Rescue; ☑570 5900; www.icesar.com) and Félag Íslenskra Bifreiðaeigenda (Icelandic Automobile Association; ☑414 9999; www.fib.is) maintain bright-orange huts on mountain passes and remote coastlines, only to be used in dire emergency (it's illegal to stay there otherwise). They are stocked with food, fuel and blankets.

FARMHOUSE ACCOMMODATION

Across Iceland, many rural farmhouses offer campsites, sleeping-bag spaces, B&Bs and chalets. Facilities vary: some farms provide meals or have guest kitchens, some have hot pots and some can organise fishing trips, sheep round-ups or horse rentals.

Around 140 farmhouses are members of Ferðaþjónusta Bænda (Icelandic Farm Holidays; ☑570 2700; www.farmholidays.is; Síðumúli 2, Reykjavík), which publishes an annual listings guide. Twenty-three are wheelchair-accessible.

GUESTHOUSES

There are various types of *gistiheimilið* (guesthouses), from private homes that let rooms to custom-built motels. Most are comfortable and homey, with kitchens, TV lounges and buffet-style breakfast (either included in the price or for around Ikr1200 extra). Some also offer sleeping-bag accommodation at a price significantly reduced from that for a made-up bed.

A high percentage of places open from June to August only. Students often take over Reykjavík guesthouses from September to May.

HOTELS

Every major town has at least one upmarket business-style hotel, usually with somewhat bland but comfortable rooms and all the expected amenities. Two of the largest home-grown chains are Fosshótels (☑562 4000; www.fosshotel.is) and Icelandair Hotels (☑444 4000; www.icehotels.is), which also runs the Edda chain.

MOUNTAIN HUTS

Sæluhús (mountain huts) sprout up on popular hiking routes, mostly in wilderness areas. Accommodation is of the rough-and-ready variety: sleeping-bag spaces (Ikr3000 to Ikr4200) in communal huts (which sometimes also have a camping ground). Some huts have cooking facilities, a warden and camping ground outside. The huts are open to anyone, but members get a discount. Book in advance, as places fill quickly.

The main mountain-hut provider is Ferðafélag Íslands (Icelandic Touring Association; ☑568 2533; www.fi.is; Mörkin 6, Reykjavík), with huts at 13 sites around Iceland.

YOUTH HOSTELS

Bandalag Íslenskra Farfugla (Icelandic Youth Hostel Association; ☑553 8110; www.hostel.is; Sundlaugarvegur 34, Reykjavík) has a network of 36 well-maintained properties – mostly youth hostels, but there are also a couple of self-catering apartments and a mountain hut. All hostels have hot showers, cooking facilities, luggage storage and sleeping-bag accommodation; almost all have family rooms. If you don't have a sleeping bag, you can hire sheets and blankets (Ikr900 per stay). Bookings are strongly recommended. About half of the hostels close over autumn and winter, so phone before rolling up out of season.

Join Hostelling International (HI; www.hihostels.com) before you arrive to benefit from HI member discounts. For a dorm bed, HI members pay around Ikr2500 (children aged five to 12 years pay half price), with a surcharge of Ikr1900, if you want a room to yourself. Breakfast (where available) costs around Ikr1100 extra.

Activities

FISHING

Salmon fishing seems like a great idea but a one-day licence may cost anything up to Ikr200,000, making your catch some of the world's most expensive fish! However, you can fish for rainbow trout, sea trout and Arctic char on a more reasonably priced voucher system. Trout fishing runs from April to mid-September, and ice fishing is possible in some areas in winter. For further information, contact the National Angling Association (☑553 1510; www.angling.is).

GLACIER WALKING

Several companies offer exhilarating guided walks, with crampons and ice axes, on the south-coast glaciers. The Icelandic Mountain

Guides (www.mountainguide.is) Reykjavík (☑587 9999); Skaftafell (☑894 2959) and the **Glacier Guides** (☑571 2100; www.glacierguides.is) both have huts in the Skaftafell visitor-centre car park in summer.

HIKING, TREKKING & MOUNTAINEERING

The best way to see the country is undoubtedly on foot, whether on an afternoon hike or a two-week wilderness trek. However, the weather can leave careful plans in tatters: rain, fog and mist are common, and snow may fall in any season at higher altitudes.

In the highlands, straightforward hiking only becomes possible in July, August and early September. At other times, routes are impassable without complete winter gear; in late spring, melting snow turns many tracks into quagmires where whole vehicles have sunk without trace! Unbridged rivers can be difficult to cross at any time of year.

There are stunning hikes and treks all over the country, including in national parks and nature reserves; only the most well-used trails are marked. The most popular walks are in the deserted Hornstrandir Peninsula, lake-dominated Mývatn area, around Skaftafell and the Landmannalaugar to Þórsmörk trek in the highlands. If you are into mountaineering, there are some serious routes, including Hvannadalshnúkur (2119m), Iceland's highest peak.

Use caution when walking with children, especially in fissured areas such as Mývatn and Þingvellir, where narrow cracks in the earth can be hundreds of metres deep. Tough boots are needed for negotiating lava fields.

For details on hiking and mountaineering, contact **Ferðafélag Íslands** (☑568 2533; www.fi.is; Mörkin 6, Reykjavík), **Íslenski Alpaklúbburinn** (www.isalp.is) or the **Icelandic Mountain Guides** (☑587 9999; www.mountainguides.is; Vagnhöfði 7b, Reykjavík).

HORSE RIDING

The Icelandic horse *(Equus scandinavicus)* was brought over by the first settlers and was prominent in the development of the country. These sweet-natured, small-but-sturdy animals are perfectly suited to the rough Icelandic terrain and are still used for farm work. They are also ridden recreationally and are known for their *tölt,* a smooth, distinctive gait that makes riding easy, even for beginners.

You can hire horses through farms and tour agencies throughout the country, with a one-hour/one-day ride costing Ikr 5000/17,000. In

September experienced riders can also volunteer for the *réttir* (sheep round-up); contact local tourist offices to arrange this.

KAYAKING & RAFTING

Paddling gently along the edges of a fjord is a fantastic way to soak up the silence and feel an intrinsic part of Iceland's wild and lovely landscape: try kayaking in Stykkishólmur, Ísafjörður and Seyðisfjörður.

Arctic Rafting (☑571 2200; www.rafting.is; ☉May-Sep) run trips in south Iceland on the Hvítá river (near Gullfoss and Geysir); and in north Iceland on two glacial rivers near to the small service town of Varmahlíð. Both bases offer gentler journeys suitable for ages 12+; but if it's wild white water that you want, head for Varmahlíð and the exhilarating three-hour trip on the **Austari Jökulsá** (East Glacial River; Ikr13,000) with Grades III to IV-plus rapids (over 18s only). If you can't get enough of this entrancing canyon with its surging green-white water, there's also a three-day adventure (Ikr70,000) that speeds you downstream from the Sprengisandur desert and the river's glacial source.

SCUBA DIVING & SNORKELLING

Visibility of 100m sounds like a crazy dream, but the glacial water in Lake Þingvellir is vision-bendingly clear. **Dive.is** (☑663 2858; www.dive.is; 2 dives at Þingvellir Ikr30,000) runs daily tours year-round to the Silfra fissure in the lake, giving you the chance to dive between the North American and European continental plates. Scuba-diving certification is required; nondivers can drift overhead with drysuits and snorkels. The company also runs three- and seven-day diving tours to other sites around the country. Just outside Akureyri, **Strýtan Divecenter** (☑862 2949; www.styrtan.is; Huldugil) visits geothermal vents and leads dives inside the Arctic Circle.

SKIING & SNOWBOARDING

Skiers who enjoy out-of-the-way slopes will find some pleasant no-frills skiing in Iceland. In winter, Nordic skiing is possible throughout the country, although drawbacks include lack of transport in rural areas, bitterly cold winds and an absence of daylight. Both Reykjavík and Akureyri have winter resorts for downhill skiing or snowboarding (one-day lift passes around Ikr2900), with rentals (Ikr3500) and instructors:

Skíðasvæðin (www.skidasvaedi.is)

Hlíðarfjall (www.hlidarfjall.is)

SWIMMING

Thanks to an abundance of geothermal heat, every town has at least one *sundlaug* or *sundhöll* (public swimming hall), some with saunas, hot pots (similar to jacuzzis) and slides. Admission costs around Ikr360/120 per adult/child. And of course there are spa centres such as the Blue Lagoon and Mývatn Nature Baths.

WHALE WATCHING

Iceland is one of the best places in the world to see whales and dolphins. Quiet oak-hulled boats minimise disruption to the creatures and can get astonishingly close. Regular sailings depart from Húsavík and Reykjavík, and on demand in the Vestmannaeyjar. A three-hour trip costs around Ikr8000. Increasingly there are sailings year-round; but the best time to see whales is still between mid-May and September (in winter, the whales migrate south).

Business Hours

Banks 9.15am-4pm Mon-Fri

Cafes & bars 10am-1am Sun-Thu, to 3am or 6am Fri & Sat

Liquor stores 11am-6pm Mon-Thu, to 7pm Fri & to 2pm Sat

Petrol stations usually until 10pm

Post offices 9am-4.30pm Mon-Fri

Restaurants 11.30am-2.30pm, 6-10pm

Shops 9am-6pm Mon-Fri, 10am–noon or 4pm Sat

Supermarkets usually until 9pm

Children

Icelanders have a relaxed attitude to kids, but there are not many activities provided especially for them. Frequent bad weather may put you off family camping, but everyone can enjoy a ride on a mild-mannered Icelandic horse or a swim in an open-air pool.

Children aged between two and 11 years pay half fare on Flugfélag Íslands (Air Iceland) flights and tours, and are charged half price for farmhouse and some other accommodation. Bus fares are half price for children aged four to 11. Reykjavík Excursions tours are free for children under 11, and half fare for those aged between 12 and 15. There's a 50% discount at pools, and admission to museums and cinemas varies from full price to free.

Food

In this chapter restaurant prices are based on the average cost of a main course, unless stated otherwise. The following price indicators apply:

€€€ more than Ikr3500

€€ Ikr1500 to Ikr3500

€ less than Ikr1500

Gay & Lesbian Travellers

Icelanders have a fairly open attitude toward gays and lesbians. Check out www.gayice.is for news and events. **Samtökin '78** (☑552 7878; www.samtokin78.is; 4th fl, Laugavegur 3, Reykjavík) is Iceland's gay and lesbian organisation; it also acts as an informal community centre and drop-in cafe (8pm to 11pm Monday and Thursday).

Internet Access

Public internet access is available in most Icelandic libraries for about Ikr200 to Ikr400 per hour. Wi-fi access is common: with a wireless-enabled laptop, you can surf in most cafes, bars, hotels and many guesthouses.

Maps

Maps are widely available from tourist offices and bookshops all over Iceland. Ask tourist offices for the free *Map of Reykjavík* and *Around Iceland* booklets (with bags of information plus town plans).

The map publisher **Ferðakort** (☑517 7210; www.ferdakort.is; Brautarholt 8, Reykjavík; ⊗9am-5pm Mon-Thu, to 4pm Fri) has a good selection of road and walking maps, available through its website or at its dedicated map shop in Reykjavík. Most drivers use the general 1:500,000 *Ísland Touring Map*. Also useful are the 1:25,000 and 1:100,000 maps of Skaftafell, the 1:50,000 map of the Vestmannaeyjar and the 1:100,000 maps of Hornstrandir, Mývatn and the Landmannalaugar to Þórsmörk trek.

Money

Currency Icelandic króna (Ikr), divided into 100 aurar. Coins: one, five, 10, 50 and 100 króna. Notes: 500, 1000, 2000 and 5000 króna.

VAT *(söluskattur)* Included in marked prices: spend over Ikr4000 in a shop offering 'Iceland Tax-Free Shopping' and you can claim back up to 15%. Shop staff will

SAFE TRAVEL

In geothermal areas avoid thin crusts of lighter-coloured soil around steaming fissures and mudpots. Snowfields may overlie fissures, sharp lava chunks or slippery slopes of scoria (volcanic slag). Don't underestimate the weather: only attempt isolated hiking and glacier ascents if you know what you're doing. The supercautious can read www.safetravel.is for further information.

give you a tax-refund form; hand it in at the tourist office, the airport or the ferry terminal for a rebate. If you spend over Ikr40,000, take your forms and goods to customs before checking in.

ATMs Accept MasterCard, Visa, Cirrus, Maestro and Electron cards. MasterCard and Visa accepted everywhere; Diners Club and Amex less commonly used.

Tipping Not required.

Public Holidays

New Year's Day 1 January

Maundy Thursday Thursday before Easter

Good Friday to Easter Monday March/April

First Day of Summer first Thursday after 18 April

Labour Day 1 May

Ascension Day May (40 days after Easter)

Whit Sunday & Whit Monday May (seventh Sunday and Monday after Easter)

Independence Day 17 June

Shop & Office Workers' Holiday first Monday in August

Christmas Eve 24 December (afternoon)

Christmas Day 25 December

Boxing Day 26 December

New Year's Eve 31 December (afternoon)

Telephone

Public phones Public phones are elusive in mobile-crazy Reykjavík: elsewhere, there's usually a phone outside the post office or in the petrol station. Many pay-phones accept credit cards. Telephone directories are alphabetised by first name.

Mobile phones 900/1800 MHz GSM network covers populated areas; NMT network covers remote regions. Most European phones are compatible with the above GSM network. US phones work on a slightly different frequency, so US visitors should check with their phone company first regarding usability. Prepaid Icelandic SIM cards (Ikr2500, including Ikr2000 of free call credit), available from grocery shops and petrol stations, allow you to make calls at local rates. You'll need an unlocked phone for this to work.

Phone codes Direct dialling is available to Europe, North America and elsewhere. After dialling the international access code (☎00 from Iceland), dial your country code, area/city code and the telephone number. For dialling into Iceland from abroad, the country code is ☎354. There are no area codes: just follow the country code with the seven-digit number. Within Iceland, just dial the seven-digit number. Most Icelandic mobile phone numbers begin with the digit '8'.

Time

Iceland is always on GMT/UTC and has no daylight-saving time. So from late October to late March, Iceland is on the same time as London, five hours ahead of New York and 11 hours behind Sydney. Between April and September, Iceland is one hour behind London, four hours ahead of New York and 10 hours behind Sydney.

Tourist Information

You'll find tourist offices with friendly staff in towns all over the country. Pick up the useful *Around Iceland* (general tourist guide) and *Áning* (accommodation guide): both are free annual publications.

Icelandic Tourist Board (☎511 4000; www.icetourist.is; Borgartún 35, Reykjavík)

Upplýsingamiðstöð Ferðamanna (Main tourist office; ☎590 1550; www.visitreykjavik.is; Aðalstræti 2, Reykjavík) Official Reykjavík tourist office.

Travellers with Disabilities

Many hotels, restaurants and large shops have facilities for people with disabilities. Airlines can take disabled passengers, as can two of the coastal ferries, the *Baldur* and the *Herjólfur*. Flugfélag Íslands offers discounts to disabled travellers. Facilities aren't available on scheduled bus services, but tours on specially equipped buses can be arranged. For details, contact the tourist information centre in Reykjavík or visit the website of the organisation for the disabled, Sjálfsbjörg (☑550 0360; www.sjalfsbjorg.is; Hátún 12, Reykjavík).

Visas

Iceland, Norway and Switzerland, plus 22 EU countries (all but Bulgaria, Cyprus, Ireland, Romania and the UK), have abolished checks at common borders under the Schengen Agreement. Citizens of the USA, Canada, Australia and New Zealand need a valid passport to visit Iceland, but do not need a visa for stays of less than three months. Citizens of EU countries and other Scandinavian countries with a valid identity card do not require visas. Other nationalities should check www.utl.is to see whether they require a visa before arriving in Iceland.

Getting There & Away

Air

Keflavík airport (☑425 6000, flight times 425 0777; www.keflavikairport.com), 48km west of Reykjavík, is Iceland's main gateway. Flights to/from Greenland and the Faroe Islands use Reykjavík domestic airport in the city centre. From June to August, there is one Saturday flight per week from Copenhagen to tiny Akureyri airport, in Iceland's northern 'second city'.

Fares in this section are general indications only, and are for average-priced high-season return tickets. Cheaper deals are available if you are flexible or if you travel in the low season.

Only a few airlines have scheduled flights to Keflavík, Reykjavík and Akureyri airports. All have great safety records.

Atlantic Airways (www.atlantic.fo)

Eagle Air (www.eagleair.is)

Flugfélag Íslands (www.airiceland.is)

Iceland Express (www.icelandexpress.com)

Icelandair (www.icelandair.com)

SAS (www.flysas.com)

CONTINENTAL EUROPE
There are regular direct Icelandair flights to Keflavík from Amsterdam (€450), Bergen (Nkr3500), Copenhagen (Dkr2200), Frankfurt (€400), Göteborg (Skr4000), Helsinki (€350), Munich (€480), Oslo (Nkr3400), Paris (€400), Stavanger (Nkr4000) and Stockholm (Skr3000), most of which take approximately 3½ hours. Icelandair also has seasonal flights between Keflavík and Barcelona, Berlin and Milan, taking between six and nine hours.

Iceland Express flies year-round between Keflavík and Copenhagen (Dkr2000, three hours) up to 13 times weekly and between Keflavík and Berlin (€350, 3½ hours) up to three times weekly. In summer, there are one to three flights weekly between Keflavík and Aalborg, Alicante, Barcelona, Basel, Billund, Bologna, Frankfurt Hahn, Friedrichshafen, Göteborg, Kraków, Oslo, Stockholm and Warsaw (all around €300, between three and four hours); and between Akureyri and Copenhagen (Dkr2500, three hours).

SAS runs direct flights from Keflavík to Oslo (Nkr2000, 2¾ hours).

GREENLAND & THE FAROE ISLANDS
In summer, Flugfélag Íslands flies from Reykjavík to the following cities in Greenland:

Kulusuk (Ikr105,000, two hours, up to 12 times weekly)

Ilulissat (Ikr150,000, 3¼ hours, up to nine times weekly)

Narsarsuaq (Ikr120,000, three hours, up to six times weekly)

Nuuk (Ikr110,000, 3½ hours, up to four times weekly)

Flugfélag Íslands and Atlantic Airways fly year-round between the Faroe Islands and Reykjavík (Ikr85,000, 1½ hours), with up to three flights weekly.

UK
Icelandair has flights to Keflavík from the following cities:

London Heathrow (£280, three hours, twice daily)

Manchester (£400, 2½ hours, up to five times weekly)

Glasgow (£360, 2½ hours)

Internet-based airline Iceland Express flies up to twice daily (less frequently in winter) from London Gatwick to Keflavík (UK£250, three hours).

From Ireland, the cheapest way is to fly with Ryanair (www.ryanair.com) from Dublin to London Gatwick, where you can catch the Iceland Express flight to Keflavík.

USA & CANADA

There are very frequent year-round Iceland-air flights between Keflavík and Boston, New York and Seattle, and several flights a week between Keflavík and Orlando (also Minneapolis and Washington from May to October). Online return fares from New York to Keflavík cost about US$900; the flight takes around six hours.

Seasonal flights also operate between Keflavík and Halifax (mid-June to mid-September) and Toronto (around CA$1000, six hours, June to mid-October).

If you're flying with Icelandair from the US or Canada to Britain or Europe, you can include a free stopover in Iceland as part of your travel itinerary.

Sea

You can travel to Seyðisfjörður in eastern Iceland from Hirtshals (Denmark) and Tórshavn (Faroe Islands) by the smart car-ferry *Norröna,* operated by Smyril Line (www.smyril-line.com). See p526 for more information.

Getting Around

Air

There's an extensive network of domestic flights in Iceland, and it's the fastest way to get from place to place. Flexible travel plans are essential since schedules are dependent on the weather.

Flight prices given in the chapter are for full-fare one-way tickets; however, there are often internet offers, and you may be able to snap up standby tickets for up to half price. There are significant discounts for senior citizens, students and children.

The main domestic airline, Flugfélag Íslands (Air Iceland; ☑570 3030; www.airiceland.is), has daily flights in summer (fewer in winter) between Reykjavík and the following cities:

Akureyri (Ikr15,000, 45 minutes)

Egilsstaðir (Ikr17,000, one hour)

Ísafjörður (Ikr14,900, 40 minutes)

Flugfélag Íslands offers four-/five-/six-sector air passes costing Ikr42,570/48,720/55,770 plus airport tax (Ikr1180). These are valid for one month and must be bought outside Iceland. There's also a Fly As You Please ticket that gives 12 days of unlimited internal flights for Ikr65,240.

Eagle Air (☑562 2640; www.eagleair.is) has flights to several other domestic airstrips (all prices include domestic airport tax):

Vestmannaeyjar (Ikr10,500, 25 minutes, daily)

Höfn (Ikr13,900, one hour, six per week)

Bicycle

Cycling is an interesting if hardcore way to view Iceland's incredible landscape. Gale-force winds, sandstorms, sleet and sudden flurries of snow add to the challenge. Bring the best waterproofing money can buy; remember, you can always put your bike on a bus if things become intolerable. A mountain bike is probably more practical than a touring rig – you can get off the Ring Rd onto minor roads and unsurfaced tracks. Bring plenty of spares and several puncture repair kits.

Domestic airline flights charge Ikr3800 per bicycle. You can carry bikes on long-distance buses (Ikr2000), but space may be a problem at busy times.

In areas best suited to cycling, such as Mývatn, Reykjavík and Akureyri, bicycle hire costs around Ikr4000 per day, plus deposit. Children under 15 must wear a helmet by law.

The Icelandic Mountain Bike Club (☑562 0099; www.fjallahjolaklubburinn.is; Brekkustígur 2, Reykjavík) and Icebike (www.icebike.net) have lots of information and links about touring in Iceland.

Boat

Main Icelandic car ferries:

Herjólfur (p296) Between Landeyjahöfn and Vestmannaeyjar

Baldur (p272) Between Flatey, Stykkishólmur and Brjánslækur

Sæfari (p280) Between Dalvík, Hrísey and Grímsey

Bus

Iceland's long-distance bus network is di-vided between several private companies who provide routes in different areas of the country. They're overseen by BSÍ (Bifreiðastöð

Íslands; ☑562 1011; www.bsi.is), based in the BSÍ bus terminal on Vatnsmýrarvegur in Reykjavík. The booking desk sells tickets and distributes the free *Ísland á Eigin Vegum* (Iceland on Your Own) brochure, which contains timetable information for some northern and southern journeys. From June to August, there are regular buses to most places on the Ring Rd and to larger towns in the Westfjords. During the rest of the year, the service is limited or nonexistent; check with BSÍ or the following major bus companies for details.

Reykjavík Excursions (Kynnisferðir; ☑580 5400; www.re.is) Reykjanes Peninsula and the Flybus to Keflavík airport, some scheduled southern routes, and summer buses across the interior.

SBA-Norðurleið (☑550 0700/70; www.sba.is) Northeast Iceland.

Sterna (Bílar og Fólk; ☑551 1166; www.sterna.is) South, west and north Iceland.

Stjörnubílar (☑456 5518; www.stjornubilar.is) Westfjords.

Various bus passes are available for June, July and August, which can reduce transport costs when used wisely. Available from Sterna (see website for full list):

Full-Circle Passport (Ikr35,000) Valid for one circuit of the Ring Rd in one direction, stopping wherever you like.

Full-Circle Passport/Western Fjords (Ikr51,000) As for the Full-Circle Passport, plus one circuit of the Westfjords, reached only via the ferry *Baldur* (from Stykkishólmur).

Snæfellsnes Passport (Ikr36,000) Valid for one circuit of Snæfellsnes Peninsula, starting and ending in Reykjavík.

West Iceland & Westfjords (Ikr25,000) Valid for one circuit of the Westfjords, to/from Reykjavík via Snæfellsnes Peninsula and Brú.

Vestmannaeyjar (Ikr8600) Includes Reykjavík–Landeyjahöfn bus journey and return ferry ticket to the islands.

Available from Reykjavík Excursions:

Highlights Passport (7-/9-/11-/13-/15-day pass Ikr37,600/46,500/53,200/59,400/65,000; mid-June to August) Unlimited travel on Reykjavík Excursions' bus routes 6, 9, 10, 11, 112, 14, 15 and 16, and SBA-

Norðurleið's bus routes 610, 641 and 661. Will get you to Þingvellir, Gullfoss, Geysir, Landmannalaugar, Þórsmörk, Lakagígar, Jökulsárlón and across the Sprengisandur route.

Highland Circle Passport (Ikr34,200; July to August) Valid for one circular route to the north of Iceland via the Sprengisandur and Kjölur routes, on Reykjavík Excursions' bus routes 10, 14 and 112 and SBA-Norðurleið's bus routes 62 and 610.

Beautiful South Passport (3-/5-/7-/9-/11-day pass Ikr19,100/28,000/34,800/41,500/47,100; mid-June to August) Unlimited travel along the south coast and to Þórsmörk and Lakagígar on Reykjavík Excursions' bus routes 6, 9, 10, 11, 112, 15 and 16.

Beautiful South – Circle Passport (Ikr17,400; mid-June to August) A more limited version of the Beautiful South Passport, this will get you as far as Skaftafell and inland to Landmannalaugar along routes 10, 11 and 112.

Car & Motorcycle
AUTOMOBILE ASSOCIATION
The Icelandic national motoring association is **Félag Íslenskra Bifreiðaeigenda** (FÍB; ☑414 9999; www.fib.is). Membership is only open to Iceland residents. However, if you already have breakdown cover with an automobile association that's affiliated to ARC Europe, you may be covered by the FÍB – check with your home association.

BRING YOUR OWN VEHICLE
It's relatively easy to bring a vehicle on the ferry from Denmark. Drivers must carry the vehicle's registration documents, proof of valid insurance, proof of ownership of the vehicle and a driving licence (EU, North American and Australian licences are fine; otherwise you may need an International Driving Permit). Contact the **Directorate of Customs** (☑560 0300; www.tollur.is) for further information. See also p526.

FUEL & SPARE PARTS
Fuel prices have risen sharply recently, with unleaded 95 octane *(blýlaust, 95 okt)* costing around Ikr212.8 per litre (diesel Ikr213.2). Outside Reykjavík, petrol station opening hours vary, but out-of-hours there's usually a self-service pump that will accept Visa/MasterCard, and sometimes Ikr500, Ikr1000

and Ikr2000 bank notes. Service stations can be quite widely dispersed; make sure you fill up when you have the chance and carry a jack, jumper leads (jumper cables), spare tyre etc.

HIRE

While rates are expensive by international standards, prices compare favourably against bus or internal air travel. The cheapest vehicles normally cost around Ikr18,000 per day, with unlimited mileage and VAT included. Rental charges for 4WD vehicles are at least twice that. The Reykjavík tourist office keeps details of special offers. It's often much cheaper to book a car over the internet before you get to Iceland – see p527.

You must be at least 20 years old to hire a car in Iceland (23 to hire a jeep), and you will need to show a recognised licence (most firms are happy with your home licence, although you could bring an International Driving Permit to be on the safe side) and pay by credit card.

HITCHING

Lonely Planet does not recommend hitching. Summer hitching is possible but can be inconsistent. The best idea is to find a petrol station, then try to charm drivers who have stopped for a break. At least if waits are long, you can get a coffee! See also p528.

ROAD CONDITIONS & HAZARDS

Icelandic highways aren't suitable for high speeds – they're two-lane affairs, often narrowing to a single lane over bridges, and there are sometimes long, unsurfaced sections. Road edges are often steeply cambered, with no shoulders or margins. Beware of oncoming cars driving in the middle of the road.

On the F-numbered (interior) highway system, 4WD vehicles are needed. If you're planning to drive through the interior, do so with an accompanying vehicle – there are no services, and glacial rivers and drifting sand pose real threats. It goes without saying that you'll need full tool/repair kits (and the expertise to use them) and emergency supplies. It's illegal to drive off-road or off-track: Icelandic soil and vegetation are extremely fragile, and damage caused by vehicles can be irreparable.

Find up-to-date weather forecasts on the Icelandic Meteorological Office (http://en.vedur.is/) website. For current road conditions, see the Vegagerðin (Icelandic Road Administration; ☑1777; www.vegagerdin.is).

ROAD RULES

Drive on the right and keep your headlights on at all times. The use of seatbelts (front and rear) is compulsory. In urban areas, the speed limit is 50km/h or less. On paved roads, the speed limit is 90km/h (80km/h on unpaved roads). Drink-driving laws are very strict in Iceland and the legal limit is set at 0.05% blood alcohol content. The penalty for driving over the limit is loss of your licence plus a large fine. Talking on a mobile phone while driving is illegal unless using a hands-free kit.

Slow down or give way at blind peaks (marked *blindhæð*) and on single-breadth bridges (marked *einbreið brú*).

Norway

Best Places to Eat

» Feinschmecker (p323)

» Potetkjelleren (p347)

» Fossheim Turisthotell
(p339)

» Pingvinen (p347)

Best Places to Stay

» Det Hanseatiske Hotel
(p343)

» Stalheim Hotel (p367)

» Utne Hotel (p352)

» Engholm Husky Design
Lodge (p402)

Why Go?

Norway is a once-in-a-lifetime destination and the essence of its appeal is remarkably simple: this is one of the most beautiful countries on earth.

The drama of Norway's natural world is difficult to overstate. Impossibly steep-sided fjords cut deep gashes into the interior. But this is also a land of glaciers, grand and glorious, snaking down from Europe's largest ice fields, and of the primeval appeal of the Arctic.

The counterpoint to so much natural beauty is found in the country's vibrant cultural life. Norwegian cities are cosmopolitan and brimful of architecture that showcases the famous Scandinavian flair for design. At the same time, a busy calendar of festivals, many of international renown, are worth planning your trip around.

Yes, Norway is one of the most expensive countries on Earth. But is it worth it? Absolutely: Norway will pay you back with never-to-be-forgotten experiences many times over.

When to Go
Oslo

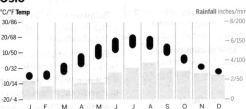

Mid-Jun–mid-Aug Summer fjords, endless days and accommodation prices fall.

Dec-Feb The aurora borealis (Northern Lights), and wonderful winter activities.

May–mid-Jun & mid-Aug–Sep Generally fine weather and without the en masse crowds.

Exchange Rates

Australia	A$1	Nkr5.71
Canada	C$1	Nkr5.50
Europe	€1	Nkr7.76
Japan	¥100	Nkr6.42
New Zealand	NZ$1	Nkr4.19
UK	UK£1	Nkr8.72
USA	US$1	Nkr5.24

Set Your Budget

» **Budget hotel room** up to Nkr750
» **Two-course evening meal** Nkr150–200
» **Museum entrance** free–Nkr80
» **Beer** Nkr50–80
» **Oslo bus or tram ticket** Nkr70 (daily pass)

Resources

» **Fjord Norway** (www.fjord norway.com) Focused on Norway's star attraction
» **Norway.com** (www.nor way.com) Links to tourist information with a practical focus
» **Norway Guide** (www. norwayguide.no) Detailed rundown on Norway's top attractions
» **Visit Norway** (www. visitnorway.com) Comprehensive Norwegian Tourist Board site

Connections

Trains and buses link Norway with Russia, Sweden and Finland. Frequent ferries head to Germany and Denmark from several Norwegian ports. Airports in Oslo and Bergen connect Norway to the world, with a handful of international flights to Stavanger, Trondheim and distant Tromsø, way up in the Arctic Circle.

ITINERARIES

One Week

Spend a day in Oslo, then take the Norway in a Nutshell tour to Bergen via Myrdal, Flåm and Nærøyfjorden. Spend two nights in Bergen before taking an unhurried jaunt around Hardangerfjord. Return to Sognefjord, stay at the Stalheim Hotel and visit glaciers around Fjærland. Return to Oslo.

Two Weeks

Instead of returning to Oslo, head back to Bergen and take the *Hurtigruten* along the coast, pausing for stays of a night or two in Ålesund and Trondheim, before continuing to the fishing villages of craggy Lofoten, where you should spend at least a couple of days exploring. Finally, take the *Hurtigruten* to Tromsø, the north's most vibrant city, before returning to Oslo.

One Month

Tromsø is your gateway to Norway's High Arctic. After a night in this engaging town, make for the prehistoric paintings of Alta, the area around Nordkapp, the activities of Kirkenes and, depending on the season, dog-sledding or hiking around the Sámi capital of Karasjok. At journey's end, allow a week in Svalbard, taking in as many activities and excursions as you can.

Essential Food & Drink

» **Reindeer** Grilled or roasted, Scandinavia's iconic species is also its tastiest red meat; you'll find it on menus from Oslo to Svalbard.
» **Elk** Call it what you like (many prefer moose), but this tasty meat appears usually as steaks or burgers.
» **Salmon** World-renowned Norwegian salmon is so popular that you'll eat it for dinner (grilled) or breakfast (smoked).
» **Arctic char** The world's northernmost freshwater fish is a star of northern Norway's seafood-rich menus.
» **Arctic menu** A popular scheme (www.arktiskmeny.no) in northern Norway that encourages restaurants to use natural local ingredients.
» **Fish markets** Often the best (and cheapest) places to eat along the Norwegian coast, with the freshest seafood at fresh-off-the-boat prices.

OSLO

POP 572, 900

To the rest of the world Norway is where Mother Nature has created one of her finest works of art. Against such a wonderful natural canvas it's easy to forget that humans can also be artistic and many a visitor has been surprised to discover that Oslo is home to world-class museums and galleries to rival anywhere else on the European art trail.

But even here Mother Nature has managed to make her mark and Oslo is fringed with forests, hills and lakes awash with opportunities for hiking, cycling, skiing and boating.

Add to this mix a thriving cafe and bar culture, top-notch restaurants and nightlife options ranging from opera to indie rock and the result is a thoroughly intoxicating place in which to forget about the fjords for a while.

History

Founded by Harald Hardråda in 1049, Oslo is the oldest Scandinavian capital. In 1299, King Håkon V constructed the Akershus Festning here, to counter the Swedish threat from the east. Levelled by fire in 1624, the city was rebuilt in brick and stone on a more easily defended site by King Christian IV, who renamed it Christiania, after his humble self.

In 1814, the framers of Norway's first constitution designated it the official capital of the new realm but their efforts were effectively nullified by Sweden, which had other ideas about Norway's future and unified the two countries under Swedish rule. In 1905, when that union dissolved, Christiania flourished as the capital of modern Norway. The city reverted to its original name, Oslo, in 1925.

◉ Sights

Many sights are clustered together within easy walking distance of Karl Johans gate. Another important concentration is the Bygdøy Peninsula, which contains the Vikingskipshuset.

TOP CHOICE **Oslo Opera House** OPERA HOUSE
(Den Norske Opera & Ballett; Map p324; www.oper aen.no; Kirsten Flagstads plass 1; admission to foyer free; ⊙foyer 10am-11pm Mon-Fri, 11am-11pm Sat, noon-10pm Sun) Hoping to transform the city into a world-class cultural centre, the city fathers have embarked on a massive waterfront redevelopment project (which is scheduled to last until 2020), the centrepiece of which is the magnificent new Opera House. Designed by Oslo-based architectural firm Snøhetta and costing around €500 million to build, the Opera House, which opened in 2008, has been designed to resemble a glacier floating in the waters off Oslo. It's a subtle building that at first doesn't look all that impressive, but give it time and it'll leave you spellbound.

Before venturing inside be sure to walk up onto the roof, which was designed to act as a 'carpet' of sloping angles and flat surfaces. The main entrance to the Opera House is

NORWAY OSLO

OSLO IN...

Two Days

Start your day at the **Nasjonalgalleriet** for a representative dose of artwork by Edvard Munch. Afterwards try an al fresco, pier-side lunch of peel-and-eat shrimp on **Aker Brygge** from one of the local fishing boats. Take a ferry from here to **Bygdøy** and spend your afternoon learning about the exploits of Norway's greatest explorers at the **Frammuseet** or **Vikingskipshuset**.

On day two head to the breathtaking new **Oslo Opera House**, after which take a look at all that's cool and modern at the **Museet for Samtidskunst**. In the afternoon, explore the medieval **Akershus Slott** and learn how to make the world a better place at the **Nobels Fredssenter**.

Four Days

With a couple of extra days you will have time to wander among the bold, earthy statues of Gustav Vigeland at **Vigeland Park**.

The energetic might also spend a day walking, skiing or cycling in the **Nordmarka** wilderness area.

Norway Highlights

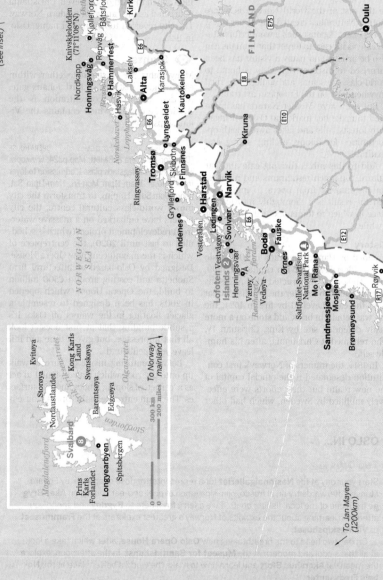

1 Take the ferry from Hellesylt to **Geiranger** (p370) through some of Norway's most spectacular fjord scenery

2 Sleep in a fisherman's *robu* (shanty) on the craggy **Lofoten Islands** (p387)

3 Journey by train from Oslo to **Bergen** (p340), arguably Norway's most attractive coastal city

4 Ride the length of Norway's jagged, beautiful coast aboard the **Hurtigruten coastal ferry** (p417)

5 Hike amid the soaring peaks and countless glaciers of **Jotunheimen National Park** (p338)

6 Draw near to the edge at **Pulpit Rock** (p356)

(Preikestolen; p364), high above glorious Lysefjord

7 Dog-sled (p402) out into the winter Arctic wilderness of Norway's far north

8 Explore the extraordinary landscapes of **Svalbard** (p403). Norway's otherworldly subpolar outpost

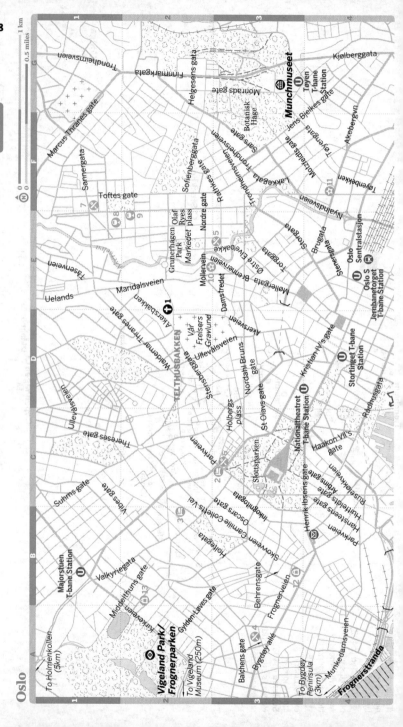

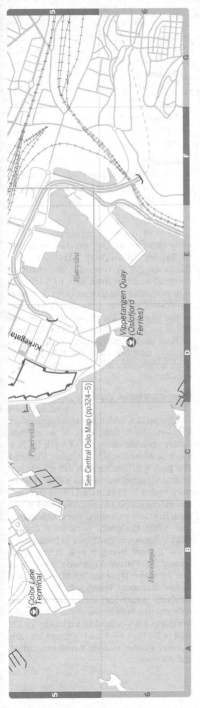

See Central Oslo Map (pp324-5)

purposefully small and unimpressive, which serves only to add to the sense of vastness that greets you on entering the main foyer (the windows alone are 15m high and flood the foyer with light).

Art Museums   ART GALLERIES

Visit the **Nasjonalgalleriet** (National Gallery; Map p324; www.nasjonalmuseet.no; Universitetsgata 13; admission free; ◷10am-6pm Tue, Wed & Fri, 10am-7pm Thu, 11am-5pm Sat & Sun) for an impressive collection featuring some of Edvard Munch's best-known works, including *The Scream,* which was brazenly stolen (and recovered) in 1994. There's also an impressive collection of European art, with works by Gauguin, Picasso, El Greco and many of the Impressionists: Manet, Degas, Renoir, Matisse, Cézanne and Monet. Contemporary collections are housed in the **Museet for Samtidskunst** (National Museum for Contemporary Art; Map p324; www.nasjonalmuseet.no; Bankplassen 4; admission free; ◷11am-5pm Tue, Wed & Fri, 11am-7pm Thu, noon-5pm Sat & Sun). Some of the 3000-piece collection is definitely an acquired taste, but it's a timely reminder that Norwegian art didn't cease with Edvard Munch.

Dedicated to the life's work of Norway's most renowned artist, **Munchmuseet** (Munch Museum; Map p318; www.munch.museum.no; Tøyengata 53; adult/child Nkr75/40, free with Oslo Pass; ◷10am-6pm Jun-Aug) contains more than 1100 paintings, 4500 watercolours and 18,000 prints that Munch bequeathed to the city of Oslo. As such, this landmark museum provides a comprehensive look at the artist's work, from dark *(The Sick Child)* to light *(Spring Ploughing).*

Bygdøy Peninsula   MUSEUMS

The magnificent **Vikingskipshuset** (Viking Ship Museum; www.khm.uio.no; Huk Aveny 35; adult/child Nkr60/30; ◷9am-6pm May-Sep, 11am-4pm Oct-Apr) houses three Viking ships excavated from the Oslofjord region. The ships had been brought ashore and used as tombs for nobility, who were buried with all they were expected to need in the hereafter, including jewels, furniture, food and servants. The impressive **Oseberg**, buried in AD 834 and festooned with elaborate dragon and serpent carvings, is 22m long and took 30 people to row. A second ship, the 24m-long **Gokstad**, is the world's finest example of a longship. Of the third ship, **Tune**, only a few boards remain.

Dirt paths wind past sturdy old barns, *stabbur* (storehouses on stilts), rough-timbered farmhouses with sod roofs sprouting wildflowers, and 140 other 17th- and 18th-century buildings at the Norsk Folkemuseum (Norwegian Folk Museum; www.norsk folkemuseum.no; Museumsveien 10; adult/child Nkr100/25 mid-May–mid-Sep, free with Oslo Pass; ⊙10am-6pm mid-May–mid-Sep). There's also a reproduction of an early 20th-century Norwegian town, including a village shop and an old petrol station. A highlight is a restored **stave church**, built around 1200 in Gol and brought to Bygdøy in 1885. Sunday is a good day to visit, as there's usually folk music and dancing at 2pm (in summer only).

Take a look a the *Kon-Tiki* balsa raft at the Kon-Tiki Museum (www.kon-tiki.no; Bygdøynesveien 36; adult/child Nkr60/25; ⊙9.30am-5.30pm Jun-Aug). Norwegian explorer Thor Heyerdahl sailed from Peru to Polynesia in 1947 on the raft to demonstrate that Polynesia's first settlers could have come from South America. Also displayed is the papyrus reed boat *Ra II*, used to cross the Atlantic in 1970.

Check out the durable *Fram* (1892) at the Frammuseet (Polar Ship Fram Museum; www.fram.museum.no; Bygdøynesveien 36; adult/child Nkr60/25; ⊙9am-6pm mid-Jun–Aug), which Roald Amundsen used for the first successful expedition to the South Pole in 1911. You can clamber around inside the boat, go down to the hold where the sled dogs were kept and view fascinating photographic displays of the *Fram* trapped in polar ice.

Ferry 91 operates from early April to early October, making the 15-minute run to Bygdøy (adult/child Nkr40/20) from Rådhusbrygge 3 (opposite the Rådhus) every 20 minutes from 8am to 8.45pm in summer; earlier final departures the rest of the year. If you buy your tickets from one of the kiosks on the departure jetties the prices are lower (adult/child Nkr26/13, or a 24-hour pass is adult/child Nkr70/35). You can also take bus 30 to the Folk Museum from Jernbanetorget, next to Oslo S train station.

Frognerparken & Vigeland Park
PARKS, SCULPTURES

Frognerparken, which has as its centrepiece Vigeland Park (Map p318), is an extraordinary open-air showcase of work by Norway's best-loved sculptor, Gustav Vigeland. The park is brimming with 212 granite and bronze Vigeland works. His highly charged work ranges from entwined lovers and tranquil elderly couples to contempt-ridden beggars. His most renowned work, *Sinataggen* (the 'Little Hothead'), portrays a London child in a mood of particular ill humour.

For a more in-depth look at the development of Gustav Vigeland's work, visit the Vigeland Museum (off Map p318; www. vigeland.museum.no; Nobels gate 32; adult/child Nkr50/25; ⊙10am-5pm Tue-Sun Jun-Aug). The museum was built by the city as a home and workshop for Vigeland in exchange for the bulk of his life's work and contains his early statuary, plaster moulds, woodblock prints, and sketches.

Nobels Fredssenter — CULTURAL CENTRE

(Map p324; www.nobelpeacecenter.org; Rådhusplassen 1; adult/student/child Nkr80/55/
free; ⊙10am-6pm Tue-Sun) Head inside the
Nobel Peace Centre for hi-tech screens
flashily exploring themes of peace and
conflict. In addition to presenting the history of the prize and its patron, Alfred
Nobel (a dynamite fellow; see boxed text,
p502), it has exhibits on winners from 1901
to present.

Akershus Slott & Festning — CASTLE, FORTRESS

King Håkon V began construction of the
earthen-walled **Akershus Festning** (Akershus Fortress; Map p324; admission free; ⊙6am-
9pm) in 1299. It's strategically positioned on
the eastern side of the harbour; clamber
up tree-lined twisting paths to stand pre-
cariously above the city and enjoy excellent
views over Oslofjord. The grounds are the
venue for a host of concerts, dances and
theatrical productions during summer. An
information centre (⊙9am-5pm Mon-Fri,
11am-5pm Sat & Sun mid-May–mid-Aug, closes 1hr
earlier rest of yr) recounts the building of the
fortress. Changing of the guard occurs at
1.30pm.

In the 17th century, Christian IV renovated **Akershus Slott** (Akershus Castle; Map
p324; adult/child Nkr65/25; ⊙10am-4pm Mon-Sat,
12.30-4pm Sun May-Aug, guided tours 11am, 1pm
& 3pm Mon-Sat, 1pm & 3pm Sun) into a Renaissance palace, though the front remains decidedly medieval. In its dungeons you'll find
dark cubby holes where outcast nobles were
kept under lock and key, while the upper
floors have banquet halls and staterooms.
The chapel is still used for army events and
the crypts of Kings Håkon VII and Olav V
lie beneath it.

FREE Rådhus — CITY HALL

(Map p324; Fridtjof Nansens plass; ⊙9am-6pm,
guided tours 10am, noon & 2pm) The Nobel
Peace Prize is awarded in the City Hall on 10
December. From the outside, its brick towers
add interest to what looks like a staid municipal building. Come inside, though, and
you'll be positively transformed by echoing monumental halls covered in colourful
murals that depict Norwegian history and
mythology.

Ibsen Museet — MUSEUM

(Ibsen Museum; Map p324; www.ibsenmuseet.no;
Arbins gate 1; adult/child Nkr85/25; ⊙guided tours
hourly 11am-6pm mid-May–mid-Sep) Housed in

the last residence of Norwegian playwright
Henrik Ibsen, the Ibsen Museum is a must-
see for Ibsen fans. The study remains exactly
as he left it and other rooms have been restored in the style and colours popular in
Ibsen's day.

FREE Historisk Museet — MUSEUM

(Map p324; www.khm.uio.no; University of Oslo,
Frederiks gate 2; ⊙10am-5pm Tue-Sun mid-May–
mid-Sep) The History Museum contains
the **National Antiquities Collection**,
displaying Viking-era coins, jewellery,
weapons and bloodthirsty plunder, as well
as medieval church art that includes the
dragon-festooned bits of the 13th-century
Ål stave church. There's also the **numis-
matic collection of coins** dating from
AD 995, and exhibits on indigenous Arctic
cultures.

Churches — CHURCHES

Oslo Domkirke (Oslo Cathedral; Map p324; Stortorget 1; admission free; ⊙24hr) dates from 1697
and is worth seeing for its elaborate stained
glass by Emanuel Vigeland, and painted
ceiling (completed between 1936 and 1950).
The exceptional 1748 altarpiece is a model
of the *Last Supper and the Crucifixion* by
Michael Rasch. The organ front and pulpit
also require your attention.

The medieval **Gamle Aker Kirke** (Map
p318; Akersbakken 26; admission free; ⊙noon-2pm
Mon-Sat) was built in stone around 1080 and
is Oslo's oldest building.

Activities

Hiking — HIKING

An extensive network of trails leads into
Nordmarka from Frognerseteren, at the end
of T-bane line 1. One good, fairly strenuous
walk is from Frognerseteren to Sognsvann
lake, where you can take T-bane line 5 back
to the city. If you're interested in wilderness
hiking, contact DNT (Den Norske Turistforening; see p328).

Cycling — CYCLING

Cyclists and mountain bikers will find
plenty of trails on which to keep themselves
occupied in the Oslo hinterland. The tourist office has free cycling maps; *Sykkelkart
Oslo* traces the bicycle lanes and paths
throughout the city, and *Idrett og friluftsliv
i Oslo* covers the Oslo hinterland. The tourist office also has a pamphlet, *Opplevelses-
turer i Marka,* which contains six possible

cycling and/or hiking itineraries within reach of Oslo.

Skiing

Oslo's ski season is roughly from December to March. There are more than 2400km of prepared Nordic tracks (1000km in Nordmarka alone), many of them floodlit, as well as a ski resort within the city limits; easy-access tracks begin right at the T-bane stations Frognerseteren and Sognsvann. The downhill slopes at Tryvann Vinterpark (✆40 46 27 00) are open in the ski season. Check out www.holmenkollen.com for more information.

☞ Tours

For the popular Norway in a Nutshell (✆81 56 82 22; www.norwaynutshell.com), book at tourist offices or at train stations. From Oslo, the typical route includes a rail trip across Hardangervidda to Myrdal, descent to Flåm along the dramatic Flåmbanen, a cruise along Nærøyfjorden to Gudvangen, a bus to Voss, a connecting train to Bergen for a short visit, then an overnight return rail trip to Oslo (including a sleeper compartment); the return tour costs Nkr2165. You can also book one-way tours to Bergen (Nkr1370).

✯ Festivals & Events

Oslo's most festive annual event is the 17 May Constitution Day celebration, when city residents descend on the royal palace in the finery of their native districts. Some other festivals:

Inferno Metal Festival   MUSIC
(www.infernofestival.net) Held in late April.

Norwegian Wood Festival   MUSIC
(www.norwegianwood.no) One of Oslo's bigger music festivals; June.

Oslo International Jazz Festival   MUSIC
(www.oslojazz.no) Jazz and long summer evenings; August.

Øya Festival   MUSIC
(www.oyafestivalen.com) Norway's largest rock and indie music festival; August.

Oslo Opera Festival   OPERA
(www.operafestival.no) Live opera for three weeks in September.

🛏 Sleeping

Oslo has plenty of accommodation, including a growing number of small B&Bs, which offer more character than the chain hotels. However, compared with many other parts of Europe, standards are generally fairly low.

CENTRAL OSLO

Grims Grenka   TOP CHOICE   HOTEL €€€
(Map p324; ✆23 10 72 00; www.grimsgrenka.no; Kongens gate 5; s/d from Nkr1395/1595; P) Oslo's answer to the exclusive, cosmopolitan experience offered by boutique hotels in London and New York, Grims Grenka has minimalist, modern-designed rooms, a hipster rooftop bar and an Asian-fusion restaurant. It is, without doubt, the most exciting hotel in Oslo.

Cochs Pensjonat   HOTEL €
(Map p318; ✆23 33 24 00; www.cochspensjonat.no; Parkveien 25; s/d Nkr580/780, without bathroom Nkr480/680) Opened as a guesthouse for bachelors in the 1920s, the very good-value Cochs has sparsely furnished, clean rooms some of which have kitchenettes. It's ideally located behind the royal palace. The rooms at the back overlooking the Slottsparken are especially spacious.

P-Hotel   HOTEL €€
(Map p324; ✆80 04 68 35; www.p-hotels.com; Grensen 19; s/d Nkr795/995; @) In addition to offering some of the best prices in central Oslo, the P-Hotel has comfortable if slightly dull rooms with decent bathrooms. A breakfast in a bag, delivered to your door, is included and there are tea- and coffee-making facilities in the rooms. It couldn't be much more central.

Anker Hostel   HOSTEL €
(Map p324; ✆22 99 72 00; www.ankerhostel.no; Storgata 55; 6-/8-bed dm with bathroom Nkr220/210, s & d from Nkr580; P@) This huge traveller-savvy hostel boasts an international atmosphere, spick-and-span rooms, a laundry, luggage room, kitchens (some rooms also contain kitchens) and small bar. Breakfast costs an extra Nkr55, linen Nkr50 and parking Nkr175 per 24 hours.

Anker Hotel   BUDGET HOTEL €€
(Map p324; ✆22 99 75 00; www.anker-hotel.no; Storgata 55; s/d from Nkr790/990; P@) Owned by the same people as the neighbouring Anker Hostel, this place could be described as a 'budget business hotel' and the plain and simple rooms are perfect for those who feel a bit too old for the hostel.

Thon Hotel Spectrum　　CHAIN HOTEL **€€**
(Map p324; ☑23 36 27 00; www.thonhotels.com;
Brugata 7; s Nkr660-1110, d Nkr925-1375; @)
Bright-purple sofas and equally purple flowers adorn the reception area. The comfortable and well-priced rooms are noteworthy
for their huge windows and fairly small
bathrooms. Sadly the staff don't exactly rush
forward to help guests.

GREATER OSLO

TOP
CHOICE **Ellingsens Pensjonat**　　PENSION **€**
(Map p318; ☑22 60 03 59; www.ellingsenspen
sjonat.no, in Norwegian; Holtegata 25; s/d
Nkr480/670, without bathroom Nkr400/580) Located in a quiet, pleasant neighbourhood,
this homey pension offers one of the best
deals in the capital. The building dates
from 1890 and many of the original features (high ceilings, rose designs) remain.
Rooms are bright and airy, with refrigera-
tors and kettles and there's a small garden
to lounge about in on sunny days.

**Holmenkollen Park Hotel
Rica**　　HISTORIC HOTEL **€€**
(☑22 92 20 00; www.holmenkollenparkhotel.no;
Kongeveien 26; r Nkr695-1135; P@▨) Founded
in 1891 as a sanatorium by Dr Ingebrigt
Christian Lund, this castle-like hotel offers
luxury, history, great views and, all things
considered, a very reasonable price.

✘ Eating

In the past, going to a restaurant in Oslo
meant parting with great wads of cash for
very little that could be called good food.
Luckily, this began to change in the late
1990s and, though costs are still high, today there are plenty of places to choose
from.

For the ultimate snack try a *polse* (hot
dog) in a *lumpe* (potato cake) for Nkr18 or
a waffle with sour cream and strawberry
jam.

CENTRAL OSLO

TOP
CHOICE **Feinschmecker**　MODERN NORWEGIAN **€€€**
(Map p318; ☑22 12 93 80; www.feinschmecker.no,
in Norwegian; Balchens gate 5; menus Nkr695) If
you're starting to think Norwegian food is
all about burgers and pizzas then this absolutely sublime restaurant, with its modern
take on old Norwegian dishes, will quickly
change your mind. The crayfish soup and
lamb with wild mushrooms are out of this
world. Despite the quality of the food and

the high prices, the atmosphere is surprisingly laidback. Book ahead.

Rust　　INTERNATIONAL **€**
(Map p318; Hegehaugsveien 22; snacks & light
meals Nkr36-59, mains Nkr119-129) On a small
side street lined with cafes and restaurants,
Rust is bright, colourful and 100% modern
Oslo. It has plenty of outdoor seating and
loads of blankets for when it gets cold. Good
for a quiet cocktail, burgers, hearty salads or
tapas late into the night.

Café Skansen　　MEDITERRANEAN **€€**
(Map p324; www.cafeskansen.no, in Norwegian;
Rådhusgata 32; pasta & salad mains Nkr90-180)
One of the new wave of sophisticated cafes
and restaurants currently taking Oslo by
storm. As in many such places this one looks
south to the Mediterranean for both style
and taste inspiration and on sunny summer
days its outdoor terrace does indeed feel
very far from the popular images of a frozen
Norway.

Grand Café　　NORWEGIAN **€€**
(Map p324; Karl Johans gate 31; mains Nkr120-275)
At 11am sharp, Henrik Ibsen would leave his
apartment on Drammensveien (now Henrik Ibsens gate) and walk to the Grand Café
for a lunch of herring, beer and one shot of
aquavit (alcoholic drink made from potatoes
and caraway liquor). His table is still there.
Don't worry though, there's more than herring on the menu. Take your pick from reindeer, Arctic char and mussels and chips.

AKER BRYGGE

Aker Brygge, the old shipyard turned trendy
shopping complex west of the main harbour, has a **food court** (☉11am-10pm) with
various eateries and a variety of waterside
restaurants.

If the weather is nice, the local meal of
choice is peel-and-eat shrimp, eaten dockside with a fresh baguette, mayonnaise and
just a touch of lemon. In summer, you can
buy shrimp from the **Fisherman's Coop**
(Map p324; Rådhusbrygge 3/4; shrimp per kg
Nkr120; ☉7am-5pm Tue-Sat) or, on Thursdays,
keep an eye out for one of Norway's richest
men, Kjell Inge Røkkes, who can be found
selling shrimp from his boat *Trygg*.

People & Coffee　　INTERNATIONAL **€**
(Map p324; Rådhusgata 21; www.peopleandcoffee.
com, in Norwegian; mains Nkr59-140, lunch specials Nkr139; ☉breakfast & lunch) Much more
than a mere coffee shop, this friendly place

Central Oslo

300 m
0.2 miles

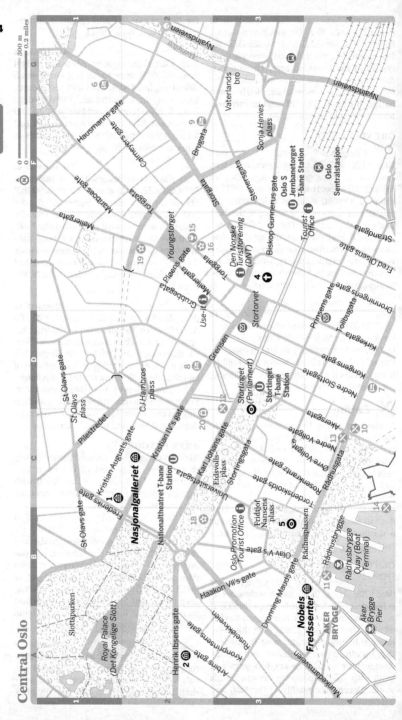

Royal Palace
(Det Kongelige Slott)

Slottsparken

Nasjonalgalleriet

Nationaltheatret T-bane Station

Nobels Fredssenter

AKER BRYGGE

Rådhusbrygge
Rådhusbrygge Quay (Boat Terminal)

Aker Brygge Pier

Rådhusplassen

Fridtjof Nansens plass

Oslo Promotion Tourist Office

Universitetsgata

Karl Johans gate

Eidsvolls-plass

Stortingsgata

Stortinget (Parliament)

Stortinget T-bane Station

Use-It

Youngstorget

Den Norske Turistforening (DNT)

Stortorvet

Grensen

Oslo S
Jernbanetorget T-bane Station

Oslo Sentralstasjon

Tourist Office

Bispop Gunnerus gate

Vaterlands bro

Sonja Henies plass

Nyland sveien

Central Oslo

offers one of the city centre's best-value lunch deals, with hot, filling meals such as chilli con carne, soups that are just the ticket on a cold winter's day, salads and the best carrot cake in Oslo.

Solsiden　　　　　　　　　　SEAFOOD €€€
(Map p324; ☎22 33 36 30; Søndre Akershus Kai 34; starters Nkt125-155, mains Nkr185-295; ◷May-Sep) Solsiden means 'sunny side' in Norwegian, which explains why this place is so popular among sun-craving Oslo dwellers. Located inside a grey warehouse, and often overlooked by massive cruise ships, on the opposite side of Pipervika from Aker Brygge, Solsiden serves up some of the city's best seafood and has an ideal view over the fjord.

GRÜNERLØKKA

Oslo's Greenwich Village, while always lively and frequented by a well-dressed, youthful crowd, is especially pleasant in summer, when life spills out onto the sidewalks from the numerous cafes, bars and restaurants around Olaf Ryes plass.

TOP CHOICE Markveien Mat & Vinhus and Dr Kneipp's Vinbar MODERN NORWEGIAN **€€€**
(Map p318; ☑22 37 22 97; www.markveien.no; Torvbakkgt 12; mains Nkr240-290, 3 courses Nkr495) With a hint of truffle oil or a dash of dill, the cooks at Markveien make Norwegian cooking unforgettable. The restaurant focuses on using local seafood and meat, as well as organic produce, to create its delectable dishes. If you're not in the mood for the formal dining room, slide into one of the dark wooden booths at Dr Kneipp's next door for finger food or a sumptuous dessert, not to mention an amazing wine list.

Sult MODERN NORWEGIAN **€€**
(Map p318; www.sult.no; Thorvald Meyers gate 26; lunch mains Nkr99-139, dinner menus Nkr355) The polished green-and-black colour scheme of Sult perfectly captures the Grünerløkka vibe with an imaginative menu replete with superb fish and pasta dishes often using local and organic ingredients. It's always packed, so get there early and wait for a table in the attached bar, appropriately called Tørst (meaning 'thirsty').

BYGDØY PENINSULA

Café Hemma Hos MODERN NORWEGIAN **€€**
(www.cafehemmahos.no; Fredrikborgsveien 16; mains Nkr165-190) The owners of the Café Hemma Hos, close to the Viking Ship Museum, know there is more to culinary life than hot dogs and stale sandwiches and have created an oasis of good food in a sea of tourist traps. Sit out in the pleasant gardens and choose from a menu that includes pickled herrings, crayfish and a variety of tapas.

🍸 Drinking & Entertainment

The tourist office's free monthly brochure *What's On in Oslo* lists current concerts, theatre and special events, but the best publication for night owls is the free *Streetwise,* published annually in English by Use-It (p328).

Bars & Clubs

Many Oslo nightspots have an unwritten dress code that expects patrons to be relatively well turned out – at the very least, don't show up in grubby gear and hiking boots. For most bars and clubs that serve beer and wine, you must be over 18 years of age, but many places, especially those that serve spirits, impose a higher age limit. On weekends, most Oslo nightspots remain open until at least 3am.

The city's best neighbourhood bar scene is along Thorvald Meyers gate and the surrounding streets in Grünerløkka. The Youngstorget area has some of the most popular places close to the city centre, while the Grønland neighbourhood has a more alternative feel.

Tea Lounge BAR
(Map p318; www.tealounge.no; Thorvald Meyers gate 33b; ⊙11am-1am Mon-Wed, 11am-3am Thu-Sat, noon-3am Sun) During the bright and cheerful daylight hours this split-personality bar is a teashop with a superb range of brews and a chilled-out soundtrack, but in the dark of night it transforms itself into one of the hippest bars in Oslo, with a list of cocktails to suit.

Bar Boca BAR
(Map p318; Thorvald Meyers gate 30) Squeeze into what is quite possibly the smallest bar in Oslo and you'll find that you have slid back in time to the 1960s. It's retro cool and has a cocktail selection as great as its atmosphere.

Fish Og Vilt CLUB
(Map p324; Pløens gate 1) With DJs rocking the crowd in the covered backyard of this barclub, and an impressive selection of beers and cocktails, this is a popular central spot. On a Monday night it's really the only place worth considering.

Villa CLUB
(Map p324; www.thevilla.no; Møllergata 23; ⊙Fri & Sat) With arguably the best sound system in the city, this is a diehard house and electro music club. In addition to the above opening hours it's also open on some Thursdays.

Live Music

Oslo has a thriving live-music scene – it's said that the city hosts around 5000 gigs a year. Keep your ear to the ground in summer to hear about outdoor concerts at Vigeland Park – a weird-and-wonderful venue.

TOP CHOICE Blå   JAZZ
(Map p318; www.blaaoslo.no, in Norwegian; Brenneriveien 9c; admission Nkr100-150) It would be a pity to leave Oslo without checking out Blå, which features on a global list of 100 great jazz clubs compiled by the savvy editors at the US jazz magazine *Down Beat*. Sometimes it veers into other musical styles such as salsa and when there's no live music DJs get the crowds moving.

Mono   ROCK
(Map p324; www.cafemono.no, in Norwegian; Pløens gate 4) An upbeat place, Mono is the rock club of choice with the cool and beautiful of Oslo. It's known for managing to book the best up-and-coming new indie bands.

Gloria Flames   ROCK
(Map p318; www.gloriaflames.no, in Norwegian; Grønland 18) In Grønland, Gloria Flames is a popular rock bar with frequent gigs and a roof-terrace bar during daylight hours.

Theatre

Oslo Opera House   OPERA
(Den Norske Opera & Ballett; Map p324; www.operaen.no; Kirsten Flagstads plass 1; admission to foyer free; ☺foyer 10am-11pm Mon-Fri, 11am-11pm Sat, noon-10pm Sun) Apart from being one of Norway's most impressive examples of contemporary architecture, Oslo Opera House is also the venue for world-class opera and ballet performances.

MS Innvik   ALTERNATIVE CULTURE
(Map p324; www.msinnvik.no, in Norwegian; Langkaia) A car ferry turned theatre and world-music concert venue, MS Innvik offers, culturally, the polar opposite to the highbrow entertainment of the next-door Opera House. See the website for a rundown of what's taking place each week.

National Theatre   THEATRE
(Nationaltheatret; Map p324; www.nationaltheatret.no, in Norwegian; Stortingsgata 15) Norway's showcase theatre, with its lavish rococo hall, was constructed specifically as a venue for the works of Norwegian playwright Henrik Ibsen, whose works are still performed here.

🛍 Shopping

Oslo excels in upmarket shopping and there are many fine shops on Grensen and Karl Johans gate. For art, try the galleries on Frognerveien, for exclusive boutiques head to Hegdehaugsveien or Skovveien, and for funky shoes or T-shirts go no further than Grünerløkka.

Vestkanttorget Flea Market   FLEA MARKET
(Map p318; Amaldus Nilsens plass; ☺10am-4pm Sat) If you're happy with pot luck and sifting through heaps of junk, take a chance here. It's at the plaza that intersects Professor Dahls gate, a block east of Vigeland Park, and it's a more than pleasant way to pass a Saturday morning.

Husfliden   TRADITIONAL CLOTHING
(Map p324; Rosenkrantz gate 19-21) Husfliden is a nationwide chain selling quality Norwegian clothing and crafts, as well as a popular place to buy a *bunad* (national costume).

Hassan og Den Dama   CLOTHES, JEWELLERY
(Map p318; www.hassanogdendama.no; Skovveien 4) One of many boutiques on Skovveien, this shop has clothing, shoes and jewellery produced by Scandinavian and international designers.

ℹ Information

Emergency
Ambulance (☎113)
Fire (☎110)
Police (☎112; Hammersborggata 10)

Internet Access
Almost all hotels and hostels in Oslo provide wi-fi access (although it's not always free) and some accomodation options also have computers with internet for guest use. Many bars and cafes also have free wi-fi for those who are eating/drinking there.

Arctic Internet Café (Oslo S; per hr Nkr40-60; ☺9am-11pm) On the 1st floor of Oslo S train station.

Use-It (Møllergata 3; free access; ☺9am-6pm Mon-Fri, 11am-5pm Sat Jun-Aug)

Medical Services
Jernbanetorget Apotek (Fred Olsens gate) A 24-hour pharmacy opposite Oslo S.

Oslo Kommunale Legevakten (Oslo Emergency Clinic; ☎22 93 22 93; Storgata 40; ☺24hr) Casualty and emergency medical clinic.

Money

There are banks with ATMs throughout the city centre, with a particular concentration along Karl Johans gate. **Forex** (www.forex.no; Fridtjof Nansens plass 6 & Oslo S; ☉9am-6pm Mon-Fri) is the largest foreign-exchange service in Scandinavia.

Tourist Information

Den Norske Turistforening (DNT; Norwegian Mountain Touring Club; Map p324; www.turistforeningen.no; Storget 3; ☉10am-5pm Mon-Wed & Fri, 10am-6pm Thu, 10am-2pm Sat, open 1hr earlier in summer) Information, maps and brochures on hiking in Norway.

Oslo Promotion Tourist Office (Map p324; ☎81 53 05 55; www.visitoslo.com; Fridtjof Nansens plass 5; ☉9am-7pm Jun-Aug, 9am-5pm Mon-Sat Apr, May & Sep)

Tourist office (Map p324; ☎81 53 05 55; Jernbanetorget 1, Oslo S; ☉7am-8pm Mon-Fri, 8am-8pm Sat & Sun May-Sep, 7am-8pm Mon-Fri, 8am-6pm Sat & Sun Oct-Apr)

Use-It (Map p324; ☎24 14 98 20; www.use-it.no; Møllergata 3; ☉9am-6pm Mon-Fri Jul & Aug, 11am-5pm Mon-Fri Sep-Jun) The exceptionally helpful and savvy Ungdomsinformasjonen (Youth Information Office, better known as Use-It) is aimed at (but not restricted to) backpackers under the age of 26. It makes (free) bookings for inexpensive or private accommodation and provides information on anything from current events to hitching possibilities.

ⓘ Getting There & Away

Air

Most flights land at Oslo's main international airport in **Gardermoen** (www.osl.no), 50km north of the city; it's the country's main international gateway and domestic hub. Oslo Torp, 123km south of the city, and Rygge Airport, 60km southeast of Oslo, are secondary airports.

Boat

For details of international ferry services, see p415.

Bus

Long-distance buses arrive and depart from the **Galleri Oslo Bus Terminal** (Map p324; Schweigaards gate 8, Galleri Oslo); the train and bus stations are linked via an overhead walkway for easy connections.

Car & Motorcycle

The main highways into the city are the E6 from the north and south, and the E18 from the southeast and west. Each time you enter Oslo,

you must pass through (at least) one of 19 toll stations and pay Nkr25.

Train

All trains arrive and depart from Oslo S in the city centre. It has **reservation desks** (☉6.30am-11pm) and an **information desk** (☎81 50 08 88; press 9 for service in English), which provides details on routes and timetables throughout the country.

Major destinations include Stavanger via Kristiansand, Bergen via Voss, Røros via Hamar, and Trondheim via Hamar and Lillehammer. For details of international schedules and prices, see p415.

ⓘ Getting Around

Oslo has an efficient public transport system with an extensive network of buses, trams, underground trains (T-bane) and ferries. In addition to single-trip tickets, day and transferable eight-trip tickets are also available. Children aged four to 16 and seniors over 67 years of age pay half price on all fares.

The Oslo Pass (see below) includes access to all public transport options within the city, with the exception of late-night buses and trams.

Trafikanten (☎177; www.trafikanten.no; Jernbanetorget; ☉7am-11pm) is located below Oslo S tower and provides free schedules and a public transport map, *Sporveiskart Oslo*.

To/From Gardermoen International Airport

Flybussen (www.flybussen.no) is the airport shuttle to Gardermoen International Airport, 50km north of Oslo. The trip costs Nkr140/240 one way/return (valid one month) and takes 40 minutes.

FlyToget (www.flytoget.no) rail services leave Gardermoen airport for Oslo S (Nkr170, 19 minutes) every 10 minutes between 4.18am and midnight. In addition, most northbound **NSB** (www.nsb.no) intercity and local trains stop at

OSLO PASS

Providing entry to most museums and attractions and free travel on public transport, the Oslo Pass (adult 1/2/3 days Nkr240/340/430, child Nkr100/120/160) is sold at tourist offices and hotels. However, note that if you are planning on just visiting city-centre museums and galleries, many of which are free, it can actually work out more expensive to buy an Oslo Pass than not to!

Gardermoen (Nkr110, from 26 minutes, hourly but fewer on Saturday).

To/From Torp Airport
To get to/from Torp Airport in Sandefjord, 123km southwest of Oslo and serviced by Ryanair and Wizzair among others, take the **Torp-Expressen** (www.torpekspressen.no; one way adult/child Nkr190/100, return adult/child Nkr320/200) bus between Galleri Oslo bus terminal and the airport (1½ hours). Departures from Oslo leave 3½ hours before scheduled departures.

To/From Rygge Airport
To get to/from Rygge, in Moss, 60km southeast of Oslo, take the **Rygge-Expressen** (www.ryg geekspressen.no; one way adult/child Nkr130/70, return adult/child Nkr230/140) bus between Galleri Oslo bus terminal and the airport (one hour). Departures from Oslo leave three hours before scheduled departures.

Bicycle
The best place to rent bicycles is the **Skiservice Sykkelutleie** (☑22 13 95 00; www.skiservice. no, in Norwegian; Tryvannsveien 2; per day Nkr350) in the Nordmarka.

One alternative if you don't plan on going too far is **Oslo Citybike** (www.oslobysykkel.no), a network of bikes that cyclists can borrow for up to three hours at a time from bicycle stands around the city. Access cards (Nkr80) can be purchased from the tourist office and last for 24 hours, but bikes must be exchanged or returned to a rack within three hours. They're convenient and well maintained.

Bus & Tram
Bus and tram lines lace the city and extend into the suburbs. There's no central local bus station, but most converge at Jernbanetorget in front of Oslo S. Most westbound buses, including those to Bygdøy and Vigeland Park, also stop immediately south of the National Theatre.

Tickets for most trips cost Nkr26/13 adult/child if you buy them in advance (at 7-Eleven, Narvesen, Trafikanten) or Nkr40/20 if you buy them from the driver. A day pass costs Nkr70/35 adult/child.

T-Bane
The six-line Tunnelbanen underground system, better known as the T-bane, is faster and extends further from the city centre than most city bus lines. All lines pass through the Nationaltheatret, Stortinget and Jernbanetorget (for Oslo S) stations. Ticket prices are the same as for the buses and trams.

SOUTHERN NORWAY

In the summer months, the curving south coast is a magnet for vacationing Norwegian families, who come to the area for its beaches, offshore islands and sailing opportunities. Unless here to pilot masted vessels, first-time foreign travellers generally visit the coast's sleepy wooden towns as a pit stop en route to more-exciting locales.

Arendal
POP 40,000
The main appeal of Arendal, one of the larger south-coast towns, is its undeniable buzz throughout summer around the harbour (known as Pollen), with outdoor restaurants and bars next to the water and a full calendar of festivals. Large enough to have an array of amenities but not too big to overwhelm, it's a nice place to spend a few days.

Just a few minutes' walk south of the train station brings you into the old harbourside area of Tyholmen, with its attractively restored 19th-century wooden buildings. In 1992 it was deservedly awarded the prestigious Europa Nostra prize for its expert restoration. Check out the Rådhus (Rådhusgata 10), which was originally a shipowner's home dating from 1815, or the Kulturhistoriste Senter (www.aaks.no, in Norwegian; Parkveien 16; adult/child Nkr20/10; ⊗9am-5pm Mon-Fri, noon-5pm Sat mid-Jun–mid-Aug), which displays objects brought home by the town's sailors. For an excellent gallery of contemporary art, the Bomuldsfabriken Art Hall (www.bomuldsfabriken.no, in Norwegian; Oddenveien 5; admission free; ⊗noon-4pm Tue-Fri) presents exhibitions and a fine permanent collection in a pretty 19th-century textile factory.

★☆ Festivals & Events

Sørlandet Boat Show BOATS
(www.sorlandetsbatmesse.no, in Norwegian) Held in late May.

Hove Festival MUSIC
(www.hovefestivalen.no) This music festival draws international acts to the island of Tromø in late June. Headliners in 2010 included the likes of Muse and Massive Attack.

Canal Street Jazz & Blues Festival

MUSIC

(www.canalstreet.no) World-class jazz and blues; late July.

🛏 Sleeping & Eating

Clarion Tyholmen Hotel   HISTORIC HOTEL **€€**

(☑37 07 68 00; www.choice.no; Teaterplassen 2; r from Nkr1126) Undoubtedly Arendal's best hotel, the Clarion combines a prime waterfront position with attractive rooms in a restored old building that seeks to emulate Tyholmen's old-world ambience. The corner suites offer magnificent sea views.

Thon Hotel Arendal   CHAIN HOTEL **€€**

(☑37 05 21 50; www.thonhotels.no; Friergangen 1; r from Nkr1050) It might not have the waterfront views, but this outpost of Thon Hotels is just 50m from the water's edge. Typical of the Thon chain, the rooms are modern, large and comfortable. There's a public pay car park nearby.

Café Victor   INTERNATIONAL **€€**

(Kirkegaten 5; light meals Nkr69-129; ⊙10am-midnight Jun-Aug, 10am-5pm Mon-Sat Sep-May) In a prime waterfront position, Café Victor is a cool choice. Apart from the antique ceiling, the decor is sleek and modern, the service friendly and the food (sandwiches and pasta) and coffee excellent.

TOP CHOICE Blom Restaurant   SEAFOOD **€€€**

(☑37 00 14 14; Lang-brygge 5; mains/menus Nkr299/599; ⊙noon-11pm Sun-Thu, noon-3.30am Fri & Sat) Perhaps the classiest bar/restaurant by the Pollen harbour, Blom is a chic place and a cut above the beer-and-yobbo culture that sometimes afflicts other waterside bars in Arendal.

ℹ Information

Tourist office (www.arendal.com; Sam Eydes plass; ⊙9am-6pm Mon-Fri, 11am-6pm Sat & noon-4pm Sun Jul–mid-Aug, 8.30am-4pm Mon-Fri rest of yr)

ℹ Getting There & Away

Nor-Way Bussekspress buses between Kristiansand (Nkr120, 1½ hours, up to nine daily) and Oslo (from Nkr350, four hours) call in at the Arendal Rutebilstasjon, a block west of Pollen harbour. Local Timekspressen buses connect Arendal with Grimstad (Nkr53, 30 minutes, half-hourly) and Risør (Nkr98, 1¼ hours, hourly).

Grimstad

POP 10,700

Unusually for a town along the coast, Grimstad, once a major shipbuilding centre, is at its most beautiful in the pedestrianised streets that lie inland from the waterfront; these streets are some of the loveliest on the Skagerrak coast. Grimstad was the home of playwright Henrik Ibsen and has a good museum. It's also officially the sunniest spot in Norway and there's a large student population.

◎ Sights

Ibsenhuset Museum   MUSEUM

(Grimstad By Museum; www.gbm.no, in Norwegian; Henrik Ibsens gate 14; adult/child Nkr75/free; ⊙11am-5pm Mon-Sat, noon-5pm Sun Jul–mid-Aug) Norway's favourite playwright, Henrik Ibsen, arrived in Grimstad in January 1844. The house where he worked as a pharmacist's apprentice, and where he lived and first cultivated his interest in writing, has been converted into the Ibsenhuset Museum. It contains a re-created pharmacy and many of the writer's belongings. The museum is closed from mid-September until late May.

Quarry Theatre   THEATRE

(☑81 53 31 33; www.fjaereheia.no, in Norwegian; tickets around Nkr250) One of the more unusual cultural experiences in Grimstad is run by Kristiansand-based Agder Theater, which performs in an old quarry up to six days a week in summer. The tourist office (and the Quarry Theatre's website) has a program of upcoming performances.

🛏 Sleeping & Eating

For camping, there are at least six nearby camping grounds that are listed on the tourist office website (www.grimstad.net), while **Grimstad Hytteutleie** (☑37 25 10 65; www.grimstad-hytteutleie.no, in Norwegian; Grooseveien 103) can book holiday cabins in the area for one night or for longer stays.

TOP CHOICE Grimstad Hotell   HISTORIC HOTEL **€€**

(☑37 25 25 25; www.grimstadhotell.no; Kirkegata 3; s/d from Nkr995/1195; 🅿) One of southern Norway's more memorable hotels, the stylish Grimstad Hotell, which spans a number of converted and conjoined timber houses, is the only in-town hotel and comes with loads of charm.

Bie Appartement & Feriesenter CAMPING GROUND €
(☎37 04 03 96; www.bieapart.no, in Norwegian; off Arendalsveien; campsites Nkr125, cabins/apt from Nkr525/1190; P ⓧ) The nearest camping option is this friendly, well-equipped site 800m northeast of the centre along Arendalsveien. As well as big grassy pitches it has a range of huts (the cheapest ones without running water) and some well-equipped apartments.

Haven Brasserie SEAFOOD €€
(Storgata 4; lunch menus Nkr95, seafood mains Nkr200-295; ⊙noon-midnight Mon-Sat, 1pm-midnight Sun) One of the few restaurants in town that allows you to sit at a table by the water, this appealing place dishes up superb seafood and a handful of pasta and pizza staples.

Platebaren SNACKS €
(Storgata 15; baguettes Nkr27-35, salads Nkr49; ⊙9am-5pm Mon-Fri, 9am-4pm Sat Jun-Aug) This highly recommended coffee bar spills out into the street in summer and is a terrific place to tuck into decent-sized snacks (baguettes, bacon and eggs etc).

❶ Information

Tourist office (www.visitgrimstad.com; Sorenskrivergården, Storgata 1A; ⊙9am-6pm Mon-Fri, 10am-4pm Sat mid-Jun–mid-Aug, 8.30am-4pm Mon-Fri Sep-May) Staff run guided tours of the town every Wednesday and Friday in July at 1pm (adult/child Nkr100/free).

❶ Getting There & Around

Nor-Way **Bussekspress** buses between Oslo (Nkr350, 4½ hours) and Kristiansand (Nkr98, one hour) call at Grimstad three to five times daily. **Nettbuss** buses to/from Arendal run once or twice hourly (Nkr53, 30 minutes).

Kristiansand

POP 77,800

Kristiansand, Norway's fifth-largest city, calls itself 'Norway's No.1 Holiday Resort'. That can be a bit misleading: sun-starved Norwegians do flock here in summer, but for everyone else it serves more as a gateway to the charming seaside villages of Norway's southern coast. What Kristiansand can offer, though, is a lively cultural and shopping scene, great restaurants and a healthy nightlife.

◉ Sights & Activities

TOP CHOICE **Kristiansand Dyrepark** ZOO
(www.dyreparken.com; admission incl all activities adult/child Nkr465/385 depending on season; ⊙10am-7pm mid-Jun–early Aug) The former Kristiansand zoo, off the E18 10km east of Kristiansand, has gradually expanded into what is probably *the* favourite holiday destination for children in Norway. There's a **funfair**, **fantasy village**, **water park**, **zoo** and the **Northern Wilderness** (Nordisk Vilmark), where visitors are transported over the habitat of moose, wolves, lynx and wolverines on elevated boardwalks.

Posebyen OLD TOWN
The Kristiansand Posebyen (Old Town) takes in most of the 14 blocks at the northern end of the town's characteristic *kvadraturen* (square grid pattern of streets measuring six long blocks by nine shorter blocks). It's worth taking a slow stroll around this pretty quarter, whose name was given by French soldiers who came to *reposer* (French for relax). The annual *Kristiansand* guide, published by the tourist office, includes a good section, 'A Stroll through Posebyen', to guide your wandering.

FREE **Christiansholm Fortress** FORTRESS
(Kristiansand Festning; ⊙grounds 9am-9pm mid-May–mid-Sep) The most prominent feature of the waterfront Strandpromenaden is the distinctive Christiansholm Fortress. It was built by royal decree between 1662 and 1672 to keep watch over the strategic Skagerrak Straits and protect the city from pirates and rambunctious Swedes. The fortress served its purpose – it was never taken by enemy forces.

One Ocean Dive Center DIVING
(www.oneocean.no; Dvergsnesveien 571, Odderhei; one/two dives with equipment from Nkr950/1300) A professional centre that runs dives to wrecks, which include a downed plane and even a minesweeper. It's 8km east of Kristiansand.

🛏 Sleeping

Kristiansand can be expensive for what you get, which may be nothing unless you book early for summer, especially during the July school-holiday period, when prices soar.

NORWAY KRISTIANSAND

Yess Hotel
HOTEL €€

(☑38 70 15 70; www.yesshotel.com; Tordenskjolds gate 12; s/d from Nkr695/795; P) This is a classic example of the kind of antiseptic but, for Norway, good-value new 'back-to-basics' hotels that seem to be slowly sprouting up in bigger towns throughout the country. The rooms at this new hotel are livened up with wall-to-wall photographs of trees. The hotel is at the western entrance of town, close to the train station.

Firmautleie B&B
B&B €

(☑91 12 99 06; www.gjestehus.no; Frobusdalen 2; s Nkr400-500, d Nkr600-800; P) Probably the most personal place to stay in Kristiansand, this small B&B in an old timber home a 10-minute walk northwest of the centre is rustic, cosy and friendly. However, the secret's out and it's often full. The B&B is west of the city centre, on the fringes of the forest that circle the city to the north.

Clarion Hotel Ernst
CHAIN HOTEL €€

(☑38 12 86 00; www.clarionernst.com; Rådhus-gaten 2; s Nkr800-1490, d Nkr1000-1695; P@) The newly renovated Clarion Hotel looks pretty dull from the outside but inside is a whole different story, with huge, pearl-string lampshades, gold and silver throne-like chairs, purple lighting and massive jet-black bedheads. It's one of the few business-class hotels in Norway with any character. Parking costs Nkr140 per day. The hotel is close to the port on the western edge of the main grid of streets in the town centre.

Scandic Kristiansand
CHAIN HOTEL €€€

(☑21 61 42 00; www.scandic-hotels.com; Markens gate 39; s Nkr1590-1790, d Nkr1790-1990; P@) If you value style as well as substance, the Scandic Kristiansand has both. The rooms and public areas are stylish, rooms have all the requisite bells and whistles, and the hotel adheres to the strictest environmental standards. Every day it lets 10 rooms go online for just Nkr530. This is another hotel at the western corner of the city centre, a block northeast of the train station.

Roligheden Camping
CAMPING GROUND €

(☑38 09 67 22; www.roligheden.no, in Norwegian; Framnesveien; campsites Nkr130 plus per person Nkr30, cabins from Nkr900; ☺Jun-Aug) Tent campers are in luck at this well-run camping ground at a popular beach site 3km east of the centre. Take bus 15 from the centre.

✗ Eating & Drinking

TOP CHOICE Bølgen & Moi
SEAFOOD €€€

(☑38 17 83 00; www.bolgenogmoi.no, in Norwegian; Sjølystveien 1A; light meals Nkr55-169, restaurant starters Nkr75-145, mains Nkr220-279; ☺3pm-midnight Mon-Sat) The best restaurant around the fish-market harbour, the supercool Bølgen & Moi does a sublime fish and shellfish soup and a tasty range of fish and seafood dishes as well as set menus. In summer the outdoor tables are packed and it's a good place for a drink after the kitchen closes.

Hos Naboen
INTERNATIONAL €€

(www.hosnaboen.no, in Norwegian; Markens gate 19A; mains around Nkr150; ☺10.30am-11pm Mon-Sat) This bustling central cafe, with a warm and sociable atmosphere, pumps out great light meals (including superb meatballs stuffed with mango chutney and melted cheese), huge doorstopper wedges of cake and decent coffee.

Sjøhuset
SEAFOOD €€

(☑38 02 62 60; Markens gate; light meals & snacks Nkr75-169, mains Nkr179-269; ☺11am-11pm) Along the waterfront next to the yacht harbour, this long-standing restaurant of quality is another fine choice for lovers of the fruits of the sea. Dishes include mussels and chips (Nkr185), shrimps (from Nkr150) or plain old fish and chips (Nkr195).

Snadderkiosken
FAST FOOD €

(Østre Strandgate 78a; dishes Nkr69-129; ☺8.30am-11.30pm Mon-Fri, 11.30am-11.30pm Sat & Sun) We don't normally direct you to the fast-food kiosks that are everywhere in Norway, but Snadderkiosken, at the eastern end of town, is one of the best of its kind. Near the town beach, this lovely tiled 1920s-style kiosk will sort you out with things such as hearty meatballs and mashed potatoes or grilled chicken with rice and salad.

TOP CHOICE Frk Larsen
BAR

(Markens gate 5; ☺11am-midnight Mon-Wed, 11am-3am Thu-Sat, noon-midnight Sun) Our favourite drinking hole in Kristiansand, this trendy place towards the southeastern end of Markens gate has retro-chic fusion decor, a mellow ambience by day and late-night music for an 'in' crowd on weekend nights. The cocktail bar opens at 8pm, but if cocktails (almost) by the seashore aren't your thing, then it's just as popular for a midday coffee.

ℹ️ Information

Tourist office (www.regionkristiansand.no; Rådhusgata 6; ⊙9am-6pm Mon-Fri, 10am-6pm Sat, noon-6pm Sun mid-Jun–Aug, 9am-4pm Mon-Fri rest of yr)

ℹ️ Getting There & Away

BOAT For information on ferries to Denmark, see p415.

BUS Departures from Kristiansand include: Arendal (Nkr130, 1½ hours, up to nine daily); Bergen (Nkr660, 12 hours, one daily); Oslo (Nkr350, 5½ hours, up to nine daily); and Stavanger (Nkr380, 4½ hours, two to four daily).

TRAIN There are up to four trains daily to Oslo (Nkr299 to Nkr631, 4½ hours) and up to five to Stavanger (Nkr199 to Nkr427, 3¼ hours).

Telemark

Most of the Telemark region is sparsely populated and rural, with steep mountains, deep valleys, high plateaux and countless lakes. Most visitors come for its incredible stave churches and the Telemark Canal.

Public transport in this region isn't particularly convenient; most buses run infrequently and train lines are largely absent, so sightseeing is best done by car. For tourist information, contact Telemarkreiser (📞35 90 00 20; www.visittelemark.com).

NOTODDEN
POP 12,200

Notodden is an industrial town of little note, but the nearby Heddal stave church (www. heddalstavkirke.no; Heddal; adult/child Nkr60/free,

entry to grounds free; ⊙9am-7pm Mon-Sat, 1-7pm Sun mid-Jun–mid-Aug) rises out of a graveyard like a scaly wooden dragon. The impressive edifice is justifiably one of Telemark's most visited attractions. Of great interest are the 'rose' paintings, a runic inscription, the bishop's chair and the altarpiece. The church possibly dates from 1242, but parts of the chancel date from as early as 1147. It was heavily restored in the 1950s. On Sundays from Easter to November, services are held at 11am (visitors are welcome, but to avoid disruption, you must remain for the entire one-hour service); after 1pm, the church is again open to the public.

Notodden's other claim to fame is the renowned and hugely popular Notodden Blues Festival (www.bluesfest.no), in early August.

Timekspressen buses run once or twice an hour between Kongsberg and Notodden (Nkr100, 35 minutes).

RJUKAN
POP 6100

Sitting in the shadow of what is arguably Norway's most beautiful peak, Gausta (1881m), Rjukan is a picturesque introduction to the Norwegian high country as well as southern Norway's activities centre par excellence.

◉ Sights

Industrial Workers Museum   MUSEUM
(Norsk Industriarbeidermuseet; www.visitvemork. com; adult/child Nkr75/45; ⊙10am-6pm mid-Jun–mid-Aug) Housed inside a hydroelectric plant dating from 1911, 7km west of Rjukan, this

---

DON'T MISS

A SLOW BOAT THROUGH TELEMARK

The 105km-long Telemark Canal system, a series of lakes and canals that connect Skien and Dalen (with a branch from Lunde to Notodden), lifts and lowers boats a total of 72m in 18 locks. The canal was built for the timber trade from 1887 to 1892.

Every day from June to mid-August, a variety of different boats (most old-fashioned steamers) chug along the canals of Telemark. One particularly good route involves catching the boat from Akkerhaugen, 24km south of Notodden, at 10am from where you travel to Lunde (adult/child Nkr300/150, 3¾ hours), where a bus takes you back to Akkerhaugen at 1.55pm. The trip can also be done in reverse by taking the 12.26pm bus to Lunde, from where you catch the boat at 1.45pm and sail serenely back to Akkerhaugen, arriving at 5pm.

For a full-day trip consider the leisurely 11-hour journey between Skien and Dalen (adult/child Nkr930/465; late June to mid-August). Boats leave Skien at 8.20am and arrive in Dalen at 6.50pm, from where you can catch a special 'canalbus' back to Skien.

For further information, contact Telemarkreiser (📞35 90 00 30; www.visittelemark.com).

museum details the Norwegian Resistance's daring sabotage of the heavy-water plant used by the Nazis in their atomic efforts.

Gaustabanen cable railway   RAILWAY
(www.gaustabanen.no, in Norwegian; adult/child Nkr350/175) For an incredible experience, ride this mind-boggling cable railway deep into a mountain core before climbing more than 1km at an improbable 40-degree angle. Built by NATO in 1952 to ensure access to a radio tower in any weather, it's expected to reopen by the time you read this. The railway's base station is 10km southeast of Rjukan.

Rjukanfossen   WATERFALL
Believed to be the highest waterfall in the world in the 18th century (Angel Falls in Venezuela now has that claim), the 104m-high Rjukanfossen is still a spectacular sight. To get the best view, take the Rv37 heading west and park just before the tun-

nel 9.5km west of town; a 200m walk leads to a fine viewpoint.

🏃 Activities

The top station of the **Krossobanen** (adult one way/return Nkr50/90, child Nkr15/30, bike Nkr30/60; ☺9am-8pm mid-Jun–Aug) cable car, above Rjukan, serves as the trailhead for a host of hiking and cycling trails.

Rjukan stands on the cusp of the bleak Hardangervidda Plateau. The range of summer activities here is seemingly endless and includes: ice climbing; Norway's highest land-based bungee jump (84m); moose safaris; and rail-biking. Winter activities include horse-drawn sleigh rides, skiing and dog-sledding. The tourist office can put you in touch with local operators organising these activities.

🛏 Sleeping & Eating

Rjukan's town centre has a few places to stay, but there are more choices up in the Gaustablikk area. For the busy winter sea-

HIKING & CYCLING FROM RJUKAN

For more information on the following routes, visit the tourist office to pick up the free *Rjukan og Tinn*.

Gausta

The most obvious goal for hikers is the summit of beautiful Gausta (1881m), from where you can see a remarkable one-sixth of Norway on a clear day. The popular, and easy, two- to three-hour, 4km hiking track leads from the trailhead of Stavsro (15km southeast of Rjukan) up to DNT's **Gaustahytta** (1830m). The summit is a further half-hour walk along the rocky ridge. A 13km road link, but no public transport, runs from the far eastern end of Rjukan to Stavsro (altitude 1173m) at Heddersvann lake. Taxis (☎35 09 14 00) charge around Nkr450 one way.

Hardangervidda

The Hardangervidda Plateau, the biggest mountain plateau in Europe and home to Europe's largest herd of wild reindeer, rises up to the north of Rjukan and offers a wealth of fantastic hikes. From Gvepseborg, the summit of the Krossobanen cable car, the most rewarding day hike is the five-hour round trip to the **Helberghytta DNT Hut**. The scenery takes in icy-cold lakes, snow-streaked hills, barren moorland and views back over towards Gausta.

For something more challenging, an eight- to nine-hour route, which can also be used by cyclists, leads from the cable car platform past the Helberghytta DNT Hut and onward to **Kalhovd Turisthytte**, where you can either catch a bus or hike nine hours down to **Mogen Turisthytte**, where you can catch the Møsvatn ferry (Nkr255) back to Skinnarbu, west of Rjukan on Rv37; ferry timetables are available from the Rjukan tourist office.

Alternatively, follow the marked route that begins above Rjukan Fjellstue, around 10km west of Rjukan and just north of the Rv37. This historic track follows the **Sabotørruta** (Saboteurs' Route), the path taken by the members of the Norwegian Resistance during WWII. From late June until mid-August, the tourist office organises three-hour guided hikes along this route (Nkr200, noon Tuesday, Thursday and Sunday).

The best hiking map to use for this part of the plateau is Telemark Turistforening's *Hardangervidda Sør-Øst* (1:60,000), available from the tourist office (Nkr98).

son, contact **Gausta Booking** (📞45 48 51 51; www.gaustatoppenbooking.com), which can help track down a spare hut.

TOP CHOICE **Rjukan Hytteby & Kro**　CABINS **€€**
(📞35 09 01 22; www.rjukan-hytteby.no; Brogata 9; cabins Nkr825-1050) Easily the town centre's best choice, Rjukan Hytteby & Kro sits in a pretty spot on the river bank and has carefully decorated and very well-equipped huts that seek to emulate the early-20th-century hydroelectric workers' cabins. The owner is exceptionally helpful. It's a pleasant 500m walk along the river bank to the town centre.

Rjukan Gjestegård　HOTEL **€€**
(📞35 08 06 50; www.rgg.no, in Norwegian; Birkelandsgata 2; dm Nkr235, s/d without bathroom Nkr385/580, d Nkr990; 🅿@) This central guesthouse occupies the buildings of the old youth hostel and is something of a travellers' centre. The rooms here are simple but fine enough, there's a guest kitchen and the location is good if you want to be in town. Breakfast costs Nkr80.

Gaustablikk Høyfjellshotell　MOUNTAIN LODGE **€€**
(📞35 09 14 22; www.gaustablikk.no; s/d from Nkr955/1350 Mon-Fri, s/d Nkr1080/1600 Sat & Sun; 🅿) With a prime location overlooking the lake and mountain off the Fv651 and 10km from town, this expansive mountain lodge is one of Norway's better mountain hotels. The rooms are modern and many have lovely views of Gausta, while the evening buffet dinner (Nkr350) is a lavish affair. Book through Fjord Pass for a cheaper one-night rate.

Roberto Gatekjokken　FAST FOOD **€**
(off Sam Eydes; snacks from Nkr35; ⊙lunch & dinner) A cut above most Norwegian roadside kiosks, this well-run little place offers fish and chips (Nkr53), hamburgers (Nkr46 to Nkr98), kebabs (Nkr55) and other heart-friendly delights. Eat at the shady adjacent tables.

ⓘ **Information**
Tourist office (📞35 08 05 50; www.visitrjukan.com; Torget 2; ⊙9am-7pm Mon-Fri, 10am-6pm Sat & Sun late Jun-late Aug, 8am-3.30pm Mon-Fri rest of yr)

ⓘ **Getting There & Away**
Regular buses connect Rjukan to Oslo (Nkr355, 3½ hours) via Notodden (where you need to change buses) and Kongsberg (Nkr240, two hours).

CENTRAL NORWAY

The central region of Norway is strewn with stunning national parks, the most spectacular of which is Jotunheimen, a popular wilderness area and national park characterised by dramatic ravines and multiple glaciers. The immensely scenic Oslo–Bergen railway line slices east to west, crossing the stark and white snowscape of the Hardangervidda Plateau, a cross-country skiing paradise. For a resort-town feel, try Lillehammer, close to several downhill slopes and host of the 1994 Winter Olympics.

Lillehammer
POP 26,400
Long a popular Norwegian ski resort, Lillehammer became known to the world after hosting the 1994 Winter Olympics, which still provide the town with some of its most interesting sights. Lying at the northern end of the lake Mjøsa and surrounded by farms, forests and small settlements, it's a laidback place with year-round attractions, although in winter it becomes a ski town par excellence.

Lillehammer's centre is small and cute. Storgata, the main pedestrian walkway, is two short blocks east of the adjacent bus and train stations.

⊙ **Sights & Activities**

TOP CHOICE **Olympic Sights**　OLYMPIC PARK, MUSEUM
Visitors can tour the main Olympic sites over a large area called the **Olympiaparken** (www.olympiaparken.no; ⊙9am-6pm mid-Jun–mid-Aug), which includes the ski jump, chairlift and bobsled simulator. The excellent **Norwegian Olympic Museum** (www.ol.museum.no; Olympiaparken; adult/student/child Nkr100/80/50; ⊙10am-5pm Jun-Aug, 11am-4pm Tue-Sun Sep-May) provides exhibits on every Olympic Games since 1896.

At Hunderfossen, 15km north of town, you can career down the Olympic Bobsled Run (Hunderfossen; ☉11am-6pm daily early Jul–early Aug, weekends only Jun & rest of August, closed rest of yr) aboard a wheelbob (adult/10-11yr Nkr220/150) under the guidance of a professional bobsled pilot. Wheelbobs take five passengers and hit a top speed of 100km/h. The real thing, taxibobs (adult around Nkr1100; ☉Nov-Easter), take four passengers, reach an exhilarating 130km/h and you won't have much time to get nervous – you're down the mountain in 70 seconds. Bookings are advisable during winter.

TOP CHOICE Maihaugen Folk Museum   MUSEUM
(www.maihaugen.no; Maihaugveien 1; adult/student/child/family Jun-Aug Nkr140/80/70/350, Sep-May Nkr100/80/50/250; ☉10am-5pm Jun-Aug) Olympics aside, Lillehammer's main attraction is the exceptional Maihaugen Folk Museum, which contains around 180 historic houses, shops, farm buildings and a stave church.

🛏 Sleeping & Eating

TOP CHOICE Lillehammer Vandrerhjem   HOSTEL €
(☑61 26 00 24; www.815mjosa.no; 1st fl, Railway Station; dm/s/d/tr Nkr325/695/840/990, 6-bed apt Nkr1650) If you've never stayed in a youth hostel, this one above the train station is the place to break the habits of a lifetime. The rooms are simple but come with a bathroom, bedlinen and free wireless internet.

Birkebeineren   HOTEL & APARTMENTS €€
(☑61 05 00 80; www.birkebeineren.no; Birkebeinervegen 24; s/d Nkr740/1020, with Fjord Pass Nkr370/740, 2-/4-bed apt Nkr1170/1620; P) This terrific place, on the road up to the bottom of the ski jump, offers a range of accommodation to suit different budgets; prices fall the longer you stay. Rooms are light-filled and modern, and there's a children's playground and sauna on-site.

Mølla Hotell   HOTEL €€
(☑61 05 70 80; www.mollahotell.no; Elvegata 12; s/d Nkr1180/1375, with Fjord Pass Nkr760/1020; P) Fully refurbished with modern rooms, the hotel has antique memorabilia in the public areas and flat-screen TVs and comfy beds in the rooms. The rooftop bar (open from 8pm to 2am Monday to Saturday) has fine views and the architecture is distinguished. Parking costs Nkr55 per day.

Svare & Berg   INTERNATIONAL €€
(Elvegata; mains Nkr139-298; ☉4-11pm Mon-Fri, 11am-11pm Sat) Right by Lillehammer's bubbling brook, this very cool cafe-restaurant serves tasty meals and great coffee. It's a popular spot for locals. The same people also run neighbouring Nikkers, where a moose has apparently walked through the wall; Nikkers does sandwiches and lighter meals.

Tid For Mat   NORWEGIAN RESTAURANT €€€
(☑61 24 77 77; Jernbanegata 1-5; tapas & starters Nkr45-125, mains Nkr200-295; ☉4-10pm Tue-Sat) This stylish restaurant attached to the First Hotel Breiseth is the domain of Siegfried Sokollek, one of Norway's more celebrated chefs. The cooking is, as you'd imagine, assured.

ℹ Information

Lillehammer tourist office (www.lillehammer.com; Lillehammer Skysstasjon; ☉8am-6pm Mon-Fri, 10am-5pm Sat & Sun mid-Jun–mid-Aug)

ℹ Getting There & Away

BUS Nor-Way Bussekspress has services to/from Oslo (Nkr315, three hours, three to four daily) via Oslo's Gardermoen airport (Nkr270, 2¼ hours), and Bergen (Nkr575, 9¼ hours, one daily). Lavprisekspressen buses run less often but are cheaper if you book online at http://lavprisekspressen.no (in Norwegian).

TRAIN Trains run to/from Oslo (Nkr339, 2¼ hours, 11 to 17 daily) and Trondheim (from Nkr661, 4¼ to seven hours, four to six daily).

Røros
POP 5600

Røros, a charming Unesco World Heritage–listed site set in a small hollow of stunted forests and bleak fells, is one of Norway's most beautiful villages. The Norwegian writer Johann Falkberget described Røros as 'a place of whispering history' and this historic copper-mining town (once called Bergstad, or mountain city) has wonderfully preserved and colourful wooden houses that climb the hillside, as well as fascinating relics from the town's mining past; the first mine opened in 1644 and operations ceased 333 years later. Røros has become something of a retreat for artists, who lend even more character to this enchanted place.

⊙ Sights

TOP CHOICE **Historic District** HISTORIC AREA

Røros' historic district, characterised by the striking log architecture of its 80 protected buildings, takes in the entire central area. The two main streets, Bergmannsgata (it tapers from southwest to northeast to create an optical illusion and make the town appear larger than it is) and Kjerkgata, are lined with historical homes and buildings, all under preservation orders.

Røros Kirke CHURCH

(Kjerkgata) Closed for major renovations when we were there, Røros' Lutheran church is one of Norway's most distinctive, not to mention one of the country's largest, with a seating capacity of 1640. The first church on the site was constructed in 1650, but it had fallen into disrepair by the mid-18th century and from 1780 a new baroque-style church (the one you see today) was built just behind the original.

Smelthytta MUSEUM

(Malmplassen; adult/student/child Nkr80/60/free; ⊙10am-6pm mid-Jun–mid-Aug) Housed in old smelting works, this mining museum is a town highlight. The building was reconstructed in 1988 according to the original 17th-century plan. Upstairs you'll find geological and conservation displays, while downstairs are some brilliant working models of the mines and the water- and horse-powered smelting processes. Displays of copper smelting are held at 3pm from Tuesday to Friday from early July to early August. In summer your entry ticket entitles you to a free guided tour at 11am, 12.30pm, 2pm (in English) or 3.30pm. The museum is on the hill next to the river at the northeastern end of the village.

Just across the stream from the museum are the protected slegghaugan (slag heaps), from where there are lovely views over town. Off the southwestern corner of the slag heaps, the historic smelting district with its tiny turf-roofed miners' cottages, particularly along Sleggveien, is one of Røros' prettiest corners.

🏃 Activities

In addition to the following activities, **canoeing**, **horse riding**, **sleigh rides** and **ice-fishing** are also possible. The tourist office has a full list of operators.

Husky Excursions

 Alaskan Husky Tours (☑62 49 87 66; www.huskytour.no; Os) and **Røros Husky** (☑72 41 41 94; www.roroshusky.no) both organise winter dog-sledding tours from a few hours to a few days. Alaska Husky Tours also operates summer tours on wheel-sleds (adult/child under 16 years Nkr700/350).

Sámi Excursions

Røros Rein (☑72 41 10 06; www.rorosrein.no; Hagaveien 17) organises a program that includes sleigh rides, getting up close and personal with reindeer and a traditional Sámi meal in a Sámi hut.

☞ Tours

Guided walking tours OLD TOWN

(adult/child Nkr60/free; ⊙tours 10am, 11.30am, 1pm & 2.30pm Mon-Sat, 11am & 1pm Sun mid-Jun–mid-Aug) Run by the tourist office, the tours take you through the historic town centre; tours at 11.30am Saturday and 1pm Sunday from mid-June to mid-August are in English and/or German.

✯✯ Festivals & Events

The biggest winter market is **Rørosmartnan** (Røros Market), begun in 1644 as a meeting place for wandering hunters to sell goods to townspeople. Thanks to an 1853 royal decree, stipulating that a grand market be held annually from the penultimate Tuesday of February to the following Saturday, it continues today with street markets and live entertainment.

Fermund Race (www.femundlopet.no), one of Europe's longest dog-sled races, starts and ends in Røros in the first week of February.

🛏 Sleeping

TOP CHOICE **Erzscheidergården** GUESTHOUSE €€

(☑72 41 11 94; www.erzscheidergaarden.no; Spell Olaveien 6; s/d from Nkr895/1190; ℗) This appealing 24-room guesthouse is up the hill from the centre and behind the church. The wood-panelled rooms are loaded with personality, the atmosphere is Norwegian-family-warmth and the breakfasts are outstanding.

Frøyas Hus B&B €€

(☑92 88 35 30; www.froyashus.no, in Norwegian; Mørkstugata 4; r without bathroom Nkr400-900) It may only have two rooms, but this gorgeous place in the village centre, off the easternmost of the two main streets running through town, has an intimacy that you won't find elsewhere. Rooms are small but, save for a lick of paint, they've scarcely changed in over 300 years – rustic in the best sense of the word.

Vertshuset Røros HISTORIC HOTEL €€
(☎72 41 93 50; www.vertshusetroros.no, in Norwegian; Kjerkgata 34; s/d from Nkr875/1050, 2-/4-bed apt Nkr1450/2250; ℗) Located in a historic 17th-century building on the main pedestrian thoroughfare, Vertshuset Røros is another wonderful choice. The all-wood rooms are generously sized, with numerous period touches: beds here are arguably the most comfortable in town.

 Eating

TOP CHOICE Vertshuset
Røros TRADITIONAL NORWEGIAN €€
(☎72 41 24 11; Kjerkgata 34; lunch mains Nkr75-145, dinner mains Nkr268-345) Lunch dishes here include fairly standard soup, sandwiches and burgers, but from 4pm onwards, the food is exquisite – the most tender fillets of reindeer or elk, as well as Arctic char and desserts such as 'blue cheese and pear marinated in cinnamon, walnuts in honey and balsamico'.

**Kaffestugu
Cafeteria** SNACKS, TRADITIONAL NORWEGIAN €
(www.kaffestuggu.no, in Norwegian; Bergmannsgata 18; lunch specials & snacks Nkr59-115, mains Nkr125-245; ⊗10am-9pm Mon-Sat, 11am-6.30pm Sun mid-Jun–mid-Aug) This historic place at the lower (southwestern) end of town offers a good range of coffee, pastries, snacks and light meals, as well as some more substantial main dishes.

ℹ️ **Information**

Tourist office (www.roros.no; Peder Hiortsgata 2; ⊗9am-6pm Mon-Sat, 10am-4pm Sun mid-Jun–mid-Aug, 9am-3pm Mon-Fri, 10am-1pm Sat rest of yr)

ℹ️ **Getting There & Away**

AIR Røros has two daily (except Saturday) **DOT LT** (www.flydot.no) flights to/from Oslo.
BUS There are up to four daily buses to Oslo (Nkr455, six hours).
TRAIN Røros lies on the eastern railway line between Oslo (from Nkr199, five hours, six daily) and Trondheim (from Nkr199, 2½ hours).

Jotunheimen National Park

The Sognefjellet road (the highest mountain road in northern Europe) between Lom and Sogndal passes the northwestern perimeter of Jotunheimen National Park, Norway's most popular wilderness destination. Hiking trails lead to some of the park's 60 glaciers, up to the top of Norway's loftiest peaks, Galdhøpiggen (2469m) and Glittertind (2452m), and along ravines and valleys featuring deep lakes and plunging waterfalls; by one count, there are more than 275 summits above 2000m inside the park. There are DNT huts and private lodges along many of the routes.

◉ **Sights & Activities**

For park information, maps and glacier-walk arrangements contact **Lom tourist office** (www.visitjotunheimen.com; ⊗9am-7pm mid-Jun–mid-Aug). Lom contains a **stave church** dating from 1170, lit to fairy-tale effect at night. It's also home to the historic **Fossheim Turisthotell**.

Dramatic **Galdhøpiggen**, with its cirques, arêtes, glaciers and summer ski centre, is a fairly tough eight-hour day hike from Spiterstulen, with 1470m of ascent, accessible by a toll road (Nkr85 per car). **Krossbu** is in the middle of a network of trails, including a short one to the **Smørstabbreen glacier**. From **Turtagrø**, a rock-climbing and hiking centre midway between Sogndal and Lom, there's a three-hour hike to Fannaråkhytta, Jotunheimen's highest DNT hut (2069m), offering panoramic views.

🛏️ **Sleeping & Eating**

Elvesæter Hotell HOTEL €€
(☎61 21 99 00; www.elveseter.no; Bøverdalen; s/d from Nkr850/1150; ℗) Run by the sixth generation of the Elvesæter family, this gorgeous hotel and restaurant (three-course dinners Nkr325) has pretty rooms, lovely architecture and is high on novelty value, adjacent as it is to the Sagasøyla, a 32m-high carved wooden pillar tracing Norwegian history from unification in 872 to the 1814 constitution.

Turtagrø Hotel MOUNTAIN LODGE €€€
(☎57 68 08 00; www.turtagro.no; dm from Nkr370, s/d Nkr1440/1900, tower ste Nkr2350; ℗) This historic hiking and mountaineering centre is a friendly yet laidback base for exploring

It's possible to engage in a wide range of activities in central Norway. For more information, contact the following tourist offices, which have a list of operators and local accommodation, and can provide advice on hiking in nearby national parks:

» **Otta tourist office & Rondane National Park Centre** (☑61 23 66 78; www.visitrondane.com; Otta)

» **Dombås tourist office & Dovrefjell National Park Centre** (Dovrefjell Nasjonalparksenter; ☑61 24 14 44; www.rondane-dovrefjell.no; Sentralplassen, Dombås)

» **Oppdal tourist office** (☑72 40 04 70; www.oppdal.com)

» **Oppdal Booking** (☑72 40 08 00; www.oppdal-booking.no; Olav Skasliens vei 12) A privately run one-stop shop for reserving activities and accommodation; booking fees apply.

Rafting

The rafting season runs from the middle of May until early October and is possible in Sjoa or Oppdal. Prices start at Nkr590 for a 3½-hour family trip; there are also five-hour trips (from Nkr990) through to seven-hour day trips (from Nkr1090); longer excursions are available on request. In addition to rafting, most of the following operators also organise **riverboarding** (from Nkr990), low-level **rock climbing** (from Nkr490), **canyoning** (from Nkr820), **caving** (from Nkr690) and **hiking**.

Operators include the following:

» **Heidal Rafting** (☑61 23 60 37; www.heidalrafting.no; Sjoa) Just 1km west of E6 along Rv257.

» **Sjoa Rafting** (☑90 07 10 00; www.sjoarafting.com; Nedre Heidal) Some 7.5km upstream from Sjoa along Rv257.

» **Sjoa Rafting Senter NWR** (☑47 66 06 80; www.sjoaraftingsenter.no; Varphaugen Gård) About 3km upstream from Sjoa along Rv257.

» **Opplev Oppdal** (☑72 40 41 80; www.opplev-oppdal.no, in Norwegian; Olav Skasliens vei 12, Oppdal)

Moose & Musk Ox Safaris

Your best chance of seeing one of Norway's last 80 musk oxen is to take a three- to five-hour morning **musk ox safari** (from Nkr300), either from Oppdal or Dombås. In both places, a three-hour evening **elk safari** is also possible.

Jotunheimen/Hurrungane whatever your budget. The main building has wonderful views and supremely comfortable rooms. Meals (three-course meal Nkr425) and full board (from Nkr1835/2690 single/double) are available.

 Røisheim

Hotel   TRADITIONAL HOTEL, RESTAURANT **€€€**
(☑61 21 20 31; www.roisheim.no; Bøverdalen; s/d incl breakfast, lunch & dinner from Nkr2100/3600, with open fireplace Nkr2275/3950; P) This charming place combines architecturally stunning buildings that date back to 1858 with modern comforts, although there are no TVs. Apart from the charming accommodation, the appeal lies in the meals, which are prepared by Ingrid Hov Lunde, one of the country's best-loved chefs. Quite simply, it's a wonderful place to stay.

Fossheim Turisthotell   HOTEL **€€**
(☑61 21 95 00; www.fossheimhotel.no; hotel s/d Nkr1100/1500, hotel annexe s/d Nkr950/1200, 4-bed apt Nkr1860; P) This historic family hotel at the eastern end of town is one of the best hotel-restaurant combinations in Norway. The all-wood rooms in the main hotel building are lovely, while there are also luxurious log cabins with modern interiors and simpler, cheaper rooms (some with good views) in the adjacent annex. But this place is equally famous for formerly being the home kitchen of the renowned Norwegian chef Arne Brimi (open 1pm to 3.30pm and 7pm to 10pm). Now under the care of Brimi's

protégé Kristoffer Hovland, the traditional Norwegian food on offer is exquisite.

Bøverdalen Vandrerhjem   HOSTEL €
(☎/fax 61 21 20 64; boverdalen.hostel@hihostels. no; Bøverdalen; dm Nkr170, s/d/f without bathroom Nkr275/420/525; **P**) This fine riverside hostel has a small cafe, tidy rooms and delightful surrounds to enjoy once the day trippers have returned home. Breakfast costs Nkr70.

Oslo to Bergen

The Oslo–Bergen railway line, a seven-hour journey past forests and alpine villages, and across the starkly beautiful Hardangervidda Plateau, is Norway's most scenic. See p350 for price information.

Midway between Oslo and Bergen is Geilo, a ski centre where you can practically walk off the train and onto a chairlift. There's also good summer **hiking** in the mountains around Geilo, where you'll find Øen Turistsenter & Geilo Vandrerhjem (☎32 08 70 60; www.oenturist.no; Lienvegen 137; dm Nkr275, huts Nkr480-825, breakfast Nkr60), a hostel near the train station that doubles as a tourist office.

From Geilo the train climbs 600m through a tundra-like landscape of high lakes and snow-capped mountains to the tiny village of Finse, near the Hardangerjøkulen icecap. Finse has year-round **skiing** and is in the middle of a network of summer **hiking trails**. One of Norway's most frequently trodden trails winds from the Finse train station down to the fjord town of Aurland, a four-day trek. There's breathtaking mountain scenery along the way as well as a series of DNT and private mountain huts a day's walk apart – the nearest is Finsehytta, 200m from Finse station. There's also a bicycle route from Finse to Flåm (six hours, downhill) on the century-old Rallarvegen railway construction road (see p366).

Myrdal, further west along the railway line, is the connecting point for the spectacularly steep Flåm railway, which twists and turns its way down 20 splendid kilometres to Flåm on Aurlandsfjorden, an arm of Sognefjorden.

BERGEN & THE WESTERN FJORDS

This spectacular region has truly indescribable scenery. Hardangerfjord, Sognefjord, Lysefjord and Geirangerfjord are all variants on the same theme: steep crystalline rock walls dropping with sublime force straight into the sea, often decorated with waterfalls, and small farms harmoniously blending into the natural landscape. Summer hiking opportunities exist along the fjord walls and on the enormous Jostedalsbreen glacier. Bergen, a lively city with a 15th-century waterfront, is exceedingly pleasing to behold, and it also contains some of Norway's finest nightlife and restaurants. Don't miss historic Bryggen.

Information on the entire region is available from Fjord Norway (www.fjordnorway.com).

Bergen

POP 256,600

Surrounded by seven hills and seven fjords, Bergen is a beautiful, charming city. With the Unesco World Heritage–listed Bryggen and buzzing Vågen harbour as its centrepiece, Bergen climbs the hillsides with hundreds of timber-clad houses, while cable cars offer stunning views from above. Throw in great museums, friendly locals and a dynamic cultural life and Bergen amply rewards as much time as you can give it. Drawback: expect rain or showers at least 275 days of the year.

Bergen is a terminus of the scenic Bergen-Oslo railway line and a convenient place to stay before excursions into fjord country. The *Hurtigruten* coastal steamer begins its six-day journey to Kirkenes from the centre.

History

During the 12th and 13th centuries, Bergen was Norway's capital and easily the country's most important city. By the 13th century, the city states of Germany allied themselves into trading leagues, most significantly the Hanseatic League; the sheltered harbour of Bryggen drew the traders in droves. They established their first office here around 1360, transforming Bryggen into one of the league's four major headquarters abroad.

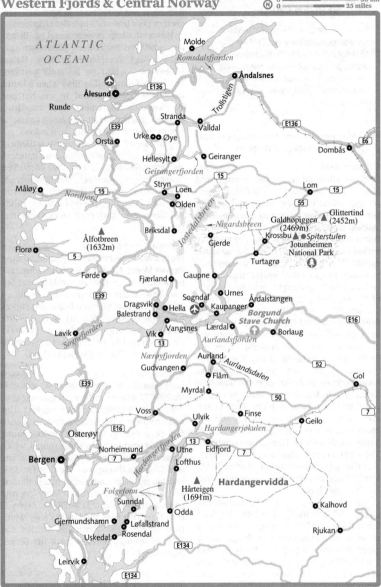

By the early 17th century Bergen was the trading hub of Scandinavia and Norway's most populous city, with 15,000 people. Bryggen continued as an important maritime trading centre until 1899, when the Hanseatic League's Bergen offices finally closed.

◉ Sights

The waterfront **fish market** at Torget is a good starting point for exploration of the city's historic district. Bergen has lots of cobblestone streets lined with older homes; one

ℹ️ BERGEN CARD

The Bergen Card (www.visitbergen.com/bergencard; adult per 24/48 hr Nkr190/250, child Nkr75/100) allows free transport on local buses, free parking and funicular-railway rides as well as admission to most sights. It's sold at the tourist office.

particularly pretty area for strolling is near the funicular station on Øvregaten.

Bryggen Area   HISTORIC AREA
Bryggen, the old medieval quarter and Unesco World Heritage site, is home to museums, restaurants and shops and its timber alleys offer an intriguing glimpse of the stacked-stone foundations and rough-plank construction of centuries past. The archaeological excavations of Bryggen, whose name means 'The Wharf', suggest that the quay was once 140m further inland than its current location. The current 58 buildings (25% of the original, although some claim there are now 61) cover 13,000 sq metres and date from after the 1702 fire, although the building pattern dates back to the 12th century.

Some of Norway's creakiest floors are in the timber building (1704) housing the Hanseatisk Museum (www.museumvest.no; Finnegårdsgaten 1a & Øvregaten 50; adult/child Nkr50/free mid-May–mid-Sep, Nkr30/free rest of yr; ⊙9am-5pm mid-May–mid-Sep). Period character flourishes, while furnishings and odd bedchambers give a glimpse of the austere living conditions of Hanseatic merchants. The entry ticket is also valid for Schøtstuene (Øvregaten 50), where the Hanseatic fraternity once met for its business meetings and beer guzzling.

The tiny Theta Museum (Enhjørningsgården; adult/child Nkr30/10; ⊙2-4pm Tue, Sat & Sun mid-May–mid-Sep) is a one-room reconstruction of a clandestine Resistance headquarters uncovered by the Nazis in 1942. Find it hidden in an upper storey at the rear of the Bryggen warehouse with the unicorn figurehead.

Rosenkrantztårnet (Rosenkrantz Tower; www.bymuseet.no; Bergenhus; adult/child Nkr50/free; ⊙10am-4pm mid-May–Aug, noon-3pm Sun Sep–mid-May) was built in the 1560s by Bergen's governor as a residence and defence post. You can climb down to bedrock and then up to the high-ceilinged bedchambers of a 16th-century tower. Detours along the way allow you to suffocate in an actual dungeon or peer into ancient toilet chambers.

Håkonshallen (www.bymuseet.no; Bergenhus; adult/child Nkr50/free; ⊙10am-4pm daily mid-May–Aug), completed by King Håkon Håkonsson in 1261 for his son's wedding, had its roof blown off in 1944 when a Dutch munitions boat exploded in the harbour. Be pleasantly disoriented while wandering through Escherian stairways, stopping to squint through blurry antique windows.

The site of Bergen's earliest settlement is now Bryggens Museum (www.bymuseet.no; Dreggsallmenning 3; adult/child Nkr60/free; ⊙10am-4pm mid-May–Aug). The 800-year-old foundations unearthed during the construction have been incorporated into the exhibits, along with pottery, human skulls and runes.

Bergen Kunst Museum   ART GALLERY
(Bergen Art Museum; www.bergenartmuseum.no; Rasmus Meyers Allé 3, 7 & 9; adult/student/child Nkr60/40/free; ⊙11am-5pm mid-May–mid-Sep, 11am-5pm Tue-Sun rest of yr) Three buildings opposite the lake fountain house this superb collection of Norwegian art from the 18th and 19th centuries, including many works by Munch and JC Dahl, as well as works by Picasso, Miró, Rodín, Klee and others.

Bergen Akvariet   AQUARIUM
(www.akvariet.com; Nordnesbakken 4; adult/child Nkr200/150 mid-Jun–mid-Aug, cheaper rest of yr; ⊙9am-7pm May-Aug, 10am-6pm Sep-Apr) This aquarium has a big outdoor tank with seals and penguins, as well as 70 indoor tanks, snakes, crocodiles and a shark tunnel, which opened in 2010. There are also penguin and seal feedings throughout the day. On foot, you can get there from Torget in 20 minutes; alternatively, take the Vågen ferry (one way/return adult Nkr40/60, child Nkr20/40; ⊙every 30 mins from 10am-6pm, late May-late Aug) which runs between the Torget fish market and Tollbodhopen at Nordnes (near the Bergen Aquarium).

Bergen Environs   MUSEUM, MANSIONS
The open-air Gamle Bergen (www.bymuseet.no; Nyhavnsveien 4, Sandviken; adult/child Nkr70/free; ⊙hourly tours 10am-5pm early May-Aug) presents around 40 buildings from the 18th and 19th centuries, including a dentist's office, bakery and houses. It's 4km north of the city centre and can be reached by city buses 20, 23 or 24.

If you want to tour the former lakeside home and workshop of composer Edvard Grieg, hop on any bus from platform 19, 20 or 21 of the bus station, get off at Hosbroen and follow the signs to **Troldhaugen** (www.troldhaugen.com; Hop; adult/child Nkr60/free; ☺9am-6pm May-Sep, 10am-4pm Oct-Apr). Although Grieg fans will best appreciate this well-conceived presentation, the main house contains some excellent period furnishings and is generally quite interesting.

🏃 Activities

Fløibanen Funicular CABLE CAR & HIKE
(www.floibanen.no; Vetrlidsalmenning 21; adult/child return Nkr70/35; ☺8am-midnight Mon-Sat & 9am-midnight May-Aug, to 11pm Sep-Apr) For unbeatable city views, take the Fløibanen funicular to the top of Mt Fløyen (320m). Trails marked with dilapidated signs lead into the forest from the hilltop station. Trails 1 and 3 are the longest, each making 5km loops through hilly woodlands. For a delightful 40-minute walk back to the city, take trail 4 and connect with trail 6.

Ulriken643 CABLE CAR & HIKE
(www.ulriken643.no; adult/child return Nkr145/75, with bus Nkr245/180; ☺9am-9pm May-Sep, 9am-5pm Oct-Apr) The Ulriksbanen cable car to the top of Mt Ulriken (642m) offers a panoramic view of Bergen, fjords and mountains. Many take the cable car one way and walk (about three hours) across a well-beaten trail to the funicular station at Mt Fløyen.

👉 Tours

📷 **Guided Tours of Bryggen** HISTORIC AREA
(☎55 58 80 10; adult/child Nkr100/free; ☺10am (German), 11am & noon (English), 1pm (Norwegian) Jun-Aug) The Bryggens Museum offers excellent 90-minute walking tours through the timeless alleys of Bryggen. The ticket includes admission to Bryggens Museum, Schøtstuene and the Hanseatic Museum.

✨ Festivals & Events

For a full list of events, see the website www.visitbergen.com.

Bergenfest MUSIC
(www.bergenfest.no) International music festival; late April to early May.

Bergen International Festival CULTURE
(www.fib.no) Held over 14 days from late May to early June, this is the big cultural

festival of the year, with dance, music and folklore presentations throughout the city.

Night Jazz Festival MUSIC
(www.nattjazz.no) Excellent jazz festival popular with Bergen's large student population; late May to early June.

Bergen International Guitar Festival MUSIC
(www.bergenguitarfestival.com) Held in late June.

Bergen Food Festival FOOD
(www.matfest.no) Showcases locally grown or caught food, which includes whale meat; early to mid-September.

Bergen International Film Festival FILM
(www.biff.no) Mid- to late October.

🛏 Sleeping

Bergen has outstanding accommodation, but *always* book before arriving in town, at least in the summer months or during festivals, when Bergen fills up fast.

The tourist office has an accommodation booking service (Nkr30 for walk-ins, Nkr50 for advance booking).

Det Hanseatiske Hotel HISTORIC HOTEL €€€
(☑55 30 48 00; www.dethanseatiskehotell.no; Finnegårdsgaten 2; d/deluxe Nkr1690/1890, ste Nkr2190-2990) The only hotel to be housed inside the old timber buildings that evoke Bryggen's bygone age, Det Hanseatiske Hotel is luxurious and like stepping back into a luxurious Bergen past. Flat-screen TVs cohabit with antique bathtubs and some extraordinary architectural features from Bryggen's days as a Hanseatic port.

TOP CHOICE **Skuteviken Gjestehus** GUESTHOUSE €€
(☑93 46 71 63; www.skutevikenguesthouse.com; Skutevikens Smalgang 11; d/attic Nkr900/1100) This authentic timber guesthouse, set on a small cobbled street in Sandviken, has traditional decoration and a few modern touches. Painstakingly restored by two artists whose work adorns the rooms, the guesthouse is quite simply charming.

Hotel Park Pension HISTORIC HOTEL €€
(☑55 54 44 00; www.parkhotel.no; Harald Hårfagresgate 35; s/d with Fjord Pass Nkr760/1020, otherwise s Nkr840-1100, d Nkr1090-1350) Filled with character and antiques, this family-run place spreads over two beautiful 19th-century buildings. Every room is different; in the main building, expect antique writing

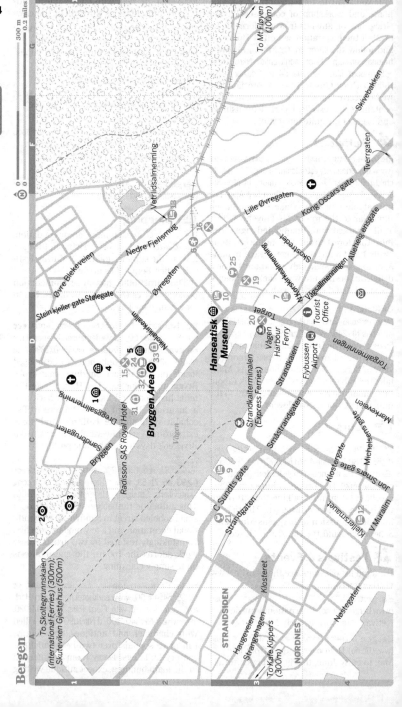

Bergen

300 m
0.2 miles

To Mt Fløyen
(100m)

Skrivebakken

Tverrgaten

Kong Oscars gate

Lille Øvregaten

Vetrlidsalmenning

Skostredet

Vågsallmenningen   Allehelg ensgate

Nedre Fjellsmug

Øvre Blekeveien

Øvregaten

Nikolaikirkeallm

Stein kjeller gate Stølegate

Hanseatisk
Museum

Bryggen Area

Vågen

Radisson SAS Royal Hotel

Dreggsalmenning

Sandbrugaten

Bryggen

Torget

Vågen
Harbour
Ferry

Strandkaiterminalen
(Express Ferries)

Strandkaien

Tourist
Office

Flybussen
Airport

Torgallmenningen

Markveien

Småstrandgaten

Småstrandgaten

C Sundts gate

Strandgaten

STRANDSIDEN

Klosteret

Haugeveien

Strangehagen

To Kafe Kippers
(300m)

NORDNES

Nøstegaten

Klostergate

Jon Smørs gate   Michels

Michels gate

Kjellersmauet

V Muralln

To Skoltegrunnskaien
(International Ferries) (300m);
Skuteviken Gjestehus (500m)

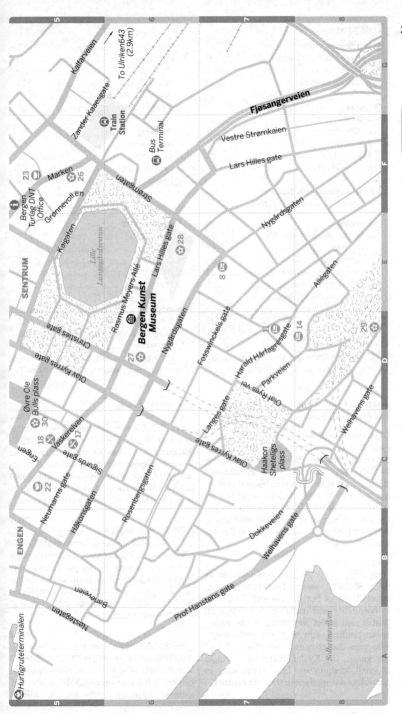

Karl Johansvei

To Ulriken643
(2.9km)

Zander Kaaesgate

R Train Station

Fjøsangerveien

Vestre Strømkaien

Bus Terminal

Lars Hilles gate

23 Marken 26

Bergen Turlag DNT Office

Grønnevollen

Strømgaten

Nygårdsgaten

1 Bergen Turlag

Kaigaten

Lille Langegårdsvann

SENTRUM

Lars Hilles gate

28

Allégaten

E

8

Nygårdsgaten

Rasmus Meyers Allé

m Bergen Kunst Museum

Christies gate

Olav Kyrres gate

Fosswinckels gate

Harald Hårfagresgate

14

27

Parkveien

D

Øvre Ole Bulls plass

30

Olaf Ryes vei

Langes gate

18 17

Vaskerelven

Sigurds gate

Engen

Olav Kyrres gate

Haakon Sheteligs plass

Welhavens gate

22

Neumanns gate

Håkonsgaten

Rosenbergsgaten

29

ENGEN

Banteveien

Nøstegaten

Dokkeveien

Welhavens gate

Prof Hanstens gate

Solheimsviken

Hurtigruteterminalen

desks, and the corner rooms are gorgeous and filled with light.

Skansen Pensjonat GUESTHOUSE €
(☎55 31 90 80; www.skansen-pensjonat.no; Vetrlidsalmenning 29; s Nkr425-475, d Nkr700-800, apt Nkr850) There are family-run guesthouses springing up all over Bergen, but this charming seven-room place is still one of our favourites. A wonderful location up behind the lower funicular station, real attention to detail and many personal touches make this a terrific choice.

Kjellersmauet Gjestehus GUESTHOUSE, APARTMENT €€
(☎55 96 26 08; www.gjestehuset.com; Kjellersmauet 22; s/d apt from Nkr700/900) This oasis of hospitality and tradition in a delightful timber-clad street southwest of the centre is outstanding. Run by the friendly Sonja, who goes the extra mile in taking care of her guests, the Kjellersmauet has a range of small, medium and large apartments in a building dating back to the 16th century.

Clarion Hotel Admiral HOTEL €€€
(☎55 23 64 00; www.clarionadmiral.no; C Sundtsgate 9; d Nkr1280-1995, Bryggen views Nkr280-380 extra) With sweeping views across the water to Bryggen from the balconies of its harbour-facing rooms, this well-appointed hotel promises the best view to wake up to in Bergen, if you can get a waterside room.

City Box HOSTEL €
(☎55 31 25 00; www.citybox.no; Nygårdsgaten 31; s/d Nkr700/800, without bathroom Nkr500/600) The best hostel in Bergen, City Box is a place where the owners do simple things well, such as bright modern rooms with splashes of colour, free wireless access, a minimalist designer feel without the price tag, and friendly young staff.

Bergen Vandrerhjem YMCA HOSTEL €
(☎55 60 60 55; www.bergenhostel.no; Nedre Korskirkealmenning 4; dm Nkr180-300, d Nkr800-900) This friendly hostel could be Norway's most central. It has that unmistakable hostel feel, same-sex or mixed dorms, kitchen facilities

and a terrific rooftop terrace. Bookings are essential year-round and, unusually, bedlinen is included in the price.

Steens Hotell HISTORIC HOTEL €€
(☎55 30 88 88; www.steenshotel.no; Parkveien 22; s/d with Fjord Pass Nkr820/1020, otherwise s Nkr760-990, d Nkr990-1340) This lovely 19th-century building oozes period charm, from the late-19th-century antiques to the gentle curve of the stairway; the bathroom facilities have recently been renovated.

✗ Eating

Bergen is the sort of place where international trends make their mark (sushi and tapas are all the rage and have been for some years) but you'll also find bastions of Norwegian tradition.

TOP CHOICE **Pingvinen** BAR-RESTAURANT €
(www.pingvinen.no, in Norwegian; Vaskerelven 14; mains Nkr69-149; ⊗1pm-3am Sun-Fri, noon-3am Sat) Devoted to small-town Norwegian cooking and with a delightfully informal ambience, Pingvinen is one of our favourite restaurants in Bergen. It's the sort of place where Norwegians come for recipes their mothers and grandparents used to cook and although the menu changes regularly, there are usually fish-cake sandwiches, reindeer, fish pie, whale, salmon, lamb shank and, our favourite, traditional Norwegian meatballs served with mushy peas and wild Norwegian berry jam.

Potetkjelleren NORWEGIAN €€€
(☎55 32 00 70; Kong Oscars gate 1A; 3-/4-/5-/6-course menus from Nkr495/565/625/685; ⊗4-10pm Mon-Sat) The 'Potato Cellar' is one of Bergen's finest restaurants, the sort of place that food critics rave about but which attracts more locals than tourists. The dining area has a classy wine-cellar ambience, the service is faultless, and the menu (which changes monthly) is based around freshest ingredients, Norwegian traditions and often subtly surprising combinations of taste. The wine list is also impeccable.

Torget Fish Market FISH MARKET €
(www.torgetibergen.no, in Norwegian; Torget; ⊗7am-7pm Jun-Aug, 7am-4pm Mon-Sat Sep-May) For price and atmosphere, it's hard to beat the fish market. Right alongside the harbour and a stone's throw from Bryggen, here you'll find everything from smoked whale meat and salmon to calamari, fish and chips, fish cakes, prawn baguettes, seafood salads, local caviar and, sometimes, nonfishy reindeer and elk.

Bryggen Tracteursted NORWEGIAN €€€
(Bryggen; lunch mains Nkr75-135, dinner mains Nkr285-375; ⊗lunch & dinner May-Sep) This is one of the great Bryggen eating experiences. Housed in a 1708 building that ranges across the former stables, kitchen and Bergen's only extant *schøtstuene* (dining hall), this fine restaurant does traditional Norwegian dishes that change regularly. It's classy and refined in the evenings, with a more informal atmosphere during the day.

Kafe Kippers INTERNATIONAL €€
(USF; Georgenes Verft 12; lunch mains Nkr65-85, dinner mains Nkr89-159; ⊗lunch & dinner) Away from the hubbub of downtown Bergen, this agreeable outdoor terrace is one of the best places for a meal or just a drink when

---

FJORD TOURS FROM BERGEN

Fjord Tours (☎81 56 82 22; www.fjordtours.com) has mastered the art of making the most of limited time with a series of tours into the fjords. Its popular and year-round **Norway in a Nutshell** tour is a great way to see far more than you thought possible in a single day. The day ticket (adult/child Nkr975/500) from Bergen combines a morning train to Voss, a bus to the Stalheim Hotel and then on to Gudvangen, from where a ferry takes you up the spectacular Nærøyfjord to Flåm, joining the stunning mountain railway to Myrdal, and a train back to Bergen in time for a late dinner (or you can continue on to Oslo to arrive around 10pm, for adult/child Nkr1345/685). From May to September, it also runs the 13-hour **Explore Hardangerfjord** (adult/child Nkr1320/780) and **Sognefjord in a Nutshell** (adult/child Nkr1150/575). It also has four-day tours that include Oslo, Sognefjorden, Geiranger and Ålesund (adult/child Nkr4410/3310).

Tide Reiser (☎55 23 87 00; www.tidereiser.no; ⊗May-Oct) runs 12-hour **Hardanger Fjord Adventure** tours that include a bus to Norheimsund, and a cruise that takes in Utne, Kinsarvik, Lofthus, Eidfjord and Ulvik (adult/child Nkr790/515) with a three-hour stop in Eidfjord (where additional sightseeing costs Nkr250/200 per adult/child).

the weather's warm. Attached to a cultural centre in an old sardine canning factory, it has an arty vibe and serves plentiful lunch dishes that include pastas and salads.

Pygmalion Økocafé
ORGANIC €

(Nedre Korskirkealmenning 4; ciabatta Nkr69-89, organic pancakes Nkr79-119, salads Nkr119-149; ⊙11am-11pm) This very cool place has contemporary art adorning its walls, a casual but classy atmosphere and tasty organic food. It's a great place at any time of the day and as good for a snack as something slightly more substantial. There are good choices for vegetarians.

Escalon
TAPAS €

(Vetrlidsalmenning 21; tapas Nkr38-108; ⊙3pm-midnight Sun-Fri, 1pm-midnight Sat) Tapas has taken Bergen by storm, but Escalon has been doing it since 1998. The friendly young waiters are happy to make suggestions on wine selection and the tapas are tasty and the closest you'll find in Bergen to what you'll get in Spain.

Naboen
SWEDISH €€

(www.grannen.no; Neumanns gate 20; mains Nkr198-252; ⊙4-11pm Mon-Sat, 4-10pm Sun) Although the cook does a range of Norwegian dishes here, Naboen is best known for its Swedish specialities, such as venison in a vanilla and port sauce. The quality is high and it has a well-earned and devoted local following.

Pølse Kiosk
SAUSAGES €

(Kong Oscars gate 1; hot dogs from Nkr45; ⊙10am-3am) If you've travelled around Norway for a while, you may be heartily sick of hot dogs bought from petrol stations, as are we. But this place has *real* sausages (including wild game, reindeer, lamb and chilli) and a better-than-average range of sauces and good-sized services.

⬤ Drinking

TOP CHOICE Altona Vinbar
WINE BAR

(C Sundtsgate 22; ⊙6pm-12.30am Mon-Thu, 6pm-1.30am Fri & Sat) Possibly our favourite wine bar in town, Altona Vinbar is in an intimate warren of underground rooms that date from the 16th century. With a huge selection of international wines, soft lighting and music that ranges from jazz to rock but never drowns out conversation, it's hard to find fault with this place.

Pingvinen
CAFE-BAR

(Vaskerelven 14; ⊙1pm-3am Sun-Fri, noon-3am Sat) As good a bar as it is as a restaurant, 'Penguin' is laidback and funky and popular with a friendly 30-something crowd. The late-night snacks are good if you get the munchies, and it has all the usual beers, as well as some boutique beers from microbreweries around Norway.

Capello
CAFE-BAR

(Marken 16; ⊙noon-5pm Mon-Wed, noon-8pm Thu, noon-1.30am Fri & Sat, noon-7pm Sun) An engaging little place that does smoothies, milkshakes, beer and, on Saturdays, pancakes, Capello is all about '50s and '60s decor and music downstairs (the jukebox is filled with Elvis, the Monkeys, the Beatles and Bob Dylan); upstairs the '70s take over. It sometimes hosts concerts and CD launches.

Sakristiet
CAFE

(Jacobsfjorden 4, Bryggen; ⊙10am-6pm) A charming little cafe in the heart of Bryggen's wooden lanes, 'Sacristy' is an oasis of calm, with comfy armchairs and good coffee, cakes, sandwiches and cookies. The setting is marvellous and it sells a carefully selected range of local food products.

Café Opera
CAFE, CLUB

(Engen 18; ⊙11am-3am Mon-Sat, noon-12.15am Sun) By day, Café Opera has a literary-cafe feel, with artworks and good coffee that attracts artists and students. On weekends, the crowd gets dancing around midnight to funk, soul, blues and disco (Wednesday and Thursday), hip hop, soul and funk (Friday) and reggae (Saturday).

Vågen
CAFE-BAR

(Kong Oscars gate 10; ⊙10am-11.30pm Mon-Wed, 10am-2am Thu-Sat, 11am-midnight Sun) This quiet cafe is where old Norwegian meets Bob Marley, with traditional Norwegian decoration, rustic wooden tables and a laidback feel helped by occasional reggae tunes. It's a cool combination and provides a great backdrop to a lazy afternoon.

☆ Entertainment

Bergen has something for everyone, from high culture to late-night live-music venues. For details and schedules, contact the tourist office.

Classical Music

Bergen has a busy program of concerts throughout summer, many of them classical

The wooden alleyways of Bryggen have become a haven for artists and craftspeople and there are stunning little shops and boutiques at every turn. Before entering the lanes, start at the waterfront with **Juhls' Silver Gallery** (see below). **Per Vigeland** (www.per-vigeland.no; Jacobsfjorden, Bryggen; ◷10am-6pm mid-May–Aug) is a local jewellery designer working with silver and gold-plated silver, while **Živa Jelnikar Design** (www.zj-d.com; Jacobsfjorden, Bryggen; ◷10am-5pm Mon-Fri, 11am-4pm Sat & Sun Jun-Aug), opposite the entrance to the Bryggen Visitors Centre, is the highly original work of Slovenian designer Živa Jelnikar; both have on-site workshops.

But it's not just about jewellery. **Kvams Flisespikkeri** (www.kvams-flisespikkeri.com, in Norwegian; Bredsgården, Bryggen; ◷9am-6pm mid-May–mid-Sep) sells lovely Bryggen-centric paintings, block prints and other artworks by Ketil Kvam. **Læverkstedet** (Jacobsfjorden, Bryggen; ◷10am-8pm mid-May–mid-Aug) is the purveyor of the softest moose leather with jackets, bags and other knick-knacks.

performances focusing on Bergen's favourite son, composer Edvard Grieg. Venues include the following:

Troldhaugen (p343; adult/student/child Nkr220/160/50; ◷6pm Wed & Sun, 2pm Sat mid-Jul–Sep)

Grieghallen (☑55 21 61 50; www.grieghallen. no; Edvard Griegs plass; ◷Aug-Jun) Performances by the respected Bergen Philharmonic Orchestra.

Nightclubs & Live Music

Garage   ROCK
(www.garage.no; Christies gate 14; ◷3pm-3am Mon-Sat, 5pm-3am Sun) Garage has taken on an almost mythical quality for music lovers across Europe. It does play live jazz and acoustic, but this is a rock venue at heart, with well-known Norwegian and international acts drawn to the cavernous basement.

Hulen   ROCK
(www.hulen.no, in Norwegian; Olaf Ryes vei 48; ◷9pm-3am Thu-Sat mid-Aug–mid-Jun) Going strong since 1968, Hulen is the oldest rock club in northern Europe and it's one of the classic stages for indie rock. Hulen means 'cave' and the venue is actually a converted bomb shelter. Sadly, it closes during summer when many of Bergen's students head off on holidays. It also hosts a heavy-metal festival in early November.

Logen   LIVE MUSIC, BAR
(Øvre Ole Bulls plass 6; ◷6pm-2am Mon-Thu, 6pm-3am Fri & Sat, 8pm-3am Sun) Upstairs above the Wesselstuen Restaurant, Logen is Bergen's antidote to its more famous heavy metal and rock scene. It has a loyal

local following for its concerts (Nkr50 to Nkr100) at 9pm on Sunday (jazz or alternative music) and Monday (Voksne Herrers Orkester) from September to May or June. At other times (including much of summer), it's a quiet bar.

Café Sanaa   LIVE MUSIC
(www.sanaa.no, in Norwegian; Marken 31; ◷8pm-3am Thu-Sat) This lovely little cafe just back from the lake spills over onto the cobblestones and draws a fun, alternative crowd with live music and some of Bergen's most creative resident DJs. Music can be jazz, tango, blues or African, depending on where the mood takes them.

🛍 Shopping

Juhls' Silver Gallery   JEWELLERY, HOMEWARES
(www.juhls.no; Bryggen 39; ◷9am-10pm Mon-Sat, noon-7pm Sun mid-Jun–Sep, 10am-5pm Mon-Fri & 10am-2pm Sat Oct–mid-Jun) This wonderful jewellery shop sells exquisite silver jewellery and other items crafted by Regine Juhls at her workshop high above the Arctic Circle (see p403).

ℹ Information

Bergen Turlag DNT office (☑55 33 58 10; www.bergen-turlag.no; Tverrgaten 4; ◷10am-4pm Mon-Wed & Fri, 10am-6pm Thu, 10am-2pm Sat) Maps and information on hiking and hut accommodation throughout western Norway.

Tourist office (☑55 55 20 00; www.visitber gen.com; Vågsallmenningen 1; ◷8.30am-10pm Jun-Aug, 9am-8pm May & Sep, 9am-4pm Mon-Sat Oct-Apr) One of the best and busiest in the country.

❶ Getting There & Away

Air

The airport is in Flesland, 19km southwest of central Bergen. Direct flights connect Bergen with major cities in Norway, plus a handful of international destinations.

Boat

Flaggruten (53 40 91 20; www.tide.no; Strandkaiterminalen) Twice-daily services from Sunday to Friday to Stavanger (one way/return Nkr750/950), with just one on Saturdays.

Fjord1 (📞55 90 70 70; www.fjord1.no; Strandkaiterminalen) At least one daily ferry from Bergen to Sogndal (Nkr570, five hours), with some services going on to Flåm (Nkr665).

The *Hurtigruten* (p417) leaves from a newly built terminal east of Nøstegaten.

Bus

Express buses run throughout the western fjords region, as well as to Stryn (Nkr489, 6½ hours, two daily), Ålesund (Nkr619, 10 hours, one to two daily), Trondheim (Nkr789, 12½ hours, two daily) and Stavanger (Nkr490, 5½ hours, five daily).

Train

The spectacular train journey between Bergen and Oslo (Nkr299 to Nkr775, 6½ to eight hours, five daily) runs through the heart of Norway. Other destinations include Voss (Nkr169, one hour, hourly) and Myrdal (Nkr253, 2¼ hours, up to nine daily) for connections for the Flåmsbana railway.

❶ Getting Around

To/From the Airport

Flybussen (www.flybussen.no) Runs up to four times hourly (45 mintues) between the airport, the Radisson SAS Royal Hotel, the main bus terminal and opposite the tourist office (adult one way/return Nkr90/150, child Nkr45/80).

Bus

City buses (📞177; adult Nkr25) Fares beyond the centre are based on distance. Free bus 100 runs between Bryggen and the bus terminal.

Car & Motorcycle

Metered parking limited to 30 minutes or two hours applies all over central Bergen. The largest and cheapest (Nkr100 per 24 hours) indoor car park is the 24-hour Bygarasjen at the bus terminal; elsewhere you'll pay Nkr200.

Voss

POP 13,900

Voss sits on a lovely lake not far from the fjords and this combination has earned it a world-renowned reputation as one of Norway's top adventure capitals. It draws both beginners and veterans of the thrill-seeking world for rafting, bungee jumping and just about anything you can do from a parasail; many of the activities take you out into the fjords.

⊙ Sights & Activities

Vangskyrkja   CHURCH
(Uttrågata; adult/child Nkr20/free; ⊙10am-4pm Mon-Sat, 1-4pm Sun Jun-Aug) Voss' stone church, the construction of which spans seven centuries, miraculously escaped destruction during the intense German bombing of Voss in 1940.

St Olav's Cross   MONUMENT
In a field around 150m southeast of the tourist office stands the weathered stone erected in 1023 to commemorate the local conversion to Christianity.

Hangursbahnen   CABLE CAR
(www.vossresort.no; adult/child Nkr100/60; ⊙11am-5pm Jun-early Sep) Above Voss, the cable car whisks you to Mt Hangur (660m) for stunning panoramic views over the town.

Prestegardsmoen Recreational and Nature Reserve   HIKING
A series of hiking tracks through elm, birch and pine forests with 140 species of plants and 124 bird species.

✦ Festivals

Vossajazz   MUSIC
(www.vossajazz.no) Held in March.

Extreme Sports Festival   SPORT
(www.ekstremsportveko.com) A week-long festival in late June that combines all manner of extreme sports (skydiving, paragliding and base jumping) with local and international music acts.

Voss Blues & Roots Festival   MUSIC
One of Norway's better music festivals; last weekend of August.

If slow boats up the fjords seem like a pretty tame response to extraordinary Norwegian landscapes, Voss may be your antidote.

For booking any of the following, your best bet is to contact the operator directly. Another option is **Destinasjon Voss** (☑40 61 77 00; www.visitvoss.no; ☺9am-5pm Mon-Fri, 9am-3pm Sat, noon-5pm Sun), a central booking service for activities and accommodation.

Paragliding, Parasailing & Bungee Jumping

Nordic Ventures (☑56 51 00 17; www.nordicventures.com; ☺Apr–mid-Oct) is one of the most professional operators of its kind in Norway, offering tandem paragliding flights (Nkr1500), parasailing (solo/dual flights Nkr575/950) and even 180m-high, 115km/h bungee jumps from a parasail (Nkr1800)!

Kayak Fjord Expeditions

If you do one activity in Voss (or even anywhere in the fjords), make it this one. The perfect way to experience stunning Nærøyfjord, the guided kayak tours offered by **Nordic Ventures** also head to Hardangerfjord and come in a range of options.

One day (nine-hour) tours cost Nkr975 (including lunch and transport to/from the fjord), while the two-day version (Nkr2195) allows you to camp on the shores of the fjord. But our favourite is the three-day kayaking and hiking expedition (Nkr2995), which explores the fjords in kayaks and then takes you high above the fjords for unrivalled views.

Nordic Ventures also rents out kayaks (one/two/three days Nkr525/825/1295) if you'd rather branch out on your own.

Rafting

Voss Rafting Senter (☑56 51 05 25; www.vossrafting.no) specialises in rafting (Nkr875 to Nkr1395) with some gentler, more family-friendly options (from Nkr575). Rafters (and riverboarders) can choose between three very different rivers: the Stranda (Class III to IV), Raundalen (Class III to V) and Vosso (Class II).

Other Activities

Voss Rafting Senter also organises **canyoning** (Nkr875), **waterfall abseiling** (from Nkr850), **riverboarding** (Nkr890), **fishing** (from Nkr575) and **hiking** (from Nkr475). Skiing is also possible from early December until April.

🛏 Sleeping & Eating

TOP CHOICE **Fleischer's Hotel**   HISTORIC HOTEL €€
(☑56 52 05 00; www.fleischers.no; Evangervegen; s Nkr845-1195, d Nkr1195-1690; **P🏊**) For historic character, the beautiful Fleischer's Hotel, opened in its current form in 1889, oozes antique charm and is the best place in town. Some rooms have lake views and there's a swimming pool with a child's pool.

TOP CHOICE **Tre Brør Café**   CAFE €
(www.vosscafe.no; Vangsgata 28; sandwiches & light meals Nkr65-135; ☺9.30am-9pm Sun-Wed, 9.30am-midnight Thu-Sat) This lovely little cafe in one of Voss's prettiest buildings is laidback and stylish all at once and the food's also fantastic. There's a small selection of sandwiches, salads and pasta dishes and a changing daily menu with the odd Asian twist.

Ringheim Kafé   TRADITIONAL CAFE €€
(Vangsgata 32; mains Nkr105-139; ☺lunch & dinner) One of numerous cafes lined up along the main Vangsgata thoroughfare, Ringheim has some real stars on the menu, including the elk burgers (Nkr139) and *hjortekoru* (Nkr125), the local smoked sausage with potato and cabbage stew.

Park Hotel Vossevangen   HOTEL €
(☑56 53 10 00; www.parkvoss.no; Uttrågata 1; s/d from Nkr875/1250; **P**) While this place lacks the elegance of Fleischer's Hotel, the modern rooms are nonetheless comfortable and many overlook the lake Vossevangen.

Voss Camping   CAMPING GROUND €
(☑56 51 15 97; www.vosscamping.no; Prestegardsalléen 40; tent/caravan sites from Nkr150/220, cabins from Nkr600; ☺Easter-Sep; **P**) Lakeside

and centrally located, Voss Camping has basic facilities and can get a bit rowdy in summer.

❶ Information

Tourist office (☎56 52 08 00; www.visitvoss. no; Uttrågata; ⊙8am-7pm Mon-Fri, 9am-7pm Sat & noon-7pm Sun Jun-Aug, 8.30am-3.30pm Mon-Fri Sep-May)

❶ Getting There & Away

BUS Frequent bus services connect Voss with Bergen (Nkr137, two hours), Flåm (Nkr126, 1¼ hours) and Sogndal (Nkr266, three hours).

TRAIN The **NSB** (☎56 52 80 00) rail services on the renowned *Bergensbanen* to/from Bergen (Nkr169, one hour, hourly) and Oslo (Nkr299 to Nkr686, 5½ to six hours, five daily) connect at Myrdal (Nkr103, 50 minutes) with the scenic line down to Flåm.

Hardangerfjord

A notch less jagged and steep than Sognefjord, Hardangerfjord's slopes support farms and wildflowers, which picturesquely enhance the green hills as they plunge into the water. Norway's second-longest fjord network, it stretches inland from a cluster of rocky coastal islands to the frozen heights of the Folgefonn and Hardangerjøkulen icecaps. The area is known for its orchards (apples, cherries and plums) and bursts into bloom from mid-May to mid-June. Helpful regional information can be found at www. hardangerfjord.com.

At the innermost reaches of Hardangerfjorden you'll find the Eidfjord area, with sheer mountains, huge waterfalls, spiral road tunnels and the extraordinary Kjeåsen Farm, a deliciously inaccessible farm perched on a mountain ledge about 6km northeast of Eidfjord. Other Eidfjord highlights include Viking burial mounds and, on the road up to the Hardangervidda Plateau, the excellent Hardangervidda Natursenter (www.hardangervidda.org; Øvre Eidfjord; adult/child/family Nkr120/60/280; ⊙9am-8pm mid-Jun–mid-Aug, 10am-6pm Apr–mid-Jun & mid-Aug–Oct) with wonderful exhibits on the plateau, and the 182m-high Vøringfoss waterfall. For information, contact Eidfjord tourist office (☎53 67 34 00; www.visiteidfjord. no; ⊙9am-7pm Mon-Fri, 10am-6pm Sat, 11am-6pm Sun mid-Jun–mid-Aug).

Tranquil Ulvik has extraordinary views from its fjord-side walking paths, while at picturesque Utne you'll find an interesting collection of old buildings at the Hardanger Folk Museum (www.hardanger.museum. no; adult/child Nkr50/free; ⊙10am-4pm May-Aug), and the pretty Utne Hotel.

For glacier hikes on the Buer arm of the Folgefonn ice sheet, contact the excellent Flat Earth (☎47 60 68 47; www.flatearth.no; adult Nkr650, incl crampons & ice axes) in Odda. The hike up to Trolltunga, a narrow finger of rock that hangs out over the void high above the lake Ringedalsvatnet, and one of Norway's most precipitous vantage points, is another highlight close to Odda. For more information, contact Odda's tourist office (☎53 65 40 05; www.visitodda.com; ⊙9am-7pm Mon-Fri, 10am-6pm Sat & Sun mid-Jun–mid-Aug).

🍴 Sleeping & Eating

🛏 Utne Hotel   HISTORIC HOTEL €€€
(☎53 66 64 00; www.utnehotel.no; Utne; s/d annexe Nkr1190/1590, main bldg Nkr1390/1790; Ⓟ) The historic wooden Utne Hotel was built in 1722, making it Norway's oldest hotel. Restored in 2003, it overflows with period touches from the 18th and 19th centuries. The hotel also has the best restaurant in town.

TOP CHOICE Eidfjord Gjestegiveri   GUESTHOUSE €
(☎53 66 53 46; www.ovre-eidfjord.com; Øvre Eidfjord; hut Nkr360, s/d without bathroom & incl breakfast Nkr590/745; Ⓟ) This delightful guesthouse run by Dutch owners Eric and Inge has a homely feel, 6.5km from central Eidfjord. There are just five double rooms and one single; the six camping huts are only open from April to October. The other huge selling point of this place is its pancake cafe (pancakes Nkr75-119; ⊙11am-8pm), with around 20 varieties of fantastic and filling, sweet and salty Dutch pancakes.

TOP CHOICE Vik Pensjonat   GUESTHOUSE €€
(☎53 66 51 62; www.vikpensjonat.com; Eidfjord; s/d/f Nkr840/1050/1480, cabins Nkr750-1100; Ⓟ) This appealing place in the centre of Eidfjord, not far from the water's edge, is set in a lovely, renovated old home. It offers a friendly welcome and an excellent range of cosy accommodation. The attached cafe (light meals Nkr65 to Nkr85, mains Nkr145 to Nkr185) is one of the better places to eat in town, with everything from soups and sandwiches to main dishes such as mountain trout.

(Continued on page 361)

Natural Wonders

Great Outdoors »
Winter Wonderland »
Summer Adventures »
Wildlife »

...ark in Skåne (p456), Sweden

Great Outdoors

The scenery in Scandinavia is one of its great attractions. Wild, rugged coasts and mountains, hundreds of kilometres of forest broken only by lakes and the odd cottage, and unspoilt Baltic archipelagos make up a varied menu of uplifting visual treats.

Iceland

1 Thrown up in the middle of the Atlantic by violent geothermal activity, Iceland offers a bleak, epic scenery that is at once both harsh and gloriously uplifting. The juxtaposition of frozen glaciers and boiling geysers make it a wild scenic ride.

Forests

2 Mainland Scandinavia has some of the world's top tree cover, and the forests stretch much further than the eye can see. Mainly composed of spruce, pine and birch, these forests are responsible for the crisp, clean, aromatic northern air.

Norway

3 Fjords are famous for a reason; coastal views here literally take the breath away. There are spectacular views the length of this long country; near the top, the Lofoten Islands present picturesque fishing villages against the awesome backdrop of glacier-scoured mountains.

Lakes

4 Once the ice melts, Scandinavia's a watery land. A Finnish or Swedish lake under a midnight sun, pines reflected in the calm, chill water, is an enduring image, with a stillness broken only by the sploshes of landing waterbirds.

Archipelagos

5 Thousands of islands lie offshore. The Baltic is the place to grab a boat and find an islet to call your own. Out in the Atlantic, the Faroes offer stern cliffs housing vast seabird colonies.

Clockwise from top left

1. Strokkur geyser in Iceland's Golden Circle (p268) **2.** Snowy beech forest, Skåne (p456), Sweden **3.** Lysefjord (p364), Norway **4.** Autumn foliage, Sweden

3

Winter Wonderland

Once the snows come, bears look for a place to sleep out the winter, but for the rest of us, there's no excuse. The ethereal beauty of the whitened land combines with numerous exciting activities to make this a great time to visit.

Landscapes

1 It's cold. But low winter light, and the eerie blue colours the winter sky takes on, make it spectacularly scenic. Trees glistening with ice crystals and snow carpeting the ground add to this magical landscape.

Skiing

2 There's not much you can teach a Scandinavian about skiing; they invented it. There are numerous places to hit the powder, with excellent facilities for all levels. Cross-country is big too, with lit trails compensating for the long nights.

Sledding

3 The whoosh of the runners as a team of huskies or reindeer whisks you through the icy northern landscapes; it's tough to beat the feeling. Don't expect a pampered ride though – learn on the job or eat snow!

Winter Activities

4 Snowmobiles are a part of life up north, and it's lots of fun to whizz about on one. More sedate is ice fishing, but you'd better pack a warm drink. Ice climbing, nights in snow hotels, the aurora borealis (Northern Lights) and snowshoe treks are other popular possibilities.

Saunas

5 If the cold has seeped into your bones, there's nothing like a log fire or, even better, a sauna, to warm the extremities again. Too hot? Get somebody to drill a hole in the lake and jump in. Good for the pores!

Clockwise from top left
1. A lake above Å (p391) in the Lofoten Islands 2. Skiing in Norway 3. Snowmobiles near Kemi (p211), Finland

Summer Adventures

When the snows melt and the sun returns, it's like a blessing bestowed upon the land. Nature accelerates into top gear, and locals pack a year's worth of fun and festivals into the short but memorably vibrant summer season.

Hiking

1 There's fabulous walking across the whole region, from the jaw-droppingly majestic Icelandic routes to the remote Finnish wildernesses. Excellent facilities mean it's easy to plan short tramps or multiday hiking adventures.

Nordic Peace

2 For many Scandinavians, summer is spent at a lakeside cottage or campsite where simple pleasures – swimming, fishing, chopping wood, picking berries – replace the stresses of urban life for a few blissful weeks.

Midsummer

3 The summer solstice is celebrated throughout the region, whether with traditional midsummer poles and dancing; or beer, sausages and a lakeside barbecue and bonfire with friends.

Kayaking & Canoeing

4 It's a perfect time to get the paddles out and explore the rivers and lakes of the interior, or the coastal serrations and islands. Throughout the region, kayaking and canoeing are extremely popular and easy to organise.

Terraces

5 Once the first proper rays bathe the pavement, coat racks in bars and cafes disappear, and terraces sprout onto every square and street, packed with people determined to suck up every last drop of the precious summer sun.

Clockwise from top left
1. Geiranger (p371), Norway 2. Tromsø (p393), Norway
3. Midsummer celebrations in Sweden 4. Kayaking in Sweden

ANDERS BLOMQVIST / LONELY PLANET IMAGES ©

Wildlife

Vast tracts of barely populated land away from the bustle of central Europe make Scandinavia an important refuge for numerous species, including several high-profile carnivores, a myriad of seabirds and lovable marine mammals.

Nordic Creatures

1 The region is stocked with other animals; lynx and wolves pace forests, while golden eagles, ospreys, ptarmigans and capercaillie add feathered glory to the mix. Seals and dolphins are aplenty, and the lonely wolverine prowls the northern wastes in search of prey or carrion.

Brown Bears

2 The ruler of the forest is deeply rooted in Finnish culture, and there's still a fairly healthy population of them in the east of the country, near the Russian border. Bear-watching trips offer a great opportunity to see these impressively large, shaggy beasts.

Polar Bears & Walrus

3 Svalbard is as close to the North Pole as most are going to get, and the wildlife is appropriately impressive. The mighty polar bear means you'll need a just-in-case weapon if you want to leave town, while the weighty walrus is also an impressive sight.

Whales & Seabirds

4 The North Atlantic islands are important seabird colonies; they breed there in huge numbers. Off these and the Norwegian coast, several varieties of whale are in regular attendance, best seen on a dedicated boat trip.

Elk & Reindeer

5 If antlers are your thing, you won't be disappointed. The sizeable but ungainly elk (moose) is widespread in the mainland forests, often blundering onto roads or into towns. In Lapland, the domesticated reindeer is the herd animal of the indigenous Sámi.

Right
1. European wolf 2. European brown bear

(Continued from page 352)

ℹ️ Getting There & Away

While thorough exploration of Hardangerfjord is best accomplished with a car, those with little time and no wheels would do well to book the 12-hour round-trip **Hardanger Fjord Adventure** tour run by Tide Reiser (☑55 23 87 00; www.tidereiser.no; adult/child Nkr790/515; ☺May-Oct), which combines bus, ferry and train with stops in Utne, Kinsarvik, Lofthus, Eidfjord and Ulvik. Try also Fjord Tours (☑81 56 82 22; www.fjordtours.com). Tickets can be purchased at Bergen's tourist office. Shorter variations on the same theme can be purchased at most tourist offices throughout Hardangerfjord.

Infrequent **Nor-Way Bussekspress** buses connect Bergen with Hardangerfjord villages, with more frequent services in summer.

Stavanger

POP 123,900

Stavanger has a lot going for it. Its centre is arrayed around a pretty harbour with the quiet streets of the old town climbing up from the water's edge and it's also home to almost two dozen museums; Stavanger is said by some to be the largest wooden city in Europe. But Stavanger's appeal is as much about atmosphere as anything else. Most nights, especially in summer, the city's waterfront comes alive and can get quite rowdy in the best tradition of oil and port cities. By Sunday morning, it's quiet and charming, for this is a place that has never lost its small-town feel. It's an excellent point from which to begin exploring the stunning Lysefjord and to surf in the cold isolation of the northern Atlantic.

◉ Sights

TOP CHOICE **Gamle Stavanger** HISTORIC AREA

Gamle (Old) Stavanger consists of cobblestone walkways passing between rows of 173 late-18th-century whitewashed wooden houses, all immaculately kept and adorned with cheerful, well-tended flower boxes. It well rewards an hour or two's ambling.

Norsk Oljemuseum MUSEUM

(Oil Museum; www.norskolje.museum.no; Kjeringholmen; adult/child/family Nkr80/40/200; ☺10am-7pm daily Jun-Aug, 10am-4pm Mon-Sat, 10am-6pm Sun Sep-May) One of Norway's best museums, the Oil Museum is filled with hi-tech interactive displays, gigantic models and authentic reconstructions. Its many highlights include the world's largest drill bit; a 12-minute documentary by former Lonely Planet TV presenter Ian Wright and another on deep-sea diving; simulators; a petrodome recreating millions of years of natural history; an escape chute that kids love; and some amazing models of oil platforms.

FREE **Stavanger Domkirke** CHURCH

(Håkon VII's gate; ☺11am-7pm Jun-Aug, 11am-4pm Mon-Sat Sep-May) This beautiful church is an impressive, but understated, medieval stone cathedral dating from approximately 1125; it was extensively renovated following a fire in 1272 and contains traces of Gothic, baroque, Romanesque and Anglo-Norman influences. Despite restoration in the 1860s and 1940, and the stripping of some features during the Reformation, the cathedral is, by some accounts, Norway's oldest medieval cathedral still in its original form. Watch out for organ recitals in summer.

Other Museums MUSEUMS

(www.museumstavanger.no; ☺11am-4pm mid-Jun–mid-Aug, shorter hr early Jun & late Aug, closed Mon rest of yr) The following museums have combined same-day admission costs of Nkr60/30 per adult/child. The main Stavanger Bymuseum (Muségata 16) reveals nearly 900 years of Stavanger's history, 'From Ancient Landscape to Oil Town'. Also in the same building is the Norwegian Natural History Museum.

More interesting is the Maritime Museum (Nedre Strandgate 17), in two restored warehouses, which gives a good glimpse of Stavanger's extensive nautical history. The fascinating Canning Museum (Øvre Strandgate 88A) occupies an old sardine cannery, where you'll see ancient machinery in action, learn about various soul-destroying jobs of the past and ogle a large collection of old sardine-can labels. There are also two 19th-century manor houses built by wealthy shipowners: the recently restored Ledaal (Eiganesveien 45), which serves as the residence for visiting members of the royal family, and the excellent Breidablikk (Eiganesveien 40A), a merchant's opulent villa built in 1881.

🛏️ Sleeping

Book well in advance. This is an oil city and prices can soar on weekdays as businesspeople arrive, but return to more reasonable levels on weekends – try to plan your visit accordingly. The tourist office website (www.regionstavanger.com) has a list of small B&Bs in and around Stavanger.

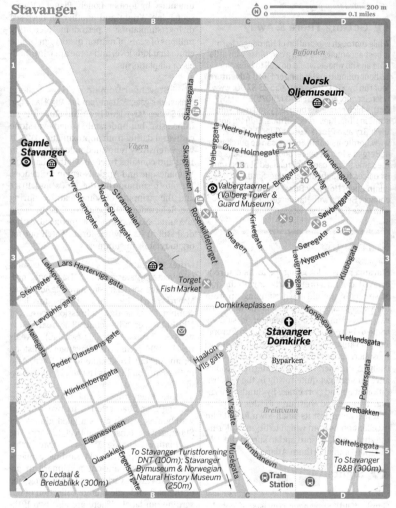

For the Mosvangen Vandrerhjem or Mosvangen Camping, take bus 78 or 79 (Nkr32) from opposite the cathedral to Ullandhaugveien, 3km to the south. Bus 4 also passes by.

TOP CHOICE Skagen Brygge Hotel HOTEL €€
(☎51 85 00 00; www.skagenbryggehotell.no; Skagenkaien 30; s/d Fri & Sat Nkr975/1275, Sun-Thu Nkr1695/1895, Jul every day Nkr1070/1370, with Fjord Pass yr-round Nkr880/1260) This large and opulent hotel (part of the Fjord Pass network) offers good weekend and summer value from its superb location right by the water. There's a range of rooms to choose from, but your best bet is to ask for a room with a harbour view and, unusually, this includes some single rooms. It also serves free waffles from 2pm to 7pm.

Myhregaarden Hotel BOUTIQUE HOTEL €€
(☎51 86 80 00; www.myhregaardenhotel.no; Nygaten 24; s/d Nkr895/995 Fri-Sun, Nkr1699/1999 Mon-Thu) Opened in 2008, the Myhregaarden Hotel is Stavanger's most stylish hotel and has a more personal touch than most chain hotels. The refurbished early-20th-century building has some original features, but the

NORWAY STAVANGER

contemporary rooms have soothing colour schemes, as all but five have chandeliers and fireplaces; the remaining five have original wooden beams.

Stavanger B&B
B&B €€

(☑51 56 25 00; www.stavangerbedandbreakfast.no; Vikedalsgata 1a; s/d Nkr790/890, with shared toilet Nkr690/790; ℗) This quiet but popular place comes highly recommended by readers and it's not hard to see why. The simple rooms are tidy and come with satellite TV, shower and a smile from the friendly owners.

Skansen Hotel
HOTEL & GUESTHOUSE €€

(☑51 93 85 00; www.skansenhotel.no; Skansegata 7; guesthouse s Nkr755-1030, d Nkr970-1190, hotel s Nkr970-1130, d Nkr1110-1290) This centrally located place, opposite the old customs house, is divided into an older guesthouse section with simple, comfortable rooms, and newer hotel rooms that are larger and more stylish.

Mosvangen Camping
CAMPING GROUND €

(☑51 53 29 71; www.stavangercamping.no; Tjensvoll 1b; campsites without/with car Nkr120/170, with caravan or camper Nkr200, huts Nkr450-650, ◎Apr-Sep) During nesting season around Mosvangen lake, campers are treated to almost incessant birdsong amid the green and agreeable surroundings.

Mosvangen Vandrerhjem
HOSTEL €

(☑51 54 36 36; stavanger.hostel@vandrerhjem.no; Henrik Ibsensgate 19; dm/s/d without bathroom Nkr275/450/525, ◎mid-May–mid-Sep) Stavanger's pleasant and simple lakeside hostel, 3km southwest of the city centre, charges Nkr60 for breakfast. It only opens in summer.

✕ Eating

Le Café Français
CAFE €

(Østervåg 30-32; sandwiches & light meals Nkr59-129; ◎9am-5pm Mon-Wed & Fri, 9am-7pm Thu, 9am-4pm Sat, 11am-5pm Sun) With the widest range of pastries and other sweet goodies in town and outdoor tables on the pedestrian street outside, Le Café Français is a good place to wind down. It also serves sandwiches, mini-quiches and good salads.

NB Sørensen's Damskibsexpedition
NORWEGIAN €€

(☑51 84 38 00; Skagen 26; mains Nkr125-329; ◎lunch & dinner) One of the better places along the waterfront, this restaurant serves everything from fish to pork ribs, with a seasonal lunch menu that's excellent value. The atmospheric indoor dining area is ideal when the weather turns, and locals swear that the food and service is better upstairs.

Charlottenlund
NORWEGIAN, FRENCH €€€

(☑51 91 76 00; www.charlottenlund.no; Kongsgate 45; mains from Nkr289, 3-/4-/5-course set menus Nkr445/510/565; ◎5-11pm Mon-Sat) One of Stavanger's classiest restaurants, Charlottenlund serves the freshest Norwegian ingredients and puts them at the service of French and Norwegian culinary traditions. The results are as impeccable as the service, and the set menus are excellent.

Kult Kafeen
CAFE €

(Sølvberggata 14; sandwiches & salads Nkr120-135; ◎10am-10pm Mon-Sat, noon-10pm Sun) Located in the Kulturhus in the centre of town, this cool place has won the affections of families and cool young professionals alike. Well-sized sandwiches and fresh salads are the high points, but many just come here for a quiet coffee.

Bølgen & Moi   NORWEGIAN €€
(Norsk Oljemuseum, Kjerringholmen; mains Nkr95-265; ⊙cafe 11am-5pm daily, bar & brasserie 6pm-1am Tue-Sat) The imaginative menus in this stylish restaurant attached to the Oil Museum include dishes such as soy-and-honey-marinated salmon with potato salad (Nkr225), and lunch specials are huge.

Emilio's Tapas Bar   SPANISH €€
(Sølvberggata 13; tapas Nkr50-190, lunch mains Nkr89-169; ⊙lunch & dinner daily Jun-Aug, closed Sun Sep-May) Opposite the Akropolis and continuing on the Mediterranean theme, this pleasant Spanish tapas bar serves good Iberian food with friendly service that comes at no extra cost.

 Drinking

Most of the livelier bars are right on the waterfront and cater to a younger crowd with a penchant for loud, energetic music. You'll hear them long before you see them and, as they're all similar, we think you're able to find them on your own.

TOP CHOICE B.brormann B.bar   COCKTAIL BAR
(Skansegata 7; ⊙4pm-2am) One of Stavanger's coolest bars, where you can actually hear the conversation and with contemporary artworks on the brick walls, this oddly named place draws a discerning over-30s crowd and serves great-value half-litre beers (Nkr63) and cocktails (Nkr96) prepared by Siv-Karin Helland, who won Norway's 2010 cocktail-mixing championship with her 'Monroe's Lemonade'.

Café Sting   CAFE-BAR, CLUB
(☑51 89 32 84; Valbergjet 3; ⊙noon-midnight Mon-Thu, noon-3.30am Fri & Sat, 3pm-midnight Sun) Just up the hill but a world away from the harbour clamour, Café Sting is at once a mellow cafe and a funky cultural space with exhibitions, live jazz whenever the mood takes it, and a weekend nightclub where the DJs keep you on your toes, spinning house, hip hop and soul.

Bøker & Brøst   CAFE-BAR
(Øvre Holmegate 32; ⊙10am-2am) There are dozens of engaging little cafes in the lanes climbing the hillside west of the oil museum, but our favourite is Bøker & Brøst with its warm and eccentric decor, great coffee

and laidback feel whatever the time of day. Special mention must be made of the toilets, which have antique wallpaper and bookshelves filled to bursting – clearly they don't mind if you linger.

❶ Information
Stavanger Turistforening DNT (off Muségata; ⊙10am-4pm Mon-Wed & Fri, 10am-6pm Thu, 10am-2pm Sat) Information on hiking and mountain huts.

Tourist office (☑51 85 92 00; www.region stavanger.com; Domkirkeplassen 3; ⊙9am-8pm Jun-Aug, 9am-4pm Mon-Fri, 9am-2pm Sat Sep-May) Local information and advice on Lysefjord and Preikestolen.

❶ Getting There & Away
To/From the Airport
Between early morning and mid- to late evening, **Flybussen** (☑51 52 26 00; www.flybussen.no/stavanger) runs every half-hour between the bus terminal and the airport at Sola (one way/return Nkr90/140).

Boat
Flaggruten (☑518 68 780) runs express passenger catamarans to Bergen (one way/return Nkr750/950, 4¼ hours, one to four daily).

Tide Reiser (www.tidereiser.no; ⊙Jun-Aug) has daily summer four-hour car ferries with tourist commentary along Lysefjord to Lysebotn (adult/child/car Nkr210/120/400) from Fiskepirterminalen.

Bus
Nor-Way Bussekspress offers services to Oslo (Nkr795, 9½ hours, up to five daily) and to Bergen (Nkr490, 5¾ hours, six daily).

Train
Trains run to Oslo (Nkr886, eight hours, up to five daily) via Kristiansand (Nkr427, three hours).

Lysefjord

All along the 42km-long Lysefjord (Light Fjord), the granite rock glows with an ethereal, ambient light, even on dull days, all offset by almost-luminous mist. This is many visitors' favourite fjord, and there's no doubt that it has a captivating beauty. Whether you cruise from Stavanger, hike up to Preikestolen (604m), or drive the switchback road down to Lysebotn, it's one of Norway's must-sees.

The area's most popular outing is the two-hour hike to the top of the incredible **Preikestolen** (Pulpit Rock), 25km east of Stavanger. You can inch up to the edge of its flat top and

For general information on the region, check out www.lysefjordeninfo.no or www.visitly sefjorden.no.

Pulpit Rock by Public Transport

From May to mid-September, five to seven ferries a day run from Stavanger's Fiskespiren Quay to Tau, where the ferries are met by a bus, which runs between the Tau pier and the Preikestolhytta Vandrerhjem. From there, the two-hour trail leads up to Preikestolen. The last bus from Preikestolhytta to Tau leaves at 7.55pm. You can buy tickets at the Stavanger tourist office or Fiskespiren Quay.

Pulpit Rock by Car

If you have your own vehicle, take the car ferry from Stavanger's Fiskespiren Quay to Tau (adult/child/car Nkr42/21/125, 40 minutes, up to 24 departures daily). From the pier in Tau, a well-signed road (Rv13) leads 19km to Preikestolhytta Vandrerhjem (take the signed turn-off after 13km). It costs Nkr60/30 per car/motorcycle to park here.

An alternative route from Stavanger involves driving to Lauvik (via Sandnes along Rv13) from where a ferry crosses to Oanes (adult/child/car Nkr24/12/59, 10 minutes, departures almost every half-hour).

Either way, the trip between Stavanger and the trailhead takes around 1½ hours.

Boat Tours to Lysefjord

Two companies offer three-hour boat cruises from Stavanger to the waters below Preikestolen on Lysefjord and back:

» **Rødne Fjord Cruise** (☑51 89 52 70; www.rodne.no; adult/senior or student/child/family Nkr380/280/200/890; ☉departures 10.30am & 2.30pm Sun-Fri & 12.30pm Sat Jul & Aug, noon daily May, Jun & Sep, noon Fri-Sun Oct-Apr)

» **Tide Reiser** (☑51 86 87 88; www.tidereiser.no; adult/senior or student/child Nkr360/280/250; ☉departures noon late May-late Aug, noon Sat Sep-late May)

Round Trips to Kjeragbolten

From mid-May to late August **Tide Reiser** (☑51 86 87 88; www.tidereiser.no; adult/child Nkr490/390; ☉departures 8am late Jun-late Aug) runs 13½-hour bus-boat-hike return trips to Kjeragbolten, which can be otherwise difficult to reach. It includes a five-hour return hike.

---

peer 600m straight down a sheer cliff into the blue water of the Lysefjord for some intense vertigo. The other option is the **Kjeragbolten** boulder (chockstone), lodged between two rock faces about 2m apart but with 1000m of empty space underneath.

Sognefjorden

Sognefjorden, Norway's longest (204km) and deepest (1308m) fjord, cuts a deep slash across the map of western Norway. In places, sheer walls rise more than 1000m above the water, while elsewhere a gentler shoreline supports farms, orchards and villages. The broad, main waterway is impressive but by cruising into its narrower arms, such as the deep and lovely Nærøyfjord (on the Unesco

World Heritage list) to Gudvangen, you'll see idyllic views of abrupt cliff faces and cascading waterfalls.

Find regional tourist information at www. sognefjord.no. **Fjord1** (☑57 75 70 00; www. fjord1.no, in Norwegian) operates a daily express boat between Bergen and both Flåm (Nkr665, 5½ hours) and Sogndal (Nkr570, 4¾ hours), stopping along the way at 10 small towns including Vik (Nkr450, 3½ hours) and Balestrand (Nkr485, 3¾ hours).

There are local ferries and buses linking the fjord towns. See www.ruteinfo.net and timetables available in tourist offices.

FLÅM
POP 550

Scenically set at the head of Aurlandsfjorden, Flåm is a tiny village of orchards and a

NORWAY IN A NUTSHELL

Although most visitors do the classic 'Norway in a Nutshell' tour (www.norwaynutshell.com) from either Oslo or Bergen (see p322 and the boxed text, p347), you can do a mini version (adult/child Nkr650/340). This circular route from Flåm – boat to Gudvangen, bus to Voss, train to Myrdal, then train again down the spectacular Flåmsbana railway to Flåm – is truly the kernel within the nutshell and takes in all the most dramatic elements. The Gudvangen boat leaves Flåm at 9am and the Flåmsbana train brings you home at 4.55pm.

handful of buildings. It's a jumping-off spot for travellers taking the Gudvangen ferry or the Sognefjorden express boat. Though it sees an amazing 500,000 visitors every summer, walk a few minutes from the centre and you'll experience solitude.

👁 Sights

Flåmsbana Railway   RAILWAY
(www.flaamsbana.no; adult/child one way Nkr240/115, return Nkr340/230) Over the course of 20km, this engineering wonder hauls itself up 864m of altitude gain through 20 tunnels at a gradient of 1:18. This, the world's steepest railway that runs without cable or rack wheels, takes a full 45 minutes to climb to Myrdal, on the bleak, treeless Hardangervidda Plateau, past thundering waterfalls (there's a photo stop at awesome Kjosfossen). It runs year-round with up to 10 departures daily in summer.

FREE Flåmsbana Museum   MUSEUM
(www.flamsbana-museet.no; ⏰9am-5pm May-Sep, 1.30-3pm rest of yr) To prepare yourself for your rail journey, browse this little museum, right beside the train platform. It's not just about railways; there are fascinating photos of construction gangs and life in and around Flåm before the car era.

🏃 Activities

Riding the Rallarvegen   BIKE DESCENT
(www.rallarvegen.com) Cyclists can descend the Rallarvegen, the service road originally used by the navvies who constructed the railway, for 83km from Haugastøl (1000m) or an easier 56km from Finse. You can rent

bicycles in Haugastøl (two days Nkr480/580 weekdays/weekend, including return transport from Flåm) and the company also offers packages that include accommodation.

Njord   KAYAKING
(www.kajakk.com) Njord operates from Flåm's handkerchief of a beach. It offers a two-hour sea-kayaking induction (Nkr350), three-hour gentle fjord paddle (Nkr450) and four-hour paddle and hike trips (Nkr590), plus multi-day kayaking, hiking and camping trips.

Fjord Safari   ZODIAC BOAT TRIPS
(www.fjordsafari.com) Bounce along in a Zodiac/RIB inflatable to see more of the fjord in less time. The team supplies full-length waterproof kit – you'll need it for this exhilarating scoot across the waters. Trips, with stops, last from 1½ hours (adult/child Nkr430/210) to three hours (adult/child Nkr640/320).

🛏 Sleeping & Eating

Fretheim Hotel   HOTEL €€€
(☎57 63 63 00; www.fretheim-hotel.no; s/d Nkr1245/1690; ⏰Feb–mid-Dec; 🅿@) Haunt of the English aristocracy in the 19th century, the vast, 121-room yet at the same time intimate and welcoming Fretheim is as much sports and social centre as hotel. In the original 1870s building, 17 rooms (Nkr400 supplement) have been restored to their former condition – including replica claw-foot retro bathtubs – while equipped with 21st-century amenities.

Flåm Camping &
Youth Hostel   HOSTEL, CAMPING GROUND €
(☎57 63 21 21; www.flaam-camping.no; car/caravan site Nkr185-195, dm Nkr200-270, s/d from Nkr330/470, cabin from Nkr685; ⏰May-Sep) This friendly spot is only a few minutes' walk from the station. In 2010, Hostelling International judged it to be Norway's best hostel and the ninth best in the world. You can see why; there's a brand-new block with en suite facilities, amenities are impeccable and the welcome couldn't be warmer.

Heimly Pensjonat   GUESTHOUSE €€
(☎57 63 23 00; www.heimly.no; s Nkr795-895, d Nkr895-1095) Overlooking the water on the fringe of the village and away from all the port hubbub, this place has straightforward rooms. There's a magnificent view along the fjord from the more expensive ones, and from the small patch of lawn.

Restaurant Arven RESTAURANT €€€
(Fretheim Hotel; mains Nkr275-290) At the Fretheim Hotel, the chefs salt and smoke their own meat and there's an 'ecological and local' menu, sourced from the region's agricultural college. You can also sample local lamb, reindeer and goat kid, grilled in the barbecue hut or featuring on the coffeehouse menu.

❶ Information
Tourist office (🖉57 63 33 13; www.alr.no; ⊙8.30am-4pm & 4.30-8pm Jun-Aug)

❶ Getting There & Away
BOAT From Flåm, boats head out to towns around Sognefjorden. The most scenic trip from Flåm is the passenger ferry up Nærøyfjord to Gudvangen (one way/return Nkr255/360). It leaves Flåm at 3.10pm year-round and up to four times daily between May and September. At Gudvangen, a connecting bus takes you on to Voss, where you can pick up the train for Bergen or Oslo. The tourist office sells all ferry tickets, plus the Flåm-to-Voss ferry/bus combination. There's also at least one daily express boat to Bergen (Nkr665, 5½ hours) via Balestrand (Nkr225, 1½ hours).
BUS Bus services also run to Gudvangen, Aurland, Sogndal and Bergen.

GUDVANGEN & NÆRØYFJORD
Nærøyfjord, its 17km length a Unesco World Heritage site, lies west of Flåm. Beside the deep blue fjord (only 250m across at its narrowest point) are towering 1200m-high cliffs, isolated farms, and waterfalls plummeting from the heights. It can easily be visited as a day excursion from Flåm.

The approach by boat is wondrous but Gudvangen itself, like a mini-Flåm only more constricted, is very missable.

Scenic ferries between Gudvangen and Flåm (one way/return Nkr215/294) via Aurland run up to four times daily. Up to eight daily buses run to/from Flåm (Nkr47, 20 minutes) and Aurland (Nkr52, 30 minutes).

STALHEIM
POP 200
This gorgeous little spot high above the valley is an extraordinary place. Between 1647 and 1909, Stalheim was a stopping-off point for travellers on the Royal Mail route between Copenhagen, Christiania (Oslo) and Bergen. The mailmen and their weary steeds rested in Stalheim and changed to fresh horses after climbing up the valley and through the Stalheimskleiva gorge, flanked by the thundering Stalheim and Sivle waterfalls.

🛏 Sleeping

TOP CHOICE **Stalheim Hotel** HISTORIC HOTEL €€
(🖉56 52 01 22; www.stalheim.com; s/d from Nkr980/1430, with Fjord Pass Nkr930/1360; ⊙mid-May–early Oct; 🅿@) Arguably Norway's most spectacularly sited hotel, this stunning place has large rooms, around half of which have glorious views. Not surprisingly, the hotel (room 324 in particular) once featured in Conde Nast's 'best rooms with a view'. The lunch/dinner buffets (Nkr250/450) are excellent, but lighter meals are available and meals work out cheaper if you pay half-board rates (Nkr1380/2180 single/double).

BALESTRAND
POP 1350
Balestrand sits comfortably beside the fjord; at its rear is an impressive mountain backdrop. Genteel and low-key, it has been a tranquil, small-scale holiday resort ever since the 19th century.

◉ Sights & Activities
Balestrand is to be home to the Norwegian Museum of Travel & Tourism (Norsk Reiselivsmuseum), destined to open in 2012 and until then showing temporary exhibitions.

It's also home to the charming wooden Church of St Olav, built in 1897 in the style of a traditional stave church, some Viking-era burial mounds and the excellent Sognefjord Aquarium (adult/child Nkr70/35; ⊙9am-5pm May-Sep).

Njord (🖉913 26 628; www.kajakk.com) explores the fjord off Balestrand in a couple of guided sea-kayak tours, lasting either two (Nkr350) or three hours (Nkr450). Reserve at the tourist office.

The tourist office's free pamphlet Outdoor Activities in Balestrand has plenty of suggestions for marked walks, ranging from easy to demanding.

🛏 Sleeping & Eating
Kvikne's Hotel HOTEL €€
(🖉57 69 42 00; www.kviknes.no; s/d from Nkr1080/1660; ⊙May-Sep; 🅿@) The majestic pale-yellow, timber-built main building of Kvikne's Hotel, with exquisite antiques in its public areas, breathes late-19th-century luxury. Of its 190 rooms, 165 are in the newer building, erected in the 1960s. **Balholm Bar og Bistro** is a reliable place for snacks and light meals. For a gastronomic delight,

invest Nkr495 in the main restaurant's outstanding dinner buffet.

Sjøtun Camping CAMPING GROUND €
(☏95 06 72 61; www.sjotun.com; per person/site Nkr30/60, 4-/6-bed cabin with outdoor bathroom Nkr250/320; ☻Jun–mid-Sep) At this green camping ground, a 15-minute walk south along the fjord, you can pitch a tent on soft grass amid apple trees or rent a rustic cabin at a very reasonable price.

Ciderhuset NORDIC, MEDITERRANEAN €€
(☏90 83 56 73; www.ciderhuset.no, in Norwegian; Sjøtunsvegen 32; mains Nkr100-200; ☻4-8pm mid-Jun–mid-Aug) Within a fruit farm that produces organic juices, jams, bottled fruits, cider and cider brandy, this delightful restaurant fuses Nordic and Mediterranean culinary traditions. Bookings advisable.

❶ Information

Tourist office (www.visitbalestrand.no; ☻7.30am-6pm Mon-Sat, 10am-5pm Sun mid-Jun–mid-Aug, 10am-5.30pm Mon-Fri May-early Jun & mid-Aug–Sep)

❶ Getting There & Away

BOAT In July and August, a car ferry (Nkr215/325 one way/return, 1¼ hours, twice daily) follows the narrow Fjærlandsfjorden to Fjærland, gateway to the glacial wonderlands of Jostedalsbreen (in May, June and September there's a daily passenger-ferry run).

BUS Express buses link Balestrand and Sogndal (Nkr94, one hour, three daily).

Jostedalsbreen

With an area of 487 sq km, the many-tongued Jostedalsbreen dominates the highlands between Nordfjord and Sognefjord and is mainland Europe's largest icecap; in some places it is 400m thick. Protected as a national park, the icecap provides extraordinary opportunities for otherworldly glacier hiking.

JOSTEDALEN & NIGARDSBREEN

The Jostedalen valley pokes due north from Gaupne, on the shores of Lustrafjord. This slim finger sits between two national parks and it's a spectacular drive as the road runs beside the milky turquoise river, tumbling beneath the eastern flank of the Nigardsbreen glacier. Of the Jostedalsbreen glacier tongues visible from below, Nigardsbreen is the most dramatic and easiest to approach.

⊙ Sights

Breheimsenteret Visitors Centre VISITORS CENTRE
(☏57 68 32 50; www.jostedal.com; ☻9am-7pm mid-Jun–mid-Aug, 10am-5pm May–mid-Jun & mid-Aug–Sep) Soaring skywards, its sweeping lines representing two abutting snow walls, this centre's a striking introduction to Nigardsbreen. Lying 34km up the valley from Lustrafjord, it has a **display** (adult/child Nkr50/35) that tells how glaciers were formed and how they sculpt the landscape. It also carries a worthwhile free pamphlet, *Walking in Jostedal,* that describes a number of short (one- to 2½-hour) walks.

SOGNEFJORDEN STAVE CHURCHES

Some 30km southeast of Lærdalsøyri along the E16, you'll find the 12th-century **Borgund stave church** (adult/child Nkr65/45; ☻8am-8pm mid-Jun–mid-Aug, 9.30am-5pm May–mid-Jun & mid-Aug–Sep). Dedicated to St Andrew, it's one of the best-known, most-photographed – and certainly the best-preserved – of Norway's stave churches. Beside it is the only free-standing medieval wooden bell tower still standing in Norway.

There are two further examples in Vik. The **Hopperstad stave church** (☻10am-5pm May-Sep), originally built in 1140 and Norway's second oldest, escaped demolition by a whisker in the late 19th century and was painstakingly reconstructed. There's also the superb **Kaupanger Stave Church**, dating from 1184.

Norway's oldest preserved place of worship, the **Urnes Stave Church** (adult/family Nkr55/120; ☻10.30am-5pm late May-Sep) is a Unesco World Heritage site. Directly across the fjord from Solvorn, it gazes out over Lustrafjord. The original church was built around 1070, while the majority of today's structure was constructed a century later. Highlights are elaborate wooden carvings – animals locked in struggle, stylised intertwined bodies and abstract motifs – on the north wall, all recycled from the original church, and the simple crucifixion carving, set above the chancel wall.

🏃 Activities

You can book directly or at the visitors centre for each of these outfits.

Ice Troll   GLACIER VISITS

(☑97 01 43 70; www.icetroll.com) Andy and his team offer a couple of truly original glacier visits. After a kayak trip, enjoy an ice walk where those without paddles never get. Both last eight to 10 hours (Nkr890). It also does longer overnight and two-day sorties.

Jostedalen Breførarlag   GLACIER VISITS

(☑57 68 31 11; www.bfl.no) Leads several guided glacier walks on Nigardsbreen. Easiest is the family walk to the glacier snout and briefly along its tongue (around one hour on the ice, adult/child Nkr200/100). Fees for the two-hour (Nkr430), three-hour (Nkr525) and five-hour (Nkr740) walks on the ice include the brief boat trip across Nigardsvatnet lake.

Riverpig   RAFTING, RIVERBOARDING

Run by the same outfit as Ice Troll, Riverpig does rafting on the Jostedalen river (Nkr650) and, for the truly hardy, riverboarding (Nkr800).

Leirdalen Bre og Juv   CANYONING, GLACIER VISITS

(Leirdal Glacier & Canyon; ☑470 27 878; www.breogjuv.no) Offers canyon clambering (Nkr500) and six- to eight-hour glacier hikes (Nkr650) on Tunsbergsdalsbreen, Norway's longest glacier arm.

Raudskarvfjellet Turriding   HORSE RIDING

(☑57 68 32 50; www.jostedal-horseguiding.no) Less strenuously, take a five-hour pony trip (Nkr700) with these stables.

🛏 Sleeping

TOP CHOICE Jostedal Camping   CAMPING GROUND €

(☑57 68 39 14; www.jostedalcamping.no; car/caravan site Nkr90/110 plus Nkr25 per person, 4-bed cabin with outdoor bathroom Nkr350-470, fully equipped bungalow for up to 6 persons Nkr1050; ☉May–mid-Oct) A trim, well-kept camping ground, right beside the Jostedal river. Facilities are impeccable and there's a lovely riverside terrace.

Jostedal Hotel   HOTEL €€

(☑57 68 31 19; www.jostedalhotel.no; s/d Nkr720/1020;@) Just 2.5km south of the visitors centre, this friendly place has been run by the same family for three generations. Meat, milk and vegetables for the restaurant come from their farm. There are also family rooms (Nkr1120) with self-catering facilities that can accommodate up to five guests.

ℹ Getting There & Around

BUS From mid-June to mid-September, Jostedalsbrebussen (No 160; The Glacier Bus; www.jostedal.com/brebussen) runs from Sogndal (with connections from Flåm, Balestrand and Lærdal) via Solvorn to the foot of the Nigardsbreen glacier, leaving at 8.45am and setting out on the return journey at 4.50pm.

CAR If you're driving, leave the Rv55 Sognefjellet Rd at Gaupne and head north up Jostedal along the Rv604.

FJÆRLAND
POP 300

The village of Fjærland (also called Mundal), at the head of scenic Fjærlandsfjorden, pulls in as many as 300,000 visitors each year. Most come to experience its pair of particularly accessible glacial tongues, Supphellebreen and Bøyabreen. Others come to bookworm. This tiny place, known as the Book Town of Norway (www.bokbyen.no), is a bibliophile's nirvana, with a dozen shops selling a wide range of used books, mostly in Norwegian but with lots in English and other European languages.

The village virtually hibernates from October onwards, then leaps to life in early May, when the ferry again runs.

◉ Sights

Supphellebreen & Bøyabreen   GLACIERS

You can drive to within 300m of the Supphellebreen glacier, then walk right up and touch the ice. Ice blocks from here were used as podiums at the 1994 Winter Olympics in Lillehammer.

At blue, creaking Bøyabreen, more spectacular than Supphellebreen, its brother over the hill, you might happen upon glacial calving as a hunk tumbles into the meltwater lagoon beneath the glacier tongue.

TOP CHOICE Norwegian Glacier Museum   MUSEUM

(Norsk Bremuseum; ☑57 69 32 88; www.bremuseum.no; adult/child Nkr110/50; ☉9am-7pm Jun-Aug, 10am-4pm Apr, May, Sep & Oct) For the story on flowing ice and how it has sculpted the Norwegian landscape, visit this superbly executed museum, 3km inland from the ferry jetty. You can learn how fjords are formed, see an excellent 20-minute multiscreen audiovisual presentation on Jostedalsbreen (so impressive that audiences often break into spontaneous applause at the end), touch 1000-year-old ice, wind your way through a tunnel that penetrates the mock-ice and even see the tusk of a Siberian woolly mammoth, which met an icy demise 30,000 years ago.

🏃 Activities

At the small fjordside shack belonging to **Fjærland Kayak & Glacier** (📞92 85 46 74; www.kayakglacier.no) you can hire a kayak, canoe, motor or rowing boat or join one of its daily guided kayaking trips (May to August), ranging from 2½ hours (Nkr400) to a full day (Nkr870).

The tourist office's free sheet, *Escape the Asphalt*, lists 12 marked walking routes, varying from 30 minutes to three hours. For greater detail, supplement this with *Turkart Fjærland* (Nkr70) at 1:50,000, which comes complete with route descriptions and trails indicated; pull on your boots and you're away.

Fjærland Kayak & Glacier offers more demanding guided glacier treks (Nkr600 to Nkr750), leaving at 8.30am each morning.

🛏 Sleeping & Eating

TOP CHOICE Hotel Mundal   HOTEL €€€
(📞57 69 31 01; www.hotelmundal.no; s/d from Nkr1120/1700; ☉May-Sep; 🅿@) Retaining much of its period furniture and run by the same family ever since it was built in 1891, this place features a welcoming lounge and a lovely round tower. The restaurant serves truly wonderful traditional four-course Norwegian dinners (Nkr360).

Mrs Haugen's Rooms   GUESTHOUSE €
(📞57 69 32 43; d Nkr400-500; ☉May-mid-Oct) In the white building behind the village church, Ms Alma Haugen rents just a couple of rooms with shared kitchen and bathroom that represent outstanding value.

Bøyum Camping   CAMPING GROUND €
(📞57 69 32 52; www.fjaerland.org/boyumcamp ing; campsites Nkr150, dm Nkr160, d without bath-room Nkr270-340, 4-/8-bed cabin Nkr710/1010; ☉May-Sep) Beside the Glacier Museum and 3km from the ferry landing, Bøyum Camping has something for all pockets and sleeping preferences.

ℹ Getting There & Away

BOAT A car ferry (Nkr215/325 one way/return, 1¼ hours) runs twice daily between Balestrand and Fjærland in July and August (in May, June and September there's a daily passenger-ferry run).

BUS Buses bypass the village and stop on the Rv5 near the Glacier Museum. Three to six run daily to/from Sogndal (Nkr73, 30 minutes) and Stryn (Nkr200, two hours).

BRIKSDALSBREEN

From the small town of Olden at the eastern end of Nordfjord, a scenic road leads 23km up Oldedalen past Brenndalsbreen, and from there on to the twin glacial tongues of Melkevollbreen and Briksdalsbreen. More easily accessible, Briksdalsbreen attracts hordes of tour buses. It's a temperamental glacier; in 1997 the tongue licked to its furthest point for around 70 years, then retreated by around 500m. In 2005, the reaches where glacier walkers would clamber and stride cracked and splintered. So for the moment, there are no guided hikes on Briksdalsbreen, but she's a fickle creature and this may change.

Melkevoll Bretun (📞57 87 38 64; www. melkevoll.no; per person/site Nkr20/100, dm Nkr110, cabin with outdoor bathroom Nkr350 plus Nkr50 per person, with bathroom Nkr650-750 plus Nkr50 per person; ☉May-Sep) is a gorgeous green camping ground with accommodation for all pockets and gorgeous views whichever way you turn.

Between June and August, buses leave Stryn for Briksdal (Nkr70, one hour) once or twice daily, calling by Loen and Olden.

Norangsdalen & Sunnmøresalpane

One of the most inspiring parts of the Western Fjords is Norangsdalen, a hidden valley west of Hellesylt. The partially unsealed Rv665 to the villages of Øye and Urke, and the Leknes–Sæbø ferry on beautiful Hjørundfjorden are served by bus from Hellesylt once daily, Monday to Friday mid-June to mid-August.

Hikers and climbers will enjoy the dramatic peaks of the adjacent Sunnmøresalpane, including the incredibly steep scrambling ascent of Slogen (1564m) from Øye and the superb Råna (1586m), a long and tough scramble from Urke.

Geirangerfjorden

Added to Unesco's World Heritage list in 2005, this king of Norwegian fjords boasts towering, twisting walls that curve inland for 20 narrow kilometres. Along the way abandoned farms cling to the cliffs and breathtakingly high waterfalls, with names such as the Seven Sisters, the Suitor and the Bridal Veil, drop straight into the sea from forests above.

The cruise by public ferry between Geiranger and Hellesylt is almost too nice to view.

Around Geirangerfjorden

High mountains with cascading waterfalls and cliff-side farms surround Geiranger, at the head of the crooked Geirangerfjorden. Although the village is tiny, it's one of Norway's most visited spots. Nevertheless, it's reasonably serene during the evening when all the cruise ships and tour buses have departed.

◉ Sights

Flydalsjuvet   VIEWPOINT
Somewhere you've seen that classic photo, beloved of brochures, of the overhanging rock Flydalsjuvet, usually with a figure gazing down at a cruise ship in Geirangerfjord. The car park, signposted Flydalsjuvet, about 5km uphill from Geiranger on the Stryn road, offers a great view of the fjord and the green river valley, but doesn't provide the postcard view down to the last detail. For that, you'll have to drop about 150m down the hill, then descend a slippery and rather indistinct track to the edge. Your intrepid photo subject will have to scramble down gingerly and with the utmost care to the overhang about 50m further along...

Dalsnibba   VIEWPOINT
For the highest and perhaps most stunning of the many stunning views of the Geiranger valley and fjord, take the 5km toll road (Nkr85 per car) that climbs from the Rv63 to the Dalsnibba lookout (1500m). A bus (adult/child Nkr180/90 return) runs three times daily from Geiranger between mid-June and mid-August.

Norsk Fjordsenter   MUSEUM
(www.verdsarvfjord.no, in Norwegian; adult/child Nkr100/50; ◔9am-6pm or 9pm mid-Jun–mid-Aug, 10am-3pm Mon-Sat rest of yr) At the Geiranger Fjord Centre learn about the essentials that shaped culture in the middle of nowhere: mail packets, avalanches and building roads over impossible terrain.

🏃 Activities

Get away from the seething ferry terminal and life's altogether quieter. All around Geiranger there are great signed **hiking** routes to abandoned farmsteads, waterfalls and vista points. The tourist office's aerial-photographed *Hiking Routes* map (Nkr10) gives ideas for 18 signed walks of between 1.5km and 5km.

🛶 Coastal Odyssey   KAYAKING, HIKING
(☏91 11 80 62; www.coastalodyssey.com) Based at Geiranger Camping, this outfit is run by Jonathan Bendiksen, who rents sea kayaks (Nkr150/400/750 per hour/half-day/day). He also does daily kayaking-with-gentle-hiking trips (adult/child Nkr800/640) lasting five to six hours to a trio of the finest destinations around the fjord.

Geiranger Adventure   CYCLING
(☑47 37 97 71; www.geiranger-adventure.com) This outfit will drive you up to Djupvasshytta (1038m), from where you can coast for 17 gentle, scenically splendid kilometres by bike down to the fjord; allow a couple of hours. It also rents bikes (Nkr50/200 per hour/day).

Geiranger Fjordservice   BOAT TOURS
(☑70 26 30 07; www.geirangerfjord.no) Does 1½-hour sightseeing boat tours (adult/child Nkr155/80, up to four sailings daily mid-May to mid-September). Its kiosk is within the tourist office.

🛏 Sleeping & Eating

Hotels here are often booked out by package tours.

Grande Fjord Hotel   HOTEL €€
(☑70 26 94 90; www.grandefjordhotel.com; d Nkr980-1150; ℗) This warmly recommended 48-room hotel does great buffet breakfasts and dinners. It's well worth paying the higher rate for a room with a balcony and magnificent view over the fjord.

Geiranger Camping   CAMPING GROUND €
(☑70 26 31 20; www.geirangercamping.no; per person/site Nkr25/125; ◔mid-May–mid-Sep; @) A short walk from the ferry terminal, Geiranger Camping is sliced through by a fast-flowing torrent. Though it's short on shade, it's pleasant and handy for an early-morning ferry getaway.

Laizas   CAFE €
(◔10am-10pm mid-Apr–Sep; @) At the ferry terminal, just beside the tourist office, the young team at this airy, welcoming place puts on a handful of tasty hot dishes, good salads and snackier items such as focaccia, wraps and sandwiches.

TOP CHOICE Villa Utsikten   HOTEL €€
(☑70 26 96 60; www.villautsikten.no; s Nkr940, d Nkr1340-1600; ◔May-Sep; ℗@) High on the hill above Geiranger (take Rv63, direction Grotli), the venerable family-owned

Utsikten, constructed in 1893, has stunning views over town and fjord.

ⓘ Information

Tourist office (☑70 26 30 99; www.visitale sund-geiranger.com; ⊙9am-6pm mid-May–mid-Sep)

ⓘ Getting There & Away

Boat

The popular, hugely recommended run between Geiranger and Hellesylt (passenger/car with driver Nkr133/278, adult/child return Nkr169/85, one hour) is the most spectacular scheduled ferry route in Norway. It has four to eight sailings daily between May and mid-October (every 90 minutes until 6.30pm June to August).

Almost as scenic is the ferry that runs twice daily between Geiranger and Valldal (adult/child single Nkr206/103, return Nkr327/157, 2¼ hours). It runs from mid-June to mid-August.

Bus

From mid-June to mid-August two buses daily make the spectacular run over Trollstigen to Åndalsnes (Nkr222, three hours) via Valldal (Nkr65, 1½ hours). For Molde, change buses in Åndalsnes; for Ålesund, change at Linge.

Åndalsnes

POP 2650

There are two dramatic ways to approach Åndalsnes: by road through the Trollstigen pass or along Romsdalen as you ride the spectacularly scenic Raumabanen. Badly bombed during WWII, the modern town, nestled beside Romsdalfjord, is nondescript, but the surrounding landscapes are magnificent.

⊙ Sights

Trollveggen   SHEER CLIFF
Near Åndalsnes, dramatic Trollveggen (Troll Wall), first conquered in 1958 by a joint Norwegian and English team, rears skywards. The highest vertical mountain wall in Europe, its ragged and often cloud-shrouded summit, 1800m from the valley floor, is considered the ultimate challenge among mountaineers.

Raumabanen   CLASSIC TRAIN JOURNEY
The rail route down from Dombås ploughs through a deeply cut glacial valley flanked by sheer walls and plummeting waterfalls; it's shadowed by the equally spectacular E136 highway. Trains run daily year-round along this spectacular route. There's also a **tourist**

train (adult/child return Nkr296/148; one child per adult travels free) with on-board commentary that runs twice daily from June to August from Åndalsnes' lakeside station up to Bjorli, at 600m. Book at the station or tourist office.

✗ Activities

The best local climbs are the less extreme sections of the 1500m-high rock route on Trollveggen and the 1550m-high Romsdalshorn, but there's a wealth of others. Serious climbers should buy *Klatring i Romsdal* (Nkr300), which includes rock and ice-climbing information in both Norwegian and English.

An excellent day hike, signed by red markers, begins in town, 50m north of the roundabout before the Esso petrol station, and climbs to the summit of Nesaksla (715m), the prominent peak that rises above Åndalsnes. At the top, the payoff for a steep ascent is a magnificent panorama.

🛏 Sleeping & Eating

TOP CHOICE ／ **Hotel Aak**   HOTEL €€
(☑71 22 71 71; www.hotelaak.no, in Norwegian; s/d Nkr850/1100; ⊙mid-Jun–Aug; ℗) This charming, comfortable place, one of the oldest tourist hotels in Norway, lies beside the E136, in the direction of Dombås, 4km from town. Its **restaurant** (mains Nkr150-190; ⊙4-10pm) is equally impressive and offers excellent traditional cuisine.

Grand Hotel Bellevue   HOTEL €€
(☑71 22 75 00; www.grandhotel.no; Åndalgata 5; s/d Nkr1030/1240; ℗@) This large whitewashed structure caps a hillock in the centre of town. Most of its 86 rooms have fine views, particularly those facing the rear. Its **restaurant** (mains Nkr135-275; ⊙dinner only) offers the town's most formal dining, but you can always nibble on a lighter dish for around Nkr100.

Kaikanten   CAFE-RESTAURANT €
(daily specials Nkr98, snacks Nkr35-78, dishes Nkr60-195; ⊙10am-11pm Mon-Sat, noon-9pm Sun mid-May–Aug) Sit back and relax here at the jetty's edge and enjoy a drink, a snack and one of Norway's prettiest panoramas in this welcoming place, run by the Grand Hotel.

Åndalsnes Vandrerhjem Setnes   HOSTEL €
(☑71 22 13 82; www.aandalsnesvandrerhjem.no; dm/s/d Nkr275/480/690; ⊙Mar-Nov) This wel-

coming, HI-affiliated, sod-roofed hostel is 1.5km from the train station on the E136, in the direction of Ålesund. It's worth staying here for the pancakes-and-pickled-herring bumper breakfast alone.

ℹ️ Information

Tourist office (☎71 22 16 22; www.visitandalsnes.com; ⊙9am-7pm mid-Jun–mid-Aug, 9am-3pm Mon-Fri rest of yr; @)

ℹ️ Getting There & Away

Bus

Buses along the spectacular National Tourist Route to Geiranger (Nkr222, three hours), via Trollstigen, the Linge–Eidsdal ferry and the steep Ørnevegen (Eagle Rd), run twice daily between mid-June and mid-August.

There are also services to Molde (Nkr127, 1½ hours, up to eight daily) and Ålesund (Nkr255, 2¼ hours, four times daily).

Train

Trains to/from Dombås (Nkr217, 1½ hours) run twice daily, in synchronisation with Oslo–Trondheim trains.

Åndalsnes to Geiranger

The Trollstigen (Troll's Ladder; www.trollstigen. net) winding south from Åndalsnes is a thriller of a road with 11 hairpin bends and a 1:12 gradient, and to add a daredevil element it's practically one lane all the way. On request, the bus makes photo stops at the thundering, 180m-high Stigfossen waterfall on its way up to the mountain pass. At the top, the bus usually stops long enough for you to walk to a lookout with a dizzying view back down the valley. The pass is usually cleared and open from late May to mid-October.

The pamphlet *Geiranger Trollstigen* (Nkr30) describes seven signed hiking trails in the Trollstigen area. You'll need to supplement this with the map *Romsdals-Fjella* at 1:80,000. The tourist office in Åndalsnes carries both.

There are waterfalls galore smoking down the mountains as you descend to Valldal. You could break your journey here – there are camping grounds, cabins and a hotel – though most travellers continue on, taking the short ferry ride from Linge across to Eidsdal. From there, a waiting bus continues along the Ørnevegen (Eagle's Hwy), with magnificent bird's-eye views of Geirangerfjorden during the descent into Geiranger village.

Ålesund

POP 23,000

The coastal town of Ålesund is, for many, just as beautiful as Bergen, if on a much smaller scale, and it is certainly far less touristy. Lucky for you, Ålesund burned to the ground in 1904. The amazing rebuilding created a fantastical downtown centre unlike anything else you'll see in Norway – a harmonious collection of pastel buildings almost entirely designed in the art nouveau tradition. All the loveliness is well staged on the end of a peninsula, surrounded by islands, water and hills.

👁 Sights & Activities

Sunnmøre Museum   MUSEUM

(www.sunnmore.museum.no, in Norwegian; Borgundgavlen; adult/child Nkr70/20; ⊙11am-5pm late Jun–Aug, 11am-3pm Mon-Fri rest of yr) Ålesund's celebrated open-air Sunnmøre Museum is 4km east of the centre of the city. Here, at the site of the old Borgundkaupangen trading centre, active from the 11th to 16th centuries, more than 50 traditional buildings have been relocated. Ship lovers will savour the collection of around 40 historic boats, including replicas of Viking-era ships and a commercial trading vessel from around AD 1000. You can take bus 613, 618 or 624 to get here.

Jugendstil Art Nouveau Centre   ART CENTRE

(Jugendstil Senteret; ☎70 10 49 70; www.jugendstilsenteret.no; Apotekergata 16; adult/child Nkr60/30; ⊙10am-5pm Jun-Aug, 11am-4pm Tue-Sun Sep-May) Everyone from serious aesthetes to kids out for fun will get pleasure from this art centre. The introductory Time Machine capsule presents 'From Ashes to Art Nouveau', a 14-minute hi-tech, very visual story of the rebuilding of Ålesund after the great fire, while the displays offer carefully selected textiles, ceramics and furniture of the genre.

Atlanterhavsparken   AQUARIUM

(Atlantic Ocean Park; www.atlanterhavsparken. no; Tueneset; adult/child Nkr130/65; ⊙10am-7pm Sun-Fri, 10am-4pm Sat Jun-Aug, 11am-4pm Tue-Sun Sep-May) At the peninsula's western extreme, 3km from the town centre, the Atlantic Ocean Park can merit a whole day of your life. It introduces visitors to the North Atlantic's undersea world with glimpses of the astonishing richness of coastal and fjord submarine life. In summer, a special

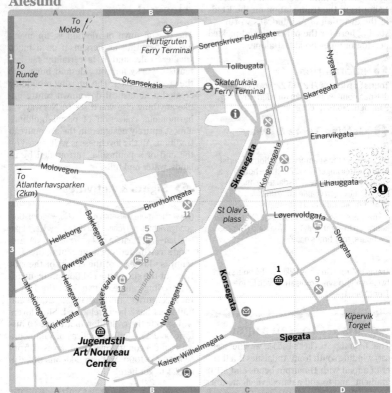

bus (adult/child Nkr35/18) leaves from beside the town hall hourly from 9.55am to 3.55pm, Monday to Saturday.

Aalesunds Museum MUSEUM
(www.aalesunds.museum.no, in Norwegian; Rasmus Rønnebergs gate 16; adult/child Nkr50/20; ⊙9am or 11am-4pm mid-Jun–mid-Aug, 11am-3pm Mon-Fri rest of yr) The town museum illustrates the history of sealing, fishing, shipping and industry in the Sunnmøre region, the fire of 1904, the Nazi WWII occupation and the town's distinctive art nouveau architecture.

Aksla VIEWPOINT
The 418 steps up Aksla hill lead to the splendid **Kniven viewpoint** over Ålesund and the surrounding mountains and islands. Follow Lihauggata from the pedestrian shopping street Kongensgata, pass the **Rollon statue** and begin the 15-minute puff to the top of the hill. There's also a road to the crest; take

Røysegata east from the centre, then follow the Fjellstua signposts up the hill.

🛏 Sleeping

TOP CHOICE **Hotel Brosundet** HOTEL €€
(☎70 11 45 00; www.brosundet.no; Apotekergata 5; s/d from Nkr1190/1390; P@) This boutique hotel, right on the waterfront, has oodles of charm. An ex-warehouse and protected building, it combines tradition with strictly contemporary comfort and style. Bedroom furnishings are of light pine, contrasting with the warm brown draperies and whitest of white sheets, while bathrooms, behind their smoked-glass walls, have the latest fittings. Rooms overlooking the harbour carry a Nkr200 supplement.

Clarion Collection Hotel Bryggen HOTEL €€
(☎70 10 33 00; www.choice.no; Apotekergata 1-3; s/d from Nkr1080/1280; @) This wonderful waterfront option occupies a converted fish

NORWAY ÅLESUND

✕ Eating & Drinking

TOP CHOICE **Maki**   SEAFOOD €€€

(☎70 11 45 00; www.maki.no; Apotekergata 5; mains Nkr285-315) The menu changes regularly at this ultracool restaurant in Hotel Brosundet. Sip a cocktail in its suave bar, then enjoy new takes on mussels, cod, and other finny delights, presented to perfection.

Sjøbua   SEAFOOD €€

(☎70 12 71 00; www.sjoebua.no, in Norwegian; Brunholmgata 1a; mains Nkr250-360; ⊙4pm-1am Mon-Fri) In yet another converted wharf-side building with thick masonry walls skewered by stout beams and posts, stylish Sjøbua is one of northern Norway's finest fish restaurants. Choose your crustacean, wriggling and fresh, from the lobster tank.

Lyst   CAFE, RESTAURANT €

(Kongensgata 12; lunch dishes Nkr75-85, dinner mains Nkr165-295; ⊙10am-11pm) This new arrival on Ålesund's gastronomic scene offers good dining within a classic converted art nouveau building. Separate lunch and dinner menus (with enticing items such as fillet of lamb gratiné in a red wine sauce) are, in fact, served throughout the day.

warehouse, artfully decorated with former tools and equipment. Rates include a light evening meal and free waffles throughout the day. There's a sauna, free to guests, too.

Rica Scandinavie Hotel   HOTEL €€

(☎70 15 78 00; www.rica.no; Løvenvoldgata 8; s/d from Nkr795/1045; P@) This fine place, Ålesund's oldest hotel, was the first to be constructed after the fire of 1904. With touches and flourishes of art nouveau – the furniture is original and in keeping with this theme, and even the lobby flat-screen TV seems to blend in – it exudes style and confidence.

Ålesund Vandrerhjem   HOSTEL €

(☎70 11 58 30; www.hihostels.no; Parkgata 14; dm/s/d Nkr255/570/790; ⊙yr-round; @) This central, HI-affiliated hostel is in an attractive building (see the murals in the vast common room) that recently celebrated its first century. There are self-catering facilities and a heavy-duty washing machine.

Hummer & Kanari
BAR, RESTAURANT €

(www.hummerkanari.no, in Norwegian; Kongensgata 19; dinner mains Nkr145-260; ☺from 4pm Mon-Fri, from 2pm Sat & Sun) Behind the bar sit row upon row of liqueur and spirit bottles for mixers and shakers. Here at the downstairs bistro, you order at the counter. Upstairs, it's waiter service. But both call upon the same kitchen, which turns out ample portions of pasta (around Nkr150) and pizza (Nkr100). For a main course, save the decision making, sit back, put yourself in the cook's capable hands and go for the best the sea can offer that day, 'Hummer & Kanari's selection of fish and shellfish' (Nkr280).

Lyspunktet
CAFE, RESTAURANT €€

(www.lyspunktet.as, in Norwegian; Kipervikgata 1; mains around Nkr200; ☺10am-10pm Tue-Fri, noon-10pm Sat & Sun) At this great-value, great-ambience, youthful place, loll back in its deep sofa. There are free refills for coffee and soft drinks, and dishes, such as the garlic turkey marinated in coconut, lime and chilli, are creative and great value.

🛍 Shopping

Celsius
GLASSWARE

(www.celsius-glass.com, in Norwegian; Kaiser Wilhelmsgata 52; ☺Tue-Sat) 'Luxury for everyday use' is the motto of this small glass studio, where each piece is designed to be stylish yet functional. The kiln is at the front, the shop at the rear.

Invit Interior
INTERIOR DESIGN

(☎70 15 66 44; Apotekergata 9) Appropriate for such a tasteful town, this shop-cum-gallery displays the very best of creative modern furniture and Scandinavian kitchenware and home appliances.

ℹ Information

Tourist office (☎70 15 76 00; www.visitalesund-geiranger.com; Skaregata 1; ☺9am-6 or 7pm Jun-Aug, 9am-4pm Mon-Fri Sep-May) Its free booklet *On Foot in Ålesund* details the town's architectural highlights in a walking tour.

ℹ Getting There & Away

AIR Ålesund has daily flights to Oslo, Bergen and Trondheim. **Flybussen** (Nkr100, 20min) departs from Skateflukaia and the bus station approximately one hour before the departure of domestic flights.

BOAT The *Hurtigruten* docks at Skansekaia Terminal.

BUS There are buses to Stryn (Nkr250, 3¾ hours, one to four daily) via Hellesylt (Nkr160, 2¾ hours, up to five daily), Bergen (Nkr610, 9¼ hours, one to three daily), Molde (Nkr130, 1½ hours, hourly) and Åndalsnes (Nkr255, 2¼ hours, four times daily).

Runde
POP 100

The squat island of Runde, 67km southwest of Ålesund, plays host to half a million seabirds of around 230 species, including 100,000 pairs of migrating puffins that arrive in April, breed and stay around until late July. There are also colonies of kittiwakes, gannets, fulmars, storm petrels, razor-billed auks, shags and guillemots, plus about 70 other species that nest here.

You'll see the best bird sites – as well as an offshore seal colony – on a **boat tour** (adult/child Nkr180/90). Three boats put out from Runde's small harbour, each two or three times daily.

Within the new **Runde Miljøsenter** (Runde Environmental Centre; www.rundecentre.no; s/d Nkr1000/1500, 5-bed apt Nkr2250), there's a seasonal **tourist office** (☺10am-6pm May-Aug) and cafe.

Goksöyr Camping (☎70 08 59 05; www.goksoyr.no, in Norwegian; per person/site Nkr20/110, 2-/4-bed cabin with outdoor bathroom Nkr250/440, 4-bed with bathroom Nkr520; ☺May-Sep) has a range of cabins and rooms around the camping ground itself, which is a fairly basic, waterside place.

NORTHERN NORWAY

With several vibrant cities and some wondrous natural terrain, you'll be mighty pleased with yourself for undertaking an exploration of this huge territory that spans the Arctic Circle. A vast plateau reaches across much of the interior, while small fishing villages cling to the incredibly steep and jagged Lofoten Islands, which erupt vertically out of the ocean. Medieval Trondheim, Norway's third-largest city, provides plenty of culture and charm, while Tromsø, the world's northernmost university town, parties year-round.

An alternative to land travel is the *Hurtigruten* coastal steamer (see p417), which pulls into every sizeable port, passing some of the best coastal scenery in Scandinavia. A good thing, too, since trains only run as far as Bodø.

MOLDEJAZZ

Every year, Moldejazz pulls in up to 100,000 fans and a host of stars, mainly Scandinavian plus a sprinkling of international top liners. Molde, northeast of Ålesund, rocks all the way from Monday to Saturday in the middle of July. Of over 100 concerts, a good one-third are free, while big events are very reasonably priced at Nkr100 to Nkr330. For the lowdown on this year's events, log onto www.moldejazz.no.

Trondheim

POP 170,000

Trondheim, Norway's original capital, is nowadays the country's third-largest city after Oslo and Bergen. With its wide streets and partly pedestrianised heart, it's a simply lovely city with a long history. Fuelled by a large student population, it buzzes with life. Cycles zip everywhere, it has some good cafes and restaurants, and it's rich in museums. You *can* absorb it in one busy day, but it merits more if you're to slip into its lifestyle.

Trondheim was founded at the estuary of the winding Nidelva in AD 997 by the Viking king Olav Tryggvason. After a fire razed most of the city in 1681, Trondheim was redesigned with wide streets and Renaissance flair by General Caspar de Cicignon. Today, the steeple of the medieval Nidaros Domkirke is still the highest point in the city centre.

◎ Sights

Nidaros Domkirke   CHURCH
(www.nidarosdomen.no; Kongsgårdsgata; adult/child Nkr50/25; ⊙9am-3 or 5.30pm Mon-Fri, 9am-2pm Sat, 1-4pm Sun May–mid-Sep) Nidaros Cathedral is Scandinavia's largest medieval building. Outside, the ornately embellished west wall has top-to-bottom statues of biblical characters and Norwegian bishops and kings, sculpted in the early 20th century. Several are copies of medieval originals, housed nowadays in the museum.

The altar sits over the original grave of St Olav, the Viking king who replaced the Nordic pagan religion with Christianity. The original stone cathedral was built in 1153, when Norway became a separate archbishopric. The current transept and chapter house were constructed between 1130 and 1180 and reveal Anglo-Norman influences (many of the craftsmen were brought in from England), while the Gothic choir and ambulatory were completed in the early 14th century. The nave, repeatedly ravaged by fire across the centuries, is mostly a faithful 19th-century reconstruction.

Music lovers may want to time their visit to take in a recital (admission free; ⊙1pm Mon-Sat early Jun-early Aug) on the church's magnificent organ.

From early June to early August, you can climb the cathedral's tower for a great view over the city. There are ascents every half-hour from its base in the south transept.

Archbishop's Palace   MUSEUM
The 12th-century archbishop's residence, commissioned around 1160 and Scandinavia's oldest secular building, is beside the cathedral. In its west wing, Norway's crown jewels (adult/child Nkr70/25) shimmer and flash. Its museum (adult/child Nkr50/25; ⊙10am-3 or 5pm Mon-Sat, noon-4pm Sun May–mid-Sep) is in the same compound. After visiting the well-displayed statues, gargoyles and carvings from the cathedral, drop to the lower level, where only a selection of the myriad artefacts revealed during the museum's construction in the late 1990s are on show. Take in too its enjoyable 15-minute audiovisual program.

Art Museums   ART GALLERIES
The eclectic Nordenfjeldske Kunstindustrimuseum (Museum of Decorative Arts; Munkegata 5; adult/child Nkr60/30; ⊙10am-5pm Mon-Sat, noon-5pm Sun Jun–mid-Aug, 10am-3pm Tue-Sun rest of yr) exhibits a fine collection of contemporary arts and crafts, including work by Hannah Ryggen, Norway's highly acclaimed tapestry artist. Trondheim Kunstmuseum (Bispegata 7b; adult/child Nkr50/30; ⊙10am-5pm mid-Jun–mid-Aug, 11am-4pm Tue-Sun rest of yr) has a corridor of Munch's lithographs and displays Norwegian and Danish art from 1850 onward.

COMBINATION TICKET

If you're planning to visit all three sights within the Nidaros Domkirke complex, it's worthwhile purchasing a combined ticket (adult/child/family Nkr100/50/200) that gives access to cathedral, palace museum and crown jewels.

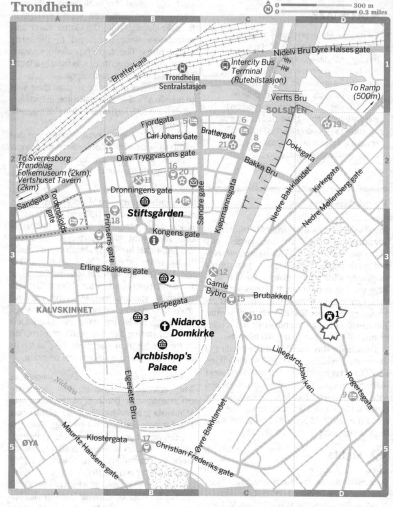

Historic Buildings & Neighbourhoods

HISTORIC BUILDINGS

Scandinavia's largest wooden palace, the late-baroque **Stiftsgården** (Munkegata 23; adult/child Nkr60/30; ⊙10am-4pm Mon-Sat, noon-4pm Sun Jun-late Aug) was completed in 1778 and is now the official royal residence in Trondheim. Admission is by tour only, on the hour.

The picturesque **Gamle Bybro** (Old Town Bridge) originally dates from 1681, but the current wooden structure was built in 1861. From here, enjoy marvellous views over the **Bryggen**, an amazingly intact collection of tall red, yellow, green and orange 18th- and 19th-century warehouses reflected colourfully in the calm river.

On the east side of the bridge lies **Bakklandet**, a neighbourhood of cobblestone streets containing cafes and plenty of revived working-class residences from the 19th century.

Puff up the hill from this neighbourhood and there's a good view of the city from the top of the 17th-century **Kristiansten Fort** (Festningsgata; ⊙10am-4pm daily Jun-Aug). Though its buildings open only during summer, the parklike grounds can be viewed year-round.

NORWAY TRONDHEIM

The **Sverresborg Trøndelag Folkemuseum** (Sverresborg Allé 13; www.sverresborg.no; adult/child incl guided tour Nkr85/35; ⊙11am-6pm Jun-Aug, 11am-3pm rest of yr), set around the ruins of a medieval castle, is one of Norway's best open-air museums. On a hill with views over town, it displays more than 60 period buildings, including a small, 12th-century stave church (visit in winter to understand how cold, dark and miserable services must have been). Catch bus 8 or 9 from Dronningens gate.

Ringve Museum MUSEUM
(www.ringve.no; Lade Allé 60; adult/child Nkr80/30; ⊙11am-4 or 5pm mid-Apr–mid-Sep, 11am-4pm Sun only rest of yr) The Ringve Museum is a fascinating music-history museum set in an 18th-century manor. Music students give tours demonstrating the antique instruments on display. Take bus 3 or 4 from Munkegaten 3km northeast of the city centre.

A lavish **botanical garden** (Lade Allé 58; admission free; ⊙24hr) surrounds the estate, covering 14 hectares near Trondheimfjord.

🏃 Activities

West of town spreads the Bymarka, a gorgeous green woodland area laced with wilderness footpaths and ski trails. Take the Gråkallbanen tram, in itself a lovely scenic ride through the leafy suburbs, from the St Olavsgata stop to **Lian**. There you can enjoy excellent views over the city and a good swimming lake, **Lianvannet**. To the east

of Trondheim, **Ladestien** (The Lade Trail) follows the shoreline of the Lade peninsula, beginning only 1km from the town centre.

The **Vassfjellet** mountains, south of town, offer both downhill and cross-country skiing. In season, a daily ski bus runs directly from Munkegata to the Vassfjellet Skisenter, only 8km beyond the city limits.

🎭 Festivals & Events

Kosmorama FILM
(www.kosmorama.no) Trondheim's international film festival occupies an intensive week in late April.

Nidaros Blues Festival MUSIC
(www.nidarosbluesfestival.com, in Norwegian) The Fabulous Thunderbirds topped the bill in 2010. Also in late April.

Olavsfestdagene CITY FESTIVAL
(www.olavsfestdagene.no) In honour of St Olav and held during the week around his saint's day, 29 July.

Trondelag Food Festival FOOD
Coincides with Olavsfestdagene. Stalls selling local fare pack Kongens gate, east of Torvet.

UKA CULTURE
(www.uka.no, in Norwegian) Trondheim's 25,000 university students stage this three-week celebration, Norway's largest cultural festival. Every other year in October and November, it's a continuous party.

> **ⓘ WI-FI IN DOWNTOWN TRONDHEIM**
>
> Trondheim is one of Europe's first wireless cities. If you're carrying your laptop, you can wi-fi (Nkr10/30 per three/24 hours) at multiple spots within the city centre. For details and to log on, go to http://tradlosetrondheim.no.

🛏 Sleeping

Britannia Hotel   HOTEL €€
(☎73 80 08 00; www.britannia.no; Dronningens gate 5; s/d from Nkr1095/1295; P@⊠) This mastodon of a hotel with nearly 250 rooms was constructed in 1897. It exudes old-world grace from the mellow, wooden panelling of public areas to the magnificent oval Moorish-revival Palmehaven restaurant – one of three places to eat – with its Corinthian pillars and central fountain.

Chesterfield Hotel   HOTEL €€
(☎73 50 37 50; www.bestwestern.no; Søndre gate 26; s/d from Nkr790/990; @) All 43 rooms at this venerable hotel are spacious. They were decorated and fundamentally renovated, with fresh beds and furniture, in 2006 following a major fire in the adjacent building. Those on the 7th (top) floor have huge skylights giving broad city views.

**Clarion Collection Hotel
Grand Olav**   HOTEL €€
(☎73 80 80 80; www.choice.no; Kjøpmannsgata 48; s/d from Nkr880/980; @) Two of Trondheim's finest hotels stare across the street at each other in perpetual competition. The Clarion offers sleek luxurious living above an airy shopping complex and the Olavshallen concert hall. It has 27 different styles among over 100 rooms, so no guest can complain of lack of choice.

**Radisson Blu Royal Garden
Hotel**   HOTEL €€
(☎73 80 30 00; www.radissonblu.com; Kjøpmannsgata 73; s/d from Nkr1095/1195; P@⊠) Opposite the Clarion, this first-class, contemporary riverside hotel (you can fish from your window in some rooms) is open and airy from the moment you step into the atrium, where the light streams in through its all-glass walls.

Singsaker Sommerhotel   SUMMER HOTEL €
(☎73 89 31 00; http://sommerhotell.singsaker.no; Rogertsgata 1; dm/s/d without bathroom Nkr230/445/685, s/d Nkr560/810; ☻mid-Jun–mid-Aug; P) On a grassy knoll in a quiet residential neighbourhood, this imposing building, usually a student hostel, was originally built as a club for occupying German officers. It represents great value. Bus 63 from the train station passes by.

Pensjonat Jarlen   GUESTHOUSE €
(☎73 51 32 18; www.jarlen.no; Kongens gate 40; s/d Nkr520/650) There's nothing fancy about this central spot but it does have price, convenience and value for money on its side. All 25 rooms have full bathroom and all except the sole single have a fridge and self-catering facilities.

Flakk Camping   CAMPING GROUND €
(☎72 84 39 00; www.flakk-camping.no; car/caravan site Nkr170/200, cabin with outdoor bathroom Nkr400-550; ☻May-Aug) Sitting right beside Trondheimfjord, this welcoming camping ground is about 10km from the city centre. Take Rv715 from Trondheim.

🍴 Eating

TOP CHOICE **Vertshuset Tavern**   NORWEGIAN €€€
(Sverresborg Allé 11; mains Nkr195-295) Once in the heart of Trondheim, this historic (1739) tavern was lifted and transported, every last plank of it, to the Sverresborg Trøndelag Folk Museum on the outskirts of town. Tuck into its rotating specials of traditional Norwegian fare or just peck at waffles with coffee in one of its 16 tiny rooms, each low-beamed, with sloping floors, candlesticks, cast-iron stoves and lacy tablecloths.

Havfruen   SEAFOOD €€€
(☎73 87 40 70; www.havfruen.no, in Norwegian; Kjøpmannsgata 7; mains around Nkr300, daily specials Nkr195, 3-course menus Nkr525; ☻5pm-midnight Mon-Sat) This characterful riverside restaurant, all odd angled pillars and rickety beams, specialises in the freshest of fish. The quality, reflected in the prices, is excellent, as are the accompanying wines, selected by the resident sommelier.

Baklandet Skydsstasjon   NORWEGIAN €€
(www.skydsstation.no, in Norwegian; Øvre Baklandet 33; mains Nkr130-245; ☻noon-1am) Within what began life as an 18th-century coaching inn are several cosy rooms with poky angles and listing floors. It's a hyper-friendly place where you can tuck into tasty dishes, such as its renowned fish soup ('the best in all Norway,' a couple of diners assured us).

Ramp
BAR, RESTAURANT €

(cnr Strandveien & Gregusgate; mains Nkr85-140; ⊙noon-midnight) Well off the tourist route and patronised by in-the-know locals, friendly, alternative Ramp gets its raw materials, organic where possible, from local sources. It's renowned for its juicy house burgers filled with lamb, beef, fish or chickpeas.

Bari
CAFE, BAR €€

(www.bari.no, in Norwegian; Munkegata 25; dishes around Nkr130) Eat in the stylish, modern, jazzy interior or choose the small streetside terrace. Bari has a reputation for, in particular, good Italian fare – pasta, superior burgers and bruschettas.

Ravnkloa Fish Market
SEAFOOD €

(Munkegata; ⊙10am-5pm Mon-Sat) You can munch on inexpensive fish cakes and other finny fare at this excellent, informal place, which also sells an impressive range of cheeses and other gourmet fare.

🍷 Drinking

As a student town, Trondheim offers lots of through-the-night life. The free papers, *Natt & Dag* and *Plan B,* have listings, mostly in Norwegian. Solsiden (Sunnyside) is Trondheim's trendiest leisure zone. A whole wharfside of bars and restaurants nestle beneath smart new apartment blocks, converted warehouses and long-idle cranes.

⌐TOP⌐ Den Gode Nabo
CHOICE   PUB

(Øvre Bakklandet 66; www.dengodenabo.com, in Norwegian; mains Nkr140; ⊙1pm-1am) The Good Neighbour, dark and cavernous within and nominated more than once as Norway's best pub, enjoys a prime riverside location. Indeed, part of it's on the water; reserve a table on the floating pontoon. There's a reproduction Wurlitzer jukebox, US visitors will find Sam Adams on draft while UK ale connoisseurs can savour Shepherd Neame's Bishop's Finger in the bottle.

Trondheim Microbryggeri
PUB

(Prinsens gate 39) This splendid home-brew pub deserves a pilgrimage as reverential as anything accorded to St Olav from all committed øl (beer) quaffers. With up to eight of its own brews on tap and good light meals (around Nkr150) coming from the kitchen, it's a place to linger, nibble and tipple. It's down a short lane, just off Prinsens gate.

Bruk Bar
BAR

(Prinsens gate 19; ⊙11am-1.30am) Inside, a stuffed elk head gazes benignly down, candles flicker and designer lamps shed light onto the 30-or-so-year-olds who patronise this welcoming joint. The music is eclectic, varying at the whim of bar staff, but guaranteed loud.

Rick's Café
BAR

(Nordre gate 11; ⊙from 11am) The ground floor here is all edgy stainless steel while upstairs, more for quiet cocktails and lingering wines, has sink-down-deep leatherette sofas and armchairs. The weekend nightclub in the basement has two zones – one for rock, the other playing house.

Studentersamfundet
STUDENT CENTRE

(Student Centre; Elgesetergate 1) During the academic year, it has 10 lively bars, a cinema and frequent live music, while in summer it's mostly a travellers' crash pad.

☆ Entertainment

There's a cluster of clubs, including Clash, Gossip and Juba Juber, at the northern end of Nordre gate.

Dokkhuset
CAFE, CULTURAL CENTRE

(⊙11am-1am Mon-Thu, 11am-3am Fri & Sat, 1pm-1am Sun) In an artistically converted former pumping station (look through the glass beneath your feet at the old engines), the Dock House is at once auditorium (where if it's the right night you'll hear experimental jazz or chamber music), restaurant and cafe-bar. Sip a drink on the jetty or survey the Trondheim scene from its roof terrace.

Olavshallen
CONCERT HALL

(☎73 99 40 50; Kjøpmannsgata 44) Trondheim's main concert hall is within the Olavskvartalet cultural centre. The home base of the Trondheim Symphony Orchestra, it also features international rock and jazz concerts, mostly between September and May.

Frakken
CLUB

(Dronningens gate 12; ⊙6pm-3am) This multistorey nightclub and piano bar features both Norwegian and foreign musicians and has live music nightly.

ℹ Information

Tourist office (☎73 80 76 60; www.trondheim.no; Torvet; ⊙8.30am-8pm Mon-Fri, 10am-6pm Sat & Sun late Jun–mid-Aug, 8.30am-6pm Mon-Fri, 10am-4pm Sat & Sun late May-late Jun & mid–late Aug, 9am-4pm Mon-Fri, 10am-2pm Sat rest of yr)

ⓘ Getting There & Away

Air

Værnes airport, 32km east of Trondheim, has both domestic and international flights.

Boat

Trondheim is a major stop on the *Hurtigruten* coastal ferry route.

Bus

The intercity bus terminal (Rutebilstasjon) adjoins Trondheim Sentralstasjon (train station, also known as Trondheim S). Nor-Way Bussekspress services run up to three times daily to/from Ålesund (Nkr596, seven hours) via Molde (Nkr450, five hours) and daily to/from Bergen (Nkr790, 14½ hours).

Train

There are two to four trains daily to/from Oslo (Nkr810, 6½ hours), while two head north to Bodø (Nkr982, 9¾ hours). You can also train it to Steinkjer (Nkr186, two hours, hourly).

ⓘ Getting Around

To/From the Airport

Flybussen (Nkr90; 45 min) runs every 15 minutes from 4am to 9pm (less frequently at weekends), stopping at major landmarks such as the train station, Studentersamfundet and Britannia Hotel.

Trains run between Trondheim Sentralstasjon and the Værnes airport station (Nkr64, 35 minutes, hourly).

Bicycle

As befits such a cycle-friendly city, Trondheim has a bike-hire scheme (Nkr70 per 24 hours). Pick up a card at the tourist office in return for a refundable deposit of Nkr200, then borrow a bike from any of 12 cycle stations around town.

Car & Motorcycle

There's a toll of Nkr60 every time you enter or leave central Trondheim. Pay up or you risk a steep fine.

Bodø

POP 47,300

Travellers generally use Bodø as a gateway to the Lofoten Islands and elsewhere in Nordland. Most get off their boat or train, poke around for a few hours and then get on the first ferry. Those that linger tend to do so to behold Saltstraumen (p384), one of the world's most impressive maelstroms.

The city's harbour is picturesque and chock-full of small fishing vessels, with steep granite islands rising behind. The town, hurriedly rebuilt after thorough destruction in WWII, is not. Even so, you'll find a pass-

---

MIDNIGHT SUN & POLAR NIGHT

Because Earth is tilted on its axis, polar regions are constantly facing the sun at their respective summer solstices and are tilted away from it in the winter. The Arctic Circle, at 66° north latitude, is the northern limit of constant daylight on its longest day of the year.

The northern half of mainland Norway, as well as Svalbard and Jan Mayen island, lie north of the Arctic Circle but, even in southern Norway, the summer sun is never far below the horizon. Between late May and mid-August, nowhere in the country experiences true darkness. Conversely, winters here are dark, dreary and long, with only a few hours of twilight to break the long polar nights.

TOWN/AREA	LATITUDE	MIDNIGHT SUN	POLAR NIGHT
Bodø	67° 18'	4 Jun to 8 Jul	15 Dec to 28 Dec
Svolvær	68° 15'	28 May to 14 Jul	5 Dec to 7 Jan
Narvik	68° 26'	27 May to 15 Jul	4 Dec to 8 Jan
Tromsø	69° 42'	20 May to 22 Jul	25 Nov to 17 Jan
Alta	70° 00'	16 May to 26 Jul	24 Nov to 18 Jan
Hammerfest	70° 40'	16 May to 27 Jul	21 Nov to 21 Jan
Nordkapp	71° 11'	13 May to 29 Jul	18 Nov to 24 Jan
Longyearbyen	78° 12'	20 Apr to 21 Aug	26 Oct to 16 Feb

Bodø

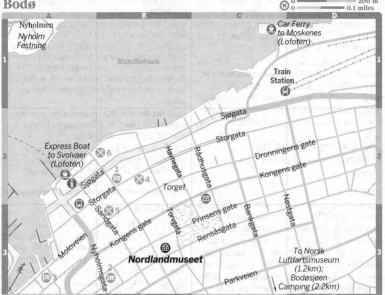

Map labels:
- Nyholmen
- Nyholm Festning
- Car Ferry to Moskenes (Lofoten)
- Rundholmen
- Train Station
- Sjøgata
- Storgata
- Dronningens gate
- Kongens gate
- Express Boat to Svolvaer (Lofoten)
- Havnegata
- Rådhusgata
- Torget
- Prinsens gate
- Bankgata
- Nestgata
- Sjøgata
- Storgata
- Sandgata
- Kongens gate
- Moloveien
- Nyholmsgata
- Torvgata
- Rensåsgata
- Nordlandmuseet
- To Norsk Luftfartsmuseum (1.2km); Bodøsjøen Camping (2.2km)
- Parkveien

able cafe, a brewery and the closest thing to nightlife for hundreds of kilometres.

⊙ Sights & Activities

Norsk Luftfartsmuseum MUSEUM OF FLIGHT
(www.luftfart.museum.no; Olav V gata; adult/child Nkr95/50; ⊙10am-6pm) Norway's aviation museum is huge fun to ramble around if you have even a passing interest in flight and aviation history. Allow at least half a day to roam its 10,000 sq metres. Exhibits include a complete control tower, hands-on demonstrations and a simulator.

Nordlandmuseet MUSEUM
(Prinsens gate 116; adult/child Nkr35/10; ⊙9am-4pm Mon-Fri, 11am-4pm Sat & Sun) Recounting the short history of Bodø, this little gem of a museum has a cheerily entertaining and informative 25-minute film with English subtitles on the town's development.

🛏 Sleeping

Skagen Hotel HOTEL €€
(☑75 51 91 00; www.skagen-hotel.no; Nyholmsgata 11; s/d from Nkr725/925; @) Rooms here are attractively decorated and a continent away from chain-hotel clones. There's a bar and free afternoon waffles and coffee. Staff can also give advice on a whole raft of vigorous outdoor activities.

Bodø

⊙ **Top Sights**

🛌 **Sleeping**

🍴 **Eating**

Clarion Collection Hotel Grand HOTEL €€
(☑75 54 61 00; www.choice.no; Storgata 3; s/d from Nkr795/980; P@) With the resources of the Glasshuset shopping centre right beside it and the shortest of strolls from the quayside, the Grand is well positioned. All rooms were radically overhauled in 2009 and have parquet flooring, new bedlinen and duvets and freshly tiled bathrooms with large sinks.

Bodøsjøen Camping CAMPING GROUND €
(☑75 56 36 80; www.bodocamp.no, in Norwegian; Kvernhusveien 1; tent/caravan site Nkr150/200 plus per person Nkr30, cabin Nkr690-840, without bathroom Nkr250-430) At this waterside

camping ground, 3km from the centre, cabins are particularly well equipped. There's an attractive grassy area with picnic tables exclusively for tent campers. Buses 12 and 23 stop 250m away.

Thon Hotel Nordlys   HOTEL €€
(☑75 53 19 00; www.thonhotels.no; Moloveien 14; s/d from Nkr850/1050) Bodø's most stylish hotel, with touches of subtle Scandinavian design throughout, overlooks the marina and runs a reasonable restaurant.

✕ Eating & Drinking

At the docks you can buy inexpensive fresh shrimp.

Kafé Kafka   CAFE €
(Sandgata 5B; daily specials with coffee Nkr125, sandwiches Nkr115; ⏲core hr 11am-1am Mon-Sat, 3pm-midnight Sun) You couldn't ask for a wider choice at this stylish contemporary cafe. It brews great coffee 12 different ways (you'll smell the aroma before you even enter) and swirls 18 distinct kinds of milkshake. Some weekends, it turns into a club with DJs.

Bjørk   CAFE-BAR €€€
(www.restaurantbjork.no, in Norwegian; 1st fl, Glasshuset; lunch specials Nkr150, mains around Nkr275) This pleasant place is a popular haunt, especially of Bodø's younger movers and shakers. It serves a variety of creative snacks, wood-fired pizzas and sushi.

Løvolds   SNACK BAR, CAFE €
(Tollbugata 9; dishes Nkr105-135, daily specials Nkr90-115; ⏲9am-6pm Mon-Fri, 9am-3pm Sat) This popular historic quayside cafeteria, Bodø's oldest eating choice, offers sandwiches, grills and hearty Norwegian fare with quality quayside views at no extra charge.

❶ Information

Backpacker Service (☑75 65 02 89; backpacker@nfk.no; Sjøgata 15-17; ⏲10am-6pm late Jun–mid-Aug; @) An excellent service that provides luggage storage, travel information, document printing, a couple of internet points, wi-fi, toilets and use of a tandem – every last one absolutely free.

Tourist office (☑75 54 80 00; www.visitbodo.com; Sjøgata 3; ⏲9am-8pm Mon-Fri, 10am-6pm Sat, noon-8pm Sun mid-May–Aug, 9am-3.30pm Mon-Fri rest of yr)

❶ Getting There & Around

AIR The airport is 2km away, with flights to Svolvær, Trondheim, Tromsø and more. Local buses (Nkr30) marked 'Sentrumsrunden' bring you to town.

BOAT Bodø is a stop on the *Hurtigruten* coastal ferry. Car ferries sail five to six times daily in summer (less frequently during the rest of the year) between Bodø and Moskenes on Lofoten (car including driver/passenger Nkr568/158, three to 3½ hours). At least one calls in daily at the tiny southern Lofoten islands of Røst and Værøy.

BUS The Nor-Way Bussekspress bus runs to/from Narvik (Nkr534, 6½ hours) via Fauske (Nkr114, 1½ hours) twice daily.

TRAIN Bodø is the northern terminus of the Norwegian train network, with a service to Trondheim (Nkr982, 10 hours, twice daily).

Around Bodø

The timber-built 19th-century trading station at sleepy Kjerringøy, by luminescent turquoise seas and soaring granite peaks 42km north of Bodø, is fantastically preserved as an open-air museum (☑75 50 35 00; www.kjerringoy.no; adult/child Nkr70/35; ⏲11am-5pm late May-late Aug) set on a sleepy peninsula. Buses run from Bodø to Kjerringøy (Nkr86, 1½ hours, one daily). In summer, it's possible to do a return trip on the same day.

The spectacular Saltstraumen Maelstrom, claimed to be the world's strongest, sufficiently boggles the mind (except on the rare off day when it appears about as powerful as a flushing toilet). At high tide an immense volume of water violently churns its whirlpool way through a 3km-long strait that empties one fjord into another. The spectacle occurs four times daily. Consult with the Bodø tourist office on when to arrive.

Narvik

POP 18,500

Narvik, whose waterfront is obliterated by a monstrous transhipment facility, is pincered by islands to the west and mountains in every other direction, while spectacular fjords stretch north and south.

◉ Sights

Water Spout   WATER SPOUT
No, Narvik can't claim geothermal activity. But locals reckon that its water is the purest in the land. Each day at 1pm and 9pm from May to September, a valve is released and a mighty, 75m-high plume of water spurts skywards.

Ofoten Museum · MUSEUM

(Administrasjonsveien 3; adult/child Nkr50/free; ☺10am-3pm or 4pm daily mid-Jun–mid-Aug, Mon-Fri rest of yr) This engaging folk museum tells of Narvik's farming, fishing, railway-building and ore trans-shipment heritage.

Red Cross War Museum · MUSEUM

(Kongens gate; adult/child Nkr50/25; ☺10am-4pm or 9pm Mon-Sat, noon-4pm or 6pm Sun) This small but revealing museum illustrates the military campaigns fought hereabouts in the early years of WWII. The presentation may not be flash but it will still move you.

✷ Activities

Narvikfjellet · CABLE CAR

(Mårveien; www.narvikfjellet.no; adult/child return Nkr100/free; ☺1-9pm or 1am Jun-Aug) Climbing 656m above town, the cable car offers breathtaking views over the surrounding peaks and fjords – even as far as Lofoten on a clear day. Several marked walking trails radiate from its top station or you can bounce down a signed mountain-bike route. From February to April, it will whisk you up high for trail, off-piste and cross-country skiing with outstanding views.

Rallarveien · HIKING TRAIL

This popular hike parallels the Ofotbanen railway, following the Rallarveien, an old navvy trail. Few walkers attempt the entire way between Sweden's Abisko National Park and the sea, opting instead to begin at Riksgränsen, the small ski station just across the Swedish border, or Bjørnfell, the next station west. It's an undemanding descent as far as Katterat, from where you can take the evening train to Narvik.

Fjord Cruise Narvik · BOAT TRIPS

(☎91 39 06 18; www.fcn.no) This outfit mounts summer fishing and sea-eagle viewing trips. From November to mid-January, when the orcas, or killer whales, gather to gorge themselves on the winter herring run, it runs trips to their feeding grounds in search of the action.

⊨ Sleeping

TOP CHOICE⟩ Norumgården Bed & Breakfast · B&B €

(☎76 94 48 57; http://norumgaarden.narvikinett.no; Framnesveien 127; s/d Nkr450/600, d with kitchen Nkr600; ☺late Jan–Nov) This little treasure of a place (it has only four rooms, so reserva-

tions are essential) offers excellent value. Used as a German officer's mess in WWII (the owner will proudly show you a 1940 bottle of Coca-Cola, made under licence in Hamburg), it nowadays brims with antiques and character.

Spor 1 Gjestegård · HOSTEL/GUESTHOUSE €

(☎76 94 60 20; www.spor1.no; Brugata 2a; dm Nkr230, s/d without bathroom Nkr500/600) This delightful place has the facilities of the best of hostels (especially the gleaming, well-equipped guest kitchen) and the comfort and taste of a guesthouse (bright, cheerful fabrics and decor and soft duvets). Next door and run by the same family is a great pub (☺Tue-Sat) with outdoor terrace.

Breidablikk Gjestehus · GUESTHOUSE €€

(☎76 94 14 18; www.breidablikk.no, in Norwegian; Tore Hunds gate 41; dm/s/d from Nkr250/995/1195; P@) It's a steep but worthwhile walk from the centre to this pleasant hillside guesthouse with rooms for all budgets and sweeping views over town and fjord. There's a cosy communal lounge and it serves a delicious buffet breakfast (Nkr50).

Best Western Narvik Hotell · HOTEL €€

(☎76 96 48 00; www.narvikhotell.no; Skistuaveien 8; s/d from Nkr850/1050; P@) This 90-room tour-group favourite, stretching long and low at the base of the cable car, offers great vistas. Accommodation is in comfortable chalet-type buildings.

✗ Eating

Fiskehallen · FISH CAFE €

(Kongens gate 42; mains Nkr80-150; ☺11am-4.30pm Mon-Fri) This tiny cafe, offshoot of the adjacent fish shop, offers tasty ready-to-eat dishes, such as fish cakes, bacalao and whale stew, to eat in or take away.

Rallar'n · BAR RESTAURANT €€€

(Kongens gate 64; daily specials NKr145, mains Nkr200-295; ☺1pm-1am) The pub/restaurant of the Quality Hotel Grand Royal is all atmospheric low ceilings, bare brick and dark woodwork. Divided into intimate compartments, it offers pizza, pasta and creative mains.

❶ Information

Tourist office (☎76 96 56 00; www.destinationnarvik.com; ☺9am-6pm Mon-Fri, 10am-5.30pm Sat & Sun mid-Jun–mid-Aug, variable hr rest of yr)

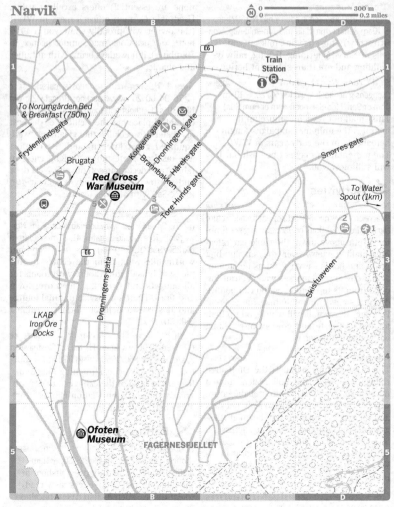

ℹ Getting There & Away

AIR Nearly all flights leave from Harstad/Narvik Evenes airport, 1¼ hours away by road. Narvik's tiny Framneslia airport, about 3km west of the centre, serves only Bodø, Tromsø and Andenes.

BUS Express buses run northwards to Tromsø (Nkr360, 4¼ hours, three daily) and south to Bodø (Nkr534, 6½ hours, two daily). For Lofoten, two Lofotekspressen buses run daily between Narvik and Svolvær (Nkr225 or Nkr425, 4¼ hours) and continue to Å. Between late June and early September, bus 91 runs twice a day up the E10 to Riksgränsen (45 minutes) in Sweden and on to Abisko and Kiruna (three hours).

Around Narvik

The spectacular mountain-hugging **Ofotbanen railway** (☏76 92 31 21) trundles beside fjordside cliffs, birch forests and rocky plateaux as it climbs to the Swedish border. Constructed by migrant labourers (navvies) at the end of the 19th century to connect Narvik with the iron-ore mines at Kiruna, in Sweden's far north, it was opened in 1903.

The train route from Narvik to Riksgränsen, the ski resort just inside Sweden (one way adult/child Nkr100/free, one hour), features some 50 tunnels and snowsheds.

Narvik

⊙ Top Sights

Activities, Courses & Tours

⊙ Sleeping

⊗ Eating

In Sweden, several long-distance trails radiate out from the railway, including the world-renowned Kungsleden, which heads south from Abisko into the heart of Sweden.

Lofoten

You'll never forget your first approach to the Lofoten Islands by ferry, especially if you've sailed from Bodø. The islands spread their tall, craggy physique against the sky like some spiky sea dragon and you wonder how humans eked a living in such inhospitable surroundings.

The main islands, Austvågøy, Vestvågøy, Flakstadøy and Moskenesøy, are separated from the mainland by Vestfjorden. On each are sheltered bays, sheep pastures and picturesque villages. The vistas and the special quality of the Arctic light have long attracted artists, represented in galleries throughout the islands.

But Lofoten is still very much commercially alive. Each winter the meeting of the Gulf Stream and the icy Arctic Ocean draws spawning Arctic cod from the Barents Sea. Although cod stocks have dwindled dramatically in recent years, fishing still vies with tourism as Lofoten's largest industry.

The four main islands are all linked by bridges or tunnels, with buses running the entire length of the Lofoten road (E10) from Fiskebøl in the north to Å at road's end in the southwest.

Tourist information is available at www.lofoten.info.

SVOLVÆR
POP 4400

A compact town of old wooden buildings and modern concrete blocks, Lofoten's principal town might be two notches less picturesque than its brothers, but it's still a pretty spot from which to base your explorations, with steep mountains rising sharply in the background and a busy harbour.

⊙ Sights & Activities

Hiking & Climbing   HIKING, CLIMBING

Daredevils like to scale Svolværgeita (the Svolvær Goat), a distinctive, two-pronged peak visible from the harbour, and then jump the 1.5m from one horn to the other – a graveyard at the bottom awaits those who miss. For phenomenal views, hikers can ascend the steep path to the base of the Goat and up the slopes behind it. There's also a rough route from the Goat over to the extraordinary Devil's Gate; ask the tourist office for details.

Trollfjord   BOAT CRUISE

(adult/child Nkr450/200) From the port, several competing companies offer sailings into the constricted confines of nearby Trollfjord, spectacularly steep and narrowing to only 100m. Take the three-hour cruise or sign on for a four-hour trip that includes the chance to dangle a line and bring home supper; the price is the same. Buy your ticket at the quayside.

Cycling   CYCLING

For 83km of breathtaking cycling, head to Holandshamn and make your way back to Svolvær along the Kaiser Route. Lonely shoreline, jagged mountains and abandoned farms will be your constant companion. Unlike the west side of Lofoten, this trip takes in parts of the islands that are largely undiscovered by tourists. A long stretch runs parallel to the Trollfjord.

Magic Ice   ICE BAR

(Fiskergata 36; adult/child Nkr95/65; ⊙noon-10.30pm mid-Jun–mid-Aug, 6-10pm rest of yr) Housed, appropriately, in what was once a fish-freezing plant, this is the ultimate place to chill out, perhaps with something to warm the spirit, served in an ice glass. The 500-sq-metre space is filled with huge ice sculptures, which illustrate life in Lofoten.

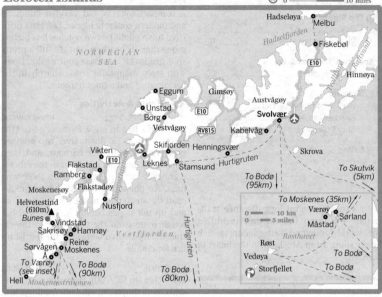

🛏 Sleeping & Eating

TOP CHOICE **Svolvær Sjøhuscamp**　SEA HOUSE €
(☎76 07 03 36; www.svolver-sjohuscamp.no; Parkgata 12; d/q Nkr540/800, d with kitchen Nkr690, all with shared bathroom) This friendly sea house straddling the water is a convivial, excellent-value place to fetch up and meet fellow travellers. There's also a gem of an apartment with balcony and full facilities (Nkr1900) that sleeps up to six.

Rica Hotel Svolvær　HOTEL €€
(☎76 07 22 22; www.rica.no; Lamholmen; s/d Nkr1195/1445; @) The Rica is built on a tiny island, above the water and supported by piles. Some rooms have balconies, while room 121 has a hole in the floor so guests in the adjacent room can drop a fishing line directly into the briny. The restaurant has attractive lightweight wooden furnishings and does a gargantuan dinner buffet (Nkr295).

Norden & Du Verden　CAFE, RESTAURANT €€
(☎76 07 70 99; www.duverden.net) Sharing premises and kitchen, these two eateries complement each other. Norden, open daily, has an airy, modern interior and waterfront terrace. It's a very congenial cafe-restaurant serving lunches of salads and sandwiches

(around Nkr150) and dinner (mains Nkr265 to Nkr290), where the house speciality is sushi. To the rear, Du Verden – open only for dinner, bookings strongly recommended – offers fine gourmet dining in a more intimate ambience with a set menu (from Nkr435) of between three and 10 courses.

Kjøkkenet　NORWEGIAN €€€
(Lamholmen; mains Nkr300-325) Kjøkkenet, originally a shack for salting fish and nowadays furnished like an old-time kitchen, is a wonderfully cosy place to dine. The cuisine is just as traditional and the recommended menu choice is of course fish – try the kitchen's signature dish, *boknafisk*, semi-dried cod with salted fat and vegetables.

Svinøya Rorbuer　CABINS €€
(☎76 06 99 30; www.svinoya.no; Gunnar Bergs vei 2; 2-/4-bed cabin from Nkr1200/1600) Across a bridge on the islet of Svinøya, site of Svolvær's first settlement, are several cabins, some historic, most contemporary, and all cosy and comfortable.

❶ Information

Tourist office (☎76 06 98 07; www.lofoten. info; Torget; ⊙9am-8pm or 10pm mid-Jun–Jul) Provides information on the entire archipelago.

ⓘ Getting There & Away

AIR Svolvær has a small airport (4km from town) where you can catch flights to Bodø.

BOAT Express boats ply the waters between Svolvær and Bodø (Nkr324, 3½ hours, one daily) and the *Hurtigruten* stops here.

BUS Buses to/from Vesterålen travel between Svolvær and Sortland (Nkr165, 2¼ hours, three to five daily). Buses to Leknes (Nkr134, 1½ hours, four to six daily) make connections to Å (Nkr242, 3½ hours, two to four daily), stopping at points west. Express buses run between Svolvær and Narvik (Nkr225, 4½ hours, two daily).

KABELVÅG

If you got off the boat and thought Svolvær's blend of traditional and modern wasn't cute enough, this pleasing village lies only 5km west and is connected by the E10 and a paved walking trail. Narrow channels lined with old warehouses lead to the circular cobbled *torget* (town square), whose pattern of paving recalls the hulls of small fishing boats, themselves docked nearby.

◎ Sights & Activities

Behind the old prison, a trail leads uphill to the statue of King Øystein, who in 1120 ordered the first *rorbu* to be built to house fishermen who had been sleeping under their overturned rowing boats.

Some of these original *rorbuer* have been excavated as part of the Lofotmuseet (www.lofotmuseet.no; adult/child Nkr60/25; ◎9am-6pm Jun-Aug; 9am-3pm Mon-Fri rest of yr), a regional history museum on the site of the first town in the polar regions.

Nearby, the seafront Lofoten Aquarium (www.lofotakvariet.no; adult/child Nkr110/55; ◎10am-6pm Jun-Aug, 11am-3pm Sun-Fri Feb-May & Sep-Nov) shows you some of the personalities that have made Lofoten great, including the heroic cod and some harbour seals in an outdoor tank.

🛏 Sleeping & Eating

Kabelvåg Hotell HOTEL **€€**
(☑76 07 88 00; www.kabelvaghotell.no, in Norwegian; Kong Øysteinsgate 4; summer s/d Nkr990/1410, winter full board Nkr1195; ◎Jun-mid-Aug & late Feb-Apr) On a small rise close to the centre of Kabelvåg, this imposing seasonal hotel has been tastefully rebuilt in its original art deco style. Rooms overlook either the port or mountains. It also functions as a centre for skiing and a host of other winter activities.

Nyvågar Rorbuhotell CABINS **€€€**
(☑76 06 97 00; www.nyvagar.no, in Norwegian; Storvåganveien 22; 4-bed rorbu incl breakfast Nkr2000) At Storvågan, below the museum complex, this snazzy, modern seaside place owes nothing to history, but its strictly contemporary *rorbuer* are attractive and fully equipped. Its acclaimed Lorchstua restaurant (mains Nkr175-300, 3-course menus Nkr395) serves primarily local specialities with a subtle twist, such as baked fillet of halibut in a cod brandade.

Ørsvågvær Camping CAMPING GROUND **€**
(☑76 07 81 80; www.orsvag.no; car/caravan site Nkr150/190, 4-bed cabin Nkr850, 7-bed sea house apt Nkr1150; ◎May-Sep) Most *rorbuer* and the sea house are right beside the fjord and offer splendid views.

Præstengbrygga PUB, CAFE **€€**
(Torget; mains around Nkr150) In central Kabelvåg, this friendly pub with all-wood interior and dockside terracing, front and rear, serves sandwiches, pizzas and tasty mains.

HENNINGSVÆR

A delightful 8km shore-side drive southwards from the E10 brings you to the still-active fishing village of Henningsvær, perched at the end of a thin promontory. Its nickname, 'the Venice of Lofoten', may be a tad overblown but it's certainly the lightest, brightest and trendiest place in the archipelago. It's also the region's largest and most active fishing port.

◎ Sights & Activities

Ocean Sounds WHALE CENTRE
(☑91 84 20 12; www.ocean-sounds.com; Hjellskjæret; adult/child Nkr200/free; ◎2-6pm Jul-mid-Aug, on request mid-Apr-Jun & mid-Aug-Oct) Beside the Henningsvær Bryggehotel, this not-for-profit research centre has a series of multimedia presentations about cod, whales and other Arctic marine mammals. Or get out and about on a three- to four-hour marine safari in the Zodiac research boat (adult/child Nkr800/600, daily departures, weather permitting).

North Norwegian Climbing School CLIMBING SCHOOL
(Nord Norsk Klatreskole; ☑90 57 42 08; www.nordnorskklatreskole.no, in Norwegian; Misværveien 10; ◎Mar-Oct) This outfit offers a wide range of technical climbing and skiing courses all around northern Norway. Climbing the peaks with an experienced guide costs Nkr2000, including equipment, for one to four people.

Lofoten Adventure OUTDOOR TOURS & ACTIVITIES
(☑90 58 14 75; www.lofoten-opplevelser.no) Based in Henningsvær, this outfit offers a cluster of maritime tours and activities between mid-June and mid-August. Advance booking is essential.

Sea-eagle safari 2.30pm, adult/child Nkr430/330, 1½ hours

Midnight safari 10pm, adult/child Nkr650/500, 2½ hours

Snorkelling 11am, Nkr650, two hours; equipment provided

Whale safaris on demand, Nkr850, three hours; November to mid-January

🛏 Sleeping & Eating

Henningsvær Bryggehotel HOTEL €€€
(☑76 07 47 19; www.henningsvaer.no; Hjellskjæret; s/d from Nkr1070/1500) Overlooking the harbour, this attractive hotel is Henningsvær's finest choice. It's modern, with comfortable rooms furnished in contemporary design, yet constructed in a traditional style that blends harmoniously with its neighbours. **Bluefish**, its award-winning restaurant, is just as stylish; serving Arctic Menu dishes and delicious desserts.

ℹ Information

Tourist office (☑91 24 57 02; www.hennings var.com; ⊙10am-6pm Mon-Fri, 11am-4pm Sat & Sun mid-Jun–mid-Nov)

ℹ Getting There & Away

In summer, bus 510 shuttles between Svolvær (40 minutes), Kabelvåg (35 minutes) and Henningsvær 10 times on weekdays (three services Saturday and Sunday).

LOFOTR VIKINGMUSEUM

This 83m-long chieftain's hall, Norway's largest Viking building, has been excavated at Borg, near the centre of Vestvågøy. The **museum** (www.lofotr.no; adult/child incl guided tour Nkr120/60; ⊙10am-4pm or 7pm May–mid-Sep) offers an insight into Viking life, complete with a scale-model reconstruction of the building, guides in Viking costume and a replica Viking ship, which you can sometimes help row.

The Svolvær–Leknes bus passes the museum's entrance.

STAMSUND

POP 1000

The traditional fishing village of Stamsund makes a fine destination largely because of its dockside hostel, a magnet for travellers who sometimes stay for weeks on end. Here,

as elsewhere on Lofoten, highlights include hiking and fishing. A popular town activity is to stare at the *Hurtigruten*'s approach.

The wonderful old beach house **Justad Rorbuer og Vandrerhjem** (☑76 08 93 34; www.hihostels.no/stamsund; dm/s/d without bathroom Nkr135/335/445, 4-bed cabin Nkr550-850; ⊙Mar–mid-Oct), 1.2km from the quay, attracts many repeat customers drawn by the waterside building, friendly manager (ask about hiking routes) and free loans of fishing gear and rowing boats. Bike rentals cost Nkr80 to Nkr100 per day.

The *Hurtigruten* coastal steamer stops en route between Bodø and Svolvær. In July and August, buses from Leknes to Stamsund (25 minutes) run three to eight times daily.

REINE

Reine is a characterless place but gosh, it looks splendid from above, beside its placid lagoon and backed by the sheer rock face of Reinebringen. You get a great view from the head of the road that drops to the village from the E10.

From June to mid-August, **Aqua Lofoten** (www.aqualofoten.com) runs three-hour **boat trips** (adult/child Nkr550/400) to the bird- and fish-rich Moskstraumen maelstrom.

In summer, the **MS Fjordskyss** (www.reinef-jorden.no, in Norwegian) runs between Reine and Vindstad (adult/child return Nkr120/60, 25 minutes, three daily) through scenic Reine-fjord. From Vindstad, it's a one-hour hike across the ridge to the abandoned beachside settlement of **Bunes**, in the shadow of the brooding 610m **Helvetestind** rock slab.

Hamnøy Mat og Vinbu (☑76 09 21 45; Hamnøy; mains Nkr175-225; ⊙May-early Sep) is a family-run place that serves stellar local specialities, including whale, bacalao and cod tongues. Grandmother takes care of the traditional dishes – just try her fish cakes – while her son is the main chef. Its fish is of the freshest, bought daily from the harbour barely 100m away.

All buses from Leknes to Å stop in Reine.

SAKRISØY

Pretty as Reine is, you'll find it hard to suppress the urge to jump out of your bus or car to snap a few pictures of its rival for visual perfection: in this instance an incredibly charming and quiet village of ochre buildings set on some rocky outcroppings and surrounded by water, mountains and cod drying racks. Here you can gawk at the scenery, grab a dockside fish cake, visit the **Museum of Dolls & Toys** (Dagmars Dukke og Leketøy Museum; adult/child Nkr50/25; ⏱10am-6pm or 8pm late May-Aug), and sleep amid the postcard setting in a fine *robuer* at Sakrisøy Rorbuer (☎76 09 21 43; www.lofoten. ws; cabin Nkr745-1640).

Sakrisøy is 1km west of Reine towards Hamnøy.

Å

Å is a very special place at what feels like the end of the world on the western tip of Lofoten. A preserved fishing village perched on forbidding rocks connected by wooden footbridges, its shoreline is lined with red-painted *rorbuer,* many of which jut into the sea. Racks of drying cod and picture-postcard scenes occur at almost every turn. Visitors enliven the tiny place in summer, while in winter it's stark, haunting and empty.

☉ Sights & Activities

Lofoten Tørrfiskmuseum MUSEUM
(adult/child Nkr50/30; ⏱11am-4pm or 5pm Jun-Aug) The Lofoten Stockfish Museum is housed in a former fish warehouse. You'll be bowled over by its enthusiastic, polyglot owner, who meets and greets every visitor. This personal collection, a passionate hobby of owner Steinar Larsen, illustrates well Lofoten's traditional mainstay: the catching and drying of cod for export, particularly to Italy.

Norsk Fiskeværsmuseum MUSEUM
(adult/child Nkr50/25; ⏱10am-6pm mid-Jun–mid-Aug, 11am-3.30pm Mon-Fri rest of yr) What is called collectively the Norwegian Fishing Village Museum is in fact a fair proportion of this hamlet: 14 of Å's 19th-century boathouses, storehouses, fishing cottages, farmhouses and commercial buildings.

Moskenesstraumen MAELSTROM
Walk to the camping ground at the end of the village for a good hillside view of Værøy island, which lies on the other side of Moskenesstraumen, the swirling maelstrom that inspired the fictional tales of Jules Verne and Edgar Allen Poe.

🛏 Sleeping & Eating

Å-Hamna Rorbuer & Vandrerhjem HOSTEL €
(☎76 09 12 11; www.lofotenferie.com; hostel s/d/t/q Nkr300/400/540/720, 4-8-bed rorbuer with bathroom Nkr800-1200) Sleep simple, sleep in more comfort; either way, this is an attrac-

tive choice. Newly affiliated to Hostelling International, it has dorms above the Stockfish Museum and in a quiet villa, set in its garden. For more space and privacy, choose one of the restored fishing huts.

Moskenesstraumen Camping CAMPING GROUND €
(☎76 09 11 48; camping for 1/2/3 persons Nkr90/140/180, caravans Nkr200, 2-/4-bed cabin from Nkr450/650, with bathroom Nkr650/750; ⏱Jun-Aug) This wonderful clifftop campground, just south of the village, has flat, grassy pitches between the rocks, just big enough for your bivouac. Cabins too have great views, as far as the mainland on clear days.

Brygga restaurant SEAFOOD €€€
(☎76 09 15 72; mains Nkr200-315, menus Nkr425, bar lunch specials Nkr125; ⏱Jun-Sep) Hovering above the water, this is Å's one decent dining choice. The menu, as is right and proper in a village with such a strong fishing tradition, is mainly of things with fins.

Å Rorbuer FISHERMAN'S HUT €€
(☎76 09 11 21; www.lofoten-rorbu.com, in Norwegian; old sea house d/tr/q per person Nkr250, new sea house d Nkr780, 2-6 person rorbuer Nkr1350-2300) *Rorbuer* accommodation is dispersed throughout Å's historic buildings, the more expensive ones are fully equipped and furnished with antiques.

ⓘ Getting There & Away

BOAT Car ferries sail five to six times daily in summer (less frequently during the rest of the year) between Moskenes (5km north of Å) and Bodø (car including driver/passenger Nkr568/158, 3½ hours).

BUS Four to five buses connect Leknes and Å daily in summer, stopping in all major villages along the E10.

VÆRØY & RØST
POP 1400

Craggy, high and rugged, Værøy has a handful of residents hugely outnumbered by 100,000 nesting seabirds. **Hiking trails** take in some of the more spectacular seabird rookeries. The main trail goes along the west coast, beginning about 300m past the island's airstrip, and continues south all the way to the virtually deserted fishing village of Måstad, passing by steep cliffs, sandy beaches and isolated settlements. This 10km hike makes for a full day's outing and is not too strenuous, but it's exposed to the elements, so is best done in fair weather.

In contrast to pointy Værøy, Røst, to the south, is pancake flat. Access to the best birdwatching requires a boat, as the largest rookeries are on offshore islands. Kårøy Rorbucamping can arrange five-hour boat trips (adult/child Nkr300/125) that cruise past major seabird colonies (especially puffins) and stop at an 1887 lighthouse and a vista point. En route it's common to see seals, and there are occasional sightings of orcas. Other than the boat trip, there's not much to do.

🛏 Sleeping & Eating

Kårøy Rorbucamping   CAMPING GROUND €
(☑76 09 62 38; www.karoy.no; per person Nkr180; ☺May–mid-Sep; @) Rooms sleep two, four or six at this authentic *rorbu*. Bathrooms are communal and there are self-catering facilities. You can borrow a rowing boat for free or rent a motor boat. This great budget choice is on the minuscule island of Kårøy; phone from the ferry and a boat will be sent to collect you.

Røst Bryggehotel   HOTEL €€
(☑76 05 08 00; www.rostbryggehotell.no; d Nkr750 Jul–mid-Aug, Nkr900 rest of yr) This modern development in traditional style is right on the quayside. It has 16 comfortable doubles, and hires out bikes, boats and fishing tackle.

Querini Pub og Restaurant   PUB, RESTAURANT €
(☑76 09 64 80) Named after the shipwrecked merchant from Venice, this is a reliable choice among Røst's few eating options.

❶ Getting There & Away

Røst, like Værøy, is served by the car ferry that runs between Bodø (passenger/car Nkr178/647) and Moskenes (passenger/car Nkr125/446).

Vesterålen

Although the landscapes here aren't as dramatic as those in Lofoten, they tend to be much wilder and the forested mountainous regions of the island of Hinnøya are a unique corner of Norway's largely treeless northern coast.

◎ Sights & Activities

Hurtigrutemuseet   MUSEUM
(www.hurtigrutemuseet.no; Markedsgata 1; adult/child Nkr90/35; ☺10am-6pm mid-Jun–mid-Aug, core hr 2-4pm rest of yr) The *Hurtigruten* coastal ferry was founded in Stokmarknes in 1893 and the Hurtigruten Museum portrays the history of the line in text and image. Hitched to the quayside is the retired ship M/S *Finnmarken,* claimed to be the world's largest museum piece, which plied the coastal route between 1956 and 1993.

Nyksund   VILLAGE
(www.nyksund-info.com) Nyksund, on Langøya, is a former abandoned fishing village that's now re-emerging as an artists' colony. There's a great walk over the headland from Nyksund to Stø (three hours return), at the northernmost tip of Langøya.

Arctic Whale Tours   WHALE-WATCHING
(☑76 13 43 00; www.arcticwhaletours.com; adult/child Nkr795/500) From the small, distinctive fishing village of Stø on Langøya's northernmost tip, boats run from late May to mid-September for six-hour whale-watching cruises. On the way to the sperm whales' feeding grounds, boats pause to view seabird and seal colonies.

Whale Safari   WHALE-WATCHING
(☑76 11 56 00; www.whalesafari.no; Andenes; adult/child Nkr830/500) Far and away the island's biggest outfit, Whale Safari runs popular whale-watching cruises between late May and mid-September. It also operates the Whale Centre. Tours include a two- to four-hour boat trip and if you fail to sight at least one sperm whale, your money is refunded or you can take another trip for free. There's a good chance of spotting minke, pilot, humpback and killer whales (orcas).

Hvalsenteret   WHALE CENTRE
(Havnegate 1; adult/child Nkr40/20; ☺8.30am-4pm or 8pm late May–mid-Sep) The Whale Centre in Andenes provides a perspective for whale-watchers, with displays on whale research, hunting and the life cycle of these gentle monsters. Most people visit the centre in conjunction with a Whale Safari.

Northern Lights Centre   NORTHERN LIGHTS EXHIBITION
(☺10am-6pm late Jun-late Aug) This impressive hi-tech aurora borealis exhibition in Andenes first featured at the 1994 Winter Olympics in Lillehammer.

🛏 Sleeping & Eating

Sjøhus Senteret   GUESTHOUSE, CABINS €€
(☑76 12 37 40; www.lofoten-info.no/sjohussen
teret; Ånstadsjøen; d/tr Nkr770/870, 3-/5-bed
cabin Nkr1345/2000) Precisely 1.4km north of
the bridge in Sortland, this appealing spot
has both comfortable rooms and waterside
cabins with views. Its **Sjøstua restaurant** (mains Nkr200-235; ⊙3-9.30pm Mon-Sat,
1-8.30pm Sun) produces a delightful range of
à la carte dishes.

Holmvik Brygge   GUESTHOUSE, CAFE €€
(☑76 13 47 96; www.nyksund.com; s/d Nkr450/800;
⊙year-round) This cosy, hugely welcoming
guesthouse and cafe in itself justifies the detour. You can either cater for yourself or eat
at its **Holmvik Stua** (lunch Nkr95-220, dinner
Nkr165-365), where the food's locally sourced
and the fish smoked on the premises.

📍 **Hotell Marena**   BOUTIQUE HOTEL €€
(☑91 58 35 17; www.hotellmarena.no; Storgata 15;
s/d incl breakfast Nkr860/1090) Hotell Marena
is an exciting and particularly tasteful recent
addition to Andenes accommodation choices. The 12 bedrooms have been individually
designed with colours that match the tones
of the blown-up photographs.

❶ Information

Andenes tourist office (☑76 14 12 03; www.
andoyturist.no; Hamnegata 1; ⊙9am-6pm mid-
Jun–Aug, 8am-3pm Mon-Fri rest of yr; @)
Sortland tourist office (☑76 11 14 80; www.
visitvesteralen.com; Kjøpmannsgata 2; ⊙9am-
5.30pm Mon-Fri, 10am-3.45pm Sat, noon-
3.45pm Sun mid-Jun–mid-Aug, 9am-2.30pm
Mon-Fri rest of yr) Covers the whole of the
Vesterålen region.

❶ Getting There & Away

Vesterålen is connected by ferry from Melbu on
Hadseløya, to Fiskebøl on Austvågøy (Lofoten).
Sortland is the main transport hub in Vesterålen.
Both Sortland and Stokmarknes are stops for
the *Hurtigruten* coastal steamer.

Tromsø

POP 67,300

Simply put, Tromsø parties. By far the largest town in northern Norway and administrative centre of Troms county, it's lively with
cultural bashes, buskers, an animated street
scene, a midnight-sun marathon, a respected university, the hallowed Mack Brewery –

and more pubs per capita than any other
Norwegian town. Its corona of snow-topped
peaks provides arresting scenery, excellent
hiking in summer and great skiing and dog-
sledding in winter.

Although the city lies almost 400km
north of the Arctic Circle, its climate is pleasantly moderated by the Gulf Stream. The
long winter darkness is offset by round-the-
clock activity during the perpetually bright
days of summer.

◉ Sights

Tromsø's city centre and airport are on the
island of Tromsøya, which is linked by bridges to overspill suburbs on both the mainland
and the much larger outer island Kvaløya.
Storgata is the principal drag.

Polaria   INTERPRETIVE CENTRE
(Hjalmar Johansens gate 12; www.polaria.no; adult/
child Nkr100/50; ⊙10am-7pm) Daringly designed Polaria is an entertaining, informative, multimedia introduction to northern
Norway and Svalbard. After a lush 14-
minute film about the latter (screened every
30 minutes), an Arctic walk leads to an aurora borealis display, aquariums of cold-water
fish and – the big draw – a trio of energetic
bearded seals.

Polar Museum   MUSEUM
(Polarmuseet; www.polarmuseum.no; Søndre Tollbodgata 11; adult/child Nkr60/10; ⊙10am-7pm
mid-Jun–mid-Aug, 11am-3pm or 5pm rest of yr)
The 1st floor of this harbourside museum,
in a restored early-19th-century customs
house, illustrates early polar research, especially the ventures of Nansen and Amundsen. Downstairs there's a well-mounted exhibition about the hunting and trapping of
fuzzy Arctic creatures on Svalbard.

Ishavskatedralen   CHURCH
(www.ishavskatedralen.no; Hans Nilsensvei 41;
adult/child Nkr30/free; ⊙9am-7pm Mon-Sat,
1-7pm Sun) The 11 arching triangles of the
Arctic Cathedral (1965), as the Tromsdalen
Church is more usually called, suggest glacial crevasses and auroral curtains. The
magnificent glowing stained-glass window
that occupies almost the whole of the east
end depicts Christ re-descending to earth.
Take bus 20 or 24.

Tromsø University Museum   MUSEUM
(Lars Thøringsvei 10; adult/child Nkr30/15; ⊙9am-
4.30pm or 6pm) Near the southern end of
Tromsøya, this museum has well-presented

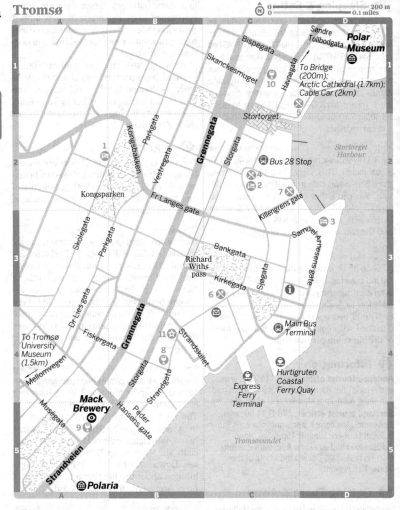

displays on traditional and modern Sámi life, a relatively small section on the Vikings (who were of lesser importance in the history of northern Norway), geology and a number of thought-provoking themes (such as the role of fire, the consequences of global warming and loss of wilderness) with plenty of touch-screen involvement. Take bus 37.

Tromsø War Museum MUSEUM
(www.tromsoforsvarsmuseum.no; Solstrandveien; adult/child Nkr50/25; ⏰noon-5pm Wed-Sun Jun–mid-Aug, Sun only May & late Aug-Sep) The cannons of a Nazi coastal artillery battery and a restored command bunker form the basis of the Tromsø Forsvarsmuseum. It also tells of the giant German battleship *Tirpitz*, sunk near the town on 12 November 1944, and the Nazi army's retreat from Leningrad, when many of its 120,000 troops were evacuated by ship from Tromsø. Take bus 12 or 28.

Mack Brewery BREWERY
(Mack Ølbryggeri; ☑77 62 45 80; www.olhallen.no; Storgata 5) This venerable institution merits a pilgrimage. Established in 1877, it produces 18 kinds of beer, including the very quaffable Macks Pilsner, Isbjørn, Haakon and several dark beers. At 1pm year-round (plus 3pm June to August) tours (Nkr150, including a beer mug, pin and pint) leave from the brewery's own **Ølhallen Pub**, Monday to Thursday. It's wise to reserve in advance.

Fjellheisen CABLE CAR
(www.fjellheisen.no; adult/child return Nkr100/50; ⏰10am-1am late May–mid-Aug, 10am-5pm rest of yr) For a fine view of the city and midnight sun, take the cable car to the top of Mt Storsteinen (421m). There's a restaurant at the top, from where a network of hiking routes radiates. Take bus 26 and buy a combination bus/cable car ticket (adult/child Nkr135/80).

🏃 Activities

In and around Tromsø (operators will normally collect you from your hotel) there's a whole range of robust activities in the winter twilight:

» Experiencing the aurora borealis
» Cross-country skiing and snowshoeing
» Reindeer and dog-sledding
» Snowshoe safaris
» Ice-fishing

To whet your winter appetite, check the tourist office website and these outfits too:

» **Arctic Adventure Tours** (www.arcticadventuretours.no)
» **Arctic Pathfinder** (www.arcticpathfinder.no)
» **Natur i Nord** (www.naturinord.no)
» **Tromsø Friluftsenter** (www.tromso-friluftsenter.no)
» **Tromsø Villmarkssenter** (www.villmarkssenter.no)

✦✦ Festivals & Events

Northern Lights Festival MUSIC
(www.nordlysfestivalen.no) Six days of music of all genres; late January.

Sámi Week CULTURE
Includes the national reindeer sledge championship, where skilled Sámi whoop and crack the whip along the main street; early February.

Midnight Sun Marathon SPORT
(www.msm.no) The world's most northerly marathon, on a Saturday in June. In addition to the full-monty 42km, there's also a half-marathon and a children's race.

Insomnia Festival MUSIC
(www.insomniafestival.no) A long, loud weekend of electronic music in October.

🛏 Sleeping

Tromsø's peak tourist time is June, when the university's still in full throe, summer tourism has begun and reservations are essential. Check out too the homestay section of the tourist office website for apartments and rooms in private homes.

Ami Hotel HOTEL €€
(☑77 62 10 00; www.amihotel.no; Skolegata 24; s/d Nkr660/870, without bathroom Nkr560/820; 🅿@) Beside a traffic-free road and park, this is a quiet, friendly, family-owned choice. There's a well-equipped kitchen for self-caterers and a couple of communal lounges, each with TV, internet access and free tea and coffee.

Clarion Hotel Bryggen HOTEL €€
(☑77 78 11 00; www.choice.no; Sjøgata 19/21; s/d from Nkr895/1095; 🅿@) This stylish 121-room waterside hotel, poking towards the sea like the prow of a ship, is architecturally stunning with its odd angles, aluminium trim, pictures on bedroom ceilings, sauna – and a top-floor jacuzzi where you can savour the

picturesque harbour and mountain views as you bubble and boil in the hot tub. Its restaurant also has great fjord views.

Rica Ishavshotel HOTEL €€
(☑77 66 64 00; www.rica.no/ishavshotel; Fredrik Langes gate 2; s/d from Nkr995/1195; @) Occupying a prime quayside position, this place is immediately recognisable by its tall spire resembling a ship's mast. It sometimes swallows as many as five tour groups per day, so summer reservations are advisable. Of its 180 attractive rooms, 74, including many singles, have superb views of the sound. Both guests and nonguests will enjoy its **Brasseriet** restaurant and **Skibsbroen** bar.

Tromsø Camping CAMPING GROUND €
(☑77 63 80 37; www.tromsocamping.no; Tromsdalen; car/caravan site Nkr205/230, 2-/4-bed cabin Nkr465/570, 4-bed with bathroom Nkr1470; P@) Tent campers enjoy leafy green campsites beside a slow-moving stream. However, bathroom and cooking facilities at this veritable village of cabins are stretched to the limit. Take bus 20 or 24.

Eating

In Tromsø, the line is blurry between restaurants, cafes and pubs and many places function in all three modes, simultaneously or at different times of the day.

Emma's Under NORWEGIAN €€
(www.emmas.as, in Norwegian; mains Nkr135-165; ⊙11am-10pm Mon-Sat) Intimate and sophisticated, Emma's Under is one of the most popular lunch spots in Tromsø, where mains include northern Norwegian staples such as reindeer fillet, lamb and stockfish. Upstairs is the more formal **Emma's Drømekjøkken** (☑77 63 77 30; mains Nkr285-345; ⊙dinner Mon-Sat), a highly regarded gourmet restaurant where advance booking is essential.

Aunegården CAFE, RESTAURANT €€
(☑77 65 12 34; Sjøgata 29; mains Nkr125-260, cakes around Nkr70; ⊙daily) You can almost lose yourself in this wonderful cafe-cum-restaurant that's all intimate crannies and cubbyholes. In a 19th-century building that functioned as a butcher's shop until 1996, it's rich in character and serves excellent salads (from Nkr140), sandwiches (from Nkr105) and mains.

Brasseriet GOURMET RESTAURANT €€€
(☑77 66 64 00; mains Nkr210-325) Rica Ishavshotel's excellent restaurant serves creative dishes, such as fried fillet of reindeer with forest-mushroom sauce and lingonberries or saffron poached cod.

Fiskekompaniet SEAFOOD €€€
(☑77 68 76 00; www.fiskekompani.no; Killengrens gate; lunch mains Nkr125-165, dinner mains around Nkr250; ⊙4-11pm) This long-standing Tromsø fish and seafood favourite has recently moved to a prime portside site. Apart from a token roast chicken dish, all starters and mains, subtly prepared and enhanced, are from the ocean.

Driv CAFE, RESTAURANT €
(www.driv.no; Tollbodgata 3; mains around Nkr120; ⊙noon-6pm mid-Jun–mid-Aug, 2pm-2am rest of yr) This student-run converted warehouse serves meaty burgers (try its renowned Driv burger, made on the spot) and great salads. It organises musical and cultural events and has a disco every Saturday. In winter you can steep yourself in good company within its open-air hot tub.

Drinking & Entertainment

Tromsø enjoys a thriving nightlife, with many arguing that it's the best scene in Norway. On Friday and Saturday, most nightspots stay open to 4am.

Ølhallen Pub PUB
(⊙9am-6pm Mon-Sat) At Mack Brewery's Ølhallen Pub you can sample its fine ales right where they're brewed. Perhaps the world's only, never mind most northerly, watering hole to be closed in the evening, it carries eight varieties on draught.

Verdensteatret CAFE
(Storgata 93b) Norway's oldest film house will satisfy both cinephiles and thirsters after great cafes. The bar is a hip place with free wi-fi and weekend DJs. At other times, the bartender spins from a huge collection of vinyl records, so expect anything from classical to deepest underground. Ask staff to let you peek into the magnificent cinema, its walls painted roof to ceiling with early-20th-century murals.

Blå Rock Café MUSIC BAR
(Strandgata 14/16; ⊙core hr 11.30am-2am) The loudest, most raving place in town has theme evenings, almost 50 brands of beer, occasional live bands and weekend DJs. The

music's rock, naturally. Every Monday hour is a happy hour.

Bastard   MUSIC & SPORTS BAR
(Strandgata 22; ⊙core hr 8pm-2am Mon-Sat, 3-11pm Sun) Bastard (with the stress on the second syllable...) is a cool basement hangout with low beams and white, furry walls (no polar bears killed during construction). It engages art-house and underground DJs (Friday and Saturday) and bands (up to three times weekly). This sports bar carries UK and Norwegian football, so it also has a faithful following of armchair sporting regulars.

❶ Information

Tourist office (☑77 61 00 00; www.visit tromso.no; Kirkegata 2; ⊙9am-7pm Mon-Fri, 10am-6pm Sat & Sun)

❶ Getting There & Away

Air

Destinations with direct SAS flights to/from **Tromsø Airport** (☑77 64 84 00), the main airport for the far north, include Oslo, Narvik/Harstad, Bodø, Trondheim, Alta, Hammerfest, Kirkenes and Longyearbyen. **Norwegian** (www.norwegian.no) flies to and from London (Gatwick), Edinburgh, Dublin and Oslo.

Boat

Express boats connect Tromsø and Harstad (2½ hours), via Finnsnes (1¼ hours), two to four times daily. Tromsø is also a major stop on the *Hurtigruten* coastal ferry route.

Bus

The main bus terminal (sometimes called Prostneset) is on Kaigata, beside the *Hurtigruten* quay. There are at least two daily express buses to/from Narvik (Nkr390, 4¼ hours) and one to/from Alta (Nkr494, 6½ hours).

❶ Getting Around

AIR Tromsø's airport is about 5km from the centre, on the western side of Tromsøya island. **Flybuss** (Nkr55, 15min) runs between the airport and Rica Ishavshotel, connecting with arriving and departing flights. Alternatively, take city bus 40 or 42 (Nkr26); when you arrive, wait for it on the road opposite the airport entrance.

BUS Local buses cost Nkr26 per ride – purchase your ticket on board.

TAXI Call ☑77 60 30 00.

All along Norway's jagged northern coast, deeply cut by forbidding fjords, you'll find numerous isolated fishing villages, as well as some of the north's star attractions: Alta with its Stone Age rock carvings; Kirkenes, a frontier-like town sharing a border with Russia; and Nordkapp, reportedly but not quite mainland Europe's northernmost point.

Those who head inland will find the vast and empty Finnmarksvidda Plateau, a stark expanse with only two major settlements: Karasjok and Kautokeino. They and Finnmarksvidda are part of the heartland of the Sámi people, where reindeer herding has occurred for centuries. At either, enjoy a dogsled journey across empty tundra half lit under the bruise-blue winter sky.

Two good sources of information about the region are www.finnmark.com and www.visitnorthernnorway.com.

Alta

POP 18,700

Although the fishing and slate-quarrying town of Alta lies at latitude 70°N, it enjoys a relatively mild climate. The Alta Museum, with its ancient petroglyphs, is a must-see and the lush green Sautso-Alta Canyon, a quick hop away, is simply breathtaking.

◉ Sights

Alta Museum   MUSEUM, PETROGLYPHS
(www.alta.museum.no; Altaveien 19; adult/child Nkr85/20; ⊙8am-5pm or 8pm) This superb award-winning museum in Hjemmeluft, at the western end of town, features exhibits and displays on Sámi culture, Finnmark military history, the Alta hydroelectric project and the aurora borealis. The cliffs around it, a Unesco World Heritage site, are incised with around 6000 late–Stone Age carvings, dating from 6000 to 2000 years ago. Themes include hunting scenes, fertility symbols, bear, moose, reindeer and crowded boats.

☞ Tours

The Altaelva hydroelectric project has had very little effect on the most scenic stretch of river, which slides through 400m-deep **Sautso**, northern Europe's grandest canyon. The easiest way to see this impressive forested gorge is to take the 3½-hour tour (adult/child Nkr545/275) that the tourist office organises each Monday, Wednesday and

Friday in July, leaving at 4pm, numbers permitting (minimum six people).

Alta is also renowned for its salmon run; several local companies organise fishing tours.

🛏 Sleeping

TOP CHOICE Park Hotell
HOTEL €€

(☎78 45 74 00; www.parkhotell.no; Markedsgata 6; s/d from Nkr895/1195; @) The 34 rooms here are spacious, each with a sofa or pair of armchairs, and bathrooms are white-tiled and sparkling. Although just off the main square, it's a tranquil spot with a roof terrace that's ideal for summer sunbathing and observing the aurora borealis in winter.

Thon Hotel Vica
HOTEL €€

(☎78 48 22 22; www.thonhotels.no/Vica; Fogdebakken 6; s/d from Nkr900/1100; P@) In a timber-built former farmhouse, the Vica beckons you in. Until recently a family-run concern but now assimilated into the Thon chain, it has, at least for the moment, preserved its originality. There's a sauna (Nkr100), steaming outdoor hot tub (wonderful in winter when all around is snow capped) and **Haldde**, Alta's finest restaurant.

Sorrisnava Igloo Hotel
ICE HOTEL €€

(☎78 43 33 78; www.sorrisnava.no; B&B per person Nkr2000; ☉mid-Jan–mid-Apr) Its 30 bedrooms – and beds too – are made entirely of ice, as are the chapel, bridal suite and stunning ice bar with its weird-and-wonderful sculptures lit by fibre optics. Then again, you might just want to drop by and visit (adult/child Nkr100/50).

Bårstua Gjestehus
GUESTHOUSE €€

(☎78 43 33 33; www.baarstua.no; Kongleveien 2a; s/d incl breakfast from Nkr630/830) This friendly B&B is set back from the E6. Its eight rooms, decorated with striking photographs, are spruce and well furnished. Each has self-catering facilities.

🍴 Eating & Drinking

🍴 Restaurant Haldde
RESTAURANT €€€

(lunch dishes Nkr100-200, dinner mains Nkr250-360) This quality restaurant within Thon Hotel Vica relies almost entirely upon local ingredients in the preparation of choice dishes such as a smoked half-leg of reindeer in red-wine sauce and its Flavour of Finnmark dessert of cloudberries and cowberry-blueberry sorbet.

Alfa-Omega
CAFE, BAR €€

(Markedsgata 14-16; mains Nkr120-280; ☉Mon-Sat) As its name suggests, this place has two parts. Omega, its contemporary cafe, open 11am to midnight, serves salads, sandwiches, pastas and cakes. Sink your teeth into its hugely popular Ole Mattis reindeer steak sandwich. Alfa, a pleasant, casual bar, comes into its own from 8pm.

Han Steike
STEAKHOUSE €€

(www.hansteike.no, in Norwegian; Løkkeveien 2; mains Nkr215-280; ☉3pm-midnight Tue-Sun) This steakhouse, all dark wood and grey flagstones, is the place to go if you're after something red and raw.

❶ Information

Tourist office (www.altatours.no; Parksentret Bldg, Sentrum; ☉9am-6pm or 8pm Jun-Aug, 9am-3.30pm Mon-Sat rest of yr)

❶ Getting There & Away

AIR The **airport** (☎784 49 555) is 4km east of Sentrum; follow the E6. Norwegian and SAS service Alta airport. Destinations include Oslo, Tromsø, Hammerfest, Lakselv and Vadsø.

BUS Buses run between Alta and Tromsø (Nkr494, 6½ hours, one daily), Kautokeino (Nkr235, 2¼ hours, daily except Sat), Karasjok (Nkr405, 4¾ hours, two daily except Saturday), Honninsvåg (Nkr405, four hours, one daily) and Hammerfest (Nkr260, 2¼ hours, two daily).

Hammerfest

POP 9700

Most visitors to Hammerfest arrive by the *Hurtigruten* and have an hour or two to poke around. Unless you have unusual interests, that's about as much time as you'll need. The fishing town's oddest experience can be found at the Royal & Ancient Polar Bear Society.

Purporting to be Norway's northernmost town (other settlements lie further north, but they are too small to qualify as towns), Hammerfest has suffered as much as the walrus in the Polar Bear Society: a gale decimated it in 1856, a fire totalled it in 1890 and the Nazis burnt it again in 1944, after which it was rebuilt in the 'Finnmark Ugly' style. At night, an awe-inspiring fire from a nearby gas plant casts the place in an eerie red glow.

Sights & Activities

Gjenreisningsmuseet MUSEUM
(Kirkegata 21; www.gjenreisningsmuseet.no; adult/
child Nkr50/free; ⊙9am-4pm mid-Jun–mid-Aug,
11am-2pm rest of yr) Hammerfest's Reconstruction Museum recounts the forced evacuation and decimation of the town during the
Nazi retreat in 1944; the hardships that its
citizens endured through the following winter; and Hammerfest's postwar reconstruction and regeneration.

Salen Hill VIEWPOINT
For panoramic views over the town, coast
and mountains, climb Salen Hill (86m),
topped by the Turistua restaurant, a couple
of Sámi turf huts and a lookout point. The
15-minute uphill walking trail begins at the
small park behind the Rådhus.

FREE **Royal & Ancient Polar**
Bear Society MUSEUM, SOUVENIR SHOP
(⊙9am-5pm Mon-Fri, 10.30am-1.30pm Sat & Sun
mid-Jun–mid-Aug, 9am-3pm Mon-Fri, 10.30am-
1.30pm Sat & Sun rest of yr) Dedicated to preserving Hammerfest culture, the Royal &
Ancient Polar Bear Society features exhibits on Arctic hunting and local history and
shares premises with the tourist office. The
place is, it must be said, a bit of a come-on.
For Nkr180, you can become a life member
and get a certificate, ID card, sticker and pin.
For a little more, you also receive a schnapps
glass and, as the demure young receptionist
will explain without blanching, get dubbed
with the bone from a walrus' penis. It's well
worth the extra for the conversation this
unique honour will generate down the pub,
once you're home.

Sleeping & Eating

Rica Hotel Hammerfest HOTEL €€
(⚑78 42 57 00; www.rica.no; Sørøygata 15; s/d from
Nkr950/1200; P@) Constructed in agreeable
mellow brick, this hotel has an attractive bar
and lounge and well-furnished rooms, most
with harbour views. Its Arctic Menu restaurant, **Skansen Mat og Vinstue**, serves excellent local fare.

Redrum CAFE, BAR €
(www.redrum.no, in Norwegian; Storgata 23; snacks
Nkr80-160; ⊙11am-5pm Mon-Thu, 11am-3am Fri &
Sat) With its attractive contemporary decor
and flickering candles, Redrum saves its
energy for weekend wildness, when there's
regularly live music. To the rear, there's a
deep, more relaxed wooden patio.

Camping Storvannet CAMPING GROUND €
(⚑78 41 10 10; storvannet@yahoo.no; Storvanns-
veien; car/caravan site Nkr155/215, 2-/4-bed cabin
Nkr400/460; ⊙late May-late Sep) Beside a
lake and overlooked by a giant apartment
complex, this pleasant site, Hammerfest's
only decent camping option, is small, so
do book your cabin in advance.

Qa Spiseri CAFE €
(Sjøgata 8; mains Nkr120-160; ⊙10am-5pm Mon-
Sat) Just off Sjøgata and run by a young
team, this popular place offers reliable
cuisine with a great price-to-quality ratio
with a choice of Norwegian, Italian and
Thai dishes.

ℹ Information

Tourist office (www.hammerfest-turist.no;
Hamnegata 3; ⊙9am-5pm Mon-Fri, 10.30am-
1.30pm Sat & Sun mid-Jun–mid-Aug, 9am-3pm
Mon-Fri, 10.30am-1.30pm Sat & Sun rest of yr)

ℹ Getting There & Away

BOAT The *Hurtigruten* coastal ferry stops in
Hammerfest for 1½ hours in each direction. A
Hurtigruten hop to Tromsø (11 hours) or Honningsvåg (five hours) makes a comfortable alternative to a long bus journey.

BUS Buses run to/from Alta (Nkr260, 2¼ hours,
two daily), Honningsvåg (Nkr390, 3½ hours, one
to two daily) and Karasjok (Nkr370, 4¼ hours,
twice daily except Saturday), with one service
extending to Kirkenes (Nkr941, 10¼ hours)
via Tana Bru (Nkr665, eight hours) four times
weekly.

Nordkapp & Magerøya

POP 3200

Nordkapp is the one attraction in northern Norway that everyone seems to visit
even if it is a tourist trap. Billing itself as
the northernmost point in continental Europe, it sucks in visitors by the busload,
some 200,000 every year. But it's the view
that thrills the most. In reasonable weather
– which is a lot of the time – you can gaze
down at the wild surf 307m below and
watch the mists roll in.

Nearer to the North Pole than to Oslo,
Nordkapp sits at latitude 71° 10' 21"N, where
the sun never drops below the horizon from
mid-May to the end of July. Long before
other Europeans took an interest, it was a
sacrificial site for the Sámi, who believed it
had special powers.

WORTH A TRIP

KNIVSKJELODDEN

Now here's a secret: Nordkapp isn't continental Europe's northernmost point. That award belongs to Knivskjelodden, an 18km round-trip hike away, less dramatic, inaccessible by vehicle – and to be treasured all the more for that. Lying about 3km west of Nordkapp, it sticks its finger a full 1457m further northwards. You can hike to the tip of this promontory from a marked car park 6km south of the Nordkapp toll booth. The 9km track, waymarked with giant cairns, isn't difficult despite some ups and downs, but it's best to wear hiking boots since it can be squelchy. When you get to the tall beehive-shaped obelisk at latitude 71° 11' 08"N, down at sea level, sign the guestbook. Allow five to six hours for the round trip.

To reach the tip of the continent, by car, by bike, on a bus or walking in, you have to pay a **toll** (adult/child Nkr235/80).

Astoundingly, you can spend the night in your motor home or caravan at Nordkapp itself (fill up on water and electricity though, because you won't find any there for the taking).

The closest town of any size is **Honningsvåg**, 35km from Nordkapp.

🛏 Sleeping

Northcape Guesthouse HOSTEL €
(☎47 25 50 63; www.northcapeguesthouse.com; Elvebakken 5a; dm Nkr250, d without bathroom Nkr600; ☺May-Aug) A 1km walk from the *Hurtigruten* quay, this bright, modern hostel is an excellent budget choice. There's a cosy lounge, washing machine, well-equipped kitchen for self-caterers – and great views over the town below. It's often full so do reserve well in advance.

Nordkapp Vandrerhjem HOSTEL €
(☎91 82 41 56; www.hihostels.no/nordkapp; dm incl breakfast Nkr330, s/d Nkr450/760; @) A 156-bed HI hostel.

Rica Hotel Honningsvåg HOTEL €€€
(☎78 47 72 20; www.rica.no; s/d from Nkr1380/1630) An excellent chain hotel with good restaurants.

ℹ Information

Tourist office (☎78 47 70 30; www.nordkapp. no; Fiskeriveien 4B; ☺8.30am-10pm Mon-Fri, noon-8pm Sat & Sun mid-Jun–mid-Aug, 8.30am-4pm Mon-Fri rest of yr) In Honningsvåg.

ℹ Getting There & Away

BOAT The *Hurtigruten* stops in Honningsvåg. Northbound ships stop for 3½ hours, long enough for the ship to offer its passengers a Nordkapp tour.

BUS Buses run to/from Alta (Nkr370, four hours, one to two daily) and Hammerfest (Nkr325, 3¼ hours, one to two daily).

ℹ Getting Around

Between mid-May and late August, a local bus (adult/child Nkr100/50, 45 minutes) runs daily at 11am and 9.30pm between Honningsvåg and Nordkapp. It sets off back from the cape at 1.15pm and 12.45am (so that you can take in the midnight sun at precisely midnight). From 1 June to 15 August, there's a supplementary run at 5pm, though this returns at 6.15pm, giving you barely half an hour at Nordkapp unless you want to hang around for the service that returns at 12.45am.

Kirkenes

POP 3500

This is it: you're as far east as Cairo, further east than most of Finland, a mere 15km from the border with Russia – and at the end of the line for the *Hurtigruten* coastal ferry. This tiny, nondescript place, anticlimactic for many, has a distinct frontier feel. You'll see street signs in Norwegian and Cyrillic script and hear Russian spoken by trans-border visitors and fishermen.

The town reels with around 100,000 visitors every year, most stepping off the *Hurtigruten* to spend a couple of hours in the town before travelling onward. But you should linger a while here, not primarily for the town's sake but to take one of the many excursions and activities on offer.

🏃 Activities

For such a small place, Kirkenes offers a wealth of tours and activities in and around town. For an overview according to season, pick up one of the tourist office's comprehensive brochures, *Summer Activities* and *Winter Activities*.

There's also a summertime **reservation point** (⌨48 18 97 97; www.incomingkirkenes.no; ⏰10am-3pm Jun-Aug) in the lobby of the Rica Hotel. Otherwise, book through the tourist office, at most hotels or directly with tour operators.

Summer Activities

» King crab safari (adult/child Nkr1290/645)

» Half-day tours of the Pasvik Valley (adult/child Nkr800/400)

» Visiting the Russian border and iron-ore mines (adult/child Nkr480/240)

» Boat trips along the Pasvik river, which demarcates the Norwegian–Russian border (from adult/child Nkr840/400)

Winter Fun

» Snowmobile safaris (from Nkr1150)

» Ice-fishing (Nkr790)

» Snowshoe walks (Nkr750)

» Dog-sledding (from Nkr1250)

» King crab safari (adult/child Nkr1290/645)

☞ Tours

Principal tour agencies:

Arctic Adventure (www.arctic-adventure.no; Jarfjordbotn)

Barents Safari (www.barentssafari.no)

Pasvikturist (www.pasvikturist.no; Dr Wessels gate 9)

Radius (www.radius-kirkenes.com; Kongens-gate 1-2)

🛏 Sleeping & Eating

TOP CHOICE **Sollia Gjestegård**   HOTEL €€
(⌨78 99 08 20; www.storskog.no; 2–6-bed cabin Nkr750-1050, d from Nkr750) The air could scarcely be purer or the atmosphere more relaxed at this wonderful getaway haven, 13km southeast of Kirkenes. The whole family can sweat it out in the sauna and outdoor tub, while children will enjoy communing with the resident huskies. Just below, beside the lake, its **Gapahuken** restaurant is just as enticing.

Thon Hotel Kirkenes   HOTEL €€
(⌨78 97 10 50; www.thonhotels.no/kirkenes; s/d from Nkr990/1190; @) This brand-new waterside hotel is Thon-boxy from the exterior. Within, though, it's open, vast and exciting, offering great views of the sound and a cluster of laid-up Russian trawlers to starboard.

Rica Arctic Hotel   HOTEL €€
(⌨78 99 11 59; www.rica.no/arctic; Kongensgate 1-3; s/d from Nkr875/1125; P@≋) The Rica Arctic, a pleasing modern block, boasts Norway's most easterly swimming pool, heated and open year-round. The other special attribute, its Arctic Menu restaurant (summer buffet Nkr295), is the best of the town's hotel dining options.

Kirkenes Snow Hotel   SNOW HOTEL €€€
(⌨78 97 05 40; www.kirkenessnowhotel.com; Nkr2250 incl transfer from Kirkenes, half-board & sauna; ⏰20 Dec–mid-Apr) Yes, the price is steep but you'll remember the occasion for life. And bear in mind that 25 tonnes of ice and 15,000 cu metres of snow are shifted each winter to build this ephemeral structure within Gabba Reindeer & Husky Park. For dinner, guests cook reindeer sausages over an open fire, then enjoy a warming main course of baked salmon.

TOP CHOICE **Gapahuken**   NORWEGIAN €€€
(⌨78 99 08 20; mains Nkr240-290; ⏰3-10pm Tue-Sun) From the broad picture windows of Gapahuken, restaurant of the Sollia Gjestegård hotel, there's a grand panorama of the lake at its feet and the Russian frontier post beyond. Discriminating diners drive out from Kirkenes to enjoy gourmet Norwegian cuisine based upon fresh local ingredients such as reindeer, king crab, salmon and halibut.

❶ Information

Tourist office (⌨78 97 17 77; www.kirkenesinfo.no; Town Sq; ⏰10am-5pm Mon-Fri, 10am-2pm Sat & Sun)

❶ Getting There & Around

AIR From **Kirkenes airport** (⌨78 97 35 20), 13km southwest of town, there are direct flights to Oslo (SAS and Norwegian) and Tromsø (Widerøe). The airport is served by the Flybuss (Nkr85, 20 minutes), which connects the bus terminal and Rica Arctic Hotel with all arriving and departing flights.

BOAT Kirkenes is the terminus of the *Hurtigruten* coastal ferry, which heads southwards again at 12.45pm daily. A bus (Nkr85) meets the boat and runs into town and on to the airport.

BUS Buses run four times weekly to Karasjok (five hours), Hammerfest (10¼ hours), Alta (10½ hours) and many points in between.

Karasjok

POP 2800

Kautokeino may have more Sámi residents, but Karasjok (Kárásjohka in Sámi) is Sámi Norway's indisputable capital. It's home to the Sámi Parliament and library, NRK Sámi Radio, a wonderful Sámi museum and an impressive Sámi theme park.

⊙ Sights

Sápmi Park   THEME PARK
(www.sapmi.no; Porsangerveien; adult/child Nkr160/70; ⊙9am-4pm or 7pm Jun-Aug, 10am-2pm Mon-Fri rest of yr) Sámi culture is big business here, and it was only a matter of time before it was consolidated into a theme park. There's a wistful, high-tech multimedia introduction to the Sámi in the 'Magic Theatre', plus Sámi winter and summer camps and other dwellings to explore in the grounds.

Sámi National Museum   MUSEUM
(Sámiid Vuorká Dávvirat; Museumsgata 17; adult/child Nkr75/free; ⊙9am-3pm or 6pm) The Sámi National Museum is also called the Sámi Collection. Devoted to Sámi history and culture, it has displays of colourful, traditional Sámi clothing, a bewildering array of tools and artefacts, and works by contemporary Sámi artists. Outdoors, you can roam among a cluster of traditional Sámi constructions and follow a short trail, signed in English, that leads past and explains ancient Sámi reindeer trapping pits and hunting technique.

FREE **Sámi Parliament**   PARLIAMENT
(Sámediggi; Kautokeinoveien 50) The Sámi Parliament was established in 1989 and meets four times annually. In 2000 it moved into a glorious new building, encased in mellow Siberian wood, with a birch, pine and oak interior. The main assembly hall is shaped like a Sámi tent, and the **Sámi library**, lit with tiny lights like stars, houses more than 35,000 volumes, plus other media. From late June to mid-August there are 30-minute tours leaving hourly, on the half-hour, between 8.30am and 2.30pm (except 11.30am). The rest of the year, tours are at 1pm, Monday to Friday.

🏃 Activities

Sven Engholm, the 11-time winner of Finnmarksløpet, Europe's longest dog-sled race, oversees the outstanding **Engholm's Husky** (www.engholm.no), which offers winter dogsled and cross-country skiing tours, as well as summer walking tours with a dog to carry most of your pack. All-inclusive expeditions range from half-day excursions to five days of dog-sledding (Nkr5700), radiating out each day, to an 11-day expedition to the Arctic sea (Nkr27,000). Consult the website for the full range of activities.

🛏 Sleeping & Eating

TOP CHOICE **Engholm Husky Design Lodge**   CABINS €€
(☑91 58 66 25; www.engholm.no; cabin Nkr400-500 plus per person Nkr300) About 6km from Karasjok along the Rv92, Sven Engholm, the owner of Engholm's Husky, has built this wonderful haven in the forest with his own hands. Each rustic cabin is individually furnished with great flair, all have kitchen facilities and two have bathrooms. A plentiful dinner costs Nkr280. Sven's place is also Karasjok's HI-affiliated youth hostel.

Rica Hotel Karasjok   HOTEL €€
(☑78 46 88 60; www.rica.no; Porsangerveien; s/d from Nkr995/1195; 🅿@) Adjacent to Sápmi Park, this is Karasjok's premier lodging, with handsome rooms and Sámi motifs throughout, plus, outside summertime, an impressive Arctic Menu restaurant. Older rooms in the hotel's more traditional **Gjestehus** (s/d Nkr795/895) are substantially cheaper.

Gammen   SÁMI €€€
(☑78 46 88 60; mains Nkr235-295; ⊙11am-10.30pm mid-Jun–mid-Aug) It's very much reindeer or reindeer plus a couple of fish options at this rustic complex of four large interconnected Sámi huts run by the Rica Hotel.

ℹ Information

Tourist office (www.sapmi.no; ⊙9am-7pm Jun–mid-Aug, 9am-4pm Mon-Fri rest of yr)

ℹ Getting There & Away

Twice-daily buses (except Saturday) connect Karasjok with both Alta (Nkr405, 4¾ hours) and Hammerfest (Nkr370, 4¼ hours). There's a service to Kirkenes (Nkr529, five hours) four times weekly.

A daily Finnish Lapin Linjat bus runs to Rovaniemi (Nkr610, eight hours) via Ivalo (Nkr240, 3½ hours), in Finland.

Kautokeino

POP 2950

While Karasjok has made concessions to Norwegian culture, Kautokeino, the traditional winter base of the reindeer Sámi (as opposed to their coastal kin), remains more emphatically Sámi; some 85% of the townspeople have Sámi as their first language and you may see a few non-tourist-industry locals in traditional costume.

◉ Sights

TOP CHOICE Juhls'

Sølvsmie   SILVER WORKSHOP & GALLERY
(www.juhls.no; Galaniitoluodda; ⊙9am-8pm mid-Jun–mid-Aug, 9am-6pm rest of yr) Juhls' Silver Gallery is on a hill above the town and clearly signed. This wonderful building, all slopes and soft angles, was designed and built by owners Regine and Frank Juhls, who first began working with the Sámi over half a century ago. Their highly acclaimed gallery creates traditional-style and modern silver jewellery and handicrafts, and displays the best of Scandinavian design.

Kautokeino Museum   MUSEUM
(Boaronjárga 23; adult/child Nkr40/free; ⊙9am-6pm Mon-Sat, noon-6pm Sun mid-Jun–mid-Aug, 9am-3pm Mon-Fri rest of yr) Outside, this little museum has a fully fledged traditional Sámi settlement, complete with an early home, temporary dwellings and outbuildings such as the kitchen, sauna, and huts for storing fish, potatoes and lichen (also called 'reindeer moss' and prime reindeer fodder). Inside is a fascinating if cluttered display of Sámi handicrafts, farming and reindeer-herding implements, religious icons and winter transport gear.

Kautokeino Kirke   CHURCH
(Suomalvodda; ⊙9am-9pm Jun–mid-Aug) The timbered Kautokeino church, which dates from 1958, is one of Norway's most frequented, particularly at Easter. Its cheery interior, alive with bright Sámi colours, has some fixtures salvaged from the earlier 1701 church that was torched in WWII.

🛏 Sleeping & Eating

TOP CHOICE Thon Hotel Kautokeino   HOTEL €€
(☑78 48 70 00; www.thonhotels.no/kautokeino; Biedjovaggeluodda 2; s/d Nkr895/1095; @) This brand-new hotel is a lovely structure with an exterior of mellow wood, built low to blend with its few neighbours. Within, rooms are cheerful and cosy. **Duottar** (lunch mains Nkr165-175, dinner mains Nkr220-335), its gourmet restaurant, serves fine cuisine.

Arctic Motell & Camping   CAMPING GROUND €
(☑78 48 54 00; www.kauto.no, in Norwegian; Suomaluodda 16; car/caravan site Nkr160/200, cabin with outdoor bathroom Nkr300, with bathroom Nkr750-1800, motel s/d Nkr500/600) At the southern end of town, this is a hyperfriendly place, where campers and cabin dwellers have access to a communal kitchen. Its *lavvo* is a warm and cosy spot to relax by a wood fire and sip steaming coffee, laid on nightly at 8pm. If you ask, the small cafe will also rustle up *bidos*, the traditional reindeer-meat stew served at Sámi weddings and other rites of passage.

ℹ Information

Tourist office (☑78 48 65 00, 957 55 199; www.kautokeino.nu; ⊙10am-6pm Mon-Fri, 10am-5pm Sun mid-Jun–mid-Aug only)

ℹ Getting There & Away

Buses run between Kautokeino and Alta (Nkr235, 2¼ hours) daily except Saturday. In July and August, the Finnish Lapin Linjat bus connects Kautokeino with Alta (1¾ hours) and Rovaniemi (eight hours), in Finland once daily.

SVALBARD

The world's most readily accessible piece of the polar north, and one of the most spectacular places imaginable, Svalbard is *the* destination for an unforgettable holiday. This wondrous archipelago is an assault on the senses: vast icebergs and floes choke the seas, and icefields and glaciers frost the lonely heights.

Svalbard also hosts a surprising variety of flora and fauna, including seals, walrus, Arctic foxes and polar bears.

Plan your trip well in advance. When you arrive, you'll almost certainly want to participate in some kind of organised trek or tour, and many need to be booked early. Since travel outside Longyearbyen is both difficult and dangerous, you miss out on a lot if you don't sign up for one.

History

Although the first mention of Svalbard occurs in an Icelandic saga from 1194, the official discovery of Svalbard (then uninhabited) is credited to Dutch voyager Willem

Barents in 1596. He named the islands Spitsbergen, or 'sharp mountains'. The Norwegian name, Svalbard, comes from the Old Norse for 'cold coast'; ancient Norse sagas referred to 'a land in the far north at the end of the ocean'. During the 17th century Dutch, English, French, Norwegian and Danish whalers slaughtered the whale population. They were followed in the 18th century by the Russians hunting walrus and seals. The 19th century saw the arrival of Norwegians, who hunted polar bears and Arctic foxes. In 1906, commercial coal mining began and is continued today by the Russians (at Barentsburg) and the Norwegians (at Longyearbyen and Sveagruva). The 1920 Svalbard Treaty granted Norway sovereignty over the islands.

Tours

View dozens of exciting options on the tourist office website. Accommodation, transport and meals are usually included in longer tours, but day tours are also available. Tour operators include the following:

Arctic Adventures ADVENTURE ACTIVITIES
(☑79 02 16 24; www.arctic-adventures.no) Small company offering the full range of activities.

Basecamp Spitsbergen ADVENTURE ACTIVITIES
(☑79 02 46 00; www.basecampexplorer.com) Mainly offers winter activities, including a stay aboard the *Noorderlicht,* a Dutch sailing vessel that's set into the fjord ice, and Isfjord Radio, the ultimate remote getaway on an upgraded, one-time radio station at the western tip of Spitsbergen island.

Poli Arctici ADVENTURE ACTIVITIES
(☑79 02 17 05; www.poliartici.com) Poli Arctici is the trading name of Stefano Poli, originally from Milan and with 13 years as a Svalbard wilderness guide.

Spitsbergen Tours ADVENTURE ACTIVITIES
(☑79 02 10 68; www.terrapolaris.com) The owner, Andreas Umbreit, is one of the longest-standing operators on the archipelago.

Spitsbergen Travel ADVENTURE ACTIVITIES
(☑79 02 61 00; www.spitsbergentravel.no) One of the giants of the Svalbard travel scene, with a staggering array of options.

Svalbard Hestesenter KAYAKING, HORSE RIDING
(☑91 77 65 95) Kayaking, horse riding and hiking.

Svalbard Husky DOG-SLEDDING
(☑98 40 40 89) Year-round dog-sledding.

Svalbard Snøscooterutleie SNOWMOBILING
(☑79 02 46 61; www.scooterutleie.svalbard.no) Winter snowmobile safaris as well as a handful of summer activities.

Svalbard Villmarkssenter DOG-SLEDDING
(☑79 02 17 00; www.svalbardvillmarkssenter. no) Experts in dog mushing, whether by sledge over the snow or on wheels during summer.

Svalbard Wildlife Expeditions ADVENTURE ACTIVITIES
(☑79 02 56 60; www.wildlife.no) Offering many of the usual and several unusual trips.

ℹ Information

Tourist office (☑79 02 55 50; www.svalbard. net; ⊙10am-5pm May-Sep, noon-5pm Oct-Apr) Produces the comprehensive *Guide Longyearbyen* and a helpful weekly activities list.

ℹ Getting There & Away

SAS (www.flysas.com) flies to/from Oslo directly in summer (three flights weekly) or via Tromsø (once or twice daily) year-round.

Longyearbyen

POP 2000

The frontier community of Longyearbyen, strewn with abandoned coal-mining detritus, enjoys a superb backdrop, including two glacier tongues, Longyearbreen and Lars Hjertabreen.

⊙ Sights

In addition to the following sights, keep an eye out for wild reindeer and even the Arctic fox in and around the town.

Svalbard Museum MUSEUM
(adult/child Nkr75/40; ⊙10am-5pm May-Sep) Museum is the wrong word for this impressive exhibition space. Themes include the life on the edge formerly led by whalers, trappers, seal- and walrus-hunters and, more recently, miners. It's an attractive mix of text, artefacts and birds and mammals, stuffed and staring. A combined ticket with the airship museum costs Nkr130/60 adult/child.

Spitsbergen Airship Museum MUSEUM
(www.spitsbergenairshipmuseum.com; adult/ child Nkr75/40; ⊙10am-5pm mid-Jun–Aug) This recently opened museum is a fascinating complement to the main museum, with a stunning collection of artefacts, original newspapers and other documents relating

to the history of polar exploration. A combined ticket with the Svalbard Museum costs Nkr130/60 adult/child.

🏃 Activities

There's a dizzying array of short trips and day tours that vary with the season. The tourist office's weekly activities list provides details of many more. All outings can be booked through individual operators (directly or via their websites; see p404) or online at the tourist office (www.svalbard.net).

Birdwatching

More than 160 bird species have been reported in Svalbard, with the overwhelming number of these present during the summer months. Some tour operators run short boat trips to the 'bird cliffs' close to Longyearbyen, while birdwatchers should buy the booklet *Bird Life in Longyearbyen and surrounding area* (Nkr50), available from the tourist office.

Boat Trips

Polar Charter (📞97 52 32 50) sends out the *MS Polargirl* to **Barentsburg** and the Esmark Glacier (adult/child Nkr1250/990, eight to 10 hours) four times a week, and to **Pyramiden** and Nordenskjöldbreen (adult/child Nkr1250/990, eight to 10 hours); prices include a lunch cooked on board. On Fridays, it also organises five-hour trips to the Borebreen glacier (adult/child Nkr950/850).

Henningsen Transport & Guiding (📞79 02 13 11; www.htg.svalbard.no) runs a near-identical service, although it's more expensive (adult Nkr1340), as well as six-hour Friday-evening trips to Tempelfjorden and the Van Post glacier (Nkr1040).

Spitsbergen Travel (3/6hr Nkr640/990) also arranges up to 13 weekly boat cruises around Isfjord, taking in **birdwatching**, **fossil-hunting** and **glacier views**.

Hiking & Fossil-Hunting

Summer hiking possibilities are endless and any Svalbard tour company worth its salt can organise half-, full- and multiday hikes.

The easiest options are three-hour **fossil-hunting hikes** (from Nkr330), some of which take you up onto the moraine at the base of the Longyearbreen glacier.

Popular destinations for other hikes, many of which include glacier hikes, include Platåberget (three/four hours Nkr300/490), up onto the Longyearbreen

glacier (five hours, Nkr590) itself, Sarkofagen (525m above sea level; five hours, Nkr590), Hiorthfjellet (900m above sea level; eight hours, Nkr1050), Nordenskjöldtoppen (1050m above sea level; seven hours, Nkr950) and the Foxfonna ice field (six hours, Nkr590).

Kayaking

Svalbard Wildlife Expeditions runs seven-hour kayaking expeditions to Hiorthamn (Nkr890) with an additional 10-hour hiking/kayaking challenge to Hiortfjellet (Nkr1100). Another option is the excursion along Adventdalen offered by Svalbard Hestesenter (6hr Nkr590).

Dog-sledding

Dedicated dog-sledding operators include Svalbard Husky and Svalbard Villmarkssenter and the standard four-hour expedition (adult/child Nkr990/690) will give you a taste. For longer excursions (including some wonderful multi-day trips), it's worth checking what Basecamp Spitsbergen (7hr adult/child Nkr1990/995) has on offer.

Snowmobiling

Spitsbergen Travel has numerous single and multi-day snowmobile expeditions. Among its single-day options are the **East Coast Snowmobile Safari** (eight to 10 hours, driver/passenger Nkr2350/1200), **Barentsburg** (seven to nine hours, Nkr1950/1200), **Pyramiden** (eight to 10 hours, Nkr2350/1200), **Coles Bay** (four hours, Nkr1250/700), **Elveneset** (four hours, Nkr1250/700) and the **Polar Night Safari** (three hours, Nkr1290/590).

Svalbard Snøscooterutleie offers many of the same routes for similar prices, as well as offering snowmobile rental. To drive a snowmobile scoot, you'll need your home driving licence.

🖙 Tours

Svalbard Maxi Taxi   MINIBUS TOURS
(📞79 02 13 05; per person Nkr250; ⊙10am & 4pm Jun-Aug) This local taxi company offers two-hour minibus tours that take you further than you might think possible around Longyearbyen.

🎉 Festivals & Events

Polar Jazz   MUSIC
(www.polarjazz.no, in Norwegian) A long winter (January or February) weekend of jazz.

Sunfest CULTURE
Week-long celebrations in early March to dispel the polar night.

Blues Festival MUSIC
(www.svalbardblues.com) Five-day jam session in late October to mark the onset of winter.

🛏 Sleeping

Basecamp Spitsbergen LODGE €€€
(✎79 02 46 00; www.basecampexplorer.com; s Nkr990-1990, d Nkr1450-2390, tr Nkr1680-3150) Imagine a re-created sealing hut, built in part from recycled driftwood and local slate. Add artefacts and decorations culled from the local refuse dump and mining cast-offs. Graft on 21st-century plumbing and design flair and you've got this place, also known as Trapper's Lodge.

Spitsbergen Guesthouse GUESTHOUSE €
(✎79 02 63 00; www.spitsbergentravel.no; dm Nkr300-365, s Nkr495-690, d Nkr795-990; ⊙mid-Mar–mid-Sep) A subsidiary of Spitsbergen Travel, this guesthouse is spread over four buildings, one of which houses the large breakfast room (once the miners' mess hall), and can accommodate up to 136. The rooms are simple, but terrific value for money.

Mary-Ann's Polarrigg HOTEL, GUESTHOUSE €€
(✎79 02 37 02; www.polarriggen.com; Skjæringa; d/f Nkr2200/2800, s/d without bathroom Nkr850/995) Run by the ebullient Mary-Ann and adorned with mining and hunting memorabilia, the Polarrigg brims with character, although most is in the public areas and rooms are quite simple. In the main wing, rooms have corridor bathrooms and doubles come with bunk beds. In the smart if somewhat overpriced annexe, rooms have every comfort.

Longyearbyen Camping CAMPING GROUND €
(✎79 02 10 68; www.longyearbyen-camping.com; campsites per person Nkr100-150; ⊙Apr & mid-Jun–mid-Sep) Near the airport on a flat stretch of turf, this particularly friendly camping ground overlooks Isfjorden and the glaciers beyond and has a kitchen and showers. You can hire a tent (per night Nkr100), mattress (Nkr10) and sleeping bag (first/subsequent nights Nkr50/20).

🍴 Eating

Huset NORWEGIAN, INTERNATIONAL €€
(cafe mains Nkr88-175, restaurant mains Nkr295-349, restaurant 3-/4-course Arctic Menus Nkr465/560; ⊙cafe 4-11pm Mon-Sat, 2-11pm Sun, restaurant 7-10pm Tue-Sun) It's something of a walk up here but it's worth it. Dining in the cafe-bar is casual, with well-priced pasta, pizza and reindeer stew on the menu; the daily specials are wonderful. In the same building, the highly regarded restaurant serves up dishes such as terrine of Svalbard reindeer, fillet of reindeer, and quail.

Kroa NORWEGIAN, INTERNATIONAL €€
(lunch mains Nkr76-139, dinner mains Nkr219-235; ⊙11.30am-2am) This pub and restaurant was reconstructed from the elements of a building brought in from Russian Barentsburg (the giant white bust of Lenin peeking from behind the bar gives a clue). Service is friendly and mains verge on the gargantuan. In high season, it's worth booking a table if you don't want to wait.

ℹ Getting Around

Longyearbyen Taxi (✎79 02 13 75) charges up to Nkr150 between the town and the airport. The airport bus (Nkr50) connects with flights.

Around Svalbard

Independent travel around Svalbard is heavily regulated in order to protect both the virgin landscape and travellers. Travel to the very few settlements is usually done as part of a tour package. One of these settlements is Barentsburg (population 400), a Soviet-era relic. Simultaneously depressing and fascinating, this tiny Russian town still mines and exports coal and a statue of Lenin still stares over the bleak built landscape that the impressive natural landscape that surrounds it. Almost-abandoned Pyramiden is a similar deal.

Tourist cruises might also bring you to Ny Ålesund, which, at latitude N79°, is a wild place full of scientists and downright hostile Arctic terns. Remnants of past glories include a stranded locomotive, previously used for transporting coal, and an airship pylon, used by Amundsen and Nobile on their successful crossing of the North Pole in 1926.

The lovely blue-green bay of Magdalen-efjord, flanked by towering peaks and intimidating tidewater glaciers, is the most popular anchorage along Spitsbergen's western coast and is one of Svalbard's prettiest corners.

UNDERSTAND NORWAY

History

Norway's first settlers arrived around 11,000 years ago with the end of the ice age. As the glaciers melted, the earliest hunter-gatherers moved in from Siberia, pursuing migrating reindeer herds. You can see the prehistoric rock drawings of these hunters in the far north on Alta. Shortly afterwards, nomadic European hunters arrived in the south of the country.

The Vikings

Norway greatly impacted Western civilisation during the Viking Age, a period usually dated from the plundering of England's Lindisfarne monastery by Nordic pirates (AD 793). Through the next century, the Vikings conducted raids throughout Europe and established settlements in the Shetland, Orkney and Hebridean islands, the Dublin area (Ireland) and in Normandy (named after the 'North men'). The Viking leader Harald Hårfagre (Fairhair) unified Norway after the decisive naval battle at Hafrsfjord near Stavanger in 872; King Olav Haraldsson, adopting the religion of the lands he had conquered, converted the Norwegians to Christianity and founded the Church of Norway in 1024. See Viking artefacts firsthand in Oslo's Vikingskipshuset and the Lofotr Vikingmuseum in Lofoten.

The Viking Age declined after 1066, with the defeat of the Norwegian king, Harald Hardråda, at the Battle of Stamford Bridge in England. Norwegian naval power was finished off for good when Alexander III, King of Scots, defeated a Viking naval force at the Battle of Largs (Scotland) in 1263.

Under Occupation

In the early 14th century, Oslo emerged as a centre of power and a period of growth followed until 1349, when the bubonic plague swept the country, wiping out two-thirds of the population. In 1380, Norway was absorbed into a union with Denmark that lasted more than 400 years.

Denmark ceded Norway to Sweden in 1814. In 1884 a parliamentary government was introduced in Norway and a growing nationalist movement eventually led to a constitutional referendum in 1905. As expected, virtually no one in Norway favoured continued union with Sweden. The Swedish king, Oskar II, was forced to recognise Norwegian sovereignty, abdicate and reinstate a Norwegian constitutional monarchy, with Håkon VII on the throne. His descendants rule Norway to this day, with decisions on succession remaining under the authority of the *storting* (parliament). Oslo was declared the national capital of the Kingdom of Norway.

Independent Norway

Norway stayed neutral during WWI. Despite restating its neutrality at the start of WWII, it was attacked by the Nazis on 9 April 1940, falling to the Germans after a two-month struggle. King Håkon set up a government in exile in England, and placed most of Norway's merchant fleet under the command of the Allies. Although Norway remained occupied until the end of the war, it had an active Resistance movement, which you can ponder in Bergen's Theta Museum and Narvik's Red Cross War Museum.

The royal family returned to Norway in June 1945. King Håkon died in 1957 and was succeeded by his son, Olav V, a popular king who reigned until his death in January 1991. The current monarch is Harald V, Olav's son, who was crowned in June 1991.

In the late 1960s, oil was discovered in Norway's offshore waters, thereafter transforming Norway from one of Europe's poorest to arguably its richest. Although Norway joined the European Free Trade Association (EFTA) in 1960, it has been reluctant to forge closer bonds with other European nations, in part due to concerns about the impact on its fishing and small-scale farming industries. During 1994 a national referendum on joining the EU was held and rejected. Norway has led many contemporary environmental initiatives, such as the creation of the Svalbard Global Seed Vault (2008), where seeds are stored to protect biodiversity. In 2007 the government declared a goal of making Norway carbon-neutral by 2030, largely by purchasing offsets from developing countries.

The Norwegians

Norway has 4.68 million people and one of Europe's lowest population densities. Most Norwegians are of Nordic origin, and are thought to have descended from central and northern European tribes who migrated northwards around 8000 years ago. In addition, there are about 40,000 Sámi, the indigenous people of Norway's far north who now make up the country's largest ethnic minority. Some Sámi still live a traditional nomadic life, herding reindeer in Finnmark.

Norway has become an increasingly multicultural society in recent years and was, at last count, home to 456,300 immigrants from 216 countries, plus 93,000 people born in Norway to immigrant parents, which together amount to 11.4% of the population (compared with 1.5% in 1970).

Around 87% of Norwegians belong to the Church of Norway, a Protestant Evangelical Lutheran denomination, but most Norwegians only attend church for Christmas and Easter. Around 1.5% of the population are affiliated with the secular Humanist & Ethical Union and there are a number of smaller Christian denominations. A growing Muslim population exists due to recent immigration.

Arts

In the late 19th century and into the early 20th century, three figures – playwright Henrik Ibsen, composer Edvard Grieg and painter Edvard Munch – tower over Norway's cultural life like no others. Their emergence came at a time when Norway was forging its path to independence and pushing the creative limits of a newly confident national identity.

Literature

In the 20th century, three Norwegian writers – Bjørnstjerne Bjørnson (1832–1910), the hugely controversial Knut Hamsun (1859–1952) and Sigrid Undset (1882–1949) – won the Nobel Prize in Literature.

One of the best-known modern Norwegian writers is Jan Kjærstad (b 1953), whose *The Seducer* (2003) combines the necessary recipes for a best seller – a thriller with a love affair and a whiff of celebrity – with seriously good writing. Among other recent Norwegian winners of the prestigious Nordic Council Literature Prize is the prolific Per Petterson (b 1952), who won the prize in 2009 and whose works include *Out Stealing Horses, To Siberia* and *I Curse the River of Time*. If you're lucky enough to get hold of a copy, Angar Mykle's *Lasso Round the Moon* (1954) might be the best book you've never read.

Cinema

Though there aren't many, Norway has produced several good films, including *Elling* (2001), *Buddy* (2003) and *Beautiful Country* (2004). For a Norwegian classic, check out *Ni Liv* (1957), a story concerning the WWII resistance. The Sámi film *Pathfinder* (1987) is a brutal adventure story set in Finnmark 1000 years ago. Information on festivals can be found at www.nfi.no.

Music

Jazz

Norway has a thriving jazz scene, with world-class festivals throughout the year and throughout the country. Jazz saxophonist Jan Garbarek is one of the most enduring Norwegian jazz personalities and is one of the biggest names on the international stage. His work draws on classical, folk and world music influences and he has recorded 30 albums. His 1994 *Officium*, with its echoes of Gregorian chants, did well in the pop charts across Europe, while his 2005 *In Praise of Dreams* received a Grammy nomination. His daughter, Anja Garbarek, is seen as one of the most exciting and innovative performers on the Norwegian jazz scene, bringing pop and electronica into the mix.

Electronica

Norway is at once one of Europe's most prolific producers and most devoted fans of electronica. Röyksopp (www.royksopp.com) in particular took the international electronica scene by storm with its debut album *Melody A.M.* in 2001 and it's never really left the dance-floor charts since.

Metal

Metal is another genre that Norway has taken to heart. Although traditional heavy metal is popular, Norway is particularly known for its black metal scene, which, for a time in the early 1990s, became famous for its anti-Christian, Satanist philosophy with a handful of members of black metal bands involved in the burning down of churches. Among the better-known Norwegian black metal bands are Darkthrone, Mayhem, Emperor, Enslaved, Gorgoroth, Satyricon and Arcturus.

Environment

The Land

Norway's geographical facts themselves tell a story. The Norwegian mainland stretches 2518km from Lindesnes in the south to Nordkapp in the Arctic north, with a narrowest point of 6.3km wide. Norway also has the highest mountains in northern Europe and a land mass of 385,155 sq km (the fourth-largest in Europe, behind France, Spain and Sweden).

Norway is also home to continental Europe's largest icecap (Jostedalsbreen), the world's second- and third-longest fjords (Sognefjorden and Hardangerfjord), Europe's largest and highest plateau (Hardangervidda) and several of the 10 highest waterfalls in the world. Norway's glaciers cover some 2600 sq km (close to 1% of mainland Norwegian territory and 60% of the Svalbard archipelago).

Wildlife

Norway has wild and semidomesticated reindeer herds, thriving elk populations and a scattering of Arctic foxes, lynxes, musk oxen, bears and wolverines. Lemmings occupy mountain areas through 30% of the country. Polar bears (population around 3000 and declining) and walrus are found in Svalbard. Several species of seal, dolphin and whale may be seen around most western and northern coasts.

Birdlife is prolific in coastal areas; puffins, fulmars and kittiwakes are commonly seen. Rarer species include ospreys, golden eagles and white-tailed sea eagles. The islands of Runde, Røst and Værøy are premier places to watch them.

National Parks

At last count, Norway had 40 national parks (including seven in Svalbard, where approximately 65% of the land falls within park boundaries). Ten new national parks have been created since 2003, with a further four new parks and three extensions to existing parks planned. National parks cover 15% of the country. In many cases, the parks don't protect any specific features, nor do they necessarily coincide with the incidence of spectacular natural landscapes or ecosystem boundaries. Instead, they attempt to prevent development of remaining wilderness areas and many park boundaries simply follow contour lines around uninhabited areas.

Norwegian national parks are low profile and lack the traffic and overdeveloped facilities that have overwhelmed other countries' parks. Some parks, notably Jotunheimen and Rondane, are increasingly suffering from overuse, but in most places pollution and traffic are kept to a minimum.

Further national park information is available at local tourist offices and from the Directorate for Nature Management (☑73 58 05 00; www.dirnat.no or www.norgesnasjonalparker.no, both in Norwegian) in Trondheim.

Green Issues

Industrial waste is highly regulated, recycling is popular and the government plans to make Norway carbon-neutral by 2030. There's little rubbish along the roadsides and general tidiness is a high priority in both urban and rural environments. Plastic bottles and cans may be exchanged for cash at supermarkets.

Loss of habitat has placed around 1000 species of plants and animals on the endangered or threatened species lists, and sport hunting and fishing are more popular here than in most of Europe. Hydroelectric schemes have devastated some mountain landscapes and waterfalls, and over-fishing perpetually haunts the economy.

Whaling in Norway is regulated by the International Whaling Commission. Norway resumed commercial whaling of minke whales in 1993, defying an international ban. The government, which supports the protection of threatened species, contends that minke whales, with an estimated population of 100,000, can sustain a limited harvest.

Norwegian Cuisine

Norwegian food *can* be excellent. Abundant seafood and local specialities such as reindeer are undoubtedly the highlights, and most medium-sized towns have fine restaurants in which to eat. The only problem (and it's a significant one) is that prices are prohibitive, meaning that a full meal in a restaurant may become something of a luxury item for all but those on expense accounts. What this does is push many visitors into eating fast-food meals in order to save money, at least at lunchtime, with pizzas, hot dogs and hamburgers a recurring theme.

Striking a balance between eating well and staying solvent requires a clever strategy. For a start, most Norwegian hotels and some hostels offer generous buffet breakfasts, ensuring that you'll rarely start the day on an empty stomach. Many restaurants, especially in larger towns, serve cheaper lunch specials (often from around Nkr79). These are often filling and well sized for those wanting more than a sandwich. Some hotels also lay on lavish dinner buffets in the evening – they're generally expensive, but excellent if it's your main meal of the day.

Staples & Specialities

Norwegian specialities include grilled or smoked *laks* (salmon), *gravat laks* (marinated salmon), *reker* (boiled shrimp), *torsk* (cod), *fiskesuppe* (fish soup), *hval* (whale) and other seafood. Roast reindeer *(reinsdyrstek)* is something every nonvegetarian visitor to Norway should try at least once; it's one of the tastier red meats.

Expect to see sweet brown goat's-milk cheese called *geitost,* and *sild* (pickled herring) with the breads and cereals in breakfast buffets. A fine Norwegian dessert is warm *moltebær syltetøy* (cloudberry jam) with ice cream. Also popular is *eplekake* (apple cake) served with fresh cream. *Lutefisk,* dried cod made almost gelatinous by soaking in lye, is popular at Christmas but it's an acquired taste.

If Norway has a national drink, it's strong black coffee. Most of the beer you'll drink is pilsner. At the other end of the taste spectrum is Norway's bitter aquavit, which does the job at 40% proof.

Where to Eat & Drink

Common throughout all of Norway is the *konditori,* a bakery with tables where you can sit and enjoy pastries and relatively inexpensive sandwiches. Other moderately cheap eats are found at *gatekjøkken* (food wagons and street-side kiosks), which generally have hot dogs for about Nkr20 and hamburgers for Nkr75. Marginally more expensive, but with more nutritionally balanced food, are *kafeterias,* with simple, traditional meals from about Nkr100. In cities, *kafes* almost always function as a hang-out, bar and restaurant. They serve filling 'small dishes' for between Nkr90 and Nkr140. Restaurants vary widely in price, with mains going for Nkr120 to Nkr350.

By international standards, Norwegian restaurant food is bland and heavy, though the cities of Oslo, Bergen, Trondheim and Stavanger have all made vast cuisine improvements.

Vegetarians & Vegans

Being vegetarian in Norway is a challenge and vegan almost impossible. In rural parts of the country, vegetarians will live out of a grocery store, though some cafes serve token dishes such as vegetables with pasta. Another easily found option is pizza, though Norwegian pizza is often bland and soggy. You'll find more options in bigger cities, though most menus are entirely based on fish and meat. About half of the kebab stands serve falafel. Norwegian restaurants aim to please, and will often attempt to make you a special order if you ask (don't expect exciting results though).

Habits & Customs

When invited to someone's house for a meal, it's polite to bring flowers or a bottle of wine. Guests should take their shoes off in the foyer. Table manners don't differ much from those in most of Europe. Locals tend to eat breakfast at home, lunch between 11.30am and 2pm (often with their coworkers) and the evening meal between 6pm and 8pm (often later in larger cities).

SURVIVAL GUIDE

Directory A–Z

Accommodation

During summer, it's wise to reserve all accommodation in advance.

The main tourist season runs from around the middle of June to the middle of August. Unusually, although this is the high season, it's also when accommodation prices are at their lowest and many hotels offer their best deals at this time. Prices are generally much higher during the rest of the year, except on weekends.

Throughout this chapter, each place to stay is accompanied by one of the following symbols (the price relates to a high-season double room with private bathroom and, unless stated otherwise, includes breakfast):

€€€ more than Nkr1400

€€ Nkr750 to Nkr1400

€ less than Nkr750

BED & BREAKFASTS

Some places operate as B&Bs, where prices (usually with shared bathrooms) start at Nkr350/500 for singles/doubles and can go up to Nkr650/900. These options can be tracked down through Bed & Breakfast Norway (www.bbnorway.com).

CAMPING

Norway has more than 1000 camping grounds. Tent space ordinarily costs from Nkr90 at basic camping grounds, up to Nkr200 for those with better facilities. Quoted prices usually include your car, motorcycle or caravan. A per-person charge is also added in some places, electricity often costs a few kroner extra and almost all places charge Nkr10 for showers.

Most camping grounds also rent out simple cabins with cooking facilities, starting at around Nkr350 for a very basic two- or four-bed bunkhouse. Bring a sleeping bag, as linen and blankets are provided only at an extra charge (anywhere from Nkr50 to Nkr100). There are also more-expensive deluxe cabins with shower and toilet facilities (Nkr750 to Nkr1200).

For a comprehensive list of Norwegian camping grounds, visit the following organisations:

Norsk Camping (www.camping.no)

NAF Camp (www.nafcamp.no)

DNT & OTHER MOUNTAIN HUTS

Den Norske Turistforening (DNT; Norwegian Mountain Touring Club; ☏22 82 28 22; www. turistforeningen.no; Storgata 7, Oslo) maintains a network of 460 mountain huts or cabins located a day's hike apart along the country's 20,000km of well-marked and maintained wilderness hiking routes. Those DNT huts include unstaffed huts with two beds, to large staffed lodges with more than 100 beds and renowned standards of service. DNT can provide lists of opening dates for each hut.

GUESTHOUSES & PENSIONS

Many towns have *pensjonat* (pensions) and *gjestehus* (guesthouses) and some, especially the latter, are family-run and offer a far more intimate option than the hostel or hotel experience. Prices for a room with a shared bathroom usually start at Nkr450/700 for singles/doubles but can cost significantly more; linen and/or breakfast will only be included at the higher-priced places.

HOSTELS

In Norway, reasonably priced *vandrerhjem* (hostels) offer a dorm bed for the night, plus use of communal facilities that usually include a self-catering kitchen (you're advised to take your own cooking and eating utensils), internet access and bathrooms. In most hostels, guests must still bring their own sleeping sheet and pillowcase, although most hire sleeping sheets for a one-off fee (starting at Nkr50) regardless of the number of nights.

Most hostels have two- to six-bed rooms and beds cost from Nkr170 to Nkr370. The higher-priced hostels usually include a buffet breakfast, while other places may charge from Nkr50 to Nkr100 for breakfast.

The Norwegian hostelling association, Norske Vandrerhjem (☏23 12 45 10; www. hihostels.no), is HI-affiliated.

HOTELS

Norway's hotels are generally modern and excellent, although those with anything approaching character are pretty thin on the ground. Aside from individual exceptions, it's always worth checking out the worthwhile De Historiske (☏55 31 67 60; www.de historiske.no) network, which links Norway's most historic old hotels and restaurants.

The main hotel chains often have hotel passes, which can entitle you to a free night if you use the chain enough times; some passes only operate in summer. These include the following:

Best Western (www.bestwestern.no)

Choice Hotels (www.choice.no) Covering Clarion, Quality and Comfort Hotels.

Fjord Pass (www.fjordpass.no) Probably the pick (and certainly the largest) of the hotel passes, the Fjord Pass costs Nkr120 (valid for two adults and any children aged under 15 years) and is available at 170 hotels, guesthouses, cabins and apartments year-round; no free nights, but the discounts on nightly rates are considerable.

Rica Hotels (www.rica.no)

Thon Hotels (www.thonhotels.com)

Activities

SUMMER

Norway is gaining traction as a favoured destination for thrill seekers thanks to its combination of highly professional operators and spectacular settings. Extreme sports include **paragliding, parasailing, bungee jumping** (including from a parasail, claimed to be Europe's highest bungee jump) and **skydiving**.

Norway has some of Europe's best **hiking**, including a network of around 20,000km of marked trails that range from easy strolls through the green zones around cities, to long treks through national parks and wilderness areas. Many of these trails are maintained by DNT and are marked either with cairns or red Ts at 100m or 200m intervals.

The hiking season runs roughly from late May to early October, with a much shorter season in the higher mountain areas and the far north. In the highlands, the snow often remains until June and returns in September, meaning that many routes are only possible in July and August.

Den Norske Turistforening (DNT; Norwegian Mountain Touring Club; ☎22 82 28 22; www.turistforeningen.no; Storgata 7, Oslo) is the Norwegian hiker's best friend and is an important resource for anyone heading out on the trail.

Norway's premier **kayaking** sites are clustered around (although by no means restricted to) the Western Fjords and there are numerous operators offering guided kayaking excursions.

The cascading, icy-black waters and whitehot rapids of central Norway are a **rafting** paradise during the short season from mid-June to mid-August. These range from short, Class II doddles to Class III and IV adventures and rollicking Class V punishment.

WINTER
Skiing (both downhill and cross-country) is possible throughout the country in winter.

Dog-sledding is easily our favourite winter activity because it enables you to experience Arctic and sub-Arctic wilderness areas by slowing you down to a pace that suits the quiet beauty of the terrain free from engine noise. Expeditions can range from half-day tasters to multiday trips with overnight stays in remote forest huts. With most operators, you'll have the option (depending on the number of travellers in your group) of 'mushing' your own sled (after a brief primer course before setting out) or sitting atop the sled and watching the world pass by as someone else urges the dogs onwards.

Life for many in the High Arctic would simply not be possible in winter without the **snowmobile**. Most operators allow travellers to ride as a passenger behind an experienced driver or (usually for an additional charge) as the driver yourself; for the latter, a valid driving licence may be required.

Business Hours

Reviews in this chapter don't list business hours unless they differ from the following standard hours. These standard opening hours are for high season (mid-June to mid-September) and tend to decrease outside that time. High-season opening hours for tourist offices and sights are listed throughout the book.

Banks 8.15am-3pm Mon-Wed & Fri, 8.15am-5pm Thu

Drinking 6pm-3am

Eating 8am-11am (breakfast), noon-3pm (lunch), 6-11pm (dinner)

Entertainment 6pm-3am

Offices 9am-5pm Mon-Fri, 10am-2pm Sat

Post offices 9am-5pm Mon-Fri, 10am-2pm Sat; large cities 8am-8pm Mon-Fri, 9am-6pm Sat

Shops 10am-5pm Mon-Wed & Fri, 10am-7pm Thu, 10am-2pm Sat

Children

Norway is a terrific destination in which to travel as a family. This is a country that has become world famous for creating family-friendly living conditions and most hotels, restaurants and many sights are accordingly child-friendly. It's worth remembering, however, that the old parental adage of not trying to be too ambitious in how far you travel is especially relevant in Norway – distances are vast and, such is the terrain, journey times can be significantly longer than for equivalent distances elsewhere.

Food

Restaurants in this chapter have been categorised by the price of an average main course, as follows:

€€€ more than Nkr200

€€ Nkr125 to Nkr200

€ less than Nkr125

Gay & Lesbian Travellers

Norwegians are generally tolerant of alternative lifestyles and on 1 January 2009 Norway became the sixth country in the world to legalise same-sex marriage. That said, public displays of affection are not common practice, except perhaps in some areas of Oslo. Oslo is generally the easiest place to be gay in Norway and it has the liveliest gay scene.

Internet Access

Internet cafes Good cybercafes that last the distance are increasingly hard to find; ask at the local tourist office. Prices per hour range from Nkr40 to Nkr75; students sometimes receive a discount.

Public libraries & tourist offices The scarcity of internet cafes is compensated for by having free internet access available in most municipal libraries (*biblioteket*). As it's a popular service, you may have to reserve a time slot earlier in the day; in busier places, you may be restricted to a half-hour slot. Internet access is also available at some tourist offices around the country; it's sometimes free but there's usually a small fee.

Money

ATMs These machines are ubiquitous, accept most international cards and are available in almost every town mentioned in this book.

Currency The Norwegian krone is most often written NOK in international money markets, Nkr in northern Europe and kr within Norway.

Changing money Don't assume that all banks will change money and in some places you may need to shop around to find one that does. Rates at post offices and tourist offices are generally poorer than at banks, but can be convenient for small amounts outside banking hours. Travellers cheques command a better exchange rate than cash (by about 2%), but may attract commissions.

Public Holidays

New Year's Day (Nyttårsdag) 1 January

Maundy Thursday (Skjærtorsdag) March/April

Good Friday (Langfredag) March/April

Easter Monday (Annen Påskedag) March/April

Labour Day (Første Mai, Arbeidetsdag) 1 May

Constitution Day (Nasjonaldag) 17 May

Ascension Day (Kristi Himmelfartsdag) May/June, 40th day after Easter

Whit Monday (Annen Pinsedag) May/June, eighth Monday after Easter

Christmas Day (Første Juledag) 25 December

Boxing Day (Annen Juledag) 26 December

Norway practically shuts down during the Christmas and Easter weeks.

Telephone
MOBILE PHONES

Close to 90% of the country has GSM mobile access; wilderness areas and national-park hiking trails are exceptions.

Norwegian SIM cards can be purchased from any 7-Eleven store and some Narvesen kiosks; prices start at Nkr200, including Nkr100 worth of calls. However, as the connection instructions are entirely in Norwegian, you're better off purchasing the card from any Telehuset outlet, where they'll help you connect on the spot.

There are three main service providers:

NetCom (www.netcom.no, in Norwegian)

Network Norway (www.networknorway.no, in Norwegian) Operates as Mobile Norway.

Telenor Mobil (www.telenor.com)

PHONE CODES

All Norwegian phone numbers have eight digits. Numbers starting with '800' usually indicate a toll-free number, while those beginning with '9' are mobile or cell-phone numbers.

International access code ⏺00

Norway country code ⏺47

Local area codes None (these are incorporated into listed numbers)

Directory assistance ⏺180 (calls cost Nkr9 per minute)

PHONECARDS

Your best bet is to go for one of the phonecards issued by private companies. Usually costing Nkr100, they allow you to make more than six hours of calls using a scratch PIN number on the back and a local access number.

For international calls, internet-connected calls (eg www.skype.com) are the way to go, although unfortunately if you're not travelling with a laptop, few internet cafes are Skype-enabled; you cannot make phone calls from municipal library computers.

Time

Time in Norway is one hour ahead of GMT/UTC, the same as Sweden, Denmark and most of Western Europe.

When telling time, note that in Norwegian the use of 'half' means 'half before' rather than 'half past'.

Norway observes daylight-saving time, with clocks set ahead one hour on the last Sunday in March and back an hour on the last Sunday in October. Timetables and business hours are posted according to the 24-hour clock.

Tourist Information

It's impossible to speak highly enough of tourist offices in Norway. Most serve as one-stop clearing houses for general information and bookings for accommodation and activities. Nearly every city and town has its own tourist office and most tourist offices in reasonably sized towns or major tourist areas publish comprehensive booklets giving the complete, up-to-date low-down on their town.

Offices in smaller towns may be open only during peak summer months, while in cities they're open year-round but with shorter hours in low season.

Visas

Norway is one of 25 member countries of the Schengen Agreement, under which 22 EU countries (all but Bulgaria, Cyprus, Ireland, Romania and the UK) plus Iceland, Norway and Switzerland have abolished checks at common borders. Citizens of the USA, Canada, Australia and New Zealand need a valid passport to visit Norway, but do not need a visa for stays of less than three months. Citizens of EU countries and other Scandinavian countries do not require visas.

Getting There & Away

Crossing most borders into Norway is usually hassle-free; travellers from non-Western countries or those crossing by land into Norway from Russia should expect more-rigorous searches.

All travellers – other than citizens of Denmark, Iceland, Sweden and Finland – require a valid passport to enter Norway.

Air

For a full list of Norwegian airports, visit www.avinor.no; the page for each airport has comprehensive information. The main international Norwegian airports are: Gardermoen (Oslo), Flesland (Bergen), Sola (Stavanger), Tromsø, Værnes (Trondheim), Vigra (Ålesund), Karmøy (Haugesund), Kjevik (Kristiansand) and Torp (Sandefjord).

Dozens of international airlines fly to/from Norwegian airports. Airlines that use Norway as their primary base include the following:

Norwegian (www.norwegian.com) Low-cost airline.

SAS (www.sas.no)

Widerøe (www.wideroe.no) A subsidiary of SAS.

BUSES

Finland–Norway

FROM	TO	PRICE (€)	DURATION (HR)
Rovaniemi	Alta	97	10
Rovaniemi	Karasjok	76.30	7
Rovaniemi	Tromsø	103.20	8-10
Rovaniemi	Vadsø	100.80	8
Saariselkä	Kirkenes	54.30	3

To Oslo

FROM	FARE	DURATION (HR)	FREQUENCY
Stockholm	from Skr283	8-13	around 5 daily
Gothenburg (Göteborg)	from Skr158	3¾	5 daily
Malmö	from Skr248	8	2-4 daily

Sweden–Norway

FROM	TO	FARE	DURATION (HR)	FREQUENCY	OPERATOR
Gothenburg (Göteborg)	Oslo	Nkr199-484	4	up to three daily	Norwegian Railways
Stockholm	Oslo	from Skr314	6-7½	up to three daily	Swedish Railways
Stockholm	Narvik	from Skr782	18-20	1-2 daily	Swedish Railways
Malmö	Oslo	from Skr401	7½	1 daily	Swedish Railways

Land

Norway shares land borders with Sweden, Finland and Russia.

FINLAND

Buses run between northern Norway and northern Finland with most cross-border services operated by the Finnish company Eskelisen Lapin Linjat (☎016-342 2160; www.eskelisen-lapinlinjat.com). See the table (p414) for options (some in summer only).

RUSSIA

Buses run twice daily between Kirkenes and Murmansk (one way/return Nkr350/Nkr600, five hours). Once in Murmansk, trains connect to St Petersburg and the rest of the Russian rail network.

To cross the border, you'll need a Russian visa, which must usually be applied for and issued in your country of residence.

SWEDEN

Bus

Swebus Express (☎0200 218 218; www.swebusexpress.se) has the largest (and cheapest) buses between Oslo and Swedish cities. GoByBus (www.gobybus.se, in Swedish or Norwegian) is also worth checking out.

Among the numerous cross-border services across the long land frontier between Sweden and Norway, there are services between Narvik and Kiruna, between Bodø and Skellefteå, and between Mo i Rana and Umeå.

Train

Rail services between Sweden and Norway are operated by Norwegian Railways (NSB; ☎81 50 08 88; www.nsb.no) or Swedish Railways (SJ; ☎in Sweden 0771-75 75 99; www.sj.se).

Sea

DENMARK

The following companies operate ferries between Norway and Denmark:

Color Line (☎in Denmark 99 56 19 77, in Norway 22 94 42 00; www.colorline.com)

DFDS Seaways (☎in Denmark 33 42 30 00, in Norway 21 62 13 40; www.dfdsseaways.com)

Fjord Line (☎in Norway 51 46 40 99, in Denmark 97 96 30 00; www.fjordline.com)

Stena Line (☎in Norway 02010; www.stenaline.no)

In the table (p416), listed passenger fares are for high season (mid-June to mid-August); at other times, fares can be half the high-season price but departures are less frequent. Depending on the route, there are a range of prices and accommodation types; check the company websites for the latest fares.

GERMANY & SWEDEN

Color Line (☎in Germany 0431-7300 300, in Norway 81 00 08 11, in Sweden 0526-62000; www.colorline.com) also connects Norway with Germany and Sweden. Check the website for different fare and accommodation types.

Getting Around

Norway has an extremely efficient public transport system and its trains, buses and ferries are often timed to link with each other. The handy *NSB Togruter,* available free at most train stations, details rail timetables and includes information on connecting buses. Boat and bus *ruteplan* (timetables) are available from regional tourist offices.

Rail lines reach as far north as Bodø (you can also reach Narvik by rail from Sweden);

FERRIES

Denmark–Norway

TO	FROM	FARE PER PERSON	DURATION (HR)	WEEKLY DEPARTURES	FERRY OPERATOR
Bergen	Hirtshals	from €30	19½	3	Fjord Line
Kristiansand	Hirtshals	from €39	2¼-3¼	up to 14	Color Line & Fjord Line
Larvik	Hirtshals	from €49.50	3¾	up to 14	Color Line
Oslo	Copenhagen	from €112	16½	7	DFDS Seaways
Oslo	Frederikshavn	from €29	12	7	Stena Line
Stavanger	Hirtshals	from €72	12	4	Fjord Line

Other Ferries to Norway

TO	FROM	FARE PER PERSON	DURATION (HR)	WEEKLY DEPARTURES
Oslo	Kiel (Germany)	from €174.50	20	7
Sandefjord	Strömstad (Sweden)	from €22	2½	up to 20

further north you're limited to buses and ferries. A fine alternative to land travel is the *Hurtigruten* coastal ferry, which calls in at every sizeable port between Bergen and Kirkenes.

Air

Due to the time and distances involved in overland travel, even budget travellers may want to consider a segment or two by air. The major Norwegian domestic routes are quite competitive, meaning that it is possible (if you're flexible about departure dates and book early) to travel for little more than the equivalent train fare.

Four airlines fly domestic routes:

DOT LT (www.flydot.no) Small planes with flights to Oslo from Røros and Fagernes.

Norwegian (www.norwegian.com) Low-cost airline with extensive network throughout the country.

SAS (www.sas.no) The largest route network on mainland Norway and the only flights to Longyearbyen (Svalbard).

Widerøe (www.wideroe.no) A subsidiary of SAS with smaller planes and a handful of flights to smaller regional airports.

Bicycle

Given Norway's great distances, hilly terrain and narrow roads, only serious cyclists engage in extensive cycle touring, but those who do rave about the experience. The long-distance cyclist's biggest headache will be tunnels, and there are thousands of them. Most are closed to nonmotorised traffic; in many (although not all) cases there are outdoor bike paths running parallel to the tunnels.

Rural buses, express ferries and non-express trains carry bikes for various additional fees (around Nkr120), but express trains don't allow them at all and international trains treat them as excess baggage (Nkr275). Nor-Way Bussekspress charges a child's fare to transport a bicycle!

Some tourist offices, hostels and camping grounds rent out bicycles to guests, while *sykkelbutikken* (bicycle shops) are another good place to ask. Rental usually starts at around Nkr60 for an hour and is rarely more than Nkr300 per day.

Boat

An extensive network of ferries and express boats links Norway's offshore islands, coastal towns and fjord districts. See specific destinations for details.

Details on schedules and prices for vehicle ferries and lake steamers are provided in the timetables published by the Norwegian Tourist Board, or *Rutebok for Norge*. Tourist offices can also provide timetables for local ferries.

For more than a century, Norway's legendary Hurtigruten coastal ferry (☎810 03 0 30; www.hurtigruten.com) has served as a lifeline linking coastal towns and villages and it's now one of the most popular ways to explore Norway. Year in, year out, one of 11 *Hurtigruten* ferries heads north from Bergen almost every night of the year, pulling into 35 ports on its six-day journey to Kirkenes, where it then turns around and heads back south. The return journey takes 11 days and covers a distance of 5200km. In agreeable weather (which is by no means guaranteed) the fjord and mountain scenery along the way is nothing short of spectacular.

On board, meals are served in the dining room and you can buy snacks and light meals in the cafeteria.

Long-haul *Hurtigruten* trips can be booked online, while all tickets can be purchased from most Norwegian travel agencies. The *Hurtigruten* website carries a full list of international sales agents.

Summer fares, which run from mid-April to mid-September, are considerably more expensive than winter prices. Prices depend on the type of cabin, which range from those without view to supremely comfortable suites.

It's also possible, of course, to book shorter legs, although you'll probably need to do this once in Norway; the *Hurtigruten* website makes shorter-haul bookings nigh-on impossible. Cars can also be carried for an extra fee. Children aged four to 16 years, students, and seniors over the age of 67, all receive a 50% discount, as do accompanying spouses and children aged 16 to 25 years.

Bus

Nor-Way Bussekspress (☎815 44 444; www.nor-way.no), the main carrier, has routes connecting every main city. Considerably cheaper are buses operated by Lavprisek-spressen (☎67 98 04 80; www.lavpriseksspressen.no, in Norwegian), which sells tickets over the internet. Its buses run along the coast between Oslo and Stavanger (via Kristiansand and most towns in between) and along two north–south corridors linking Oslo with Trondheim. If you're online at the right moment, fares between Oslo and Trondheim can cost as little as Nkr49. There's a host of local bus companies; most of them operate within a single county.

To get a complete listing of bus timetables (and some prices) throughout the country, pick up a copy of the free *Rutehefte* from any reasonably sized bus station and some tourist offices.

Advance reservations are almost never required in Norway, and Nor-Way Bussek-spress even has a 'Seat Guarantee – No Reservation' policy. Unless there's more than nine in your party – then you might be stuffed.

Car & Motorcycle

If you plan to drive through mountainous areas in winter or spring, check first to make sure the passes are open, as some are closed until May or June. The Road User Information Centre (☎175) can tell you about the latest road conditions. Main highways, such as the E16 from Oslo to Bergen and the E6 from Oslo to Kirkenes, are kept open year-round. Cars in snow-covered areas should have studded tyres or carry chains.

If you plan to travel along Norway's west coast, keep in mind that it isn't only mountainous, but deeply cut by fjords. While it's a spectacular route, travelling along the coast requires numerous ferry crossings, which can be time-consuming and costly. For a full list of ferry schedules, fares and reservation phone numbers, consider investing in a copy of *Rutebok for Norge*, the comprehensive transport guide available in larger bookshops.

AUTOMOBILE ASSOCIATIONS

Norges Automobil-Forbund (NAF; ☎92 60 85 05; www.naf.no)

24-hour breakdown assistance (☎08505)

DRIVING LICENCE

Short-term visitors may hire a car with only their home country's driving licence.

FUEL

Leaded and unleaded petrol and diesel are available at most petrol stations. Although prices fluctuate, prevailing prices at the time of research ranged from around Nkr11 per litre up to Nkr13. Diesel usually costs around Nkr1 per litre less. You can pay with major credit cards at most service stations.

In towns, petrol stations may be open until 10pm or midnight, but there are some 24-hour services. In rural areas, many stations close in the early evening and don't open at all on weekends.

MINIPRIS – A TRAVELLER'S BEST FRIEND

On every long-distance train route, for every departure, Norwegian State Railways sets aside a limited number of tickets known as *minipris*. Those who book the earliest can get just about any route for just Nkr199. Once those are exhausted, the next batch of *minipris* tickets goes for Nkr299 and so on. These tickets cannot be purchased at ticket counters and must instead be bought over the internet (www.nsb.no) or in ticket-vending machines at train stations. Remember that *minipris* tickets may only be purchased in advance (minimum one day), reservations are nonrefundable and cannot be changed once purchased.

HIRE

Major international car-rental agencies operate in Norway, but Norwegian car hire is costly and geared mainly to the business traveller. Walk-in rates for a compact car with 200km per day free typically approach Nkr1000 per day (including VAT, but insurance starts at Nkr60 per day extra). In summer, always ask about special offers.

If you'll be using the car for a while, you should seriously consider hiring your car in Sweden and either return it there afterwards, or negotiate a slightly more expensive one-way deal. This is possible through the following online rental agencies, which act as clearing houses for cheap rates from major companies and offer a host of pick-up and drop-off options in Norway and across Europe:

Auto Europe (www.auto-europe.com)

Autos Abroad (www.autosabroad.com)

Ideamerge (www.ideamerge.com)

INSURANCE

Third-party car insurance (unlimited cover for personal injury and Nkr1 million for property damage) is compulsory, and if you're bringing a vehicle from abroad, you'll have fewer headaches with an insurance company Green Card, which outlines the coverage granted by your home policy. Make sure your vehicle is insured for ferry crossings.

ROAD RULES

Blood-alcohol limit 0.02%

Headlights The use of dipped headlights (including on motorcycles) is required at all times and right-hand-drive vehicles must (in theory) have beam deflectors affixed to their headlight in order to avoid blinding oncoming traffic.

Legal driving age for cars 18 years

Legal driving age for motorcycles & scooters 16 to 21 years (depending on the motorcycle's power); a licence is required.

Motorcycle parking Motorcycles may not be parked on the pavement (sidewalk) and are subject to the same parking regulations as cars.

Red warning triangles Compulsory in all vehicles for use in the event of breakdown.

Side of the road Drive on the right.

Speed limits 80km/h on the open road, but pass a house or place of business and the limit drops to 70km/h or even 60km/h. Through villages limits range from 50km/h to 60km/h and, in residential areas, they're 30km/h. A few roads have segments allowing 90km/h or 100km/h. The speed limit for caravans (and cars pulling trailers) is usually 10km/h less than for cars.

Train

Norwegian State Railways (Norges Statsbaner, NSB; ☎81 50 08 88, press 9 for English; www.nsb.no) operates an excellent, though limited, system of lines connecting Oslo with Stavanger, Bergen, Åndalsnes, Trondheim, Fauske and Bodø; lines also connect Sweden with Oslo, Trondheim and Narvik.

Most long-distance day trains have 1st- and 2nd-class seats and a buffet car or refreshment trolley service.

Reservations sometimes cost an additional Nkr50 and are mandatory on some long-distance routes.

There's a 50% discount on rail travel for people aged 67 years and older, for travellers with disabilities, and for children aged between four and 15 years; children under four travel free. Students get discounts of between 25% and 40%.

Sweden

Best Places to Eat

» Mathias Dahlgren (p436)
» Tranan (p436)
» Nystekt Strömming (p435)
» Hambergs Fisk (p450)
» Bakfickan (p490)

Best Places to Stay

» Hotel Hellsten (p434)
» Vandrarhem af Chapman & Skeppsholmen (p433)
» Slottshotellet (p483)
» Växjö Vandrarhem (p480)
» Vadstena Klosterhotel (p479)

Why Go?

As progressive and civilised as it may be, Sweden is a wild place. Its scenery ranges from barren moonscapes and impenetrable forests in the far north to sunny beaches and lush farmland further south. Its short summers and long winters mean that people cling to every last speck of sunshine on a late August evening – crayfish parties on seaside decks can stretch into the wee hours. In winter locals rely on candlelight and *glögg* to warm their spirits. But lovers of the outdoors will thrive here in any season: winter sees skiing and dog-sledding while the warmer months invite long hikes, swimming and sunbathing, canoeing, cycling, you name it – if it's fun and can be done outdoors, you'll find it here. For less rugged types, there's always shopping and nightclub hopping. And in most Swedish cities you'll find top-notch museums dedicated to local and national history, art and culture.

When to Go
Stockholm

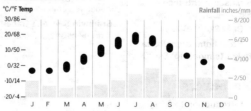

Jun-Aug Sweden's summers are short but intense, and room prices drop.

Sep-Oct Nothing's open, but the countryside is stunning in autumn.

Dec-Feb Winter sports and the aurora borealis (Northern Lights) keep Norrland towns buzzing.

Exchange Rates

Australia	A$1	Skr6.54
Canada	C$1	Skr6.30
Europe	€1	Skr8.90
Japan	¥100	Skr7.35
New Zealand	NZ$1	Skr4.81
UK	UK£1	Skr9.99
USA	US$1	Skr6.00

Set Your Budget

» **Budget hotel room** from Skr800

» **Two-course evening meal** Skr250

» **Museum entrance** Skr70–100

» **Beer** Skr50–60

» **Stockholm tunnelbana ticket (single trip)** Skr30

Resources

» **Introduction to Sámi people** (http://boreale. konto.itv.se/samieng.htm)

» **The Local** (www.thelo cal.se)

» **Smorgasbord** (www. sverigeturism.se/smorgas bord/index.html)

Connections

Trains and buses link Sweden with Norway, Finland and Denmark. Flights connect Göteborg and Stockholm to Iceland. Stockholm-Arlanda Airport connects Sweden with the rest of the world, and domestic flights connect the capital with the country's northern- and southernmost cities. Direct flights link Umeå to various points in the UK. Frequent overnight ferries sail between Stockholm and Helsinki in Finland. Ferries and the Öresund bridge connect Sweden and Denmark.

ITINERARIES

One Week

Spend three days exploring Stockholm and Uppsala, and two days in and around Göteborg before continuing south to the dynamic cities of Malmö and Lund. Alternatively, explore the Stockholm region more thoroughly, including day trips to Drottningholm and Birka and a couple of days in the archipelago, before heading to Uppsala via Sigtuna.

Two Weeks

As above, but include a trip northwards to the Lake Siljan region, then further up towards Sundsvall to explore the dramatic cliffs of Höga Kusten. Outdoorsy types may opt to cycle on Gotland or head up to Abisko for great hiking.

Essential Food & Drink

» **Köttbullar och potatis** Meatballs and mashed potatoes, served with *lingonsylt* (lingonberry jam).

» **Gravlax** Cured salmon.

» **Sill & strömming** Herring, eaten smoked, fried or pickled and often accompanied by capers, mustard and onion; beware the pungent *surströmming* (fermented Baltic herring).

» **Toast skagen** Toast with bleak roe, crème fraiche and chopped red onion.

» **Brännvin** Sweden's trademark spirit, also called aquavit and drunk as *snaps* (vodka).

Sweden Highlights

1 Touring the urban waterways, exploring top-notch museums and wandering the labyrinthine Old Town of **Stockholm** (p422)

2 Hiking through wild landscapes, seeing herds of reindeer, absorbing Sámi culture and sleeping in the world-famous **Ice Hotel** in Jukkasjärvi (p498)

3 Digging into the art, fashion and originality that make Sweden's 'second city' of **Göteborg** (p465) first-rate

4 Celebrating Midsummer in the heartland villages surrounding lovely **Lake Siljan** (p453)

5 Admiring the picturesque farmsteads and cosmopolitan cities that dot the green fields of **Skåne** (p456)

STOCKHOLM

📞08 / POP 809,000

Beautiful capital cities are no rarity in Europe, but Stockholm must surely be near the top of the list for sheer loveliness. The saffron-and-cinnamon buildings that cover its 14 islands rise starkly out of the surrounding ice-blue water, honeyed in sunlight and frostily elegant in cold weather. The city's charms are irresistible. From its movie-set Old Town (Gamla Stan) to its ever-modern fashion sense and impeccable taste in food and design, the city acts like an immersion school in aesthetics.

History

Legend has it that when the town of Sigtuna burned to the ground in 1187, the burghers put all their money into a hollow log and set it afloat, saying, 'Wherever this log washes up, that's where we'll settle next.' An equally reliable story holds that a rebellious fisherman in ancient times caught the biggest fish of his life and swore that it would grace the table of no bishop; so he swam off with the salmon, and where they landed became Stockholm.

Whichever origin story you believe, it's clear that the waterways had a hand in establishing Stockholm's location. Vikings moved their trade centre here from northern Mälaren lake for easier sea–lake trade. Around 1250, Stockholm's leaders wrote a town charter and signed a trade treaty with the Hanseatic port of Lübeck. Stockholm's official founder, Birger Jarl, commissioned the Tre Kronor castle in 1252.

A century later, Stockholm was hurting. The Black Death of 1350 wiped out a third of the population, and in 1391 the Danish Queen Margareta Valdemarsdotter besieged the city for four years. This led to the Union of Kalmar, which linked the crowns of Sweden, Norway and Denmark in 1397. But Sweden soon began to chafe under the union. Discontent peaked with the Stockholm Bloodbath of 1520, when Danish King Christian II tricked, trapped and beheaded 82 Swedish burghers, bishops and nobles on Stortorget in Gamla Stan. One of the 82 victims was the father of Gustav Eriksson Vasa; Gustav Vasa's quest to retaliate eventually led to widespread rebellion against Danish rule – and he became King of Sweden on 6 June 1523. These days, Swedes view Gustav Vasa as equal parts 'father of the country' and ruthless tyrant.

By the end of the 16th century, Stockholm included 9000 people and had expanded beyond Gamla Stan to the neighbouring islands of Norrmalm and Södermalm. The city was officially proclaimed Sweden's capital in 1634, and by 1650 the city had a thriving artistic and intellectual culture and a grand new look, courtesy of father-and-son architects the Tessins. The next growth spurt came in 1871, when Sweden's northern and southern train lines met at Centralstationen (Central Station) and started an industrial boom. The city's population reached 245,000 in 1890.

Sweden's famed neutrality left it and its capital city in good shape through both world wars, but modern times have seen some blemishes on Stockholm's rosy reputation – including the still-unsolved murder of Prime Minister Olof Palme in 1986 and the stabbing death of foreign minister Anna Lindh in 2003. These days, the capital is part of a major European biotechnology region, not to mention a rising star on the world stages of fashion and culinary arts.

⊙ Sights

Stockholm is a compact, walkable city, with sights distributed across all central neighbourhoods. The modern city spreads out from its historic core, Gamla Stan, home to the Royal Palace. Two smaller, satellite islands are linked to it by bridges: Riddarholmen, whose church is home to the royal crypt, to the west, and Helgeandsholmen, home of the Swedish parliament building, to the north. The tourist office is just across the street from Centralstationen, on the main island.

Many of Stockholm's best museums are on Djurgården, east of Gamla Stan, and the small island of Skeppsholmen. Södermalm, the city's funky, bohemian neighbourhood, lies south of Gamla Stan, just beyond the rather baffling traffic interchange called Slussen.

GAMLA STAN

Once you get over the armies of tourists wielding ice-cream cones and shopping bags, you'll discover that the oldest part of Stockholm is also its most beautiful. The city emerged here in the 13th century and grew with Sweden's power until the 17th century, when the castle of Tre Kronor, symbol of that power, burned to the ground. While ambling along Västerlånggatan, look out for Mårten Trotzigs Gränd (Map p428) by No 81: this is Stockholm's narrowest lane, at less than 1m wide.

Kungliga Slottet
CASTLE

(Royal Palace; Map p428; www.royalcourt.se; Slottsbacken; adult/child each attraction Skr100/50, combined ticket Skr140/70; most attractions ⊙10am-5pm daily Jun-Aug) The 'new' palace is built on the ruins of Tre Kronor, which burnt to the ground in the 17th century. Its 608 rooms make it the largest royal palace in the world still used for its original purpose. Many visitors find the Royal Apartments (Map p428) the most interesting, with two floors of royal pomp and princely portraits.

The Swedish regalia and other royal items are displayed at Skattkammaren (Royal Treasury; Map p428), by the southern entrance to the palace near Slottskyrkan (Royal Chapel; Map p428). Gustav III's Antikmuseum (Map p428) displays the Mediterranean treasures, particularly sculpture, acquired by the eccentric monarch. Descend into the basement Museum Tre Kronor to see the foundations of 13th-century defensive walls and exhibits rescued from the medieval castle during the fire of 1697.

The **Changing of the Guard** takes place in the outer courtyard at 12.15pm Monday to Saturday and 1.15pm Sunday and public holidays from June to August, and 12.15pm Wednesday and Saturday and 1.15pm Sunday and public holidays from September to May.

Nobelmuseet
MUSEUM

(Map p428; http://nobelmuseet.se; Stortorget; adult/child Skr70/free; ⊙10am-5pm Wed-Mon, to 8pm Tue mid-May–mid-Sep) On nearby Stortorget is this excellent museum, presenting the history of the Nobel Prize and past laureates as well as changing exhibitions about art, science, creativity and inspiration. Befitting a museum dedicated to the spirit of creativity and invention, it's a beautifully designed space, with long sleek rows of information panels and subtly placed multimedia nooks.

Livrustkammaren
MUSEUM

(Royal Armoury; Map p428; www.livrustkammaren. se; Slottsbacken 3; adult/child Skr90/free; ⊙10am-5pm daily Jun-Aug) The large collection of royal memorabilia includes ceremonial costumes and colourful carriages. Kungliga Myntkabinettet (Royal Coin Cabinet; Map p428; ☑51 95 53 04; Slottsbacken 6; adult/child Skr60/free; ⊙10am-4pm), opposite the palace, covers the history of money and finance.

Riddarholmskyrkan
CHURCH

(Map p428; ☑402 61 30; adult/child Skr30/15; ⊙10am-5pm daily Jun-Aug) The island of Riddarholmen has some of the oldest buildings in Stockholm, most prominently this church with its striking iron spire, home to the royal necropolis. Guided tours (in English at 3pm) include lots of detailed stories and are recommended.

Storkyrkan
CHURCH

(Map p428; adult/child Skr40/free, admission free Oct-Apr; ⊙9am-6pm mid-May–Oct) Near the palace is the Royal Cathedral of Sweden, consecrated in 1306. The most notable feature is the life-sized *St George & the Dragon* sculpture, dating from the late 15th century.

FREE Medeltidsmuseet
MUSEUM

(Medieval Museum; Map p428; www.medeltidsmuseet.stockholm.se; Strömparterren; ⊙noon-5pm Tue-Sun, noon-7pm Wed, noon-5pm Mon Jul & Aug) This atmospheric, kid-friendly place is situated on the opposite side of Helgeandsholmen from the parliament building. While preparing to build a Riksdag car park here in the late 1970s, construction workers unearthed foundations dating from the 1530s. The ancient walls were preserved as found, and a museum was built around them.

DJURGÅRDEN

The royal playground, Djurgården is an urban oasis of parkland with some of Stockholm's best attractions. To get here, take bus or tram 47, or the Djurgården ferry from Nybroplan or Slussen. Beyond the large tourist haunts are plenty of small gems, including some excellent art collections. You can rent bikes near the bridge in summer, and cycling is the best way to explore the island.

Skansen
MUSEUM

(Map p424; www.skansen.se; adult/child Skr120/50, less in low season; ⊙10am-8pm May–late Jun, 10am-10pm late Jun–Aug, 10am-8pm Sep) The world's first open-air museum, Skansen was founded in 1891 by Artur Hazelius to give visitors an insight into how Swedes lived once upon a time. You could easily spend a day here and still not see it all. It's meant to be 'Sweden in miniature', complete with villages, nature, commerce and industry. The glass-blowers' cottage is a popular stop; watching the intricate forms emerge from glowing blobs of liquid glass is transfixing. The **Nordic Zoo**, with moose, reindeer, wolverine and other native wildlife, is a particular highlight, especially in spring when baby critters scamper around. Check the website for individual workshop closing times.

Stockholm

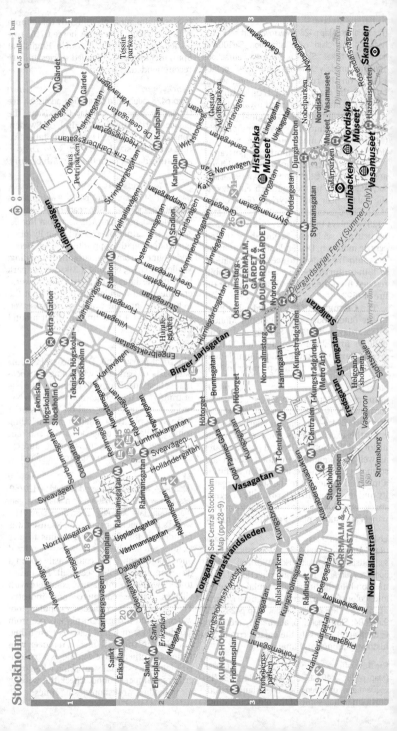

1 km
0.5 miles

Tessin-parken

Gärdet

Gärdet

Rindögatan

Olaus Petriparken

Erik Dahlbergsgatan

Hedinsgatan

Askrikegatan

De Geersgatan

Valhallavägen

Karlaplan

Karlaplan

Gustav Adolfsparken

Banérgatan

Karlavägen

Nobelparken

Nordiska

Linnégatan

Limnégatan

Witstocksgatan

Narvavägen

Historiska Museet

Nordiska Museet

Skansen

Rosendalsvägen

Hazeliusporten

Vasamuseet

Djurgårdsbrunnsviken

Djurgårdsbron

Museet · Vasamuseet

Galärparken

Junibacken

Vasamuseet

Lidingövägen

Valhallavägen

Strindbergsgatan

Valhallavägen

Karlavägen

Karlaplan

Strandvägen

Skeppargatan

Grevgatan

Riddargatan

Styrmansgatan

Styrmansgatan

Nobelparken

Stadion

Stadion

Östermalmsgatan

Karlavägen

Kommendörsgatan

Linnégatan

Strandvägen

ÖSTERMALM, GÄRDET & LADUGÅRDSGÄRDET

Djurgårdsfärjan (Summer Only)

Djurgårdsfärjan Ferry (Summer Only)

Norrström

Teknisk Högskolan Stockholm Ö

Tekniska Högskolan-Stockholm Ö

Östra Station

Valhallavägen

Engelbrektsgatan

Humle-gården

Villagatan

Floragatan

Braheg.

Grev Turegatan

Sturegatan

Humlegårdsgatan

Östermalmstorg

Östermalmstorg

Nybroplan

Berzelii

Nybroplan

Strandvägen

Birger Jarlsgatan

Brunnsgatan

Norrmalmstorg

Hamngatan

Kungsträdgården

Strömgatan

Helgeands-holmen

Sveavägen

Norrtullsgatan

Odenplan

Odenplan

Rehnsgatan

Kungstensgatan

Rådmansgatan

Luntmakargatan

Sveavägen

Holländergatan

Surbrunnsgatan

Odengatan

Rådmansgatan

Hötorget

Hötorget

Olof Palmes Gata

Kungsgatan

Vasagatan

T-Centralen

T-Centralen

Kungsträdgården (Metro Art)

Fredsgatan

Strömgatan

Vasabron

Strömsborg

Klara Sjö

Stockholm

See Central Stockholm Map (pp428–9)

Vanadisvägen

Karlbergsvägen

Freigatan

Sankt Eriksplan

Sankt Eriksplan

Dalagatan

Upplandsgatan

Västmannagatan

Rådmansgatan

Torsgatan

Klarastrandsleden

Kungsholmsstrandsstig

Kungsbron

Kungsbron

Klarabergsviadukten

NORRMALM & VASASTAN

Centralstationen

Stockholm Centralstationen

Sankt Eriksplan

Sankt Eriksgatan

Atlasgatan

Kungsholms-parken

Kronobergs-parken

Polhemsgatan

KUNGSHOLMEN

Fridhemsplan

Fridhemsplan

Hantverkargatan

Fleminggatan

Kungsholmsgatan

Polishusparken

Rådhuset

Rådhuset

Bergsgatan

Kungsholmstorg

Norr Mälarstrand

Norr Mälarstrand

Pipersgatan

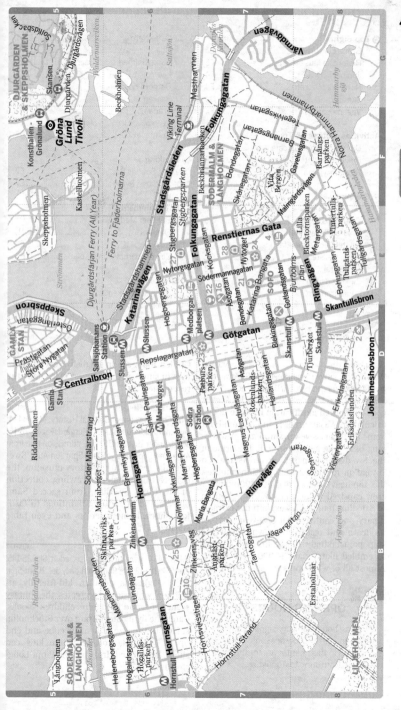

Stockholm

Vasamuseet   MUSEUM

(Map p424; www.vasamuseet.se; Galärvarvsvägen 14; adult/under 19yr Skr110/free, adult Skr80 5-8pm Wed Sep-May; ☉8.30am-6pm Jun-Aug) A good-humoured glorification of some dodgy calculation, Vasamuseet is the custom-built home of the massive warship *Vasa*. A whopping 69m long and 48.8m tall, the pride of the Swedish crown set off on its maiden voyage on 10 August 1628. Within minutes, the top-heavy vessel and its 100-member crew capsized tragicomically to the bottom of Saltsjön. Tour guides explain the extraordinary and controversial 300-year story of its death and resurrection, which saw the ship painstakingly raised in 1961 and reassembled like a giant 14,000-piece jigsaw. Almost all of what you see today is original.

OPENING HOURS

Opening hours can vary significantly between high and low seasons. Hours provided in this chapter are for the high season, from June to August.

Guided tours are in English every 30 minutes in summer, and at least twice daily the rest of the year.

Nordiska Museet   MUSEUM

(National Museum of Cultural History; Map p424; www.nordiskamuseet.se; Djurgårdsvägen 6-16; adult/under 19yr Skr80/free, admission free from 4pm Wed Sep-May; ☉10am-5pm Jun-Aug) Sweden's largest cultural history museum, the epic Nordiska has a sprawling collection of all things Swedish, from sacred Sámi objects and Strindberg paintings to fashion, shoes, home interiors and even table settings.

Junibacken   MUSEUM

(Map p424; www.junibacken.se; adult Skr125-145, child Skr110-125; ☉9am-6pm daily Jul, 10am-5pm Jun & Aug) This popular, kid-friendly attraction whimsically recreates the fantasy scenes of Astrid Lindgren's children's books. Catch the flying Story Train over Stockholm, shrink to the size of a sugar cube and end up in Villekulla cottage where kids can shout, squeal and dress up like Pippi Longstocking.

Gröna Lund Tivoli AMUSEMENT PARK

(Map p424; www.gronalund.com; admission/under 7yr Skr90/free; ⊗noon-10pm Mon-Sat, to 8pm Sun Jun, 11am-10pm Sun-Thu, to 11pm Fri & Sat Jul–early Aug, varies May & early Aug–mid-Sep) This fun park has dozens of rides and amusements – the Åkband day pass (Skr289) gives unlimited rides, or individual rides range from Skr20 to Skr60. Big-name concerts are often held here in summer.

CENTRAL STOCKHOLM

The fashionable, high-heeled heart of modern-day Stockholm beats in bustling Norrmalm. Near T-Centralen station is Sergels Torg (Map p428), a severely modern public square (actually round) bordered on one side by the imposing Kulturhuset. Norrmalm is also home to the beloved public park Kungsträdgården (Map p428), where locals gather in all weather. The park is home to an outdoor stage, winter ice-skating rink and restaurants, cafes and kiosks. Vasastan is the somewhat quieter, more residential area that extends to the north of Norrmalm.

Nationalmuseum MUSEUM

(Map p428; www.nationalmuseum.se; Södra Blasieholmshamnen; adult/under 19yr Skr120/free; ⊗11am-5pm Wed-Sun, to 8pm Tue Jun-Aug) Sweden's largest art museum, the excellent Nationalmuseum houses the national collection of painting, sculpture, drawings, decorative arts and graphics, from the Middle Ages to the present. Don't miss the immense and once-controversial 'Midwinter Sacrifice,' one of several Carl Larsson paintings gracing the walls above the main stairway.

Historiska Museet MUSEUM

(Museum of National Antiquities; Map p424; www.historiska.se; Narvavägen 13; adult/under 19yr Skr70/free; ⊗10am-5pm daily May-Sep) Sweden's main national historical collection is at the enthralling Historiska Museet. Displays cover prehistoric, Viking and medieval archaeology and culture; don't miss the incredible **Gold Room** with its rare treasures, including a seven-ringed gold collar.

Kulturhuset LEISURE COMPLEX

(Map p428; www.kulturhuset.stockholm.se; Sergels Torg) This glass-fronted community centre in Sergels Torg houses temporary exhibitions (often with entry fee), a theatre, bookshop, design store, reading room, several cafes, a comics library and bar. It's open daily, although some sections are closed on Monday.

SKEPPSHOLMEN

Moderna Museet MUSEUM

(Map p424; www.modernamuseet.se; Exercisplan 4; adult/under 19yr Skr100/free; ⊗10am-8pm Tue, 10am-6pm Wed-Sun) Across the bridge by the Nationalmuseum is the sleek, impressive Moderna, which boasts a world-class collection of modern art, sculpture, photography and installations, temporary exhibitions and an outdoor sculpture garden. The adjacent

---

STOCKHOLM IN...

Two Days

Beat the crowds to the labyrinthine streets of **Gamla Stan** for a coffee in an atmospheric, ancient cafe on Stortorget, the main square. Watch St George wrestle the dragon inside **Storkyrkan**, then join a tour of **Kungliga Slottet**, the royal palace, or simply watch the midday changing of the guard. Wander down to Slussen and catch a ferry across to Skeppsholmen for lunch and Lichtenstein at **Moderna Museet**, then walk back to Södermalm for dizzying views atop **Katarinahissen** and an evening of dinner and drinks in funky Södermalm (try the bar-lined street Skånegatan). Spend the next day exploring **Skansen**, before dinner and drinks at **Sturehof** – and if you have energy left, check out some of the clubs around Stureplan.

Four Days

As above, but with a little detour out of town on the third day – if the weather's nice, rent a bicycle and follow the bicycle path to **Drottningholm Slott**. Keep the Swedish-history theme going with a meal at **Den Gyldene Freden**. Next day, take a boat tour onto the archipelago, then dine at the Grand Hôtel's **Verandan** restaurant and finish in style with a drink at **Operan**.

SWEDEN STOCKHOLM

Central Stockholm

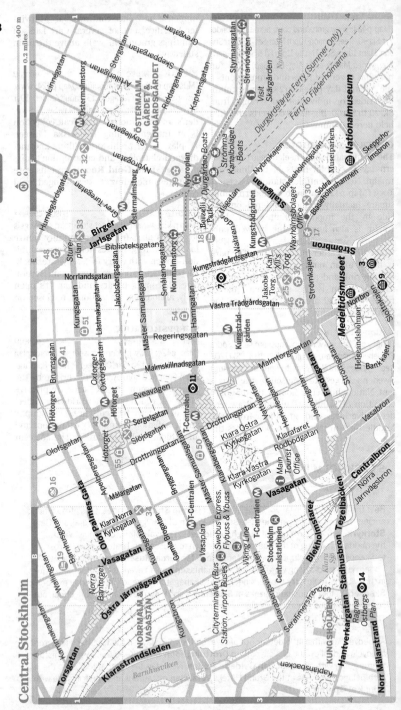

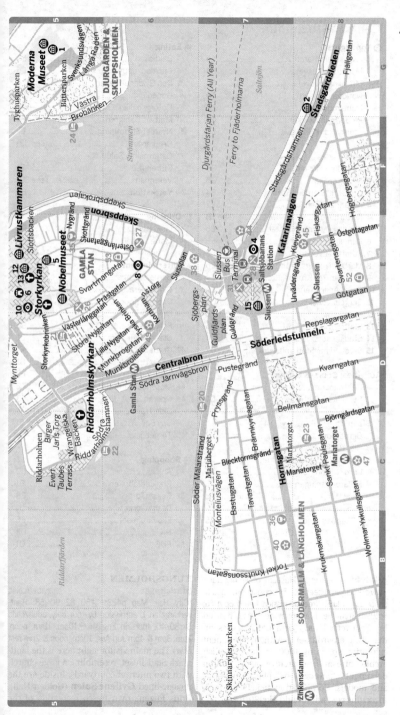

Moderna Museet 1

DJURGÅRDEN & SKEPPSHOLMEN

Tyghusparken

Stenshundsvägen

Långa Raden

Battenparken

Västra Brobänken

24

Strömmen

Djurgårdsfärjan Ferry (All Year)

Ferry to Fjäderholmarna

Saltsjön

Stadsgårdsleden

Stadgårdshamnen

2

Fjällgatan

Högbergsgatan

Högbergsgatan

Katarinavägen

Klevgränd

Fiskargatan

Östgötagatan

45

Svartensgatan

Slussen

52

Götgatan

Repslagargatan

Kvarngatan

Söderledstunneln

Livrustkammaren

Slottsbacken

Skeppsbron

Skeppsbrokajen

Nygrand

Skottgränd

Skeppsbrokajen

Österlånggatan

GAMLA STAN

Svartmangatan

Prästgatan

35

27

Slussen Bus Terminal

Slussplan

38

31

Slussen

Saltsjöbanans Station

Nobelmuseet

12 13

5

Storkyrkan

10 6

Storkyrkobrinken

Västerlånggatan

Stora Nygatan

Lilla Nygatan

26

Köpmangatan

Köpmanbrinken

Tyska Brinken

Trångsund

8

Sjöbergs-plan

Sjöbergs-plan

Guldfjärds-plan

Guldgränd

15

Uvädersgränd

Riddarholmskyrkan

Munkbrogatan

Munkbroleden

Gamla Stan

Centralbron

Södra Järnvägsbron

Pusegränd

Söderledstunneln

Riddarholmen

Birger Jarls Torg

Evert Taubes Terrass

Wrangelska Backen

Södra Riddarholmshamnen

22

20

Prysgränd

Söder Mälarstrand

Mariaberget

Bellmansgatan

Björngårdsgatan

Mariatorget

23

Söder Mälarstrand

Blecktornsgränd

Brännkyrkagatan

Hornsgatan

Mariatorget

Mariatorget

47

Montelíusvägen

Bastugatan

Tavastgatan

Sankt Paulsgatan

Riddarfjärden

36

SÖDERMALM & LÅNGHOLMEN

40

Torkel Knutssonsgatan

Krukmakargatan

Wollmar Yxkullsgatan

Skinnarviksparken

Zinkensdamm

Mynttorget

Central Stockholm

Arkitekturmuseet (Museum of Architecture; www.arkitekturmuseet.se; Exercisplan 4; adult/under 19yr Skr50/free, admission free 4-6pm Fri; ⊗10am-8pm Tue, 10am-6pm Wed-Sun), housed in a converted navy drill hall, focuses on the built environment, with a permanent exhibition spanning 1000 years of Swedish architecture and an archive of 2.5 million documents, photographs, plans, drawings and models. Combination tickets for both museums cost adult/child Skr130/free.

KUNGSHOLMEN

Stadshuset CIVIC BUILDING
(City Hall; Map p428; ☎50 82 90 58; Hantverkargatan 1; admission by tour only, adult/child Skr80/40; tours in English ⊗10am, 11am, noon, 2pm, 3pm & 4pm Jun-Aug, 10am, noon & 2pm rest of yr) The main visitor sight here is the landmark Stadshuset, resembling a large church with two internal courtyards. Inside are the mosaic-lined **Gyllene Salen** (Golden Hall), Prins Eugen's own fresco recreation of the

lake view from the gallery, and the **Blå Hallen** (Blue Hall), where the annual Nobel Prize banquet is held. You can walk down the staircase just like the Nobel laureates do, only without putting in all that hard work. The tower (admission Skr30; ⊙9am-5pm Jun-Aug, 9am-4pm May & Sep) offers stellar views and a great thigh workout.

SÖDERMALM
Once-working-class 'Söder' is Stockholm's coolest neighbourhood, jammed with up-and-coming boutiques and galleries, hip cafes and bars and a museum of city history. 'SoFo' (the area south of Folkungagatan) is the trendiest district.

Fotografiska   GALLERY
(Map p428; Stadsgårdshamnen 22; http://foto grafiska.eu; adult/child Skr95/free; ⊙10am-9pm) This 2500-sq-metre gallery space, housed in an old customs building, hosts several major photography exhibitions each year, all of them impressively thorough and atmospherically staged. Those with even a passing interest in photography should make a point of stopping in. The upstairs cafe has the most artfully arranged display of sandwiches imaginable.

FREE Stockholms Stadsmuseum   MUSEUM
(City Museum; Map p428; www.stadsmuseum. stockholm.se; Slussen; ⊙11am-5pm Tue-Sun, 11am-8pm Thu) The city museum covers Stockholm's development from fortified port to modern metropolis via plague, fire and good old-fashioned scandal. Fans of Stieg Larsson's *Girl with the Dragon Tattoo* novel trilogy can take the museum's Millennium tour (in English at 11.30am Saturday, tickets Skr120; self-guided tour map Skr40).

Katarinahissen   ELEVATOR
(Map p428; Slussen; admission Skr10; ⊙8am-10pm mid-May–Aug, 10am-6pm rest of yr) Start any visit to this neighbourhood with a panoramic view over Stockholm from the top of this lift, dating from the 1930s. It takes you up 38m to the heights of Slussen. If you prefer, zigzagging wooden stairs also lead up the cliffs to the balcony. At the top is one of the city's best restaurants, **Gondolen** (p436).

LADUGÅRDSGÄRDET
The vast parkland of Ladugårdsgärdet is part of the 27-sq-km Ekoparken (www. ekoparken.com), the world's first national

STOCKHOLM CARD   431

Available from tourist offices, camping grounds, hostels, hotels and Stor-stockholms Lokaltrafik (SL) public transport centres, the Stockholm Card (www.stockholmtown.com; adult 24/48/72/120hr Skr395/525/625/895, accompanying child Skr195/225/245/285) gives free entry to about 75 attractions (including Skansen), free city parking in metered spaces, free sightseeing by boat and free travel on public transport (including Katarinahissen, but excluding local ferries and airport buses).

park within a city. An impressive 14km long, its combo of forest and open fields stretches far into the capital's northern suburbs. This section of it, reached by bus 69 from Centralstationen or Sergels Torg, boasts three fine museums and one of Stockholm's loftiest views.

FREE Etnografiska Museet   MUSEUM
(Museum of Ethnography; www.etnografiska.se; Djurgårdsbrunnsvägen 34; ⊙10am-5pm Mon-Fri, 11am-5pm Sat & Sun) Brings the world under one roof.

Sjöhistoriska Museet   MUSEUM
(National Maritime Museum; www.sjohistoriska.se; Djurgårdsbrunnsvägen 24; adult/under 18yr Skr50/ free, admission free Mon; ⊙10am-5pm) Exhibits maritime memorabilia.

Tekniska Museet   MUSEUM
(Museum of Science & Technology; www.tekniska museet.se; Museivägen 7; adult/child Skr80/40, admission free from 5pm Wed; ⊙10am-5pm Mon-Fri, to 8pm Wed, 11am-5pm Sat & Sun) Exhibits on Swedish inventions and their applications.

Kaknästornet   VIEWPOINT
(☑667 21 80; www.kaknastornet.se; adult/child Skr40/20; ⊙9am-10pm Jun-Aug) This 155m-high TV tower has an observation deck with stunning 360-degree views, plus a restaurant.

Activities
Summer sees many head for the coast and the islands of the archipelago (with good swimming spots). Winter also sees some outdoor activity, including ice-skating on a rink set up in Kungsträdgården.

ℹ️ STOCKHOLM À LA CARTE

Destination Stockholm (📞663 00 80; www.destination-stockholm.com; from Skr465) offers discount hotel-and-sightseeing packages that can be booked online. Its Stockholm à la Carte package is available weekends year-round and throughout the summer.

Swimming Pools   SWIMMING
Eriksdalsbadet (Map p424; 📞50 84 02 58; Hammarby slussväg 8; adult/4-19yr Skr90/40) has indoor and open-air swimming pools in the far south of Södermalm, plus gym, aerobics and other activities. For more atmospheric splashing there's art nouveau **Centralbadet** (Map p428; www.centralbadet. se; Drottninggatan 88; adult Skr130, Skr180 Fri & Sat after 3pm; ⏰6am-9pm Mon-Fri, 8am-9pm Sat, 8am-6pm Sun), where entry includes pool, sauna and gym access. Treatments, including massage, facials and body wraps, are available for an additional fee and are best booked two weeks ahead.

Strandbryggan   BOATING
(Map p424; www.strandbryggan.se; Strandvägs-kajen 27) Opposite Djurgårdsbrons Sjöcafe, this floating resto-bar rents out sailing and motor boats from April to September. Sailing boats cost around Skr500 per hour, and all boats can be rented for a day, weekend or week.

Djurgårdsbrons Sjöcafe   OUTDOOR ACTIVITIES
(Map p424; 📞660 57 57; canoes per hr/day Skr80/300; ⏰9am-9pm mid-Apr–mid-Sep) Next to the bridge leading to Djurgården, this place rents out bicycles, in-line skates, kayaks, canoes, rowing boats and pedal boats.

Stockholm City Bikes   CYCLING
(www.stockholmcitybikes.se) Has 67 self-service bicycle-hire stands across the city. To use, purchase a bike card (three days/season card Skr125/250) from the tourist office.

🚌 Tours

Stockholm Sightseeing (Map p428; 📞12 00 40 00; www.stockholmsightseeing.com) operates frequent cruises from early April to mid-December around the central bridges and canals from Strömkajen (near the Grand Hôtel), Nybroplan or Stadshusbron;

you'll find ticket booths at these departure points. Some of the one-hour tours are free for Stockholm Card holders, but the two-hour tour, Under the Bridges of Stockholm (Skr200), covers more territory and passes under 15 bridges and through two locks, with a recorded commentary in several languages to fill in the history of the areas you pass by.

🎉 Festivals & Events

Smaka På Stockholm   FOOD
(www.smakapastockholm.se) Taste samples from some of Stockholm's top kitchens and watch cooking duels at this weeklong annual festival in Kungsträdgården, held in the first week of June.

Stockholm Jazz Festival   MUSIC
(www.stockholmjazz.com) Held on the island of Skeppsholmen in late July, this internationally known jazz festival brings artists from all over, including big names such as Van Morrison and Mary J Blige; evening jam sessions at famed Stockholm jazz club Fasching are a highlight.

Stockholm Pride   GAY & LESBIAN
(www.stockholmpride.org/en/) This annual parade and festival in late July to early August is dedicated to creating an atmosphere of freedom and support for gay, lesbian, bisexual and transgender people.

Stockholm International Film Festival   FILM
(www.stockholmfilmfestival.se) Screenings of new international and independent films, director talks and discussion panels draw cinephiles to this important annual festival in mid-November. Tickets go quickly, so book early if you're interested.

🛏️ Sleeping

Whether you slumber in youth hostels, B&Bs, boutique digs or big-name chains, you can expect high-quality accommodation in Stockholm. The trade-off is that it can be an expensive city to sleep in, but deals do exist! Major hotel chains are invariably cheaper if booked online and in advance, and most hotels offer discounted rates on weekends (Friday, Saturday and often Sunday night) and in summer (mid-June to mid-August), sometimes up to 50% off the listed price. Unless otherwise noted, we list standard weekday prices here, but for most accommodation, the price you'll pay will depend on several variables, including demand at time of booking.

A number of agencies, including Bed & Breakfast Service (☑660 55 65; www.bedbreakfast.se; info@bedbreakfast.se) and Bed & Breakfast Agency (☑643 80 28; www.bba.nu; info@bba.nu), can arrange apartment or B&B accommodation from around Skr300 per person per night.

Stockholm has several HI-affiliated Svenska Turistföreningen (STF) hostels, as well as Sveriges Vandrarhem i Förening (SVIF) and independent hostels (no membership cards required). Many have options for single, double or family rooms. Many hostels have breakfast available, usually for an additional Skr65 to Skr80. Sheets are almost always required; if you don't have your own, you'll need to rent them (around Skr50).

Finding midrange rooms (with a standard rate of Skr800 to Skr1600 per room) can be a bit of a struggle, but note that many of the top-end choices fall into this category with the summer/weekend discounts.

TOP CHOICE Vandrarhem af Chapman & Skeppsholmen HOSTEL €

(Map p428; ☑463 22 66; www.stfchapman.com; dm from Skr215, s & d from Skr530; ❷) The legendary af Chapman is a storied vessel that has done plenty of travelling of its own. It's now well anchored in a superb, quiet location, swaying gently off Skeppsholmen. Bunks in dorms below decks have a nautical ambience, unsurprisingly. Staff members are friendly and knowledgeable about the city and surrounding areas. Apart from showers and toilets, all facilities are on dry land in the Skeppsholmen hostel, where you'll find a good kitchen with a laidback common room and a separate TV lounge. Laundry facilities and 24-hour internet access are available.

Rival Hotel HOTEL €€€

(Map p428; ☑54 57 89 00; www.rival.se; Mariatorget 3; s/d Skr2295/2495; ❷) Owned by ABBA's Benny Andersson and overlooking leafy Mariatorget, this ravishing design hotel is a chic retro gem, complete with vintage 1940s movie theatre and over-the-top art deco cocktail bar. The super-comfy rooms feature posters from great Swedish films and a teddy bear to make you feel at home. Both the smoking and nonsmoking rooms boast flat-screen TVs and good-sized bathrooms, and there's a scrumptious designer bakery–cafe beside the foyer.

Zinkensdamm Hotell & Vandrarhem HOTEL, HOSTEL €€

(Map p424; ☑616 81 00; www.zinkensdamm.com; Zinkens väg 20; dm Skr230, hostel s/d Skr430/600, hotel r from Skr1505; ❷) With a foyer that looks like one of those old Main St facade recreations you find in cheesy museums, the Zinkensdamm STF is unabashedly fun. It's attractive and well equipped – complete with an ubersleek guest kitchen and personal lockers in each room – and caters for families with kids as well as pub-going backpackers; so it can be crowded and noisy, but that's the trade-off for an upbeat vibe. While the hostel breakfast buffet isn't spectacular, you can buy breakfast in the attached restaurant-pub, which also serves lunch and dinner.

STF Vandrarhem Gärdet HOSTEL €

(☑463 22 99; gardet@stfturist.se; Sandhamnsgatan 59; dm/s/d from Skr340/540/680; ❷) Located in quiet Gärdet, a quick metro ride from Östermalm, Stockholm's first 'designer hostel' ditches low-cost drab for smart, contemporary rooms featuring red pin chairs and clever use of space. Some rooms are almost comically tiny, but each comes equipped with a flat-screen TV, comfy beds and a hotel-grade private bathroom. Sheets and towels are included in the price. Several walking trails through lush parkland pass nearby. Take bus 1 from Centralstationen (or Gärdet tunnelbana stop) to Östhammarsgatan bus stop.

Bed & Breakfast 4 Trappor B&B €€

(Map p424; ☑642 31 04; www.4trappor.se; Gotlandsgatan 78; apt s/d Skr725/850, incl breakfast Skr800/1000) For elegant slumming, it's hard to beat this sassy, urbane apartment, complete with cosy, floorboarded bedroom (maximum two guests), modern bathroom and well-equipped kitchen (espresso machine included!). Breakfast is served in the wonderful owners' next-door apartment, and the SoFo address means easy access to Stockholm's coolest shops and hang-outs. There's a two-night minimum stay and a discounted rate for stays of more than five nights. It's a huge hit, so book months ahead.

Columbus Hotell HOTEL €€

(Map p424; ☑50311200; www.columbus.se; Tjärhovsgatan 11; budget annexe s/d/tr Skr795/925/1150, s/d Skr1295/1595; ❷) Family owned and highly recommended, Columbus Hotell is nestled in a quiet part of Södermalm, near

T-Medborgarplatsen, and set around a cobblestone courtyard by a pretty park. Accompanying the budget rooms (which have TV, telephone and shared bathroom facilities) are comfortable hotel-standard rooms.

TOP CHOICE Hotel Hellsten   HOTEL €€

(Map p424; ☎661 86 00; www.hellsten.se; Luntmakargatan 68; s/d from Skr1190/1390; @) Hip Hellsten is owned by anthropologist Per Hellsten and features objects from his travels and life, including Congan tribal masks and his grandmother's chandelier. Rooms are supremely comfortable and individually styled, with themes spanning rustic Swedish to Indian exotica; some even feature original tile stoves. The sleek bathrooms sport phones and hand-cut Greek slate. Hotel extras include a sauna and small fitness room, as well as live jazz in the ethno-chic lounge on Thursday evenings.

Långholmen Hotell & Vandrarhem   HOSTEL, HOTEL €

(☎668 05 10; www.langholmen.com; hostel dm adult/child Skr240/115, 2-/4-bed cells per person Skr295/240, hotel s/d Skr1590/1950; @) Guests at this hotel/hostel, in a former prison on Långholmen island, sleep in bunks in a cell. The friendly, efficient staff members assure you they will not lock you in. The kitchen and laundry facilities are good, the restaurant serves meals all day, and Långholmen's popular summertime bathing spots are a towel flick away.

Den Röda Båten – Mälaren/Ran   HOTEL, HOSTEL €€

(Map p428; www.theredboat.com; Söder Mälarstrand, Kajplats 6; dm Skr260-290, s/d from Skr480/620, hotel s/d from Skr900/1200; @) 'The Red Boat' is a hotel and hostel on two vessels, *Mälaren* and *Ran*. The hostel section is the cosiest of Stockholm's floating accommodation, thanks to lots of dark wood, nautical memorabilia and friendly staff. Linens are included. Hotel-standard rooms are also excellent.

City Backpackers   HOSTEL €

(Map p428; ☎20 69 20; www.citybackpackers. org; Upplandsgatan 2A; dm Skr230-280, d from Skr650; @) The closest hostel to Centralstationen has clean rooms, friendly staff, free bicycle hire and excellent facilities, including sauna, laundry and a kitchen (with a free stash of pasta). City tours are also offered, from a free weekly neighbourhood

walk to themed, payable options such as 'Historic Horror'.

Bredängs Vandrarhem & Camping   HOSTEL, CAMPING GROUND €

(Map p444; ☎97 62 00; www.bredangvandrar hem.se; Stora Sällskapetsväg 51; campsites Skr265, dm/s/d Skr210/380/550, 4-bed cabin Skr980) A lakeside option 10km southwest of central Stockholm. It's well equipped, with a hostel and cabins. Take the metro to T-Bredäng, then walk 700m. If you're driving, it's well signposted from the E4/E20 motorway.

Mälardrottningen   HOTEL €€

(Map p428; ☎54 51 87 80; www.malardrottningen. se; Riddarholmen; s/d cabins from Skr1200/1450) At one time the world's largest motor yacht, this stylish, cosy option features well-appointed cabins, each with en suite. Launched in 1924, it was once owned by American heiress Barbara Hutton (a modest gift from her father for her 18th birthday). Upper-deck, sea-side rooms offer the best views, and three rooms come with queen-sized beds for spacious slumber.

Crystal Plaza Hotel   HOTEL €€€

(Map p428; ☎406 88 00; www.crystalplazahotel.se; Birger Jarlsgatan 35; standard s/d Skr1600/1800; @) Flaunting an eight-storey tower and neoclassical columns, this friendly hotel, housed in an 1895 building, routinely offers early-booking discounts. Its wonderfully cosy (albeit smallish) rooms have all the standard mod-cons.

Rex Hotel   HOTEL €€€

(Map p424; ☎16 00 40; www.rexhotel.se; Luntmakargatan 73; s/d from Skr1990/2190; @) While a little less luxe than its sibling Hotel Hellsten across the street, Rex's stylish, functional rooms likewise deliver flat-screen TVs and svelte, Greek-stone bathrooms. Rooms in a more recent extension sport urbane concrete walls, walnut furniture and lush velvet textiles. Other positives include a fab glassed-in breakfast space and fascinating travel photography by the affable owner.

Lord Nelson Hotel   HOTEL €€

(Map p428; ☎50 64 01 20; www.lordnelsonhotel. se; Västerlånggatan 22; s/d from Skr1290/1590; @) Yo-ho-ho, me scurvy barnacles! It's a tight squeeze but this pink-painted, glass-fronted building feels like a creaky old ship loaded with character. At just 5m wide, the 17th-century building is Sweden's narrowest hotel. Its nautical theme extends to brass and mahogany furnishings, antique sea-captain trappings and a model ship in each of the small rooms. Some are in need of a little TLC, but all are comfy and clean, and we adore the little rooftop sundeck.

Berns Hotel   HOTEL €€€
(Map p428; ☏56 63 22 00; www.berns.se; Näckströmsgatan 8; small/medium r Skr2950/3650; @) Popular with rock stars, the rooms at forever-hip Berns come equipped with CD players and styles ranging from 19th-century classical to contemporary sleek. Some rooms are more impressive than others (the balcony rooms get our vote); Room 431 was once a dressing room used by the likes of Marlene Dietrich and Ella Fitzgerald. Part of a historical entertainment complex, with buzzing restaurants, bars and live acts, it's a sparkly choice for the party crew.

Hostel Bed & Breakfast   HOSTEL €
(Map p424; ☏15 28 38; info@hostelbedandbreakfast.com; Rehnsgatan 21; dm from Skr330, s/d Skr540/780; @) Near T-Rådmansgatan, north of the city centre, this pleasant, informal basement hostel comes complete with a kitchen and laundry. Rates include breakfast.

✖ Eating

Stockholm, with its six Michelin-starred restaurants, has certainly earned its reputation as a foodie destination. For top-notch seafood with human scenery to match, head toward Östermalmstorg. Candlelit cafes dripping in history and charm line the crooked little streets of Gamla Stan. For solid everyman cuisine, head to Odenplan, and for inventive vegetarian fare try Södermalm's bohemian joints or Luntmakargatan and surrounding streets.

Östermalms Saluhall   MARKET €€
(Map p428; Östermalmstorg; ⊙9.30am-6pm Mon-Thu, to 6.30pm Fri & 4pm Sat) Stockholm's historic, blue-ribbon market spoils taste buds with fresh fish, seafood and meat, as well as fruits, vegetables and hard-to-find cheeses. In addition to the market, it's full of small eateries serving everything from sushi to pasta. The building itself is a Stockholm landmark, designed as a Romanesque cathedral of food in 1885.

WANT MORE?   **435**

For in-depth information, reviews and recommendations at your fingertips, head to the Apple App Store to purchase Lonely Planet's *Stockholm City Guide* iPhone app.

Alternatively, head to Lonely Planet (www.lonelyplanet.com/sweden/stockholm) for planning advice, author recommendations, traveller reviews and insider tips.

Hötorgshallen   FOOD HALL €€
(Map p428; Hötorget; ⊙10am-6pm Mon-Thu, 10am-6.30pm Fri, 10am-4pm Sat, 10am-6pm Mon-Fri, 10am-3pm Sat Jun & Jul) Below Filmstaden cinema, multicultural Hötorgshallen sells everything from fresh Nordic seafood to fluffy hummus and fragrant teas. Squeeze into galley-themed dining nook **Kajsas Fiskrestaurang** for soulful *fisksoppa* (fish stew) with mussels and aioli (Skr85).

Chokladkoppen   CAFE €
(Map p428; Stortorget; cakes & snacks Skr30-70) Arguably Stockholm's best-loved cafe, hole-in-the-wall Chokladkoppen sits slap bang on the Old Town's enchanting main square. It's a gay-friendly spot, with cute, gym-fit waiters, a look-at-me summer terrace and yummy grub such as broccoli-and-blue-cheese pie and scrumptious cakes.

Nystekt Strömming   FAST FOOD €
(Map p428; Södermalmstorg; combo plates Skr35-65; ⊙generally 10am-6pm Mon-Fri, 11am-4pm Sat & Sun) Pick up some authentically Swedish fast food – fried *(stekt)* herring – at this humble cart outside the metro station at Slussen. The *strömming* burger makes a great snack on the go, but the full dinner combos are excellent if you want something more substantial.

Pelikan   SWEDISH €€
(Map p424; Blekingegatan 40; mains Skr80-180; ⊙dinner daily, lunch Sat & Sun) Lofty ceilings, wood panelling and no-nonsense waiters in waistcoats set the scene for classic *husmanskost* (traditional home cooking) at this century-old beer hall. The herring-and-cheese platters are particularly good (try the 'SOS', Skr98), and there's usually a vegetarian special. There's a minimum age of 23.

STOCKHOLM EATING

Den Gyldene Freden
SWEDISH €€€

(Map p428; www.dengyldenefreden.se; Österlånggatan 51; lunch specials Skr125, starters Skr145-225, mains Skr185-395; ☺lunch & dinner, closed Sun) Opened in 1722, this venerable barrel-vaulted restaurant is run by the Swedish Academy, and is where (rumour has it) Academy members meet to decide the winners of the Nobel prize. Personally, we think it should go to the chefs, whose sublime offerings include civilised *husmanskost* dishes such as quail stuffed with duck liver, celeriac purée and Gotland truffles.

Tranan
SWEDISH €€€

(Map p424; www.tranan.se; Karlbergsvägen 14; starters Skr120-185, mains Skr145-325; ☺11.30am-midnight Mon-Thu, 11.30-1am Fri, 5pm-1am Sat, 5-11pm Sun, 6pm-midnight Mon-Sun late Jun-Aug) The food at this upmarket neighbourhood bistro combines Swedish *husmanskost* with savvy Gallic touches; if fried herring is available, you'd be mad not to try it. On weekends, DJs hit the decks in the pumping, 30-something basement bar (note that the bar is closed in July and August).

Örtagården
VEGETARIAN €€

(Map p428; Nybrogatan 31, 1st fl, Östermalms Saluhall Bldg; lunch/dinner buffets Skr95/135; ☺10.30am-9.30pm Mon-Fri, 11am-9pm Sat & Sun) Perched above Östermalms Saluhall, this popular, casual restaurant has an extensive (mostly) vegetarian lunch and dinner buffet; there are some token meat dishes, but the vegie stuff is where the kitchen shines – plus it's guilt-free, though decadent. Arrive before noon or after 2pm if you want to avoid the lunch stampede.

Östgöta Källaren
PUB, RESTAURANT €€

(Map p424; Östgötagatan 41; starters Skr56-95, small plates Skr80-116, mains Skr125-212; ☺5pm-1am Mon-Fri, 3pm-1am Sat & Sun) The regulars at this soulful pub-cum-restaurant span multi-pierced rockers to blue-rinse grandmas, all smitten with the dimly lit romantic atmosphere, amiable vibe and hearty Swedish, Eastern European and French-Med grub.

TOP CHOICE Rosendals Trädgårdskafe
CAFE €€

(Rosendalsterrassen 12; cakes Skr30-45, soups Skr85, mains Skr125-145; ☺11am-5pm Mon-Fri, 11am-6pm Sat & Sun May-Sep, 11am-4pm Tue-Sun Oct-Dec, closed Jan) Rosendals is an idyllic spot for heavenly carrot cake and an organic wine in summer or a warm cup of *glögg* (spicy mulled wine) and a *lussekatte* (saffron roll) in winter. Much of the produce is biodynamic and grown on-site. To get here, take bus 47 from Norrmalmstorg, in Vasastan; it's a 15-minute walk (about 1km) from Djurgårdsbron.

Vurma
CAFE €

(Map p424; www.vurma.se; Polhemsgatan 15; sandwiches Skr45-75, salads Skr70-85, ☺8am-6pm Mon-Fri, 9am-6pm Sat & Sun) Squeeze in among the chattering punters, fluff up the cushions and eavesdrop over a vegan latte at this kitsch-hip cafe–bakery. The scrumptious sandwiches and salads are utterly inspired; try the chèvre cheese, marinated chicken, tomato, cucumber, walnuts, apple and mustard salad. Other branches include those in Vasastan (Gästrikegatan 2) and Södermalm (Bergsunds Strand 31; ☺to 7pm).

Bakfickan
SWEDISH €€€

(Map p428; www.operakallaren.se; starters Skr140-150, mains Skr149-279; ☺11.30am-11pm Mon-Fri, noon-10pm Sat) A more relaxed corner of the Opera House's bar-and-dining complex, the 'back pocket' of Operakällaren is crammed with opera photographs and art deco–style lampshades. Old-school waiters serve elevated versions of traditional Swedish comfort food, from cured salmon or pickled herring to meatballs and mash, and the counter seats make it a perfect spot for solo diners – a rare find in Sweden.

Lao Wai
VEGETARIAN €€

(Map p424; Luntmakargatan 74; lunches Skr85, mains Skr135-195; ☺lunch Mon-Fri, dinner Tue-Sat) Tiny, herbivorous Lao Wai does sinfully good things to tofu and vegetable combos, hence the faithful regulars. Nosh virtuously on dishes such as Sichuan-style smoked tofu with shitake, chillies, garlic shoots, snow peas and black beans.

Gondolen
SWEDISH €€€

(Map p428; www.eriks.se; Stadsgården 6; seasonal menus Skr495, mains Skr195-295; ☺lunch Mon-Fri, dinner Mon-Sat) Perched atop the iconic Katarinahissen (the vintage Slussen elevator), Gondolen combines killer city views with contemporary Nordic brilliance from chef Erik Lallerstedt. Play 'spot the landmark' while carving into gems like thyme-roasted halibut with lobster sauce and root vegetable cake.

TOP CHOICE Mathias Dahlgren
INTERNATIONAL €€€

(Map p428; ☎679 35 84; www.mathiasdahlgren.com; Grand Hôtel Stockholm, Södra Blasieholmshamnen 6; Matbaren mains Skr245-395, Matsalen mains Skr325-455; ⊘Matbaren noon-2pm Mon-Fri & 6pm-midnight Mon-Sat, Matsalen 7pm-midnight Tue-Sat) Chef Mathias Dahlgren's namesake restaurant, set in the Grand Hôtel, consists of the casual Matbaren (the Food Bar) and the more formal Matsalen (the Dining Room). The latter is where Dahlgren really delivers, wowing critics and mortals alike with his ever-changing menu: think foie gras terrine with mango black sesame and black pepper, or fried apple with goat's milk ice cream, vanilla cream and rye bread. Book ahead.

The Grand Hôtel's more casual **Verandan** (☑679 35 86; www.grandhotel.se; ⊘7am-11pm) restaurant has a traditional Swedish smörgåsbord year-round.

Caffé Nero   ITALIAN €
(Map p428; Roslagsgatan 4; coffee & pastries from Skr35; ⊘7am-10pm Mon-Fri, 8am-10pm Sat, 8am-6pm Sun) Architect Tadao Ando would approve of the brutal concrete interiors at this Vasastan hang-out, where local hipsters down mighty caffé, grappa shots, salubrious panini and Italian home cooking, from sublime veal meatballs to tiramisu.

Sturehof   SWEDISH, SEAFOOD €€€
(Map p428; www.sturehof.com; Stureplan 2; starters Skr115-220, mains Skr125-365; ⊘11-2am Mon-Fri, noon-2am Sat, 1pm-2am Sun) Superb for late-night sipping and supping, this buzzing, convivial brasserie sparkles with gracious staff, celebrity regulars and fabulous seafood-centric dishes (the bouillabaisse is brilliant). Both the front and back bars are a hit with the eye-candy brigade and perfect for a post-meal flirt.

Brasserie Elverket   SWEDISH-EXPERIMENTAL €€
(Map p424; www.brasserieelverket.se; Linnégatan 69; lunches Skr79-145, starters Skr79-125, mains Skr99-225; ⊘lunch Mon-Fri, brunch 11am-3pm Sat & Sun, dinner Tue-Sat) In an old electricity plant reborn as an experimental theatre, this slick, dimly lit resto-bar peddles bold, adventurous grub such as melon and vanilla consommé served with cardamom pannacotta and a pineapple-sage salsa. Starters are a pick-and-mix tapas-style affair, and the weekend brunch buffet (Skr199 to Skr239, depending on drinks) is one of Stockholm's best.

Kungsholmen   INTERNATIONAL €€€
(Map p424; ☑50 52 44 50; www.kungsholmen.com; Norr Mälarstrand, Kajplats 464; sushi 150-325, grill Skr160-295, specialities Skr220-350; ⊘5pm-1am Mon-Sun) Owned by celebrity chefs Melker Andersson and Danyel Couet, this hip, sexed-up 'food court' features seven open kitchens cooking up different specialities, including Swedish standards, sushi, bistro grub, 'fast food' and fruit-and-cheese plates. Add a sleek, cocktail-savvy bar, weekend DJ sessions and a waterside location, and you'll understand why it's best to book.

Grill   INTERNATIONAL €€€
(Map p428; www.grill.se; Drottninggatan 89; daily lunches Skr110, dinner mains Skr180-475; ⊘11.15am-2pm & 5pm-1am Mon-Fri, 11.15am-2pm & 4pm-1am Sat, 3-10pm Sun, closed Jul–early Aug) Kick-started by culinary stars Melker Andersson and Danyel Couet, this outrageous restaurant–bar looks like a furniture showroom, with various themed nooks, from Miami art deco to Astroturf garden party. The menu is a global affair, arranged by grill type. Vegetarians aren't overlooked, service is casual and accommodating, and there's a popular Sunday grill buffet (Skr295).

Vetekatten   CAFE €
(Map p428; Kungsgatan 55; tea & coffee/snacks from Skr25/35; ⊘7.30am-8pm Mon-Fri, 9.30am-5pm Sat, noon-5pm Sun) A cardamom-scented labyrinth of cosy nooks, antique furnishings and oil paintings, Vetekatten is not so much a cafe as an institution.

🍷 Drinking

From concrete-and-bare-bulb industrial spaces to raucous vintage beer halls and bricked-in underground vaults, there's a bar for every taste in this town – the only thing you might struggle to find is a grimy dive bar with bad lighting. Good neighbourhood hang-outs *(kvarterskrog)* abound, but generally, the shiny-miniskirt crowd hangs out in Östermalm, while the hipsters and arty types slink around Södermalm – any of the bars along Skånegatan are a good bet.

Marie Laveau   BAR
(Map p428; www.marielaveau.se; Hornsgatan 66; cocktails Skr79-99; ⊘5pm-midnight Tue & Wed, 5pm-3am Thu-Sat) Sip on vaguely New Orleans–flavoured drinks, from a Sazerac to a Hurricane, at this designer-grunge bar on one of the main drags through Södermalm – think chequered floor and subway-style tiled columns. The basement bar hosts raucous theme DJ nights on Saturdays.

Pet Sounds Bar BAR

(Map p424; www.petsoundsbar.se; Skånegatan 80; ⊙from 5pm, closed Mon) A SoFo favourite, this jamming bar pulls in music journos, indie culture vultures and the odd Goth rocker. While the restaurant serves decent Italo-French grub, the real fun happens in the basement. Head down for a mixed bag of live bands, release parties and DJ sets.

Soldaten Svejk PUB

(Map p424; www.svejk.se; Östgötagatan 35; beers from Skr58; ⊙from 5pm) In this crowded, amber-windowed, wooden-floored pub, decorated with heraldic shields, regulars pine for Prague with great Czech beer, including the massively popular Staropramen, on tap. Line your stomach with simple, solid Czech meals (Skr102 to Skr185); the smoked cheese is sublime. Head in early or prepare to queue for a table.

Le Rouge BAR

(Map p428; ☑50 52 44 30; www.lerouge.se; Österlånggatan 17; ⊙11.30am-2pm & 5pm-1am Mon-Thu, 11.30am-2pm & 4pm-1am Fri, 5pm-1am Sat) Fin de siècle Paris is the inspiration for this decadent melange of rich red velvet, tasselled lampshades, inspired cocktails and French bistro grub in Gamla Stan. Operated by two of Stockholm's hottest chefs (Danyel Couet and Melker Andersson), the adjoining restaurant prepares luxe French and Italian dishes in period-glam surrounds. DJs hit the decks and will get you dancing from Thursday to Saturday.

☆ Entertainment

Scan the local papers for up-to-date listings of entertainment events, particularly the Friday *På Stan* section of *Dagens Nyheter* newspaper. The monthly *What's On Stockholm* brochure, available free from the tourist office, is a more general guide.

Nightclubs

Berns Salonger CLUB

(Map p428; ☑56 63 22 22; www.berns.se; Näckströmsgatan 8; ⊙bar/nightclub 11pm-4am Thu-Sat, midnight-5am Thu-Sat) A Stockholm institution since 1862, this glitzy entertainment palace remains one of the city's hottest party spots. While the gorgeous ballroom hosts some brilliant live music gigs, the best of Berns' bars is the intimate basement bar–club 2.35:1, packed with cool creative types, top-notch DJs and projected art-house images. It's occasionally also open on Wednesday and Sunday.

Spy Bar CLUB

(Map p428; www.thespybar.com; Birger Jarlsgatan 20; admission from Skr160; ⊙10pm-5am Wed-Sat) Set in a turn-of-the-century flat (spot the tiled stoves), this party stalwart pulls in a 20- and 30-something media crowd, as well as the odd American heiress (yes, Paris partied here). Expect three bars, electro, rock and hip-hop beats and no entry after 2am (unless you're well connected, darling).

Café Opera CLUB

(Map p428; ☑676 58 07; www.cafeopera.se; Operahuset, Karl XII's Torg; admission from Skr150; ⊙10pm-3am Wed-Sun) Rock stars and wannabe playboys need a suitably excessive place to schmooze, booze and groove, one with bulbous chandeliers, ceiling frescos and a jet-set vibe. This bar/club combo fits the bill. The adjoining bar is a bartenders' hang-out, meaning a mediocre martini is strictly out of the question.

Grodan CLUB

(Map p428; ☑679 61 00; www.grodannattklubb.se; Grev Turegatan 16; admission from Skr150; ⊙10pm-3am Fri & Sat) At street level it's a packed bar and mock-baroque restaurant. Down in the cellar, A-list DJ talent from Stockholm, London and beyond spins the vinyl, pumping out house and electro tracks for sweat-soaked clubbers.

Gay & Lesbian Venues

For club listings and events, pick up a free copy of street-press magazine *QX*, found at many clubs, stores and cafes around town. Its website (www.qx.se) is more frequently updated. *QX* also produces a free, handy Gay Stockholm Map.

Torget BAR

(Map p428; www.torgetbaren.com; Mälartorget 13) Gamla Stan's premier gay bar has eye-candy staff, mock-baroque touches and a civilised salon vibe.

Roxy BAR

(Map p424; www.roxysofo.se; Nytorget 6; ⊙from 5pm) Chic resto-bar popular with lipstick lesbians, publishing types and SoFo's creative set.

Lady Patricia FLOATING BAR

(Map p428; ☑743 05 70; Stadsgårdskajen 152; ⊙Sun) The perennial Sunday-night favourite has a superb seafood restaurant, two crowded dance floors, drag shows and a Schlager-loving crowd, all on board a docked yacht.

Side Track
BAR

(Map p428; ☑641 16 88; www.sidetrack.nu; Wollmar Yxkullsgatan 7; ☺Wed-Sat) A hit with down-to-earth guys for its low-key, pub-like ambience and decent grub.

Live Music

Debaser
INDIE ROCK

(Map p428; ☑462 98 60; www.debaser.se, in Swedish; Karl Johanstorg 1, Slussen; ☺7pm-1am, to 3am club nights Sun-Thu, 8pm-3am Fri & Sat) The king of rock clubs hides away under the Slussen interchange. Emerging or bigger-name acts play most nights, while the killer club nights span anything from rock-steady to punk and electronica. One metro stop further south, Debaser Medis (Map p424; Medborgarplatsen 8) is its sprawling sister venue, with three floors rocking to live acts and DJ-spun tunes.

Mosebacke Etablissement
ECLECTIC

(Map p428; ☑55 60 98 90; www.mosebacke.se, in Swedish; Mosebacketorg 3; tickets free-Skr250; ☺to 11pm Mon & Tue, to 1am Wed & Sun, to 2am Thu-Sat) Eclectic theatre and club nights aside, this historic culture palace hosts a mixed line-up of live music. Tunes span anything from home-grown pop to antipodean rock. The outdoor terrace combines dazzling city views with a thumping summertime bar.

Glenn Miller Café
JAZZ, BLUES

(Map p428; ☑10 03 22; Brunnsgatan 21A; ☺5pm-1am Mon-Thu, 5pm-2am Fri & Sat) Loaded with character, this tiny jazz and blues bar draws a faithful, fun-loving crowd. It also serves excellent French-style classics like mussels in white wine sauce. Take bus 1, 43 or 56 to get here.

Concerts, Theatre & Dance

Dramaten
THEATRE

(Map p428; ☑667 06 80; www.dramaten.se; Nybroplan; tickets Skr170-400) The Royal Theatre stages a range of plays in a sublime art nouveau environment. Dramaten's experimental stage Elverket (Map p424; Linnégatan 69, same contact details) pushes all the boundaries with some edgier offerings that are performed within a converted power station.

Operan
OPERA

(Map p428; ☑791 44 00; www.operan.se; Operahuset, Gustav Adolfs Torg; tickets Skr135-500) The Royal Opera is the place to go for thunderous tenors, sparkling sopranos and classical ballet. It also has some bargain tickets in seats with poor views for as little as Skr40, and occasional lunchtime concerts for Skr180 (including light lunch).

Konserthuset
CLASSICAL MUSIC

(Map p428; ☑50 66 77 88; www.konserthuset.se; Hötorget; tickets Skr100-350) Head here for classical concerts and other musical marvels, including the Royal Philharmonic Orchestra.

Folkoperan
THEATRE

(Map p428; ☑616 07 50; www.folkoperan.se; Hornsgatan 72; tickets Skr260-450) Folkoperan gives opera a thoroughly modern overhaul with its intimate, cutting-edge and sometimes controversial productions. Those aged under 26 years enjoy half-price tickets.

Sport

Bandy matches, a uniquely Scandinavian phenomenon, take place all winter at Stockholm's ice arenas. Catch a game at Zinkensdamms Idrottsplats (Map p424; Ringvägen 16; ☺Nov-Feb 8am-2pm Tue-Thu, 8am-11pm Sat, 1-4pm Sun). The sport, a precursor to ice hockey but with more players (11 to a side) and less fighting, has grown massively popular since the late-1990s rise of the Hammarby team. The season lasts from November to March, so make sure you bring your own thermos of *kaffekask* – a warming mix of coffee and booze.

For the ultimate Scandi sport experience, head to an ice hockey game at Globen (☑50 83 53 00; www.globen.se; Arenavägen, Johanneshov; tickets Skr90-270); matches take place here up to three times a week from October to April.

🔒 Shopping

A design and fashion hub, Stockholm offers shoppers everything from top-name boutiques to the tiniest secondhand shops. Good local buys include edgy street wear, designer home decor and clever gadgets, and edible treats such as cloudberry jam, pickled herring and bottles of *glögg*. Södermalm's SoFo district (the streets south of Folkungagatan) is your best bet for home-grown fashion, while Östermalm is the place for high-end names like Marc Jacobs and Gucci.

For all-in-one retail therapy, scour department store giant Åhléns (Map p428; ☑676 60 00; Klarabergsgatan 50) or its upmarket rival NK (Map p428; ☑762 80 00; Hamngatan 12-18).

Ekovaruhuset
FAIR-TRADE

(Map p428; 22 98 45; www.ekovaruhuset.se; Österlånggatan 28; 11am-6pm Mon-Fri, 11am-4pm Sat & Sun) This enlightened concept store stocks fair-trade, organic products, from cosmetics and chocolates to trendy threads and too-cute baby wear. Expect anything from Edun T-shirts from Peru to in-the-know labels like Zion and Misericordia.

Chokladfabriken
CHOCOLATE

(Map p424; 640 05 68; www.chokladfabriken. com; Renstiernas Gata 12; 10am-6.30pm Mon-Fri, 10am-5pm Sat) For an edible souvenir, head straight to this chocolate peddler, where seasonal Nordic ingredients are used to make some amazingly heavenly cocoa treats. There's a cafe for an on-the-spot fix, and smaller branches in Norrmalm (Regeringsgatan 58) and Östermalm (Grevgatan 37).

DesignTorget
DESIGN

Götgatan (Map p428; 462 35 20; Götgatan 31, Södermalm; 10am-7pm Mon-Fri, 10am-5pm Sat, noon-5pm Sun); Sergels Torg (Map p428; 50 83 15 20; Basement, Kulturhuset, Sergels Torg B; 10am-7pm Mon-Fri, 10am-6pm Sat, 11am-5pm Sun) If you love good design but don't own a Gold Amex, head to this chain, which sells the work of emerging designers alongside established denizens. There are several branches around the city.

Tjallamalla
CLOTHING

(Map p424; 640 78 47; www.tjallamalla.com; Bondegatan 46; noon-6pm Mon-Fri, noon-4pm Sat) Raid the racks at this fashion icon for rookie designers like Hot Sissy, Papagaio and organic Malmö street wear label Kärleksgatan. Graduates from Stockholm's prestigious Beckmans College of Design School sometimes sell their collections here on commission.

PUB
DEPARTMENT STORE

(Map p428; 402 16 11; Drottninggatan 72-6; 10am-7pm Mon-Fri, 10am-6pm Sat, 11am-5pm Sun) Historic department store PUB famously once employed Greta Garbo.

❶ Information

Emergency
24-hour medical advice (32 01 00)
24-hour police stations Kungsholmen (401 00 00; Kungsholmsgatan 37, Kungsholmen); Södermalm (401 03 00; Torkel Knutssonsgatan 20, Södermalm)
Emergency (112) Toll-free access to the fire service, police and ambulance.

Internet Access
Most hostels and many hotels have a computer with internet access for guests, and nearly all also offer wi-fi access in rooms (usually free, but sometimes for a fee of up to Skr120 per 24hr). Wi-fi is also widely available in coffee shops and bars and in Centralstationen. Those without their own computer have more limited options, but the ubiquitous Sidewalk Express terminals are handy.

Sidewalk Express (www.sidewalkexpress.se; per hr Skr19) Rows of computer monitors and tall red ticket machines mark out these self-service internet stations, which roam the city. They're found at various locations, including City Bus Terminal, Centralstationen, Stockhom-Arlanda Airport, and numerous 7-Eleven locations around town.

Media
The best overall guide for visitors is the monthly *What's On Stockholm*, available free from tourist offices and online at www.stockholmtown.com. Tourist offices also carry two separate accommodation guides in English – one for camping, the other for hotels and hostels – both free.

Medical Services
Apoteket CW Scheele (454 81 30; Klarabergsgatan 64) 24-hour pharmacy.
CityAkuten (412 29 00; Apelbergsgatan 48; 8am-8pm) Emergency health and dental care.
Södersjukhuset (616 10 00; Ringvägen 52) The most central hospital.

Money
ATMs are plentiful, with a few at Centralstationen; expect queues.

The exchange company Forex has more than a dozen branches in the capital and charges Skr15 per travellers cheque. Two handy locations:
Stockholm-Arlanda Airport (Terminal 2; 5.30am-10pm Sun-Fri, to 6pm Sat)
Forex Bank (10 49 90; Vasagatan 16; 9am-7pm Mon-Fri, 10am-5pm Sat, noon-4pm Sun)

Post
You can buy stamps and send letters at a number of city locations, including newsagents and supermarkets – keep an eye out for the Swedish postal symbol (yellow on a blue background). There's a convenient outlet next to the Hemköp supermarket in the basement of central department store **Åhléns** (Klarabergsgatan 50).

Telephones
Coin-operated phones are virtually nonexistent; payphones are operated with phonecards purchased from any Pressbyrån location (or with a credit card, although this is ludicrously

expensive). Ask for a *telefonkort* for Skr50 or Skr120, which roughly equates to 50 minutes and 120 minutes of local talk time respectively. International calls are charged at a higher rate; for calls abroad, you're better off buying a long-distance calling card, available at many Pressbyrån outlets.

Tourist Information

Tourist office (Map p428; ✆508 28 508; www. stockholmtown.se; Vasagatan 14; ⏰9am-7pm Mon-Fri, 10am-5pm Sat, 10am-4pm Sun May–mid-Sep) The main tourist office has moved to a new location just across the street (Vasagatan) from Centralstationen. There's a Forex currency-exchange counter next-door.

Websites

Stockholm Visitors Board (www.stockholm town.com) Excellent tourist information in English (and many other languages).
The Local (www.thelocal.se) News and features about Sweden, written locally, in English.
Visit Stockholm (www.visit-stockholm.com) A helpful source for travellers, with nearly 500 pages of information on sights, food, accommodation, shopping and getting out of town.

ⓘ Getting There & Away

Air

Stockholm Arlanda Airport (✆797 60 00; www.arlanda.se) Stockholm's main airport, 45km north of the city centre, reached by bus and express train.
Bromma Stockholm Airport (✆797 68 00) Located 8km west of Stockholm, used for some domestic flights.
Stockholm Skavsta Airport (✆0155-28 04 00) 100km south of Stockholm, near Nyköping, mostly used by low-cost carriers such as Ryanair.
Västerås Airport (✆21 80 56 10) About 100km northwest of Stockholm on the E18 motorway, this tiny airport is used by Ryanair.
Scandinavian Airlines System (SAS; ✆0770-72 77 27; www.sas.se) Network serves 28 Swedish destinations from Arlanda airport and has international services to Copenhagen, Oslo, Helsinki and a host of other European cities including Amsterdam, Barcelona, Brussels, Berlin, Dublin, Frankfurt, Geneva, Hamburg, London, Manchester, Milan, Moscow, Paris, Rome, St Petersburg and Zagreb. It also flies direct to Chicago, New York, Bangkok and Beijing.
Finnair (✆0771-78 11 00; www.finnair.com) Flies several times daily to Helsinki.
Blue1 (✆0900-102 58 31; www.blue1.com) Has direct flights to Helsinki, as well as to Tampere, Turku/Åbo and Vaasa.

Boat

Both **Silja Line** (✆22 21 40; www.silja.com) and **Viking Line** (✆452 40 00; www.vikingline.se) run ferries to Turku and Helsinki. **Tallink** (✆22 21 40; www.tallink.ee) ferries head to Tallinn (Estonia) and Riga (Latvia).

Bus

Cityterminalen (Map p428; www.citytermina len.com) The main bus station, connected to Centralstationen. The ticket counter (open 7am to 6pm) sells tickets for several bus companies, including Flygbussarna (airport coaches), Swebus Express, Svenska Buss, Eurolines and Ybuss.
Swebus Express (✆0771-21 82 18; www. swebusexpress.com; 2nd level, Cityterminalen) Runs daily to Malmö (9¼ hours), Göteborg (seven hours), Norrköping (two hours), Kalmar (six hours), Mora (4¼ hours), Örebro (three hours) and Oslo (eight hours). There are also direct runs to Gävle (2½ hours), Uppsala (one hour) and Västerås (1¾ hours).
Ybuss (✆020 033 44 44; www.ybuss.se; Cityterminalen) Runs services to the northern towns of Sundsvall, Östersund and Umeå (see relevant sections for details).

Car & Motorcycle

The E4 motorway passes through the west of the city, on its way from Helsingborg to Haparanda. The E20 motorway from Stockholm to Göteborg via Örebro follows the E4 as far as Södertälje. The E18 from Kapellskär to Oslo runs from east to west and passes north of central Stockholm.

For car hire close to Centralstationen head to **Avis** (✆20 20 60; Vasagatan 10B) or **Hertz** (✆454 62 50; Vasagatan 26).

Left Luggage

There are three sizes of **left-luggage boxes** (per 24hr Skr50-120) at Centralstationen. Similar facilities exist at the neighbouring bus station and at major ferry terminals.

Train

Stockholm is the hub for national train services run by **Sveriges Järnväg** (SJ; ✆0771-75 75 75; www.sj.se) and **Tågkompaniet** (✆0771-44 41 11; www.tagkompaniet.se, in Swedish).

Centralstationen (Stockholm C; Map p428; ⏰5am-midnight) is the central train station. In the main hall you'll find the **SJ ticket office** (⏰domestic tickets 7.30am-7.45pm Mon-Fri, 8.30am-6pm Sat, 9.30am-7pm Sun, international tickets 10am-6pm Mon-Fri, general customer service 6am-11pm Mon-Fri, 6.30am-11pm Sat, 7am-11pm Sun). You'll also find automated ticket machines (from 5am to 11.50pm Monday to Sunday).

Direct SJ trains to/from Copenhagen, Oslo and Storlien (for Trondheim) arrive and depart from Centralstationen, as do the overnight services from Göteborg (via Stockholm and Boden) to Kiruna and Narvik; the Arlanda Express; and the SL *pendeltåg* commuter services that run to/from Nynäshamn, Södertälje and Märsta. Other SL local rail lines (Roslagsbanan and Saltsjöbanan) run from Stockholm Östra (T-Tekniska Högskolan) and Slussen, respectively.

In the basement at Centralstationen, you'll find lockers costing Skr40, Skr60 or Skr120 (depending on size) for 24 hours, toilets for Skr10 and showers (next to the toilets) for Skr35. These facilities are open 5am to 12.30am daily. There's also a left-luggage office, open daily, and a **lost property office** (☑50 12 55 90; sj.lostproperty@bagport.se; ◷9am-7pm Mon-Fri); look for the 'Hittegods' sign.

Follow the signs to find your way to the local metro (T-bana) network; the underground station here is called T-Centralen.

ℹ️ Getting Around

To/From the Airports

The **Arlanda Express** (☑020-22 22 24; tickets from Skr240) train from Centralstationen takes 20 minutes to reach Stockholm-Arlanda Airport; trains run every 10 to 15 minutes from about 5am to 12.30am. The same trip in a taxi costs around Skr450.

The cheaper option is the **Flygbuss** service between Stockhom-Arlanda and Cityterminalen. Buses leave every 10 or 15 minutes (Skr119, 40 minutes). Tickets can be purchased on arrival at the Flygbuss counter at Stockholm-Arlanda's main terminal.

Bicycle

Stockholm boasts a wide network of bicycle paths, and in summer you won't regret bringing a bicycle with you or hiring one to get around. The tourist offices have maps for sale, but they're not usually necessary if you have a basic city map.

Trails and bike lanes are clearly marked with traffic signs. Some long-distance routes are marked all the way from central Stockholm: Nynäsleden to Nynäshamn joins Sommarleden near Västerhaninge and swings west to Södertälje. Roslagsleden leads to Norrtälje (linking Blåleden and Vaxholm). Upplandsleden leads to Märsta, which is north of Stockholm, and you can ride to Uppsala via Sigtuna. Sörmlandsleden leads to Södertälje.

Bicycles can be carried free on SL local trains, except during peak hour (6am to 9am and 3pm to 6pm weekdays). They're not allowed in Centralstationen or on the metro, although you'll occasionally see some daring souls.

Boat

Djurgårdsfärjan city ferry services connect Gröna Lund Tivoli on Djurgården with Nybroplan and Slussen as frequently as every 10 minutes in summer (less frequently in low season); a single trip costs Skr30 (free with the SL transport passes).

Car & Motorcycle

Driving in central Stockholm is not recommended. Skinny one-way streets, congested bridges and limited parking all present problems; note that Djurgårdsvägen is closed near Skansen at night, on summer weekends and some holidays. Don't attempt driving through the narrow streets of Gamla Stan.

Parking is a major problem, but there are *P-hus* (parking stations) throughout the city; they charge up to Skr60 per hour, though the fixed evening rate is usually lower. If you do have a car, one of the best options is to stay on the outskirts of town and catch public transport into the centre.

Public Transport

Storstockholms Lokaltrafik (SL; www.sl.se) runs all tunnelbana (T or T-bana) metro trains, local trains and buses within the entire Stockholm county. There is an SL information office in the basement concourse at **Centralstationen** (◷6.30am-11.15pm Mon-Sat, 7am-11.15pm Sun) and another near the Sergels Torg entrance (open until 6.30pm weekdays, 5pm weekends), which issues timetables and sells the SL Tourist Card and Stockholm Card. You can also call ☑600 10 00 for schedule and travel information.

The **Stockholm Card** (see p431) covers travel on all SL trains and buses in greater Stockholm. There are also 24-hour (Skr100) and 72-hour (Skr200) SL Tourist Cards; the latter is especially good value if you use the third afternoon for transport to either end of the county – you can reach the ferry terminals in Grisslehamn, Kapellskär or Nynäshamn, as well as all of the archipelago harbours. If you want to explore the county in more detail, bring a passport photo and get yourself a 30-day SL pass (Skr690, or Skr420 for children aged seven to 18 and seniors).

On Stockholm's public transport system the minimum fare costs two coupons, and each additional zone costs another coupon (up to five coupons for four or five zones). Coupons cost Skr30 each, but it's better value (and handier) to buy strips of 16 tickets for Skr180. Coupons are stamped at the start of a journey and are good for two hours. Travelling without a valid ticket can lead to a fine of Skr600 or more. Coupons, tickets and passes can be bought at metro stations, Pressbyrån kiosks, SL train stations and SL information offices. Some bus stops now have ticket-vending machines, but plan ahead, as tickets cannot be bought on buses.

International rail passes (eg Scanrail, Inter-Rail) aren't valid on SL trains.

BUS Bus timetables and route maps are complicated but worth studying as there are some useful connections to suburban attractions. Inner-city buses radiate from Sergels Torg, Odenplan, Fridhemsplan (on Kungsholmen) and Slussen.

Bus 47 runs from Sergels Torg to Djurgården, and bus 69 runs from Centralstationen and Sergels Torg to the Ladugårdsgärdet museums and Kaknästornet. Useful buses for hostellers include bus 65, which goes from Centralstationen to Skeppsholmen, and bus 43, which runs from Regeringsgatan to Södermalm.

Inner-city night buses run from 1am to 5pm on a few routes. Most leave from Centralstationen, Sergels Torg, Slussen, Odenplan and Fridhemsplan to the suburbs.

TRAIN Local *pendeltåg* trains are useful for connections to Nynäshamn (for ferries to Gotland), to Märsta (for buses to Sigtuna and the short hop to Stockholm-Arlanda Airport) and Södertälje. SL coupons and SL travel passes are valid on these trains, and should be bought before boarding.

TRAM The historic **No 7 tram** (and its sleek, modern new siblings) connects Norrmalmstorg and Skansen, passing most attractions on Djurgården. Both the Stockholm Card and SL Tourist Card as well as regular SL tickets are valid on board.

METRO The most useful mode of transport in Stockholm is the tunnelbana, run by SL. Its lines converge on T-Centralen, connected by an underground walkway to Centralstationen. There are three main tunnelbana lines with branches.

Taxi

Taxis are readily available but expensive, so check for a meter or arrange the fare first. The flag fall is Skr45, then about Skr10 to Skr13 per kilometre. Reputable firms include **Taxi Stockholm** (☎15 00 00), **Taxi 020** (☎020 20 20 20) and **Taxi Kurir** (☎0771-86 00 00).

AROUND STOCKHOLM

Most locals will tell you one thing not to miss about Stockholm is leaving it – whether for a journey into the lovely rock-strewn archipelago or an excursion into the surrounding countryside. Within easy reach of the capital are idyllic islands, Viking gravesites, cute fishing villages and sturdy palaces.

Suburbs

One of Stockholm's loveliest attractions is Millesgården (Map p444; www.millesgarden.se; Carl Milles väg 2, Lidingö island; adult/child Skr90/free, ☺11am-5pm mid-May-Sep), a superb sculpture park and museum of works by Carl Milles and others. It's on Lidingö island with great views to the mainland; take the metro to T-Ropsten then bus 207.

The extensive Naturhistoriska Riksmuseet (Map p444; www.nrm.se; Frescativägen 40; adult/child Skr80/free; ☺10am-8pm Tue, 10am-7pm Wed-Fri, 11am-7pm Sat & Sun) was founded by Carl von Linné in 1739. There are hands-on displays about nature and the human body, as well as whole forests' worth of taxidermied wildlife, dinosaurs, marine life and the hardy fauna of the polar regions. The adjoining Cosmonova (Map p444; adult/child Skr90/50, no children under 5yr) is a combined planetarium and Imax theatre. Take the metro to T-Universitetet.

Haga Park (Map p444) is also pleasant for walks and bicycle tours, with attractions including the royal Gustav III's Pavilion, Butterfly House and colourful Copper Tent. To reach the park, take bus 515 from Odenplan to Haga Norra.

One of Stockholm's more unusual attractions, Skogskyrkogården (Map p444; Söckenvagen; admission free; ☺24hr) is an arrestingly beautiful cemetery set in soothing pine woodland. Designed by the great Erik Gunnar Asplund and Sigurd Lewerentz, it's on the Unesco World Heritage list and famed for its functionalist buildings. Residents include Stockholm screen goddess Greta Garbo. To get here, take the metro to T-Skogskyrkogården.

Fjäderholmarna

Located on the eastern side of Djurgården, these tiny, delightful islands ('Feather Islands') offer an easy escape from the city. They're just 30 minutes away by boat and are a favourite swimming spot for locals. Boats (adult/child return Skr85/50) to the islands depart hourly from Nybroplan between May and early September. There are a couple of craft shops and restaurants here, though the main activity is low-key chilling. The last boats leave the islands at around midnight, making them a perfect spot to soak up the long daylight hours.

SWEDEN AROUND STOCKHOLM

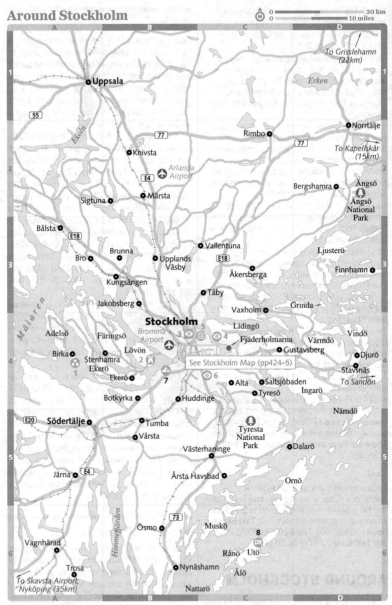

Ferry Ports

Nynäshamn, 50km south of Stockholm, is the main gateway to Gotland; there are also regular ferries to Gdańsk (Poland). Regular local (SL) trains run from Stockholm to Nynäshamn; you can use SL passes, but international rail passes are not valid. There are also direct bus services from Stockholm's Cityterminalen to connect with the Gotland ferries (Skr90), leaving 1¾ hours before ferry departure times.

Around Stockholm

Ferries sail between tiny Kapellskär (90km northeast of Stockholm) and Turku (Finland) via the Åland islands. The ferry companies offer a direct bus from Stockholm Cityterminalen to meet the ferries (Skr65), but SL pass holders can take bus 640 from T-Tekniska Högskolan to Norrtälje and change there to 631, which runs every two hours or so (infrequent at weekends).

For more information on reaching the Åland islands, check www.visitaland.com or contact the main companies operating between Sweden and Åland. Of these, Viking Line (www.vikingline.aland.fi) and Silja Line (www.silja.com) continue on to Finland, while Eckerö Linjen (www.eckerolinjen.fi), Ånedin Linjen (www.anedinlinjen.com) and Birka Cruises (www.birkacruises.com) operate only between the islands and Sweden. Once on the islands, you can happily pedal almost anywhere thanks to the bridges and handy network ferries.

Vaxholm

◎08 / POP 9500

Vaxholm, located about 35km northeast of the city, is the gateway to the central and northern reaches of Stockholm's archipelago and it positively swarms with tourists in summer. It has a collection of quaint summer houses that were fashionable in the 19th century. The oldest buildings are in the Norrhamn area, a few minutes' walk north of the town hall, but there's also interesting architecture along Hamngatan (the main street).

Bus 670 from Stockholm's T-Tekniska Högskolan metro station runs regularly to the town. Waxholmsbolaget (Map p428; ☑679 58 30; www.waxholmsbolaget.se) boats sail fre-

quently between Vaxholm and Strömkajen in Stockholm (about 40 minutes). Strömma Kanalbolaget (Map p428; ☑12 00 40 00; www.strommakanalbolaget.com) sails between Strandvägen and Vaxholm three times daily from mid-June to mid-August (one-way/return Skr100/200) and infrequently the rest of the year.

Stockholm Archipelago

◎08

The archipelago is the favourite time-off destination for Stockholm's locals, and summer cottages on rocky islets are popular among the well-to-do. Depending on whom you ask, the archipelago has between 14,000 and 100,000 islands (the usual consensus is 24,000).

Visit Skärgården (Map p428; ☑10 02 22; www.visitskargarden.se; Kajplats 18, Strandvägen; ⊙9am-5pm Mon-Fri, 10am-4pm Sat, 11am-4pm Sun), a waterside information centre, can advise on (and book) accommodation and tours.

The biggest boat operator is Waxholmsbolaget (Map p428; ☑679 5830; www.waxholmsbolaget.se). Timetables and information are available from its offices outside the Grand Hôtel on Strömkajen in Stockholm, at the harbour in Vaxholm, and online. It divides the archipelago into three areas: Norra Skärgården is the northern section (north from Ljusterö to Arholma); Mellersta Skärgården is the middle section, taking in Vaxholm, Ingmarsö, Stora Kalholmen, Finnhamn, Möja and Sandhamn; and Södra Skärgården is the southern section, with boats south to Nämdö, Ornö and Utö. The Båtluffarkortet pass (Skr420 for five days) gives you unlimited boat rides plus a handy map with suggested itineraries.

If time is short, consider taking the Thousand Island Cruise, which is offered by Stromma Kanabolaget (Map p428; ☑12 00 40 00; www.strommakanalbolaget.com; Nybrokajen) and runs daily between late June and early August. The full-day tour departs from Stockholm's Nybrokajen at 9.30am and returns at 8.30pm; the cost of Skr975 includes lunch, dinner, drinks and guided tours ashore. (A slightly fancier, two-course-dinner version costs Skr1110.) The tour includes three island stops and swimming opportunities.

Sandhamn village on Sandön is popular with sailors and day trippers. The historic

Sandhamns Värdshus (☎57 15 30 51; s/d Skr795/1290) serves a lip-smacking fish and shellfish casserole (mains Skr100 to Skr245).

The 900m-long Finnhamn, northeast of Stockholm, combines lush woods and meadows with sheltered coves, rocky cliffs and visiting eagle owls. While it's a popular summertime spot, there are enough quiet corners to indulge your inner hermit. Vandrarhem Finnhamn (☎54 24 62 12; info@finnhamn.se; dm Skr260; ☺year-round; ☺) is an STF hostel in a large wooden villa, with boat hire available. It's the largest hostel in the archipelago; advance booking is essential.

A cycling paradise in the southern archipelago, Utö has it all: sublime sandy beaches, lush fairy-tale forests, sleepy farms and abundant birdlife. Reception for the STF hostel (dm Skr325; ☺Sep-May) is at the nearby Utö Värdshus (Map p444; ☎50 42 03 00; receptionen@utovardshus.se; 2-person chalets incl breakfast per person from Skr995), whose restaurant (lunches Skr89-125, mains around Skr215; ☺closed Jan) is ranked among the best in the archipelago.

Ekerö District

☎08 / POP 22,600

The pastoral Ekerö district, 20km west of Stockholm, is home to the romantic Drottningholm castle as well as several large islands in Mälaren lake, a dozen medieval churches and the Unesco World Heritage site at Birka.

DROTTNINGHOLM

Still the royal family pad for part of the year, the Renaissance-inspired Drottningholm Slott (Map p444; www.royalcourt.se; adult/child Skr80/40; ☺10am-4.30pm May-Aug, noon-3.30pm Sep, closed mid-Dec–early Jan), with its geometric baroque gardens, was designed by architectural great Nicodemius Tessin the Elder and begun in 1662, about the same time as Versailles palace in France. You can walk around the wings open to the public on your own, but we recommend the one-hour guided tour (no additional charge; English tours at 10am, noon, 2pm and 4pm daily from June to August, reduced schedule rest of the year). A combined ticket including Kina Slott costs Skr120/60 adult/child.

The unique Drottningholms Slottsteater (www.dtm.se; admission by tour adult/child Skr90/free; tours ☺hourly noon-4pm May, 11am-4pm Jun-Aug, 1-3pm Sep) is the original 18th-century court theatre and is well worth a tour, especially the backstage sound-effects department; ask about opera, ballet and musical performances here in summer.

At the far end of the gardens is the 18th-century Kina Slott (adult/child Skr65/35; ☺11am-4.30pm daily May-Aug, noon-3.30pm Sep), a lavishly decorated 'Chinese pavilion' that was built as a gift to Queen Lovisa Ulrika. Admission includes an entertaining guided tour. A combined ticket including Drottningholm Slott costs Skr120/60 adult/child.

Given the separate admission charges for each attraction, it's a good idea to use the Stockholm Card. If you're not short of time, you could cycle out here, otherwise take the metro to T-Brommaplan and change to bus 301 or 323. The most pleasant way to get to Drottningholm is by boat: Strömma Kanalbolaget (Map p428; www.strommakanalbolaget.com) will take you there. Frequent services (one-way/return Skr115/160) depart from Stadshusbron (Stockholm) daily between May and mid-September, with less-frequent daily departures mid- to late September, and weekend-only services in October. A *kombibiljett* (combined ticket, Skr280) includes return travel and admission to the palace and Kina Slott.

BIRKA

At the fascinating Viking trading centre of Birka (Map p444; ☎12 00 40 00; ☺11am-6.30pm late Jun–mid-Aug, 11am-3pm May–late Jun & mid-Aug–early Sep), a Unesco World Heritage site on Björkö in Mälaren lake, archaeologists have excavated the ancient settlement's cemetery, harbour and fortress. Daily cruises to Birka run from early May to early September; the round trip on Strömma Kanalbolaget's *Victoria* from Stadshusbron, Stockholm, is a full day's outing (Skr295). The cruise price includes a visit to the museum and a guided tour in English of the settlement's burial mounds and fortifications. Call ☎12 00 40 00 or visit www.stromma.se for details; boats leave around 9.30am. Ferries do not run during the midsummer holidays.

Sigtuna

☎08 / POP 6500

About 40km northwest of Stockholm is the picturesque lakeside town of Sigtuna, the oldest surviving town in Sweden. It was founded in about 980; the first Swedish coins were struck here in 995. There's a popular Medieval Festival in July and good holiday markets throughout December.

Ten rune stones still stand in various places around Sigtuna, and 150 more dot the surrounding landscape. Storagatan is probably Sweden's oldest main street, and there are ruins of 12th-century churches around town. The mid-13th-century Mariakyrkan, Sigtuna's most arresting sight, contains restored medieval paintings. The friendly Sigtuna Museum (☑59 12 66 70; Storagatan 55; adult/child Skr20/free; ☉noon-4pm Tue-Sun Sep-May, noon-4pm Jun-Aug) displays finds from excavations of the area.

There's little budget accommodation in town. Those with their own wheels should look for signs advertising *stugor* (cabins) at local farmhouses (usually Skr300 to Skr500) or ask at the tourist office. Sigtuna Stadshotell (☑59 25 01 00; www.sigtunastads hotell.se; Stora Nygatan 3; s/d Skr2090/2490; ☑) features pale, uberstylish interiors, spa treatments and a restaurant hailed as a rising star.

There are a number of good cafes and restaurants to choose from, plus supermarkets for picnic supplies (and tables by the lake, among the ducks). Don't miss the delightful Tant Brun Kaffestuga (☑59 25 09 34; Laurentii gränd 3; cakes Skr30, pie Skr33), a 17th-century cafe with a worryingly saggy roof and pretty courtyard just off Storagatan. (A painted sign above the door says, roughly,

'It's better to bend the neck than hit the head', an apt proverb.)

The friendly tourist office (☑59 48 06 50; Storagatan 33; ☉10am-5pm Mon-Fri, 11am-4pm Sat & Sun) inhabits an 18th-century wooden house.

Travel connections are easy from Stockholm. Take a local train to Märsta, from where there are frequent buses to Sigtuna (570 or 575).

SVEALAND

This area, the birthplace of Sweden, offers evidence of the region's long history, including rune stones so plentiful you might stumble over them. Pre-Viking burial mounds in Gamla Uppsala light the imaginations of myth-builders and history buffs. There's also the old mine in Falun, which accidentally provided the red paint for all those little cottages dotting the landscape. And in Mora, the definitive Swedish king's path towards the crown is still retraced today, by thousands of skiers each year in the Vasaloppet.

Uppsala

☑018 / POP 182,000

Drenched in history but not stifled by the past, Uppsala has the party vibe of a university town to balance its important buildings and atmosphere of weighty cultural significance. It's a good combination, one that makes the

---

WORTH A TRIP

SIGURDSRISTNINGEN

The vivid, 3m-long Viking Age rock carving Sigurdsristningen (admission free; ☉24hr) illustrates the story of Sigurd the Dragon Slayer, a hero whose adventures are described in *Beowulf* and the Icelandic sagas. The story inspired Wagner's *Ring Cycle*, and *The Hobbit* and *Lord of the Rings* also borrow from it.

Carved into the bedrock around AD 1000, the carving shows Sigurd roasting the heart of the dragon Fafnir over a fire. Sigurd's stepfather, Regin, has persuaded him to kill Fafnir for the dragon's golden treasure. Sigurd touches the heart to see if it's cooked, then sucks his finger, and voila – he suddenly understands the language of birds. They warn him that Regin is plotting to kill him and keep the treasure, so Sigurd attacks first, chopping off his stepfather's head; the unfortunate fellow is shown in the left corner of the carving, among his scattered tools.

The carving is situated near Sundbyholms Slott and Mälaren lake, 12km northeast of Eskilstuna; take bus 225. Get more details at the Eskilstuna tourist office (☑710 23 75; www.eskilstuna.se; Nygatan 15; ☉10am-6pm Mon-Fri, 10am-2pm Sat, plus 10am-2pm Sun May-Aug).

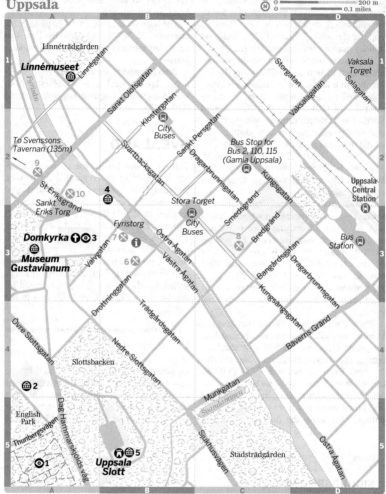

town both fun and functional, not to mention rewarding to the interested visitor.

On the edge of the city is Gamla (Old) Uppsala, the original site of the town, which was once a flourishing 6th-century religious centre.

◉ Sights

Gamla Uppsala RUINS

A great excursion for imaginative history buffs, especially in nice weather, is Gamla Uppsala – the city's beginnings. The site's three grave mounds are said to be those of legendary pre-Viking kings (although recent evidence suggests that at least one of the occupants is a woman) and lie in a field including about 300 smaller mounds and a great heathen temple. Even more fascinating is all the myth-making that has grown up around the grave mounds. A 17th-century professor, Olof Rudbeck, argued that Gamla Uppsala was actually the ancient sunken city of Atlantis, for example. The site is located 4km north of the modern city; take bus 2 from Stora Torget.

For more myths, rumours and some of the actual science surrounding the site, visit **Gamla Uppsala Museum** (adult/child

Uppsala

◉ Top Sights

◉ Sights

⊗ Eating

Skr60/35, under 6yr free; ⊙11am-5pm daily May-Aug). The museum has exhibits of ancient artefacts excavated from Gamla Uppsala and the nearby archaeological sites. Guided tours will help you get more out of your visit – these are held at 3pm daily from May to August and are included in the entry price of the museum.

Christianity arrived in the 11th century and with it the bishops and other church officials. From 1164 the archbishop had his seat in a cathedral on the site of the present **church**, which, by the 15th century, was enlarged and painted with frescos.

Uppsala Slott
CASTLE

(www.uppsalaslott.se; admission by guided tour only, adult/child Skr80/15; ⊙tours in English 12.45pm & 2.45pm Mon-Fri, 12.45 & 3.15pm Sat & Sun Jun-Aug) Originally constructed by Gustav Vasa in the mid-16th century, Uppsala Slott features the state hall where kings were enthroned and a queen abdicated. Midsummer and other holidays are frequently marked by ringing the nearby, freestanding **Gunilla klockan**.

The castle is accessible through the **Uppsala Art Museum** (Castle Entrance E); museum admission is included in the tour price. The **Botanical Gardens** (Villavägen 6-8; admission free; ⊙7am-9pm daily May-Sep), below the castle hill, show off more than 10,000 different species and are pleasant to wander through.

Museum Gustavianum
MUSEUM

(www.gustavianum.uu.se; Akademigatan 3; adult/child Skr40/free; ⊙11am-4pm Tue-Sun) The shelves in this pleasantly musty wonder cabinet hold case after case of obsolete tools and preserved oddities; also at Museum Gustavianum is a cleverly tucked-away anatomical theatre in the dome. The musuem offers tours in English at 1pm Saturday and Sunday.

Linnémuseet
MUSEUM

(www.linnaeus.se; Svartbäcksgatan 27; adult/child Skr50/free; ⊙11am-5pm Tue-Sun May-Sep) Memorabilia of von Linné's work in Uppsala. The gardens, with more than 1000 herbs, were designed according to an 18th-century plan.

FREE Domkyrka
CHURCH

(www.uppsaladomkyrka.se; ⊙8am-6pm May-Sep) The Gothic cathedral dominates the city, just as some of those buried there dominated their country, including St Erik, Gustav Vasa, Johan III and Carl von Linné.

Treasury
MUSEUM

(adult/child Skr30/free; ⊙10am-5pm Mon-Sat & 12.30-5pm Sun May-Sep) Gustav's funerary sword, silver crown and shiny golden buttons are kept in the north tower of the Domkyrka.

Carolina Rediviva
LIBRARY

(Dag Hammarskjölds väg 1; adult/child Skr20/free; ⊙9am-5pm Mon-Fri, 10am-5pm Sat, 11am-4pm Sun mid-Jun–mid-Aug) The old university library has a display hall that contains maps and historical and scientific literature, the pride of which is the 6th-century *Codex Argentus* (aka 'Silver Bible').

FREE Upplandsmuseet
MUSEUM

(www.upplandsmuseet.se; Sankt Eriks Torg 10; ⊙noon-5pm Tue-Sun) County collections from the Middle Ages, housed in an 18th-century mill.

🛏 Sleeping

There are several top-end chain options in the city centre, including Scandic and the newly renovated Clarion Gillet, with its hopping bar; budget options are a little further from the action.

UPPSALA KORTET

This handy little three-day **discount card** (Skr125) gives free or discounted admission to many of the town's attractions, plus free local bus travel and parking. There are also discounts at participating hotels, restaurants and shops. The card is valid from June to August, and can be bought from the tourist office. It covers one adult and up to two children.

STF Vandrarhem Sunnersta Herrgård
HOSTEL €

(☎32 42 20; www.sunnerstaherrgard.se; Sunnerstavägen 24; dm Skr225, hotel s/d Skr630/740; ☺Jan–mid-Dec; @) This hostel in a historic manor house about 6km south of the city centre has a parklike setting at water's edge and a good on-site restaurant. You can rent bikes (per day/week Skr50/200) or borrow a boat. There's free wi-fi. Hotel-standard rooms, including breakfast buffet, are also available. Take bus 20 to get here.

Uppsala Vandrarhem
HOSTEL €

(☎10 00 08; www.uppsalavandrarhem.se; Kvarntorget 3; dm/s/d from Skr190/400/500; ☺year-round; @) A 10-minute walk from the city centre, Uppsala Vandrarhem is an ultra-tidy STF hostel built around an interior courtyard reminiscent of a gym or swimming hall. Rooms are modern and in good shape (although dorms suffer from traffic and level-crossing noise). A breakfast buffet is available, and there's a nearby supermarket for self-caterers.

Fyrishov Camping
CAMPING GROUND €

(☎727 49 60; www.fyrishov.se; Idrottsgatan 2; campsites Skr130, 4-bed cabins Skr895; ☺year-round) This camping ground, situated 2km north of the city, is great for families with water-babies: it's attached to one of Sweden's largest water parks, with discounted swim-and-stay packages (cabins from Skr995). Take bus 1 from Dragarbrunnsgatan.

✖ Eating

Casual dining options can be found inside Saluhallen (Sankt Eriks Torg; ☺Mon-Sat), an indoor market between the cathedral and the river. Find groceries at the central Hemköp supermarket (Stora Torget; ☺to 10pm).

Eko Caféet
CAFE €

(Drottninggatan 5; lattés Skr15, specials Skr89) This funky little place with retro and mismatched furniture serves some of the best (and least expensive!) coffee in town. It does Italian-style wholefood, turns into a tapas bar on Wednesday to Saturday evenings, and frequently hosts live jazz/folk, as well as changing art exhibits and general studenty goings-on. Things quiet down somewhat in the summer, when it just opens for lunch Monday to Friday.

Ofvandahls
CAFE €

(Sysslomansgatan 3-5; cakes & snacks around Skr40) Something of an Uppsala institution, this classy *konditori* (bakery/confectionery/cafe) dates back to the 19th century and is a cut above your average coffee-and-bun shop. It has been endorsed by no less a personage than the king, and radiates old-world charm; somehow those faded red-striped awnings just get cuter every year.

Hambergs Fisk
SEAFOOD €€€

(Fyristorg 8; lunches from Skr80, mains Skr150-240; ☺11.30am-10pm Tue-Sat) No need to ask at the tourist office about where to eat: if you're there, you'll be close enough to smell the aromas of dill and seafood tempting you into this excellent fish restaurant. Self-caterers should check out the fresh fish counter inside.

Svenssons Tavernan
SWEDISH €€

(Sysslomansgatan 14; pizzas from Skr109, mains Skr135-195) US furniture chain Pottery Barn meets the Ancient Mariner in the decorating scheme of this upmarket eatery, with a nice outdoor patio and a menu of gourmet Swedish staples as well as a long list of pizzas.

❶ Information

Forex (Fyristorg 8; ☺9am-7pm Mon-Fri, 9am-3pm Sat) Currency exchange next to the tourist office.

Tourist office (☎727 48 00; www.uppsalatourism.se; Fyristorg 8; ☺10am-6pm Mon-Fri, 10am-3pm Sat, also noon-4pm Sun mid-Jun–mid-Aug) Pick up the *Walking Tour of Uppsala* leaflet, and *What's On Uppsala* for event listings.

❶ Getting There & Away

The **Flygbuss** (bus 801) departs at least twice an hour around the clock for nearby Stockholm Arlanda Airport (one-way Skr100, 45 minutes); it leaves from outside Uppsala Central Station.

Swebus Express (☑0200-218 218; www. swebusexpress.se) runs regular direct services to Stockholm (Skr57, one hour, at least hourly), Gävle (Skr70, 1½ hours, two daily), Västerås (Skr122 to Skr222, 3½ hours, six daily), Örebro (Skr114 to Skr164, 4½ hours, four to seven daily) and Falun (Skr200, 5½ hours, one daily).

For car hire, contact **Statoil** (☑20 91 00; Gamla Uppsalagatan 48), next to the Scandic Uppsala Nord. There are also three petrol stations with car hire, 1.5km along Vaksalagatan: **OKQ8** (☑29 04 96; Årstagatan 5-7) often has good deals.

There are frequent **SJ** (www.sj.se) trains to/ from Stockholm (Skr30 to Skr70, 40 minutes), Gävle (from Skr188, 50 minutes, at least seven daily), Östersund (Skr436 to Skr595, five hours, at least two daily) and Mora (Skr224 to Skr572, 3¼ hours, two daily).

🛈 Getting Around

Upplands Lokaltrafik (☑0771-14 14 14; www. ul.se) runs traffic within the city and county. City buses leave from Stora Torget and the surrounding streets. Tickets for unlimited travel for 90 minutes cost from Skr30.

Örebro

☑019 / POP 127,000

A substantial, culturally rich city, Örebro buzzes around its central feature, the huge and romantic castle surrounded by a moat filled with water lilies. The city originally grew as a product of the textile industry, but it's now decidedly a university town – students on bicycles fill the streets, and relaxed-looking people gather on restaurant patios and in parks.

⊙ Sights

Slottet CASTLE
(☑21 21 21; guided tours adult/child Skr50/free; ⊙daily Jun-Aug, 1pm Sat & Sun rest of yr) The magnificent **Slottet** now serves as county governor's headquarters. Parts of the interior are open for exhibits, but to really explore you'll need to take a tour – there's a historical one at 4.30pm (in Swedish or English, depending on numbers), or a 'Secrets of the Vasa Fortress' option at 2.30pm (in English) in summer. Tickets can be purchased from the tourist office. The castle's northwest tower holds a small **history exhibition** (admission free; ⊙10am-5pm daily May-Aug).

Wadköping MUSEUM
(per person Skr20; ⊙tours 1 & 3pm Jun-Aug) A pleasant stroll east of the castle along the river will take you through Stadsparken, where the Stadsträdgården greenhouse precinct has a great cafe. Further east is the excellent Wadköping museum village, an open-air museum with craft workshops, a bakery and period buildings. Bikes are available to rent from May to September from the kiosk (Hamnplan) on the river's edge.

St Nikolai Kyrka CHURCH
(⊙10am-5pm Mon-Fri, 11am-3pm Sat) The commercial centre and some grand buildings are around Stortorget, including the 13th-century St Nikolai Kyrka, where Jean Baptiste Bernadotte (Napoleon's marshal) was chosen in 1810 to take the Swedish throne.

FREE **Länsmuseum & Konsthall** MUSEUM
(www.orebrolansmuseum.se; Engelbrektsgatan 3; ⊙11am-5pm Tue & Thu-Sun, 11am-9pm Wed) Outside the castle grounds is this combined regional and art museum. Exhibits include a treasury and a collection from medieval churches in the area.

🛏 Sleeping & Eating

Behrn Hotell HOTEL €€€
(☑12 00 95; www.behrnhotell.se; Stortorget 12; s/d Skr1295/1595; ✳@) Excellently situated on the main square, Behrn Hotell goes the extra mile, with homey rooms each individually decorated, ranging from strictly business to farmhouse to edgy modern Scandinavian. Do it right and get a room with a balcony, or a suite with old wooden beams, chandeliers and jacuzzi. There's also a spa, and a restaurant that serves dinner from Tuesday to Friday.

STF Vandrarhem Livin HOSTEL €
(☑31 02 40; www.livin.se; Järnvägsgatan 22; dm from Skr200, s/d Skr450/540, hotel s/d Skr900/1100) The STF hostel has moved closer to the town centre, about 300m from the train station, and is now part of a modern budget-hotel building; hostel rooms have the same basic features as the hotel rooms, including private bathroom and TV, but prices don't include sheets or breakfast. A good self-catering kitchen, laundry room and bicycle hire are also available.

Gustavsvik Camping CAMPING GROUND, CABINS **€€**
(☎19 69 50; www.gustavsvik.se; Sommarrovägen; campsites Skr295, cabins from Skr1035; ☺mid-Apr–early Nov; ☒) This camping facility is 2km south of the city centre; take bus 11 to get here. It's huge and family-oriented, with pools, mini-golf, a cafe, gym, restaurant and bike rental (Skr60 per day).

Hälls Konditori Stallbacken CAFE **€**
(Engelbrektsgatan 12; coffees Skr20, pastries Skr15-45, lunch specials Skr74-89) One of two locations of this bakery–cafe (the other's in Järntorget), Hälls is a classic old-style *konditori*. Sensible light meals (salads, quiche, sandwiches) are available, plus there's tee-tering piles of creamy cakes and pastries.

Cafe Deed CAFE-BAR **€**
(www.cafedeed.se; Järnvägsgatan 8; snacks from Skr30; ☺3-8pm Tue-Thu, 6pm-1am Fri & Sat) This cool hang-out for local youth is run by vol-unteers, and everything on offer is made of certified-organic ingredients, from the eggs and milk to the souvenir T-shirts. Locally made artwork covers the walls, and there's usually live music in the evenings.

Rosali's Deli CAFE **€**
(Stortorget 16; lunch mains Skr79; ☺11am-6pm Mon-Fri, 11am-4pm Sat) This bright-coloured corner cafe serves hearty takeaways and quick, casual lunches of pasta bowls and salads.

☆ Entertainment

Liquid CLUB **€**
(☎10 42 20; Storgatan 20; ☺5pm-late) A local arts publication recently dubbed this hipster hang-out 'Örebro's answer to Williamsburg' (in NYC). See what you think.

ℹ Information

Tourist office (☎21 21 21; www.orebro.se; ☺10am-6pm Mon-Fri, 10am-4pm Sat & Sun Jun-Aug) Inside the castle.

ℹ Getting There & Away

Long-distance buses, which leave from opposite the train station, operate pretty much every-where in southern Sweden. From here, **Swebus Express** (☎0200-21 82 18; www.swebus express.se) has connections to Norrköping, Karlstad and Oslo, Mariestad and Göteborg, Västerås and Uppsala, and Eskilstuna and Stockholm.

Train connections are also good. Direct SJ trains run to/from Stockholm (Skr212, two hours) every hour, some via Västerås (Skr100, one hour); and Göteborg (Skr250, 2¾ hours). Other trains run daily to Gävle (Skr290, three to four hours) and Borlänge (Skr190, 2¼ hours), where you can change for Falun and Mora.

Falun
☎023 / POP 55,000
An unlikely combination of industrial and adorable, Falun is home to the region's most important mine and, as a consequence, the source of the deep-red paint that renders Swedish country houses so uniformly cute. It's the main city of the Dalarna region, put-ting it within easy striking distance of some of Sweden's best attractions – including the home of painter Carl Larsson, a work of art in itself.

◉ Sights & Activities

Kopparberget copper mine MINE, MUSEUM
(☎78 20 30; www.kopparberget.com; ☺daily) The Kopparberget copper mine was the world's most important by the 17th cen-tury and only closed in 1992 (it's now on Unesco's World Heritage list). As a by-product, the mine also provided the red coating that became the characteristic house paint of the age and is still in popular use today. The mine museum (adult/child Skr50/free; ☺10am-6pm) contains everything you could possibly want to know about the history, administration, engineering, geolo-gy and copper production of the mine. The complex is west of town at the top end of Gruvgatan (take bus 709). One-hour tours (adult/child Skr190/70) explore the bowels of the disused mine (bring warm clothing); call in advance to find out the times of English-language tours. On weekdays from October to April tours must be booked in advance.

Carl Larsson-gården HISTORIC HOME
(☎600 53; www.carllarsson.se; Sundborn; admis-sion by guided tour only adult/child Skr120/50; ☺10am-5pm May-Sep) Carl Larsson-gården is the beautiful early 20th-century home of the artist Carl Larsson and his wife Karin in the pretty village of Sundborn (13km from Falun; bus 64). It's a bright, lively house with superb colour schemes, decoration and furniture. Tapestries and embroidery woven by Karin Larsson reveal she was a skilled artist in her own right. Admission is by

45-minute guided tour only; call in advance for times of English tours.

There's more folk culture at **Dalarnas Museum** (☑76 55 00; www.dalarnasmuseum.se; Stigaregatan 2-4; admission free; ☺10am-5pm Tue-Fri, noon-5pm Sat-Mon), plus Nobel Prize-winning author Selma Lagerlöf's preserved study and library and some cutting-edge temporary exhibits of Swedish artists.

Stora Kopparbergs Kyrka CHURCH
(Kyrkbacksvägen 8; ☺10am-6pm Mon-Fri, 10am-6pm Sat, 9am-6pm Sun) This late 14th-century church is Falun's oldest building, with brick vaulting and folk-art flowers running round the walls.

Hopptornen TOWER
(☺10am-6pm Sun-Thu, 10am-11pm Fri & Sat mid-May–mid-Aug) This tower and ski jump in the hills behind the town has great views; you can either walk or take a lift to the top (Skr20).

🛏 Sleeping & Eating

As ever, kebab shops and pizza joints abound. For self-caterers, there's a centrally located **ICA supermarket** (Falugatan 1) and a **Systembolaget** (Åsgatan 19).

Falu Fängelse Vandrarhem HOSTEL €
(☑79 55 75; info@falufangelse.se; Villavägen 17; dm/s/f Skr250/350/650; @) The SVIF hostel really feels like what it is – a former prison. Dorm beds are in cells, with heavy iron doors and thick walls, concrete floors, steel lockers for closets etc. The place is extremely friendly, and common areas are spacious and full of well-worn, den-like furniture. The shower and toilet facilities are somewhat limited, so it's worth asking for a room with bathroom if available.

Kopparhattan Café &
Restaurang CAFE €€
(☑191 69; Stigaregatan 2-4; specials Skr80, mains from Skr130) An excellent choice is this funky, arty cafe–restaurant, attached to Dalarnas Museum. Choose from sandwiches, soup or good vegetarian specials for lunch, and light vegie, fish and meat evening mains. There's an outside terrace overlooking the river, and live music on Friday nights in summer.

Hotel Falun HOTEL €€
(☑291 80; Trotzgatan 16; s Skr650-750, d Skr800-950; @) There are some good hotel choices right by the tourist office, including this place, which has comfortable modern

rooms (cheaper rooms have private toilet and shared shower).

🛈 Information

Tourist office (☑830 50; www.visitfalun.se; Trotzgatan 10-12; ☺9am-7pm Mon-Fri, 9am-5pm Sat, 11am-4pm Sun)

🛈 Getting There & Away

Falun isn't on the main train lines – change at Borlänge when coming from Stockholm or Mora – but there are direct trains to and from Gävle (Skr130, 1¼ hours, roughly every two hours), or regional buses (Skr100, two hours) equally often.

Swebus Express (☑0200-21 82 18; www.swebusexpress.se) has buses on the Göteborg–Karlstad–Falun–Gävle route, and connections to buses on the Stockholm–Borlänge–Mora route.

Regional transport is run by **Dalatrafik** (☑0771-95 95 95; www.dalatrafik.se), which covers all corners of the county of Dalarna. Tickets cost Skr22 for trips within a zone and Skr15 extra for each new zone. A 31-day *länskort* (county card) costs Skr1250 and allows you to travel throughout the county; cards in smaller increments are also available. Regional bus 70 goes approximately hourly to Rättvik (Skr52, one hour) and Mora (Skr82, 1¾ hours).

Lake Siljan Region

This pretty, traditional area in the county of Dalarna is a popular summer- and winter-sports destination, with reasonable-sized towns offering good facilities and attractions. The area is a very popular summer destination, with numerous outdoor festivals and attractions. Maps of **Siljansleden**, an excellent network of walking and cycling paths extending for more than 300km around Lake Siljan, are available from tourist offices for Skr20. Another way to enjoy the lake is by boat: in summer, **MS Gustaf Wasa** (☑070-542 10 25; www.wasanet.nu; cruises Skr100-275) runs a complex range of lunch, dinner and sightseeing cruises from the towns of Mora, Rättvik and Leksand. Ask at any tourist office or go online for a schedule.

LEKSAND
☑0247 / POP 15,500

Leksand's claim to fame is its Midsummer Festival, the most popular in Sweden, in which around 20,000 spectators fill the bowl-shaped green park on the first Friday evening after 21 June to sing songs and watch costumed dancers circle the maypole. Leksands Kyrka (☑807 00; Kyrkallén), with its distinctive onion dome, dates from the early 13th century. The tourist office (☑79 61 30; leksand@siljan.se; Norsgatan 40; ☺9am-7pm Mon-Fri, 10am-5pm Sat & Sun mid-Jun–mid-Aug) is on the main drag.

Tiny Tällberg, midway between Rättvik and Leksand, is a pretty village of wooden buildings scattered like a handful of rubies along a hillside, and it's nearly as expensive if you want to stay the night. It has a population of around 200 and eight upmarket hotels. But it's a lovely place to enjoy lunch and have a wander. The Tällberg website (www.infotallberg.nu, in Swedish) has links to all the hotels. Bus 58 between Rättvik and Leksand stops in the village regularly, and it's worth going just for the scenic landscape along the route.

There are a couple of direct intercity trains every day running from Stockholm to Leksand (Skr240, three hours). Bus 58 regularly connects Leksand with Tällberg (Skr35, 20 minutes), and bus 258 goes to Rättvik (Skr50, 20 to 50 minutes).

RÄTTVIK & AROUND
☑0248 / POP 10,900

Laidback Rättvik has sandy lakeside beaches for summer and ski slopes for winter. Don't miss the longest wooden pier in Sweden, the 625m Långbryggan. Views from surrounding hills are excellent.

By the lake northwest of the train station, the 13th-century church, rebuilt in 1793, has 87 well-preserved church stables, the oldest dating from 1470.

Inviting all sorts of bad puns about rocking out, Dalhalla (www.dalhalla.se) is an old limestone quarry 7km north of Rättvik used as an open-air theatre and concert venue in summer; the acoustics are incredible and the setting is stunning.

On the lake shore near the train station is Siljansbadets Camping (☑516 91; www.siljansbadet.com; campsites low/high season Skr95/235, 4-bed cabins from Skr400/950). Across town, Enåbadets Camping (☑561 00; www.enan.se; Furudalsvägen 1; campsites low/high season Skr135/255, 4-bed cabins from Skr890) is by the river off Centralgatan (1km from the train station). There's a swimming pool (adult/child per day Skr60/40) and bicycle hire available.

By Enåbadets camping ground is the highly rated hostel STF Vandrarhem Rät-tvik (☑105 66; Centralgatan; dm Skr150; ☺reception 8-10am & 5-6pm; P@), in a charming complex of old wooden buildings. Reception for the hostel is at the camping ground office.

The picturesque, church-run B&B Stiftsgården Rättvik (☑510 20; www.stiftsgarden.org; Kyrkvägen 2; s without bathroom Skr375, s with/without shower Skr696/475, d with/without shower Skr970/830) is by the lake, away from the hustle and bustle of town but within easy walking distance and near footpaths and outdoor activities. Rooms are simple but pleasant; breakfast is included, and lunch/dinner is available for Skr85/95. Canoes and cycles can be hired.

Pizza joints abound, and Storgatan is home to a few supermarkets. Frick's Konditori (Torget; coffee & roll Skr30, sandwiches Skr30-60), in the square across from the train station, has great pastries and sandwiches and is a social hub for locals.

More information on the culture and history of the surrounding area can be found in Rättvik's library, Kulturhus (Storgatan 2; ☺11am-7pm Mon-Thu, 11am-4pm Fri, 11am-2pm Sat, 1-4pm Sun). The tourist office (☑79 72 10; rattvik@siljan.se; Riksvägen 40; ☺10am-7pm Mon-Fri, 10am-5pm Sat & Sun mid-Jun–mid-Aug) is at the train station.

Buses depart from outside the train station. Dalatrafik's bus 70 runs regularly between Falun, Rättvik and Mora. A couple of direct intercity trains per day from Stockholm (Skr354, 3½ hours) stop at Rättvik (otherwise you have to change at Borlänge). Local trains run often between Rättvik and Mora (Skr65, 25 minutes).

MORA
☑0250 / POP 20,100

Legend has it that in 1520 Gustav Vasa arrived here, in a last-ditch attempt to start a rebellion against the Danish regime. The people of Mora weren't interested, and Gustav was forced to put on his skis and flee for the border. After he left, the town reconsidered and two yeomen, Engelbrekt and Lars, volunteered to follow Gustav's tracks, finally overtaking him in Sälen and changing Swedish history.

Today the world's biggest cross-country ski race, Vasaloppet, which ends in Mora, commemorates this epic chase. Around 15,000 people take part on the first Sunday in March. In summer, you can walk the route on the 90km Vasaloppsleden.

Sights

Zornmuseet   MUSEUM
(✎59 23 10; www.zorn.se; Vasagatan 36; adult/
child Skr60/free; ⏰9am-5pm Mon-Sat, 11am-
5pm Sun mid-May–mid-Sep) One of Mora's
big draws, this museum displays many of
the best-loved portraits and characteristic
nudes of the Mora painter Anders Zorn
(1860–1920), one of Sweden's most renowned artists. Next door, the Zorn family
house Zorngården (✎59 23 10; Vasagatan 36;
admission & tour adult/child Skr70/30; ⏰10am-
4pm Mon-Sat, 11am-4pm Sun mid-May–mid-Sep)
reflects Zorn's National Romantic aspira-
tions (check out the Viking-influenced hall
and entryway). Access is by guided tour (every 15 minutes in summer; phone ahead for
English tours).

Around Mora   AREA
Traditional wooden Dala horses are painted
in bright, cheerful colours; to many they're
the ultimate symbol of Sweden. A good
place to see how they're made, and pick up
some of your own, is Nils Olsson Hemslöjd
(✎372 00; www.nohemslojd.se; ⏰8am-6pm Mon-
Fri, 9am-5pm Sat & Sun mid-Jun–mid-Aug) at Nus-
näs, 10km southeast of Mora (bus 108, three
per day Monday to Friday).

Outside the town of Orsa (16km north
of Mora) is Grönklitt Björnpark (✎462
00; www.orsagronklitt.se; adult/child/fam-
ily Skr150/120/400; ⏰10am-6pm mid-Jun–Aug),
where you can see bears, wolves and lynxes
in fairly natural surrounds. The bears are
usually fed around noon, when you'll get a
great view of them. Bus 118 runs from Mora
to Grönklitt, via Orsa (twice daily weekdays,
once on Sunday).

Vasaloppsmuseet   MUSEUM
(✎392 25; www.vasaloppet.se; Vasagatan; adult/
child Skr40/15; ⏰10am-5pm mid-Jun–mid-Sep)
Even if you have no interest in skiing,
you may be pleasantly surprised by this
excellent museum, which really commu-
nicates the passion behind the world's
largest cross-country skiing event.

Sleeping & Eating

Målkull Ann's Restaurang, B&B &
Vandrarhem   HOSTEL, HOTEL €€
(✎381 96; www.maalkullann.se; Vasagatan 19; dm/
s/d Skr190/400/580, B&B s/d from Skr600/830,
with bathroom Skr650/880, pensionat r from
Skr680; @) This hostel–B&B near the Vasaloppet museum is housed in a series of
variously rustic buildings. The STF hostel
(at Fredsgatan 6) is part of the same com-

plex. Call ahead, as reception hours vary a
lot depending on the season.

Restaurang Vasagatan 32   SWEDISH €€
(✎102 27; www.restaurangvasagatan32.se; Vasagatan 32; daily lunches Skr85; ⏰lunch daily, dinner
Fri-Sun) This classy new restaurant, a white-
tablecloth-and-wineglasses kind of place
next to the Vasalopps museum, serves meaty
main dishes such as beef roasts and grilled
salmon on the weekends and a lunch special
daily.

Mora Parken   CAMPING GROUND, CABINS €€
(✎276 00; moraparken@mora.se; tent & car
Skr175, 2-/4-bed cabins from Skr275/500, hotel
s/d Skr995/1295; @) This camping ground
and hotel are combined in a great waterside spot, 400m northwest of the church,
and both have solid facilities.

Mora Kaffestuga   CAFE €
(Kyrkogatan 8; lunches from Skr75; ⏰7am-7pm
Mon-Sat) Along the main pedestrian shopping street are a few small cafes; this is
the pick of them, for its stylish interior and
heavenly baked goods and sandwiches.

ℹ Information

Tourist office (✎59 20 20; mora@siljan.se;
⏰10am-5pm Mon-Fri, 10am-2pm Sat; closed
Mon mid-Sep–mid-Nov) At the train station.

ℹ Getting There & Away

All Dalatrafik buses use the bus station at
Moragatan 23. Several buses run frequently to
Rättvik, Falun and Orsa. Once or twice daily, bus
170 goes to Älvdalen, Särna, Idre and Grövelsjön,
near the Norwegian border.

Mora is an SJ (✎0771-75 75 75; www.sj.se) train
terminus and the southern terminus of Inlandsbanan (Inland Railway), which runs north to Gällivare (mid-June to mid-August). The main train
station is about 1km east of the town centre. The
more central Mora Strand is a platform station in
town, but not all trains stop there, so check the
timetable. When travelling to Östersund, you can
choose between Inlandsbanan (Skr414, 6¼ hours,
one daily, June to August only) or bus 45 (Skr182,
5¼ hours, two daily).

SKÅNE

Artists adore southern Sweden. Down here,
the light is softer, the foliage brighter and the
shoreline more dazzling and white. Sweden's
southernmost county, Skåne (Scania) was
Danish property until 1658 and still flaunts
its differences. You can detect them in the
strong dialect (skånska), in the half-timbered

houses and in Skåne's hybrid flag: a Swedish yellow cross on a red Danish background.

Malmö

♪040 / POP 280,800

Once dismissed as crime-prone and tatty, Sweden's third-largest city has rebranded itself as progressive and downright cool. Malmö's second wind blew in with the opening of the Öresund bridge and tunnel in 2000, connecting the city to bigger, cooler Copenhagen and creating a dynamic new urban conglomeration. Such a cosmopolitan outcome seems only natural for what is Sweden's most multicultural metropolis; 150 nationalities make up Malmö's headcount. Here, Nordic reserve is countered by hot cars with doof-doof stereos and exotic Middle Eastern street stalls.

◉ Sights & Activities

The cobbled streets and interesting buildings around **Lilla Torg** are restored parts of the late-medieval town – the oldest of the half-timbered houses here was built in 1597. Many are now occupied by galleries, boutiques and restaurants.

Malmö Museer   MUSEUM COMPLEX
(www.malmo.se/museer; Malmöhusvägen; combined admission adult/child Skr40/10, free with Malmökortet; ⊙10am-4pm Jun-Aug) Various museums in and around **Malmöhus Slott** (castle) make up the Malmö Museer. There are cafe–restaurants inside all the museums. You can walk through the royal apartments, see the **Stadsmuseum** with its Malmö collection, and see works by important Swedish artists such as John Bauer and Sigrid Hjerten at the **Konstmuseum**.

Malmö

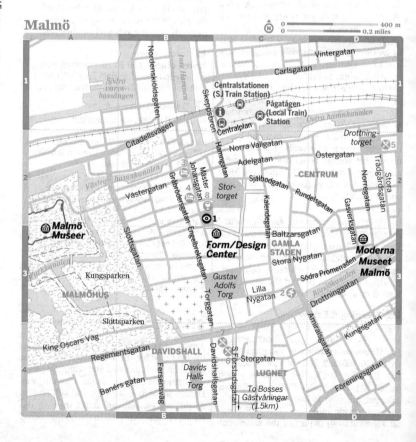

MALMÖ CARD

The **Malmökortet discount card** covers free bus transport, street parking, entry to several museums, and discounts at other attractions and on sightseeing tours. It costs Skr130/160 for one/two days – the price includes one adult and up to two children aged under 16 years. Buy it at the tourist office.

Moderna Museet Malmö MUSEUM
(www.modernamuseet.se; Gasverksgatan 22; adult/child Skr50/free; ⊙11am-6pm Tue-Sun, 11am-9pm Wed) This southern outpost of Stockholm's modern art museum is currently home to several favourites from the larger museum, by major players such as Robert Rauschenberg, Öyvind Fahlström and Niki de Saint Phalle.

FREE **Form/Design Center** ART GALLERY
(Lilla Torg 9; ⊙11am-5pm Tue, Wed & Fri, 11am-6pm Thu, 11am-4pm Sat, noon-4pm Sun) This research and exhibition centre showcases cutting-edge design, architecture and art. The surrounding cobbled streets are restored pockets of the late-medieval town; the half-timbered houses now house **galleries** and **boutiques** selling arts and crafts.

Turning Torso ARCHITECTURE
The northwest harbour redevelopment is home to the Turning Torso, a striking skyscraper that twists through 90 degrees from bottom to top. Designed by Spaniard Santiago Calatrava and inaugurated in 2005, it's now Sweden's tallest building (190m).

FREE **Malmö Konsthall** ART GALLERY
(www.konsthall.malmo.se; St Johannesgatan 7; ⊙11am-5pm, to 9pm Wed) This gallery about 500m south of central Malmö is one of Europe's largest contemporary art spaces, with exhibitions spanning both Swedish and foreign talent. To get here, follow Davidshallsgatan south across Triangeln, and continue south along Rådmansgatan.

City Boats Malmö PEDAL BOATS
(☎0704-71 00 67; www.cityboats.se; Amiralsbron, Södra Promenaden; per 30/60min Skr80/130; ⊙daily 11am-7pm May-Aug) To scoot around Malmö's canals in a pedal boat, head to this place just east of Gustav Adolfs Torg.

🛏 Sleeping

Private rooms or apartments from Skr395 per person are available through **City Room** (☎795 94; www.cityroom.se); bed sheets and towels cost an additional Skr100 per set. The agency has no office address but can be reached by phone on weekdays from 9am to noon. Otherwise, contact the tourist office.

STF Vandrarhem Malmö City HOSTEL €
(☎611 62 20; malmo.city@stfturist.se; Rönngatan 1; dm Skr190, s/d from Skr390/460; @) This huge hostel has spotless, brand-new facilities, and several rooms include TV and private bathroom. There's a big kitchen, spacious dining room, TV lounge and very helpful staff, and most sights are within easy walking distance. To reach the hostel, take bus 29 to Triangeln, then walk up Östra Rönnholmsvagen to Rönngatan.

Bosses Gästvåningar HOSTEL €
(☎32 62 50; info@bosses.nu; Södra Förstadsgatan 110B; s/d/tr/q from Skr375/525/625/850; @) The quiet, clean rooms in this central SVIF hostel are like those of a budget hotel, with proper beds, TVs and shared bathrooms. Service is helpful and it's close to Möllevångstorget

and opposite the town hospital (follow the signs for 'Sjukhuset' if arriving by car).

Hotel Duxiana
HOTEL €€€

(☎607 70 00; www.malmo.hotelduxiana.com; Mäster Johansgatan 1; s/d from Skr1290/1890; @) Close to Centralstationen, ubersleek Hotel Duxiana is one for the style crew. In a palate of white, black and gunmetal grey, design features include Bruno Mattheson sofas and the same heavenly beds supplied to the world's first seven-star hotel in Dubai. Single rooms are small but comfy, while the decadent junior suites feature a clawed bathtub facing the bed.

Mäster Johan Hotel
HOTEL €€€

(☎664 64 00; www.masterjohan.se; Mäster Johansgatan 13; s/d Skr2575/2775; P@) Just off Lilla Torg is one of Malmö's finest slumber spots, with spacious, elegantly understated rooms featuring beautiful oak floors and snowy-white fabrics. Bathrooms flaunt Paloma Picasso–designed tiles, there's a sauna and gym, and the immaculate breakfast buffet is served in a glass-roofed courtyard.

✖ Eating & Drinking

Malmö isn't short on dining experiences, whether it's vegan grub in a grungy left-wing hang-out or designer supping on contemporary Nordic flavours. One sure-fire strategy is to try whichever kebab stand in Möllevångstorget has the longest line. For atmosphere and conviviality, head to the restaurant-bars on Lilla Torg: Victors (☎12 76 70), Moosehead (☎12 04 23) and Mello Yello (☎30 45 25) are all great spots with varied menus (from Thai to Tex-Mex), affable service and alfresco seating (complete with heaters and blankets in cold weather).

Solde
CAFE €

(Regementsgatan 3; panini from Skr45; ⊙7.15am-6.30pm Mon-Fri, 9am-4pm Sat) Malmö's coolest cafe is a grit-chic combo of concrete bar, white-tiled walls, art exhibitions and indie-hip regulars. The owner is an award-winning barista; watch him in action over lip-smacking Italian panini, biscotti and *cornetti* (croissants).

Glassfabriken
CAFE €

(Kristianstadsgatan 16; mains around Skr50; ⊙11am-8pm, closed Mon) Easy to miss, this grungy, arty, alcohol-free hang-out serves cheap, tasty grub such as vegan salads, ciabatta and freshly baked cakes; locals like the weekend brunch (Skr45). Play board

games over mango milkshakes, check out the local art on display or catch the occasional music or theatre gig. To get here, walk south along Södra Förstadsgatan towards Möllevångstorget.

Krua Thai
THAI €€

(☎12 22 87; Möllevångstorget 14; mains Skr79-115; ⊙11am-3pm Mon, 11am-3pm & 5-10pm Tue-Fri, 1-10pm Sat, 2-10pm Sun) Anchoring one corner of the buzzing Möllevångstorget is this authentic, long-standing Thai joint, a reliable if less than thrilling choice. The family also runs a central **takeaway** with longer hours (Södergatan 22; Skr60 for two-dish combo).

🌿 Salt och Brygga
ORGANIC €€€

(☎611 59 40; www.saltobrygga.se; Sundspromenaden 7, Västra Hamnen; lunches Skr99-169, dinner mains Skr129-250; ⊙lunch & dinner Mon-Sat) Overlooking the Öresund bridge, this stylish, contemporary Slow Food restaurant serves contemporary Swedish cuisine with a clear conscience. Everything is organic (including the staff's uniforms), waste is turned into bio-gas, and the interior is allergen-free. Flavours are clean and strictly seasonal – think smoked reindeer with dill meringue and chanterelles, or Jerusalem artichoke soup with apples and langoustine tails. Book ahead.

Dolce Sicilia
GELATO €

(Drottningtorget 6; gelato from Skr25; ⊙11am-9pm May-Aug) Run by certified Sicilians. Head here for fresh, organic Italian-style gelato (the chilli-chocolate and fig flavours are divine). Savoury edibles include ciabatta (Skr60) and salads (Skr70).

☆ Entertainment

Debaser
LIVE MUSIC

(Norra Parkgatan 2; ⊙7pm-3am Wed-Sun) Stockholm's music club heavyweight has opened shop in Malmö, with live gigs and club nights spanning anything from indie, pop and hip hop to soul, electronica and rock. There's a buzzing outdoor bar–lounge overlooking Folkets Park and decent grub till 10pm for a preparty feed. To get here, follow Amiralsgatan about 600m south towards Möllevangstorget.

❶ Information

Forex (Centralstationen; ⊙7am-9pm) Currency exchange; several branches around town.

Skånegården (☎040-20 96 00; www.skane.

com; Stortorget 9, SE-21122 Malmö; ⊙9am–
8pm Mon-Fri, 9am-4pm Sat & Sun mid-Jun–
mid-Aug) Tourist office, on the E20, 800m
from the Öresund bridge tollgate. Designed for
motorists entering from Denmark.
Tourist office (☑34 12 00; www.malmo.se;
⊙9am-7pm Mon-Fri, 10am-4pm Sat & Sun mid-
Jun–early Sep) Inside Centralstationen, has
free internet hotel-booking service (with fee).

❶ Getting There & Away
To/From the Airport
Trains run directly from Malmö to Copenhagen's
main airport (Skr95, 35 minutes, every 20 minutes), which has a much wider flight selection.
Flygbuss (☑0771-77 77 77; www.flygbus
sarna.se) runs from Centralstationen to Sturup
airport (adult/child Skr99/79, 40 minutes)
roughly every 40 minutes on weekdays, with six
services on Saturday and seven on Sunday; a
taxi shouldn't cost more than Skr400.

Air
Sturup airport (☑613 10 00; www.malmoair
port.se) is situated 33km southeast of Malmö.
SAS (☑0770-72 77 27; www.sas.se) has up to 11
non-stop flights to Stockholm Arlanda Airport
daily. **Malmö Aviation** (☑0771-55 00 10; www.
malmoaviation.se) flies several times daily to
Bromma Stockholm Airport. International destinations include Antalya, Budapest, Gran Canaria
and Heraklon.

Bus
There are two bus terminals with daily departures to Swedish and European destinations.
Travelshop (Malmö Buss & Resecenter; ☑33 05
70; www.travelshop.se; Skeppsbron 10), north
of the train station by the harbour, services (and
sells tickets for) several companies, including **Swebus Express** (☑0771-21 82 18; www.
swebusexpress.com), which runs two to four
times daily to Stockholm (Skr400 to Skr600,
8½ hours), four times to Jönköping (Skr285,
4½ hours) and up to 10 times daily to Göteborg
(Skr268, three to four hours); five continue to
Oslo (Skr445, eight hours).

The second long-distance bus terminal,
Öresundsterminalen (☑59 09 00; Terminal-
gatan 10) is reached via bus 35 from Centralstationen to Arlöv (Skr16; 30 minutes). From
here, **Svenska Buss** (☑0771-67 67 67; www.
svenskabuss.se) runs a service to Stockholm
(Skr370, 11 hours) via Karlskrona, four times
weekly.

GoByBus (☑0771-15 15 15; www.gobybus.se,
in Swedish) has six buses on the Copenhagen–
Malmö–Göteborg route per day, with a couple
originating from Berlin and continuing on to Oslo.

Train
Skånetrafiken (www.skanetrafiken.se) runs
local trains, called Pågatågen, regularly to
Helsingborg (Skr96, one hour), Landskrona
(Skr78, 40 minutes), Lund (Skr42, 15 minutes),
Simrishamn (Skr96, 1½ hours), Ystad (Skr78, 50
minutes) and other destinations in Skåne (bicycles are half-fare, but not allowed during peak
times, except from mid-June to mid-August).
The platform is at the end of Centralstationen
and you buy tickets from the machine. International rail passes are accepted.

The integrated Öresundregionen transport
system operates trains from Helsingborg via
Malmö and Copenhagen to Helsingør. The Malmö
to Copenhagen Kastrup airport or Copenhagen
central station trips take 20 and 35 minutes,
respectively (both journeys Skr95); trains leave
every 20 minutes. Driving a car across the Öresund bridge costs Skr395 one-way.

High-speed X2000 trains run several times
daily to/from Göteborg (Skr289, 2½ hours) and
Stockholm (Skr772, 4½ hours).

❶ Getting Around
The customer service desks in Centralstationen, at Gustav Adolfs Torg and at Värnhemstorget (at the eastern end of Kungsgatan)
provide bus information and tickets. Local
tickets cost Skr16 for one hour's travel. The
bus hubs are Centralplan (in front of Centralstationen), Gustav Adolfs Torg, Värnhemstorget
and Triangeln. The Malmökortet includes city
bus travel.

Lund
☑046 / POP 105,300
Centred around a striking cathedral (complete with a giant in the crypt and a magical clock), learned Lund is a soulful blend
of leafy parks, medieval abodes and coffee-
sipping bookworms. Like most university
hubs, however, it loses some of its buzz during the summer, when students head home
for the holidays.

◉ Sights & Activities
Kulturen MUSEUM
(www.kulturen.com; Tegnerplatsen; adult/child
Skr70/35; ⊙11am-5pm mid-Apr–Sep) The spectacular Kulturen, opened in 1892, is a huge
open-air museum filling two whole blocks.
Its 30-odd buildings include everything from
the meanest birch-bark hovel to grand 17th-
century houses. The popular outdoor cafe
flanks several **rune stones**.

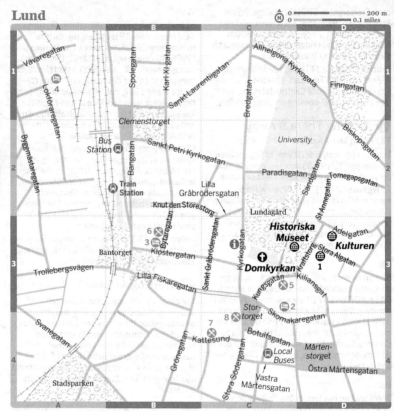

Domkyrkan
CHURCH

The magnificence of Lund's Romanesque cathedral is well publicised, but for a surprise, visit at noon or 3pm (1pm and 3pm Sunday and holidays), when the astronomical clock strikes up.

Historiska Museet
MUSEUM

(☑222 79 44; Kraftstorg; adult/child Skr50/free; ⏰11am-4pm Tue-Fri, noon-4pm Sun) Behind the cathedral, Historiska Museet has a large collection of pre–Viking Age finds, including a 7000-year-old skeleton. It's joined with **Domkyrkomuseet**, which explores the history of the church in the area; the rooms filled with countless statues of the crucified Christ are supremely creepy.

🛏 Sleeping & Eating

The tourist office can book private rooms from Skr300 per person plus a Skr50 fee.

STF Vandrarhem Lund Tåget
HOSTEL €

(☑14 28 20; www.trainhostel.com; Vävaregatan 22; dm Skr160) This quirky hostel is based in old railway carriages in parkland behind the station. The triple bunks and tiny rooms are okay if you're cosying up with loved ones, but a little claustrophobic with strangers. Less novel are the hot-water vending machines in the showers (have a few Skr1 coins handy). Reception is open for check-in from 5pm to 8pm, and reservations are recommended.

Hotel Ahlström
HOTEL €€

(☑211 01 74; info@hotellahlstrom.se; Skomakaregatan 3; s/d without bathroom Skr670/850, d Skr1100) Lund's oldest hotel is friendly and affordable, and on a quiet, central street. Rooms have parquet floors, cool white walls and washbasins (most have shared bathrooms). Breakfast is brought to your door.

Lund

Hotell Oskar   HOTEL €€
(☑18 80 85; www.hotelloskar.com; Bytaregatan 3; s/d Skr1395/1595; @) This dinky place in a 19th-century townhouse has smashing rooms filled with sleek Scandi design. It's also well equipped, with DVD players, kettles and stereos. Breakfast is served in the nearby Hotel Lundia.

Café Ariman   CAFE €
(Kungsgatan 2B; snacks around Skr40, mains from Skr65; ⊙11am-midnight Mon, to 1am Tue-Thu, to 3am Fri & Sat, 3-11pm Sun, closed Sun in summer) Head to this hip, grungy hang-out for cathedral views, strong coffee and cafe fare like ciabatta, salads and burritos. It's popular with left-wing students: think nose-rings, dreadlocks and leisurely chess games. From September to May, DJs hit the decks on Friday and Saturday nights.

Gattostretto   ITALIAN €€
(Kattesund 6A; salads Skr59, mains Skr170-210; ⊙9am-11pm Mon-Sat) Located over medieval ruins and co-run by an affable Roman chef, this breezy cafe–restaurant serves a tasty slice of dolce vita. Guzzle down proper Italian espresso, have a slice of *torta rustica,* or long for Rome over hearty *ragú,* zesty artichoke salad or *pollo alla cacciatore.*

Ebbas Skafferi   CAFE €
(Bytaregatan 5; lunches Skr65; ⊙9am-7pm Mon-Fri, to 6pm Sat & Sun) Ebbas is the perfect cafe: think warm wooden tables, green plants and flowers, odd bits of artwork, a laidback courtyard, scrumptious coffee and teas, and tasty grub such as hearty risotto and moreish cheesecake.

Glasskulturen   ICE CREAM €
(Stortorget; 1/2/3 scoops Skr19/26/31) The locals will wait all afternoon for samples of the frozen delights this little ice-cream nook churns out; 50,000 Lundites can't be wrong, right?

ℹ Information

Tourist office (☑35 50 40; www.lund.se; Kyrkogatan 11; ⊙10am-7pm Mon-Fri, 10am-3pm Sat, 11am-3pm Sun mid-Jun–Aug) Opposite the cathedral.

ℹ Getting There & Away

Flygbuss (☑0771-77 77 77) runs regularly to Malmö's Sturup airport (Skr99).

Long-distance buses leave from outside the train station. Most buses to/from Malmö (except buses to Trelleborg and Falsterbo) run via Lund.

It's 15 minutes from Lund to Malmö by train, with frequent local Pågatågen departures (Skr39). Some trains continue to Copenhagen (Skr125, one hour). Other direct services run from Malmö to Kristianstad and Karlskrona via Lund. All long-distance trains from Stockholm or Göteborg to Malmö stop in Lund.

Trelleborg

☑0410 / POP 41,000
Trelleborg is the main gateway between Sweden and Germany, with frequent ferry services. It's not really on the tourist trail: if you're entering Sweden from here, consider heading on to Malmö or Ystad.

Trelleborgen (☑460 77; admission free) is a 9th-century Viking ring fortress, discovered in 1988 off Bryggaregatan (just west of the town centre).

Simple and functional with shared bathrooms, **Night Stop** (☑410 70; Östergatan 59; s/d Skr250/350; P) has the cheapest beds in town. Open 24 hours, it's about 500m from the ferry (turn right along Hamngatan after disembarking), diagonally opposite the museum. Bathrooms are shared, and breakfast costs Skr50.

The **tourist office** (☑73 33 20; www.trelleborg.se/turism; Hamngatan 9; ⊙9am-7pm Mon-Fri, 10am-6pm Sat, 10am-5pm Sun Jun-Aug) is near the harbour.

Bus 146 (Skr55, 45 minutes) runs roughly every half-hour between Malmö and Trelleborg's bus station, some 500m inland from the ferry terminals. Bus 165 runs frequently Monday to Friday (five services Saturday and four services Sunday) from Lund (Skr45, 15 minutes).

Scandlines (☑650 00; www.scandlines. se) ferries connect Trelleborg to Sassnitz (Skr145, five daily) and Rostock (Skr210, two or three daily). TT-Line (☑562 00; www.ttline. com) ferries shuttle between Trelleborg and Travemünde (Skr320) three to five times daily, and between Trelleborg and Rostock (Skr320) up to three times daily. Buy tickets inside the building housing the tourist office (Hamngatan 9).

Ystad

☑0411 / POP 27,700

Half-timbered houses, rambling cobbled streets and the haunting sound of a nightwatchman's horn give this medieval market town an intoxicating lure. Fans of writer Henning Mankell know it as the setting for his best-selling Inspector Wallander crime thrillers, while fans of drums and uniforms head in for the spectacular three-day Military Tattoo in August. Ystad is a terminal for ferries to Bornholm and Poland.

⊙ Sights

Sankta Maria Kyrka   CHURCH
(Stortorget; ⊙10am-6pm Jun-Aug) Ever since 1250, a nightwatchman has blown his horn through the little window in the clock tower here (every 15 minutes from 9.15pm to 3am). The watchman was traditionally beheaded if he dozed off!

Klostret i Ystad   MUSEUM
(☑57 72 86; St Petri Kyrkoplan; adult/child Skr30/ free; ⊙noon-5pm Tue-Fri, noon-4pm Sat & Sun) Located in the Middle Ages Franciscan monastery of Gråbrödraklostret, this place features local textiles and silverware. The monastery includes the 13th-century deconsecrated St Petri Kyrkan, now used for art exhibitions, which has around 80 gravestones from the 14th to 18th centuries. Included in the same ticket, and with the same opening hours, is the Ystads Konstmuseum.

FREE Ales Stenar   RUINS
(☑57 76 81; admission free, tours adult/child Skr20/10; ⊙24hr) One of Skåne's most intriguing and remote attractions, this place has all the mystery of England's Stonehenge

without the commercialism. It's Sweden's largest stone ship setting, gorgeously located on a grassy knoll by the sea, 19km east of Ystad. Guided tours can be arranged through Ystad's tourist office. To get here, take bus 322 from Ystad (three times daily from June to August). At other times, take bus 570 from Ystad to Valleberga kyrka, and then walk 5km south to Kåseberga.

🛏 Sleeping & Eating

STF Vandrarhem Ystad   HOSTEL €
(☑665 66; kantarellen@turistlogi.se; Fritidsvägen 9; dm/s/d Skr200/300/400) In a charming sky-blue building, this beachside hostel has good facilities, including bike rental for covering the 2km into the town centre. The same folks also run the Station B&B (Spanienfararegatan 25; www.turistlogi.se; dm from Skr295), on the 1st floor of the historic train station.

Bryggeriet   PUB €€
(☑699 99; Långgatan 20; mains Skr95-198; ⊙5-10pm Mon-Thu, 5-11pm Fri, noon-11pm Sat, 1-10pm Sun) Unique and relaxed, this meat-leaning restaurant–pub is in an old brewery. The courtyard is an excellent spot to linger over a well-cooked meal and Ystad Färsköl, a beer brewed on the premises.

Book Café   CAFE €
(Gåsegränd; ⊙11am-3.30pm Tue-Sat) For soup and sandwiches, seek out the charming Book Café – inside there's a room full of mismatched furniture and books; outside is a leafy courtyard.

ℹ Information

The tourist office (☑57 76 81; www.ystad.se; St Knuts Torg; ⊙9am-7pm Mon-Fri, 10am-6pm Sat & Sun mid-Jun–mid-Aug) is opposite the train station. Pick up an 'In the Footsteps of Wallander' brochure to follow along with everyone's favourite gloomy detective, created by author Henning Mankell.

ℹ Getting There & Away

Boat

Unity Line (☑55 69 00; www.unityline.se) and Polferries (☑040-12 17 00; www.polferries. se) operate daily crossings between Ystad and Świnoujście. Ystad's ferry terminal is within walking distance of the train station (drivers follow a more circuitous route).

Bornholmstrafikken (☑55 87 00; www.born holmstrafikken.dk) runs frequent ferries and catamarans between Ystad and Rønne, on the

Danish island of Bornholm. Catamarans operate from a terminal directly behind the train station.

Bus

Buses depart from outside Ystad train station. Bus 190 runs from Ystad to Trelleborg (Skr65, one hour) via Smygehuk 12 times daily on weekdays, six times on Saturday and twice on Sunday. The direct bus to Simrishamn (Skr48, one hour) via Löderup runs three to nine times daily.

SkåneExpressen bus 6 runs to Lund (Skr85, 1¼ hours, hourly on weekdays, infrequently on weekends), and bus 4 runs three to nine times daily to Kristianstad (Skr65, 1¾ hours). Local train is the only way to get to Malmö.

Train

Pågatågen trains run roughly every hour (fewer on weekends) to/from Malmö (Skr80, 50 minutes). Other local trains run up to 12 times daily to Simrishamn (Skr45, 40 minutes).

Helsingborg

☎ 042 / POP 125,000

At its heart, Helsingborg is a sparkly showcase of rejuvenated waterfront, metro-glam restaurants, lively cobbled streets and lofty castle ruins. With Denmark looking on from a mere 4km across the Öresund, its flouncy, turreted buildings feel like a brazen statement.

⊙ Sights & Activities

Dunkers Kulturhus   MUSEUM
(www.dunkerskulturhus.se; Kungsgatan 11; exhibitions adult/child Skr70/free; ⊙10am-5pm Tue-Sun, to 8pm Thu) Just north of the transport terminals, the crisp, white Dunkers Kulturhus houses an interesting town museum and temporary art exhibitions (admission includes entry to both). The building's creator, Danish architect Kim Utzon, is the son of Sydney Opera House architect Jørn Utzon.

Fredriksdals Friluftsmuseum   MUSEUM
(www.fredriksdal.helsingborg.se; off Hävertgatan; adult/child Skr80/free May-Sep, admission free Oct-Mar; ⊙10am-6pm May-Aug) Just 2km northeast of the centre, the Fredriksdal area is well worth a visit. It's home to this place, one of Sweden's best open-air museums, based around an 18th-century manor house, with a street of old houses, children's farm, graphics museum and blissfully leafy grounds. Take bus 1 or 7 to the Zoégas bus stop.

Norra Hamnen   HARBOUR
Saunter along Norra Hamnen (the North Harbour), where sleek apartments, restaurants and bars meet docked yachts and preened locals in one rather successful harbour-redevelopment project.

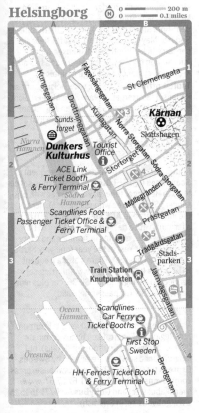

Helsingborg

◎ **Top Sights**

🛏 **Sleeping**

🍴 **Eating**

Kärnan   RUINS

(adult/child Skr20/10; ☉10am-6pm Jun-Aug,
closed Mon rest of yr) Dramatic steps and
archways lead up from Stortorget to this
square tower, all that remains of the
medieval castle.

🛏 Sleeping

Villa Thalassa   HOSTEL €

(☎38 06 60; www.villathalassa.com; Dag Ham-
marskjöldsväg; dm from Skr200, 2-/3-bed r
Skr595/795) This SVIF option is a lovely early
20th-century villa situated in beautiful gardens. Hostel accommodation is in huts, but
the hotel-standard rooms (with or without
private bathroom) are a cut above if your
budget will stretch. The villa lies 3km north
of central Helsingborg in the Pålsjö area.
Bus 219 stops 500m short, at the Pålsjö-
baden bus stop.

Hotel Maria   HOTEL €€

(☎24 99 40; www.hotelmaria.se; Mariagatan 8A;
s/d from Skr850/1150; @) Tucked away behind Olsons Skafferi, Hotel Maria is utterly
inspired, with each room flaunting a different historical style. Themes include National
Romantic, art deco and 1970s disco. Beds
are divinely comfy, the staff are friendly, and
there's a tapas bar downstairs.

Helsingborgs Vandrarhem   HOSTEL €

(☎14 58 50; www.hbgturist.com; Järnvägsgatan
39; dm from Skr195, s/d Skr395/595) Despite
the somewhat anonymous vibe, this central hostel offers clean, comfortable rooms
located about 200m from Knutpunkten.
Reception is open between 3pm and 6pm.

🍴 Eating & Drinking

Koppi   COFFEE HOUSE €

(Norra Storgatan 16; sandwiches/salads Skr58/68
☉closed Sun) This bright-white cafe and
microroastery is your best bet for top-notch
coffee. The savvy young owners sell their
own roasted beans, alongside scrumptious
edibles such as fresh salads and gourmet
ciabatta.

Ebbas Fik   CAFE €

(Bruksgatan 20; sandwiches Skr25-75; ☉9am-6pm
Mon-Fri, 9am-4pm Sat) It's still 1955 at this
kitsch-tastic retro cafe, complete with jukebox, retro petrol pump and hamburgers
made to Elvis's recipe. The extensive cafe
menu also includes (huge) sandwiches, baked
potatoes and crazy cakes and buns.

Vegeriet   VEGETARIAN €

(☎24 03 03; Järnvägsgatan 25; lunches around
Skr75; ☉11.30am-6pm Mon-Fri, 11am-3pm Sat)
Vegetarians adore the appealing cafe–
restaurant Vegeriet for tasty, flesh-free
versions of quiche, lasagne, tortilla and
stir-fries. Vegans aren't forgotten, either.
Note that this place usually shuts for a
month in summer.

Olsons Skafferi   CAFE €€

(Mariagatan 6; lunches Skr75-95, dinner mains
Skr129-235; ☉lunch & dinner Mon-Sat) Olsons
is a super little spot, with alfresco seating
on the pedestrian square right in front of
Mariakyrkan. It doubles as an Italian deli
and cafe, with rustic good looks, spangly
chandeliers and pasta that would make Bologna proud. The dinner menu offers more
elaborate Mediterranean flavours.

ℹ Information

First Stop Sweden (☎10 41 30; www.first
stopsweden.com; Bredgatan 2; ☉9am-8pm
Mon-Fri, 9am-5pm Sat & Sun late Jun–mid-Aug,
9am-6pm Mon-Fri, 9am-4pm Sat, 9am-2pm
Sun late May-late Jun & rest of Aug) Near the
car-ferry ticket booths, it dispenses tourist
information on the whole country and has an
X-Change currency exchange counter.

Tourist office (☎10 43 50; www.helsingborg.se;
Rådhuset, Stortorget; ☉9am-8pm Mon-Fri, 9am-
5pm Sat & 10am-3pm Sun mid-Jun-Aug, 10am-
6pm Mon-Fri, 10am-2pm Sat Sep–mid-Jun)

ℹ Getting There & Away

Boat

Knutpunkten is the terminal for the frequent
Scandlines (☎18 61 00; www.scandlines.se) car
ferry to Helsingør (one-way Skr35, car with passengers Skr345, free with rail passes). Across
the inner harbour, **ACE Link** (☎38 58 80) has
a terminal with a passenger-only ferry to Helsingør every 20 minutes in summer and every
30 minutes the rest of the year (one-way Skr50,
free with rail passes). There's also a frequent
HH-Ferries (☎19 80 00; www.hhferries.se)
service to Helsingør (adult Skr30, car plus nine
people Skr385, rail passes not valid).

Bus

The bus terminal is at ground level in Knutpunkten. Regional Skånetrafiken buses dominate
(see respective destinations for details), but
long-distance services are offered by **Swebus
Express** (☎0771-21 82 18; www.swebusexpress.
com), **Svenska Buss** (☎0771-67 67 67; www.
svenskabuss.se) and **GoByBus** (☎0771-15 15 15;
www.gobybus.se, in Swedish).

All three companies run north to Göteborg (Swebus Express and GoByBus) services continue to Oslo) and south to Malmö. Swebus Express and GoByBus also operate services northeast to Stockholm via Karlstad. Fares to Stockholm cost around Skr500 (7½ hours), to Göteborg Skr250 (three hours) and to Oslo Skr300 (seven hours).

Train

Underground platforms in Knutpunkten serve Öresundståg trains, which travel across the Öresund bridge into Denmark, SJ and Pågatågen, which depart daily for Stockholm (Skr750, five to seven hours), Göteborg (Skr320, 2½ to three hours), nearby towns including Lund (Skr79), Malmö (Skr95), Kristianstad (Skr95) and Halmstad (Skr115) as well as Copenhagen and Oslo.

GÖTALAND

This region has a rich history and plenty to offer the visitor. For one, it's home to Sweden's second city, Göteborg (also known as Gothenburg), with an amusement park for the kids and a huge range of grown-up entertainment. Norrköping, an urban-restoration achievement, has turned its workmanlike heart into a lovely showpiece. Linköping's medieval cathedral is one of Sweden's largest, and in Vadstena there's the abbey established by the country's most important saint, Birgitta. There's also the overwhelming natural beauty of the Bohuslän coast.

Varberg

📞 0340 / POP 56,100

A town built for sunsets, Varberg has plenty of hang-out space along the waterfront and some gorgeous views from the **medieval fortress** (adult/child Skr50/free; ⊙10am-5pm mid-Jun–mid-Aug), which has guided tours and excellent museums. You might also want to brave the brisk Nordic weather and swim at **Kallhusbadet** (adult/child Skr60/30; ⊙1-8pm Wed mid-Jun–mid-Aug), a striking bathing house built in Moorish style on stilts above the sea.

Fästningens Vandrarhem (📞 868 28; vandrar hem@turist.varberg.se; dm/s/d from Skr195/360/440) is within the fortress and offers single rooms in old prison cells or larger rooms in other buildings. Call ahead, as reception hours are limited.

Most dining options are along the pedestrianised Kungsgatan, but the fortress cafe offers the best sea views in town.

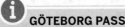
The brilliant Göteborg Pass discount card is well worth bagging, at least if you're planning to park in Göteborg (home to Sweden's priciest street parking and most dedicated traffic wardens). Perks include free or reduced admission to a bundle of attractions (including Liseberg and the museums), plus free city sightseeing tours, and travel by public transport within the region. The card costs Skr245/170 per adult/child for 24 hours, Skr390/270 for 48 hours. You'll need to efficiently cram in your museum time to get the most out of the pass; those planning to take the sightseeing tour will save the most. It's available at tourist offices, hotels, Pressbyrån newsagencies and online at www.goteborg.com.

The **tourist office** (📞 868 00; www.turist.varberg.se; Brunnparken; ⊙9.30am-7pm Mon-Sat, 1-6pm Sun late Jun–early Aug, 10am-6pm Mon-Fri, 10am-3pm Sat Apr–late Jun & early Aug–Sep) is in the centre of town.

Buses depart from outside the train station; local buses run to Falkenberg, but regular trains are your best bet for Halmstad, Göteborg and Malmö. Stena Line ferries operate between Varberg and the Danish town of Grenå; the ferry dock is next to the town centre.

Göteborg

📞 031 / POP 493,500

Often caught in Stockholm's shadow, gregarious Göteborg (Gothenburg in English) socks a mighty good punch of its own. Some of the country's finest talent hails from its streets, including music icons José González and Soundtrack of Our Lives. Ornate architecture lines its tram-rattled streets and cafes hum with bonhomie. West of Kungsportsavenyn (dubbed the 'Champs Élysées' in brochures and a 'tourist trap' by locals), the Haga and Linné districts buzz with creativity. Fashionistas design fairtrade threads while artists collaborate over mean espressos. Stockholm may represent the 'big time', but many of the best and brightest ideas originate in this grassroots town.

SWEDEN GÖTALAND

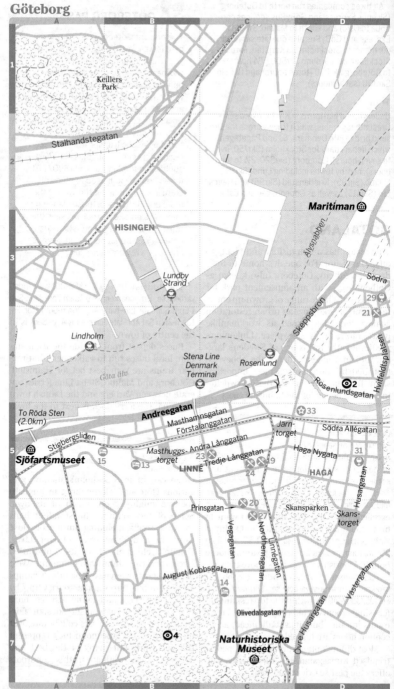

Keillers Park

Stalhandstegatan

HISINGEN

Maritiman 🏛

Älvsnabben

Södra

29

21

Lundby Strand

Lindholm

Skeppsbron

Göta älv

Stena Line Denmark Terminal

Rosenlund

◉2

Rosenlundsgatan

Hvitfeldtsplatsen

To Röda Sten (2.0km)

Andreegatan

Masthamnsgatan
Förstalanggatan

33

Järntorget

Södra Allégatan

Stigbergsliden

15

Masthuggs-torget

Andra Långgatan

Haga Nygata

31

Sjöfartsmuseet 🏛

13

23

Tredje Långgatan

19

24

LINNÉ

HAGA

Husargatan

Prinsgatan

20

27

Skansparken

Skans-torget

Vegagatan

Nordhemsgatan

Linnégatan

Västergatan

August Kobbsgatan

14

Olivedalsgatan

Övre Husargatan

◉4

Naturhistoriska Museet 🏛

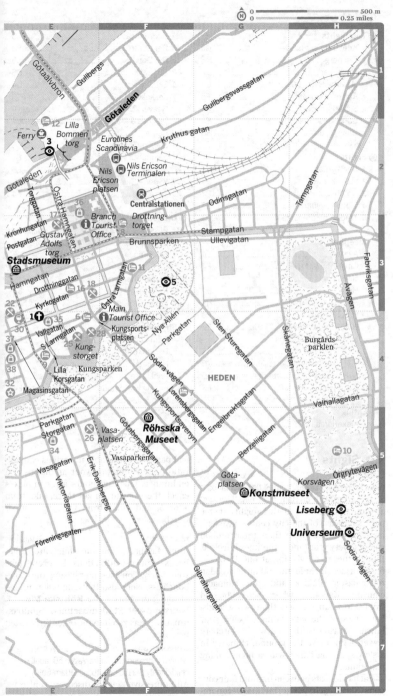

0   500 m
0   0.25 miles

Götaälvbron

Gullbergs

Götaleden

Gullbergsvassgatan

Kruthus gatan

Ferry

Lilla Bommen torg

Eurolines Scandinavia

Nils Ericson Terminalen

Nils Ericson platsen

Tampgatan

Götaleden

Östra Hamngatan

Torggatan

Centralstationen

Odinsgatan

Branch Tourist Office

Drottning-torget

Kronhusgatan

Postgatan

Gustav Adolfs torg

Drottningtorget

Stampgatan

Ullevigatan

Brunnsparken

Stadsmuseum

Fabriksgatan

Avägen

Harngatan

Drottninggatan

Kyrkogatan

Östra Larmgatan

Main Tourist Office

Kungsports-platsen

Sten Sturegatan

Burgårds-parken

Vallgatan

S Larmgatan

Kungs-torget

Nya Allén

Parkgatan

Skånegatan

Lilla Korsgatan

Kungsparken

Södra vägen

HEDEN

Vaihallagatan

Magasinsgatan

Lorensbergsgatan

Engelbrektsgatan

Parkgatan

Storgatan

Vasa-platsen

Göteborgsgatan

Kungsportsavenyn

Berzeligatan

Örgrytevägen

Röhsska Museet

Vasagatan

Erik Dahlbergsg.

Vasaparken

Göta-platsen

Korsvägen

Konstmuseet

Viktoriagatan

Liseberg

Föreningsgatan

Universeum

Gibraltargatan

Södra Vägen

◉ Sights

Liseberg   AMUSEMENT PARK
(www.liseberg.se; tickets from Skr80, annual pass
Skr195; ⊘to 10pm or 11pm most days May-Aug)
Scream yourself silly at this mighty theme
park southeast of the city centre. Sweden's
largest, it draws more than three million
visitors every year (and sometimes it feels as
though they're all visiting at once!). Blockbuster rides include the 90km/h wooden
rollercoaster Balder and the stomach-
churning Kanonen, where you're blasted
from 0 to 75km/h in less than two seconds.
For views of the city without losing your
lunch, the ride to the top of the Liseberg
Tower, 83m above the ground, climaxes in
a slow spinning dance with a breathtaking
panorama.

Each ride costs between one and four coupons (Skr20 each) per go, but more econom-

ical passes are available in various configurations, depending on your ambitions and
endurance. Opening hours are complex –
check the website. To get there, take tram
4 or 5, and enter from Örgrytevägen or
Getebergsled.

Museums   MUSEUMS
After Liseberg, the museums are Göteborg's strongest attractions. If several take
your fancy, consider purchasing the Göteborg Pass. Note also that admission to one
of four museums – the **Röhsska Museet**,
Konstmuseet, **Stadsmuseum** or **Sjöfartsmuseet** – gets you into the other three listed
here free.

Universeum   SCIENCE CENTRE
(www.universeum.se; Södra Vägen 50; adult/
child/family Skr155/99/465; ⊘10am-6pm)
An impressive 'science discovery centre'

featuring everything from rainforests to a shark tank.

Stadsmuseum
MUSEUM

(Östindiska huset, Norra Hamngatan 12; adult/under 25yr Skr40/free; ⏰10am-5pm May-Aug) Archaeological, local and historical collections, including Sweden's only original Viking ship.

Konstmuseet
MUSEUM

(www.konstmuseum.goteborg.se; Götaplatsen; adult/under 25yr Skr40/free, during special exhibitions adult Skr60; ⏰11am-6pm Tue & Thu, 11am-9pm Wed, 11am-5pm Fri-Sun) Works by the French Impressionists, Rubens, Van Gogh, Rembrandt, Picasso, as well as Scandinavian masters like Bruno Liljefors, Edvard Munch, Anders Zorn and Carl Larsson, plus the Hasselblad photo collection.

Röhsska Museet
MUSEUM

(www.designmuseum.se; Vasagatan 37; adult/under 20yr Skr40/free; ⏰noon-8pm Tue, noon-5pm Wed-Fri, 11am-5pm Sat & Sun) Covers modern Scandinavian design and decorative arts, but also contains classical and oriental items, and a design store and popular cafe.

Maritiman
MUSEUM

(www.maritiman.se; Packhuskajen; adult/child Skr90/50; ⏰10am-6pm May-Sep) Historical crafts, including fishing boats, a light vessel and a firefighter, linked by walkways.

Sjöfartsmuseet
MUSEUM

(www.sjofartsmuseum.goteborg.se; Karl Johansgatan 1-3; adult/under 25yr Skr40/free; ⏰10am-5pm Tue-Sun, to 8pm Wed) The main museum of maritime history, near Stigbergstorget about 2km west of the city centre. There's an interesting aquarium attached. Take tram 3, 9 or 11.

Naturhistoriska Museet
MUSEUM

(Natural History Museum; www.gnm.se; Slottsskogen Park; adult/under 25yr Skr40/free; ⏰11am-5pm Tue-Sun) Contains the world's only stuffed blue whale. In the lead-up to Christmas, visitors are occasionally allowed to step inside its mouth.

Other Sights
OTHER SIGHTS

The classical domkyrkan (Gustavi Cathedral; Västra Hamngatan; ⏰9am-6pm Mon-Fri, 11am-5pm Sat, 10am-3pm Sun Jun-Aug) was consecrated in 1815 – two previous cathedrals were destroyed by town fires.

It's hard to miss the skyline-altering, giant Göteborgs Hjulet (Wheel of Gothenburg; Kanaltorget; adult/child Skr85/60; ⏰11am-9pm

GöteborgsPaketet is an accommodation package offered at various hotels, with prices starting at Skr545 per person per night. It includes the Göteborg Pass for the number of nights you stay. Book online at www.goteborg.com or through the tourist office. More expensive packages include theatre or concert tickets, casino passes, spa visits etc.

daily, limited hr on holidays & during strong winds), which opened in May 2010 – a Ferris wheel of gondolas, it offers astonishing views for the non-acrophobic.

Feskekörka (Rosenlundsgatan; ⏰9am-5pm Tue-Fri, 9am-6pm Fri, 10am-2pm Sat), or 'Fish Church', isn't a church at all – it's a fish and seafood market, and a perfect stop for lunch or a snack.

The Haga district, south of the canal, is Göteborg's oldest suburb, dating back to 1648. In the 1980s and '90s, the area was thoroughly renovated and is now a cute, cobblestone maze of precious cafes and boutique shops.

There are some lovely green oases in the city, including Trädgårdsföreningen (Nya Allén; adult/child mid-Apr–mid-Sep Skr15/free, other times free; ⏰7am-6pm Mon-Fri, 9am-6pm Sat & Sun), laid out in 1842 and home to a couple of pretty cafes, a rosarium and a palm house. In Göteborg's southwest is Slottsskogsparken, the 'lungs' of the city; the Botanic Gardens – the largest in Sweden – are nearby.

🛏 Sleeping

Göteborg has several high-quality hostels near the city centre. Most hotels offer decent discounts at weekends and in summer.

STF Vandrarhem Slottsskogen
HOSTEL €

(✆42 65 20; www.sov.nu; Vegagatan 21; dm Skr215, s/d Skr360/440; @) Unlike many Swedish hostels, big, friendly Slottsskogen is a cracking place for meeting other travellers. For a small extra payment there's access to a laundry, sauna and sunbed, and the buffet breakfast (Skr65) is brilliant. Parking spaces can be booked for a fee. Reception is closed between noon and 2pm. Take tram 1 or 6 to Olivedalsgatan.

Kvibergs Vandrarhem & Stugby HOSTEL €
(☎43 50 55; www.vandrarhem.com; Kvibergsvägen 5; d/tr/q Skr490/600/720; @) This sterling SVIF hostel, a few kilometres northeast of the city centre (tram 6, 7 or 11), boasts super amenities, including flat-screen TVs, sauna, sunbeds, laundry, table tennis, two kitchens and two lounges. There are no dorms; you rent out the entire room. Hotel-style rooms and cabins are also available. Rates drop in low season.

Masthuggsterrassens Vandrarhem HOSTEL €
(☎42 48 20; www.mastenvandrarhem.com; Masthuggsterrassen 10H; dm/d Skr195/500; @) If you're after a good night's sleep, try this clean, quiet, well-run place, whose long hallways are plastered with vintage film posters. Facilities include three lounges, three kitchens and a little library (mostly Swedish books), and it's handy if you're catching an early ferry to Denmark. Take tram 3, 9 or 11 to Masthuggstorget and follow the signs up the hill.

STF Vandrarhem Stigbergsliden HOSTEL €
(☎24 16 20; www.hostel-gothenburg.com; Stigbergsliden 10; dm/d from Skr160/400; @) In a renovated seamen's institute (tram 3, 9 or 11 to Stigbergstorget), this hostel has history. Staff are helpful, and there's a big kitchen, laundry and TV room. Perks include a sheltered garden and bike rental (per day Skr50).

Vanilj Hotel, Kafé & Bar BOUTIQUE HOTEL €€
(☎711 62 20; www.vaniljhotel.se; Kyrkogatan 38; s/d Skr1145/1295; @) On a quiet, central street, this petite slumber spot is cosy, homelike and adorable. There are individually decorated rooms and breakfast is served in the buzzing cafe downstairs. Get there early to grab one of the five parking spaces.

Hotel Flora BOUTIQUE HOTEL €€
(☎13 86 16; www.hotelflora.se; Grönsakstorget 2; s/d Skr1395/1695; @) An extreme makeover took Flora from frumpy to fabulous, with uberslick rooms flaunting black-and-white interiors, designer chairs, flat-screen TVs and sparkling bathrooms. Top-floor rooms have air-conditioning, several rooms offer river views and the chic split-level courtyard is perfect for sophisticated chilling.

Hotel Royal HOTEL €€
(☎700 11 70; www.hotelroyal.nu; Drottninggatan 67; s/d Skr1395/1595; @) Göteborg's oldest hotel (1852) has aged enviably. The grand entrance has been retained, complete with painted glass ceiling and sweeping staircase, and the elegant, airy rooms make necessary 21st-century concessions like flat-screen TVs and renovated bathrooms. There's also homemade cake for guests.

Avalon HOTEL €€€
(☎751 02 00; www.avalonhotel.se; Kungstorget 9; s/d from Skr1890/2290; @☀) The showy, design-conscious Avalon is steps away from the main tourist office. Rooms are sleek and uncluttered, with flat-screen TVs and heavenly pillows. Some rooms feature a mini spa (three even have their own gym equipment), and the upmarket resto-bar is an after-work hot spot. The ultimate highlight is the rooftop pool (open May to September), which leans out over the edge for a dizzying dip. Check the website for package deals.

City Hotel Vid Avenyn BUDGET HOTEL €
(☎708 40 00; www.cityhotelgbg.se; Lorensbergsgatan 6; s/d without bathroom from Skr695/795) The City represents excellent value for such a central hotel. Staff are friendly, rooms are comfy and for about Skr300 extra you can have a private bathroom. A continental breakfast is included, or you can opt to buy the breakfast buffet at the in-house restaurant–pub (which boasts 80 varieties of beer).

Hotel Eggers HOTEL €€
(☎333 44 40; www.hoteleggers.se; Drottningtorget; s/d around Skr1270/1590; P@) Elegant Eggers would make a great set for a period drama. Founded as a railway hotel in 1859, its rooms are a Regency-style treat. A good few have private balconies overlooking the bustling square, and nearby parking spots (per 24 hours Sk120) can be booked at reception.

Hotell Barken Viking HOTEL €€€
(☎63 58 00; barken.viking@liseberg.se; Gullbergskajen; s/d Skr1595/2150; @) *Barken Viking* is an elegant four-masted sailing ship, converted into a stylish hotel and restaurant and moored near Lilla Bommen harbour. Rooms are smart and suitably nautical, with handsome blue carpet, Hamptons-style linen and warm wood panelling. The discounted May to September rate includes entry to Liseberg.

Hotel Gothia Towers
HOTEL €€€

(☎750 88 10; hotelreservations@gothiatowers.
com; Mässans gata 24; s/d from Skr1895/2095;
P@) Sweden's largest hotel is the 23-storey
Gothia Towers (take tram 5). Its 704 rooms
ooze Nordic cool, especially the 'Design' options: all sharp, clean lines and bathroom
windows for a vista-friendly soak. More
bird's-eye views await at the hotel's bar and
restaurant Heaven 23, a hit with non-guests
too and home to Göteborg's best shrimp
sandwich (Skr189).

✖ Eating

Cool cafes, cheap ethnic gems and foodie favourites abound around the Vasastan, Haga
and Linné districts, often with lower prices
than their more obvious rivals along Kungsportsavenyn (Avenyn). Many places are
closed on Sundays.

For something quick, the Nordstan
shopping complex has loads of fast-food
outlets.

Bar Doppio
CAFE €

(Linnégatan; double espresso Skr20, breakfast
packets Skr50-80; ⊗7am-6.30pm Mon-Fri, 8am-
5pm Sat & Sun) Class-A caffeine awaits at this
Scandi-cool cafe, where regulars keep track
of their tabs on a giant blackboard. The tiny
space has a great neighbourhood vibe and
fresh grub such as homemade muesli, soup,
focaccia and fruit smoothies.

Publik
GASTROPUB €€

(Andra Långgatan 20; lunches Skr75, mains
Skr100-145; ⊗11.30-1am Mon-Sat) Arguably
Göteborg's coolest hang-out (think grit-chic
interiors, local art exhibitions, DJ-spun
tunes and creative indie crowds), this cafe-
bar hybrid also serves brilliant, great-value
food such as goat cheese-stuffed auber-
gines with red pesto potatoes. The well-
priced house wine is perfectly drinkable
and there's a backyard courtyard for fine-
weather lounging.

Bar Italia
CAFE €

(Prinsgatan 7; panini Skr30-40; ⊗7.30am-6pm)
In the Linné district, this is another cultish
espresso bar, complete with Italian baristi
and suspended Vespa. In warm weather,
watch the hip brigade squeeze onto the
pavement banquette for perfect caffeine,
cornetti, gourmet calzoni and gossip.

Smaka
SWEDISH €€

(Vasaplatsen 3; mains Skr125-225; ⊗5pm-2am
Mon-Thu & Sun, 5pm-3am Fri & Sat) This lively,
down-to-earth restaurant–bar cooks up
brilliant, old-school Swedish *husmanskost* such as the speciality meatballs with
mashed potato and lingonberries. Modern
adaptations might include a goat's-cheese
soup with roasted beetroot and asparagus.

Tranquilo
GRILL €€€

(Kungstorget 14; meals Skr140-235; ⊗11.30am-late
Mon-Sat, from 9pm Sun) Complete with glowing pink-and-blue bar and a giant Rio-style
Jesus on the ceiling, this hip, bombastic
resto-bar peddles grilled meats and tropical-
flavoured brilliance such as grilled mango
and goat's cheese burger with grilled corn
and rhubarb chutney.

Magnus & Magnus
FRENCH, SWEDISH €€€

(www.magnusmagnus.se; Magasinsgatan 8;
2-/3-course menus Skr395/495; ⊗from 6pm) A
hit with VIPs, this ever-fashionable restaurant serves inspired Euro-fusion flavours.
The summer courtyard – complete with
bar, DJs and different club nights from
Wednesday to Monday – draws an ubercool
crowd.

Bar Centro
CAFE €

(Kyrkogatan 31; focaccias Skr30-60; ⊗6am-6pm
Mon-Fri, 7am-5pm Sat, 8am-5pm Sun) Fans of
this iconic, retro espresso bar spill out
onto the street, downing smooth espresso
and tasty focaccias. The few window seats
are perfect for urban voyeurs.

Andrum
VEGETARIAN €

(Östra Hamngatan 19; large plates Skr70; ⊗11am-
9pm Mon-Fri, noon-8pm Sat & Sun) Vegetarians
love this casual, meat-free spot with its
value-for-money, all-day lunch buffet. It's
simple, tasty, wholesome stuff, and cheerfully recommended.

Alexandras
SOUP €

(Kungstorget) Located in the central Saluhallen, this famous Greek soup kitchen
dishes out excellent hearty soups and
pasta (around Skr40), particularly welcoming on a chilly day.

Super + Sushi
SUSHI €

(Prinsgatan 4; ⊗to 9pm) Close to several of
the hostels, this cubby hole offers excellent Japanese lunch deals, including miso
soup, green tea and 10 pieces of sushi for
Skr65.

Self-Catering

Saluhall Briggen
FOOD HALL €€

(Nordhemsgatan 28; ⊗9am-6pm Mon-Fri, 9am-2pm
Sat) It might lack Saluhallen's size and buzz,

but this covered market (in an old fire station) will have you drooling over its bounty of fresh bread, cheeses, quiches, seafood and ethnic treats. It's particularly handy for the hostel district.

Saluhallen FOOD HALL €€
(Kungstorget; ⊙9am-6pm Mon-Fri, 9am-3pm Sat) Göteborg's main central market is jammed with tasty budget eateries and food stalls, and is the perfect place to stock up that picnic basket.

Ekostore SUPERMARKET €€
(☏13 60 23; Ekelundsgatan 4; ⊙10am-8pm Mon-Fri, 10am-4pm Sat) An eco-chic grocery store selling organic and fair-trade products.

Drinking

Kungsportsavenyn brims with beer-downing hordes; try the following places for a little more character. The Linné district is home to several student hang-outs serving extremely cheap beer!

Lokal BAR
(Kyrkogatan 11; ⊙4pm-1am Mon-Sat) Awarded best bar in Göteborg and run by the team from Publik, this cool hang-out pulls everyone from artists and media types to the odd punk rocker. The drinks are inspired (think kiwi and ginger daiquiri), the pick-and-mix menu (Skr145 to Skr160) brims with fusion flavours, and music spans soul, jazz and electro. Best of all, staff donate 10% of their tips to a Cambodian orphanage.

Sjöbaren PUB
(Haga Nygata 25; ⊙11am-midnight) One of the few old-school pubs in Göteborg, this friendly but unfussy nautical-themed place in Haga often has what look to be real fishermen smoking outside the front door. Beer pours out of a copper diving helmet, and the menu covers the full range of seafood.

Bliss COCKTAIL LOUNGE
(Magasinsgatan 3; ⊙11.30am-2.30pm Mon-Fri, 6pm-1am or 2am Tue-Thu & Sat, 5pm-1am or 2am Fri) Bliss boasts one of the hippest interiors in Göteborg, with low designer seats and slick contemporary tones. It's a long-standing nocturnal favourite: if you're not up to a main meal (lunch Skr79, dinner mains around Skr200; they're usually delicious), you can nibble on tapas-style snacks and groove to live DJs until late.

☆ Entertainment

Clubs have varying minimum-age limits, ranging from 18 to 25 years, and many may charge admission depending on the night.

Röda Sten CLUB, ART GALLERY
(www.rodasten.com; Röda Sten 1; admission Skr60-100 for events; ⊙Fri & Sat) Paging Berlin with its post-industrial look, this power station turned art gallery cranks up the party vibe with a variety of pan-European DJs, live music and club nights on Fridays and Saturdays. Check the website for a schedule. There's also a restaurant (lunch Skr80, mains Skr79 to Skr119) known for its fish soup. To get here, follow Oscarsleden southwest about 700m.

Nefertiti CLUB
(www.nefertiti.se; Hvitfeldtsplatsen 6; admission Skr95-350) A Göteborg institution, this effortlessly cool venue is famous for its smooth live jazz, blues and world music, usually followed by kicking club nights spanning from techno, deep house and soul to hip hop and funk. Times vary, so check the website.

Pustervik CLUB-THEATRE
(☏368 32 77; Järntorgsgatan 12) Culture vultures and party people pack into this hybrid venue, with its heaving downstairs bar and upstairs club and stage. Gigs range from independent theatre and live music gigs (anything from emerging singer-songwriters to Neneh Cherry) to regular club nights spanning hip hop, soul and rock.

🔒 Shopping

Prickig Katt Boudoir CLOTHING
(Magasinsgatan 19; ⊙closed Sun) Trendsetting guys come here for non-conformist labels like Denmark's Humor and Göteborg's Gissy. Sharing the same address, local label **Velour** (⊙closed Sun) and Stockholm legend **Acne Jeans** stock slick, stylish street wear for guys and girls.

DesignTorget DESIGN
(Vallgatan 14) Cool, affordable design objects from both established and up-and-coming Scandi talent.

Prickig Katt CLOTHING
(Magasinsgatan 17; ⊙closed Sun) The 'Spotted Cat' sports retro-clad staff, idiosyncratic fashion from Dutch, Danish and home-grown labels, as well as kitschy wares and out-there handmade millinery and bling.

DEM Collective CLOTHING

(☑12 38 84; Storgatan 11; ⊖closed Sun) Head to this bite-sized boutique for Scandi cool, fair-trade threads. Completely organic, designs are minimalist, street-smart and supremely comfortable.

ℹ Information

Internet Access

Sidewalk Express (www.sidewalkexpress.se; per hr Skr29) For internet access, at Central-stationen and the 7-Eleven on Vasaplatsen.

Medical Services

Apotek Vasan (☑0771-45 04 50; Nordstan complex; ⊖8am-10pm) Late-night pharmacy.

Östra Sjukhuset (☑343 40 00) Major hospital about 5km northeast of central Göteborg, near the terminus at the end of tramline 1.

Money

Forex (☑0200-22 22 20; www.forex.se) Centralstationen (⊖7am-9pm Mon-Sun); Kungsportsavenyn 22 (⊖9am-7pm Mon-Fri, 10am-4pm Sat); Kungsportsplatsen (⊖9am-7pm Mon-Fri, 10am-4pm Sat); Landvetter airport (⊖5am-9pm Mon-Fri, 5am-8pm Sat, 5am-7pm Sun); Nordstan shopping complex (⊖9am-7pm Mon-Fri, 10am-6pm Sat, 11am-5pm Sun) Foreign-exchange office with numerous branches.

Tourist Offices

Main tourist office (☑61 25 00; www.goteborg.com; Kungsportsplatsen 2; ⊖9.30am-8pm daily mid-Jun–mid-Aug, 9.30am-6pm Mon-Fri, 10am-2pm Sat & Sun May–mid-Jun & end Aug) Central and busy, it has a good selection of free brochures and maps.

Branch tourist office (Nordstan shopping complex; ⊖10am-6pm Mon-Fri, 10am-6pm Sat, noon-5pm Sun)

ℹ Getting There & Away

Air

About 25km east of the city, **Landvetter airport** (☑94 10 00; www.swedavia.se) has up to 22 direct daily flights to/from Stockholm's Arlanda and Bromma airports (with SAS and Malmö Aviation), as well as daily services to Umeå and several weekly services to Borlänge, Luleå and Sundsvall.

Direct European routes include Amsterdam (KLM), Brussels (Brussels Airlines), Copenhagen (SAS), Frankfurt (Lufthansa and SAS), Helsinki (Finnair and Blue1), London (SAS), Manchester (City Airline), Munich (Lufthansa), Oslo (Wideroe) and Paris (Air France).

Göteborg City Airport (☑92 60 60; www.goteborgairport.se), some 15km north of the city at Säve, is used for budget Ryanair flights to destinations including London Stansted, Rome and Frankfurt.

Boat

Göteborg is a major entry point for ferries, with several car and passenger services to Denmark, Germany and Norway.

Nearest to central Göteborg, the **Stena Line** (☑704 00 00; www.stenaline.se) Denmark terminal near Masthuggstorget (tram 3, 9 or 11) has around eight daily departures for Frederikshavn in peak season, with a 20% discount for rail-pass holders.

Further west is the Stena Line terminal for the daily car ferry to Kiel (Germany; from Skr1100 one-way). Take tram 3 or 9 to Chapmans Torg.

Bus

The bus station, Nils Ericson Terminalen, is next to the train station. There's a **Västtrafik information booth** (☑0771-41 43 00; ⊖6am-10pm Mon-Fri, 9am-10pm Sat, 9am-7pm Sun) here, providing information and selling tickets for all city and regional public transport within the Göteborg, Bohuslän and Västergötland area.

Eurolines (☑10 02 40; www.eurolines.com; Nils Ericsonplatsen 17) has its main Swedish office at the bus station in central Göteborg.

Swebus Express (☑0771-21 82 18; www.swebusexpress.com) has an office located at the bus terminal and operates frequent buses to most of the major towns. Services to Stockholm (Skr260 one-way, seven hours) run five to seven times daily. Other direct destinations include Copenhagen (Skr179 one-way, four to five hours), Halmstad (Skr78, 1¾ hours), Helsingborg (Skr113, three hours), Jönköping (Skr72, 1¾ hours), Oslo (Skr173, four hours), Malmö (Skr131, three hours) and Örebro (Skr181, four hours).

Svenska Buss (☑0771-67 67 67; www.svenskabuss.se) has daily departures for Stockholm (Skr430, 7½ hours) via Jönköping (Skr120, 2¼ hours).

As always, prices are lower for advance bookings, especially for Swebus Express and GoByBus.

Car & Motorcycle

The E6 motorway runs north–south from Oslo to Malmö just east of the city centre and there's also a complex junction where the E20 motorway diverges east for Stockholm.

International car-hire companies Avis, Europcar and Hertz have desks at Landvetter and Göteborg City airports. For car hire in town, contact one of the petrol stations, for example **Statoil** (☑41 11 62; Marklandsgatan 2), in southwestern Göteborg.

Train

Centralstationen is Sweden's oldest train station and now a listed building. It serves SJ and regional trains, with direct trains to Copenhagen (Skr395, four hours) and Malmö (Skr289, 3¼ hours), as well as numerous other destinations in the southern half of Sweden.

High-speed X2000 trains to Stockholm depart approximately every one to two hours (Skr1240, three hours); book online in advance (at www. sj.se) and the price can drop to less than half that, depending on time of day.

❶ Getting Around

Buses, trams and ferries run by **Västtrafik** (🖉0771-41 43 00; www.vasttrafik.se) make up the city's public transport system; there are Västtrafik information booths selling tickets and giving out timetables inside **Nils Ericson Terminalen** (◷6am-10pm Mon-Fri, 9am-10pm Sat, 9am-7pm Sun), in front of the train station on **Drottningtorget** (◷6am-8pm Mon-Fri, 8am-8pm Sat & Sun) and at **Brunnsparken** (◷7am-7pm Mon-Fri, 9am-6pm Sat).

Holders of the Göteborg Pass travel free, including on late-night transport. Otherwise a city transport ticket costs adult/child Skr25/19 (Skr50 on late-night transport). A 24-hour Dagkort (day pass) for the whole city area costs Skr65, or Skr130 for 72 hours.

The easiest way to cover lengthy distances in Göteborg is by tram. Lines, numbered 1 to 13, converge near Brunnsparken (a block from the train station).

Västtrafik has regional passes for 24 hours/30 days (adult Skr240/1350, under 26 years Skr240/1150) that give unlimited travel on all *länstrafik* buses, trains and boats within Göteborg, Bohuslän and the Västergötland area.

Cykelkungen (🖉184300; Chalmersgatan 19) offers bike rental for Skr120/500 per day/week.

Marstrand

🖉0303 / POP 1300

Pretty **Marstrand** (www.marstrand.nu), with its wooden buildings, island setting and relaxed air, conveys the essence of the Bohuslän fishing villages that dot the coast from Göteborg to the Norwegian border, and provides an idyllic area for sailing, cycling or driving. Car traffic is banned on the island itself, so those with their own wheels should take the frequent passenger ferry from Koön, 150m to the east.

The 17th-century **Carlstens Fästning** (www.carlsten.se; adult/child Skr75/25; ◷11am-

6pm early Jun–mid-Aug, 11am-4pm rest of Aug) fortress reflects the town's martial and penal history; entry price includes a guided tour.

Marstrands Varmbadhus Båtellet (🖉600 10; marstrandsvarmbadhus@telia.com; Kungsplan; dm from Skr225, r Skr675; @⊠) offers simple hostel accommodation. Turn right after disembarking from the ferry and follow the waterfront for 400m. Only dorm accommodation is available in the summer.

There are numerous eating options along the harbour, including fast-food stalls (one sells fresh fish and chips for about Skr50), cafes and upmarket restaurants.

From Göteborg you can take bus 312 to Arvidsvik (on Koön) then cross to Marstrand by frequent passenger-only ferry. The complete journey takes about an hour. Buy a Maxirabbat 100 carnet (Skr100) from the Västtrafik information booth at Nils Ericson Terminalen in Göteborg and validate it on the bus.

Strömstad

🖉0526 / POP 11,600

A resort, fishing harbour and spa town, Strömstad is laced with ornate wooden buildings echoing nearby Norway. Indeed, Norwegians head here en masse in summer to take advantage of Sweden's cheaper prices, lending a particularly lively air to the town's picturesque streets and bars. One of Sweden's largest, most magnificent **stone ship settings** (admission free; ◷24hr) lies 6km northeast of Strömstad; ask for details at the tourist office.

No, **Crusellska Hemmet** (🖉101 93; info@crusellska.com; Norra Kyrkogatan 12; s/d Skr400/600; ◷Mar-Sep; 🅿@) is not a Disney villain; it's an exceptional hostel. Drifting white curtains, pale decor and wicker lounges lend the place a boutique vibe. The kitchen is seriously spacious, and there's a peaceful garden for alfresco contemplation, as well as a range of pampering spa treatments. Make sure you book ahead.

Try the fresh local *räkor* (shrimp) and delicious seafood in the many restaurants, or purchase from local fishmongers. Next to the tourist office is **Laholmens Fisk** (🖉102 40; Torget), selling seafood baguettes (from Skr45), along with fish fresh off the boats. You'll find it just off the main square, next door to Restaurang Bryggan – also a cosy harbour restaurant.

The tourist office (📞623 30; www.strom stad.se; Gamla Tullhuset, Norra hamnen, Ångbåts-kajen 2; ⊙9am-8pm Mon-Sat, 10am-7pm Sun Jun-Aug), between the two harbours on the main square, also offers internet access (per 15 minutes Skr20).

Buses and trains both use the train station near the southern harbour. The Swebus Express (📞0771-21 82 18; www.swebusexpress.com) service from Göteborg to Oslo calls here up to two times daily and Västtrafik operates buses to Göteborg (Skr185) up to five times daily. Strömstad is the northern terminus of the Bohustág train system, with around six trains every day to/from Göteborg (Skr200).

Norrköping

📞011 / POP 126,700

The envy of industrial has-beens across Europe, Norrköping has managed to cleverly regenerate its defunct mills and canals into a posse of cultural and gastronomic hang-outs fringing waterfalls and locks. Retro trams rattle down streets that are lined with eclectic architecture, while some 30km to the northeast, the animal park at Kolmården swaps urban regeneration for majestic Siberian tigers.

◉ Sights

Summer-only attractions include short guided tours on vintage trams; enquire at the tourist office.

Kolmården   ZOO
(www.kolmarden.com; adult/child Skr379/289; ⊙10am-6pm Jul–mid-Aug, 10am-5pm May, Jun & rest of Aug) Kolmården zoo is Scandinavia's largest, with around 750 residents from all climates and continents. It's divided into two areas: the main Djurparken, with a dolphin show in Marine World, an ape hang-out and a whole section devoted to the famed Swedish teddy bear Bamse; and Safariparken, home to lions, tigers and bears. The ticket gets you into both the zoo and safari park.

Kolmården lies 35km north of Norrköping, on the north shore of Bråviken (regular bus 432 or 433 from Norrköping; Skr60, 40 minutes).

FREE Arbetets Museum   MUSEUM
(Laxholmen; ⊙11am-5pm) Sweden's Museum of Work is just across the bridge from the Stadsmuseum in a 1917 building designed

to mirror the island it sits on; named Strykjärnet (flatiron), it has seven sides, seven floors and a total of 7000 sq metres of floor space. The permanent displays on work culture over the years are engrossing for kids and adults alike; don't miss the permanent exhibit about political cartoonists, primarily Ewert Karlsson, or EWK, whose work appeared in the *New York Times* and *Le Monde*.

Louis de Geer Konserthus   CONCERT VENUE
(📞15 50 30; www.louisdegeer.com; Dalsgatan 15) A modern addition to the riverside scenery is this extraordinary 1300-seat concert house, in a former paper mill. Still containing the original balconies, it's a superb setting for orchestral, jazz and pop concerts.

FREE Stadsmuseum   MUSEUM
(Holmbrogränd; ⊙10am-5pm Tue, Wed & Fri, to 4pm Jun-Aug, 10am-8pm Thu, 11am-4pm Sat & Sun) The industrial past is exhibited here at the city museum.

FREE Konstmuseum   MUSEUM
(Kristinaplatsen; ⊙noon-4pm Tue & Thu-Sun, noon-8pm Wed Jun-Aug, 11am-5pm Wed & Fri-Sun, 11am-8pm Tue & Thu Sep-May) Boasts important early 20th-century works as well as Carl Larsson's dreamy *Frukost i det gröna*.

🛏 Sleeping

Norrköpings Camping   CAMPING GROUND €
(📞17 11 90; www.norrkopingscamping.com; Camping-vägen; campsites Skr200, 2-/4-bed cabins Skr350/450) This little camping ground sits on the south bank of Motala ström, approximately 2.5km from the city. It's short on bells and whistles, but there's a small cafe on site. Public transport is nonexistent.

STF Vandrarhem Abborreberg   HOSTEL €
(📞31 93 44; abborreberg@telia.com; dm/s/d Skr195/300/550; ⊙Apr–mid-Oct) Stunningly situated in a coastal pine wood 6km east of town, this sterling hostel offers accommodation in huts scattered through the surrounding park. The associated ice-cream parlour is a hit with gluttons. Take bus 116 to Lindö.

Hotell Hörnan   HOTEL €
(📞16 58 90; www.hotellhornan.com; cnr Hörn-gatan & Sankt Persgatan; s/d Skr620/765) The only central budget option, with comfy rooms above a busy pub and restaurant. All rooms come with cable TV. Breakfast is an additional Skr65.

SWEDEN GÖTALAND

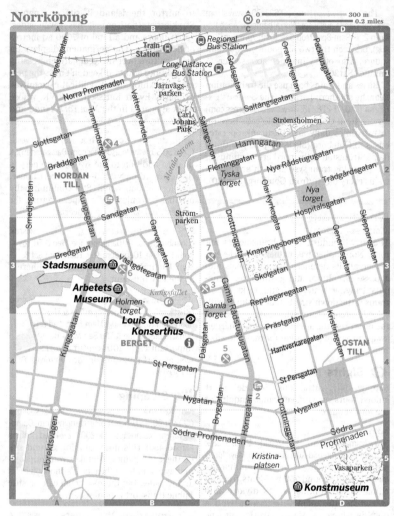

Norrköping

| | | 0 | 300 m |
| | | 0 | 0.2 miles |

Hotel Drott HOTEL €
(☎18 00 60; www.hoteldrott.se; Tunnbindaregatan
19; s/d Skr825/975; @) Peaceful Hotel Drott
serves up old-fashioned but comfy rooms,
as well as a kitchen for self-caterers.
Breakfast includes meatballs and sausage,
and light evening meals are an option.

✖ Eating & Drinking

There are plenty of eateries in the shopping
district along Drottninggatan and in the
student quarter around Kungsgatan. This is
also where you'll find supermarkets.

Cafe Broadway CAFE €
(Bråddgatan 26; sandwiches from Skr55) This casually funky, kid-friendly cafe is decked out
with jukeboxes and album covers. The menu
includes hot and cold sandwiches (Skr55 to
Skr75) large enough to satisfy the hungry
students who fill the place at lunchtime.
Good coffee, too.

Jolla Choklad & Dessert DESSERTS €
(☎12 61 61; Prästgatan 3) Head to this chocolate shop and cafe for exquisite homemade
gelato (try a white chocolate, lime and chilli
combo), desserts, pralines and truffles. As
for the real-deal espresso served in the

Norrköping

cafe, it could make an Italian barista weep happy tears.

Knäppingen CAFE €
(☎10 74 45; Västgötegatan 21; lunches Skr70-90; ☺10am-5pm Tue-Fri, 11am-4pm Sat & Sun) The Stadsmuseum's cafe makes a refreshing change from other dining options, offering focaccia, tacos, crêpes and better vegie options than boring pasta; there's an extensive salad bar during lunch. In summer, you can munch away in a bright, sunny courtyard that is neatly tucked between stately old mills.

Pappa Grappa Bar & Trattorian ITALIAN €€€
(☎18 00 14; Gamla Rådstugugatan 26-28; pizzas Skr92-109, mains Skr150-295; ☺6pm-late Mon-Sat, pizzeria also open Sun) Gobble up a brilliant wood-fired pizza in the pizzeria, or slip into the vaulted restaurant for scrumptious antipasto and meat and fish mains. Established by an Italian ballroom-dancing champion, it also has an on-site deli for take-home treats.

Bagarstugan BAKERY-CAFE €
(☎470 20 20; Skolgatan 1A; sandwiches Skr40-50, salads Skr59-75; ☺10am-6pm Mon-Fri, 10am-4pm Sat, noon-4pm Sun) This stylish, floorboarded bakery–cafe peddles freshly baked cookies, cinnamon buns, muffins and scones, as well as tasty salads, sandwiches and takeaway homemade marmalades. There's a courtyard for alfresco noshing.

ⓘ Information

The well-stocked **tourist office** (☎15 50 00; www.destination.norrkoping.se; Dalsgatan 16; ☺10am-5pm Mon-Fri, 10am-2pm Sat & Sun Jul–mid-Aug) has free internet access.

ⓘ Getting There & Around

Sweden's third-largest airport (Nyköping Skavsta) is 60km away. To get there take the train to Nyköping, then catch a local bus. **Norrköping airport** (www.norrkopingflygplats.se) has direct flights from Copenhagen, Munich and Helsinki.

The regional bus station is next to the train station, and long-distance buses leave from a terminal across the road. **Swebus Express** (☎0771-21 82 18; www.swebusexpress.com) has very frequent services to Stockholm (Skr107, 2¼ hours) and Jönköping (Skr165, 2½ hours), and several services daily to Göteborg (Skr204, five hours) and Kalmar (Skr170, four hours). **Svenska Buss** (☎0771-67 67 67; www.svenska buss.se, in Swedish) runs similar, though less frequent, routes.

Norrköping is on the main north–south railway line, and SJ trains depart every one to two hours for Stockholm (Skr95 to Skr400, 1½ hours) and Malmö (Skr550 to Skr910, 3¼ hours). Trains run roughly every hour north to Nyköping (Skr60 to Skr75, one hour) and every 20 minutes south to Linköping (Skr80, 25 minutes).

Linköping

☑013 / POP 140,400

Most famous for its mighty medieval cathedral, Linköping is also the site of yet another regime-changing bloodbath in Swedish history. In 1600, civil war flared between the Polish, Catholic King Sigismund, Sweden's legitimate but way-too-busy ruler, and his Protestant uncle, Duke Charles, who'd been administering the country. Charles won, becoming King Charles IX and promptly beheading five of Sigismund's supporters, cementing Protestant dominance in Sweden and making way for the nation-shaping reign of his son, Gustavus Adolphus (r 1611–32).

◎ Sights & Activities

Domkyrkan CHURCH
(cathedral; ☺9am-6pm) The enormous, copper-roofed *domkyrka* with its 107m spire is the landmark of Linköping and one of Sweden's oldest and largest churches. Learn more about its history and architecture at the museum inside the castle just across the way, the **Slotts & Domkyrkomuseum** (Castle &

Cathedral Museum; adult/under 7yr Skr40/free; ⊙11am-4pm Tue-Fri, noon-4pm Sat & Sun Apr-Sep).

FREE **Gamla Linköping** MUSEUM

Some 2km west of the city is Gamla Linköping, one of the biggest open-air living-museum villages in Sweden. Among the 90 quaint houses are about a dozen theme museums, many handicraft shops, a small chocolate factory, a restaurant and a cafe. You can wander among the 19th-century buildings at will – the village and most museums are open daily. Just 300m through the forest behind the old village is the Valla Fritidsområde (admission Skr20), a recreation area with domestic animals, gardens, a children's playground, minigolf, a few small museums and old houses. To get here, take bus 202 or 214.

Kinda Canal CANAL CRUISES

Upstaged by the Göta Canal, Linköping boasts its own canal system, the 90km Kinda Canal. Opened in 1871, it has 15 locks, including Sweden's deepest. Cruises include evening sailings, musical outings and wine-tasting trips. For a simple day excursion, from late June to early August **MS Kind** (☎0141-23 33 70; cruises from Skr95 ⊙May-Sep) leaves Tullbron dock at 10am on Tuesday, Thursday and Saturday, and travels to Rimforsa (Skr330, return by bus or train included).

Östergötlands Länsmuseum MUSEUM

(Vasavägen; adult/child Skr50/free; ⊙10am-4pm Tue-Sun, to 8pm Tue & Thu Sep–mid-Dec & mid-Jan–May) Just north of the cathedral, this museum houses an extensive collection of art by a variety of European painters, including Cranach's view of Eden, *Original Sin*.

🛏 Sleeping

Hotell Östergyllen HOTEL €€

(☎10 20 75; www.hotellostergyllen.se; Hamngatan 2B; s/d Skr745/895, ste from Skr1095) Despite the forlorn ambience (lino floors and anonymous corridors), this budget hotel just east of the train station offers cheap, comfy-enough rooms not far from the train station. You can save around Skr200 by opting for a shared bathroom.

Park Hotel HOTEL €€

(☎12 90 05; www.fawltytowers.se; Järnvägsgatan 6; s/d Skr990/1190; P @) Billed as Sweden's 'Fawlty Towers', this hotel at the corner of the park across from the train station resembles that madhouse in appearance only (yes, there's a moose head at reception). A smart family-run establishment close to the train station, it's peppered with chandeliers, oil paintings and clean, parquet-floored rooms. There's a restaurant on site and afternoon tea is served daily.

Linköping STF Vandrarhem & Hotell HOSTEL €

(☎35 90 00; www.lvh.se; Klostergatan 52A; dm from Skr255, s/d Skr465/580; @) A swish central hostel with hotel-style accommodation too, mostly with kitchenettes. All rooms have private bathroom and TV. Book ahead. To get here, head south of town along Drottninggatan.

🍴 Eating & Drinking

Most places to eat and drink are on the main square or nearby streets, especially along buzzing Ågatan.

Barista COFFEE HOUSE €

(Tanneforsgatan 11; sandwiches Skr55-75; ⊙9am-8pm Mon-Fri, 10am-5pm Sat, 11am-4pm Sun) This hip cafe chain (attached to the DesignTorget store just off Stora Torget downtown) peddles fair-trade coffee and other treats, such as chai, organic focaccia and pick-me-up chocolate bars, under fashionable low-slung lamps.

Stångs Magasin SWEDISH €€€

(Södra Stånggatan 1; lunches around Skr90, mains Skr245-295; ⊙lunch Mon-Fri, from 6pm Mon-Fri & from 4pm Sat Sep-Jun, from 2.30pm Tue-Sat Jul & Aug) In a 200-year-old warehouse down near the Kinda Canal docks, this elegant award winner fuses classic Swedish cuisine with continental influences – think glazed duck breast with almond potato puree and artichoke ragout in a wine balsamic sauce. The lunch specials are good value.

Kikko ASIAN FUSION €€

(www.kikko.se; Ågatan 39; lunch buffets Skr88, mains Skr145-280; ⊙lunch & dinner) Head to this place on the main pedestrian drag for zen designer details and Japanese classics like tempura, *gyoza* and sushi, as well as spicier Southeast Asian numbers such as tom yum soup and Penang curry.

Riva ITALIAN €€€

(Ågatan 43; mains Skr178-279; ⊙from 5pm Tue-Fri, from 6pm Sat) Trendy Riva serves Italian-with-a-twist bistro grub like rack of lamb with pancetta and pecorino, scampi with sesame-marinated seaweed, and pizza with shellfish toppings.

❶ Information

Tourist office (☎20 68 35; www.linkoping. se; Östgötagatan 5) Inside the library, not far from the cathedral; there's also free internet access here.

❶ Getting There & Away

The **airport** (☎18 10 30) is only 2km east of town. **Skyways** (☎0771-95 95 00; www. skyways.se) flies direct to Stockholm Arlanda Airport on weekdays. **KLM** (☎08-58 79 97 57; www.klm.com) flies daily to Amsterdam. There's no airport bus, but taxi company **Taxibil** (☎14 60 00) charges around Skr150 for the ride.

Regional and local buses, run by **Östgöta-Trafiken** (☎0771-21 10 10; www.ostgotatrafiken. se), leave from the terminal next to the train station; route maps and timetables are available at the information office. Journeys cost from Skr20; the 24-hour *dygnskort* (adult/under 26 years Skr140/110) is valid on all buses and local trains within the region. Tickets can be purchased at Pressbyrån outlets or at the train station. Tickets purchased on board cost an extra Skr10.

Up to five express buses per day go to Vadstena; otherwise change at Motala.

Long-distance buses depart from a terminal 200m northwest of the train station. Swebus Express runs 10 to 12 times daily to Jönköping (Skr97, 1½ hours) and seven to eight times daily to Göteborg (Skr191, four hours), and north to Norrköping (Skr53, 45 minutes) and Stockholm (Skr145, three hours).

Linköping is on the main north–south railway line. Regional and express trains run to Stockholm roughly every hour; express trains go to Malmö. Frequent regional trains run north to Norrköping (Skr85, 25 minutes). Kustpilen SJ trains run every few hours to Norrköping, Nyköping and Kalmar.

Vadstena

☎0143 / POP 7540

On Vättern lake, Vadstena is a legacy of both church and state power, and today St Birgitta's abbey and Gustav Vasa's castle compete for admiration. The atmosphere in the old town (between Storgatan and the abbey), with its wonderful cobbled lanes, evocative street names and wooden buildings, makes the place a satisfying pit stop.

◉ Sights & Activities

Vadstena Slott CASTLE
(☎315 70; Slottsvägen; tours adult/child Skr90/60; ⊙11am-4pm, longer hr Jul & Aug) The Renaissance castle looks straight over the harbour and lake beyond. It was the mighty family project of the early Vasa kings, and in the upper apartments are some items of period furniture and paintings. There are daily tours from mid-May to mid-September.

Klosterkyrkan CHURCH
(abbey church; ⊙9am-8pm Jul, 9am-7pm Jun & Aug) The superb 15th-century Klosterkyrkan, consecrated in 1430, has a combination of Gothic and some Renaissance features. Inside are the accumulated relics of St Birgitta and medieval sculptures.

Near the church is the **Sankta Birgitta Klostermuseum** (Lasarettsgatan; adult/8-18yr Sk50/20; ⊙10.30am-5pm Jul–early Aug, 11am-4pm Jun & rest of Aug), the old convent founded by St Birgitta.

Cycling CYCLING
The area around Vadstena is full of history and deserves a closer look. Cycling is an option, as the scenic flatlands around Vättern lend themselves to the pedal. A series of ancient legends is connected with **Rökstenen**, Sweden's most famous rune stone, by the church at Rök, just off the E4 on the road to Heda and Alvastra.

⏣ Sleeping & Eating

STF Vandrarhem Vadstena HOSTEL €
(☎103 02; Skänningegatan 20; dm Skr190, s from Skr290; ℗) A short walk from the town centre sits this big hostel, with affable staff, sunny dorms and a large underground kitchen decorated with cheery Dala horses. Book ahead from late August to early June.

Vätterviksbadet CAMPING GROUND €
(☎127 30; campsites Skr200, simple r & cabins from Skr400; ⊙May–mid-Sep; ❄) A quality camping ground near the lake, 2km north of town, with family-friendly amenities including a beach with shallow waters, minigolf, boule, sauna, waterslide, kiosk, cafe and pub.

Vadstena Klosterhotel BOUTIQUE HOTEL €€€
(☎315 30; hotel@klosterhotel.se; r Skr890-1750; ℗@) History and luxury merge at this wonderfully atmospheric hotel in St Birgitta's old convent. The bathrooms are a wee bit dated, but the medieval-style rooms are

great, with chandeliers, high wooden beds, and heaven-sent coffee makers. Most rooms boast lake views.

Rådhuskällaren   RESTAURANT-BAR €€€
(Rådhustorget; mains Skr155-195) Under the old courthouse, this affable 15th-century cellar restaurant dishes out simple but filling burger, pasta and fish meals. Its outdoor area is a favourite afternoon drinking spot in summer. On weekends, the cellar becomes a nightclub, with international DJs and live music.

Restaurant Munkklostret   SWEDISH €€€
(☑130 00; lunches from Skr85, mains Skr200-324; ☺from noon in summer, shorter hr in winter) The Klosterhotel's ravishing restaurant is the best nosh spot in town. Seasonal game, steak, lamb and fish dishes are flavoured with herbs from the monastery garden, and served in the monks' old dorms. It's wise to book ahead.

❶ Information

Tourist office (☑315 70; www.vadstena.com; ☺10am-6pm Jul, 10am-6pm Jun & early Aug) Located in Rödtornet (Sånggatan).

❶ Getting There & Around

See Linköping (p479) for regional transport information. Only buses run to Vadstena – you must take bus 610 to Motala (for trains to Örebro) or bus 661 to Mjölby (for trains to Linköping and Stockholm). Swebus Express runs on Fridays and Sundays to/from Stockholm (Skr235, 4¼ hours). **Blåklints Buss** (☑0142-121 50; www.blaklintsbuss.se, in Swedish) runs one to three services daily from the Viking Line terminal in Stockholm to Vadstena (Skr170).

SMÅLAND

The region of Småland is one of dense forests, glinting lakes and bare marshlands. Historically it served as a buffer zone between the Swedes and Danes; the eastern and southern coasts in particular witnessed territorial tussles. Today it's better known for the Glasriket (Kingdom of Crystal) in the central southeast.

Växjö
☑0470 / POP 79,600

A venerable old market town, Växjö (pronounced *vak*-choo, with the 'ch' sound as in the Scottish 'loch'), in Kronobergs *län* (Kronoberg county), is an important stop for Americans seeking their Swedish roots. In mid-August, Karl Oscar Days commemorates the mass 19th-century emigration from the area, and the Swedish-American of the year is chosen.

◉ Sights

Smålands Museum   MUSEUM
(www.smalandsmuseum.se; Södra Järnvägsgatan 2; adult/child Skr40/20; ☺10am-5pm Tue-Fri, 11am-5pm Sat & Sun) This museum has an absorbing exhibition of glassworks that are accompanied by good explanations in English setting out the development of each phase of the art form. Don't miss the record-holding collection of glass cheese-dish covers – hard to beat for obscure notoriety – or the strangely affecting examples of 'glass sickness'. There are also temporary exhibitions (for instance, at time of research: 'Can Swedishness be at an end?'), events and lectures. There is an attached cafe, Kult, which serves good coffee (Skr19) and traditional Swedish staples such as herring with potatoes (mains Skr80 to Skr125).

Utvandrarnas Hus   MUSEUM
(Emigrant House; www.utvandrarnashus.se; Vilhelm Mobergs gata 4; adult/child Skr40/free; ☺9am-5pm Tue-Fri, 11am-4pm Sat & Sun May-Aug) Has archives, information and historical exhibitions on the beckoning USA. It's just behind the train-and-bus station.

🛏 Sleeping

Växjö Vandrarhem   HOSTEL €
(☑630 70; www.vaxjovandrarhem.nu; dm from Skr200; P @) At Evedal, this pretty former spa hotel with a picturesque lakeside setting dates from the late 18th century. All rooms have washbasins; there's a big kitchen, laundry and a wonderful lounge in the attic. It's well loved, so book early. Take bus 1C from town.

❶ Information

Tourist office (☑414 10; www.turism.vaxjo.se; Västra Esplanaden 7; ☺9.30am-6pm Mon-Fri, 10am-2pm Sat Jun-Aug) Shares a building with the library, which offers free internet access.

❶ Getting There & Away

Småland airport (☑75 85 00; www.smaland airport.se) is 9km northwest of Växjö. **SAS** (☑0770-72 77 27; www.flysas.com) has direct flights to Stockholm Arlanda Airport, **Fly Småland** (☑0771-71 72 00; www.flysmaland.com) to

Stockholm's Bromma airport, Berlin and Vilnius, and **Ryanair** (☑0900-20 20 240; www.ryanair.com) to Düsseldorf Weeze. An airport bus (Flygbussen) connects with flights (Skr20); otherwise take a **taxi** (☑135 00).

Länstrafiken Kronoberg (☑0771-76 70 76; www.lanstrafikenkron.se, in Swedish) runs the regional bus network, with daily buses to Halmstad, Jönköping and Kosta. Long-distance buses depart beside the train station. Svenska Buss runs one or two services daily to Eksjö (Skr220, 1½ hours), Linköping (Skr310, 3¼ hours) and Stockholm (Skr410, 6½ hours).

Växjö is served by SJ trains running roughly hourly between Alvesta (on the main north–south line; Skr37 to Skr55, 15 minutes) and Kalmar (Skr146, 1¼ hours). A few trains run daily directly to Karlskrona (Skr123, 1½ hours), Malmö (Skr220, two hours) and Göteborg (Skr265, 3¼ hours).

Glasriket

One of the most impressive things to see in Sweden is traditional glass-blowing, and there's no better place to see it than here, in its birthplace, the so-called 'Kingdom of Crystal'. The rest of the scenery's not bad either – dense forests, quaint red houses and intricately winding roads. It's no surprise that the area known as Glasriket (www.glasriket.se) is the most visited part of Sweden outside Stockholm and Göteborg. There are at least 11 glass factories (look for *glasbruk* signs), most with long histories: Kosta, for example, was founded in 1742.

The glassworks have similar opening hours, usually 10am to 6pm Monday to Friday, 10am to 4pm Saturday and noon to 4pm Sunday. Expert glass designers produce some extraordinary avant-garde pieces, often with a good dollop of Swedish wit involved. Factory outlets have substantial discounts on seconds (around 30% to 40% off), and larger places can arrange shipping to your home country.

NYBRO
☑0481 / POP 19,600

The biggest town in Glasriket, Nybro makes a good base for exploration. It was once an important centre for hand-blown light bulbs(!), and still has two glassworks on its doorstep. Of the two glassworks, 130-year-old Pukeberg (www.pukeberg.se; Pukebergarnas väg), just southeast of the centre, is perhaps more interesting for its quaint setting. Ny-bro (www.nybro-glasbruk.se; Herkulesgatan) is

smaller and laced with quirky items (think Elvis Presley glass platters).

There's a superior homestead museum, **Madesjö Hembygdsgård** (adult/child Skr30/10; ☺10am-5pm Mon-Fri, 11am-5pm Sat & Sun mid-May–mid-Sep), about 2.5km west of Nybro. Housed inside the 200m-long *kyrkstallarna* (former church stables), it contains an admirable collection, with cannonballs, clothing, coffins, carpenters' tools, a classroom and a fantastic (ice-) cycle – and they're just the things beginning with 'C'.

Nybro Lågprishotell & Vandrarhem (☑109 32; Vasagatan 22; dm/s/d Skr225/350/450, hotel s/d Skr490/790; ℗) The local STF hostel, near Pukeberg, is clean and comfortable, with a kitchen on each floor as well as a sauna. More expensive hotel rooms have cable TV, non-bunk beds and private showers and toilets, with breakfast included. You can also rent bicycles.

Nybro isn't exactly a hotbed of culinary action; for sandwiches, light meals and coffee, try **Lilla Café** (Torget 1; sandwiches from Skr20, coffee Skr15; ☺10am-6pm Mon-Fri, 10am-3pm Sat) on the main square.

Nybro's **tourist office** (☑450 85; www.nybro.se, in Swedish; Stadshusplan; ☺10am-6pm Mon-Fri, 10am-4pm Sat mid-Jun–Aug) is inside the town hall.

SJ trains between Alvesta and Kalmar stop here every hour or two. Regional bus 131 runs to/from Kalmar.

KOSTA, BODA & ORREFORS

These three tiny Småland villages are home to the three biggest names in Swedish glass production. Each namesake company is open daily and each factory complex has an outlet store, museum or gallery, glass-blowing demonstrations and tourist information for the area.

The **Kosta Boda** (www.kostaboda.se) complex pulls in coachloads of visitors, who raid the vast discount outlets (there's even discounted designer threads these days). Funnily, Sweden even manages to make its tourist traps pleasant places. The exhibition gallery (Skr30) contains some inspired creations, and there are plenty of glass-blowing demos in the old factory quarters.

Orrefors (www.orrefors.se) was founded in 1898. The factory complex is impressive (make sure you check out the gallery) and there's a good hostel nearby.

The friendly, well-equipped **Vandrarhem Orrefors** (☑300 20; Silversparregatan 14; dm/

s/d from Skr170/320/390; ☻May-Sep) is located conveniently near the factory. Quaint red houses surround a grassy garden, and the peaceful rooms have proper beds. Breakfast is available on request.

If you're here from June to August, ask about *hyttsill* parties at the glass factories, where meals are prepared using the furnaces and cooling ovens. The menu includes herring, smoked sausage, bacon and baked potatoes, as well as the regional speciality *ostkaka* (cheesecake). The cost starts at around Skr495 per person including drinks. Contact the regional tourist offices or the glassworks for more information.

ⓘ Getting There & Around

Apart from the main routes, bus services around the area are practically non-existent. The easiest way to explore is with your own transport (beware of elk). Bicycle tours on the unsurfaced country roads are excellent; there are plenty of hostels, and you can camp almost anywhere except near the military area on the Kosta–Orrefors road.

Kalmar Länstrafik's bus 139 runs from mid-June to mid-August only and calls at a few of the glass factories. The service operates four times per day on weekdays and once on Saturday, and runs from Nybro to Orrefors and Målerås. Year-round bus services connect Nybro and Orrefors (up to nine weekdays), and Kosta is served by regular bus 218 from Växjö (two or three daily).

Oskarshamn

☎0491 / POP 26,300

Oskarshamn is useful mostly for its regular boat connections with Gotland.

The well-run **STF Vandrarhem Oskarshamn** (☎158 00; info@forumoskarshamn.com; Södra Långgatan 15-17; hostel dm/s/d Skr180/305/410; Ⓟ@) is a brilliant budget option, with sleek modern rooms and private bathrooms, a snazzy TV lounge and dining room, and a tidy kitchen for self-caterers.

The **tourist office** (☎881 88; www.oskarshamn.se; Hantverksgatan 18; ☻9am-6pm Mon-Fri, 10am-3pm Sat & Sun Jun-late Aug, 9.30am-4.30pm Mon-Fri late Aug-May) is in Kulturhuset, along with the **library**, which has free internet access and a small museum dedicated to the wooden sculptures of Axel Petersson (1868–1925) illustrating traditional Småland life.

Oskarshamn airport is 12km north of town, and **Skyways** (☎0771-95 95 00; www.skyways.se) flies direct to Stockholm Ar-

landa Airport three times daily Monday to Wednesday and twice daily Thursday and Friday. An extra flight each weekday flies to Stockholm Arlanda via Linköping.

Long-distance bus services stop at the very central bus station. Regional bus services run up to six times daily from Oskarshamn to Kalmar (Skr75, 1½ hours) and Västervik (Skr67, one hour).

Swebus Express has three daily buses between Stockholm and Kalmar calling in at Oskarshamn. The closest train station is in Berga, 25km west. Here, regional trains run from Linköping and Nässjö. Local buses connect Berga and Oskarshamn.

Boats to Visby depart from the ferry terminal near the now-disused train station, daily in winter and twice daily in summer. Boats to Öland depart from the ferry terminal off Skeppsbron.

Kalmar

☎0480 / POP 61,500

Not only is Kalmar dashing, it also claims one of Sweden's most spectacular castles, where the crowns of Sweden, Denmark and Norway agreed to the short-lived Union of Kalmar in 1397. Other local assets include Sweden's largest gold hoard, from the 17th-century ship *Kronan,* and the storybook cobbled streets of Gamla Stan (Old Town) to the west of Slottshotellet.

⊙ Sights & Activities

Kalmar Slott   MUSEUM

(☎45 14 90; adult/child/under 7yr Skr80/20/free; ☻10am-6pm daily Jul, 10am-5pm Aug, 10am-4pm May, Jun & Sep) The once-powerful Renaissance Kalmar Slott, located in a magnificent setting by the sea south of the railway, was the key to Sweden before the lands to the south were claimed from Denmark. The panelled **King Erik chamber** is the highlight of the castle's interior. **Guided tours** (☻in English 2.30pm late Jun, plus 11.30am & 1.30pm Jul–mid-Aug, 11.30am only mid-Aug–early Sep) are included.

Kalmar Konstmuseum   MUSEUM

(www.kalmarkonstmuseum.se; Stadsparken; adult/child Skr40/free; ☻noon-5pm Tue-Sun, to 8pm Wed) This modern-art museum, in its pretty setting of Gamla Stan, is worth a look.

Kalmar Länsmuseum   MUSEUM

(County Museum; www.kalmarlansmuseum.se; Skeppsbrogatan; adult/child Skr60/30; ☻10am-6pm mid-Jun–mid-Aug) In the old steam mill by the harbour is this exhibition of finds

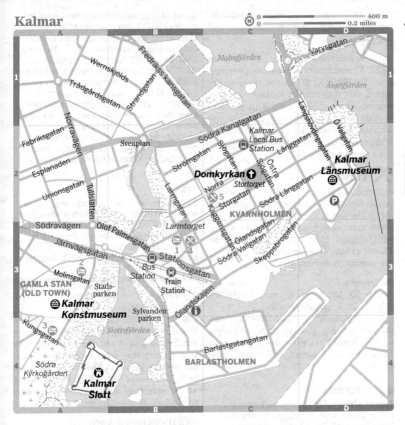

from the flagship *Kronan,* which sank controversially off Öland in 1676.

Domkyrkan CHURCH

(Cathedral; Stortorget) Home to a spectacular pulpit, the baroque Domkyrkan was designed by Tessin, King Karl X Gustav's favourite architect.

🛏 Sleeping

Slottshotellet HOTEL €€€

(✆882 60; www.slottshotellet.se; Slottsvägen 7; s/d Skr1390/1790; 🅿@) Kalmar's top pick is this wonderfully romantic, cosy hotel based in four buildings in a gorgeous green setting near the castle. Most rooms have antique furnishings and some feature vintage Swedish tile stoves. Staff are wonderful and there's an onsite summer restaurant.

Söderportshotellet HOTEL €

(✆125 01; www.soderportsgarden.se; Slottsvägen 1; d/tr/q Skr795/1150/1450; ⊙mid-Jun–mid-Aug)

Kalmar

⦿ Top Sights

🛏 Sleeping

🍴 Eating

With a location right outside of the castle, Söderportshotellet offers nice summertime accommodation in student digs. Rooms are modest yellow-washed affairs; some of the rooms on the upper floor have castle views. There's an award-winning cafe–restaurant downstairs with regular blues and jazz gigs.

Frimurarehotellet HOTEL €€
(☎152 30; www.frimurarehotellet.com; Larmtorget 2; s/d Skr1290/1490; @) In the heart of the action, this 19th-century building contains spacious, personable rooms with polished wooden floors. The plant-filled lounge comes with complimentary tea, coffee and biscuits, while one cheaper room (about Skr200 less) has a shower off the corridor.

✖ Eating

Kullzenska Caféet CAFE €
(☎288 82; 1st fl, Kaggensgatan 26; snacks from Skr35) The pick of the town's cafes is this gorgeous maze of genteel 19th-century rooms, with original tiled stoves and furniture. There's a range of sandwiches and cakes (try the yummy fruit crumbles).

Da Ernesto ITALIAN €€€
(☎200 50; Larmtorget 4; mains Skr148-248; ⊙lunch Sat & Sun, dinner daily) Run by a real-deal Neapolitan, this Italian cafe, restaurant and bar attracts scores of people with its baristi, extensive menu (including Neapolitan-style pizzas), and well-mixed drinks.

❶ Information

Tourist office (☎41 77 00; www.kalmar.se/turism; Ölandskajen 9; ⊙9am-9pm Mon-Fri, 10am-5pm Sat & Sun late Jun–mid-Aug, shorter hours other times) About 100m south of the train station.

❶ Getting There & Away

Air

The **airport** (☎45 90 00; www.kalmarairport.se) is 6km west of town. **SAS** (☎0770-72 77 27) flies several times daily to Stockholm Arlanda Airport, while **Kalmarflyg** (www.kalmarflyg.se, in Swedish) flies to Stockholm's Bromma airport. An airport bus (bus 402; Skr40, 20 minutes) provides connections to central Kalmar.

Bus

All regional and long-distance buses depart from the train station; local town buses have their own station on Östra Sjögatan. Regional buses are run by **Kalmar Länstrafik** (☎0491-76 12 00; www.klt.se, in Swedish), including buses to Öland (Skr28, 35 minutes).

Roughly three **Swebus Express** (☎0771-21 82 18; www.swebusexpress.com) services daily

run north to Västervik (Skr121, two hours), Norrköping (Skr213, four hours) and Stockholm (Skr239, 6½ hours); and one to three services daily run south to Karlskrona (Skr57, 1¼ hours), Karlshamn (Skr73, two hours), Kristianstad (Skr121, three hours), Lund (Skr164, four hours) and Malmö (Skr152, 4½ hours). **Svenska Buss** (☎0771-67 67 67; www.svenskabuss.se, in Swedish) has four services per week on the same route; journey times and prices are similar. **Silverlinjen** (☎0485 261 11; www.silverlinjen.se, in Swedish) runs one to three daily direct buses from Öland to Stockholm (adult/child Skr300/200), calling at Kalmar; reservations are essential.

Train

SJ trains run every hour or two between Kalmar and Alvesta (from Skr150, 1¼ hours), where you can connect with the main Stockholm–Malmö line and with trains to Göteborg. Trains run to Linköping up to nine times daily (from Skr220, three hours), also with connections to Stockholm.

Öland

☎0485 / POP 25,000

Like a deranged vision of Don Quixote's, Öland is covered in old wooden windmills. Symbols of power and wealth in the mid-18th century, they were a must-have for every aspiring man about town and the death knell for many of Öland's oak forests. Today, 400 or so remain, many lovingly restored by local windmill associations.

FÄRJESTADEN & AROUND

South of Färjestaden the entire island is a Unesco World Heritage site, lauded for its unique agricultural landscape, in continuous use from the Stone Age to today, and peppered with rune stones and ancient burial cairns.

The bridge from Kalmar lands you on the island just north of Färjestaden, where there's a well-stocked **tourist office** (☎56 06 00; www.olandsturist.se) at the Träffpunkt Öland centre. Staff can book island accommodation (for a fee). There are few hotels, but more than 25 camping grounds and at least a dozen hostels (book ahead). Camping between midsummer and mid-August can cost up to Skr300 per site.

Silverlinjen (☎261 11; www.silverlinjen.se, in Swedish) runs one to two daily direct buses from Öland to Stockholm (Skr300, 6½ hours), calling at Kalmar – reservations are essential.

BORGHOLM & AROUND

Öland's 'capital' and busiest town, Borgholm exudes a vaguely tacky air with its discount shops and summer hordes of teens on the pull. The most dramatic (and satisfying) sight is the enormous ruined castle on its outskirts.

◉ Sights

Borgholms Slott   CASTLE
(www.borgholmsslott.se; adult/child Skr50/20; ◎10am-6pm May-Aug) Northern Europe's largest ruined castle looms just south of town. This epic limestone structure was burnt and abandoned early in the 18th century, after life as a dye works. There's a terrific museum inside and a nature reserve nearby, as well as summer concerts and children's activities. The grounds outside the castle are open for wandering year-round.

Solliden Palace   PALACE
(adult/child Skr70/40; ◎11am-6pm mid-May–mid-Sep) Sweden's most famous 'summer house', 2.5km south of the town centre, is used by the Swedish royals. Its exceptional gardens are open to the public in summer and well worth a wander.

⌂ Sleeping

The tourist offices in Borgholm and Färjestaden can help you find inexpensive private rooms in the area.

Ebbas Vandrarhem &
Trädgårdscafé   CAFE-HOSTEL €
(✆103 73; ala-catering@glocalnet.net; Storgatan 12; dm Skr270, s/d Skr350/520; ◎May-Sep) Right in the thick of things, Ebbas cafe has a small STF hostel above it. Five of the cosy lemon-yellow rooms overlook the gorgeous rose-laced garden, and four the bustling pedestrianised main street. There's a kitchen for self-caterers...or just pop downstairs for decent hot and cold grub (lunch Skr85), served until 9pm in the summer (earlier at other times). Book ahead.

Guntorps Herrgård   HOTEL €€
(✆130 00; www.guntorpsherrgard.se; Guntorpsgatan; s/d from Skr1095/1295) This is a delightful old farmhouse east of town. The accommodation is excellent and unintentionally camp, with peachy tones and chandeliers above the beds. The restaurant, with its decadent, multicourse tasting menus (3-/5-course Skr430/555) offering superb samples of local dishes, is an added draw.

✗ Eating & Drinking

Nya Conditoriet   CAFE €
(Storgatan 28; pastries from Skr17, coffee Skr20) For a cosy hang-out during low season, try this cafe next door to Ebbas, with an awesome bakery that draws enthusiastic locals by the dozen. Sandwiches are available, but we recommend something sweet.

Pubben   PUB €€
(Storgatan 18; ◎dinner) There are snacks and light meals here, but punters mainly come to this English-style pub for the beer and hefty selection of whiskies.

❶ Information

Tourist office (✆890 00; Sandgatan 25) At the bus station.

Karlskrona

✆0455 / POP 62,300

If you like your Swedes in uniform, you'll appreciate Karlskrona. Marine cadets pepper the streets of what has always been an A-league naval base. In 1998 the entire town was added to the Unesco World Heritage list for its impressive collection of 17th- and 18th-century naval architecture.

◉ Sights & Activities

Kungsholms Fort   FORT
(guided tours adult/child Skr195/50; ◎10am-2.30pm Jul & Aug) Karlskrona's star is the extraordinary offshore Kungsholms Fort, with its curious circular harbour, established in 1680 to defend the town. Four-hour boat tours, including a visit to the fortress, depart from Fisktorget; book at the tourist office or Marinmuseum (bring ID).

Drottningkärs kastell   CASTLE
Bristling with cannons, this tower on the island of Aspö was described by Admiral Nelson of the British Royal Navy as 'impregnable'. You can visit it on a **Skärgårdstrafiken boat** (return adult/child Skr140/70; ◎Jun-Aug), departing from Fisktorget.

Cruises   ISLAND CRUISES
Pick a sunny summer afternoon for a tour around Karlskrona's **archipelago**, made up of almost 1000 islands. A three-hour tour costs Skr140/70 per adult/child; contact the Skärgårdstrafiken office at Fisktorget or check www.affarsverken.se for timetables and information.

FREE Blekinge Museum   MUSEUM
(Fisktorget 2; ⊙10am-6pm Jun-Aug) This evocative museum explores the local fishing, boat-building and quarrying trades.

Marinmuseum   MUSEUM
(Stumholmen; adult/under 19yr Skr60/free; ⊙10am-6pm Jun-Aug) The national naval museum has interesting ship and historical displays.

🍴 Sleeping & Eating

Dragsö Camping   CAMPING GROUND €
(☑153 54; www.draggso.se; Dragsövägen; campsites from Skr155-215, 2-bed cabins Skr400-500, 4-bed from Skr500; ⊙Apr–mid-Oct) This large, good-looking camping ground, 2.5km northwest of town, is situated on a scenic bay. Facilities include boat rentals (per hour/day Skr60/200) and bicycle hire (half-/full day Skr45/80), as well as a Karlskrona-themed minigolf course. Bus 7 stops about 1km short of the camping ground.

First Hotel Ja   HOTEL €€€
(☑555 60; www.firsthotels.se; Borgmästaregatan 13; s/d from Skr1400/1600; P@) Karlskrona's top slumber spot boasts slick, hip, recently renovated rooms in white and charcoal hues, with blissful beds and flat-screen TVs. Hotel perks include a sauna, bar–restaurant and a great breakfast buffet.

Montmartre   FRENCH €€
(Ronnebygatan 18; pizzas Skr75-95, pastas Skr79-89, mains Skr105-209; ⊙4-11pm Mon-Fri, 1-11pm Sat & Sun) Next door to the Museum Leonardo da Vinci Ideale, atmospheric Montmartre evokes a French bistro with its wine-red drapes, tasselled lampshades and oil paintings. The menu is a more worldly affair, with pizzas, Swedish favourites and fusion numbers like grilled tuna with wasabi, lime and chilli.

STF Vandrarhem Trossö
Karlskrona   HOSTEL €
(☑100 20; www.karlskronavandrarhem.se; Drottninggatan 39; dm/s/d from Skr150/250/350) Modern, clean and friendly, this hostel has a laundry, TV room and backyard for kids to play in; parking on the opposite side of the street is free.

Glassiärens Glassbar   ICE CREAM €
(Stortorget 4; ⊙May-Sep) The queues at this legendary ice-cream peddler are matched by the mammoth serves. Piled high in a heavenly waffle cone, the two-flavour option (Skr33) is a virtual meal.

ℹ Information

Tourist office (☑30 34 90; www.karlskrona.se/tourism; Stortorget 2; ⊙9am-8pm Jun-Aug) Has internet access.

ℹ Getting There & Away

The bus and train stations are just north of central Karlskrona.

Air

Ronneby airport is 33km west of Karlskrona; the Flygbuss leaves from Stortorget (Skr80), near the tourist office. SAS flies to Stockholm Arlanda Airport daily, and Blekingeflyg flies to Bromma Stockholm Airport Sunday to Friday.

Boat

Stena Line ferries to Gdynia (Poland) depart from Verkö, 10km east of Karlskrona (take bus 6).

Bus

BlekingeTrafiken (☑0455-569 00; www.blekingetrafiken.se) operates regional buses.

Svenska Buss runs four times a week from Malmö to Stockholm, calling at Kristianstad, Karlshamn and Karlskrona. Swebus Express service 834 runs once to twice daily from Malmö to Kalmar, calling at Kristianstad, Karlshamn and Karlskrona.

Kustbussen runs six times daily on weekdays (twice daily on weekends) each way between Karlskrona and Kalmar (around Skr150; 1½ hours).

Trains

Direct trains run at least 13 times daily to Karlshamn (Skr75, one hour) and Kristianstad (Skr120, two hours), at least seven times daily to Emmaboda (Skr60, 40 minutes), and 10 times to Lund (Skr185, 2¾ hours) and Malmö (Skr185, three hours). Trains also run at least a couple of times to Göteborg (Skr395, five hours). Change at Emmaboda for Kalmar.

GOTLAND

Gorgeous Gotland has much to brag about: a Unesco-lauded capital, truffle-sprinkled woods, A-list dining hot spots, talented artisans, and more hours of sunshine than anywhere else in Sweden. It's also one of the country's richest historical regions, with around 100 medieval churches and countless prehistoric sites.

The island is situated nearly halfway between Sweden and Latvia, in the middle of the Baltic Sea. Just off its northeast tip you'll find the island of Fårö, most famous as the home of Sweden's great director, the late

Ingmar Bergman. The island national park of Gotska Sandön is located 38km further north, while the petite islets of Stora Karlsö and Lilla Karlsö sit just off the western coast.

Information on the island abounds; www.gotland.net and www.guteinfo.com (in Swedish) are good places to start. Keep in mind that it's primarily a summer holiday destination, and much of the island shuts down between September and May, including many restaurants, museums and accommodation – so plan ahead if you're thinking of a low-season visit.

Getting There & Away

Air

There are regular **Skyways** (☑0771-95 95 00; www.skyways.se) flights between Visby and Stockholm's Arlanda and Bromma airports (up to 10 times a day for each airport). Flights between Stockholm and Visby generally cost Skr760 and up; click on the 'Low fare calendar' link on the website to check for the best prices (starting around Skr495).

The cheaper local airline is **Gotlands Flyg** (☑22 22 22; www.gotlandsflyg.se), with regular flights between Visby and Bromma airport (one to 10 times daily). Prices start at around Skr400 one-way; book early for discounts, and enquire after cheaper stand-by fares. Popular summer-only routes include Göteborg, Hamburg, Oslo and Helsingfors.

The island's **airport** is 4km northeast of Visby. No buses serve the airport directly; your best bet is to catch a taxi into/from town (around Skr150).

Boat

Year-round car ferries between Visby and both Nynäshamn and Oskarshamn are operated by **Destination Gotland** (☑0771-22 33 00; www.destinationgotland.se). There are departures from Nynäshamn one to five times daily (about three hours). From Oskarshamn, there are one or two daily departures in either direction (three to four hours). Ferry passengers are allowed two pieces of luggage, one to check; there are also lockers in the ferry terminals (small/large per 24hr Skr50/60).

Regular one-way adult tickets for the ferry cost between Skr152 and Skr499, but from mid-June to mid-August there is a far more complicated fare system; some overnight, evening and early-morning sailings in the middle of the week have cheaper fares.

Transporting a bicycle costs Skr50; a car usually costs from Skr269, although again in the peak summer season a tiered price system operates. Booking a non-refundable ticket, three weeks in advance, will save you money. If you're thinking of taking a car on the ferry between mid-June and mid-August, make sure you reserve a place well in advance.

Getting Around

Many travel agents and bike-rental places on the island also rent out camping equipment. In Visby, hire bikes from Skr100 per 24 hours at **Gotlands Cykeluthyrning** (☑21 41 33), behind the tourist office (on the harbour).

Kollektiv Trafiken (☑21 41 12) runs buses via most villages to all corners of the island. The most useful routes, which have connections up to seven times daily, operate between Visby and Burgsvik in the far south, Visby and Fårösund in the north (also with bus connections on Fårö), and Visby and Klintehamn. A one-way ticket will not cost you more than Skr68 (although if you take a bike on board it will cost an additional Skr40), but enthusiasts will find a monthly ticket good value at Skr675.

Visby

☑0498 / POP 22,200

The port town of Visby is medieval eye candy and enough to warrant a trip to Gotland all by itself. Inside its thick city walls await twisting cobbled streets, fairy-tale wooden cottages, evocative ruins and steep hills with impromptu Baltic views. The city wall, with its 40-plus towers and the spectacular church ruins within, attest to the town's former Hanseatic glories.

Sights

Medieval ruins   RUINS

Visby's 13th-century wall of 40 towers makes for an impressive sight; savour a leisurely walk around the perimeter (3.5km). Ask at the tourist office about guided walking tours, conducted in English a few times a week in summer (Skr85), or buy a copy of *Visby on Your Own* (Skr35) for a self-guided tour.

Within the town walls are the ruins of 10 medieval churches, as well as the stoic Sankta Maria kyrka (Cathedral of St Maria; ⊗8am-9pm Sun-Fri, to 7pm Sat late Jun–early Aug, 8am-7pm early-late Jun & early Aug–Sep), built in the late 12th and early 13th centuries and heavily touched up over the centuries.

Gotlands Fornsal   MUSEUM

(www.lansmuseetgotland.se; Strandgatan 14; adult/child Skr80/50; ⊗10am-6pm Fri-Wed, to 7pm Thu Jun–mid-Sep) Gotlands Fornsal is one of the mightiest regional museums in

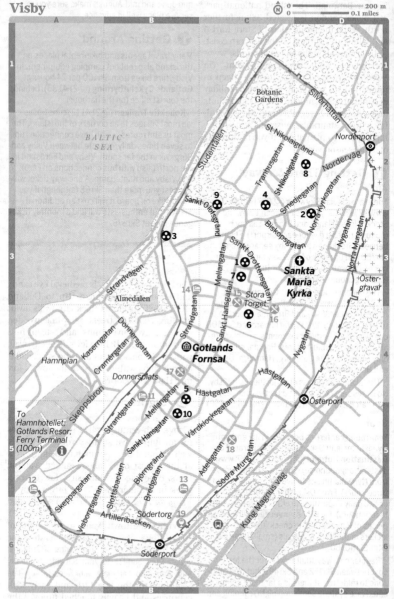

Sweden. Highlights include amazing 8th-century pre-Viking picture stones, human skeletons from chambered tombs and medieval wooden sculptures. The star is the legendary Spillings hoard. At 70kg, it's the world's largest booty of preserved silver treasure.

The museum's cafe, **Fornsalens**, serves a surprisingly gourmet daily lunch (Skr75), as well as coffee and snacks.

SWEDEN NORRLAND

🛏 Sleeping

Moderately priced accommodation in and around Visby is in demand; we recommend booking well in advance if possible. Gotland's hotel prices work opposite to most hotel rates in Sweden: prices increase on summer weekends and in the peak tourist months.

Fängelse Vandrarhem   HOSTEL €

(☎20 60 50; Skeppsbron 1; dm/s/d from Skr200/350/450) As hard to get into as it once was to get out of, this hostel offers beds year-round in the small converted cells of an old prison. It's in a handy location, between the ferry dock and the harbour restaurants, and there's a cute terrace bar in summer. Reserve well in advance and call ahead before arriving to ensure someone can let you in.

Gotlands Resor   APARTMENTS, COTTAGES €€

(☎20 12 60; www.gotlandsresor.se; Färjeleden 3; apt from Skr795, cottages from Skr780) This travel agency, in Hamnhotellet, books stylish, fully equipped cottages in eastern and northern Gotland, as well as apartments in the Visby area. Bookings for the summer should be made around six months in advance. The agency also organises bike hire (per day from Skr70) and rents camping equipment.

Värdshuset Lindgården   HOTEL €€

(☎21 87 00; www.lindgarden.com; Strandgatan 26; s/d Jun-Sep Skr1250/1450, Oct-May Skr875/1025; @) This is a sound central option, with rooms set facing a soothing garden beside a popular restaurant. In summer, you can dine outdoors and listen to music in the romantic courtyard.

Hotel Villa Borgen   HOTEL €€

(☎20 33 00; www.gtsab.se; Adelsgatan 11; s/d Skr1036/1276; @) On the main shopping street in the town centre, this place has satisfying rooms set around a pretty, quiet courtyard and an intimate breakfast room with French doors and stained glass for that boutique feeling.

Clarion Hotel Wisby   HOTEL €€€

(☎25 75 00; cl.wisby@choice.se; Strandgatan 6; s/d from Skr1770/2190; @🏊) Top of the heap in Visby is the luxurious, landmark Wisby. Medieval vaulted ceilings and look-at-me candelabra contrast with funky contemporary furnishings. The gorgeous pool – complete with medieval pillar – occupies a converted merchant warehouse.

🍴 Eating & Drinking

There are more restaurants per capita in Visby than in any other Swedish city. Most are clustered around the Old Town squares, on Adelsgatan or at the harbour. Wherever you choose, do not pass up a chance to try the island's speciality – a saffron pancake *(saffranspankaka)* with berries and cream.

Skafferiet   SWEDISH €€

(Adelsgatan 38; quiches Skr69, lunch specials Skr95) This old-school Swedish cafe, with its low ceilings, stubby candles, rough-hewn wood tables and copper saucepans on the walls, is equally good for lingering over coffee or a quick, convenient lunch of the quiche-and-salad variety. Staff are adorable and cheery.

Cafe Amalia
CAFE €

(Hästgatan 3; coffee Skr25, pastries Skr35, lunch mains Skr65-85) This friendly hang-out is sweet and spacious, with big people-watching windows, good music, breakfast served all day, and possibly the best coffee in Sweden. Pasta bowls and sandwiches are huge and satisfying; try a cold salmon-and-gorgonzola panini. Sweets are all homemade.

Bakfickan
SEAFOOD €€€

(www.bakfickan-visby.nu; Stora Torget; lunch specials Skr85, mains Skr148-258; ☺lunch & dinner) White tiled walls, merrily strung lights and boisterous crowds define this foodie-loved hole in the wall, where you'd be foolish not to try the rich, hearty seafood stew flavoured with saffron and aioli.

Bolaget
FRENCH €€€

(Stora Torget 16; mains Skr179-225; ☺lunch & dinner to 2am, closed Mon) Take a defunct Systembolaget shop, chip the 'System' off the signage, and reinvent the space as a buzzing, bistro-inspired hot spot. Top-notch seasonal flavours shine through in French-inspired dishes such as duck with cherry sauce, cocoa beans and walnut-roasted potatoes.

Tretton Tinnar
PUB €€

(Adelsgatan 2; snacks Skr29-69, mains Skr75-180) This pub, formerly called Effes, is used as a venue for live music and events as well as a regular, grungy pub with a menu of inexpensive bar grub. It's built into the town wall and is a good place to grab a drink and check out the vaguely rockish party crowd (as opposed to the shiny-shirts-only party crowd found in most Visby bars). There's an outdoor courtyard in summer.

❶ Information

Library (Cramergatan, ☺10am-7pm Mon-Fri, noon-4pm Sat & Sun) Free internet access (Skr20 mid-June to mid-August), plus a small coffee shop for study breaks.

Gotland City (☎08-406 15 00; www.gotland city.se, in Swedish; Kungsgatan 57) A central travel agency in Stockholm, useful if you're planning your trip from the capital.

Tourist office (☎20 17 00; www.gotland.info; Skeppsbron 4-6; ☺8am-7pm in summer, 8am-4pm Mon-Fri rest of yr) At the harbour.

Around the Island

Renting a bicycle and following the well-marked Gotlandsleden cycle path is one of the best ways to spend time on Gotland. It loops all around the island, sometimes joining the roadways but more often winding through quiet fields and forests. You can hire cycles at several locations in Visby. There's an excellent hostel network along the cycle route, with particularly good facilities in Bunge, Lummelunda, Lärbro and the small northern islet of Fårö.

NORRLAND

Norrland, the northern half of Sweden, is remote enough for travellers here not to see much of the tour-bus crowd – or, for that matter, much of anyone else. The population is sparse – reindeer outnumber cars on the roads, and much of the landscape consists of deep-green forest. It's a paradise for nature lovers who enjoy hiking, skiing and other outdoor activities. The north is home to the Sámi people, and several villages have well-preserved open-air museums that demonstrate traditional Sámi lifestyles.

Norrland also rewards quirk-seekers: it boasts a rarely glimpsed monster lurking in a lake, a disappearing hotel made of ice, and a golf course that flits between Sweden and Finland. Inlandsbanan, the historic railway line from Mora to Gällivare via Östersund, Storuman, Arvidsjaur and Jokkmokk, is a fun if not particularly fast way to see the north in summertime.

Sundsvall

☑060 / POP 93,300

When Sundsvall burned to the ground in 1888, civic leaders made a decision that left behind the city's small-town feel and gave it a new sense of weight and significance: on the sites of the old wooden houses, they rebuilt the town in stone. This forced poorer residents to the city's outskirts, while wealth and power collected in the centre, but it also meant that modern Sundsvall, which might have been just another architecturally bland coastal city, is today not only historically significant but also quite pretty.

Kulturmagasinet, on Sjögatan down near the harbour, is a magnificent restoration of some old warehouses. The buildings now contain the library and Sundsvall Museum (adult/child Skr20/free; ☉10am-7pm Mon-Thu, 10am-6pm Fri, 11am-4pm Sat & Sun), which has exhibits of local art, natural history, Iron Age archaeology and geology. The tiny Café Skonerten (☉10am-4pm) serves a humble, meat-and-potatoes buffet lunch (Skr75).

🛏 Sleeping & Eating

STF Vandrarhem Sundsvall　　HOSTEL €
(☑61 21 19; www.gaffelbyn.se; Gaffelbyvägen; dm with/without bathroom Skr290/225) The STF hostel is above the town on Norra Stadsberget, and has both older rooms and more expensive modern rooms with private bathroom. The 20-minute walk (about 1km) up a hill to the hostel from the city centre is pleasant, but not much fun with heavy bags – guests can telephone for a bus (☑744 90 10) from the train and bus stations.

Lilla Hotellet　　HOTEL €
(☑61 35 87; Rådhusgatan 15; s/d Skr595/795) In a stone building designated a historical monument, this small family-run hotel is in a great location and has a friendly vibe. Rooms have interesting architectural details, many including ceramic tile stoves.

🍴Tant Anci & Fröcken Sara　　CAFE €€
(Bankgatan 15; soups/pastas/sandwiches/soups/pastas Skr60/65/75; ☉10am-10pm Mon-Fri, 10am-5pm Sat, 11am-5pm Sun) Humongous bowls of soup or salad are the speciality at this adorable organic cafe, where you can also get hearty sandwiches, giant bowls of pasta and pastries. The space has expanded, allowing for more tables, but takeaway is also available. The restaurant also contains a small health-food shop with organic tea and coffee, chocolate, snacks and cooking supplies.

Barista　　COFFEE HOUSE €
(Storgatan 11; espresso drinks Skr32-37, mains from Skr79; ☉9am-9pm Mon-Fri, 10am-9pm Sat & Sun) This sleek little coffee shop is part of a small chain bringing fair-trade organic espresso drinks to Sweden; nestle in one of its hanging basket chairs with a frothy cappuccino.

❶ Information

Tourist office (www.sundsvallturism.com; Stora Torget; ☉10am-5pm Mon-Fri, 10am-2pm Sat, longer hr Jul & Aug) Has information on activities including summer boat tours.

❶ Getting There & Away

Midlanda airport is 22km north of Sundsvall; buses run from the bus station three to nine times daily (Skr85) to connect with SAS and Skyways flights to Göteborg, Luleå and Stockholm.

Buses depart from the Sundsvall bus station, near Kulturmagasinet. Ybuss runs to Östersund (Skr190, 2½ hours, twice daily) and Stockholm (Skr275, six hours, four to five daily). Länstrafiken Västerbotten bus 100 runs several times daily to Umeå (Skr295, 3¾ hours), Luleå (Skr440, eight hours) and most other coastal towns.

Trains run west to Östersund and south to Söderhamn, Gävle and Stockholm. The station is just east of the town centre, on Köpmangatan.

Höga Kusten
☑0613

Some of the most dramatic scenery on the Swedish coastline is found here, on the Höga Kusten (High Coast). The secret to its spectacular beauty is elevation; nowhere else on the coast do you find such a mountainous landscape, with sheer rocky cliffs plunging straight down to the sea, as well as lakes, fjords and islands. The region was recently recognised as geographically unique and listed as a Unesco World Heritage site.

In addition to the striking landscapes, the other major attractions around the region are the many well-preserved fishing villages – with the pick of them being Barsta, Bönhamn and Norrfällsviken – and the delightful offshore islands, especially Högbonden and Ulvön.

Norrfällsviken is a picture-perfect half-circle of red-and-white fishing huts around a narrow inlet. There's a hilltop chapel from 1649, and the friendly Fiskar Fänget (fish plates Skr75-225; ☉late Apr–mid-Sep) sells smoked fish to take away, as well as more substantial meals in its cosy wood-panelled restaurant–pub; the weekend seafood buffet (Skr200) in summer is a treat. Next door is a tiny fishing museum (☉11am-4pm late Apr–mid-Sep) where you can learn the history of *surströmming,* the fermented herring that's famously an acquired taste, including how (and more to the point *why*) it's made.

Skuleberget Naturum (☑401 71; admission free; ☉9am-7pm May-Sep, 10am-5pm Wed-Sun Oct-Apr), by the E4 north of Docksta, has exhibitions and lots of information on hiking routes on and around Skuleberget (285m), the looming mountain.

🍴 Sleeping & Eating

STF Vandrarhem Docksta
HOSTEL €

(🖉130 64; dm Skr130-200, s/d from Skr170/260; ⚏) This attractive and busy hostel is 3km south of Docksta at Skoved, right along the Höga Kustenleden (High Coast Trail). Facilities include a restaurant and an outdoor stage for summer concerts. Campsites (Skr130) are available; reservations recommended.

Norrfällsviken Camping
CAMPING GROUND €

(🖉213 82; tent Skr185, 3-bed cabins Skr495, self-catering cabins Skr995, hotel r Skr1295) This popular summer complex includes a huge camping ground, cabins and a few hotel-grade rooms, plus activities such as minigolf and fishing. In summer, staff bring fresh-baked bread around in the morning. Self-catering cabins sleep four and include a sitting room, dining room, kitchen and full bathroom and shower.

Vandrarhem Högbonden
HOSTEL €

(🖉230 05, 420 49; www.hogbonden.se; dm from Skr300; ⊘May-Oct) A relaxing getaway on the little island of Högbonden. There's a kitchen here, and the cafe is open from June to August. Book well in advance.

❶ Information

The regional **tourist office** (🖉504 80; www.hogakusten.com) can help you with information on exploring the region by bus, car or on an organised tour; it's located inside Hotell Höga Kusten, just north of **Höga Kustenbron**, the spectacular E4 suspension bridge over Storfjärden.

Unfortunately, there's little by way of public transport (buses cruise along the E4 highway but don't make it into the region's villages). Hence, this area is virtually impossible to explore without having your own set of wheels – unless you opt to **hike** the Höga Kustenleden (High Coast Trail).

❶ Getting There & Around

Bus 217 runs one to six times daily between Nordingrå, the bridge and Kramfors. Länstrafiken Västerbotten bus 100 runs along the E4.

Ferries to Högbonden (🖉0613-230 05, winter 231 00; www.hogbonden.se; adult/child return Skr150/50) go from Barsta only mid-May to mid-June and mid-August to October (noon Friday to Sunday), and from both Barsta and Bönhamn in peak summer (mid-June to mid-August). During this period boats leave from Barsta at 9.30am, 11.30am, 2.30pm and 5.30pm, and from Bönhamn at 10am, noon, 3pm and 6pm.

Ferries to Ulvön (🖉070-651 92 65; ⊘Jun-Aug) leave year-round from Köpmanholmen (Skr70 one-way, twice daily) and mid-June to August from Ullånger (9.30am) and Docksta (10.15am), both adult/child Skr125/50 one-way.

Östersund

🖉063 / POP 58,400

This pleasant town by Storsjön lake, in whose chilly waters is said to lurk a rarely sighted monster, has good budget accommodation and is a relaxed and scenic place; it's an excellent gateway town for further explorations of Norrland.

◎ Sights & Activities

Östersund is a major winter sports centre. You can also ask at the tourist office about monster-spotting lake cruises (adult/child Skr100/45; ⊘Jun-Sep). Bring your binoculars.

Jamtli
PARK, MUSEUM

(www.jamtli.com; adult/child mid-Jun–Aug Skr110/25, rest of yr Skr60/20; ⊘11am-5pm) Don't miss Jamtli, 1km north of the town centre. It combines an open-air museum park (à la Skansen in Stockholm) with a first-rate regional culture museum. In the outdoor section, guides wearing period costumes explain the traditions of the area. Indoors, the regional museum exhibits the **Överhogdal tapestry**, a Viking relic from around 1100 that's perhaps the oldest of its kind in Europe.

FREE Färgfabriken Norr
ART GALLERY

(www.fargfabrikennorr.se; Byggnad 33, Infanterigatan 30; ⊘noon-4pm Thu-Sun during exhibitions) An offshoot of Färgfabriken in Stockholm, Färgfabriken Norr is a huge gallery space across E14 from Jamtli. It's a cavernous room with an ambitious curatorial scope; exhibitions change frequently, and there are occasional live music performances. Take bus 14 or 8 to get here.

Frösön
ZOO

Several attractions lie on the adjacent island of Frösön, reached by road or footbridge from the middle of Östersund. These include **Frösöns Djurpark** (www.frosozoo.se; adult/child/family Skr180/90/500; ⊘10am-4pm mid-late Jun & Aug, 10am-6pm Jul). There are slalom and Nordic ski runs on the island at Östberget, plus a **viewing tower** (adult/child Skr10/5;

⊙9am-9pm mid-Jun–mid-Aug) and cafe. Bus 5 will bring you here.

🛏 Sleeping & Eating

STF Vandrarhem Jamtli   HOSTEL €
(☑12 20 60; vandrarhemmet@jamtli.com; Museiplan; dm Skr150, s/d from Skr245/300) Right inside the gates of Jamtli museum park is this comfortable hostel, housed in a low, barn-like wooden building with a huge kitchen. Dorms are in two- to five-bed rooms, and facilities are all top-notch. Reservations are recommended. Take bus 5 to get here.

Hotel Emma   HOTEL €€
(☑51 78 40; www.hotelemma.com; Prästgatan 31; s/d Skr940/1090; ℗ @) Emma couldn't be better located: it's on the main pedestrian shopping street, right above a whisky bar. The hotel has all the comforts of a fancy chain but with personality: its rooms are nestled into crooked passages on two floors, with homey touches like squishy armchairs and imposing ceramic stoves; some rooms have French doors facing the courtyard and buttery wood floors. Parking costs Skr75.

Volos   GREEK, SWEDISH €€
(Prästgatan 38; daily lunches Skr79, pasta Skr115, mains Skr159-179; ⊙11am-9pm, to midnight weekends & Jul & Aug) This upmarket Greek restaurant, under new ownership, emphasises locally produced, organic ingredients, including beef from Jämtland, potatoes from Härjedalen and char from nearby Landö lake, which is served fried with onions and potatoes in traditional Jämtland style.

Brunkullans   SWEDISH €€€
(Postgränd 5; starters Skr55-149, mains Skr124-250; ⊙11am-2pm Mon-Fri, from 5pm Tue-Sat, from 4pm Fri) A local favourite for its outdoor patio, Brunkullans also has a wonderfully atmospheric, candlelit 19th-century interior space. The menu features Swedish classics and upmarket versions of basic bar food.

ℹ Information

Tourist office (☑1440 01; www.turist.oster sund.se; Rådhusgatan 44; ⊙9am-5pm Mon-Thu, 10am-3pm Fri-Sun) Opposite the town hall; has free internet access.

ℹ Getting There & Away

The **airport** is on Frösön, 11km west of the town centre, and the airport bus leaves regularly from the bus terminal (adult/child Skr70/20). SAS

flies several times daily to Stockholm; Fly Nordic and Nordic Regional serve Luleå and Umeå.

The train station is a short walk south from the town centre, but the main regional bus station is central on Gustav III Torg; local buses usually run to both. Local buses 1, 3, 4, 5 and 9 go to Frösön (Skr20). Most city buses stop in front of the tourist office.

Länstrafiken bus 45 runs to Mora (5½ hours, two to four daily). Bus 155 runs west to Åre (1½ hours); bus 63 runs northeast to Umeå (six hours, two to four daily).

SJ trains run from Stockholm (from Skr607, six hours) via Gävle, and some continue to Storlien (from where you can catch trains to Trondheim, Norway). You can also catch a train east to Sundsvall (Skr272, 2½ hours). In summer the Inlandsbanan train runs once daily, to Gällivare (Skr962) or Mora (Skr414).

Åre & Around

☑0647 / POP 9700
A fun, outdoorsy place to hang out in the low season, Åre is beautifully situated in a mountain valley, but it gets crowded in winter, thanks to its famed ski area (www.ski star.com/are). The place has 45 ski lifts, 100 pistes and 1000 vertical metres of skiable slopes, including a 6.5km downhill run. The skiing season is from November to mid-May, but conditions are best from February, when daylight hours increase.

🛏 Sleeping & Eating

Note that accommodation fills up quickly in winter, so plan well ahead. Not all hotels stay open in summer, but those that do offer bargains.

STF Vandrarhem Åre   HOSTEL €
(☑301 38; www.brattlandsgarden.se; dm Skr200, s/d from Skr300/400) A lovely spot on an old farmstead with dorm rooms tucked into red wooden buildings and a huge living room and dining area. The place is 8km east of Åre, in Brattland; once-daily buses connect it to town, although service is spotty.

Fjällgården   HOTEL €€€
(☑145 00; www.fjallgarden.se; r from Skr1495) Up on the hillside, this is as much an activity centre as a hotel. It offers fishing, mountain biking, golf, horse riding, paddling and a chance to try the 'zipline', which lets you fly across the valley on a tiny string. Suites and large double rooms are available (plus

luxury versions of each), decorated in faux-rustic, après-ski style.

TOP CHOICE Åre Bageri — BAKERY €

(Årevägen 55; sandwiches Skr50-60, breakfast buffet Skr85; ⊙7am-3.30pm) A sprawling organic cafe and stone-oven bakery with a comfy, shabby-chic atmosphere, this place lends itself to lingering. In addition to great coffee, pastries and huge sandwiches, it does a fairly epic all-you-can-eat breakfast spread.

Werséns — PIZZA €€

(www.wersens.se; Årevägen 101; lunches Skr115, pizzas from Skr115, mains Skr125-295; ⊙5-10pm Sun-Fri & noon-11pm Sat) This white-tablecloth brasserie and pizzeria has takeaway options and half-portions available. There's a bar and, in good weather, outside tables.

ⓘ Information

The **tourist office** (☑177 20; www.visitare.se), above the train station, has free internet access. The same building contains luggage lockers (small/large Skr30/70 per day), a sporting-goods store and an ICA supermarket.

ⓘ Getting There & Away

Regional bus 157 runs from Östersund and connects Åre to the nearby winter-sports centre of Duved (Skr28, 15 minutes, several daily). Bus 571 connects Duved to Storlien (Skr90, one hour). Regular trains between Stockholm and Storlien, via Östersund, stop at Åre (Skr939, seven hours).

Umeå

☑090 / POP 114,000

With the vibrant feel of a college town (it has around 30,000 students), Umeå is a welcome outpost of urbanity in the barren north. It's one of the fastest-growing towns in Sweden and an agreeable place to hang out, wind down or stock up for an outdoor adventure.

◉ Sights & Activities

There are interesting offshore islands plus a number of activities in the surrounding area, including fishing, rafting, jet-boating and canoeing in or on the local rivers, horse riding and a variety of walking trails. The tourist office can help organise these.

FREE Gammlia — MUSEUM COMPLEX

(☑17 18 00; ⊙10am-5pm mid-Jun–mid-Aug) This cluster of museums 1km east of the town centre includes the cultural and historical exhibits and Sámi collections of the regional **Västerbottens Museum**; the modern art museum, **Bildmuseet**; and the **Maritime Museum**. These are surrounded by **Friluftsmuseet**, an open-air historic village where staff wear period clothes and describe traditional homestead life.

🍴 Sleeping & Eating

Hotel Aveny — HOTEL €€€

(☑13 41 00; Rådhusesplanaden 14; s/d Skr1595/1795) Hotel Aveny has a techno-sleek decor scheme, vivid with all the colours of the neon rainbow. Rooms are modern and comfortable; suites contain jacuzzis. There's a bar and an Italian restaurant on the grounds.

STF Vandrarhem Umeå — HOSTEL €

(☑77 16 50; info@umeavandrarhem.com; Västra Esplanaden 10; dm Skr160, s/d from Skr260/320;@) Rooms are tiny but comfortable at this busy and efficient youth hostel, one of the few in the region that's actually occupied by youth. It's in a great location, a residential neighbourhood at the edge of the town centre.

Hotel Pilen — HOTEL €€

(☑14 14 60; Pilgatan 5; s/d Skr695/895) This smallish boutique hotel has comfortable, unfussy rooms located in a quiet area some 600m from the town centre and close to the river. There's also a good restaurant attached.

Rost Mat & Kaffe — COFFEE HOUSE €

(Rådhusesplanaden 4B; soups Skr65; ⊙11am-6pm Mon-Fri, 11am-4pm Sat) This teeny industrial-chic coffee shop is covered in tiles and doles out good espresso and light meals.

ⓘ Information

Tourist office (☑16 16 16; www.visitumea.se; Renmarkstorget 15)

ⓘ Getting There & Away

Air

The **airport** is 4km south of the city centre. SAS and Malmö Aviation each fly to Stockholm up to seven times daily; there are also direct flights to Luleå, Göteborg and Örebro.

Boat

RG Line (www.rgline.com) operates ferries between Umeå and Vaasa (Finland) once or twice daily (Sunday to Friday). A bus to the port leaves from near the tourist office an hour before RG Line's departures.

Bus

The long-distance bus station is directly opposite the train station. Ybuss runs services south up to three times daily to Gävle (Skr375, seven hours) and Stockholm (Skr415, nine hours), via the coastal towns of Örnsköldsvik, Härnösand, Sundsvall, Hudiksvall and Söderhamn.

Umeå is the main centre for **Länstrafiken i Västerbotten** (020-91 00 19; www.ltnbd. se), the regional bus network. Direct buses to Mo i Rana (Norway) run once daily (bus 300, eight hours), but buses going as far as Tärnaby (Skr250, 5½ hours) run up to four times a day. Other destinations include Östersund (Skr350, 6½ hours, three daily), Skellefteå (Skr175, two hours, several daily) and Luleå (Skr300, 4¾ hours, several daily).

Train

Tågkompaniet trains leave daily from Umeå, to connect at Vännäs with the north–south trains between Stockholm (Skr1300, eight hours, four daily) and Luleå (Skr278, five hours, once daily); northbound trains stop in Boden, from where there are connections to Kiruna (Skr604, nine hours, twice daily) and Narvik (Norway).

Luleå

0920 / POP 45,100

Luleå is a pretty town with several parks and a sparkling bay surrounded by a marina. It's the capital of Norrbotten, chartered in 1621; the town centre moved to its present location in 1649 because of the falling sea level (9mm per year), due to postglacial uplift of the land. An extensive offshore archipelago contains some 1700 large and small islands.

Unesco World Heritage–listed Gammelstad (45 70 10; www.lulea.se/gammelstad; admission free; 24hr), or 'Old Town', contains row after zigzaggy row of cute little red-and-white cottages. This was the medieval centre of northern Sweden. The stone church (from 1492), 424 wooden houses (where the pioneers stayed overnight on their weekend pilgrimages) and six church stables remain. Many of the buildings are still in use, but some are open to the public, and the site is lovely to walk around.

Guided tours (Skr30) leave from the Gammelstad tourist office (25 43 10; worldheritage.gammelstad@lulea.se; 9am-6pm mid-Jun–mid-Aug) every hour on the hour between 10am and 4pm, mid-June to mid-August. (Tours are given in the language

of whoever booked first, so you may have to wait an hour for one in English.) Bus 32 runs hourly from Luleå.

Norrbottens Museum (24 35 02; Storgatan 2; admission free; 10am-4pm Mon-Fri, noon-4pm Sat & Sun), inside the pretty Hermelins park, is worth a visit for the Sámi section, but there are also exhibits about the Swedish settlers, plus films and musical performances, an outdoor maze and a kids' playground.

Boat tours of the archipelago depart from Södra Hamn daily between June and August; typical prices are around Skr350 to Skr500 for adults, Skr150 to Skr200 for children. Evening cruises are also popular; pick up a brochure at the tourist office.

🛏 Sleeping & Eating

SVIF Vandrarhem Kronan/ Luleå   HOSTEL €

(43 40 50; www.vandrarhemmetkronan.se; Kronan H7; dm/s/d/tr Skr175/270/390/560; @) About 3km from the centre, this year-round hostel is the best budget option in the area, with good facilities set in a forested location. To get here, take any bus heading towards Kronanområdet.

Amber Hotel   HOTEL €€

(102 00; www.amber-hotell.se; Stationsgatan 67; s/d Skr790/980) The pick of the city-centre hotels is this small wooden guesthouse; its spacious rooms have all the modern touches, flat-screen TVs etc, but still feel homey. It's just a few steps from the train station.

Cafe Mat & Prat   CAFE €

(28 11 90; Storgatan 51; mains Skr50-80; 10am-6pm Mon-Fri, 10am-4pm Sat) Sure, it's inside a shopping mall, but practically everything this far north is inside a shopping mall; it's dark and freezing most of the year here. This cheery cafe is pleasant and homey, serving real espresso as well as pasta, focaccia, sandwiches, salads and a good Thai curry.

ℹ Information

Tourist office (45 70 00; www.lulea.se; 10am-7pm Mon-Fri, 10am-4pm Sat & Sun) Inside Kulturens Hus.

ℹ Getting There & Around

The airport is 9km southwest of the town centre. SAS, Direktflyg and Nordic Airways fly regularly to Stockholm, Sundsvall and Umeå. Other airlines serve smaller destinations, including

Pajala. Take the **airport bus** (📞122 00; Skr45) from outside the Comfort Hotel on Storgatan.

Bus 100 operates between Haparanda, Luleå, Skellefteå, Umeå and Sundsvall at least four times daily. Buses run frequently to Boden (Skr55, one hour), Arvidsjaur (Skr170, three hours, via Boden and Älvsbyn) and Jokkmokk (Skr185, three hours) and on to Gällivare (via Boden and Vuollerim).

Direct Tågkompaniet trains from Stockholm and Göteborg operate at night only. Most trains from Narvik and Kiruna via Boden terminate at Luleå.

Haparanda
📞0922 / POP 10,500

Bargain-hunters' alert! Haparanda has become a full-scale shoppers' paradise, thanks to a 2005 decision to build an Ikea store in this tiny town nestled up against Finland. The furniture giant's arrival rescued the town's economy and encouraged other businesses (mainly big-box retail stores) to invest as well.

Haparanda's primary attraction, other than shopping, is its Green Zone Golf Course (📞106 60), on the border with Finland. During a full round of golf the border is crossed four times. Around Midsummer you can play under the midnight sun; book in advance.

The tourist office can arrange rafting trips on the scenic Kukkolaforsen rapids. There's a small tourist village here, which includes a camping ground and cabins (📞310 00; campsites Skr190, 4-bed cabins from Skr590), plus there is a restaurant, a cafe, fish smoke-house, saunas and a museum.

The waterfront Vandrarhem Haparanda (📞611 71; www.haparandavandrarhem.com; Strandgatan 26; dm/s/d from Skr200/325/480; ⊙year-round, reception 4-7pm) is at the edge of a park close to the town centre. Some rooms have private bathroom and TV.

The main tourist office (📞120 10; www.haparandatornio.com; Green Line; ⊙8am-8pm Mon-Fri, 10am-6pm Sat & Sun) in Haparanda is shared with the office in Tornio (in Finland) on the 'green line'.

Tapanis Buss (📞129 55; www.tapanis.se) runs express coaches from Stockholm to Haparanda two to three times a week (Skr600, 15 hours). Regional buses reach Luleå (Skr134, 2½ hours, three daily) and towns further south.

Arvidsjaur
📞0960 / POP 7000

The small settlement of Arvidsjaur, on Inlandsbanan, was established as a Sámi marketplace, but it's most famous now as a testing ground for fast machines. Local companies specialise in setting up test tracks on the frozen lakes in the area, then putting vehicles through their paces.

The first church was built in Arvidsjaur in 1607, in hopes of introducing the Sámi to Christianity. Church attendance laws imposed a certain amount of pew time upon the nomadic Sámi, so to make their church visits more manageable they built small cottages, or *gåhties,* for staying overnight. Some 80 of these are preserved now in Lappstaden (admission free, tours Skr30; ⊙10am-7pm, tours 5pm Jun-Aug), just across Storgatan from the modern church. The buildings are owned by the forest Sámi and are still in use.

Friendly accommodation can be found at Lappugglans Turistviste (📞124 13; lappugglan@hem.utfors.se; Västra Skolgatan 9; dm Skr150; 🅿), a hostel with a likeable hippie vibe, or at Hotell Edström (📞96 01 71 00; www.hotelledstrom.se; cnr Stationsgatan & Skomakargatan; s/d from Skr800; 🅿), a 52-room hotel off the main drag with a flowery, vaguely British style, amiable staff and a trio of restaurants (Scottish pub, steakhouse, Japanese grill) to choose from.

The tourist office (📞175 00; www.arvidsjaur.se; Östra Skolgatan 18C; ⊙9.30am-6pm Mon-Fri, noon-4.30pm Sat & Sun Jun-Aug) is just off Storgatan.

Länstrafiken Norrbotten bus 45 goes daily between Gällivare and Östersund, stopping at the bus station on Storgatan. Bus 200 runs daily between Skellefteå and Bodø (Norway) via Arvidsjaur. In summer the Inlandsbanan train can take you north to Gällivare (Skr352) via Jokkmokk, or south to Mora via Östersund (Skr610).

Jokkmokk
📞0971 / POP 5600

Jokkmokk is an important town in Sámi culture, not only due to the definitive Sámi museum but also because it is home to an enormous annual market gathering. Just north of the Arctic Circle, it's a quiet little town that makes a nice base for visitors to the Laponia World Heritage site; ask for information about the area at the tourist office.

The illuminating Ájtte Museum (☎170 70; Kyrkogatan 3; adult/child Skr60/ free; ⊙9am-6pm mid-Jun–mid-Aug, 10am-4pm Tue-Fri & 10am-2pm Sat & Sun rest of yr) gives a thorough introduction to Sámi culture, including traditional costume, silverware and some 400-year-old magical painted shamans' drums. Look for replicas of sacrificial sites and a diagram explaining the uses and significance of various reindeer entrails. One section details the widespread practice of harnessing the rivers in Lappland for hydroelectric power and the consequences this has had for the Sámi people and their territory. There are extensive notes in English.

🛏 Sleeping & Eating

STF Vandrarhem Åsgård HOSTEL €
(☎559 77; asgard@jokkmokkhostel.com; Åsgatan 20; dm Skr125, s Skr310; ⊙reception 8-10am & 5-8pm; @) The STF hostel has a lovely setting among green lawns and trees, near the tourist office; it's a comfortable place with numerous bunk beds, kitchen, TV lounge and showers in the basement. Thin walls make the place a little noisy when crowded.

Hotell Gästis HOTEL €€
(☎100 12; www.hotell-gastis.com; Herrevägen 1; s/d/tr from Skr950/1195/1300; P) This place has pleasant rooms in a small grey building. Meals are available.

Café Glasskas CAFE €
(Porjusvägen 7; mains Skr35-75) A coffee shop, bar and internet cafe, Glasskas has a great, wide patio for warm-weather dining, casual but filling meals (salads, quiches, sandwiches etc) and friendly service.

TOP CHOICE **Ájtte museum restaurant** SÁMI €€
(mains Skr85-120; ⊙noon-4pm) At the museum cafe, it's possible to enhance what you've learned about the local wildlife by sampling some of them as a lunch special. Sámi cooking generally involves smoked or salted reindeer and fish, as well as elk and other game and locally picked berries. The cafe serves a daily lunch special as well as à la carte meals.

ℹ Information

Tourist office (☎121 40; www.turism.jokk mokk.se; Stortorget 4; ⊙9am-7pm Mon-Fri, 10am-6pm Sat & Sun mid-Jun–Aug) Has internet access.

ℹ Getting There & Away

Buses arrive and leave from the bus station on Klockarvägen. Buses 44 and 45 run twice daily to and from Gällivare (Skr110, one to three hours), and bus 45 goes to and from Arvidsjaur once a day (Skr170, two to three hours). Bus 94 runs to Kvikkjokk (Skr140, two hours) twice daily.

In summer, Inlandsbanan trains stop in Jokkmokk. For main-line trains, take bus 94 to Murjek via Vuollerim (Skr70, one hour, up to six times daily) or bus 44 bus to Boden and Luleå (Skr170, two to three hours).

Gällivare & Malmberget

☑0970 / POP 19,500

Gällivare and its northern twin, Malmberget, are surrounded by forest and dwarfed by the bald Dundret hill. After Kiruna, Malmberget ('Ore Mountain') is the second-largest iron-ore mine in Sweden; the town belongs to government-owned mining company LKAB. And like Kiruna, the area's sustaining industry is simultaneously threatening the town with collapse: all that digging around below the surface has weakened the foundations beneath Malmberget, so buildings are gradually being shifted to sturdier ground. The populace seems unfazed.

◎ Sights & Activities

Dundret (821m) is a nature reserve with excellent views, and you can see the midnight sun here from 2 June to 12 July. In winter there are four Nordic courses and 10 ski runs of varying difficulty, and the mountaintop resort rents out gear and organises numerous activities. If you have your own car, it's a rather hair-raising drive to the top. You can also book a tour by taxi, via the tourist office or online at www.gellivaretaxi.se.

In Malmberget, 5km north of Gällivare, **Kåkstan** (admission free) is a historical 'shanty town' museum village, dating from the 1888 iron-ore rush. Contact the Gällivare tourist office for details of the **LKAB iron-ore mine tour** (from Skr250; 9.30am-1pm mid-Jun–mid-Aug, by appointment in winter), which takes you down on a bus. And if you like that, you'll love the **Gruvmuseum** (Puoitakvägen; adult/child Skr50/ free; ⊙2-6pm Tue-Thu mid-Jul–late Aug, by appointment otherwise), covering 250 years of mining. Bus 1 to Malmberget departs from directly opposite the Gällivare church; outside summer hours, contact the Gällivare tourist office to arrange a visit.

🛏 Sleeping & Eating

Grand Hotel Lapland
HOTEL €€

(☑77 22 90; www.grandhotellapland.com; Lasarettsgatan 1; s/d from Skr1295/1675) A modern hotel opposite the train station, with comfortable rooms and a restaurant–pub on site.

Restaurang Husmans
ARABIC €

(Malmbergsvägen 1; mains from Skr65; ⊘9am-9pm Mon-Fri, 11am-8pm Sat & Sun) Close to the tourist office and behind Hotel Lapland; serves kebabs and salads and in the evenings has a small dining nook where you can get Arabic food.

ℹ Information

Tourist office (☑166 60; turistinfo@gellivare.se; Centralplan 3; ⊘8am-6pm daily mid-Jun–mid-Aug, Mon-Fri rest of yr) Near the train station.

ℹ Getting There & Away

Regional buses depart from the train station. Bus 45 runs daily to Östersund (Skr465, 11 hours) via Jokkmokk and Arvidsjaur; bus 93 serves Ritsem (Skr200, three hours) and Kungsleden in Stora Sjöfallet National Park (mid-June to mid-September only); buses 10 and 52 go to Kiruna (Skr130, two hours); and bus 44 runs to Jokkmokk and Luleå (Skr230, three hours).

Tågkompaniet (☑0771-44 41 11; www.tagkompaniet.se, in Swedish) trains come from Luleå and Stockholm (sometimes changing at Boden), and from Narvik in Norway. More exotic is the summer-only **Inlandsbanan** (☑0771-53 53 53; www.inlandsbanan.se), which terminates at Gällivare.

Kiruna

☑0980 / POP 23,400

Kiruna's citizens live up to their nickname – 'the no-problem people' – by remaining unperturbed at the news that their city is on the verge of collapsing into a mine pit. A few years back, it became clear that years of iron-ore extraction was sucking the stability out of the bedrock underneath the town. In 2007 the town voted to shift itself a couple of miles northwest in order to allow the mining activity to continue; LKAB, the mining company, is largely funding the project. Plans are to move the railway, church and about 450 homes by 2013, with the rest of the town centre to follow gradually.

A visit to the depths of the LKAB iron-ore mine, 540m underground, is recommended – some of the stats you'll hear on a tour are mind-blowing. Tours leave daily from the tourist office, more frequently from mid-June to mid-August (from Skr195; prices vary depending on time of year, group size and tour length). Tours in English happen only a few times a week (currently, 3pm Wednesday and Friday); make bookings through the tourist office.

Every winter at Jukkasjärvi, 18km east of Kiruna, the amazing Ice Hotel (www.icehotel.com) is built from hundreds of tonnes of ice from the frozen local river. This custom-built 'igloo' has a chapel and a bar – you can drink from a glass made of ice – and ice-sculpture exhibitions. It also has 50 'hotel rooms' outfitted with reindeer skins and sleeping bags guaranteed to keep you warm despite the –5°C temperatures (and in winter that's nothing; outside the hotel it can be as low as –30°C). You can also book activities through the hotel, such as snowmobiling tours and classes, night hikes, dogsled tours and winter wildlife safaris (from Skr550 per person).

Also in Jukkasjärvi is Gárdi (adult/child Skr60/30; ⊘tours 10am-6pm mid-Jun–mid-Aug), a reindeer yard that you can tour with a Sámi guide to learn about reindeer farming and Sámi culture. Regular bus 501 runs between Kiruna and Jukkasjärvi (Skr29, 30 minutes, several daily).

🛏 Sleeping

Rådhusbyn Ripan Hotell & Camping
CAMPING GROUND, HOTEL €€

(☑630 00; www.ripan.se; Campingvägen 5; campsites/s/d from Skr135/1450/1610, cabins from Skr995; @≋) In the northern part of town, this is a large and well-equipped camping ground with hotel rooms and chalets in addition to its caravan and campsites. Ask about the organised walk to Samegården, the museum of Sámi culture (Skr450, 1pm Fridays), and other interesting activities.

Hotel Vinterpalatset
HOTEL €€

(☑677 70; info@vinterpalatset.se; Järnvägsgatan 18; s/d from Skr800/950; @) Inside this dark-brown wooden building near the train station are pretty, spacious B&B rooms, each with a TV and modern bathroom, plus an upstairs lounge and a breakfast room almost flowery enough to make you think you're in the Cotswolds. The decadent breakfast buffet includes cured salmon and roast game.

Ice Hotel
HOTEL €€€

(☎98 06 68 00; www.icehotel.com; Jukkasjärvi; cold rooms s/d from Skr1900/2800, warm rooms s/d from Skr1600/2300) From early December to late April you can snuggle up between reindeer furs on a bed of snow and ice in the igloo-like 'cold rooms' of the Ice Hotel. The hotel promises the rooms never get colder than about −8°C, but it's advisable to book only one night at a time in the cold room and spend the rest in the toasty main building.

SVIF Yellow House
HOSTEL €

(☎137 50; www.yellowhouse.nu; Hantverkaregatan 25; dm/s/d Skr170/350/440) The SVIF hostel also has budget hotel rooms; the excellent facilities include a sauna, kitchen and laundry, a TV in each room, and a nice, quiet enclosed garden.

✗ Eating

Café Safari
CAFE €

(Geologsgatan 4; sandwiches/focaccia/pasta salads Skr35/60/68; ☺lunch & dinner daily, to 9pm Thu-Sat) This is the nicest cafe in town, a long skinny room with good French-press coffee, cakes and light meals such as sandwiches, quiche and baked potatoes.

Café Rost
CAFE €

(Folkets Hus, upstairs; mains Skr58-75) This cool, designy cafe above the tourist information office churns out filling lunch fare such as quiche and salad, as well as coffee and cakes.

❶ Information

The **tourist office** (☎188 80; www.lappland. se; Lars Janssonsgatan 17, in Folkets Hus; ☺8.30am-9pm Mon-Fri, 8.30am-6pm Sat & Sun Jun-Aug), on the main square, has computers for internet access (per hour Skr20) and can book mine tours and accommodation as well as various activities, including rafting, dog-sledding and snow-scooter trips. There's a cafe upstairs.

❶ Getting There & Away

The small airport, 7km east of the town, has two to three daily non-stop flights to Stockholm with SAS, and to Umeå (weekdays only) with Skyways. The **airport bus** (☎156 90) operates during peak summer season.

Regional buses to and from the **bus station** (Hjalmar Lundbohmsvägen), opposite the Stadshus, serve all major settlements around Norrbotten. Bus 10 runs twice daily to Gällivare (Skr140) and Luleå (Skr280), and 92 goes two to four times daily to Nikkaluokta (Skr75) for the Kebnekaise trailhead. To reach Karesuando and Finland, take bus 50 (Skr180, not Saturday).

Trains between Kiruna and Narvik have earned a reputation as unreliable and often late, so you'll want to plan around a flexible schedule. SJ connects Kiruna with Luleå (Skr316, four hours), Stockholm (from Skr920, overnight) and Narvik, Norway (Skr180, three hours). Trains to Narvik call at Abisko (Skr93, 1½ hours) and Riksgränsen.

Abisko
☎0980

Spectacular scenery, friendly people, a long tradition of Sámi culture and extremely easy access to all of the above make Abisko one of the highlights of any trip to Lappland. The 75-sq-km **Abisko National Park** spreads out from the southern shore of scenic Torneträsk lake. It's framed by the striking profile of Lapporten, a 'gate' formed by neighbouring hills that serves as the legendary gate to Lappland.

Abisko is less rugged than either Sarek or Padjelanta, and easier to get to by trains, buses and the scenic mountain motorway between Kiruna and Narvik. This is also the driest part of Sweden, giving the area a completely distinct landscape – it's wide open and arid, and consequently has a relatively long (for northern Sweden) hiking season.

Abisko has two train stops: Östra station puts you in the centre of the tiny, tiny village, while Abisko Turiststation is across the highway from the STF lodge.

The **STF Turiststation/Abisko Mountain Lodge** (☎402 00; www.abisko.nu) provides information on local hikes; **guides** (☺9am & 7-8pm) are available for consultation, and several **tours** (per person Skr395-995, Sámi camp tours Skr170; ☺8.40am-5pm) leave from here. There's a small shop with supplies, snacks and **equipment rentals** (☺8am-8pm Jun, 8am-10pm Jul & Aug), as well as a restaurant and hostel. From December through March, a chairlift takes you up local mountain Nuolja to the **Aurora Sky Station** (www.auroraskystation.se; round trip Skr690; ☺8pm-midnight Tue-Sat), one of the best places on earth to see the Northern Lights. It's safest to book in advance; overnight stays (Skr2390) can also be booked.

Naturum (☎401 77; ⊙9am-5pm mid-Jun–Sep) has an office and exhibition space next to STF Turiststation; staff can suggest hikes and answer questions about where to hike and what to bring. Various guided tours are available, mostly family oriented and free of charge, and a simple map offers suggestions based on available time ('if you have two hours...' etc).

🏃 Activities

Hiking is the big activity here – trails are varied in both distance and terrain, and they're easy to reach. Between the STF Turiststation and Naturum, you'll find all the expertise and equipment you need for everything from a day hike to a months-long trek along the popular Kungsleden.

The **Kungsleden** trail follows the Abiskojåkka valley, and day trips of 10km to 20km are no problem from Abisko. Kungsleden extends 450km south from Abisko to Hemavan, with STF huts serving most of the trail; the hut at Alesjaure is 15km from the trailhead.

For hikes in this area, use the map *Fjällkartan BD6* (Skr120), available at the STF lodge, Naturum and most sporting-goods stores.

🛏 Sleeping & Eating

Abisko Fjällturer   HOSTEL €
(☎401 03; www.abisko.net; dm from Skr200) Just behind the town, this is a backpackers' delight. The small hostel has basic accommodation and a wonderful wooden sauna. Brothers Tomas and Andreas keep a large team of sled dogs; one package includes a night's accommodation plus skiing, snowshoeing, a sauna and a dog-sled tour (Skr900). There are also very popular week-long sled trips (around Skr8000), which include all of your meals and accommodation – you will need to book very early for these. Follow signs from Abisko Östra to the 'Dog Hostel'.

STF Abisko Turiststation   HOSTEL €€
(☎402 00; www.abisko.nu; dm/d/q Skr250/720/960; ⊙8am-9pm 22 Dec–3 Jan, 15 Feb–4 May, 6 Jun–21 Sep; @) This huge place, which also serves as local information centre, has 300 beds in various configurations, from dorms to self-catering 'cabins', all kept to the usual high STF standards. Breakfast/lunch/dinner

are available for Skr85/85/295 (lunch is noon to 2pm, dinner 6pm to 8pm, à la carte 8pm to 9pm).

Self-service **STF huts** (dm Skr220-295) along Kungsleden are spread at 10km to 20km intervals between Abisko and Kvikkjokk; you'll need a sleeping bag. Campers are charged Skr40; non-members pay an extra Skr50 to Skr100 per night.

Lapporten Stormarknad (⊙9am-8pm Mon-Fri, shorter hr Sat & Sun), in Abisko village, is a grocery store that also carries a range of outdoor supplies, such as batteries, candles, bug spray and basic camping gear.

ℹ Getting There & Away

SJ trains run frequently between Luleå and Narvik and stop at both stations, Abisko Östra and Abisko Turiststation (Skr91, 1½ hours, four daily).

UNDERSTAND SWEDEN

History

Written records in Sweden survive only from the late Middle Ages, but the number of ancient fortifications, assembly places, votive sites and graves is impressive.

The Viking Age was under way by the 9th century, and vast repositories of Roman, Byzantine and Arab coins attest to the wealth and power that Swedish Vikings accumulated.

Internal squabbles whiled away the bulk of the Middle Ages until Denmark intervened and, together with Norway, joined Sweden in the Union of Kalmar in 1397, resulting in Danish monarchs on the Swedish throne.

A century of Swedish nationalist grumblings erupted in rebellion under the young nobleman Gustav Vasa. Crowned Gustav I in 1523, he introduced the Reformation and a powerful, centralised nation state. The resulting period of expansion gave Sweden control over much of Finland and the Baltic countries.

King Karl XII's adventures in the early 18th century cost Sweden its Baltic territories. The next 50 years saw greater parliamentary power, but Gustav III led a coup that brought most of the power back to the crown. An aristocratic revolt in 1809 fixed that (and lost Finland to Russia). The constitution produced in that year divided leg-

Sweden's approximately 15,000 indigenous Sámi people (sometimes incorrectly called Lapps) are a significant ethnic minority. These hardy nomadic people have for centuries occupied northern Scandinavia and northwestern Russia, living mainly from their large herds of domestic reindeer. These days, around 10% of Sámi live from reindeer husbandry, with many more having migrated to Sweden's urbanised, industrialised south in search of employment. The total population of around 60,000 Sámi still forms an ethnic minority in four countries: Norway, Sweden, Finland and Russia. The Sámi people refer to their country as Sápmi.

The history of relations between the Sámi and Nordic peoples is often dark. Until recently, the Sámi religious practice of shamanism was denigrated, and *noaidi* (Sámi spiritual leaders) were persecuted. Use of the Sámi language was discouraged. Today, despite improved mainstream attitudes, many Sámi still encounter prejudice. At an international Sámi youth conference held in October 2008, participants demanded that more be done to address the high level of youth suicide in the Sámi community.

Nature plays a crucial role in Sámi religious traditions, as does the singing of the *yoik* (also spelt *joik*), or 'song of the plains'. Briefly banned, it's now enjoying a resurgence in popularity. Sámi education is now available in government-run Sámi schools or regular municipal schools. Of the 6000 Sámi who still speak their mother tongue, 5000 speak the North Sámi dialect.

The booklet *The Saami – People of the Sun & Wind*, published by Ájtte, the Swedish Mountain and Saami Museum in Jokkmokk, describes Sámi traditions in all four countries of the Sápmi region and is available at tourist shops around the area.

islative powers between king and *riksdag* (parliament).

The Bernadottes & Beyond

During a gap in royal succession, Swedish agents chose Napoleon's marshal Jean-Baptiste Bernadotte (renamed Karl Johan) as regent. He became king of Norway and Sweden in 1818, and the Bernadotte dynasty still holds the Swedish monarchy.

Sweden declared itself neutral at the outbreak of WWI, but a British economic blockade caused food shortages and civil unrest. Consensus was no longer possible, and in 1921 a Social Democrat and Liberal coalition government took control for the first time. Reforms followed quickly; the new government introduced the eight-hour work day and suffrage for all adults over the age of 23.

The Social Democrats dominated politics after 1932. After the hardships caused by the Depression, they reworked the liberal tendencies of the 1920s and combined them with economic intervention policies to introduce Sweden's famed welfare state.

These trends were scarcely interrupted by Sweden's officially neutral (but in practice ambiguous) stance in WWII. The Social Democrats sponsored models for industrial bargaining and for full employment, which allowed the economy to blossom. The 1950s and '60s saw rapidly improved living standards for most Swedes.

Recent Years

Effects of the world recession of the early 1990s provoked frenzied speculation against the Swedish krona, forcing a massive devaluation of the currency. With both their economy and national confidence shaken, Swedes voted narrowly in favour of joining the European Union (EU), effective 1 January 1995.

Since then, Sweden's welfare state has undergone tough reforms and the economy has improved considerably, with falling unemployment and inflation. The country has remained outside the single European currency; a 2003 referendum on whether Sweden should adopt the euro resulted in a 'no' vote.

In October 2006, the long-entrenched Social Democrats lost their leadership position in parliament. The centre-right Alliance Party won the election, with new Prime Minister Fredrik Reinfeldt campaigning on a 'work first' platform.

The global economic crisis again affected Sweden towards the end of 2008; that year the Swedish krona dropped to its

PEACE, YO

In his will, Alfred Nobel (1833–96), the inventor of dynamite, used his vast fortune to establish the Nobel Institute and the international prizes, in 1901. This idea was reportedly sparked by an erroneous report in a French newspaper, a premature obituary in which the writer condemned Nobel for his explosive invention ('the merchant of death is dead,' it declared). Prizes are awarded annually for physics, chemistry, medicine and literature, as well as the Peace Prize. An awards ceremony is held in Stockholm on 10 December, while the Peace Prize is awarded in Oslo in the presence of the King of Norway.

weakest level since 2002. As ever, economic tensions fed social anxieties. An annual survey about ethnic diversity, conducted by Uppsala University researchers, indicated twice as many Swedes had an 'extremely negative' attitude towards racial diversity in 2008 than in 2005. (Researchers added, however, that Sweden is still well ahead of the rest of Europe in terms of encouraging diversity.)

The Swedes

Sweden's population is relatively small given the size of the country – with 9.4 million people spread over the third-largest area in Western Europe, it has one of the lowest population densities on the continent. Most Swedes live in the large cities of Stockholm, Göteborg, Malmö and Uppsala. Conversely, the interior of Norrland is sparsely populated.

The majority of Sweden's population is considered to be of Nordic stock, thought to have descended from central and northern European tribes who migrated north after the end of the last Ice Age, around 10,000 years ago.

About 30,000 Finnish speakers form a substantial minority in the northeast, near Torneälven (the Torne river). More than 160,000 citizens of other Nordic countries live in Sweden.

Circa 17% of Sweden's population are either foreign born or have at least one non-Swedish parent. Most immigrants have come from other European countries, including Russia, the former Yugoslavia, Poland and Greece. The largest non-European ethnic group consists of Assyrian/Syriac people. Chile and Somalia also have a sizeable presence, and there are around 45,000 Roma.

Swedish music stars José González and Salem Al Fakir and film director Josef Fares are testament to Sweden's increasingly multicultural make-up. In 2007, the small town of Södertälje, 30km south of Stockholm, welcomed 1268 Iraqi refugees; the USA and Canada combined accepted just 1027 the same year. Some 200 languages are now spoken in Sweden.

Sweden first opened its borders to mass immigration during WWII. At the time it was a closed society, and new arrivals were initially expected to assimilate and 'become Swedish'. In 1975 parliament adopted a new set of policies that emphasised the freedom to preserve and celebrate traditional native cultures.

Not everyone in Sweden is keen on this idea, with random hate crimes – including the burning down of a Malmö mosque in 2004 – blemishing the country's reputation for tolerance. As hip-hop artist Timbuktu (himself the Swedish-born son of a mixed-race American couple) told the *Washington Post,* 'Sweden still has a very clear picture of what a Swede is. That no longer exists – the blond, blue-eyed physical traits. That's changing. But it still exists in the minds of some people.'

The Arts

Art

Sweden's 19th-century artistic highlights include the warm art nouveau oil paintings of Carl Larsson (1853–1919), the nudes and portraits of Anders Zorn (1860–1920), August Strindberg's violently moody seascapes, and the nature paintings of Bruno Liljefors (1860–1939). Carl Milles (1875–1955) is Sweden's greatest sculptor, once employed as Rodin's assistant.

Literature

Well-known Swedish writers include the poet Carl Michael Bellman (1740–95), playwright August Strindberg (1849–1912) and children's writer Astrid Lindgren (1907–2002). Vilhelm Moberg (1898–1973) won international acclaim with *Utvandrarna*

(The Emigrants; 1949) and *Nybyggarna* (The Settlers; 1956). More recently, Stieg Larsson's Millennium trilogy (*The Girl with the Dragon Tattoo* et al) has been a worldwide phenomenon and has inspired at least two feature-film adaptations.

Swedish Design

Sweden is a living gallery of inspired design, from Jonas Bohlin 'Tutu lamps' to Tom Hedquist milk cartons. While simplicity still defines the Nordic aesthetic, new designers are challenging Scandi functionalism with bold, witty work. A claw-legged 'Bird Table' by Broberg Ridderstråle and a table made entirely of ping-pong balls by Don't Feed the Swedes are two examples of playful creations from design collectives such as Folkform, DessertDesign and Defyra.

Aesthetic prowess also fuels Sweden's thriving fashion scene. Since the late 1990s and continuing today, local designers have aroused global admiration: Madonna dons Patrik Söderstam trousers, and Acne Jeans sell like hot cakes at LA's hip Fred Segal. In fact, these days Sweden is exporting more fashion than pop.

Swedish Cinema

Swedish cinema is inextricably linked with the name of Ingmar Bergman. His deeply contemplative films *(The Seventh Seal; Through a Glass Darkly; Persona)* explore alienation, the absence of god, the meaning of life, the certainty of death and other light-hearted themes. Recently, Trollhättan and Ystad have become film-making centres, thanks to younger directors like Lukas Moodysson, whose *Lilja 4-Ever, Fucking Åmål* and *Tillsammans* have all been hits. Director Tomas Alfredson's atmospheric teen-vampire film *Let the Right One In* also became a cult hit and inspired an American remake.

Pop Music

Any survey of Swedish music must at least mention ABBA, the iconic, dubiously outfitted winners of the 1974 Eurovision Song Contest (with 'Waterloo'). More current Swedish successes are pop icon Robyn, indie melody-makers Peter Björn & John, and the exquisitely mellow José González, whose cover of the Knife's track 'Heartbeats' catapulted the Göteborg native to international stardom.

Sweden occupies the eastern side of the Scandinavian peninsula, sharing borders with Norway, Finland and Denmark (the latter a mere 4km to the southwest of Sweden and joined to it by a spectacular bridge and tunnel).

Sweden's surface area (449,964 sq km) is stretched long and thin. Around one-sixth of the country lies within the Arctic Circle, yet Sweden is surprisingly warm thanks to the Gulf Stream: minimum northern temperatures are around –20°C (compared with –45°C in Alaska).

The country has a 7000km-long coastline, with myriad islands – the Stockholm archipelago alone has up to 24,000. The largest and most notable islands are Gotland and Öland on the southeast coast, and the best sandy beaches are down the west coast, south of Göteborg.

Forests take up 57% of Sweden's landscape. The Swedes aren't short of inland lakes, either, with around 100,000 lakes in all across the country. Vänern is the largest lake in Western Europe, at 5585 sq km. Kebnekaise (2111m), part of the glaciated Kjölen Mountains along the Norwegian border, is the highest mountain in the entire country of Sweden.

Wildlife

Thanks to Sweden's geographical diversity, it has a great variety of European animals, birds and plants. The big carnivores – bear, wolf, wolverine, lynx and golden eagle – are all endangered species. The elk (moose in the USA), a gentle, knobby-kneed creature that grows up to 2m tall, is the symbol of Sweden. Elk are a serious traffic hazard, particularly at night: they can dart out in front of your car at up to 50km/h. Around 260,000 domesticated reindeer, also no fun to run into on a highway, roam the northern areas, under the watchful eyes of Sámi herders. Forests, lakes and rivers support beaver, otter, mink, badger and pine marten, and hundreds of bird species populate the country.

National Parks

Sweden had the distinction of being the first country in Europe to establish a national park (1909). There are now 29, along with around 2600 smaller nature reserves; together they cover about 9% of the country. The organisation Naturvårdsverket oversees and produces pamphlets about the parks in Swedish and English, along with the excellent book *Nationalparkerna i Sverige* (National Parks in Sweden), which you can buy or download from www.swed ishepa.se.

Four of Sweden's large rivers (Kalixälven, Piteälven, Vindelälven and Torneälven) have been declared National Heritage Rivers in order to protect them from hydroelectric development.

Green Sweden

Ecological consciousness in Sweden is very high and reflected in concern for native animals, clean water and renewable resources. Swedes are fervent believers in sorting and recycling household waste – you'll be expected to do the same in hotels, hostels and camping grounds. Most plastic bottles and cans can be recycled – supermarket disposal machines give Skr0.50 to Skr1 per item.

Sweden makes it easy to be a responsible traveller: recycling is practically effortless, as bins and sorting instructions are everywhere, from hotel rooms to highway rest stops. There's a high level of general environmental consciousness in the country. Two organisations that set standards for labelling products as ecologically sound are the food-focused KRAV (www.krav.se), a member of the International Federation of Organic Agriculture Movements, and Swan (www.svanen.se), which has a wider scope and certifies entire hotels and hostels.

Aside from environmental concerns, one of Sweden's biggest challenges is protecting the cultural heritage of the Sámi people. The two issues are closely linked: the harnessing of rivers for hydroelectric power can have massive (negative) impact on what has historically been Sámi territory, whether by flooding reindeer feeding grounds or by diverting water and drying up river valleys. In general, the mining, forestry and space industries have wreaked havoc on Sámi homelands. Travellers interested in learning more and experiencing Sámi culture are encouraged to look for the 'Naturens Bäst' logo, which indicates that an excursion or organisation has been approved by Svenska Ekoturismföreningen (www.ekoturism.org, in Swedish), the country's first ecotourism regulating body.

Swedish Cuisine

Epicureans around the world are smitten with Sweden's new-generation chefs and their inventive creations. Current luminaries include Bocuse d'Or recipient Mathias Dahlgren, TV chef Niklas Ekstedt and New York–based Marcus Samuelsson.

Staples & Specialities

While new-school Swedish nosh thrives on experimentation, it retains firm roots in Sweden's culinary heritage. Even the most avant-garde chefs admire simple, old-school *husmanskost* (everyman cuisine) like *toast skagen* (toast with bleak roe, crème fraiche and chopped red onion), *köttbullar och potatis* (meatballs and potatoes, usually served with lingonberry jam, or *lingonsylt*), and *pytt i panna* (similar to hash). Seafood staples include caviar, gravlax (cured salmon) and the ubiquitous *sill* (herring), eaten smoked, fried or pickled and often accompanied by capers, mustard and onion. The most contentious traditional food is the pungent *surströmming* (fermented Baltic herring), traditionally eaten in August and September in a slice of *tunnbröd* (thin, unleavened bread) with boiled potato and onions and ample amounts of *snaps* (vodka).

Where to Eat & Drink

Most hotels and some hostels provide breakfast buffets laden with cereals and yogurt plus bread, fruit, cold cuts, cheese and the like. Many cafes and restaurants serve a daily lunch special called *dagens rätt* or *dagens lunch* at a fixed price (typically Skr75 to Skr95) between 11.30am and 2pm. The price includes main course, salad, bread, cold drink and coffee.

To counter the mid-afternoon slump, Swedes enjoy *fika,* an almost mandatory coffee break. *Konditori* are old-fashioned bakery–cafes where you can get a pastry or a *smörgås* (sandwich) from Skr35, but there are also many stylish, modern cafes where you can enjoy people-watching over pricier Italian coffees, gourmet salads, bagels and muffins.

Pure vegetarian restaurants (especially buffets) are increasingly common, and there will usually be at least one vegetarian main-course option on the menu at ordinary restaurants.

Habits & Customs

Generally speaking, dining traditions in Sweden don't differ much from the rest of Europe. When invited to someone's house for a meal, it's polite to bring flowers or a bottle of wine. Guests should remove their shoes in the foyer.

Locals tend to eat breakfast at home, lunch between 11.30am and 2pm and the evening meal between 6pm and 8pm, often later in larger cities.

Drinking

Lättöl (light beer, less than 2.25% alcohol) and *folköl* (folk beer, 2.25% to 3.5% alcohol) account for about two-thirds of all beer sold in Sweden and can be bought in supermarkets everywhere. *Mellanöl* (medium-strength beer, 3.6% to 4.5% alcohol), *starköl* (strong beer, over 4.5% alcohol) and wines and spirits can be bought only at outlets of the state-owned alcohol store, called Systembolaget, which is open until about 6pm on weekdays and slightly shorter hours on Saturday.

Sweden's trademark spirit, *brännvin*, also called aquavit and drunk as *snaps*, is a fiery and strongly flavoured drink that's usually distilled from potatoes and spiced with herbs.

The legal drinking age in Sweden is 18 years, although many bars and restaurants impose significantly higher age limits.

SURVIVAL GUIDE

Directory A–Z

Accommodation

Most hotels in Sweden offer steep discounts (up to 50%) on Friday and Saturday nights and from mid-May through August. Many hotels have also started using 'flexi' prices, discounts for rooms booked online ahead of time. In this chapter we list the standard price; what you'll actually pay may vary significantly. For the best deals, book early and online. Our Sleeping entries are listed by author preference and labelled according to the price of a standard double room with private bathroom in high season (June to August). Throughout this chapter, each place to stay is accompanied by one of the following symbols:

€€€ more than Skr1600

€€ Skr800 to Skr1600

€ less than Skr800

CABINS & CHALETS

Daily rates for *stugor* (cabins and chalets, often found at camping grounds or in the countryside) offer good value for small groups and families, and range in both quality and price (Skr350 to Skr950). Some are simple, with bunk beds and little else (you share the bathroom and kitchen facilities with campers); others are fully equipped with their own kitchen, bathroom and living room. Local and regional tourist offices have listings of cabins and cottages that may be rented by the week; these are often in idyllic forest, lakeside or coastal locations. See the Stuga (www.stuga.nu) website for more.

CAMPING

Sweden has hundreds of camping grounds; a free English-language guide with maps is available from tourist offices. Some are open year-round, but the best time for camping is from May to August. Prices vary with facilities, from Skr150 for a basic site to Skr350 for the highest standards. Most camping grounds have kitchens and laundry facilities, and many have the works – swimming pool, minigolf, bike and canoe rental, restaurant, store etc.

You must have a Camping Card Scandinavia to stay at most Swedish camping grounds. Apply for one in advance by writing to Sveriges Camping & Stugföretagares Riksorganisation (fax 0522-64 24 30; info@scr.se; Box 255, SE-45117 Uddevalla) or fill in the form on the website www.camping.se; otherwise pick up a temporary card at any Swedish camping ground. The card costs Skr125 a year. One card covers the whole family.

Visit www.camping.se for lots of useful information.

HOSTELS

Sweden has well over 450 hostels *(vandrarhem)*, usually with excellent facilities. Outside major cities, hostels aren't backpacker hang-outs but are used as holiday accommodation by Swedish families, couples or retired people. A related oddity is the frequent absence of dormitories, meaning you often have to rent a room rather than a bed. Some hostels also have singles and doubles with en suite bathrooms that are almost of hotel quality, for very reasonable rates. About 50%

of hostels open year-round; many others open from May to September, while some open only from mid-June to mid-August.

Be warned: Swedish hostels are virtually impossible to enter outside reception opening times, and these hours are frustratingly short (except in Stockholm and Göteborg): generally between 5pm and 7pm, occasionally also between 8am and 10am. The secret is to pre-book by telephone or online – reservations are highly recommended in any case, as hostels fill up fast.

Some 315 hostels are affiliated with Svenska Turistföreningen (STF; ☑08-463 21 00; www.svenskaturistforeningen.se), part of Hostelling International (HI). Holders of HI membership cards pay the same rates as STF members. Non-members can pay Skr50 extra (Skr100 at some mountain lodges), or join up at hostels. In this book we quote prices at STF hostels for members. Children aged under 16 years pay about half the adult price.

Around 190 hostels belong to STF's 'rival', Sveriges Vandrarhem i Förening (SVIF; ☑0413-55 34 50; www.svif.se). No membership is required and rates are similar to those of STF hostels. Most SVIF hostels have kitchens, but you sometimes need your own utensils. Pick up the free guide at tourist offices or SVIF hostels.

HOTELS

Sweden is unusual in that hotel prices tend to *fall* at weekends and in summer, sometimes by as much as 40% or 50%. In this book, we list standard rates unless noted. Many hotel chains also offer flex rates, which let you change your reservation details until the last minute, and lower rates for early booking online. Hotel prices include a breakfast buffet unless noted in individual reviews. Ask at tourist offices for the free booklet *Hotels in Sweden* or visit the website www.hotelsinsweden.net.

Activities

Sweden is a **canoeing and kayaking** paradise (canoes are more common). The national canoeing body is Svenska Kanotförbundet (Swedish Canoe Federation; ☑0155-20 90 80; www.kanot.com; Rosvalla, SE-61162 Nyköping). It provides general advice and produces a free, annual brochure listing 75 approved canoe centres that hire out canoes (for around Skr350/1500 per day/week).

Swedes love **hiking**, and there are thousands of kilometres of marked trails. European Long Distance Footpaths Numbers One and Six run from Varberg to Grövelsjön (1200km) and from Malmö to Norrtälje (1400km), respectively.

Nordkalottleden runs for 450km from Sulitjelma to Kautokeino (both in Norway), but passes through Sweden for most of its route. Finnskogleden is a 240km-long route along the border between Norway and the Värmland region in Sweden. The Arctic Trail (800km) is a joint development of Sweden, Norway and Finland and is entirely above the Arctic Circle; it begins near Kautokeino in Norway and ends in Abisko, Sweden. The most popular route is Kungsleden, in Lappland. Overnight huts and lodges are maintained by Svenska Turistföreningen (STF).

The best hiking time is between late June and mid-September, when trails are mostly snow-free. After early August the mosquitoes have gone.

Mountain trails in Sweden are marked with cairns, wooden signposts or paint on rocks and trees. Marked trails have bridges across all but the smallest streams, and wet or fragile areas are crossed on duckboards. Avoid following winter routes (marked by poles with red crosses), as they often cross lakes or marshes.

Large ski resorts cater mainly to downhill (alpine and telemark) **skiing and snowboarding**, but there's also cross-country. For resort reviews in English, visit www.goski.com and www.thealps.com. SkiStar (www.skistar.com) manages two of the largest places, Sälen and Åre, and has good information on its website.

Cross-country (Nordic) skiing opportunities vary, but the northwest usually has plenty of snow from December to April (but not much daylight in December and January). Kungsleden and other long-distance tracks provide great skiing. Practically all town areas (except those in the far south) have marked and often illuminated skiing tracks.

Business Hours

General opening hours are listed here, but there are variations (particularly in the largest cities where opening hours may be longer). Hours are listed in individual reviews where they differ substantially from these.

Banks 9.30am to 3pm Monday to Friday; some city branches open 9am to 5 or 6pm

Department stores 10am to 7pm Monday to Saturday (sometimes later), noon to 4pm Sunday

Government offices 9am to 5pm Monday to Friday

Museums Generally short opening hours, even in July and August; see individual destinations for more details

Restaurants Lunch from 11.30am to 2pm, dinner between 6pm and 10pm; often closed on Sunday and/or Monday

Shops 9am to 6pm Monday to Friday, 9am to 1pm Saturday

Supermarkets 8am or 9am to 7 or 9pm

Systembolaget (State-owned alcohol stores) 10am to 6pm Monday to Friday, 10am to 2pm (often to 5pm) Saturday, sometimes with extended hours on Thursday and Friday evenings

Tourist offices Usually open daily Midsummer to mid-August, 9am to 5pm Monday to Friday mid-August to Midsummer; see individual destinations for specific hours

Children

Sweden is a very easy, friendly place to travel with children. Museums almost always have dedicated playrooms with hands-on learning tools; restaurants are happy to bring out high-chairs and kids menus for parents; and people are just generally fond of kids here. Particularly in larger cities such as Stockholm and Göteborg, you'll have no trouble finding entertaining things to do with the family. Hostels generally have family rooms and camping grounds are often equipped with swimming pools and playgrounds so kids don't get bored.

Discount Cards

Seniors normally get discounts on entry to museums and other sights, cinema and theatre tickets, air tickets and other transport. No special card is required, but show your passport if asked for proof of age (the minimum qualifying age is generally 60 or 65).

Food

Restaurants in this chapter have been categorised by the price of an average main course, as follows:

€€€ more than Skr185

€€ Skr75 to Skr185

€ less than Skr75

Gay & Lesbian Travellers

Sweden recognises civil unions or 'registered partnerships' that grant general marriage rights to gay and lesbian couples.

Riksförbundet för homosexuellas, bisexuellas och transpersoners rättigheter (RFSL; ☎08-457 13 00; forbund@rfsl. se; Sveavägen 59, Box 350, SE-10126 Stockholm) National organisation for gay and lesbian rights.

QX (www.qx.se) Free monthly magazine in Stockholm, Göteborg, Malmö and Copenhagen.

Internet Access

Most hotels have wireless LAN connections, and some even have laptops you can borrow. Hostels and tourist offices frequently have at least one internet-enabled computer available for use, occasionally with a fee of Skr10 to Skr25 per hour.

Nearly all public libraries offer free internet access, but often the timeslots are booked for days in advance by locals.

Internet cafes typically charge around Skr1 per online minute, or Skr50 per hour. Wireless internet is almost universal at coffee shops, train stations, bars, cafes and hotels, although often there's a fee for access.

Money

ATMs are everywhere and easy to find.

Currency The Swedish krona (plural: kronor), usually called 'crown' by Swedes speaking English, is denoted Skr (or SEK in Sweden) and divided into 100 öre. Coins are 50 öre (obsolete) and one, five and 10 kronor, and notes are 20, 50, 100, 500 and 1000 kronor.

Exchanging Money Forex (☎0200-22 22 20; www.forex.se) is the biggest foreign money exchange company in Sweden; it has branches in major airports, ferry terminals and city centres. There's a service fee of Skr15 per travellers cheque exchanged.

Taxes At shops that display the 'Tax Free Shopping' sign, non-EU citizens making single purchases of goods exceeding Skr200 are eligible for a VAT refund of up to 17.5% of the purchase price. Show your passport and ask the shop for a 'Global Refund Cheque', which should be presented along with your unopened purchases (within three months) at your departure point from the country (before you check in), to get export validation. You can then cash your cheque at any of the refund points, which are found at international airports and harbours. Ask at tourist offices about tax-free shopping through Global Refund, or call ☎545-284 40 for more information.

Tipping At restaurants, round up to nearest Skr10; in taxis, add Skr10 to Skr15.

Public Holidays

Many businesses close early the day before and all day after official public holidays, including the following:

Nyårsdag (New Year's Day) 1 January

Trettondedag Jul (Epiphany) 6 January

Långfredag, Påsk, Annandag Påsk (Good Friday, Easter Sunday & Monday) March/April

Första Maj (Labour Day) 1 May

Kristi Himmelsfärds dag (Ascension Day) May/June

Pingst, Annandag Pingst (Whit Sunday & Monday) Late May or early June

Midsommardag (Midsummer's Day) First Saturday after 21 June

Alla Helgons dag (All Saints' Day) Saturday, late October or early November

Juldag (Christmas Day) 25 December

Annandag Jul (Boxing Day) 26 December

Telephone

Most Swedes own a mobile phone, so there aren't many public phones and even fewer coin phones; all public telephones take Telia phonecards (Skr50 or Skr120 for 50 or 120 units), available at Pressbyrå shops.

For directory assistance dial ☎118118 (for numbers within Sweden) or ☎118119 (international), but note that these services aren't free.

Calls to Sweden from abroad require a country code (☎46) followed by the area code and telephone number (omitting the first zero in the area code). For international calls dial ☎00 followed by the country code and the local area code.

Swedish phone numbers have area codes followed by varying numbers of digits. You must use the area code when dialling from outside that area. Numbers beginning ☎020 or ☎0200 are free (but not from public phones or mobiles). Numbers beginning ☎077 are roughly the same price as a local call. Mobile phone numbers usually begin with ☎070.

Time

Sweden runs on Central European Time and generally uses the 24-hour clock. The country observes daylight-saving time (with changes in March and October).

Toilets

Public toilets in parks, shopping malls, libraries and bus or train stations are rarely free in Sweden. Except at the larger train stations (where an attendant is on duty), pay toilets are coin operated, and usually cost Skr5 to Skr10 (so keep coins handy). The exception is museums, where toilets usually are free and well maintained.

Tourist Information

Sweden has about 350 local tourist information offices. Most are open long hours in summer and short hours (or not at all) during winter.

FörTur (www.turism.se) Lists Sweden's tourist information offices and their contact details.

Swedish Travel Tourism Council (www.visitsweden.com) Useful information in many languages.

Travellers with Disabilities

Sweden is one of the easiest countries to travel around in a wheelchair. People with disabilities will find transport services with adapted facilities, ranging from trains to taxis, but contact the operator in advance for the best service. Public toilets and some hotel rooms have facilities for people with disabilities; **Hotels in Sweden** (www.hotelsinsweden.net) indicates whether hotels have adapted rooms.

De Handikappades Riksförbund (☎08-685 80 00; www.dhr.se; Katrinebergsvägen 6, Box 47305, SE-10074 Stockholm) National association for people with disabilities.

Visas

Sweden is one of 25 member countries of the Schengen Agreement, under which 22 EU countries (all but Bulgaria, Cyprus, Ireland, Romania and the UK) plus Iceland, Norway and Switzerland have abolished checks at common borders. Citizens of the

USA, Canada, Australia and New Zealand need a valid passport to visit Sweden, but do not need a visa for stays of less than three months. Citizens of EU countries and other Scandinavian countries with a valid passport or national identification card do not require visas. Other nationalities should check www.migrationsverket.se to see whether they require a visa before arriving in Sweden.

Getting There & Away

Air

The main airport is Stockholm Arlanda, which links Sweden with major European and North American cities. Göteborg Landvetter is Sweden's second-biggest international airport. Stockholm Skavsta (actually 100km south of Stockholm, near Nyköping) and Göteborg City both act as airports for the budget airline Ryanair. Stockholm's Västerås airport also serves Ryanair. For travelling between international airports and city centres, see Getting Around in the relevant sections in this chapter.

Göteborg City Airport (www.goteborgcityairport.se)

Göteborg Landvetter Airport (www.lfv.se)

Stockholm Arlanda Airport (www.arlanda.se)

Stockholm Skavsta Airport (www.skavsta-air.se)

Scandinavian Airlines System (SAS) is the regional carrier and has a good safety record. Most of the usual airlines fly into Sweden, including the following:

Air France (www.airfrance.com)

Blue1 (www.blue1.com)

British Airways (www.britishairways.com)

Lufthansa (www.lufthansa.com)

Ryanair (www.ryanair.com)

SAS (www.scandinavian.net)

Land

Direct access to Sweden by land is possible from Norway, Finland and Denmark (from Denmark via the Öresund toll bridge). Border-crossing formalities are nonexistent.

Train and bus journeys are also possible between Sweden and the Continent – these vehicles go directly to ferries. Include ferry fares (or Öresund tolls) in your budget if you're driving from continental Europe.

Long-distance bus operator Eurolines (www.eurolines.com) has an office inside the bus terminals in Sweden's three largest cities: Stockholm, Göteborg and Malmö. Full schedules and fares are listed on the company's website.

CONTINENTAL EUROPE

Eurolines services run between Sweden and several European cities. The Göteborg–London service (Skr1319, 30 hours, one to four times weekly) goes via Malmö, Copenhagen, Hamburg and Amsterdam or Brussels. There are also services from Göteborg to Berlin (Skr709, 17 hours, three weekly).

DENMARK

Eurolines runs buses between Stockholm and Copenhagen (Dkr285, nine hours, at least three per week), and between Göteborg and Copenhagen (Dkr205, 4½ hours, daily). Swebus Express (☑0200-21 82 18; www.swebusexpress.se) and GoByBus (☑0771-15 15 15; www.gobybus.se, in Swedish) both run regular buses on the same routes, and have discount fares for travel from Monday to Thursday. All companies offer student, youth (under 26) and senior discounts.

Öresund trains operated by Skånetrafiken (www.skanetrafiken.se) run every 20 minutes from 6am to midnight (and once an hour thereafter) between Copenhagen and Malmö (one-way Skr105, 35 minutes) via the bridge. The trains usually stop at Copenhagen's Kastrup airport.

From Copenhagen, it's necessary to change in Malmö for Stockholm trains. Six or seven services operate directly between Copenhagen and Göteborg (Skr330, four hours). Trains every hour or two connect Copenhagen, Kristianstad and Karlskrona. The X2000 high-speed trains are more expensive.

You can drive from Copenhagen to Malmö across the Öresund bridge on the E20 motorway. Tolls are paid at Lernacken, on the Swedish side, in either Danish or Swedish currency (single crossing per car Skr375), or by credit or debit card.

FINLAND

Frequent bus services run from Haparanda to Tornio (Skr15, 10 minutes). Tapanis Buss (☑0922-129 55; www.tapanis.se, in Swedish) runs express coaches from Stockholm to Tornio via Haparanda twice a week (Skr570, 15 hours).

Länstrafiken i Norrbotten (☎020-47 00 47; www.ltnbd.se) operates buses as far as Karesuando, from where it's only a few minutes' walk across the bridge to Kaaresuvanto (Finland). There are also regular regional services from Haparanda to Övertorneå (some continue to Pello, Pajala and Kiruna) – you can walk across the border at Övertorneå or Pello and pick up a Finnish bus to Muonio, with onward connections from there to Kaaresuvanto and Tromsø (Norway).

NORWAY

GoByBus (☎0771-15 15 15; www.gobybus. se, in Swedish) runs from Stockholm to Oslo (Skr425, 7½ hours, fives times daily) via Karlstad, and from Göteborg to Oslo (Skr265, four hours, seven daily). Swebus Express (☎0200-21 82 18; www.swebusexpress. se) has the same routes with similar prices.

In the north, buses run once daily from Umeå to Mo i Rana (eight hours) and from Skellefteå to Bodø (nine hours, daily except Saturday); for details, contact Länstrafiken i Västerbotten (☎0771-10 01 10; www.tabussen. nu) and Länstrafiken i Norrbotten (☎0771-10 01 10; www.ltnbd.se), respectively.

The main rail lines run from Stockholm to Oslo, from Göteborg to Oslo, from Stockholm to Östersund and Storlien (Norwegian trains continue to Trondheim), and from Luleå to Kiruna and Narvik.

Trains run daily between Stockholm and Oslo (Skr500 to Skr700, six to seven hours), and there's a night train from Stockholm to Narvik (Skr810, about 20 hours). You can also travel from Helsingborg to Oslo (Skr750, seven hours), via Göteborg. The X2000 high-speed trains are more expensive.

Sea

Ferry connections between Sweden and its neighbours are frequent and straightforward. Most lines offer substantial discounts for seniors, students and children, and many rail-pass holders also get reduced fares. Most prices quoted in this section are for single journeys at peak times (weekend travel, overnight crossings, mid-June to mid-August); at other times, fares may be up to 30% lower.

DENMARK
Helsingør to Helsingborg

This is the quickest route and has frequent ferries (crossing time around 20 minutes). HH-Ferries (☎042-19 80 00; www.hhferries.se) 24-hour service. Pedestrian/car and up to nine passengers Skr30/385.

Scandlines (☎042-18 63 00; www.scandlines. se) Similar service and prices to HH-Ferries.

Göteborg to Frederikshavn

Stena Line (☎031-704 00 00; www.stenaline. se) Three-hour crossing. Up to six ferries daily. Pedestrian/car and five passengers/ bicycle Skr195/1535/375.

Stena Line (Express) Two-hour crossing. Up to three ferries daily. Pedestrian/car and five passengers/bicycle Skr300/1795/400.

Varberg to Grenå

Stena Line (☎031-704 00 00; www.stenaline. se) Four-hour crossing. Three or four daily. Pedestrian/car and five passengers/bicycle Skr195/1535/285.

Ystad to Rønne

BornholmsTrafikken (☎0411-55 87 00; www. bornholmstrafikken.dk) Conventional (1½ hours) and fast (80 minutes) services, two to nine times daily. Pedestrian/car and five passengers/bicycle from €24/141/26.

EASTERN EUROPE

To/from Estonia, Tallink (☎08-666 6001; www.tallink.ee, in Estonian) runs the routes Stockholm–Tallinn and Kapellskär–Paldiski.

Scandlines (☎08-5206 02 90; www.scand lines.dk) operates Ventspils–Nynäshamn ferries around five times per week.

To/from Lithuania, Lisco Line (☎0454-33680; www.lisco.lt) operates daily between Karlshamn and Klaipėda.

To/from Poland, Polferries (☎040-121700; www.polferries.se) and Unity Line (☎0411-556900; www.unityline.pl) have daily Ystad–Świnoujście crossings. Polferries also runs from Nynäshamn to Gdańsk. Stena Line (☎031-704 0000; www.stenaline.se) sails from Karlskrona to Gdynia.

FINLAND

Helsinki is called Helsingfors in Swedish, and Turku is Åbo.

Stockholm–Helsinki and Stockholm–Turku ferries run daily throughout the year via the Åland islands (exempt from the abolition of duty-free within the EU, making them a popular outing for Swedes). These ferries have minimum age limits; check before you travel.

Stockholm to Helsinki

Silja Line (☎08-22 21 40; www.silja.com) Around 15 hours. Ticket and cabin berth from about €130.

Viking Line (☎08-452 40 00; www.vikingline. fi) Operates the same routes with slightly cheaper prices (from €100).

Stockholm to Turku

RG Line (☎090-18 52 00; www.rgline.com) Runs the routes Sundsvall–Vaasa and Umeå–Vaasa.

Silja Line (☎08-22 21 40; www.silja.com) Eleven hours. Deck place €11, cabins from €45; prices are higher for evening trips. From September to early May, ferries also depart from Kapellskär (90km northeast of Stockholm); connecting buses operated by Silja Line are included in the full-price fare.

Viking Line (☎08-452 40 00; www.vikingline. fi) Operates the same routes as Silja Line, with slightly cheaper prices. In high season it offers passage from both Stockholm and Kapellskär.

Stockholm to Åland Islands (Mariehamn)

Prices quoted are for passenger-only return trips.

Ånedin-Linjen (☎08-456 22 00; www. anedinlinjen.se, in Swedish) Six hours, daily. Couchette Skr115, berth from Skr355.

Birka Cruises (☎08-702 72 00; www.birka cruises.com) A 22-hour round-trip. One or two daily. Berth from Skr480. Prices include supper and breakfast.

Eckerö Linjen (☎0175-258 00; www.eckero linjen.fi) Runs to the Åland islands from Grisslehamn.

GERMANY
Trelleborg to Sassnitz

Scandlines (☎042-18 61 00; www.scandlines. se) A 3¾-hour trip. Two to five times daily. Pedestrian/car and up to nine passengers/ passenger with bicycle Skr145/1050/210. A fuel surcharge of Skr50 to Skr80 may be added.

Trelleborg to Rostock

Scandlines (☎042-18 61 00; www.scandlines. se) Six hours (night crossing 7½ hours). Two or three daily. Pedestrian/car and up to nine passengers/passenger with bicycle

Skr210/1160/245. A fuel surcharge of Skr50 to Skr80 may be added.

TT-Line (☎0410-562 00; www.ttline.com) Operates the same as Scandlines, with similar prices.

Trelleborg to Travemünde

TT-Line (☎0410-562 00; www.ttline.com) Seven hours. Two to five daily. Car and up to five passengers from Skr1350, Skr50 surcharge for bicycle. Berths are compulsory on night crossings.

Göteborg to Kiel

Stena Line (☎031-704 00 00; www.stenaline. se) 14 hours. One crossing nightly. Pedestrian/car and up to five passengers from Skr520/1390. Rates are flexible depending on how early you book and which cabin level you choose.

NORWAY

There's a daily overnight DFDS Seaways (☎031-65 06 80; www.dfdsseaways.com) ferry between Copenhagen and Oslo (from €120 per passenger), via Helsingborg. Passenger fares between Helsingborg and Oslo (14 hours) start at Skr1100 and cars Skr475, but the journey can't be booked online; you'll need to call. DFDS also sails from Göteborg to Kristiansand (Norway), three days a week (from seven hours); contact DFDS for prices.

A Color Line (☎0526-620 00; www.color line.com) ferry between Strömstad (Sweden) and Sandefjord (Norway) sails two to six times daily (2½ hours) year-round. Tickets cost from Nkr180 (rail passes get 50% discount).

Getting Around
Air

Domestic airlines in Sweden tend to use Stockholm Arlanda Airport (www.arlanda. se) as a hub, but there are 30-odd regional airports. Flying domestic is expensive on full-price tickets (usually between Skr1000 and Skr3000 for a single ticket), but substantial discounts are available on internet bookings, student and youth fares, off-peak travel, return tickets booked at least seven days in advance and low-price tickets for accompanying family members and seniors. It's worthwhile asking about standby fares.

Sweden's internal flight operators and their destinations include the following:

Malmö Aviation (☎040-660 29 00; www.malmoaviation.se) Göteborg, Stockholm and Umeå.

Scandinavian Airlines System (SAS; ☎0770-72 77 27; www.flysas.com) Arvidsjaur, Borlänge, Gällivare, Göteborg, Halmstad, Ängelholm-Helsingborg, Hemavan, Hultsfred, Jönköping, Kalmar, Karlstad, Kiruna, Kramfors, Kristianstad, Linköping, Luleå, Lycksele, Norrköping, Malmö, Mora, Örebro, Örnsköldsvik, Oskarshamn, Skellefteå, Stockholm, Storuman, Sundsvall, Sveg, Torsby, Trollhättan, Umeå, Vilhelmina, Visby and Västerås.

Skyways (☎0771 95 95 00; www.skyways.se) Arvidsjaur, Borlänge, Göteborg, Halmstad, Hemavan, Jönköping, Karlstad, Kramfors, Kristianstad, Linköping, Lycksele, Norrköping, Mora, Örebro, Skellefteå, Stockholm, Storuman, Sundsvall, Trollhättan, Vilhelmina and Visby.

Boat

CANAL BOAT

The canals provide cross-country routes linking the main lakes. The longest cruises, on the Göta Canal from Söderköping (south of Stockholm) to Göteborg, run from mid-May to mid-September, take at least four days and include the lakes between.

Rederiaktiebolaget Göta Kanal (☎031-15 83 11; www.gotacanal.se) operates three ships over the whole distance at fares from Skr9775 to Skr17,275 per person for a four-day cruise, including full board and guided excursions. For shorter, cheaper trips on the canal, contact tourist offices in the area.

FERRY

An extensive boat network and the five-day Båtluffarkortet boat passes (Skr420) open up the attractive Stockholm archipelago. Gotland is served by regular ferries from Nynäshamn and Oskarshamn, and the quaint fishing villages off the west coast can normally be reached by boat with a regional transport pass – enquire at the Göteborg tourist offices.

Bus

Swebus Express (☎0200-21 82 18; www.swebusexpress.se) has the largest network of express buses, but they serve only the southern half of the country (as far north as Mora in Dalarna). **Svenska Buss** (☎0771-67 67 67; www.svenskabuss.se) and **GoByBus** (☎0771-15 15 15; www.gobybus.se, in Swedish), formerly Säfflebussen, also connect many southern towns and cities with Stockholm; prices are often slightly cheaper than Swebus Express, but services are less frequent.

North of Gävle, regular connections with Stockholm are provided by several smaller operators, including **Ybuss** (☎0771-33 44 44; www.ybuss.se, in Swedish), which has services to Sundsvall, Östersund and Umeå.

You don't have to reserve a seat on Swebus Express services. Generally, tickets for travel between Monday and Thursday are cheaper, or if they're purchased over the internet, or more than 24 hours before departure. If you're a student or senior, it's worth asking about fare discounts; however, most bus companies will only give student prices to holders of Swedish student cards.

BUS PASSES

Good-value daily or weekly passes are usually available from local and regional transport offices, and many regions have 30-day passes for longer stays, or a special card for peak-season summer travel.

REGIONAL NETWORKS

The *länstrafik* bus networks are well integrated with the regional train system, with one ticket valid on any local or regional bus or train. Rules vary but transfers are usually free if used within one to four hours. Fares on local buses and trains are often identical.

Car & Motorcycle

Sweden has good-standard roads, and the excellent E-class motorways rarely have traffic jams.

AUTOMOBILE ASSOCIATIONS

The Swedish national motoring association is **Motormännens Riksförbund** (☎020-21 11 11; www.motormannen.se).

BRING YOUR OWN VEHICLE

If bringing your own car, you'll need your vehicle registration documents, unlimited third-party liability insurance and a valid driving licence. A right-hand drive vehicle brought from the UK or Ireland should have deflectors fitted to the headlights to avoid dazzling oncoming traffic. You must carry a reflective warning breakdown triangle.

DRIVING LICENCE

An international driving permit isn't necessary; your domestic licence will do.

HIRE

To hire a car you have to be at least 20 (sometimes 25) years of age, with a recognised licence and a credit card.

Fly-drive packages may save you money. International rental chains (such as Avis, Hertz and Europcar) are more expensive but convenient; all have desks at Stockholm Arlanda and Göteborg Landvetter airports and offices in most major cities. The best car-hire rates are generally from larger petrol stations (such as Statoil and OK-Q8) – look out for signs saying *biluthyrning* or *hyrbilar*.

Avis (☎0770-82 00 82; www.avisworld.com)

Europcar (☎020-78 11 80; www.europcar.com)

Hertz (☎0771-21 12 12; www.hertz-europe.com)

Mabi Hyrbilar (☎08-612 60 90; www.mabirent. se) National company with competitive rates.

OK-Q8 (☎020-85 08 50; www.okq8.se, in Swedish) Click on *hyrbilar* in the website menu to see car-hire pages.

Statoil (☎08-429 63 00; www.statoil.se/bilu thyrning, in Swedish) Click on *uthyrningssta- tioner* to see branches with car hire, and on *priser* for prices.

ROAD HAZARDS

In the northern part of Sweden, privately owned reindeer and wild elk are serious road hazards, particularly around dawn and dusk. Look out for black plastic bags tied to roadside trees or poles – this is a sign from local Sámi that they have reindeer herds grazing in the area. Report all incidents to police – failure to do so is an offence. Sandboxes on many roads may be helpful in mud or snow. Also, if driving in Göteborg and Norrköping watch out for trams.

ROAD RULES

The basic rules of the road conform to EU standards. In Sweden, you drive on and give way to the right. Headlights should always be dipped, but must be on at all times when driving. Seatbelt use is obligatory for the driver and all passengers. The maximum blood-alcohol limit is a stringent 0.02%, and random breath tests are not uncommon. The speed limit on motorways and remote highways is usually 110km/h. Police often use hand-held radar equipment and cam-

In Sweden, local transport is always linked with regional transport (*län- strafik*). Regional passes are valid both in the city and on the rural routes. Town and city bus fares are around Skr20, but it usually works out cheaper to get a day card or other travel pass.

Swedish and Danish trains and buses around the Öresund area form an integrated transport system, so buying tickets to Copenhagen from any station in the region is as easy as buying tickets for Swedish journeys.

Stockholm has an extensive underground metro system, and Göteborg and Norrköping run tram networks. Göteborg also has a city ferry service.

eras to detect speeding, and will impose on-the-spot fines.

On many highways you will see broken lines defining wide-paved edges. The vehicle being overtaken is expected to move into this area to allow faster traffic to pass by safely.

Train

Sweden has an extensive and reliable railway network, and trains are certainly faster than buses. Many destinations in the northern half of the country, however, cannot be reached by train alone, and Inlandsbanan, the historic train line through Norrland, runs only during summer.

COSTS

Travel on the super-fast X2000 services is much pricier than on 'normal' trains. Full-price 2nd-class tickets for longer journeys cost about twice as much as equivalent bus trips, but there are various discounts available, especially for booking a week or so in advance (*förköpsbiljet*), online, or at the last minute. Students (with a Swedish CSN or SFS student card if aged over 26), pensioners and people aged under 26 get a steep discount on the standard adult fare.

Tickets on X2000 services include a seat reservation. All SJ ticket prices are reduced in summer, from late June to mid-August. Most SJ trains don't allow bicycles to be taken onto trains (they have to be sent as freight), but those in southern Sweden (especially Skåne) do; check when you book your ticket.

TRAIN OPERATORS

Sveriges Järnväg (SJ; ☎0771-75 75 75; www. sj.se) National network covering most main lines, especially in the southern part of the country. Its X2000 fast trains run at speeds of up to 200km/h.

Tågkompaniet (☎0771-44 41 11; www.tagkompaniet.se, in Swedish) Operates excellent overnight trains from Göteborg and Stockholm north to Boden, Kiruna, Luleå and Narvik, and the lines north of Härnösand.

In summer, various **tourist trains** offer special rail experiences. The most notable is **Inlandsbanan** (☎0771-53 53 53; www.inlandsbanan.se), a slow and scenic 1300km route from Kristinehamn to Gällivare, one of the great rail journeys in Scandinavia. Several southern sections have to be travelled by bus, but the all-train route starts at Mora. It takes seven hours from Mora to Östersund (Skr414) and 15 hours from Östersund to Gällivare (Skr962). A pass allows two weeks' unlimited travel for Skr1595.

TRAIN PASSES

ScanRail no longer exists, but several other options provide similar benefits. The Sweden Rail Pass, Eurodomino tickets and international passes, such as Inter-Rail and Eurail, are accepted on SJ services and most regional trains.

The **Eurail Scandinavia Pass** (www.eurail.com) entitles you to unlimited rail travel in Denmark, Finland, Norway and Sweden; it is valid in 2nd class only and is available for four, five, six, eight or 10 days of travel within a two-month period (prices start at youth/adult US$235/315). All rail-pass holders are required to pay a supplement of Skr65 (including the obligatory seat reservation) for X2000 trains. The pass also provides free travel on Scandlines' Helsingør–Helsingborg route, and 20% to 50% discounts on the following ship routes (check www.eurail.com/countries/sweden/benefits-in-sweden for additional routes):

ROUTE	OPERATOR
Frederikshavn-Göteborg	Stena Line
Grenå-Varberg	Stena Line
Helsinki-Åland-Stockholm	Silja Line
Turku-Åland-Stockholm/ Kappelskär	Silja Line
Turku/Helsinki-Stockholm	Viking Line
Stockholm-Tallinn	Silja Line
Stockholm-Riga	Silja Line

Survival Guide

Directory A–Z

This chapter gives a general overview of the entire Scandinavian region. For information relevant to a particular country, see the Directory section at the end of each country chapter.

Some subjects are covered in *both* places (eg general accommodation options are discussed following, but price ranges and contact details for useful accommodation organisations appear in each country Directory).

Accommodation

Throughout this book, accommodation is divided into budget, midrange and top-end categories. Our choices are listed in order of preference, with our favourites first. See each individual country Directory for an overview of local options, prices and useful associations.

Cheap hotels are virtually unknown in far-northern Europe, but hostels, guesthouses, pensions, private rooms, farm accommodation and B&Bs can be good value. Self-catering cottages and flats are an excellent option if travelling in a family or group.

If you arrive in a country by train, there's often a hotel-booking desk at the station. Tourist offices tend to have extensive accommodation lists and the more helpful ones will go out of their way to find you somewhere to stay. There's usually a small fee for this service, but it can save a lot of running around.

Agencies offering private rooms can be good value; you may lack privacy, but staying with a local family brings you closer to the spirit of the country.

B&Bs, Guesthouses & Hotels

There's a huge range of accommodation above the hostel level. B&Bs, where you get a room and breakfast in a private home, can often be real bargains. Pensions and guesthouses are similar but usually slightly more upmarket.

Most Scandinavian hotels are geared to business travellers and have prices to match. However, excellent hotel discounts are often available at certain times (eg at weekends and in summer in Finland, Norway and Sweden) and for longer stays.

Breakfast in hotels is usually included in the price of the room.

If you think a hotel is too expensive, ask if they have a cheaper room. In nonchain places it can be easy to negotiate a discount in quiet periods if you're with a group or are planning to stay for any length of time.

Camping

Camping is cheap and immensely popular throughout the region. There's usually a charge per tent or campsite, per vehicle and per person. National tourist offices have booklets or brochures listing camping grounds all over their country. See p518 for information on camping cards that offer good benefits and discounts.

In most larger towns and cities, camping grounds are some distance from the centre. If you're on foot, the money you save by camping can quickly be outweighed by the money spent commuting in and out of town.

Nearly all mainland Scandinavian camping grounds rent simple cabins and sometimes more upmarket cottages – a good budget option if you're not carrying a tent.

Camping other than in designated camping grounds is not always straightforward but in many countries there's a right of common access that applies. See the Directory of the relevant country chapter for additional information. Tourist offices usually stock official publications in English explaining your rights and responsibilities.

Hostels

Hostels generally offer the cheapest roof over your head in Scandinavia, and you don't have to be young to use them. In Scandinavian countries, hostels are geared for budget travellers of all ages, including families with kids, and most have dorms and private rooms.

Most hostels are part of national YHAs (Youth Hostel Associations), known collectively throughout the world as **Hostelling International** (HI; www.hihostels.com). Technically you're supposed to be a YHA or HI member to use affiliated hostels (indicated by a blue triangle symbol) but in practice most are open to anyone. Without an HI card you may have to pay a bit extra, but this can be offset against future membership. Prices given throughout this book are HI member prices. To join HI, ask at any hostel, contact your local or national hostelling office, or register over the internet. If you'll be spending more than four or five nights in hostels in Scandinavia, it's worth doing. There's a particularly huge network of HI hostels in Denmark and Sweden.

Travellers with disabilities Specially adapted rooms for visitors with disabilities are becoming more common, but check with the hostel first.

Linens You must use a sleeping sheet and pillowcase or linen in hostels in most Scandinavian countries; sleeping bags are not permitted. It's worth carrying your own sleeping sheet or linen, as hiring these at hostels is comparatively expensive.

Breakfast Many hostels (exceptions include most hostels in Iceland and the Faroe Islands) serve breakfast, and almost all have communal kitchens where you can prepare meals.

Bookings Some hostels accept reservations by phone; they'll often book the next hostel you're headed to for a small fee. The HI website has a booking form you can use to reserve a bed in advance – however, not all hostels are on the network. Popular hostels in capital cities can be heavily booked in summer and limits may be placed on how many nights you can stay.

Many hostel guides are available, including HI's annually updated *Official International Youth Hostels Guide*. For further information on Scandinavian hostels, including price ranges, see the Directory section in individual country chapters.

Self-Catering

Across the region, but especially in Norway, Sweden, Denmark and Finland, there's a huge network of rental cottages that make excellent, peaceful places to stay and offer a chance to experience a traditional aspect of Scandinavian life. See specific country chapters for details of booking agencies.

University Accommodation

Some universities and colleges rent out their students' rooms to tourists from June to mid-August. These are sometimes called 'summer hotels' and are usually single or twin rooms with a kitchenette (but often no utensils). We've listed many of these throughout the guide; for more, enquire directly at the college or university, student information services or local tourist offices.

Children

Child-friendliness Most of Scandinavia is very child-friendly, with domestic tourism largely dictated by children's needs. Iceland and the Faroes are exceptions: children are liked and have lots of freedom, but they're treated as miniadults, and there aren't many attractions tailored particularly for children.

Activities In Denmark, Finland, Norway and Sweden you'll find excellent theme parks, water parks and holiday activities. Many museums have a dedicated children's section with toys, games and dressing-up clothes.

Accommodation The bigger camping grounds and spa hotels are particularly kid-conscious, with heaps of facilities and activities designed with children in mind. Cots (cribs) are standard in many hotels but numbers may be limited.

Transport Car-rental firms hire out children's safety seats at a nominal cost, but advance bookings are essential.

Restaurants High chairs are standard in many restaurants but numbers may be limited.

Food Choice of baby food, infant formulas, soy and cow's milk, disposable nappies (diapers) etc is wide in Scandinavian supermarkets.

Customs Regulations

From non-EU to EU countries For EU countries (ie Denmark, Sweden, Finland and Tallinn), travellers arriving from outside the EU can bring duty-free goods up to the value of €300 (€430 if you arrive by air or sea) without declaration. You can also bring in up to 16L of beer, 2L of wine and 1L

BOOK YOUR STAY ONLINE

For more accommodation reviews by Lonely Planet authors, check out hotels.lonelyplanet.com/Europe. You'll find independent reviews, as well as recommendations on the best places to stay. Best of all, you can book online.

of spirits, 200 cigarettes or 250g of tobacco, and 50g of perfume. These allowances vary slightly by country and change regularly so check before departure. Check out http://ec.europa.eu/taxation_customs and follow the 'Travellers' menu for details.

Within the EU If you're coming from another EU country, there is no restriction on the value of gifts or purchases for your own use.

Åland islands Although technically part of the EU, arriving on or from the Åland islands carries the same import restrictions as arriving from a non-EU country.

Other Nordic countries Norway, Iceland, the Faroe Islands and St Petersburg have lower limits. See country chapters for details.

Discount Cards

Camping Cards

Camping Card Scandinavia (www.camping.se) acts as an ID card, offers discounts at many camping grounds and attractions, and has built-in third-party insurance. In Denmark and some Swedish camping grounds, it's obligatory to have this or a similar card. If you're just getting a camping card to use in Scandinavia, we recommend this one, as it's accepted in more places than others.

Validity It's valid in Denmark, Norway and Finland and at most Swedish camping grounds, and in some other European countries. One card covers you whether you're an individual, a couple or a family with children under 18.

Purchasing You can order the card through the website before you leave home, or buy it from campsites throughout the region (this is sometimes cheaper). It costs €7 to €20 depending

on what country and whereabouts you get it.

The similar Camping Card International (www.campingcardinternational.com) is also widely accepted in the region, though not in Iceland or the Faroes.

Hostel Card

While not mandatory in Scandinavia, a Hostelling International (HI; www.hihostels.com) card gives a sizeable discount every time you check in to an affiliated hostel. It's best to buy the card from your national hostelling association before you set off, although in Scandinavia some hostels will issue one on the spot or after six stays (generally more expensive than getting one at home). See p516 for more details on hostelling in the region.

Seniors

Museums and other sights, public swimming pools, spas and transport companies frequently offer discounts to retirees, pensioners and to those over 60 (sometimes slightly younger for women; over 65 in Sweden). Make sure you bring proof of age.

See the Transport section of the individual country chapters for details.

Student & Youth Cards

International Student Identity Card (ISIC; www.isic.org) The most useful of these is a plastic ID-style card with your photograph, which provides discounts on many forms of transport, reduced or free admission to museums and sights, and cheap meals in student cafeterias – a worthwhile way of cutting costs. Check the website for a list of discounts by country. Because of the proliferation of fake ISIC cards, carry your home student ID as back up. Some places won't give student discounts without it.

Euro26 Card (www.eyca.org) and International Youth Travel Card (IYTC; www.isic.org) offer discounts to those aged under 26. These cards are available through student unions, hostelling organisations or youth-oriented travel agencies. There's also the International Teacher Identity Card (ITIC) for teachers and academics. The discounts for flashing these cards have reduced over the years due to widespread fraud, but you'll still be able to make a few savings here and there.

Local student cards If you are studying in Scandinavia, a local student card will get you megadiscounts on transport and more.

Electricity

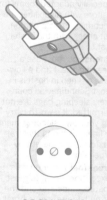

230V/50Hz

Embassies & Consulates

Travellers can visit the website of their home country's national department or ministry of foreign affairs to locate embassies and consulates in Scandinavia.

US Department of State www.usembassy.gov

UK Foreign & Commonwealth Office www.fco.gov.uk/en/travel-and-living-abroad/find-an-embassy

Foreign Affairs & International Trade Canada www.international.gc.ca/ciw-cdm/embassies-ambassades.aspx

Australian Department of Foreign Affairs & Trade www.dfat.gov.au/missions

New Zealand Ministry of Foreign Affairs & Trade www.nzembassy.com

French Ministry of Foreign Affairs www.diplomatie.gouv.fr/en/ministry_158/embassies-and-consulates_2052/index.html

German Federal Foreign Office www.auswaertiges-amt.de/EN/AAmt/Auslandsvertretungen/Uebersicht_node.html

Irish Department of Foreign Affairs www.dfa.ie/home/index.aspx?id=285

Netherlands Ministry of Foreign Affairs www.mfa.nl

Gay & Lesbian Travellers

This book lists contact addresses and gay and lesbian venues in the individual country chapters, and your national gay and lesbian organisation should be able to give you more information before you travel.

Denmark, Finland, Iceland, Norway and Sweden are very tolerant nations, although public displays of affection are less common in rural areas, particularly Lapland.

It's a good idea to be discreet in the Faroe Islands, where a conservative society and strongly held religious beliefs may cause problems for gay and lesbian couples. Both Tallinn and St Petersburg have lively scenes, but public affection outside those cities is not yet the norm.

Health

Travel in Scandinavia presents very few health problems. The standard of health care is extremely high and English is widely spoken by doctors and medical clinic staff. Tap water is safe to drink, the level of hygiene is high and there are no endemic diseases.

Health issues The main health issues to be aware of are extreme climates (with the potential for such nasties as hypothermia, frostbite or viral infections such as influenza) and biting insects such as mosquitoes, though they're more of an annoyance than a real health risk.

Vaccinations Specific travel vaccinations are not required for visitors to Scandinavia but you should be up to date with all normal childhood vaccinations.

Insurance (EEA) Citizens of the European Economic Area (EEA) are covered for emergency medical treatment in other EEA countries (including Denmark, Finland, Iceland, Norway and Sweden) on presentation of a European Health Insurance Card (EHIC), which replaced the old E111 form. Enquire about EHICs at your health centre, travel agency or (in some countries) post office well in advance of travel.

Insurance (non-EEA) Citizens from countries outside the EEA should find out if there is a reciprocal arrangement for free medical care between their country and the country visited. If not, health insurance is recommended.

Insurance

A travel insurance policy to cover theft, personal liability, loss and medical problems is recommended. There are a variety of policies available and travel agencies will have recommendations. Travel insurance also usually covers cancellation or delays in travel arrangements, for example, if you fall seriously ill two days before departure. For car insurance, see (p527).

Timing Buy insurance as early as possible. If you buy it the week before you are due to fly, you may find that you're not covered for delays to your flight caused by strikes or other industrial actions that may have been in force before you took out the insurance.

Policies Make sure you get a policy that covers you for the worst-possible health scenario if you aren't already covered by a reciprocal health-care agreement. Make sure your policy also covers you for any activities you plan to do, like skiing – check the small print. Find out in advance if your insurance plan will make payments directly to providers or reimburse you later for overseas health expenditures.

Credit cards & banks Paying for your airline ticket with a credit card often provides limited travel accident insurance, and you may be able to reclaim the payment if the operator doesn't deliver. Certain bank accounts also offer their holders automatic travel insurance.

Worldwide travel insurance is available at www.lonelyplanet.com/travel_services. You can buy, extend and claim online anytime – even if you're already on the road.

Internet Access

You'll find internet cafes throughout Scandinavia: many are listed in the country chapters in this book. In general, libraries provide a free or very cheap internet service, although there may be a waiting list and locals may have priority. You can also find public internet access in some post offices, tourist offices, hostels, hotels and universities.

Wireless (wi-fi) hot spots are rife in Scandinavia. An astonishing number of cafes, bars, hostels and hotels offer the service for free. So many, in fact, that we've decided not to clog up the text of this guide by mentioning it. A growing number of towns and cities in the region have free public wi-fi across the centre.

It can also be reasonably priced to buy a USB modem and pay-as-you-go SIM card, though in some countries you'll need to register an address.

Money

Changing money All Scandinavian currencies are fully convertible.

Debit & credit cards Scandinavians love using plastic, even for small transactions, and you'll find that debit and credit cards are the way to go here.

ATMs Widespread, even in small places.

Foreign currencies Easily exchanged, but you're better off going to exchange offices rather than banks. Always ask about the rate and commission before handing over your cash.

Travellers cheques Rapidly disappearing but still accepted in big hotels and exchange offices.

Cash-cards A good alternative to travellers cheques. These are much like debit or credit cards but are loaded with a set amount of money. They also have the advantage of lower withdrawal fees than your bank might otherwise charge you.

Charge cards Includes cards like American Express and Diners Club. These are less widely accepted than credit cards because they charge merchants high commissions.

Tipping For the most part, tipping isn't required in Scandinavia, although if you round up the bill or leave a little something in recognition of good service, it won't be refused.

Tax A value-added tax (VAT) applies to most goods and services throughout Scandinavia. International visitors from outside the European Economic Area can claim back the VAT above a set minimum amount on purchases that are being taken out of the country. The procedure for making the claim is usually pretty straightforward. For guidance, see the relevant country chapters.

SCANDINAVIAN CURRENCIES

COUNTRY	CURRENCY
Denmark	Danish krone (Dkr)
Faroe Islands	Faroese króna (Fkr) & Danish krone (Dkr)
Finland	euro (€)
Iceland	Icelandic króna (Ikr)
Norway	Norwegian krone (Nkr)
St Petersburg	rouble (R)
Sweden	Swedish krona (Skr)
Tallinn	euro (€)

Telephone

Emergencies The emergency number is the same throughout Scandinavia: ☑112.

Phone boxes Almost nonexistent in much of Scandinavia.

Mobile phones The best solution to stay connected is to bring a mobile that's not tied to a specific network (unlocked) and buy a local SIM card in each country you visit. If coming from outside Europe, check that the phone will work in Europe's GSM 900/1800 network.

Phonecards Easily bought for cheaper international calls.

Internet Calling via the Internet is another practical and cheap solution for making international calls.

Reverse-charge (collect) calls Usually possible, and communicating with the local operator in English should not be much of a problem.

Calling abroad To call abroad dial the international access code (IAC) for the country you are calling from (most commonly 00 in Europe), the country code (CC) for the country you are calling, the local area code (usually dropping the leading zero if there is one) and then the number. If, for example, you are in Norway (which has an international access code of ☑00) and want to make a call to Sweden (country code ☑46) in the Stockholm area (area code ☑08, number ☑123 4567), dial ☑00-46-8-123 4567.

Time

Scandinavia sprawls across several time zones. See the individual country Directory sections for details. The 24-hour clock is widely used.

Tourist Information

Location Tourist information offices in Scandinavia tend to be located at train stations or centrally (often in the town hall or central square) in most towns.

Opening hours Tourist information offices tend to be open for longer hours over the summer and reduced hours over the winter; smaller offices may be open only during the peak months of summer.

Facilities Generally excellent, with piles of regional and national brochures, helpful free maps and friendly employees. Staff are often multilingual, speaking several tongues including Scandinavian languages, English, German and French.

Services Most offices will book hotel and transport reservations and tours; a small charge may apply.

Travellers with Disabilities

Scandinavia leads the world as the best-equipped region for the traveller with disabilities. By law, most institutions must provide ramps, lifts and special toilets for people with disabilities; all new hotels and restaurants must install disabled facilities. Most trains and city buses are also accessible by wheelchair.

Some national parks offer accessible nature trails, and

TELEPHONE CODES

COUNTRY	☑CC	☑IAC
Denmark	45	00
Faroe Islands	298	00
Finland	358	00
Iceland	354	00
Norway	47	00
St Petersburg	7	810
Sweden	46	00
Tallinn	372	00

Use the country code (CC) to call into that country. Use the international access code (IAC) to call abroad from that country.

cities have ongoing projects in place designed to maximise disabled access in all aspects of urban life.

Iceland and the Faroes are a little further behind the rest of the region – check access issues before you travel. Scandinavian tourist office websites generally contain good information on disabled access.

Before leaving home, get in touch with your national support organisation – preferably the 'travel officer' if there is one. They often have complete libraries devoted to travel and can put you in touch with agencies that specialise in tours for the disabled. One such in the UK is **Can Be Done** (☎+44 (0)20-8907 2400; www.canbe done.co.uk).

Visas

See p15 for a summary of visa information. For more specific visa information, refer to the individual Directory sections in the country chapters.

Women Travellers

Scandinavia is one of the safest places to travel in all of Europe and women travellers should experience little trouble. In smaller towns, and especially in the north of Sweden and Finland, bars can be fairly unreconstructed places, and women sometimes get a bit of nonthreatening but unpleasant hassle from drunk locals.

Transport

This chapter gives a general overview of the entire Scandinavia region. For information relevant to one particular country, see the Directory section at the end of each country chapter.

GETTING THERE & AWAY

Scandinavia is easily accessed from the rest of Europe and beyond. There are direct flights from numerous destinations into Sweden, Norway, Denmark and Finland, and less choice to the Faroe Islands and Iceland. Denmark, Sweden and Norway can be accessed by train from Western Europe, while Baltic and Atlantic ferries are another good option for accessing these countries.

Flights, tours and rail tickets can be booked online at lonelyplanet.com/bookings.

Air

As well as the many national carriers that fly directly into Scandinavia's airports, there is a host of budget options. These change frequently, and are best investigated on the website www.whichbudget.com. They have the extra advantage of well-priced one-way tickets, making it easy to fly into one of the region's cities and out of another.

Major hubs in Scandinavia:

Arlanda Airport (www.arlanda.se) Stockholm, Sweden.

Helsinki-Vantaa Airport (www.helsinki-vantaa.fi) Helsinki, Finland.

Kastrup International Airport (www.cph.dk) Copenhagen, Denmark.

Keflavík Airport (www.kefair port.is) Reykjavík, Iceland.

Oslo Airport (www.osl.no) Oslo, Norway.

Land

Bus

Without a rail pass, the cheapest overland transport from Europe to Scandinavia is the bus, though a cheap flight deal will often beat it on price. **Eurolines** (www.euro lines.com), a conglomeration of 32 coach companies, is the biggest and best-established express-bus network, and connects Scandinavia with the rest of Europe. Most buses operate daily in summer and between two and five days per week in winter; advance ticket purchases are usually necessary. There's a 10% discount for those under 26 or over 60 years.

The Eurolines Pass allows unlimited travel to 40 cities across Europe; the Scandinavian cities included are Copenhagen, Göteborg, Oslo, Stockholm and Tallinn. Between late June and mid-September, a 15-/30-day pass costs €345/455

CLIMATE CHANGE & TRAVEL

Every form of transport that relies on carbon-based fuel generates CO_2, the main cause of human-induced climate change. Modern travel is dependent on aeroplanes, which might use less fuel per kilometre per person than most cars but travel much greater distances. The altitude at which aircraft emit gases (including CO_2) and particles also contributes to their climate change impact. Many websites offer 'carbon calculators' that allow people to estimate the carbon emissions generated by their journey and, for those who wish to do so, to offset the impact of the greenhouse gases emitted with contributions to portfolios of climate-friendly initiatives throughout the world. Lonely Planet offsets the carbon footprint of all staff and author travel.

(€290/375 for those under 26 years and over 60; cheaper at other times).

Car & Motorcycle

Driving to Scandinavia means driving into Denmark from Germany (and then on across to Sweden via the bridge and tunnels), going through Russia or taking a car ferry.

See p526 for more information about required paperwork.

Hitching & Car-Ride Services

For local hitching conditions and laws, see the individual country chapters.

After hitching, the cheapest way to head further north in Europe is as a paying passenger in a private car. Car-sharing is particularly well organised in Germany. After paying a reservation fee to a city-based **Mitfahrzentrale agency** (www.mitfahrzentrale.de, in German), you're then linked up with people driving in your direction (petrol money is also due to the driver). Local tourist information offices can help you locate agencies.

Train

From Germany Apart from trains into Finland from Russia, the rail route into Scandinavia goes from Germany into Denmark, then on to Sweden and thence Norway via the Copenhagen–Malmö bridge and tunnel connection. Hamburg and Cologne are the main gateways in Germany for this route. There are several direct Hamburg–Copenhagen trains daily (2nd class from €39, five hours); the hour-long ferry trip between Puttgarten and Rødby is included in the ticket price (the train actually boards the ferry). Overnight trains head from Cologne to Copenhagen (11 hours) via Odense.

From London There are various options. See the exceptional **Man in Seat 61** (www.seat61.com) for details. Contact **Deutsche Bahn UK** (☎08718 808066; www.bahn.com) for details of frequent special offers and for reservations and tickets. For more information on international rail travel (including Eurostar services), contact the **Rail Europe Travel Centre** (☎08448 484 064; www.raileurope.co.uk; 178 Piccadilly, London W1). You can also book via their website.

For further information about rail passes, see p528.

Sea

Prices given in this section are sample starting prices, based on a foot-passenger travelling one way in high season, using the cheapest available sleeping option (usually a reclining seat or couchette). Booking a cabin, travelling on weekends or night boats, or taking a vehicle will obviously increase the cost; travelling outside June to August will lower it. Book as early as possible to take advantage of limited cheaper tickets.

See the Transport sections of the country chapters for information about boat-train links within Scandinavia. See also p528 for rail passes and their validity on ferries.

Ferry Companies

The following is a list of the main ferry companies operating to and around Scandinavia, with their websites and major routes. See their websites and the Transport sections of individual countries for contact telephone numbers, times, durations and sample fares.

BornholmerFærgen (www.bornholmerfaergen.dk) Denmark–Sweden, Denmark–Germany.

Color Line (www.colorline.com) Norway–Denmark, Norway–Germany, Norway–Sweden.

DFDS Seaways (www.dfdsseaways.com) Norway–Sweden–Denmark, Denmark–UK.

Eckerö Line (www.eckeroline.fi) Finland–Tallinn, Finland–Sweden.

Finnlines (www.finnlines.com) Finland–Sweden, Finland–Germany, Finland–Poland.

Fjord Line (www.fjordline.com) Norway–Denmark.

Linda Line (www.lindaliini.ee) Finland–Estonia.

Polferries (www.polferries.pl) Sweden–Poland, Denmark–Poland.

RG Line (www.rgline.com) Finland–Sweden.

St Peter Line (www.stpeterline.com) Finland–St Petersburg.

Scandlines (www.scandlines.com) Sweden–Germany, Sweden–Latvia, Sweden–Denmark, Denmark–Germany.

Smyril Line (www.smyrilline.com) Denmark–Faroe Islands–Iceland.

Stena Line (www.stenaline.com) Denmark–Norway, Denmark–Sweden, Sweden–Germany, Sweden–Poland.

Tallink/Silja Line (www.tallinksilja.com) Finland–Sweden, Finland–Tallinn, Sweden–Tallinn, Finland–Germany.

TT-Line (www.ttline.com) Sweden–Germany.

Viking Line (www.vikingline.fi) Finland–Sweden, Finland–Tallinn.

Baltic Countries

There are numerous sailings between Tallinn, Estonia and Finland (see p235). Tallink/Silja also sails from Tallinn to Stockholm and from Paldiski (Estonia) to Kappelskär (Sweden).

Scandlines runs from Nynäshamn, Sweden to Ventspils, Latvia several times weekly. Tallink/Silja does a Stockholm–Riga run.

Lisco Line (www.lisco.lt) operates daily between Karlshamn (Sweden) and Klaipėda (Lithuania).

0 — 250 km
0 — 150 miles

Railways
Ferry Routes
• Major Stations/
Interchanges

Germany

Denmark Bornholmer Færgen runs between the island of Bornholm and Sassnitz, in eastern Germany. Scandlines runs from Rødby, on the island of Lolland, to Puttgarten, and between Gedser, on the island of Falster, and Rostock.

Finland Finnlines runs from Helsinki to Travemünde with a connecting bus to Hamburg. Tallink/Silja runs Helsinki–Rostock.

Norway Color Lines runs daily Oslo–Kiel.

Sweden Scandlines runs Trelleborg–Rostock and Trelleborg–Sassnitz. TT-Line runs Trelleborg–Travemünde and Trelleborg–Rostock. Stena Line runs Göteborg–Kiel.

Poland

Denmark Polferries operates to Świnoujście from both Copenhagen and Rønne on Bornholm.

Finland Finnlines runs from Helsinki to Gdynia.

Sweden Polferries runs Ystad–Świnoujście, as does **Unity Line** (www.unityline.pl). Polferries also links Nynäshamn with Gdańsk. Stena Lines run between Karlskrona and Gdynia.

United Kingdom

DFDS Seaways has ferries from Harwich to Esbjerg in Denmark but no longer runs to Norway or Sweden.

GETTING AROUND

Getting around the populated areas of Scandinavia is generally a breeze, with efficient public transport systems and snappy connections. Remote regions usually have trustworthy but infrequent services.

Air

Flights around Scandinavia are safe and reliable. They can be expensive, but they're often cheaper than land-based alternatives for longer journeys, and of course can save days of travelling time. Companies running internal airline routes offer reduced rates for internet bookings. There are several budget operators offering domestic and intra-Scandinavian flights. For carriers, see the country Transport sections of individual chapters.

Travelling between airports and city centres isn't a problem in Scandinavia, thanks to good bus and train networks.

Visitors flying **SAS** (www. flysas.com) or code-shared flights on a return ticket to Scandinavia from Asia or the USA can buy Visit Scandinavia/Europe Airpass coupons (starting at US$51 each plus taxes). These can be decent value.

The passes allow one-way travel on direct flights between any two Scandinavian cities serviced by SAS, Blue1 and other operators, with stopovers limited to one in each city. Children fly for around 70% of the adult price. Tickets can be purchased after arriving in Scandinavia if you have a return SAS international ticket.

Bicycle

Bike-friendly Scandinavia is exceptionally bike-friendly, with lots of cycle paths, courteous motorists, easy public transport options and lots of flattish, picturesque terrain.

Bike shops These are widespread in towns and cities, but it's worth taking sufficient tools and spare parts if you're visiting more remote areas.

Bike theft Take a decent lock and use it when you leave your bike unattended; theft is not uncommon in places like Helsinki and Copenhagen.

Bike club One organisation that can help you gear up is the wonderful **Cyclists' Touring Club** (www.ctc.org. uk), which offers cycling conditions, routes, itineraries, maps and specialised insurance.

Bike hire It's easy to hire bikes throughout Scandinavia, sometimes from train station bike-rental counters, and in some cases it's possible to return them to another outlet so you don't have to double back.

Bikes on transport On slower trains and local

buses in Scandinavia, bikes can usually be transported as luggage, either free or for a small fee. For taking bikes on faster trains and long-distance buses, see the country Transport sections in individual chapters.

Bike no-no Cycling across the Øresund bridge between Denmark and Sweden is prohibited.

Boat

Ferry

You can't really get around Scandinavia without using ferries extensively. The shortest routes from Denmark (Jutland) to Norway and from southern Sweden to Finland are ferry routes. Denmark is now well connected to mainland Europe and Sweden by bridges.

Ferry tickets are cheap on competitive routes, although transporting cars can be costly. Bicycles are usually carried free. On some routes, train-pass holders are entitled to free or discounted travel (see p528).

Weekend ferries, especially on Friday night, are significantly more expensive. Teenage travellers are banned from travelling on some Friday night ferries due to problems with drunkenness.

For further information about the many ferry options available between the destinations in this book, see the Transport sections of the individual country chapters. Also see p523 for ferry companies running services between Scandinavian countries.

Steamer

Scandinavia's main lakes and rivers are served by both diesel-powered boats and steamers during the summer. Treat these extended boat trips as relaxing, scenic miniholidays; if you view them merely as a way to get

THE NÖRRONA FERRY

The popular *Nörrona* ferry travels from Denmark to the Faroe Islands and on to Iceland. Faroes author Mark Elliott has some handy hints:

It can be confusing to piece together the reality from the Smyril Line (www.smyrilline.com) website. Standard fares include a bed in a claustrophobic 'couchette' (windowless six-bed dorm) in the bowels of the ship, but neither linen nor pillow is provided. Upgrading to a two-person cabin (linen, pillow, TV etc included) offers a vast improvement in comfort and means you have somewhere to leave your luggage during the day without paying Dkr20/40 for small/large lockers every time you need something. If driving, note that the car deck is inaccessible during the voyage. Buffet meals (breakfast/lunch/dinner Dkr98/99/195) are ample and beers cost from Dkr25 on the 8th-floor deck bar, but bring plenty of drinking water if you don't want to pay Dkr10 per 500mL bottle once aboard. Wi-fi (for €9.50/25/32 per hour/24 hours/full trip) is available by credit/debit card and there are power points in the corridors and cafeteria (coffee/sandwich Dkr15/35). Live music and evening magic shows are free as is use of the deck 1 swimming pool (bring your own towel).

A massively important thing is to realise that when they suggest that passengers should arrive two to three hours ahead of time for check-in they are dead serious – I arrived just over two hours before departure and was only just in time to board.

from A to B, they can seem quite expensive.

Sweden has the largest fleets in Scandinavia. Most leave from Stockholm and sail east to the Stockholm archipelago (p445) – a maze of 24,000 islands and islets – and west to historic Lake Mälaren (p446) – home base of the Swedish Vikings a millennium ago. You can also cruise the Göta Canal (p512), the longest water route in Sweden.

The legendary Hurtigruten ferry (p417) provides a link between Norway's coastal fishing villages. In Finland, steamships ply Lake Saimaa (p186) and its canal; there are also diesel-engine boats.

Bus

Buses provide a viable alternative to the rail network in Scandinavian countries, and are the only option in Iceland, the Faroes and parts of northern Sweden, Finland and Norway. See the Transport sections in the country chapters for details of routes, bus operators and internal bus passes.

Cost Compared to trains, they're usually cheaper (Finland is the exception) and slightly slower. Connections with train services (where they exist) are good.

Advance reservations Rarely necessary. However, you do need to prepurchase your ticket before you board many city buses, and then validate your ticket on board.

Routes There are regular bus services between Denmark and Sweden, and Sweden and Norway. Services between Finland and Norway run in Lapland, and there's a bus between Finland and Sweden at the border towns of Tornio/Haparanda. Buses connect Helsinki and other southern Finnish towns with St Petersburg.

Bus pass Eurolines offers the Eurolines Pass – see p522 for more details.

Car & Motorcycle

Travelling with your own vehicle is the best way to get to remote places and gives you independence and flexibility. Drawbacks include cost, being isolated in your own little car bubble and stressful city-centre driving.

Scandinavia is excellent for motorcycle touring, with good-quality winding roads, stunning scenery and an active motorcycling scene – just make sure your wet-weather gear is up to scratch. The best time for touring is May to September. On ferries, motorcyclists rarely have to book ahead as they can generally be squeezed in.

Bringing Your Own Vehicle

Documentation Proof of ownership of a private vehicle should always be carried (this is the Vehicle Registration Document for British-registered cars) when touring Europe. You'll also need an insurance document valid in the countries you are planning to visit (Russia has separate requirements from the rest of the countries in this book). Contact your local automobile association for further information.

Border crossings Vehicles crossing an international border should display a sticker showing their country of registration. (The exception is cars with

Euro-plates being taken into another EU country.)

Safety It's compulsory to carry a warning triangle in most places, to be used in the event of breakdown, and several countries require a reflective jacket. You must also use headlamp beam reflectors/converters on right-hand-drive cars.

Driving Licence

An EU driving licence is acceptable for driving throughout Scandinavia, as are North American and Australian licences, for example. If you have any other type of licence, you should check to see if you need to obtain an International Driving Permit (IDP) from your motoring organisation before you leave home.

If you're thinking of going snowmobiling, you'll need to bring your driving licence with you.

Fuel & Spare Parts

Fuel is heavily taxed and very expensive in Scandinavia. Most types of petrol, including unleaded 95 and 98 octane, are widely available; leaded petrol is no longer sold. Diesel is significantly cheaper than petrol in most countries. Always check the type of fuel being supplied – usually pumps with green markings and the word *Blyfri* on them deliver unleaded fuel, and black pumps supply diesel.

Hire

Cost Renting a car is more expensive in Scandinavia than in other European countries. Be sure you understand what's included in the price (unlimited or paid kilometres, injury insurance, tax, collision damage waiver etc) and what your liabilities are.

Insurance Always take the collision damage waiver, although you can probably skip the injury insurance if you and your passengers have decent travel insurance.

Companies The big international firms – Hertz, Avis, Budget and Europcar – are all present, but using local firms can mean a better deal. Big firms give you the option of returning the car to a different outlet when you've finished with it, but this is heavily charged.

Booking Try to prebook your vehicle, which always works out cheaper. Online brokers often offer substantially cheaper rates than the company websites themselves.

Fly/drive combinations SAS and Icelandair often offer cheaper car rentals to their international passengers.

Borders Ask in advance if you can drive a rented car across borders.

Age The minimum rental age is usually 21, sometimes even 23, and you'll probably need a credit card (or a mountain of cash) for the deposit.

Motorcycle and moped rental Not particularly common in Scandinavian countries, but it's possible in major cities.

Insurance

Third-party motor insurance A minimum requirement in most of Europe. Most UK car-insurance policies automatically provide third-party cover for EU and some other countries. Ask your insurer for a Green Card – an internationally recognised proof of insurance (there may be a charge) – and check that it lists all the countries you intend to visit.

Breakdown assistance Check whether your insurance policy offers breakdown assistance overseas. If it doesn't, a European breakdown-assistance policy, such as those provided by the AA or the RAC, is a good investment. Your motoring organisation may

also offer reciprocal coverage with affiliated motoring organisations.

Russia Has its own insurance requirements, and you'll need to organise to insure your car before you enter.

Road Conditions & Hazards

Conditions and types of roads vary widely across Scandinavia, but it's possible to make some generalisations.

Motorways Primary routes, with the exception of some roads in Iceland, are universally in good condition.

Minor roads Road surfaces on minor routes are not so reliable, although normally adequate.

Norway Has some particularly hair-raising roads; serpentine examples climb from sea level to 1000m in what seems no distance at all on a map. These roller coasters will use plenty of petrol and strain the car's engine and brakes, not to mention your nerves! Driving a campervan on this kind of route is not recommended.

Tolls In Norway, there are tolls for some tunnels, bridges, roads and entry into larger towns, and for practically all ferries crossing fjords. Roads, tunnels, bridges and car ferries in Finland and Sweden are usually free, although there's a hefty toll of €40 per car on the **Øresund bridge** (www. oresundsbron.com) between Denmark and Sweden.

Winter During winter in Scandinavia, snow tyres are compulsory. Chains are allowed in Norway but are illegal elsewhere.

Livestock on roads Suicidal stock, including sheep, elk, horses and reindeer, is a potential hazard. If you are involved in an animal incident, by law you must report it to the police.

Right Drive on the right-hand side of the road in all Scandinavian countries.

Seatbelts Compulsory for driver and all passengers.

Headlights Must be switched on at all times.

Give way Priority is usually given to traffic approaching from the right.

Helmets It's compulsory for motorcyclists and their passengers to wear helmets.

Speed Take care with speed limits, which vary from country to country.

Fines Many driving infringements are subject to on-the-spot fines in Scandinavian countries. Drink-driving regulations are strict: see individual country chapters.

Hitching

Safety Hitching is never entirely safe in any country in the world. Travellers, particularly women, who decide to hitch are taking a small but potentially serious risk – even in 'safe' Scandinavia.

As transport Hitching is neither popular nor particularly rewarding in most of the region. In fact, it's some of the slowest in the world. That said, with a bit of luck, hitchers can end up making good time in some areas, but obviously your plans need to be flexible.

Car sharing It's sometimes possible to arrange a lift privately: scan student notice boards in colleges or contact car-sharing agencies (see p523).

Train

Trains in Scandinavia are comfortable, frequent and punctual. As with most things in the region, prices are relatively expensive, although European train passes can make travel af-

fordable. There are no trains in Iceland or the Faroes, nor in most of far-northern Norway.

Schedules If you plan to travel extensively by train, get the **Thomas Cook European Rail Timetable** (www.thomascookpublish ing.com), which gives a complete listing of train schedules and indicates where supplements apply or where reservations are necessary.

Costs Full-price tickets can be expensive, but there are generally lots of discounts, particularly if you book ahead. European rail passes are worth buying if you plan to do a reasonable amount of intercountry travelling within a short space of time. Seniors and travellers under 26 years of age are eligible for discounted tickets, which can cut fares by between 15% and 40%.

Reservations It's a good idea (and sometimes obligatory) to make reservations at peak times and on certain train lines, especially long-distance trains. In some countries it can be a lot cheaper to book in advance. Check the individual country chapters for particulars.

Express trains There are various names for fast trains throughout Scandinavia: see individual chapters. Supplements usually apply on fast trains and it's wise (sometimes obligatory) to make reservations at peak times and on certain lines.

Overnight Trains

If you don't fancy sitting upright all night with a stranger dribbling on your shoulder, overnight trains usually offer couchettes or sleepers.

Reservations Advisable, particularly as sleeping options are generally allocated on a first-come, first-served basis.

Couchettes Basic bunk beds numbering four (1st

class) or six (2nd class) per compartment that are comfortable enough, if lacking a little privacy. In Scandinavia, a bunk costs around €25 to €50 for most trains, irrespective of the length of the journey.

Sleepers The most comfortable option, offering beds for one or two passengers in 1st class and two or three passengers in 2nd class. See the country chapters for regional variations.

Food Most long-distance trains have a dining car or snack trolley – bring your own nibbles to keep costs down.

Car Some long-distance trains have car-carrying facilities.

Train Passes

There are a variety of passes available for rail travel within Scandinavia, or in various European countries including Scandinavia. There are cheaper passes for students, people under 26 and seniors. Supplements (eg for high-speed services) and reservation costs are not covered by passes, and terms and conditions change – check carefully before buying. Passholders must always carry their passport on the train for identification purposes.

EURAIL PASSES

Eurail (www.eurail.com) now offers a good selection of different passes available to residents of non-European countries, which should be purchased before arriving in Europe.

Discounts Most of the passes offer discounts of around 25% for under 26 year olds, or 15% for two people travelling together. On most Eurail passes, children aged between four and 11 get a 50% discount on the full adult fare. Eurail passes give a 30% to 50% discount on several ferry lines in the region; check the website for details.

Eurail Scandinavia Pass
Gives a number of days in a two-month period, and is valid for travel in Denmark, Sweden, Norway and Finland. It costs €241 for four days, and up to €375 for 10 days. A similar but cheaper pass includes Sweden and one of the following: Norway, Denmark or Finland. There are also single-country passes.

Eurail Global Pass Offers travel in 22 European countries – either 10 or 15 days in a two-month period or unlimited travel from 15 days up to three months.

Global Pass Much better value for under 26s, as those older have to buy a 1st-class pass.

INTERRAIL PASSES
If you've lived in Europe for more than six months, you're eligible for an InterRail (www.interrailnet.com) pass. InterRail has scrapped its complex zonal system and now offers two passes valid for train travel in Scandinavia.

InterRail One Country Pass Offers travel in one country of your choice for three/four/six/eight days in a one-month period, costing €115/145/195/235 in 2nd class for Denmark or Finland, and €175/199/259/301 for Sweden or Norway.

Global Pass Offers travel in 30 European countries and costs from €259 for five days' travel in any 10, to €619 for a month's unlimited train travel.

Discounts On both the above passes, there's a 33% discount for under 26s. InterRail passes give a 30% to 50% discount on several ferry lines in the region; check the website for details.

WANT MORE?

For in-depth language information and handy phrases, check out Lonely Planet's *Scandinavian Phrasebook*. You'll find it at **shop.lonelyplanet. com**, or you can buy Lonely Planet's iPhone phrasebooks at the Apple App Store.

Language

This chapter offers basic vocabulary to help you get around Scandinavia, as well as in Tallinn and St Petersburg. If you read our coloured pronunciation guides as if they were English, you'll be understood. Note that the stressed syllables are indicated with italics.

Some of the phrases in this chapter have both polite and informal forms (indicated by the abbreviations 'pol' and 'inf' respectively). Use the polite form when addressing older people, officials or service staff. The abbreviations 'm' and 'f' indicate masculine and feminine gender respectively.

DANISH

Danish has official status in Denmark and the Faroe Islands.

All vowels in Danish can be long or short. Note that aw is pronounced as in 'saw', eu as the 'u' in 'nurse', ew as 'ee' with rounded lips, oh as the 'o' in 'note', ow as in 'how', and dh as the 'th' in 'that'.

Basics

Hello.	Goddag.	go·*da*
Goodbye.	Farvel.	faar·*vel*
Excuse me.	Undskyld mig.	*awn*·skewl mai
Sorry.	Undskyld.	*awn*·skewl
Please.	Vær så venlig.	ver saw *ven*·lee
Thank you.	Tak.	taak
Yes.	Ja.	ya
No.	Nej.	nai

What's your name?

| Hvad hedder De/du? (pol/inf) | va *hey*·dha dee/doo |

My name is ...

| Mit navn er ... | mit nown ir ... |

Do you speak English?

| Taler De/du engelsk? (pol/inf) | *ta*·la dee/doo *eng*·elsk |

I don't understand.

| Jeg forstår ikke. | yai for·*stawr* i·ke |

Accommodation

campsite	campingplads	*kaam*·ping·plas
guesthouse	gæstehus	*ges*·te·hoos
hotel	hotel	hoh·*tel*
youth hostel	ungdoms- herberg	*awng*·doms· *heyr*·beyrg

Do you have a ... room?	Har I et ... værelse?	haar ee it ... *verl*·se
single	enkelt	*eng*·kelt
double	dobbelt	*do*·belt

Signs – Danish

Indgang	Entrance
Udgang	Exit
Åben	Open
Lukket	Closed
Forbudt	Prohibited
Toilet	Toilets

Numbers – Danish		
1	*en*	in
2	*to*	toh
3	*tre*	trey
4	*fire*	feer
5	*fem*	fem
6	*seks*	seks
7	*syv*	sew
8	*otte*	aw·te
9	*ni*	nee
10	*ti*	tee

How much is it per ...?	*Hvor meget koster det per ...?*	vor *maa*·yet *kos*·ta dey peyr ...
night	*nat*	nat
person	*person*	per·*sohn*

Eating & Drinking

What would you recommend?
Hvad kan De/du anbefale? (pol/inf) — va kan dee/doo an·bey·fa·le

Do you have vegetarian food?
Har I vegetarmad? — haar ee vey·ge·*taar*·madh

I'll have ...
..., tak. — ... taak

Cheers!
Skål! — skawl

I'd like the ..., please.	*Jeg vil gerne have ..., tak.*	yai vil *gir*·ne ha ... taak
bill	*regningen*	*rai*·ning·en
menu	*menuen*	me·*new*·en

beer	*øl*	eul
coffee	*kaffe*	*ka*·fe
tea	*te*	tey
water	*vand*	van
wine	*vin*	veen

breakfast	*morgenmad*	*morn*·madh
lunch	*frokost*	*froh*·kost
dinner	*middag*	*mi*·da

Emergencies

Help!	*Hjælp!*	yelp
Go away!	*Gå væk!*	gaw vek

Call ...!	*Ring efter ...!*	ring *ef*·ta ...
a doctor	*en læge*	in *le*·ye
the police	*politiet*	poh·lee·*tee*·et

I'm lost.
Jeg er faret vild. — yai ir *faa*·ret veel

I'm ill.
Jeg er syg. — yai ir sew

Where's the toilet?
Hvor er toilettet? — vor ir toy·*le*·tet

Shopping & Services

I'm looking for ...
Jeg leder efter ... — yai *li*·dha *ef*·ta ...

How much is it?
Hvor meget koster det? — vor *maa*·yet *kos*·ta dey

That's too expensive.
Det er for dyrt. — dey ir for dewrt

market	*marked*	*maar*·kedh
post office	*postkontor*	*post*·kon·tohr
tourist office	*turist-kontoret*	*too*·reest·kon·toh·ret

Transport & Directions

Where's ...?
Hvor er ...? — vor ir ...

What's the address?
Hvad er adressen? — va ir a·*draa*·sen

Can you show me (on the map)?
Kan De/du vise mig det (på kortet)? (pol/inf) — kan dee/doo *vee*·se mai dey (paw *kor*·tet)

One ... ticket (to Odense), please.	*En ... billet (til Odense), tak.*	in ... bee·*let* (til oh·*dhen*·se) taak
one-way	*enkelt*	*eng*·kelt
return	*retur*	rey·*toor*

boat	*båden*	*baw*·dhen
bus	*bussen*	*boo*·sen
plane	*flyet*	*flew*·et
train	*toget*	*taw*·et

ESTONIAN

Double vowels in written Estonian indicate they are pronounced as long sounds.

Note that air is pronounced as in 'hair', aw as in 'law', ea as in 'ear', eu as in 'nurse', ew as ee with rounded lips, oh as the 'o' in 'note', ow as in 'how', uh as the 'a' in 'ago', kh as in the Scottish *loch*, and zh as the 's' in 'pleasure'.

Basics

Hello.	*Tere.*	*te*·re
Goodbye.	*Nägemist.*	*nair*·ge·mist
Excuse me.	*Vabandage.* (pol)	va·ban·da·ge
	Vabanda. (inf)	va·ban·da
Sorry.	*Vabandust.*	va·ban·dust
Please.	*Palun.*	pa·lun
Thank you.	*Tänan.*	*tair*·nan
Yes.	*Jaa.*	yaa
No.	*Ei.*	ay

What's your name?
Mis on teie nimi?   mis on *tay*·e *ni*·mi

My name is ...
Minu nimi on ...   *mi*·nu *ni*·mi on ...

Do you speak English?
Kas te räägite   kas te *rair*·git·te
inglise keelt?   *ing*·kli·se keylt

I don't understand.
Ma ei saa aru.   ma ay saa *a*·ru

Eating & Drinking

What would you recommend?
Mida te soovitate?   *mi*·da te *saw*·vit·tat·te

Do you have vegetarian food?
Kas teil on taimetoitu?   kas tayl on *tai*·met·toyt·tu

I'll have a ...
Ma tahaksin ...   ma *ta*·hak·sin ...

Cheers!
Terviseks!   *tair*·vi·seks

I'd like the ...,	*Ma sooviksin*	ma *saw*·vik·sin
please.	*..., palun.*	... *pa*·lun
bill	*arvet*	*ar*·vet
menu	*menüüd*	me·newt
beer	*õlu*	*uh*·lu
coffee	*kohv*	kokv
tea	*tee*	tey
water	*vesi*	*ve*·si
wine	*vein*	vayn
breakfast	*hommikusöök*	*hom*·mi·ku·seuk
dinner	*õhtusöök*	*uhkh*·tu·seuk
lunch	*lõuna*	*luh*·u·na

Emergencies

Help!	*Appi!*	*ap*·pi
Go away!	*Minge ära!*	*ming*·ke *air*·ra

Call ...!	*Kutsuge ...!*	*ku*·tsu·ge ...
a doctor	*arst*	arst
the police	*politsei*	po·li·*tsay*

I'm lost.
Ma olen ära eksinud.   ma o·len *air*·ra ek·si·nud

Where are the toilets?
Kus on WC?   kus on *ve*·se

Shopping & Services

I'm looking for ...
Ma otsin ...   ma o·tsin ...

How much is it?
Kui palju see maksab?   *ku*·i *pal*·yu sey *mak*·sab

That's too expensive.
See on liiga kallis.   sey on *lee*·ga *kal*·lis

bank	*pank*	pank
market	*turg*	turg
post office	*postkontor*	*post*·kont·tor

Transport & Directions

Where's the ...?
Kus on ...?   kus on ...

Can you show me (on the map)?
Kas te näitaksite   kas te *nair*·i·tak·sit·te
mulle (kaardil)?   *mul*·le (*kaar*·dil)

One ... ticket (to Pärnu), please.	Úks ... pilet (Pärnusse), palun.	ewks ... *pi*·let (pair·nus·se) pa·lun
one-way	úhe otsa	ew·he o·tsa
return	edasi-tagasi	e·da·si·*ta*·ga·si

boat	laev	laiv
bus	buss	bus
plane	lennuk	*len*·nuk
train	rong	rongk

FAROESE

In front of two or more consonants, vowels are pronounced shorter and have a more open quality than their long equivalents. Note also that air is pronounced as in 'hair', eu as the 'u' in 'nurse', iew as in 'view', oh as the 'o' in 'note', ow as in 'how', and uh as the 'a' in 'ago'.

Basics

Hello.	Góðan dag.	goh·wuhn dair
Goodbye.	Farvæl.	far·*vairl*
Excuse me.	Orsaka.	o·shair·kuh
Sorry.	Orsaka.	o·shair·kuh
Please.	Ger so væl.	jer so vairl
Thank you.	Takk.	tuhk
Yes.	Ja.	yair
No.	Nei.	nai

What's your name?
Hvussu eita tygum?   kvus·se ai·tuh tee·yun

My name is ...
Eg eiti ...   e ai·ti ...

Do you speak English?
Tosa tygum enskt?   toh·suh tee·yun enkst

I don't understand.
Eg skilji ikki.   e shil·yi i·chi

Eating & Drinking

What would you recommend?
Hvat kunnu tygum   kvairt *kun*·nu tee·yun
mæla til?   me·luh til

Do you have vegetarian food?
Hava tygum nakran   he·vuh tee·yun ne·kruhn
mat fyri vegetarar?   mairt fi·ri ve·ge·*tuhr*·ruhr

I'll have a ...
Eg hevði fegin ...   e he·yi fay·yin ...,

Cheers!
Skál!   skwuhl

I'd like the ..., please.	Kann eg fáa ..., takk?	kuhn e fwuh ... tuhk
bill	rokningina	rok·nin·ji·nuh
menu	matseðilin	mairt·say·i·lin

bottle of (beer)	eina fløsku av (øli)	ai·nuh *fleus*·ku airv (eu·li)
(cup of) coffee/tea	(ein kopp av) kaffi/te	(ain kop airv) *kuhf*·fi/te
glass of (wine)	eitt glas av (víni)	ait glairs airv (vui·ni)
water	vatn	vatn

breakfast	morgun-matur	*mor*·gun mair·tur
lunch	døgurði	deuv·ri
dinner	nátturði	not·ri

Emergencies

| Help! | Hjálp! | hyolp |
| Go away! | Far burtur! | fair *bush*·tur |

Call ...!	Ringið eftir ...!	*rin*·ji et·tir ...
a doctor	lækna	lek·nuh
the police	løgregluni	*leug*·reg·lu·ni

I'm lost.
Eg eri vilstur/vilst. (m/f)   e e·ri vils·tur/vilst

Where are the toilets?
Hvar eru vesini?   kvair e·ru vair·si·ni

Shopping & Services

I'm looking for ...
Eg leiti eftir ...   e *lai*·ti et·tir ...

How much is it?
Hvussu nógv kostar   kvus·se negv kos·tuhr
hetta?   het·tuh

That's too expensive.
Tað er ov dýrt.   tair er oh dusht

Where's the ...?	Hvar er ...?	kvair er ...
bank	bankin	*buhn*·chin
post office	posthúsið	*post*·hiew·si
shopping centre	sølumið-støðin	*seu*·lu·mi·steu·yin

Numbers – Faroese

1	eitt	ait
2	tvey	tvay
3	trý	trui
4	fýra	fui·ruh
5	fimm	fim
6	seks	seks
7	sjey	shay
8	átta	o·tuh
9	níggju	nu·je
10	tíggju	tu·je

Transport & Directions

Where's ...?
Hvar er ...?   kvair er ...

Can you show me (on the map)?
Kunnu tygum visa   kun·nu tee·yun vee·suh
mær tað (á kortinum)?   mair tair (wuh kosh·ti·nun)

Please take me to (this address).
Koyr meg til (hesa   koyr may til (he·suh
adressuna), takk.   uh·dres·su·nuh) tuhk

One ... ticket (to Klaksvík), please.	... (til Klaksvíkar), takk.	... (til kluhks·vui·kuhr) tuhk
one-way	Einvegis ferðaseðil	ain·vay·yis fair·ruh·say·il
return	Ferðaseðil aftur og fram	fair·ruh·say·il uh·tur oh fruhm

Is this the ... to (Tórshavn)?	Er hetta ... (til Tórshavnar)?	er het·tuh ... (til torsh·how·nuhr)
boat	báturin	bwuh·tu·rin
bus	bussurin	bus·su·rin
plane	flogfarið	floh·fair·ri

FINNISH

Double consonants are held longer than their single equivalents. Note that eu is pronounced as the 'u' in 'nurse', ew as 'ee' with rounded lips, oh as the 'o' in 'note', ow as in 'how', and uh as the 'u' in 'run'.

Basics

Hello.	Hei.	hay
Goodbye.	Näkemiin.	na·ke·meen
Excuse me.	Anteeksi.	uhn·tayk·si
Sorry.	Anteeksi.	uhn·tayk·si

Please.	Ole hyvä.	o·le hew·va
Thank you.	Kiitos.	kee·tos
Yes.	Kyllä.	kewl·la
No.	Ei.	ay

What's your name?
Mikä sinun nimesi on?   mi·ka si·nun ni·me·si on

My name is ...
Minun nimeni on ...   mi·nun ni·me·ni on ...

Do you speak English?
Puhutko englantia?   pu·hut·ko en·gluhn·ti·uh

I don't understand.
En ymmärrä.   en ewm·mar·ra

Eating & Drinking

What would you recommend?
Mitä voit suositella?   mi·ta voyt su·o·si·tel·luh

Do you have vegetarian food?
Onko teillä   on·ko teyl·la
kasvisruokia?   kuhs·vis·ru·o·ki·uh

I'll have a ...
Tilaan ...   ti·laan ...

Cheers!
Kippis!   kip·pis

I'd like the ..., please.	Saisinko ...	sai·sin·ko ...
bill	laskun	luhs·kun
menu	ruoka-listan	ru·o·kuh·lis·tuhn

bottle of (beer)	pullon (olutta)	pul·lon (o·lut·tuh)
(cup of) coffee/tea	(kupin) kahvia/teetä	(ku·pin) kuh·vi·uh/tay·ta
glass of (wine)	lasillisen (viiniä)	luh·sil·li·sen (vee·ni·a)
water	vettä	vet·ta

breakfast	aamiaisen	aa·mi·ai·sen
lunch	lounaan	loh·naan
dinner	illallisen	il·luhl·li·sen

Signs – Finnish

Sisään	Entrance
Ulos	Exit
Avoinna	Open
Suljettu	Closed
Kielletty	Prohibited
Opastus	Information

Emergencies

Help!	*Apua!*	*uh·pu·uh*
Go away!	*Mene pois!*	*me·ne poys*
Call ...!	*Soittakaa*	*soyt·tuh·kaa*
	paikalle ...!	*pai·kuhl·le ...*
a doctor	*lääkäri*	*la·ka·ri*
the police	*poliisi*	*po·lee·si*

I'm lost.
Olen eksynyt.   *o·len ek·sew·newt*

Where are the toilets?
Missä on vessa?   *mis·sa on ves·suh*

Shopping & Services

I'm looking for ...
Etsin ...   *et·sin ...*

How much is it?
Mitä se maksaa?   *mi·ta se muhk·saa*

That's too expensive.
Se on liian kallis.   *se on lee·uhn kuhl·lis*

Where's the ...?	*Missä on ...?*	*mis·sa on ...*
bank	*pankki*	*puhnk·ki*
market	*kauppatori*	*kowp·pa·to·ri*
post office	*posti-*	*pos·ti-*
	toimisto	*toy·mis·to*

Transport & Directions

Where's ...?
Missä on ...?   *mis·sa on ...*

Can you show me (on the map)?
Voitko näyttää sen   *voyt·ko na·ewt·ta sen*
minulle (kartalta)?   *mi·nul·le (kar·tuhl·tuh)*

Please take me to (this address).
Voitko viedä minut   *voyt·ko vi·e·da mi·nut*
(tähän osoitteeseen).   *(ta·han o·soyt·tay·sayn)*

One ... ticket,	*Saisinko*	*sai·sin·ko*
please.	*yhden*	*ewh·den*
	... lipun.	*... li·pun*
one-way	*yksisuun-*	*ewk·si·soon·*
	taisen	*tai·sen*
return	*meno-paluu*	*me·no·pa·loo*

Where does	*Minne tämä ...*	*min·ne ta·ma ...*
this ... go?	*menee?*	*me·nay*
boat	*laiva*	*lai·vuh*
bus	*bussi*	*bus·si*
plane	*lentokone*	*len·to·ko·ne*
train	*juna*	*yu·nuh*

Numbers – Finnish		
1	*yksi*	*ewk·si*
2	*kaksi*	*kuhk·si*
3	*kolme*	*kol·me*
4	*neljä*	*nel·ya*
5	*viisi*	*vee·si*
6	*kuusi*	*koo·si*
7	*seitsemän*	*sayt·se·man*
8	*kahdeksan*	*kuhk·dek·suhn*
9	*yhdeksän*	*ewh·dek·san*
10	*kymmenen*	*kewm·me·nen*

ICELANDIC

Double consonants are given a long pronunciation. Note that eu is pronounced as the 'u' in 'nurse', oh as the 'o' in 'note', ow as in 'how', öy as the '-er y-' in 'her year' (without the 'r'), dh as the 'th' in 'that', and kh as the 'ch' in the Scottish loch.

Basics

Hello.	*Halló.*	*ha·loh*
Goodbye.	*Bless.*	*bles*
Please.	*Takk.*	*tak*
Thank you.	*Takk fyrir.*	*tak fi·rir*
Excuse me.	*Afsakið.*	*af·sa·kidh*
Sorry.	*Fyrirgefðu.*	*fi·rir·gev·dhu*
Yes.	*Já.*	*yow*
No.	*Nei.*	*nay*

What's your name?
Hvað heitir þú?   *kvadh hay·tir thoo*

My name is ...
Ég heiti ...   *yekh hay·ti ...*

Do you speak English?
Talar þú ensku?   *ta·lar thoo ens·ku*

I don't understand.
Ég skil ekki.   *yekh skil e·ki*

Eating & Drinking

What would you recommend?
Hverju mælir þú með?   *kver·yu mai·lir thoo medh*

Do you have vegetarian food?
Hafið þið   *ha·vidh thidh*
grænmetisrétti?   *grain·me·tis·rye·ti*

I'll have a ...
Ég ætla að fá ...   *yekh ait·la adh fow ...*

Cheers!
Skál!   *skowl*

I'd like the ..., please.	Get ég fengið ... takk.	get yekh fen·gidh ... tak
bill	reikninginn	rayk·nin·gin
menu	matseðillinn	mat·se·dhit·lin

bottle of (beer)	(bjór)flösku	(byohr)·fleus·ku
(cup of) coffee/tea	kaffi/te (bolla)	ka·fi/te (bot·la)
glass of (wine)	(vín)glas	(veen)·glas
water	vatn	vat

breakfast	morgunmat	mor·gun·mat
lunch	hádegismat	how·de·yis·mat
dinner	kvöldmat	kveuld·mat

Emergencies

| Help! | Hjálp! | hyowlp |
| Go away! | Farðu! | far·dhu |

Call ...!	Hringdu á ...!	hring·du ow ...
a doctor	lækni	laik·ni
the police	lögregluna	leu·rekh·lu·na

I'm lost.
Ég er villtur/villt. (m/f)   yekh er vil·tur/vilt

Where are the toilets?
Hvar er snyrtingin?   kvar er snir·tin·gin

Shopping & Services

I'm looking for ...
Ég leita að ...   yekh lay·ta adh ...

How much is it?
Hvað kostar þetta?   kvadh kos·tar the·ta

That's too expensive.
Þetta er of dýrt.   the·ta er of deert

Where's the ...?	Hvar er ...?	kvar er ...
bank	bankinn	bown·kin
market	markaðurinn	mar·ka·dhu·rin
post office	pósthúsið	pohst·hoo·sidh

Numbers – Icelandic

1	einn	aydn
2	tveir	tvayr
3	þrír	threer
4	fjórir	fyoh·rir
5	fimm	fim
6	sex	seks
7	sjö	syeu
8	átta	ow·ta
9	níu	nee·u
10	tíu	tee·u

Transport & Directions

Where's ...?
Hvar er ...?   kvar er ...

Can you show me (on the map)?
Geturðu sýnt mér (á kortinu)?   ge·tur·dhu seent myer (ow kor·ti·nu)

Please take me to (this address).
Viltu aka mér til (þessa staðar)?   vil·tu a·ka myer til (the·sa sta·dhar)

One ... ticket (to Reykjavík), please.	Einn miða ... (til, Reykjavíkur) takk.	aitn mi·dha ... (til Reykjavíkur) rayk·ya·vee·kur) tak
one-way	aðra leiðina	adh·ra lay·dhi·na
return	fram og til baka	fram okh til ba·ka

Is this the ... to (Akureyri)?	Er þetta ... til (Akureyrar)?	er the·ta ... til (a·ku·ray·rar)
boat	ferjan	fer·yan
bus	rútan	roo·tan
plane	flugvélin	flukh·vye·lin

NORWEGIAN

There are two official written forms of Norwegian, *Bokmål* and *Nynorsk*. They are actually quite similar and understood by all speakers. It's estimated that around 85% of Norwegian speakers use *Bokmål* and about 15% use *Nynorsk*. In this section we've used *Bokmål* only.

Each vowel can be either long or short. Generally, they're long when followed by one consonant and short when followed by two or more consonants. Note that aw is pronounced as in 'law', eu as the 'u' in 'nurse', ew as 'ee' with pursed lips, and ow as in 'how'.

Basics

Hello.	*God dag.*	go·*daag*
Goodbye.	*Ha det.*	*haa*·de
Excuse me.	*Unnskyld.*	ewn·shewl
Sorry.	*Beklager.*	bey·*klaa*·geyr
Please.	*Vær så snill.*	veyr saw snil
Thank you.	*Takk.*	tak
Yes.	*Ja.*	yaa
No.	*Nei.*	ney

What's your name?
Hva heter du?   vaa *hey*·ter doo

My name is ...
Jeg heter ...   yai *hay*·ter ...

Do you speak English?
Snakker du engelsk?   *sna*·ker doo *eyng*·elsk

I don't understand.
Jeg forstår ikke.   yai fawr·*stawr* i·key

Accommodation

campsite	*campingplass*	*keym*·ping·plas
guesthouse	*gjestgiveri*	*yest*·gi·ve·ree
hotel	*hotell*	hoo·*tel*
youth hostel	*ungdoms-herberge*	*ong*·dawms·heyr·beyrg

Do you have a single/double room?
Finnes det et   *fi*·nes de et
enkeltrom/dobbeltrom?   *eyn*·kelt·rom/*daw*·belt·rom

How much is it per night/person?
Hvor mye koster det   vor *mew*·e *kaws*·ter de
pr dag/person?   peyr daag/*peyr*·son

Eating & Drinking

I'd like the menu.
Kan jeg få   kan yai faw
menyen, takk.   me·*new*·en tak

What would you recommend?
Hva vil du anbefale?   va vil doo *an*·be·fa·le

Do you have vegetarian food?
Har du vegetariansk   har doo ve·ge·ta·ree·*ansk*
mat her?   maat heyr

I'll have ...
Jeg vil ha ...   yai vil haa ...

Cheers!
Skål!   skawl

I'd like the bill.
Kan jeg få   kan yai faw
regningen, takk.   *rai*·ning·en tak

Signs – Norwegian

Inngang	Entrance
Utgang	Exit
Åpen	Open
Stengt	Closed
Forbudt	Prohibited
Toaletter	Toilets

beer	*øl*	eul
coffee	*kaffe*	*kaa*·fe
tea	*te*	te
water	*vann*	van
wine	*vin*	veen

breakfast	*frokost*	*fro*·kost
lunch	*lunsj*	loonsh
dinner	*middag*	*mi*·da

Emergencies

Help!	*Hjelp!*	yelp
Go away!	*Forsvinn!*	fawr·*svin*

Call a doctor/the police!
Ring en lege/politiet! ring en le·ge/po·lee·*tee*·ay

I'm lost.
Jeg har gått meg vill. yai har gawt mai vil

I'm ill.
Jeg er syk.   yai er sewk

Where are the toilets?
Hvor er toalettene?   vor eyr to·aa·*le*·te·ne

Shopping & Services

I'm looking for ...
Jeg leter etter ...   yai *ley*·ter e·*ter* ...

How much is it?
Hvor mye koster det?   vor *mew*·e *kaws*·ter de

That's too expensive.
Det er for dyrt.   de eyr fawr dewrt

market	*marked*	*mar*·ked
post office	*postkontor*	*pawst*·kawn·tawr
tourist office	*turist-informasjon*	tu·*reest*·in·fawr·ma·*shawn*

Transport & Directions

boat	*båt*	bawt
bus	*buss*	bus
plane	*fly*	flew
train	*tåg*	tawg

Numbers – Norwegian

1	*en*	en
2	*to*	taw
3	*tre*	trey
4	*fire*	*fee*·re
5	*fem*	fem
6	*seks*	seks
7	*sju*	shoo
8	*åtte*	*aw*·te
9	*ni*	nee
10	*ti*	tee

Where is ...?
Hvor er ...? vor ayr ...

What is the address?
Hva er adressen? va ayr aa·*dre*·seyn

Can you show me (on the map)?
Kan du vise meg kan du vee·se ma
(på kartet)? (paw *kar*·te)

One one-way/return ticket (to Bergen), please.
Jeg vil gjerne ha yai vil *yer*·ne haa
enveisbillett/ en·veys·bee·*let*/
returbillett re·*toor*·bi·*let*
(til Bergen), takk. (til *ber*·gen) tak

RUSSIAN

Most Russian sounds are also found in English, so just follow our pronunciation guides for the following phrases and you don't even need to know how to read the Cyrillic alphabet.

Note that kh is pronounced as in the Scottish *loch* and zh as the 's' in 'pleasure'. Also, r is rolled in Russian and the apostrophe (') indicates a slight y sound.

Basics

Hello.	Здравствуйте.	*zdrast*·vuyt·ye
Goodbye.	До свидания.	da svee·*dan*·ya
Excuse me./ Sorry.	Извините, пожалуйста.	eez·vee·*neet*·ye pa·*zhal*·sta
Please.	Пожалуйста.	pa·*zhal*·sta
Thank you.	Спасибо.	spa·*see*·ba
Yes./No.	Да./Нет.	da/nyet

What's your name?
Как вас зовут? kak vaz za·*vut*

My name is ...
Меня зовут ... meen·*ya* za·*vut* ...

Do you speak English?
Вы говорите vi ga·va·*reet*·ye
по-английски? pa·an·*glee*·skee

I don't understand.
Я не понимаю. ya nye pa·nee·*ma*·yu

Accommodation

campsite	кемпинг	*kyem*·peeng
guesthouse	пансионат	pan·see·a·*nat*
hotel	гостиница	ga·*stee*·neet·sa
youth hostel	общежитие	ap·shee·*zhi*·tee·ye

Do you have a ... room?	У вас есть ...?	u vas yest' ...
single	одноместный номер	ad·nam·*yes*·ni *no*·meer
double	номер с двуспальней кроватью	*no*·meer z dvu·*spaln*·yey kra·*vat*·yu

How much is it ...?	Сколько стоит за ...?	*skol*'·ka *sto*·eet za ...
for two people	двоих	dva·*eekh*
per night	ночь	noch'

Eating & Drinking

What would you recommend?
Что вы shto vi
рекомендуете? ree·ka·meen·*du*·eet·ye

Do you have vegetarian food?
У вас есть овощные u vas yest' a·vashch·*ni*·ye
блюда? *blyu*·da

I'll have ...
..., пожалуйста. ... pa·*zhal*·sta

Cheers!
Пей до дна! pyey da dna

I'd like the ..., please.	Я бы хотел/ хотела ... (m/f)	ya bi khat·*yel*/ khat·*ye*·la ...
bill	счёт	shot
menu	меню	meen·*yu*

beer	пиво	*pee*·va
coffee	кофе	*kof*·ye
tea	чай	chey
water	вода	va·*da*
wine	вино	vee·*no*

Signs – Russian

Вход	Entrance
Выход	Exit
Открыто	Open
Закрыто	Closed
Запрещено	Prohibited
Туалет	Toilets

breakfast	завтрак	zaf·trak
lunch	обед	ab·yet
dinner	ужин	u·zhin

Emergencies

| Help! | Помогите! | pa·ma·gee·tye |
| Go away! | Идите отсюда! | ee·deet·ye at·syu·da |

Call a doctor!
Вызовите врача! — vi·za·veet·ye vra·cha

Call the police!
Вызовите милицию! — vi·za·veet·ye mee·leet·si·yu

I'm lost.
Я потерялся/ потерялась. (m/f) — ya pa·teer·yal·sa/ pa·teer·ya·las'

I'm ill.
Я болею. — ya bal·ye·yu

Where are the toilets?
Где здесь туалет? — gdye zdyes' tu·al·yet

Shopping & Services

I'd like ...
Я бы хотел/ хотела ... (m/f) — ya bi khat·yel/ khat·ye·la ...

How much is it?
Сколько стоит? — skol'·ka sto·eet

That's too expensive.
Это очень дорого. — e·ta o·cheen' do·ra·ga

market	рынок	ri·nak
post office	почта	poch·ta
tourist office	туристическое бюро	tu·rees·tee·chee·ska·ye byu·ro

Transport & Directions

Where's the ...?
Где (здесь) ...? — gdye (zdyes') ...

What's the address?
Какой адрес? — ka·koy a·drees

Can you show me (on the map)?
Покажите мне, пожалуйста (на карте). — pa·ka·zhi·tye mnye pa·zhal·sta (na kart·ye)

One ... ticket (to Novgorod), please.
Билет ... (на Новгород). — beel·yet ... (na nov·ga·rat)

| one-way | в один конец | va·deen kan·yets |
| return | в оба конца | v o·ba kant·sa |

Numbers – Russian

1	один	a·deen
2	два	dva
3	три	tree
4	четыре	chee·ti·ree
5	пять	pyat'
6	шесть	shest'
7	семь	syem'
8	восемь	vo·seem'
9	девять	dye·veet'
10	десять	dye·seet'

boat	параход	pa·ra·khot
bus	автобус	af·to·bus
plane	самолёт	sa·mal·yot
train	поезд	po·yeest

SWEDISH

Swedish is the national language of Sweden and it also has official status in Finland.

Vowel sounds can be short or long – generally the stressed vowels are long, except when followed by double consonants. Note that aw is pronounced as in 'saw', air as in 'hair', eu as the 'u' in 'nurse', ew as 'ee' with rounded lips, oh as the 'o' in 'note', and fh is a breathy sound pronounced with rounded lips, like saying 'f' and 'w' at the same time.

Basics

Hello.	Hej.	hey
Goodbye.	Hej då.	hey daw
Excuse me.	Ursäkta mig.	oor·shek·ta mey
Sorry.	Förlåt.	feur·lawt
Please.	Tack.	tak
Thank you.	Tack.	tak
Yes./No.	Ja./Nej.	yaa/ney

What's your name?
Vad heter du? — vaad hey·ter doo

My name is ...
Jag heter ... — yaa hey·ter ...

Do you speak English?
Talar du engelska? — taa·lar doo eng·el·ska

I don't understand.
Jag förstår inte. — yaa feur·shtawr in·te

Accommodation

| campsite | campingplats | kam·ping·plats |
| guesthouse | gästhus | yest·hoos |

Signs – Swedish

Ingång	Entrance
Utgång	Exit
Öppet	Open
Stängt	Closed
Förbjudet	Prohibited
Toaletter	Toilets

hotel	*hotell*	hoh·*tel*
youth hostel	*vandrarhem*	van·drar·hem

Do you have a single/double room?
Har ni ett enkeltrum/ har nee et en·kelt·rum/
dubbeltrum? du·belt·rum

How much is it per night/person?
Hur mycket kostar det hoor mew·ket kos·tar de
per natt/person? peyr nat/*peyr*·shohn

Eating & Drinking

I'd like the menu.
Jag skulle vilja ha yaa sku·le vil·ya haa
menyn. me·*newn*

What would you recommend?
Vad skulle ni anbefalla? vaad *sku*·le nee an·be·fa·la

Do you have vegetarian food?
Har ni vegetarisk mat? har nee ve·ge·*taa*·risk maat

I'll have ...
Jag vill ha ... yaa vil haa ...

Cheers!
Skål! skawl

I'd like the bill.
Jag skulle vilja ha yaa *sku*·le vil·ya haa
räkningen. *reyk*·ning·en

beer	*öl*	eul
coffee	*kaffe*	ka·fe
tea	*te*	tey
water	*vatten*	va·ten
wine	*vin*	veen
breakfast	*frukost*	froo·kost
lunch	*lunch*	lunsh
dinner	*middag*	mi·daa

Emergencies

Help!
Hjälp! yelp

Go away!
Försvinn! feur·*shvin*

I'm ill.
Jag är sjuk. yaa air fhook

I'm lost.
Jag har gått vilse. yaa har got vil·se

Call a doctor!
Ring efter en doktor! ring ef·ter en dok·tor

Call the police!
Ring efter polisen! ring ef·ter poh·*lee*·sen

Where are the toilets?
Var är toaletten? var air toh·aa·le·ten

Shopping & Services

I'm looking for ...
Jag letar efter ... yaa ley·tar ef·ter ...

How much is it?
Hur mycket kostar det? hoor mew·ke kos·tar de

That's too expensive.
Det är för dyrt. de air feur dewrt

market	*torghandel*	tory·han·del
post office	*posten*	pos·ten
tourist office	*turistbyrå*	too·rist·bew·raw

Transport & Directions

Where's ...?
Var finns det ...? var finns de ...

What's the address?
Vilken adress är det? vil·ken a·dress air de

Can you show me (on the map)?
Kan du visa mig kan doo vee·sa mey
(på kartan)? (paw kar·tan)

A one-way/return ticket (to Stockholm), please.
Jag skulle vilja ha en yaa sku·le vil·ya haa eyn
enkelbiljett/returbiljett en·kel·bil·yet/re·toor·bil·yet
(till Stockholm). (til stok·holm)

boat	*båt*	bawt
bus	*buss*	bus
plane	*flygplan*	flewg·plaan
train	*tåg*	tawg

Numbers – Swedish

1	*ett*	et
2	*två*	tvaw
3	*tre*	trey
4	*fyra*	few·ra
5	*fem*	fem
6	*sex*	seks
7	*sju*	fhoo
8	*åtta*	o·ta
9	*nio*	nee·oh
10	*tio*	tee·oh

behind
the
scenes

SEND US YOUR FEEDBACK

We love to hear from travellers – your comments keep us on our toes and help make our books better. Our well-travelled team reads every word on what you loved or loathed about this book. Although we cannot reply individually to postal submissions, we always guarantee that your feedback goes straight to the appropriate authors, in time for the next edition. Each person who sends us information is thanked in the next edition – and the most useful submissions are rewarded with a free book.

Visit **lonelyplanet.com/contact** to submit your updates and suggestions or to ask for help. Our award-winning website also features inspirational travel stories, news and discussions.

Note: We may edit, reproduce and incorporate your comments in Lonely Planet products such as guidebooks, websites and digital products, so let us know if you don't want your comments reproduced or your name acknowledged. For a copy of our privacy policy visit lonelyplanet.com/privacy.

OUR READERS

Many thanks to the travellers who used the last edition and wrote to us with helpful hints, useful advice and interesting anecdotes:

Masso, Walter Bertschinger, Chris Bourne, Erica Brennen, Nienke Coehoorn-buma, Johan Collberg, Henry Dare, Nick Dillen, Anton Krivtsun, Nelson Ricardo Da Silva Duarte, Deborah Schubert, John Soar, Marco Sommariva, Jason Stewart, Monique Teggelove, Rinus Van Hoogenhuizen, Tony Wheeler, Lance Wilson.

AUTHOR THANKS

Andy Symington

Andy owes a big debt of thanks to many Finnish friends for numerous kindnesses and warm hospitality. Staff at tourist offices throughout the country were extremely helpful and patient – *kiitos*! – while Oscar Jackson Hevia and his parents David and Carmen provided an excellent Swedish base camp. Thanks too, to the brilliant team of authors and editors that made coordinating this book a very light task. Jorma Hynninen was kind enough to take time in a busy period to answer my questions and my family, as ever, endure my long absences without a murmur.

Cristian Bonetto

On the ground, an epic 'Tak' to Søren Rose, Rune RK, Tue Hesselberg Foged, Toke Lykkeberg, Jens Martin Skibsted, Trine Wackerhaus, Peter Kreiner, René Redzepi, Rasmus Kofoed, Aaron Giles, Julie Sanders, Søren Knudsen Moller, Christina Catharina Friis Blach and Susanna Greve. Thanks also to the many locals who offered time, tips and humour along the way. At Lonely Planet, many thanks to Jo Potts, Imogen Bannister, Sally Schafer, Darren O'Connell, Laura Stansfeld, Kirsten Rawlings, Andy Symington, Herman So, Kim Hutchins and Andi Lien.

Mark Elliott

Heartfelt thanks to Tom Masters for honouring his gentleman's agreement, to Solarn Solmunde, Jon Tyril, Ken in Eiði, Johan in Saksun, Sigrid & Wieland in Viðareiði, Árant Hansen in Gøta, Gert and friends in Tvøroyri and to the impromptu 'welcoming committee' in Skarvanes. And above all, never-ending thanks to my parents, sibling and beloved wife Danielle Systermans without whose love and constant assistance I wouldn't have the astonishing opportunities that make my life so blessed.

Anthony Ham

Just about every Norwegian I met was a friendly and unfailingly helpful ambassador for their country – there are too many to name, but I am deeply grateful to all of them. Thanks to Miles Roddis, a long-standing companion of the road, and Stuart Butler. And this book is dedicated to Marina and our two girls Carlota and Valentina (who was born not long after I returned home from Norway) – one day we'll explore Svalbard together.

Becky Ohlsen

Becky Ohlsen would like to thank her fellow authors, especially Cristian Bonetto for his work on the Sweden chapter in the previous edition of this book and Andy Symington for putting it all together; Matt and Lindy in Tärnaby; and Peter Kvarnestam and family in Skåne.

Fran Parnell

A huge thank you to everyone who helped during the research and writing of the Iceland chapter of this book. This includes all the tourist office, museum and activity guide staff, particularly Auður from Reykjavík TI, Svanhvít at BSÍ, Svala at Air Iceland and Erlendur at Strýtan Divecenter. It's always fun catching up with Jón Trausti Sigurðarson

at *Grapevine*. On a personal note, I am very grateful to the people who helped when my car fell to pieces on a mountain pass, especially Dagur from Sixt. And thanks to Kristján for being a calm presence before the marathon.

Simon Richmond

Bolshoi spasibo to Mirjana Vesentin, Leonid Ragozin, Sasha and Andrey, my fabulous hosts in St Petersburg, and Peter and Valery for their company and input.

ACKNOWLEDGMENTS

Climate map data adapted from Peel MC, Finlayson BL & McMahon TA (2007) 'Updated World Map of the Köppen-Geiger Climate Classification', *Hydrology and Earth System Sciences*, 11, 163344.

Cover photograph: Rape field, red house and forest, Kullaberg, Skåne, Anders Blomqvist/Lonely Planet Images. Many of the images in this guide are available for licensing from Lonely Planet Images: www.lonelyplanet images.com.

THIS BOOK

Many people have helped to create this 10th edition of Lonely Planet's *Scandinavia* guidebook, which is part of Lonely Planet's Europe series. Other titles in this series include *Western Europe*, *Eastern Europe*, *Mediterranean Europe*, *Central Europe* and *Europe on a Shoestring*. Lonely Planet also publishes phrasebooks for these regions. This guidebook was commissioned in Lonely Planet's London office, and produced by the following:

Commissioning Editors Jo Potts, Anna Tyler

Coordinating Editor Andi Lien

Coordinating Cartographer Hunor Csutoros

Coordinating Layout & Colour Designer Wendy Wright

Managing Editors Kirsten Rawlings, Tasmin Waby McNaughtan

Managing Cartographers Amanda Sierp, David Connolly

Managing Layout Designer Jane Hart

Assisting Editors Andrew Bain, Cathryn Game, Kim Hutchins, Helen Koehne

Assisting Cartographer Enes Basic

Cover Research Naomi Parker

Internal Image Research Aude Vauconsant

Language Content Branislava Vladisavljevic

Thanks to Trent Paton, Lisa Knights, Annelies Mertens, Chris Girdler, Helen Christinis, Susan Paterson, Jacqui Saunders, Averil Robertson, Juan Winata, Carol Jackson, Kerrianne Southway, Paul Iacono,

NOTES

index

000 Map pages
000 Photo pages

000 Map pages
000 Photo pages

how to use this book

These symbols will help you find the listings you want:

⊙	Sights	🎊	Festivals & Events	☆	Entertainment
🏃	Activities	🛏	Sleeping	🛍	Shopping
🎓	Courses	🍴	Eating	ℹ	Information/Transport
👉	Tours	🍷	Drinking		

These symbols give you the vital information for each listing:

☎	Telephone Numbers	🌐	Wi-Fi Access	🚌	Bus
⊘	Opening Hours	🏊	Swimming Pool	⛴	Ferry
P	Parking	🍃	Vegetarian Selection	Ⓜ	Metro
⊖	Nonsmoking	📋	English-Language Menu	Ⓢ	Subway
❄	Air-Conditioning	👪	Family-Friendly	Ⓛ	London Tube
@	Internet Access	🐾	Pet-Friendly	Ⓣ	Tram
				Ⓡ	Train

Reviews are organised by author preference.

Look out for these icons:

TOP CHOICE	Our author's recommendation
FREE	No payment required
🌿	A green or sustainable option

Our authors have nominated these places as demonstrating a strong commitment to sustainability – for example by supporting local communities and producers, operating in an environmentally friendly way, or supporting conservation projects.

Map Legend

Sights
- ⊙ Beach
- ⊙ Buddhist
- ⊙ Castle
- ⊙ Christian
- ⊙ Hindu
- ⊙ Islamic
- ⊙ Jewish
- ⊙ Monument
- ⊙ Museum/Gallery
- ⊙ Ruin
- ⊙ Winery/Vineyard
- ⊙ Zoo
- ⊙ Other Sight

Activities, Courses & Tours
- ⊙ Diving/Snorkelling
- ⊙ Canoeing/Kayaking
- ⊙ Skiing
- ⊙ Surfing
- ⊙ Swimming/Pool
- ⊙ Walking
- ⊙ Windsurfing
- ⊙ Other Activity/Course/Tour

Sleeping
- ⊙ Sleeping
- ⊙ Camping

Eating
- ⊙ Eating

Drinking
- ⊙ Drinking
- ⊙ Cafe

Entertainment
- ⊙ Entertainment

Shopping
- ⊙ Shopping

Information
- ⊙ Post Office
- ⊙ Tourist Information

Transport
- ⊙ Airport
- ⊗ Border Crossing
- ⊙ Bus
- Cable Car/Funicular
- Cycling
- Ferry
- Ⓜ Metro
- Monorail
- Ⓟ Parking
- Ⓢ S-Bahn
- ⊙ Taxi
- Train/Railway
- Tram
- Ⓣ Tube Station
- Ⓤ U-Bahn
- • Other Transport

Routes
- Tollway
- Freeway
- Primary
- Secondary
- Tertiary
- Lane
- Unsealed Road
- Plaza/Mall
- Steps
- ⊱⊰ Tunnel
- Pedestrian Overpass
- Walking Tour
- Walking Tour Detour
- Path

Boundaries
- International
- State/Province
- Disputed
- Regional/Suburb
- Marine Park
- Cliff
- Wall

Population
- ⊙ Capital (National)
- ◉ Capital (State/Province)
- ⊙ City/Large Town
- ⊙ Town/Village

Geographic
- ⊙ Hut/Shelter
- ⊙ Lighthouse
- ⊙ Lookout
- ▲ Mountain/Volcano
- ⊙ Oasis
- ⊙ Park
-)(Pass
- ⊙ Picnic Area
- ⊙ Waterfall

Hydrography
- River/Creek
- Intermittent River
- Swamp/Mangrove
- Reef
- Canal
- Water
- Dry/Salt/Intermittent Lake
- Glacier

Areas
- Beach/Desert
- +++ Cemetery (Christian)
- ××× Cemetery (Other)
- Park/Forest
- Sportsground
- Sight (Building)
- Top Sight (Building)

Mark Elliott

Faroe Islands Elliott's previous 'great north' guidebook assignments have seen him getting trapped in Greenland's offshore ice floes and crossing Siberia's deepest (frozen) lake in a truck. In the comparative warmth of the Faroes, more manageable excitement included dodging dive-bombing skuas and avoiding dizzying chasms that cut invisibly across certain hiking trails. Sudden gales at Kallur lighthouse almost gusted Mark off the clifftops but he was equally 'blown away' by the Faroes' vibrant music scene and by many stimulating encounters with local artists.

Read more about Mark at:
lonelyplanet.com/members/markelliott

Anthony Ham

Norway Anthony fell in love with Norway the first time he laid eyes on her and there aren't many places in Norway he hasn't been. His true passion is the Arctic north whether dog-sledding and spending time with the Sámi around Karasjok or drawing near to glaciers and scouring the horizon for polar bears in the glorious wilderness of Svalbard. When he's not travelling for Lonely Planet, he lives in Madrid and writes for magazines and newspapers around the world.

Read more about Anthony at:
lonelyplanet.com/members/anthonyham

Becky Ohlsen

Sweden Becky has travelled in Sweden since the age of two. She's constantly amazed that no matter how often she visits, she still finds things she's never seen before, whether it's an underground cafe in Södermalm or a Viking-era stone ship hidden away in the forest. Becky's favourite things about Sweden include fried herring and saffron ice cream (not together), the art of John Bauer, the diaries of August Strindberg, the films of Ingmar Bergman, the hiking trails of Norrland and the little red huts everywhere. She also writes about the Pacific Northwest for Lonely Planet. Becky lives in Portland, Oregon.

Read more about Becky at:
lonelyplanet.com/members/beckyohlsen

Fran Parnell

Iceland Fran's passion for Scandinavia began while studying for a masters degree in Anglo-Saxon, Norse and Celtic. Fran travels to Iceland as often as possible and always finds something new to appreciate. This year, she ran the Reykjavík marathon for the first time, and would recommend the experience to everyone. Fran has worked on other Lonely Planet guides to Scandinavia, including *Iceland*, *Sweden*, *Denmark*, *Reykjavík* and previous editions of *Scandinavia*.

Read more about Fran at:
lonelyplanet.com/members/franparnell

Simon Richmond

St Petersburg After studying Russian history and politics at university, Simon's first visit to St Petersburg was in 1994. He's since travelled the breadth of Russia from Kamchatka in the far east to Kaliningrad in the far west. An award-winning writer and photographer, Simon is the coauthor of the first and subsequent editions of Lonely Planet's *Trans-Siberian Railway* as well as editions 3, 4 and 5 of *Russia*. Read more about him at www.simonrichmond.com.

Read more about Simon at:
lonelyplanet.com/members/simonrichmond

OUR STORY

A beat-up old car, a few dollars in the pocket and a sense of adventure. In 1972 that's all Tony and Maureen Wheeler needed for the trip of a lifetime – across Europe and Asia overland to Australia. It took several months, and at the end – broke but inspired – they sat at their kitchen table writing and stapling together their first travel guide, *Across Asia on the Cheap*. Within a week they'd sold 1500 copies. Lonely Planet was born.

Today, Lonely Planet has offices in Melbourne, London and Oakland, with more than 600 staff and writers. We share Tony's belief that 'a great guidebook should do three things: inform, educate and amuse'.

OUR WRITERS

Andy Symington

Coordinating Author, Finland Andy hails from Australia, lives in Spain, learnt to ski in Norway, was entranced by wintertime Finland as a backpacking teenager and has been a regular visitor to the Nordic lands ever since. He's travelled widely throughout the region, and is a frequent contributor on Finland and Scandinavia to Lonely Planet guides and other publications. Personal highlights have included close encounters with bears and a near-terminal swim in a seriously cold Arctic Ocean. Constantly seeking honorary northern citizenship, his bedtime books include Icelandic sagas and Finnish grammars, while his huge Scandi-CD stockpile ranges from entrancing contemporary Sámi *yoik*s to epic '80s Viking metal.

Read more about Andy at:
lonelyplanet.com/members/andysymington

Carolyn Bain

Tallinn Melbourne-based Carolyn has investigated great pockets of northern Europe in the name of work, including Sweden, Denmark and the Baltic countries. For this book she returned to the northeast, where Estonia combines the best of Eastern Europe and Scandinavia and delivers something heart-warmingly unique.

Read more about Carolyn at:
lonelyplanet.com/members/carolynbain

Cristian Bonetto

Denmark A weakness for svelte design, adventurous chefs and cycle-toned bodies first drew Cristian Bonetto to Denmark. Years later, the country's effortless cool continues to inspire this one-time soap scribe, whose musings on travel and popular culture have appeared in Australian, British and Italian publications. When Cristian isn't hunting down Denmark's best *kanelsnegle* (cinnamon 'snail'), you're likely to find him scouring Sweden, Italy, New York or his hometown Melbourne for decent espresso, cheap chic and the perfect shot to post on Facebook.

Read more about Cristian at:
lonelyplanet.com/members/cristianbonetto

OVER MORE
PAGE WRITERS

Published by Lonely Planet Publications Pty Ltd
ABN 36 005 607 983
10th edition – Oct 2011
ISBN 978 1 74179 680 3
© Lonely Planet 2011   Photographs © as indicated 2011
10 9 8 7 6 5 4 3 2 1
Printed in China